PENGUIN BOOKS

HOSTAGE TO FORTUNE

Amanda Smith is Joseph P. Kennedy's granddaughter. A graduate student at Harvard University, she lives in Washington, D.C.

Praise for *Hostage to Fortune*

"A unique written legacy . . . these rare first-hand accounts not only create a fascinating historical panorama but also provide a side of Kennedy never before seen as he progressed in his public and private life."
—*The Indianapolis Star*

"Superb"   —*The New York Review of Books*

"This authoritative book fills a void and is a dazzling portrait of an American original. [Amanda Smith] had done a yeoman's work discovering, compiling, and preserving this trove of materials. This volume will satisfy a thirst for documentation and fill out the histories of business, diplomacy, and politics yet to be written . . . it also fills out the biographies of his children. In all those that exist . . . none captures the poignance of their young lives more than this volume."   —*Chicago Sun-Times*

"These documents are worth having; for the reader familiar with the Kennedy literature, they do much to fill out a portrait of a fascinating clan and a fascinating man."   —*Publishers Weekly*

"As broker and motion picture producer, head of New Deal agencies and ambassador to the Court of St. James, and patriarch of a large, lively clan of future activists, Kennedy had an unusual perspective on twentieth-century history, a perspective well captured in this collection."
—*Booklist*

"Uncluttered by secondary excuses or analysis, *Hostage to Fortune* opens a unique window on history."   —*Los Angeles Times Book Review*

HOSTAGE TO FORTUNE

The Letters of Joseph P. Kennedy

EDITED BY

Amanda Smith

PENGUIN BOOKS

PENGUIN BOOKS

Published by the Penguin Group
Penguin Putnam Inc., 375 Hudson Street,
New York, New York 10014, U.S.A.
Penguin Books Ltd, 80 Strand, London WC2R 0RL, England
Penguin Books Australia Ltd, 250 Camberwell Road, Camberwell, Victoria 3124, Australia
Penguin Books Canada Ltd, 10 Alcorn Avenue, Toronto, Ontario, Canada M4V 3B2
Penguin Books India (P) Ltd, 11 Community Centre, Panchsheel Park, New Delhi – 110 017, India
Penguin Books (N.Z.) Ltd, Cnr Rosedale and Airborne Roads, Albany, Auckland, New Zealand
Penguin Books (South Africa) (Pty) Ltd, 24 Sturdee Avenue,
Rosebank, Johannesburg 2196, South Africa

Penguin Books Ltd, Registered Offices: Harmondsworth, Middlesex, England

First published in the United States of America by Viking Penguin,
a member of Penguin Putnam Inc. 2001
Published in Penguin Books 2002

1   3   5   7   9   10   8   6   4   2

Selections from this book first appeared in *The New Yorker.*

Exerpts from the diplomatic journals of Jay Pierrepoint Moffat reprinted
by permission of the Houghton Library, Harvard University

THE LIBRARY OF CONGRESS HAS CATALOGED THE HARDCOVER EDITION AS FOLLOWS:
Kennedy, Joseph P. (Joseph Patrick) 1888–1969.
Hostage to fortune : the letters of Joseph P. Kennedy / edited by Amanda Smith.
p.   cm.
Includes bibliographical references (p.) and index.
ISBN 0-670-86969-4 (hc.)
ISBN 0 14 20.0037 X (pbk.)
1. Kennedy, Joseph P. (Joseph Patrick), 1888–1969—Correspondence.
2. Amassadors—United States—Correspondence.   3. Politicians—United States—
Correspondence.   4. Businesspeople—United States—Correspondence.   5. United Sates—
Foreign relations—1933–1945—Sources.   6. United States—Politics and government—
1933–1945—Sources.   7. Kennedy, Joseph P. (Joseph Patrick), 1888–1969—Family.
8. Kennedy family.   I. Smith, Amanda.   II. Title.
E748.K376 A4 2000
973.9'092—dc21
[B]   00–036786

Every effort has been made to ascribe appropriate credit and to locate the
proprietors of the photographic material that appears in this book.

Printed in the United States of America
Set in Photina
Designed by Jaye Zimet

To my mother

. . . I have a great stake in this country. My wife and I have given nine hostages to fortune. Our children and your children are more important than anything else in the world. The kind of America that they and their children will inherit is of grave concern to us all. In the light of these considerations, I believe that Franklin D. Roosevelt should be reelected president of the United States.

—Joseph P. Kennedy,
radio address on behalf of
Franklin Roosevelt's third-term election,
October 29, 1940

ACKNOWLEDGMENTS

A great many people assisted me in the process of assembling and editing the manuscript. I'm not sure that these acknowledgments are sufficient thanks for their help and kindness to me over the past several years.

A number of people associated with various libraries and repositories in the United States and abroad made easier the process of tracking stray letters and finding documents that would illuminate those I had already found. I would like to thank first and foremost the staff of the John F. Kennedy Library, particularly Maura Porter and Alan Goodrich. I would also like to thank Dr. B. S. Benedikz at the University of Birmingham; Katherine Bligh; Dr. John Booker of the Lloyds Bank Archive in London; John Bowman; Jennifer Campbell; Nicholas Coney at the Public Record Office (PRO); Peter Dalleo and Vin Watchorn for their fascinating material on the Bethlehem Steel Baseball League; Christina Deane at the University of Virginia; J. M. Fewster; Sam Gill at the Margaret Herrick Library at The Motion Picture Academy of Arts and Sciences in Los Angeles; Kurt Hasselbach at the Massachussets Institute of Technology; Alan Kucia at Churchill College; Helen Langley; David Linton; Breandán MacGiolla Choille for his help with the de Valera papers; Verne Newton at the Roosevelt Library in Hyde Park; Dr. David Smith at the Borthwick Institute at the University of York; Andrej Suchcitz at the Polish Institute in London; Martin Tyson; and Timothy Wiles at the National Baseball Hall of Fame.

I would particularly like to thank my mother, Jean Kennedy Smith, for her unflinching support and unflagging enthusiasm for the project, especially at moments when it faced stumbling blocks and when her own attentions were occupied not with the past, but with weightier present-day matters. I would also like to thank Senator Edward Kennedy, Ethel Skakel Kennedy, Patricia Kennedy Lawford and Eunice and Sargent Shriver for sharing their own papers and recollections and for their encouragement. The duke and duchess of Devonshire were extremely generous in sharing family correspondence and memories, as were the queen, the Queen Mother and Princess Margaret, Lula Percey and Lady Soames. I would like to thank John Seigenthaler for his suggestions and recollections, and Christie, Viscountess Simon, and Page Huidekoper Wilson for sharing their memories of both London immediately before the war and the American ambassador of the time. Doris Kearns Goodwin, David Nasaw and Jeff Shesol were all extremely kind in suggesting or making available other relative manuscript collections and sources. I am also grateful to Sir Robert Fellowes, Edie Ferrante, Melody Miller, Amy Seigenthaler and Gwen Urdang-Brown for making the process of securing permissions and tracking down sources a great deal easier.

I would also like to thank Bob Corcoran, Greg Craig, Joe Hakim, Paul Kirk, Joanne Nestor, Father Charles O'Byrne, Carolyn Osteen, Arthur M. Schlesinger, Bobby Shriver and Stephen Smith for their advice and suggestions. I am grateful to Fritzie and Jack Goodman, Scott Nathan, Fern and Jonathan Oppenheimer, Bridie Sullivan and Sir Mark Tennyson-d'Eyncourt for putting me up and feeding me (!) while I was doing research away from home. Louis Caldarella, Nick Halper and Laura Hundley were invaluable for their comments on the original proposal, and I am indebted to Carter Hood for going beyond the call of duty in helping me with the bibliography and endnotes for the final version of the manuscript. Matthew Bergstresser, Carrie Klotz, Joe Kusnan, Rob McKeon, Rachel Schlesinger, Michael Warnick and Randi Wolkenbriet were extremely helpful in helping me compile the documents that would form the basis of this book and in shedding light on some of the many (occasionally obscure) characters who appear among its pages. I would particularly like to acknowledge Kim Foster for having performed the Herculean task of transcribing the original documents onto discs. I am also especially grateful to Ian Gold and Nancy Mehegan for their tireless and unrelenting efforts to help me track down information on the material and people described in the documents that follow and for their help keeping track of such an overwhelming amount of bibliographical material. Finally I would like to thank Tina Bennett, Lynn Nesbit, Ray Roberts and Al Silverman for all their advice and encouragement.

CONTENTS

INTRODUCTION

Negotiating the lawn between our aunt's and our grandparents' houses, I watched my shadow's progress across the grass while our baby-sitters reminded us that girls curtsy and boys bow. Familiar distances have shrunken apace with my own growth since then; that path across what seemed to me an endless expanse at two is a matter of only a few dozen paces today. As we set out that morning during what must have been the summer of 1969, the summer before Grandpa's death, my cousin and I had been promised that we were going to see Grandpa—and only Grandpa. To my exasperation, however, I began to gather from the conversation around me that in addition, we would be paying a visit not only to a Mr. Kennedy but to someone (or something) known as the ambassador as well. Such unexpected changes to our plans, I suspected, could only lead to more walking.

I have no recollection of having seen my adoptive grandfather either before or after that day, although my growing anticipation as we climbed the stairs to his bedroom, toward the source of bustle and hum in that otherwise still house, suggests that at the time I remembered visiting him before.

His room was filled with people, all of them orbiting his bed, all of them busy on his behalf. My cousin and I were led through the crowd of knees until we found ourselves at his bedside. With some prompting, I duly performed my curtsy and climbed and craned to kiss Grandpa. At eighty, he was likely the oldest person I had ever seen; left immobile and mute by a stroke several years earlier, he was certainly the most infirm. Other than the fact that he wore red pajamas, the aura that he created in that room is far more vivid and immediate to me in memory than is his image. I was struck, then as now, that the center of activity in that busy room, the figure who commanded so much whispered reverence, whom everyone called by a different name—Daddy, the ambassador, Mr. Kennedy, Grandpa—was himself silent, motionless, pale and (most impressively, it seemed to me) spectacularly freckled.

It was my cousin's turn then to say hello. Mistaking the gesticulation and prodding to "bow to Grandpa, *bow* to Grandpa," for a concept more familiar to him from cartoons, I suppose, my cousin approached the bed and then, grinning, launched a tiny fist toward Grandpa's jaw with a screech of "Pow!" Beyond this single memory I have no other recollection or knowledge of Grandpa that is wholly my own.

Although I hadn't given much concerted thought to that lone memory until recently, I am amazed by the degree to which it has so insistently governed and organized my subsequent knowledge of our grandfather. Just as I had assumed so crankily that morning that we would be paying visits to several apparently unconnected people who turned out to be the same man, so had I always found it difficult to reconcile the father and grandfather whom I learned about at home with his various and evolving incarnations in print and over the airwaves as father, speculator, film producer, bootlegger, chairman, ambassador, appeaser, philanderer, philanthropist, kingmaker.

As I've grown older, I have begun to marvel, too, at how much of my life I have spent among ghosts. These are no malevolent presences. They rattle no chains. They make no Old Hamlet-style demands. Rather, they are such restless spirits as only the strange twentieth-century cocktail of celebrity, technology and collective memory could produce. My mother's relatives, the ones I never met or don't remember, are never and yet always distant. They lend their names to street signs, schools, VFW posts, expressways, a national center for the performing arts, an airport, a space center. They manifest themselves on the faces of coins and postage stamps. I have heard them invoked in history class and in schoolyard fights. They find themselves revivified for eternity in documentaries, news footage, miniseries and their reruns. In docudramas, those modern history plays with all the traditional accommodations of fact to histrionics, they bark witty repartee at one another in Katharine Hepburn accents through choreographed touch-football games.

When I was small, I took the media for a mirror of my own reality, reflecting back to me the expanse of my tiny world. The figures whom I saw in photographs around the house and heard about in my mother's stories of her own childhood also looked back at me from the television set and from the pages of magazines. It was a small world indeed, and it was peopled almost entirely, quite naturally, by Mom's relatives. As I grew and the parameters of my consciousness began to expand beyond my family, it occurred to me that I recognized and remembered those particular images over the many thousands that presented themselves largely *because* they were familiar. Like newly learned vocabulary words, I noticed them everywhere. Familiarity, it seemed to me, bred ubiquity. More recently, I have had the occasional impression of looking at a family portrait in a sideshow mirror; clearly these are figures whom I recognize, although with some features grotesquely distorted, others shrunken to near invisibility. Public personas, grown in the rich hosts of film, print, biography and gossip column, and further fed by continued interest, are capable of leading existences autonomous from those who gave them life. Unlike their mortal originals, however, they are capable of continuing on, reinvigorated, ever mutating and metastasizing after death. Such is celluloid immortality.

There is a kind of immortality too, though, in private memory. Dozens of people have told me of their experiences meeting these figures or seeing one of them in the flesh long ago in Newport or Cork, Washington or Paris. Two days after my grandmother died, I was moved inexpressibly to see the number of people who had come to stand out in the January cold on the streets of Boston with their hands over their hearts, waiting for her to pass by for the last time as her funeral procession made its way from the church to the cemetery. One summer evening in Cambridge, England, after finishing my research for the day, I went running to the nearby cemetery for the American war dead. Waiting for me there, too high up for me to touch, graven in the stone of a wall commemorating those still missing in action after more than half a century, was the name of an uncle I had never met. Beyond his personal effects, his correspondence and some scattered written recollections, the very letters that form his name on that stone slab make up his only physical remains; no trace of his body has ever been found. On another occasion, when my immediate family was having lunch in a restaurant in New York, an elderly Englishman who had lost both of his legs in the war approached our table to ask if Mom had had a sister named Kathleen Kennedy— they were so much alike. Rather taken aback, Mom said that she had, and he went on to relate that Kathleen had been one of his dearest friends. Not a day had passed, he said, since they had met in the late thirties or since her early death in 1948, that he hadn't thought about her. Another shy English octogenarian once took me aside to relate that Kathleen had had "the most 'sex-appeal' (as the young say nowadays) of any woman" he had ever known. Not, he said, because she was beautiful, but because she was so kind.

A few weeks after my father died of lung cancer, I moved into a new apartment and got ready to start graduate school. Unable to sleep, I began to watch TV early one morning, and came upon a documentary based on the news coverage of the election of 1960. Intermingled with the footage of the candidates and the up-to-the-moment returns, of Mom and her sisters serving tea and resplendent in their John F. Kennedy poodle skirts, I saw to my delight and sadness clips of Dad. He had told me a few years before that in marrying my mother he had become part of a new family. His own father had died when he was five, and he had taken on her father very much as his own; her brothers had become his brothers and his best friends. In the footage—delivering messages, working behind the scenes, at the convention or on the telephone—he was nearly a decade younger than I had ever known him and about a decade older than I was at the time, almost my peer. On film, he would be eternally young—or for as long, at least, as anyone would see fit to transfer such images to successive technologies. Like the family he had taken as his own, he (or rather his image) had entered the realm of two-dimensional immortality, and like them, having departed life, would remain forever alive, healthy and young, however intangible. *So long as men can breathe, or eyes can see, So long lives this, and this gives life to thee,* I guess. I went to sleep in the early hours of that morning by the blue light of the television set with the odd, one-sided relief of having had a chance sighting of a lost and much-missed friend.

And yet, for all of this simultaneous access to, and distance from, family members that the media and collective or individual memory provided, there remained one figure more distant than all of the others. Curiously, it was he who had been largely responsible for sparking public interest in his family, and yet he was also the most elusive, the most stubbornly unyielding to examination both in life and after death.

Visiting Grandma at Easter and in the summers during the years that followed Grandpa's death, we learned that she had "married for love" over her father's objections that "Joe Kennedy didn't have a collar button to his name." We asked her over and over again to tell us how they used to meet clandestinely in the Christian Science church in order to avoid the notice of other Catholics who might reveal to her father the growing frequency of her meetings with her beau. My mother told me of her delight at discovering a cache of butterscotch crunch buried in a stack of sweaters while playing in her own father's closet one day when she was little. A decade or so later, after my mother's eldest brother and godfather died as a pilot toward the end of the Second World War, Grandpa (both a lifelong dieter and the closeted consumer of that butterscotch) would insist that she reduce if she hoped to christen a battleship in her brother's name. With some annoyance, she did. And in the same shipyard where their father had served as assistant general manager during the First World War, rejecting active duty because of his objections to the slaughter of American boys as the result of any entangling foreign alliances, she went on to crack open a bottle of early postwar champagne substitute against the hull of a destroyer intended to memorialize a life lost in the war following the war to end all wars.

At home I learned that Grandpa was a parent who encouraged kindness to younger siblings, legible penmanship, civic activism, "keeping out of the columns," thorough knowledge of current affairs, eloquence, punctuality. My mother's sister, twenty minutes late for lunch at "21", met him coming out of the revolving door, where he left her. She was seldom late afterward. After the queen ate her asparagus with her fingers at dinner one night at the American Embassy in London, Ambassador and Mrs. Kennedy's efforts to dissuade their children from engaging in the practice were in vain. With war looming throughout 1939, Grandpa pestered dozens of American ambassadors and consuls around the globe to send my mother dolls typical of their regions so that she would have an extensive, educational (and, as we might say nowadays, multicultural) collection. I learned of countless acts of loyalty, friendship and generosity, offers to take in children who found themselves in difficult circumstances (in addition to the nine at home), loans that snatched several from the jaws of bankruptcy. With time, I learned, too, of defeat, calumny, loss and grief.

And with time, I began to learn of him from sources beyond my home. In articles, successive biographies (either of himself or in which he figures peripherally), television programs and conversations that I overheard from strangers, his life began to take on a fairy-tale quality. In his younger incarnations he was a real-life Jay Gatsby, ever reinventing and legitimizing himself, ever shrouding and distancing himself from a whispered, glittering past among gangsters, flappers and starlets. In his later manifestations he materialized as a man who realized that ultimate power would never be his in a single lifetime, and so he struck a Faustian bargain to allow his precious children to fulfill his dreams. One succeeded, but only at the cost of the lives of four. And, broken physically and spiritually, the story goes, the father who launched them all into the limelight died under the weight of his own grief. He appeared other times as a kind of allegorical character in a twentieth-century morality play, a human embodiment of a single quality—Rapaciousness, Adultery, Isolationism, Anti-Semitism, Living-Vicariously-Through-One's-Children—any and all of which resulted in his own well-deserved demise. If others saw him as the incarnation of these and myriad other traits, I would learn later from his letters and writings that he saw in his own family an embodiment of America itself. The rhetoric that has come to characterize and define his family has on occasion made use of that theme, although often in ways I'm not sure that the founding father would have anticipated.

While Joseph Kennedy was transforming himself from a young bank examiner into the assistant manager of a wartime shipyard, and making his first killings on Wall Street and forays into the nascent motion picture business, unbeknownst to him his Viennese contemporary Dr. Werner Heisenberg was attempting to pry into the atom itself, to fathom and delineate its inner workings once and for all, definitively and objectively. Rather than illuminate the mechanics and movements within those particles that he attempted to observe, however, Heisenberg had stumbled upon the ultimate tautology of objective observation: any apparatus devised to probe the atom necessarily interfered with its natural and accustomed inner workings. All attempts at observation necessarily imposed upon, and therefore altered the observed. The only truth—objective or otherwise—to emerge from his efforts was the certainty of inescapable subjectivity. As with subatomic particles, so, I have come to think, with biographical subjects.

One estimate has it that the family that Joseph Kennedy generated has itself generated more words than anyone or any phenomenon besides Christ and the War Between the States. Reading over family biographies, I am always struck by how much they say about the nation and the particular generation for whom they were written as much as by what they reveal about the family itself. If these works can be said to share anything beyond their subject matter, it might be their curious lack of self-consciousness. That is, they serve as the very vehicles for the evolution and unflagging propagation of the mythology that they seek variously to perpetuate, recast or debunk, all the while leaving largely unexamined the role that media, public scrutiny or indeed works like themselves might play in contributing to the situational oddities or personal shortcomings on which they often focus. And with the exceptions of the only three works to draw directly on material from Joseph P. Kennedy's archive (Arthur M. Schlesinger, Jr.'s *Robert Kennedy and His Times*, Michael Beschloss's *Kennedy and Roosevelt: The Uneasy Alliance* and Doris Kearns Goodwin's *The Fitzgeralds and the Kennedys*), accounts of the paterfamilias share a hollow center. Without access to his papers, biographers have been forced to rely on a more or less finite body of contemporaneous news clippings, documentary archives, oral histories and interviews. Occasionally writers discover something not yet uncovered or someone new to interview, thereby adding a little more "explosive" or "shocking" information to the mix in order to echo or repudiate existing scholarship and rework that still-elusive figure for public consumption by successive generations of Americans. His own voice remains largely unheard despite the controversies that continue to surround him decades after his death.

During his lifetime and especially from the late thirties onward, Joseph Kennedy's press clippings reflect a man who inspired either admiration or hatred, but very little in between. His family tended (at least until recently) to fare somewhat better. Articles, newsreels and photospreads parade the images of happy, healthy affluence at weddings and parties, in the street, on horseback, under sail. By the early sixties, a series of close examinations seem to mirror the unprecedented and growing intimacy with public figures that television by then permitted. These works, reflecting by and large better on the family than on its progenitor, speak perhaps as much about the last vestiges of the now proverbial Eisenhower-era, Cleaver-family normality as they do of a growing antipatriarchy and questioning of authority. Beginning in the late fifties, television, along with related technological advances in telecommunications, film and sound recording, swept his family further into the public realm much as it did the likes of Elvis Presley, Marilyn Monroe and the Beatles, transforming, multiplying and universalizing their images and depositing them all in the Oz of superstardom. When Joe Kennedy returned from London late in 1940, it was his intention to do everything in his power to prevent the United States from entering the war. His isolationism hastened the political downfall that the widening rift between himself and the Roosevelt administration had already set in motion. And yet, it was his very noninterventionism that the writer of his obituary praised in one New York paper on the day after his death at the height of the war in Vietnam. In the roaring and self-indulgent eighties he reappeared as the adulterer and the speculator on the unregulated market of the roaring twenties in talk-show psychiatric diagnoses and *Lifestyles of the Rich and Famous* accounts of his life. More recently he has become a crushing, incestuous father figure at a moment when adult children of monstrous parents have begun to reexamine their own childhoods.

Seeing himself described as "Irish Catholic" in the paper one morning late in his life, my mother's father (a third-generation Bostonian) asked with some bitterness, "How long do you have to be in this country before they consider you an American?" Joseph Kennedy was a man who has been often (and quite accurately) characterized as self-conscious and hyperconcerned about the image that he and his family projected. But his very self-consciousness reveals also a man who understood with equal measures of pride and outrage that everything he had accumulated, all that he and his family had managed to achieve, was possible for Irish Catholics almost for the first time in the moment and nation of his birth. Inasmuch as he and others have characterized his family as an embodiment of the American Dream, so too has that family continued to reflect a changing America, even after death.

During my first year in graduate school my mother mentioned to me that her family still had her father's papers and were interested in opening them. I knew something about rare document preservation and went to the JFK Library, where my grandmother had sent the bulk of the papers in anticipation of their opening, to have a look. I found there more than two hundred linear feet of documents, largely uncataloged and in so advanced a state of decay that the earliest weren't merely fraying around the edges, but crumbling. Crammed in no particular order into overtaxed cardboard boxes and deteriorating from within due to their own high acidity, most of these documents were the diaphanous carbon copies of his dictations and the letters to which they responded. Other hands had reordered the papers over the years prior to their arrival at the JFK Library in a variety of ways—alphabetically, according to where they had been written, or (as far as I was able to tell) by simply stuffing them arbitrarily into file cabinets and manila envelopes.

Out of this motley, decaying entropy I began to piece together the fragments of a life in the sequence in which it had been lived. The papers chronicle his adulthood, the eventual growth of his family and his many metamorphoses—from bank examiner to speculator to film producer, to politico as Securities and Exchange and Maritime Commission chairman, to diplomat, to retirement (partly enforced, as he saw it), to first father. They chart in personal terms the course of the twentieth century in America. The number and variety of his correspondents is astonishing. I was surprised to discover that he kept up with childhood and school friends throughout his life, all the while courting the friendship (and sometimes the eventual animosity) of the likes of Herbert Hoover, Harpo Marx, William Randolph Hearst, Babe Ruth, (more notoriously) Gloria Swanson, Felix Frankfurter, Cecil B. DeMille, Hedda Hopper, Bernard Baruch, Marlene Dietrich, the Roosevelt family, Clare Boothe Luce, Will Hays, Lord Beaverbrook, Eric von Stroheim, Harry Truman, the Princesses Elizabeth and Margaret, William Hillman, Ed Sullivan, William O. Douglas and J. Edgar Hoover, to name only a few.

Punctuating the correspondence were also trivial, although telling, artifacts accumulated over the course of a lifetime. A certificate from a home-county golf course commemorates the newly arrived American ambassador's hole in one in March 1938. I found grains of sand still lodged in the folds of a crumpled telegram received in Biarritz in 1926. Stuffed into a metal file cabinet among some old school notebooks was the casing of a (detonated) aerial bomb that had landed near the American Embassy in London during the terrible summer of 1940. Strangely, it bears the inscription "JPK." A diet, prescribed in 1920 both to combat a lifelong stomach ailment and to promote healthful eating generally, encourages the use of "plenty of butter on toast and vegetables," while warning against "cabbage, cauliflower, brussels sprouts, fruit and raw vegetables." A tiny black and white cylindrical box marked "Mr. Kennedy—Good Crown" yielded a tooth. Evidently, the unvarnished and plain-speaking ambassador brought a great deal of newfangled Americana with him to the Court of St. James's. Birthday cards and their sober, accompanying thank-you notes indicate that he gave Princess Elizabeth cells of Walt Disney's *Pinocchio* for her thirteenth birthday. The duchess of Kent and the queen received phonographic recordings of the latest American hits, "My Heart Belongs to Daddy," "You Must Have Been a Beautiful Baby," "You're a Sweet Little Headache," "Get Out of Town," "Jeepers Creepers," and that curious A- and B-side pairing "Thanks for Everything" and "Do You Remember Last Night?"

As I came to gain a sense of what his archive contained, I began to wonder about its evident holes. The shortcomings and gaps in Grandpa's correspondence were most apparent, curiously, during the period when he generated by far the greatest number of letters: his tenure in London as American ambassador between 1938 and 1940. He was so careful to save copies of current parliamentary debates, and yet I could find little trace of the correspondence he must have conducted with the two prime ministers of the era, Chamberlain and Churchill. There were a few notes exchanging pleasantries between himself and some of the other political figures of the day, Lord Halifax, Sir John Simon, Anthony Eden, and Leo Amery among them, but strangely, there was little of any substance. I knew from the State Department's tomes, *Foreign Relations of the United States*, that diplomatic telegrams bearing the name "KENNEDY" were dispatched from Grosvenor Square at least daily during peacetime and every few hours, in some cases, after war had been declared. And yet I was unable to find even a fragment of a draft of any of these.

Before the papers arrived at the JFK Library in the late seventies, they had been in office storage first on Third Avenue in Manhattan and later in a warehouse in Queens. Hoping that some documents had been left behind rather than lost—sunken during their wartime passage to the United States or burned up (a number of documents and notations among the surviving papers recorded a devastating warehouse fire)—I went to Long Island City to see if anything was still there. In that stifling garret amid the clutter of more recent office records, old movie reels devolving into goo and chrome-yellow powder, opened and unopened copies of the *Warren Commission Report*, a card catalog of address lists for the intended recipients of *I'm for Roosevelt* (a businessman's 1936 boost for the New Deal), and a tailcoat made in the late thirties in Cambridge, Massachusetts, for one "J. F. Kennedy" (the breast pocket still containing a dirty handkerchief), I found much more than I had expected.

There were about twenty boxes (fifty linear feet or so) of documents that dated from the thirties to the sixties. The material seemed to concentrate, however, on the decade between 1938 and 1948. The diplomatic dispatches that I had looked for were there. Grandpa's correspondence with Chamberlain and Churchill was there, along with more letters both to and from members of the Roosevelt family, Felix Frankfurter, Clare and Henry Luce and William Randolph Hearst. There was also a great deal of material whose existence I hadn't anticipated. There was a copy of the notorious telegram Franklin Roosevelt had sent to Neville Chamberlain as the latter set off for Munich in September 1938 that reads simply, "GOOD MAN." I found diaries that Grandpa kept fairly faithfully while working at the embassy in London, and sporadically otherwise. Parts of the secret correspondence between Churchill and Roosevelt form a curious counterbalance within the microcosm of this cache of documents to those handwritten letters from Charles Lindbergh prophesying the invincibility of the *Luftwaffe*.

Among all of these was a huge family correspondence as well. My mother's eldest brother, Joe, left England for Spain in the spring of 1939, writing his father on a nearly daily basis of his experiences during the fall of Madrid and the last days of the Spanish Civil War. Ever hopeful to bring public notice and acclaim to his children (and especially to his namesake), Grandpa had encouraged Joe to rework and publish the letters as *Dear Dad*. After a single modified installment appeared in the *Atlantic Monthly* and another was translated for publication in France, Joe's attention turned elsewhere. Joe himself returned to law school, and the letters were filed and eventually presumed lost. My mother's sister Kathleen, alias Kick, recorded her experiences as a London debutante during one of the last seasons before that six-year war swept away and reduced to vestiges a way of life and a social order that had been in place for centuries. Indeed, family letters and written recollections of balls, parliamentary debates on appeasement or war, the coronation of a pope, house parties and presentations at court give a curious sense of time warp. That is, the very presence at those events of such a family of Americans as descended long ago from a line of now nearly mythical warrior kings, but more recently from destitute, hungry and illiterate Irish farmers, ragged immigrants, saloon keepers, ward bosses and Boston politicians, was in many ways a harbinger of things to come in the postwar world.

Not long after I came across these documents in Long Island City, I heard that more documents had surfaced at what had been Grandpa's office in Manhattan. A secretary who had worked there for decades was retiring, and in the process of cleaning out her office, discovered hundreds of family letters that had been filed and forgotten about a quarter century before. Most of these are early childhood letters from each of the nine Kennedy children to their parents, describing variously dances, boyfriends, dogs, regattas and pimples. These papers, then, along with those left in Long Island City, those housed at the JFK Library and those still kept in the attic above the room where Grandpa died, make up the bulk of what remains of Joseph P. Kennedy's papers.

A man who sat next to me at a dinner once when I was in college asked, "So, your grandfather made his money in bootlegging?" It is certainly accurate, as it has often been said and as his letters reveal, that Grandpa supplied his tenth college reunion with alcohol in 1922 at the height of Prohibition. It is equally true, however, that he was a man who guarded his privacy zealously and covered his tracks impeccably. And so, rumors of his deeper or more organized involvement in violations of the Eighteenth Amendment, of his waiting in the darkness on the North Shore of Boston for his rumrunners to come in, remain in the limbo of myth, finding neither confirmation nor denial. At least his own papers reveal very little, even to a curious granddaughter with unlimited access. Neither do his letters, diaries or memoirs shed much light on meetings—unsanctioned by the State Department though meticulously recorded by others—with German bankers and government officials in the year leading up to the outbreak of war in Europe. He makes little mention either of meetings in Hollywood during which he was reported (by the likes of Douglas Fairbanks, Jr., and others) to have warned studio executives in the gravest terms against the production of films that might be offensive to the Reich. By the same token, however, he detailed very little of what were, according to contemporary press accounts, his elaborate negotiations to evacuate Jewish refugees from the ever-expanding boundaries of the German state; instead, the best sources of information about his efforts come down through Chaim Weizmann and Rabbi Stephen Wise. His own accounts of his interactions with Gloria Swanson never stray from the realm of business and film production; he seems to have written far more often and extensively, in fact, to her husband of the moment, the marquis de la Falaise. And yet, it has always struck me as unfortunate that any life, especially one as varied and momentous as his own (however exemplary or contemptible) could be reduced to a single word—bootlegger.

Joseph Kennedy's letters reveal a man who grew increasingly guarded with age and in proportion to his own burgeoning notoriety. His interactions with the press were as much the cause as the reflection of his fame (or infamy) and his eventual, sometimes crotchety reserve. The man who saw in the infant motion picture industry "another telephone" understood equally well the persuasive powers of that other branch of the mass media family tree, the syndicated column. He cultivated relationships, it is well known, with the most influential pundits, commentators and press barons of the day on either side of the Atlantic—Boake Carter, Westbrook Pegler, Louella Parsons, Da-mon Runyon, William Randolph Hearst, Hedda Hopper, Arthur Hays Sulzberger, Alsop and Kintner, Henry Luce, George Bilainkin, Pearson and Allen, Lord Beaverbrook, Colonel McCormick and his cousins Joseph and Cissy Patterson, Herbert Bayard Swope, O. O. McIntyre, and the two Walters who are said to have represented the midcentury's polarities of high- and lowbrow American culture: Lippmann and Winchell. "I may have lighted your Federal path, but I never started you on it," his particular friend *The New York Times'* Arthur Krock noted magnanimously to the chairman of the Maritime Commission on July 1, 1937. "Every inch of the way you won yourself, and splendidly. I am happy to believe that I called the public attention to you in an effective way. But that is all I concede." The Joseph Kennedy papers contain countless thank-you notes not only to reporters and columnists who made favorable mention of him, but also to their papers' editors and owners as well, whether he knew any of them personally or not. Having observed and imitated the practice early in his public life and adhered to it assiduously into middle age, he attempted to pass it on to his children as a means of bolstering their own political futures. "I would suggest," he wrote to Jack, then a month away from being elected to a first term in Congress, "that from now on you write a personal note to any magazine or newspaper making a kind reference to you. [Bernard] Baruch has always done that and has built a terrific newspaper support out of it. These fellows are like everyone else; they will appreciate hearing from you." Prone to holding, and even nursing grudges, Joseph Kennedy was unusually and surprisingly forgiving of members of the press.

From Joe Kennedy's earliest national appearances in the Hearst papers at twenty-five as "America's Youngest Bank President" until his stroke at seventy-three, his letters reveal a man who was hyperaware and ever jealous of the public persona that he had engendered, but that others came increasingly to shape. From his thirties onward, and especially after coming to know many members of the Washington press corps on the Roosevelt campaign train in 1932, his public self reflected back to him from a growing number of sources. Write-ups in motion picture trade journals and business publications in the twenties gave way to profiles in magazines of national circulation, such as *The Saturday Evening Post*, the *American Magazine*, *Liberty*, *Fortune* and even a cover story in *Time*, as he took command of the Securities and Exchange and Maritime Commissions in the thirties. By then, the clipping services he had engaged had come to serve him as a sort of 360-degree mirror.

Ambassador Kennedy's letters from London between 1938 and 1940, as well as those that followed America's entrance into the war, however, reflect a growing concern that his public image in the United States (influenced increasingly by others, separated as it was from its original across the ocean) was assuming a new intractability. His distance from home, coupled with the administration's growing impatience with his indiscreet and apparently self-aggrandizing leaks to those members of the press with whom he had built cordial and symbiotic relationships, greatly curtailed his accustomed means of counterbalancing negative stories about himself. In addition, his mushrooming unpopularity in governmental and press circles on both sides of the Atlantic—due to associations he had formed in England, his stance on America's entrance into the war and his pessimism about Britain's chances of winning—left his public image largely (he feared) in the hands of hostile forces. By the end of his two and a half years in London, he had come to believe that his ambassadorship had been as much the administration's reward to him for services rendered as it was a gilded exile. He returned to the United States amid wild and mutually contradictory rumors of his hawkishness and isolationism, of his profascist, fawningly Anglophilic and anti-British leanings and of his imminent betrayal of the president for Wendell Willkie in the rapidly approaching election of 1940. He intended an interview and a series of speeches supporting Roosevelt's third-term election and "all aid to Britain short of war" to set the record straight about his views and intentions. The result of these, however, was to cloud public perception of him further and to add hypocrisy and equivocation to a growing list of actual or presumed failings. His own political career ended with his resignation; his public persona would never fully recover from his ambassadorship. Two decades later, he would abandon his nearly finished diplomatic memoir (and self-vindication) after working on it intermittently and with various researchers and ghostwriters partly, it is often said, to avoid passing on the stigma of that period of his life to his sons. His few oblique remarks on the subject suggest that he was perhaps concerned instead about stealing their thunder. "I have come to the conclusion that I will not write anything for publication," he wrote a family biographer in 1957. "With Jack and Bobby and Teddy coming along, I feel since I have withdrawn from most everything that I'd better just stay out of it."

I mention his interactions with the press in such detail here for two reasons. First, because an examination of his life, as his letters show, is equally a case study of the interdependent growth of mass media and celebrity (and indeed its pitfalls) in the twentieth century. Second, his fortunes in the press, in newsreels, in syndicated columns and over the radio, and the frequency of his appearances in all of these, seem to bear an inverse relation to the degree of his self-revelation in his letters. Over the years, the space between the concentric circles of intimacy in his life widened. As he grew more famous he came increasingly to reserve self-expression for those closest to him, although those letters that he dispatched to acquaintances, colleagues or strangers are characteristic of their author in their own more impersonal way.

His earliest surviving letters, dating from the mid-1910s, demonstrate a lack of the very self-consciousness that would grow in all but his most intimate correspondence and diary entries as he aged. Among affectionate, if mundane letters written while he was traveling on business to his wife and small children and dutiful letters to his own parents are those notes that he sent to his secretary requesting her to transact business for him. These survive, it seems, only because she disregarded his notations to "kindly destroy this letter . . . [a]fter you understand this transaction thoroughly, and make out your records . . ." Others, written as he involved himself increasingly in the theater and film worlds in the twenties, suggest flirtations, boys' nights out and a growing worldliness. By the time he took his posts within the Roosevelt administration in the thirties, such instances of careless self-exposure on paper all but disappeared (only to return again as he neared the age of seventy), with a few exceptions such as a diary entry of June 17, 1943, in which he recounted that Madame Chiang Kai-shek "appeared to be horrified when I told her that she had sex appeal and immediately asked if I meant like Gypsy Rose Lee." Generally, however, by the thirties, he had begun to reserve personal, epistolary reflection almost exclusively for close friends and family.

His letters from that period onward reflect an increasingly panoramic view of the world, of economics, of trade and diplomacy. Yet their very generality, the global nature of these official letters, is as reflective in a way of his changing character (and career) as the more personal expressions that he sent to friends and his children at home or boarding school. His gloomy dispatches from the embassy in London, assessing Britain's dwindling odds of winning a war without material aid from the United States, are likewise projections of a personality that grew increasingly conservative and "bearish" (as he would put it) over time. Letters that he wrote following his return from London in late October 1940 maintain the global viewpoint he had developed over the course of the previous decade, but convey the perspective of an isolated outsider rather than the earlier command of one who influenced or had direct access to the mechanisms underlying the events described.

His letters and writings, and particularly those that date from his entrance into government service, convey a weird sense of anticipation that at some future date eyes like mine or yours would read his thoughts, that his "prognostics" and actions would be of historical interest both to his family and to the public alike. He recorded his recollection of informing Roosevelt of the Supreme Court's Gold Decision in February 1935, noting, "I am writing this memorandum because I feel the occasion is a historical one and I feel that the opportunity of being the person to relay this information to the President would be of value historically to my family." He punctuated his diary entries routinely with notations like "(Add children's and Rose's impressions to mine—here)" or "(See also my cable to [the State] Department)," expecting to flesh them out and colorize them later for public consumption.

For one so savvy (or craven, as some say) about financial matters, political jockeying and the media, he was remarkably ingenuous in many respects. He was as easily flattered, seemingly, as he was thin-skinned. His diaries, diplomatic memoir, and notations reveal that he seldom passed up an opportunity to record a compliment paid either to himself or to his family. On May 23, 1939, for example, he noted in his diary, "Prime Minister last night. He listened to Joe's letter from Spain and thought it excellent." While Germany menaced Poland with invasion in late August 1939, the American ambassador was called upon for consultation in the highest of circles. "When I left No. 10[,] I thought to myself that incident has probably been the most important thing that ever happened to me," he recorded in his diary.

> Here I was an American Ambassador, called into discussion with the P.M. and Foreign Secretary over probably the most important event in the history of the British Empire. I had been called in before the cabinet and had been trusted not only for my discretion but for my intelligence. It was a moving experience.

In spite of his attempts to keep America from sending another generation of young men to the slaughter far from home and his assiduous efforts not to go native in London—by declining to wear the traditional knee britches at court or by never forgetting (as he would put it) that it was his duty to represent American interests in Britain rather than the reverse as some of his predecessors had done—I have wondered sometimes whether he didn't share Gladstone's sneaking fondness for a lord. He seems to have been especially susceptible to kind words from peers and royals, noting that the lords Derby or Beaverbrook ("a great admirer of mine, and a terribly smart man") had found his counsel sensible and useful or that the queen had requested specifically to dance with him. On the other hand, he reported to a friend at the Vatican in 1961, "I am not like my older son who makes up to the people who attack him. When I have a bad experience, I remember it forever. It is very bad, I realize, and I know I should be more charitable in my old age, but I seem to get worse instead of better."

Having formed an impression of Grandpa as something of a misanthrope and a loner from reading about him over the years, I was surprised to discover from his letters that throughout his life he cultivated a series of mentoring relationships. As a young man, he seemed to seek out those whose financial acumen might serve as an example to him in his professional life; many of these relationships became genuine friendships. Although the overtures that he made to the younger J. P. Morgan seem to have been rebuffed unceremoniously, he met (and apparently impressed) Eugene Grace of Bethlehem Steel while working as assistant general manager of the Fore River Shipyard during the First World War. In that capacity he also came to know Galen Stone, who gave him his first job as a broker at Hayden, Stone & Co. in Boston after the war. Indirectly, Stone made possible the young broker's entrees into both Hollywood and Wall Street and would remain a friend until his death in 1926. To a request for financial advice in 1960, the father of the president-elect replied "[o]ne of the greatest stock market operators I ever knew of was a man named Galen Stone. He operated at a time when it was legal to operate so-called stock market pools. Yet, he told me that over a period of 40 years he would have been just as well off i[f] he had invested his money at 5%." James Fayne, a friend from Harvard, Wall Street and the SEC, observed that Kennedy ". . . was the type who would grasp an older man that he admired and go to him for his advice constantly." Fayne remembered particularly his admiration of Louis Brandeis and Herbert Hoover. Although Kennedy sided with Roosevelt in 1932, taking active steps to defeat the incumbent president, he would grow close to Hoover over the coming decades, asking advice and offering his own assessments of world affairs, and serving on both Hoover Commissions for the reorganization of government in the 1950s. Although his relations with Roosevelt would sour irrecoverably by the time the United States declared war, he noted to Lady Halifax at dinner at Windsor Castle in 1938,

> If you want [Roosevelt] in one word, it is gallantry. The man is almost paralyzed yet he ignores it and forces others to overlook it. He dominates a room. I have seen him when he is determined to win an argument, rise to his full height and, bearing his weight solely upon his arms braced against the desk, make the point to bring him to victory. This always brings a lump to my throat, although I consider myself pretty hard boiled.

He confessed in a farewell letter to Neville Chamberlain, which he drafted on the train to Plymouth while leaving England for good in late 1940, that the former prime minister and Cardinal Pacelli (by then Pope Pius XII) were the two men he most admired. He came to know William Randolph Hearst (whom he continued to address as "Mr. Hearst" until an oddly advanced age) through his involvement in the infant motion picture industry, and eventually persuaded the publisher to make a very generous eleventh-hour donation to the Roosevelt war chest in 1932. His letters to Hearst ring with an uncharacteristic deference bordering on obsequiousness. Bernard Baruch, with his immigrant background, his history of successful speculation and his entree into both domestic and international politics, seems to have been another role model. Among New Dealers, Baruch and Kennedy seem to have found in each other (relatively conservative) kindred spirits. Their letters from the early thirties record jokes and gags, and often close with "Love and Kisses," Wilson's chairman of the War Industries Board signing off as "Chairman," Roosevelt's head of the new Securities and Exchange Commission replying as "Little Chairman." Relations between the two became strained, according at least to the younger man's letters, once the Little Chairman became the ambassador. Even late in life, Grandpa continued to cultivate the notice and advice of older men, as his curious (or perhaps wise) deference to J. Edgar Hoover indicates.

In middle age he began to take on younger protégés as well. Often these were the children of extraordinary, famous and very busy parents. He made efforts to cultivate friendships and mentoring relationships with Franklin and Eleanor Roosevelt's children; James and Anna seem to have been his favorites while his efforts with Elliott, for example, were less successful. In a letter to his wife from London after the outbreak of war and the return of his family to the United States, he described Randolph Churchill (with whom his relations appear to have been almost entirely stormy otherwise) coming to him for advice about proposing to an actress. Within a week of being turned down, Churchill would propose again, this time to the nineteen-year-old Pamela Digby, who accepted him. "Nuts! I call it," was the ambassador's only comment about the first marriage of the notorious future American ambassador to France. Grandpa's diplomatic diary entries describing the young English princesses, Elizabeth and Margaret Rose, ring with an unwonted delight; their relationship with their parents fascinated and charmed him. Orphaned as teenagers, his wife's sister's children came to live with the family. Along with his correspondence to a small group of friends, to fond colleagues from the Fore River shipyard, Hollywood, the Roosevelt campaign train, the SEC, the Maritime Commission or London, his letters to mentor figures and protégés form the outermost circle to whom he was generally willing to express himself in personal terms. "As a parent," he wired a friend in 1959, "I picked out some men of great character whom I had known and tried to teach my children to follow them." Such documents convey the distinct sense that his emulation, counsel and close observation served as meticulous practice for fathering his own children.

His letters to his family and his diaries seem to be the most intimate accounts of himself that he left behind, both explicitly in statements about himself and indirectly in his commentary on national or world affairs. His letters to his children, especially when they were very young, often contain civic or self-improving messages, exhorting them to work on their handwriting, their grades, their attitudes or their eating habits. Although he had often been accused of living through his children, those who survive remember him with profound affection, gratitude, fierce loyalty and love. In his occasionally stern counsel to them as children and young adults, they recall not an effort to groom them to enact his dreams, but his single demand: that each child fulfill his or her own potential through the rigorous cultivation of his or her own particular gifts. In the height of the Depression, he wrote to Jack, then fourteen and at boarding school,

> In looking over the monthly statement from Choate, I notice there is a charge of $10.80 for suit pressing for the month of March. It strikes me that this is very high and while I want you to keep looking well, I think that if you spent a little more time picking up your clothes instead of leaving them on the floor, it wouldn't be necessary to have them pressed so often.
>
> Also, there are certain things during these times which it might not be a hardship to go without, such as the University hat.

A series of letters to his children, all written on September 10 and 11, 1940 reveal his efforts to develop political consciousness in them, whatever their ages. "I don't know whether you would have very much excitement during these raids," he wrote to Teddy, who was eight at the time.

> I am sure, of course, that you wouldn't be scared, but if you heard all these guns firing every night and the bombs bursting you might get a little fidgety. I am sure you would have liked to be with me and seen the fires the German bombers started in London. It is really terrible to think about, and all these poor women and children and homeless people down in the East End of London all seeing their places destroyed. I hope when you grow up you will dedicate your life to trying to make people happy instead of making them miserable, as war does today.

On the same day, he wrote a similar letter to fourteen-year-old Bobby. Its realism—or pessimism—makes it more accessible to the teenager than to the child, but reveals in its commentary much about the author's attitudes toward the government, the status quo and the prime minister.

> The Government is still very popular, and Churchill is, of course, the God of all. Now how long that will last when people, like those in the East End of London today, are homeless and jobless, it is difficult to say. My opinion is that the people who just see this bombing from afar and who aren't direct sufferers from it, are standing up very well, but those who have lost their homes, their friends and their jobs, are not much different from other poor unfortunates who suffered this air attack. Therefore, what the future of the Government here will be one can't say, at least for the time being.

As his children grew to adulthood and he went into semiretirement, his political career having halted abruptly following the resignation of his ambassadorship, his letters recount in his characteristic staccato the whereabouts and activities of the other children, changes in the neighborhoods of Palm Beach or Hyannis Port, the course of the war, the present administration's blunders, marriages, births and deaths. Punctuating these accounts are confidences made to his children as adults. When Kick returned to England to join the Red Cross in 1943 (and to be nearer the Englishman with whom she had fallen in love five years before), he wrote,

> Don't get too upset if you hear the British taking about your Dad. After all, the only crime I can be accused of is that I was pro-American instead of pro-English. I don't blame them for being mad at me for not wanting America to go into the war to help them out, but that wasn't my job, any more than I could be critical of Churchill for having such a terrific influence in our affairs. I resent him as an American, but I don't blame him as an Englishman. But oftentimes the British aren't that tolerant. I don't care what they say, so don't let it bother you. You have your own life to live and you needn't answer any of my problems, responsibilities or difficulties—so just smile and say, "Fight with him; he can take care of himself." After all, no one has been more sympathetic to the British cause than you, so you shouldn't have to take any of the criticism, but I'm just saying this so you'll be prepared for it. I don't mind; don't you.

As Kick met with various members of the Anglican and Roman Catholic clergy in London in a desperate effort to remain part of her Church while marrying outside of it, her father wrote her in March 1944,

> Everyone who comes home from England seems to know you . . . Scarcely a day goes by that I don't hear some report about you. The last one was that you were making converts. Maybe if you made enough of them a couple of them could take your place. If Mother ever saw that sentence I'd be thrown out in the street.

Once Kick finally decided to marry, bringing the opprobrium of Catholics and Anglicans, laity and clergy alike upon herself and her husband, Mom, who was then a teenager, remembers her father coming unexpectedly to talk to her at the convent boarding school that she attended in Connecticut. As they walked alone beside the campus lake, he told her that he wanted to be sure that she understood—whatever the nuns, her classmates, other Catholics or anyone else told her—that Kick's marriage was not a sin. He would remain adamant to the last that in marrying the man she loved she had never imperiled her soul and would eventually find her way to heaven. Among those papers that had been forgotten at the bottom of a drawer at his office, I found a crumpled scrap bearing his handwriting that read:

To Kick

No one who ever met her didn't feel that life was much better that minute. And we know so little about the next world we must think that they wanted just such a wonderful girl for themselves. We must not feel sorry for her but for ourselves.

(Written 1/2 hr after being notified of Kick's death)

As absorbing as reading and processing the letters has been, the project and my feelings about the ghosts I have come to know quite intimately through it are never unmingled with a sense of voyeurism. I have spent much of my time reading other people's mail and pouring eagerly and unceremoniously over their diaries. I have come to recognize handwriting at a glance, to be shocked, to share in the humor, joy and grief of people I don't remember well or never knew, most of whom will never know me. Growing up as I did, jointly among the living and the dead, I have seen that privacy resembles nothing so much as Pandora's box. Since Gutenberg's day, and exponentially since then, privacy once lost can never be fully recaptured. Once broadcast, utterances about lives public and private resonate either clearly and accurately or else, with even the slightest misrepresentation, can echo and amplify from one source to another, assuming a ring of veracity which they might not otherwise have had.

Grandpa's letters represent not an objective viewpoint (if such a thing can be said to exist), but rather the seminal vision of a disputed personality. They may not be the last word on Joe Kennedy, but they are unquestionably the first. While they leave certain rumored aspects of his life neither proved nor overturned, they contribute not only to what it is possible to know about him but also to the body of documentation available on such topics as Wall Street or Hollywood in the twenties, the Roosevelt administration, the nation's first systematic efforts to regulate its stock market or to create a merchant marine, the mainstreaming of Irish-Catholicism into American politics and "society," Anglo-American relations in the late thirties, America's entrance into World War II, the study of mental retardation and the development of those children to whom he gave life and helped to shape.

He was a man known not to mince words, and as such is said to have coined a number of adages: "There are no big shots," "You make your money when you buy," and "Don't get mad, get even" among them (some of which I suspect of being dubious attributions). One thing that I know him to have said, however, was "Never write anything down that you wouldn't want published on the front page of the *New York Times*." And so, in betraying a sense of expectancy in his diaries that others in successive generations would read his writings, he seems to have been as much the original editor of his posterity as he was its author.

These decaying reams of paper along with their curious (and sometimes touching) appendages have become for me a one-way mirror. They are my only direct glimpses beyond that single early memory into either Grandpa's life or the lives that he engendered, unfiltered as they are yet through the idolatry, prurience, loyalty, affection or contempt of anyone either inside or outside the family. Letters, and especially family letters, are at once the most faithful and the most distorting representations of the relations between individuals. They transfix for all time (or at least for as long as the paper holds up) those sentiments that characterize an instant in history. And yet the very need to correspond springs from the unusual circumstance of friends or family members—people who are ordinarily close to one another—being separated. They report far more completely and evocatively on the extraordinary and the unusual than they do on the most familiar and mundane aspects of life. It is odd but often moving, I have found, to touch these documents, these chronicles of lives now ended, these harbingers not only of ordinary news but occasionally of joy or inexorable grief. It is even odder, though, to read them without feeling the electric jolt that some of them—announcements of engagements, births or deaths—must have conveyed when the eyes of their intended recipients first saw them. Able to view the people and events that appear in these documents only in retrospect, watching decisions made decades ago backward through their results, I have read the letters with the clairvoyance of hindsight, knowing at every moment, as their authors and recipients did not and could not, what would happen to them next.

My mother and her surviving siblings knew their father *as a father* firsthand from the moments of their births. They grew to adulthood as he went into retirement and learned directly from his own recollections about the life he led before their lives began. I first came to know of his life from their memories of his memories, then from the investigations, assessments and impressions of others, and finally, in a way, from him. Reading those papers that he left behind—letters sent and received, diaries, receipts, stock ticker tape, V-mail, reminders, condolences, and tickets to Hialeah, the Albert Hall, or the inaugurals of 1933 or 1961—I have caught glimpses of his life as he saw it: vivid, immediate and still unretouched by hindsight.

His generation of these papers, however, was not always constant. My understanding of his life (at least from his own point of view) is circumscribed as much by his willingness to record his reflections as by his decision to save a particular document at any given moment fifty or seventy-five years in the past. And while I have come to have some sense of him through his papers, my understanding is bounded eternally by the fact that I will never know *him*. I would not recognize his voice, for example, if I were to hear it. And while I know that he had red hair and blue eyes, I can picture him as a young man only in black and white, ambling with the mechanical jaunt of the silent film star. The various and incongruous characters who appeared to me under his name as I was growing up have become a single man. While my mother's generation knew him in life, I have come to know him—and to understand my only memory dating from his lifetime—after his death.

Reading over the residua of a lifetime of activity and thought, I have often felt that in death the individual takes on a humpty-dumpty quality: the life can never be wholly or conclusively reconstructed, despite our best efforts. Once the soul or animating force quits the body, whatever trappings of that life that remain above ground are scattered to the winds—personal effects to intimates, documents to storage, memories divvied up unequally among hundreds or thousands according to their familiarity with the deceased. Finding and reading Grandpa's papers has been for me an excavation of the only remains of the life of a mind.

EDITOR'S NOTE

As the author and subject of these assembled papers recedes in hindsight with the passage of time and interest, I suspect that whatever lasting value or curiosity these documents might hold for posterity will result less from any insights that they provide into Joseph Kennedy's personality than from the vistas that his documentary record opens onto both the nation and the century that gave rise to a character such as his. My initial intention in gathering these documents together from the various places where they languished for decades was to reassemble as completely as I was able, and to preserve from imminent decay and ultimate loss, the only firsthand record of a life that has been both celebrated and condemned, but which—for better or worse—can only be called extraordinary. Having begun to reconstruct the order in which he and his many correspondents wrote them, I found them engaging, revealing, amusing, upsetting and often moving. I hope others will find them interesting as well.

Early on, I became wedded to the notion that any published by-product of my searches and squirrelings should take the form of an edition of annotated letters rather than of biography. The difference between the two, to my mind, is very much the difference between showing and telling. The letters, telegrams, cards and diary entries I collected recount the unfolding of events and the growth of personalities far more immediately, evocatively and precisely than my own descriptive powers would permit and, with all due respect to those who have treated these subjects in the past, than do any secondhand accounts I have read. The documents record his life and those lives that his touched in their own terms. In reproducing uncut versions of Joseph Kennedy's letters and journal entries, I have attempted to present them to the reader in their original state, without their truncation or mutilation, without the overlay of my own assessment. This format, I hope, allows readers to make up their own minds and the dead— about whom much has been said and supposed—to speak for themselves.

The inadvertent upshot of the concept of fair use within copyright jurisprudence was another factor in my choice of annotated letters over biography. The vast majority of the papers that Joseph Kennedy saved in his own files over the course of his lifetime are the carbons of the letters he dictated. While his own copies were filed, stored and occasionally forgotten, he sent the originals to his thousands of correspondents, who in many instances (particularly if they themselves were well known) gave their papers to various libraries and repositories over the course of time. In those archives, along with their own correspondence, letters that they received from Joseph Kennedy have been open and available (although as sources of material relating to him, many have gone untapped). It is from a few of these sources that journalists and biographers have tended to draw much of the documentary material that had previously been published about him.

Without explicit permission from a copyright holder (or from that person's estate or heirs, and so forth), historians, biographers, journalists or anyone else wishing to quote in print are limited by law either to excerpting only a small portion of any given document or to its paraphrase. In many instances the selection or paraphrase suffices to represent the spirit of the document as a whole—or, indeed, the spirit of the life as a whole. In some cases, however, a comparison of the original document in its entirety with the fractional or described counterpart that appears in print reveals disparities in emphasis: bald statements bereft of qualifying remarks, irony read literally. The selection or characterization of quotation has the potential to be as interpretive, as subjective as analysis itself. And although intended as a means of balancing the literary rights of the authors of documents such as these against the First Amendment rights of those who would assess or make use of them in print "for purposes such as criticism, comment, news reporting, teaching, . . . scholarship, or research," adherence to the doctrine of fair use results in the occasional distortion or disfiguration of the very documents at issue. It is for this reason, more than any other, that I decided to leave the documents that follow for the most part raw.

Having read both sides of Joseph Kennedy's correspondence, letters both sent and received, and whatever notes friends, enemies, colleagues and family made of their interactions with him, it occurred to me that publishing his letters and diaries by themselves would result in a somewhat lopsided and sadly anemic rendition of his life and times. For that reason, I have attempted on occasion to amplify his own writings with letters responding to his letters, notes that others made about him or their shared experiences, contemporaneously recorded gossip, newspaper clippings, memoranda—insofar at least as the copyright holders of such documents, their heirs, their estates or (barring those) fair use would permit. By this triangulation, I tried to map more precisely not only his life, but also his interactions with the many others whose lives he touched and influenced.

For one who grew increasingly circumspect about self-revelation on paper as he aged, he was explicit and unabashed perhaps more about his hopes and ambitions for his children than about any other personal characteristic. He linked his own "prestige" (to use his word) inextricably to theirs; his fortunes, his contacts, the benefit of his experience and sometimes his enemies were theirs. He would be mutely inconsolable until the end of his life at losing them. As I read over his correspondence, it became increasingly evident that to create a portrait of him through his own writings would be impossible without his children's. Inasmuch as this project is an attempt to allow the dead to speak for themselves, it is also an attempt to permit the dead—whose interrelations have been sources of veneration, controversy, analysis and speculation—to speak to one another.

Early on I lost track of the number of documents I read while compiling from attics, warehouses, archives and libraries in the United States and abroad any documents by or about Joseph Kennedy, but I believe that from start to finish I went through upward of six hundred thousand pages. In the interest of avoiding the production of a tome whose spine would be several hundred feet wide, therefore, I have not included herein a number of letters from the original assemblage.

On a few occasions throughout his life, Joseph Kennedy's circumstances both official and private required that he compose and dispatch what amounted to form letters. During his stints in government service, first as chairman of the Securities and Exchange Commission and later of the Maritime Commission, and later still as ambassador to the Court of St. James's, his daily duties demanded that he draft letters that might be applicable to numerous recipients, whether insisting on compliance with new regulations or offering invitations to tea or dinner. His files include entire boxes devoted to letters and telegrams proclaiming hearty agreement or disgust with his latest speech. He answered each, but often by drafting a few versions that might be sent interchangeably to his many unsolicited correspondents. Some of the most interesting and touching material that he saved, both in his office files and in the attic above the room where he died, are the condolence cards that he and his remaining family members received in response to the early and untimely deaths of the first two of the four children whom he was to survive. Unable to read or digest these except in small doses, he responded personally to only a few that touched him especially and left the rest to a secretary to answer. Rather than include every letter sent as part of these voluminous bulk mailings, I have instead selected prototypical documents to represent the larger corpus.

His datebooks reveal that regardless of his presence in Washington or at Grosvenor Square, his official correspondence continued unabated. Whether in or out of the office himself, legions of commissioners, diplomats, clerks and secretaries (along with his own children, in a few instances) drafted letters on his behalf, leaving their own initials in the bottom left-hand corners of the carbon copies. For the most part, such missives fell within the drafter's area of jurisdiction or expertise, or addressed routine matters taking the form of thank-you notes, requests for compliance with the commissions' regulations, or overviews for the Departments of State or Treasury of local press comment or developments in the City.

When considering letters to include in this collection, I gave preference to those he composed himself over those that, although bearing his name, were drafted (and occasionally signed) for him by others—with a few exceptions. As war approached and eventually arrived, his scheduled official duties, meetings and social engagements left him without sufficient time to draft all of his own dispatches to the State Department. On occasion he managed to write part of the wire before being called away again, at which point he would leave the rest in the hands of Herschel Johnson (the counselor of the embassy), Walton Butterworth (the Treasury representative in London), or another embassy official within whose jurisdiction the telegram fell. In other instances, particularly after Chamberlain's declaration of war in September 1939, it seems that he had only time enough to report his latest talks with government officials or diplomats to Johnson before leaving the embassy again for scheduled or impromptu engagements. His own diaries and date books often place him at meetings, luncheons or dinners at the very times that Johnson (or some other official) drafted a number of dispatches detailing the ambassador's experiences in the first person, signed them "KENNEDY," had them encoded and sent them over the wire. While I had decided in general to give preference to letters Joseph Kennedy drafted himself, I have included letters written partly or wholly for him by others when their omission would disrupt the unfolding of significant events from his own point of view—albeit once removed through the prose of another. In all such instances, I have included the names or initials of the drafter(s) as they appeared on the bottom left-hand corner of the original.

As Joseph Kennedy grew famous, and fabulous, variant estimates of his fortune were whispered, broadcast and published; and many solicitors—both known and unknown to him—began to appeal for material aid especially at a moment when America's own fortunes were temporarily, although perilously, in decline. His responses to these requests in a few instances, particularly when he had known the supplicant since his boyhood in East Boston, include advice extending beyond the realm of mere subsistence or finance into the sad personal affairs of his correspondents. Because these few letters reveal far more about the lives, medical conditions and familial relationships of people who were never public figures than they do about Joseph Kennedy himself, I have chosen to exclude them categorically from this volume. Since my early childhood I have come to regard privacy as precious and irretrievable. Having chosen to collect and publish the writings of one who managed briefly to harness the force of twentieth-century technological celebrity to his own ends, I do not believe it to be within my rights to invite the public scrutiny (however glancing) of dead men and women who never made the choice to do so for themselves—whatever their connection to him.

Given the limitations of available space in a single volume I have attempted to create a portrait of his life from a representative sampling of his papers. Overall, I have tried to select documents that contribute to a narrative continuum illustrated with documents particularly characteristic of moments or figures in history. My access to any of Joseph Kennedy's papers was in no way restricted. Further, no documents were restricted from publication in this volume. For that I am very grateful.

Among his letters to his children I have inserted in a number of instances their responses to him (and occasionally their letters to one another) insofar as these address issues raised in his letters, describe him or in some cases their authors' impressions of historical events. Because the typescripts on the pages that follow obliterate any visual clues about the authors (especially when the documents were originally handwritten), I thought it might be useful for the reader to know the ages of both writer and recipient—at least until one or other or both could safely be said to have entered adulthood at the age of, say, thirty. I have also included a number of what Rose Kennedy called her round-robin letters. With her characteristic efficiency, she acted as a sort of clearing house for information and family news while her children were in the service, abroad, working or away at school during the Second World War. In addition to providing individualized reminders about spelling or English grammar and directives to get new underwear, the letters summarize the latest news of each child for the others and, when not coauthored by their father, track his movements and activities.

Whenever possible, I have attempted to remain as faithful to the original document as possible. While leaving the substance of each intact, for the sake of uniformity I have standardized the letters by setting the author's location and the date (whenever these were available) in the upper right-hand corner. Because Joseph Kennedy dictated the bulk of his surviving correspondence, the collection exhibits a wide range of spelling variations resulting from his own peculiar pronunciation or the stenographer's particular spelling abilities and familiarity with the places, terms or figures in question. For the sake of readability, therefore, I have standardized spellings throughout the documents. That said, however, I have left intact the children's particular letter choice (to the age of fifteen) as well as spellings current and acceptable at the time that the document was written. For the sake of legibility I have separated words that ran together in the original documents and have added appropriate letters whenever an expiring typewriter ribbon or the inopportune edge of a page prevented their original recording. When it was possible to decipher words that had been scratched out, I included mistakes and rethought phrases in strikethrough. The authors' handwritten addenda or corrections to documents appear *in italics* between square brackets at the authors' intended insertion points within the bodies of a number of documents. My own addenda (for the most part words that the author left out and that I have added for the sake of readability) appear in square brackets in *plain type*. The text of each letter appears here in the sequence in which it was written, not necessarily in the order in which it appears on the original document. That is to say that I have placed postscripts and afterthoughts (often scrawled across envelope backs or above the "Dear Whoever") at the ends of letters.

Like their parents, when the Kennedy children attended memorable events, met famous people or traveled, they often recorded their experiences and afterward brought their handwritten recollections to be typed professionally at their father's office in New York. The typescripts of those documents, however, are only as reliable, as faithful to the original as the handwriting was legible and the typist adept at its decipher. One of these retyped documents—partly handwritten in his graceful hieroglyphs around the margins and across the backs of pages typed on a portable—was the travel diary that John F. Kennedy wrote during his trip to Europe in 1945 while visiting his sister in London and covering the British elections for the Hearst papers. The professionally typed version of one entry reads:

In Frankfurt deep underground in the salt mine was found nearly $300,000,000 in gold, silver, securities, and other loot. There was gold from Hungary and France. France is claiming most of it.

There were securities from France and the other countries of the world. We visited it and it was piled brick on brick — bag on bag — in the cellar of the Reichsmarch. Its ultimate disposal is still undecided.

Note:

So far, there has been no negotiation with the Russians about how much Occupation money will be printed. They have been printing marks wholesale in Berlin, they pay 4,000 marks for a watch which we have been changing at the rate of 10 for a dollar.

From Frankfurt we flew to Salzburg, where King Leopold was detained, and drove to the town of Berchtesgaden. It is a beautiful town in the mountains — the houses are alpine in architecture, and the people are well-fed and healthy. There is no bomb damage and there is plenty of wood to take the place of coal. It is a town apart from the destruction of war. We stayed at a beautiful inn for the evening after dining with the local General at the lavishly furnished building that was formerly the headquarters of General Kietal. It was reported that there were six miles of corridors underneath the main building.

The dinner consisted of about six courses — Rhine wines and champagne. After dinner they brought out some cigars taken from Goering's armored car.

In the morning we went up to Hitler's mountain home. It was completely gutted, the result of an air attack from 12,000 pound bombs by the R.A.F. in an attempt on Hitler's life.

Leaving the chalet, we drove to the very top of the mountains (about 7,000) feet) where the famed Eagle's lair was located. The road up was covered with solid rock in many places and was cleverly camouflaged. On arrival at the top, we entered a long tunnel carved through the rocks and came to an elevator which took us up through solid rock for the last 600 feet. The elevator was a double-decker — a space being left on the lower deck for the SS guard.

The lair itself had been stripped of its rugs, pictures, and tapestries, but the view was beautiful — the living room being round and facing out on every side on the valley below.

After visiting these two places, you can easily understand how that within a few years Hitler will emerge from the hatred that surrounds him now as one of the most significant figures who ever lived.

He had boundless ambition for his country which rendered him a menace to the peace of the world, but he had a mystery about him in the way he lived and in the manner of his death that will live and grow after him. He had in him the stuff of which legends are made.

At what had been their father's office, I found the handwritten version of the same events, misfiled and forgotten among hundreds of letters that the younger Kennedys had written home over the course of nine childhoods. While traveling, Jack had scribbled the account of his visits to the Reichsbank and to Berchtesgaden underneath and across the back of the description of landing in Dublin that he had typed on his portable. In his own handwriting it reads:

Note on the Reichsbank—
In Frankfurt, deep underground in a salt-mine was found nearly 300,000,000 in gold & silver and other loot. There is gold from Hungary, France, (France is claiming most of it) — securities from France and the other countries of the world. We visited it and it was packed brick on brick, bag on bag in the cellar of the Reichsbank Its ultimate disposal is still contested
Note: So far there has been no negotiations with the Russians about how much occupation money will be printed. They have been printing marks which we have been cashing in for dollars!

In the morning, we went up to Berchtesgarden, Hitler's mountain home, It was completely gutted — the result of an air-attack with 12,000 pounders by the R.A.F. in an attempt on Hitlers life. Leaving that we drove to the very top of the mountain — (about 7,000 ft.) where the former Eagle's ~~Nest~~ Lair was located. The road was carved through solid rock in many cases—and ~~at the~~ on arrival at the top, you entered a long tunnel carved through the rocks and entered an elevator which took you up the last 600 ft. The elevator was a double-decker—a space being left for the S.S. guard.

The "Lair" itself ~~was~~ had been stripped of its rugs, pictures and tapestries, but he the view was beautiful — and the living room was round and faced out everywhere on the valley below.

After visiting those two places, you can easily prophesy that within a few years Hitler will emerge as one of the most significant figures that ever lived. He was evil with boundless ambition for his country, but he had a mystery about him and the way that he lived, and at the end in his death that will live after him. He has the stuff of which legends are made.

Whatever accounts for the distinctions between these two texts (and others like them)—subsequent editing, added or merged descriptions, misread handwriting—in an effort both to demonstrate the evolution of rewritten documents and to avoid compounding misunderstandings made decades ago, I have attempted to include within this volume the earliest existing or available version of each document, to note subsequent alterations and to indicate whenever evidence suggested the disappearance of a version earlier than the one that I have used. Any new misreadings or misinterpretations of the documents on the pages that follow are therefore my own.

This book, as I have said, represents a distillation of my larger, original project of reassembling and staving off the decay of the Joseph Kennedy papers. As such, it is less an attempt to account for the life as a whole (an endeavor that I consider to fall within the province of biography) than it is an effort to reconstruct the existing documentary record of that life from within. Neither is it an attempt at objectivity, except to the extent the documents present one man's vision of himself directly rather than through the retrospective evaluations of others who never knew him or knew him only briefly—myself included. By reassembling the mosaic of his surviving writings, I hope to have reconstructed in some measure not only the portrait that he left behind of himself but also his vision of the nation that made his life possible and upon which he left his mark. And by intermingling his own writings with the records of those who—loving or hating him—knew him well, I hope that the texts themselves have given rise to a sort of documentary cubism showing the multiple facets and variant contemporaneous viewpoints of the figures who appear, and the situations that arise, on the pages that follow.

His geographical movements and his ever evolving career divided his life into a few (fairly) discrete periods; it is along these lines that I have organized his correspondence. What survived of his earliest correspondence dates from the First World War in Boston, where the family remained until the autumn of 1927 when they moved to New York and his involvement in the market as a broker gave way to the pull of the motion picture industry. His activities between 1927 and 1932 were bicoastal, spent between Hollywood and New York. After Henry Morganthau brought him into the Roosevelt camp during the election of 1932, he became increasingly involved in national politics, taking on two (in his estimation vaguely disappointing) governmental posts until the illness and death of the American ambassador to the Court of St. James's in 1937 vacated the most desirable and prestigious of the postings that the Department of State had to offer. He would begin in London at the pinnacle of his career in 1938 and leave in 1940 under a cloud. During his two and a half years as ambassador, he generated at least half the correspondence that he sent over the course of his entire lifetime and documented his dealings with what was for him an unprecedented precision and regularity. He documented his ambassadorship initially with an eye to his legacy for posterity, but eventually, as his relations with the administration deteriorated, his writings became an effort to detail what he felt was its dishonesty regarding intervention abroad and misuse of its ambassador for his anticipated self-vindication. During the period between 1941, when the president finally accepted his resignation, and 1961, when he suffered the stroke that would immobilize him until his death in 1969, he entered a state of semiretirement characterized by initial frustration at what he felt were the administration's efforts at preventing him from taking a meaningful part in the war effort and his despondency at the unexpected consequences of surgery on one of his children and the deaths of two others in the middle and late forties. He entered business again with a few ventures, such as the purchase of the Merchandise Mart in Chicago in 1945, started a charitable foundation in memory of the son he had lost during the war, and began to devote himself with renewed vigor to his remaining children's careers and through them, once again, to politics—in spite of his rather conspicuous efforts to remain behind the scenes.

Since letters, memoranda and diaries are both the most exact, immediate accounts of moments in time and the patchiest in the irregularity of their recording, I have included introductions to each section—Boston, New York and Hollywood, Washington, London and his semiretirement—that attempt to provide background information and make connections between the documents and the individuals mentioned in them that might not be self-evident. These brief introductions are by no means intended to serve as a comprehensive biographical account of his life. Rather, through them I have attempted to provide an overview (if only an impressionistic one) of the documents that follow. I hope I have done justice both to the documents and to the figures who authored and appear in them.

PART I

Boston

1914–1927

Given the volume of paper that Joseph Kennedy generated and kept over the course of his eighty-one years—miles of carbon copies, letters received from a staggering variety of correspondents, newspaper clippings, diaries, nearly completed drafts of the ghostwritten diplomatic memoir that he never published, pamphlets and speeches in support of the first three presidential candidacies of Franklin Roosevelt, private memoranda repudiating "the bastard" at the time of the fourth, detailed narratives recounting meetings with "Important People"; cards, telegrams and V-mail from his nine children—it is unfortunate as well as surprising that the earliest surviving documentation of his life dates from his late twenties, during the First World War, when he was assistant general manger of the Fore River Shipyard near Boston. Even his wife, who had known him since her childhood, saved family mementos and letters with a fortuitous jealousy and who took decades' worth of diary notes in anticipation of someday publishing an autobiography, began to document their relationship only at the time of their wedding, in October 1914. Her husband's sole surviving reflections upon his childhood, schooling and youth are retrospective, appearing in a few interviews and among many thousands of letters written decades later as occasional glimpses of a favorite teacher or priest, a baseball game, after-school or summertime jobs, advice imparted by his father. What remains of the young Joseph Kennedy has survived for the most part through others as a composite portrait drawn from memory, contemporaneous sources varying in their familiarity with the figure in question (and sometimes ungaugeable in their accuracy) and layer upon layer of ongoing reassessment.

The surviving documents that predate the family's move from Boston to New York in September 1927 are unusual among the larger aggregate of Kennedy family papers. The earliest, dating from the mid-1910s, were filed and saved only haphazardly. Many of the events described in the letters of the period—business deals, stock purchases, initial acquaintances with individuals who appear throughout the later correspondence—survive in their own documentary archipelago, the underlying connective geography submerged, almost impenetrable and unchartable except by means of speculation. A number of events known or rumored to have occurred during the period—his witnessing the Wall Street bombing of 1920, his manipulation of the Yellow Cab Company stock in the spring of 1924 or his involvement in the sale of "intoxicating liquors" during Prohibition, to mention only a few—come down to posterity through interviews he granted some time later, through independent documentation, later revelations or the recollections of others. Little or no mention is made contemporaneously of such events or of his involvement in them among the papers that he kept. Likewise, little of the professional correspondence he must have generated in the late 1910s and early 1920s remains among his own papers. Nothing pertaining to him has survived in the archives either of Bethlehem Steel's Fore River Shipyard or of the brokerage firm of Hayden, Stone and Company, where he worked during the First World War and immediately after the Armistice. The family correspondence, which was to become an extensive epistolary web over the coming decades (particularly before the postwar boom in long-distance telephone usage in the late 1940s), did not yet exist as such. Before 1927 the younger Kennedy children were toddlers, infants or not yet born, their elder siblings only just then in the throes of learning to write. Their mother, conscious of the unusual opportunities she had been afforded as the daughter of the mayor of Boston in meeting dignitaries and celebrities, in witnessing important events and in traveling and attending school abroad, had kept extensive diaries as a young girl and would do so again in middle age as her children left for school and her husband's changing career allowed her more time both to travel and to reflect. As a young mother managing a series of ever-growing households, however, her diary-keeping dwindled and all but lapsed in the decade and a half following her wedding. She managed to write with some regularity throughout 1923 and occasionally in 1924 and 1926, but her daily recollections and reflections amounted to no more than several lines each. Moreover, because her husband's business interests tended to take him only as far as New York until the midtwenties, the couple seemed seldom to have the need to correspond in the early years of their marriage. As a result, Joseph Kennedy's personal and professional life is far more scantily documented in the period leading up to the family's move out of Boston (both from within and without) than it was to become over the coming decades.

"I think he could have been a showman had he started out that way," the journalist Mark Sullivan would observe soon after meeting the new chairman of the Securities and Exchange Commission during the infernal Washington summer of 1934. "[B]ut I suspect," Sullivan continued, "[that] all that characteristic of him has been rather submerged by the traits of mind he developed in business." Sullivan it seems, had either forgotten or had never seen the flamboyant Film Booking Offices posters outside a growing number of movie palaces or the full-page advertisements so prominent in the film industry trade journals during the previous decade. "Master Showman Joseph P. Kennedy," these announced, was proud to present FBO's latest feature beneath an enthusiastic cameo of the master showman himself, grinning and bespectacled after the manner of Harold Lloyd. Showmanship had in fact been Joseph Kennedy's business until only a few years earlier, and indeed, even his honeymoon had been devoted in large part both to sporting and theatrical entertainments and to forming (or perhaps to strengthening) contacts in the industry that would make him much of his fortune through midlife.

With a recently declared war in Europe and a newly opened series of locks permitting maritime travel across the Americas' narrowest span rather than around their southernmost point, William Cardinal O'Connell of Boston married twenty-six-year-old Joseph Patrick Kennedy to twenty-four-year-old Rose Elizabeth Fitzgerald in the private chapel of his residence on the morning of October 7, 1914. Returning from their honeymoon, the couple settled into their new home in Brookline, Massachusetts, the groom resuming the presidency of the Columbia Trust Company (a small bank that his father had helped to found that catered to the financial needs of the immigrant communities of the Kennedys' native East Boston), the bride awaiting the "precious little package" who would arrive during the following summer to take his father's name. Two years later, shortly after Congress's declaration of war, the second of the Kennedy children (this one named for his ebullient maternal grandfather, former Boston Mayor John Fitzgerald) would follow.

Objecting as he would throughout his life to the slaughter of American boys in conflicts not directly touching upon American interests, the young banker did not volunteer for active duty but rather resigned his post at Columbia Trust to become assistant general manager of Bethlehem Steel's Fore River Shipyard, a fact which resulted in cooled relations between himself and a number of his friends and contemporaries. Among the earliest and most fragile of the Joseph P. Kennedy papers is a crumbling conscription questionnaire entitled "Claim for Exemption or Deferred Classification."

In it, "Series X: Dependency," is demarcated with large, handwritten Xs. Series X applied to those having "a wife, or child or aged, infirm, or invalid parents or grandparents, or brother under 16 or sister under 18 years of age, or a helpless brother or sister of whatever age mainly dependent on [the registrant's] physical or mental labor for support." Despite having a wife, two small children and a third on the way, and despite Bethlehem's arguments about the young Kennedy's indispensability to the yard and thereby to the war effort itself, the District 5 Board continued proceedings to draft the assistant general manager into active duty, perhaps because of his admission to having "absolutely no technical knowledge of shipbuilding." The district board's efforts were only halted, apparently, by appeal to higher authority. On February 25, 1918, Joseph Powell, Bethlehem Shipbuilding's vice president, wired the chief of the Emergency Fleet Corporation's Industrial Service Department, Meyer Bloomfield, the prewar pioneer of the personnel management and vocational training movements, "the new profession of handling men":

> MR. KENNEDY WHO IS ASSISTANT GENERAL MANAGER OF FORE RIVER PLANT TELLS ME THAT HE HAS BEEN PLACED IN CLASS 1 OF THE DRAFT IN SPITE OF MY PERSONAL APPEAL TO THE BOARD STOP THERE ARE NOT OVER SIX MEN IN THIS ESTABLISHMENT WHOSE LOSS AT THIS TIME WOULD BE FELT AS MUCH AS KENNEDY'S AND FOR HIM TO BE PUT IN CLASS 1 IS INEXCUSABLE FROM ANY POINT OF VIEW STOP WHAT CAN YOU DO TO HELP US OUT STOP

Evidently Bloomfield did help them out and Joseph Kennedy remained assistant general manager until seven months after the Armistice.

What remains of the assistant general manager's correspondence survives largely because it was, like his and the management's appeals to the draft board, partly personal in nature and was filed therefore among his own papers. Bethlehem Steel's papers, by contrast, were divided up after the company's sale to General Dynamics in 1964 and parceled out to suitable repositories near the company's various shipbuilding plants on either coast, almost entirely weeded of correspondence in order to make room for blueprints, plans and photographs of the ships themselves. With the discarded papers likely went whatever correspondence may have existed, for example, between the assistant general manager of the Fore River plant and the assistant secretary of the navy, Franklin Delano Roosevelt. "We never got along then," Kennedy recalled on the Roosevelt campaign train shortly before Election Day in 1932. "He would laugh and smile and give me the needle, but I could not help but admire the man. We had great confidence in him . . . and we made millions of dollars worth of supplies for the government with no more authority than a telephone call from him." Gone too (perhaps as a result of archival weeding or perhaps because the negotiations were carried out face-to-face and over the ephemeral medium of the telephone) is nearly all documentation, save Joseph Kennedy's recollections recorded by interviewers some years later, regarding a payment dispute over two Argentine dreadnoughts returned to the Fore River Yard for premature repairs only a few years after their launchings. Argentina refused to pay for the improvements; Bethlehem Steel refused to release the ships. Roosevelt and Charles Schwab squabbled over the issues of payment and release. The assistant secretary of the navy made the case that the Argentine government should be made to feel "secure" doing business in the United States and that the Department of State would collect fees. The president of Bethlehem Steel argued (through Assistant General Manager Kennedy of the Fore River yard, whom he had deputized to negotiate) for immediate settlement. "Roosevelt was the hardest trader I ever came up against," the ambassador to the Court of St. James's would recall of the president who had recently appointed him, two decades after armed marines arrived to remove the battle ships from Fore River and conduct them into the hands of the Argentine government, ". . . I was so disappointed and angry that I broke down and cried." Indeed these initial interactions between the two men would prefigure their last.

The corpus of documentation available on the assistant general manager's official duties at Fore River has survived, therefore, pale and thin alongside its more robust and intact unofficial counterpart, much of it concerning the fortunes of the Fore River baseball team relative to the rest of the Bethlehem Steel League. Kennedy's immediate superior, dismayed by what he described as the "amateur stuff" that he had witnessed on the yard's baseball diamond over the summer of 1918, strongly encouraged him to improve both the team's roster and its results. The upshot was a flurry of letters revealing heated intramural jealousies on all sides, careful accountings of the number of genuine work days that the opposing teams' best players (many of them prewar professional stars, including Shoeless Joe Jackson and Babe Ruth) had spent in their respective shipyards, attempts to backdate the documentation of players' arrivals, indignant protests and ingratiating appeals.

Over the course of the autumn of 1918, as the influenza epidemic decimated the shipyard's workforce and as the assistant general manager worked around the clock attempting to find available space that might be converted to house and treat the sick, a clipping in Rose Kennedy's scrapbook announced that on Friday, September 13, 1918,

> a dainty daughter was added to the nursery which previously sheltered two sturdy sons . . . Rose Marie was the name bestowed upon the infant, who was christened Thursday, its sponsors being the father's sister, Miss Margaret Kennedy, of Winthrop, and Mr. Edward Moore.

"A brilliant future is predicted for the baby," the clipping added.

With peace restored, the father of three small children began looking for new opportunities. Returning from the three-month convalescence that had resulted from nervous and physical exhaustion in the spring of 1919, he attempted to interest Galen Stone, the cofounder of the brokerage house of Hayden, Stone and Company, in some of the yard's surplus ships. The interview, conducted on board a New York–bound train, resulted not in the sale of the ships but rather in Stone's hiring a new broker and manager for the firm's Boston office. On June 30, 1919, Assistant General Manager Kennedy resigned his post at Fore River, leaving the plant as "one of its greatest rooters," a sentiment which would be transformed into something of a "hostile mental attitude" in the wake of the fracas over the yard management's early termination of his contract to run the plant's restaurant a year later.

Like so many of the Bethlehem Steel papers, much of the routine daily correspondence that Hayden, Stone's Boston brokers must have generated over the course of the early 1920s appears to have been weeded and discarded before arriving at its present home in the Harvard Business School Archives. Likewise, most of what survives of Joseph Kennedy's Hayden, Stone–related correspondence among his own papers is partly personal in nature. His trading many of the stocks with which he became familiar at work on behalf of family and friends, his exchanging (perhaps overly well-informed) tips with colleagues in the financial realm, and his continued intervention into the management of the Columbia Trust Company, all the while acting in the capacity of broker and manager at Hayden, Stone, were indicative not only of the nebulous boundaries between his personal and professional financial interests, but also of the freedom which both the firm and contemporary banking and securities law (or lack thereof) permitted brokers in the early 1920s. Much of his correspondence from the period concerns favors extended and received, a form of financial patronage not unlike that practiced by his father and father-in-law in Boston's political realm. For friends and their family members there were job recommendations, thank-you notes for suggesting pay raises to a number of employers, appointments or promotions resulting from the right words whispered in the right ears, travel reservations secured through hotel managers whose investments he oversaw. He offered investment opportunities to uncles and cousins. As his parents and in-laws grew older, the business of paying hospital bills and settling estates fell increasingly to him. To old family friends he suggested investments with which he had first become acquainted at Hayden, Stone and of which he had taken advantage himself. "As to Eastern Steamship," he told Dr. John Bottomley, a summertime friend from the seaside village of Cohasset, "I think it is a remarkably cheap stock at this price and I have bought some myself from $85. down and would not hesitate to advise its purchase." At the close of his first full year at Hayden, Stone, on New Year's Eve 1920, he wrote a friend in Palm Beach, "I really ought to be ashamed of myself for not acknowledging your great kindness in sending us the grapefruit and oranges, but, to be truthful, I have spent most of the days scheming how to keep my friends and myself cut out of the hands of the ever watchful creditors." To colleagues and associates in finance he pointed out opportunities, exchanged tips with them and followed their leads. At the market's low during the depression of 1921, he wrote Alfred Wellington at Columbia Trust, "Confidentially, I am not sure but what the Shawmut Bank stock that we own should be sold." Bob Potter, his old college friend and the current vice president of Shawmut itself, he explained, ". . . had 100 shares with us at Hayden's here, and with all secrecy proceeded to dispose of it the other day at around 198." To his friend Matt Brush, widely known in the 1920s as the "prince of speculators," he suggested, "more and more it occurs to me that there are unlimited possibilities with you[r] connections to make a lot of money. I wish sometime we could sit down for an hour or so and perhaps I could point out numerous ways. Up to date, I have been fairly successful in doing that."

Although he had resigned from the Columbia Trust Company's presidency "on forty-eight hours notice" to be succeeded by his father in October 1917, he maintained close ties to the bank and its management throughout the early 1920s. Indeed, the Columbia Trust letterhead continued to bear his name as president for some time after his official departure. Making use of the bank examiner's training that he had received shortly after graduating from college, he paid careful attention to Columbia's books, took it upon himself to strategize about the collection of overdue loans and attempted to alert the present management to potential legal or financial liabilities, particularly in instances that might affect his father. In addition to suggesting friends' investments and placing buy and sell orders for their stocks, he encouraged the bank to provide loans to them and intervened occasionally to extend their credit past the originally agreed upon deadlines. His energy for keeping himself, his family and friends "out of the hands of the ever watchful creditors" while holding down his job at Hayden, Stone; maintaining his involvement with Columbia Trust; overseeing the affairs of both his extended and (constantly growing) immediate families and looking for business opportunities on the side abated occasionally, it seems. "Tim Reardon is obliged to raise $900 and I am prepared to give it to him," he wrote his old mentor, Alfred Wellington, Columbia Trust's treasurer, in October 1921, "but I have been taking care of so many people lately that I would rather get out of it if I can. He has security for this $900 and if you can see your way clear to make him a loan I would appreciate it." The Columbia Trust secretarial staff handled his bank-related correspondence, kept him abreast of bank affairs and overdue loans, and acted as private bankers and accountants to his immediate family, transacting his suggested tinkerings between their accounts and the investments he made for them, and occasionally transferring funds which were in effect short-term loans from the bank itself. So closely bound up were his personal financial affairs with the bank's, in fact, that he filed his family's financial correspondence under the heading of "Columbia Trust Co. - Family Finances."

The Columbia Trust secretarial staff oversaw the paperwork for his and his family's sideline business ventures, keeping his accounts not only for his early forays into the local entertainment industry but also for his efforts to sell off the alcohol that his father had stored immediately before the Eighteenth Amendment took effect in 1920 and rendered the manufacture, sale and transportation (although, oddly, as it has often been noted, not the possession) of "intoxicating liquors" unconstitutional. Over the course of the early twenties, the surviving alcohol-related correspondence indicates that he acted as an agent of sorts in selling off some of his father's sherry, port and brandy stores as well as a number of vintage French wines and champagnes to his business associates, friends and former Harvard classmates (who would enthusiastically, dub him "decennial Santa Clause" amidst the hilarity of their tenth reunion in 1922).

As Hayden, Stone diversified its interests in the postwar boom, the firm began to investigate new technologies and allowed a number of its young brokers not only the apparent freedom to pursue their personal financial affairs, but also to specialize within the firm according to their own interests. Soon after starting at Hayden, Stone in the summer of 1919, "Joe made a week-end trip to Maine with me to visit Bill Gray, who was one of the original pioneers in moving pictures," a friend, Joe Conway, would recall three decades later.

> Within the previous two years Gray had started several small picture houses [the Maine and New Hampshire Theatres Company], first at Portsmouth, New Hampshire, later at several cities in Maine including Lewiston, the headquarters. At that time the picture business had no credit standing with the banks, and all transactions were for cash.
>
> On Sunday of the week-end, Gray discussed the picture business with Joe and I recall Joe's remark to me after listening to Gray. He said, "What's this fellow Gray giving me, good stories for all[,]" and my answer to Joe was "I have known Gray several years and never knew him to exaggerate". About then Gray returned to join us and in Joe's presence I told him what Joe sayd [sic]. Gray then insisted we leave the cottage at the lake, go to Lewiston and seek his books. His results were astounding and our drive back to Boston Joe, with his great insight into the future said, "Joe[,] this is another telephone and we must get into this business."

The young financier attempted immediately to join Gray in Maine and New Hampshire's management, expansion and financing, but because of Gray's partner's unwillingness to sell, came only as close as serving the company as an intermittent adviser over the course of the 1920s. His interest in the film industry piqued, but with no outlet for his cash or for what seem to have been his budding managerial aspirations, he continued to search out moneymaking opportunities for Hayden, Stone, for his family, his friends, his associates and himself (although perhaps not necessarily in that order) in a field which held little interest at the time for the banking or brokerage communities at large. He became involved in various phases of the industry through a number of small concerns, acting as an investor in and adviser to the Boston-based Columbia Film Company, operating the local Universal Film franchise briefly in 1920 and 1921, and attempting without success to interest Babe Ruth (whom Harry Frazee, Red Sox owner and financially strapped theatrical producer, had recently sold to the New York Yankees) in a picture contract. In late 1919 he invested no less than eighty-six thousand dollars in the Hallmark distribution concern, which promptly declared bankruptcy, and served as treasurer throughout the early twenties to the newly formed Fred Stone Production Company, in which, he lamented, "there isn't any money . . ."

"[M]y experience in the picture business with my own money, and, in some instances, with that of my friends, has been very disastrous, due, very likely, to our ignorance of the business and our childlike simplicity in taking stock in anybody in the motion picture business," he confessed in September 1920 in response to one Rufus S. Cole's request for his services in refinancing (and hopefully selling off) the floundering Robertson-Cole Film Company on behalf of Graham's of London and the failing Anglo-Indian merchant bank, Cox and Co. Despite his official role as financial adviser, the young financier involved himself almost immediately in the minutiae of Robertson-Cole's daily operations, overseeing story lines and casting decisions, hiring directors and writers, insisting on distribution arrangements and plotting "propaganda" and "exploitation" strategies.

At home in Brookline, his family continued to grow. On February 20, 1920, Joe Junior and Rosemary received their new sister, Kathleen. On the day of her birth, however, two-year-old Jack came down with scarlet fever, requiring that he be treated both for his own and for the newborn's safety "At City Hospital Boston - with Dr. Hill - Dr. Reardon," rather than at home, their mother's card catalog of childhood illnesses recorded. By early March, Jack was out of danger, but not yet fully recovered and so was sent to the Mansion House Hotel in Poland Springs, Maine, where a number of his relatives visited him in the care of one Mrs. Sara Miller. Returning home two months later, only a few weeks before his third birthday, his nurse reported to his parents that he had been "an excellent little patient" and that after meeting his baby sister at last, seemed "very happy."

The family correspondence as well as the diary that Rose Kennedy kept as a young mother in the early 1920s, while scanty compared with similar documents generated in later decades, record the "great extravagance" of summers spent at the beach on Boston's South Shore (where they continued to vacation even after the rejection of the family's application to the largely Episcopalian Cohasset Golf Club in the summer of 1922); the purchase of a pony for Christmas in 1920; thumb sucking; discussions of "bedbugs and cooties"; the arrival of Eunice, who would become "the best little talker of all" in 1921; and the budding personalities of each of the children. Edward Moore, the former assistant to Boston Mayors Fitzgerald, Curley and Peters, became Joe Kennedy's assistant and confidant from the mid-1920s onward. At the same time Moore became the Kennedy children's honorary uncle, mentor and occasional baby-sitter and would go on to record their early lives before they were themselves capable of writing, or indeed of speaking or remembering. When Joe Junior was "about 7 months old," Moore recalled, the infant accompanied his parents to Poland Springs "for winter sports."

They decided one day to take Joe for a ride on a sled, so they got a soap box, had it nailed to the sled, bundled Joe up as it was pretty cold, in shawls, and put their snow shoes on and started off. After they had traveled a little distance across the fields they looked back to see how Joe was getting along but here was no Joe, the sled had turned over at one of the rough spots and Joe had fallen out. They went back about an eighth of a mile and there was Joe lying on his back laughing and cooing.

One day in Brookline,

The Governess had Jack all dressed and they were all ready for a walk. She left him for a minute to get her coat and hat and while she was gone Jack climbed through the nursery bathroom window on the roof of an ell. When the nurse returned she couldn't find him but she could hear his voice calling to some of his little friends in the street. She spied Jack and tried to coax him to come in, but he was having too much fun to pay any attention to her. She called his mother and they tried to entice him in with candy and toys, but he refused to budge. They were afraid to go out and get him, because they thought he might try to fun [sic] away and fall off the roof. When he had all the fun he wanted out there he came in himself. Everyone was pretty much disturbed about it, because it was a 30 feet [sic] drop to the ground.

When Galen Stone retired at the end of 1922, his protégé realized his long-held aspiration of going into business for himself, setting up shop down the hall from Hayden, Stone at 87 Milk Street in Boston as "Joseph P. Kennedy, Banker" in the new year. While continuing the attempted sale of Robertson-Cole to several parties, he took on new, varied and occasionally unorthodox ventures, ranging from theatrical advertising to stock manipulation. In early 1924 Walter Howey, the editor of the Hearst papers' *Boston American* which had looked favorably upon former Mayor John F. Fitzgerald's unsuccessful gubernatorial bid in 1922, approached Fitzgerald's financier son-in-law for financial help. The apparent operation of a hostile pool threatened not only the value of John Hertz's Yellow Cab stock or the company's imminent expansion to New York from Chicago, but also Howey's investment of the bulk of his savings in the company. Hertz and his vice president, Charles McCullogh, provided the young banker and Edward Moore with $5 million, borrowed in Chicago. They then attempted to thwart the raiders' efforts by secretly driving the stock up and down at random, ultimately supporting and buoying its price through its countermanipulation from a room at the New York Waldorf-Astoria. Having been holed up in the Waldorf-Astoria for more than a month, Kennedy returned home in late May 1924 suffering from acute neuritis and not yet having met his newest daughter Patricia.

The refinancing of Robertson-Cole completed but with no offers forthcoming for its purchase, Kennedy began to attempt to buy it himself. In the summer of 1925 he boarded that "regular floating palace," the *Aquitania*, amidst a group of fellow passengers who "would make any one sick even if the ocean didn't," and set sail for England in order to discuss the purchase of Robertson-Cole and its renamed distribution arm, Film Booking Offices of America, by a syndicate he had assembled in Boston. Despite "extensive palaver" with Lord Inverforth of Lloyd's, however, there would be no sale in 1925. In February 1926, however, while leaving the Harvard Club in New York after a stopover on his way to Palm Beach for a vacation, a bellboy called him back to the telephone. Reappearing after several minutes, *The Irish World and American Industrial Liberator* reported him to have said, " 'You go ahead, Ed.' (meaning his chum Mr. E. Moore), 'I think I've just bought a moving picture concern.' " By summertime, FBO's first feature entirely produced under the company's new ownership was ready for release. *Bigger than Barnum's* (along with the vaudeville accompaniment of the clairvoyant Princess Wah-Leh-Kah, "an Indian girl, . . . ready to tell whatever you wish to know") opened at the newest of the Olympia Theatres on Boston's Washington Street on August 3, 1926. "We will produce photoplays filled with fast action, drama, comedy, romance and thrills—and worthy always of being witnessed by every member of an American family," the new president and chairman of the board of directors of FBO announced at the premiere. "[The motion picture industry] is no longer a 'game,' as it once was, but a well-balanced conservatively operated enterprise, and I see nothing at all incongruous in a banker and business man like myself being also a showman," he told his audience.

Having come to think of himself as a bona fide "picture man," he devised the idea of the Harvard Business School's examining those aspects of the motion picture industry that he had encouraged to be "conducted along sound, common sense lines" according to traditional business principles over the course of his eight years' involvement. He counted on Harvard's participation by agreeing to endow a film archive within the university's fine arts department and by providing the university itself with favorable publicity. He managed to flatter and cajole some of his colleagues, many of them the industry's pioneers (and many of them then in the throes of litigation with one another), into addressing "the oldest of American universities" on "the youngest of . . . arts." Will Hays (the new motion picture "czar" who had been appointed to oversee the industry's self-regulation in the wake of a series of scandals and lurid revelations) addressed the class on "Supervision from Within." Paramount-Famous-Lasky was particularly well represented at the lectures with Jesse Lasky, the executive vice president, speaking on "Production Problems"; Adolph Zukor, the president, on "The Origin and Growth of the Industry"; and the general manager, Sydney R. Kent, on "Distributing the Product." Robert Cochrane, the Universal vice president who had "invented the 'big splash' and 'loud colors' and other devices for attracting attention," addressed the class on "Advertising Motion Pictures." Dr. Attilio H. Giannini, president of the Bowery and East River National Bank and a pioneer in film finance, spoke on "Financial Aspects." An "outspoken advocate of free competition" and the president and founder of the then-independent Fox Film Corporation, William Fox would recount his "Reminiscences and Observations" of the short history of the film industry. Although seriously ill, Marcus Loew, then president of both Metro-Goldwyn Pictures and of Loew's Incorporated, the theater chain he had founded, would describe the historical relationship between "The Motion Picture and Vaudeville" only a few months before his death. In his lecture on "Future Developments," Harry Warner, the president of Warner Brothers, described a device that would "revolutionize the industry by adding one more miracle, greater than all the rest" in bringing sound to the motion picture. Using Vitaphone, Warner announced to the class ". . . we intend to bring out the actors' singing and the actual performance of each person on the stage," and revealed, "[o]ur first picture embodying that feature will be 'The Jazz Singer,' with Al Jolson." At thirty-three, Sam Katz, who ran his Publix Theaters "as carefully as a Ford factory" and went so far as to issue "printed manuals of instruction for employees," was the youngest of the speakers to appear before the class in his lecture on "Theatre Management." After an "unavoidable" spring break of three weeks to accommodate the remaining speakers' schedules, Cecil B. DeMille would describe the process of "Building a Photoplay"; Earl Hammons, the president of Educational Pictures, would address "Short Reels and Educational Subjects"; and finally, Milton Sills, one of the most luminous stars in First National's firmament, would cover "The Actor's Part."

The lectures' organizer and president of FBO would in the coming autumn find his renown to have overspilled the bounds of the film and financial press for the first time since he was elected "America's Youngest Bank President" at Columbia Trust more than a decade earlier. The journalist John B. Kennedy wrote him in late August 1927,

> I'm writing your story for the *American Magazine,* which means that the press department of F.B.O. should take care not to personalize you in any but movie publication[s] until they have time to print it. You know the *American Magazine* has a whale of a circulation, more than 2,400,000 and is the paradise of self-made men.

"[I]ncidentally," Kennedy added, "I'll have to sign it with another name, to prevent it looking like a brother act." The result, "Joe Kennedy Has Never liked any Job He's Tackled," (published under John B. Kennedy's real name) appeared in the May 1928 issue, and marked a turning point in Joseph Kennedy's sense of personal publicity. Not long after, he would engage a clipping service to track similar appearances in the national press. Through his experience with film publicity, advertising and politics over the course of the decade, he had begun to develop an instinct for the possibilities of promotional cross-pollination that the media and new technologies were increasingly providing.

In the theater, for example, he saw not only the potential for theatrical or cinematic profit, but also, in effect, a new source of billboard space. One of the sideline ventures that he founded following his departure from Hayden, Stone specialized in "theatrical scenic advertising." The Columbia Advertising Agency arranged for the names and logos of a variety of companies (many of whose stocks he had traded at Hayden, Stone) to be painted directly onto the backdrops that formed the street scenes for the vaudeville entertainments that preceded the picture shows. By 1924, Columbia Advertising operated in cinemas throughout the Northeast and the South as well. "With newspapers being filled up the way they are with advertising, and billboards being abolished, theatre advertising offers the big solution of the problem," he wrote a colleague at the Maine and New Hampshire Theatres Company in October 1924. Although his Columbia Advertising endeavors were not ultimately especially successful, new methods of generating publicity, such as the English Cineplex and Multiplex machines that allowed for the rotation and display of several advertisements on the same billboard, continued to attract his attention.

Throughout the Joseph Kennedy correspondence files from the early twenties, there are notes to priests, local theater managers and scriptwriters alike thanking them for inserting a good word about former Mayor Fitzgerald's latest candidacy into their sermons or musical comedies. His philosophy of publicity and his promotional practices would continue to evolve over the course of his life. In the thirties, after the repeal of Prohibition, Kennedy would encourage popular mystery writers to make mention in their latest thrillers of some of the spirits that his Somerset Importers represented. "[A]s I have said a thousand times," he would remind his son Bobby in 1955, by way of advising the young prosecutor with larger political aspirations how best to publicize the latter's upcoming trip with Justice William O. Douglas, "things don't happen, they are made to happen in the public relations field." In an effort to give a ring of historical veracity to FBO's 1927 production of *Jesse James* (and to quell Will Hays's concerns the film might appear to promote lawlessness and banditry), the financier hired the outlaw's grandson as a consultant. Attempting to generate publicity for the film's release, he went to some trouble to ascertain whether any members of the original James gang were still alive and available to attend the premiere.

By the twenties the young banker with far-flung interests seems to have conceived of fame as a transitive property; earned in one realm, renown could be exploited in many others. From the time of his early and unsuccessful efforts to cast Babe Ruth, he gravitated toward featuring athletes, celebrities, politicians or national heroes—people who were already nationally well-known in their respective fields—in his films. Increasingly, it seems, he attempted to enlist the support of celebrities in promoting his product, whether his motion pictures or his father-in-law. Of a 1927 FBO premiere, the *Exhibitor's Herald* noted that

> [u]nusual tribute was paid to a motion picture and its producers when Mayor James J. Walker attended a private showing of "Red" Grange's football picture, "One Minute to Play," in the Film Booking Offices projection room . . . as the guest of Joseph P. Kennedy, F.B.O. President. Always a lover of sports, "Jimmy" was delighted with the picture. "It is real thrilling entertainment, and bound to please everyone," the Mayor said. "Red" is great!

If a political figure could rally publicity and support for popular entertainment, then a popular entertainer could, by the same token, lend interest to politics, as Frank Sinatra's "High Hopes" for Jack's 1960 campaign would demonstrate. While Fred Stone's reputation and popularity in musical comedy helped him make the natural transition from stage to screen, the former treasurer of Fred Stone Productions continued to attempt to capitalize on fame earned outside the cinematic realm. He cast prominent young athletes such as track and field star and former Nevada State Boy Scout Commissioner Fred Thomson and football All-American Red Grange (in whom he envisioned "a fine manliness" and the potential to develop "into a splendid motion picture player").

His instinct for what were in the twenties called "exploitation" and "propaganda" would serve him and become increasingly refined throughout his life. In the late summer of 1927, as the family prepared to move from Massachusetts to New York, Kennedy also attempted (unsuccessfully as it turned out) to engage young Captain Lindbergh, recently landed at Le Bourget, in a film contract. "I think [Lindbergh] has the most tremendous hold on the country that any individual has ever had," he remarked that summer, prefiguring the telegram that his friend Lord Beaverbrook would send to Winston Churchill about his own son shortly before election day in 1960: "IT SEEMS TO ME THAT AMERICA REGARDS KENNEDY WITH SIMILAR HYSTERIA SHOWN FOR LINDBERGH HALF A CENTURY AGO AND HE WILL WIN."

Rose Kennedy: *"Early Life"*

Before we were married we bought a small home[1] — a simple wooden dark green building — in fact rather a common looking little house in Brookline — a town about 20 minutes by subway from Boston — It had a living room — a small dng *[sic]* room and kitchen downstairs. Upstairs there was our bedroom two other bedrooms & on the top floor two maid's rooms. It was not as luxurious as any of my friends' houses, who had had new houses given them, but it was very compact & comfortable, and in a pleasant neighborhood & more accessible to Boston than it would have been living near to my parents. One of my friends sent me her maid — a gay neat Irish girl who cooked & served & made the beds at 7-00 a week & made us quite happy. It was not long before we realized that a precious little package was on its way to bless our house & we started making plans — we decided to take a little home near the sea for the summer — a great extravagance it seems to me now as we had no money at the time.[2]

Now that my several children have grown up to be over twenty yrs. old — I suppose I have arrived at the blissful state which so many people talked about when they were little and I was a young matron, namely, "You have such a wonderful family & it will be so lonely when they are grown up." But I wonder sometimes if it is quite as nice as I thought it would be & as they told me it would be. When I look back now, I wonder at the colossal size of the job & I think that when we stood as a blushing radiant gay young bride & groom [*it was lucky*] we were not able to look ahead & see nine little helpless infants with our responsibility to turn them into men & women who were mentally morally & physically perfect, how would we have felt — But as the pious old Irish nun in the Convent used to say — Pray to our dear Lord & that is what we did — as that is all we could do.

Rose Fitzgerald Kennedy, 24: *Wedding Log*

Married at the Cardinal's Chapel at nine o'clock on Wednesday, October seventh.[3] Wedding pictures taken at home before and after the ceremony. Bouquet of white orchids and lilies of the valley. Pictures for papers snapped outside Cardinal's house. Reception at house. Later left for New York on one o'clock stopped at Hotel Belmont. Had luncheon at Claridge's went to ride in Arthur Goldsmith's[4] machine. Later dined with him at ——— [*sic*]. Went to see Douglas Fairbanks in "He Comes Up Smiling."[5] Father[6] & John[7] arrive on way to World Series Games.

Left on Friday morning for Philadelphia where we met all the Royal Rooters,[8] led by father. Took in the game in the afternoon and waited for the second game on Saturday

1. On August 20, 1914, JPK had made a two-thousand-dollar down payment on the nine-room house at 83 Beals Street in Brookline, Massachusetts.
2. Joseph Patrick Kennedy, Jr. (1915–44), would be born on July 25, 1915 in his parents' rented summer home at Nantasket Beach, Massachusetts.
3. They were married at the cardinal's residence by William Cardinal O'Connell (1860–1944), archbishop of Boston, 1911–44.
4. After graduating along with JPK in the Harvard College Class of 1912, Arthur Jacob Goldsmith (1891–1964) had joined his father's jewelry manufacturing firm, Goldsmith, Stern & Co., the source of the bride's engagement ring.
5. Douglas Fairbanks, Sr. (1884–1939), had opened on Broadway at The Liberty a month earlier.
6. Under the cloud of scandal arising from his kissing a cigarette girl known as "Toodles" Ryan, John Francis "Honey Fitz" Fitzgerald (1863–1950) was at the time of his daughter's wedding a month away from losing the Boston mayoral seat which he had held since 1910 (and before that in 1906 and 1907) to fellow Democrat, James Michael Curley.
7. Her brother, John Francis Fitzgerald, Jr. (1897–1979).
8. The Boston Braves' boisterous fan club.

taking the train for White Sulphur Springs in the evening. We arrived Sunday morning October eleventh. There we met some delightful as well as distinguished people include Mr. John Hays Hammond,[9] Mr. & Mrs. George Watters,[10] Mr. & Mrs. Clarence Hellman of Louisville and many others. Dr. Karlo, who had charged of the "Kur," [sic] was most interesting, as well as reliable. We rode every day, and also enjoyed the tennis and golf. One of the most pleasant evenings was that spent with Mr. & Mrs. Watters when we dined with them.

We left White Sulphur on Wednesday October twenty-second[11] in the evening and reached Atlantic City Thursday afternoon. After trying the bathing we went to the theatre to see Nazimova in a new play which was not especially good.[12] The next morning we promenaded on the boardwalk and "had our picture took" in the afternoon. We went back to New York and went to the theatre to see "On Trial."

Saturday we went to see Montgomery & Stone in Chin Chin.[13] Later supped and danced at the Biltmore. We returned home Sunday and went to live at Beals Street Wednesday, October twenty-eighth.

Joseph P. Kennedy, 29, to District Draft Board No. 5[14]

Quincy, Mass., February 18, 1918

Gentlemen:

In order that there may be no misunderstanding in the minds of you gentlemen as to my claim for deferred classification on industrial grounds, I respectfully request that the following statement be admitted as evidence:

About October 1, 1917,[15] I was invited by Mr. Joseph W. Powell then President of the Fore River Shipbuilding Corporation and now Vice-President of the Bethlehem Shipbuilding Corporation, Ltd.,[16] to a conference at Young's Hotel, Boston, which conference I attended and at which I met Mr. Guy Currier, attorney for the Fore River Shipbuilding Corporation,[17] Mr. Joseph W. Powell and Mr. Samuel W. Wakeman, then the General Superintendent and now the General Manager of the Fore River plant.[18] Mr.

---

9. John Hays Hammond (1855–1936), mining engineer, intimate of former President Taft, Republican Party enthusiast and international peace movement activist.
10. Playwright and former Chicago vaudeville manager, George Manker Watters (1893–1943).
11. October 22, 1914, was in fact a Thursday.
12. *That Sort*, then playing at Nixon's Apollo Theatre, Atlantic City, and featuring the brooding Crimean, Alla Nazimova (1875–1945), was scheduled to open on Broadway a month later.
13. Producer C. B. Dillingham's most recent extravaganza, *Chin Chin*, featuring the acrobatic musical comedy team of Dave Montgomery (1870–1917) and Fred Stone (1873–1959), had opened on Broadway at Dillingham's Globe Theatre (later the Lunt-Fontanne) a few days earlier.
14. JPK had received word from his district draft board that he had been placed in Class I Division A, generally represented by single men of appropriate age, ineligible for industrial deferment and without dependents.
15. The date was probably Saturday, September 29, 1917.
16. Joseph W. Powell (1878–1954), the new vice president of Bethlehem Shipbuilding, of whose Fore River Shipyard in Quincy, Massachusetts, JPK was assistant general manager. In 1921 and 1922 Powell would become president of the Emergency Fleet Corporation and would go on to serve both of Franklin Roosevelt's wartime secretaries of the navy, Frank Knox and James Forrestal, as special assistant two decades later.
17. Boston politico, lobbyist and lawyer, Guy Currier (1867–1930) had left state office before becoming the Fore River Corporation's counsel and serving on a number of directorates, most of them railway and transportation concerns. JPK would maintain contact with Currier throughout the coming decade, convincing him in February 1926 to take a 50 percent share in the syndicate that JPK had assembled to buy the Robertson-Cole film production company and its distribution arm, Film Booking Offices of America.
18. Under the management of Samuel Wiley Wakeman (1876–1940), the twenty-six thousand employees

Powell then proposed to me that I should come with the Fore River Shipbuilding Corporation. I told him that I had absolutely no knowledge of shipbuilding and could not realize how I might be of any great service to them. However, he informed me that he, Mr. H. G. Smith and Mr. Harry E. Brown, both Vice-Presidents of this corporation, and Mr. E. B. Hill, the Treasurer, were all going to leave Fore River and it was necessary for someone to take up the business end of this undertaking occasioned by their absence.

On the occasion of the leasing of the Fore River Shipbuilding Corporation, which was to become effective November 1, 1917, the offices of President, Vice-President and Treasurer for the individual companies were to be done away with and in their place there was to be a General Manager and an Assistant General Manager. The latter position Mr. Powell offered to me. When he convinced me that there was work here to be done, I asked him how soon it would be necessary for me to take up my new duties. This was of a Saturday. He told me the following Monday. Of course, I informed him that it was absolutely impossible for me to leave the bank, of which I had been President for three years, on forty-eight hours' notice, but that I would endeavor to wind up my business in such manner that I could leave the following Wednesday or Thursday. I found that it would require at least a week to do this, so that my coming with the Fore River Shipbuilding Corporation was postponed until the 15th or 16th of October.

I resigned as President of the Columbia Trust Company at a regular directors' meeting, and was asked to continue as chairman of the Executive Committee until certain matters that were then being handled could be finished. My father[19] was elected President in my place and I agreed to assist the Bank in getting matters straightened out as best I could. For the first month or two it was necessary for me to give them about five hours a week, three of which hours were usually given on Saturday nights, when the Bank was open, the other two hours when I could give them during the week. For the last month or six weeks it has been possible for me to give this up entirely, and my visits are very infrequent, once in every two weeks and then only about an hour at a time.

Since coming here at the plant on October 15th, I have taken up various duties of the gentlemen who have left. I have been giving an average of sixty to sixty-five hours a week to this establishment. I will briefly outline some of the duties which I perform:

First: The Compensation insurance is handled by the United States Mutual Liability Insurance Company, which is a corporation absolutely controlled by the Fore River Shipbuilding Corporation, and the conduct of this business is entirely in my hands, without supervision from anyone else. This company will take in premiums this year a matter of about $800,000, and the income, disbursement, and investment of funds are left entirely to my discretion.

Second: The Fore River Shipbuilding Corporation has what is termed a plant railroad. This railroad is now being incorporated and the matter is under my jurisdiction. I have appeared before the Railroad Committee of the Massachusetts Legislature asking for incorporation and I am handling the entire railroad situation, which, in a plant doing a business such as we are now doing, is of considerable importance.

---

of the Fore River and Squantum Plants (constructed in record time) would produce as many destroyers as all of the other plants in the country combined, with thirty-six and thirty-five, respectively.

19. In addition to helping to found the Columbia Trust Company of East Boston in 1895, ward boss Patrick Joseph Kennedy (1858–1929) had served in the Massachusetts House of Representatives between 1889 and 1891 and in the Massachusetts State Senate from 1892 to 1893.

Third: I have had charge of all business arrangements in connection with the bills of sale of the so-called "Luckenbach boats," which were built by the Fore River Shipbuilding Corporation for the Luckenbach Company of New York and subsequently commandeered by the Emergency Fleet Corporation. I have prepared all the papers in this case and personally handled both transactions with Mr. Arringdale, the Resident Inspector, and Mr. H. O. Trowbridge, the Division Head. I was also sent by Mr. Powell to the Harlan & Hollingsworth plant, one of the subsidiaries of the Bethlehem Shipbuilding Corporation, Ltd., to assist Mr. Weaver, formerly President, now General Manager of that plant, in preparing his bill of sale in accordance with the one we prepared at this plant for the approval of the Emergency Fleet Corporation.

Fourth: All the contracts and business arrangements connected with the Boston Elevated Railway, Edison Electric Company and other companies, for the new Victory plant at Squantum, have been turned over to me, and I have had frequent conferences with Mr. Brush[20] of the Elevated Railway, and within a few days have appointed Mr. John E. Benton[21] to act as our arbitrator in the arbitration hearings on the question of extra compensation for the Boston Elevated Railway Company, in which matter I will represent the Fore River Shipbuilding Corporation. All the business matters, contracts and questions of policy have been turned over to me.

Fifth: The United States Government authorized the Fore River Shipbuilding Corporation to double track Washington Street from Quincy Square to our plant. This entire operation, outside of the engineering end, has been under my supervision and will be until it is finished, late in the spring. This involves an expenditure of the United States Government's money of from $750,000 to $1,000,000.

Sixth: The entire question of housing at both the Fore River plant and the Squantum plant has been entirely left with me. I have prepared all the data and have submitted the same at three conferences I have had with Mr. Eidlitz at Washington, Chairman of the National Housing Committee,[22] and with Admiral Bousseau, representing the Navy Department. We have asked for an appropriation of $2,500,000 and I expect to be the Fore River representative to look after the Government's interests.

Seventh: The insurance proposition at this plant, which is an item of well over $100,000,000, is under my jurisdiction.

Eighth: I am at the present time endeavoring to negotiate a contract for the restaurant accommodations at the Squantum plant, involving an expenditure of from $700,000 to $1,000,000 a year, and at the same time am preparing plans and looking for companies to take the business at our Fore River plant, which would be a much larger item.

I am Treasurer of the Mutual Benefit Association, which looks after the interests of the 14,000 men we have now on our payroll and the 20,000 men we expect to have within the next six months.[23]

20. Matthew Chauncey Brush (1877–1940), president of the Boston Elevated Railroad Company and later president of the American International Corporation, which *The New York Times* would describe as "one of the largest investment trusts in history" by 1940. He would remain a close friend and associate of JPK's throughout the 1920s, trading investment advice on matters that would land him in front of the Senate Banking and Currency Committee in 1929 to testify about the practice of short selling, during which he observed that "[n]o one is in Wall Street for his health" and that "[t]he stock market could be turned into a racket which would make Al Capone look like a piker."

21. John Edwin Benton (1875–1948), solicitor for the Interstate Commerce Commission's Bureau of Valuation.

22. Civil engineer Otto Marc Eidlitz (1860–1928).

23. *The Fore River Log* would report in January 1919 that under JPK's tutelage the association would pay out eighty-three thousand dollars in "accident, sick and death claims" over the course of 1918.

Mr. Wakeman's duties call him for numerous conferences in Bethlehem, Pa. and New York, trial trips, etc., at which times I am left with authority to act.

I am very free to admit that I have had absolutely no technical knowledge of ship-building. I am just beginning to acquire a little knowledge of it from our daily Board meetings, and I expect to make myself as conversant with it as possible. I have never had a technical training. My experience has been entirely in the business field.

I am a Trustee of the Massachusetts Electric Companies, acting with men like Philip Dexter,[24] C. E. Cotting,[25] Gordon Abbott[26] and others. I am a director of the Boston Morris Plan Company, having been invited there by Mr. Eugene V. R. Thayer,[27] then President, and associated with men like Mr. McElwain, Mr. Sterns, Mr. Edgar of the Edison Electric Company, and others of that kind.

I am one of the six men at this plant who are on a bonus scheme in addition to their salaries, the other five men being absolutely technical men.[28]

I have submitted this information to you as evidence to show that I am trying to perform the duty which I feel incumbent upon me. My inclination to enter the ship-building business was absolutely prompted by a desire to feel that I was doing something worth while.

Trusting that you will give this evidence some consideration, I am

Very respectfully yours,

Subscribed and sworn to before me this [18th] day of February, 1918.

Joseph P. Kennedy to James Richards[29]

9 September 1918

Dear Mr. Richards:

I wish to express to you my sincere appreciation of your kindness in offering me a Directorship in the Citizens' Gas Company of Quincy.

I regret very much that I could not in justice to the Gas Company and the Ship-building Corporation by whom I am employed accept it.

My short experience, however, has taught me that the attitude of labor to-day towards management in charge of enterprises is not improved much by having labor think that there is too close a connection between the employers and those that sell them the commodity that they use. This was brought home to me very strongly when it became necessary to stagger the hours of the shifts here at the Quincy Works from one opening at seven o'clock in the morning to an opening at seven and one at eight, in order that the Bay State Street Railway, which was carrying our men, might take care

---

24. Boston lawyer Philip Dexter (1868–1934) served not only as trustee and manager of various railroad and manufacturing interests, but also of several real estate trusts, including that of the Tremont Building, site of the District Five Draft Board Offices.
25. Charles Edward Cotting (1889–1985), a contemporary of JPK's at Harvard and a stockbroker at the Boston firm of Lee, Higginson.
26. Gordon Abbott (1863–1937), chairman of the board of directors of the Old Colony Trust Company.
27. Eugene Van Rensselaer Thayer, Jr. (1881–1937), president of the Chase National Bank of New York. Three years earlier, as president of the Merchants National Bank of Boston, Thayer had made the fifteen-thousand-dollar loan to JPK that saved the Columbia Trust Company from absorption into the First Ward National Bank and launched JPK to Columbia's presidency in January 1914 at the age of twenty-five.
28. JPK was to be paid "$4,000⁰⁰ per annum, beginning as of date of employment," and would receive a bonus of "0.01% (percent) of the total manufacturing profits of the Quincy Works of the Fore River Plant."
29. Financier James Lorin Richards (1858–1955), director and chairman of the board of the Boston Consolidated Gas Company.

of the constantly increasing number of employees. However, the committee of the men which rose to protest against this action did not hesitate to openly charge that the officials of the Shipbuilding Corporation were interested in the Bay State Street Railway, and the shift in hours was made to help the Railway Company to get more money by being able to use the same crew twice in the morning instead of being obliged to hire additional help to take care of our men in one shift. The fact that I was a trustee of the Massachusetts Electric Company did not add to our comfort in the situation.

Realizing, therefore, how necessary it was for you to increase your rates for gas here in Quincy, which would necessarily affect many of our employees, I felt the fair thing to do was to relieve your Company as well as the Shipbuilding Corporation from any charge of working together to this end.

I want you to know, however, that I appreciate the offer of the Directorship and the opportunity it gave me of becoming connected with one of your companies, -something which I have looked forward to for a long time.

Thanking you again for the opportunity, I remain,

Sincerely yours,

Joseph P. Kennedy to Joseph Larkin[30]

16 Sept. 1918

Dear————: [sic]
In re: Leonard[31] Case

Let me relate the facts leading up to Leonard's employment, so that this whole matter will be clear in your mind.

About June 15th, Leonard, being in Class IV of the draft and having a premonition that he was going to be moved up to Class I, left the Red Sox in St. Louis and came to Fore River to be hired.[32] He showed us his card entitling him to a place in Class IV and said he would like to work at Fore River. We asked him if the Baseball Manager of the Boston team[33] was willing to have him come here and leave his team at mid-year, and he said, "Yes, that they were satisfied."

This all happened about the 17th of June.

The following morning the story appeared in the Boston papers that it was rumored that Leonard was coming to Fore River. Immediately under the story appeared the notice of his Local Board in California that he had been reclassified in the draft and put in Class I.

Leonard pitched the afternoon of the 20th against Philadelphia and was taken out of the game as a result of a bad blow to his hand, which would have made it impossible for him to pitch on the 22nd for us, even had there been a game.

---

30. Joseph Maurice Larkin (1888–1970), assistant to Eugene Grace, president of Bethlehem Steel.
31. Boston Red Sox pitcher Hubert Benjamin "Hub" or "Dutch" Leonard (1892–1952). Over the course of the war, Bethlehem Steel made a particular effort to recruit some of the era's best professional baseball players to its various plants, offering industrial deferment for what appears to have been light work and extensive play during the rigorous Bethlehem baseball season.
32. On May 23, 1918, the office of the Provost Marshall General issued its revised selective service regulations for the classification of draft registrants, withdrawing deferment from any and all "registrants found to be idlers or engaged in nonproductive occupations." According to this "work or fight order," as of July 1 of that year, "[p]ersons, including ushers and other attendants, engaged and occupied in and in connection with games, sports, and amusements, excepting actual performers in legitimate concerts or operas, or theatrical performances" would no longer be able to claim deferment.
33. Edward Grant "Cousin Ed" Barrow (1868–1953).

When Leonard was here on the 17th he told us that he would report immediately after the game on the 20th, that is, on the morning of the 21st, so on the 21st of June we telegraphed Gheen at Bethlehem to place his name on the list.

However, the papers rode him so hard that we believed that Leonard had changed his mind, and this was substantiated by the fact that we did not hear a word from him about his coming from the time he was here on the 17th up to and including the 22nd. On Monday, the 24th of June, our baseball manager, not Mrs. Leonard, who said that "Dutch" had decided not to come to Fore River and was then out purchasing the tickets for a trip to the Coast, in order that he might enlist in the Naval Reserves with his friend "Duffie" Lewis.[34] O'Hara, the baseball manager,[35] got Leonard on the phone later that day and had this confirmed, Leonard telling him that he had decided not to go to Fore River. O'Hara thereupon wired Bob Steele of Pittsburgh, a pitcher,[36] to come here and work because we understood Mamaux[37] was going into Aviation and we would be left without a pitcher.

All these facts have been substantiated by Leonard himself in the conversation I have had with him in the past week, when the question of additional salary came up, and he admitted the truth of the statements so far mentioned.

During the latter part of the week of June 24th, Leonard called up O'Hara and said that he had heard from Lewis and that there was nothing doing on the Coast and asked whether or not he could take on again with Fore River. When he rung up this time he was worried not about salary but about the draft. We told him that we certainly could not promise exemption from the draft but that we were willing to put his name up to Mr. Amos Little, the District Representative of the Emergency Fleet, who would decide whether he was entitled to the protection of this list or not.

Leonard reported here the morning of the 29th and pitched that afternoon against Steelton, with the understanding that his salary was to begin the Monday of that week, that is, the 24th, at the rate of $250 per month.

When Leonard says, as he does on page 2 of his letter, that "O'Hara notified him by phone that there was no game with Lebanon" he is not telling the truth. O'Hara was with me the morning the Lebanon game was called off and had not heard from Leonard since the 17th.

In regard to Leonard's salary for June, I am quoting the telegram sent to Mr. Gheen regarding Leonard's employment, dated July 25th:

"Referring your telegram twenty second regarding time of Leonard's employment would say that negotiations were carried on with Leonard during early part of June and it was decided to take him up on the rolls of June twenty first stop Inadvertently the employment card was dated June sixth stop Upon investigation it has been found that Accounting Department took Leonard up on the rolls on June sixth and received no time card for him until June twenty second stop Accounting Department not knowing Leonard from any other

34. Red Sox outfielder George Edward "Duffy" Lewis (1888–1979).

35. The May 1918 issue of the *Fore River Log* noted that "Fore River has been particularly fortunate in securing the services of Jack O'Hara, who last year managed the Springfield team in the Eastern League. Jack has played with the Philadelphia Athletics, Jersey City, and has been one of the most successful minor league managers in the country for the last five years. He has surrounded himself with some former stars of the major leagues and Fore River is going to have baseball of a major league caliber."

36. Steele (1894–1962) pitched left-handed not only for the Pirates but also for the Cardinals and the Giants during his professional career, which spanned 1916 to 1919.

37. Pittsburgh Pirates pitcher and vaudeville performer, Albert Leon "Al" Mameaux (1894–1963), the "Golden Voiced Tenor."

employee requested information as to whether he was actually employed from date shown on employment card stop Baseball Manager through error submitted time card on request of Accounting Department for entire period stop This is borne out by fact that no payment on salary was made to Leonard until within a week stop If it had been our intention to employ him as of June sixth we would have entered his name before June fifteenth when the thirty day time limit went on, thereby making him available for baseball which action we did not take because at no time did we consider Leonard actually at work in Plant until after June twenty second."

It was our intention, in the case of Leonard, to pay him $200 a month from the Plant and I was willing to make up the $50 in his case myself, thinking that with the acquisition of this man it would make the pennant sure.

The question of Leonard's being paid for the month of June at no time ever came up, as far as I know, until the day that he was leaving here, and when he said I "reassured him that it was a matter for form," he tells an absolute falsehood.

It is true that Leonard worked hard at Fore River while he was here and there is not the slightest complaint about his work.

It is true that on August 30th he was notified that he had been taken off the Emergency Fleet list, not because, as he says, "that he had not been employed a year at Fore River," but because the Naval Intelligence Officers and the Emergency Fleet officers felt that he was here for no other reason than to "duck the draft," and they refused to keep him, as well as the other baseball players, on the list any longer.

Leonard pitched August 31st because there was nothing else for him to do, and his insinuation that "Mr. Lewis might be pleased because he had pitched and won from Bethlehem [Steelton] and felt that he should offer the same opposition to Steelton," reflects no great credit on him, because after the 4th inning he begged Kopf the Captain[38] to take him out because his arm was tired, but as we had to save Mamaux for Monday it was impossible to relieve him.

When I informed Leonard on August 30th that he had been taken off the list our relations were very friendly. In fact he said that he had been treated very well and went so far as to offer Mr. Wakeman and me, or rather stated that he would procure for us some seats for the World's Series, but we told him that we did not think we would have a chance to go. He offered some very pertinent remarks regarding the conduct of the men at the Plant and they impressed me so strongly that I asked him to tell them to Mr. Wakeman, which he did. They were regarding the men's attitude toward the work in the shop.

I told Leonard how sorry I felt about his being taken off the Emergency Fleet list without our being notified and told him that we were perfectly willing to keep him here until he received notice from his Local Board that he must report for draft duty. He informed me that Mr. Frazee, owner of the Red Sox,[39] had asked him to pitch a World Series game, and he said that he did not think that he was in shape. I told him that I was perfectly willing, and out of my own pocket, to pay him his own salary up to and including the World's Series and allow him to leave the Plant immediately after the game on the 31st and get in shape. His salary was to go on up to the time that he was called.

---

38. After playing second and third bases and shortstop variously for the Cleveland Naps and for the Philadelphia Athletics, from 1916 to 1921 (with the exception of 1918 when he captained the Fore River team), William Lawrence "Larry" Kopf (1890–1986) played for the Cincinnati Reds before spending his last two professional seasons in Boston.
39. Theatrical producer Harry Herbert Frazee (1880–1929).

He said he appreciated this and would think it over. On August 31st, however he told me that he had talked with Frazee and had decided that he would not be able to get into shape.

Tuesday, September 3d, Leonard called at my office and requested his back salary. I did not know what his back salary was and asked Scollard,[40] the Baseball Manager, to make up what was due him and to let me know and I would pay it. The statement that he puts in his letter of money received is absolutely right, but it includes three weeks, that is the weeks of June 8, 15 and 22nd, to which he has no claim at all. The reason that these amounts were allowed to run on was because Leonard had asked my help in getting him enlisted as an officer in the Navy, which I gave him most cordially, and in view of the fact that he attempted to get a commission and that we knew that he was trying, made us feel that his services with us would be terminated at any moment, and we felt that the question of this over-payment could be straightened out when it was found just how much would be due him when he left.

I did not attempt to offer him $39.64 as payment in full for all back salaries but told Scollard to give him the money, as that was all that was due him and I do not understand that Mr. O'Hara "could not remember ever having promised to pay me for June," because Mr. O'Hara flatly denies he ever made any such statement, and Mr. O'Hara goes on to say that if any statement had ever been made, Leonard's actions on the 24th of June of calling off all arrangements made up to that time in order that he might go to the Coast would certainly not prejudice any one in his favor to think that he might receive $250 for just pitching one game in July.

I resent Mr. Leonard's insinuation that the payments made in June were simply a scheme to disguise the real facts of his salary, and I feel that Leonard is taking advantage of an error which he knew took place when the Leonard-Mamaux incident was thrashed out, by claiming money that is not due him in any sense of the word.

I think that he is a first class hypocrite when he appeals to Mr. Lewis that it is the "principle" of the matter which he insists on righting, for on the first page of his letter he says that it is a matter of "gravest importance to me."

I think that positively no steps should be taken to pay him any more than we have told him is due, because to do that would be a decided reflection on everything that I have told him, and I feel that everything has been done for Leonard that could be done. Mr. Wakeman and others at the Plant will testify that he has been treated by me as well as anybody possibly could be, and I consider his letter a distinct criticism of my action, and I would consider that any payment made to him would be backing him up, and I feel sure that you will not stand for this kind of business being put over.

With very best regards, believe me,

Yours very truly,
FORE RIVER PLANT
By
Assistant General Manager

---

40. The Fore River works accountant, Clinton J. "Pat" Scollard, had replaced Jack O'Hara as baseball manager after O'Hara's dismissal in July. Scollard would rejoin his former Fore River colleague, JPK, in the management of a number of the latter's film concerns in the 1920s.

Joseph P. Kennedy and Babe Ruth: *Agreement*

Hayden, Stone & Co.[41]

Referring to agreement made between Henry Tagler [?] & Geo Ruth assigned to me. I hereby agree with Geo Ruth that the contract outlined in this agreement will be signed & the picture started both within 3 weeks from due date or both parties are released from the agreement with no damages

J P Kennedy
G. H. Ruth[42]

Joseph P. Kennedy to Andrew Peters[43]

Boston, May 7, 1920

Dear Mr. Mayor:-

I have just returned from the South, and have tried to get you on the telephone, but find you are very busy indeed.

I want you to know that I appreciate more than I can express, your kindness in my affair, and I only hope that at some time I may have the chance to reciprocate.[44]

Yours very truly,

Joseph P. Kennedy to Galen Stone[45]

Boston, May 18, 1920

Dear Mr. Stone:

Last Christmas I received a pony from the Dupont stables for my son, Joe. It is about 32 inches high, and I have had considerable difficulty trying to arrange to get a pony cart. I finally heard that Mr. Lawson had one, and I tried to buy it, but for some reason I could make no arrangements with the stableman. I asked Mr. Fitzgerald if he would be good enough to get in touch with Mr. Lawson and find out if the pony cart was in the market. The attached is a letter received this day from Mr. Lawson.

Any doubt that you may have as to his mental condition, I imagine will be quickly dispelled after reading this letter.

Yours very truly,

41. Leaving Fore River in 1919, JPK had become a manager at the Boston brokerage house of Hayden, Stone, where he had begun to investigate investment opportunities in new technologies such as film distribution and production.
42. On October 31, 1919, the Boston Red Sox pitcher (who would shortly be sold to the New York Yankees), would respond "[m]ust have full amount before I start Victure [*sic*]" and added "must hear from you at once or will call everything off." No further correspondence remains among the JPK papers and the picture appears never to have been made.
43. Beating out such formidable opponents as James Michael Curley and Peter Tague, Andrew James Peters (1872–1938) served as Democratic mayor of Boston from 1918 to 1922.
44. A post at Treasury would elude JPK throughout his life. On April 21, Peters had endorsed JPK's (ultimately unsuccessful) candidacy for the post of assistant secretary of the treasury in charge of fiscal bureaus.
45. Galen Luther Stone (1862–1926), financier, trustee, cofounder of the Boston brokerage house of Hayden, Stone & Company and JPK's mentor during his tenure at the firm between 1919 and 1922.

Joseph P. Kennedy to Dr. Place

Boston, July 2, 1920

Dear Doctor Place:

I am enclosing herewith my check for $150 — payment of your bill.

I would indeed be an ingrate if I let this chance pass by without telling you how much I appreciate your wonderful work for Jack during his recent illness.[46] I had never experienced any very serious sickness in my family previous to this case of Jack's, and I little realized what an effect such a happening could possibly have on me. During the darkest days I felt that nothing else mattered except his recovery, and you must have some notion of what the gratitude of a parent can be to have his boy returned in the wonderful shape that Jack seems to be now.

My only hope in the whole matter is that you might always feel that I am indebted to you, and if at some future time I can be of any service to you whatsoever, I only wish that you will allow me to serve.

With best wishes from Jack and myself, I remain,

Sincerely yours,

Joseph P. Kennedy to Christopher Dunphy[47]

Boston, August 12, 1920

Dear Chris:

Eastern may look tough but its better than I ever told you it was. Keep up your courage! Some day you will make plenty on that.[48]

With best regards,
Sincerely,

Joseph P. Kennedy to Robert Potter[49]

Boston, August 17, 1920

Dear Bob:

As regards that account you have requested a number of times:

I finally got some figures today from my father's head man, and he tells me that you owe $212, for $16\frac{1}{2}$ gals. of one and 10 gals. of the other, each at $8 a gal.

Sincerely yours,

---

46. The couple's second child, John Fitzgerald Kennedy (1917–1963), had come down with scarlet fever on February 20, the date of his sister Kathleen's birth. Dr. Place had overseen his care at the Boston City Hospital. Once out of immediate danger, Jack convalesced at the Mansion House in Poland Springs, Maine, returning home to Brookline in April, a month before his third birthday and after two months' absence, to meet his new sister for the first time.

47. JPK and Dunphy had met when the latter was assistant manager of the Copley Plaza Hotel in Boston. Dunphy had since become the summer-season manager of the Mt. Pleasant Hotel in Bretton Woods, New Hampshire, and winter-season manager of the Royal Poinciana in Palm Beach, Florida. JPK and family were frequent guests at both.

48. Eastern Steamship's common stock would trade at a high of $28\frac{5}{8}$ in 1920; by 1923 it would soar to $127\frac{1}{2}$.

49. JPK's Harvard 1912 classmate, Robert Sturgis Potter (1890–1947), a former fellow member of the Crimson freshman and varsity baseball squads and the current vice president of the National Shawmut Bank of Boston. Potter had ordered sherry and port from among the stores that P. J. Kennedy (a former publican in addition to ward boss and banker) had set aside shortly before the Eighteenth Amendment had taken effect in January.

Joseph P. Kennedy to Rufus Cole[50]

Boston, August 30, 1920

Dear Mr. Cole:

In the first place, I want you to know that I appreciate very much your having me in mind in the consideration of the re-financing of your business.

I had a talk with Mr. Stone today, with the idea of trying to get over to New York tonight, but it is just as I told you over the telephone, — we are frightfully busy, due to a fight for control of the Mathieson Alkali Works, which management we control today, and it is taking all of the time of Mr. Stone and his lieutenants.

Mr. Stone said, however, that it was very likely that you probably would not contemplate an immediate issue, because he doubted very much if any house would be able to handle it just at this time.

I told him that you and I had discussed it from that point of view, and that our idea at the present time, was to get the proposition in shape so that it might be submitted for financing, if you thought it advisable after you had some notion on what basis the proposition might be floated. So, if Thursday, Sept. 9th, is not too late, I will arrange to be in New York on that date.

With kindest regards, I am,
Very truly yours,

Joseph P. Kennedy to Rufus Cole

Boston, September 24, 1920

Dear Mr. Cole:

I regret very much that I have not been able to get to New York to further discuss with you the various picture matters, but, as you can very well appreciate, the banking situation in Boston has made anybody with any banking connections feel very uneasy. It is my present intention to be in New York on Wednesday next, but as I have had to disappoint you so many times recently, I even now hesitate to make this definite.

Now as to the propositions which you so very kindly offer me: As I told you, my experience in the picture business with my own money, and, in some instances, with that of my friends, has been very disastrous, due, very likely, to our ignorance of the business and our childlike simplicity in taking any stock in anybody in the motion picture business. For that reason, I am very loath to try and interest any of my friends in the picture proposition, except in a small way, so that they might get the benefit of a good proposition at least. At the same time, the banking situation has contributed to make the raising of money just a bit more difficult, and it is my own notion that I would not care to ask them to become interested in any proposition, with the possible exception of THE STEALERS. However, I note that you say you would not care to set aside an interest in less than two of the pictures, so I have not even put the proposition up to them.

If, however, you would be interested in just doing business with THE STEALERS, I will be glad to talk it over with you on my next visit to New York.

50. During the First World War, Rufus Cole (1879–1954) became the American representative to the English banking house of Graham's & Co. In conjunction with the ailing Anglo-Indian banking house of Cox & Co. (later subsumed by Lloyd's Bank), Cole formed the Robertson-Cole Corporation of America, producers and distributors of motion pictures and exporters of American automobiles to the United Kingdom, India and Java. By the summer of 1920 Robertson-Cole was operating at a loss and had fallen deeply into debt, and Cole had been forced to approach Hayden, Stone in an effort to sell the concern.

25

I want you to appreciate, however, that there is not the slightest obligation on your part to do this, and I can give you no assurance that we could get together even on the terms you suggest, but I do say that we are, I hope, going to do some business together in the very near future. It has been a great pleasure to know you and I do want to have the satisfaction of having a motion picture deal with a man in whom I have the confidence I have in you.

Yours very truly,

***

Joseph P. Kennedy to Louis Coolidge[51]

Boston, October 16, 1920

Dear Mr. Coolidge:

I very much appreciate your invitation to join the Middlesex Club, and, in accordance with your suggestion, have sent my application to Mr. Ramsay.

I sincerely hope that I can be of some assistance to you and the Club.

With kindest regards,

***

Joseph P. Kennedy to Ethel Turner[52]

Boston, December 23, 1920

My dear Miss Turner:

I put through a deal yesterday, which I will outline to you so that your records may be clear.

I had formed a Massachusetts corporation called the Robertson-Cole Distributing Corporation of New England, with $100,000 preferred and $200,000 common stock. Yesterday I bought $60,000 worth of the preferred. The $40,000 left of the preferred is still in the treasury, and I have not decided how the common will be divided.

To get the $60,000 I made the following arrangements:

With the Brookline Trust Company: I withdrew from my loan there 100 Eastern Steamship, Preferred, and substituted therefor, 2100 shares Columbia Trust and 10 shares United States Envelope Company. With the 200 Todd which you sent me, I took this 100 Eastern Steamship, Preferred, and placed it as part of the collateral in a loan that John F.[53] has at the Shawmut Bank, and received a check from his account with Hayden, Stone & Co. for $20,000, with the understanding that when I either sold some of my Robertson-Cole Preferred, or got some additional cash, I should pay back the $20,000 to his account and take back my 200 Todd and 100 Eastern Steamship, Pfd.

In addition to that, I withdrew $5,000 from the account of Mary A. Kennedy[54] and placed it to her account in the Columbia Trust Company, and then put through a charge ticket against it for $5,000.

I also put through a charge ticket against my own account in the Columbia Trust Company for $5,000.

51. Louis Arthur Coolidge (1861–1925), former private secretary to Massachusetts Senator Henry Cabot Lodge, assistant secretary of the treasury in charge of finance under Theodore Roosevelt and Republican Party activist. In a recent letter, Coolidge had encouraged JPK to join the Middlesex Republican Club of New England.
52. JPK's former secretary during his tenure as president of the Columbia Trust Company.
53. Fitzgerald, JPK's father-in-law.
54. His mother, Mary Augusta Hickey Kennedy (1857–1923).

I also arranged to borrow from the Columbia Trust Company, $20,000 with miscellaneous collateral furnished by Mr. Fitzgerald, not signed by J. J. Shinkwin.

After you understand this transaction thoroughly, and make out your records, kindly destroy this letter.

Sincerely yours,

Joseph P. Kennedy to Ethel Turner

Boston, January 21, 1921

My dear Miss Turner:

Please charge Mary A. Kennedy's account $2500 and credit my father's account, as part of the $10,000 borrowed the other day.

Mr. Fitzgibbon[55] will, within a few days, send you a check for $5,000, which he will receive from the sale of stock, which you will also credit to my father's account.

The balance of $2500 I will take care of when I return.

While I am gone, Miss Fitzpatrick will probably send you a check for $12,500. Will you please hold this in a special account and if Mr. Fitzgibbon needs it to make up any deficit in Robertson-Cole, he is authorized to use it.

Yours very truly,

Joseph P. Kennedy to Eugene Thayer[56]

Boston, February 14, 1921

Dear Hughie:

I can't tell you how sorry I am to hear that you are forced to take a vacation as a result of poor health. When I last saw you in New York, I knew it was only a question of time — that your physical strength could not stand the strain much longer.

I hesitate to presume that any of the rumors I hear concerning how bad you have been personally hit are true, but I want you to know this, that in the past few years I have been able to get together, where I could lay my hands on it today, $50,000 to $75,000. This, of course, I know is only a very small amount but I want to assure you that any or all of it is yours for the asking, on 72 hours' notice.

I mean this, Hughie, because I figure that the start you gave me at the Columbia Trust Company has made all the rest of the things possible, and I would more than like to show my appreciation. I would consider it a great favor if you can feel that this can be of any service to you whatsoever.

With best regards and a hope for a speedy return to your normal self, I am,

Sincerely yours,
Joe Kennedy

---

55. JPK's former assistant in a Fore River Shipyard private cafeteria venture, Stephen Fitzgibbon (1880–1954). Fitzgibbon would continue to work for JPK intermittently throughout the 1920s, both in the restructuring and attempted sale of Robertson-Cole Pictures and at JPK's Columbia Advertising Agency, a "theatrical-scenic advertising agency" that arranged for customers' advertisements to be painted into the scenery that formed the backdrops of the vaudeville shows that at the time preceded the film screenings.

56. Thayer, the former president of the Merchants National Bank of Boston whose fifteen-thousand-dollar loan had rescued the Columbia Trust Company (thereby securing JPK's presidency of the institution) in 1914, had since become president of the Chase National Bank of New York. Thayer had recently suffered a nervous collapse under the strain of the pressures of a hostile working environment. A handwritten note on the original document reads *"Not Sent—(Mr. Thayer away)."*

Joseph P. Kennedy to Albert Garceau[57]

Boston, June 14, 1921

My dear Mr. Garceau:

The following account has probably missed your attention, due to the many mistakes made in the original bill. As I am very anxious to get the matter cleaned up and out of the way, I would appreciate your sending me a check as soon as you conveniently can.

7 - 16 oz bots.	Charteau	$15.05
24 - 24 " "	Pommerner	36.00
12 - 24 " "	Chat. Gircour	20.00
8 - 24 " "	" Carmeil	11.20
7 - 24 " "	" Macon	20.42
5 - 12 " "	" Giscours	10.34
14 - 24 " "	" Ruat	14.00
4 - 12 " "	" "	8.00
3 - 24 " "	" Olivier	3.44
100 - 12 " "	" Perrier	14.50
50 - 24 " "	" "	10.50
		$163.45

Yours very truly,

Joseph P. Kennedy to Joseph Godsol[58]

Boston, June 17, 1921

Dear Mr. Godsol:

I was unable to reach Mr. Hearst[59] yesterday afternoon, but have an appointment with him on Wednesday next, unless detained out of the city. I have talked to Thayer and hope to get in touch with you, after I have seen Hearst, sometime Thursday morning, and will telephone you and make an appointment.

Regarding the New England situation: I think that with the R-C franchise and the Goldwyn franchise, I could get the best men in this district to give their personal attention to a combination of this kind, which would insure first-runs in Boston and which would guarantee holding up the percentage of your business as well as ours.

If you will let me know whether it interests you at all, and along what lines, I will get some proposition and bring it with me when I go to New York next week.

Yours very truly,

---

57. According to JPK's papers, a Boston attorney.
58. Chairman of the board of the short-lived Goldwyn Pictures Corporation.
59. Throughout the early 1920s, JPK attempted (without success) to interest a number of parties in Robertson-Cole. One such party was William Randolph Hearst (1863–1951), who, JPK felt, might share his vision of the potential for conglomeration within the film industry. By the early 1920s, Hearst had extended his media empire to include not only print journalism but film as well. Following the successes of his *Perils of Pauline* serials and the Hearst-Selig weekly newsreels, Hearst had established Cosmopolitan Pictures to produce the films of Marion Davies (1897–1961), the young actress whom he had met in 1917 and who would become his lifelong companion.

Joseph P. Kennedy to Grenville MacFarland[60]

Boston, June 18, 1921

Dear Grenville:

Confirming my conversation with you over the telephone this morning, I have been representing the Grahams of London, one of the biggest trading houses in England and India, and Cox's Bank of London, who have an investment in the Robertson-Cole Company of over $5,000,000. I have just reorganized the company and we are going to go on. My own notion is, however, that all these smaller companies are on their way to the poorhouse and nothing can stop them unless a consolidation goes through.

I have talked with some people in Goldwyn's, and I feel sure that if we could make some deal with Mr. Hearst he could get hold of an organization that would consist of Goldwyn, Metro, Robertson-Cole and Selznick,[61] and would, to my mind, make a really worth while proposition. He is turning over enough product and of calibre sufficient to warrant his own organization, and sooner or later, when Paramount gets control, if they do, they will take all the cream that he has made for himself.[62]

What I would like to do is to have a talk with Mr. Hearst personally, not with one of his lieutenants, to find out whether he would be interested and whether we could get something started. My present plan is to be in New York next Wednesday and Thursday, and I would like to see Mr. Hearst sometime Thursday morning, if possible, or Wednesday morning if more convenient for him. Will you first see whether he would be interested and, if so, if you can make an appointment?

Sincerely yours,

Joseph P. Kennedy to Vera Murray[63]

Boston, August 15, 1921

Dear Vera:

Not having heard from you at 12:15 to-day, I tried to get you on the phone but they told me that you have left for the station. I talked with Jack Potter[64] and he said you were coming up with Mr. Dillingham and that he knew nothing of your plans.

Not knowing what the functions are of the right-hand man to the powers that be, I don't know how close you will be obliged to stick to your boss tonight. I know how close you would have to if I were your boss. However, Messrs. Conway, Moore[65] and Kennedy will arrive at the Plaza Hotel at 7 o'clock to take you to dinner—the aforesaid gentlemen not being in evening clothes, by the way, and, up to date, without theatre tickets.

Now, if it becomes necessary for you to spend the evening in the seat next to your

60. Attorney Grenville MacFarland (1878–1924), the editor of Hearst's *Boston American* and the local general counsel to the Hearst papers.
61. The Lewis J. Selznick Pictures Corporation. Selznick (1870–1933), the child of Russian immigrants from the East Side of New York, had founded the company in the 1910s with less than a thousand dollars. In fewer than ten weeks it would turn a profit of some $105,000, prompting its founder to observe to the Wheeler Motion Picture Investigating Committee in 1917 that "less brains are necessary in the motion picture industry than in any other."
62. Between 1919 and 1923, Paramount distributed the product of Hearst's Cosmopolitan Pictures. In 1924, however, Marion Davies and Cosmopolitan would leave Paramount for the Goldwyn Company, which was to be subsumed within the newly formed Metro-Goldwyn-Mayer a year later.
63. Vera Murray (1885–1956), executive secretary to theatrical producer and manager C. B. Dillingham.
64. Theatrical manager John Potter (1888–1966).
65. Edward E. Moore, the former assistant to JPK's father-in-law, John F. Fitzgerald, during his tenure as mayor of Boston, had become JPK's assistant as well as his close friend and confidant.

boss, by all means do it. If, however, it is not necessary, please buy us some seats so we four can sit together.

At this dinner at 7 o'clock you might state what is your pleasure for the balance of the evening, and the three Boston youths will try, insofar as they can, to make things pleasant for you during your stay. If you feel, however, that your duty requires your presence in other quarters, while the gentlemen will regret it, they realize that business must come first. So feel no obligations at all — but we will be at the Plaza at 7 o'clock.

If you have made other arrangements for dinner, just leave a note and tell us when and where we can see you later on. In the meanwhile I will try and lick the other two gentlemen at the Braeburn Country Club in a very exciting game of golf.

See you later.

Sincerely yours,

Joseph P. Kennedy to Alfred Wellington[66]

Boston, August 22, 1921

Dear Alfred:

Confidentially, I am not so sure but what the Shawmut Bank stock that we own should be sold. Bob Potter had 100 shares with us at Hayden's here, and with all secrecy proceeded to dispose of it the other day at around 198.[67] There is no question but what this bank is taking terrible losses and I am almost inclined to suggest selling, even though we take a loss, with the idea that the banks have not taken all their losses yet and we may be able to pick it up cheaper later on.

I am just setting these facts forth as I know them, and you can judge what you want to do about it.

Sincerely,

Joseph P. Kennedy to Arthur Houghton[68]

Boston, September 19, 1921

Dear Arthur:

I have your wire today and if you are surprised that I am not dead, the shock is as great to me to find that you are still among the living. However, I have been working on

---

66. Vice president and treasurer of the Columbia Trust Company.
67. JPK's former baseball teammate and college classmate was vice president of the Shawmut Bank at the time.
68. In an undated memorandum entitled "Joe in Show Business and Movies" (written, evidently, many years after his associations with the entertainment industry had ended), Rose Kennedy recalled that Joe has always more or less been attracted to show business as it is called. That is, the world of the theater. One night when he was buying tickets at the Colonial Theater in Boston, he was introduced to the manager of the then-current production, the famous "Chin Chin," of which the shining star was Fred Stone, an actor who was more or less a comedian, an acrobat, and a popular star of the 1916's [*sic*]. His manager, Arthur Houghton, was a man about 16 years older than Joe who had been born in Boston of a saintly Irish mother and father and who had become a successful and a popular manager of the Fred Stone Company, and Joe and he became great friends. Consequently, from Arthur's experiences, he had had a life full of interesting and amusing incidents in the theatrical world which he narrated with an amusing twist of his own imagination. From that year until now, he has been a great friend and a close companion of Joe's. After he retired and his wife passed away, he spent his winters with us at Palm Beach and his summer at Hyannis or abroad. Always gay, always full of anecdotes or amusing personal experiences, and distracting Joe from the serious heavy baffling problems of business. Joe always liked to have someone gay around him, so that he would have relief from his heavy cares and responsibilities.

a lot of things, like the Stone pictures, that there isn't any money in, and I hope to get straightened away pretty soon.

Rogers will probably not be in Chicago until the latter part of the week, so look for him then. We have a fairly decent contract with Robertson-Cole and I think we can eventually get our money out, provided we do not get sewed up in too much litigation with the crowd of thieves with whom we formerly had the contract, the Federated.

Wiley is out of town so I don't know whether they intend to give up the stills or not. If you have any receipts or evidence that they have them, let me have it all because I may have use for it.

I have asked Rogers to arrange to release both pictures while Stone is in Chicago, and I think that Fred, to help us out, would make a personal appearance at least with the first picture, because that would give us a lot more money and start the picture on its way in good shape.

R-C think the pictures are very good pictures. The only trouble is that they have been kicked around so much. I am inclined to agree with them. However, do what you can to send them along.

I have had Ahern in to see me regarding your mother's house. He thinks that perhaps he could get an offer of $6200. I have checked this up and the consensus of opinion is that this is a fairly reasonable price, but, of course, I don't want to take the responsibility of having her sell it unless that is your desire.

Vera tells me that the show is going excellently in Chicago, and I am tickled to death for your sake and Fred's, because everything here is going terribly.[69] She also says that we needn't look for you before Christmas. By that time the snow will be on the ground and the only satisfaction about that is that you will be saved from a licking at golf because, I want to tell you, I am getting very good.

I hope you have all the good-looking girls in your company looking forward, with anticipation, to meeting the high Irish of Boston, because I have a gang around me that must be fed on wild meat lately, they are so bad. As for me, I have too many troubles around me to both[er] with such things at the present time. Everything may be better, however, when you arrive.

Give my best to Fred, and behave yourself.

Sincerely,

Joseph P. Kennedy to Arthur Houghton

Boston, November 25, 1921

Dear Arthur:

I have your note and you have probably received a wire from me by this time as to what I have been able to do. At any rate, I start this afternoon to try and dig you up an apartment. I will surely land something that will be satisfactory.

Rose and I went to see John Charles Thomas Wednesday night, and while their business was good, there has arisen a terrible prejudice against Thomas in this town.[70] His overbearing manner is plainly discernible on the stage and the play is hopelessly

69. Between 1920 and 1923, while not filming *The Duke of Chimney Butte* or *Billy Jim* for Fred Stone Productions (of which JPK was treasurer), Stone appeared in both the Broadway and the traveling productions of Dillingham's *Tip Top*. The show's enormous success made up for the financial failures of some of the other Dillingham productions of the period, such as *The Love Letter* of 1921.
70. Wholesome American baritone John Charles Thomas (1887–1960) was at the time playing the lead in Victor Jacobi's unsuccessful adaptation of Molnár's *The Love Letter*.

weak. I understand that the show is to be disbanded a week from Saturday night, and if that is true and you are in need of girls for your show, I would suggest your getting in touch with Dillingham to see if some of these could not be shifted to your show. The two Bradys are in it and they would be a notable addition to your company.

I am tickled to death that you are coming on so early as things are horribly dull, and if it were not for the fact that we have had some Yale money to spend for the last few days, life would not be worth living.

The Stone pictures are coming along first rate and the Orpheum Circuit of the West has booked them in all the big cities that they control.[71] When Fred comes to Boston we are going to put the thing over right, if it is the last thing we do, as I have control of the New England agency for these pictures.

If you could arrange to get in at a little more reasonable hour on Monday, I will be there to meet you; otherwise I will have to postpone it until some time later in the day.

I think it would be a good idea if you would wire the fat-headed Lothian who now runs the Colonial Theatre, and who is as big a fool as he ever was, that it would be well to save four front row seats for all performances, subject to your order. He won't have brains enough to do that and we may need them from time to time.

If there is anything you want taken care of in Boston before your arrival, send me a wire and Moore and I will see that it is done.

Best regards to you and Fred.

Sincerely yours,

Joseph P. Kennedy to Ethel Turner

Boston, December 28, 1921

My dear Miss Turner:

I enclose check for $20. Will you please see that $10 is deposited to Joe's savings account and $10 to Jack's, — this being from their uncles.

Yours,

Joseph P. Kennedy to P. J. Kennedy

Boston, January 12, 1922

Dear Father:

It has occurred to me that some immediate step should be taken on the question of getting additional collateral from John L. Bates.[72] I went to see him some months ago and he told me at that time that he had a lot of International Trust and United States Trust stock which, when it came back to its normal price, he would be able to send over to us. There has been a marked appreciation in these stocks and I do not know whether you have heard from them or not. My own feeling is that Bates is not on the level about paying these loans or reducing them. He owes everybody and unless we get after him very hard, the first thing we know he is going into bankruptcy or is going to die, and we are going to take some very heavy losses.

---

71. Martin Beck's Orpheum Circuit dominated the West Coast (and to some degree the Midwestern) vaudeville circuit much as the Keith Circuit controlled the East.
72. John Lewis Bates (1859–1946), former Republican speaker of the Massachusetts House of Representatives, 1897–99; lieutenant governor, 1903–04; and president of the Massachusetts Constitutional Convention, 1917–19.

There is no sense in letting up on this, because if we do it is going to be a very serious matter. I would suggest that in the first place you check up the loans that he has secured by real estate, and see if we are protected, or not. Then I would go after him in very strong fashion and get additional security or make him pay off some of his loans.

I cannot impress you too much with the seriousness of this matter. I have some inside information that makes it very apparent that we must do something, or otherwise we will be burdened with an enormous loss.

Yours,

Joseph P. Kennedy to Thomas Croak

Boston, February 7, 1922

Dear Mr. Croak:

I am sorry that we were not able to get together last week for lunch, and as I am leaving for Florida this week, it looks as though we would have to postpone our date until after my return.

What I particularly wanted to talk with you about is the question of Father's salary. I am writing to Mr. McClellan also,[73] as I feel that you two are the most interested in him and in me of any that are in the Bank. You know, as well as I, that to pay Father a salary such as the Bank is now paying him — less than some of their bookkeepers — is really a disgrace. Although I realize that he has fought consistently against it, nevertheless the Bank should pay him at least $300 a month.

I feel that you and Father are really responsible for the Bank being organized, and it seems too bad that you both do not get more out of it. If there is any way that it could ever be arranged, nothing would please me more.

The increase in salary for Father would, for the most part, come out of me, as the largest stockholder, so I am sure there certainly would be no objections from the stockholders.

I wish you would give this your attention and try to put the matter through, even with the opposition of my father. It means a lot to me and I am more than interested in it.

Thanking you for all past favors and kindnesses to me, I remain,

Joseph P. Kennedy to Matthew Brush

June 26, 1922

Dear Matt:

Eddie Moore spoke to me about some gin that you would like to get hold of. Before selling it to you I would like you to get the whole story on it.

The committee on our Decennial at Harvard bought 190 proof alcohol, and had it blended and fixed up by a Mr. Dehan, who formerly worked for my father, and who really is one of the best men on this in this part of the country. The stuff turned out very well indeed, and was perfectly satisfactory to all the fellows in the class who are, of course, used to the best — and the worst. Twenty-five dollars is the actual cost of the

---

73. Both Thomas Croak and William McClellan (whom JPK had sent substantially the same letter) had been elected to the board of directors of the Columbia Trust Company at the time of JPK's election to the institution's presidency in January 1914.

stuff, and I would be very happy to have you have it, if you think it would be satisfactory.

I would appreciate it if you would let me know at once, because the committee itself will take all of it that is not used.

With best regards.

Sincerely yours,

Joseph P. Kennedy to Matthew Brush

June 29, 1922

Dear Matt:

I have sent over to the address you gave me two cartons, each containing forty half-pints. I think that everything is O.K.

Very truly yours,

Joseph P. Kennedy to Father Toma

Boston, November 1st, 1922

Dear Father Toma:

My sister Loretta,[74] who called on you yesterday, has told me how very kind you were concerning your willingness to help Mr. Fitzgerald in his candidacy.[75] I do not know how well you know Mr. Fitzgerald or his record, but it has been a very progressive one, and one which has recognized all the newer bloods in this country.

I want you to know that we very much appreciate your kindness in this matter.

Yours very truly,

Joseph P. Kennedy to Christopher Dunphy

Boston, December 20, 1922

Dear Chris:

Your voice sounded just as snappy as ever over the telephone.

You were always good in delivering on matters in which you had some connection, but the one I am putting up to you now required "big league" work. As you know, the bill to purchase the Cape Cod Canal has been in Congress for some months. It received the recommendation of three secretaries of the Harding Cabinet and passed the Senate as a rider to the Rivers and Harbors Bill. The bill was lost in the House because sufficient work was not done on it.[76] The bill should have been reported by Congressman Winslow from Massachusetts, who was Chairman of the Interstate Commerce Com-

---

74. Mary Loretta Kennedy, later Connolly (1892–1972).
75. On September 12, 1922, John F. Fitzgerald had won the Democratic nomination for the upcoming Massachusetts gubernatorial race by 89,831 votes to Peter F. Sullivan's 53,697. On November 7, however, Republican Channing Cox would be reelected governor of Massachusetts, receiving 464,873 votes to John F. Fitzgerald's 404,192.
76. In December 1921, Representative Samuel Winslow (1862–1940), chairman of the Committee on Interstate Commerce and a Republican of the Fourth Massachusetts District, proposed a bill to permit the federal government to buy the Cape Cod Canal. Since then, however, the bill had languished in committee.

mission and has told everybody in Massachusetts that he is doing all he can for the bill. Confidentially, I believe that he has done his best to put the bill in his pocket and give us as little help as possible, but, of course, I cannot prove this except by the fact that, up to date, he has accomplished nothing. The only course left for the bill now, in order to get it before the present Congress, is to have a special rule adopted, and the only way to get that rule would be by request from the President to Representative Campbell[77] that he would like the special rule for the Canal Bill. Of course, if the President feels, and rightly so, that Winslow is not sufficiently interested to go to him and ask that the special rule be adopted, it is very unlikely that Harding will go to the bother to ask Representative Campbell for the rule. The President may very properly feel that until Winslow comes to him he will not feel like interfering in the matter. Winslow, on the other hand, is kidding everybody up here that everything is all right, but I know down deep in my heart that it is far from being all right, and the first thing we know the time will have elapsed in which the special rule could be put across. What we want, of course, is to get the bill introduced into the House. Now it is no good for you to send back word that we must get Winslow, because we will always give you the same answer—he tells us he is all right, but he gets nothing done. Is there not some way we can get the President to assume that Winslow is anxious, in view of his public statements, to get the special rule? Now we do not want Harding to use one iota of influence as far as the passage of the bill is concerned. We feel that if it gets introduced into the House we have a very good chance of getting it passed. What we do want, however, is to get this special rule, and to my way of thinking the only one who can do this is somebody who plays poker with Harding, or who can talk to him outside of any political connection. Lodge[78] and Weeks and all those fellows are, of course, friendly, but, to my way of thinking, they are not the men to do it. Therefore, I fall back on you to suggest how it can be done. Of course Mr. McLean[79] could do it if he so desired, but this is a personal matter with me, as my boss has put it up to me to see if anything can be done, and I am out to make good. My other suggestion is Will Hays, for whom I did a number of favors during the censorship fight, and who would be very glad, I am sure, to say a word to the President if it would be of any help.[80] Unfortunately, Hays is now on the west coast and will not be in New York before the 2nd or 3rd of January and it is possible this may be too late. Will you give this some thought, and when you have decided on a plan of campaign give me a call on the telephone. Of course any expense incurred in this I will be more than glad to meet.

   With best regards,

Yours very truly,

77. Guy Edgar Campbell (1871–1940), Republican from the Thirty-sixth District of Pennsylvania.
78. Historian, essayist, jurist, Republican member of Congress, 1880–87, and U.S. senator from Massachusetts, 1893–1924, Henry Cabot Lodge (1850–1924). Lodge had defeated the Democratic contender, John F. Fitzgerald, in his reelection bid of 1916. In 1919, the same year that Lodge led the opposition to the League of Nations Covenant as Senate majority leader, he had sponsored a bill proposing that the federal government purchase and operate the Cape Cod Canal, which had failed to pass the Commerce Committee.
79. Edward B. McLean, editor of the *Washington Post*.
80. William Harrison Hays (1879–1954), the recently appointed president of the new Motion Pictures Producers and Distributors of America, and President Harding's former postmaster general. Hays had spent much of autumn of 1922 attempting to combat state-by-state film censorship measures in the wake of a number of lurid industry scandals that had shocked public sensibilities nationally. The Massachusetts film censorship referendum had been defeated on November 7.

Rose Kennedy: *Diary*

[Brookline] January 1, 1923

Came up to Poland Springs, [Maine,] December 27th, with Joe and Jack and Mary Moore.[81] Eddie and Joe came later. Two horribly snowy days and boys had to stay in the house. Very gay crowd. College boys and girls. Went to Mass at Lewiston and had dinner at Bill Gray's,[82] then coasted at Auburn on Sunday. Stormy on Monday. Joe and Ed went home in afternoon. Masquerade at night.

January 2, 1923

Joe and I went home on afternoon train leaving Jack and Mary, as I think Jack needs a few days longer. Train 1/2 hour late. Jack said he had to put his hand over Mrs. Moore's mouth last night, cause she was humming (she really was snoring).

January 3, 1923

Put adhesive on Kathleen's thumb, so she would not suck it. She took it off and in the morning when I asked her where it was she said, "A little mouse took it".

January 7, 1923

Took care of children. Miss Brooks, the governess, helped. Kathleen still has bronchitis and Joe sick in bed. Great life.

January 14, 1923

Miss Brooks went home as her father was sick. Mrs. Banks and Mrs. Moore over to help with children. Ed and Joe went to Winthrop to see Grandma who is sick[83] and Uncle John.

January 16, 1923

Joe left on 5 o'clock for Palm Beach with Bill Spargo,[84] Eddie, and Ted O'Leary. They joined him in New York and left there about 5 o'clock Wednesday, the 17th.

January 27, 1923

Came home from Poland Springs.[85] Heard that Jack took a drink of ammonia instead of Poland Water. Did not swallow it, so he is okay.

February 8, 1923

Joe home on 1 o'clock today train, very late yesterday coming to New York.

February 14, 1923

Eunice[86] walking alone and talking a lot. Best little talker of all. Also tries to make a bow and say, "Little Partner, dance with me," etc. Joe in Washington. Sent him "Bear" valentine.

February 21, 1923

Went in to hear Hilare Belloc,[87] English lecturer, with Mrs. [Mary] Moore. Ed in Washington. Joe went to Hockey game.

81. Mrs. Edward Moore.
82. William P. Gray (1879–1927), founder and president of the Maine and New Hampshire Theater Companies, who had introduced JPK to film in 1919. Since then, JPK had served as treasurer and financial adviser to the company.
83. Her mother-in-law had stomach cancer.
84. William Spargo (1878–1925), the owner, editor and publisher of the *Quincy* (Massachusetts) *Evening Telegram*.
85. She had taken four-year-old Rosemary and two-year-old Kathleen to Maine on January 17 because of what she described as a "grippe epidemic" among children in Brookline.
86. Eunice Mary Kennedy, later Shriver (1921–).
87. Poet, satirist, critic and former MP, Joseph Hilaire Pierre Belloc (1870–1953) was currently on a speaking tour of the United States. He would publish his reflections on his journey and on the differences between America and Britain as *The Contrast* in the same year.

February 22, 1923

Joe working on Canal Bill. Joe played squash in A.M., later we all went coasting. Stayed home evening, Kathleen goes out now in her little sleigh.

February 23, 1923

Joe went inside altar rail today at early Mass to practice being altar boy, but has not been one yet. Has Cassock all ready.

February 25, 1923

The boys have a new song about the Bed Bugs and the Cooties. Also a club where they initiate new members by sticking pins into them.

March 7, 1923

Joe helped serve Mass today with other older boy.

March 30, 1923

Jackie did not care much about wishing for happy death, but thought he would like to wish for two dogs. Joe went to Stations[88] all dirty.

April 4, 1923

Little Aggie[89] and I left for California at 10 A.M. from South Station. Joe Malloy, Eddie, Bill Spargo, Father and Joe down. Mother at Saranac.[90]

Joseph P. Kennedy to Rose Kennedy:[91] *Telegram*

APR 8 1923

ROSA DEAR I STILL MAINTAIN A REPUTATION AS THE GREATEST MANAGER IN THE WORLD THE CHILDREN ARE FINE JACK IS SLEEPING EVERY NOON AND IS GREATLY IMPROVED STOP THE MOORES HAVE BEEN THE BUSIEST PEOPLE IN THE WORLD AND TONIGHT MAY IS GOING TO THE MISSION STOP JOE IS GREAT AND THE LITTLE GIRLS LOOK FINE STOP WE GO OUT FRIDAY NIGHTS SO THE COOK IS GREAT AND ALL IN ALL WE ARE DOING NICELY STOP MY MOTHER IMPROVING TOO STOP YOUR MOTHER AND EUNICE ARE FINE STOP YOUR FATHER SAYS EVERYTHING IS FINE WITH THEM STOP I HOPE YOU ARE HAVING A REAL GOOD TIME BECAUSE YOU RICHLY DESERVE IT PLEASE DO NOT THINK TOO MUCH ABOUT US AND SPOIL YOUR PARTY STOP I AM NOT LONESOME BECAUSE I FIND MYSELF VERY HAPPY IN THE THOUGHT THAT YOU ARE ENJOYING YOURSELF LOTS OF LOVE FROM US ALL

JOE

Joseph P. Kennedy to Rose Kennedy: *Telegram*

1923 APR 16 AM 3 46

RECEIVED WIRE AFRAID YOU STILL THINKING OF BOSTON TOO MUCH STOP[92] WE ARE GETTING ALONG SPLENDIDLY STOP JOE AND JACK WENT TO OREARDON PARTY

---

88. Of the Cross, that is.
89. Her sister, Mary Agnes Fitzgerald, later Gargan (1892–1936).
90. While ministering to returning servicemen in the great tented hospitals that covered Boston Common at the end of World War I, Rose's younger sister, Eunice Fitzgerald (1900–1923), had contracted tuberculosis. Their mother, Mary Josephine Hannon Fitzgerald (1865–1964), had accompanied Eunice to Saranac Lake, New York, in order to make use of the area's extensive facilities for consumptives.
91. Rose and her sister Agnes had made their way westward, arriving in Chicago on April 5, Kansas City on the 6th, and Albuquerque on the 7th. They spent April 8 at the Grand Canyon and arrived at Riverside, California, the following day, where they "Stopped at Mission Inn."
92. None of Rose Kennedy's telegrams or letters from her 1923 trip to California appear to have survived.

YESTERDAY JACK SAYS THEY WERE ROTTENEST DANCERS THERE LITTLE GIRLS FINE
WE START MISSION TONIGHT WAS EVERYTHING ALL RIGHT SO FAR WITH YOU MY
FAMILY AND YOURS STILL IMPROVING BANK ACCOUNT AND INSTRUCTION IN YOUR
LETTER FIXED UP SEND NIGHTLETTER OCCASIONALLY TO MY OFFICE I LIKE TO
KNOW HOW YOU ARE STOP SAW SCHOOL TEACHERS THEY REPORT BIG IMPROVE-
MENT WEATHER VERY COOL MARY WRITING YOU TODAY LOVE FROM US ALL

JOE

Joseph P. Kennedy to Rose Kennedy: *Telegram*

23 APR 20 AM 12 02

DEAR ROSE TODAY IS HOLIDAY AND FATHER TOOK BOYS TO MARATHON I WENT THE
GOLF TOURNAMENT AT WOODLAND SO STOP JOE JACK AND ROSE[93] WENT OVER TO
BUNKER HILL YESTERDAY AND THE BOYS WENT TO THE TOP STOP GOT YOUR TWO
LETTERS AND PICTURE YOU LOOK FINE MOTHER AND DWYER HAVE BOXES AND
WERE PLEASED YOU WERE VERY THOUGHTFUL IS THERE ANYTHING I CAN DO FOR
YOU AT LOSANGELES STOP I AM GOING TO NEWYORK NEXT WEEK TO MATT BRUSH
DINNER STOP[94]TONIGHT I WISH IT WAS IN LOSANGELES STOP EVERYBODY FINE
AND WE ALL SEND OUR LOVE PARTICULARLY ME

JOE

Joseph P. Kennedy to Rose Kennedy: *Telegram*

1923 MAY 9 AM 2 17

DEAR ROSA I AM LOOKING FORWARD TO THE NINETEENTH LIKE I DID FOR OCTOBER
SEVENTH SOME YEARS AGO EVERYBODY STILL FINE BUT I THINK THE HELP WILL
WELCOME YOU BACK YOUR CLUB[95] HAD THEIR PICNIC TODAY EVERYBODY MEN-
TIONED THAT YOU SENT THEM POSTAL STOP I THINK IT WAS VERY THOUGHTFUL
STOP I SUGGEST TAKING THE TRAIN FROM CHICAGO THAT ARRIVES BOSTON ABOUT
NOON YOUR SCHEDULE TRAIN ARRIVES LATE IN AFTERNOON AND IS TERRIBLE
TRIP STOP YOUR DRESS ARRIVED SAFELY YOUR LETTERS ARE FINE WE ALL SEND
OUR LOVE

JOE

93. That is, four-year-old Rosemary.
94. Matthew Brush had invited JPK to a dinner celebrating his elevation to the presidency of the American
    International Corporation on April 6.
95. After graduating from college in June 1910, Rose Fitzgerald had returned to Boston and founded a club
    ". . . composed of young women who had been to school abroad and were interested in studying and
    discussing world wide history and meaningful current events. Thanks to my father, we were able to get
    all sorts of visiting dignitaries to address us." One of these was the English Jesuit, Bernard Vaughn, who
    suggested the name "the Ace of Clubs . . . meaning the first and the foremost and the most important of
    all clubs."

Joseph P. Kennedy to Dr. Frank Lahey[96]

June 11, 1923

Dear Dr. Lahey:

I appreciate very much your very frank and considerate letter of June 5th, regarding my mother's operation. Fortunately probably this is my first experience with a major operation, and I am just as much at a loss to know what fee should be charged as you were. May I suggest $1,000.00 as what I feel in my mind is fair, considering what I feel that I could afford to pay. I am frank to say that I feel this is more than my father could pay. However, if this does not meet with your approval, kindly let me know, and I will adjust it to your satisfaction.

I appreciate very much the work that you and your staff did in this case, and I feel that I should make any sacrifice to live up to any just obligations.

Joseph P. Kennedy to Dr. Frank Lahey

June 14, 1923

Dear Dr. Lahey:

Enclosed please find my check for one thousand dollars in payment of your fee. I want to take this opportunity to express to you and your assistants the deep appreciation of myself and family for your many kindnesses and great care shown my mother.

We feel keenly her loss, but we have the consolation of knowing that she was in the best hands possible, and that everything was done for her that possibly could be. It was just God's Will.[97]

Kindest personal regards.

Sincerely yours,

Rose Kennedy: *Diary*

[Beach Island, Massachusetts] June 15, 1923

Up to town. Florence with me. Shopped. Joe up all night on business. Boys down for good.

June 19, 1923

Eunice going back, cannot sleep at home.[98]

September 11, 1923

Boys went to school. Staying with Moores. Jack said at night, "Well, here I have been home only a few hours and the cops are chasing me already." He later explained he was teasing a little girl who told policeman and he hid in a cellar.

---

96. Lahey (1880–1953), a professor of clinical surgery at the Harvard Medical School and surgeon in chief at the New England Baptist Hospital, was at the time attempting to establish a new clinic in Boston under his own name.
97. Following her operation, Mary Hickey Kennedy had died at the New England Baptist Hospital of uremia on May 20, at the age of sixty-five.
98. On September 25, *Boston Evening Transcript*'s "Recent Deaths" section would announce that
    Miss Eunice Fitzgerald, youngest daughter of former Mayor and Mrs. John F. Fitzgerald, died this morning at her parents' home, 39 Welles Avenue, Dorchester, of tuberculosis, which was first contracted while she was doing war work for the Red Cross on Boston Common. On several occasions during the last two years and a half Miss Fitzgerald has been at Saranac Lake and her condition had grown so serious the last few days, that she was brought home from there only yesterday.

Boys went to store and saw "No dogs allowed in this Restaurant" and they put in front of it "Hot".

October 28, 1923

Boys stole false mustaches for Halloween from shop — Anna Shop.

November 21, 1923

Boys were down cellar collecting milk bottles to sell when I found them.

December 5, 1923

Jack said, "Daddy has a Sweet Tooth, hasn't he? I wonder which one it is?" His teacher is coming to tell on him (?) [*sic*]. He says, "You know I am getting on all right and if you study too much, you're liable to go crazy".

Joseph P. Kennedy: *Memorandum for Matthew Brush*

December 14, 1923

I feel very strongly that the market will not last much longer than another three weeks. I feel that the top has been on Industrials and I figure that the margin of profit will be greatly reduced from now on. Rails may stay at present prices unless we have some radical legislation in Congress. There may be a little hope for oils, and sugars but unless your friends in New York strong-arm this market and elect Calvin Coolidge president, I think we are in for it.

Rose Kennedy: *Diary*

February 28, 1923 [1924]

Agnes sent boys alligators from South at this time. They named them after their best friends Jerry Berman and Charlie Driscoll. Charlie has a dog whose name is Brandy, because his father is a bootlegger.

Joseph P. Kennedy to Vera Murray[99]

March Fourteenth 1924

Dear Vera:

I just returned from Chicago this morning, and while there I saw the second act of the Duncan Sisters' show.[100] The show itself is not particularly good, at least what I saw of it, but the Duncan sisters have made an unqualified hit. I think a good deal of this talk is bunk, because there seems to be a very good disposition of the company towards the two of them.

Also, I feel that Harris is still interested with Wilkes of San Francisco, and that they are grossing about $20,000 a week. The Duncan sisters are getting about $2200 a week and as they have written all the music in the show their royalties are about $700 per week.

---

99. Assistant to producer C. B. Dillingham.
100. Despite having been panned by critics as the "freak of the season" and "a terrible thing," *Topsy and Eva*, the unlikely musical comedy extravaganza based on *Uncle Tom's Cabin* had opened in Chicago at the Selwyn Theatre in December 1923. The show would gross nearly half a million dollars during its six-month run in Chicago before moving on to Broadway and then to Europe. Rosetta Duncan (1896–1959), in blackface, played Topsy to her sister Vivian's (1899–1986) Little Eva St. Clair.

They have a score for a new show, and the numbers I heard are simply knock-outs. You know I am pretty tough on criticisms, but I think this pair have got something if they can be handled at all. They are still crazy to get back to Dillingham management, and regardless of what feelings you may have, from a money-making point of view they should be considered. I should judge that the pay roll for the show as it now stands, hardly amounts to anything at all, and the show would have to be strengthened a great deal to be brought into New York. I think, however, that they would like to get in line with C. B.[101] again, and it is well to have this in mind in considering them.

While out there they introduced me to a boy named Martin Downey [sic] an Irish kid from Connecticut, who was singing with the Leviathan Orchestra.[102] He has a very agreeable personality, and I think he is a wonderful singer. He is a tenor of the first water, and somebody is going to grab him soon. He makes voices like John Steele's[103] and all that type just after the top-notchers, go into the discard. They are playing for Grand Rapids this week and are gradually moving East. He can sing an Irish song better than anyone I ever heard with the one exception of John McCormack.[104] Don't lose sight of him.

I hope to be in New York the week after next.

Love and kisses,

Rose Kennedy: *Diary*

April 19, [1924]

Met Joe at Providence after his week in New York on Yellow Cab and Harny [sic] matter.[105] Dinner at Duck Inn.

101. Dillingham.
102. The "King of Jazz," bandleader Paul Whiteman, had discovered Morton Downey (1901–1985), an Irish-American tenor from Connecticut, in 1919 and would feature him with the Whiteman Orchestra throughout the early 1920s. In the 1930s and 1940s Downey's national broadcasts over WABC would make him one of the best-known and most highly paid entertainers in the United States. Downey would go on to sing both at the Roosevelt White House and at George VI's coronation in 1936.
103. The veteran of numerous Ziegfeld's Follies, tenor John Steel (1900–1971) was the first to sing the beauty pageant standard, "A Pretty Girl Is Like A Melody" in the Follies of 1919.
104. The Irish-born tenor John McCormack (1884–1945) had made his American debut at the St. Louis Exposition of 1904; soon after, he embarked on a successful operatic and recording career on both sides of the Atlantic.
105. Over the previous few years, Walter Crawford Howey (1882–1954), editor of the Hearst Papers' *Boston American* (and the model for the city editor in Ben Hecht and Charles McArthur's *The Front Page*) had invested much of his savings in the Yellow Cab Company of Chicago. Yellow Cab, the first enterprise to provide a fleet of clean, reliable taxis that the customer could hail from the street, had been an overwhelming success in Chicago and by early 1924 was attempting to break into the New York market. At Howey's request, JPK and Eddie Moore had spent several weeks in April and May attempting to defend the stock of the Yellow Cab Company of Chicago (and by extension, Howey's savings) from an anonymous hostile pool's attempts to drive its price down. In secrecy JPK and Eddie Moore spent several weeks in April and May at the Waldorf-Astoria in New York, where they attempted to countermanipulate and defend the stock against the pool's efforts to drive it down.

Joseph P. Kennedy to John Borden[106]

June Nineteenth 1924

Dear John:

I was sorry to have missed you in Chicago. We tried to locate you a couple of times, but there didn't seem to be much trace. I waited around the Yellow Cab meetings on Monday, but you didn't show up.

I went in on that "Drive-it-Yourself" scheme for $25,000.[107] I am going to work along with it, not to the exclusion of my other business however, and see how it turns out.

I also received a check for $20,000 for which also please accept my thanks. The Yellow stocks are acting rather better, and I take some credit for this as I suggested very strongly that they stop trying to sell stocks and let them take a natural course, and hence the rise yesterday. I think it was necessary to keep the present holders of the stock interested in what they had.

I will keep you posted if I have any news from around here, and would appreciate your letting me know if anything is going on. I will be in Chicago sometime next month, and wish you would let me know when you plan to come East.

With kindest regards, I am

Very truly yours,

Joseph P. Kennedy to Sherman Bowles[108]

October 22, 1924

Dear Sherman:

I have been thinking over our bet, and it occurs to me that we should each estimate the percentage of the total vote cast that LaFollette will get, and I suggest that, if this meets with your approval, we mail to one another, say on next Monday night, just what we figure the percentage will be. That is, if there will be a million votes cast, and you think that LaFollette will get 150,000, your guess will be 15%.

You mail me your figure Monday night, and I will mail you mine Monday night. We will both keep them for reference, and the loser buys the hat.

Very truly yours,

Joseph P. Kennedy to Sherman Bowles

October 27, 1924

Dear Sherm:

My guess on the La Follette vote in the State of Massachusetts is 18% (eighteen) of the total vote cast.[109]

---

106. John Borden (1884–1961), joint founder and secretary of the Yellow Cab Company.
107. Following the stabilization of the Yellow Cab Stock, John Hertz (1879–1961) established the Drive-Ur-Self Corporation (the precursor to Hertz Rent-a-Car) and effected the merger of Chicago Motor Coach Company that he had founded in 1922 with the Fifth Avenue Coach Company to form the Omnibus Corporation of America, all of which General Motors would buy the following year for some $16 million.
108. Sherman Hoar Bowles (1890–1952), the 1912 business manager of the *Harvard Crimson* and the publisher of Western Massachusetts's *Springfield Republican*.
109. According to LaFollette's running mate, Senator Burton Wheeler, JPK had made a $1,000 contribution to the Progressive campaign. On October 29, Bowles bet that Progressive presidential candidate

I always wear a brown hat, and usually a Stetson or a Dobbe.
With best regards,

Very truly yours,

John F. Kennedy, 7, to Rose Kennedy

Mansion House South Poland, ME. Dec. 29, 1924

Dear Mother

we are haveing a very nice time we go skiing we go sliding and we go to bed the same time that we go at home and we have a very nice time and we go out avry day and the horse are good. and one of the horse are lazy and is name is Happy he can run if he wants to. but hees a good horse just a same. love frome

Jack

Joseph P. Kennedy, Jr., 9, to Joseph P. Kennedy

Dec. 1924

Dear Dadey

we are getting along fine we went skiing this morning and I think we are going again this aafternoon. We went a little to toboganing this morning. And we are gaing a very nice time we go to bed at half past seven. We get up at quarter to eight I wish you would send me some letters. Can't we go out ten above. Please sent that answer.

love from
Joe

John F. Kennedy, 7, to Rose and Joseph P. Kennedy

Dec. 29, 1924

Dear dady

and mother we went skiing to day and we hade raceses and Joe one the first one and Eddie one the second one and one the third one and we skied down a hill that was a quarter of a mild long and I fell and I hat to chase it down too the bottom of the hill. And we went toboganing.

love from Jack

Joseph P. Kennedy, Jr., 9, to Joseph P. Kennedy

Feb. 10, 1925. Brookline Mass

Dear Dady

I am very well. Jack is all right now and so is the little girls. I got a ten all ~~the~~ last week in arithmetic and I am doing better in oral arithmetic and I am getting a little poor in English. This week in reading I got two tens, On Monday we do not have Reading we ~~have~~ have drawing instead. In Spelling I got two 9+ and one ten. In a arithmetic I got, a nine plus and one nine and a ten. I hope you are enjoying your trip.[110]

Love from
Joe

Senator Robert Marion La Follette of Wisconsin (1855–1925) would garner 10 percent of the Massachusetts vote. On November 4, La Follette received 141,225 votes in Massachusetts, or 12.5 percent.

110. JPK was vacationing at the Royal Poinciana Hotel in Palm Beach.

Joseph P. Kennedy to Rose Kennedy

HARVARD CLUB [New York], August 18, 1925

Rosa dear,

I am getting ready to go now & when you get this I will be on my way, but I will be coming back soon so please don't be too lonesome & have a great time.[111]

I just want you to know that going away on trips like this makes me realize just how little anything amounts to except you as years go on I just love you more than anything in the world and I always wonder whether I ever do half enough for you to show you how much I appreciate you.

Well dear this is just a little love letter from a husband to wife married 11 years. Break 50 if you have to take a lesson morning & night.

The "Popper"[112] said today he would be down soon so you'll be busy & I'll be home before you know it.

Love to you & my wonderful family.

Joe

Joseph P. Kennedy to Rose Kennedy

Sunday Morning [August 23, 1925]

Rosa dear,

We have just finished Mass celebrated by an Italian priest in the 2nd cabin. They do give you service on these boats.

Yesterday we ran into a lot of fog and it was fairly rocky and today promises no better.

Jack[113] & I have taken up deck tennis to save us from reading every book in the library.

We haven't met any people on the boat probably because they don't look interesting enough.

We had a concert last night with a Mr. Carl Fishcher of Vienna Opera Co & Sophie Tucker the American coon shouter entertaining and it was quite good.[114]

I have found a strawberry jam that I am sure you will like. It is made in England by "Cairns" and it tastes fine.

I showed all the kids' pictures to Mrs. Potter yesterday (at her request), and of course she thought they were grand.

She is a splendid type, of fine family gone absolutely broke but she still shows breeding while the old man would stay tight the whole trip if he could find someone to stay tight with.

111. Having assembled a Boston syndicate interested in buying Film Booking Offices, JPK was traveling to Europe, eventually making his way to London, in order to discuss the offer with Lord Inverforth of the merchant bank of Graham's and Company. Since Robertson-Cole had lost some $7 million over the past five years, however, the syndicate's offer of $1 million would be unacceptable to Graham's for the time being.

112. Presumably her father, John F. Fitzgerald.

113. JPK was traveling with theatrical producer Jack Potter and Potter's parents. James Potter, the producer's father, was a former manager of the Philadelphia Phillies.

114. "The last of the red-hot mamas," Sophie Tucker (1884–1966) achieved her initial theatrical successes in blackface on the East Coast Park Circuit in 1907 and 1908. Soon after, she began billing herself as the "World-Renowned Coon Shouter" and a "Manipulator of Coon Melodies." After a smash season on the London stage at the Metropole in *The Midnight Follies*, of 1922, she would return to London three years later to play "the fashionable Kit-Kat Klub" in the Haymarket.

We sleep at Cherbourg tomorrow night the Potters leave us for Paris and we arrive in Southampton Tuesday noon, arriving London that afternoon. We will probably stay there a few days in order to order suits & then move on to Paris returning in about a week or so.

I miss you all like the deuce.

Love,
Joe

Joseph P. Kennedy to Rose Kennedy

Monday night [August 24, 1925]

Rosa dear,

We are just getting near Cherbourg & expect to be in London tomorrow. The trip has been rather lazy and I miss you all so much. I loved the pictures and yours is great except I think you have a better nose than they gave you. I was tickled to get it but you should have put it in the first envelope. You know that's where you belong and always will. Love to all.

Joe

Joseph P. Kennedy to John F. Kennedy, 8: *Postcard*

9-1-25 Paris

Hello Jack:

You must learn French and come over here. The little French boys roll a hoop instead of playing football.

Love,
Joe [sic]

Joseph P. Kennedy to William Gray[115]

February 5, 1926

Dear Bill:

I just closed the deal fifteen minutes ago and I am now on my way.[116] I have read your letter, and I intend to make it a bible of good common sense for the administration of the organization. I realize better than ever just what you advise in this proposition, and I do hope you will get well enough so I can confer with you.

I have been damn miserable for the past year on account of the misunderstanding that caused you and I to keep apart.[117] I felt that I had always demonstrated my actual feelings towards you so that you would never think I would do anything to slight you or make you unhappy. But these things do come up once in a while, and people get too proud to discuss them. I sincerely hope that you will just blot out this year as I have, and

---

115. Founder and president and treasurer of the Maine and New Hampshire Theater Companies of which JPK had served as an investment adviser since 1919.
116. Having been hired originally to sell Cox's and Graham's interests in the Robertson-Cole Pictures Corporation five years earlier, JPK finished by buying it for $1.1 million through the syndicate he had formed (consisting mainly of himself and Boston attorney, Guy Currier, and of lesser investors including his father-in-law).
117. The details of their misunderstanding went unrecorded.

we can resume the relationship where we left off some time ago. I am naturally interested in the businesses in which I put my money, but I have got by the point where I think about them to the exclusion of every other thought that I should have.

Just discount 99% of the things I am supposed to have said, and I have already discounted 99 9/10ths of those you are supposed to have said, and lets call it off. As I have said before, I appreciate your advice, and I hope I may call on you from time to time for further suggestions that you care to give me.

With kindest regards,

Yours sincerely,

Joseph P. Kennedy to Joseph Schnitzer[118]

[New York] February 11, 1926

Dear Joe:

After having sat in your chair for the past four days, and using your office and your efficient secretary, I am beginning to think I am a "picture" man.

There has been nothing particularly exciting here. I brought over with me from Boston an expert accountant and we have been going over the financial situation, trying to familiarize ourselves with it. However, I feel there are a few things that can be done to improve the situation.

I met most of the office people and was very much impressed with everything I have seen of the organization up to the present time.

We ran into a few situations which were not quite in accord with our expectations on several Balance Sheet items, but we are trying to adjust them now.

It appears unlikely that the stock[119] from England will get here much before the end of the month so that I will probably not be able to leave for the Coast before the first week in March. Everybody seems to feel that I should stay for the convention. However, I will be guided by your opinion of the matter.

I received a wire from Mr. Powers,[120] congratulating me on the deal and telling me that Mr. McCormick wishes me to get in touch with Mr. Rowland[121] for the sale of the studios for $1,500,000. I have done nothing on it as yet and will, of course, not make any trade until you are informed about it. It really does not look serious at all, however.

Will Hays has been very anxious that I should join the organization, but I told him of our financial position and that we haven't the means to join the organization at the present time although we are anxious to do so.

If you wish to send me any telegrams you may send them in care of the Harvard Club.

Mr. Yates sent me his resignation today, as a member of the Board.

I wonder if it would be possible for someone out there in the studios to give me an idea, in advance, of what our financial requirements will be for the next four or five weeks. I am contemplating a very comprehensive plan for financing our next year's

---

118. Joseph Schnitzer (1887–1944), Robertson-Cole's vice president in charge of Production and Distribution.
119. Robertson-Cole's film stock.
120. Patrick Anthony Powers (1869–1948), treasurer of Robertson-Cole.
121. Richard Rowland (1881–1947), founder of the Metro Picture Corporation, had sold out his holdings in 1919 to Marcus Loew and had since become general production manager and vice president of First National Pictures.

product, although I understand the finances will not be needed until April. I will discuss this with you when I reach the Coast.

I think I have practically covered all the happenings since my arrival at the office. I also want to reiterate at this time what I already told you; I have the greatest confidence in the world in your ability and I am interesting people in this Company, with me, who have unlimited financial resources and there is no reason why we shouldn't just be starting on our upward climb.

If you have any suggestions to offer, I certainly want them. If there is anything you feel I can do for you just let me know and it will be done.

With kindest regards, I am

Sincerely yours,

Joseph P. Kennedy to John F. Kennedy, 8: *Telegram*

NEW YORK NY 1926 MAY 19 AM 8 58

DEAR JACK GOOD LUCK TO THE TEAM IN YOUR GAME WITH RIVERS THIS AFTER-
NOON AND HOPE YOU ALL PLAY WELL   DADDY
CAPTAIN JACK KENNEDY
NOBLE AND GREENOUGH LAW SCHOOL [*SIC*]
PLEASANT ST BROOKLINE MASS

Joseph P. Kennedy to Joseph P. Kennedy, Jr., 10

July 13, 1926

Dear Joe:

I had planned to write you last week but when I returned to New York I received word that Uncle Jim died suddenly and I had to go back for the funeral.[122]

You remember Uncle Jim was the Police Captain in Boston and I feel very sad about his death.

I went down to the Cape, Saturday, and everybody was delighted that you were writing so many letters, particularly Grandpa Kennedy. He was very much surprised to get your note and tickled to pieces to hear you won the swimming race.

Jack, I think, is really very lonesome for you and he wants me to be sure and promise him that he will go to camp next summer. He is taking swimming lessons to see if he can improve his stroke.

Fred Thomson's new picture THE TWO GUN MAN is showing on Broadway, New York, this weekend I am sure you will like it when you see it.[123]

Mother and I are planning to go up there around the 25th, that is a week from Saturday and we, perhaps, will get up there at lunch time. Jack wants to go but I am not sure we can take him.

Drop me a line telling me how things are going with you.

Love,
Your dad

122. James Hickey (1861–1926), JPK's maternal bachelor uncle, had died on July 7.
123. Fred Thomson (1890–1928), former Nevada state Boy Scout commissioner and football and track and
 field star, had opened in FBO's newest release atop his gray stallion, Silver King, at Warner's Theatre on
 July 12. The Robertson-Cole production company had recently taken the name of its former distribution wing, Film Booking Offices of America, or FBO.

Joseph P. Kennedy to Joseph P. Kennedy, Jr., 10

July 28, 1926

Dear Joe:

After we left the Camp Sunday we went over to Gray's Camp in Augusta. It took us about five hours. We left there Monday morning and I just had time to get the boat to New York and I had to go in my white knickers as there wasn't enough time to go to Eddie's house to get my blue suit, so Mother and Mrs. Moore had a great laugh.

Eddie is sending up the things you wanted, from Boston, and you should have them tomorrow or the next day at the latest; that includes the tennis racket.

I am getting busy on that picture proposition and hope to have a special KRAZY KAT cartoon made up; when it is completed I will drop you a line.

I just want to tell you again that Mother and I were more than pleased that you were enjoying it up there and I certainly think you were wonderful to Mother to remember her on her birthday and to show her such attention at Camp and it made me very happy indeed.

Don't worry about the lessons because, after all, there isn't much time left and you will be much better prepared in the Fall and then you will be thankful that you did a little work. Remember that Jack is practicing at the piano each day an hour and studying from one-half to three-quarters of an hour on his books so that he is really spending more time than you are.

As I said before, we were all tickled to death with the way you seem to be getting along and I am going to try to get up to Camp once more before we sail for Europe.

> *Love,*
> *Your*
> *Dad*

P. S. While I am making up the Krazy Kat picture, send me the names of some of the counselors and boys and let me know some of the funny things that have happened to them and I will try to have them incorporated in this picture.

Kathleen Kennedy, 6, to Santa Claus

Dear Santa Claus i want a doll and a doll carriage tea set and paper doll little book are little blck boad your little friend Kathleen 131 naple rd brookline mass

---

Joseph P. Kennedy to Will Hays: *Telegram*

JAN. 13, 1927

HAVE COMPLETED NEGOTIATIONS WITH HARVARD AND HAVE ANNOUNCEMENT TO GO OUT WHICH I WILL SUBMIT TO WHOEVER YOU DESIGNATE IN YOUR OFFICE.[124] THINK IT SPLENDID. CALLS FOR US TO GET HAYS, ZUKOR,[125] KENT,[126] JOE

---

124. He was attempting to organize and publicize a lecture series on the origins and present state of the burgeoning film industry at the recently opened Harvard Business School.
125. Adolph Zukor (1873–1976), president of the Paramount-Famous Players-Lasky Corporation, would lecture on "The Origin and Growth of the Industry."
126. Sydney Raymond Kent (1882–1942), general manager in charge of distribution for the Famous Players–Lasky Corporation, would cover "Distributing the Product."

SCHENCK,[127] DEMILLE,[128] LASKY,[129] LLOYD[130] OR FAIRBANKS AND WHOEVER ELSE YOU THINK OF OR YOU MIGHT ELIMINATE ANY OF THESE. WOULD APPRECIATE WIRE CONFIRMING THESE NAMES AND HOW WE ARE TO GET THEIR CONFIRMATION. LECTURES BEGIN MARCH FIFTEENTH THREE PER WEEK FOR THREE WEEKS. THINK THIS WILL BE TREMENDOUSLY IMPORTANT THING AS THEY ARE MAKING IT PART THEIR REGULAR CURRICULUM WILL SEND YOU COPY BY AIRMAIL. THEY ARE ANXIOUS RELEASE STORY FOR MONDAY MORNING THEREFORE SHOULD HAVE ACCEPTANCES IMMEDIATELY.

JOS. P. KENNEDY

Joseph P. Kennedy to Adolph Zukor

January 22, 1927

My dear Mr. Zukor:

I am enclosing your copy of the letter that the Fine Arts Department of Harvard is writing to General Hays. This, I feel, will be a step of world-wide importance and should be a matter of great interest to Mr. Lasky and your production department. It means a recognition of the artistic work that this gentleman has been doing by the oldest university in the United States and by a department that is second to none in the world.

Very truly yours,

Joseph P. Kennedy to Will Hays: *Telegram*

JAN. 22, 1927

THINK IT WOULD BE OF GREAT INTEREST TO HARVARD IF NEW YORK TIMES COMMENTED ON THEIR PROGRESSIVE STEPS EDITORIALLY. I MERELY MAKE THIS SUGGESTION FOR YOUR CONSIDERATION. BELIEVE TIMES WOULD DO IT FOR YOU.

JOE KENNEDY

Joseph P. Kennedy to Fred Thomson

February 25, 1927

Dear Fred:

This is dictated over the phone before I catch my train to Boston. I just left Will Hays' office and the General tells me he is a little bit disturbed about the title JESSE JAMES. He is afraid to glorify the bandit because of the criticisms that will come from the preacher element. On the other hand, he is afraid that if the bandit is not glorified, the picture will lose so much of its interest that it will not be a good proposition for either of us.

127. Joseph Schenk (1887–1961), president of United Artists, did not participate in the lecture series.
128. Director, producer, screenwriter and president of DeMille Studios, Cecil Blount DeMille (1881–1959) would discuss the process of "Building a Photoplay."
129. Jesse Louis Lasky (1880–1958), Famous Players–Lasky's executive vice president, would cover "Production Problems."
130. First National's Milton Sills (1882–1930), rather than Harold Lloyd (1893–1971), whose bespectacled, mild-mannered and accident-prone screen persona had achieved spectacular box-office success in the mid-1920s, would eventually cover "The Actor's Part."

The General says you are the idol of the small boys of the country and he does not want you to make any mistake. On the other hand, Kent[131] appreciates it is the best title in the picture business. Will you give me some word, so that I can have the General feel easy, because I want to have him perfectly satisfied that we can go thru and not do anything harmful to his very strict law. Up to date, he has refused to allow anybody to make this picture and the only reason he is considering it now is on your account.[132]

With kindest regards,

Sincerely,

Joseph P. Kennedy to Cecil B. DeMille

March 18, 1927

Dear Mr. DeMille:

If you had any idea how anxious the Harvard authorities are to see you, you would forgive my keeping after Hays to have you come here. I spent most of my first lecture at Harvard telling them about the marvelous work you have done in "The King of Kings". In talking with President Lowell, I told him of some of the events which took place during the making of the picture. He was tremendously interested, and is very anxious to meet you personally.

The Fine Arts Department have agreed to make a selection of the best films each year, and have really put the stamp of Harvard University on the industry as a new development in art.

Mr. Lasky was here yesterday, and Mr. Zukor comes tomorrow. Mr. Lasky told me he had had the best day in a good many years. I realize how terrifically busy you are, and I sincerely hope that somehow or other you may find a chance to come here for a day. I am planning to go to the coast with Mrs. Kennedy on the third of April, arriving there about the seventh, and if you have not left for the east by that date I should be very glad to meet you, and tell you all about what has been done here.

Assuring you of my appreciation for your interest in the matter, and with the best wishes in the world for the success of the greatest motion picture ever imagined. I am

Very truly yours,

Joseph P. Kennedy, Jr., 11, to Rose Kennedy[133]

131 Naples Road Brookline May 15, 1927

Dearest Mother,

I thank you and dad for the lovely telegram. The most important thing I have to tell you that I was confirmed yesterday by Cardinal O'conell. I served and received Holy Communion at seven o'clock mass, then I came home and had breakfast, changed my clothes and was back at the hall at nine About ten o'clock we started for the church in a prosession. Confirmation was a ten-thirty prompt. Eddy, Mrs Moore, Rose, and Ennice

---

131. General manager in charge of distribution for Famous Players–Lasky.
132. Despite Hays's initial reservations, Fred Thomson Productions (under JPK's management) would release *Jesse James* in October 1927. Although Hays had worried about the "preacher element's" objections to bandit glorification on the screen, upon the film's release the *New York Times* theater critic Mordant Hall lamented that "[n]ot much is made of Jesse James's train robbing exploits or his attacks on stage coaches," and expressed disappointment at what little marauding the film did portray, finding, for example, "[t]he train hold-up . . . not especially impressive."
133. She was in California, visiting JPK.

Aunt Loretta, grandpa and grandma Fitzgerald and Aunt Agnes were there. Grandpa Kennedy had to go to a funeral (Dr. Gibline) The church was pretty well crowded.

The services were over at quarter past eleven and then we had our picture taken. Then I went home and changed my clothes and went out to Billy Butler's

I thank you very much for the prayer book you gave me. Grandpa Kennedy gave me a five dollar gold piece and Aunt Agnes and grandma gave me some rosary beads, Grandpa Fitzgerald gave me a signet ring. I went out to Billy Butlers who was having a party and then went with him to the movies.

The weather has been rainy and chilly every day since you left. Kathleen is going to receive her first communion next Sunday. I hope you are feeling well every body around here is feeling good. I will have to close now with best love to you and daddy

Your Loving Son
Joe

Kathleen Kennedy, 7, to Rose Kennedy

May 19, 1927

Dear Mother,

I got your letter to-day. and I was glad to hear that you and Daddy are having a nice time. I go to church every day to prepare for communion. Helen and Elinor played with us to-day. Eunice went to Evelyns. Bobby says "Stop" to everybody now when he is teased. I gained a pound and a half Eunice gained some too. Rose is as fat as ever. When Pat[134] gets cross she says "Bold stump" to us.[135] Bobby's bangs are getting long.

Love from all
Kathleen

Joseph P. Kennedy et al. to Will Hays: *Telegram*

JUNE 10TH, 1927

WE THE MEMBERS OF YOUR ASSOCIATION HAVE TODAY SENT THE FOLLOWING NIGHTLETTER TO JOSEPH SCHENCK[136] QUOTE WE THE UNDERSIGNED IN MEETING ASSEMBLED TODAY DESIRE TO VOICE THE STRONGEST PROTEST OF WHICH WE ARE CAPABLE AGAINST THE MAKING OF RAIN EITHER UNDER THE NAME OF SADIE THOMSON OR ANY OTHER NAME OR THE MAKING OF THIS STORY EVEN WITH VARI-ATIONS AND CHANGES STOP[137] A YEAR AGO IT WAS AGREED THAT THIS STORY WAS BANNED AND ON THE STRENGTH OF THIS EVERY PRODUCER LAID OFF THE MAKING OF CERTAIN MATERIAL STOP IT WAS FURTHER UNDERSTOOD THAT IF SUCH MATE-RIAL WAS PRODUCED BY ANY ONE THAT MEMBERS OF THE ASSOCIATION IN ORDER TO PROTECT THEMSELVES SHOULD REFUSE TO EXHIBIT THE SAME STOP FOR THIS SUBJECT TO BE PRODUCED AT THIS TIME WILL OPEN UP THE ENTIRE QUESTION

---

134. Patricia Kennedy, later Lawford (1924–), the couple's sixth child and fourth daughter.
135. "Bold stump" was the epithet that Kikoo, the children's governess, used to scold them.
136. President of Union Artists.
137. Unbeknownst to her industry colleagues, one of Joseph Schenk's united artists, Gloria Swanson (1899–1983), had secretly bought the rights to W. Somerset Maugham's controversial short story "Miss Thomson" some months earlier. Although hotly contested, the various studios had agreed that the rights to the story should be mutually off-limits; its depiction of a fallen missionary ran afoul of the Hays Office's Production Code. Swanson (who, unlike her protesting colleagues, was not a signatory to the Code) had purchased the rights to Maugham's short story (on which there was no ban as there was for its stage adaptation, *Rain*), and had begun production of the screen version, *Sadie Thomson*, in which she had already invested some two hundred thousand dollars by June 1927.

AGAIN AND CERTAIN BOOKS AND PLAYS NOW BANNED WILL BE PRODUCED BY THIS
ASSOCIATION AND WE WILL LOSE FOR OURSELVES EVERYTHING WE HAVE GAINED
IN PUBLIC RESPECT AND CONFIDENCE FOR THE PAST FOUR OR FIVE YEARS STOP AS
MEMBERS OF THE ASSOCIATION AND AS PERSONAL FRIENDS OF YOURS WE BEG YOU
TO STOP THE PRODUCTION OF THIS PICTURE AT ALL COSTS STOP WE DO NOT BE-
LIEVE THAT ANY INDIVIDUAL MEMBER HAS THE RIGHT TO JEOPARDIZE THE INTER-
ESTS OF ALL THE OTHER MEMBERS NO MATTER WHAT THE FINANCIAL GAIN MIGHT
BE BY TAKING AN ACTION WHICH WILL PUT OUR ENTIRE ASSOCIATION AND ALL OF
ITS MEMBERS IN DISREPUTE WITH THE PUBLIC OF THE COUNTRY STOP OUR REFUSAL
TO PRODUCE SALACIOUS BOOKS AND PLAYS AGAINST WHICH THERE IS AN OVER-
WHELMING PUBLIC OPINION AT THIS TIME HAS BEEN THE CORNER STONE UPON
WHICH THE PRODUCERS ASSOCIATION HAS BEEN BUILT AND TO DESTROY THAT AT
THIS TIME WOULD IN OUR OPINION BE AN ACTION UNFORGIVABLE AND UNWAR-
RANTED AND A DIRECT VIOLATION OF PROMISES WE HAVE MADE THE PUBLIC THAT
MATERIAL OF THIS KIND WOULD NOT BE MADE UNQUOTE END OF WIRE STOP WE
WISH TO PROTEST [SIC] TO YOU WITH ALL THE FORCE OF WHICH WE ARE CAPABLE
AGAINST UNITED ARTISTS MAKING OR RELEASING THE PRODUCTION RAIN UNDER
ANY CHANGE OR SUBTERFUGE STORY BY ANOTHER TITLE AND WITH OR WITHOUT
THE ORIGINAL CHARACTERS OF THE STAGE PLAY STOP THIS PLAY WAS BANNED A
YEAR AGO AND THE AGREEMENT WAS THAT IF IT WAS MADE BY ANYONE OUTSIDE
IT WOULD NOT BE EXHIBITED BY THE MEMBERS OF THE ASSOCIATION STOP IF THIS
PLAY IS PRODUCED IN ANY FORM OTHER MEMBERS OF THE ASSOCIATION WILL PRO-
DUCE OTHER PLAYS AS DETRIMENTAL AND HARMFUL AS THIS ONE AND WE FEEL
THE ENTIRE WORK OF OUR ORGANIZATION WHICH WE HAVE STRUGGLED TO BUILD
UP WILL BE LOST AND THAT WE WILL FORFEIT PUBLIC CONFIDENCE STOP WE RE-
QUEST THAT IF THIS PLAY IS PRODUCED THAT YOU USE EVERY POWER THAT YOU
POSSESS TO PREVENT ITS EXHIBITION BY THE EXHIBITORS OF THIS COUNTRY AS ITS
RELEASE WOULD BE A BLOW AGAINST EVERY MEMBER OF THE ASSOCIATION WHO
HAS ABIDED BY THE POLICIES THAT YOU HAVE OUTLINED FOR US ALL STOP WE BE-
LIEVE THAT NO ACTION IS TOO STRONG FOR US TO TAKE TO PROTECT OUR INDIVID-
UAL AND COLLECTIVE INTERESTS IN THE HANDLING OF A MATTER THAT IS A
DIRECT VIOLATION OF EVERY UNDERSTANDING AND EVERY PLEDGE THAT WE ALL
MADE TO YOU AND THAT YOU IN TURN MADE TO THE PUBLIC AND WE ARE DETER-
MINED INDIVIDUALLY AND COLLECTIVELY THAT NO ONE SHALL RISK THE INVEST-
MENT THAT WE HAVE MADE IN TRYING TO WIN PUBLIC OPINION PUBLIC GOODWILL
AND RESPECT AND FURTHER INSIST THAT NO ONE HAS A RIGHT EITHER FOR FI-
NANCIAL GAIN OR ANY OTHER REASON TO JEOPARDIZE THE STRUCTURE OF THE EN-
TIRE BUSINESS BECAUSE OF THE DISREGARD OF A PROMISE OR POLICY OF ANY ONE
MEMBER EITHER DIRECTLY OR INDIRECTLY ASSOCIATED WITH THIS ORGANIZATION
STOP WE ALL HAVE IN OUR POSSESSION MATERIAL BOUGHT AND PAID FOR IN TIMES
GONE BY WHICH AT YOUR REQUEST WE HAVE REFRAINED FROM MAKING AND
THERE ARE ALSO IN THE MARKET MANY PLAYS NO MORE OFFENSIVE THAN THIS
ONE THAT THERE CAN BE NO JUSTIFICATION FOR REFUSING TO MAKE IF THIS ONE
GOES THROUGH BECAUSE THE MAKING OF THIS WILL TEAR DOWN IN OUR OPINION
EVERYTHING THAT WE HAVE ALL STOOD FOR KINDEST REGARDS
WILLIAM FOX[138]
WINNIE SHEEHAN[139]

138. William Fox (1879–1952), founder and president of the Fox Film Corporation.
139. Winfield Richard Sheehan (1883–1947), vice president and general manager of Fox.

ABE WARNER[140]

J.J. MURDOCK[141]

~~NICHOLAS SCHENK~~ MARCUS LOEW[142]

ROBERT RUBIN[143]

ROBERT COCHRANE

JOE KENNEDY

SAM KATZ[144]

JOHN MCGUIRK

S. R. KENT

ADOLPH ZUKOR

JESSE L. LASKY

SAM SPRING

RICHARD ROWLAND

Joseph P. Kennedy to Gene Tunney[145]

June 23, 1927

Dear Gene:

I got this memorandum from the Coast on Fred's[146] athletic record. I am sending it to you to read over and advise me what you think you can do on it or how I can be of any service. Grantland Rice, I am sure, would be a help.[147]

With kindest regards, I am

Very truly yours,

Joseph P. Kennedy to Albert Brunker[148]

July 22, 1927

Dear Al:

I quite agree with all your conclusions regarding Lindbergh.[149] I think he has the most tremendous hold on the country that any individual has ever had, but after he

---

140. Albert Warner (1883–1967), cofounder of Warner Brothers Pictures.
141. The Scottish-born John J. Murdock (1865–1948), general manager of the B. F. Keith Corporation, had been assistant to the president, E. F. Albee, on the Keith vaudeville circuit in New York from its inception. Murdock had become president of Pathé in the wake of the recent merger between the Keith-Albee theatrical holdings and the Pathé-DeMille film interests. Throughout the 1920s, Murdock had tried without success to persuade Albee to integrate and welcome new motion picture technologies into the Keith Circuit, and would eventually sell his own Keith holdings to JPK in the company's takeover in the spring of 1928.
142. Marcus Loew (1870–1927), president of Metro-Goldwyn Pictures, would be succeeded by his vice president, Nicholas Schenck (Joseph Schenck's brother), in September, when Loew would succumb to what *Variety* would describe as "complications arising from a long disordered stomach culminating in a complication that bore too strongly upon an already weakened heart."
143. Robert Rubin (1882–1958), film industry attorney.
144. Sam Katz (1891–1961), president of the Paramount-Publix Theatres.
145. By defeating Jack Dempsey, the reigning champion and four-to-one favorite, Gene Tunney (1898–1978) had become Heavyweight Boxing Champion of the World in September 1926.
146. Fred Thomson's.
147. The *New York Tribune*'s syndicated sports columnist, Grantland Rice (1880–1954), had in the past contributed to building the reputations of a number of the sports heroes of the 1920s, among them Babe Ruth, Red Grange, and Notre Dame's backfield, whom he had likened to the Four Horsemen of the Apocalypse after their victory over Army in 1924.
148. Albert Ridgely Brunker (1883–1959), chairman of the board of the Liquid Carbonic Company of Chicago, who seems to have been an acquaintance of Lindbergh's.
149. Attempting to capitalize on Charles Lindbergh's (1902–1974) worldwide popularity following his un-

has made this trip (which will take two months) and has been in so very many places, I have very grave doubts that we could get the kind of picture we would want from him, or that it would sell nearly as well as we had hoped.

At any rate, drop in to see me when you are in town and we will talk it over. With kindest regards, I am

Sincerely yours,

Joseph P. Kennedy to Fred Thomson: *Telegram*

SEPT 20, 1927

DEAR FRED ROSE AND CHILDREN ARRIVE NEWYORK SATURDAY[150] BECAUSE OF THE NEWNESS OF THE PLACE AND NUMBER THINGS TO BE DONE TO GET THEM SETTLED IN HOUSE I FEEL I REALLY SHOULD BRING THEM OVER OR AT LEAST TAKE CARE OF THEM WHEN THEY ARRIVE WOULD IT BE POSSIBLE FOR YOU TO JUMP ON HERE AND KENT[151] YOU AND I COULD LOOK AT PICTURE ALONE[152] KENT WIRING YOU TODAY THINK IT TREMENDOUSLY IMPORTANT FOR YOUR SUCCESS AS WELL AS THAT OF PICTURES TO BE HERE IN NEWYORK AND MEET THE HALF DOZEN HEAD SALES EXECUTIVES AFTER ALL THE SUCCESSFUL LAUNCHING OF THIS PICTURE MEANS EVERYTHING TO BOTH OF US HATE TO UPSET YOUR PLANS BUT THINK THIS BY FAR THE BETTER PLAN BEST TO ALL

JOE

Joseph P. Kennedy to Thomas Jefferson Newbold

September 22, 1927

Dear Jeff:

As I plan to be out of Boston for at least the next year, and as the boys are not attending school at Dexter, I feel that I should tender you my resignation, so that you can fill in with somebody who will be available when you need him.[153]

I certainly have many regrets in pulling out of Boston, but there doesn't seem very much else for me to do.

I am enclosing formal letter of resignation.

If, in the meantime, you find somebody who wants to buy my Second Mortgage Bonds, I will be very glad to sell them.

Sincerely yours,

---

precedented trans-Atlantic flight in May, FBO had joined the fray among film companies attempting to sign the aviator to an exclusive film contract.

150. On September 24, the family would move from Brookline to 5040 Independence Avenue at 252nd Street in Riverdale, New York.

151. The general manager in charge of distribution for Famous Players–Lasky, who would be handling *Jesse James.*

152. *Jesse James* was scheduled to open in October.

153. Former Undersecretary of the Treasury Thomas Jefferson Newbold (1886–1939). Newbold was treasurer of the Dexter School for boys, which had been established jointly by a group of parents (JPK among them) who had purchased the former Nobles and Greenough campus in Brookline in the summer of 1926.

PART II

New York and Hollywood

1927–1932

By the mid-1930s Joseph Kennedy would transform himself into a figure of national reputation. His involvement in the first two Roosevelt election efforts would result not only in a pair of administration posts, but in increased contact with both high government officials and with the national political press. Behind the scenes at speeches and rallies, at the convention in Chicago or on board the westbound *Roosevelt Special* during the 1932 campaign, he cultivated associations and friendships with journalists from across the political spectrum. By the middle of the decade he would begin to read of himself with growing regularity in syndicated columns and in papers from coast to coast. For the first time in his life he would be moved to record his own impressions of events and characters—not as incidental inclusions within his correspondence—but for their own sake. The occasional, careful narratives in which he began to detail his interactions with the president in the mid-1930s were to grow into the extensive daily diaries he would keep in London by the end of the decade. These recorded reflections were the apparent result of a growing sense not only of the historical significance of his circle of acquaintances and the events he witnessed, but also of the place he saw himself occupying in the annals of twentieth-century America.

In the late 1920s, however, when he divided his professional life between Hollywood and Wall Street, he had not yet developed the self-consciousness that would lead him to document his thoughts and activities with an eye to posterity. Indeed, perhaps given the nature of the whisperings that were to follow him to Washington and London, it might have served him well not to maintain such documentation. Insofar as he recorded his activities in the late 1920s, his accounts relate almost exclusively to his dealings in Hollywood rather than on Wall Street, and take the form of fragmented correspondence rather than of personal memoranda or diaries. With the exception of his family letters, very little correspondence survives to document the period spanning his departure from Hollywood in 1930 to his involvement with the Roosevelt campaign two years later. Almost none of what remains among his papers relates to his notorious trading and short-selling practices from a desk at the offices of Halle & Steiglitz in New York before and after October 1929. Much of what does survive to document his life between 1927 and 1932 was recorded haphazardly by others. A legion of accountants, lawyers and lieutenants (loyal, reticent Irish-Catholics recruited from the Fore River Ship Yard and from his previous ventures in Boston) attended to and recorded the minutiae of his varied interests—mergers and vertical integration, the introduction of talking picture technology, Gloria Swanson's precarious financial situation and staggering tax liabilities, the IRS's queries about the nature of his film partnership in the wake of settlement of Guy Currier's estate. Breathless accounts of his dealings in the Hollywood trade press—a spectacular merger, a new or rumored advisory role in resuscitating an ailing production company, a lavish promotional campaign—help to chart his approximate course through the film colony at the end of the decade. The most reliable and consistent (if clinical) accounts of his professional activities and the events, encounters and transactions in which he involved himself are the minutes of meetings that were filed alongside (and outnumber) his correspondence from the period. Recorded by a designated secretary, these note his and others' presence, and detail resolutions adopted, stock sales and purchases, new appointments, progress, developments and amendments since the last meeting. In the aggregate they plot the unfolding of events and delineate agreements, understandings and exchanges of cash or stock between individuals and entities. Nevertheless, for the most part such documents only hint at strategy and intention, reducing to mere letters on a page the identities of those involved, his own included.

"A banker?" vaudeville and film pioneer Marcus Loew is reputed to have exclaimed in what *Variety* described as one of his "waggish moments" upon first meeting Joseph Kennedy. "I thought this business was just for furriers." By late 1927 the banker had begun to extend his film interests beyond the bounds of the FBO Studios. Over the next three years he would come to oversee not only FBO's management, but the reorganization, refinancing and indeed the establishment of a number of other entities, among them Pathé, Gloria Productions, RKO, and (for only a few acrimonious days) First National Studios. Under his tutelage the corporate structures of several of these were to become linked and their interests and holdings aligned and intermingled, bringing them in the aggregate ever closer to the vertically integrated conglomerate that he had envisioned since his earliest forays into the industry. Between 1927 and 1930 the time he spent on the opposite coast from his family would expand dramatically, as would his interactions, personal and financial, with the reigning screen siren of the day, Gloria Swanson. He would leave the industry in 1930, however, just as abruptly and completely as he had been thrown into it by the somewhat unexpected purchase of Robertson Cole four years earlier. Leaving Hollywood for good, his sights would turn almost exclusively to market activity in New York (to the near neglect, some of his associates would complain, of his few remaining obligations in Hollywood), and from there to politics in the wake of the financial cataclysm of 1929.

On December 13, 1927, Kennedy and Guy Currier, still the majority owners of the renamed Robertson-Cole Company, which they had purchased nearly two years earlier, incorporated the Gower Street Company in Delaware. "It was Mr. Currier's idea," explained a memorandum outlining the company's subsequent transactions to a curious Internal Revenue Service several years later,

> that a holding company such as the Gower Street Corporation should be formed so as to handle . . . FBO transactions in a simplified manner, thereby dispelling any form of partnership between Mr. Kennedy and Mr. Currier.

Soon after, the first of a number of transactions that would eventually liquidate the company's holdings took place when the Gower Street Company sold twenty thousand shares of FBO to the Radio Corporation of America. Valued at ten dollars at the time of the sale of R-C Pictures to Currier and Kennedy in February 1926, the Radio Corporation of America bought the stock at twenty-four on the final day of 1927.

As promised in Harry Warner's lecture at Harvard seven months earlier, Vitaphone technology had indeed "revolutionize[d] the industry" by bringing sound to film. Vitaphone's "sound-on-disc" synchronization was at best haphazard, however. Inevitably human error would affect its operation because the projectionist was required to begin playing the Vitaphone system discs at the moment a "start" frame passed through the gate of the projector. In the interim, such imprecision had allowed for the emergence of several rival sound-on-film technologies that produced what were in effect presynchronized talking pictures. Over the course of the middle and late

1920s, David Sarnoff of RCA had overseen the acquisition of a number of entertainment-related companies and the rights to various new technologies, including the Photophone sound-on-film talking picture device. In meeting with the president of the moderately sized FBO Studios in late 1927, Sarnoff was seeking an existing film outfit to make use of the Photophone devices in the production of talking films, thereby assuring a market for the manufacture of the devices themselves by General Electric, RCA's parent company. With the outlet for RCA's Photophone machines secured by the December 31 Gower Street stock purchase, and the production of Photophone films guaranteed at the FBO Studios both on Gower Street in Los Angeles and in northern Manhattan, Photophone talking films lacked only a distribution network to make them available to an eager movie-going public by the advent of 1928.

As part of the wave of conglomerations and mergers that was at the time sweeping the West Coast film colony, the corporate components of the B. F. Keith vaudeville empire had merged with Pathé-DeMille Pictures earlier in 1927. While Kennedy and Sarnoff concluded their December 1927 negotiations, the new Keith entity entered into a subsequent merger with the Orpheum vaudeville circuit. The result was the Keith-Albee-Orpheum Corporation. E. F. Albee, former assistant and protégé to showman B. F. Keith, would maintain the by-then nominal presidency he held at the Keith organization. The general management of K-A-O would fall to Albee's own former assistant and protégé, a shrewd Scot named J. J. Murdock who had foreseen vaudeville's decline in the growth of film and had attempted for some time with little success, to persuade Albee to embrace the new industry.

FBO's, RCA's and K-A-O's financial interests would become increasingly intermingled by similar stock transfers over the coming months; their corporate structures would follow suit. On February 14, 1928, the directors of the Gower Street Company, Currier and Kennedy, ratified an agreement with Murdock of Keith-Albee-Orpheum. In exchange for six hundred thousand dollars, due in installments over the course of the coming year, the Keith Corporation would acquire forty thousand shares of FBO class B common stock, complete with voting rights. Kennedy and Currier agreed additionally to amend the Gower Street Company's certificate of incorporation so that "all such [B shares] shall be given the same voting power and in all other respects the same rights as the Class A stock." Exercising the voting rights that had accompanied K-A-O's stake in FBO, Murdock would nominate himself and Sarnoff to the company's board. Soon after Gower Street's ratification of the Keith agreement in mid-February 1928, K-A-O's Pathé-DeMille (of which Murdock was the current president) would hire Joseph P. Kennedy as special adviser.

Over the spring of 1928, Kennedy attempted likewise to acquire a substantial interest in K-A-O. He assembled a syndicate comprised of East Coast bankers, including the Blair Company's president, Elisha Walker, the Lehman brothers, Richard C. Hunt and Jeremiah Milbank, which was prepared to offer $4.2 million for 200,000 shares of K-A-O common stock. Despite Murdock's urgings, Albee, still at the helm, refused to sell—until May 10 when the banking syndicate offered $21 per share while the stock traded at $16. "There is no truth in any rumor abroad," a K-A-O press release insisted on May 16, "that Mr. Albee, the president of the Circuit, is to retire or be less active in the affairs of the Keith-Albee-Orpheum Circuit than he has been for the past forty years." Nevertheless, the stock purchase had given the syndicate a controlling interest in K-A-O, and had altered substantially not only the company's function and mission but its management structure as well. The Kennedy-Murdock management would streamline K-A-O, sweeping away many of the vestiges of the old vaudeville operation, including Albee himself (rather unceremoniously, the story goes) some months later.

On June 7, 1928, Sarnoff, Kennedy and the banking syndicate jointly established a "New Holding Company." In exchange for its recently acquired two hundred thousand shares of K-A-O common stock, the banking syndicate was to receive two hundred thousand A and two hundred thousand B shares in the as-yet-unnamed holding company. For 4.2 million, the purchase price of the K-A-O stock, RCA was likewise to receive two hundred thousand shares of the holding company's A and B stock, respectively. RCA was to guarantee that the holding company would act as "sole and exclusive agent for the leasing or sale" of the Vitaphone apparatus, and would make any "improvements in the art of sound films and the apparatus therefor" available as well. Moreover, on RCA's behalf Sarnoff agreed to transfer both the exclusive right to manufacture Vitaphone films to the holding company as well as the "further right" to allow the holding company to extend Vitaphone filmmaking equipment and privileges to "associated companies" like FBO, Pathé and any others "in which the new holding company at any time has an investment." In return, the Walker-Kennedy-Murdock group agreed to provide the holding company with a guarantee not only to install Photophone's projection apparatus in all theaters owned or controlled by K-A-O but also to "use its best efforts to cause the Photophone apparatus to be installed in theatres which it does not control but with which it has friendly relations of one sort or another."

Concurrently, the B. F. Keith Corporation bought fourteen thousand shares of FBO from the Gower Street Company. In July 1928, Murdock, Marcus Heiman (K-A-O's vice president) and (despite what seem to have been Murdock's and Kennedy's efforts at his exclusion and circumvention) Albee took their seats on the FBO board of directors. In August, K-A-O amended its bylaws to allow for the election of Elisha Walker and Richard Hunt to its board of directors. The sale of K-A-O shares to the likes of the Shubert Theatres Corporation, Harry Black's Hippodromes, Publix and even the early proponents of the rival Vitaphone system, Warner Brothers, allowed for the expansion of the Photophone system into the studios and theaters of these newly "associated companies."

By late October 1928, the film industry's largest merger to date would be complete. The former FBO Studios would produce Photophone talking films for distribution throughout the network of some two hundred old Keith and Orpheum vaudeville theaters across the country under the new heading of Radio-Keith-Orpheum. Management of RKO would fall to RCA. Kennedy would resign from active operations and cash out his stock. By the end of 1928, his only remaining connections to Hollywood would be through Pathé and Gloria Productions.

In early November 1927, Joseph Kennedy received requests from both Dr. Attilio Giannini, who as president of the Bowery and East River National Bank had been one of the earliest bankers to finance motion pictures, and from Robert Kane, president of Robert Kane Pictures at First National Studios, to meet with Gloria Swanson in order to discuss her financial predicament. Two years earlier, Swanson had become the first star to reject a million-dollar offer from Famous Players-Lasky in favor of establishing her own production company under the aegis of United Artists. The two films that she had produced since then had drawn her deeply into debt, however. *The Love of Sunya* had failed to make up in box office revenues the sum it had lost in late production. The same *Sadie Thompson* that had drawn the protests of her colleagues some months earlier was at the moment stymied by censors and would spend the next several months mired in expensive litigation intended to free it for distribution. In addition to the large production debts that she had incurred and the lavish salaries that she paid an extensive staff, her situation had become further complicated by the fact that the Internal Revenue Service had taken exception to a number of stock-in-trade deductions that she had made to her income taxes (including, for example, nearly fifty thousand dollars for "Apparel," "Appearance," and "Entertaining" alone) in the period spanning 1921 to 1926.

"Gloria needs handling, needs being properly financed and having her organization placed in proper hands," Kane informed Kennedy. "I have taken the liberty," he added, "of asking her to see you, and am writing you now asking you, to see her and find out if there is some way that we can get together on taking her over as a producing asset." After a first Armistice Day meeting with the starlet, however, Kennedy, then in the midst of preliminary negotiations with David Sarnoff, responded that he envisioned little "possibility of doing business there." By late December, as RCA prepared to purchase its first block of FBO stock, FBO's president underwent an evident change of heart, for unrecorded reasons, with regard to the Swanson matter. "I told Miss Swanson that it would be ridiculous for me to make a trade with her to look out for any of her affairs," he informed her lawyer, Milton Cohen. He added nebulously, however, that he would gladly put himself and "some people in [his] organization" at her disposal in restructuring her finances. "If, at some later day, it looks like the services we might render have been of any value, we could at that time take up with you the consideration of any further deal." Eventually he would propose what Swanson described as a "whopping deal." Swanson would trade Joseph Schenck the rights to *The Love of Sunya* and *Sadie Thomson* for the cancellation of her debts to the studio. Additionally, Schenck would permit Swanson (who owned one fifth of United Artists) to use some of her UA stock toward repaying her debts and back taxes.

The accounts that Joe Kennedy and Gloria Swanson left of their interactions between 1928 and 1930 are in many respects inverses; where one is detailed and expansive, the other is mute. Written after the passage of half a century, Swanson's autobiography recalls trysts at Palm Beach and on Rodeo Drive, and paints a scene of deepening emotional attachments and discussions of love and marriage against a murky backdrop of troublesome financial liablilties, sorted and settled by her lover's henchmen. By contrast, the contemporaneous documentation relating to Gloria Swanson among the Joseph Kennedy papers addresses almost exclusively (if clinically) the professional interactions between the star and the financier, and the legal and monetary arrangements that underpinned their working relationship. Their correspondence survives among his papers in the form of a number of curt and jovial (if businesslike) telegrams, often arranging for later telephone conversations of which no record survives. Swanson's financial adviser and producer appears to have corresponded somewhat more extensively, and indeed in greater detail—on matters ranging from business at Pathé to recent filming progress (or lack of it, as would become the case on the set of *Queen Kelly*) to Swanson's physical and emotional condition—with her current husband, the marquis de la Falaise.

Among the Joseph Kennedy papers there are boxes of file folders presenting extensive accounts of Swanson's assets and liabilities, notes indicating settlements with impatient dressmakers and coiffeurs, and drastic, ill-received reductions to her staff. Several files devoted to the "Client's Tax Record" detail his staff's efforts to make sense of her financial records (which one bewildered assistant described as "not the best") and to mollify the Internal Revenue Service, seemingly by any means possible. "I cried all afternoon on [an I.R.S. agent's] shoulder" the same assistant reported after extensive wrangling over the client's jewelry, Beverly Hills real estate and stock, "and after he slept on it, he started crying with me the next morning." In her autobiography Swanson would recall signing a "single power of attorney," after which she "would not be plagued with a thousand problems [she] was not equipped to deal with." Later, after Kennedy's departure from Hollywood, she would remember resenting the discovery that a number of items she had believed had been gifts—fur coats and a lavish bungalow dressing room on the Pathé lot—had in fact been charged to Gloria Productions. Nevertheless, there are a number of desiccated contracts and legal documents among Joseph Kennedy's "Gloria Productions" files, signed in Swanson's hand. These less often detail the actress's and her adviser's legal or financial obligations to each other than they delineate her obligations to him and to entities connected to him—a guarantee to repay the Columbia Trust Company for desperately needed cash infusions (at the current rate of interest), an agreement to remunerate Pathé for the use of both its lot during filming and of the lavish dressing room upon it befitting a star of Swanson's magnitude.

While E. F. Albee considered the sale of the K-A-O stock that would permit the final alignment of the corporate components of the New Holding Company in May 1928, Gloria Pictures, the streamlined reincarnation of United Artists' Gloria Swanson Productions, newly incorporated in Delaware, embarked on its first project. Since March, Kennedy and Swanson had been negotiating with Erich von Stroheim to write and produce his proposed part talkie, *The Swamp.* Although best known ultimately as a director, von Stroheim had arrived in Hollywood from Vienna during the First World War, and had begun in the industry acting the role of the stock Teutonic villain, "the man you love to hate," at a moment of vehement anti-German sentiment. As a director, in the wake of a series of exacting, expensive and longer-than-epic productions that had extinguished the patience and goodwill of a number of studio executives, von Stroheim had become as widely renowned for his genius as for his excesses by the mid-1920s. "I have arranged to get von Stroheim to direct," Kennedy wrote Louis B. Mayer. Mayer had been involved in the director's productions of both *The Merry Widow* of 1925, and *Greed* of 1924, from which von Stroheim had been removed as director before the film could be cut from more than nine hours' running time to 140 minutes. "I can already hear you saying: 'You have had no troubles in the picture business yet—they have just started.'" By way of encouragement, Mayer responded weakly, "[a]t least, if you weather the storm you will have something worth talking about."

"Our story opens in Reginenburg, capital of the imaginary state of Cobourg-Nassau in the German Empire," von Stroheim announced in his synopsis of the photoplay. He had chosen Seena Owen to play Regina V, the "spinster queen" who becomes morbidly besotted with her cousin, His Highness Prince Wolfram-Erhart von Honenberg-Felsenburg, "a wild, roistering, typical old-world cavalier," to be played by Walter Byron. Swanson was to play the female lead as Patricia Kelly, "a most charming, beautiful and impudent-nosed girl of Irish extraction, [who] catches the eye of His Highness" while walking among her fellow pupils from the local Convent of the Sacred Heart as the prince's regiment rides by. Although betrothed to his cousin, he is unable to forget Patricia Kelly, and so kidnaps her that night during the commotion caused by the "fake fire" that he sets at the convent. After an intimate dinner and moonlit declarations of love, the queen enters, surprising the lovers, and flies into a jealous rage. Following both the ingenue's expulsion from the palace at the lash of the angry queen and a thwarted attempt at suicide, Kelly receives word that her aunt and benefactress is near death in Dar es Salaam, and sets off promptly for German East Africa. She finds her aunt at The Swamp, which von Stroheim envisioned as "a typical seaport dive, dance hall and saloon downstairs and transient rooms upstairs." Her aunt reveals to

Kelly the true identity of her benefactor, one "Poto-Poto Jan," a "lascivious, Lecherous Looking [*sic*], emaciated and malaria ridden" European multimillionaire planter, played by Tully Marshall. Having, unbeknownst to Kelly provided for her education and upbringing, he now expects to marry her forthwith. She rebuffs his advances, however, and he leaves her in Dar es Salaam, hoping that "the associations afforded by the 'Swamp' will soon wear down her resistance." Eight months later, Prince Wolfram arrives in town in search of the young woman now known as Queen Kelly of The Swamp. Spying them during their tempestuous reunion, Jan becomes jealous and forces Kelly to accompany him to remote Poto-Poto. Wolfram follows, only to be captured by Jan and his minions, and lashed with Kelly to a rotting ebony tree. "Tied together in the middle of the swamp with rain pouring over them and crocodiles snapping below them they await the inevitable but with happy hearts." Having been informed of the prince's sudden departure for deepest Poto-Poto, however, the local colonial governor intercedes to rescue the lovers from the brink of certain death and to bring Jan to justice. The nefarious planter manages to escape briefly before meeting a fitting end among Poto-Poto's crocodiles, and the prince, now the king (his cousin and fiancée Regina V having suddenly and conveniently died), marries his sweetheart in the local garrison. "The King looks at his bride" in the last scene "and says 'Well, Your Majesty!' and she, poking her nose impudently in the air, replies 'Majesty my foot: Just plain Queen Kelly!'"

Production of *The Swamp*, whose title von Stroheim had decided to change to *Queen Kelly*, began in November 1928 on a generous budget and a tight schedule. Within a few weeks it became clear, however, that the pace of production, punctuated by numerous retakes to insure exactly the effect von Stroheim sought, was too slow by half. Furthermore, the working atmosphere was becoming charged in large part as a result of von Stroheim's production-lot embellishments to the original script. To the treatment of the initial meeting and flirtation between the prince and Kelly, von Stroheim added the touch of Kelly's pantaloons falling to her ankles for no discernible reason. Unbeknownst at first to Swanson and to much of the production staff, von Stroheim then edited in his direction to Walter Byron to pick up the fallen undergarment and to smell it before stuffing it into his pocket and riding off. It was von Stroheim's direction to Tully Marshall to drool tobacco juice on to the heroine's hand while attempting to force a wedding ring upon it, however, that finally prompted Swanson to walk off the set and the senior production staff to seek a new director in order to finish filming. Not only was *Queen Kelly* grossly over-budget and off schedule by late January 1929, but it was also becoming questionable whether the scenes that von Stroheim had shot would be acceptable to the Hays Office even if another director were able to work them into a completed film.

By late spring, Kennedy and Swanson agreed to abandon *Queen Kelly* for the time being (at a loss of some eight hundred thousand dollars) and begin work on Swanson's first all-talking picture. *The Trespasser*, written by Swanson and Edmund Goulding and directed by Goulding for Gloria Pictures, premiered in London in September 1929. Production of *Queen Kelly*, however, would never be resumed. Although the film was never released (except in a cut-and-paste video version in 1985), some of its footage of young Gloria Swanson appeared in *Sunset Boulevard* in 1950. The film reunited Swanson, playing Norma Desmond, the aging silent star, and her former director von Stroheim, playing Max, Desmond's chauffeur-butler (and husband) who is also, as it turns out, her former director.

Completion of *Queen Kelly* had been further complicated by the illness and death of P. J. Kennedy from carcinoma of the liver, which had necessitated his son's absence from Hollywood during much of the winter and spring of 1929. With the film shelved temporarily, the younger Kennedy made the four-day cross-country train trip from Los Angeles to Boston to visit his father in the Deaconess Hospital in early May. He had returned to California, shortly after, however, to attend to business during what proved to be only a temporary improvement in his father's condition. "I FEEL PROUDER OF THE CHARACTERIZATION THAT I WAS THE SON OF A GREAT MAN AND A MAN OF CHARACTER THAN ANYTHING THAT HAS EVER BEEN SAID TO ME OR ABOUT ME IN MY LIFE," he wired J. J. Murdock after having been informed of his father's death immediately upon his return to Los Angeles. "I HAD HOPED TO BE ABLE TO GET BACK STOP THEY TOLD ME I COULD AND THE SHOCK OUT HERE IS TREMENDOUS." Without time to return for the funeral, he was represented instead by thirteen-year-old Joe Junior.

Despite his business and personal interests, his attentions in 1928 and 1929 were evidently not entirely focused on the West Coast. In 1928, as production began on *Queen Kelly* and its producer maneuvered toward his eventual exit from the film industry in tying up the RKO deal, he bought Malcolm Cottage, the substantial summer home on Nantucket Sound that he and his family had rented since 1925. The following spring, while Kennedy was on the East Coast visiting his father, the family would move from Riverdale to a larger home in the nearby New York suburb of Bronxville. Although many of his activities and dealings went unrecorded in his spotty business-related correspondence between 1927 and 1932, his protracted absences from home and family gave rise to a burgeoning (and for the period, atypically well-preserved) archive of family letters. As the younger children learned to write and as Joe and Jack set off for boarding school (from which they were obliged to write home weekly), the volume of family correspondence grew dramatically. The children evidenced less care in saving letters received from their parents than did their parents in saving letters from them. Their father's correspondence with them survives largely because he dictated it and filed the letters he received from them along with the carbon copies of the letters he had sent. Their mother's correspondence, which at the time was often handwritten, appears to be less complete.

A month to the day before the Wall Street crash, young Joe would begin his freshman year at a largely Episcopalian boys' boarding school in Wallingford, Connecticut. At Choate, he would report, his studies were rigorous ("[a]ll my subjects are going good except Latin and I think I can get that up"), his athletic activities vigorous ("I am taking an exercise called body building. It is composed of fellows who do not have much muscle . . ."), and his pleasures simple ("[m]y roommate brought an electric toaster back with him so we have a lot of fun at night making toast"). Although Joe had been away to camp before, at Choate he would correspond regularly and extensively with his parents for the first time in his life, allowing glimpses not only of his sporting activities, but also an overview of his growing character. He was a dutiful, hardworking, goal-oriented (if occasionally domineering) teenager who kept careful accounts for his parents of his expenses, sports scores and grades.

Jack, by contrast, had tendencies toward sloppiness, infirmity and wit. Although Jack's marks were more erratic than his elder brother's, with an evident love of literature and history, he began to emerge early on as the more intellectual of the two. "We are reading Ivanhoe in English," he wrote his father, "and though I may not be able to remember material things such as tickets, gloves and so on I can remember things like Ivanhoe and the last time we had an exam on it I got a ninety eight." Indeed, the same boy who would later adapt Churchill's title to his own first published work, and echo

John Keats in teasing his mother ("I look like hell, but my stomach is a thing of beauty—as are you, Ma,—and you, unlike my stomach—will be a joy forever"), had early on developed an ear for rhetoric and a facility for its adaptation to his own purposes. Although almost all of his siblings would at some time hit up their father for an increased allowance, none of their requests would be so elegant as Jack's Pauline "Plea for a Raise." "My recent allowance is .40¢," he reminded his father. "This I used for aeroplanes and other playthings of childhood, but now I am a scout and I put away my childish things." Throughout his childhood and youth Jack would suffer (and nearly die) from a number of illnesses, as yet not fully diagnosed. Indeed, his detailed, often plaintive, correspondence from school shows a marked preoccupation with infirmity, both his own and others'. "I have hives," he told his mother in January 1931, "that is a sickness which everything begins to itch. . . . My knees are very red with white lumps of skin," he continued, adding bravely, "I guess I will pull through." "I see things blurry even at a distance of 10 feet." "I just about fainted and everything began to get black . . . Joe fainted twice in church so I guess I will live." Over the summer of 1930, the thirteen-year-old would transfer from the Riverdale Country Day School to the Catholic boys' boarding School, Canterbury, but would be forced to withdraw before the end of the school year due to illness before following his brother to Choate as a freshman in the fall of 1931.

"I like Jean very much," eight-year-old Kick would inform her father, referring to her new baby sister, who had arrived in February 1928. Kick and Jean, along with the other younger children, would remain at home with their mother in Bronxville as their father left Hollywood and Wall Street for Washington. Kick, like her sisters, attended the local public school. Growing into adolescence, she began to develop an interest in boys, parties and her appearance. "I had my hair waved," she told her mother shortly after Roosevelt's inauguration and a few days before her twelfth birthday, "and it looked hot." Although seventeen months older than Kick, Rosemary, it had become clear by the late 1920s, was beginning to lag behind developmentally. Nevertheless, with the assistance of special tutors and governesses Rosemary had managed to learn to read, do mathematical problems, speak a little French and with a little assistance correspond with her parents during their absences.

"Politically, I inherited a Democratic label at birth," the chairman of the U.S. Maritime Commission would record on the occasion of his twenty-fifth Harvard reunion in 1937, "and that label I still proudly wear . . . ." Nevertheless, he had wavered in his loyalty to the Democratic Party in the past, having both flirted with joining the Massachusetts Republican Party in the early 1920s and made a substantial donation to the La Follette-Wheeler Progressive ticket in 1924. For almost a decade the former assistant general manager of the Fore River Shipyard had heard nothing from the former assistant secretary of the navy who had made him break down and cry in anger and frustration during the war. In September 1928, however, Franklin Roosevelt contacted the film industry financier confidentially on Governor Smith's behalf. Believing Kennedy to support his coreligionist's candidacy, Roosevelt requested his "suggestions and counsel." No response survives either among the Kennedy or the Roosevelt papers. Some months into 1929, however, Kennedy sent a note of congratulations to Charles Francis Adams, the newly appointed secretary of the navy who had changed party affiliations from Democrat to Republican nearly a decade earlier, telling him, ". . . I considered your appointment was reason enough for President Hoover's election and sufficient justification for a good Democrat like myself to vote for him again." By 1932, however, he no longer saw sufficient reason for a good Democrat to reelect Hoover. "I was really worried," he would tell a *New York Times* reporter in 1934, "I knew that big, drastic changes had to be made in our economic system and I felt that Roosevelt was the one who could make those changes. I wanted him in the White House for my own security and for the security of our kids—and I was ready to do anything to help elect him."

As early as 1930, Henry Morgenthau, Governor Roosevelt's Duchess County neighbor, old friend and sometime business partner, approached the financier for a quiet exploratory luncheon in Albany. A more publicized meeting in Warm Springs, Georgia, in May 1932, would make public the financier's intention to support the governor the following month at the party convention in Chicago. While there, (although worried that he might not be accorded full credit for the maneuver in the "history books") he secured the pivotal, eleventh-hour support from William Randolph Hearst that would make his candidate the nominee. Not long afterward he delivered the publisher's contribution of $25,000 as well. Over the course of the campaign Kennedy would bring in an estimated $150,000 in donations, public and anonymous, giving $25,000 of his own money to the candidate and loaning another $50,000 to the party. On board the California-bound campaign train with Eddie Moore in September, he kept his ear to the ground at the various stopping points along the route, plotted strategy, galvanized support in Hollywood and helped draft speeches. He also became acquainted with the press corps and the Roosevelt children. He began making friends (and indeed a few enemies) among future members of the administration, and threw a small victory celebration for the Roosevelt family and a few intimates on the evening following the election.

Although the financier had begun to predict a 1932 Roosevelt victory among his friends and associates shortly after his 1930 meeting in Albany, other reports indicate that early on he had reservations about the candidate. On July 11, 1932, he had called on Roy Howard, chairman of the board of the Scripps-Howard papers, "to endeavor to do a little selling work in Roosevelt's behalf," Howard would write Newton Baker, whom Roosevelt had recently defeated at the convention. Kennedy, Howard reported, "is quite frank in his very low estimate of Roosevelt's ability." It seems that he held some members of the governor's inner circle, particularly Louis Howe (the governor's longtime secretary and adviser) and Jim Farley (then chairman of the New York State Democratic Committee), in equally low regard, and voiced concern about the candidate's susceptibility to their influence. As a result, Howard added, Kennedy intended to be present at as many of Roosevelt's post-convention strategy sessions as possible, so as to prevent others from "unmak[ing] Roosevelt's mind on some of the points which Kennedy has made it up for Roosevelt."

Ambivalence would characterize Kennedy's attitude toward the president until the end of their relationship. Roosevelt found in Kennedy not only a means of fortifying the presidential war chest, but a rare, and indeed a staunch ally in the world of finance. In Roosevelt, Kennedy saw a means of preserving peace and private property in the face of drastic economic upheaval, and through him would (eventually) find an entrée into politics. The two were not merely mutually useful, however. Through the midthirties each would seem to demonstrate genuine feeling for the other; they shared a sense of humor and evidenced appreciation for the other's abilities. The financier's enthusiasm and support would always be tempered and punctuated by critical outbursts like his remarks to Roy Howard, however. Indeed, such indiscretions would come to undermine their relationship and contribute substantially to its eventual, hostile stalemate. In the wake of the 1932 election, Kennedy would protest that he had supported Roosevelt for the good of the country rather than for his own political advancement. Nevertheless, after what he felt were substantial contributions to the campaign, financial and otherwise, in private he would be astonished, hurt and resentful that the president would make him no offers for more than a year after the inauguration. Although he would occasionally hire out his management and consulting services (to the likes of Paramount Pictures and William Randolph Hearst), after he had struck out on his own as Joseph P. Kennedy, Banker, in 1923, he would never again work for anyone else—with one exception. The two chairmanships and the ambassadorship that Franklin Roosevelt would offer were not the cabinet post at Treasury that Kennedy had hoped for, but did make it possible for him to contribute his services to his country. The posts would open new doors to the Irish Catholic from East Boston and confer the "prestige" that he had hoped for upon his children. His chairmanships would allow him to work in the manner that best suited his talents, attention span and interests—short, intensive bursts of managerial and reorganizational activity. He would not, however, be suited temperamentally or ideologically (as it turned out) to the ambassadorship that would eventually extinguish what remained of the friendship between the two men. And so in Roosevelt's offers, and in Kennedy's acceptances of the posts that were to come, the two men had set in motion the events that would eventually end their relationship and Joseph Kennedy's public career.

Joseph P. Kennedy to Robert Kane[1]

November 15, 1927

Dear Bob:

I called to see Gloria, at her invitation, and I can't find out if there is any possibility of doing business there, as she practically has her financing straightened out with Schenck.

I advised her that what she needed most was another picture with United artists, and she could not afford to be too particular on what terms or on what basis they wanted it, as she was not in any position to trade; furthermore, if she turned out another picture like SADIE THOMPSON, she was on the way up again.

I think the trouble is that she got herself all spread out with debts and one thing or another, and told too many people about it.

She seemed to be very well pleased with her talk with me. As far as I know, I can do nothing further.

With kindest regards, I am

Sincerely yours,

Joseph P. Kennedy to E. F. Albee

[November 27, 1927]

Dear Mr. Albee:

I am sending you a copy of "The Story of the Films," which is a compilation of the lectures given last Spring at the Harvard Business School.

I would esteem it a great honor and privilege to have you read this book.

I am sending you one of the first copies, because from my earliest recollections of the amusement business, I have always connected the name of "Albee" for the successful development of it, and I feel that the changes, due to take place in the industry in the next few years, must be guided greatly by your hand.[2]

With kindest regards,

Sincerely yours,

Joseph P. Kennedy to Milton Cohen[3]

December 20, 1927

Dear Mr. Cohen:

Miss Gloria Swanson has come to me at the suggestion of Mr. Robert Kane, and later at that of Dr. Giannini,[4] to discuss her motion picture business situation. From the

---

1. In a letter of November 7, Robert Kane (1890–1957), president of Kane Pictures at First National Studios, had suggested that Gloria Swanson contact JPK about the possibility of his restructuring her precarious finances. Kane had also proposed taking the Swanson organization off United Artists' hands, Kane handling the star's future productions, and JPK her finances.
2. Earlier in 1927 the corporate components of the B. F. Keith theatrical empire (which oversaw the extensive Keith vaudeville circuit as well as its talent management and booking services) had merged with Pathé-DeMille Pictures. In December, a subsequent merger with the Orpheum Circuit would form the Keith-Albee-Orpheum Corporation under the presidency of Edward Franklin Albee (1857–1930), formerly president of the Keith enterprises and assistant and protégé to showman B. F. Keith himself.
3. Milton Cohen (1881–1950), Gloria Swanson's attorney, also represented a number of prominent film stars of the 1920s, among them Fatty Arbuckle, whom he had assisted in defending against charges of manslaughter in connection with the lurid death of a young actress at a California party in 1921.
4. Former Spanish-American War army surgeon and current president of the Bowery and East River Na-

very sketchy outline I am able to obtain from Miss Swanson, it rather appears to me as if she has so heavily mortgaged her future that very drastic steps must be taken if she hopes to straighten herself out.

Because of the condition I think the motion picture business is in at the present time, I am firmly of the belief that it will be impossible for any of the companies to gross anywhere near as much on the pictures this year as their past experience would lead them to believe they might. From the expectancy of SUNYA,[5] I would say that her equity in that was rather a liability than an asset, and while I am of the opinion that SADIE THOMPSON is a very good picture, from the figures she has given me I am afraid that she will have gross $1,000,000. or $1,200,000. to get herself out even.

The maintenance of her overhead also seems to me to be a very difficult one in her present financial condition. I think her earning power is still very great, and if she were not saddled to take care of those obligations that have gone by, it might not be long before she would be in a sound financial position.

I told Miss Swanson that it would be ridiculous for me to make a trade with her to look out for any of her affairs, but I would be very glad, after receiving word from you, to put myself and some people in my organization at her disposal to work out her problem as best we could without any cost to her until we found out whether it was really possible to work it out or not. If, at some later day, it looks like the services we might render have been of any value, we could at that time take up with you the consideration of any further deal.

Would you be good enough to have compiled for me a list of all her obligations, and also the market value of her assets as you view them?

To me, the very difficult thing seems to be that she has mortgaged her future. If, by any chance, SADIE THOMPSON or LOVES OF SUNYA represent any serious loss and it would be necessary for her to work for considerable time before those obligations are paid off, it might be possible to make some kind of an arrangement with Mr. Schenck (dating from the picture she is on now), whereby, for some consideration, he would call his present contract on her third picture, and all future ones, free from all liability. From the conversation I have had with Miss Swanson, she would then be obliged to face only her personal obligations and settlement of her contract with Mr. Moore.[6] In that event, it might not be necessary to consider bankruptcy; but if nothing can be accomplished with Mr. Schenck, it would seem to me rather desirable to consider some method of cleaning up the slate without a serious loss to her present picture prestige.

I am not at all sure that prices Miss Swanson is getting on her pictures are not less than I would reasonably expect they would be in proportion to some of the other artists on the United Artists program, and would not seem conducive to working out successfully her personal guarantee on both these contracts.

It may be that you have some very definite plans in mind as to how all these things can be done, and because you know so much better than I do, I hesitate to make any suggestions at all; but if you so desire, I will be very glad to cooperate to help work out some plan if in yours and Miss Swanson's mind this seems desirable.

Believe me to be

Sincerely yours,

---

tional Bank, Dr. Attilio Henry Giannini (1874–1943) had been among the first bankers to finance motion pictures.

5. *The Love of Sunya* was currently under production and would open in March 1928.

6. Thomas Alan Moore of the Guaranty Trust Company of New York, an officer of Gloria Swanson Productions.

Joseph P. Kennedy to the Marquis de la Falaise[7]

March 3, 1928

Dear Henry:

I know you must be terribly disappointed at getting the news on the passport, but immediately upon receipt of your original cable, I got in touch with Jerry Hurley, who was in charge of that work in Boston and who is now at Washington. He looked up the matter and found the records unsatisfactory. We asked him to continue a further search and he found that the papers had been received but were incomplete and had been sent back to California, presumably to Milton Cohen, from whose office I suppose they came. I know nothing, of course, about the original papers and this is my only guess.

As you know, diplomatic relations between Milton and me for the present are rather strained,[8] but I am leaving for California next week and I will have no hesitancy in calling upon him myself and ask him what has been done on the papers, and at least see that they are put into proper form and returned to Washington.

Gloria has left for the West and it is possible that she may see Cohen before I get there and may have the matter straightened out before my arrival, which will be not later than next Saturday or Sunday. Immediately upon their receipt in Washington, Mr. Hurley promises that he will expedite the matter at once, and unless there are some complications that I am unaware of, we should get very prompt action. I shall keep on the job myself and will hurry it every way that I can.

I am enclosing copies of Gloria's correspondence with Somerset Maugham.[9] The only thing that I can see that might still be done at this time is to have a talk with him and get an idea of what he has for material. The price seems to have been fixed by Gloria at $25,000; therefore, the price does not seem to enter into it at this time. However, after talking with him, you might have an idea of whether the material sizes up right, also get a general opinion of it, so that we could discuss it when you get back.

There is one other matter I spoke to Gloria about that you could do. As you know, there is a very beautiful blonde actress by the name of Lily Demiti.[10] She has appeared in some films that have come to America and everybody here is very much impressed with her. I understand, however, that she has a very rich sweetheart in business abroad, and, for that reason, cannot be tempted to come to America. It might be possible, because of his business relations, to interest him to come also, on the ground that we might be able to do something to help him. I have no idea whether she can be tempted to come, for how long or for how much, but she looks like the best European prospect yet. I thought, possibly, (without going out of your way) that you might get me some idea as to whether anything could be worked out. I expect to stay at the Ambassador in Los Angeles, and you might cable me there or c/o FBO Studios.

---

7. Swanson's third husband, Henri James La Bailly, marquis de la Falaise de la Coudraye (b. 1898), had become European director of Pathé Studios in Paris in January 1928. JPK had been appointed special adviser to Pathé in Hollywood in February in order to liquidate the company's American holdings and terminate the distribution contract between Pathé and Cecil B. DeMille Pictures.
8. The dismissal of a number of Swanson's former employees and associates, Cohen among them, had accompanied the dissolution of Gloria Swanson Productions and JPK's recent establishment of a new Delaware Corporation, Gloria Productions, in its place.
9. She had been negotiating with Maugham for several months to write the sequel to *Sadie Thomson.*
10. The French actress and former music hall dancer, Lili Damita (1901?–1994), would make her American screen debut later in 1928 in Goldwyn's *Rescue.*

We have four or five stories that Gloria is interested in, but, up to date, none of them appeals very much to me. I think she looks like she had gained some weight and seems perfectly reconciled to go back to work.

We are still fighting on the settlement of her various propositions but are not making half the headway I feel we should have made. However, I hope to have the matters fairly well adjusted before you get back.

Ted is in New York now all the time and offers to serve as a reception committee for you on your return.

Eddie is coming to the Coast with me, also Derr.

I trust you are having a good time and I shall be glad to see you back in California, which I hope will be before I leave there.

With kindest regards, I remain

Sincerely yours,

Joseph P. Kennedy to Elisha Walker:[11] *Memorandum*

March 27, 1928

Talked with DeMille today. We have got to put the original deal back again, and he is instructing McCarthy to draw the papers, which I hope to forward you as quickly as possible. Another suggestion has come up, and I wish you would give it very careful consideration before turning it down because I, personally, believe it to be of a tremendous importance to the company.

As you know, the one thing we will have to fight against this year is that with DeMille gone the standard of pictures will be very cheap. I will try some ways to offset it, but nevertheless it will be the charge of the exhibitors against us.

DeMille has a contract with United Artists, altho not yet signed, whereby he gets a guaranty of about as much money as he got with us. He still has tremendous pride, and dislikes very much to go to United Artists. He figures that somewhere in this whole picture a reorganization will take place in which he will figure for the type of thing that he feels he does best — that is the making of big pictures.[12]

In my discussion with him today he has suggested that if a deal could be made whereby he could supervise one picture a year for Pathe, similar to "Chicago," for which he would receive fifty thousand and 5% of the gross.[13] From a business point of view of Pathe I, personally, consider this a very good piece of business.

Second, that he would make one picture a year not to exceed one million dollars. I think he would agree, altho he has not definitely said he would, to put up his own money for the cost running over one million. Of this million, two hundred thousand would go to him for direction and the rest of his services, and he would expect 5% of the gross. I think both these gross figures could be changed to percentage of net profits, altho I have not any reason for saying so.

11. The president of Blair & Company, Elisha Walker (1879–1950), formed part of the syndicate of financiers that JPK had assembled to attempt to purchase Keith-Albee-Orpheum. Walker was perhaps best known in the 1920s and 1930s for his financing of a number of spectacular oil industry transactions including Standard Oil's purchase of Pan American Petroleum in 1925.
12. DeMille would sign a three-picture deal with MGM in August, selling off his Pathé stock, as he described it, at a "very handsome" profit.
13. In the previous year DeMille had overseen Frank Urson's direction of the screen adaptation of Maurine Watkin's spectacularly successful play.

Now altho the proposition sounds terribly wild, I know, nevertheless, it is not. In the first place, I have not any hesitancy in believing that Doctor Giannini's bank in New York, or any of the banks that do motion picture financing, would be glad to loan seven hundred or seven hundred fifty thousand on this picture, which means that an independent financing company would only have to be formed with two hundred fifty or three hundred thousand capital. The advantages accruing to Pathe would be tremendous.

In the first place we would ballyhoo the fact that he was still with the company. Second, as "The Godless Girl" seems to be a tremendous hit,[14] and I think it is, we would have a big special to carry the following year's program.

If you decided you wanted to continue to operate the company or else that you wanted to sell it out because, as I have told you before, this would be the time to make the trade with "The King of Kings" and "The Godless Girl" in the offing, so that for a very reasonable investment, and to me not a tremendously big gamble, considering everything at stake, we could get practically at least another three quarters or a million dollars gross on our regular program, which of course, would be net to us.

Joseph P. Kennedy to Guy Currier

April 7, 1928

Dear Mr. Currier:-

At the suggestion of Mr. William Danforth I am writing to you to give you a very brief picture of the F B O Productions, Inc. and its allied companies. Of course, you realize it is very difficult to set forth on paper just what we are doing or hope to do. I should be very glad to go into this with anybody interested, if you would care to have me do so.

The high spot of the whole situation seems to me to be the fact that we have a very definite niche in the film business of this country. For producers who own the high-class theatres there is a satisfactory outlet for their pictures. For producers who make high-class pictures without a theatre outlet it is a very unsatisfactory condition. For the producer who makes a middle class product there is no outlet whereby he can get his cost back. This may seem strange and yet very elucidating, but it would take too long to explain it. I ask you to accept this as a fact.

We go into none of these classes at all. We make what we call the low cost productions; i.e. our average negative cost is approximately fifty odd thousand dollars, consisting of twelve to fourteen Western pictures averaging sixteen thousand dollars; a series of dog pictures, and another series of outdoor pictures, twelve in all, averaging twenty thousand dollars. The balance of our program is made up of features, some of which cost as high as seventy five thousand dollars. On this type of product there is a very definite market. Even assuming that we cannot get the so-called first runs, by our wide distribution we are able to maintain a very satisfactory gross. It is in this field that Fox and Universal, who had absolute control of this type of business, made their reputations and their fortunes. They have subsequently moved out of this field. Fox is now entirely making high-class productions to satisfy his large theatres, and Universal is still straddling the fence; i.e. trying to make both classes of product.

---

14. Pathé had released DeMille's depiction of the inmates, conditions and rampant atheism within a juvenile reformatory a month earlier.

We follow this principle of low cost production in our short product also so that we are not dependent on any particular group for support in order to get representation for our product.

Our company, as you know, has been in existence for eight or ten years. Previous to our time the original owners are reported to have lost over seven million dollars in trying to establish a policy. We have been able to pick up a business that was losing a good deal of money, and with a finance company on the side with approximately five hundred thousand dollars paid in, we have been able to carry on a business which last year did approximately nine million dollars worth of income.

We have through out the United States thirty-three offices through which we distribute film to the various theatres in that locality. In Canada we have six offices, and we also have offices in London, Paris and Berlin.

We have not attempted to follow the ordinary principles of motion picture accounting, which are themselves of an arbitrary method because the industry is so new, whereby the value of a released film is set month by month by a table of amortization fixed by Price-Waterhouse. We, on the contrary, take our profits only when they are received in cash, and charge off all probably losses on the basis of sales.

As the income of our pictures run to as long as eighteen months, and as we have only been in the business two years, we are not yet beginning to feel any great advantage from this conservative method of taking up profits.

In the absence of exactly definite figures as to the amount of common stock issued, I would suggest that you get the correct capitalization from the New York office.

During the past six months we have added as stockholders the General Electric and Radio Corporations with whom we hope to be associated in the development of their talking motion picture machines, and with the Keith-Albee Company from whom we have hope of getting first run representation in all of their houses and those affiliated with them.

I would consider that our business fundamentally is sound. We feel that there is still great opportunity for improvement in its development on the basis of selling prices of other motion picture companies.

In consideration of what we hold this company at we still have a very great margin in market values.

As to the question of policy of production and distribution, it would really take too long to go into this in detail, but I would be very glad to discuss it any time you see fit.

I think that our organization in all branches of the business is highly respected by the rest of the industry, and it is on this manpower that we have great hopes for the future.

We feel that, as we enter on our third year of program, very satisfactory advancement has been made in all branches of our business, and from the present outlook of the industry and conditions of some of the other motion picture companies we feel that the field will be narrowed and greater opportunities will accrue to those who are able to remain.

Sincerely,

Kathleen Kennedy, 8, to Joseph P. Kennedy

April 7

Dear Daddy

I hope you have got rid of your cold. I like Jean very much.[15] We are all fine and we miss you very much. I went to see Rio Rita on Wed the 4th of April. rose and Joe and Jack went to. We liked it very much. We go back to school on the 9th of April.

Love from all
Kathleen

Joseph P. Kennedy to E. F. Albee: *Draft Agreement*

May 10, 1928

I hereby offer to buy from you 200,000 shares of common stock of Keith-Albee-Orpheum Corporation at a price of $21.00 per share,[16] payable against delivery of certificates therefor, duly endorsed and stamped for transfer, at the office of Blair & Company, 25 Broad Street, New York City, on such day on or before [*sic*] 1928, as I shall designate in written notice to you.

This offer is conditioned upon and subject to all of the present Directors of the Keith-Albee-Orpheum Corporation, or such of said Directors as I may require, signing a letter to me assuring me of their co-operation, which letter has already been approved by J. J. Murdock and Maurice Goodman.

If this offer is acceptable to you, kindly note your acceptance at the place left below for that purpose, whereupon this offer, so accepted, will constitute an agreement for the sale by you and purchase by me of the said shares on the terms above set forth.[17]

A C C E P T E D:_____

Joseph P. Kennedy to Louis B. Mayer

May 25, 1928

Dear Mr. Mayer:

As you may or may not know, I have taken unto myself the responsibility of financing and producing the next Swanson picture. I have arranged to get von Stroheim to direct, and I can already hear you saying: "You have had no troubles in the picture business yet — they have just started."[18] However, we shall try to do the best we can under the circumstances.

As both of these people have expressed a desire to borrow Ollie Marsh from you (your cameraman),[19] they have asked me if I would write you to see whether it would

---

15. Her baby sister, Jean Ann Kennedy, had been born on Kick's eighth birthday, February 20, 1928, at St. Margaret's Hospital in Dorchester, Massachusetts.
16. The stock was currently trading at sixteen.
17. JPK had made Albee an earlier offer of $4.2 million (financed by the syndicate he had assembled) for the two hundred thousand K-A-O shares, but had been refused. Albee would accept the offer of May 10, however, and would remain president of KAO (for the immediate future); JPK would become chairman of the board of directors.
18. Discussions had been underway for several months of a screen epic for which JPK was to produce, Gloria Swanson was to act and Erich von Stroheim (1885–1957) was to write and direct under the working title of *The Swamp*. As vice president in charge of production at Metro-Goldwyn-Mayer, Louis Burt Mayer (1885–1957) had produced von Stroheim's versions of *Greed* in 1924 and *The Merry Widow* in 1925.
19. Like Oliver Marsh (1893–1941) many of the members of the *Queen Kelly* technical staff had worked with von Stroheim previously on *The Merry Widow*.

be possible. I realize you are very busy, but if it would be possible for us to use him in about nine weeks from now for the shooting of the Swanson picture, I would regard it as a personal favor.

As you probably know, not feeling that there was enough excitement in the picture business, I have gone into the vaudeville game — God knows what will happen there.

With kindest regards, believe me
Cordially yours,

Joseph P. Kennedy to John F. Fitzgerald

June 4, 1928

Dear Mr. Mayor:

I am in receipt of a letter from Blair & Co., two (2) copies of which I am enclosing, which sets forth our agreement regarding the Keith-Albee Circuit. I will sign the original letter that they have written me for our three participations, because, as it stands today, you have 500 shares, George Lane[20] 200 and I have 5500. If this is agreeable to you and you will be good enough to return me a copy of the enclosed, signed, I will forward it to Blair & Co. with the original, bearing my signature.

I am at present holding 12,500 shares of stock in a deposit box at the Bowery & East River Bank, and Mr. Scollard, of my office, has a memorandum setting forth your participation.

I will also write a letter to Blair & Co. upon receipt of your signed copy of enclosure, setting forth that you have participation in this pool, and probably by that time, they will ask me to return the stock to them, giving me a receipt, which I, in turn, will send to you for your proportionate part.

Very truly yours,

Joseph P. Kennedy to Eric von Stroheim

June 11, 1928

Dear Von:

As your letter of June 6th to Bill[21] arrived here after he had left, it was turned over to me.

I have taken up with Winnie Sheehan regarding the possibility of getting Lowe and he told me that he would let me know within forty-eight hours what the Coast commitment were on Lowe. I will advise you by phone.

Powers had already asked about the concluding scenes on THE WEDDING MARCH being taken at FBO, but not realizing that there was anything particular at stake or that you had any particular desire, and because of the fact that the other scenes had been shot at Famous Players, and because there might be a great deal of dispute about any

20. Lane was president of the Lewiston (Maine) Trust Company and had taken an earlier financial interest in William Gray's Maine and New Hampshire Theatres.
21. Von Stroheim had written William Le Baron (1883–1958), vice president in charge of production at FBO, with a number of suggestions and requests regarding the upcoming production. The director hoped, for example, to cast screen idol Edmund Lowe, then under contract to Fox, as the male lead in *The Swamp*. Additionally, he requested that Le Baron hire Gordon Pollack as cameraman, and wondered (given his deteriorating relations with Famous Players) whether he might finish filming his current project on the FBO lot.

bills that might be incurred, I thought it much the wiser to say that the scenes had better be shot at Famous. I am sorry, however, that I did not know you felt the way you do about it.

Pollack looks very interesting to me.[22] I am planing to be in California within the next month and if he is not under contract and I can talk to him when I get there, I am sure we could work something out. He sounds like a very interesting man and one that we can very well use in our organization.

With kind regards,

Very truly yours,

Joseph P. Kennedy to J. J. Ford[23]

July 2, 1928

Dear Johnnie:

I am afraid that I have fallen down on the talk with Albee. I tried up to the last minute on Friday to see him but was not successful.

I would suggest that you find out just how far we are obligated to pay him his salary; then go in and have a talk with him, explaining conditions and discuss with him the cuts on the ground that Mr. Goodman[24] said he was considering the matter. I think he should be cut to $25,000.[25]

Also take up all the other things you suggest, and at the same time the question of the marquee in Boston. Whichever way you want it is O. K.

J. P. K.

Joseph P. Kennedy to J. J. Ford

July 2, 1928

J. J. F.

I think you should get busy at once setting forth the theatres we will want PHOTOPHONE installed in for the Keith Company all over the country and for Maine and New Hampshire.[26] It is very necessary to do this, in order that we will be protected for the fall openings.

Have Mr. Murdock follow up the Evansville deal with the Lowe Company.

J. P. K.

---

22. Von Stroheim had also suggested hiring Gordon Pollack (". . . the most intelligent, ingenious expert on sound photography") as cameraman.
23. General manager of William Gray's Maine and New Hampshire Theatre Company.
24. The former general counsel to the Keith Exchange, Maurice Goodman (1883–1939) had assumed the same position at K-A-O.
25. More than a decade later, unnamed K-A-O employees would recall that Albee's figurehead presidency came to an end one day when he came to JPK to make a suggestion. JPK's reported response was simply, "Didn't you know, Ed? You're washed up, you're through."
26. That is, Gray's Maine and New Hampshire Theatres.

Joseph P. Kennedy to Al Lichtman[27]

August 17, 1928 (Dictated 10:45 PM)

Dear Al:

I am sorry that I did not get back in time to see you and have a chat with you about the next Swanson picture. When I told you that I hoped the budget would be reasonably low, I had every reason to believe that it would be. The figures now approximate $800,000. without any sound expense, so please be as generous as you can in trying out prices.

We have retained Barney Glazer (who you know is the best scenario man on the Coast and who supervised the MERRY WIDOW) to work on sound in this picture.[28]

Now that QUEEN KELLY has been decided on for a title, every one feels that you have picked by far the best one, and in talking with Kent yesterday, he feels it is one of the best of the year.

Sorry I did not have a chance to talk to Shapiro on publicity, but immediately upon my return, I want to get in touch with you, so that we can outline a campaign and run it in conjunction with you.

I appreciate very much everything you are doing and if any problem comes up while I am gone, please get in touch with Mr. Derr at my office, who will take care of it for you.

Very truly yours,

Franklin Roosevelt[29] to Joseph P. Kennedy

Sept. 13, 1928

Dear Sir:

As both candidates for the Presidency have now clearly stated where they stand upon all the important issues in this campaign, every voter is in a position to determine his choice. Information comes to me, that, having weighed the attitude of the two candidates you have decided to support Governor Smith. I sincerely hope this is correct and if so, won't you write me confidentially, as there are some matters upon which I would appreciate your suggestions and counsel.

One of the interesting and gratifying developments of the campaign thus far, is the assurances of support coming to us from men in all sections of the country, who are finding in the present situation sufficient reasons for supporting Governor Smith, regardless of their previous party affiliation. I sincerely hope that you will let me know frankly and confidentially where you stand.

This is a personal letter. I am not writing you as a member of the Democratic National Executive Committee, nor am I leading up to the matter of a campaign contribution, as I have nothing whatever to do with the financial end of the campaign.

Please address your reply to No. 49 East 65th Street, New York City, New York.

Very sincerely yours,
Franklin D. Roosevelt

27. Alexander Lichtman (1888–1958), president of United Artists.
28. The former head of the Famous Players–Lasky Story Department, Benjamin Glazer (1887–1958) had written the script for von Stroheim's *The Merry Widow* in 1924 and had won the Academy Award for his screenplay *Seventh Heaven* in 1927. He would become Pathé's head of production later in 1928.
29. As Alfred E. Smith's convention floor manager, Franklin Delano Roosevelt (1882–1945) had delivered the Roman Catholic's nomination speech at the recent Democratic Convention. Roosevelt would succeed Smith as governor of New York when the Happy Warrior's presidential bid would fail in November.

Joseph P. Kennedy and David Sarnoff[30]
to the Employees of Keith-Albee-Orpheum

October 1928

TO ALL EMPLOYEES OF KEITH-ALBEE-ORPHEUM CORPORATION:

To dispel any anxiety or unrest there may be in the organization, the Committee of Stockholders under the Plan for the formation of <u>Radio-Keith Orpheum</u> Corporation, which is to acquire at least a controlling interest in Keith-Albee-Orpheum Corporation and F. B. O. Productions Inc., has authorized the undersigned to make the following statement:-

It is the desire of the new management to augment and strengthen, rather than reduce or disturb the present organization, and efficient heads of departments and members of the staff need have no concern about being replaced.

You are urged to attend conscientiously to the duties of your position, and pay no attention to any rumors there may be in circulation as to changes contemplated in the Company,

DAVID SARNOFF
JOSEPH P. KENNEDY

Joseph P. Kennedy to the Marquis de la Falaise: *Radiogram*

OCT 31, 1928

IF OWNER HAS BONAFIDE OFFER LET SCENARIO GO GLORIA STARTS SHOOTING THURSDAY SHE SEEMS CONSIDERABLE UPSET OVER CABLE FROM YOU EVERYTHING HERE PERFECTLY OKEY FAR AS YOU CONCERNED HAVE NO ANXIETY AND DONT UPSET HER BECAUSE WE NOW ALMOST THREE MONTHS LATE REGARDS

JPK

E. B. Derr to Edward Moore: *Telegram*

JANUARY 25 1929

FOLLOWING IS WALTERS[31] OPINION WHICH I HAVE BRIEFED FOR TELEGRAM QUOTE CLIENTS[32] OBJECTION TO ORIGINAL DIRECTORS[33] ENDING IS JUSTIFIED STOP I THEN RAN APPROXIMATELY THIRTY REELS OF ENTIRE ROUGH CUT TO DATE AND MY OPINION IS THAT ORIGINAL DIRECTOR IN AN ATTEMPT TO BE BIZARRE AND UNUSUAL HAS BEEN VULGAR GROSS AND FANTASTICALLY IMPOSSIBLE IN THE CON-

---

30. David Sarnoff (1891–1971), vice president and general manager of General Electric and Westinghouse's jointly owned marketing and development arm, Radio Corporation of America. Following recent negotiations between Sarnoff and JPK, RCA had acquired a substantial interest in FBO. With the use of RCA's Photophone technology, the former FBO Studios would produce talking films for distribution throughout the extensive K-A-O theater chain under the management of the new Radio-Keith-Orpheum Corporation.
31. Because of the substantial, impromptu and occasionally lewd changes that von Stroheim had made to the original *Queen Kelly* script, E. B. Derr, JPK's former Fore River colleague, had hired Eugene Walters to make an assessment of the existing footage with an eye to determining not only how much might be salvageable for eventual release, but also the likelihood of a completed film's passage by the censors.
32. Swanson's.
33. With a highly charged working atmosphere on the set and the film itself vastly overbudget, long overdue and far from completion, Derr and JPK had replaced von Stroheim with a series of directors, including scenarist, songwriter and director Edmund Goulding and screenwriter Benjamin "Barney" Glazer to rewrite the ending and finish shooting.

CEPTION AND EXECUTION OF SITUATIONS CHARACTERS INCIDENTS OF NARRATIVE AND THEIR RELATIONSHIPS AND IN DOING SO LOST EVERY ELEMENT OF HUMAN NATURAL CHARACTERIZATION STOP I AM SATISFIED THAT ORIGINAL DIRECTOR AND BARNEY LACK KNOWLEDGE OF FUNDAMENTAL RUDIMENTS OF STORY CON-STRUCTION STOP CLIENT DURING THIRTY REELS WHICH INCLUDE ENTIRE PART OF STORY PLAYED IN MYTHICAL KINGDOM NEVER IS GIVEN ONE SITUATION FOR HER-SELF STOP HER CHARACTERIZATION AS DEPICTED IS NEGATIVE AND RETREATING AND PASSIVE AND AT NO TIME DOES ONE SINGLE SOLITARY THING WHICH WOULD SHOW ANY EVIDENCE OF STRENGTH OR INDIVIDUALITY OR OF CHARM OR OF ANY OF HER ATTRIBUTES STOP HER CHARACTERIZATION AS WRITTEN COULD BE PLAYED BY ANY THIRD CLASS LEADING WOMAN STOP UP TO END OF FIRST HALF SHE IS DEPICTED AS EITHER THE MOST EXASPERATING SAP OR A POTENTIAL PROS-TITUTE STOP WITHOUT HAVING SHOWN ANY ROMANTIC LOVE SCENES OR WITH-OUT ANY PERSONAL CONTACT OF ANY DESCRIPTION OTHER THAN A SIMPLE ACCIDENTAL MEETING ON ROADWAY WITH A SOLDIER[34] SHE IS KIDNAPPED FROM CONVENT BY CLUMSY DEVICE AND BROUGHT TO CASTLE WHERE ELABORATE PREP-ARATIONS WERE MADE FOR SEDUCTION STOP SHE CONVENIENTLY GOES INTO FAINT AFTER KIDNAPPING AND REMAINS IN FAINT UNTIL AWAKENING IN CASTLE WHICH IS SUBTERFUGE OF AMATEUR IN WRITING AND THEN UPON AWAKENING SHOWS NO RESENTMENT AT BEING THERE STOP PRINCE NEVER SHOWS TENDER-NESS NOR SLIGHTEST INDICATION OF AFFECTION BEYOND DESIRE TO CONQUER VIRGIN STOP AFTER QUEEN[35] DISCOVERS SEDUCTION AND USES WHIP THE PRINCE DOES NOT LIFT A FINGER TO PROTECT STOP DURING ENTIRE THIRTY REELS NOT ONE SITUATION IS GIVEN TO CLIENT STOP WE KNOW HER CHARACTER NAME BUT WHO SHE IS OR WHERE SHE CAME FROM OR HOW SHE HAPPENED TO BE IN CON-VENT OR WHO THE AUNT IS AND WHAT HER ATTITUDE TOWARD HER NIECE IS BE-YOND FACT SHE PAID FOR EDUCATION IS NOT TOLD NOR HINTED AT NOR CAN YOU DETERMINE STOP ENTIRE PREMISE OF STORY IS OMITTED STOP STORY AS SCREENED SLOVENLY GROSS OFTEN REVOLTING WITH NAKED QUEEN FROTHING AT MOUTH INDICATING RAGE SHOULD CAUSE LAUGHTER FROM NORMAL AUDIENCE PROVIDED CENSORS DO NOT DELETE QUEEN FROM PICTURE STOP I MADE REPORT TO THIS EFFECT WHICH RESULTED IN NEW DIRECTORS MIND WORKING TO RECON-STRUCT PREMISE STOP AFRICAN SCENES ARE CLUMSY AND UNBELIEVABLE EXPEDI-ENCE FOR TELLING STORY STOP THEY SHOW REVOLTING SPECTACLE OF MADAM ON DEATHBED BEING GIVEN LAST RIGHTS BY COLORED PRIEST WHO ENTERS WITH VESTMENTS TRAILING THROUGH IMPROPER ATMOSPHERE WITH COLORED ACOLYTES BEARING HOST AND CHALICE IN WHAT WAS PROBABLY INTENDED TO BE IMPRESSIVE PROCESSION AND THIS CONTINUES WITHOUT REVERENCE TO END OF MARRIAGE OF CLIENT AND DEATH OF AUNT AND ENDS REVOLTINGLY AND SMACKS OF SACRILEGE STOP THE CLIENT MARRIES A TOBACCO SPITTING INDESCRIBABLY REPULSIVE CHARACTER WHO IS THE MENACE IN AFRICAN SEQUENCE AND WHO IN-DUCED COLORED PRIEST TO MARRY HIM TO UNWILLING BRIDE STOP I HAVE NEVER BEEN SO SHOCKED AND SO REVOLTED STOP IT WAS IN EXECRABLE TASTE STOP FOL-LOWING THOSE SCENES SHOWS HUSBAND AS REPULSIVE REPUGNANT MAN ENTER-ING BRIDES CHAMBER WHILE HE BECKONING TO CROWD OF THIRTY OR FORTY

34. Walter Byron had been cast in the role of Prince Wolfram.
35. Played by Seena Owen.

79

PROSTITUTES TO ACT AS AUDIENCE STOP AS DRAMATIST AND AS MAN SCHOOLED IN FORMS OF STORY CONSTRUCTION AND PLAYWRITING AND IN STAGING PLAYS IT IS MY OPINION THERE IS NO CHARACTERIZATION GIVEN TO CLIENT AT ANY TIME TO SHOW WHAT KIND OF WOMAN OR WHERE SHE CAME FROM OR WHAT HER STATE OF MIND IS STOP AS FAR AS PICTURE SHOWS ALL SHE DOES IS YIELD AND WEEP WHICH BECOMES DEADLY MONOTONOUS IN SPITE OF CLIENTS SKILL STOP A FUNDAMENTAL RULE IS THAT IF A CHARACTER IS TO DOMINATE STORY THAT CHARACTER MUST CONTROL SOME SITUATIONS IN MOST INSTANCES AND MAJOR-ITY BUT AS FAR AS PICTURE SHOWS TO DATE CLIENT NEITHER CONTROLS NOR IS GIVEN SINGLE SITUATION STOP IN TRYING TO KEEP HER PURE AND CLEAN AND A VIRGIN TO MARRY HER PRINCE WHEN HE COMES TROTTING ALONG THEY KEEP HER CLEAN BUT HAVE HER OPERATE DIVE LIVING OFF EARNINGS OF PROSTITUTES STOP IN MY OPINION A WOMAN WHO TAKES PROFIT FROM OPERATING HOUSE OF PROS-TITUTES COULD SCARCELY BE CREDITED WITH POSSESSING ANY OF HIGH VIRTUES OF HER SEX STOP PICTURE IS NOT COHERENT NOR BELIEVABLE NOR IN GOOD TASTE NOR HUMAN BUT PRODUCTION IS MAGNIFICENT BUT IN MY HUMBLE OPINION IT IS MOSTLY GUILDING TO THE MANURE PILE STOP PROBLEM OF CONSTRUCTION IS TO ESTABLISH INTRODUCTION OF STARS CHARACTER AND TO SHOOT SOME LOVE SCENES IN FIRST SEQUENCE BEFORE SEDUCTION THAT WILL GIVE HER SITUATIONS AND SCENES WHICH WILL PALLIATE HER SEDUCTION BY PRINCE STOP I SUGGEST INSTEAD OF GOING INTO SOUND IN MIDDLE OF AFRICAN SEQUENCE THAT SOUND BE INTRODUCED FROM VERY BEGINNING OF AFRICAN SEQUENCE BY REWRITING AND DISINFECTING WHAT HAS BEEN DONE AND WITH DRAMA DOMINATING PRO-DUCE ENTIRE AFRICAN SEQUENCE ALMOST WITH AS MUCH INTENSITY AS A PLAY STOP UNQUOTE PRESENT THEORY INCLUDES POSSIBILITY OF OPENING PICTURE IN AFRICA ESTABLISHING STAR CHARACTERIZATION AND HAVE AUNT RUN HOUSE OF DANCE GIRLS BAR AND GAMBLING BUT NOT PROSTITUTES NECESSARILY AND HAVE CHARACTER OF JAN NOT BE A REPULSIVE CRIPPLE ON CRUTCHES WITH SLIMY MOUTHSPITTING TOBACCO JUICE AND MAYBE NEVER RELATED TO STAR AND HAVE STAR SENT FROM AFRICA TO CONVENT AND THEN USE SEQUENCES OF MEETING ON ROAD AND CONVENT AND ALL OTHER OF FIRST HALF SCENES SHOT WITH ADDED LOVE SCENES TO PREVENT SEDUCTION FROM BEING SO SUDDEN THEN BRING DISIL-LUSIONED GIRL BACK TO AFRICA WHERE NEW ENDING IS BEING CONCEIVED AND WRITTEN WITH POSSIBILITY OF RESHOOTING ALL REMAINING SCENES IN LESS TIME THAN PREVIOUSLY ANTICIPATED IF OLD SCRIPT AND DIRECTOR HAD BEEN MAINTAINED AND WITHIN OR POSSIBLY LESS THAN REMAINING MONEY WHICH WOULD HAVE BEEN SPENT HAD FORMER PROCEDURE CONTINUED STOP AFTER COMPLETE VERSION REWRITTEN AS COMPLETE STORY LINE WE WILL AGAIN USE WALTERS AND C B[36] STOP MY CONCLUSION IS THAT AT LEAST WE WILL NOT BE CRIMINALLY NEGLIGENT IN KILLING STAR VALUE FOR STAR WITH KIND OF CHAR-ACTERIZATION FORMER COMPLETE STORY MIGHT HAVE CAUSED STOP IF THIS PRO-CEDURE IS BELIEVED TO BE PROPER THEN FORMER DIRECTORS SERVICES AND CUTTING REGARDLESS OF WILLINGNESS CANNOT BE USED AS CUTTING TO FIT TO NEW STORY ENDING REQUIRES ONE IN SYMPATHY WITH ATTEMPT AT UTILIZATION OF MATERIAL SHOT STOP I SUGGEST NO ADDITIONAL MONEY OF REMAINING TWENTY THOUSAND BE PAID FORMER DIRECTOR WHICH PROBABLY HAS BEEN ASKED OF YOU STOP APPRECIATE THAT MANAGER OF FORMER DIRECTOR HAS

36. DeMille.

ONLY ONE COMPLAINT IN THAT I DID NOT APPROACH HIM FIRST BUT CIRCUM-
STANCES PREVENTED THEREFORE FORMER MANAGER ON THIS PETTY GROUND WAS
QUITE BELLIGERENT STOP I SUGGESTED TO MANAGER TWO METHODS TERMINATION
CONTRACT OF FORMER DIRECTOR ONE TO SIGN OFF MUTUALLY AND THE OTHER TO
SEND LEGAL NOTICE OF TERMINATION ACCOUNT VIOLATION CONTRACT IN TIME
AND MONEY AND MANAGER SAID TO ME QUOTE WHICH WAY DO I GET THE MOST
MONEY UNQUOTE STOP I SUGGEST YOU DO NOT CONSIDER ANY FURTHER PAYMENT
TO FORMER DIRECTOR IN VIEW FLAGRANT VIOLATION CONTRACT TERMS STOP
PLEASE BE CAREFUL LEGALLY NOT TO STATE ANY DISSATISFACTION IN STORY AND
PICTURE AS YOU HAVE NO LEGAL GROUNDS ALONG THOSE LINES FOR TERMINA-
TION STOP WILL DO EVERYTHING HUMANLY POSSIBLE TO START SHOOTING MON-
DAY OR TUESDAY AND SUGGEST WE NO LONGER LOOK FOR ANY JUDGMENT FROM
ANY OF THOSE FORMERLY CONNECTED WITH STORY OR DIRECTION STOP CLIENT
CONSTANTLY FAMILIAR AND ACQUIESCING IN MINUTEST PROCEDURE.

E B.

Joseph P. Kennedy, Jr., 13 to Joseph P. Kennedy

Sunday Feb. 25, 1929 Riverdale N.Y.

Dear Dad,

I hope you will be back soon we all miss you. Everybody is fine here. I was playing with a boy who got the mumps so I <u>might</u> have to stay out of school for a week. We had quite a snowstorm and nearly everybody (all except Jean) were out helping build a snowhouse. I went to Reed Handy's party on Friday and we all had on costumes me as a pirate and Jack as a prince. First we had a ventriloquist who was very good then we saw a clown and a policeman on stilts. Then we had dancing. Larry and the other boys wouldn't dance but Mrs. Handy took me over and introduced me to two girls and I danced a little while. Then we had supper after supper we went home. Yesterday I went to Hughes party they had two pictures. Hands up & Rinn Tin Tin The Lighthouse by the sea both were very good. One of the boys said Rin Tin Tinn was dead is he? I went ski-ing yesterday too with Mac & his father. It was awfully funny to see his father ski. Some cups were stolen from school that were given by the parents and it was quite a loss. Mrs. Moore was up here to-day and weighed her self she lost a few pounds and was quite joy-full about it. Give my best regards to Eddie and tell him if he sees some good horses to please bring them back to us as Jack is getting homesick without one and wants to go to a horse back riding camp. I ~~will~~ have to go to bed now. Always

Your loving son
Joe

Joseph P. Kennedy to the Marquis de la Falaise

March 13, 1929

Dear Henry:

I suppose you are interested to know what is happening on QUEEN KELLY. I will give you just a brief outline of what the situation has been and now is:

As you know, Gloria stopped production just before you sailed for Europe. We got into quite a discussion about it over the telephone and she became considerably upset.

After working for two or three weeks, things seemed to be getting more hectic than ever, and I went out there and found Gloria in very bad shape in the hospital, as the result of practically a nervous collapse. She was down to 108 in weight and her attitude towards the picture, and everybody connected with it, was quite hostile.

I looked at the picture and agreed that it certainly could not be released in its present form and tried to get another ending. We worked on this for ten days and it was a seemingly impossible task. Goulding was hopeless and Gloria suggested four or five other people who seemed equally hopeless on this problem.

There is no need to go into the personal reaction of Gloria toward owing me considerable money on the picture but it was far from a pleasant one. She went so far as to see Lasky with the idea of doing pictures there. I think her entire attitude was due to her overwrought condition and the discouragement over the whole situation. We had a very drastic showdown after the Lasky incident, and I insisted that some sort of a finish must be made because there was too much money at stake and too much loss of prestige if the picture was not finished.

Gloria was perfectly willing then to acquiesce and Barney Glazer, whom she hates, loathes and despises, got a boy to write a finish, which seems a very excellent one. That finish is now in preparation and it will be shot all-dialogue by Paul Stein.[37] Whether it will ever get started, whether it will ever see a finish, whether (when it is finished) it will be any good, I can give you no information whatsoever. If there is a reasonable chance of finishing the picture and my presence in California will help, Rose and I will go out there again. It is the chief concern now, as there is already over a million dollars invested with nothing to show. I am not giving you this story to annoy you but just to keep you posted on what is going on.

As far as Pathe is concerned, it is doing very beautifully. We have an excellent program lined up for next year, and, in the meantime, I have taken over the reorganization and refinancing of United Artists, although this is not publicly known.

FBO's production and distribution situation seems to me to be in a very critical state — but then the whole industry is in a critical state.

Hurel met me at the train on Monday and I am planning to see him this week.

If anything comes up that you think would interest me, drop me a line and I will keep you advised, as well as possible, as to what the developments are here.

Gloria has got back a lot of her weight and seems to be in rather a cheerful mood at the present time. Virginia[38] stayed with her a couple of weeks but had to come back owing to the illness of her mother.

Harry d'Arrast[39] may direct the Ina Claire picture[40] and I am working out a confidential deal with Hearst.

I am as busy as ever and have not had a chance to talk much with Dowling.[41] From all accounts, he lies as much as ever.

Regarding the two plays that you wrote me about, would FAME be any good for Gloria? I will see the other people when they arrive.

With kindest regards, I remain
Sincerely yours,

---

37. Austrian director Paul Stein (1892–1952).
38. Swanson's confidante and occasional assistant, Virginia Bowker.
39. Director Harry d'Abbadie d'Arrast (1897–1968) was currently under contract to Fox.
40. After a series of musical comedy successes on the Broadway and London stages, Ina Claire (1892–1985) would make her screen debut in Pathé's talking version of The Awful Truth later in 1929.
41. Writer, producer and actor Eddie Dowling (1894–1976).

Joseph P. Kennedy to Charles Francis Adams[42]

April 13, 1929

Dear Mr. Adams:

I have waited until the rush of your duties had subsided a little before writing and telling you how happy and proud I am that you are our new Secretary of the Navy.

I told Mr. Milbank[43] at lunch the other day that I considered your appointment was reason enough for President Hoover's election and sufficient justification for a good Democrat like myself to vote for him again.

I cannot tell you how great an appointment it has been for President Hoover and how satisfied I am that the Navy is in the finest hands it has been for a great many years.

With kindest regards and best wishes for the greatest success ever, I remain
Sincerely yours,

Joseph P. Kennedy to the Marquis de la Falaise: *Telegram*

APRIL 15 1929

LOOKS VERY MUCH LIKE NEW FINISH[44] UNSATISFACTORY TO GLORIA AND PICTURE LIKELY BE SHELVED APPROXIMATE LOSS BETWEEN EIGHT HUNDRED AND MILLION STOP NOW CONTEMPLATING SECOND STORY HAVE BEEN UNABLE GET TO CALIFORNIA TO FIND OUT HOW THINGS ARE BECAUSE MY FATHERS ILLNESS WHICH IS DRAGGING ON STOP[45] NOTHING CAN BE DONE JUST KEEPING YOU ADVISED STOP CONFIDENTIALLY CONTEMPLATING REMOVING SMITH IN LONDON REPLACING HIM WITH RUSSELL OF IDEAL IF POSSIBLE IN YOUR OWN WAY WISH YOU WOULD GET LINE ON WHETHER THIS ACTION SEEMS WISE OR NOT THINGS OTHERWISE MOVING ALONG NICELY HERE LOOKING FORWARD CONSTANCES[46] ARRIVAL BEST REGARDS
KENNEDY

Joseph P. Kennedy to Russell Ayres[47]

May 1, 1929

Dear Russ:

In the course of business over here, a letter like yours is like a breath of fresh air in a stuffy atmosphere. It was terribly nice of you to bother interesting Mr. St. John[48] and

---

42. Financier, philanthropist and leading American yachtsman of his day, Charles Francis Adams (1866–1954) had changed party affiliations from Democrat to Republican in 1920, and would serve as Hoover's secretary of the navy until 1933.
43. Financier Jeremiah Milbank (1887–1972), the majority Pathé stockholder until 1928, the financial backer of DeMille's *King of Kings* and a member of the previous year's syndicate to purchase K-A-O, had served as East Coast treasurer for the Republican Committee during the 1928 election.
44. I.e., to *Queen Kelly.*
45. Suffering from degenerative liver disease, P. J. Kennedy had entered the Deaconess Hospital in Boston, where JPK had gone to visit him.
46. After appearing in a few roles for MGM and Pathé in 1924, Constance Campbell Bennett (1904–1965) had retired (temporarily) from films in order to move to Paris with her son and her new husband, millionaire Philip Morgan Plant. She would return to the United States in 1929 under contract to Pathé.
47. A member of the Harvard College Class of 1915 and a former captain of the Crimson baseball squad, Russell Romeyn Ayers (1893–1959) coached baseball and chaired the history department at the Choate School for boys in Wallingford, Connecticut.
48. The Reverend George Clair St. John (1877–1966), headmaster of Choate.

yourself about the boys and I have definitely made up my mind to send them to Choate, provided I can get them in. I will fill out the applications to spend three years there, instead of two as I had planned, and I expect to forward the forms this week.

If for no other reason than you are there, it would make me most happy to have the boys with you. When I spoke to Mrs. Kennedy originally about writing to you, she said she had always felt that it would be difficult for me to have a boy whom I cared more for than I did for Russ Ayres, so the association of my boys with you at Choate would bring me great pleasure.

I am afraid that I must leave for California this week, to be gone for possibly a month. If I get back before school closes, I will make it my business to get up there and spend some time. If I don't leave for California this week, I will certainly come up and visit next week.

Again assuring you of my great appreciation of your kindness in writing to me, I am, as ever,

Your old friend,

Joseph P. Kennedy to John F. Fitzgerald: *Telegram*

MAY 22, 1929

DEAR MISTER MAYOR THANKS VERY MUCH FOR YOUR WIRE IT WAS KIND OF YOU TO SEND THAT WIRE AND BUCK ME UP A LITTLE[49] STOP MY GREATEST SATISFACTION OUTSIDE OF MY MARRIAGE TO ROSE HAS BEEN THAT I HAVE BEEN THE SON OF SUCH A GREAT FATHER I WILL NEVER FORGET IT THANK YOU FOR YOUR KINDNESSES

JOE KENNEDY

Joseph P. Kennedy to Joseph P. Kennedy, Jr., 13

June 3, 1929

Dear Joe:

I want to tell you of the lovely reports I got from Boston about you at Grandpa's funeral. Everybody says you were perfectly fine and handled yourself splendidly. I was terribly disappointed not to be there myself, but I was more than proud to have you there as my own representative and delighted everybody liked you so much. It is reports like this that are most encouraging.

By the time you get this letter you will be getting ready to go to the beach and will have finished school. I want to take this opportunity to congratulate you on the splendid record you have made this year at school. Your making up those subjects was a real worthwhile achievement, and while we may have had a little disagreement once in a while about some particular thing, I am very proud of your efforts and results.

I do not know how long I will have to stay here to finish the job I came out to do, but in the meanwhile, help mother and everybody out as much as you can and I will be with you as soon as possible.

Love to all.

---

49. During what proved to be only a temporary improvement in P. J. Kennedy's condition, JPK had left to attend to business in California, not managing to return to Boston before his father's death at the Deaconess Hospital on May 18.

Joseph P. Kennedy to John F. Kennedy, 12

June 3, 1929

Dear Jack:

I have been pretty busy since I arrived here trying to get things straightened out so I could get home and have a little fun with you all at the beach. As it looks now, I may be out here the balance of this month, but you may be sure I will get home as quickly as possible and when I do I will get busy on that horse arrangement so that you can do some regular horse back riding.

I hope everything finished up well at school and that you are helping mother out as much as possible.

I read your letter to a lot of the people out here and they thought it was very smart indeed.

Sorry I was not with you on the birthday party, but we will have a little party of our own when I get back.[50]

Love to all.

Patricia Kennedy, 5, to Joseph P. Kennedy

DEAR DADDY

I HOPE YOU COME HOME SOOn I THINK OF YOO EVERY night I WAnT kISS YOU
LOVE
PaT.
XXXXXXXXX

Joseph P. Kennedy to Gloria Swanson: *Radiogram*

AUGUST 16 1929

DEAR GLORIA STOP KELLY CABLED ME THAT AS SYNCHRONIZED PRINT WILL NOT GET THERE UNTIL LATE SEPTEMBER IT IS QUITE UNLIKELY THERE WILL BE ANY OPENINGS OUTSIDE OF ENGLAND[51] MAYBE IN YOUR DISCUSSION WITH HIM YOU CAN MAKE DIFFERENT PLANS WOULD YOU CARE CONSIDER MAKING APPEARANCES IN VARIOUS COUNTRIES IN ANTICIPATION OF OPENING IN ORDER TO START PUBLICITY OVER YOU AND YOUR NAME THINK THIS MIGHT BE WISE FOR NEXT WEEK OR SO AND THEN LATER ON BEFORE LONDON OPENING HENRY HAS ALWAYS FELT THAT MOST OF EUROPE THOUGHT YOU WERE OFF SCREEN STOP SHIPPING FOUR DIALOGUE PRINTS TODAY ON LEVIATHAN AND FOUR COLORED MAIN TITLES SEPARATELY YOU CAN DECIDE WHETHER YOU WANT USE THEM OR NOT STOP SHOWED PICTURE TO MORE PEOPLE AND THEY WILDLY ENTHUSIASTIC HOPE YOU HAD A FINE TRIP BEST TO YOUR TRAVELING COMPANION HENRY AND YOURSELF

JPK

---

50. Jack had turned twelve on May 29.
51. With *Queen Kelly* abandoned temporarily, Swanson had recently completed her first talking picture, *The Trespasser,* directed by Edmund Goulding and produced for Gloria Productions by JPK. After a single preview of the film at the New York Rialto on July 30, United Artists had scheduled a much ballyhooed London premiere (at which Swanson, Falaise, JPK and Rose Kennedy were to be present) before the film's general release in the United States in the fall of 1929.

Joseph P. Kennedy to Joseph P. Kennedy, Jr., 14

October 1, 1929

Dear Joe:

I have written the school about horseback riding and your teeth. I was wondering how you are going to do horseback riding if you are going to be out playing football. I think it would be lots more fun (and you would have a better time) if you went out with the team instead. Perhaps both of these things can be done but I would not give up the chance of participating in school athletics for the sake of riding horseback.

I also have written the school for permission for you to attend First Friday, and I know you will fix this up so that you can go.

I think you have a great chance down there and I am terribly anxious to see how it will work out. As you can imagine, the reports on the summer were not particularly pleasing to either mother or me and I wish you would give it the effort that I know you can to make the record down there an outstanding one.

Drop me a line when you have a chance and tell me how things are going. I will try to get up there within the next couple of weeks, possibly for one of the football games.

Everybody's fine and send their love.

Joseph P. Kennedy to the Marquis de la Falaise

October 2, 1929

Dear Henry:

Got your cable yesterday about Corniglion.[52] Looks to me like you were demonstrating your power. I had a long talk with Kane when I returned home and told him the facts. I agreed with him, pending cleaning up a few necessary details here, to form a separate unit and send it abroad, in which you, he, and Steve Fitzgibbon would be considered as participating parties.

I am hoping to get the equipment and organization on the boat within the next week or ten days, with the idea of shooting a French and a Spanish picture immediately. I have gone over our talks with Kane and he has some very good ideas for production. I think the thing to do is to wait until he arrives and then you and he work out a plan which you think will prove successful. You might tell Hurel that we are on the matter and will probably have something very definite by cable almost as soon as you get this letter.

Without saying anything to anybody, I am considering again another change in foreign management, but I don't want you to mention it.

Gloria has been living at the Plaza and has not been at all well. In fact, she is in bed now and will probably remain there for the balance of the week. Little Gloria and Brother are here with her,[53] and although we have not told her yet, it looks very much as though little Gloria might have to be operated on for throat trouble.

The picture has opened in Detroit and Buffalo and it seems to be doing very well.

Got a wire from Constance but have not had a chance to talk with her. They say her second picture is very good; the first one [is] only ordinary, although I have not seen either.[54]

---

52. Through Falaise and Robert Kane, Pathé had entered into negotiations in the late summer of 1929 with French producer Edouard Corniglion-Molinier for financing, producing and distributing Photophone films in Europe.
53. Swanson's children: Gloria Somborn (1920–), by her second marriage, and Joseph "Brother" Swanson, whom she had adopted as an infant in 1922.

Variety today carries an article that there is a rift between you and Gloria. Can't imagine where they got this information, unless somebody in Paris talked. Gloria has had no further discussion about the matter since she arrived, having remained in bed on the boat the whole trip, with the exception of one night.[55]

She is now talking about appearing in a stage play while her vogue is still great in pictures, and if a good German or French play turns up, think it would be well for you to notify me at once before some of the American producers had a chance to buy it up. This is about all the information at the present time.

I am enclosing the receipt you wanted on the French Line.

Behave yourself and keep out of trouble and don't gallivant around too much in Leaping Lens.

With kindest regards, I am
Sincerely yours,

Joseph P. Kennedy to Cornelius Keating[56]

November 1, 1929

Dear Neal:

I am leaving for California on Monday. Mr. Scollard will be here in New York and you can get in touch with him for anything. If you need me, you can reach me at the Pathe Studio, Culver City, California.

The crash in the stock market left me untouched; I was more fortunate this time than usual.

I appreciate the fine work you are doing.

With kindest regards, I remain

Sincerely yours,

Joseph P. Kennedy to Rosemary Kennedy, 11

13 November 1929

Dear Rosemary:-[57]

I cannot tell you how excited and pleased I was to get your letter. I arrived here today with your report, and I think you were a darling to write me so soon.

Miss Swanson is sending you a picture and writing you a letter so that you should receive it a few days after this letter.

Mother went over to Boston to see Grandma Fitzgerald, but she will be back soon and she is coming down to see you.

I was very glad to see a lot of improvement in the report card, and I am sure that within the next couple of months it will be even better.

Thanks again, my sweetheart, and if you have some time write me another letter.

Lots of love,

---

54. Bennett made her first two talking pictures, *This Thing Called Love* and *Son of the Gods,* for Pathé in 1929.
55. *Variety*'s brief "Rift in Falaise Ménage" had reported from Paris on October 1 that Swanson and Falaise were "at odds . . . according to stories going the rounds here." The article went further to say that "[d]ifferences came up just before [Swanson's] sailing, aggravated by a telegram to the marquis from another celeb who is not named in the gossip, which peeved Gloria." In December 1929, Bennett would divorce her husband; two years later she would marry the recently divorced marquis de la Falaise.
56. Keating, a Boston attorney, had been charged with the settlement of P. J. Kennedy's estate.
57. She was attending the Devereux School in Berwyn, Pennsylvania.

Joseph P. Kennedy to the Marquis de la Falaise: *Telegram*

DECEMBER 14 1929

KELLY STARTED AND STOPPED AGAIN AFTER THREE DAYS GYPSY CURSE STILL ON
IT HAVE NOW DECIDED TO MAKE MUSICAL OPERETTA WITH THE STUDIO NOT MAK-
ING ANY PICTURES [due to] THE FIRE IN NEW YORK[58] THE STOPPING OF QUEEN
KELLY AND VARIOUS AND SUNDRY OTHER ITEMS IT IS STILL A GREAT LIFE WOULD
LIKE TO GET A GREAT WALTZ FROM FRANZ LEHAR[59] WHO I UNDERSTAND IS IN VI-
ENNA IF HE KNOW WE WANTED IT HE WOULD NOT SELL IT OR WOULD ASK PRO-
HIBITIVE PRICE COULD YOU GO AND SEE HIM OR GET IN TOUCH WITH HIM AND SEE
WHETHER THERE IS ANY POSSIBILITY OF BUYING WALTZ TO USE AS THE BIG FEA-
TURE OF KELLY PICTURE AT NOT TOO PROHIBITIVE COST LEAVING TODAY FOR NEW
YORK CABLE ME THERE BEST

JOE

Joseph P. Kennedy, Jr., 14, to Joseph P. Kennedy

Jan. 14, 1930, Choate School

Dear Dad,

We are [*sic*] awful weather up here, there is no hockey, the Sport I go out for so
there isn't much to do. I went down town yesterday but we couldn't go to the movies.
Three boys ran away last week, and they haven't been able to find them. One of them
was one of Dr. Cloney's patients. I am doing well in my studies and I think I will pass
everything these two weeks. I will show you what I have been spending money for.

church	20c	
chapel	5c	
haircut	50c	
watch fixed	30c	
Tuck shop	25c	
Footes (ice cream)	15c	20
needles (for victrola)	25c	<u>160</u>
		1.60

I am going to keep a notebook of what I spend and I will show it to you when I get
home. The best way to do I think, is to get what I need because some weeks I spend more
than others.

Mother has probably told you that I have moved houses. They are not half so strict
over here. I have not had any hours in hall for about a month, so I guess I am pretty
good. That's about all the news. Dr. Crosby every three weeks.

Joe

---

58. The Pathé Sound Studios at Park Avenue and 134th Street had gone up in flames on the morning of December 10, when a spark from a carbon lamp near the set ignited a velvet curtain, leaving ten dead and
eighteen injured.
59. Hungarian composer Franz Christian Lehár's (1870–1948) light operetta, *The Merry Widow* of 1905,
had been an international sensation and had served as the basis for von Stroheim's 1925 film for MGM.

Joseph P. Kennedy, Jr., 14, to Joseph P. Kennedy

Dear Dad,

It has been very cold up here the last few days and we have had good skating. Yesterday the varsity played Storm King in hockey and beat 4 to 0. The captain of Choates hockey team last year was on the Storm King team. In fact three of the fellows that went here last year were either kicked out or resigned and then went to Storm King. We had a picture here last night. Harold Loyd in <u>Welcome Danger</u>. it was a silent version, the fellows liked it a lot. If you come up again, I wish you would speak to Mr. St. John about it. I have a very nice room here and the roomate is all right. Thats about all the news.

Joe

Dad

I just had this letter already and sealed when I got a letter from J. Alden <u>Yacht Broker</u>. I had asked him to send me some of the particulars of some of his boats. I am sending you details of one which I think is an excellent buy. I know you won't have hardly any time to look at it, but when you consider Crosby's 25 foot boats 2nd hand for $1,200 and they have a rotten cabin and no motor. I have had the Junior designes for three years and I am sure I will be able to sail this.

Just to show you what a studious boy I am going to work right after I mail this letter.

Joseph P. Kennedy to Sime Silverman

Dear Sime:

I can't go away tonight without writing and thanking you most sincerely for your very kind article in VARIETY today, and for your many, many kindnesses to me during my stay in the business.[60]

You have been a most loyal friend and a most helpful confidant. I have depended upon your advice and suggestions more than you will ever know. It has been a great pleasure and privilege to have known you and to have had you as a friend. I sincerely hope that our paths will cross as frequently in the future as they have in the past.

Again expressing my very deep and appreciative thanks, and with kindest wishes to Mrs. Silverman and Sid,[61] I remain

Sincerely yours,

Joseph P. Kennedy to Dr. Frederick Keyes

Dear Freddie:

I have your letter of October 2nd regarding the fact that you do not need any new bus, at least for the present. Also note what you say about the Catholic Medical Mission Board.[62]

---

60. Sime Silverman (1872–1933), founder, editor and publisher of _Variety_. That day the trade weekly had published an article entitled, "Jos. P. Kennedy Leaving Films to Re-enter Banking Business; Going With Elisha Walker," which described JPK as having done "the miraculous" during his short career in the film industry.
61. Silverman's son and eventual successor, Sidne (1898–1950).
62. Ten years earlier, upon Jack's recovery from scarlet fever, JPK had donated a bus to the Guild of St. Apolonia, a group of 250 dentists who volunteered their services to underprivileged children. It was founded and headed by Dr. Frederick Keyes (1886–1938). Recently Keyes had approached JPK for a do-

Now, to be very honest with you, Freddie, I have a very great interest in our situation right here in the United States and no place else. This may seem unfair and unreasonable but not to my way of thinking. There is plenty of work to be done right here and anything I contribute I expect to confine to "local" charities.

I regret that I probably do not see this in the same way that you do, but I have had strong feelings about this for a great many years.

I shall be up in Boston within a month or two and, perhaps, we can talk things over. With very kindest regards to yourself and family, I remain

Sincerely yours,

Joseph P. Kennedy to George St. John

October 23, 1930

Dear Mr. St. John:

Replying to your letter of October 15th, I feel terribly badly to have to say that it will be impossible for me to visit Joe again over the weekend of November 1st.

This comes at a very bad time for me, because, usually, I am in California from the middle of October until Christmas. This year, however, I have stayed East a little later but I am planning to leave the first of next week. I realize what a great loss this is to me but I just cannot find it possible to attend. With kindest personal regards, believe me

Sincerely yours,

Joseph P. Kennedy to B. P. Schulberg[63]

November 29, 1930

Dear Mr. Schulberg:

Referring to your letter of November 24th, I greatly appreciate the honor conferred upon me by the Academy of Motion Picture Arts and Sciences, but inasmuch as I am now definitely out of the motion picture industry, I feel that I must decline the invitation to become a member.

Very truly yours,

Joseph P. Kennedy to Elisha Walker: *Telegram*

DECEMBER 4 1930

DEAL SIGNED SIX FORTY FIVE TONIGHT THINK IT MAGNIFICENT ONE FOR US I AM HAPPIEST BECAUSE I KNOW YOU WILL LIKE IT[64] VERY BEST

J P KENNEDY

---

nation toward replacing the original bus, but later requested a donation to establish a similar program overseas instead.

63. Benjamin Percival Schulberg (1892–1957), vice president in charge of Production at Paramount and chairman of the Academy of Motion Picture Arts and Sciences.

64. At the time of the formation of RKO, JPK had remained chairman of the board of the ailing Pathé. Having attempted unsuccessfully to interest various parties, including Howard Hughes, in Pathé's substantially devalued assets over the course of 1930, he managed to sell them to RKO for a sum approaching $5 million, causing Pathé's stock price to plummet and a number of stockholders to bring suit against him.

Joseph P. Kennedy to J. J. Murdock

December 9, 1930

Dear J. J.:

I am enclosing a copy of the agreement of the deal with R-K-O and a copy of the letter that was sent out today to the stockholders.

I can't tell you what a relief it is to me to get this cleaned up. It was so loaded with dynamite over the last three or four years that anything could have happened at any time.

I think we have worked out a deal for the Pathe security stockholders which can't help but make them all more than satisfied.

I believe this has probably taken another five years off my life. I am going to stay around until the Stockholders' Meeting in January and if there is anything left of me then, I am going away for three or four months.

With kindest regards to the family and Pat, believe me

Sincerely yours,

John F. Kennedy, 13, to Rose Kennedy

Dear Mother,

I got the suit the other day but I did not not like the color and it was a pretty itchy looking material so if it is alright with you when I go to the occulist I can pick out a suit. Is that OK.

Doctor Hume said he was going to write to you about my right eye. I see things blurry even at a ~~dr~~ distance of ten feet. I cant see much ~~coolo~~ color through that eye either. So if you make the appointment with the occulist I can get my suit fitted and kill two birds with one stone.

I was going coasting the other day on a place like this [illustration]. I went first but did not make and went into ditch. The other two boys went past me. The hill is all ruts and all icey for (mi. You go from 35 mi. to 40 mi. As I turned in on a ten foot ~~rdd~~ radius I smashed into a sled that was lying on the ground and I saw the other boy, Brooks lyi[ng?] on the ground holding his stoma[ch?]. We lifted him up, he began to faint and so we put him on my sled and towed him (mi up a hill and then a (of a mile to school. He was all gray and as we carried him up stairs he fainted. He went to the hospital a hour later and he was just ~~as~~ a white grayish color. I think maybe he was operated on yesterday but I am not sure. He had internal ~~injury~~ injuries and I liked him a ~~lole~~ lot.

That about all.

Love to everybody

Joseph P. Kennedy to Margaret Welsh

December 19, 1930

Dear Miss Welsh:

I have your letter of the 15th and I am deeply appreciative of the confidence you showed in buying stock of a company with which I was affiliated; nevertheless, I must make it clear to you that I never urge any of my friends to buy securities of any company in which I may be interested.[65]

65. Welsh, a native of Brighton, Massachusetts, had written to say that she had invested and had persuaded her friends and family to invest some one thousand dollars collectively in Pathé because of JPK's reputation and asked for his assurance that the principal would not be lost.

My own feeling is that the proposed sale to R-K-O of assets that at the present time are losing money for us is by all means the best thing for the stockholders of Pathe, in that they will retain an interest in the equity of a company that is very prosperous (i.e., 49% of the Pathe-DuPont Co.) and get rid of the losing assets for a substantial amount of money.

Replying to your question as to why we did not let all the holdings go and swap them for RKO stock, I think that our judgment in not taking the stock is vindicated by the action of the amusement securities in the stock market last week, because had we made a trade of the stock while securities are wild, then our equity in the above company would have been severely handicapped.

I honestly believe that this proposed trade will be of great benefit to the corporation and I urge you to send along your own proxies with those of your friends.

Very truly yours,

Robert Kennedy, 5, to Joseph P. Kennedy

Dear Daddy

I hopE you aRE wElL I Miss you VERY much Please bring me home a fire engine
Best love
from Bobby

John F. Kennedy, 13, to Rose Kennedy

Canterbury School, New Milford, Connecticut[66]

Dear Mother,

I have only lost a pound up here. I have hives, that is a sickness which everything begins to itch. My face ~~had~~ hands <u>knees</u> and feet. I also have a cold. Outside of that I am O.K. When ever I go out the Doc jumps ~~one~~ on me for not wearing enough even though all the other boys arent either. Our Hockey team got licked to-day 2-1.

The icheting is ferocious and it is hard to sleep. The doctor up here just painted it ~~whith~~ with idione and that has done no good. [illustration] He is an old country doctor with a collo about three zizes too big for him. It is spreading ~~for~~ from the bottom of my chin to my cheeks and to my head. My face is hot to. Anything I can put on it. Two fellows almost died of pneumonia, ~~bee~~ with temperatures of 105° and oxygen tanks. One fellow who cracked his head to pieces and broke his collor bone sledding was one of them. They patched up his arm and then let him out two days later. He was a little fellow in the first form two days later he was down with pnemonia. They should not have let him out because he was weak and white. The other boy went to the infirmay with a slight cold and then he got pnemonia.

It is not much fun taking a rest because it breaks up my basket ball by half. Also with my milk and crackers I cannot have any tea because I have to take them at recess. That with my tonic results in recieving some kidding about my delicay though I suppose that does not make any difference it is not exactly comfortable. I am made out to be an awful baby. About my eye I did speak to you in vacation about it and you said you would have me examined the next time I came to the dentist. It has gotten worse and everything is a blur at over eight feet but if you ~~do~~ want me to wait till Easter I will if you

---

66. Jack had entered the Catholic boys' boarding school in September 1930.

think it best. I just saw Mrs. Hume and the doctor is coming to see me because my face has grown red from top to bottom and is very not.

My knees are very red with white lumps of skin but I guess I will pull through.

Love

Jack

P.S. I started this letter on Thursday is now Sunday. Have been to infirmary with Hives. Please thank Bobby and Pat for there letter. I will write them tomorrow.

Received ink-well. It is keen

PS. Love to everybody.

Joseph P. Kennedy, Jr., 15, to Joseph P. Kennedy

February 15, 1931

Dear Dad:

I am heeling the BRIEF which is the annual school publication. I have to get advertisements and think up wise cracks, I am not very good thinking up wise-cracks, but I have written letters to advertisers for some of the board. I am enclosing the price list for advertisements, many people put for their advertisement COMPLEMENTS OF A FRIEND. Would you like to put in a half-page? If you know of anybody that might put in an advertisement will you please tell me. It usually takes two competitions to get on the BRIEF each competition takes a quarter so I ought to get on by the end of the year.

I am getting good marks this week and if I keep it up I will have the best marks since I have been here. Give my love to Mother.

Love

Joe

P.S. Do you think the Rolls Royce would put one in?

John F. Kennedy, 13, to Rose and Joseph P. Kennedy

Canterbury School [postmarked March 5, 1931]

Dear, Dad and Mother,

I recieved your letter this morning. You know that I went up to one hundred and one and then back to 98. This week I went back up to 101. I have sat with Dr. Hume for a four weeks and am entering the fifth week straight. Every week the boys draw numbers to see which table they will go to for that week. The Dr. makes me sit with him and Mrs. Hume along with about three or two sixth formers and one other fellow who is usually a upper former. I dont have a very live time and he tells the same line of talk to every table and so soon I will be able to give a full and interesting took [talk(?)] for morning, noon or night a là Hume. Mrs. Hume says something and you cant hear it so you laugh and nod your head. I We are practicing the singink of the Kyrie Santus, Agnus Dei and so on. There are about fifteen of the younger boys who sit seperate and are supposed to sing an octave higher than the rest. We had some tryouts for voices and as I looked as if I had a good voice when I sing, he asked me to go O ^{Ooooo} I went O-O! x-x-x so he thought I was only fooling and he said so. "You are only fooling" said he. I had done my best note and so he thought I could sing and left me alone. My voice must by changing because when I go up it sounds as if Buddy was howling. I go up another note and Buddy is choking another note and Buddy and me have gasped our last. He will find out some day!!! We had a pretty big snowstorm. We beat the Yale Freshmans first team last night. We one sevan meets and lost one in the relay because our relay team could not swim, and the first and third men were out of it. The fellows who beat us were hill House — 2,000 boys. Our regular relay team did much better time than they did. The swimming season is over and the pool is now open for a hour. They have relays and every thing. Dr. Hume wont let me go in till I weigh 105. Wont you please write him saying O.K. I guess that is about all. The Latin is going faster and faster now that the deadwood is out of the class as the teacher calls them. It is too fast for me and some others. I am the Last of the Mohicans or at least thats what Mr. Malony ~~says~~. He takes me for the worst ride and he is tough Tough. He coaches basketball and baseball. He is a BRUTE.

That is about all
Lots of Love — Jack
My other envelope would not hold the letter so I had to use this bigger one

---

John F. Kennedy, 13, to Rose and Joseph P. Kennedy

Dear Dad and Mother,

The weather up here is pretty warm and about all of the snow is melted. I wish you would write to Dr. Hume, Dad, to say that you have given me permission to swim as long as I do not loose weight. Today we had a latin test, I handed in ~~y~~ my paper the last one and I thought he had it because I gave it to him. He was also handing out some corrected papers so he must have handed out mine because I have not seen it around and I cant convince him that I gave it to him so he gave me a zero which pulls my mark down to about 40 and so I guess my average will be very very low this month. In all my other subject after the first weeks bad start I am doing pretty well but the first week counts 1/5 so my average will be around 69 or maybe higher. What a mess! I am getting my algebra now and so if the term of grading was longer I think I could pull my mark up. Im going to get that Latin though. I spend 45 minutes to a hour on Latin and I get my days assignment right but when he give us sentances————[*sic*].

The other day we had a test of 23 words. Giving the Nomnative Genative, Gender and declension. I got my words all right but I either made a mistake in the gender or declension and then I got someworong in the sentences. He takes five or sevan off for each mistake no matter how much or how little we have and so I flunked. It wont be this month and maybe not next but I am going to pass Latin for at least one month if it in possible. This is a pretty gloomy letter. We play a lot of bridge up here in spare time and I have improved quite a lot. I am going to learn how to play contract if I can. Thanks again for the oranges. I hope Eddie did not see my letter. Did he?

Lots of Love
Jack

John F. Kennedy, 13, to Joseph P. Kennedy

Dear Dad,

We have had a thaw up here at Canterbury and the temperature went up to fifty five. We had mass said this morning by a missionary who gave us one of the most interesting talks that I ever heard, about India. When he was saying the confieton, I began to get sick dizzy and weak. I just about fainted and everything began to get black so I went out and then I fell and Mr. Hume caught me. I am O.K. now. Joe fainted twice in church so I guess I will live.

The Latin had gone up about twelve points. My marks are approximately now as far as I can tell.

Math — 93   Average 78.80
English — 75   These marks may be higher or lower.
History — 80
Science — 78
Latin — 68

We are reading Ivanhoe in English and though I may not be able to remember material things such as tickets, gloves and so on I can remember things like Ivanhoe and the last time we had an exam on it I got a ninety eight.

There goes the bell and that is not just a form of finish because it really did ring.

Love
Jack

John F. Kennedy, 13, to Rose and Joseph P. Kennedy

[Choate][67] *J.F.K. 12/6/31*

Dear Mother and Dad:

Sir William Grenfellcame today and lectured on Labrator and it was very good.[68] I received Communion this morning and am going to Churchon Tuesday. ireceived the prayer-booo and would you please send me a puff because it is very cold. You will find enclosed an extract from this weeks News about Mr. Ayres. Mr. Brien was up here the other day and Ibought a pair of skates and he sent youhis best. Every thing is going fine and Iwish you would send me my reports. The other reports you will probably receive with this letter. What did you think of my marks?Love to all.

WITHLove
Jack

P.S. Please excuse all misprints[69]

John F. Kennedy, 13, to Joseph P. Kennedy

Dec 9

Dear Dad,
Football season ended with our first snowstorm. The snow was a foot high and then it turned to ice. When you walked, you were at any minute liable to go on your ear. I am going out for basketball and I think I can make it. Studies have been going neat. Last week I was not recalled and I got a B2 for French and a jump from D4. I am doing my Christmas shopping Saturday with another boy. Due to fiancalnil difficulties at Wall

---

67. Due to illness, JFK had been forced to withdraw from Canterbury before the end of the spring term and had begun the subsequent 1931–32 school year at Choate.
68. As president of both the London Chamber of Commerce and the British Imperial Council of Commerce, William Henry Grenfell, Baron Desborough (1855–1945), had been offered but had declined the post of governor-general of Canada in 1921.
69. He had typed the letter himself.

Street we will not be encumbered by any weight in that direction. Woolworths five and ten cent store will probably be our object Saturday. I had a whole lot of boys up Sunday and we had a good game of football. The football was used at Dartmouth in 1913 but nethertheless we had a good game. I know a lot of boys around here. What do you want for Christmas? When I was talking about that ice I forgot to tell you that I am sure you would have likeed because you always enjoyed slipping around. When Joe came home he was telling me how strong he was and how tough. The first thing he did to show ~~of~~ me how tough he was was to get sick so that he could not have any thanksgiving dinner. Manly Youth. He was then going to show me how to Indian wrestle. I then through him over on his neck. Did the sixth formers lick him. Oh Man he was all blisters, they almost paddled the life out of him. He was roughousing in the hall a sixth former caught him he led him in and all the sixth formers had a swat or two. What I wouldn't have given to be a sixth former. They have some pretty strong fellows up there if blisters have anything to do with it.[70]

Joseph P. Kennedy, Jr., 16, to Joseph P. Kennedy

[Choate] January 10, 1932

Dear Dad:

The weather here has been very warm, and so we haven't had any hockey. However we have indoor hockey in the new gym. There are seventeen squash courts, and squash is quite the thing here. Everybody plays it. I have played it four or five times, and like it very much. I am taking an exercise called body building. It is composed of fellows who don't have much muscle, and they have a man come up from New Haven to give the exercises. Mr. Massie, the physical director here, suggested that I take it after my operation, and I think it does me a lot of good. Are you having good weather down there. I am looking forward to Spring Vacation, I think it begins March 18.

Love
Joe

P.S. I got an ad from Hallle & Stieglitz.

Rose and Kathleen Kennedy, 11, to Joseph P. Kennedy

Jan. 24, 1932

Dear Daddy,

Everybody's fine here. How are you? Grandma[71] went home Friday. It was raining yesterday, but it is lovely today. I went to The Taming OF The Shrew & Local Boy Makes Good with Joe Brown. They both were good but I liked Local Boys makes Good best. Feb 5 our goal cards come out so I am studying hard I go in to 7B then too every thing is changed we have some different teachers ~~and~~ at different times. Hope to see you soon.

Love From all
Kathleen

Joe dear — I love you very much & would like to see you this minute

Rosa

---

70. The original letter is incomplete.
71. Her maternal grandmother, Mary Josephine Hannon Fitzgerald (1865–1964).

Kathleen Kennedy, 11, to Rose Kennedy

February 13, 1932

Dear Mother,

How are you feeling[72] Daddy did not come home last night. we do not know when he is coming. Will you please let Bride know if Rose is coming home for my party and send the games ~~home.~~ for my party.

I went to the dance at school last night I had a very nice time I had ~~my~~ hair waved and it looked hot. We had this sort of lucky number dance where the boys got a number which was printed on a card then the man called out numbers like from 90 to 125 and so on. The boy that chose me ~~to~~ had about five hearts and we were into the last. the lucky number was 22 and we had 27.

Jean got a darling costume for the party at the Field club this afternoon.

Love From All

Kick

P.S. At Margery Callman's where I had supper before the dance, she had a party they had peanuts and they were throwing them at everybody so I am not having peanuts for my party

X X X

John F. Kennedy, 14, to Rose Kennedy

[Choate]

Dear Mother,

It is the night before exams so I will write you Wednesdy.

Lots of Love.

P.S. Can I be Godfather to the baby[73]

Kathleen Kennedy, 12, to Joseph P. Kennedy

294 Pondfield Road
Bronxville, New York.
March 8, 1932

Dear Daddy,

How are you? Everyone is fine. Mother called up last night and everyone spoke to her. On Saturday Night Iwe_nt to a party. There were no boys, we play~~ed~~ games and had a lot of fun. I am going to a party March 18 too. Do you think during Easter Vacation we all could go to see the musical comedy "Hot-Cha". Margery callman is going to see it too. Every body thinks that the baby Should have been called George After Washington mother said she didn't like it though. Dr. Good told Mother she ouhgt to buy me a horse. He saw me at the horse show down at the Cape. Iam writing This on a ~~typewritere~~ type writre because I am tryng xxxxxx xxx TO learn to type. I hope you can read it.

Much love from~~e~~ all
Kathleen

P. S. Is'nt it terrible about the Lind bergh baby.

---

72. REFK had gone to Boston to deliver her ninth child in the care of her longtime obstetrician, Dr. Frederick Good.
73. Jack would become godfather, and Rosemary godmother to Edward Moore Kennedy, who had been born on February 22.

Joseph P. Kennedy to John F. Kennedy, 14

April 12, 1932

Dear Jack:

In looking over the monthly statement from Choate, I notice there is a charge of $10.80 for suit pressing for the month of March. It strikes me that this is very high and while I want you to keep looking well, I think that if you spent a little more time picking up your clothes instead of leaving them on the floor, it wouldn't be necessary to have them pressed so often.

Also, there are certain things during these times which it might not be a hardship to go without, such as the University hat. I think it would be well to watch all these expenditures in times like these, in order that the bills will not run too high.

I am leaving today for California on business and expect to be gone about three weeks. My plans were very sudden; otherwise, I would have come up to see you and Joe. Mother is home and is feeling very well. I suggest that you drop her a note and tell her about Palm Beach.

Love,

Joseph P. Kennedy to Roy Howard[74]

Dictated by Mr. Kennedy, via telephone, from Cape Cod, Mass. August 16, 1932

Dear Roy:

Now that your former "baby" has seen the light of day on Prohibition,[75] I imagine we will have to step pretty hard to interest you in our Candidate. I have seen very little of him the last month but have been trying to keep him in my mind.

My own impression is that if Hoover is able to put two and one-half million people back to work, his chances will be excellent; otherwise, I think our Candidate is still the favorite.

I expect to be at Hyannis for the next month. If you have planned on anything, I will be more than interested to hear about it.

With kindest regards, believe me

Sincerely yours,

Joseph P. Kennedy to A. P. Giannini: *Telegram*

SEPTEMBER 8 1932

AM SUFFERING AT THE MINUTE WITH HAYFEVER BUT IF BETTER BY MONDAY WILL GO WEST WITH ROOSEVELT STOP[76] WILL SEE YOU IN SANFRANCISCO STOP THE EAST IS THE ONLY SPOT THERE IS ANY WEAKNESS IN HIS CAMPAIGN I FEEL VERY CERTAIN AND I ASSURE YOU CONFIDENTIALLY THAT SMITH WILL COME OUT FOR

---

74. Although traditionally liberal editorially, the Scripps-Howard papers tended to follow the political leanings of their chairman, Roy Wilson Howard (1883–1964). The chain had supported La Follette's Progressive candidacy in the 1924 presidential race, but had endorsed Hoover's Republican ticket in 1928 and would go on to support Roosevelt against Hoover in 1932.

75. Having praised the "noble experiment" four years earlier, President Herbert Clark Hoover (1874–1964) had admitted the failure of the Eighteenth Amendment and began advocating state-by-state repeal in the course of accepting the Republican Party's renomination on August 11.

76. On September 13, in Albany, JPK and Eddie Moore would board the Democratic campaign train, the *Roosevelt Special*, bound for Missouri, Kansas, Utah, Montana, Washington, Oregon and California.

ROOSEVELT AND WILL BE OF GREAT VALUE TO HIM HERE STOP BIG INDUSTRIES ARE
STILL NO PUTTING MEN TO WORK AND TO ME THAT IS HOOVERS ONLY POSSIBLE
CHANCE STOP FROM ALL REPORTS CALIFORNIA SEEMS RATHER STRONG FOR ROO-
SEVELT AS DO A NUMBER OF THE WESTERN STATES STOP I THINK THE SLIGHT TEN-
DENCY TOWARD HOOVER IN THE LAST TWO WEEKS WILL BE CHECKED BY NEXT
WEEK AND I LOOK TO SEE ROSSEVELT GET MUCH STRONGER STOP IF I FINALLY DE-
CIDE TO GO ON THE WESTERN TRIP I WOULD LIKE TO HAVE YOU MEET HIM IN SAN-
FRANCISCO I KNOW HE WOULD BE ANXIOUS TO HAVE A CHAT WITH YOU BEST
REGARDS

JOE

Joseph P. Kennedy, Jr., 16, to Rose Kennedy

[Choate] Oct. 9, 1932 Sunday

Dear Mother:

Received your letter to-day. I can easily understand how busy you must be buying antiques and clothes. We had our first game yesterday with Hartford High who are supposed to have a very good team, in fact, they were picked to beat us. I was not in the first team line-up but after about the first three minutes of the first quarter the coach sent me in for right-end, and I played there until the last two minutes of the game. They were a pretty tough bunch, and were always arguing with the referee and trying to get us sore. I wish Dad had come up yesterday, because I might not play so long next week, but that is to be seen. I am enclosing some of the articles of different papers written about the game. Will you please send them back to me as I want to put them in my scrap-book. There was no secret about me getting a ticket, I was waiting until I saw how I came out before writing you. It seems that I was hurrying along a wide cement road with no cars in sight right near New Haven, a town called Orange, when a cop came alongside and told me to pull into the curb. He said that we would have to put up a bond of $25 or we would have to leave the car there. We went to the chief's house, and the boy I was with happened to have $24 and I had $1 so we put up the bond. We also got a summons calling us to court Monday last. I got in touch with a policeman up here I know, and he went down and talked to the captain of the Wallingford police force who went to Orange and talked to the Judge, but he couldn't do a thing, you know the judges in small towns. Well, the captain knew a certain judge to town that knew the judge in Orange very well, he got the case off the list and had it annulled for the costs which amounted to $15. I am going down town sometime this week to get my $10 back. I am not sure of the time Jim came but I think is was on the 20th, maybe a day or two before. One of the masters up here would like to know if there are any 16 milometer films on Switzerland views etc. If it isn't too much bother I wish you would ask Dad or Paul Murphy about it and let me know. I dropped Vergil and took up French 4 instead. I will have a much better chance to pass the French board, and I also like French a lot better. I have to work pretty hard though most courses are very interesting. We are reading Hardy's <u>Mayor of Casterbridge</u>, and <u>The Woodlanders</u> which I like very much. Jack is in the same house that I was last year, and he seems to be getting along fine I have a fine roomate, plays left end on the football team, but a rotten corridor. I guess thats about all the news.

Love
Joe

P.S. Please be sure to show this letter to Dad.

I made a mistake in my letter last week, it is the <u>New York Times</u> instead of the <u>New Yorker.</u>

Joe

The best games of the season will be the last three.

Joseph P. Kennedy to William Randolph Hearst

October 19, 1932

My dear Mr. Hearst,-

I know that I speak for everyone in the campaign when I say that you were most generous in your contribution.[77] Considering the fact that there are only two contributions equal to yours, you can well understand what a terrific sensation this check made, and as I told Mr. Willicombe this morning when it arrived there was just $1402. left in the treasury so that it was thrice welcome.

I sent word to the Governor at Buffalo by his son Jimmy[78] about the check and he just could not realize it.

As far as I am concerned and as I told the Colonel this morning, I appreciate personally, more than I can ever express to you, your kindness in mailing it to me because I realize that this check coming to the Committee through me helps a great deal in having consideration paid to any suggestions that I might want to make.

You may be rest assured, and this I want to say in order to go on record, that whenever your interests in this administration are not served well, my interest has ceased.

I am so glad to hear that you are getting well rapidly and hope that you will be back West in the very near future and feel your usual self.[79]

With kindest regards,

Sincerely yours,

Franklin Roosevelt to Joseph P. Kennedy: *Telegram*

1932 OCT 24 PM 6 44

BEEN HAVING A GREAT TRIP STOP WHY DONT YOU JOIN UP WITH US AT RICHMOND WASHINGTON OR BALTIMORE=

FRANKLIN D ROOSEVELT

Joseph P. Kennedy to Edward Flynn[80]

October 26, 1932

Dear Ed,-

I have sent my check for the bill to the El Tovar Hotel and suggest that your half be donated to the Bronx Democrats to get a big vote out for Roosevelt.

---

77. On October 14, William Randolph Hearst had communicated through his secretary, Colonel Willicombe, to JPK that he wished to contribute $25,000 toward the Roosevelt campaign's "broadcasting program."
78. James Roosevelt (1907–1991), the Roosevelts' second child and eldest son.
79. Hearst was recuperating from esophageal surgery at the Cleveland Clinic.
80. Bronx Democratic boss Edward J. Flynn (1891–1953) had succeeded Robert Moses as the secretary of state of New York in 1929, shortly after Roosevelt's election to the governorship.

I haven't bothered you because I know that you are busy, but after the 7th of November — mind you I say the 7th — let's have a reunion.

Was with the Governor last night in Baltimore and he is still in great shape. Talked with some of the Washington newspaper men who were with us on the Western trip but who have been with Hoover on his present trip, and they say he is in very bad physical shape and felt that they were all lucky to get out of Detroit last week without an assassination.[81] I really feel very badly for him. It is a bitter price our high officers must pay.

With kind regards,

Joseph P. Kennedy to Elliott Roosevelt[82]

[November 10, 1932][83]

My dear Elliott:

I just left Jimmie at the boat and he told me, in a roundabout way, that you were quite hurt about missing the party last night. I want to set the facts before you and then let you judge.

In the first place, there was no party settled. It was discussed on Monday with Jimmie over the telephone, presumably for a party of eight. At that time, however, Jimmie was so indefinite about his plans that nothing further was said about the matter. On the night of election, I talked to Anna[84] about it and she said a big crowd of newspapermen and every one else had been invited by Jimmie, and I said: "All right, go ahead on that and let us not bother about a party of our own."

Jimmie joined up with me about 3 to 4 o'clock in the morning following election, and at that time, he decided that he had not invited anybody and that we would go ahead with our party. He did not know whom he was going to ask and agreed to call me at 12 o'clock on the following day.

I heard nothing at 12 o'clock, and Anna called me some time after lunch, presumably around 2:30, and said she had talked with Jimmie and Jimmie had decided he had not asked anybody and that we should go ahead on our plans. I asked Anna at that time whether Curt[85] was coming or not, and she said it was rather indefinite, as he had a date to play tennis. I said it would be rather necessary to know how many were going, so that I could get theatre tickets. I asked whether she had any idea as to how many might come and she said "No." I said I would try to locate Jimmie and see what could be arranged.

On dropping the telephone after my talk with Anna, I immediately called your office and asked for you. Your telephone operator said that you had left word that you would not be in at all during the day and that you had left no message as to where you

---

81. The motorcade carrying the president from Detroit's Union Station to the Olympic Arena, where he was scheduled to deliver a campaign speech on October 22, had met with what the *New York Times* described as "the first hostile demonstration of his campaign." Hundreds of jobless men and boys believed to be connected with the Workers Ex-Servicemen's League lined the route, jeering and waving placards bearing such slogans as "Down with Hoover" and "Hoover — Baloney and Applesauce."
82. Elliott Roosevelt (1910–1990), the third of Eleanor and Franklin Roosevelt's five surviving children.
83. Two days earlier Roosevelt had been elected president with 60.7 percent of the popular vote to Hoover's 36.4 percent.
84. Anna Roosevelt Dall (1906–1975), the eldest of the Roosevelts' children and only daughter.
85. Anna Roosevelt's first husband, stockbroker Curtis Bean Dall (1896–1991), from whom she would be divorced in 1934.

could be reached. If you will call your operator, you will find out that this message was left at your office.

I then called your home and asked if they knew where I could locate you. The person who answered the phone told my operator (so my operator reports) that they did not know where you were. This got to be about 4 o'clock.

At 5 o'clock I had an appointment that was to keep me until about 7 P. M. I left Eddie Moore and Arthur Houghton to try and get theatre tickets and to make arrangements as soon as they found out how many people were going to be there.

The party was got together on just these plans. Nobody else was notified. Jonas Lee was notified as late as 6 o'clock last night by, I think, Mrs. Cushing.[86] We finally located Louis Ruppel[87] and he arrived too late to have dinner with us.

If I knew anywhere else to have tried to locate you, besides your home and office, I certainly would have done so. I know you feel, and I know that Isabel definitely knows, that the farthest thought from my mind was to have a party (to which you might have come) and not have had you included.

It was one of those things that was got together within the time that I have specified, so please don't feel that I was neglectful or inconsiderate, because I assure you that the first person I called after my talk with Anna was yourself.

I may be rated sometimes as not particularly thoughtful, but never unappreciative, and I am sure you know that I would not have had knowledge of the folks who were to be there and considered for a minute not inviting you, or whomever you might have liked to have brought along.

Please believe me, Elliott, because your annoyance gives me great concern.

Sincerely yours,
Joe Kennedy

Joseph P. Kennedy to Frank Walker[88]

November 21, 1932

Dear Frank:

When I made my gifts, I told you that while I would like very much to be able to help defray the past loans of the National Committee (because I felt that I would like that same kind of treatment to get mine paid off), it was my intention that my contributions were to be devoted wholly to the expenses of the Roosevelt Campaign and not to be applied to the old loans, inasmuch as I felt it would be very difficult to raise enough money to even meet our legitimate expenses. Therefore, I want to have this as a record, so that there cannot be any question over the County Trust Company.

I would also like to point out that the $50,000 I advanced is a loan, and no part of that money should be used to pay any previous obligations. This was thoroughly understood when I gave it, and with that understanding, I can't see where there should be any questions about it.

I trust this will make my record clear with you.

Sincerely yours,

86. James Roosevelt's mother-in-law, Katherine Crowell Cushing (1870–1949).
87. *New York Daily News* political correspondent Louis Ruppel (1903–1958) had covered the campaign from aboard the *Roosevelt Special.*
88. The former vice president and general counsel to the East-Coast Comerford Theatre chain. Frank Comerford Walker (1886–1959) had become treasurer of the Democratic Committee in 1932.

Joseph P. Kennedy to Will Hays

November 22, 1932

Dear General:

Just returned to my office this morning, as I have been suffering from a slight cold since election; consequently, I am just getting around to answering my telegrams.

The only secretarial job that I would ever consider would be one to General Will Hays.[89] I have no desire for political preferment, and I still feel that some spot in the reorganization of the picture business would give me much more pleasure, and probably would be more in line with something I might be successful at. However, we will talk that over one of these days.

With kindest regards, believe me

Sincerely yours,

Joseph P. Kennedy to Hiram Brown[90]

November 22, 1932

Dear Hiram:

I was very happy to get your note of the 17th. I have had about the same experience as you have had, but in the last analysis, it doesn't make very much difference what people say; they all adjust themselves finally.

Of course, I am terribly pleased that Roosevelt won, but the responsibility is sufficient to make all of his enthusiastic supporters shake with fright. As far as my accepting any position under him, I can assure you that it is the farthest thing from my mind. I went into the fight for the fun it gave me, and there is no hope of an ultimate reward. I still feel that the next four years are going to be bad, and one had better hop from one foot to the other to try and hang on to what he has got. However, if they are going to be good, it will be very important to be in a position to support one's family.

With kindest regards,

Yours sincerely,

89. On November 9, the day after the election, Hays had wired JPK to congratulate him for his part in the Roosevelt victory, addressing him as "Mr. Secretary."
90. Hiram Staunton Brown (1882–1950), president of RKO.

PART III

Washington

1933–1937

"There is nothing I would like better than to attend that party with you at this time, but a week ago Sunday, I was thrown from a horse," Kennedy wrote Louis Ruppel, the former *New York Daily News* political writer whom he had met aboard the *Roosevelt Special*, in mid-May 1934.

> The horse started to go along with me, and broke my left leg, smashing my right ankle. I know you will be happy to hear, however, that nothing happened to the horse . . .
>
> By a strange coincidence, the horse's name was "Louis", named after you I hope, not after the president's secretary, Mr. Howe. But then, after all, I have been thrown pretty consistently by Louises this year. I will recover, however, and press on to greater efforts. Moore suggests that I ride one of those horses that they put in swimming pools, and when I fall off, I can only get wet.

Although protesting to friends and acquaintances that he entertained no political ambitions, that he had supported Roosevelt's candidacy solely for the good of his country and his children, Kennedy had brooded privately for more than a year over the fact that the president had made him no offer of an administration post. Many of the friends and associates whom he had met on the campaign and aboard the *Roosevelt Special* had accepted the call (including Louis Ruppel, who had been appointed U.S. deputy commissioner of narcotics after the inauguration). The financier's long-held hopes of a cabinet position at Treasury had been dashed twice. William Hartman Woodin had been appointed in 1933, only to resign the following year. Woodin's successor had been the man who had brought Kennedy into the Roosevelt camp initially, the president's old friend and erstwhile business associate, Henry Morgenthau. Although Kennedy had been considered briefly for the post of treasurer of the United States, he had been passed over for that position as well. In the spring of 1934 the president would finally offer ministries in Uruguay and the Irish Free State, but Kennedy would dismiss them as being of no particular interest. In the eighteen months following the election he had maintained occasional contact with the president and his immediate staff, but the correspondence on both sides, although often jocular, was politely distant. Privately, Kennedy's criticisms of the president and the administration grew increasingly vociferous. He had provided the election effort not only with loans, funds he had solicited and his own donations but he felt he had given generously of his time and his counsel as well. Believing not only that he had shared a genuine camaraderie with the candidate and with many members of the entourage, but also that the governor had appreciated his plainspoken advice, he was fundamentally hurt that he had been so easily forgotten. In the spring of 1934, however, his growing suspicions would be confirmed. The very rapport that he had shared with Roosevelt had in fact been largely responsible for sparking not only Louis McHenry Howe's jealousy, but also the president's faithful, gnomelike, watchful assistant's opposition to a Kennedy post as well.

In the meantime, with his political hiatus from business at an apparent end and the repeal of Prohibition imminent, the financier would resume looking for new business opportunities both on the stock market and in liquor importation and distribution. Amidst both intensive federal investigations into unethical stock trading practices and rumors of the increased demand for bottles in the face of repeal, he joined a pool in trading, generating interest in, and then selling short the stock of the Libbey-Owens-Ford Company. Although indeed a glass manufacturer, Libbey-Owens-Ford did not in fact produce bottles and would therefore not stand to benefit from the ratification of the Twenty-first Amendment. The pool, soon to come under the scrutiny of the Senate Banking and Currency Committee, was also composed of Henry Mason Day, a partner of the firm of Redmond and Company (of which Kennedy's Harvard friend Arthur Goldsmith had recently also become a partner); Elisha Walker of Kuhn, Loeb and Company (who had participated in the 1928 syndicate to purchase K-A-O); the Lehman Brothers and Walter P. Chrysler. Netting an estimated sixty to sixty-five thousand dollars from the pools' transactions (conducted through an account in the name of Edward Moore at Redmond and Company), Kennedy's trading during the period is likely to have been more extensive. His business activities in the early 1930s, however, are almost impossible to reconstruct. Accounts of the Libbey-Owens-Ford pool's actions (and of Joseph Kennedy's participation in them) survive largely because they had been scrutinized and recorded as part of the Senate Banking and Currency Committee's investigations into stock exchange practices at the time. Whatever his other contemporaneous securities interests and trading practices might have been, having escaped public notice at the time, they remain obscure. Almost no mention survives of Libbey-Owens-Ford among the Joseph Kennedy papers beyond a few passing references to the committee's chief counsel, Ferdinand Pecora, and the latter's reported objections to serving on the new Securities and Exchange Commission with a speculator who had participated in a pool that the latter had recently investigated.

Although Kennedy maintained cordial but distant (if resentful) relations with the president in 1933 and early 1934, his friendship with the president's son Jimmy and his wife, the former Betsey Cushing, had remained close since the westward trip aboard the *Roosevelt Special* in the fall of 1932. Indeed, by 1937 the elder man would come to consider himself a "foster-father" of sorts to the younger. The young Roosevelts had visited Hyannis Port in the summer of 1933 and would take a house in nearby Marion, Massachusetts, the following summer. The couple paid a visit to Palm Beach at the end of 1933, not long after returning from a European trip with the Kennedys. In September of that year Jimmy and Betsey Roosevelt, Rose, Joseph and young Joe Kennedy embarked for Southampton aboard the *Europa*. With the ratification of the Twenty-first Amendment expected within the coming months, Kennedy joined the heated competition to secure American franchises for a variety of liquors, particularly Scotch whiskeys. Assisted, no doubt, by the cachet of traveling with the president's son, Kennedy's Somerset Importers would become the American agent for John Dewar's, Gordon's Gin, Haig & Haig and Black and White. Like Kennedy's participation in the Libbey-Owens-Ford pool, the story of his role and intentions in Somerset's origins and early operations survives primarily through sources other than himself and beyond his own papers. Some five years after the trip, out of the few known facts and many rumors that had developed in the interim, journalist Alva Johnston wrung a short narrative, almost incidental to the article in which it figures, that still serves as the basic account of Somerset's establishment. In a *Saturday Evening Post* piece deeply critical of Jimmy Roosevelt and the extent to which he was alleged to have taken advantage of his position as the president's son in various business dealings, Johnston asserted that "Jimmy has helped Kennedy to reach the two great positions which he now holds—that of Ambassador to London and that of premier Scotch-whiskey salesman in America." Having secured import licenses for medicinal alcohol in Washington before leaving the United States, Johnson contended, Somerset had stockpiled large quantities of alcohol in American warehouses immediately before repeal. Rumors of the way in which Somerset had procured its contracts and begun its operations, of Jimmy Roosevelt's conduct and role in the company's origins, and of Kennedy's stake in involving Roosevelt would persist and indeed evolve for many years to come. "In April, 1942," a 1955 FBI memorandum noted,

> A source of unknown reliability advised that James Roosevelt traveled to England just prior to the repeal of prohibition and secured exclusive U.S. liquor rights from the company which controlled almost the entire Scotch whiskey output in England. Due to pressure from U.S. liquor interests, James Roosevelt allegedly transferred these contacts to Kennedy who was reportedly appointed Ambassador to England so he could handle the contracts. It was further alleged that Senator Nye had been advised of the above but was reluctant to act on the information since its disclosure would likely have created disunity while the Nation was at war. In October, 1953, the Antitrust Division of the Department requested the Bureau to conduct investigation [*sic*] concerning the importation and distribution of Scotch whiskey in the United States, stating that allegations had been received implying that the United States Ambassador to England probably designated the agencies in the United States. It was further alleged that members of the Roosevelt family possibly owned interests in the Somerset Company, Inc., Scotch whiskey importers, formerly owned by Joseph P. Kennedy.

"Extensive investigation which was concluded in April 1954," the memo's author, Agent Boardman, noted, however, "failed to develop any information substantiating allegations or revealing possible antitrust violation." Nevertheless, although typically little remains among Joseph Kennedy's own papers to document his negotiations with British distillers in late 1933, he wrote his namesake on December 4 that "I closed with the Englishmen for the distribution of Haig & Haig and Dewar's." Two days later Utah would ratify the Twenty-first Amendment, thereby repealing Prohibition, and Somerset's imports would be made available for sale to a thirsty general public unable to buy alcohol legally since 1920.

The 1933 trip to England had not been all business, however. Having won Choate's Harvard Prize for the senior best combining scholarship and athleticism the previous spring, Joe Junior would take the coming school year abroad before matriculating at Harvard as a freshman in the fall of 1934. During his last months at Choate, Joe had toyed with the ideas of joining either the well-known wild game collector, explorer, author and RKO star, "Bring 'Em Back Alive" Frank Buck, on safari in Africa, or radio personality Phillips Lord on a round-the-world broadcasting cruise. After consulting with Felix Frankfurter at the Harvard Law School, however, his father had arrived at another plan. "I am taking Joe to Europe with me . . . to get an appreciation of the tremendous problems facing the world, by getting first-hand information of the foreign problems," Kennedy reported to George St. John, Choate's headmaster, the evening before sailing with the Roosevelts. Frankfurter (who, after meeting young Joe, had reported to the proud father that the boy exhibited "brains and . . . sticktoitiveness . . . entirely absent in this day and age") had suggested that Joe spend the year studying under his friend, political scientist and Fabian Socialist, Harold Laski, at the London School of Economics.

Living on his own in London for the first time in his life, Joe made a wide variety of new acquaintances. He would witness events that had far-reaching consequences for world affairs over the next decade and be exposed to ideologies that he had only read and theorized about at Choate. His father encouraged him to pursue his own new contacts among British and Scottish distillers, and to seek out Frankfurter (then spending the academic year at Oxford) for guidance. Joe reported that at Laski's famous Sunday teas, frequented as they were by intellectuals of every persuasion, Marxist to Nazi, "you certainly can learn a lot . . ." He visited the houses of Parliament, engaged in regular sporting activity and made dogged, conscientious efforts to consider and inform himself of a variety of viewpoints. "Read two newspapers in the morning," he told his father shortly after his arrival,

> the "Times" and the Manchester "Guardian", a socialist paper, so I get both points of view; also read the "New York Herald" and the "Evening Standard", so you see I'm getting pretty well posted. Besides, read "Literary Digest" and "The Nation", "What everyone wants to know about money" by G. D. H. Cole, "A tract on monetary reform" by Keynes and am in the midst of many books on economics, international relations and British politics.

He found his English contemporaries stimulating. "It is more interesting to talk to them than an American boy, because they talk about important things and not on dances, etc. and it gives me a chance to get their point of view," he told his father after six weeks in London, adding with some satisfaction, "I am just getting to the point where I can discuss matters intelligently and not be like a dumb ham."

During his Christmas holiday he skied in Zermatt before making his way to Geneva accompanied by his tutor, Richard Greaves, to observe the League of Nations at work. In the spring he traveled extensively on the Continent, writing his father a startling letter from Germany containing his observations on the Nazi state and its new chancellor. "Before starting on my trip I had heard the greatest condemnation of Hitler and his party. I had been to Laski's many times to tea, and heard him and many German Socialists tell of the frequent brutalities in Germany," he confided. After meeting an innkeeper in Munich who assured him that "there was no brutality to speak of," he reported in an odd, if characteristic effort to maintain an open mind, "I am not willing to accept her statement or the statements I heard in London in full, but I think a 50% discount in both is pretty fair." Attempts at objectivity aside, he would be impressed with sterilization as a means of "do[ing] away with many of the disgusting specimens of men which inhabit this earth," and although "regrettable," he would argue that the German "dislike of the Jews . . . was well founded" as they were reportedly "quite unscrupulous." Overall, however, the eighteen-year-old would see in National Socialism "a remarkable spirit which can do tremendous good or harm, whose fate rests with one man alone." The boy who would volunteer, and indeed give his life a decade later in an effort to eradicate both the state and the mushrooming abuses he had described with some enthusiasm in April 1934, would decide for the time being not to reveal his opinions to Laski or Greaves. "It might hurt their feelings," and in any case, "Laski would probably give me examples which might change me back again." Joe's ongoing efforts to "see the other point of view" led him to travel to the Soviet Union with Laski and Frankfurter in June, despite his father's concerns about the open talk he had heard in Washington of Frankfurter's suspected communist sympathy. Tending toward impressionability over objectivity in his efforts at open-mindedness, Joe embarked eastward proclaiming it "a pretty discraceful [sic] state of affairs" that the young Americans he had met on board ship had been forced to seek work in the Soviet Union. He would return home, however, with an enthusiasm for leftist ideology and for much of what he had seen that rivaled his sentiments on Germany of two months earlier.

During Joe's travels in the spring of 1934, his father had begun to spend more time in Washington and was in the process of renewing his former cordial relations with the president. In the years since Kennedy's participation in the Libbey-Owens-Ford pool, the widespread abuses in stock exchange practices unearthed by Ferdinand Pecora and the Senate Banking Committee had resulted in the Truth in Securities Act of 1933 and the following year's Securities and Exchange Bill.

On the evening of the Gridiron Dinner in mid-April 1934, the president invited Rose and Joe to stay at the White House (where Howe, upon spying Kennedy for the first time in almost a year "looked . . . as if he were looking at the devil himself"). The following morning the president suggested not only Kennedy's appointment to the new commission that was to regulate the securities industry, but his chairmanship. The suggestion did not come as a surprise, apparently, as the financier had arrived with a prepared statement defending his business practices on Wall Street. The issue (and indeed the sensitivity it provoked) would resurface at a subsequent meeting in June, at which, presidential adviser Raymond Moley would recall, "[w]ith a burst of profanity he defied anyone to question his devotion to the public interest or to point to a single shady act in his whole life."

> The President did not need to worry about that, he said. What was more, he would give his critics—and here again the profanity flowed freely—an administration of the S.E.C. that would be a credit to the country, the President, himself, and his family—clear down to the ninth child. (And in the job he made good on all he said that night.)

Despite the president's suggestion of his choice for chairman, the bill required the appointed members of the commission to select their chief from among their own number. With the passage of the bill into law in late June, the issue of who would fill the chairmanship became contentious—both within the commission and without. Both Kennedy and Pecora were determined to have the chairmanship (indeed, William Randolph Hearst counseled the former to take "nothing but"). Ray Moley had characterized Kennedy to the president as "[t]he best bet for Chairman because of executive ability, knowledge of habits and customs of business to be regulated . . ." Bernard Baruch and former *New York World* editor Herbert Bayard Swope concurred. The suggestion of a Kennedy chairmanship had met with antipathy from Roy Howard, who ran an editorial excoriating the administration for the proposed appointment, and from Postmaster General and Democratic Party Chairman James Farley and Louis Howe, who likened such an appointment to setting a cat to guard the chickens. The president would respond that it takes a thief to catch a thief, and sensed, correctly, that having made his fortune, the financier hoped that the respectability of civic service might transmit to his children. Further, Wall Street might be less threatened by and, therefore, recalcitrant to regulation by one of its own. With no little wrangling and delay, the commissioners (Pecora and Kennedy as well as James Landis, George Matthews and Robert Healy, all of the Federal Trade Commission) would finally emerge into the overwhelming July 2 heat, having chosen Kennedy as their chairman.

Despite the initial public outcry at his appointment, the job suited the chairman's talents well, requiring the same intense, exhausting, relatively short-term managerial work at which he had excelled in the past. As with much of the work that he had performed throughout his life—at Fore River, at the Columbia Trust Company or in Hollywood—he was faced with a specific mandate and granted broad authority toward its implementation. Characteristically, he assembled much of his own staff. Eddie Moore joined him as a dollar-a-year man. His former Boston Latin baseball teammate, Joseph Sheehan; his Harvard contemporary and Boston banking colleague from his days at Hayden, Stone, James Fayne; and his own Boston counsel, Bartholemew Brickley, also entered the commission's ranks. For legal counsel he hired both John J. Burns, who at twenty-seven had become a Harvard Law School professor and at thirty, the youngest superior court justice in Massachusetts history, and a young, liberal Yale Law professor named William O. Douglas. The commission would be responsible for ending the abusive and deceptive trading practices of the previous decade in addition to registering and regulating not only the twenty-four formerly self-governing exchanges, but also their members (who numbered some twenty-five hundred at the time) and the more than five thousand securities that the exchanges traded collectively as well. In order to facilitate local enforcement, the commission established a number of branch offices throughout the country; refusing to comply with federal regulation, the exchanges in Boston, Denver and California were closed. Although not mandated by law, it fell to the chairman to promote the reformed regrowth of the securities industry as part of recovery generally. The former speculator announced in his maiden address to the National Press Club and a coast-to-coast radio audience that "not all the old practices are wrong, and there is no belief . . . in the minds of the Securities and Exchange Commission that business is to be viewed with suspicion; that it must be harassed and annoyed and pushed around." "We of the SEC do not regard ourselves as coroners sitting on the corpse of financial enterprise," he assured members of the securities industry, who had awaited his comments anxiously at exchanges across the country. "On the contrary, we think of ourselves as the means of bringing new life into the body of the securities business."

His tenure at the SEC would usher in a new era in his relationship with the president. Believing at first that his family would accompany him to the capital, he had rented Marwood, a sprawling estate in Maryland. Rose and the younger children remained undisrupted in Bronxville, however. Over the course of 1934–35, Marwood became the site of a number of glittering dinners and informal gatherings hosting a variety of public officials and notables, the president, Congressman Truman and Janet Auchincloss, Jack's future mother-in-law, among them. Relations between the president and his chairman would revert to the easy camaraderie of 1932, a fact that would begin to arouse the jealousies of administration members beyond Louis Howe.

Having told the president upon his appointment that he intended to stay in the position only so long as it would take to get the commission on its feet, Kennedy attempted to resign in May 1935. After a few months' delay resulting from the Supreme Court's declaration that the National Recovery Administration was unconstitutional and the congressional fight over the Public Utilities Holding Company Bill's "death sentence" clause, he would finally submit his resignation in September 1935. The end of his chairmanship was heralded with the almost universal (albeit sometimes incredulous or grudging) acclaim of the press and the administration alike for having done ". . . one of the best jobs of anyone connected with the New Deal." "No man has ever held an important post in Washington who has had more praise and less abuse than Mr. Kennedy," the *Baltimore Sun*'s Frank Kent noted. Kennedy's tenure at the SEC had brought him not only the kudos of the Washington political press, but also increased contact with many of its number as well. Despite his own conservatism, his friendships throughout his life would be politically ecumenical. Likewise, at the time of his retirement from the SEC he enjoyed both the congratulations and in some cases the intimacy of prominent journalists and commentators from across the political spectrum. He was the single administration member to escape the opprobrium that Father Coughlin generally reserved for New Dealers. And, indeed (for the time being) he had impressed such staunch liberals as Walter Lippmann and John T. Flynn of *The New Republic*. The campaign had made Arthur Krock a close friend; in the intervening years the *New York Times* political columnist had become his most avid and consistent public champion. He had also cultivated friendships with the duo of Drew Pearson and Robert Allen, as well as Walter Winchell, Colonel McCormick, the Pattersons and Henry Luce.

Protesting as he would many times throughout his public life that he was "out of politics" for good, he returned to Europe in September 1935. This time he would be the president's unofficial observer on European economic conditions and, with his wife, would accompany Jack to England to follow his elder brother to the London School of Economics, and Kick to Paris to enroll in boarding school. At Choate, Jack had attempted to keep up his grades and participate in sports in whatever way he could despite ill health, intermittent hospitalization and near expulsion. "Mr. Ayres told me that he has one of the few great minds he has ever had in history," his worried father told his elder brother in London in November 1933, "and yet they all recognize the fact that he lacks any sense of responsibility and it will be too bad if with the brains that he has he really doesn't go as far up the ladder as he should." Despite Jack's obvious proclivities for history and literature, his overall performance at Choate had not matched Joe's; he won no prizes at graduation. And yet, at sixteen he had appeared to outstrip his elder brother in sensitivity and empathy. On the same day that Joe noted his observations on the Reich, Jack, assigned to write "Justice" from within the walls of Choate during the height of the Depression, would begin to consider the fairness of class and economic disparity. As at Choate, Jack's studies under Harold Laski in London would be interrupted and finally cut short by the recurrence of a jaundicelike condition that had plagued and hospitalized him previously. Returning to the United States in October, he would recuperate sufficiently to join his Choate friends Rip Horton and Lem Billings at Princeton as a freshman. His tenure at Princeton would be short-lived as well, however. Ill again, he would be forced to withdraw shortly after Thanksgiving, and would spend much of the coming year recuperating in Palm Beach, at the Peter Bent Brigham Hospital in Boston and at a ranch in Arizona before joining Joe at Harvard in the fall of 1936.

Before arriving in Neuilly-sur-Seine, Kick had attended "that old firetrap," the Convent of the Sacred Heart, overlooking Long Island Sound in Noroton, Connecticut. Only about thirty miles from Jack, the two (accompanied by a variety of friends) had managed to visit each other fairly frequently. In Neuilly, despite her initial loneliness, she made friends, saw the sights of Paris, learned some French and, with hard-won permission from the nuns, attended a few parties and balls. She skied in Gstaad during the Christmas holidays of 1935 and spent her spring vacation of 1936 traveling in fascist Italy with some of her schoolmates before her mother's welcomed arrival in Paris in late April ("it does get kinda' lonely here"). In May, following young Joe's lead, mother and daughter set off for the Soviet Union and Eastern Europe before Kick's return to Noroton in the fall.

In the meantime, the elder Joe Kennedy had returned to the private sector. He oversaw the recapitalization of RCA in the early winter of 1936 and would begin to suggest restructuring strategies to save the Hearst empire from imminent bankruptcy and dissolution by the end of the year. In the interim, Adolph Zukor had commissioned his assessment of Paramount Pictures as the studio lurched toward bankruptcy. Kennedy and a crew of familiar associates spent several intense weeks in Hollywood in May examining the studio's books and operations. The resulting Paramount Report would provide an intimate view both of the studio itself and of practices and operations common in the film industry generally at the time. Perhaps unintentionally, the report would take the form of a general financial history of Hollywood chronicled by one who had spent much of his professional life observing, and intermittently participating in, the young industry's growth. Typically, he would encourage budget cutting wherever possible, particularly in the areas of agents' and executives' salaries, and in studio overhead. Additionally, he would offer advice gleaned, certainly, from his recent observations of the studio, but mostly from personal experience. Cautioning the Paramount board of directors against "Total Write-Offs," "Extravagance in Scenario Preparation," "Failure to Prepare Scripts, Final Cost Estimates and 'Shooting' Schedules on Time," and "Unfortunate Experiences with Producers and Directors," he was no doubt conscious that he would have done well to implement his own recommendations on the set of *Queen Kelly* eight years earlier.

During his stay in California, he had set his friend and former SEC associate John J. Burns to ghostwriting the first draft of the campaign pamphlet that he had mulled over with the president some months earlier. Over the summer, a number of journalists, including Mark Sullivan, reworked Burns's draft before Arthur Krock (on a five-thousand-dollar retainer) produced the finished manuscript. By the time of its publication in September, the originally envisioned pamphlet had grown into a booklet entitled *I'm for Roosevelt*, a businessman's overall endorsement both of the New Deal and of a second Roosevelt election victory in the fall of 1936. In the meantime, the consultant published a series of offshoot pro-Roosevelt articles in the *Review of Reviews* and *The New York Times Magazine*. He delivered radio addresses on behalf of his candidate and took up the onerous and apparently thankless task of attempting to interest his business colleagues (who ranged generally from reluctant to hostile) in attending Roosevelt fund-raising dinners across the country.

Shortly after the second inauguration, he was called to Washington again to head the newly established United States Maritime Commission. He accepted, leaving the private sector again with some hesitancy, both genuine and studied. In March 1937 he became chairman after the passage of a special resolution in Congress, allowing him to serve while continuing to hold the 1,200 shares of Todd Shipyards stock that he had accumulated during his time at Hayden, Stone. As chairman, his job would in some ways resemble the consultancy and managerial work that he had so often done before. He would be responsible for overseeing the implementation of the Maritime Act of 1936, designed to revivify the American shipping industry. Working seven days a week with a staff that he had once again contributed to assembling, he would settle some $73 million in languishing mail contracts for $750,000 before the July 1 deadline set by law. During his tenure, the commission would also settle a number of heated labor disputes. By November, the body would produce its report on American shipping prescribing arbitration in labor disputes and maritime schools to educate seamen.

His press at the Maritime Commission was, once again, overwhelmingly positive. Nevertheless, as his tenure in Washington neared its end he would experience with some shock, indignation and hurt the professional criticism and ad hominem digs that would come increasingly to characterize his appearances in the media over the coming decade. Presented with the first draft of Harry Looker's feature article on him for *For-*

tune magazine's survey of U.S. shipping, he bristled not only at the aspersions cast upon his past and his qualifications to hold his present chairmanship, but also at Looker's crude, glib stereotyping of his origins and ethnicity. During the summer of 1937 the chairman wrangled with *Fortune*'s senior editorial staff, eventually prevailing upon them to publish a fairer (or indeed more favorable) portrait for its September issue. In the process he made a new, friendly acquaintance of Russell Davenport, *Fortune*'s managing editor.

By the end of 1937 he would be offered the post that he felt was at last fitting repayment for the contributions and efforts he had made on behalf of Franklin Roosevelt and the administration. Having acquitted himself by most accounts admirably in his previous two administration posts despite initial criticism, the outcry over his appointment as ambassador to the Court of St. James's was much dampened and diminished comparatively. Indeed, its announcement was heralded as groundbreaking and was received with pride in the Irish-American community. There was some griping among administration colleagues with whom the chairman shared a mutual suspicion and dislike. Others, however, saw the appointment as portending ill both for international relations and for Joe Kennedy personally. "If, as a matter of fact, Joe accepted the appointment to the Maritime Commission with the understanding that he would only remain until the organization was completed, and will in any event soon return to his business," Senator James F. Byrnes of South Carolina allowed to Arthur Krock after an apparent disagreement over the appointment at the Gridiron Dinner a few evenings earlier, "then it is better for him to go to London because he will have an opportunity to render some public service."

> I am contentious enough, however, to still argue that under any other circumstances the appointment was unwise. I do not believe he has rendered so much public service that he should, like Andrew Mellon, retire to the drawing room of the Embassy in London.
>
> Nor would I have you believe that I agree Joe can render a great service as Ambassador because of wars and rumors of wars. I do not believe you can promote peace on earth by sending an Irishman to London.
>
> Woodrow Wilson once told me that you could send an American to London, but it was difficult to keep an American there. I am willing to admit that no matter how long Kennedy stays there, we will still have an American there. However, I fear he will never again speak the same language. You know what kind of language that fellow speaks. When he returns, he will be able to qualify for the "Holy Name Society". It may promote his spiritual welfare, but it will take a lot of joy out of our lives.
>
> I agree to withdraw my statement that I would object to his confirmation. I am for him, and I hope to secure for him a copy of Emily Post's latest book in order to assist him in qualifying for service at Saint James and for entrance to the sacred portals of Claridge's.

The new ambassador himself would embark not only for London but also on a new career in diplomacy as the international situation grew steadily darker, joking with his colleague John Cudahy, the United States minister in Dublin, that "[t]he nicest thing about [the appointment] . . . is that you and I will be able to settle the affairs of the world either on horseback, or the golf course."

Joseph P. Kennedy to John F. Kennedy, 15

Palm Beach, Florida, February 10, 1933

Dear Jack:

Mother and I got your letter of the fourth with your examination and daily marks. It looks to me very much as if you were starting on the toboggan again, and the only possible result is grief and a bad summer.

I am just as sure, however, that you are trying lots harder now than you ever did before, but for some reason or other you evidently are missing again, and as it is now only February, you have plenty of time either to slide down or pull yourself up. I am much more hopeful that you can pull yourself up than I have ever been any other year, because I think your attitude is much better and I think that not only do you want to do well, but that you are really trying to; so, for goodness sake, don't spoil your spring and summer by not doing the job as well as you might.

The weather has been fine down here, and I am sure that by the time you arrive, it will be beautiful. We have a very nice place, and the food is so good that I don't think you will have to make [*sic*] that waffle iron much this year.

Give my love to Joe, and best to yourself, and stay in there and hustle.

Joseph P. Kennedy to Franklin Roosevelt: *Telegram*

NEW LONDON, CONN., MARCH 14, 1933. 415 PM

THE PRESIDENT:

I JUST STOPPED OFF AT PROVIDENCE TO SEE MY OLDEST DAUGHTER AT THE SACRED HEART CONVENT. THE MOTHER SUPERIOR OF THE CONVENT, A REAL SAINTLY WOMAN, SAID THE NUNS WERE PRAYING FOR YOU AND THEN MADE A REMARKABLE STATEMENT FOR A RELIGIOUS WOMAN TO MAKE "THAT SINCE YOUR INAUGURATION PEACE SEEMED TO COME ON THE EARTH; IN FACT IT SEEMED LIKE ANOTHER RESURRECTION." MORTAL MEN CAN PAY YOU NO HIGHER COMPLIMENT.

JOE KENNEDY

Joseph P. Kennedy to Missy LeHand[1]

May 19, 1933

Dear Missy,-

I am enclosing a letter for the president in answer to a note he so kindly sent me. I would appreciate it if you would see that he got it.

I read and hear about you all of the time and know that you must be terribly happy to think that things are going so well for your Boss and the country.

I do miss seeing you and having a laugh, but maybe that will come one of these days.

With very best wishes to Grace[2] and yourself,

Sincerely yours,

---

1. Marguerite Alice LeHand (1898–1944), Franklin Roosevelt's personal secretary, 1922–43.
2. Grace George Tully (1900–84), Roosevelt's private secretary and confidential stenographer, 1929–45.

Joseph P. Kennedy to Franklin Roosevelt

May 19, 1933

Dear Governor:

I was honored by your letter and flattered by the thought that prompted it.[3] It is pleasant to any of us to know that we are remembered by those in high places. And you have made your place high—in the respect, admiration, faith and gratitude of the people you saved from despair, or worse, and high in history, for, I feel sure, your work will go on, widening in scope and results. It is not a flash in the pan; it is lasting and important.

I knew you capable of that sort of thing when first I joined your forces; I have continued to think that ever since.

I owe you a debt for the privilege I feel it was to have come into contact with you, and to have been of such slight aid in your battle as was in my power. I shall always look upon that period as one of the most satisfactory in my life.

It was good of you to invite me to a cruise on the Sequoia. I appreciate your consideration, but I am rarely in Washington. If I am, however, I shall certainly join you. Thanks, anyway.

Faithfully,

Joseph P. Kennedy to Joseph P. Kennedy, Jr., 17

May 29, 1933

Dear Joe,-

Mother and I are very proud of the whole job you have done at Choate as I feel that you have accomplished certainly more than I had hoped you would and the awarding of the prize on Friday is a fine finish to a very worth-while prep school career.[4]

I know that the attitude that has made a success of your Choate career, will make one of your college career. There is not much that a father can do to make his boy's career a success—it rests entirely upon the boy. You can look for help and suggestions—that you know I am prepared, willing, and anxious to give at all times.

All the family are terribly proud of you.

Love,

Joseph P. Kennedy to John F. Kennedy, 16: *Telegram*

MAY 29, 1933

DEAR JACK MOTHER AND I SEND LOVE AND CONGRATULATIONS ON YOUR BIRTHDAY I AM REALLY VERY MUCH PLEASED WITH THE WAY YOU HAVE TAKEN HOLD OF THINGS THIS YEAR AND IT IS A GREAT SATISFACTION TO BOTH OF US TO FEEL THAT YOU REALLY ARE DOING THE JOB WE KNEW YOU WERE CAPABLE OF REAL HONEST EFFORT SOMETIMES IS DISAPPOINTING IN ITS RESULTS BUT IN THE LONG RUN NEVER MISSES WISH YOU ALL KINDS OF GOOD LUCK ON THE EXAMS TRY AND CLEAN THEM UP SO WE CAN HAVE A NICE PEACEFUL SUMMER LOVE

DAD

---

3. The president had written to thank him for his help during the campaign, but had offered no administration appointments.
4. Joe had been awarded Choate's Harvard Trophy as the senior best combining "scholarship and sportsmanship."

Rose Kennedy to George St. John

July 3, 1933

My dear Mr. St. John:

Jack and I were delighted to hear that he passed the English and Mathematics. His tutor and he were extremely doubtful about the Latin—so he was not too disappointed. I am arranging for him to work down here every day with an experienced teacher, and I hope and I will make sure that by the end of September, he will know his first year Latin. As a matter of fact, he hates routine work but loves History and English—subjects which fire his imagination.

Again let me thank you for your interest and patience with Jack. He has a very attractive personality, we think, but he is quite different from Joe for whom we feel you have done so much.

Sincerely yours,
Rose Kennedy

Joseph P. Kennedy to George St. John

September 25, 1933

Dear Mr. St. John:

I received the enclosed check from The Choate School Foundation Endowment, with a letter setting forth that it was impossible to carry the idea thru to a successful conclusion. I regret this exceedingly but feel sure it is only temporarily postponed. I am endorsing the check to you for your Scholarship Fund, and leave it to your good judgment and discretion as to the use you may care to make of it.

I am taking Joe to Europe with me tomorrow night, to put him in school there for a year to study German and French, and to get an appreciation of the tremendous problems facing the world, by getting first-hand information of the foreign problems. We have a number of friends there in high capacities, who, I am sure, will aid him in his quest.

I feel very pleased and satisfied with the development Joe has shown since he has been under your care, and I am sincerely hopeful of Jack coming out with the same results. Jack, unquestionably, improved tremendously last year, but I feel that the fundamental thing to watch is the absolute necessity of keeping him employed in various enterprises. I feel definitely sure that he can do things very well, provided he has enough of them to do and feels that he is getting results. Unfortunately, he has not gained any weight this Summer; therefore, football is not a possibility. I think he must be very carefully watched to see that he is heeded into other enterprises, such as [the] [B]rief, rowing, and other things to keep his mind active.

He still has a tendency to be careless in details, and really is not very determined to be a success. Occupation in a number of things seems to be, to me at least, one of the important steps for his future.

Mrs. Kennedy and I will be back around the middle of November. We shall come up to see you at that time to learn how he is getting along.

With kindest regards,

Sincerely yours,

Joseph P. Kennedy to Rose Kennedy: *Telegram*[5]

CANNES, 10-18-33

YOUR CARD MADE ME TERRIBLY HAPPY WITH YOU FEELING THAT WAY ITS GREAT
TO BE ALIVE YOU ARE EVERYTHING ROLLED INTO ONE DO HAVE A GOOD TIME BEST
LOVE = JOE

Joseph P. Kennedy, Jr., 18, to Felix Frankfurter[6]

October 22, 1933, South Kensington

Dear Professor Frankfurter:

In reading today's *Times*, I noticed that you had been elected to a Supernumery Fellowship, and I want to take this opportunity of sending my congratulations.

Dad left for America Wednesday on board the "Majestic," so I have really settled down to work. So far, I like the school a lot and think I will learn a great deal. Professor Laski[7] has been awfully nice to me and has introduced me to a Canadian boy with whom I am now rooming. We have a swell flat and are very comfortable, so comfortable in fact, that I am not yet a bit lonesome. They boy knows quite a few fellows as he was here last year so I have succeeded in meeting quite a few.

I began athletics yesterday for the first time, in the morning, went to Barnes Bridge for some rowing and in the afternoon went to Malden for rugger. We had a match, and although I wasn't much good to our team I had a lot of fun. They have athletics here twice a week and on other afternoons you can play badminton. There are also many outside clubs which I have not yet attended, but which look very interesting.

As far as my studies are concerned, I have not had much of a chance to judge them, but my favorite subject at the time is the "British Constitution" with Professor Laski.

Give my best to your wife and your secretary and thank her again for the delicious luncheon. Lots of good luck, and I am hoping to see you sometime soon.

Yours sincerely
Joe Kennedy

Joseph P. Kennedy to Rose Kennedy: *Telegram*

NEW YORK 31 x 1933

YOU ARE MISSING NOTHING HERE CHILDREN ARE FINE HOPE YOU ARE ENJOYING
YOURSELF I MISS YOU TERRIBLY BEING WITH YOU IS ALL THAT COUNTS LOVE YOU
MORE THAN EVER — JOE[8]

---

5. They had arrived in London with Jimmy and Betsey Roosevelt on October 2. Rose had traveled on to France alone.
6. Harvard's Byrne Professor of administrative law, Felix Frankfurter (1882–1965) was to spend the 1933–34 academic year at Baliol College, Oxford, as Eastman Visiting Professor.
7. London School of Economics professor of political science and Fabian Society executive committee member, Harold Joseph Laski (1893–1950).
8. She received the telegram in Naples; after JPK's return to the United States she had continued on to Italy.

Joseph P. Kennedy to George St. John

Nov. 21, 1933

Dear Mr. St. John:-

I went down to see Jack play football about a week or ten days ago and I have been meaning to write you ever since, but I have been laid up at home with a cold.

As I wrote you some time ago, I told you I felt that Jack was at a very critical stage in his career, that it would be quite easy for him to go ahead and be very much worthwhile or else slide off and get in with a group which regarded everything as a matter of fact.

I felt then, as I do now, that you and the instructors feel that this is very definitely a serious factor in Jack's development and I can't tell you how unhappy I felt in seeing him and talking with him and feeling that he certainly is not on the right track. The observations that I made are not much different than I made before, that the work he wants to do he does exceptionally well, but he seems to lack entirely a sense of responsibility, and that to my way of thinking must be developed in him very quickly, or else I am very fearful of the results.

The happy-go-lucky manner with a degree of indifference that he shows towards the things that he has no interest in does not portend well for his future development. I feel very, very sure that if responsibility can be pushed on his shoulders, not only in studies but in other things, that he may decide to observe them. He has too many fundamentally good qualities not to feel that once he got on the right track he would be a really worthwhile citizen.

I realize that you have many problems and that each parent's problem seems to him to be the most important one of the day. Nevertheless, I do wish you would give this some extra consideration to see if we can't devise some method of developing Jack's sense of responsibility.

Joe you would be proud of. I have left him in London at the branch of the University of London, a school of economics and political science and he is doing a remarkable job. I would very much like to have Jack follow in his footsteps and he can only do that if he senses his own responsibilities.

I am not sending Jack a copy of this letter, but if you feel that it suits your purpose best, I have no objection to your showing him this.

With kindest regards to Mrs. St. John and yourself, I remain,

Sincerely yours,

Joseph P. Kennedy, Jr., 18, to Rose and Joseph P. Kennedy

November 26, 1933

Dear Mother and Dad:

Got your cable[9] at twelve last night and was very happy to hear the good news, won a bet of five shillings. Had been expecting a letter from Dad for about two weeks, as in the first cable he said he was writing the next week. Anxious to know what he thinks is going to happen in the States, you get all sorts of pessimistic reports here. Laski asked me to-day if you were still pro Roosevelt, also asked me to remember him to you when I wrote.

Had two quite interesting days yesterday and to-day, in that yesterday I got my first taste of driving and to-day my first of riding. Rented a small car, and what a time I had.

9. The document does not survive.

The gear shift is different, they have four gears ahead, and the reverse is where our high is. The horn is about half way down to the floor, and what is more every time the engine was slowed up it began to stall. Drove to Hyde Park Corner to see about riding, had a great time in the traffic, but after going way out of my way, finally arrived there. In the afternoon, planned to drive to the rugger field with another boy, he couldn't find the house, and I started out about half an hour late. Had a terrible time finding it as it was a little town about an hour from here. Luckily the game was late, and I breezed in about the middle of the first half. Played very well yesterday, although we were up against a very poor team. Went out to Wimbledon last night with Ben and succeeded in losing about ten shillings, used the choices of the Evening Standard, and only one dog won out of six races. Went to early Mass and then went horseback riding. Met a girl and another man, and had a swell ride in Rotten Row. Going to take a few lessons in jumping. The riding master thought I rode very well. Look very spiffy in my new riding outfit, and will send you a snapshot if they are out. By the way, Dad, did you ever get the pictures that we had taken in the park in Westchester?

Went to Laski's to tea, it was extremely interesting to-day because there were two Nazis there, who were attacked by Laski and another German, a Socialist. Thought the Nazis answered them very well, they have certainly got a lot of faith in Hitler. Met a Professor Fletcher from Amherst who is studying Political Science at the school and is going to teach it next year.

Mr. Greaves[10] told me he had written you concerning Christmas Vacation. It doesn't look like we are going to see much of the Disarmament Conference or the League, but can see the buildings, and a few committees. He seems like a nice fellow, so I ought to have a swell time.

Am being kept very busy with my studies, and time is flying. Don't know which one I like best yet, they are all different than any work I have previously done, that they are all terribly interesting. Have spent quite a little time writing letters, and have now written to every one. Have bought some attractive Christmas cards that I'm going to send to everybody.

The flat is fine, and we have now got a radio.[11]

Joseph P. Kennedy to Felix Frankfurter

Dec. 5, 1933

Dear Felix:-

You don't know what a joy it is to received one of your letters. I save all your very formal ones and expect that Joe will be showing them to his grandchildren when he talks about that great man Professor Frankfurter, or Judge Frankfurter, whatever your pleasure is to be.

If I were to send you a short summary of the whole situation in the country I would just say "confusion".

Al, as you know, was invited to the White House.[12] Not one word was mentioned as to policies. Al told Herbert[13] that he was absolutely convinced it was merely a gesture

---

10. Harold Richard Goring Greaves (1907–1981), Joe's tutor and a former student and protégé of Laski's, had been appointed an assistant lecturer in political science at the London School of Economics in 1930.
11. What remains of the original document ends at this point.
12. On November 14, Al Smith and Franklin Roosevelt met for the first time since the former's failed renomination attempt in Chicago in 1932. Pleasantries exchanged over tea notwithstanding, Smith (who had since become a leading figure in the anti-Roosevelt American Liberty League) had gone on to assail the

to seemingly have Al in line, hence the smash against the monetary policy and against the public works policy.

The same thing happened to Baruch who was invited to the White House the night before Woodin's resignation and not one word was mentioned to him about what was to happen.[14]

Personally, I can't see a bit of sense in feeding your own ego by having public recognition, but at least you speak to the "little white father" and yet know in your heart that your advice is not wanted.

Father Coughlin, who has made terrific attacks on Smith, is becoming a very dangerous proposition in the whole country.[15] He has the most terrific radio following that you can imagine and to my way of thinking he is becoming an out and out demagog with a rather superficial knowledge of fundamentals, but a striking way of making attacks that pleases the masses, with a beautiful voice that stirs them frightfully.

Of course, I believe that if Roosevelt would turn against any of the policies that Coughlin is advocating, Coughlin would turn at once against Roosevelt unless he felt that the Apostolic Delegate at Washington might demand his silence. He has his own Bishop on his side and the Catholic Hierarchy are unable to do anything with him whatsoever.

Roosevelt seems to be taking all the criticisms smiling and I doubt if he has lost any of his popularity with the people. They are all convinced he is a good man trying to do the best he can for all.

What the future holds in store for us God only knows. I am keeping my mouth shut and sitting on the rails, not even pretending to know anything.

As far as the McKee defeat is concerned, it had little, if any, effect on Roosevelt.[16]

The appointment of Conboy as Federal Attorney in this district was not at all pleasing to the political powers, but seemed to be a compromise appointment.[17]

Acheson looks like he was just bodily kicked out of the Treasury and didn't even get a letter from the president one way or the other.[18]

---

administration and its monetary policy. On November 24, Smith declared himself to be "for gold dollars as against baloney dollars," and on December 1 excoriated the Public Works Administration as incompetent.

13. Herbert Henry Lehman (1878–1950), Roosevelt's successor as governor of New York, 1933–42.
14. Financier and former chairman of Wilson's War Industries Board, Bernard Mannes Baruch (1870–1965) had spent the night of November 14 at the White House. The following day William Hartman Woodin (1869–1934) had tendered his resignation as secretary of the treasury for the second time in a month, the president having refused to accept the first. Woodin had been dogged by both ill health and growing demands for his resignation that followed the Senate Banking Committee's discovery of his name on the "Morgan preferred list" of customers to whom the banking house had offered securities at prices below market value.
15. Since late November, "the radio priest," Father Charles Edward Coughlin (1891–1979), had decried Al Smith's support of the gold standard. Further, he had accused the former New York governor not only of "Morganism" and "banking minded[ness]," but of impropriety in approaching the House of Morgan several years earlier (Coughlin claimed) to request a loan for the construction of the Empire State Building.
16. Following Jimmy Walker's resignation as mayor of New York amidst a highly publicized municipal graft investigation in September 1932, Joseph Vincent "Holy Joe" McKee (1889–1956), then president of the City Board of Aldermen, took up the mayoral post, instituting sweeping measures to counteract city-wide corruption. In November 1933, McKee had offered himself as a mayoral candidate on the Recovery Party ticket, but had been defeated, despite widespread popularity, by Fiorello LaGuardia.
17. Martin Conboy (1878–1944), United States attorney for the Southern District of New York.
18. Convinced of the unconstitutional nature of Roosevelt's recent gold-purchase policy, Undersecretary of the Treasury Dean Gooderham Acheson (1893–1971) (who was at the time acting secretary in Woodin's absence) had learned from the press of the acceptance of his resignation in November 1933.

Judge Lowell in Boston died Friday and there is a mad scramble for the appointment.[19] I do not know any good outstanding Democrats (good ones if you will) that have been mentioned for the new appointment.

The liquor situation in the country is causing some talk, but it is really only a minor bit of excitement.

I got a letter from Joe's supervisor at school and he was quite pleased with Joe's work. I am delighted that I sent him there and I agree with you that it will do him a world of good.

This seems to be about all the items I think you would be interested in, but I will keep you posted from time to time.

With my best to Mrs. Frankfurter and yourself, believe me always,

Sincerely yours,

Joseph P. Kennedy to William Randolph Hearst: *Telegram*

DECEMBER 23 1933

DEAR MISTER HEARST I REGRET EXCEEDINGLY I HAVE NOT BEEN OUT TO SEE YOU AND PAY MY RESPECTS BUT WITH A LARGE FAMILY WE HAVE HAD QUITE A BIT OF SICKNESS THIS FALL AND I AM TAKING TWO OF MY YOUNG CHILDREN AWAY FOR A MONTH OR SIX WEEKS POSSIBLY ENDING UP IN ARIZONA STOP MY INTEREST IN POLITICS AND NATIONAL AFFAIRS HAS NOT CEASED MY CONTACT CEASED FROM THE DAY A CERTAIN GENTLEMAN NEGLECTED TO SEND A TELEGRAM TO YOU URGING YOU TO COME TO NEWYORK WHICH HE TOLD ME HE WOULD DO STOP IN SPITE OF MY VERY CLOSE CONNECTIONS DURING THE CAMPAIGN I HAVE NEVER SEEN HIM FROM THAT DAY TO THIS STOP I AM VERY HOPEFUL THAT YOUR STAND ON PUBLIC QUESTIONS WILL IN THE NEXT YEAR AS IT HAS SO EXTENSIVELY IN THE PAST YEAR KEEP THE SHIP ON AN EVEN KEEL IT IS THE ONLY INFLUENCE LEFT IN AMERICA THAT CAN TAKE A DEFINITE STAND PEOPLE NOW ARE NOT CARRIED AWAY BY PREJUDICES STOP MAY I EXTEND TO YOU MY SINCERE WISHES FOR A MERRY CHRISTMAS AND A HAPPY NEWYEAR AND YOUR CONTINUED INFLUENCE FOR THE GOOD OF THE NATION

JOE KENNEDY

Kathleen Kennedy, 13, to Joseph P. Kennedy

Sacred Heart Convent, Noroton, Conn. January 8, 1934

Daddy dear,

Now I suppose you are glad you have me stuck back behind convent walls I am all safe and sound now and can't go skipping around to "El Studio" or the "Everglades" etc. When we are back it doesn't seem any time that we were away. I am already counting the days until our week-end Feb. 16. In fact the whole school is. And then spring vacation and Palm Beach again. Thanks loads for the wonderful vacation Daddy. It was the best one I have ever had. Each one gets better. I hope we go to Palm Beach next Xmas again in fact anytime is alright with me.

---

19. Republican James Arnold Lowell (1869–1933), United States district court judge, 1922–33.

Jack confided to me that he would rather go to Palm Beach than stay in Bronxville. So I guess you will have no peace in Florida any more. I feel very rested and everyone thinks I look very well so a few parties never did anyone any harm.

It has been very warm here with quite a fog so I am getting used [to] the climate slowly. But when the cold weather comes I don't see how I will stand it. Br-r-r.

Thanks again for the swell vacation. I am thinking about flying to Washington for Feb. 16. What do you think? Don't work to hard.

Oceans of love from
Your debutaunte daughter
Kick

Joseph P. Kennedy to Felix Frankfurter

New York, Feb. 14, 1934

Dear Felix:-

I have been down South since Christmas taking a rest from the mental strain, as a result of the policies that you established in the country before you walked out of it.

I have just come back because of the illness of my boy Jack, but he seems to be getting better today.[20]

Joe has been in constant communication with us and I really feel he is doing a fine job over there. At least his letters give us great hope and confidence.

On my return to New York I found that another bombshell had been dropped, in the form of the new stock exchange bill and while I agree with 85% of it, (which, by the way, is quite an acknowledgment from an old conservative like myself) I still think that it is unnecessarily severe in the other 15%.[21]

Business unquestionably is a good deal better throughout the States. Of course, people like myself, who are not yet convinced that the ultimate goal is a safe one, feel that this rise in business is the result of the Government expenditures, or at least promises of extraordinarily large future expenditures. The President, on the other hand, from my informants, is very optimistic that business will be improved as a result of the Government spending these huge sums. The premise is excellent, it is the conclusion I question.

There seems to be a general feeling around that Jim Farley is in not as good repute with the White House or with a great many people throughout the country.[22] The whole feeling is that Jim is not able to deliver to those who felt they are entitled to something and he has come in for great condemnation.

The throwing out of all the lawyers has met on the whole with a rather popular reaction. The boys felt that some of the group were making too much.

20. Suffering from fatigue and hives, Jack had been admitted to the New Haven Hospital.
21. Earlier in the month, Senator Duncan U. Fletcher and Speaker of the House Sam Rayburn had introduced identical bills intended to enforce the Securities Act of the previous year (which Frankfurter himself had drafted in large measure). A number of Frankfurter's former students, Benjamin V. Cohen, James Landis and Thomas Corcoran, as well as the Senate Banking and Currency Committee's legal counsel, Ferdinand Pecora, had drafted the Fletcher-Rayburn bill of 1934. In its initial form the 1934 bill proposed empowering the Federal Trade Commission to regulate the exchanges, forbid members to trade on their own behalf and establish strict margin requirements. Wall Street immediately attacked the bill as overzealous and deliberately punitive, resulting in its evolution over the next four months into the less severe Securities Act of 1934, which would establish a Securities and Exchange Commission independent of the FTC.
22. James Aloysius Farley (1888–1976), chairman of the Democratic National Committee, 1930–44, and postmaster general of the United States, 1933–40.

I had lunch with Flynn[23] the other day and he told me that he thought the Democratic situation in New York City was going to straighten itself out, but that he definitely was not going to be the head of the new Tammany, although with the Bronx and Brooklyn tied up he would be a very important factor. I talked with Jimmy the other night and he told me that he was definitely sure that Ely[24] will not be a candidate for Governor and the two outstanding candidates at the minute are Hurley[25] and Curley,[26] with Stanley King, President of Amherst[27] and Joe Carney, Internal Revenue Collector,[28] a couple of stand-by candidates. This might be a good year for your friend, Judge Burns, to be the compromise candidate.[29]

If Roosevelt continues strong certainly Bacon could not lick a Liberal candidate.[30] Walsh[31] will practically be unopposed from present indications, but in New York it looks very much like Washington would not favor Senator Copeland's return.[32]

Baruch's attitude hasn't changed at all. He is not having anything to do with the situation in Washington, not through choice, however, but rather through circumstances.

Ray Moley is on the Coast and he is hopeful of his newspaper,[33] but I am not very optimistic about it.

The Frankfurter Liberals are still in the saddle. I hope when the revolution comes, my knowing you will at least get me a sergeantcy, if they have any sergeants now in your prospective Armies.

Give my very best to Mrs. Frankfurter and tell her that in spite of all I say about you I will be most happy when you come home.

Best always,

23. The Bronx Democratic boss.
24. Joseph Buell Ely (1881–1956), Democratic governor of Massachusetts, 1930–34.
25. William Hurley (1875–1957), postmaster of Boston, 1931–35.
26. Former Massachusetts representative and current mayor of Boston, James Michael Curley (1874–1958), would be elected governor in November.
27. Stanley King (1883–1951), president of Amherst College, 1932–46, and chairman of the Massachusetts Commission on the Stabilization of Employment, 1931–34.
28. Joseph Patrick Carney (1876–1971) would vacate the post of state internal revenue collector later in 1934 to head the New England Reconstruction Finance Corporation.
29. A full professor at Harvard Law School and an associate justice of the Massachusetts Supreme Court before the age of thirty, John Joseph Burns (1901–1957) would become general counsel to the newly formed Securities and Exchange Commission five months later.
30. The current lieutenant governor of Massachusetts, Gaspar Bacon (1886–1947), would be defeated in his 1936 gubernatorial bid by Democrat James Michael Curley.
31. The Massachusetts senator.
32. A conservative and increasingly anti-New Deal Democrat, Senator Royal Samuel Copeland of New York (1868–1938) would be reelected to a third term in November 1934, despite initial party opposition to his renomination.
33. The former Columbia University political science professor and preeminent Brains Trust member, Raymond Charles Moley (1886–1975), had advised Roosevelt both officially and informally since the New York gubernatorial campaign in 1928. After brief stints as assistant secretary of state in 1933 and at the Justice Department, Moley began editing the initially pro–New Deal *Today* magazine and continued to serve as an adviser, drafting many of the president's addresses and fireside chats until 1935. In the mid-1930s Moley would become increasingly distanced from the administration, breaking with the president over court packing in 1937, and finally joining the Republican Party in 1940.

Feb. 14, 1934

Dear Joe:-

I have been up North here for the past ten days, due to the very serious sickness of Jack's. He was in the infirmary at the school and all of a sudden he seemed to be losing a lot of ground and they rushed him to the New Haven Hospital. His blood count and high temperatures frightened us all very badly and we called in a conference of Boston doctors and doctors from Mayo Clinic. He is recovering now and the tail end of his sickness seems to be a case of jaundice. He has been having a very miserable time and has handled himself very well.

I went up to the school and saw Mr. Steele[34] and Mr. St. John and they were delighted with the way he has improved the last quarter and I am sorry that he has been laid up. It has resulted in the slowing up of a lot of his activities.

The doctors have very definitely told me that he has got to go very light on all athletics for at least six months, in order to get his strength back, but he is a good sport about it and seems pretty well reconciled.

As to the trip with Phil Lord, I certainly would have no objection to you making this trip. If your judgment warrants you believing that it is to your best interests, I would certainly be agreeable to it.[35] However, I want to set before you the facts as I have found them out in New York. Lord's boat is still traveling up and down the Atlantic Coast. He is now in Bloomington, N. C., doing commercial broadcasts, but Lord himself is in New York trying to complete financial arrangements for the second 13 weeks of his contracts, his original broadcasting contract only running 13 weeks.

I have tried to locate him but have not been able to do so. I have also tried to get an itinerary of his future trip, but his office says this is uncertain at the minute. I talked with John Royal, Executive Head of the National Broadcasting Co.[36] and he very definitely told me that he saw nothing in the trip whatsoever, that it had turned from one of adventure to one of commercialism. I understand that he leaves Florida some time around the middle of March and proposes then to sail the Caribbean Sea, where he finally makes his last two broadcasts some time around the middle of April. After that, the trip is uncertain. Nobody knows what he is going to do, including himself.

With this kind of a setup I cannot see where he has anything at all to offer you, even assuming that he would be willing to have you. Of course, he would like to have me make a financial underwriting. At that, I would be willing to try and work something out with him if I thought it was the trip that we originally thought he was going to make, but I am thoroughly convinced that you wouldn't have any real fun out of the whole situation.

I have made a very careful study and a very careful check before I wrote you this, because I knew that if it were all right you would like to go.

In addition to that, I think you should really be back in the States somewhere around the latter part of July or the first of August to sort of get lined up on your courses next year in Harvard and the Freshman Football Training Camp this year begins rather early in September. Walter Cleary, the Head Coach, called me up the other

34. The assistant headmaster at Choate.
35. In November 1933, former high school principal, radio personality, producer and writer Phillips Haynes Lord (1902–1975) would embark on a midcareer, round-the-world cruise aboard the *Seth Parker,* a schooner equipped for remote radio broadcasts and named after one of Lord's radio characters.
36. John Francis Royal (1886–1978), former midwestern general director of Keith-Albee-Orpheum, vice president in charge of radio programming at the National Broadcasting Company, 1930–1940, and later NBC's first vice president in charge of television, 1940–1953.

day to ask if you were coming back. Also, I think it would be nice to spend a month at home at least with the family.

I am sure that with all the excitement abroad you can find plenty of thrilling things to do to fill out this year. The French and Italian situations seem to me to be most interesting and I can arrange for you to meet Mussolini through Breckinridge Long, the American Ambassador to Italy and also arrange an audience with the Pope. I think also that it would be highly educational and instructive to go into Germany and see something of Russia. Bill Bullitt, American Ambassador to Russia, will be there in a couple of months and I am sure you will see some worth while things there, so summing up the whole situation, I certainly would not have any objection to your taking the trip if I thought the trip itself was worth while. I am thoroughly convinced that it isn't and I would get as much as I could cut of that foreign situation. You would be surprised how interested friends of ours are to see what you are going to learn out of this year abroad.

I met Sir James Calder,[37] Lady Calder and Jack yesterday and they are leaving for Palm Beach today. They are going to stay with us at the house. They are really very fond of you and they are looking forward to seeing a good deal of you on their return.

The situation in America still remains rather exciting. Business is improving, but all the people are afraid of what the result is going to be. Perhaps one shouldn't bother looking that far ahead, nevertheless, I think there is a serious problem facing us over the horizon.

I suppose you know Kathleen was operated on for appendicitis and is now down at Palm Beach with Eunice, who also has not been feeling very well. In fact, we have had quite a run of sickness this Fall.

Jack tells me that your roommate has left and that you are rooming with an American. I know you will be smart enough to keep your contacts with the foreigners as much as possible. You have Americans to live with the rest of your life.

We are all delighted to get your letters and everybody is very pleased to hear from you. I think you have done a great job on keeping contacts.

Everyone sends their love and I will be very interested to hear what your reaction is.

Love,

Joseph P. Kennedy: *Memorandum*

Around the 20th of April of 1934,[38] Mr. James Roosevelt urged me to take a position as Minister to Uruguay, South America, with the idea of representing new trade treaties. I told him I was not at all interested in this position. He reported this to his father, who was vacationing off the Miami Coast. He then sent Jimmie back to me with the suggestion that I become Ambassador to Ireland. This I also declined to consider, and the matter was bracketed for the time being.

The President landed in Miami around the 18th of April, or approximately at this time, and Jimmie sent me a cable to meet the train when it went through the Palm Beach Station. As I had only seen the president once since Election Day, I thought it would be nice to go over and say "How do you do." The train stopped there and I went

---

37. Sir James Calder (1869–1962), director of the Distillers Company, Ltd., of Edinburgh, with whom JPK had negotiated the previous fall for Somerset's distribution contracts.
38. The date was in fact April 14.

in to see him. He was most cordial, and asked when I was going home. I said on the following day with Rose. He said he wanted to talk about a certain matter, and urged me to spend the weekend at the White House with Rose, which I very gladly accepted.

On the following day, we left Palm Beach, arrived in Washington on Saturday, and got to the White House about eleven o'clock in the morning. Jimmie and his wife, Betsey,[39] were there and said they had made plans for us to go to the race track in the afternoon, returning to Washington in time for me to attend the Gridiron Dinner. We all went out to the race track and had a very enjoyable afternoon. On our return to the White House, Jimmie told me to be ready at seven thirty, as I would go with the Presidential Party to the Willard Hotel where the Dinner was to be held. I was dressed at about quarter past seven, and waited in the upper hall while the President talked with Jimmie and somebody else in his study. Up to this time, I had not seen the President at all. About seven twenty, he came out (being wheeled in his chair) with two secret service men and Mr. Louis Howe, who looked at me as if he were looking at the devil himself, and as if he thought I was probably the last man whom he would expect to see in the White House after our numerous disputes.[40] We merely looked at each other without any recognition and moved to the elevator.

The President called to me to ride down with him and the rest of his party. This brought me face to face with Howe and we merely exchanged "how do you dos". Our party was divided into two groups. We went to the dinner and stopped at the head of the elevator where they had set up cocktails for the President's party. We then went in and had the usually entertaining dinner. At the close of the dinner, the Toastmaster announced that everybody would remain in his place until the President and his party had left. With that, I went out, joined the Presidential Party, and went back to the White House. We arrived there about twelve o'clock.

We went upstairs and there were Louis Howe, Jimmie, the President, and myself. The President was wheeled into his study. Louis Howe bade him good-night, and I bade him good-night. As I turned to go into my room, he called out, "Joe, I want to talk with you." As he said this, Louis Howe turned and came back into the President's study. Jimmie also came back and we sat down there until a quarter past three Sunday morning. We talked over all the prospective legislation that was before Congress, including the Silver Bill.[41] We also discussed at some length income taxes and inheritance taxes; in fact, we went over all important steps of legislation, but nothing was said about what he wanted me down for. At about three o'clock, he decided to go to bed, and we all went to our rooms, Jimmie going with his father. When I was undressed, Jimmie came in and told me that the President wanted to see me the following morning in his bedroom at eleven o'clock. Therefore, I decided that Rose and I had better go to nine o'clock Mass in order to be available. We got up Sunday morning and went to nine o'clock Mass, getting back to the White House a little after ten. We began to pack because we planned to

39. Betsey Cushing Roosevelt (later Whitney) (1908–1998), the second of eminent Boston neurosurgeon Dr. Harvey Cushing's three glamorous, beautiful and well-married daughters.
40. JPK had suspected for some time that the efforts and personal antipathy of Colonel Louis McHenry Howe (1871–1936), Roosevelt's longtime assistant and adviser, were at the root of his not yet having been offered what he considered to be a substantial administration post.
41. On January 30 the president had signed into law the Gold Reserve Act, empowering him to fix the price of gold at thirty-five dollars an ounce. Encouraged, and believing that a similar remonitization of silver would improve agricultural purchasing power within their western constituencies, the bloc of so-called Silver Senators continued their agitation for bimetallism throughout the spring of 1934. On March 19 the Silver Purchase Bill (mandating silver purchases until government holdings achieved a value of one third of its gold holdings) passed in the House with little opposition, and by mid-April had emerged from the Senate Agriculture Committee, slightly modified, but unopposed. Despite the president's reservations, the bill would pass into law on June 19.

get back to New York to see the children right after my interview. About eleven fifteen, he sent for me and I went to his bedroom. He was being treated for a cold by Dr. McIntyre of the Naval Service,[42] and was still in bed. He asked me to sit down and wait for a few minutes. McIntyre, the Doctor, finished in about five or ten minutes. At that, the President started to talk to me about general matters, mentioning the two previous positions I had spoken about. He told me he thought the time had come when I should come to Washington. I told him I was perfectly happy and willing to come to Washington to be of service to him, but reiterated what I had told him on the train coming up from Baltimore six months earlier — that my only interest was my personal affection for him, and that I was not interested in taking a position for any other reason. I said I had been rather annoyed at the coolness that had sprung up between us, and for which I blamed Louis Howe. He passingly referred to my connection with Wall Street,[43] and at that time, I begged him to take a look at my statement which I had with me, showing that the bulk of all my money had been made by business acumen rather than Wall Street operation. However, he didn't seem to want to discuss anything about the past. He wanted me to forget all that and urged me to come to Washington. He suggested that it might be a very great idea to have me come down as charge of the Securities Commission, which bill was before Congress at that time. He made me no direct offer, and I made him no promise of acceptance. I told him the only possible interests I would have were first, if I could aid him by so doing, and second, if it meant something to my family. I told him my own impression was very much against taking it. He pressed me to stay for lunch, as he said, "I have had no chance to talk with Rose." I said that we would be very happy to. After another short talk, he sent for Rose and asked her to urge me to be willing to come to Washington. We had lunch with the President and Mrs. Roosevelt, Secretary of State Hull, and Mrs. Hull. After that, we left for New York.[44]

John F. Kennedy, 16, to Rose Kennedy

[Choate] Saturday [April 21, 1934]

Dear Mother:

Things are going OK except I have ~~g~~ a great cold. I've lost 2 lbs. since I have come back but I hope I'll gain them back. Exams just ended and while I did not come out with flying colors still I passed which is in itself a small acomplishment. History 73, Plane- 65, French 67 - English 75 - I've been working harder than I have worked for a long time and its helping. I had a blood count taken today and will write when I hear about it. After I had a talk with Dad the other night I went down and had an hours' talk with Mr. Steele and straightened a lot of things out. I got 11 pages for the year on The Brief so it ought to help me I'm not doing anything this spring except going for walks so I can't figure out why I'm not gaining. However, I will, I hope.

Best love to all

Jack

P.S. Got your White House letter. It must have been swell.

---

42. Commander Ross McIntyre (1889–1959), Roosevelt's physician.
43. Ferdinand Pecora (1882–1971), legal counsel to the Senate Banking and Currency Committee since January 1933, had led the Committee's recent sweeping investigations of securities, tax and banking fraud, which had unearthed, among other things, JPK's participation in the Libbey-Owens-Ford Glass stock pool.
44. Because the document appears to have been written some time later, I have broken it into two parts in order to allow the correspondence from the period to keep pace with the events described in the memorandum. The conclusion of the document appears among the correspondence for June 1934.—AS

Joseph P. Kennedy, Jr., 18, to Joseph P. Kennedy

London, April 23, 1934

Dear Dad:

I thought I would write you a few of my impressions of Germany, as it is the most talked of country at the present time. Before starting on my trip, I had heard the greatest condemnation of Hitler and his party. I had been to Laski's many times to tea, and heard him and many German Socialists tell of the frequent brutalities in Germany. Before actually being inside the German frontier I had the opportunity of talking with two different men, one in Pisa, who was travelling by automobile. He was quite a learned man, did a lot of business in the States, and was pretty well informed all around. I discussed the usual points with him, and I was very much impressed by the enthusiasm and confidence which he had in the policies of Hitler. He of course agreed that it was regrettable that the Jews had to be driven out, but he said that the methods they employed in business were appalling. The other German with whom I talked was a Baron somebody in Rome who was translating a German book about the Jews into English. He ~~loaned~~ lent me the book, but I had very little time to look through it as we were leaving the next day, however my talk with him made me more skeptical than ever about the talk I had heard in London.

On arriving in Munich which is very close to the Austrian border, I was much impressed by the quietness of the city. Everybody was more than anxious to show us our route which is much more than the French would offer. The only signs of a Nazi Germany were the brown shirts, who were very numerous, parading the streets. They have snappy brown open touring cars, and they get quite a kick out of driving through the streets at a high speed. They are very nice and polite, however, at least to foreigners, and one sees no sign of ~~the~~ brutality. In fact, one of them came into a beer garden with us, and although he could not speak English, we had a great time amusing ourselves with the sign language, which by the way, worked quite successfully. Another brown shirt in Heidelberg on a motorcycle drove up to us and asked if he could do anything to help us. ~~Throught~~ Throughout the country, one is struck by the number of people marching. They march to their celebrations, the children march to school. They seem to love it. The troops seem to have a great spirit, and they sing songs as they march. Just to watch them one feels he would like to join them, so it is not strange that the small boy wants to be a soldier. In all parts of the country, as in Italy, the children give you the Hitler salute as you pass, thus showing the appeal even to the children. Nobody is required to salute, but nearly everyone does, and I'm sure if I was a German and valued my health I would expound [*sic*] that slight effort which is required to raise my arm. It is almost comical the number of times the two words "Heil Hitler" are used. Before a brown shirt speaks to another he says Heil Hitler, and always he ends by this expression. Many people talking to each other use it, and it means Hello, How are you, Good bye in fact it can mean nearly anything. Hitlers pictures fill shop windows, and you see nobody's picture with him except Hindenberg which ~~rare~~ is a rarity. The German people are not allowed to forget him for a minute. Celebrations and fetes are going on at all times in the different towns, and there the Nazi leaders keep up their enthusiasm. At Heidelberg, I went to a big celebration held in the castle overlooking the town. The people began marching about seven o'clock in the morning, and paraded through the streets till about eleven when they ascended the steep hills under the boiling sun. The heat was terrific, but the whole town came, and waited hours listening to the speakers, and what speakers! Although I could understand very little I was carried away by the fury to which these men worked themselves. Many people fainted, but I did not see any walk out until after the last speech was finished. The guards which kept the crowd in order were very amicable, and did get angry or ugly when the people broke the line. That afternoon twenty-five Nazis got married together, and they had a big celebration with many friends. The pension where we stayed in Munich was run by an Austrian family which had lived in Munich some years, and the lady spoke quite openly to us. From what I learned, there was no brutality to speak of, and the government itself tried its best to discourage it. I am not willing to accept her statement or the statements I heard in London in full, but I think a 50% discount in both is pretty fair. I have tried to give you a brief and varied account of outside appearances, and now I will try to analyze the spirit of the whole thing.

In talking with the Germans, both inside and out, they wish to impress on you their feeling before the coming of Hitler. They had tried liberalism, and it had severely failed. They had no leader, and as time went on Germany was sinking lower and lower. The German people were scattered, despondent, and were divorced from hope. Hitler came in. He saw the need of a common enemy. Someone of whom to make the goat. Someone, by whose riddance the Germans would feel they had cast out the cause of their predicament. It was excellent physchology, and it was too bad that it had to be done to the Jews. This dislike of the Jews, however was well founded. They were at the heads of all big business, in law etc. It is all to their credit for them to get so far, but their methods had been quite unscrupulous. A noted man told Sir James the other day that the lawyers and prominent judges were Jews, and if you had a case against a Jew, you were nearly always sure to lose it. It's a sad state of affairs when things like that can take place. It is extremely sad, that noted professors, scientists, artists etc so should have to suffer, but as you can see, it would be practically impossible to throw out only a part of them, from both the practical and physchological point of view. As far as the brutality is concerned, it must have been necessary to use some, to secure the whole hearted support of the people, which was necessary to put through this present program. I can see how a great deal of brutality was on private lines, as those supporters of Hitler felt so strongly that they lost their heads over the non-supporters. It was a horrible thing, but in every revolution you have to expect some bloodshed. Hitler is building a spirit in his men that could be envied in any country. They are not thinking of war, but of Germany through Hitler. They know he is doing his best for Germany, they have tremendous faith in him, and they will do whatever he wishes. This spirit could very quickly be turned into a war spirit, but Hitler has things well under control. The only danger would be if something happened to Hitler, and one of his crazy ministers came into power, which at this time does not seem likely. As you know, he has passed the sterilization law which I think is a great thing. I don't know how the Church feels about it, but it will do away with many of the disgusting specimens of men which inhabit this earth. He has made the whole movement a brotherhood in which both rich and poor mingle. A brown shirt that travelled with us from Munich to Cologne was always welcomed by brown shirts in other parts, and was taken in as a friend. Many different types of badges where proceeds go to the working man or something similar, are always bought by everyone. In all, I think it is a remarkable spirit which can do tremendous good or harm, whose fate rests with one man alone.

(The latest developments of the financial situation for the month in Germany shows a vast improvement.)

I am sending this to you, Dad, to see how you think I have sized it up. It is not taken from any reading, but from what I have actually seen and heard. I would not like to discuss it with Laski, or with Greaves as a matter of fact, as it might hurt their feelings. Laski would probably give me examples which might change me back again. Anyway

I'm sending this to you. It is in bad order and bad sequence, but I think you will be able to grasp my impressions.

Returned from Sir James this morning after a delightful weekend. They seem to have enjoyed their stay at the house immensely, and were crazy about the whole family. I am seeing Laski tomorrow morning about the Russian trip, I am fairly sure I can go with him. He will leave the 26th of May and will be gone about five weeks. I may take off a few days in Berlin, and would like to see the Passion Play at Oberammergau, but I will work this out later. Will go up and see Frankfurter either this week or next. He went to Palestine and liked it very much. Wants to go there for a year.

There was a painter doing several portraits of Sir James and Lady Calder. He is one of the rising ones in England and has done some remarkable pictures. Wants to get to America to finish some battle pictures of the War showing Americain troops in action. If he finishes them over there he will not have to pay duty! If he could get ten or fifteen portraits to do over there he would do them very cheaply to pay for his expenses, about $450 to $500 apiece. He is going to give me 10% commission, so if you hear of some let me know. He really has the stuff. You and Mother both ought to get one done.

Ambassador Long[45] was swell to us. He doesn't seem like the ambassador type, at least not on the English lines, but seems more the "regular guy" type. Had quite a long talk with him.

Love
Joe

John F. Kennedy, 16: *"Justice"*

John F. Kennedy
English V
Theme "Justice"
April 23, 1934
Mr. Tinker

Justice

We read in the news-paper, periodicals and in most of the other products of the printing press; we hear from the pulpits, soap-boxes and the other numerous locations that orators choose; about the word justice. Justice is pictured as a lady holding scales in her hand on which is weiged right and wrong. Always is the word linked with God until it has come to have an almost synonimous meaning. But should this be so? To quote Webster Justice means "The rendering to everyone his just due." But does God render to everyone his just due?

A boy is born in a rich family, brought up in [a] clean environment with an excellent education and good companions, inherits a fool-proof business from his father, is married and then eventually dies a just and honest man. Take the other extreme. A boy is born in the slums, of a poor family, has evil companions, no education; becomes a loafer, as that is all their is to do, turns into a drunken bum, and dies, worthless. Was it because of the ~~poor~~ [rich] boys' abylity that he landed in the lap of luxery, or was it the poor boys fault that he was born in squalor? The answer will often come back "The poor boy will get his reward in the life hereafter if he is good. While that is a dubious

---

45. Samuel Miller Breckenridge Long (1881–1958) U.S. ambassador to Italy, 1933–36, and assistant secretary of state, 1940–44. Long's tenure in Italy had been marked by criticism of his initial enthusiasm for the fascist state.

prospect to many of us, yet there's something in it. But how much better chance has [the] boy born with a silver spoon in his mouth of being good than the boy who from birth is surrounded by rotteness and filth. This even to the most religious of us can hardly seem a "square deal." Thus one see that justice is not always received from "The Most Just" so how can we poor motals ever hope to attain it.

Joseph P. Kennedy to Joseph P. Kennedy, Jr., 18

May 4, 1934

Dear Joe:

Mother and I received your two letters this morning, and we were delighted to see how much you got out of the trip through the Continent. Mother wishes you to get an enlarged picture with the Coliseum as a background. If you can, bring it home when you come.

I was very pleased and gratified at your observations of the German situation. I think they show a very keen sense of perception, and I think your conclusions are very sound. Of course, it is still possible that Hitler went far beyond his necessary requirements in his attitude towards the Jews, the evidence of which may be very well covered up from the observer who goes in there at this time.

I am interested in following out your impressions to see what reason you give for his present attitude towards the Catholics. If he wanted to re-unite Germany, and picked the Jew as the focal point of his attack, and conditions in Germany are now so completely those of his own making, why then is it necessary to turn the front of his attack on the Catholics? When you go in there next time, I think it would be interesting to make some observations on this point. At any rate, I think you show a great development in your mind in the last six or seven months. It is most gratifying to both Mother and me.

Now as to the situation here. Mother and I have spent the week-end at the White House with the president and, after we attended the Gridiron Dinner, he and I sat down in his study from twelve o'clock until three o'clock in the morning and talked over all the prospective legislation. He definitely does not want to turn to anything inflationery, if he can help it. He is of the opinion that industry in America has received a tremendous impetus, and of its own strength, should carry on to a successful conclusion. He feels that the so-called conservatives such as Jim Wadsworth[46] and Casper Beacon of New York, who ordinarily would be expected to stand with the conservative element, voted to override his veto on the soldiers' payment, and he pointed out that was evidently what the conservative interests were doing in this country—playing politics in order to cause him embarrassment rather than go through some legislation that would help solve present social problems[47] He is very hopeful to present his Tariff Bill which gives him the power to regulate tariffs on his own say so.[48]

46. James Wolcott Wadsworth (1877–1952), Republican representative from New York, 1932–51, and a founding member of the antiadministration American Liberty League.
47. The onset of the Depression had prompted large numbers of World War I veterans to agitate for the premature disbursement of the bonus established for them under the Adjusted Compensation Act of 1924. Like Hoover before him, Roosevelt objected to placing "a special class of beneficiaries over and above all other citizens" under current economic conditions, and had therefore vetoed those bonus bills that had appeared on his desk annually before 1935.
48. On June 7, the president would sign into law the Reciprocal Trade Agreements Act, permitting the chief executive to enter into international bilateral trade agreements and to reduce tariffs without the specific approval of Congress.

He talked with me about going to South America as the head of the Commission to regulate tariffs for South America, where he feels the great bulk of the prospects for foreign trade lies. I told him that I did not think the kind of work I was particularly interested in; in fact, I told him that I did not desire a position with the Government unless it really meant some prestige to my family, that I felt my responsibilities with my large family were so great that I would be obliged to remain out of the Government's activities.

He said that he thought I had an obligation to do something, and then suggested that I go to Ireland as Minister because there is a very strained situation between the Irish Free State and the English Government. He thought it would be a very nice thing for me to go back as Minister to a country from which my grandfather had come as an immigrant. But Mother and I talked it over, and we decided that this wasn't of any particular interest, and I told him so. Now, he has in mind another position in Washington which he hasn't made clear to me as yet, but unless it fills the very definite requirements that I deem necessary, I will probably not be interested.

We had lunch the following day with Secretary of State Hull and Mrs. Hull and Mother and I had a very enjoyable visit. He sent Mother a very personal photograph of himself, very nicely inscribed to her.

The situation in this country is still one of great uncertainty. People feel that they are a great deal better off since the President came in, but like everything else, when you feel a little better, you begin to take more liberties with yourself. I talked with him on the 'phone the other night and he is frankly worried about the big drop in commodity prices, and it is my belief that sooner or later he will do something about silver in the hope that it will work the thing out.

There is a terrific agitation and feeling against the so-called Frankfurter group in Washington and, even the topside Jews of the country are very much worried about the situation in Washington. In fact, in my conversation with Ray Moley and Swope[49] the other day I told them that you were contemplating a trip into Russia with Felix and Laski. They both told me that they were going to urge Felix not to go because of the many charges that have been made against him of being a Communist. I am inclined to agree somewhat with their judgment, and knowing Felix's absolute intelligence and honesty of purpose, I can see his indignation on being advised against doing it, but he is smart enough to know that we here in America are seeing and hearing a lot of things that he cannot possibly get abroad. So much for politics.

We all had a very lovely winter at Palm Beach. I think you have heard all about the place now from Sir James. It really did all the children a lot of good. We had eight of them down there for about a month, and at one time, we had a total of twenty-six in the house including the help, so you can see we really ran a small-size hotel.

Jack came down there in terrible shape weighing about 125 pounds, but he gained 15 pounds in the five weeks he was there, and went back in reasonably good condition. His case is the subject of an article now being prepared by Doctor William P. Murphy of the Peter Bent Brigham Hospital in Boston for discussion before the American Medical Association, because it is only one of the few recoveries of a condition bordering on leuchemia, and it was the general impression of the doctors that his chances were about five out of one hundred that he ever could have lived. He is still taking the treatments, and I am going to have him go to the Mayo Clinic at the close of school.

49. Publicist, former Pulitzer Prize–winning journalist and executive editor of the *New York World*, Herbert Bayard Swope (1882–1958) had recently become chairman of the New York State racing commission.

Eunice has improved a good deal too, and that is very gratifying. Kathleen is back at the Convent. She has been suffering from a very bad cold, so we are rather of the mind that we will not be able to send her back to Noroton next year, but probably to a convent further South.

Tommy Deane was taken to the hospital last week with Scarlet Fever, which developed into Spinal Meningitis. Bobby came down a couple of days later with a temperature of 102, and frightened us half to death, but he has recovered and Tommy is getting better.

I turned your car, which was in the South, in and got an allowance of $500 on it against delivery of a new car in Boston. I think you might drop me a line right away as to what type and color your would like to have, so that it may be broken in before you get home. I think probably you would need a Coupe like mine for use in Boston in the winter as the type of car you had might not be very practical for four or five months in the cold winter. However, send me your suggestions, and I will get a car and have it broken in so that when you come home, you will be all set.

As to the bags you wrote Mother about, I think it much wiser to buy all these things abroad, remembering all the time that their leather goods are usually of marvelous wearing qualities, but very heavy to carry, so I'd definitely try and get light weight bags, as they will be much more serviceable.

The liquor business is in a state of absolute chaos. The high taxes and custom duties make the cost of Scotch almost prohibitive, and until Roosevelt reduces the taxes or the duties, I am not inclined to think there will be much more business. The State Control Liquor commissions are all back on their payments, and I look for an absolute state of chaos in the next sixty or ninety days, although to date, we have done surprisingly well with contracts.

I think it would be wise for you to go with Laski, particularly because it would give you a very favorable view point in consideration of things here, and with rounding out your year there, it strikes me that you would have a great start on any of your contemporaries, and you should be able to keep up very important contacts, so I am very hopeful that you will be able to make the trip.

Houghton is still the same with plenty of trouble with his stomach and back. Eddie is going down tomorrow to see the Darby in Louisville, Kentucky.

We have sold the TENOVUS[50] for $2,750 as is, with a very small commission, and I think considering everything, it is just as well.

Jim and Betsey Roosevelt have taken a house at Marion, and have bought the boat called Wianno from Crosby Yacht Building & Storage Company, and he is very anxious to get into the racing of the various boats down at Wianno this summer, so maybe you will have a crew for August.

I think this concludes about all the news and information I have. Oh, I received a letter from Ambassador Long in which he stated he hadn't seen any youngster who showed more intelligence or a finer grasp of the situation, and he was tremendously pleased with you. Galeazzi[51] wrote and said he was sorry not to have been able to give you more time.

I am delighted that you are having such an enjoyable time, and at the same time, as worthwhile as I know this is for you. We will be delighted to have you back and talk

---

50. The sixteen-foot Wianno Junior in which JPK, Jr., had learned to sail.
51. Enrico Pietro Galeazzi (1896–198?), secretary and intimate of Papal Secretary of State Cardinal Pacelli, later director general of Technical and Economic Services at the Vatican, and chief architect of the Holy See.

the whole thing over, but we don't want to hurry you home as long as there is a chance of adding something to your general knowledge.

I dictated this letter in order to get it on the boat tonight, won't be able to sign it, as I thought you would rather have it right away.

Love to all.

Joseph P. Kennedy, Jr., 18, to Rose and Joseph P. Kennedy

S. S. Rykov, June 1, 1934

Dear Mother & Dad:

We arrive tomorrow morning after a very pleasant trip. We started a day and a half late on account of a strike at the pier. The boat is quite small, but comfortable and good food. There should be four in my cabin but because of the scarcity of passengers there is only one other, a Russian.

There are all sorts of people aboard, and many interesting characters. Third class costs only about eight pounds and is the cheapest way to get to Russia. All passengers are given the full run of the ship, however the third class have a dining room of their own. The Laskis are travelling first, I'm second, but we eat at the same table, so it is just about the same.

There are no deck games, but most of the day is occupied by discussions on Marx, Communism etc. There are several Americans, young fellows who are going to Russia for a job, because they can't get anything at home. It's a pretty discraceful state of affairs. Everybody is either a bolshevist or a Communist, and I'm all alone. I wish you could hear some of their conversations. It is really an education and an enlightenment.

Laski is very amusing, and some other people are screams, so it's darn good fun. Looking forward to landing there, and also to getting home.

Love
Joe

Joseph P. Kennedy: *Memorandum*[52]

I heard nothing one way or another from the president until around the 22nd of June. In the meantime, Congress had delayed about the Securities Bill, and for a while, it looked as if it would be in the control of the Federal Trade Commission. Finally, a separate Commission was set up, and everybody queried who would be members. James Landis, of the Federal Trade Commission,[53] was generally named by all interests as the new chairman, but I had made up my mind that unless it was the chairmanship for me, I was not at all interested.

The Sunday previous to the 28th of June,[54] Jimmie Roosevelt, in a conversation with his father at Albany, was requested by him to ask me to come to Washington on the following Thursday to discuss the Commission. At this time, I had been laid up with a broken leg and had made no trips anywhere at all. On being urged strongly by Jimmie, I came to New York. On Wednesday night or Thursday morning, I was called by Herbert Swope on the telephone. He told me that, after a conversation with Moley the night

---

52. The document forms the conclusion of the memorandum concerning exploratory discussions of an administration post for JPK around the time of the Gridiron Dinner on April 14.—AS

53. Federal Trade Commission member and former Harvard Law professor, James McCauley Landis (1899–1964), had been one of the joint drafters of the Securities Acts of 1933 and 1934.

54. June 24.

before, it looked very much as if Ferdinand Pecora was to be elected Chairman in consideration of the work he had done in connection with the Senate Investigation, and that the President was afraid he could not offer me the Chairmanship for the first year, but at the end of the first year, I was to receive it. I told Swope I was not interested in any way whatsoever. He said that Roy Howard of the Scripps-Howard Newspapers told him he had heard my name mentioned for the Commission, and in spite of the fact that he had a great appreciation of my honesty and ability, and personally liked me very much he thought it would be a terrific mistake for me to accept the Commission as I was regarded as a Wall Street man. Swope said that this accusation crystalized itself that there would be many less blows on my head if I left someone else take the Chairmanship for a year. I told him I was not at all interested in any job but the Chairmanship, and I was becoming less interested in that.

I arrived in Washington Thursday afternoon and Ray Moley came to see me four times, saying he hoped I would be Chairman, but even if I were not, I should go on if the president made it a personal matter. I called the White House and told them I was available. I was told I would be notified on Friday morning what time the appointment was to be. My conversation with Moley lasted all Thursday afternoon and night and I got the distinct impression that he thought the Commission, which would consist of four men beside myself, would place me in a very enviable position.

The following morning Frank Walker, head of the Executive Committee, came to see me and urged me to take the position regardless of the Chairmanship. I told him the same thing I had told the others. I then called Mr. Randolph Hearst in Wales, England and told him the situation. He urged me to take nothing but the Chairmanship, and even questioned that. However, he promised me his undivided support if I took it, based on the fact that somebody was getting it who knew his business.

At about eleven o'clock, I got a call from the White House making an appointment for five o'clock Thursday afternoon.[55] Thursday afternoon at five o'clock, I appeared at the Executive Offices and was ushered in to see the President about five thirty. He was extremely agreeable and had me sit there while he had conferences with Lewis Douglas[56] and other executives. He signed a great many bills that had been passed by the outgoing Congress. He was about to make a speech over the radio that night and at six thirty, having said nothing to me about the matter he had called me down for, he invited me to have a swim with him in the pool and stay for dinner, which of course, I was very happy to do. While the two of us were swimming around, Herman Oliphant, General Counsel for the Appraisal Department[57] brought over the bill for the Embargo on Silver.[58] The President swam to the end of the pool, wiped his hands, and signed the bill. I dressed and went over to the White House and he sent for me to come to his study. We had a cocktail and still nothing was said about what I was there for. We went down to dinner about eight o'clock. Mr. Baruch was there with several others for dinner and we had a lot of light conversation. At the close of the dinner, Mrs. Roosevelt upon rising, said to the President, "Franklin, when are you going to talk to Joe?" And he said, "About two o'clock tomorrow morning." Everybody smiled and he went away to prepare his radio speech. I stayed and talked with Baruch and Moley.

55. June 28.
56. Lewis William Douglas (1894–1974), director of the Office of the Budget, 1933–34.
57. Herman Enzla Oliphant (1884–1939), general counsel to the department of the treasury, 1934–39.
58. Henry Morgenthau, Jr. (1891–1967), Woodin's successor as secretary of the treasury, had ordered an embargo on the export of silver in a preemptive attempt to halt speculative efforts to remove it from the country, hold it abroad, and then sell it back to the government at a profit under the silver purchase program.

137

After that, I sat and talked with Baruch, while Moley went upstairs with the President. About fifteen minutes later, he sent for me and asked me to come up and bring Baruch with me. When we got there he said, "Joe, sit down and just pretend you are not here while we discuss the make-up of committees I have to appoint before I leave on my vacation tomorrow." These, the Securities Commission and the Commodities Commission. He then read a copy of a telegram he had received from Pecora in which Pecora indicated he would be willing to accept the Chairmanship for one year. The President was rather indignant about this and resented the tone of the telegram. He then took up a sheet of paper on which he had the names in the following order: Kennedy, Mathews,[59] Landis, Healy,[60] and Shaughnessy.[61] He said, "This is a list I made up two weeks ago, and I see no reason to change it except to put Pecora in Shaughnessy's place, because I have a sort of agreement with Fletcher[62] to give Pecora one of the places." He talked on for about fifteen or twenty minutes without indicating that was what he intended to do, or that he intended to make me the Chairman. He finally said in a jocular manner, "I think you can be a great liberal on that, and I think you would do a great job running it." At that, Baruch and Moley both got up and shook hands with me. I said, "Mr. President, I appreciate this honor more than I can tell you, but before I accept it, I'd like to tell you what my observations are, and the dangers to you in offering me this position." First of all, I told him about Howard of the Scripps-Howard Newspapers, that he regarded the appointment as ridiculous, and threatened to attack it bitterly.[63] I told him that I had been involved in Wall Street, and, over a business career of twenty-five years, had done plenty of things that people could find fault with. He listened to my speech which lasted fifteen minutes and then put out his hand and said, "If you are happy, it is perfectly satisfactory to me." After that, we entered into a general discussion, and stayed there until two o'clock in the morning. The following morning I went to the White House, saw McIntyre[64] and told him I had to go back and make some arrangements for disposing of my business, and asked him to ring up the Attorney's General's office to see if there could be a week's delay in swearing me in, in order that I might have time to do what I wished. He said he would, and upon receipt of the word, he would advise me at home. I then got a plane and came back to Cape Cod.

On Saturday night[65] at six o'clock McIntyre called from the White House and said the President was then giving out a list of the members of the Securities Commission which gave me five years, Mathews four, Landis three, Healy two, and Pecora one. I said that was lovely, but what mention was made of the Chairmanship. He said no mention was made, as the President had no authority to name the Chairman, that it was the duty of the Commission to make the selection. He had indicated to the newspaper men that I was to be Chairman, and he was going to notify Landis and Mathews to that ef-

59. Federal Trade Commissioner and former Wisconsin Public Utilities Commissioner George C. Mathews (1886–1946).
60. Robert E. Healy (1883–1946), chief counsel to the Federal Trade Commission, 1928–34.
61. Frank C. Shaughnessy, president of the San Francisco Stock Exchange.
62. As chairman of the Senate Banking and Currency Committee, Duncan Upshaw Fletcher of Florida (1859–1936) had jointly sponsored both the 1933 and 1934 Securities Acts and had supervised Pecora's securities fraud investigations.
63. Earlier in the week Howard had voiced his opposition to JPK's chairmanship not only to Moley and Roosevelt, but to JPK himself as well, assuring them of the hostility of the Scripps-Howard papers should he accept. On Saturday morning, June 30, an editorial in the Scripps-Howard *Washington News* duly lamented that the president might "with impunity administer such a slap in the face to his most loyal and effective supporters that reported to be contemplated in the appointment of Joseph P. Kennedy."
64. Marvin Hunter McIntyre (1878–1943), the president's personal secretary.
65. June 30.

fect. I said it was perfectly agreeable to me. He told me, however, that I would have to be there Monday morning[66] to be sworn in and to organize the Commission. On Sunday afternoon, I came down and saw Herbert Swope, and met him, Ray Moley, and Baruch Sunday night. Moley had had a talk with the President and had received a letter of instructions to give to Landis and Mathews if it became necessary to elect me Chairman, but in the meantime, a great uproar had started on the ground that Pecora would not serve with me on the Commission unless he was elected Chairman, because I had been involved in a pool which he had investigated.

I arrived in Washington Monday morning, saw McIntyre at the White House, and asked him what the setup was. He said they had heard nothing from Pecora, and didn't know whether he would accept or not. In the meantime, the newspaper men were all geared up at the prospect of a fight. I went over to the Trade Commission and had a talk with Landis and met Mathews and Healy. Pecora, in the meantime, sent word that he would not be there until two o'clock. About two o'clock, Pecora arrived, was ushered into Landis' room, and he and I were introduced to each other. He then said he had nothing personal against me, but felt he had been treated very badly by Roosevelt and wanted to return to private practice unless I agreed to let him have the Chairmanship. I told him that since Roosevelt had decided that I was to be Chairman, I had no authority to make the trade. I urged him strongly to stay with us, so did Landis. He finally said if we would give him the Chairmanship for sixty days he would then resign and [give] up the position. I turned this down also, and after a three-hour conference, he finally agreed to stay for a while, and as we were going into the room to organize, he said, "I think I will stay a year." And they voted unanimously to make me Chairman.

Joseph P. Kennedy to Arthur Krock

July 16, 1934

Dear Arthur:

I received your letter with enclosure from Miss Colman of 220 West 57th Street. For your own information I will take up her charges.[67]

Page 2: In connection with paragraph numbered 1, Robertson & Cole was owned by the Grahams & Company of England; Hayden, Stone never had a dollars worth of interest in the proposition. The Grahams control was bought by me personally so that the first statement that Hayden, Stone represented English money is wrong.

Paragraph 2: There never was any investing public in Robertson & Cole Company before I bought it as it was owned exclusively by Grahams, and there never was any investing public before or after I bought it outside of two or three of my personal friends, and as a matter of interest, the Company never had a loss after the first month.

Paragraph 3 and Paragraph 4 are, I think, the result of some confusion in Miss Colman's mind. While I was operating F. B. O. Radio Corporation bought an interest in the Company because they were in process of exploiting their talking picture machines and they felt that they would like to have a laboratory in which to experiment. While still heading the F. B. O. Company, I was invited by the Chase Bank, Blair and Company,

66. July 2.
67. Arthur Krock (1887–1974), the *New York Times* Washington correspondent and JPK's close friend since 1932. Krock had received a number of unsolicited letters, such as one Stella Coleman's, expressing disgust both with JPK's nomination and with Krock's laudatory editorials on the subject in the *Times* on July 4 and 6.

and Jeremiah Milbank to take over the management of the Pathe' Company, which company had three months previously sold seven million dollars worth of bonds. I think that my compensation for straightening out that proposition was a little more than a customers' man receives as it amounted to approximately five hundred thousand dollars. While still in process with both of these companies, I was invited by an entirely different banking group consisting of Edward B. Smith and Company and Hayden, Stone to take over the management of the First National Pictures, now reorganized into the present Warner Bros. Company, at that time one of the largest motion picture companies in the industry. As to acquiring control, by a piece of inside business, of Keith-Albee-Orpheum, that I cannot understand at all, because the Keith-Albee-Orpheum Company had already acquired a substantial interest in my F. B. O. Company and the only transaction that I ever had in the purchase of stock was from Mr. Albee himself, who sold me approximately four million dollars worth of his own stock. Now as to the big "coup" idea, Miss Colman is right in saying that the Keith circuit was not in nearly as good a condition due to the decline of vaudeville as it had been in years previous. However, they had managed to refinance themselves before I ever entered into the picture, and they were still making substantial profits although I felt that they were not keeping up with the parade. What actually happened was that the Radio Corporation which had an interest in F. B. O. and the Keith Company which had an interest in F. B. O. all felt that because of Mr. Owen Young's[68] and Mr. David Sarnoff's desire to enter the picture business, principally because the Western Electric Company had managed to tie up all the first class picture and Radio people felt that they wanted to make an entry in the amusement business and it was their desire to do so. If you will gaze at the personnel of the directorate of the Radio Corporation and also their attorneys I am afraid that Miss Colman attributes too much to my ability in selling them something that did not look attractive to them.

In Paragraph 5 she said "Look at Mr. Kennedy's mergers and manipulations". The only merger that I was in was the one cited above and the same thing has happened to that as has happened to almost all motion picture companies. I do not think there is anything peculiar to that particular company that it got into difficulties. At the price that they bought the property they had about 50% appreciation, the value of the securities thereafter. I haven't any idea what she means by manipulation.

Paragraph 6: My short career in the movies was a matter of about four years. I was retained in practically every instance for straightening out the management. Experienced executives seemingly were not getting along very well.

As to the charge that Mr. Schwab[69] and Mr. Grace[70] permitted Mr. Kennedy to get away,[71] that does not deserve much comment. I was employed when my sphere of activity was entirely management and all things to do with the conduct of business and not with building ships, and after the war the organizations shrunk so in size that there was little occasion for practically the next eight or ten years for anybody in that capacity or it was not anything I would have cared to stay with.

Paragraph 7, as to whether I will play ball with the "money-changers", time alone will prove whether I will to the detriment of Miss Colman's interest. I feel very definitely that this is just loose talk. I resent very much the fact that anybody made me in Wall

68. Owen D. Young (1874–1962), former chairman of the board of General Electric and chairman of RCA, had also devised the interwar German reparations plan that bore his name.
69. Charles Schwab, World War I director general of the United States Shipping Board and former president of Bethlehem Steel.
70. Eugene Gifford Grace (1876–1960), Schwab's successor as president of Bethlehem Steel.
71. From the Fore River Shipyard in 1919.

Street. I have never been a director of any corporation or bank in the country except the ones I personally managed. I have yet to be indebted to anybody or Wall Street for any hand-out.

As to whether the Senate will confirm me, that is in the future.[72] I haven't any desire to get into any arguments with Miss Colman and on the other hand I appreciate your confidence expressed in your article, and it is my obligation and duty to see that you never have any reason to regret it.

With very kindest regards, I am

Sincerely yours,
Joseph P. Kennedy

Joseph P. Kennedy to Lou Ordway[73]

July 26, 1934

Dear Lou:

Thanks for your telegram of approval of my speech,[74] but I cannot agree with your suggestion of continuing to make them. I lost eight pounds over this one and plenty of sleep — no more for me. I will let well enough alone.

I hope that your health is in good shape and that it is not as hot up your way as it is here. It is terrible.

Sincerely yours,

Joseph P. Kennedy to LeMoyne Billings

September 24, 1934

Dear Le Moyne:

I think you are a very good sport and I appreciate your attitude in the matter of the bill, but as I told your mother, I did that because I wanted to and not because I felt I should.[75] Therefore, I insist upon your spending this money some other way than paying doctor's bills for yourself. The only thing I insist upon is that you do not run any more cheese parties for Jack and yourself at Choate this year.

My very kindest regards to your Mother and yourself,

Sincerely,

John F. Kennedy, 17, to Joseph P. Kennedy

[Choate] Sunday

Dear Dad:

Things are going pretty well up here. We are up on Mr. Mahers[76] corridor right next to him and everything we say he lobs in and adds his comments. We are practi-

---

72. The Senate would confirm all five members of the commission at once with no debate after reconvening on January 16, 1935.
73. Lucius Pond Ordway (1890–1964), a partner at the Wall Street firm of Clark, Childs & Keech.
74. The day before, JPK had delivered his maiden speech as chairman (a fifteen-minute account of the commission's mission and philosophy coupled with his frequent assurances of its "good will" toward business) to the National Press Club and a nationwide radio audience.
75. During a visit to Hyannis Port over the course of the summer, Jack's best friend at Choate, (Kirk) LeMoyne Billings (1915–1981) had been hospitalized for three weeks with second- and third-degree burns as well as severe lacerations after a newly installed shower head doused him with scalding water and fell on him.

cally rooming with him which is more than we bargained for. However, it really isn't so bad. We start our foot-ball season tomorrow and it looks as if we would have a pretty fair season. I'm a cheer leader. The golf is going good and I have a slight chance for the team because it is rather sad this year. Do you think you can come up some week-end. It would be swell if you could come up for Father's weekend which is about the 28 of October.

I suppose it is pretty hot in Washington. Take it easy down there.

My studies are going pretty hard and I have a rather tough schedule. However it will work out allright I think. Le Moyne wants to be remembered to you.

Love

Jack

Pardon the penmanship, I'm afraid it is as bad as ever.

Joseph P. Kennedy to Father Nilus McAllister

October 2, 1934

Dear Father Nilus:

Mrs. Kennedy sent me your letter regarding two boys. I agree with you quite completely about both of them.[77] I think they have great potentialities, but I think they are also very critical and rather of an inquisitive frame of mind. I believe Joe, who is attending Harvard, will be the less inclined to become careless now that he is in an atmosphere where he can have direct contact with the St. Paul Catholic Club at Harvard and will be associated with people of a more rational point of view. As far as Jack is concerned, I am very worried. I did try him at a Catholic school — Canterbury — and feel I completely wasted a year of his life. We made every effort to interest parish priests near the Choate School, which he attends, but with no help or cooperation whatsoever — a fact I believe, to be a disgraceful proceeding on the part of the clergy. I am pleased, however, to get your ideas and suggestions because it will make both Mrs. Kennedy and me more insistent on attention being paid to this obligation on the part of both boys. They both felt they got a great deal out of the retreat and are very appreciative of your attention.

Joe is going to be at Stoughton Hall, Harvard University, and I think if you have time once in a while to drop a line to him it might be helpful. I am sure Jack would appreciate hearing from you. He is at Choate School, Wallingford, Connecticut.

I am writing Joe today telling him you have his things and suggesting he arrange to get them.

I am enclosing a check which I hope will defer some of the expenses of this retreat. Assuring you of our appreciation, and with my warmest regards, I am

Sincerely yours,

---

76. Joe's former housemaster.
77. Although McAllister, director of the Gabriel Laymen's Retreat of Brighton, Massachusetts, had found Joe and Jack to be "fine manly boys—so sincere" during their recent stay, he had informed their mother not only that he feared for their piety, but worried moreover that they might assume indifferent or even critical stances toward their faith.

Joseph P. Kennedy to Rose Kennedy: *Telegram*[78]

OCTOBER 6, 1934

DARLING THIS IS YOUR TWENTIETH ANNIVERSARY I CANNOT TELL YOU HOW HAPPY THESE YEARS HAVE BEEN FOR ME AND WHAT A MARVELOUS PERSON YOU HAVE BEEN THROUGH IT ALL THE THING THAT MAKES THIS SO TRUE IS PROVEN BY THE FACT THAT I LOVE YOU MORE NOW THAN EVER STOP I HAVE TAKEN THE CHILDREN TO LUNCH AT THE PLAZA AND MOVIES AND THEY ARE ALL IN FINE SHAPE EUNICE HAS GAINED ONE AND HALF POUNDS AND THE REST CORRESPONDINGLY JACKS BLOOD COUNT WAS CHECKED YESTERDAY AND IT IS BACK TO NORMAL HIS EYES WERE CHECKED AND THEY HAVE TAKEN AWAY HIS GLASSES HE ONLY NEEDS VERY LIGHT ONES JOE STARTED WITH THE FIRST TEAM AT HARVARD TODAY ROSEMARY RAISED CAIN FIRST WEEK BUT MISS NEWTON AND HER MOTHER HAVE BOTH WRITTEN ME SAYING YOU WOULD NEVER KNOW THE CHILD I AM PLANNING TO GO UP AND VISIT THEM NEXT SATURDAY STOP HAD DINNER WITH THE PRESIDENT WEDNESDAY NIGHT AND SPENT THE EVENING ALONE WITH HIM UNTIL ONE OCLOCK IN THE MORNING STOP HAVE YOU HEARD FROM AMBASSADOR[79] I WISH I WERE WITH YOU IN PARIS TODAY TO CELEBRATE OUR UNIVERSARY LOVE FROM ALL

JOE

Rose Kennedy to Joseph P. Kennedy: *Telegram*

[PARIS] 1934 OCT 6 PM 6.18

THANK YOU TWENTY YEARS RARE HAPPINESS ALL MY LOVE ALWAYS=

ROSA

Joseph P. Kennedy to Felix Frankfurter

October 9, 1934

Dear Felix:

I am not really as courteous as you are in answering letters by hand, but I know you will excuse under the pressure of business.

As to Joe's course of study, I agree entirely with your point of view.[80] I very likely did not make myself clear to your bride about what I hoped you would be able to do as far as Joe goes. The assistant graduate manager of athletics sent me word that he thought Joe was taking a much too difficult course and his Mother received a letter from the Passionist priests with whom Joe had made a retreat, stating that his point of view was not what they had hoped it would be and his Mother became unduly concerned. Judge Burns said that the philosophy course in his first year might not be the best thing for him. I wrote him and told him all these facts, but said, of course, I would be governed by his decision and made no suggestions as to what I thought he should do. He told me he was going to consult with you just the minute he had time, but with

---

78. She received the wire in Paris.
79. Philanthropist and former Macy's department store president Jesse Isidor Straus (1872–1936) had been an ardent Roosevelt supporter since the 1920s and served as United States ambassador to France between 1933 and 1936.
80. In a note of October 7, Frankfurter (who had returned to Harvard Law School from Oxford) had informed JPK (diplomatically) that he wished to maintain an independent friendship with Joe and would not therefore intercede in his choice of Freshman courses.

courses in the morning and football in the afternoon I really think he has been fairly busy. I certainly would not urge you to take any position other than the one you outline, because in the first place I know you wouldn't and in the second place I really want to do the best thing for Joe. By that I mean that I don't wish to force on him anything he can't see himself. I still hope to be able to make suggestions and possibly help direct him. That's as far as I ever want to go.

I read in the papers that he is starting the game for the freshmen tomorrow. They tell me he is the best end there but too light. If he starts the game a week from Saturday I think I will come up to Boston and visit him and my oldest daughter who is there, and also visit with you.

I had dinner with the President Wednesday and stayed with him until after 1 o'clock in the morning, just the two of us, and I know no one in my life who seems so anxious to do a real job for everyone as he does. If he fails it will be because those that give him advice are not competent to do so.

Give my love to your wife and to that very intelligent and charming mother-in-law of yours my warmest regards. I must have words with her when I come up. You do know I am sincerely appreciative of your interest in the Kennedy family.

Sincerely,

Joseph P. Kennedy to John F. Kennedy, 17

October 10, 1934

Dear Jack:

I thought you would be interested to read the enclosed clippings which you may not have received, and also, Bob Fisher's[81] letter to me about Joe.

I understand the game was called off last Saturday because of very disagreeable weather, and I have not heard anything of what he is going to do this week. I am planning to go up to Boston on Saturday to see how Rose[82] and Joe are getting along, and to see the game, if there is one. Last Sunday I saw Kathleen at Noroton and she told me she had heard from you. She seems to be getting along very well. I am not at all sure, however, that she will be able to stick it out up there because she is complaining of attacks of asthma at night. However we will see in another month or so. I think it would do Rose good if you would write to her — 29 Powell Street, Brookline, in care of Helen Newton.[83] You know it is very important that we have a good job done up there this year.

I was delighted to get your note, and even though it was not particularly newsy, I judge you and LeMoyne start off by considering that one of the first problems facing you is the battle between you two and Mr. Mahar. My suggestion is to try to get all you can out of the association this year. After all, you do hope to get to Europe next year, and it would be well to develop as fast as you can this year.

I strongly urge you to pay a little more attention to penmanship. Mine has always been pretty bad, so I am not a very good authority to speak about it, but yours is disgraceful and should get some attention. I feel about that as about most things you do —

---

81. JPK's Harvard classmate, sophomore class president and three-year all-American, Robert Thomas Fisher (1888–1942) had coached Crimson football from 1919 to 1925 (leading Harvard to its only Rose Bowl victory—or indeed appearance—in his first season) before becoming a broker at Spencer, Trask in Boston in 1931.
82. Rosemary, that is.
83. Her tutor and companion.

that is, you could do them very well if they interested you sufficiently to warrant your wanting to do them.

I was delighted to hear from Mrs. S. John that the test for your eyes seemed to show them getting much stronger. I think that is a development that will take place in all the weaknesses. I have sent the blood count out to Dr. O'Leary at Mayo's.[84]

Drop me a line occasionally and let me know your views on things and how you are getting along.

For my part, I think that with the help and cooperation of the business interests of the country, we are on the verge of a big business improvement. We have been in liquidation for six years and I believe if everybody got together, we could really start things on their way. I am hopeful that this will take place in the near future.

I would like to come up on Father's Day, the 27th, but I have a tentative appointment to dine with the Apostolic Delegate in Washington. If I can get out of that, I will come up then.

Give my kindest to the teachers I know up there, and tell LeMoyne I expect the two of you to do a very good job this year.

Love,

Joseph P. Kennedy to Dr. Frederick Good

October 15, 1934

Dear Fred:

Some years ago when you came down to Hyannis Port we discussed the gland theory as affecting Rosemary. She is in Boston studying with a Miss Helen Newton, 29 Powell Street, Brookline, Massachusetts, and is still suffering from backwardness.

Miss Newton told me yesterday that Dr. Charles H. Lawrence,[85] 520 Commonwealth Avenue, Boston had done wonders for a couple of her pupils, and I wondered if it would be too much trouble to have a talk with Miss Newton, then check up and see whether her suggestion is of any value and whether Dr. Lawrence is the one to start with. I thought I should like to have this investigated before Rose got back on the twenty-eighth. We do not want to leave a stone unturned if there is anything possible to be done.

Sincerely yours,

Joseph P. Kennedy to Helen Newton

October 15, 1934

My dear Miss Newton:

I had a very firm talk with Rosemary and told her that something must be done, and I am sure she really wants to do it. It is something else besides herself that must be blamed for her attitude. By that I mean, it is her inherent backwardness, rather than a bad disposition. She was pleased because you felt she had improved with her studying, and I think the other things will show an improvement too.

I have asked Dr. Frederick Good, a personal friend of the family, to contact you in order to discuss the gland situation and make a survey as to its possibilities affecting

---

84. Dr. Paul Arthur O'Leary (1891–1955), chief of the dermatology and syphilology department at the Mayo Clinic in Rochester, Minnesota, 1924–53.
85. Chief endocrinologist at the New England Medical Center.

Rosemary, so that it may be considered when her mother returns from Europe the 27th or 28th.

Sincerely,
Joseph P. Kennedy

Rosemary Kennedy, 15, to Joseph P. Kennedy[86]

October 15, 1934

Dear Daddy

I had a lovely time on Saturday.

Thank you ever so much for coming down to see me Sunday I also had good time. I would do anything to make you so happy. I hate to Disapoint you in any way.

Come to see me very soon. I get very lonesome everyday.

See you soon I hope.

It was Raining to-day. We could not play hockey. So we went to Franklin Park. We had lots of fun. I bought A New Hockey Stick for $4.35. Most Sticks cost $6.00. I got a very good one.

give my love to everyone at Home. looking forward to seeing you again some time soon. lots Of love kisses, Your loving Daughter,

Rosemary.

John F. Kennedy, 17, to Joseph P. Kennedy

[Choate] Sunday [December 2, 1934]

Dear Dad:

I thought I would write you right away as Le Moyne and I have been talking about how poorly we have done this quarter, and we have definitely decided to stop any fooling around. I really do realize how important it is that I get a good job done this year if I want to go to England. I really feel, now that I think it over, that I have been bluffing myself about how much real work I have been doing.

We saw Kathleen for quite a time, and we had a swell visit. Rose was able to see her for a short time, and then Frank took her to the train while we stayed up there till he came back with Butch. It is quite an attractive place, and Kathleen was looking very well. I want to thank you and Mother for the swell vacation, as I had a great time.

I really feel that we will get something done this quarter as Lemoyne seems to feel the same way as I do.

Love
Jack

Joseph P. Kennedy to John F. Kennedy, 17

December 5, 1934

Dear Jack:

I got a great satisfaction out of your letter. In fact, I think the improvement started when you made up your mind to write, [*and*] there seems to be a forthrightness and directness that you are usually lacking. In addition to that, the penmanship was immensely improved.

---

86. She had written the letter with Miss Newton's help.

Now Jack, I don't want to give the impression that I am a nagger, for goodness knows I think that is the worst thing any parent can be, and I also feel that you know if I didn't really feel you had the goods I would be most charitable in my attitude toward your failings. After long experience in sizing up people I definitely know you have the goods and you can go a long way. Now aren't you foolish not to get all there is out of what God has given you and what you can do with it yourself. After all, I would be lacking even as a friend if I did not urge you to take advantage of the qualities you have. It is very difficult to make up fundamentals that you have neglected when you were very young and that is why I am always urging you to do the best you can. I am not expecting too much and I will not be disappointed if you don't turn out to be a real genius, but I think you can be a really worthwhile citizen with good judgment and good understanding.

I like LeMoyne and think he is a very fine boy, with great possibilities, and I know that if both of you really made up your minds to do what you honestly could do with your talents, you would both be surprised and pleased. I think your letter shows that you have an appreciation of the problem and I am sure you will work it out with satisfaction both to yourself and to Mother and me. Good luck to you both.

Love,

Joseph P. Kennedy to Joseph P. Kennedy, Jr., 19

December 7, 1934

Dear Joe:

First of all, I think you have gone back to your poor penmanship. It seems to be as bad as it ever was and I think you really should do something about improving it. Second, as to the allowance — I realize that there are a great many expenses incident to your being there that you are not able to set down and as I have made provision for a certain income a year for you, after all you will be taking it out of your own pocket, but I would suggest for the sake of trying to keep an even balance that the allotment be made on the basis of $125 a month merely for the moral effect of trying to live as reasonable as possible. If you try this for a couple of months and it doesn't work, let us look into the subject again. If this is satisfactory I would write a letter to Paul and straighten the matter out with him.

I think your suggestion on the balance of your time until Christmas is very wise. I would try, however, to get some outdoor exercise if you could possibly work it in.

I stopped in and spent an hour and a half with the President this morning and he is looking very well and is feeling quite optimistic about conditions. I am very hopeful that if we get set to a good start when Congress comes in we will be well on our way toward recovery. I had my first baptism this afternoon with the Congressional Committee, as I went before the Appropriations Committee on my budget. We are struggling here to get out as many forms as possible before Christmas and I think we will have some very constructive ones popping before I leave for the South.

I am looking forward to a fine vacation. Be sure and bring your golf sticks and we will take on Jack.

Love,

Joseph P. Kennedy to Rosemary Kennedy, 16

December 8, 1934

Dear Rosemary:

Mother sent me your letter and I was delighted to hear from you. It showed a lovely spirit for you to write and pleased both Mother and me very much to think you are so appreciative and also to feel that you are now studying as hard as I know you can and are doing.

I hope the skating turns out to be lots of fun and I will be anxious to hear just what happened to you. Be sure to wear a big pillow where you sit down so that when you sit on the ice (as I know you will) you won't get too black and blue.

I am looking forward to the fun we will have at Palm Beach, so do a good job on your work and we will talk it all over at Christmas time.

Love,

Joseph P. Kennedy to George Steele

January 5, 1935

Dear Mr. Steele:

I regret exceedingly that it was necessary to urge you to let Jack go to Palm Beach ahead of the time he should have gone, but I thought that a few extra days would really be worthwhile for him. It was impossible to get other airplane reservations, and he would have had to go by train. As you know, I am still considerably concerned about his health and want to do the best for him.

However, I agree definitely that he still lacks the proper attitude toward the consideration of his problems. I feel, and have always felt, as you know, that he has a fine mind. He is quite kiddish about his activities and although I have noticed a tremendous improvement this year, I still feel that what he needs to be trained in most is the ability to get a job done. We have possibly contributed as much as anybody in spoiling him by having secretaries and maids following him to see that he does what he should do, and he places too little confidence on his own reliance. If this subject can be stressed the next four or five months, I am sure a lot of good can be accomplished.

Sincerely yours,

Joseph P. Kennedy to Felix Frankfurter

February 6, 1935

Dear Felix:

I have decided that one of the reasons I insist on typewriting a letter to you is because I am really a worse penman than you are, and I would hate to have you go to the bother of deciphering my letters as I do in deciphering yours. While I apologize every time I write to you, nevertheless I am delighted to breach correspondence etiquette in the joy of telling you what a really swell person you are.

Rose and I had dinner with the President the other night and he talked about Joe. Rose made it very clear that the great improvement was due to your "benevolent influence" (quote from the New York Times' description of one Kennedy, Sunday last). Most people have to keep doing spectacular things to make people realize they are somebody — but you have so many voices in the world of young men, whom you have been swell to, hollering for you, that you just have to continue being yourself.

Of course, when I pay you this tribute, I know you will have sense enough to convey it to the two women who live with you[87] and who are responsible for it.

All my love to them and best wishes for yourself,

Sincerely,

Joseph P. Kennedy to John F. Kennedy, 17

February 6, 1935

Dear Jack:

Was glad to get your nite.[88] That Fourth Group is a step up, but after all this is your last year and you should try to finish in a blaze of glory. There are college examinations to be passed, you know, and it would be an awful bore to have one of them hanging over you this summer, particularly as you will be considering your trip to Europe. So regardless of everything, I would try to work very hard.

Of course, I would be delighted to have Barlow and Billings down there, and I hope they have luck in their hitch-hiking. Mother thought it might be a good experience for you, but with that $750 bank-roll of yours in the bank, I suppose you would be very hard to sell.

We had lunch with Kathleen on Sunday and she looks fine. She really thinks you are a great fellow. She has a love and devotion to you that you should be very proud to have deserved. It probably does not become apparent to you, but it does to both Mother and me. She thinks you are quite the grandest fellow that ever lived, and your letters furnish her most of her laughs in the Convent. She is coming up to stay with me on the 16th on February, and I have told her that if you and LeMoyne or another of your gang can get off, I will blow you all to a party. I dare say she has got in touch with you before now.

Mother has had a very interesting week since she came up from the South. I am expecting her back Sunday, as she is up with Joe and Rose this week.

I am leaving for Chicago tomorrow to make a speech on Friday and back to Washington Saturday morning.

I received a letter from Paul O'Leary in which he was very much pleased with your great improvement — he advised that Mr. Watkins said to continue the marrow until late Spring, and thought the only thing that was annoying you now was your "schnozzle". At least that is what he told me; he also was very insistent that this was a matter that would be cleaned up very quickly as soon as you get yourself into shape.

My best to the boys and love from Mother, and

[Dad]

Joseph P. Kennedy: *Memorandum*

Monday, February 18, 1935

From all indications, copies of newspapers attached, the Supreme Court of the United States will today announce the Gold Decision.[89]

---

87. Frankfurter's wife (Marion Denman Frankfurter) and his mother-in-law.
88. That is, Jack's night letter (telegram).
89. "The Gold Decision" consisted in fact of the Court's rulings on four cases collectively testing the constitutionality of both the Emergency Banking Act and the Joint (gold) Resolution of 1933 by which the United States had abandoned the gold standard.

I arrived at the office about 9 o'clock and called a meeting of the Commission to see if they had any ideas as to what action should be taken regarding the closing of the exchanges. They all agreed that there was certainly no purpose in closing the exchanges before the decision and that we would have to govern ourselves as to what action we can take when the decision is made. The meeting adjourned then until 12 o'clock, when the supreme Court was to come in. At 10:30 I called up the President and got Mr. McIntyre, his secretary, on the line, who told me the President was shaving. I asked him if the President had any ideas or suggestions and he said that after talking with him the President would be available, with everything cleaned up, at 12:00, and I could get in touch with him from then on, if anything arose.

The Secretary of the Treasury called me on the phone as to the status of the arrangements at the Supreme Court and I notified him that we had the only line out of the marshall's office, and Judge Burns and Ike Stokes of our legal department would be there. He said Mr. Laylan[90] from the Treasury would go along with them, and he would be with the President at the White House.

At 11:15 Miss LeHand called up, and in a very serious tone announced that since it was a very nice day the President had decided to take a nice, long automobile ride and would return sometime later in the afternoon or evening and was sure that everything would be well handled. I am citing this to show that while the whole world was on the verge of nervous prostration at the possibilities of the Gold Decision, the President of the United States, the one most vitally interested, was not so upset that he couldn't have a little joke, thus demonstrating his capacity to take this along with everything else in stride and to relieve the tension that anyone might feel.

The newspaper men notified me that there was no question about the Decision, as special passes had been issued at 11:45. Judge Burns then called me from the Supreme Court, saying that the Marshall in charge of the court had a little bun on and everything looked like it was getting started in the right direction. Promptly at 12:00 we opened our telephone lines to the Court and at 12:07 Judge Burns called me and notified me that upon the first case the Supreme Court had decided in favor of the Government. I immediately took up the private line to the White House, connected with line 33, which was the line direct to the President. The phone was answered by Secretary Morgenthau, to whom I delivered the first message. He turned the phone over to the President and I relayed the first message from the Supreme Court. About two minutes later Judge Burns notified me that on the second case the Court had decided also with the Government and then announced this over the line to the President, who in turn relayed it to the group sitting with him at the White House.

The stock market started to rise very rapidly, some gains going as high as ten points. There were 1,000,000 shares dealt in between 12:00 and 1:00. The Chicago Board of Trade closed down because of the volume of orders. I called the President and advised him of all these facts. With a full victory in sight, I called the President to remark on the amazing similarity of the legal point he made in his speech that he had read to me a week ago Sunday, which would have been a classic in American history and which he would have delivered if the Supreme Court had decided against the Government in the Gold Case.[91] He seemed to put his finger on the proper solution of the

90. As special assistant undersecretary of the treasury from 1933 to 1935, John Gallup Laylin (1902–1979) had drafted the Gold Clause Resolution of 1933.
91. Had the Court decided otherwise, the president planned to issue an executive order voiding the unfavorable ruling. Further, Roosevelt had intended to authorize the chairman of the SEC to close the exchanges, justifying his actions by arguing that "[t]o stand idly by and to permit the decision of the Supreme Court to be carried through to its logical, inescapable conclusion would so imperil the eco-

problem that the Supreme Court should have taken, and in spite of all the guesses that had been made as to how it would be decided, it was on the basis of his outline that the Supreme Court finally determined the fact. I suggested to him that when he wrote his memoirs this speech should find a place somewhere in it. He was in marvelous humor and his only regret was his inability to deliver the speech.

About 2 o'clock Judge Burns notified me from the Supreme Court that the vote was five to four, and that Mr. Justice McReynolds was sounding off in a Fourth of July campaign speech.[92] I relayed that immediately to the President.

Later in the day, I called Miss LeHand and assumed that since the victory was the President's, now was the good time to get that week's vacation. She said the President was then in swimming and due consideration would be given to my proposal.

I left the office about 8 o'clock, and the President tried to reach me on the phone. I went to keep an appointment, and called him about 9:45 at the White House from a drug-store. He told me to take the week off, after I had convinced myself that there were no jitters in the stock market, and that he, himself, was going to Boston on Saturday to attend Franklin's dinner,[93] then going to Hyde Park to sleep for four days.

I am writing this memorandum because I feel the occasion is a historical one and I feel that the opportunity of being the person to relay this information to the President would be of value historically to my family.

Joseph P. Kennedy to Kathleen Kennedy, 15

February 20, 1935

Dear Kick:

I know you want to do all you can for Jack, but I think I should tell you that one of the serious difficulties he found himself in was his characterization of "public enemy" and that group of his with the frightful name "muckers". I really don't think there is anything smart about it and I hope it won't be the cause of having him expelled from school.[94] Therefore, I want to urge you to stop all this talk [in] letters and telegrams to him and LeMoyne, so that we can dismiss the whole matter. The Headmaster told me of the wire you sent him last Sunday and it merely added fuel to the fire. It has all been smoothed out temporarily, but have this in mind.

Love,

---

nomic and political security of this nation that the legislative and executive officers of the Government look beyond the narrow letter of contractual obligations so they maintain its substance."

92. Speaking extemporaneously for the conservative minority, James Clark McReynolds (1862–1946) assailed the outcome of the cases and the resulting repudiation of the gold cause, lamenting that "[a] debased currency is nothing new. Nero undertook to exercise that power," and that "[t]he Constitution as many of us have understood it, the Constitution that has meant so much, is gone!"

93. On February 23 the president was to attend his fourth son and namesake's initiation into The Fly, his own former final club at Harvard.

94. On February 17, the day before the Supreme Court's Gold ruling, JPK had been called to Choate for a conference in order to discuss what headmaster George St. John feared to be growing insubordination on campus. During the course of the previous weekend's sermon, St. John had denounced as "public enemies" those boys who comprised the Muckers' Club, namely Jack, Lem Billings and several others, who had banded together (as Jack described it in his scrapbook) to "put over festivities in our own little way and to buck the system more effectively." Jack and Lem had reveled briefly in the headmaster's dismay in a volley of correspondence with Kick, until St. John managed to intercept a congratulatory telegram from Noroton, and notified JPK.

Kathleen Kennedy, 15, to Rose and Joseph P. Kennedy

[Noroton] Thursday — [February 21, 1935]

Dearest Daddy and Mother,

Thanks just heaps for the check and perfume. I had a very happy birthday alltough I missed everyone too much. It was the first birthday away from home and its quite hard. I had a birthday cake though. I received the telegram from Dad which was very sweet.

I had a swell time at Ann's. We had our hair done at Bests, undressed at her aunt's apartment. Daddy certainly can take in the nicest places. We really had more fun. Sunday we went to 12:30. mass and went to the movies in the afternoon. We also went Sun. night. Monday we went into New York and met Moria O'Connell and one of my roomates. We all had lunch at Maillards and then went to Radio City. Leslie Howard was there in "The Scarlet Pimpernel" It was simply marvelous. I got the pass and we had wonderful seats. The girls were all very excited. On our way down in the elevator it got stuck for five minutes. The man took our name etc. More fun. Had supper in Greenwich with two roomates and back to firetrap[95] — I really had a wonderful time — Ann's aunt is awfully sweet and she took us every place. Pressed my evening dress etc. I hope Dad wasn't too tired because we certainly did it up brown.

My birthday present from Joe is that he is driving up here today on way to New York so am looking forward to seeing him. give my love to everyone and please thank Eunice for her letter.

All my love,
Kick

<u>P.S.</u> Please prepare Palm Beach for my arrival around Mar. 20th Incidentlly we better prepare Ma Fitz[96] too.

<u>P.S. Jr.</u> Mother Fitzgerald has just asked me if it would be possible to get a movie for the Shrove Days before Lent. They are the last two days we are allowed to have candy, dancing etc. One afternoon she thought if possible. "David Copperfield" is the one or any other good one. It would be wonderful if you could Daddy and Mr. Ford[97] or anyone else can call me about it. Thanks piles.

Kathleen Kennedy, 15, to Joseph P. Kennedy

NOROTON, Friday [February 22, 1935]

Daddy dear,

I have written Mother a letter telling all the news but I wanted to write you privately about the letter you wrote me. (In case you have not told Mother).

I am really awfully sorry Daddy that we sent the telegram if I got Jack into more trouble. I guess it was very stupid but we thought it would cheer them up. I never thought the head-master would read it. Ann really feels badly too because Mary Alice talked to Jack about it and he thinks pretty badly of both of us. It seems to have reached such a point that we tried to call Jack yesterday and tell him how sorry we were. He was not there but may call him again. He hasn't written or anything so I think it is the best thing to do. I hope it will then be over and finished.

The school is in estacy over the picture Daddy and it was sweet of you to send it. Mother Fitzgerald said she has never known such a quick man.

95. Noroton.
96. That is, Mother Fitzgerald, mother superior at Noroton.
97. Family trustee and manager of JPK's New England theater interests, John J. Ford.

I hope everything is O.K. now and I really want to help Jack. Hoping to see you all soon

All my love,
<u>*Kick*</u>

Joseph P. Kennedy, Jr., 19, to Joseph P. Kennedy: *Telegram*

1935 APR 19 AM 7 09

BROKE MY ARM PLAYING FOOTBALL TODAY IT FEELS PRETTY WELL SO DONT WORRY WILL SEE YOU MONDAY OR TUESDAY WHEN YOU COME UP LOVE=

JOE

Rose Kennedy: *Jean's First Communion*

[April 28, 1935]

Joe unable to come home so phoned from White House about 7-30 — was down Potomac on with Pres. writing speech for his radio address to-night on spending of four billion dollar fund.[98] Pres. talked to me & said Joe was great help as editor & that Jimmie was going to house with Joe for dinner

Spoke with President

He then asked to speak to Jean. Said her father was helping him tremendously but was sorry he could not be home. His voice fascinating on phone — so deep — so full so resonant —

Children all excited.

Paul Murphy[99] to Dr. Paul O'Leary

May 7, 1935

Dear Doctor O'Leary:

As Jack Kennedy is now starting to go out to dine and dance, Mrs. Kennedy would like to have you recommend a drink that you think would be the least harmful to him. She would like to know if you approve of any of the following: Lemonade, Orangeade, White Rock, Apollinaris Water, or beer.

His skin is broken out quite a bit and Mrs. Kennedy thought it might possibly be his age and nothing could be done about it; however, she would greatly appreciate anything you might suggest.

Very truly yours,
Secretary

---

98. On April 22, Roosevelt had asked JPK to serve as his secretary in overseeing expenditures in the administration of the recently signed $4.88 billion Emergency Relief Appropriation Act. Sighting an inability to work with Secretary of the Interior and PWA head Harold Ickes (whom the president had chosen to chair the relief fund's Allotment Board), JPK had declined the secretarial position in favor of an advisory role in matters concerning the financing of public works projects. On April 27, the evening before Jean's First Communion, he attended the White House Correspondents' Dinner, at which the president was guest of honor.
99. JPK's personal secretary.

Joseph P. Kennedy to Sam Rayburn[100]

Dear Sam:

I feel very badly about adding to your present troubles, but two things are on my mind.

One is, I wish you could see your way clear to make the effective date of your Act the first of December, rather than the first of November. We still have a tremendous amount of work to be cleaned up under the Securities Act and there is an enormous amount of detail to be made ready for the Utility Act. The four of us have been carrying the load here for the last six months and we frankly are all shot to pieces, and need to get some rest before we take on this terrific new job. It may not seem to be a very good reason for asking for a delay of a month, but I am anxious to start this bill off well, in order to get as favorable public reaction as we can. I just do not see how we can start off by the first of November.

The second is, I talked with the President yesterday about certain details of both bills that made the administration rather difficult. I suggested that Thomas Corcoran[101] and I appear before the conferees, if that is practical, with our suggestions as to just what the administrative tangles might be as the result of certain language now present in the bill. Beyond that, of course, I have no suggestions.

Now I know you are busy and I know you realize that both of these things are important, at least from our point of view. If you think neither of them should be done, or can be done, then just forget it. I am planning to go home to Cape Cod over the Fourth of July, to be gone until the following Monday. On the other hand, you may want me back here right after the Fourth if I am to appear before the conferees.

I will appreciate very much if you can give me any light on this. I know how hectic things are, and I feel like hell bothering you, but I found I just had to.

Best,

Arthur Krock: *Memorandum*

FOR THE SECRET ARCHIVES OF JOSEPH P. KENNEDY

Protector of the Poor in his office at the Securities and Exchange Commission, in Washington, D.C., and from his estates at Hyannis, Palm Beach, Bronxville and Potomac;[102] and, practically, The Father of His country.

Washington, July 2, 1935.

For Joseph P. Kennedy, who has now learned that as friends, sharing hospitality, Presidents and some forms of newspaper men won't mix; and is going to be more careful about his week-end invitations in the future.

---

100. As chairman of the House Committee on Interstate and Foreign Commerce, Texas Democrat Samuel Taliaferro Rayburn (1882–1961) had sponsored the Public Utility Holding Company Bill, which sought to restructure electric utility holding companies to prevent them from defrauding the public and evading regulation. In its current form the bill contained the so-called death sentence, which required the SEC to dissolve any utility holding company unable to demonstrate its usefulness to the local community by the start of 1940.

101. A former Frankfurter protégé and the special counsel to the Reconstruction Finance Corporation, 1934–41, Thomas Gardiner "Tommy The Cork" Corcoran (1900–81) had jointly drafted not only the Utilities Bill (including its "death sentence" clause), but also the recently passed Wealth Tax Act, the 1934 Securities Act and the legislation which created both the Tennessee Valley Authority and the Federal Housing Administration.

102. In 1934–35 and again in 1937, JPK leased the thirty-three-room Marwood on 125 acres overlooking the Potomac in Maryland.

The attached is Mr. Kennedy's exclusive property, not the author's, who signs himself, with high regard, and the hope of dining on the terrace [at Marwood] once before he dies—

—*Arthur Krock*

Washington, July 1, 1935

Memorandum:

The time may come when this notation on the personality of Franklin D. Roosevelt ~~may~~ [*can*] be [*made*] available to some historian of these days, ~~possibly even myself~~

I spent the week-end at "Marwood," fourteen miles northwest of Washington on the Potomac River, a large estate leased by Joseph P. Kennedy, chairman of the Securities and Exchange Commission. It happened that in the previous few days I ha~~ve~~d been obliged to write critically of the President's methods in trying to drive the wealth-tax, so-called, through Congress without hearings and in defiance of Constitutional procedure. Therefore it was with a shock [*at noon Sunday*] that I learned from my host, Mr. Kennedy, that the President had decided to come out for dinner.

Clearly, my presence might be embarrassing to him and to me, since relaxation was his aim. Somewhat confused, Mr. Kennedy had failed to mention that I was in the house. The day being intensely hot, I decided to stay in my quarters upstairs, instead of returning to town, a voluntary prisoner. I was to be served my dinner on the second floor of this amazing chateau. The only other person present during this week-end, beside the servants, was "Eddie" Moore, Mr. Kennedy's private secretary and companion.

At 7 p.m. I saw two White House cars coming up the drive and fled upstairs. Little did I realize how truly imprisoned I was to be. Five secret service men accompanied the President, and, since Mr. Kennedy had failed to mention that I was in the house, my escape would have been noticed [*by the cordon*] and there might have been a scene of some sort. This situation forced me- because of the design of the house- to be an involuntary eavesdropper on the fete. Although I moved, each time the party on the terrace moved, to the most distant room on my floor, it was impossible not to hear much of what went on.

The President was accompanied by his private secretary, Miss Marguerite LeHand; her assistant, Miss Grace Tully; John Burns, general counsel of the SEC; and Thomas Corcoran, chief drafter of the utilities holding company bill which is to be voted on in Congress, amid great controversy, today and tomorrow. Mr. Roosevelt is striving to enforce the so-called "death sentence;" the House is resisting.

The party soon became very merry. The President's laughter rang out over all, and was most frequent. After a reasonable number of mint juleps, which the President said would be "swell," they dined in the same mood. At dinner, though I was trying not to listen, the President said one thing so loudly it was impossible not to overhear him.

"If I could," he said, "the way I'd handle Huey Long would be physically. He's a physical coward. I've told my fellows up there that the way to deal with him is to frighten him. But they're more afraid of ~~what he'll say about them~~ him than he is of them."[103]

After dinner, there was a movie on the lawn, "Ginger," starring a child actress whose name was [*Jane Withers*]. The President thought her excellent, and said the movie was one of the best in years.

Then Mr. Corcoran took out his accordion, and the real merriment began. The

103. Although instrumental in Roosevelt's nomination in 1932, the former governor and present senator from Louisiana, Huey Pierce Long (1893–1935), had grown increasingly critical of both the president and the administration. Calling for a national redistribution of wealth, Long had already announced his intention to run against Roosevelt in 1936. He would be assassinated by a young doctor in Baton Rouge nine weeks later.

President joined in all the songs, in a rather nice tenor-baritone, and finally he took the instrument and performed creditably for one unfamiliar with it.

"The night after the Chicago convention," he said, "we decided we needed some campaign songs. After working all evening the only thing we turned out went "The old G.O.P., it ain't what it uster be." This moved Mr. Corcoran to improvise: "Old George Huddleston, he ain't what he uster be," a reference to a member of Congress from Alabama, a Democrat, who had recently defied the President on the "death sentence" provision.[104] The President, when this was concluded, burst out with "Old Carter Glass,[105] he ain't what he uster be" etc. No further inspiration coming, someone remarked "Did you know Huddleston once posted his wife for debt?" There were cries of horror from the ladies, and then the company turned back to their favorite song of the evening Kipling's "Gentlemen Rankers." On the repetitions of "baa, baa, baa," the President's voice was remarkably distinguishable. One song he called for was "When I fit with Gen'rul Grant."

Mr. Roosevelt, as if without a care in the world, which continued to impress an unwilling but fascinated eavesdropper — for he had been battered all week by Congress and the press — began telling stories of his college life, of sailing adventures when a young man, in which a number of dull-pated classmates, notably one Tom Beale of Boston, now a banker,[106] figured in a series of amusing anecdotes. "Your taste in dumb cruisemates doesn't seem to have changed," said Mr. Kennedy, referring to the Nourmahal group with whom the President goes fishing every year- Vincent Astor,[107] Will Stewart,[108] Milton Holden[109] and others. A hearty roar of Presidential laughter at this.

The favorite jest of the evening seemed to deal with the Yankee pronunciation of "boat." The President gave this as "bhutt." From that time on, whenever he said "boat" or "float" or any similar word, Miss LeHand would chime in with "bhutt" or "flutt." This must have happened twenty times. The President sometimes paid no attention to the interruption, which must have grown tiresome to him, but at times he conceded the jest with a laugh.

They discussed the holding company bill briefly, and Mr. Corcoran at one point said: "I've never been drunk in my life, but if this amendment[110] goes through tomorrow, I'm going to get stinking." The President laughed heartily at this.

His stories of New England sailor and fisher folk were very amusing, and very well told. He aped the Yankee accent impressively.

104. In June, George Huddleston (1869–1960) had headed the recent defeat of the "death sentence" clause in the House.
105. Although Virginia Democratic Senator George Carter Glass (1858–1946) had initially cooperated with the administration, particularly on emergency banking measures, he had grown increasingly suspicious of what he feared to be growing government bureaucracy and federal encroachment upon individual and states' rights, likening the New Deal to "transplant[ed] Hitlerism" as early as the summer of 1933.
106. Thomas Prince Beale (1883–1977), who had served as an usher at Roosevelt's wedding a year after their graduation from Harvard, was president of the Second National Bank of Boston, 1923–1950.
107. In both 1933 and 1934, Roosevelt had cruised aboard the Nourmahal, a $2.5 million yacht belonging to financier and philanthropist William Vincent Astor (1891–1951). Although initially an enthusiastic and generous Roosevelt supporter in 1932, like Ray Moley (his partner in founding Today magazine), Astor had grown increasingly disaffected with the administration (particularly after the announcement of the proposed wealth tax on June 19, 1935) and with what he described as the president's "irresponsible radical[ism]" by the midthirties.
108. Often called the most attractive man in New York by hostesses and debutantes, William Rhinelander Stewart (1889–1945) was a director of Rhinelander Real Estate and vice president of the John C. Paige insurance brokerage.
109. Milton Holden (1890–1974), a partner at the brokerage of Bull, Holden & Co.
110. The "death sentence."

The singing and talk went on until well after midnight. About that time I fell asleep, pondering over the Presidential type and not decided in my own mind whether it was a good or bad thing for the country that its chief executive could relax in this fashion, and that his familiars could be induced to deal with him as if he were only a merry gentleman [*with whom*] they ~~know~~ were in a party ~~with~~.

Arthur Krock

Joseph P. Kennedy to Burton Wheeler[111]

July 8, 1935

My dear Senator:

In accordance with your request of this morning, I am writing to express my views regarding the Holding Company Bill as it passed the House. This is to be taken merely as an expression of my individual views on the administrative features of this Bill and is in no sense intended to be an expression of opinion regarding the legislative policy implicit in the draft passed by either branch of Congress.

As you know, the Bill which passed the Senate and the House Bill propose to give our Commission a variety of duties and confer, even apart from Section 11, wide powers of discretion in the administration of this Act. These Bills, among other things, require us to register holding companies, to regulate all security transactions, with power to supervise even the underwriting arrangements. In addition, the Commission is to regulate the acquisition of all securities and capital assets of companies subject to the Act.

These duties while enormous can be discharged, I believe, with reasonable efficiency, by a trained and competent personnel; but the burden cast upon us by Section 11 of the House Bill is simply staggering. I cannot be too vehement in urging upon you my feeling that this Section, as now drawn, is most unfortunate. I urge my objections to this Section upon two grounds. The first is simply the limitations on human capacity to achieve results. The second objection is based upon my conception of what is wisdom in government.

The task with which the Commission is confronted under Section 11 of the House Bill is that of determining whether it is "necessary in the public interest" to limit the operations of a holding company system to a single "integrated" public-utility system. If the Commission finds that such limitation is not necessary it is then under a duty to require limitation to "such number of integrated public-utility systems as it finds may be included in such holding company system consistently with the public interest."

The phrase "public interest" is not defined in the House Bill. Thus this bill furnishes no effective standard to guide the Commission in the momentous decisions it must make as to which of the Holding Company systems are to be broken up, and how such process is to be effected. I do not believe it is fair or practical to expect any five men to shoulder the grave responsibility for deciding which of these systems are to be reorganized and into what size and character the ultimate groupings shall evolve.

The administrative burden involved in the duties required under Section 11 will just be overwhelming, no matter what the appropriation, no matter the size or the technical equipment of the staff.

---

111. As chairman of the Interstate Commerce Committee, Wheeler had sponsored the Senate version of the Public Utilities Holding Bill, which had passed in the Senate by a single vote in June, despite the utility industry's extensive efforts and expenditures. The House, however, had recently rejected the death sentence clause, 216 to 146.

The second reason and by far the more important one is my strong conviction that it is not a wise public policy to vest in any one group of men the tremendous responsibility involved in this grant of power. Certainly, this is true unless such a grant is hedged with precise and defined standards set up by the Congress itself.

I have an appreciation of the great need in our modern life of flexible language in statutes, so that the administration of the law may be responsive to an everchanging existence. Both bills wisely contain grants of discretionary power over the details of implementing the statute. This discretion is desirable in order to attain a practical and efficient administration. But so far as the vital decisions as to the size and character of the Holding Company systems of the future are concerned, which decisions will affect the interests of millions of people, investors and the consuming public alike, I do not believe that any Commission should be given unfettered discretion to decide matters of such transcendent importance.

It is also my opinion that from an administrative point of view Section 13 of the House Bill is open to serious objection. The comparable section in the Senate Bill was very definite and explicit to the effect that intra-system service transactions should be on a cost or mutual basis. The administration of such a law involves no great burden. Section 13 of the House Bill, however, while intending doubtless to reach a similar result provides that profits may be realized in inter-company transactions. The language of Section 13 seems to indicate that our Commission is required to pass on inter-company service contracts to determine whether their terms are fair and involve no unreasonable profit. It appears to me that this task which will devolve upon the Commission will be an impossible one. There is no objective standard as to what is a fair and reasonable profit. There are not comparable precedents on which the Commission may rely. As you know, most of the large holding companies have an elaborate system of service contracts and the companies furnishing the services are merely corporate shells controlled by the group dominating the holding company system. These service companies have little capital and normally there is a complete absence of arm's length dealing. All these factors prompt me to urge very strongly the undesirability of retaining the language of the House Bill in these sections.

One further thought occurs to me in connection with the attainment of the statutory objectives to-wit: the simplification of holding company structures. The Senate Bill provides machinery whereby voluntary reorganizations and simplifications can be attained under the control of the Commission. The House Bill has no such provision. This omission is unfortunate because it appears to me to be highly desirable that efficient and expeditious machinery be made available in order to facilitate the voluntary simplification of the corporate structures of holding companies.

I am sure that if the machinery for voluntary reorganizations were enacted into law many systems promptly upon passage of the bill would proceed to simplifying their organizations on their own initiative under the Commission's direction. This should have a beneficial effect upon the investors whose anxieties would thereby be resolved. It should be advantageous to the companies themselves whose permanent status will thereby the sooner be determined.

The Commission will be prepared at a later date, if requested, to furnish specific recommendations affecting the administrative problems of the proposed legislation.

Respectfully submitted,

Joseph P. Kennedy,

Chairman.

[John J. Burns]

Franklin Roosevelt to Robert Kennedy, 9

July 12, 1935

Dear Bob:-

Your Dad has told me that you are a stamp collector and I thought you might like to have these stamps to add to your collection. I am also enclosing a little album which you may find useful.

Perhaps sometime when you are in Washington you will come in and let me show you my collection.

My best wishes to you,

Very sincerely yours,

Robert Kennedy, 9, to Franklin Roosevelt

HYANNISPORT, MASSACHUSETTS, July 19, 1935

Dear Mr. President,

I liked the stamps you sent me very much and the little book is very useful. I am just starting my collection and it would be great fun to see yours which mother says you have had for a long time.

I am going to frame your letter and I am going to keep it always in my room.

Daddy, Mother, and all my brothers and sisters want to be remembered to you.

Bobby Kennedy

Joseph P. Kennedy to Franklin D. Roosevelt

September 6, 1935

Dear Mr. President:

At the time of my appointment to the Securities and Exchange Commission in 1934, for which signal honor I shall always be grateful, I indicated to you the probability that I could not remain in office much longer than a year. For personal reasons it is now necessary for me to ask you to relieve me by September 23, 1935.

My decision to ask to go at this time is made easier by the realization that the Commission is now strongly established as a going concern and that the lines of policy for the administration of these two great measures, the Securities Act and the Securities Exchange Act, have been firmly laid. There remain a few major problems in this first phase of the work of the Commission, but as to these also general principles have been agreed upon and the Commission is working toward an early announcement of conclusions, with which I am in agreement.

The Public Utility Act of 1935 (which you have just signed) places additional large responsibilities upon the Commission. For quite some time the energies of the Commission in this field will be devoted largely to studies of the various holding company systems. Many of the most vital problems arising out of this legislation will not be imminent for a year and beyond. It seems most important that in working out the policies of the New Act, there should be a continuity of administration. Therefore, the private exigencies which compel me to ask you to relieve me coincide with the Commission's requirements for administration direction of long duration.

To discontinue my official relations with you is not an easy task. Rather is it one involving genuine regret assuaged only by the privilege of your friendship. As a Chief you have been unfailingly considerate and stimulating. In the pioneer work of the Commission, my colleagues and I have had your whole-hearted and enthusiastic support.

Without your backing, our accomplishments for the protection of the investors would not have been possible.

You know how deeply devoted I am to you personally and to the success of your Administration. Because of this devotion after retiring from the post of Chairman of the Securities and Exchange Commission I shall still deem myself a part of your Administration.

I suggest this particular date of September 23 because, as you know, Mrs. Kennedy and I plan to go abroad with the children the latter part of the month and it seems wiser for me to terminate my official relations prior to leaving.

Faithfully yours,

Joseph P. Kennedy to George Steele

September 6, 1935

Dear Mr. Steele:

I am very happy to get your letter of August 29th.

Jack has really demonstrated more this summer than ever before. Of course, as I have always told you, I would place a bet that he has everything to go a long distance, and I am convinced now that he is on his way. It was more than kind of you to write this and I am very pleased that his handling of the matter showed real intelligence, which I know he possesses, and cooperation with you who have been so helpful.

We are sailing for England on the 25th and I plan to have Jack meet the high officials of three or four countries before he starts school.

My kindest regards to you and my appreciation for all the Choate School has done for Jack,

Sincerely,

Joseph P. Kennedy to Cissy Patterson[112]

September 23, 1935

Dear Mrs. Patterson:

I have read and re-read with the keenest satisfaction the splendid editorial in the HERALD on Saturday. It is a tribute that I shall always value. I want to thank you for the fairness and sympathy which the HERALD has manifested ever since the establishment of the Commission. It has helped enormously to make our work understandable and effective.

I am now through with public life forever, but I expect to be in Washington soon after my return from Europe and hope to see you then.

In the meantime, let me say once more how gratified I am by the HERALD'S attitude towards the Commission and the fine send-off you gave me personally.

With kindest regards, I am,

Sincerely,

---

112. Eleanor Medill "Cissy" Patterson (1884–1948), editor and publisher of the *Washington Times-Herald*, 1930–46.

Joseph P. Kennedy to Ogden Mills Reid[113]

September 23, 1935

Dear Mr. Reid:

I think I have already told you how I appreciate the eminently fair and cordial treatment accorded the Securities and Exchange Commission by the Herald Tribune. As I leave the Commission and public life I want to express once more my gratitude. At the same time, may I tell you that your editorial regarding my departure gave me the greatest personal satisfaction and you may be sure that I will keep and value it as long as I live.[114]

I have already told Bob Kintner[115] several times how highly I regard him as a reporter and I want to let you know that his sympathetic curiosity and clear understanding of the problems of the Commission make him outstanding among the many newspaper men I have known.

It looks as though the log-jam of financial advertising is breaking — this is good news for me and I trust for you as well.

Although I speak of the Herald Tribune my gratitude goes directly to you and Mrs. Reid, to whom the credit directly belongs.

Please give my kindest regards to Mrs. Reid.

Sincerely yours,

Rose Kennedy: *Recollection*

An incident aboard the "Normandie"[116] some years later (1935) emphasized my husband's deep concern about family unity. Lawrence Fisher,[117] one of the famous Fisher brothers of General Motors fame, was introduced to my husband while we were enjoying a "stretch" on Deck Chairs. Immediately, we sent for "Jack" who was making the trip with us. When "Jack" came to his father's chair, hair tossed, and necktie askew from playing in a game of deck tennis, his father greeted him as follows: "Jack, I sent for you because I want you to meet Mr. Lawrence Fisher, one of the famous Fisher Body family. I wanted you to see what success brothers have who stick together."

Joseph P. Kennedy to Franklin Roosevelt: *Cablegram Draft*

[London] *2/10/35*

DON'T WORRY ABOUT ELECTION IN AMERICA YOU COULD BE ELECTED ANYTHING IN ENGLAND. IF THE PAPERS AND BUSINESS MEN OF AMERICA GAVE YOU TEN PER-

---

113. Ogden Mills Reid (1882–1947), managing editor and president of the *New York Herald Tribune*; his wife, Helen Rogers Reid (1882–1970), was the *Herald's* vice president.
114. On September 21, the *Herald's* financial editor, C. Norman Stabler, had described JPK's resignation as "a real blow to the Roosevelt administration."
115. Robert Edmonds Kintner (1909–1980) had covered the Treasury Department and general economic matters from the *Tribune's* Washington bureau since 1933.
116. On September 25, JPK, Rose, Jack and Kathleen had embarked for Europe. JPK would be reporting upon European economic conditions for the president. Jack would enroll at the London School of Economics and Kathleen would board for the school year at a convent near Paris.
117. Lawrence Peter Fisher (1888–1961), president of the Cadillac Motor Corporation and vice president and director of General Motors, which had purchased a controlling interest in the Fisher Body Corporation that Fisher had cofounded with his brothers in 1908.

Rose Kennedy: *"Visit to Churchill"* [*sic*]

At last the coveted invitation arrived to visit Mr. And Mrs. W̲ [*Churchill*] at their home outside of London. It was in 1933 when he did not hold any office but he had been a glamorous figure and was expected to have influence later.[118] We were very excited and delighted at the prospect of meeting him en famille as we motored through the lovely English countryside on a typical English rainy day and arrived at the simple comfortable country house for lunch. Mr[s]. W ____ [*Churchill*] met us clad in her tweeds, topped by a most becoming shade of rose sweater which heightened the color of her fresh English complexion. Mr. W̶ [Churchill] with his puckish face was clad also in tweeds and looked more like a country squire than an English statesman. Of course the crowning event of the visit was to sit at lunch and listen to him talk. That privilege is not always possible when one is invited to dine with one of the great men of the generation because it is only in a small intimate group of four at best or of six at the most that a man usually expands and discloses his real thoughts and feelings. At a large lunch when many are present he of necessity talks to the lady on either side and usually indulges in banalities as he cannot trust a large group. But today with only four people a rapid exchange of thoughts and ideas took place. The characteristic which thrilled me was the ease and facility and satisfaction with which W _ spoke and the wealth of ideas he expressed. His dominating thought at that time was to have England and U.S.A. develop a sufficiently strong navy so that they would dominate the world and police it and keep the other nations in their present status quo. Mr_____ [*Smith from the U.S.A*] felt the idea impractical to "sell" in the U.S.A. and felt that there were too many isolationists especially through the middle west. Too many Irish haters of England, too many people that would prefer to remain outside England's sphere. But that idea dominated W__ 's manner compared with Lord B[*eaverbrook*] whom we had met two nights previously.[119] B asked countless questions, volunteered little information and W_____ on the other hand talked expansively narrating, explaining and trying to convince us of the wisdom of his points.

Mrs. W̶ ___[*Churchill*] was quiet and charming looking with characteristic English features as we know them through paintings, thin facial qualities, pink fresh coloring and soft grey hair. She was intensely interested in just what people really thought of Mrs. Roosevelt as at that time people in this country as well as abroad felt that the President's wife was an exhibitionist and was using her husband's high office to court pub-

118. The meeting between the Kennedys and Winston Spencer (1874–1965) and Clementine Ogilvy Hozier Churchill (1885–1977) at Chartwell took place, most likely, on October 7, 1935. There is no reference to a meeting either in 1933 or 1935 among the Churchill papers, and since the only other reference to such a meeting among the Kennedy papers appears in a wire from JPK to Bernard Baruch of October 9, 1935, it seems likely that the luncheon took place in 1935 rather than during JPK's trip to England with James Roosevelt two years earlier.

119. Churchill's close friend, William Maxwell Aitken, first Baron Beaverbrook (1879–1964), politician, author and owner of the pro-empire *Daily Express, Sunday Express* and *Evening Standard*. JPK had come into contact with Beaverbrook (who had held a substantial interest in Pathé in Britain) in the late 1920s while seeking out film distribution possibilities abroad.

licity for herself. I tried to convince her that I thought Mrs. Roosevelt was sincere and I felt people would accept her in her self-appointed role, would value her sincerity and unselfish devotion ~~and become accustomed to her unconventional~~ to the common man as she had always been interested in social service. Gradually people would become accustomed to her unconventional approaches.

After lunch we walked to Mr. W ___ [*Churchill*]'s paint shop, a small room on the other end of the garden. There he had several paintings which he worked upon in his leisure time thereby finding recreation. There were flowers, vegetables, other simple little homely subjects which he found it easy to draw upon.

More amazing than this hobby was our trip to the brick wall which surrounded the house and which Mr. ~~W~~_____ [*Churchill*] had laid brick upon brick and put the mortar in between patiently, slowly. It seemed a queer avocation for a man to have, a man of letters, a man who had been brought up to shoot, to ride, to fish like all other Englishmen but there was his hobby and there was the wall to bear mute testimony.

I wonder if he has built any walls since and if often he does not have a nostalgic longing for the quiet country garden filled with blooms and with his retreat where he worked with his hands and rested his brain now so war-weary and so wracked with the tragedies of the world.

Joseph P. Kennedy to James Farley

9th Oct. 1935

Dear Jim,

I want to express my appreciation for your thoughtfulness in sending us a wire before sailing.

I have not taken much of a vacation yet, as I have been rather busy gathering a lot of material that may be of some help to us when I get home.

I am leaving for the Continent on Thursday and hope to get back to the States early in November. One thing we can be sure of and that is if all the newspaper and business men of America had one tenth of the confidence in the President that they have here in England, he could be President for the rest of his life. His recent proclamation of the Neutrality Resolution has made him tremendously popular in both England and France.[120]

It may be well to observe at this time that the business men in Europe are going to have more trouble to the square inch than the American men will have to the square mile.

Anyway, I will tell you all about it when I get back.

Warmest regards,

Very sincerely,

Joseph P. Kennedy to Joseph P. Kennedy, Jr., 20: *Cablegram*

14/10/35

JACK BEEN QUITE ILL BETTER NOW[121] SEND NIGHT LETTER OUTLINING FOOTBALL TO DATE VERY INTERESTED LOVE DAD

---

120. On August 31 the president had signed the first in a series of neutrality bills that would go into effect over the next six years, this one providing for an embargo on arms to all belligerents and their allies, establishing a munitions control board to oversee exports of American armaments and withdrawing protection from Americans traveling on belligerent vessels.

121. He appeared to have suffered a relapse of the agranulocytosis with which he had been diagnosed in 1934. Shortly afterward, Jack would be forced to withdraw from the London School of Economics and

Joseph P. Kennedy to John F. Kennedy, 18

November 11, 1935

Dear Jack:

I had a nice talk with Doctor Raycourt[122] on the 'phone this morning and he couldn't have been any nicer. He is very much interested in your case and we have decided to go along on the proposition as outlined by Doctor Murphy[123] and see how you get along until Thanksgiving. Then, if no real improvement has been made, you and I will discuss whether or not it is best for you to lay off for a year and try and put yourself in condition.

After all, the only consideration I have in the whole matter is your happiness, and I don't want you to lose a year of your college life (which ordinarily brings great pleasure to boy) by wrestling with a bad physical condition and a jam in your studies. A year is important, but it isn't so important if it's going to leave a mark for the rest of your life. So let's give it a try until Thanksgiving and see if you are showing any improvement, then you and I will discuss what's best to do.

You know I really think you are a pretty good guy and my only interest is in doing what is best for you.

Love,

Joseph P. Kennedy to Robert Worth Bingham[124]

November 11, 1935

My dear Mr. Ambassador:

I cannot tell you how much I appreciate the letter I received from you on the Berengaria. You were more than kind to write it and I shall save it as a remembrance of a most pleasant trip to London.

Jack is far from being a well boy and as a result I am afraid my time for the next six months will be devoted to trying to help him regain his health with little or not time for business and politics.

I came back on the boat with Sir Ronald Lindsay[125] and we had some very interesting talks.

I wish to express to you again my gratitude for the many kindnesses to me while I stayed in London and for the great help you gave me in making contacts that I know will be of service to me. Mr. Atherton[126] couldn't have been more helpful and my respect for him and the work he is doing for the United States is of the greatest.

The Kennedy family join me in wishing you a continuation of the brilliant work you are doing for us all over there.

With warmest regards.

Very sincerely yours,

---

return to the United States. In the last week of October, he had recovered sufficiently to matriculate at Princeton, where he joined his Choate roommate Lem Billings.
122. The university doctor at Princeton.
123. The doctor who had treated him at the Peter Bent Brigham Hospital in Boston.
124. Robert Worth Bingham (1871–1937), owner and former publisher of the pro–New Deal *Louisville* (Kentucky) *Courier Journal* and the *Louisville Times*, and United States ambassador to the Court of St. James's, 1933–37.
125. Sir Ronald Charles Lindsay (1877–1945), British ambassador to the United States, 1930–1939.
126. Ray Atherton (1883–1960), counselor of the American Embassy in London.

Kathleen Kennedy, 15, to Rose and Joseph P. Kennedy

[Neuilly sur Seine] November 17, 35 —

Mother and Daddy dear —

Received your letter and was so glad to hear from you. Also received Eunice's —

The French is going quite nicely but it still is rather discouraging at times. Time will tell though. I am trying to read as much as possible as I think it is the greatest help besides talking — It still is a great temptation to talk English and the only way to keep from it is to leave the party and go and read —

I now have a roomate. An English girl who talks French rather well. When she first came she was with a French girl who was quite impossible so they had to change her. She is quite nice and if we talk French all day we are allowed to talk English an hour at night — Most of the French girls are very strange but there is a Belgium girl I like who I go out with as much as possible — It is quite disheartening though to go into a shop and ask for something in perfect French and they don't understand and when a French girl says seemingly the same thing and they do understand her —

Went to Paris last Tuesday for my injection. The doctor is very nice and he said Mrs. Straus[127] had been talking to the other doctor — the first one we went to — Did a little shopping — it has been raining every day here so I had to get a good raincoat. Got a nice English one — on Monday, Armistice. Hope was out for the day and so I went to tea at Mrs. Larkin's apartement — Hope has lost ten lbs. and looks awful — Of course, her parents don't know — Mrs. Larkin is still the same — She asked me if this school was more expensive than St. Maur. I nearly collapsed. She is taking Hope to some small place in Switzerland for Xmas — gosh, I am glad I got out of her clutches —

My history and Latin are still going fine and I am reading as much as possible for the literature. The nun, Mother Bernadette who teaches me is keeping account of all my studies. Terribly nice —

Armistice day — saw all the parades and soldiers and was in Paris during the two minutes silence — It really was marvelous although you couldn't get within a mile of the Arc D'Triomphe — I have never been so squashed in my life — In the afternoon there were alot of Communist parades and policemen lined all the residential parts of Paris — Went to the Louvre and studied all the paintings — Very interesting. The nun explains in French and if we don't understand goes over it in English — Saw Eleanor Clark, a girl from Palm Beach — The other one that was in that picture with Joe, Jack and Mimi Baker — Every place you go you see so many girls' schools —

I haven't received any answer from the cable yet but expect an answer tonite or tomorrow — I wrote you two letters about it Mother and didn't hear so I cabled as the two Irish girls want to know as we must engage our rooms before long. I am enclosing a picture of the hotel we have chosen as it is the best and the girls that have been there say by far the best. It is only 200 francs more for three weeks which isn't bad — The list is also here made by the nun for the expenses — Our chaperon is going to be a sister of one of the nuns. She is married, and American but speaks French excellently — If this is all O.K. I think I may have to get another evening dress as the hotel is big. Eleanor Hoguet is coming the day after Xmas — so everything is daisy — Please write soon and let me know about the evening dress etc.

Eva, the lady from Patou wrote and asked me to tea with her neice but I told her I was sorry I couldn't go —

127. The American ambassador's wife.

A big piece was on the front page of Paris Herald Tribune Friday the 15th — Am enclosing it —

Mon. nite —

Just a few lines before going to bed. All the Frenchies including the nuns say I have made great progress so I feel very well about it all — I can understand quite well but have to wait a while longer before I begin jabbering — Forgot to mention I saw the "Symphonie Inachevée" in German — It was the original version of Shurburt's life in German. They had undertitles in French and I understood it all —

By the way, if there are any interesting clippings in the paper I wish you would send them as they are very interesting over here —

That is about all the news up-to-date — Please write soon and give my love to all —

Loads of love and kisses to mon cher père et ma chère mère

Kick

Kathleen Kennedy, 15, to Rose Kennedy

Royal Hotel, GSTAAD SUISSE Mon. Jan. 7

Mother dear —

This is a rush note to give you more details about why and where I should like to go to England. This boy, Derek Richardson is very nice and I met him through the Mac-Donnell's in Southampton. He wants me to try to get to Cambridge for the Oxford game the 22nd. I thought I could stay with Lady Calder as I want to see her before she leaves for the States. I could fly over quite easily from Le Bourget — I suppose this sounds fantastic but it would be so much fun and I wouldn't miss anything as Thurs. is free that is the 23rd. in Paris. I would just go to the game and then stay with Lady Calder. If she is in London all the better. Will you please cable immediately so I can let him know and tell Rev. Mother Derek will take me to and from the game so I shall not bother Lady Calder.

Most everyone has left the hotel and we leave Thurs. for Lausane for the day and Paris on Friday. Will write more later — Love to all — Thanks piles for the New Year's cable —

Kick

Joseph P. Kennedy to John F. Kennedy, 18

Palm Beach, Florida, January 11, 1936

Dear Jack:

I heard from Mother, who arrived last night after a very nice flight down (By the way, I arranged to send a small plane to bring her from Miami to Palm Beach but the small ones were out and they sent a big three-motored plane, which holds about 10 or 12 passengers, and she arrived in that in the dark last night, but was a very good sport about it.) [Heard (?)] that you were a little bit downhearted over the fact you might have to spend two months at the Hospital.[128] Of course, I realize Palm Beach is much more attractive than it is there, but after all you have given up a year of your time to try and arrive at a definite idea of what is the matter with you and should spend the balance of

---

128. After two months at Princeton, Jack's health had again failed, forcing his withdrawal from the university and his admission to the Peter Bent Brigham Hospital in Boston with suspected leukemia.

the time making up for a period of bad health. So, definitely our first problem is to arrive at a definite conclusion regardless of how much time it takes because we must settle this matter once and for all on this occasion. Your future and your happiness depend entirely on how well you feel. Of course if over a period of two months (I hope it may be less, but assuming it is not) they come to a definite conclusion how they can help you, you would still have five or six weeks down here, which is more than most people could look forward to, so I would not feel discouraged because I really cannot agree with you that you should as I still think you can have a very enjoyable time in Boston and a productive one for yourself, besides accomplishing what we are all trying to do.

My golf is getting a little better. I had two 81s at the Seminole this week and I plan to stay here until about Friday and then go North to work on the radio plan. While in New York I will jump to Boston to see you, Joe and Rosemary. By the way, if you see Rosemary I think Mother would like it if you would jolly her in to putting on more weight. Mother thinks she is too thin, but she should be jollied into it, and I think you, or Joe, can do it much better than Mother and I.

Buck up old boy, and lets look this situation over once and for all.

Love to all,

Joseph P. Kennedy to Robert Kennedy, 10

January 11, 1936

Dear Bob:

First of all, why didn't you drop Margaret a little note and thank her for the present she sent you, rather than for me to do it for I am sure she would love to hear from you and it would be very good practice.

I hope you are really doing a very good job on the studies so that you will have a very good report when I get back in a week or so, and I certainly expect to get an excellent report from Miss Kail because Joe, Jack and I talked it over the other night and decided we really depended on you to do a good job in the house now that you are with the only man left in it.

Lots of love,

Rosemary Kennedy, 16, to Rose and Joseph P. Kennedy

HOTEL BELLEVUE, BOSTON[129] Sunday Jan 12, 1936

Darling Mother and Daddy,

Last Monday on the train with Mrs McCarthy. We saw the publicity man of RKO was on the train. Director of this railroad. Whitney sons were in the drawing room.

Jackie Coogan engaged to a movie Acress. they were both on the train.

Tuesday, Christine took to see "A Tale of Two Cities." also RoNald Colman and Elizabeth Allan. Wednesday, I played Badminton with Mary O Keefe.[130] Thursday, I went to girl Scouts, I am taking Nature up. Friday, went to Dr. Lawrence. Sorry to say I have to take Injections 3 times a week till I go South. Then he waunts to see me in Febuary. Sat-

---

129. The Fitzgeralds' address.
130. Rosemary was currently living near her grandparents in Swampscott, Massachusetts, with the O'Keefe family under the care and tutelage of Mrs. Ruth O'Keefe.

167

urday, I went to see Aunt Loretta, Aunt Margarette, Aunt Katie, at Night Mary O Keefe, Christine, Edward O Keefe, and I played Bridge. Mrs O Keefe played with us.

Sunday, Joe, and Jack, and I, Grandma, Grandpa, went to Aunt Agnus for lunch then Jack took Grampa, Grandma, and I to St. Joseph Cermtory. Also Grandma took me to the movies. Miss Cahill[131] wrote me a letter. I answer it already. Sunday, mary O O Keefe and I went skating at the Arena in Boston. I took a lesson from miss Muller. Wounderful teacher. Jack is taken me to the next dance and I dont know who is taking mary O Keefe. He is going to take me in his new car.

How is it down in Florida, I hear Aunt Agnus and Uncle Joe is going down. I was so glad to hear your voice the other night. thanks loads for calling me up. I miss you so much. I had a lovely time at home at Christmas. I try to keep my spirit up all the time. I have a new gurdle which costs 5$. my other white one was torn. It was a sight, so Mrs O Keefe bought me one. I gave Jack 1$ he diddn't ask for it either 2 cents. I paid for his papper. Lots of love kisses your darling daughter, Rosemary.

John F. Kennedy, 18, to Rose and Joseph P. Kennedy

*PETER BENT BRIGHAM HOSPITAL,
BOSTON, MASSACHUSETTS*

Dear Mother and Dad:

Things are going pretty well. As I said Joe's blood-count was 9400 mine for comparison was 4000 which makes him just twice as healthy. They are doing quite a number of things, but I am rather a difficult subject. Milk and wheat to which I used to have a bad reaction are now all right and something else is bad. However, Dr. Murphy seems to know what he is doing. Am going to the symphony tomorrow I think and have been looking up the Emerson School. Go over to the Harvard gym everyday when I am not busy. Johnny Ford has been very kind. I suppose it's pretty jolly down there and I envy you greatly. Asked Dr. Murphy to drop you a line at the end of this week. Going out Sunday and get the real low-down on the Irish persecution in Boston.

Dr. Murphy says it will probably be necessary for me to stay 2 months, the thought of which makes me rather ill. Have a radio but all that seems to come out is that song the music goes round & round which is having a bad effect on me. Thats about all the news.

Best Love

Jack

P.S. A nurse told me she thought Olive[132] the luckiest girl in the world

---

Joseph P. Kennedy to Kathleen Kennedy, 15: *Telegram*

JANUARY 18, 1936

MOTHER AND I BOTH FEEL YOU SHOULD NOT GO LONDON THIS TIME PLENTY OTHER OPPORTUNITIES AND WE'LL ARRANGE IT LATER EXPLAINING MORE FULLY IN LETTER LOVE

DAD

---

131. Her younger siblings' governess in Bronxville.
132. His girlfriend, Olive Field Cawly.

Kathleen Kennedy, 15, to Rose and Joseph P. Kennedy

Dearest Mother & Daddy —

Received the wire about London this morning. Understand perfectly — Really didn't expect to go but thought I might as well ask. It would be more fun to go later when everything could be arranged. Everyone says the crew races are better than the hockey match anyway —

It has been raining nearly every day since we have been back — Went to the docter last week for an injection — I still have had no asma so everything is daisy. He wanted to know if I gotton any fatter — I don't know why he should want me any bigger.

Have received gifts from Bunty Holbrook and Betty Broome on which the duty was terrible — Shall be completely wiped out in another month. Am starting to attend some French lectures on the history of my period which are quite expensive. Going to see La Bôheme this coming Sat. Really, I shall be educated.

Mother, have you thought anymore about coming over — If we go to Italy which no one knows we shall leave around the 25th of March — for pretty nearly three weeks. If you did come I think it would be better around the 10th of March. If we don't go to Italy I should rather take a trip some place with you for ten days instead of going with the school to Spain or someplace. If Sir James and Lady Calder — why not go home with them.

Plus-tard-

Went to a lecture by Henri Robert this afternoon on Henry IV. It was excellent and I understand it quite well — There isnt much news at the minute but will write more later — Enclosed are the pictures which I took in Gstaad — Will you please send them back as soon as possible — thanks very much. Loved the clippings of Palm Beach and would like to receive them all

Love to all,
Kick

<u>P.P.S. Important!!</u> Mother, there is going to be a military ball at the Opera. Is it alright for me to go if Reverend Mother says it is alright. A chaperon is going to take a group of us to see it — Rev. Mother just wants to be sure of your O.K. Its all going to be with a chaperon and the girls — Will you please wire Reverend Mother saying it is O.K. for Kick to go to the dances — Thanks very much

---

Joseph P. Kennedy to Franklin D. Roosevelt

January 20, 1936

Dear Mr. President:-

I received your letter of the 15th this morning, with Roper's enclosures,[133] and I am terribly sorry that we didn't get far in our talk yesterday, but with the rush for the Church and the bad weather and my arguments, it seems that the point of the visit was entirely lost.

Maybe I just don't express myself correctly about what I sense is the attitude of the

---

133. The secretary of commerce, Daniel Calhoun Roper (1867–1943), had prepared a list of some fifty businessmen whom he believed to be "friendly" (to varying degrees) toward the administration, with an eye to enlisting them in the president's upcoming reelection campaign.

people we are seemingly trying to get hold of, but I do sense the difficulty, and I am frank to say it is very difficult for me to suggest to you a manner of handling it. Every time I try to it seems merely a repetition of past arguments. I keep thinking of ways and means and I still believe that at least my contribution toward the Campaign will be a constructive one and be of some value. How I am going to do it or what it is I do not know. I do know we will get something done that will really mean something.

About the list you sent me, I feel it is not at all strong enough to do what we thought of, but I will go ahead and try to think out some plan and if any of your people have a suggestion as to how it can be well used, I wish they would let me know.

It isn't that I am stubborn or stupid, but I am anxious to get a result that will merely not be just a superficial gesture. I still think I can do it.

Always with my great respect and warmest regards, I am,

Sincerely,

Joseph P. Kennedy to Kathleen Kennedy, 15

January 20, 1936

Dear Kathleen:-

I got your letter of January 6th upon my arrival here from Palm Beach and I sent you a wire.

You know, mother and I have no objection to your seeing as many things as you can over there and we want you to, but the idea of merely going over for a game was not quite the thing to do.

The Calders, you know, are planning to come to America, but I do not know on what date and what the relationship is at the present moment. My business relationship with Sir James and the other gentleman is a bit strained just now and it will be a little difficult for me, at the moment, to send word that you are coming on such short notice and on such an occasion. I am sure you will understand this.

Mother is still planning to come over there toward the end of March or the first part of April and there will be plenty of opportunity on your visit to England with Mother to get up to the games at Oxford and Cambridge, and see all there is to be seen.

I am terribly proud of the way you handled yourself over there and your whole attitude toward everything and I am sure that you will get a great deal out of your year abroad.

Jack, as you probably know, is at the Peter Bent Brigham Hospital in Boston for a period of two months, as we are trying to find out what is the matter with him.

Mother was down to Palm Beach with me last week and is staying there with Aunt Agnes and Uncle Joe and I am here doing some work on the Radio reorganization and will be here for another ten days.

The weather has been quite cold at Palm Beach and there was lots less doing at Christmas than a year ago, so you didn't miss much. I am sure you had a much better time.

Try to get all you can out of this trip, because it will be of great help to you in everything you do hereafter.

Lots of love,

Joseph P. Kennedy to Robert Rutherford McCormick[134]

Personal January 31, 1936

Dear Colonel McCormick:

I have no desire to joust with your editorial writers, who have mis-dubbed me "The Wall Street Member of the Administration", but I do wish to write to you personally to voice my sentiments on The Tribune's editorial of January 18th.[135]

You will permit me, I am sure, to cherish some pride for my part in the creation and the organization of the Securities and Exchange Commission. I shall not lose that feeling of satisfaction, nor would I willingly permit anyone unfairly to besmirch the record which has been made.

I believe you are aware of the fact that there has never been any adverse criticism of even slight consequence against the manner in which the exchange markets of the country and the sale of securities have been brought under a proper control. There is no word of criticism in your editorial concerning any official act of mine or my erstwhile associates. We rejoice in the fact that from all manner of persons, of whatever political or economic belief, has come gratifying praise for the work done. This commendation has been generously voiced by the investing public, by bankers, by stock brokers, exchange officials, newspapers of varying political faiths and by men in public office. Whatever you may think of the other acts of the present Administration, won't you concede that this was a praiseworthy job?

The views which I held as Chairman of the Securities and Exchange Commission, regarding stock market practices, I still hold to firmly today. But even if my convictions in this respect were not sincerely held, I still would follow them to the letter, so that I might continue to cherish my reputation and my record to the point of defending them aggressively against unfair attacks. I engaged in public service at a great financial sacrifice to my family and during the period of my service I resolutely refrained from entering into any transactions affecting my investments, even to the point of suffering large losses which I could easily have avoided.

When the work which I had agreed to undertake had been completed — that is, the organization of the Securities and Exchange Commission — I sought and obtained the consent of the President that I might return to private business. If the President requires my further service at some future date, I shall be impelled, as a citizen, to respond again to such a call. It goes without saying that should I be required to give further service to the Government, I should again divest myself of all private business activities.

At the present time, however, I am definitely and completely a private citizen, pretending to no official influence or connection whatsoever. I believe you should concede to every citizen the right to pursue a lawful and proper private activity. It ought not be expected of me that because I have given a service to the Government, which has been universally commended, I should thenceforth forever be barred from following a career which I have pursued since my first entry into the business world. I have engaged in various business enterprises for many years, and long before the advent of the present Administration I was engaged frequently to offer advice and counsel to officials and stockholders of corporations. This I am continuing to do now.

134. Colonel Robert Rutherford McCormick (1880–1955), editor and publisher of the *Chicago Tribune*, 1910–1955.
135. The editorial had asserted (among other things) that "President Roosevelt . . . had appointed a stock market manipulator to stop stock market manipulation" and took issue with the advisory role that JPK had played over the previous month in restructuring RCA's finances so soon after his resignation from the SEC.

For your further information, the work I have engaged in for the Radio Corporation of America, and the recommendations I have made, have no possible relationship to the Securities and Exchange Commission or to any other branch of the Government.

I am enclosing herewith a copy of my report which I made to the Directors of the Radio Corporation which has not been made public and also a copy of the letter going to the stockholders which makes some small changes in the plan as originally reported to the Board of Directors and which has been made public this afternoon. The Directors Report, of course, has not been made public.

The Directors, having under consideration numerous plans affecting the capital-ization of the company, and in particular with reference to the accumulations on the reference "B" stock, retained me to make a study of the Corporation and to make a re-port, with recommendations, which would be fair to all classes of security holders. If you will read the report, you will see for yourself that the services which I was asked to give, and did perform, were entirely ethical in character and that they were sought, not because of political or financial relationships at all, but because the Directors believed I was capable of giving them detached, objective recommendations which would be to the interest of the Corporation and the stockholders.

I earnestly commend you to a reading of the report, the recommendations of which should convince you that your editorial, with its suggestions of political fixing, market manipulation and abuse of public office, is wholly false and most unfair.

Those who know me best know well that I will not now, as a private citizen, com-promise any ideals that I held as a public official, and that I will not at any time seek im-properly to bring the slightest influence to bear upon any official of the Securities Exchange Commission or of the Federal or any other Government.

I am willing to stand on the integrity of my future conduct. Will you be fair and not condemn me in advance?

Sincerely yours,

Kathleen Kennedy, 15, to Rose Kennedy

Neuilly S/Seine February 8 — 36

Dearest Mother —

I hope this letter reaches you in Florida as you seem to jump around like a frog be-tween N.Y. and Florida — One minute in New York the next in Florida —

Have you received a letter from Rev. Mother saying I do not eat enough — What I don't eat exactly is soup and potatoes. We have plenty of other things to make up for them such as tea and cakes in the afternoon — As all the French girls are very much larger and most of the other girls in the school are fatter she expects me to be also — I certainly do not want to get fat now and try to take it all off when I go home — As I hardly get any exercise except for walking it's silly to eat alot of stuff. I weigh exactly the same so there is no cause to worry — Rev. Mother thinks I am rather stuck on my own ideas and won't listen to any one else — She may be right but anyway I receive all my lectures in French so maybe I don't know the half of it —

Went to tea at Mrs. Larkins apartement Thurs. She is very well but misses Hope quite a bit — Marie Celeste O'Malley and her sister arrived Thurs. You remember her as the one whom Mrs. Green said was coming here in her ~~last~~ "Normandie" letter — Graduated from Noroton last year and is trying to make up some subjects here before going to Manhattanville next year — Taking Latin and Math — More advanced than

172

me — The two sisters are on their way to Garmish for the Olympics[136] — Marie Celeste is then coming here and her sister who is quite a bit older is going home — I think I am going out for lunch and to see the Malmaison where "Josephine" lived tomorrow — they are both very sweet — Grandpa gave a card to Marie introducing her to me — Not knowing of course that I knew her —

Miss Clyne called me yesterday and I am going to lunch with her Thursday. She said you were all fine and I am getting the skirts and sweaters then —

Suppose you know James Hoquet is getting better due to the knowledge of Jack's case which Eleanor wrote her mother of —

The only people who are going to Italy now are Eleanor, my English roomate and two rather strange French girls — one of the English room girls who was going is no longer on account of the condition in Italy.[137] Rev. Mother still says it is alright but some people say there are rations on food and if any revolution should break out it was silly — Wish you could perhaps find out the view-point and whether it is really worth the while to go — If not would much rather go to England with you — Would almost rather I think anyway but suppose it is better to go to Italy and take the trip while I can go and see all the museums etc. The dates on the trip to Italy are March 25th to April 20th about — Mother please come over if it isn't too much trouble —

Is Miss. Cahill sending me any records or should I buy a few here and also my tennis raquet which someone could bring if there is someone else coming over —

Jim MacColl sent me a clipping from some paper about the article which Dad wrote for the "Saturday Evening Post" Have ordered it so I can read the article — Ought to have it tomorrow morning — It looks very thrilling with a name like "Shielding The Sheep"[138]

The American boy I met who was at Cambridge wrote and said he saw the funeral of the king — He said it was the most impressive sight he had seen while in London — We heard some of it over the radio — The English girls attended a service and now all wear black strips — Have never seen anything like the love they had for the old king and more than love for the new king — That reminds me Mrs. Larkin herd some stories of the new Prince King[139] — She has plenty of scandal —

Truly never in my life have I seen anything like the weather now in Paris — It has rained every day since we have been back from Suisse — It really is ghastly hardly ever seeing the sun — Just hope for the "Paris In The Spring" —

Did I tell you in my last letter that Earl of Dudley[140] and Lady Patricia Ward were at Gstaad — The Earl's son[141] took a fancy to the little Irish girl — He was only 16 and told her she was only 15 — She is really 18 — Was she mad —

Thats about all the news Mother — My love to all and hope to see you soon —
Much love
Kick —

---

136. Reich Chancellor Hitler had presided over the opening of the eleventh winter Olympiad in Garmisch-Partenkirchen, Germany, on February 6.
137. The League of Nations had imposed limited sanctions upon Italy in response to Mussolini's invasion of Ethiopia on October 3, 1935.
138. An election-year recapitulation of the president's, the administration's and the SEC's successes in protecting the investor, JPK's "Shielding the Sheep" (as told to journalist John B. Kennedy) had appeared in the January 18 issue of the *Saturday Evening Post.*
139. George V (1865–1936) had died of a long-term heart ailment complicated by "bronchial catarrh" on January 20. David, prince of Wales (1894–1972), had succeeded his father as Edward VIII on January 22.
140. William Humble Eric Ward, third earl of Dudley, Baron Ward and Viscount Ednam (1894–1969), president of the British Iron and Steel Federation.
141. William Humble David Ward (1920–).

Joseph P. Kennedy to Louis Ruppel[142]

Dear Lou:

Miss Christian, and I think your camera man, are coming to lunch with me to-day. We made one appointment before, but it was called off on account of the Mdivani wedding.[143] I will be very happy to be of any assistance I can to make their stay a very profitable one.

I also notice your very strange comment: "I never make passes at lasses who work for you." It strikes the little doctor and myself we heard some comment on this subject when I was in Chicago making a speech, and even then we excused you so are not going to believe you about this, as we do about everything else, and will try to get at the truth, before you have received this letter so you will not have a chance to tell her again, as you have fifty times before she left — not to say anything to Moore or me. However, old boy, we will do the best for you, you know that.

The weather is not exactly perfect, but it is warm. It must be lovely in Chicago.

Best always,
Joseph P. Kennedy

Joseph P. Kennedy to Eunice Kennedy, 14

February 11, 1936

Dear Eunice:

By this time I suppose Bobby has that bugle and the house is pretty nearly a mad house. However, maybe you could arrange to send him down near the railroad station and let him play when the trains come in. I cannot imagine Kiku permitting that noise with Teddy and Jean trying to sleep; however, I think it will probably work out for the best.

As I told Bobby, we are still having lots of cold and rainy weather here, but I hope it will get all right.

I talked with ~~Mamma~~ [*Mother*], Grandpa, Jack and Joe and Grandpa's birthday and they all seem to be having a fine time. I understand ~~Mamma~~ [*Mother*] and Jack are planning to come down on Sunday and you will be coming in March. We will have everything ready for you and will turn on the nice warm weather.

Now that those orals are over, I suppose you are taking it nice and easy. I suggest getting plenty of practice writing. I am quite discouraged with the penmanship of the Kennedy children — Joe, Jack, Rosemary, you and Bobby. It is almost like mine — pretty bad, so I suggest, although you have shown marvelous improvement, that you practice a little more for I would hate to have you as bad a penman as your Dad. Anyway, you were sweet to write and I love hearing from you.

Give my love to all.

---

142. The former *New York Daily News* political reporter and U.S. deputy commissioner of narcotics, whom JPK had met during the 1932 campaign, had become managing editor of the *Chicago Times* in 1935.
143. In a private ceremony held in Palm Beach on February 8, Princess Louise Astor Van Alen Mdivani married Serge Mdivani, the younger brother of Prince Alexis Mdivani of Georgia (whom the bride had divorced four years earlier). Five weeks later, her second husband and former brother-in-law (who himself had previously been married both to actress Pola Negri and to opera star Mary McCormic) would die of cranial injuries sustained after a fall from a polo pony.

Joseph P. Kennedy, Jr., 20, to Joseph P. Kennedy

Dear Dad:

I felt that I did fairly well in exams. I had hoped to get a B in Govt, but missed it by a couple of points. However it is a full years course, and I think I will get a B for the year. I have decided to take five courses this half year. I never could get a very good mark in Fine Arts, but still would like to take, so I added two courses and dropped French because now I have passed my language requirements. I have added National Govt under Holcombe and a very interesting course on Russia under Hopper.[144] [*I think they are both very good, especially the latter*]

I talked with a captain yesterday, and am enclosing two of his references. He has had experience in both rowing and with motors. He has been on several good yachts, in the New York Yacht Club Cruise, in the Bermuda Race etc. and seems to like children a great deal. His references seem to be unlimited and unusually good. However the drawback is that, as he has a family, he will consider only a year around job. He has been accustomed to receiving more than doc paid Eric, $250, but I think we could get him for the same price $200 if we would pay all year around. I think he would do work on the boats for seven months. It seems to me a question whether you would consider taking the boat South with you. He has had experience down there, and would be very capable. I told him I would let him know within ten days, as he has to give a month's notice on the job he has now. You might talk to Jack about him as Jack has received a letter from him, and has probably talked to other men.

Reggie Boardman[145] said he saw you, and that you were looking fine. I haven't been doing any exercise because of my arm. I cut it skiing and had to have eight stitches, but it is healing well. Spring Football is going to last four weeks, with three weeks of scrimmage which will be mighty jolly. Not sure of rugby trip, but think I might go to Bermuda. Downes[146] is out on probation, but if his marks don't improve he will be kicked out at the end of the year, which isn't so hot. Weather has been terrible. Saw Dr. Murphy. Think I will take Felix & Mrs Frank — to dinner at the Ritz next week on you if its O.K. Tell Mother that one of the boys that I saw at a deb party last week ~~saw~~ had met Rose at the Fly Assemblies and thought she was very nice. Bob Downes also thought she was good looking as did Francis Shea, so I think she is coming along finely. All these came from a clear sky, so they were not meant to be the old bunk.

By the way Barbara Cushing[147] & a friend of hers who was out with you in N.Y. hearing Toscanini, Persian Room etc. till 3 o'clock were up here and gave me the low down on you. They said they nearly went South. I think Mother ought to keep a better eye on you. I told Barbara that I would call her up for a date which thrilled her no end (Yes it did!) but when I called her up she had gone to N.Y. to see Betsy. She looked pretty good.

The House Dance is tomorrow night & Pat Kennedy is coming up from N.Y. it ought to be pretty good. Give Mother my love, and please let me know about the skipper.

Love

Joe

P.S. Our house was broken into at Hyannisport, but nothing was taken.
~~I have misplaced the references, but Jack has copies.~~

---

144. Professor Arthur Norman Holcombe (1884–1977) taught "The National Government of the United States: Administration" and Assistant Professor Bruce Campbell Hopper (1892–1973), "Problems in Soviet Foreign Relations" during the spring term of 1936.
145. Joe's classmate and a resident of Palm Beach.
146. Robert Choate Downes, a sophomore.
147. Barbara "Babe" Cushing (later Paley) (1915–1978), the youngest of Dr. Harvey Cushing's three daughters and James Roosevelt's sister-in-law.

Joseph P. Kennedy to Missy LeHand: *Telegram*

PALM BEACH. FEB. 25, 1936

THAT WAS NOT A CASE OF MISTAKEN IDENTITY. CHURCHES DOWN HERE FILLING UP WITH LIBERTY LEAGUERS. UNDERSTAND THAT CAMPAIGN SONG FOR THIS INSTEAD OF HAPPY DAYS ARE HERE AGAIN WILL BE QUOTE I'LL BE GLAD WHEN YOU'RE DEAD, YOU RASCAL, YOU, WHEN ARE YOU COMING DOWN? LOVE AND KISSES.

JOE

Joseph P. Kennedy to Joseph P. Kennedy, Jr., 20

February 27th, 1936

Dear Joe:

I am enclosing the letters you sent to me — recommendations of Captain Anderson. He seems to be a very worthwhile man, but I see no chance of using him for the winter. I doubt very much if I would have a boat down here because it would be an additional expense which to me would be entirely unnecessary. However, if he is the type that could work on the boats, getting them ready and putting them away, I should think that would take six or seven months, and I would be willing, probably, to pay him $50 extra and just sign him up for that period, but I would not want the responsibility of having him for the winter months. So, if he seems the right type to you and can do all the work that Eric did, why I am perfectly willing to have you hire him on a seven months' basis.

Jack and Mother arrived and Jack rather intimates your financial condition is rather precarious. He is not at all specific but I judge some of those bills have piled up much faster than your allowance would warrant; however, I will stand the expense of the dinner to Felix and Mrs. Frankfurter, so let me know what it cost and I will have Paul send you a check.

Don't worry too much about Barbara Cushing and her pal as 21 or 22 is still a little too young for me. I still play nursemaid for Jimmie.

Talked with Dr. Good last night. He told me you were planning to have Dr. Ober look at your arm. I think you are very wise to follow them up and get it corrected because it should not bother you now.

I was wondering whether it might not be very good experience for you to get yourself signed up and possibly make some speeches in the fall in the campaign throughout Massachusetts. It would be a very interesting experience and you could work up two or three subjects you wanted to discuss and go out through the State. Of course, the trouble is football may be on and it may be very difficult, but you might think it over anyway — you might have some chance late in the summer.

I thought, if you also had some time, you might drop in at the bank and see Mr. Porter[148] and look around. There may be some points of interest there you would like to follow up.

It is possible I may have to come to New York within a couple of weeks, and if I do I will get over to see you and talk things over.

Give my best to Bob and tell him to hustle now as we do not want to see him lose out.

Love,

---

148. Drew Porter, current president of the Columbia Trust Company.

Joseph P. Kennedy to Eunice, 14, Patricia, 11, and Jean Kennedy, 8

[Palm Beach] February 27, 1936

Dear Girls:

I got so many letters and Valentines I have to write to all three of you at the same time because otherwise I would not have news to go around.

Ever since Mother, Jack, Grandpa and Grandmother arrived the weather has been fine, so I think they brought us all good luck.

Mother and Jack went to Lake Worth this morning to take a golf lesson and they are talking about bringing the golf professor from there to Cape Cod this year so that you all can take lessons every day and become good golfers — and that means Jeannie, too.

You were all very kind to drop me a note and to send the Valentines, and I am saving them all and keeping them in my office.

My love to you all,

Joseph P. Kennedy to Robert, 10, and Edward Kennedy, 4

February 27, 1936

Dear Bobby & Ted:

I do not think you two boys would like to get a letter with the girls so am writing you one separately.

As for old Ted telling me he would not come down until the crowd comes, he left me pretty lonesome here so I will probably have to come up in ten days or so to see how the two of you are getting along. Maybe then we will have to go into town to lunch and the movies. Perhaps we will take the girls with us — what do you say?

Thanks for the Valentines and letters. You were both very kind and I like very much to hear from you.

The girls will tell you about the golf lessons Mother and I were talking about. I think Teddy would be a little too small, don't you?

Love to you both,

Rosemary Kennedy, 17, to Rose and Joseph P. Kennedy

[Boston] March 1st, 1936

Dear Mother and Daddy.

The Chauffer drove mary O Keefe and I to Adams House on Friday night. Thats where we met Joe and John O Keefe at ten past eight. Then Mary went with Joe in his car to the dance. I went with John O Keefe. He told the chauffer how to go. It was a costume party but we diddn't know it. I wore my red evening dress, red shoes, 2 red bows on my hair, black evening coat. Mary wore her red evening dress, red evening coat And we both had our nails polished. Christine did them.

O Keefe did a backward somersault at the dance. They had punch to drink there. and Joe went to a Deb Party after the dance. Saturday, Babe Kaughlin a friend of mary's, and I and mary went down on the Beach and cooked sausage's and put it in a sandwich, cooked stake and Bacon, and brought gingerbread to eat. We made a fire, and got wood for it. Paper too. And we came home, Mary had coca, I had tea, babe, had coca. We all had gingerbread with it. I played Christine in ping pong, and mary and babe also. We also played three handered bridge. At night mary and I played Monopoly with Christine. Sunday Aunt Agnas envited Joe and I to lunch. I stayed over night. Aunt Agnas took me to school Monday Morning.

Mrs O Keefe has been in a Automobile Accident. She has her two knees bandaged. The ford had much repears to make. We had to borrow another ford for the time being. Mary and I went also skating Sunday. We both had a lesson. The chauffer took us up to the Arena. Miss Sipple has taught me to do the tango. I showed the doctor, Christine, Mrs O Keefe Mary, Babe Kaughlin, Joe, and I told John O Keefe.

Christine took me to Dr. Lawrences Friday. He took my pulse, my blood pressure. I weight 121 in a 1/2 there. but Uncle Joe weighed me and I weigh 124 in a half.

I take my red pills, injections in my arm 3 times a week.

My new white shoes are ready. I have a new necktie red and white the color.

I am going to study Napoleon, Mary O Keefe has a new red and white bathing suit, new white shorts, new blue evening dress. I tried the bathing suit on me, also the new silk dress she bought. I tried it on me. I get 3 dollars allowance a week. I have had my hair waved and my eyebrows plucked.

I got a letter from Jean thanking me for her present. talked to Aunt Pappe on the phone since she got home. Aunt Agnas took me to see "The Bride come home."

lots of love and kisses to the best Mother and father in the world. Your loving daugher.

Rosemary

Kathleen Kennedy, 16, to Rose and Joseph P. Kennedy

Hotel Gabrielli Sandwirth, Venezia March 29

Darling Mother and Dad —
Venice is too wonderful to give you all a good idea of how we are doing here — Left Paris Thurs nite — nun and all. The first incident was when we had to sneak into the nun's room next door and opened the door to the bathroom which we were sharing with her — after she locked it again we finally gave up — The next event was when the French girl sat up all nite making notes — Passed through quite a few snow-capped alps — Passed through Milan and Verona. Arrived in Venice at two, pouring rain took two gondolas down the Grand Canal to hotel — Went to see some "Marano" glass works which was the most lovely glass and Mosaics I have ever seen. It is not very funny here as all the men talk to the girls on the street — we had about 6 in a cavalcade following us all over Venice today — It makes one feel so very ignorant here where everyone from the gondolier up speaks either French or English and lots of times both. They teach the French in the schools — The first night we were here I didn't finish eating my pea soup so the nun proceeded to tell me that since the country was at war I must eat everything — It is the funniest thing to be with a nun in a hotel. Sat. afternoon morning we visited a great many churches and saw the academy of Venice with a great many lovely pictures in it. In the afternoon went out in a boat to visit the three islands of Murano (glass works) Burano (lace works and Torcello noted for old cathedral of ninth century — We walked for awhile after dinner and it was the most perfect night — This morning went to Mass at San Marco and the Italian priest told Marie O'Malley while she was receiving communion that her lips were too red. So thats that — attended a Fascist demonstration for a Dominican priest who was killed in Ethiopia in the Palais des Doges — His brother spoke — Never seen such a collection of uniforms — very thrilling.

Last nite we all went out in gondola for an hour Never have I seen such a night — We have all decided to come back here on our honeymoon. The gondolier sang and the nun tried to help him along — she thought the gondola was tipping over every other minute — We sleep and are awoken by the sound of singing gondoliers — This morning visited San Marco and the Palais des Doges — Perfectly marvelous. Yesterday afternoon after fighting to get on the ferry for one hour we finally managed and went out to the ~~Louvre~~ Lido. Took about 15 minutes and it was very crowded although no one was swimming — This afternoon visited three churches and bought a Facist hat which will certainly make a big hit —

The hotel is quite small and owned by a German. Strange as it may be for a French convent to stay with Germans — Hardly any Americans in Venice at all — A terrific amount of Germans coming down from the winter sports —

Really no sign of war here at all except of course the sanctions have closed down a great deal of the glass and lace works —

Sorry this letter is so very mixed up but trying to write it in a few moments —

Shall write more but this should go on "Rex" —

Happy Easter to all and hope to see Mother very soon — Never thank you enough for this trip —

Love to all —
Kick —

Joseph P. Kennedy, Jr., 20, to Joseph P. Kennedy

April 11, 1936

Dear Dad:

I took the 1:55 train back Sunday night after a swell time in New York, and was greeted at the House by a great number of bills. I am writing Paul to-day to advance me a month's allowance, and it looks like I will have to pay you back July 26th. If this is not O.K., I guess I'll have to write Jack or go over to your bank in East Boston and get a loan. After reading of your $120,000 profit in the N.B.C. deal I feel that I am ready to offer myself as one of your business partners. Couldn't you employ me as one of those accountants to whom you payed $30,000 and it would save you trouble on your income tax.

The big reason for my finances being in such a state is my trip to Bermuda. I bought some clothes, and with other incidentals it about finished a month's allowance. In spite of our talk of last week, I would like to impress the fact that you gave Jack and myself quite a talk last Spring about doing what the College demands, rather than what you yourself wanted to do. I would just as soon gone to Florida, it would have cost you $120 anyway for plane trip, so I should think the sporting thing to do would be to pay me the difference, for carrying the name of Kennedy and Harvard to foreign lands. I think Jack and Mother will remember well the discussion last Spring on this subject.

Have been out for football the past week. There are plenty of big and good ends. I should say that there are about four ends ahead of me. I'm not looking like any ball of fire, but I think I can give them a run. We were supposed to play a rugby game to-day against a Boston Rugby Team, but it was called off on account of rain. Football is plenty tough, with four scrimmages last week, and plenty to come. It is going to last about three weeks more. Chances for a good team next year look pretty good.

The S.E.C. decision last week seemed fair enough to me.[149] It looked like Burns just wanted to get Jones behind the boss so badly that he wouldn't stop. Supposing a person had applied for registration, and then found something wrong which he hadn't known of before, he wouldn't be able to withdraw. What do you think?

My marks, so far so good. Whacked off another A in my written report for Gov. 7B, Holcombes course. Got a B- in my Gov. 30 hour exam, also in Gov I. My marks are on the good side of Dean's list, but a little drop in two of them would throw me off.

Wrote a letter to Mother, and told her about the trip to Russia. We get a holiday the 20th of April, and I thought I might go to N.Y. during that weekend, to see Mother before she left. Personally I can't afford it, but if you think Mother would like to see me, O.K.

Sir James was here, and I had dinner with him. I received a letter from the Head of the Associated Harvard Club asking me to assist in the arrangements at one of the gatherings in the Tercentenary Celebration.[150] Some fellows from every class are selected.

Thats about all the news, please let me know as soon as possible about the first item.

Love
Joe

Joseph P. Kennedy to Joseph P. Kennedy, Jr., 20

April 13, 1936

Dear Joe:

I read your letter with great interest and note your financial predicament. As I see it, I am afraid discussions of general policy between us must in the future be limited to each particular occasion so that there can be no misunderstanding. However, I am glad you went to Bermuda and I will have Paul send you a check for $120 which I hope will ease your financial difficulties. All I want you to do is to look at the total amount spent one way or another and I'll trust your good judgment to keep it in line.

As to my fee for the RCA deal, it is unfortunate that the newspapers misquoted it. My fee was $150,000 and the $30,000 was for the statisticians. Of course, the Government will get 70% of that. As you are still unable to qualify as an expert, I am very much afraid I cannot get you on the payroll, but if you will hurry up and get through while I am still able to do any work, maybe we can work out something for you.

I note that there are four ends ahead of you. I should think, with your usual determination to get what you want, that some intensive work this summer might put you in shape where you could at least be within the four — which would probably get you into the games. However, I will leave that to your usual persistence.

Your point on the S. E. C. is a very good one, but it has never been the policy of the Commission to issue a stop order or have an examination made where the error appeared to be anything but a flagrant steal, and in the case of Jones, that is exactly what it was. The unfortunate part of it all is that with a limited number of men to examine

---

149. In *J. Edward Jones v. the Securities and Exchange Commission* the Supreme Court had found that the commission did not have the right to deny the withdrawal of issues once they had been submitted for registration. Earlier in the year, rather than submit to a subpoena to appear before the SEC at a hearing intended to ascertain the legitimacy of oil royalty certificates that he had attempted to register for sale, Jones had chosen to withdraw the issue and ignore the subpoena. The commission's insistence that Jones appear in any case, had prompted Jones's counsel to bring suit, arguing government persecution.

150. Harvard College's three-hundredth anniversary festivities were scheduled for the coming fall.

the statements, it is quite possible that a statement might get by that contained a great many untruths and the securities would get into the hands of the public who would get mulcted.

I congratulate you on your excellent report. I think it would be most creditable to get on the Dean's list. Besides doing a good job it means additional prestige and that all helps in the long run.

It might be well to come over that weekend and see Mother about Russia — I'll stand the expenses of the traveling.

I think it would be very nice for you to aid in one of the gatherings in the Tercentenary Celebration because it may bring you in touch with a great many interesting people.

I expect Jack up this weekend. He will be in Boston next week to see Doctor Murphy and then I hope to start him West. I think he has made a great deal of improvement down south, but don't think he did nearly as well as he should have done. Of course I realize that it is a great temptation to want to go out nights especially when one doesn't feel very sick, but after all, he has sacrificed a year of his life to get himself into condition, and I think he could have done a whole lot better. However, I think the Arizona trip will build him up in real good fashion.

I am expecting Mother this afternoon and will look forward to seeing you over the weekend — Jack will be here too.

Rose will be in Boston around Wednesday or Thursday I think, so give her a ring and tell her you understand she was swell down South.

Love,

Kathleen Kennedy, 16, to Joseph P. Kennedy

Hotel Metropole & Ville, Naples <u>*Monday — April 15*</u>

Dearest Dad —

As Mother will probably have left for this side of the ocean by the time this reaches you —

We arrived in Naples today, leaving ~~Pari~~ Rome this morning at ten — This afternoon we visited a small volcano which is one of the most interesting sights yet seen. Tomorrow we are going to Capri and Dame Rumor has it that it is quite a ruff voyage but I think that if I stood the English Channel I can stand that — Hope so anyway. Wednesday we are taking that Amalfi drive through Pompeii along the Mediterranean coast. The hotel here is suitaited in quite a nice place right on the river front and we have a huge balcony from which we can see the whole bay of Naples and a corner of Vesuvius — Going to have breakfast there tomorrow morning as special treat — The sun is as hot as blazes and tonight I look quite Palm Beachey. Ever since I made the remark about Venice resembling Palm Beach I have been taking a great deal of teasing as all the girls ask me if everything doesn't look like Palm Beach —

Not having written since in Rome I had better relate the big news. Arrived in Rome the seventh and the convent is perfectly beautiful — another convent of the same order from Switzerland are also there — nine girls all English and are they English! Visited an old Roman church and the colesseum Wed. morning — Tried to get Mr Galeazzi but had quite a time trying to understand the Italian, French and English all at the same time of his maid — The maid also spoke of him as "she" so thought maybe he was married. But found out later it was just the English of the maid — In the afternoon visited St. Peter's and St. Paul's — It certainly was a thrill to see St. Peter's — Wanted to go to the mass

Holy Thursday in the Sistine Chapel said by the Pope but as I couldn't get a hold of Mr. Galeazzi went along with the other girls to the corridor there where one can see the Pope pass to and from the Chapel — As only fifty people attend Mass in the chapel besides all the clergy the nuns could not get them — We all had our little camp stools and sat out-side during the mass. What a crowd we were all nearly squashed to death — Met two girls from the Normandie while being shoved from side to side — Thursday afternoon went to the Tenebrae at St. Peter's — Three wonderful relics were ~~being~~ shown — (Veronica's veil, part of the true cross and the spear that pierced our Lord's heart) — I was lost for an hour so had quite a time — Never have seen so many American priests all together at once M. Galeazzi called that night at the convent and I talked with him for a few minutes — He is one of the most charming men I have ever met — The nuns knew him at school as he has done a great deal for different Americans who have been here — He got me three tickets for the Mass on the Sistene Chapel Good Friday said by the Pope by calling the Vatican that night — We all wore black and he sent a man with car and chauffeur with us to the Vatican — Went through the apartments of Cardinal Pacceli[151] which are magnificent — The Mass was most impressive — After it was over we had quite a time getting out as no one understood and the Swiss guards speak only German — We had a little man in black velvet shorts running around for us — When we arrived as guests of Cardinal Pacceli, who is the Secretary of State in the Vatican there was plenty of excitement — Sat. morning on our way to the Capitoline Hill we stopped to see a demonstration by some visiting Frenchies ~~on~~ in the huge square, Victor Emmanuel — ~~The~~ A policeman told us that Mussolini would probably appear from his office in re-sponse to cheering and yelling — Lo and behold we had only been there about an hour when they stood outside his offices and made plenty of noise. "Il duce" came out with a big stride and a bigger grin — I was wedged in trying to take his picture and was so nerv-ous my hand was going up and around — No one else had their camera so mine was their only hope — He is magnificent and one cannot help liking him after seeing the pa-triotism of the Italians. Seeing him was what we all had hoped for and it was an excep-tional chance. We then went into a church where a man came up to me and another girl for not having coats on in church. I told him to calm down in English which he did not understand so I thought I should promptly get bounced on my ear — From there we climbed to the very tip-top of St. Peter's — climbed up in the ball which was very hot — Did it by a ladder and it is the last time any of us will do it. One of the girls thought she was going to faint and nothing would be more jolly than trying to get out of the ball — Saw the giant bells ring at twelve — In the afternoon we were all at a fountain drinking sodas when a priest came in blessing the place -We all hopped off our stools and knelt down — It is a very inspiring thing really but it seemed so funny to see a priest blessing a soda fountain It seems they bless every store, restaurant etc. in Italy on Holy Saturday — When the clerk, who had gone to make change came back we yelled "Benite" meaning "Blessing" at him — He didn't know what to make of it all and started to yell "Benito Mussolini." We laughed for hours at that[.] Also visited the Forum and tried to recall all my ancient history. Some German film company was making a movie there which I must confess interested us more than the ruins. Nancy Cochrane, Boston girl who was in my class last year at Noroton is traveling here with a group of girls and invited all the Noroton girls of Neuilly to dinner so we had a jolly reunion — Mr Galeazzi wanted to take me on the drive to Tivoli Sat. but the nun thought it better to go on the day the oth-ers went and not miss the Forum — so am going on my return from Naples — He very

151. Eugenio Giuseppe Giovanni Pacelli (1876–1958), papal secretary of state, 1930–39 and later Pope Pius XII, 1939–58.

kindly sent five tickets for the Cardinal's Easter Sunday mass at St. Peter's — The Pope did not say it this year — The church was crammed full — Had a nice Easter Sunday and received the cable — Hope you received mine — The nuns even gave us wine for dinner — The food is delicious in Rome and one wouldn't think there were sanctions at all — we heard it was going to be quite to the contrary —

If this letter arrives before Mother leaves please do not bring too much warm clothing as I am afraid it will be quite warm in Paris and light clothes are the best — In fact we wear only light blouses outside now —

Am still getting very fat and spaghetti is helping plenty — Love to all —

Kick

P.S. All the soldiers who go to Abysinnia leave from here and there are ships going out every day -

P.S. Mother please bring blue straw hat — and stockings —

P.P.S. Nuns very impressed with Mr. Galeazzi

Joseph P. Kennedy to John F. Kennedy, 18

April 25, 1936

Dear Jack:

This looks good, so work hard and build yourself up for the rest of your life.[152]

Love,
Dad

Joseph P. Kennedy to John F. Kennedy, 18

April 28, 1936

Dear Jack:

I am enclosing a letter from Mr. Van Ness. He spoke to me about this place the other day and it looks very interesting. You might drop over there and see them.

I am also enclosing letters of introduction from Lew Douglas — you can use them at your convenience.[153]

Joe has hurt his knee rather badly and there is a question in my mind as to whether or not he will ever play again. It isn't decided yet, but it looks that way to me, so you will have to get big and strong and be ready to uphold the traditions of the Kennedy family in the athletic fields.

Love,

Rose Kennedy to Joseph P. Kennedy

[Ritz Hotel, Paris] Sunday [May 3, 1936]

Dear Joe,

I was quite overwhelmed by the length of your message this A.M., and of course I loved every word of it. I had counted my words very carefully as you saw. I just wished I might have been with you to-day darling.

---

152. Jack's grades had arrived.
153. Lewis Douglas, vice president of the American Cyanamid Corporation (as well as former director of the Office of the Budget, 1933–34), had written letters of introduction on Jack's behalf to several large-scale ranchers in Lewis's native state of Arizona, where Jack planned to spend part of the summer recuperating.

We have no special news from Paris. The clothes are the same as at home and very expensive. I ordered a lace dress, good for N.Y. and Palm Beach & may get a coat or I may go to London Wednesday. To-day we went to Notre Dame and did some sightseeing. Last night we went to a French movie. It is quite different from what I have been doing here lately. We both talk French entirely, and we are going to a French movie again to-nite. I love it, because it is a different view of Paris. We did have the "sole" at La Rue's. Happened to meet Forteviot[154] in the lobby. May go to Scotland but it seems far.

Much, much love to you my dearest.

Rosa

Robert Kennedy, 10, to Joseph P. Kennedy

Bronxville, May 11, 1936

Dear Daddy,

Have you seen any Movie stars?

Do you like California?[155] I took my baby Rabbits out to day And I am going to start selling them. Have you seen Jack? give my love to him and tell him I'll write him. Ask him if he thinks I will like the wild and wooly west.

I went to Doctor Cloney on Sat. and he said I will not need a turtle[156] any more

I got a post card from Mother We also got a cable from her and she said she was very excited

We are having are final tests in school and I hope I pass

Lots of love to Jack and yourself Bobby

Edward Kennedy, 4, to Joseph P. Kennedy

Dear Daddy,[157]

Everybody in the world is good but Jeannie. Jean is good sometimes too. Bobby sold some rabbits and when you come home you'll see. Kikoo is home now. When are you going to telephone me again? Eddie took me to see the fishes, but, the place wasn't open, so we fed the pigeons and they came right near me. That's all XX XXX

Love,

Teddy

Joseph P. Kennedy to Adolph Sabath[158]: *Telegram*

JUNE 2, 1936

I HAVE JUST LEARNED OF THE HEARING OF YOUR COMMITTEE SCHEDULED IN WASHINGTON ON THURSDAY CONCERNING THE REORGANIZATION AND PRESENT

---

154. John Dewar, second Baron Forteviot (1885–1947), director of John Dewar & Sons, distillers, and chairman of the Distillers Company, Ltd., whose whiskeys were represented by Somerset Importers in the United States.
155. JPK would spend most of the month in Los Angeles; Adolph Zukor, chairman of the board of Paramount Pictures, had commissioned his assessment of the company's dire financial condition.
156. A retainer for his teeth.
157. He had dictated the letter to his nanny, Kikoo.
158. Adolph Joachim Sabath (1866–1952), Chicago Democrat, dean of the House of Representatives and chairman of the Select Committee to Investigate Bondholders Reorganization. The committee had been examining allegations of collusion and other irregularities in the Paramount bankruptcy proceedings, which had resulted in defaulted bond issues on Paramount theaters nationwide.

ACTIVITIES OF THE REORGANIZED PARAMOUNT PICTURES CORPORATION STOP IT
IS VERY EVIDENT TO ME AND I AM SINCERELY OF THE OPINION FROM THE INVESTI-
GATION THAT I HAVE JUST CONCLUDED FOR THE COMPANY THAT A HEARING AT
THIS TIME WILL CONFUSE MATTERS TO A GREATER EXTENT IN SO FAR AS THE
BONDHOLDERS AND SECURITY HOLDERS ARE CONCERNED I THEREFORE RESPECT-
FULLY REQUEST THAT THIS HEARING BE POSTPONED UNTIL AT LEAST AFTER THE
STOCKHOLDERS MEETING ON JUNE SIXTEENTH AT WHICH TIME I HOPE THAT A
PROGRAM WILL BE INITIATED BASED UPON DEFINITE RECOMMENDATIONS THAT I
AM MAKING THAT WILL REMEDY THOSE CONDITIONS IN THE COMPANY NOW SUB-
JECT TO CRITICISM WHICH COMPANY I CONSIDER ONE OF THE FINEST PROPERTIES
IN THE MOTION PICTURE INDUSTRY STOP THE SENDING OF ANONYMOUS COMMU-
NICATIONS REFLECTING UPON THE PURPOSE OF THE INVESTIGATION BY YOUR
COMMITTEE IS INSPIRED IN MY OPINION BY PERSONS WISHING TO UNNECESSAR-
ILY COMPLICATE THE PARAMOUNT SITUATION FURTHER STOP PERSONALLY I AM
DEEPLY APPRECIATIVE OF THE CONSTRUCTIVE WORK THAT YOUR COMMITTEE IS
DOING I AM VERY ANXIOUS TO COOPERATE WITH YOUR COMMITTEE AND I AM EN-
DEAVORING TO DO A CONSTRUCTIVE JOB FOR THE ULTIMATE GOOD OF THE SECU-
RITY HOLDERS WHICH I KNOW IS YOUR VIEWPOINT TOO AND THAT PURPOSE
WOULD BEST BE SERVED BY ADJOURNING THIS MATTER WITH AN OPPORTUNITY TO
WORK OUT THEIR PROBLEM STOP I ASSURE YOU THAT I SHALL BE THE FIRST TO EX-
POSE ANY ACTS WHICH ARE NOT FOR THE BEST INTERESTS OF THE SECURITY
HOLDERS

JOSEPH P. KENNEDY

Joseph P. Kennedy to Missy LeHand

June 15, 1936

Dear Missy:

The copy of the manuscript I sent the President was the only one I had, but I managed to scrape some working sheets together to make another copy, so of course he's
perfectly welcome to it.[159]

I should like to hear from you when he thinks it should be published, with his suggestions of course, or whether he thinks it should just be forgotten. Unless he feels that
there is some value in releasing it, it won't hurt my feelings at all if he just says, "Let's
use it in some other way", but if he really feels that it is worthwhile, I should appreciate
hearing from you as to whether or not to go ahead with it.

I sent in my report to Paramount last Friday and I am fairly free now of any business activities, so if he thinks I can be of any service to him, please let me know.

I am going to take up the "bum's life" again. I am taking all the children to the Cape
Wednesday of this week, but shall be available if there is anything he wants me to do.

With warmest regards.

Very sincerely yours,

159. During the time that JPK had spent in California working on the Paramount report, his former SEC associate, John J. Burns, had been ghostwriting the first draft of the campaign pamphlet that JPK had discussed with the president some months earlier. Reworked over the course of the summer by a number
of JPK's friends and associates in the press, Arthur Krock in particular, the pamphlet (an enthusiastic
endorsement of the New Deal from the businessman's point of view) would evolve into the 141-page
I'm for Roosevelt at the time of its publication in September.

Joseph P. Kennedy to Arthur Krock

June 24, 1936

Dear Arthur:

I suppose by this time Johnnie Burns has sent a copy of the outline of the book to you.

I am enclosing copy of a letter I received from the President last week. I gather from it that he is anxious to have it done, and if it is done, I should like to have it done in bang-up shape.

I imagine that you are going on your vacation after this convention, and I wonder if you could give some of your time each week for, say the next five weeks, to help put it in shape. I shall only avail myself of your services, however, if you will permit me to pay you for the work you do on it.

I should like to make a deal with you for $1,000 a week for five weeks, if that is worth your while. Your time and efforts are worth a lot to me, and if you can see your way clear to doing it, I should love to have you. I am sure it will not require much time and can be done wherever you are.

I am going to the Cape today and do not expect to go to Philadelphia, but you can get in touch with me at Hyannisport.

The Paramount situation is still in a mess, and I am not at all impressed with their idea of working it out.

With warmest regards.

Very sincerely yours,

Joseph P. Kennedy to Robert S. Allen[160]

August 8, 1936

Dear Bob:

You know when I go on a vacation I don't ever write letters. I answer an occasional telephone call, and become a first-class bum that my instincts tell me to be, but I thought I had better write an answer to you, because I have a distinct recollection that came to me.

As I was leaving Washington you made me make you one promise, and that was that I would never write a book, but, My God, I have gone and done it. My only excuse is that it wasn't about the SEC but it was conceived in righteous indignation and born of strict determination to take a crack at the people who should be down on their knees thanking Roosevelt instead of abusing him and everybody connected with him.

I have fiddled around with it now for six or seven months, and I promise you now, without a GTC that I will never do another. When it comes off the press I'll send you one and think that on the whole you will like it pretty well. I am doing a couple of articles, one for *Review of Reviews* and one for the Magazine Section of the *New York Times*.[161]

---

160. Robert Sharon Allen (1900–1981), coauthor of the United Features syndicated "Washington Merry-Go-Round" column.

161. "Why I'm for Roosevelt; A Business Man's Estimate of the New Deal" would appear in the September issue of the *Review of Reviews*. On September 6, JPK's "The Administration and Business" (in which, "Kennedy, Asserting That Prosperity Is Here, Defends Policies of the President") would appear on the front page of the *New York Times Magazine*.

As I seem to be a voice crying in the wilderness I expect to get my head kicked off. I am anxious to have Frank Kent[162] and Mark Sullivan[163] do a job on these writings to solve their conscience for all the nice things they said about me. Well anyway, Bob, it is done, and I only hope it will do some good.

You were damned nice to write me and I got more kick out of it than any of the hundreds of letters I got, which by the way, I did.

Give my best to Drew[164] and tell him that I am an economic royalist of the loafing type.

Warmest regards.

Yours sincerely,

Joseph P. Kennedy to Father Charles Coughlin

August 18, 1936

Dear Father Coughlin:

Thanks for all the kind things you are saying about me.[165] I feel like the fellow on his vacation who sends the postal card back to his friends saying, "Wish you were with us".

Very respectfully yours,

Joseph P. Kennedy to Delmar Leighton[166]

August 28, 1936

My dear Dean Leighton:

Thank you very much for your letter of August 14.

Jack was graduated year before last from Choate School, Wallingford, Connecticut, and I intended to enter him in the University of London as I did his older brother, Joe. I took him abroad last year but he had a recurrence of a blood condition and I brought him home to be near his doctors. He entered Princeton university where he stayed for about two months. His condition got no better and I sent him to the Peter Bent Brigham Hospital. After a period of two months there, I sent him South and then to Arizona. He seems to have recovered now and is in very good health.

Jack has a very brilliant mind for the things in which he is interested, but is careless and lacks application in those in which he is not interested. This is, of course, a bad fault. However, he is quite ambitious to try and do the work in three years. I know how the authorities feel about this and I have my own opinion, but it is a gesture that pleases me very much because it seems to be the beginning of an awakening ambition. If possible, I should like very much to have one of your assistants confer with Jack to decide whether or not this three-year idea is to be encouraged. He will be available at any time

---

162. The *Baltimore Sun*'s Frank Richardson Kent (1877–1958) had made a number of favorable references to JPK in his syndicated "Great Game of Politics" column since the latter's tenure at the SEC.
163. Mark Sullivan (1874–1952), columnist for the *New York Herald Tribune*.
164. Andrew Russell "Drew" Pearson (1897–1969), Allen's "Washington Merry-Go-Round" coauthor.
165. The August 16 edition of the *Boston Sunday Post* had reported that, despite Father Coughlin's vocal hostility toward both the president and the administration generally, he had recently described JPK as "a shining star among the dim 'knights' of the present administration's activities."
166. Dean of freshmen at Harvard College.

at Hyannisport, Massachusetts, and could come immediately to Boston if such a meeting can be arranged. I should like to have Jack do this before his adviser is appointed if possible.

I am leaving for Europe on business and shall be back in about a month, and at the beginning of the college term, I shall make it my business to go to Boston and talk with the teachers from whom Jack will receive instruction in his freshman year.

Assuring you of my willingness to help in any way possible, I am,

Very truly yours,

Joseph P. Kennedy to Robert Worth Bingham

October 6, 1936

My dear Ambassador:

I must apologize for not dropping you a line on my return to America, but I received word on the boat of the sudden death of Mrs. Kennedy's sister,[167] and was taken off the boat at quarantine where I took a plane for Boston.

After I had recovered from this shock, my son, while playing on the Harvard football team, smashed his knee and had to have it operated on. Last Friday, when he was about to leave the hospital, he slipped in the bathtub and re-opened the wound, so that in the rush of events, I didn't have a minute to do anything either in politics or in business.

I talked with the President on Saturday morning and I am going to Washington for a couple of days. The campaign looks to me distinctly Roosevelt, but it will be by no means an easy fight. Father Coughlin has definitely made bother [*sic*] in the states that we need to carry, and the Communist cry has been raised rather successfully among the Catholics, I believe to the damage of Roosevelt. There is nothing new in the situation — it's the same old stuff — and I am convinced more than ever that Roosevelt will win the election with his own speeches and appearances.

I shall be delighted to keep you posted if anything interesting comes up. In the meantime, may I thank you for the kindness and courtesy which you extended to me during my visit in London.

My warmest regards to Mrs. Bingham and yourself.

Very sincerely yours,

Joseph P. Kennedy to Ellin Mackay Berlin: *Telegram*

OCTOBER 17, 1936

SWOPE TURNED OVER YOUR WIRE TO ME TODAY REGARDING TAXES STOP I HAVE NEVER MADE ANY SUCH STATEMENT AS APPEARS IN YOUR TELEGRAM[168] ON THE CONTRARY WOULD SAY EMPHATICALLY THAT HERE IS CERTAINLY NO INCREASE IN TAXES CONTEMPLATED OR NECESSARY. THE BUDGET I BELIEVE WILL BE BALANCED THE NEXT GOVERNMENT FISCAL YEAR STOP IT IS ALL MERELY ANOTHER RIDICULOUS STATEMENT MADE TO SCARE PEOPLE HALF TO DEATH YOU MIGHT ADD ALSO THAT IN SPITE OF INCREASE IN TAXES MADE IN ROOSEVELT ADMINISTRATION AS I

---

167. The mother of three children all under the age of six, forty-three-year-old Agnes Fitzgerald Gargan had died in her sleep of an embolism on the night of September 17.
168. In giving out copies of *I'm for Roosevelt* to friends, Ellin Mackay Berlin, Mrs. Irving Berlin, had been met with "second and third hand" rumors of JPK's predictions both of vastly increased taxes in the second Roosevelt administration and of his own imminent appointment as secretary of the treasury.

POINTED OUT IN MY ARTICLE IN THE NEWYORK TIMES MAGAZINE OF SEPTEMBER
SIXTH ACTUAL TAXES WERE INCREASED IN MUCH GREATER PROPORTION IN
HOOVER THAN IN ROOSEVELT ADMINISTRATION STOP INCIDENTALLY ROOSEVELT
IS BECOMING STRONGER HERE EVERY DAY LOVE TO YOU AND IRVING

JOE KENNEDY

Joseph P. Kennedy to Harpo Marx: *Telegram*

OCTOBER 27, 1936

PRESIDENTS PHOTOGRAPH SENT TO YOU FROM WHITE HOUSE ONLY THE TERRIFIC
PRESSURE DELAYED IT AS LONG AS IT HAS HE WAS MORE THAN GLAD TO SEND IT
TO YOU STOP WE ALWAYS DELIVER KID COME ON EAST AFTER TUESDAY AND HELP
US CELEBRATE LOVE AND KISSES

JOE KENNEDY

Joseph P. Kennedy to G. A. Richards[169]

November 9, 1936

Dear Dick:

I am looking forward to the program you are sending me under a separate cover, although it hasn't arrived yet.

I guess the old saying, "Unto everyone that hath shall be given" still holds true. I am delighted though that we were all on the winning end.

I called Frank Murphy[170] and he told me that he was coming here soon and I am looking forward to seeing him.

I didn't hear the Padre Saturday night, but I read his speech. I think he's very wise in discontinuing.[171] I certainly don't feel that he has helped the cause very much during this campaign. It's a shame to have a man of his capabilities, energy and capacity on the wrong side.

I am looking forward to seeing you on your next visit here.

With warmest regards.

Very sincerely yours,

John F. Kennedy, 19, to Joseph P. Kennedy

32 Weld Hall, Cambridge, 22/11/36

Dear Dad:

Enclosed is a check for $40.00 — and one for Ed for $20.00. Times are getting tough and I shall have to reduce my scale of living. Will see you Wednesday —

Love

Jack

---

169. President of the Goodwill Station of Detroit, Michigan, a competitor to the CBS affiliate from which Father Coughlin made his weekly broadcasts.
170. Frank Murphy (1890–1949), governor of Michigan, 1936–39.
171. During his broadcast on November 7, Coughlin had admitted the decisive defeat of his National Union for Social Justice in the wake of the Democratic landslide on November 3. Further, Coughlin asserted that he was "hereby withdrawing from all radio activity in the best interests of all the people," and that the remnants of the NUSJ would assume an unaccustomed "policy of silence" with regard to the administration.

Joseph P. Kennedy to James Roosevelt

Dear Jimmie:

If I were a real gentleman I would be writing this letter to you by long hand. I know that if you or Betsy were writing to me it would be by hand and if you should write to me I am hoping you would not write by hand so that the crime would not be too great.

This introduction is to begin to thank you for your very swell Christmas gift. The studs arrived and there was no card so I had to call the Brooks Bros., to find out who sent them. Hence the delay in the acknowledgment. You know as far as I am concerned you are young people and struggling to get along and I am your foster-father, so as far as I am concerned it will always make me happy if you are doing well and not spending all your money on an old guy like me.

I'll drop in on you one of these days and see how things are going in Washington. My love to you both,

Sincerely,
JOSEPH P. KENNEDY

Rosemary, 18, Kathleen, 16, Eunice, 15, Patricia, 12, Robert, 11, Jean, 8, and Edward Kennedy, 4: *"President Roosevelt's Second Inauguration."*[172]

We arrived in Washington, D.C., about 6.30, January 19th, 1937. We went immediately to the Hotel. After cleaning up we went to the Mayflower for dinner, while we were there we saw Postmaster General Farley, Jack Demsey[173] and other well-known people.

On Wednesday we went to the luncheon in the Ball room of the WhiteHouse. There were about three thousand guests. We saw Secretary of Commerce Roper, Secretary of State, Cordell Hull, Vice presidend Garner, Senator Robinson[174] and the President's Mother.[175]

We talked with the President's secretary, Mr. Mc Intire, and James Roosevelt, who took us in for an Interview with his father. President Roosevelt said, "It is about time you came. How is your father? How can I put my arm around any of you?. Which is the oldest? You are all so big."

The Inaugaration.

On Tuesday, the 19th of January, six of us Kennedy's took a trip to Washington to be present at the Inauguration of President Roosevelt the next day. On arriving in Washington we went to the Mayflower Hotel where we had dinner. Afterwards we drove around the city, admiring the handsome buildings and beautiful parks of Washington.

The next day we felt very excited for we were going to meet the President himself in person, and witness the Inauguration which was very interesting. The President made a splendid speech, but the ceremony was in a great measure spoiled by the heavy rain which lasted all day. We enjoyed our visit with the President very much. He and Mrs. Roosevelt were very friendly with us, and we all had a great time.

172. The Moores and Miss Dunn, the governess, had accompanied them to Washington.
173. Jack Dempsey (1895–1983), World Heavyweight Champion, 1919–1926.
174. Joseph Taylor Robinson (1872–1937), Senate majority leader and a native of Arkansas.
175. Sara Delano Roosevelt (1885–1941).

After the luncheon we went to see the Inaugural parade. Mr. Moore did not think we should stand in the rain to hear the President's speech. We saw Mr. Morganthau at the Parade. He said "Hello," to us.

At five o'oclock we all went to the reception in the Grand Ball room in the White House. Mrs. Roosevelt and some others were in the receiving line. Mrs. Roosevelt did not realize who we were until we had almost gone by. She spoke to us and said, "This is the Kennedy's, isn't it?"

Later we talked with Barbara Cushing and Betsy Roosevelt. We met Postmaster General Farley, Rear Admiral Grayson,[176] Secretary of Treasury, Morganthau, Frankfurter of Harvard, and Postmaster Tatue[177] of Boston.

On the train coming back we met Mr. McSweeney of Boston.

Jean Kennedy, 8, to Rose and Joseph P. Kennedy

Bronxville, Jan — 26, 1937

Dear Daddy & Mother,

This is to tell you about my trip to Washington. After coming from the train, we went to the Brighton Hotel. Then we went to the mayflower Hotel for supper. While there, we met monisighor Lavalle,[178] Postmaster Tauge of Boston; Mr & Mrs Joseph Maynard. After supper Bob & I went back to the Hotel and went to bed with Miss Dunn. The next day we woke up and had Breakfast in our room. We couldn't here the President's speech because it was raining so hard. Then we hired a car and rode to the whitehouse. We talked a while with some people then we formed in a line to meet Mrs Roosevelt. Then we went to lunch. There we met the Postmaster Farley, Betsey and Jimmie & The President. He shook hands with us. and said well it was about time. He asked who was the oldest We all said Hello. We went to the reception and saw the Parade and then we went home.

Thank you very much for letting us go Daddy.

Much   Love   Jean

XXXXXXXXXXXXXXXXXXXXXXXXXXXXXXXXXXXXXXXXXXXXXXXXXXOOOOOOO
OOOOOOOOOOOOOOOOOOOOOOOOOOOOOOOOOOOOOOOOOOOOOOOOO

Jean

John F. Kennedy, 19, to Joseph P. Kennedy

Weld Hall, Thursday afternoon, Feb. 11, 1937

Dear Dad:

Mother told me you were rather upset about my not getting back on time. However, when I found Mother wanted me to stay over due to the cold, I wired up and found that it made no difference as & it was not like the end of vacation — so it turned out allright.

Had dinner with Sir Paul[179] Monday night and went out with him a bit. He certainly enjoyed himself down there.

---

176. Rear Admiral Cary Travers Grayson (1879–1938), chairman of both the American Red Cross and of the Roosevelt Inaugural Committee.
177. That is, Peter Francis Tague (1871–1941), former Democratic Massachusetts congressman, 1915–1919, and postmaster general of Boston, 1936–41.
178. Monsignor Michael Lavelle, rector of St. Patrick's Cathedral, 1887–1939.
179. That is, Paul Murphy, his father's secretary and assistant.

The swimming has been going O.K. and I'm now in a strict training due to having five meets the next four weeks. Football begins two days later. Went down and met Dick Harlow[180] yesterday who was very friendly

Going in tonight for Grandpa's birthday. Mother came up with me and I think is going back to-morrow. The whole family is looking well. Rose was out with us Monday, and had a good time I think, and was up to see Kik Sunday — The nuns had great reports about her. Thats about all the news except got 2 C+'s and 2 Bs with 3 B's and a 1 C+ so we came out all-right. Please ~~rember~~ remember me to Ed & Mrs. Moore etc. and thanks very much for the vacation, as I had a great time.

Love

Jack

Joseph P. Kennedy to Joseph P. Kennedy, Jr., 21

Palm Beach, February 15th, 1937

Dear Joe:

I was delighted to get your wire and talk with you on the phone the other night. It really was tough luck to miss the Dean's list by such a close call, but it was a real worth while effort and I am sure you will make it later on. Incidentally it is much closer than your father ever got to it.

I am still a little bit concerned about your going back and trying foot-ball again. I know how anxious you are to make your letter, but after a fellow has been banged up the way you have, and as you have only one more year to go before you go out in the world, you should think very seriously whether it is worth while or not. I do not want to be in the position of telling you not to, but all my judgment urges me to at least ask you to give it grave consideration. I would by all means talk to Dr. Richards before I made any plans, because in his conversation with me he thought the knee should be taken care of still some time to come.

We have had a bad week here in the weather, but now it is coming along beautifully. I certainly have no objection to having Tom come down for Easter, he is a very nice boy and I am sure we can fit him in very nicely. Let me know your plans and I will talk it over with Mother.

You are doing a swell job there and I am proud of you.

Love,

Joseph P. Kennedy to John F. Kennedy, 19

Palm Beach, February 15th, 1937

Dear Jack:

I was not particularly upset about your not getting back on time as I feel you are doing such a good job up there, but some little thing like that might put you off on the wrong foot and then again it may give people the idea that you were expecting privileges that other people could not enjoy. However, I am glad you are back and I think you and Joe did a swell job on your marks.

I am impressed with the almost complete turn around you have made in yourself in the last year, you know I always felt you had great possibilities and I think now you are starting to avail yourself of them. You are making a great hit with the older people

---

180. Richard Cresson Harlow (1891–1962), Harvard football coach, 1935–48, Ivy League Coach of the Year for 1937, and custodian of birds' nests and eggs at Harvard's Museum of Comparative Zoology.

and they are very much impressed with your discussions and looking on you with a great deal of respect. For your own satisfaction this is really worth-while.

I talked with Mother on the phone last night, she is coming down this week. Said she had a grand time in Boston and she was more than pleased with you and Joe. Rosemary had a marvelous time also and really does not require many gestures like this to make her life worth while.

The weather after you left was bad for almost the whole week, in fact it was raining for three days, so you were most fortunate in the break you got on the weather.

I went to the Colony Saturday night and I saw Mrs. Dewar smiling and shaking all over the floor. My golf is completely gone, I can't beat anybody but O'Leary[181] and Heffernan. Arthur Brown, the artist,[182] is staying here with LeRoy Ward[183] for a couple of days and he again told me that he would take care of you and Joe for any original drawings that you want for your rooms. Maybe you can get some of the originals of Olive from some of the artists that are doing them.

Good luck to you on the swimming and as to foot-ball, remember to be as good as the spirit is. You ought to weigh somewhere about 170.

Love,

Joseph P. Kennedy to Kathleen Kennedy, 16

February 15th, 1937

Dear Kick:

You were a darling to send the valentine. The children sent me a box of candy from Bailey's in a valentine heart, but as I have sworn off candy for Lent I will have to be generous in passing it out or take a chance on it's not spoiling before Easter Monday.

I got a letter from Jack saying he had been up to see you and that the Nuns thought you were pretty good. I think that is really a great tribute to you, knowing how you felt about going back to the convent, to have made as big a success as you have of it. But then I always knew you had lots of grand qualities and have only harped on one or two bad ones and I am sure you will fix them up.

Both Joe and Jack did very well on the examinations at Harvard and I have just written them congratulating them. I am expecting Mother right after the birthdays this week and then we will plan about Easter. I think it would be nice if we were all down here, but we will see.

Thanks again for the valentine and loads of love,

Joseph P. Kennedy to Louise Regan[184]

February 15th, 1937

Dear Louise:

I can quite understand your anxiety about the future of your young sons. I have it to a greater degree than you for I am now planning for quite a group and I become more conscious of the fact that it is very difficult to lay out a program for a boy without having the slightest idea of how his tendencies run. To have a boy say he wants to go in

---

181. Edward J. O'Leary (d. 1964), president of JPK's Somerset Importers.
182. Magazine illustrator Arthur William Brown (1881–1966).
183. Society architect and interior designer LeRoy Pierrepont "Sport" Ward, whom JPK had met through Gloria Swanson in 1928.
184. A fellow native of East Boston.

business or be an architect or be a painter is really not enough to pass a judgment on the type of thing that he can do best.

While I would be delighted to help you I do not know just where to start in. I am completely at a loss as to my older boy myself because while he has taken about the same course that Herbert has and seems to have the same tendencies, I am still not at all sure I can pick out the thing that would suit him best.

When I was at college I had the same indecision as I had no well defined plan until I got out and tried on my own to see what I fitted into best. I know that this is not very helpful advice it is very honest and is the result of my own experience and the result of my planning for young Joe.

Of course I will be delighted to help him if he gets an idea as to just what particular place he would like to go and I think I will do both him and yourself the greatest service by trying to help along that line.

In the meantime, I will be in Boston sometime late in the spring and will be pleased to have a talk with him. With warmest regards to Neil and yourself, I am

Sincerely,

Joseph P. Kennedy to Missy LeHand: *Telegram*

FEB 17 1937

IF AFTER WHAT I CALLED THE AIR PLANE COMPANY YESTERDAY MORNING THEY DONT THROW THE STONE CRABS OFF THE PLANE FOR SPITE YOU WILL HAVE THEM IN WASHINGTON TOMORROW AFTERNOON THEY ARE BEING COOKED AND PACKED IN DRY ICE AND LEAVING HERE AT NINE THIRTY THURSDAY MORNING IN FACT THE HEAD OF THE AIR PLANE COMPANY SAID HE WOULD MUCH RATHER CARRY STONE CRABS THAN CARRY ONE KENNEDY THE WORST CRAB HE EVER KNEW FOR A WHILE YESTERDAY IT LOOKED LIKE THEY WERE GOING TO PUT A SEAT ON ONE OF THE WINGS THEY TOLD ME TODAY THEY WISHED I'D GONE BECAUSE THE PLANE CAME DOWN IN RALEIGH AND STAYED THERE ALL NIGHT I CERTAINLY WOULD HAVE ENJOYED THAT ANYHOW THE CRAB WILL BE THERE TOMORROW AND THEY BETTER BE GOOD BEST TO ALL[185]

JOE

Joseph P. Kennedy to Franklin Roosevelt

March 2, 1937

My dear Mr. President:-

I am deeply honored by the suggestion in your letter of February twenty-sixth that I accept the appointment as Chairman of the Maritime Commission.[186]

As I have told you many times, I felt that I was through with the Government service, but if you feel that I can be of any help at all in the present situation, of course, I am delighted to serve.

185. By way of thanking JPK on behalf of the president, Missy and Betsey, James Roosevelt wired, "Wish to report stone crabs spent comfortable night in interior in spite previous reports they became air sick at Richmond. All greatly enjoyed your treat . . ."

186. The Merchant Marine Act of 1936 had provided for the establishment of an independent regulatory body to implement, oversee and regulate the Law's attempts to subsidize, and thereby modernize a flagging American merchant shipping and shipbuilding industry. On February 26, the president had asked JPK to chair the commission.

I think, however, that there is one thing you should know about my holdings of securities that might affect my appointment under Section 201-B of the Act.

I am the holder of record of eleven hundred shares of Todd Ship Yards, Incorporated, whose business primarily is ship repairs. This stock has been in my family approximately twenty years. It pays $2.00 a year and sells at approximately $55.00 a share. The assets of the Todd Corporation are approximately between twenty and twenty-five million dollars and there are approximately 220 odd thousand shares of stock, so that my holdings are less than 1/2 of 1%. However, I feel that you and the Senate should know of my ownership of this block before any steps are taken for my appointment.

If this does not bar me as a member I shall be pleased to serve.

Very respectfully yours,

Joseph P. Kennedy to Royal Copeland

March 12, 1937

My dear Senator Copeland:

On my return to New York I had a survey made of all my holdings that might affect my appointment to the Maritime Commission. I think you should have this information when consideration of my name comes up. The restrictions as to qualifications are so far reaching that I am quite concerned about my eligibility. With this in mind, I sent today to Mr. James Roosevelt for the attention of his father the following telegram:

On my return to my office yesterday I had my secretary go over all my securities and holdings stop one of my assets is a twenty thousand mortgage on a sixty-five foot oil carrier with a capacity of fifty thousand gallons stop this is operated privately by my brother-in-law in Boston Harbor and is not a member of any system or any company stop I own this as a result of a twenty thousand dollar loan I made him and he put a mortgage on the oil tanker of his own volition I have never received any interest on this mortgage stop I also own Three Hundred shares Union Pacific Railroad stock it is possible they may have some steamships, I don't know stop Mrs. Kennedy owns in her own name Five Thousand Atlantic Gulf and West Indies Steamship Lines Bonds which have been in our family for many years stop Mrs. Kennedy has owned them for fifteen years stop I understand also that you and Mr. Black[187] have been informed that a Trust established for the benefit of my children in Nineteen Hundred and Twenty Six owns entire stock of Fred Thomson Productions Inc. Which in turn owns Thirty Three Hundred shares Todd Shipyards which stock has also been in my family for a number of years stop this Trust is irrevocable and I have no control over it and it was so decided by the Treasury Department some years back stop these seem to be the only possible links connecting me with the industry stop I believe before the Committee takes action on my appointment that you should be informed of all the above facts.

187. Although he would object to the confirmation of three of the five prospective maritime commissioners, on March 26 Senator Hugo Lafayette Black (1886–1971), chairman of the Committee on Education and Labor, would voice no opposition to the Senate resolution declaring JPK eligible to assume the chairmanship despite his long-held shipping and shipbuilding interests.

If in the judgment of the Committee they see fit to recommend me and I am approved by the Senate, it is my desire to rid myself of my holdings of 1,100 shares of Todd Shipyards, of which you have already been advised. This will necessitate my paying a rather substantial income tax because a fairly sizable profit has accrued.

The procedure I should like to follow, if agreeable to your Committee, is to turn the stock over to Mr. Elisha Walker, senior partner of Kuhn, Loeb & Co., with instructions to dispose of it within the next sixty days. The reason for my putting a time limit on it is because very rarely if ever is any of the stock sold, and as the newspapers have already given notice that I propose to sell it, I feel there will be a thin market and it would take a little time to dispose of it. I shall put it beyond my control, however, before taking the oath of office. I think an understanding of these facts will clear my position much more satisfactorily, at least in my own mind.

Very respectfully yours,
Joseph P. Kennedy

Rosemary, 18, Eunice, 15, Patricia, 12, Robert, 11, Jean, 9, and Edward Kennedy, 5, to Joseph P. Kennedy

Daddy Dear:

> Here's a ship from
> us, one and all,
> Guaranteed to last
> thru waves that
> rise and fall.
> Though it only
> cost a dime
> It's for the <u>Best</u>
> Commissioner of
> the Maritime.

> Ted
> Rosemary
> Jean
> Robert
> Patricia
> Eunice

Joseph P. Kennedy to James F. Byrnes[188]

March 15, 1937

Dear Jim:

Thank you very much for your note.

To be very honest with you I had a great hesitancy in taking this job. I had received a couple of large assignments which were along the lines I like and they would have proved very profitable, but the President made his appeal on such a personal basis that

---

188. James Francis Byrnes (1879–1972), Democratic senator of South Carolina.

there was nothing for me to do but go back into Government service. I know it's a hectic job but I'll give it all I have, with the hope that we will get good results.

I am planning to take the same house I had before if possible. If by any chance the boys hold you in Session for the summer we'll at least have some nice cool mint juleps and Boston lobster. If I am confirmed, I expect to be in Washington from next Friday on, and then I'd like to see you as often as you can find time to see me.

With warmest regards.

Very sincerely yours,

Joseph P. Kennedy to John Boettiger[189]

March 22, 1937

Dear John:

Thanks to the Post-Intelligencer and thank to the publisher for his kind words, but boy, is this a job! I should love to tell you the story how I got into this mess and you and Anna would have plenty of laughs. I give up my business, give up my leisure to take up the most unworkable bill I ever read in my life, but you know that man's winning ways.

It is pretty good when you can give up a perfectly good reputation and throw it in the ash can when you can be of service, but you know. If you are going through with a guy you must go all the way through.

Arthur Krock just telephoned me and he does not think my luck will hold and I probably will be confirmed, although there is still a great doubt.[190] I will be with you the first chance I get.

Love to Anna and yourself.

Sincerely,

John F. Kennedy, 19, to Joseph P. Kennedy

32 Weld [April 19, 1937]

Dear Dad:

Things are going pretty well up here, though am very busy. Play football twice a week and swim the other times. In the University handicap championships got second — The man who beat me having seven seconds which was a bit too much. Talked with mother about a week ago and she said that there was a mix up over my not phoning the night before. I did not get in to N.Y. until six thirty and was under the impression that you both were in town going to the Ballet. Therefore, I thought I would phone the next night when you were both there. However, I should have phoned the house anyway though, and am sorry I didn't.

Went in last Sat. Night to see "The Gondoliers" D'Oly Carte productions with Dent Friedberg. It was much better that I thought it would be and I think that someone should tell the Head that the school productions are certainly no way to get anyone to like G & S. Have been pretty busy on the Smoker[191] — went with Mr Sternberg and we

---

189. John Boettiger (1900–1950), publisher of the *Seattle Post Intelligencer*, 1936–45, and (having married the recently divorced Anna Roosevelt Dall in January 1935) son-in-law of the president.
190. On March 30 the president would sign into law the unprecedented joint resolution allowing JPK to take the Maritime Commission chairmanship despite his interest in Todd Shipyards.
191. Jack was on the committee to organize the Harvard Freshman Smoker, as Joe had been before him.

are going to get the show out from the Met. Also we may be able to get Gertrude Niesen who should be rather good.[192] Thought I would get Grandpa to get Bill Cunningham[193] & Clarence De Mar[194] and I was wondering if you could get Neal O'Hara, or should I get Grandpa to try & do this too. It is going to take place two weeks from tomorrow that is Tuesday — May 4th I would like to get O'Hara to go go on for about ten or fifteen minutes [*around 9:15 to 10:00*]. Could you let me know right away if you are going to contact him or whether Grandpa should and if you do contact him what the results are as we will have to make out a schedule.

We wanted to get some sort of Ginger ale or Coco-Cola for a refreshment and due to the expense was wondering about ~~contacting~~ getting in touch with Hartman about seeing if there is some ~~Ct~~ company that would donate their ginger-ale for advertising purposes or some cookie company that ~~is~~ would do the same. I shall ask Johnny Ford about it anyway but if you have any ideas I wish you would let me know as quickly as possible.

When do you think you will be up here? Please remember me to Ed.

Love
Jack

We are planning our trip abroad. Both Lem and I think that the best part of its trip would be getting into Spain either as newspaper correspondents or as members of the Red Cross for about 3 weeks. If we can get in there it will ~~change~~ effect our plans so hope you will be able to work it. Could you let me know the chances of it being O.K. Am writing Jack Kennedy.[195]

Joseph P. Kennedy to Marion Davies: *Telegram*

APRIL 23, 1937

DEAR MARIAN THERE IS NOTHING IN THE WORLD I WOULD LIKE BETTER THAN TO ATTEND THE CIRCUS TO BE GIVEN FOR MR HEARST STOP BUT FIND MYSELF COMPLETELY IMMERSED IN THE AFFAIRS OF THE MARITIME COMMISSION IN WASHINGTON AND THE WEEKENDS ON MATTERS IN CONNECTION WITH MR HEARSTS INTERESTS SO THINK I HAD BETTER WORK A WHILE LONGER AND GET OUT AS SOON AS POSSIBLE STOP YOU WERE SWEET TO THINK OF ME AND I APPRECIATE IT VERY MUCH

JOE KENNEDY

Joseph P. Kennedy to Arthur Houghton: *Telegram*[196]

MAY 4, 1937

BERNARD BARUCH IS ON HIS WAY TO HOLLYWOOD. I HAVE ADVISED HIM TO WIRE YOU THE TIME OF HIS ARRIVAL. I AM SURE EVERYBODY OUT THERE WILL BE PLEASED TO ENTERTAIN HIM. INCIDENTALLY THEY SHOULD BE [*SIC*] HE IS A GREAT

---

192 Singer and radio personality Gertrude Niesen (1910–75).
193. Radio Commentator, *Boston Post* sportswriter, and after-dinner speaker Elijah William "Bill" Cunningham (1896–1960).
194. Clarence De Mar (1888–1958), seven-time Boston Marathon winner and three-time Olympian.
195. The RKO representative in London.
196. He was currently working at the Hays Office.

CITIZEN. HE IS STILL PARTIAL TO BEAUTIFUL BLONDES, HOWEVER. I HAVE TOLD HIM YOU WOULD MEET HIM ON RECEIPT OF A TELEGRAM AND SEE THAT EVERYTHING IS DONE TO HIS HEART'S CONTENT. BEST TO YOURSELF AND JOE.[197]

JOE KENNEDY

Joseph P. Kennedy to Robert Fisher

May 12, 1937

Dear Bob:

I can't say your invitation comes as a surprise because I have been given warning about it for about four months.[198] I won't be like a coy debutante but will say I'll be there. It is certain, however, I'll not talk more than fifteen minutes, and for the honor and glory of Kennedy, [*Campbell*],[199] Fisher and Company. I'll do the best I can.

Rose is in Boston this week and I told her to contact somebody to talk to seriously as to the arrangements to be made for the children there. As I have told you before, I lack the enthusiasm I should have but maybe you can stir me up.

With best regards.

Sincerely,

Joseph P. Kennedy to Russell Davenport[200]

May 17, 1937

Dear Mr. Davenport:

Generally, my comment on this article is that it is permeated with distrust of my character, dislike of my occupations and social prejudice against my origin. If that is the kind of attitude Fortune wants to reflect, the choice is within your right to make.

If, however, you prefer to have the article written objectively, without precise aspersions and nasty insinuations, I have marked fifty-four inaccuracies in as many places. These I should be glad to point out to you if and when you come to see me on that understanding. I can then also answer the question you say FORTUNE must answer: "Are you in there just to organize a commission, or is this shipping business a career?"

Awaiting your reply, I am

Sincerely yours,

---

197. Joseph Ignatius Breen (1890–1965), director of Production Code Administration at the Hays Office, which vetted and censored scripts for production and completed films for release.
198. Fisher had proffered the official invitation for JPK to speak at their upcoming twenty-fifth Harvard College reunion dinner. On June 23, JPK's short, enthusiastic review of the New Deal before his fellow members of the class of 1912 was to be met by boos and catcalls.
199. Thomas Joseph Campbell (1866–1972), JPK's former German A classmate, Crimson baseball teammate and fellow Institute of 1770 member, was the current vice president of the Norfolk County Trust Company.
200. Russell Wheeler Davenport (1899–1954), managing editor of *Fortune* magazine, had agreed to send JPK the first completed draft of the biographical article on him that journalist Harry Looker was preparing for September's "monumental survey of U.S. shipping."

Joseph P. Kennedy to Russell Davenport: *Draft*

May 24, 1937

Dear Mr. Davenport:

I am taking you at your word and give you the trust you asked for by enclosing a number of examples of the inaccuracies I mentioned paralleled with the correct statement in such instances as I wished to make it. In the case of certain personal references, I do not wish to make the facts public but am pointing to the inaccuracies in these instances also.

I shall expect you at the end of the month with the rewritten manuscript which I assume you can leave with me for a few days.

Very truly yours,
Joseph P. Kennedy

Statement[201]

Observation[202]

Page 2. "[. . . when shortly ago, March eighth, Mr. Roosevelt, after delaying the naming of a permanent Maritime Commission from the end of October to the beginning of March, announced his appointments, and the name of Joseph Patrick Kennedy led all the rest, there was hardly a ripple or repercussion] except where the New York *Times* column of the administration's innocuous [Arthur Krock ran for the day a nice little personality piece all about how the President's card-index mind had remembered Joe and given him another hard job.]"

Frank R. Kent in the Baltimore Sun was among several others who commented kindly and favorably, and if you could prove that Mr. Krock belongs to the Administration, that is his business.

Page 3. "* * * he was manifestly without real experience with ships (despite a wartime job with Bethlehem Shipbuilding), less with shipping and none with labor."

As Assistant General Manager of the Fore River Shipyards during the war I had experience with ships and labor of a very practical and thorough kind.

Page 4. "The three men [Kennedy, Landis and Pecora] sweated, cajoled, argued, fought for an hour to decide which of two of them was to be elected Chairman of the Commission," etc. "The swart Sicilian Pecora did not wish to serve if Kennedy was to be Chairman."

There was no fighting, cajoling, or arguing. Pecora did not take the position that he did not wish to serve if Kennedy was to be Chairman. Nor did he at any time attempt to prevent the naming of Kennedy as Chairman.

Page 4. "[He (JPK) had been one of the operators of the Libbey-Owens-Ford pool which Pecora had investigated as chief in-

If out of Pecora's findings, as you say, had come all these laws, and remembering the testimony of the Morgan partners, how

201. Here, I have expanded on some of these excerpted "Statements" taken from the first (and only) draft of Looker's "Kennedy" article in order to make them more immediately accessible to the reader.—AS
202. He had drafted these "Observations" (or retorts to Looker) with Arthur Krock's help.

quisitor of the Norbeck Senate investigation. Begun by a Republican Committee and revitalized by Democratic desire to put the 'money changers' on the spot, this inquiry had revealed the sometimes stupid, sometimes scandalous details of banking, industrial finance and the mainsprings of the Stock Exchange;] its high news point had been the episode of the midget [manoeuvered by a press agent to suddenly appear upon the broad knee of a witness, the startled Mr. J. Pierrepont Morgan. Out of Pecora's findings had come the Securities Act of 1933, the national blue-sky law, and the Securities and Exchange act of 1934 which had created this Securities and Exchange Commission.]"

can you rate the parallel statement as a responsible appraisal?

Page 4. "as a lawyer [Pecora] preferred the lean, energetic Landis * * * for the Chairmanship", etc.

Pecora never preferred Landis.

Page 5. "Editors asked [their reporters after JPK's emergence as Chairman of the SEC], "Just who is Kennedy; all about him.?' The reporters could only answer[: ... he's some kind of a corporation organizer, financial expert and speculator who seems to have made a lot of money . . . He rode F.D.'s electioneering train . . .]"

Kennedy was known throughout the campaign to all the important Washington correspondents whose business it is to follow Presidential candidates while on tour. There had been a good deal of publicity about Kennedy at that time.

Page 5. "Told to 'Go back and get more from Kennedy himself,' the correspondents were met by little more than his statement than he was 'no sucker.'"

I never made any such remark in my life.

Page 5. "* * * Kennedy was a 'cold blooded Bear of exceptional shrewdness who, in the period 1928–1932, seems to have cleaned up nearly five millions.'"

The facts: the amount ridiculous. Mr. Looker was so informed.

Page 6. "* * * his Chairmanship was fought, within the Commission on grounds of integrity;" etc.

His Chairmanship was never fought on any grounds within the Commission.

Page 6. "To repeat: ships, shipbuilding, ship operation, the handling of labor are unknown to him."

Same answer as to previous statement of similar kind.

Page 7. "A place in the government of the Commonwealth made, then as now, more common the opportunities for the acquisition of wealth and [his father] Patrick Kennedy, who was a partner in Kennedy & Quigley's Saloon on Border Street in East Boston, became a liquor wholesaler and part owner of another saloon * * *".

The inference here is mean and contemptible. My father's reputation could never be touched by any such aspersion.

Page 7. "The voices raised were the shrill ones of Joe's sisters, [. . . in the excitement of Ward Club and Church Society outings at the near Boston Beaches . . .]

This speaks for itself.

. . . in the midst of the swarming crowds about the clam shucking tables, on the fringes of the pushing about beer barrel [bunging, awed by the perfervid periods of political speechmaking.]"

It may seem strange, but I have yet to attend a meeting such as you describe.

Page 9. "[But Joe Kennedy was not ashamed . . .] that he and his room mate, Bill Donovan[203][, had run a rubberneck charabank from Boston to Lexington] ." etc.

I never had a room mate named Bill Donovan, and the man I was associated with in the sight seeing business was Joe Donovan.

Page 9. "[While Joe was in college . . . the family moved to . . .] dismal Winthrop".

I never heard that description of a delightful Boston suburb.

Page 9. [the Kennedy home in Winthrop was a] "gay place Sunday mornings when it was filled with Joe's friends and joyous Irish laughter, * * *."

The gatherings of half a dozen of my friends was on a Sunday night, and I dislike the descriptive term.

Page 10. "As for the rest of Harvard he made the Hasty Pudding Club * * *."

I also made the Institute of 1770, the Dickey, and D.U.

Page 10. "There is a persistent legend of a real estate venture during his senior year in college* * *" etc.

I never was in the real estate business while I was in college, and I never heard of any legend that I shoe-stringed the largest suburban development at Boston to that date. I was interested in a company after I finished college that did some of the large suburban development, one of them may be seen at the present time in Newton near Boston College.

203. Joseph Daniel Donovan (1888–1947), JPK's fellow Boston Latin alumnus, and best man at his wedding.

Page 10. "[But tangible evidence of a sizeable (college real estate) business there is none, though Joseph Patrick Kennedy] with that engaging Irish as well as Broadway and Hollywood actor's failing, of coming to believe as true most of what has been told about yourself, [half believes now that it may have been so.]"

I never heard it was particularly Irish, and I think it entirely inaccurate description of myself.

Page 11. "It was through the good offices of 'John F.' [Who viewed (JPK's bank examinership) as helping a likely lad to get a sure financial footing, the first requirement of the establishment of a political as well as any other kind of a family.]".

Mr. Fitzgerald may think and hope he secured this position, but it was really secured by Alfred P. Wellington, Treasurer of the Columbia Trust Company.

Page 11. ["In January, 1914, at the age of twenty-five, Joseph Patrick Kennedy became President of the Columbia Trust Company, the bank of which his father was a director. Since overnight he was publicized as the 'Boy Banker', the facts of his election became confused. Certainly he was not selected for his attainments nor the voting power : it was Irish Proxies."]

The entire paragraph of my election at the Columbia Trust Company is completely wrong. I was elected President of Columbia Trust Company because I went out and borrowed some money and bought stock which put me in a responsible position and the directors considered that I had the personal qualifications to carry out its functions.

Page 11. Paragraph beginning "And who, reasoned the Honorable the Mayor 'John F.'", etc.

This entire paragraph is completely wrong-down to the bottom of page 12.

Page 13. "[His selection for an executive position at the Fore River yards of Bethlehem Shipbuilding was due,] not to a 'discovery' by Mr. Charles Schwab as legend now would have it, [but to Guy Currier, Boston Attorney for Bethlehem, who had been ordered to find, if possible among the Boston banks, a man who could organize and watch the disbursements of large war allotments as well as one who was aggressive, quick and decisive . . .]"

I am reading this story for the first time in my life.

Page 13. "The record shows that he was the General Manager's general utility man, * * *".

I was the Assistant General Manager of the plant with the duties and responsibilities usually pertaining to such a position.

Page 13. "* * * and the launchings of Bethlehem's quota of the $3,000,000,000 ex-

The plant was not given over to building of freighters. It built destroyers and sub-

travagantly built battlecraft and the so-called 'one trip' freighters, [many of which were not ready for service until long after the Armistice]."

marines particularly; laid down practically no freighters.

Page 15. [At Hayden, Stone,] "Kennedy's concern was entirely with the execution of customers' orders and had nothing to do (as again legend now has it) with the investment banking business, new financing or syndicates.

I have never read that it ever did.

Page 16. "[. . . it was not long before Kennedy was found to be a remarkable market operator . . . His own comment on how to make money:] 'Toss a coin, you know what happens? Toss the coin and if the public calls it, you'll make money.'"

First, I never said any such thing, and second, I don't think it can be true because I don't yet understand quite what it means.

Page 16. "* * * he still sends flowers to Mrs. [Galen] Stone on her birthday."

I'm sorry — I don't. But I send them to her on Easter and Christmas.

Page 17. "Shortly thereafter Kennedy called [Walter] Howey" etc.

The complete story of the Yellow Cab incident as outlined here is 100% untrue.

Page 18. "Not incidentally it was, again, a case of pure personal politics: Kennedy saves his father-in-law with Howey;", etc.

This is also 100% untrue.

Page 19. "Obviously now, Kennedy's justifiable ambition to become a member of the firm [of Hayden, Stone] was not to be realized."

Kennedy never had any ambition to be partner of Hayden-Stone & Co. Therefore in fact, that conclusion drawn by the author is completely wrong.

Page 19. "The places where he looked were naturally those with which he was familiar at Hayden-Stone . . . and one of these was in the entertainment field, since the investment banking houses had acted as fiscal agent for British motion picture interests in America."

If it did, I never heard of it. It never had anything to do with what I went into.

Page 19. "Later he was to say, "I entered the amusement business [with the viewpoint of a banker. If, after the organization of a new corporation is running smoothly, I look around and get a good offer for my holdings, I will make a trade.]"

I just never said any such thing.

Page 19. "The details of Kennedy's purchase of FBO, like many other Kennedy details, are obscure."

What is strange about that? I dare say there are a great many enterprises being conducted by individuals in the United States, the details of which are not known to the public. This corporation was privately owned and had no public participation.

Page 20. "Certainly at the time FBO was one of the largest producers and heaviest losers in the industry."

It was neither.

Page 20. "The third [Gloria Productions film], 'Queen Kelly', which cost $800,000, was suppressed because Gloria, after all the work was done, wondered whether or not it might be offense [sic] to the Church."

This is completely wrong.

Page 21. Sentence beginning "For example:" to end of paragraph. [" . . . when Kennedy took over the active management of FBO he was so excited with its possibilities, though it was a million dollars in the red, that his immediate rushing reorganization of it turned it so quickly into a money-maker that Radio Corporation of America bought a block of stock in it. 20,000 shares, in 1927 and Keith Albee Orpheum . . . followed suit in 1928."]

This is a very inaccurate and poor description of me at work.

Page 21. "Kennedy was making 'conservative cost' pictures, averaging $70,000 * * *".

They averaged about $30,000.

Page 21. "From now on, such was the glamor of his action, Kennedy became more and more of a legendary figure, if not to his own immediate family than surely to even his sisters, his father-in-law the ex-mayor and all the collaterals."

Contacts with my immediate family have never ceased to be intimate and continuous.

Page 21. "He was busy and increasingly dictatorial, for as President and Chairman of the FBO (1926-29) he was exhibiting to the motion picture industry an amazing ability for organization and management."

I don't believe it—what is the evidence.

Page 22. "DeMille's salary was a million dollars a year and his contract was so ac-

"Allowed" is a very inaccurate and misleading word.

cordion-pleated that he was allowed to run the company [Pathé] into the ground if he wished and then take equipment * * *", etc.

Page 23. "As for Pathe, [JPK] liquidated its various stock holdings for a total of about four and a half millions [and with it bought Keith-Albee-Orpheum stock—the exact amount not known.]"

I haven't the slightest idea what this means. The description of the discussion is completely a mystery to me.

Page 23. "In February, 1928, Kennedy appeared on the board of directors of the aforementioned K.A.O. presumably to represent this interest purchased for Pathe."

What interest? I have no knowledge that they ever had one.

Page 23. "* * * in May, 1928, Kennedy together with J. J. Murdock President of Pathé [. . . bought on their own account some 200,000 shares of K.A.O. stock."]

Did not buy in their own account 200,000 shares of K.A.O. stock but were very incidental members of the group that did.

Page 23. "At K.A.O. Kennedy wielded the ax", etc., "making more of a shambles of organization."

If you save $900,000 a year is your organization a shambles?

Page 24. "The next step and the most involved situation, Kennedy thus explains [with the simplicity of omission: 'Early in 1928, some FBO stock was sold to KAO and RCA. Within six months RCA bought FBO from myself and my associates. In October I sold KAO to RFC—and RCA was now in stock control of the works.' These four sentences cover the whole of the complexities of the famous FBO-KAO merger to form the Radio Keith Orpheum Corporation]."

I never thus explained this in my life.

Page 24. "There seems to be no question that the merger" etc., to end [" . . . was Kennedy's conception from the beginning; the *denoument* being the joint achievement of himself and Sarnoff of the RCA. There is of course a legend in connection with it; Kennedy and Sarnoff settled it over a plate bluepoints, Sarnoff saying 'I'll swallow this,' and Kennedy 'I'll swallow that . . .'"]

This is all wrong.

Page 29. "[He was dangerous fighter (sic); often when he seemed most to fight] it was just Irish fun. As often when it seemed to be fun it was an attack by indiscretion. He could bellow like an Irish cop * * *."

I leave the taste and justice of this to you.

Page 29. "The only stock transactions were sales for personal cash needs;" etc.

There were no stock transactions while I was at the S.E.C.

Page 29. "Within the offices of the SEC in Washington [he was accomplishing much by off-hand methods which confounded the lengthy legal policy discussions of his colleagues, saying, as Counsel was upon the door-sill poised for departure, 'Oh, by-the-way, I want you to change that provision so it reads "may" instead of "may not" . . .]."

This never happened.

Page 30. "His resignation from the Commission held no hidden meaning, though an attempt was made to connect it with the President's appointment of J. D. Ross, [one of the Commissioners, to handle public utility matters exclusive of other business; this limited Kennedy; he was not having his way entirely and he could not get it]."

This was too trivial to call an attempt and since there was no truth in the suggestion what is the point of saying this. Also, the President's letter at the end of the S.E.C. period stated the prior understanding that I was to serve only a limited time.

Page 30. "[Certainly his first interest and enthusiasm had long since worn off;] he was tired with his first experience with drudgery; * * *"

Untrue.

Page 30. "There was reason to believe that never had he worked with such concentration."

Who says so and how does he know it?

Page 31. "In New York he kept easy office hours, often disappeared."

Not true.

Page 32. "[If you] want a ship or a line, cash or credit to build one or the other, or to raise your own pay, or to settle your ports of call, [or what freight you shall carry if at all, do not make the mistake of thinking Mr. (Edward) Moore supercargo]."

I make my own decisions as Chairman of this Commission.

Page 32. "He describes [his business in the private sector] as that of 'consultant,

This is untrue.

207

financial consultant' [or, better, finance and management adviser . . . I've been engaged in this business since I left the SEC, but my SEC duties and SEC views didn't affect my relations with those who became my clients afterwards; they're too big for that . . .]".

Page 33. "Upon his retirement [from the SEC]" etc., "Kennedy was back again in his bear market operations [giving financial and management advice . . . he was making large money in the market again, which adding to his consultant fees]."

This is untrue.

Page 33. "Kennedy had one great advantage[: RCA had ample resources; its fiscal year of 1934 ended with $23,679,000 in cash and securities; plus $5,000,000 for the sale, October, 1935 [sic] of half of RCA's interest in RKO to the Atlas Corporation and Lehman Brothers . . .]".

So had Owen Young, Gerard Swope[204] and representatives of both firms being on the R.C.A. Board in their attempt over a period of two years to work out a plan.

Page 35. "The net of Kennedy's report[, for which he received $50,000; ' . . . An inexcusable waste of your money to proceed further with the work of survey (sic) . . . unless such changes are made in management as I deem and essential preliminary . . .']."

Many more constructive quotations could be made than this one.

Page 36. "Some months after February, 1936[, a change became more and more apparent in Kennedy's whole make-up . . . A sharp, quick, realistic mind seemed to be dulling . . . In seven months he succeeded in composing 30,000 words. The result was a slim 149 page book, 'I'm for Roosevelt' . . . Kennedy wrote his book at Palm Beach and elsewhere, with Arthur Krock of the New York *Times* to polish the language and Mrs. Kennedy to revise the last third of the manuscript]."

This is all bunk of the whole writing of the book.

Page 36. "It was his main contribution to the second Roosevelt, 1936, campaign,

I didn't.

204. Gerard Swope (1872–1957), president of RCA's parent company, General Electric, 1922–39.

though he gestured another loan of $38,000."

Page 38. "So it is Kennedy***" etc. To end of paragraph. ["The sequence to bank president, general utility executive with Bethlehem Shipbuilding, Hayden Stone, motion pictures, speculation and counseling covers twenty-two years of searching for and successfully finding sources of quick profit rather than applying himself to constructive work where the results would bring profit . . ."]

What is one supposed to do who has normal ambition? As far as constructive work is concerned, I think my average will stand inspection. The sentence "As against twenty-two years of quick profit taking there are fourteen months of public service with the SEC" is an obvious and unjust slur.

Page 38. "Then there is a quality of mind which is a hazard — his willingness to be the hero."

I'd like to see the proof of that one.

Page 38. "Today he says of his Bethlehem Shipbuilding experience: ['I've built subs, destroyers, freighters and I know about the building of battleships']."

I never said any such thing — I said the yards built the ships.

Page 39. "Of the operation of ships he says, 'operating problems [are like those of the utility holding companies, aren't they?].'"

This is nonsense and I never said it.

Page 39. "Yet it would seem likely he possesses this ability. [Unquestionably he knows enough about men and management, the falsity of figures, corporation finance, evasion, trickery, the cracks which lie behind the facades of corporation structures, and is possessed of the personal intelligence service, built up through years of building the house that Joe builds, to inform himself of much which . . . would be a library of closed books to the honest and honorable Admirals of the Commission.]"

The use of the words "evasion" and "trickery" leave an unpleasant implication. I protest this picture of myself by Mr. Looker.

Page 39. "Obviously he was a profiteer."

By what standards is this conclusion arrived at and how can it be proved,

Page 39. "He is perfectly tailored [but . . . he used wire hangers which spoiled the shoulders of his coats; he is perfectly successful but, in his rise, he used a kind of intelligence which spoils the legend of public service . . .]."

I regard this as a prejudicial and slurring statement.

Page 40. "The financial and business community is looking to Kennedy to overcome his predilection to drop a situation the moment he has milked the profit out of it for himself [—in this case the kudos derived from establishing the Commission —and to follow through until the job is actually accomplished.]"

I have the same estimate of this as of the previous passage.

Page 40. "But if Kennedy has taken the Chairmanship of the Commission as another stepping stone to another place of power, [then it is a common situation which may be called Kennedy common —desiring a place in the Cabinet if a vacancy occurs, which Kennedy must know is a probability, and from there, looking forward to being addressed as His Excellency, the Honorable Joseph Kennedy, Governor of New York]."

I don't need this for a stepping stone to anything. And the suggestion about the governorship of New York is puerile.

Page 41. "Or does he wish to be a civilian Czar of U. S. Shipping?"

This is the bunk. What appeal would there be in that for me? You seem to be the only one who has any misunderstanding as to how I happened to come into this job.

Generally, may I reiterate my comment on this article that it is permeated with distrust of my character, dislike of my motives, and social prejudice against my origin. It is nonobjective and its facts are misleading and wrong.

Joseph P. Kennedy to Robert Benchley:[205] *Telegram*

MAY 24, 1937

DEAR BOB THERE ARE FORTY-SIX MAIL CONTRACTS WHICH HAVE TO BE SETTLED FOR THE UNITEDSTATES GOVERNMENT IN THE AMOUNT OF FOUR HUNDRED MILLION DOLLARS BEFORE JUNE THIRTIETH BUT THEY ARE SELLING ME THE IDEA OF COMING TO THE REUNION IF ONLY FOR A COUPLE OF DAYS. NOW THEY ARE BEGGING ME TO TRY TO SELL YOU THE IDEA TO COME. IF I HAVE TO BE THERE THERE IS NO ONE I'LL MISS MORE IF HE ISN'T THERE THAN YOU. I COULD TALK WITH ALL YOUR BOSSES AND GET YOU A LEAVE OF ABSENCE IF YOU WANTED IT. IT IS A LONG TOUGH HOT TRIP HERE AND I KNOW WHAT YOU ARE UP AGAINST BUT AFTER ALL YOU ARE THE GREAT BOY OF THE CLASS AND MY PARTICULAR PET SO LEAVE ALL THE BEAUTIFUL WOMEN OR BRING TWO ON IF YOU WANT TO AND TRY TO COME IF ONLY FOR SATURDAY NIGHT DINNER. I HAVE TO MAKE THE ADDRESS AND I WANT YOU TO INTRODUCE ME. MY PAST IS SAFE IN YOUR HANDS. WARMEST REGARDS SINCERELY YOURS

JOE

205. Critic, humorist, actor, Algonquin Round Table member and JPK's fellow 1912 Harvard alumnus, Robert Charles Benchley (1889–1945) had published a collection of sketches, *My Ten Years in a Quandary, and How They Grew*, in the previous year and was at the time screenwriting for Metro-Goldwyn-Mayer.

Joseph P. Kennedy to Russell Davenport

May 25, 1937

Dear Mr. Davenport:

I have no trouble in trusting you. The trouble is with Looker whose presentation of me is so cheap and tawdry that a rereading of the script sickened me. There are so many deliberate misrepresentations that I believe that either Looker has an ingrained hatred of the Irish, or a resentment against me personally. The only basis for personal antagonism I could think of might be Looker's anger at my failure to arrange for him a sale of his book to a moving picture company. This request was made to me in writing while he was engaged in [*sic*] Wilkin on the present draft. If such is the explanation for the article, the word "blackmail" despite all its ugly imputations is not too extreme a characterization.

After consulting with some friends in Washington, I am convinced that it would be useless to attempt to revise a draft so permeated with bias and incompetence.

However, when you come to see me I shall be glad to point out the numerous errors which have made this article unfair and dishonest.

Sincerely yours,

[John J. Burns]

Joseph P. Kennedy to Russell Davenport

May 28, 1937

My dear Mr. Davenport:

I am indeed very sorry that the whole subject of this article has come up. I am convinced, after talking with your Mr. Wood,[206] that it is just the brain-child of a psychopathic case and as such I am trying to forget.

I will be delighted to see you next Wednesday if you will notify my office on Tuesday what time you expect to arrive.

Sincerely yours,
Joseph P. Kennedy

Joseph P. Kennedy to Kathleen Kennedy, 17: *Telegram*

1937 JUN 9

CONGRATULATIONS TO MY DARLING ON HER GRADUATION STOP SATISFACTION YOU ARE GETTING OUT OF HAVING DONE A TOUGH JOB BEAUTIFULLY CANNOT COMPARE WITH THE HAPPINESS I AM GETTING OUT OF YOUR FINAL ACCOMPLISHMENT OF THIS YEARS WORK STOP YOU HAVE PROVED TO ME VERY DEFINITELY THAT YOU ARE MADE OF FINE STUFF AND I AM MORE THAN PROUD OF YOU STOP ALL KINDS OF GOOD LUCK AND LOVE STOP JUST FINISHED TALKING WITH MOTHER AND SHE TOLD ME YOU GRADUATED TODAY THE WISHES STILL GO AND YOU MAY ALSO WANT TO KNOW THAT THE UNITEDSTATES GOVERNMENT TODAY LAUNCHED ITS NEW BUILDING PROGRAM FOR THE MERCHANT MARINE AND IT WAS STARTED ON YOUR GRADUATION DAY LOVE=

DAD

---

206. As a peace offering, Davenport had sent a member of *Fortune*'s editorial staff to hear out JPK's grievances.

211

Joseph P. Kennedy to Russell Davenport

August 6, 1937

My dear Mr. Davenport:

I want to tell you how very much I appreciate the picture.[207] It will remind me of a great many things, not least of which is your masterful handling of a very difficult situation with a very irritable young man named Kennedy.

Please don't, by any chance, forget that Toscannini party.[208] It is the only shrine at which I worship today. The feet of clay become so apparent in most others.

My warmest personal regards and assuring you it has been a great pleasure working with you, I am

Sincerely yours,
Joseph P. Kennedy.

Joseph P. Kennedy to Eric Hodgins[209]

[August 13, 1937]

My dear Mr. Hodgins:

I have examined the September issue of Fortune with interest born of recent but close contact with our Merchant Marine, and I hope, a candid appreciation of our problems in securing what the president has told us the American Government owes its people—"ships in keeping with our national pride and national needs."

You people have done a grand job, the first concise, comprehensive, and colorful presentation of that many-sided venture heretofore vaguely known as "the Merchant Marine". Your work is especially valuable because it will cause people generally to realize that the Merchant Marine must be considered as the business investment not only of the stockholders in the various companies but of the nation. Your survey is an unbiased statement of facts based upon which the reader can formulate a sound opinion of his own. And the only firm foundation upon which the American Merchant Marine can rest is the opinion of the American people that they need a Merchant Marine and are willing to pay for it.

We in the Commission realize the proportions and ramifications of the job we have to do. We are concerned with delicate questions of international relations and the fluctuation of trade between the nations. We must deal with the labor problem so that passengers and shippers, as well as operators and crews, can count upon a square deal at all times. We are faced with the financial and operating problems of an industry in which hundreds of millions have been invested and in which more millions must be invested if it is to remain a going concern. And we must remember always that we are charged with the responsibility of securing one hundred cents of value for every dollar we spend.

We are attempting to do this job in an intelligent way. We have found that many fundamental questions which should have been answered before any attempt was made to build a Merchant Marine have received scant attention in the past. We are going to find the answers to those questions and base our policy for the future upon the hard facts of today. In so doing we are necessarily aided by investigations such as your representatives made in preparing this issue of Fortune. They made a conscientious inquiry, and have, I think, succeeded in developing genuine and helpful information. The

---

207. Before embarking for Europe with David Sarnoff, Davenport had sent a copy of the color photograph that was to appear in the September issue of *Fortune* along with the rewritten feature on JPK.
208. Arturo Toscannini (1867–1957) would be conducting at the Salzburg Festival that summer.
209. Eric Francis Hodgins (1899–1971), publisher of *Fortune*, 1937–41.

dissemination of such information, in my opinion, is not only of value to the Maritime Commission, but constitutes a real service to the American Merchant Marine.

I am sure that the entire personnel of the Commission joins me in wishes Fortune the very best of fortune for a splendid piece of work.

Very sincerely yours,
Joseph P. Kennedy,
Chairman

Joseph P. Kennedy to Enrico Galeazzi

August 25, 1937

Dear Mr. Galeazzi:

I just received a note from Jack telling me how kind you were to him during his stay and how honored he was with meeting Cardinal Pacelli and having an audience with the Pope.

The only trouble with all of this is that I have such a large family that those who have enjoyed your hospitality insist upon their return that the others must go to Rome to meet Mr. Galeazzi. So, if your patience will hold out, I will send the little Kennedys along as they gradually get old enough to travel.

Congress adjourned two days ago and the President is taking a holiday for about a month. In the meantime, I feel his appointment of Senator Black to the Supreme Court has started a rather prejudicial feeling against him, particularly in Catholic states. It is understood that Black has been a member of the Ku Klux Klan.[210] I have informed Jimmy Roosevelt that I thought that steps like we contemplate would be very helpful in the not too far distant future. Just as soon as there are any developments here, I will advise you.

Again thanking you for your kindness and hospitality to Jack, and with best regards to my friends in Rome, I am

Yours very sincerely,

Joseph P. Kennedy to William Reid

August 31, 1937

Dear Mr. Reid:

Your letter of August 19th showing American shipments for July is acknowledged and while our standing for July is fourth, the recent orders sent to you during July and August amounting to over 72,000 cases, will improve our position.

Due to various reasons, we carried over an excessive inventory which curtailed our purchases the early part of this year, but now that this situation has been corrected, our orders will be comparable with our sales. Our fiscal year begins December 1, 1936 and for the first nine months ending with September 1st, we shipped and billed 136,000 cases of Haig as against 98,000 for the same period the year previous. Our sales in August also show substantial increases; the figures are 20,139 cases as against 14,166 cases for the month of August last year. I still believe my estimate of approximately 220,000 cases for this year will be realized. This will show us an increase of 60,000 cases over last year.

---

210. On August 12, the president had nominated Senator Hugo Black of Alabama to the Supreme Court. Shortly after Black's confirmation and swearing-in, however, the *Pittsburgh Post Gazette* revealed that Black had been a member of the Klan from 1923 to 1925.

Canada Dry, taking advantage of their differential in cost of 5 shillings per case on Johnnie Walker Black, have recently taken some orders giving the jobber the benefit of this differential. Inasmuch as our wholesale and retail prices are identical and we both sell the same jobbers in many instances, the jobber is exerting more effort on Johnnie Walker because his profit is considerably greater — namely $1.25 per case. This is quite an incentive. As I have stated on numerous occasions, if this situation is not corrected it will be impossible for us to maintain our position on Pinch in competition with Johnnie Walker Black. The additional $100,000 they have to spend for advertising and sales promotion gives them a decided advantage. This we can discuss in person if my proposed trip to Europe materializes.

I realize fully Mr. Herd's illness and death has delayed our agreement and trust we will have it very soon.

I appreciate your feelings having recently taken over the responsibilities of Haig & Haig. You want to make a success. Your worries and mine are identical and you have my assurance that the entire Somerset organization is exerting its very best efforts to increase the sale of your brand in this market and I feel very definitely that when the year has passed, you will be pleased with the result of our showing.

Sincerely,
SOMERSET IMPORTERS, Ltd.,

Joseph P. Kennedy to Joseph Schenck[211]

October 13, 1937

Dear Joe,

A year ago last summer you were kind enough to come to my office and ask me to go along with you at the Twentieth Century-Fox. At that time I was unable to accept your offer because I was tied up with the Paramount situation, but I took the liberty of telling you what a difficult problem I thought you and Mr. Zanuck[212] had before you in disposing of any substantial blocks of your stock in Twentieth Century unless business continued at top speed and earnings were very substantial.

I am taking the liberty of writing you today to tell you the impression of a picture, which I have just seen, has made on me and the possible effect on your holdings. I refer to "Wife, Doctor and Nurse". I know this has received good notices, but I also know that in the church there is a feeling the bars are liable to come down on the decency problem again and it is felt that this picture has enough things about it to indicate such a situation exists.[213] Now, with the present market conditions, if anything like that should happen or any agitation should start again, your holdings would be not at all secure. I write you this because of our friendship and because of my admiration of Mr. Zanuck. I think it would be a good idea to watch this subject very closely. You have too much at stake to have something like that pull the props from under you.

With warmest personal regards.

Sincerely yours,

---

211. In 1933 the former chairman of United Artists cofounded Twentieth Century Pictures with Daryl Zanuck; in 1935 the company merged with Fox Studios.
212. The former writer for FBO and executive producer of the *Jazz Singer* at Warner Brothers, Darryl Francis Zanuck (1902–1979) was vice president and chief of production at Twentieth Century-Fox.
213. The National Legion of Decency had given Fox's *Wife, Doctor, Nurse* a B rating, which is to say that the organization had found the film to be "Morally Objectionable." "Films in this category are considered to contain elements dangerous to Christian morals or moral standards."

Kathleen Kennedy, 17, to Rose and Joseph P. Kennedy:
Spiritual Bouquet

Spiritual Bouquet

October 17, 1937

Masses –	100
Communions –	100
Rosaries –	100
Acts –	25

From
Kathleen
with much
love

Joseph P. Kennedy to Joseph Curran[214]

November 4, 1937

Dear Sir:

This will acknowledge receipt of your letter of October 30, 1937, repudiating certain newspaper accounts attributing to you a statement that you were "going to get Kennedy's scalp."

I concur wholeheartedly in the desire you express not to engage in a personal dispute and believe that neither the interests of the Government nor those of maritime labor will be served thereby. Your hope of building a strong American merchant marine of which all Americans can be justly proud is most encouraging.

I am forced, however, to disagree with you—in a purely impersonal manner—with respect to the merits of the ALGIC case. I shall only point out that the Commission has not attempted "to render a decision on what is obviously a labor dispute" with respect to this vessel but has merely exercised one of the attributes and duties of her ownership in instructing its employee, the Master of the ALGIC, to enforce discipline on his ship in accordance with the law. The cable sent by unanimous vote of the Commission was not approved without investigation, but only after detailed telephonic reports from the American Consul in Montevideo and the ship's Master had disclosed that her crew had continuously refused and were then refusing to obey the Master's lawful commands.

Upon the return of the ALGIC to Baltimore, the Commission placed the facts within its knowledge before the Bureau of Marine Inspection and Navigation which, after investigation, referred the case to the Department of Justice for criminal prosecution. The lawfulness of the conduct of the Master and the unlawfulness of the seamen's

---

214. On October 30, newspaper accounts reported that the founder and president of the militant National Maritime Union, Joseph Edwin Curran (1896–1981), had threatened to "get Kennedy's scalp—and get it soon" in the wake of the *Algic* affair. On September 10, as chairman of the Maritime Commission, JPK had wired instructions to the captain of the SS *Algic* to place in irons any crew members refusing to obey orders out of sympathy for longshoremen striking in the port of Montevideo, where the U.S. government-owned freighter had recently landed. Although the crew complied temporarily, instances of insubordination, desertion and indeed murder punctuated the ship's return voyage. Some fourteen crew members had been arrested upon their arrival in Baltimore on October 20, promoting both a Senate inquiry into "communistic influences" on American maritime labor and the NMU's call for JPK's "summary dismissal."

conduct are questions which will have to be determined by the orderly processes of the courts and cannot be resolved in the public press by either you or me.

The Commission proposes to continue to see that maritime labor receives a "square deal" and is protected in all its lawful rights but at the same time it proposes to assure the public, which is contributing so heavily to the support of the American merchant marine, an equally square deal.

I am glad to note that your organization has no desire to promote strikes or irresponsible action in foreign ports and that it is willing to dispose reasonably of any disputes that may arise. There is a proper method and proper time and place, however, for such reasonable disposition of disputes and it is not by refusing to obey lawful commands aboard a vessel as in the case of the ALGIC at Montevideo.

Very truly yours,
Joseph P. Kennedy
Chairman

Joseph P. Kennedy to Wesley Stout[215]

November 7, 1937

My dear Mr. Stout:
Here is the Maritime article. If you like it, use it, and if you don't, I'll understand perfectly.

"March of Time" is making a special issue for release around January first on the survey that we made on Maritime affairs, and that, in addition to the fact that at this special session of Congress, the Senate and the House will be adopting the suggestions that I am working on now, may make it a timely subject.[216] However, please believe me when I say that I'd much rather not have it published unless you think it really worth while and not just another article.

A writer whom I regard very highly has suggested that the first two pages be rewritten. I am therefore enclosing another opening for your notation. You may use either one you prefer. If you do decide to use it, it will precede the pencil marks on Page 2.

Very truly yours,

Joseph P. Kennedy to Robert Hague[217]

November 24, 1937

Dear Bob:
Thanks so much for the tickets to the Lambs Gambol Dinner and Ball. We will all be on tap for the cocktail party and dinner later. I will send the list of names just as soon as I get organized.

I am quite right in my understanding, am I not, that I do not have to make any speeches of any nature? You told me you know that I shouldn't have to but I just want

215. Wesley Winans Stout (1890–1971), the recently named editor of the *Saturday Evening Post*, 1937–42.
216. The Maritime Commission's survey would be released two days later, concluding, in essence, that the American Merchant Marine was "a very sick industry." It would suggest further that Congress amend the Merchant Marine Act of 1936 to provide greater government subsidies to American shipping lines and establish both training facilities for merchant seamen and an arbitration board to oversee labor disputes.
217. Robert Lincoln Hague (1880–1939), manager of the Marine Department of Standard Oil of New Jersey, had reorganized the theatrical supper club, The Lambs, preventing it from closing during the Depression, and had invited JPK to preside over its December 4 annual dinner.

to be sure that a quick one will not be pulled on me so that all the brilliant lights of New York will be there to see me make a mug of myself.

I told my wife you were going to get me the most beautiful blonde in New York, so with her permission, you will have to make good.

With warmest regards—

Sincerely,

Joseph P. Kennedy to Joseph P. Kennedy, Jr., 22

December 9, 1937

Dear Joe:

In talking with Joe Sheehan[218] he asked me if I knew whether or not you had received the material for your thesis which you had requested from him.

I want to point out to you that it is most important whenever you have asked people to do things for you that you acknowledge receipt of any material received and to thank them for their efforts. I am suggesting this as a very good habit to acquire. People like to do things and flourish under a little consideration.

I know this has been an oversight on your part but I want to impress this upon you so that you might establish it in your mind for the future. In the meantime, please write to Joe.

I will see you Sunday.

Love,

Joseph P. Kennedy to Alice Cahill Bastien[219]

Dec. 21, 1937

My dear Miss Cahill-

Well, we are all back in Palm Beach and on receipt of your letter I told all the crowd right down to Teddy that you sent your best love. Teddy is growing big now and I am afraid that he has got out of the baby class and I will have to look forward to grand-children to fill the void.

I am delighted that you liked the picture and I think the one in LIFE was very cute. Of course, I am getting a bit fed up with hearing that my wife looks so very young, because to really understand that it means that I look like her father and that is a terrible state of affairs after all these years struggling to keep my youthful figure, so I am going right back to chocolate ice cream and plenty of chocolate cake.

I hope everything is well in Marlboro and remember we are always prepared to furnish the news so that you can be our envoy in that district.

With best wishes to you both from all the Kennedys for a Merry Christmas and a Happy New Year, I am,

Sincerely,

---

218. A contemporary of JPK's at both Boston Latin and Harvard, Joseph Raymond Sheehan (1888–1940) had served as director of employment research at the SEC. After JPK's resignation, Sheehan became his personal assistant and had accompanied him to the Maritime Commission as executive director. Upon the departure of the newly appointed Ambassador Kennedy for London, Sheehan would become president of the Dollar Line (soon to be renamed American President Lines).
219. Miss Cahill, the children's former nanny, had left to marry and had settled in Marlboro, Massachusetts.

Joseph P. Kennedy to Ralph Lowell[220]

December 21, 1937

Dear Ralph —

I would like to be as considerate as you are and write this letter in long hand, but I know you will forgive me at this time because work is piling up very fast and though I haven't yet received the appointment as Ambassador I appreciate your note of congratulation.

I wouldn't consider the position unless I felt that there was some chance of doing a really worthy job. I made up my mind that, unless for family reasons or an emergency financial crisis prevents, I would spend my time in the government service until Roosevelt retires, so what I do in the meantime is only dependent on whether I think I can be of any service and whether I get enough pleasure out of the job to keep me doing a good deed.

If I do take this job and I don't feel that I am doing as much in it as I would like, then I am through with that.

I feel very deeply about your note and it is most encouraging to receive these from time to time as you have been kind enough to write them.

My very best wishes to the whole family for a Merry Christmas and a Happy New Year.

Sincerely,

Joseph P. Kennedy to Joseph Breen

Dec. 21, 1937

Dear Joe —

I suppose you remember the night you were down at my house in Washington, when you stood by the radio and said—"Why don't you get that job as Ambassador to England and I will come over to visit you." Well, boy, although I haven't taken it yet, if I do, I will hold you to your promise.

I am planning, although you are not supposed to know it, to take that Irishman out there away from you and get him assigned to the London office, to be sure that I have somebody over there that I can have a laugh with, even though he doesn't do any work for that great motion cause. I have already broached this in great secrecy to the Honorable General[221] and he was impressed with the idea but he is handling it in his own good order. I hate like hell to take him away from you but, my God, London is cold, dreary and foggy during the winter and I haven't heard anybody complaining of being sick since I last saw Houghton.

It is a bare possibility that I may go to California in January end if I do I expect a little time from your arduous duties to devote to real entertainment. Anyway, remember we are still going to be in some business deal together before years are past. In the meantime, give my best wishes for a Merry Christmas and a Happy New Year to all the family. My very best to you.

Sincerely,

---

220. JPK's Harvard classmate, Boston philanthropist and banker, Ralph Lowell (1890–1978).
221. Will Hays.

Joseph P. Kennedy to Joseph Tumulty[222]

December 21, 1937

My dear Mr. Tumulty:-

Although I have not received the appointment as Ambassador to Great Britain I would like to tell you that under the law of inherent probability I may, I do not expect to get a letter from any one in this country that will move me as much as your letter has done.

After all, you blazed the trail for the Irish lads in America with your great service to the country and Woodrow Wilson. As I read over your feelings when you took your position I have had the same feeling on both the jobs I have taken in Washington and I feel that only by giving my best efforts can I keep faith with my dear father and mother.

I, too, have a hostage to the future in my large family, as you have, and my only personal satisfaction is that I will leave the heritage to them that I did the best I could for a great nation. I assure you that if I do take the position I will have in mind all the things that you had when you took your great position and will try to do the very best I can.

With best wishes to your family for a very Merry Christmas and a Happy New Year, I am,

Most sincerely,

Joseph P. Kennedy to James F. Byrnes

Dec. 23, 1937

Dear Jim:-

To strike a serious note for a minute, your conversation on the night of the Gridiron dinner struck a very serious cord in my make-up. Whether for good or bad I have always made up my own mind and paid very little attention to criticism, except from very, very few friends. I wouldn't really give a damn what most people think of the new appointment if in my own heart I thought it was the thing too, but for your opinion I have the greatest respect. If you had misgivings about the new appointment there would be reason for me to have.

I came down here to Palm Beach and I have thought the thing over very seriously. If the premise were correct that I could exert all the influence that I am supposed to have, then I would have no feeling but to stay here and do everything I can, but you are as good a judge of that as any one and you know that no individual possesses that much influence. To continue where I am is certainly a waste of whatever talents I possess, because, with the five man commission and the outline that we have made for the future, it is silly for me to sit around there and waste my time. Now, while there may be a change made in the Cabinet, that is going to take a long time and I would be unhappy waiting around with not enough to do. You say there is plenty to do, but when you try to particularize, it is much more difficult.

I haven't any idea how well I will get along abroad, either from the point of view of doing very much for the country, or doing a job of which my friends will feel proud, but if I don't get the results that I feel are necessary I would get out at once.

I will stick along with this administration as long as I can do any good or as long as I have the confidence of the leaders, regardless of the inconveniences that accrue to me.

I have never had political ambitions and have none now. I am only vitally con-

---

222. Joseph Patrick Tumulty (1879–1954), secretary and adviser to Woodrow Wilson.

cerned with where we are headed. If fellows like yourself think I can help, I will stay and help in whatever job I can do the most good. If I can't help, I can always go back to my own private affairs and be quite happy.

I have talked with Washington since talking with you and I understand everything is held up until I get back for another talk. I do want you to know, however, that you are one of those fellows whom I have met in the last five years whose opinion I respect and whose affection I always want to retain.

All the Kennedys send to you and Mrs. Byrnes very best wishes for a Merry Christmas and a Happy New Year.

Sincerely,

Edward Kennedy, 5, to Santa Claus

Dear Santa Claus,

Thank you very much for the toys you gave me you can give me some more any time you want to. I liked the watch best. Thank you again.

Lot of
Love
ted dy

P.S. Happy new year—

PART IV

London

1938–1940

The questions perhaps most fundamental to Joseph Kennedy's ambassadorship are also those that frame the two and a half years he spent in London. Why was a man who by his own admission lacked both diplomatic experience and a diplomatic nature appointed to the primary listening post in Europe in late 1937 as the international situation grew rapidly darker? And why, despite the administration's growing dismay at his outspokenness, his hosts' mounting resentment at his bearishness, and his own requests to be allowed to return home in 1940, was he never recalled?

Presenting his credentials to the king in the early spring of 1938, the new ambassador to the Court of St. James's gratefully accepted his posting, believing its "prestige" to be of eventual benefit to his children's careers and fitting repayment at last for services rendered to both the Roosevelt election efforts and to the administration over the previous five years. His hopes of the position at Treasury dashed by the appointment of Henry Morgenthau (with whom he had come to share only a mutual loathing), he had accepted and indeed had thrown himself into the chairmanships that he had been given, despite feeling vaguely disappointed by them. When it became clear that Ambassador Bingham would not recover from Hodgkin's disease in late 1937, Roosevelt had originally rejected the idea of sending the chairman of the Maritime Commission to London as his replacement, but then reconsidered. "I certainly will be glad to have him out of Washington," the secretary of the treasury confessed gleefully to his diary, "and I take it that is the way the President feels." Although Morgenthau's account of the president's rationale was perhaps not unmingled with some combination of his own feelings and the president's well-known skill at mirroring his listener's sentiments, it is telling nonetheless:

> The President . . . made a startling remark that he considered Kennedy a very dangerous man and that he was going to send him to England as Ambassador with the distinct understanding that the appointment was only for six months and that furthermore by giving him this appointment any obligation that he had to Kennedy was paid for.
> . . . The President said, "I have made arrangement to have Joe Kennedy watched hourly and the first time he opens his mouth and criticizes me, I will fire him." He said two or three times, "Kennedy is too dangerous to have around here."

Dangerous or not, Kennedy would be a good candidate to negotiate the upcoming Anglo-American Trade Agreement, and there was perhaps no American better suited to conduct the related film negotiations as British protectionist measures of a decade earlier expired. He was wealthy enough to supplement the department's budget in order to maintain the position and entertain in fitting style. As for the seeming incongruity of sending an Irish Catholic to London, with the same flippancy with which he had set "a thief to catch a thief" three years earlier at the SEC, the president reportedly chuckled that the appointment was "a great joke, the greatest joke in the world." Kennedy himself would recall in his memoir that "[i]n many quarters my appointment was applauded for the very reason that my Irish and Catholic background, my self-made qualities and lack of homage to old-fashioned protocol, my bluntness and outspokenness, would render me proof against British wiles." And so, for better or worse, the appointment was made.

Once installed in London, the new ambassador to the Court of St. James's faced challenges almost entirely unlike those he had dealt with previously in his professional life. In the past he had seemed to thrive upon the cycle that he had repeated throughout middle age: intense, relatively short-term round-the-clock focus and activity followed by periods of recuperation in Palm Beach or Hyannis Port. Until late 1940, his term in London, by contrast, was indefinite, despite his own and the president's occasional testy assertions to the contrary. A few breaks for vacation and debriefing at home notwithstanding, his duties were ongoing and continuous. The post of ambassador came with specific powers—and limitations. Diplomacy would call for the curtailment of his accustomed volubility and unrestrained (occasionally four-lettered) expansiveness.

After two years in London, constantly shifting international events, the resulting uncertainty in the direction of American foreign policy and the ambassador's diminishing stature in both Washington and London would leave him ill informed and, uncharacteristically, somewhat rudderless. From the outset of his ambassadorship he appears to have sought a presidential mandate to guide his course; his later reflections upon his tenure in London would focus particular attention on Roosevelt's parting advice—or lack of it. Insofar as he recalled the president providing him with direction, the mandate (as the ambassador recalled and reported it) bore a close resemblance to his own views on American intervention, on the world economy and on the democracies' interactions with the dictatorships. Moreover, his recollections of the president's farewell advice would evolve markedly over the course of time.

On February 22, 1938, the newly appointed United States ambassador to the Court of St. James's had taken his leave of the president at Hyde Park before sailing and recorded in his diary the simple, final instructions that he had received. The president, he recalled,

> . . . discussed the foreign situation in general. . . . He indicated his firm intention of keeping our country out of any and all involvements or commitments abroad. He considered the situation too uncertain for the United States to do anything but mark time until things have settled down. He did not seem to resent the position Chamberlain has taken of trying to make deals with Germany or Italy in order to fend off a crisis. . . .

Having reached the zenith of his public career, the ambassador began recording with some pride his daily activities in London, his interactions and growing intimacy with notable figures and the evolution of his political and geopolitical ruminations. The memoranda that had chronicled some of his activities in Washington grew into several volumes of reflections on his life in London. Punctuated with his own editorial notations, these private daily recollections appear to have been intended for public consumption, both immediately and eventually. It was not uncommon for his observations, and even for whole sentences or passages from his diaries and dispatches, to find their way into his correspondence with political, financial and journalistic associates. From there, his reflections more than occasionally made their way into print. The ambassadorial diaries reflect not only on the private man, but also on the private man's reflections on himself, both as a public and as a potentially historical figure.

Besides diaries and correspondence, the new American ambassador generated a number of other documents that suggest a growing interest in his posterity. Judging by the "Chapter I" fragments that survive among his files, it appears that from the outset he fully intended to publish an autobiographical article or perhaps a memoir of the historic, inaugural ambassadorship of an Irish-American at the Court of St. James's. At Arthur Krock's suggestion he had hired *New York Times* reporter Harold Hinton to be his personal (and press) secretary at the embassy. Shortly after arriving in March 1938, it appears that Hinton set to work ghostwriting his boss's reflections on the first few weeks of the ambassadorship. Hinton made use, it appears, of the earlier Hyde Park diary entry, presenting the president's hope of "keeping the United States out of any and all involvements abroad" verbatim. Although the 1938 diary entry implies that the president's attitude of neutrality *was* his mandate to his new envoy, Hinton's fragmentary draft appears to have generated some uncertainty on the subject. "The president had given me no instructions," it notes, adding "(amplify—there must have been some)," and concludes, "I was on my own, and one of my major tasks was going to be that of representing American sentiments to the British."

More than a decade after Ambassador Kennedy's angry return from London, after his relationship with the president had ended in mutual recrimination and after his eldest son had been lost in a war that he had devoted all of his engeries to preventing the United States from entering, he would rework his account of the farewell meeting in Hyde Park for a third and final time. Between 1949 and 1955, under his supervision, his old friend and former SEC associate James Landis would refashion the ambassadorial diaries, diplomatic dispatches and correspondence into the memoir that the former ambassador had long intended to write. Despite the elapse of more than a decade, the memoir records the farewell meeting, the president's sentiments and, more particularly, his instructions on that day in late February 1938 in far greater detail than do its earlier counterparts.

"To tell you the truth, Joe," [the president] said, "I still have not lost heart. If Chamberlain succeeds in pacifying the Dictators the time may soon come when my [late 1937 peace] plan can be put into effect. The United States, of course, cannot participate in any political settlements, but it can, and I believe it will be able to, lead the world out of the economic morass in which it is floundering. In my opinion, the economic distress of the world these last nine years has been the root cause of most of the other troubles . . ."

"I agree completely," I told the President. "Economic maladjustment is one of the principal reasons for the world's unrest. One of my chief tasks as I see it, will be to try and gauge the economic pulse of England and Europe. If any remedies occur to me I'll try to let you know at once."

"Be careful about one thing, Joe. Don't forget that this country is determined to be neutral in the event of any war. The United States must be kept out of any and all involvements abroad. That means that no matter how much we might favor or dislike the objective of any of the nations, we must not show our likes or dislikes. We shall have to mark time until we see whether or not Chamberlain accomplishes anything. If he does we might have an opportunity to play a part in an overall economic settlement. But to do so, we shall have to remain in a position where our sincerity of purpose to help all nations could not be doubted."

"The President's emphasis on neutrality had my fullest concurrence," the envoy concluded, "and I told him so."

The London diaries and first memoir draft had begun as a breezy chronicle of the new ambassador's first forays into international politics and society. The final version of the memoir, by contrast, would emerge after the war in large part as a careful accounting of what he had come to see as the Roosevelt administration's increasing circumvention, intentional public humiliation and general ill usage of its ambassador in London as Europe staggered toward war. The manuscript would also chronicle the president's quiet movement away from neutrality while the American public remained uninformed. Although never published, the completed "Diplomatic Memoir" would highlight in particular the ideological rift that was to develop between the ambassador and the president over the issue of intervention. "Peace above all," the ambassador's stance and the source, he felt, of much of the eventual public outcry against him, had not only been his unwavering conviction from the outset of his tenure in London, but also, he would insist, his presidential mandate as well.

Although the new American ambassador would always be regarded with suspicion and disdain in some quarters for his background and ethnicity, his informality (or vulgarity, as some put it) and his new money, both he and his sizable photogenic family met with overwhelming and immediate popularity in London. Within the first month of his arrival, the press on both sides of the Atlantic ballyhooed the new ambassador's hole in one at Stoke Poges. A number of articles and editorials touted his egalitarianism and lack of pretense both in declining to wear knee breeches while presenting his credentials to the king and in discontinuing the practice of presenting ambitious American debutantes at court. His children and his wife, likewise, appeared on the society pages, in a flattering *Vogue* feature and in snippets in a variety of English and American publications large and small.

Joe and Jack would remain at Harvard until their respective graduations but often spent their longer vacations in London. Following Jimmy Roosevelt's example, Joe Junior would work as his father's secretary after finishing his undergraduate thesis on the Spanish Civil War and graduating in June 1938. In the spring of 1939, young Joe would travel to Spain to witness the fall of Madrid, writing a series of journalistic letters home that his father hoped he might later publish. Bobby and Teddy were enrolled in day schools in London. Eunice, Pat and Jean boarded at the Convent of the Sacred Heart nearby in Roehampton. Kick and Rosemary, eighteen and nineteen, respectively, at the time of their arrival, lived at Prince's Gate with their parents. Their father's recent decision to end the presentation of American debutantes had only applied to girls coming from the United States for the privilege, not to Americans living in England. As a result, the elder Kennedy girls were presented shortly after their arrival in London. Eunice would make her debut the following year, in the last months of peacetime, during what was said to be the most lavish and spectacular of London seasons. Following the declaration of war, Rose and the children, with the exception of Rosemary, would return to the United States. Over the course of her stay in England, Rosemary had been placed under the guidance and supervision of Miss Dorothy Gibbs at a Montessori training school in Hertfordshire, where she had begun to flourish. Rather than uproot her and disrupt her progress in wartime, her parents had decided that she should remain in Hertfordshire within easy reach of her father and the Moores.

If the Kennedys were welcome and popular in London at the outset of their stay, then it was Kick who, from the start, was most at home there. Congenial and affectionate, she made quick and deep friendships that would weather her father's declining popularity and eventual disrepute among the English, and last to the end of her short life. The number of her beaux had early on engendered rumors of her marrying in England, despite her religion, a fact that prompted her dinner companion, Evelyn Waugh, to inquire as to the size of her "dot" one evening. Uncertain, but presuming that he referred to her belly button, she could only respond that she didn't think hers was any larger than anyone else's. Waugh pressed the subject, however, arguing that with a noted financier for a father, hers must surely be substantial. It took her several minutes to realize that he was speaking of her dowry. The correspondence with her father that followed upon her abrupt return home after the declaration of war shows a particular fondness and concern for one Billy Hartington, the duke of Devonshire's eldest son.

Despite the new ambassador's lack of diplomatic experience, both the president and the State Department found that initially his characteristic frankness served him well as an extremely candid and observant reporter of events—at least so long as Chamberlain remained in power. The ambassador's ideological affinity with and personal fondness for the prime minister and for several members of his cabinet (particularly the foreign secretary, Lord Halifax, and the chancellor of the Exchequer, Sir John Simon) made his dispatches and reports the most immediate and reliable that had been received from London in years. The dispatches from London, however, would soon come to reflect the ambassador's diminishing ability to prevent his own convictions from coloring his reporting of events and his suggestions to the White House and the State Department as Britain (and potentially the United States) were drawn to the precipice of war.

Ambassador Kennedy's two major addresses of 1938 and the reactions they provoked, publicly and officially, would become milestones on his and the president's divergent philosophical paths. Two and a half weeks after his arrival the new envoy delivered his maiden speech at the Pilgrims Society dinner, traditionally held in honor of incoming American ambassadors. Rather than treat the customary topics of the common bonds uniting the English Speaking Peoples, he chose instead to focus on the potential limits of those bonds in light of the uncertain international situation. "I feared that the admitted fact of Anglo-American friendship was being wishfully and perhaps artfully interpreted to mean that our common bonds also held us together in the fashioning of our national policies," he would recall of his frame of mind while drafting the speech. "It would be unfair to the British folk, I thought, not to disabuse them of that thought." The draft he had sent to Washington for approval would return to him much corrected and diluted, the secretary of state having found the original to be ". . . entirely too isolationist in its every implication, or virtually so." Although the speech was well received at home, its reception in London was tepid. He would record in his diary the next morning, "I got the feeling that parts of it fell flat. The speech was intended primarily for home consumption, as I am very anxious that my friends there should not think I have gone over to the British." Nevertheless, he had achieved his aim of telling his "British hosts a few homely truths," and realized that they "could not be expected [to] cheer their heads off."

If his audience for the Pilgrims' speech had failed to cheer for his first major statement, his second, seven months later, would provoke outrage. On October 19 he informed the Navy League at its annual Trafalgar Day dinner that

[i]t has long been a theory of mine that it is unproductive for both the democratic and dictator countries to widen the divisions now existing between them by emphasizing their differences, which are now self-apparent . . . But

there is simply no sense, common or otherwise in letting these differences grow into unrelenting antagonisms. After all, we have to live in the same world. . . .

The speech unleashed a furore in Washington and London, in American missions around the world and in the press. A radical departure from the president's "Quarantine" speech of a year earlier, it was unclear whether the Navy League speech represented a new direction in American foreign affairs. Although he had submitted a draft to the department for approval just as he had done with the Pilgrims' speech, in the confusion resulting from the recent Munich Agreement, both the secretary and undersecretary erroneously believed the other to have read and corrected the address. As a result, it had been returned to London unchanged. The following week, the president delivered his own radio address criticizing the fascist states, publicly repudiating the sentiments expressed in the Trafalgar Day speech and leaving his ambassador feeling stabbed in the back.

Kennedy's correspondence would be an additional source of irritation to the president. Over the course of the spring of 1938, the ambassador sent a series of "Private and Confidential" letters (which were in reality virtually identical) containing his observations on the international situation. The recipients were a number of his friends, colleagues and associates "in every walk of life, in government, in business, in newspaper work." Although the list varied slightly from letter to letter, the recipients generally included Arthur Krock; Walter Lippmann; Boake Carter; the outspokenly antiadministration columnists John O'Donnell and Hugh Johnson; Roy Howard; Frank Kent; Felix Morley of the *Washington Post*; *Fortune*'s Russell Davenport; Paul Block; Paul Mallon; William Randolph Hearst; Bob Allen; Bernard Baruch; Justice McReynolds; James Roosevelt; Jay Pierrepont Moffat of the State Department's European section; T. J. White of the Hearst organization; and Senators Wheeler, Byrnes, Harrison and Pittman. The president, however, was not among the recipients.

The letters coincided with what the ambassador would come to call his "presidential boomlet." As it was still unclear that Roosevelt would run for an unprecedented third term in 1940, the capital rumor mill had already begun churning out potential successors. The political letters appeared to many (the president included, apparently) to be the ambassador's naked attempt to generate favorable publicity and perhaps a new position for himself from abroad. "Mr. Roosevelt . . . had a quality—a failing some have called it," Kennedy would recall in the diplomatic memoir, "of resenting the suggestion that he was to be succeeded and cooling perceptibly towards a man who might be considered by his friends a worthy successor." Never alluding to the letters, the president debriefed the ambassador and shared a "pleasant dinner" with him at Hyde Park during the latter's short visit home in June 1938. Thus it would come as a shock to Kennedy not only to learn from the headlines the following day of a reported rift between the president and himself (resulting, it was alleged, from his own presidential aspirations), but also to discover that the White House itself had been the source of the leak. Returning to London, he would recall, "deep within me I knew something had happened."

Such rebukes would affect the ambassador sufficiently to secure his early off-the-cuff public support of a third Roosevelt election bid. Returning to the United States for Christmas in 1939, Kennedy told a Boston reporter, "I cannot go against the guy. He's done more for me than my own kind. If he wants it I'll be with him." Nevertheless, he would find his loyalties to the president tested increasingly in the time remaining until his resignation. Having long advocated closer diplomatic relations between the United

States and the Holy See, he would serve with pride and gratitude as the president's personal representative at the coronation of Pope Pius XII in March 1939. In most other matters, however, the president withdrew his confidence from the ambassador in London. As the ambassadorship progressed, Kennedy would come to discover increasing instances of the circumvention of his authority. Circumvention would not only embarrass and irritate him, it would also make him increasingly prone to indiscreet and unflattering outbursts about the president. Just as his authority and counsel would come to be largely ignored by mid-1940, so both the State Department and the White House would often leave him uninformed of the latest nuances in American foreign policy. In the vacuum, he would cling to American neutrality as both his conviction and his original presidential mandate, and would attempt to fill the void with his own extemporaneous pronouncements on the subject.

Although Kennedy had been the first to conceive of the enormous public relations benefits to Anglo-American friendship that a royal visit to the United States might yield, the Department of State did not invite him to accompany the royal couple on their triumphal North American tour in the early summer of 1939. The ambassador was aware of the secret correspondence between the president and the first lord of the Admiralty that had begun in 1939, long before Churchill's ascendancy to the post of prime minister, largely because it had fallen to him, as ambassador, to deliver and retrieve the exchanges. In March 1940, without consulting the secretary of state or the American ambassadors in Paris or London, the president sent his childhood friend and undersecretary of state, Sumner Welles, to investigate possibilities for a peaceful settlement. Although Kennedy liked Welles personally (at least as much as he liked anyone at the State Department), he would resent the intrusion and be embarrassed as much by the president's manifest lack of confidence in him as by the fact that he had only been invited to attend a few of the undersecretary's meetings with British officials in London. Some months later the insult would be compounded when the president sent a series of observers, among them "Wild Bill" Donovan and reporter Edgar Mowrer, on special missions to London to investigate Britain's military strength and need for destroyers. Not having been consulted, the ambassador would complain bitterly to his diary that Donovan's presence could "do nothing but complicate the situation," and went on to dismiss the colonel's recommendations as "ridiculous." Regarding the concurrent destroyers-for-bases negotiations that had been carried out largely through the British Embassy in Washington, he would complain to the president, "I would have no knowledge whatsoever of the situation had it not been for the fact that the Prime Minister has seen fit to send some cables back through me." Questioning his usefulness as ambassador if he were to remain uninformed and unable to contribute, he threatened to resign, telling the president in no uncertain terms, "Frankly and honestly I do not enjoy being a dummy."

Inasmuch as the ambassador's identification with Chamberlain and the policy of appeasement had resulted in his exceptionally penetrating early dispatches, Churchill's rise to power in May 1940 would severely limit his ability to report accurately. Indeed, his very closeness to the former prime minister, personally and philosophically, would estrange him not only from Churchill but also from many members of the wartime coalition as well. Although Churchill had been one of his earliest British political contacts, and had even suggested Kennedy's name for an award celebrating freedom and peace as recently as 1938, the war had engendered mutual suspicion between the two men. Perhaps not without some infusion of personal sentiment into his reportage,

Kennedy peppered his diaries, dispatches and correspondence increasingly as the war progressed with anecdotes relating the president's professed long-standing dislike of the prime minister as well as the prime minister's wartime drinking habits and admitted pessimism in the face of the German enemy. His growing dislike of Churchill did not prevent him from seeing the place that the prime minister might come to occupy in history, however. Several notes to Brendan Bracken indicate the ambassador's persistent efforts to secure nine poster-sized excerpts of the rousing post-Dunkirk "we shall never surrender" oration, signed personally by the prime minister—whenever he had a spare moment. Autographs notwithstanding, the ambassador saw in the gorgeous Churchillian rhetoric celebrating the common bonds of the English Speaking Peoples little more than an effort to ennoble an ill-fated attempt to preserve the empire by entangling the United States in the conflict.

Although Joseph Kennedy often appears in modern invocations as almost congenitally anti-British, his relations with his hosts both during and after his ambassadorship were somewhat more complicated. He was indeed mindful of appearing at home to have been taken in by "British wiles." In matters of protocol he seems to have borne in mind Woodrow Wilson's dictum regarding American ambassadors, ". . . you could send an American to London, but it was difficult to keep an American there." The ambassadorial stances on knee breeches and debutantes were orchestrated as deliberate and self-conscious gestures of polite independence. "[T]he more I see of things here, the more convinced I am that we must exert all of our intelligence and effort toward keeping clear of any involvement," he would write the like-minded Senator Borah shortly after both his arrival and the completion of the Austrian *Anschluss*. Decades later, the former ambassador would insist that, far from being anti-British gestures, his objections to American intervention had always been objections not only to the economic devastation that he envisioned after a global war but also to the loss of American life in a conflict he believed initially to be unrelated to American interests. He would maintain as well that he had never hoped for a British defeat, as it was sometimes charged. He would attribute his unpopularity after September 1939 to his realism (which he believed the British took for defeatism) in predicting the unlikelihood of a British victory in the face of what were estimated at the time to be superior German forces.

Nevertheless, a number of his American contemporaries from across the ideological spectrum in politics and the press worried that his unwavering concurrence with the Chamberlain government, especially on matters relating to foreign policy, might ultimately entangle the United States in another European war. In April 1939, before the Senate Foreign Relations Committee, former New Dealer and increasingly conservative and isolationist General Hugh Johnson would liken the ambassador to Walter Hines Page, a Kennedy predecessor whose Anglophilia had been popularly faulted at home for embroiling the United States in the Great War. The leftward-leaning former Wisconsin governor, Philip LaFollette, would demand Kennedy's recall a few months later. Having recently returned from a European tour, LaFollette reported that he had found the American ambassador in London to have grown too close to Chamberlain to be able to represent American interests there. Kennedy's unerring and insistent outspokenness on the issue of nonintervention notwithstanding, by mid-1939 he would begin to advocate both financial aid to Britain and repeal of the Neutrality Act, albeit as a means of keeping America *out of* war. In the wake of Dunkirk he would come to support both the sale of American firearms and Churchill's requests for destroyers. His wartime correspondence would demonstrate a heartfelt (if somewhat surprised) admiration for British courage, resilience and determination in the face of the German onslaught.

On a personal scale he seems to have developed a genuine, slightly awed admiration and affection for his British hosts. Undoubtedly, his feelings were not unmingled with a certain pride in the social standing that his position and his new acquaintances conferred. His diaries are replete with anecdotes regarding gestures of friendship made to him and his family by aristocrats and royals, and trust placed in him by high-ranking British government officials. Besides family photos, the pictures that he kept in his homes in Palm Beach and Hyannis Port until the end of his life were almost exclusively of friends and acquaintances he had made while in England, in some cases, independent of his agreeing with, or even liking, their subjects. Churchill, Eden, Hull and Roosevelt, for example, appear alongside Chamberlain, Halifax, de Valera and members of the royal family.

Both throughout his life and after his death he would suffer from facile characterization, particularly of his political views. In many respects his political leanings sprang from (or perhaps *were* at bottom) the economic views of a staunch capitalist who had experienced the extremities and upheavals of the previous two decades as a financier. He would often augment such political beliefs as he held with tenets and aspects borrowed from incongruous ideological sources to arrive at his own, sometimes seemingly inconsistent stances. He was a capitalist who had given his support to the Roosevelt campaign in 1932, believing that a modicum of socialism administered at the heart of the Great Depression might avert revolution, thereby safeguarding private property and helping to secure his children's futures. In the months following his return from England in 1940, he would be popularly excoriated as an isolationist. Although he shared the isolationist horror of intervention, he would tell a national radio audience in January 1941 that he could not "sympathize" with the isolationist point of view; he *supported* aid to Britain as the means of averting war. Throughout his ambassadorship he would be characterized variously as isolationist, hawkish, Anglophilic, anti-British, pro-German, anti-Semitic and sympathetic to appeasement by many who followed his career. The father of two sons of draft age, his objections to intervention, however, were perhaps less partisan or ideological at their roots than they were personal and economic. "I hate to think how much money I would give up rather than sacrifice Joe and Jack in a war," he told his father-in-law shortly after his arrival in London. He envisioned only economic devastation for the British Empire (resulting in enormous American reconstructive aid) in the unlikely event of a British victory, and "chaos beyond anybody's dreams" should the United States intervene in a global conflict so close upon the heals of a global depression. Of the polarities of totalitarianism, as a Catholic and a capitalist he objected more strenuously to communism, which he feared would grow unchecked in Europe in the wake of the defeat of fascism. He encouraged aid to Britain with no ultimate expectation of repayment beyond her acting as a first line of defense for the United States against inevitable and insatiable Axis expansion. He saw little hope for the British rearmament effort when compared with Charles Lindbergh's late-1938 estimates of German military and technological might, particularly in light of Britain's economic fortunes over the course of the previous decade and the default on her earlier war debt to the United States.

With an independence that annoyed (and occasionally alarmed) the State Department and the White House, he would practice and preach "getting along with the dictators" on both a personal and international scale in the interest, he argued, of preserving peace and keeping the United States uninvolved. On a number of occasions throughout his tenure in London, he requested permission to enter into exploratory peace discussions with a number of high-ranking German officials. Official permission from the United States was always withheld. In June 1938 the German ambassador, Herbert von Dirksen, would send the first in a series of dispatches in which he reported at length (albeit with some muddling of the verifiable facts) that he had found his American counterpart sympathetic both to the Reich and to its racial policies. Of the events of the same day, by contrast, the American ambassador, pressed for time before his imminent departure for the United States, would only record that he had seen "the German ambassador, the French ambassador, Sir Horace Wilson, Mr. Chamberlain, Lord Halifax, Oliver Stanley and Sir John Simon—an awfully crowded day." Later, when such captured German documents as von Dirksen's dispatches would be published, the former American ambassador (whose 1939 diary remarks upon von Dirksen's admitted lack of fluency in English) would pronounce his former colleague's account of the interview "complete poppycock."

Nevertheless, a number of the friendships and associations that Kennedy formed in England would contribute to his reputation for pro-German leanings. Reports in the Communist press of his visits to Cliveden, the Astor's Buckinghamshire home and the reputed epicenter of fascist sympathy in England, would soon find their way into American political columns and, elements within the administration ensured, to the president's desk. His friendship with the Lindberghs and the gloomy view he took of Allied air strength, based upon the aviator's firsthand assessment of the *Luftwaffe*, would further such impressions. The American ambassador's contacts and defeatism prompted no little scrutiny in British official circles. The Foreign Office kept an ongoing file of "Kennediana," consisting of short (sometimes second- or third-hand) reports regarding the ambassador's latest public and confidential pronouncements on Britain, Germany and American neutrality. Often such reports were accurate and verifiable; sometimes they were more far-fetched. During the American ambassador's wintertime trip to the United States in 1940, the Ministry of Information intercepted a telegram signed KENNEDY requesting the press secretary at the American Embassy in London to "RUSH PACIFIST LITERATURE" to the sender in the United States at once. "More Kennediana! Becoming a Pacifist!" an incredulous foreign officer scribbled, not noticing apparently that the telegram had originated in Cambridge, Massachusetts, where twenty-two-year-old Jack Kennedy was in the frantic last stages of finishing his undergraduate thesis, *Appeasement at Munich*, which would be published six months later as *Why England Slept*. Suspecting the American ambassador's possible involvement in the passage of classified embassy documents (including the president's and prime minister's now-famous secret correspondence) to fifth columnists in London, MI5 and Scotland Yard would delay for some months the arrest of the code clerk responsible in order to keep the American Embassy and its ambassador under surveillance.

His stance on refugees and his gestures toward them would appear similarly conflicted. Although George Rublee, chairman of the International Committee on Refugees, would complain to the State Department about the ambassador's lack of interest in the plight of refugees from the Reich, the ambassador would personally oversee the emigration of a number of German Jews. He would develop his own alternative to Rublee's efforts, but among the extensive collection of papers, clippings and memorabilia that he took home from London, curiously little information would survive about his plan or its proposed implementation. The ultimately unfulfilled Kennedy Plan, intended, apparently, to repatriate refugees in distant, sparsely populated regions of the empire or the Americas, received far greater coverage in the press than it did in his own diaries or correspondence.[1] His attitudes toward other refugees, however, were somewhat more clear-cut, and his efforts better documented. At the request of the mother superior at his younger daughters' school, he enlisted the help of the prime minister and the Anglo-Catholic foreign secretary in the successful evacuation of a number of Sacred Heart nuns from war-torn Barcelona. Describing his reasons for releasing news of their rescue to the papers, he noted in his diary on July 20, 1938, "I wanted to emphasize that the Jews from Germany and Austria are not the only refugees in the world, and I wanted to depict Chamberlain and Halifax as human, good-hearted men, capable of taking an active interest in such a bona fide venture."

Accusations of anti-Semitism would follow him throughout his life. His experience in film, business and government had brought him into contact to a far greater degree than many of his contemporaries, Irish Catholic or otherwise, with people of differing recent-immigrant backgrounds, particularly Eastern European Jews. Although rumors persist of dismissive cracks that he made in the 1920s regarding the backgrounds of his Hollywood colleagues ("a bunch of pants-pressers"), typically these survive as secondhand or overheard comments recollected by others years later and are for that reason difficult to trace or substantiate. His own preambassadorial papers make little mention of Judaism except insofar as they record genuine friendships with a number of prominent Jewish figures. In New York he had come to admire and emulate Bernard Baruch, interacting and corresponding with him jovially and even affectionately until the beginning of the ambassadorship. He would encourage Harvard repeatedly to confer an honorary degree on Justice Brandeis, whom he was said to have admired immensely. His initially friendly interactions with Henry Morgenthau had been responsible for his entrée into the Roosevelt camp in 1932 and for his introduction to Felix Frankfurter's circle. Although by 1940 he would come to regard both Morganthau and Frankfurter as central among the elements hostile to him within the administration, in the early and middle thirties his relations with Frankfurter had been close, admiring and jocular, despite their differing political stances. Indeed, he had paid Frankfurter the supreme compliment of consulting him about young Joe's education.

During the course of his ambassadorship, however, he would come to express a growing suspicion that his declining stock within the administration and his bad press at home (the "Jew influence in the papers in Washington") had an ethnic basis. Walter Lippmann, he would tell his wife in the spring of 1940, "hasn't liked the US Ambassador for the last 6 months. Of course the fact he is a Jew has something to do with that." The belief that he was under attack in influential Jewish circles for his reported anti-Semitism, indifference to the refugee issue and support of appeasement seems to have prompted him, curiously, to record his views on Judaism and on some of his Jewish colleagues far more explicitly and pejoratively than he had ever done before. In the wake of his Trafalgar Day speech, *Kristallnacht* and the recent leak of Rublee's complaints about him to the press, he would tell William Randolph Hearst's deputy, T. J. White, that "75% of the attacks made on me by mail were by Jews, and, yet, I don't suppose anybody has worked as hard for them as I have or more to their advantage." Almost entirely absent from his papers before his ambassadorship, such comments would

---

1. Evidently, he had conceived of the plan jointly with Malcolm MacDonald, the secretary of state for both the colonies and for dominion affairs. Unfortunately, MacDonald's own papers offer no illumination on the Kennedy Plan either; the secretary's only surviving diary from the period deals exclusively with the subject of bird-watching.

afterward become commonplace among his writings. Nevertheless, he would always insist that his dislike was not categorical but individual. "It is no secret that I have not a high opinion of Felix Frankfurter—or of Henry Morgenthau, Jr., or of a number of Jews in high places," he would later tell Joseph Dinneen of the *Boston Globe*, "but that doesn't mean that I condemn all Jews because of my personal feelings for some."

By 1940 he would find himself politely ostracized by the British and increasingly isolated. Citing ill heath, the stress of living apart from his family for more than a year and the fact that the administration had reduced him to little more than a "glorified errand boy," he requested on a number of occasions over the course of 1940 to be allowed to come home. He embarked at last in October amidst speculation that he would abandon the president for Wendell Willkie in the imminent election. Along his return route he received a number of telegrams from the president and the secretary, emphasizing their happiness at his return and suggesting strongly and repeatedly that he come to the White House to talk to the president before speaking to members of the press. There the ambassador would finally vent his outrage and frustration. The president would express his astonishment and sympathy. With the northeastern Catholic vote flagging in the face of the president's suspected growing willingness to fight for Britain, the chief executive would eventually prevail upon his ambassador to make a national broadcast on behalf of the third-term election effort.

The ambassador would offer his resignation on November 6 in the wake of the third-term election victory, although the president would not accept it until a successor could be found. In the midst of ongoing confusion about his views, the outgoing ambassador attempted, with disastrous results, to explain his stance. An interview on November 9 with the *Boston Globe*'s Louis Lyons (with whom he disagreed as to whether his remarks had been made off-the-record) would result in the publication of a number of astonishing statements across the United States and eventually in Britain. "Democracy is finished in England. It may be here, because it comes to a question of feeding people. It's all an economic question," Lyons (who made no written notes during the interview) reported him to have said. The ambassadorial comments ranged from democracy and economics to his opinions of the first lady and the queen. Although he left no recollections in his files regarding his subsequent trip to California to visit William Randolph Hearst and a number of his former associates in Hollywood, Douglas Fairbanks, Jr. (among others) would report that the ambassador had cautioned studio executives against the production of films that might offend the Reich. He intended his address of late January 1941, advocating "all aid to Britain short of war" and rearmament without intervention, to both explain his views and set the stage for his imminent testimony at the Lend-Lease hearings. Press comment, however (some of it, he believed, directed by the White House), would revive accusations of defeatism, appeasement and isolationism that would dog him throughout the semiretirement that he would afterward enter.

Joseph P. Kennedy to John Cudahy[2]

January 10, 1938

Dear John:

Just before leaving for the West Coast I talked with the President and it looks like London the first of February.

I haven't been educated in all the things I may or may not do, and I'm sure I'll be a rotten student. But I am hoping that when I get there you will find an excuse to come over and give me a few pointers — primarily on how to avoid going to dinners and teas.

The nicest thing about it, though, is that you and I will be able to settle the affairs of the world either on horseback, or the golf course.

With warmest regards, I am

Yours very sincerely,

Joseph P. Kennedy to William Gonzales

January 10, 1928 [1938]

My dear Mr. Gonzales:

I returned to the office from Palm Beach only to pack my bag and leave for the West Coast.

I can't let the opportunity go by without saying some word about the editorial which you were so generous to write and so kind to send to me.[3]

I have no misgivings about my training as a diplomat. If whatever success I have for the country is to be determined by the standards of a regular diplomat I am afraid it looks rather hopeless. But I always remember a course I took at Harvard called Ec. 18 in accounting. By the end of the term I gave it up because it seemed I was making no headway. Strangely enough, six months later I took up bank examining as a profession and most of my activities since then have been based on a knowledge of accounting. So it may be that this will hold true in the new job.

All I can promise is to do the best I can, and if I feel that I cannot deliver, then, in the words of John Sharp Williams, "Home holds no terror for me."[4] I'll be back on a boat.

With best wishes, I am

Yours sincerely,
Joseph P. Kennedy
Chairman

Joseph P. Kennedy to Franklin Roosevelt: *Telegram*

SHELBY, MONTANA, JANUARY 13, 1938

MY DEAR MR. PRESIDENT: MOORE AND I ARE ON OUR WAY HOME BY TRAIN. THE LAST CRACKUP OUT OF SEATTLE SCARED US A BIT.[5] JUST GOT NEWS OF MY CON-

---

2. John Clarence Cudahy (1887–1943), United States minister to the Irish Free State, 1937–39.
3. In his editorial of December 15, Gonzales, editor of the *Columbia* (South Carolina) *State,* had challenged criticism of JPK's lack of diplomatic experience by praising what he described as JPK's "genius of adaptability."
4. John Sharp Williams (1874–1932), Democratic senator from Mississippi, 1911–23, had declined renomination in 1922 and retired to his native Yazoo City, citing dismay at the congressional defeat of the Wilsonian postwar program.
5. Amidst intensifying West Coast maritime labor unrest, JPK had spent the past five days in the Pacific Northwest delivering his final series of addresses as chairman of the Commission. He had spoken before

FIRMATION. WILL THANK YOU PERSONALLY WHEN I GET HOME. I WANT TO SAY NOW THAT I DON'T KNOW WHAT KIND OF A DIPLOMAT I SHALL BE, PROBABLY ROTTEN, BUT I PROMISE TO GET DONE FOR YOU THOSE THINGS THAT YOU WANT DONE. ROSE AND I ARE DEEPLY GRATEFUL.

JOE KENNEDY

Joseph P. Kennedy: *Diary*

Feb. 18, 1938

Today I resigned as chairman of the Maritime Commission and was sworn in as ambassador to Great Britain. The ceremony took place in President Roosevelt's private office. Mr. Justice Reed[6] administered the oath of office. Eddie Moore, Miss LeHand, Marvin McIntyre, Mrs. James Roosevelt and Mrs. Stanley Reed were there.

From the White House, I went to pay a few last calls at the Capitol. Representative McReynolds of Tennessee, chairman of the Foreign Affairs Committee, Senator Pat Harrison and Senator Jimmy Byrnes were all nice enough to say they were sorry to see me leave the country in the difficult times which they saw facing us. Pat Harrison spoke of his plans to modify any radical tax legislation which might come over from the House.

My last visit, before I had to tear to the airport to take a plane to New York, was to Vice President Garner. He told me that he hated to fight with the President, but that he had to do so yesterday in the presence of Harrison and others over the proposed debt settlement with Hungary. He told the President it would pass only over his dead body.[7] He said to me he was sorry I was leaving the country, and expressed the wish that we could get the strongest men in the United States for advice and for the Cabinet. He thought we now have the worst he has ever seen. He said he was more worried now than at any time in forty years.

Feb. 22, 1938

At Hyde Park, President Roosevelt received me for the last talk I could have with him before sailing. He discussed the foreign situation in general and the break between Eden and Chamberlain in particular.[8] He indicated his firm intention of keeping our country out of any and all involvements or commitments abroad. He considered the situation too uncertain for the United States to do anything but mark time until things have settled down. He did not seem to resent the position Chamberlain has taken of trying to make deals with Germany and Italy in order to fend off a crisis, but he seemed to regret Eden's passing from the picture.

He told me of his mother's worry that I shall not wear knee breeches[9] and suggested that, if she brought up the matter at luncheon, I might say I am waiting until I

---

the Seattle Chamber of Commerce the previous day as tensions mounted between the local Waterfront Employers Association of Seattle and the International Longshoremen's Union.

6. Former Solicitor General Stanley Forman Reed (1884–1980) had himself been sworn in as an associate justice of the Supreme Court on January 31.

7. The previous morning the president had convened a secret (and as it turned out, contentious) meeting in the Oval Office at which he suggested readjusting past-due wartime loan payments from the United States' small-debtor nations. Those present were the secretaries of State and of the Treasury; the chairman of the House Ways and Means Committee; the chairman of the Senate Finance Committee, Byron Patton Harrison (1881–1941); and vice president, John Nance Garner (1868–1967).

8. On February 20, 1938, (Robert) Anthony Eden (1897–1977) had resigned as foreign secretary over objections both to the prime minister's rejection of President Roosevelt's secret peace proposal in late 1937 and to his recent concession of de jure recognition of the Italian annexation of Ethiopia.

9. Some years later Rose Kennedy would recall that,

get to London to decide. If I didn't do something of the kind, the President warned me, no lunch might be eaten. However, the subject never came up.

In addition to the President and his mother, young Mrs. James Roosevelt, Mrs. Eleanor and Missy were there. The President told newspaper men that I was to be his only guest during this stay at Hyde Park. He gave me a beautiful picture of himself — the best I have ever seen.

Feb. 23, 1938

The sailing today on the *Manhattan* was a nightmare. All of the children, except Jack, were there to see me off, but I couldn't get to them. Newspaper men, casual well-wishers, old friends and strangers by the thousand, it seemed to me, pressed into my cabin until we all nearly suffocated. Joe Guffey[10] was seeing someone off and I shook hands with him. Jimmy Roosevelt managed to get to my cabin and I took him into the bedroom for a brief chat. Even there, the photographers had to snap us as we sat on the bed trying to make sense.

Finally, I got up to the deck and the children. The professional photographers were reinforced by all of the passengers who had cameras. I sent them ashore just before the gangplank was raised, Eddie Moore promising to get them a place on the dock where they could wave to me as the ship got under way. I waited on the promenade deck and saw them clearly, standing on the uncovered portion, in the rain, waving and throwing kisses.

I put off what mail I get to [*sic*] by the time the pilot left the ship at Ambrose. I am very tired and intend to rest for the entire seven days. My cabin is comfortable and the general arrangements seem excellent.

Joseph P. Kennedy to James Roosevelt

Personal & Confidential London, March 3, 1938

Dear Jimmy:

Well, I am here after a very nice trip in the "Manhattan." The ship rolled all the way across, but I have had much worse trips on larger liners in the middle of the summer. The sailors and the stewards couldn't have been nicer — no trouble and no Mickey Finns.

Yesterday I called on Lord Halifax[11] and told him frankly about the situation as I viewed it in America. I am seeing the Prime Minister tomorrow and expect to repeat the

---

[w]hen Joe went to England, there was considerable discussion, serious and fictitious, as to whether or not he would wear velvet knee breeches, which were the regular "tenue" or dress worn when the men went to Court or to a dance where the King and Queen were to be present . . . Joe thought about the matter carefully and tried to weigh all the reasons. He did not want to start off badly in the eyes of the British, nor did he want to jeopardize his respect in the eyes of his fellow Americans who might say he was unduly influenced by the British. The slang expression was, "they are going to put the American Ambassador right in their vest pocket."

Though this subject seems unimportant now, his first appearance at Court was watched and commented on with this feature in mind. After careful consideration, he decided that he could best serve his country and England by appearing in his white tie and tails—the accredited dress for evening affairs in the United States. He then explained his attitude to the British Government and the Royal Family, saying that if the United States felt he was independent in thought and in action, he could then act for the best interests of England as well as of the United States in a crisis, and then America would not feel that he had been unduly influenced by the British.

10. Joseph Finch Guffey (1870–1959), Democratic senator from Pennsylvania, 1935–47.
11. Eden's successor as secretary of state for foreign affairs, Edward Frederick Lindley Wood (1881–1959), third Viscount Halifax, later first earl of Halifax.

same story. Today, by appointment, I went to Buckingham Palace and saw Sir Sidney Clive[12] and made arrangements for being received by the King on Tuesday.

I straightened out with him too the fact that I do not have to wear knee breeches — Praise be to Allah — but I am afraid I shocked him very much when I told him I didn't want to present any American debutantes. Much to my amusement, he was quite stunned and asked for a little time to talk it over with the Lord Chamberlain.[13]

I am of the opinion that they think this is a great ad in America and they don't want to lose its effect. Frankly, I told them that it was just the opposite and was the cause of considerable trouble, so I am waiting to hear from them to see what the next move is. I want to get these things on the record so when I write you in another week or two about cutting out debutantes' introductions, some wise mug over there won't say, "Ah! Kennedy is pro-British." I have already delivered myself to the Foreign Minister on that.

Got a wire from Secretary Hull today asking for a copy of my speech and telling me that he liked it.[14] The trouble was that the speech was prepared ten days ago and a great many parts of it are out of date and I have so cabled him. Just as soon as I feel I have a final draft of the speech, it will be on its way to the Secretary.

Being reasonably an expert in economic matters, I can tell you, after forty-eight hours in this place, that England is faced with an economic problem that makes ours look like a tea party. The armament program is keeping the wolf from the door, but underneath is a condition that seems to me to be as dangerous as ours was during the year 1929. England has used up practically all of its aces. First of all, its debt is large; second, it's taxing about as much as it can; third, its cost of carrying the debt has been marked down; it has already got the benefit of a tariff imposition and it is now spending all its money on armament and, boy, when this stops they're in for it, and I believe that this factor, considering our own situation in America, will be the determining factor in writing the fate of the world rather than the political side. And you can put this right in the little book along with the prophecy I made you last March or April that we're headed for the ashcan, and I feel that attention to this subject and a point of view on the American subject as viewed from here may have some value.

Incidentally, please tell the President that I think it quite inadvisable for him to write Harold Laski. He is too likely to quote him. Today, at a luncheon, two gentlemen, one of whom was Ferdinand Kuhn, Correspondent of the New York Times, told [Laski] about having received a letter from the President in which the President first said that the Chicago speech had not done what he hoped it would do,[15] and concluded by some comments on the Eden situation. Now it is quite likely the President never did and if he did it was very innocuous, but Harold has the happy faculty of wanting to make himself important, so, without saying anything to Laski when he sees him, because he is going to America very soon, that he has heard it from anywhere, it seems to me that it would be very wise not to have him as a correspondent, because we have one of two

12. Lieutenant General Sir (George) Sydney Clive (1874–1959), marshal of the diplomatic corps, 1934–45.
13. Rowland Thomas Baring, second earl of Cromer (1877–1953), lord chamberlain of the Royal Household and official play censor (1922–38).
14. Cordell Hull (1871–1955), secretary of state, 1933–44. JPK was due to deliver his maiden speech as ambassador before the Pilgrims Society on March 18.
15. The president had delivered his "Quarantine" speech on October 5, 1937, in the wake of the bombing of Nanking on September 21 and amidst mounting Japanese aggression in China generally. An apparent softening of the American attitude of nonintervention, the president had told his Chicago audience that "the epidemic of world lawlessness is spreading. When an epidemic of physical disease starts to spread, the community approves, and joins in a quarantine of the patients in order to protect the health of the community against the spread of disease."

choices — either to tell the powers that be here that we are going to deal straightforward with them and expect them to deal that way with us, or not bother much with them at all. But I am sure that they hear that Laski has a line in to the White House and it causes some little difficulty. I am sure that the President wants me to comment on these things as I see them.

Also tell him that I have a beautiful blue silk room and all I need to make it perfect is a Mother Hubbard dress and a wreath to make me Queen of the May. If a fairy didn't design this room, I never saw one in my life. I have Joe Choate looking down at me in a red gown and tell the President every time I look at him, I think I can hear him say, "Call me a cab."[16] I just made my first trip around through the building. Not only was the designer a fairy, but he was probably the most inefficient architect I have ever seen. If there was ever a badly laid out building for which the United States Government has to pay regular money, this tops it all. But as Sokowski[17] [sic] says at the bottom of his Hollywood column, "Don't get me wrong. I love London."

Well, old boy, I may not last long over here, but it is going to be fast and furious while it's on.

My love to Missy and tell her the minute I get any scandal, I'll start a social column for her, and tell the boss that, leaving aside the Kennedy family, there are two things I am for — the U.S.A. and F.D.R. and you can put this last paragraph on the last letter I write when I leave here.

Love and kisses,

Joseph P. Kennedy: *Diary*

March 4, 1938

The Foreign Office telephoned to say the Prime Minister would receive me, so I dropped everything and went to Downing Street. I found him a strong, decisive man, evidently in full charge of the situation here. Perhaps those at home who regretted the departure of Anthony Eden are backing the wrong horse.

Mr. Chamberlain was apparently prepared as Lord Halifax had been, for my assurance that the United States must not be counted upon to back Great Britain in any scrape, right or wrong. He said he was making his plans for pacification or fighting, as things might develop, without counting on us, one way or the other. I talked to him quite plainly and he seemed to take it well.

March 8, 1938

Today, I became a full fledged ambassador by presenting my letters of credence to King George VI. The coaches, with their scarlet-coated drivers and footmen, came for us at the Embassy a little after eleven. Herschel Johnson[18], Millard,[19] Williamson,[20]

16. Joseph Hodges Choate (1832–1917), United States ambassador to the Court of St. James's, 1899–1905. In a letter of March 4, 1938, Rabbi Stephen Wise, president of the American Jewish Congress and founder of the World Jewish Congress, described a recent meeting with JPK to the president: "After Joe K. told me that he was the first Catholic to hold the London Embassy post, I pointed to Choate's portrait and said: 'I suppose you know, J.K., that Choate was nastily anti-Irish at times?' J.K.'s answer was: 'I'll ring for the porter and have the portrait removed at once.' We both noted that Choate was frowning at us, Joe for being an Irish Ambassador, and at me on general principles as Jew and Rabbi. But Joe is going to give the earlier Joe a chance to hang on the wall if he adapts himself to his new Irish American surroundings."
17. Show business reporter Sidney Skolsky (1905–83), author of the nationally syndicated "Tintypes" column.
18. Herschel Vespatian Johnson (1894–1966), counselor of the American Embassy in London, 1937–41.
19. First secretary of the U.S. embassy.
20. Second secretary.

Butterworth,[21] Capt. Willson,[22] Col. Lee,[23] Meekins[24] and Dr. Taylor[25] accompanied me as my staff.

Sir Sidney Clive was in charge, and rode with me in my coach. I discussed again with him the matter of court presentations, and found that he had the jitters more than ever. It appears they feel any refusal on my part might mean the United States is snubbing the new King.

The show at Buckingham Palace was set up to expectations, and I chatted informally with the King for five minutes. I found him charming in every way. Lord Halifax was there. The King said he liked to play golf, but could not for the moment because of an infected hand. He mentioned that he plays tennis left-handed.

As soon as I could change, I went to the Savoy to lunch with the American Correspondents' Association. I told the men quite frankly that I was by no means sure that an American ambassador could accomplish anything here just now; that I would go home very shortly if I found that to be the case; that I had no political aspirations whatever and any reports they had seen to the contrary were unfounded; that I would deal with them exactly as I had done with their colleagues in Washington, as soon as I discovered what custom and ethics were prescribed for such relations.

The Pilgrim speech is in shape for final polishing tomorrow. I want to make it a good speech, saying something and thereby breaking a precedent of many years' standing.

I tried to clean up the great number of good-will letters, telegrams and cables which reached me during the past two weeks. Tony Biddle[26] called to pay his respects on the new ambassador, but I was out paying my own calls. He was described to me as a symphony in a black jacket, striped trousers, a blue cross-striped, stiff-bosomed shirt and stiff collar. He said he had put them on to do me honor.

Joseph P. Kennedy to Franklin Roosevelt

London, March 11, 1938

Dear Mr. President:

I am writing this at noon, after just having made three courtesy calls on the French, Spanish and Argentine Ambassadors. This afternoon I have the Turkish Embassy, the Cardinal Archbishop of Westminster, the Russian Embassy and the Brazilian Embassy and, if I get anything interesting, I will add it on to this letter.

I don't expect that I will be able to tell you anything you are not familiar with or that you will consider very deeply a judgment formed after ten days here, but there are certain definite signs that would help me to make up my mind in America on a given condition and I think I am justified in drawing the same conclusions here.

First of all, I am impressed in talking with the various Government officials of foreign countries that they regard the situation as acute in Central Europe, but, in the words of the French Ambassador this morning, nothing is likely to happen except to have Schuschnigg eventually give in unless there is some indication that France and

---

21. Financial attaché.
22. Naval attaché and naval attaché for air.
23. Military attaché.
24. Commercial attaché.
25. Agricultural attaché.
26. Anthony Joseph Drexel Biddle, Jr. (1896–1961), U.S. ambassador to Poland, 1937–40. In 1941 Biddle would be voted one of the ten best-dressed men in the world.

England are prepared to back him up.[27] The Spanish Ambassador, of course, feels that if a strong position had been taken in the Spanish situation, it would not now be necessary to have to take one in Central Europe in order to save Europe.

My own impression is that Hitler and Mussolini, having done so very well for themselves by bluffing, they are not going to stop bluffing until somebody very sharply calls their bluff. They have made considerable capital in their own countries of the fact that Eden was more or less persona non grata to both; they have persuaded their own people that they were strong enough to force Eden out of the British Cabinet. This is psychologically the worst result that has been obtained; this and the fact that the small countries of Europe are impressed with the fact that England is considerably moved by the positions of Spain and Italy.

The French Ambassador feels that the real point of difference between the Eden and Chamberlain policies was that Eden maintained a policy always looking at the outside of Britain and Chamberlain makes his policy looking at the political situation here. If Chamberlain is successful in working out some kind of a deal with either country, he will be a hero; if he isn't successful, he will probably say, "I have done the best I could to avert war; I have used every facility at my command to make a trade with these two nations; I can't do anything." The impression seems to be pretty general among the banking and financial interests that this is probably the way he will finally work himself out.

With all due respect to all these ideas, I am thoroughly convinced and the heads of the various departments in the Government and outside of the Government all feel that the United States would be very foolish to try to mix in. All they are interested in is to have the United States stay prosperous and build a strong navy, and they feel that time will take care of their position with the United States. This feeling is almost unanimous among the top-side people.

However, as I say, I am more convinced than ever that the economic situation in Europe is becoming more and more acute and if our American business does not pick up so that trade is generated for these countries, we will have a situation that will far overshadow any political maneuverings. Great Britain has the same kind of stock market we have; it is thin and nobody is anxious to buy anything. Armament is keeping industry going and they are looking around for methods of increasing taxation. There is some feeling in the industrialist's mind that there is always a potential danger from Germany by air raids, because London's political, financial and industrial centers are practically all one and the same and a hostile air fleet hit into a small part of London would put the whole place out of commission. In a discussion yesterday with Inskip, Minister of National Defense,[28] the question was brought up as to the possibility of this same air fleet keeping off ships carrying food to England, but even though they think about this incidentally, the bankers see the handwriting on the wall and are frightfully disturbed. The standard of living, of course, is getting much worse in all the countries of Europe, except England, and they are finding themselves more and more dependent on America's prosperity than they ever believed possible.

27. Later that day, Arthur Seyss-Inquart, Austrian minister of the interior and local Nazi Party leader, would replace federal Chancellor Kurt von Schuschnigg (1897–1977) as the Austrian head of state. At Berchtesgaden a month earlier, Hitler had pressured Schuschnigg to legalize the Austrian Nazi Party and appoint Seyss-Inquart to a cabinet position. Defying the führer upon his return to Vienna, however, Schuschnigg had announced a plebiscite to determine Austria's fate: independence or absorption into the greater Reich. Nevertheless, under mounting German pressure Schuschnigg had been forced to cancel the referendum and resign. On March 12, the day after the writing of this letter, German troops, which had been gathering along the Austrian border for weeks, would invade unopposed.
28. Sir Thomas Walker Hobart Inskip, later First Viscount Caldecote (1876–1947), minister for the Coordination of Defense (the British rearmament effort), 1936–1939.

My own belief, on that plan you discussed with me, is that the time is going to come, after Chamberlain has made the political offers necessary, for you to make a worldwide gesture and base it completely on an economic stand, but it should be entirely a question of proper timing. There is nothing, I believe, that could possibly be done at the moment. The obligation of finding a way to accelerate trade and get business started in all these countries should come when there is a mad desire on their parts to have you do it. To my thinking, that is bound to come, and the proper entrance into the field at the right time will make world history never to be forgotten, and it isn't something that may have to be done, it is something that will have to be done.

I am getting some rather strong convictions on personnel and methods of organization, but that will wait for a while.

I think I have made a fairly good start here with the people and seem to be getting along reasonably well with the Government so far.

On the 31st of this month I am going to take the American point of view on the Merchant Marine at a banquet here in London of all the steamship operators and builders. I think I have a chance to answer the criticism that has always been so prevalent as to why America should have a Merchant Marine.

I don't know that you want to be bothered with this kind of letter, but, if you do, just let me know and I will send them along to you when I have any personal observations. A great deal of the stuff that will go forward, it seems to me, might be interesting, but not particularly important. Nobody is going to fight a war over here unless Germany starts shooting somebody. Nobody wants it.

I miss seeing you all very, very much.

Faithfully yours,

P.S. — On my trips this afternoon, there was nothing interesting at the Turkish Embassy. The Cardinal[29] told me that the Apostolic Delegate in Spain, although an Italian, had informed him that there were approximately twenty thousand Italian troops still in the Franco army, but that there is a general feeling that the war is coming to a close.

At the Russian Embassy I had a very interesting time. I told him[30] point blank that America was frankly amazed at the so-called trials in Russia[31] and wondered if he cared to tell me something about them. He told me that they all date back to the original break of the Trotsky-Stalin philosophy; Stalin contending on one hand that Russia was big enough to maintain a social system of her own; Trotsky, on the other hand, saying that Russia could never prosper under a Communistic system unless they worked to make the rest of the world Communistic. This fight went on in a proper way between the ordinary political opponents for five or six years.

Then came time to lay out the Five Year Plan around 1938, and things started to be very bad in 1932 and 1933. Since they were not able to get outside capital, they were obliged to lay out their own money and, of course, this capital did not earn them any money and therefore conditions were extremely bad. But the Trotsky group, representing a great many men in high places, contended among themselves that there was still a good spot here for planning and plotting and Stalin recognized that this was taking place, but, because of the unsettlement and unrest, did not want to take dire steps.

---

29. Arthur Cardinal Hinsley (1865–1943), archbishop of Westminster and primate of the Roman Catholic Church in England, 1935–1943.
30. Ivan Mikhailovich Maisky (1874–1975), Soviet ambassador in London, 1932–43.
31. In its efforts to stamp out the alleged Nazi-Trotskyite conspiracy against Stalin in the wake of the assassination of party chief Sergei Kirov in December 1934, the Communist Party had interned, exiled or executed thousands of members of the Soviet hierarchy and the Red Army.

Then conditions started to improve in 1934, '35, '36 and '37, and this group, seeing that they would lose the advantage gained by unrest of the people, now decided to carry on with Japan and Germany, going so far as to pledge the Ukraine to Germany and the maritime port to Japan.

I said all this might be true, but why did these men hold these high places. He said that in a great many cases Stalin knew of their leanings, but tried to win them over, but finally decided it was impossible and took these steps.

He would like to go into this more at length later and I will have a talk with him. To be very frank, he looks scared to death of himself. My own belief is that, if the telephone had rung and said "Come back to Russia," he would have died right on my hands.

I don't know whether any of this makes any sense, and, as I say, I never have had any experience as to what you want in news, so please don't hesitate to tell me not to bother sending this and just keep up with the quick bulletins, but, if you take my word, these quick bulletins will be newsy but still unimportant as far as the United States of America's policy goes.

J.P.K.

Cordell Hull to Joseph P. Kennedy: *Diplomatic Dispatch*

March 14, 1938

In view of the events in Europe in the last few days the President and I have thought it would be well to reconsider the draft of your Pilgrim dinner speech further in the light of special significance which will be given to what you say just at this critical time. We are inclined to think that the tone of the speech is a little more rigid, and hence subject to possible misinterpretation, than would appear advisable at this precise moment.[32] Furthermore, with the President's approval, I am making within a few days a speech which will set forth as our Governmental policy our effort to avoid the extremes of isolationism and internationalism, indicating our desire to see established the fundamental principles which should govern relationships between nations and, while having no idea of policing the world, indicating that we should cooperate in every practical way with peace seeking nations in the establishment of these principles.

The following changes are suggested for your consideration:

Where you say "all the endless combinations one could imagine would be clamoring for preferential treatment" substitute "sectional" for "preferential."[33]

---

32. At his first official speaking engagement, the Pilgrims Dinner, JPK had decided to break with custom by addressing foreign affairs. In his Diplomatic Memoir he would recall:

> I thought it would be wise to specify within the framework of our policy, as it was being worked out by Mr. Roosevelt and Mr. Hull, those elements that might be of vital concern to the British mind and on which I felt certain that there was some confusion. I feared that the admitted fact of Anglo-American friendship was being wishfully and perhaps artfully interpreted to mean that our common bonds also held us together in the fashioning of our national policies. It would be unfair to the British folk, I thought, not to disabuse them of that thought.

33. Describing the "average American" as having "little interest in foreign affairs," JPK had written the original version to read:

> To give some picture of the situation to those who have less personal knowledge of the extent and variety of our country, I can only ask them to visualize that the entire British Empire were placed on one continent — on contiguous territory. All of the endless combinations one could imagine would be clamoring for preferential treatment. Group interests would be, or would appear to be, conflicting with each other and with the general interest. I think you will all agree that it would be difficult, under such conditions to evolve any semblance of a long-range foreign policy.

In the sentence "The ordinary American, the man in the street, whose collective thinking we describe as public opinion, has his mind on domestic matters these days" insert "primarily" before "on domestic matters these days."[34]

Omit the words "The lack of interest of the American people, by and large, in foreign political developments was brought home to me" and begin the next sentences with the phrase "When I was Chairman of the Securities and Exchange Commission in Washington one of the first things I had to do", etc.[35]

Omit the sentence "It is only when our vital interests are definitely affected that we are moved to action, and that is as it should be."

In the sentence beginning "We believe it is wise to make clear that any stand the American people takes" substitute "national interest" for "self-interest."[36]

In the sentence beginning "It must be realized, once and for all, that the great majority of Americans *oppose* any alliance" omit the words "once and for all", and insert "entangling" between "any" and "alliance", making the latter word plural to read "any entangling alliances"; place a period after "alliances" and omit the rest of that sentence.[37]

Omit the sentence "While many of us understand that other dilemmas confront the statesmen of Europe, we are still convinced in my country that the economic difficulties facing the world are more fundamental than the current political frictions which must, of course, be eased."

Omit the following three sentences: "The United States, as this now stands, has no plans to seek or offer assistance in the event that war — and I mean, of course, a war of major scope — should break out in the world. My country will endeavor to prepare itself for its own defense against any possible attack. Further than this, our present foreign policy does not attempt to go."

I have shown this to the President and he heartily approves.

Hull

---

34. The original version had read,
> Obviously, another factor of great importance at the present time is our own economic situation. As you know, we have by no means solved our internal difficulties. The every-day business of making a living has recently become harder for our people, following a period in which they had begun to breathe a bit more easily. The ordinary American, the man in the street, whose collective thinking we describe as public opinion, has his mind on domestic matters these days.

35. JPK's draft read,
> The lack of interest of the American people, by and large, in foreign political developments was brought home to me when I was chairman of the Securities and Exchange Commission in Washington.
> One of the first things I had to do was to make a comprehensive study of the operation of the various exchanges and speculative activities of our country. I learned, among other things, that speculation in foreign exchange is almost non-existent in the United States. The arbitrage dealers and the skilled professionals have this field practically to themselves.

36. "Nothing constructive can be built on false hopes and false fears," JPK had written. "We believe it is wise to make clear that any stand the American people takes will be based on the fundamental and firm ground of self-interest, which is the soundest basis for relations between nations."

37. JPK's original had read,
> It must be realized, once and for all, that the great majority of Americans oppose any alliance, agreement or understanding for joint action with any foreign country, even though the arrangement might be temporary and designed only for the prevention of war. Most Americans insist that their country retain its independent and unmortgaged judgment as to the merits of world crises as and when they arise. This viewpoint has dominated the whole foreign policy of the United States and it endures to this day. My country is unwilling to bind itself to any course of action in the future without an opportunity to examine the situation in the light which then envelops it. It seems to me, to judge from conflicting and contradictory reports which reach us from abroad, that this attitude of the United States is not well understood.

Joseph P. Kennedy: *Diary*

March 18, 1938

This morning, I presented my wife to the Queen at Buckingham Palace. The Queen was very gracious. Tonight, I faced the Pilgrims. Lord Halifax made a long and complimentary introduction, which put me in a bad spot to follow.

I ad libbed a few comebacks to his jokes about the hole-in-one,[38] the influence of my shining countenance on the Britain [*sic*] weather (there has been uninterrupted sunshine ever since we landed at Plymouth on March 1) and my horsemanship. At the last minute, we wrote in a paragraph or two of thanks to the Pilgrims and to Lord Derby,[39] who presided.

As soon as that was over, I launched into the set speech. Much of it was applauded, especially where I said it was a mistake to assume the United States would not fight unless actually invaded.

However, I got the feeling that parts of it fell flat. The speech was intended primarily for home consumption, as I am very anxious that my friends there should not think I have gone over to the British. Under the circumstances, I had to tell my British hosts a few homely truths, and they could not be expected to cheer their heads off. The note of frank dealing which I set in the speech seems to have aroused some favorable reaction at the Foreign Office.

Joseph P. Kennedy to Cordell Hull: *Diplomatic Dispatch*

228, March 18, 7 p.m. Confidential for the President and the Secretary.

I have discussed on several occasions confidentially the question of presenting American ladies at Court with the officials directly concerned. They have apparently given careful thought to the matter and there is no doubt in my mind that they are seriously concerned at the possible effect of our adopting a rule of no presentations. What they fear is that it will in some way be considered a reflection on the King and the Court here and lose for them a means of friendly propaganda in the United States. Our position has been fully explained to them and they have suggested a compromise that the presentations might be strictly confined to young ladies of debutante age, whether residents of the United States or daughters of Americans in England representing American business enterprise. There have already been a large number of applications for this year's Courts which begin in May and it will therefore be necessary for a definite decision one way or the other to be reached very shortly. My feeling on presentations is no different from what it was when I left America. Their opinion as to possible effect on the King is a matter that is beyond my scope and one that you should decide. Because it seemed to me to involve a serious question, I am sending you this message. All I want from you is an intimation as to whether this is serious enough, or not, to change all our minds.[40]

KENNEDY

The Ambassador, Mr. Johnson

38. On March 5, after a round of golf at Stoke Poges, JPK recorded in his diary that "[o]n the second hole, 128 yards, I holed my tee shot." The incident had received extensive coverage in the press both in Britain and in the United States.

39. Statesman and horse racing enthusiast, Edward George Villiers Stanley, seventeenth earl of Derby (1865–1948).

40. On March 21, the president would inform Hull, "I agreed with Kennedy's position in regard to the presentation of American ladies at the British Court—and I still do."

Joseph P. Kennedy to Arthur Krock

Private & Confidential[41] *London, March 21, 1938*

Dear Arthur:

The march of events in Austria made my first few days here more exciting than they might otherwise have been, but I am still unable to see that the Central European developments affect our country or my job. After three weeks in London, I still find myself able to evaluate European events against the background of our public opinion at home, as I understand it, and not against the semi-hysterical attitude which the professional diplomats here adopt whenever another foreseen step occurs.

My early talks with British and other diplomats convince me more than ever that there is no war in the immediate offing. Nobody is prepared to talk turkey to Messrs. Hitler and Mussolini, and nobody is prepared to face the risk of war by calling their bluffs. At this writing, it seems to be fundamental that the British will not do anything to check either one of them unless they actually fire guns. If that guess is correct, I am sure I am right that none of these various moves has any significance for the United States, outside of general interest. If and when a general European war breaks out, our people will review the situation and will decide that things are serious enough to face, but not before, as I see it. Therefore, I have been to no great pains thus far in reporting to the State Department the various bits of information and gossip which have come my way, because they don't mean anything as far as we are concerned.

The more I talk with people in the City, with diplomats, and with British Cabinet members, the more convinced I am in my own mind that the economic situation in Europe, and that includes Great Britain, is the key to the whole situation. All of the playing house they are doing on the political fronts is not putting people back to work and is not getting at the root of the situation. An unemployed man with a hungry family is the same fellow, whether the swastika or some other flag floats above his head.

Chamberlain and his close friends either do not realize or are trying to conceal that Great Britain is on the verge of serious economic difficulties. Unemployment is mounting and would do so at a faster rate if it were not for the armament program. The armament program, which is temporarily serving to retard the decline, they cannot afford.

The British press is discussing the possibility of war quite frankly and calmly, weighing the advantages and disadvantages in a more or less dispassionate manner. The conclusions are that Great Britain has no interest in a preventive war (in Czechoslovakia, for example).

I talked to Winston Churchill on the opening day of the debates in the House following the Austrian annexation. He seemed to think that sentiment is growing in the House in favor of Eden's policy of strict adherence to League procedure to curb aggressions such as Herr Hitler has just put across, not to mention the Poles. I must say that I am not sure he is right — or at least, that the House opinion he describes represents the country in any large measure. Chamberlain's policy of waiting to see what happens would appear to me to be the popular course, so far as an outsider can judge.

I hoped you liked my speech before the Pilgrims. I worked very hard on it, and intended it to reassure my friends and critics alike that I have not as yet been taken into the British camp. It seemed to me that it was imperative, just now, to tell our British

---

41. Despite its private and confidential designation, the document constitutes the first in the series of almost identical "political letters" that JPK sent to influential friends and associates in politics, journalism and business over the course of the spring of 1938.

cousins that they must not get into a mess counting on us to bail them out. We might or might not. But it hardly seems fair to let them assume that we will be ready, as last time, to come to their rescue if they get in a jam. I, personally, am by no means sure our people would consider it.

Chamberlain, Halifax, Inskip, and others to whom I have talked privately assured me that they understand this public opinion in the United States and approve of it. Therefore, it seemed to me, there could be no harm in speaking out. However, as I gave my set speech, it seemed to me that there was an awful let-down after I had said that no one must assume the United States would not fight except if invaded. That, of course, they cheered. But when I told them that it was also highly probable that our country would remain neutral in another world war, they cooled off.

The dinner was well done. Lord Halifax made a charming and friendly introduction, and the atmosphere was such that it was difficult to let them have the unpalatable truth I had to offer. On the whole, I think it went off quite well. By the way, I heard Halifax described the other day as "an efficient saint." He seems to be a man of great parts — a scholar, sportsman and everything that an upper class Englishman who gives his life to public service ought to be.

These remarks of the amateur diplomat will not inform you very much, but I felt that I must not let my self-imposed exile lose me the friendship of men I value as much as I do you. From time to time, as the spirit moves me, I shall inflict on you such oddments of information of opinion as come my way.

On your side, I hope you will keep me informed as to what is going on at home. Our sources of information here are, as you know, lamentably scarce, and it would be a real favor if you help me to keep from losing touch. Our ambassadors here probably go native from lack of news as much as from British influence.

To revert to the war situation, Jan Masaryk, the Czech Minister here and son of the old President, gave me to understand that his country will make its deal with Germany, unpalatable as it may be, unless it is assured of British protection. It does not consider the proffered French assistance as valuable enough to justify putting up resistance against Berlin. I am not sure how well he represents the official views of Prague, but I was struck by the fact that their Minister in Paris, who has been conducting the conversations at the Quai d'Orsay, said practically the same thing to the Anglo-American Press Association there the other day.

My wife and five of the children have arrived and are more or less well installed. We are trying to sort them out into the various schools which will be best for their minds and souls. As soon as that is all settled, I shall feel a load off of my mind and shall settle down to the more serious side — if there is one — of the diplomatic career.

With best wishes, I am,

Sincerely yours,

Joseph P. Kennedy to Arthur Krock

Private & Confidential London, March 28, 1938[42]

Dear Arthur:

Every time I see an intimation in the papers that the uncertainties of the foreign situation are factors in the American market's nose-dive and the general industrial pes-

---

42. This March 28 letter constituted the second in JPK's series of "political letters."

simism in the United States,[43] I don't know whether to be sad or mad. I wish our fellows at home would attend to the worries they have on their own doorsteps and keep Europe out of their minds until they made some headway in their own country.

Of course, I appreciate that war scares are usually more acute in the United States than they are in Europe, but even at that I can't see how anyone could (a) believe that a general war will break out during the remainder of this year or (b) could figure it would affect the United States very adversely if it did.

I am more than ever convinced there is not fight in prospect. Chamberlain's speech last Thursday was a masterpiece. I sat spellbound in the diplomatic gallery and heard it all. It impressed me as a combination of high morals and politics such as I had never witnessed.[44]

Now that the initial indignation of certain elements of the public here has worn off, following Eden's resignation, I have the distinct feeling that Chamberlain is gaining in general popularity. His speech last week, it seemed to me, simply slew the Opposition. I listened to Major Attlee when he attacked the Government's position, as Chamberlain had just outlined it, and could not see that he made any points at all.[45]

All this means, as I size it up, that there will be no war if Chamberlain stays in power with strong public backing, which he seems to be acquiring day by day. A deal will be made with Italy (it may be practically complete by now) which will include a trade agreement and arrangements for restricting naval force in the Mediterranean. Germany will get whatever it wants in Czechoslovakia without sending a single soldier across the border. The Czechs will go, hat in hand, to Berlin and ask the Führer what he wants done, and it will be done.

As a matter of fact, it has already started. On instructions from Berlin, the Foreign Office in Prague called in the foreign newspaper men and told them that they could not send from there any news about Germany or Austria. The press associations, which had formerly used Vienna as a clearing house for their Central European news, had intended to transfer their large organizations to Prague — indeed, many of them are there already.

With Prague cut off, some of them are going to try Budapest, but they know they won't last long there. The same instructions will come to Admiral Horthy[46] as were sent to Prague. As far as I can gather, press associations, The New York Times, and other organizations of large scope, will probably end up in Zurich as a center for Balkan and Central European news. They believe that the Germans will not try to intimidate the Swiss or, if they do, the Swiss will not give in.

The Germano-Czech situation will solve itself without interference by France or Russia, it appears from here. As long as Great Britain will not give unconditional promises to back them up in a fight, the French will not do anything rash to stop the German

---

43. Over the course of the month of March, fear of impending war in Europe coupled with setbacks in economic recovery generally had caused Wall Street stock prices to fall, dragging the Dow-Jones Industrials average down nearly 25 points to a yearly low of 69.7.

44. On March 24, the prime minister described "the fundamental basis of British foreign policy [as] the maintenance and preservation of peace . . ." Referring to direct and indirect British commitments to defend other states (including Czechoslovakia) against unprovoked aggression, however, he went on to suggest that "that does not mean that nothing would make us fight."

45. "I could not find any approach to any policy to establish peace on firm foundations," the Labour Party leader, Clement Richard Attlee (1883–1967), had responded. "I found the Prime Minister stating very strongly the principle that the rule of force should give way to the rule of law," he continued. "[Chamberlain] did not believe in the arbitrament of force, but in actual fact he yields to force all the time . . . and he is proceeding on a policy of negotiating with persons who have shown their belief in force and who exercise force even while he is negotiating with them."

46. Admiral Miklós Horthy de Nagybánya (1868–1957), regent and dictator of Hungary, 1920–44.

domination of Czechoslovakia and the Czechs in power know that. The Russians are too disorganized and too far away.

So where is your war? The Spanish revolution seems about to fold up in favor of Franco. Chamberlain made it plain that neither Great Britain nor France will take any steps to bolster up the government forces, so Franco ought to be able to finish it off this spring. That will be at least temporarily the end of that danger spot.

All of this is merely to illustrate how I find it ridiculous that an American investor in his own country's securities should worry that war in Europe will tilt his apple cart further on the bias. You know as well as I do that the vast majority of speculators don't know a damned thing about foreign affairs and usually care less. Why are they concerned about them now?

Great Britain ought to be in for something of a mild boom soon, I should think. Chamberlain has given the rearmament program full priority over the ordinary commerce of the country, practically as in war-time. This means that money will be spent and in large amounts. The stimulation of the heavy industries ought to induce an acceleration of general trade at even a greater rate than we experienced in 1935, after the bonus and other spending measures had been adopted.

Now, if we could just start a comeback in the United States to coincide with this movement over here, perhaps the two countries could establish the basis of some kind of permanent prosperity, for a period, at least. But if we keep lagging behind, Britain can't make the grade alone. Our capital would begin to move over here as things got better in London, until prices would get too high and there would be a break in the market here.

That would probably be the finishing touch for all of us, and we would be in a tailspin from which there would be no pulling out. We must do something in our country to get going. I should be sorry if the needle had to be a revival of governmental spending, but I am beginning to think that might not be so bad as letting this thing go to what appears to be its inevitable end.

A few more months of depression of values will have us and the rest of the world so deeply in the doghouse that war might seem to be an attractive out. That is the danger in world-wide depressions such as we have nowadays. Everybody gets to feeling poor and put upon at the same time. International tempers flare up. Pressure is brought to bear on those in authority to do something drastic to better the economic lot of their subjects.

I am sorry I haven't any more cheerful news for you at the moment. Britain seems to be the only really bright spot, but they can't go on much further unless there is a general pick-up. After all, the armament program will have to be financed with borrowed money. They have practically reached the limit of taxation, they seem to think.

They are shooting the works in the hope that they can work out a general appeasement, once they are strong enough to stand up to the bargaining table with a few aces in the hole, and from that situation general prosperity may be revived. That is a long shot, perhaps, but at least they think they know what they are doing. Are any of the rest of us conscious of what we are doing, if anything?

With best wishes, I am,

249

Joseph P. Kennedy: *Diary*

Monday, April 4, 1938

I attended dinner (list attached) given by Lord and Lady Astor.[47] (I like her very much, a hard worker and a great heart.)

My dinner companion was Mrs. Churchill and I had a very interesting discussion with her. I told her my idea of an Ambassador was to do some work, such as telling America, Chamberlain's part in Irish negotiations, etc. She told me her husband liked me very much and would see me any time that I cared to see him.

The Archbishop of Canterbury,[48] whom I met, told me he knew of no one who had met the success I had since my arrival and wanted to have me for lunch.

Had a long talk with Duke of Kent[49] who is crazy to go to America for the Fair.[50] Told me of talk with the President some time ago at Bermuda, who told him he knew that King George hated Americans. Kent said he really didn't but was mad that the brothers had all had affairs with Americans.

He thought that Mrs. Simpson,[51] who he said hated him, was bitch [*sic*] and would try to go over herself in order to spoil it for him. Asked me to try and arrange it from America.

Talked with Montagu Norman[52] who characterized the Whitney affair as a suicide, just somebody out of his mind.[53]

Talked with Brazilian Ambassador, Lord Halifax and many others.

Left at 11:45. Went to Ball to see Kathleen.

Joseph P. Kennedy: *Diary*

April 9, 1938 (Written evening of April 10, 1938)

Rose and I arrived by car[54] sharply at 7, were met by _____ [*sic*] in a gray suit and escorted to our rooms after he commented on our usual promptness.

We were shown to a beautiful sitting room with gorgeous paintings of Queen Mary, Duke of Windsor (then Wales) King Edward, Queen Alexandra, Duke of Cambridge and numerous miniatures. A lovely green room.

We were served sherry, dressed and went to reception room at 8:20. There we saw Mr. & Mrs. Neville Chamberlain (Prime Minister) Lord Elphinstone and his wife (a sister of Queen Mary)[55] and the Court List.

---

47. Waldorf Astor, second Viscount Astor (1879–1952), chairman of the Royal Institute of International Affairs, 1935–49, and his wife, Nancy Witcher Langhorne Astor, Viscountess Astor (1879–1964), a native of Virginia and the first woman to take her seat in the House of Commons, as a Conservative for the Sutton Division of Plymouth.
48. The Most Reverend and Right Honorable Cosmo Gordon Lang, first Baron Lang of Lambeth (1864–1945), archbishop of Canterbury, 1928–42.
49. George Edward Alexander Edmund (1902–42), the king's youngest brother.
50. The 1939 New York World's Fair, that is.
51. In December 1936, Edward VIII, Kent's eldest brother, had abdicated in order to marry the twice-divorced American socialite (Bessie) Wallis Warfield Simpson (1896–1986).
52. Montagu Collet Norman (1871–1950), governor of the Bank of England, 1920–44.
53. That month, Richard Whitney (1888–1974), the former four-term president of the New York Stock Exchange, 1930–35, would plead guilty to charges of grand larceny for embezzlement and misuse of both family and customer funds at the Wall Street brokerage house that bore his name.
54. At Windsor Castle.
55. The former Lady Mary Frances Bowes-Lyon (1883–1961) was in fact the elder sister of the then queen, Elizabeth, and the wife of Sydney Herbert, sixteenth Baron Elphinstone (1869–1955). As King George V's queen consort, Queen Mary (1867–1953) was the mother of the present king and his brothers, the dukes of Windsor, Gloucester and Kent.

I sat on the Queen's[56] right. She was dressed in pearls and on her left sat the Prime Minister. On my right sat Lady Halifax, Lady-in-Waiting to the Queen.

The Queen started talking to me and lost her napkin. I looked down. She told me it was gone but I found it sticking up and retrieved it.

We discussed American Press, relations of England and America. She impressed me as a most charming person with a fine head.

Lady Halifax and I discussed the story of Lord Halifax and my efforts to get the nuns out of Spain.[57] She sincerely hoped it would be done. I told her and the Prime Minister later that it would be a great stroke and the Prime Minister observed he hoped it would happen, but they had had such bad luck trying to get people out that he was holding his breath.

As dinner closed a Scotch bag-piper walked through the room playing. A red-coated orchestra played all through dinner and after dinner.

After dinner we walked through the room, bowing to the Queen, and followed in after the King into another room.

He called me aside on a sofa and we had a talk.

I told him they should come to America. He told me of the Music Hall joke about Kennedy being father of his country, which amused him no end. I told him publicity and propaganda was bad in America for British and suggested the right people contact American press so that both sides of all questions should get proper hearing. He seemed to have trouble concentrating.

After our talk we joined the ladies and I mentioned to Chamberlain I had written to Rome about Austria and would advise him if I heard anything.

The Queen took Rose and me into a room and showed us some things of Mary Queen of Scots [sic], necklace.

Talked with one of King's secretaries, who handles press. Said he had seen debutante letter, thought the King and Queen might stop off in America, at Washington, New York and Boston after they had visited Canada in a couple of years. I insisted they would help Great Britain immensely.

Talked with a descendant of General Gage, great General of Revolutionary War, offered to show me some relics of his.

Prime Minister commenting on election in Fulham said doctor was hard to beat and times were not very exciting, or the Government might have won.[58] People never vote for you out of gratitude but they do sometimes if they were frightened.

While I was talking with the Queen somebody mentioned we had to push our clocks ahead an hour. I said it was unfortunate it had to happen tonight and the Queen thought that was a "very sweet thought."

We retired about 12:30. I stopped the clocks in both rooms, mine by pushing a towel down in back, Rose's by just stopping it.

After I had retired, Rose wanted her window opened. I got up and tried by no luck, and as I looked out the window the guard was marching up the long walk, and so to sleep.

---

56. Elizabeth, formerly Lady Elizabeth Bowes-Lyon (1900–), daughter of the fourteenth earl of Strathmore, queen consort of George VI (1936–1952), and afterward Queen Mother.

57. In March, while JPK paid a visit to Jean, Pat and Eunice at the Convent of the Sacred Heart in Roehampton, the mother superior appealed to him for assistance in the evacuation of thirty-four Sacred Heart nuns from war-torn Barcelona.

58. Despite low voter turnout, on April 6, Labour candidate Dr. Edith Summerskill had beaten out her Conservative opponent by some 1,421 votes in the West Fulham by-election. The general election of 1935, by contrast, had returned a Tory majority of 3,483.

April 10th, 1938

Dear Pat,

We have just spent a most delightful day here after a very brilliant dinner party last night. I sat on the right of the King, and I was so thrilled. We shall be returning in the morning. Much love.

Mother

Pat — Please keep this note, dear   M

Joseph P. Kennedy: *Diary*

Sunday Morning [April 10]

Awoke about eight o'clock, bathed, shaved and Rose and I had breakfast in living room. They had omelet, grilled sole and bacon on a heater moved into the room. After breakfast read papers and wrote letters to Eddie and Mary, Betsy, Missy, Ruth Greene,[59] Bobby, Teddy. (Last night I wrote Joe and Jack, Margaret, Loretta[60] and Aunt Katie.)

Left at 10:50 for Mass at church in Windsor. Greeted by priest on arrival on street and there were four guards, in red coats, to salute us at entrance of church.

The priest escorted us down to two separate kneeling benches in front of church. Rose on left and I on right.

Palm Sunday. Read the long gospel in English. We had to stand. After church went back to see him and say good-bye. Then back to Palace. Rose and I took a walk for a half hour over beautiful lawns. We both felt the whole thing wasn't real, it was like playing soldier and turning back pages of history. While we were walking Princess Elizabeth walked out of bushes, smiling. I didn't recognize her but Rose did.

We returned and got ready for lunch. We started at 1:15 but King and Queen, with the two Princesses, had stopped in the long corridor. We all joined up and I talked with the Princesses. We all went into lunch. I sat on Mrs. Chamberlain's right and Princess Elizabeth on my right.

Princess said she liked movies, loved Seven Dwarfs, particularly the animals when Snow White talked to them, liked Silly Symphonies. When I asked her if she had seen Yank at Oxford[61] she said they hadn't seen many.

Mrs. Chamberlain asked her what her favorite study was and she said geography. She had just finished studying the Atlantic Coast of U.S.A.

She liked swimming and horseback riding. She batted a ball around with King and Queen, whom she called Daddy and Mummy, but it was too hot. We were laughing at her little sister, who was eating fast across the table. Princess Elizabeth said she only came down Sundays and as the grown-ups always finished first they always were embarrassed. She is charming — they both are.

Mrs. Chamberlain discussed Boake Carter[62] and I told her and the King about what a gallant figure Roosevelt was even after Infantile.[63]

---

59. His former secretary in Washington.
60. His sisters, Margaret Burke and Loretta Connelly.
61. MGM's first British production, starring Robert Taylor, Lionel Barrymore and Maureen O'Sullivan had opened in February.
62. British-born former *Daily Mail* reporter, (Harold Thomas Henry) "Boake" Carter (1898–1944), had come to prominence in the United States first as a syndicated columnist for the *Philadelphia Public Ledger* in the 1920s and then as a radio commentator in the following decade. The enormous popularity of his nationwide coverage of the Lindbergh kidnapping for CBS had given rise by 1933 to a polemical weeknight news show. Carter's sensational broadcasts (often excoriating the Roosevelt administration, or-

After lunch we looked out window, heard band, saw crowd and flowers, and King joined Chamberlain and me and said he was thinking over what I said last night about American Press getting all sides. We all three agreed it was important.

Chamberlain told me Italy agreement O.K. but important country though [*sic*]. The Germany agreement not too promising. Every time he tried to get the Germans to say what they wanted they became very indefinite. For instance, they holler for colonies and when he gets them in to discuss it they say O.K. six or ten years from today. He said they always were that way even back in Bismark's time.

He said how purposeless it all was. He thought six years ago they had made good financial agreements and now a war scare made everything impossible.

King and Queen invited us to walk and look at flowers and have tea, so we started out. I walked with the Queen and, as always, found her most charming. We walked down from the castle, went to the Tomb of Old Duchess of Kent (Mother of Victoria) and looked at her statue, marveling at the sculpture of lace on her dress. Trees and flowers were beautiful. Then the Queen took us over to the house where Queen Victoria did most of her work, sitting outside in the air. Queen commented it didn't sound very attractive to her.

I am impressed by the willingness of the English to jolly about the old Kings and Queens. They pay them all homage when alive, but when they die they are fair subjects for kidding.

The old house is a model of Victorian period to the nth degree — no electricity or any conveniences. The Queen told me she and the King spent their honeymoon there.

We then all took cars and went to see a new garden that the King is interested in.

I commented on the fact that the King with half a dozen equerries carried a big bunch of keys and let us all in a big gate and locked it after us, like a watchman.

After passing through pretty gardens we took the cars and went to the King's house where he spends his week-ends when they are in residence at Buckingham. It's just like a modern home and not like a palace. They've just built a swimming pool and we went through the miniature house presented by the people of Wales to the two children. You bend down to get in, but it is quite complete. The little Princess wanted to clean off everybody's shoes.

We then went over to the house for tea. Rose sat with the children. They are darlings, very smart, well-mannered and intelligent and industrious. They showed us the garden they planted and how neatly they hung up all their tools.

During tea Lady Elphinstone had a heart attack and it was quite terrible. The Queen retained her composure, said good-bye to the Chamberlains who were leaving, handled herself like a Queen that one reads about. Rose rushed the children out of doors and took care of them and earned the gratitude of both the King and Queen who spoke very feelingly of it to me. The Queen said that Rose has established a bond between them.

We finally came back to the Castle, bring the children, and suggesting to Lady Halifax we should go back to London because of the happening, but she telephoned later that the King and Queen wanted us to stay and that Lady Elphinstone was better.

---

ganized labor and the British Empire while celebrating the virtues of conservatism and isolationism) made him the most widely listened to radio commentator of the mid-1930s, but promoted stormy relations with his sponsors.

63. Poliomyelitis, then commonly known as infantile paralysis.

Tonight we dined again, I on the Queen's right, Rose on King's right. I explained the presentation idea to the Queen. She agreed it was snobbery and was glad I did what I did.

I had another talk with the King after dinner. He asked about Lewis[64] and Green.[65] Told me about Jack Morgan shooting in Scotland.[66] Would never permit his guests to have their morning mail or papers before they went shooting because it would upset them.

Saying good-night to Queen she invited Rose and me to her own apartment to show us some beautiful Gainsboroughs, and then to Victoria's private sitting room. Said good-night and good-bye and she said we must meet again soon.

Wrote to Ford, et als.

In the afternoon Sir Richard Molyneaux ("Dick" to me)[67] who knows all about paintings and the Castle took Rose and me around and showed us all the beauties, and so ends a great week-end.

Joseph P. Kennedy to T. J. White[68]

London, April 27, 1938

Dear Tom:

You were a peach to write me all that news, and I got your hint on the Head situation.[69] She is very sweet and is most helpful to me, and, of course, she is almost heart-broken about this donkey over here who represents some bank and says they are running the business now and that Tom White is out. My only discomforting thought is of that swell guy out there in California in the hands of those sharpshooters in New York. Of course, the only thing I blame him for is that he didn't take my advice, but, in his mental state, I can understand that.[70]

I hope David and his wife got along well down in Rome, but I am sure they did.

I am still getting along very nicely, but hope to come home and report to you directly in June.

Keep playing along with those monkeys and remember that piece of advice I gave you — I don't pay any attention to it myself, but you have sense enough to — and that is, never get so mad that it costs you money.

---

64. John Llewellyn Lewis (1880–1969), president of the United Mine Workers of America, 1920–60, and former vice president of the American Federation of Labor, 1934–35, had broken with the AFL and went on to found the Committee for Industrial Organization (later the Congress of Industrial Organizations) in 1935.

65. William Green (1870–1952), president of the American Federation of Labor, 1924–52, and former secretary-treasurer of the United Mine Workers, 1912–22.

66. The king considered financier John Pierpont Morgan, Jr. (1867–1943), not only a friend, but also "the world's greatest gentleman," and had hunted with him, both at Balmoral and at Morgan's Gannochy Lodge in Scotland.

67. Major the Honourable Sir Richard Molyneux (1873–1954), groom-in-waiting to Kings George V and Edward VIII, and extra equerry to Queen Mary.

68. Thomas Justin White (1884–1948), general manager of Hearst Enterprises.

69. Reputedly the highest paid British female executive of the 1920s and 1930s, Alice Maud Head (1886–1981) served as both managing director of William Randolph Hearst's National Magazine Company of London and editor of its *Good Housekeeping*, 1924–39. Since her earliest association with Hearst in the late 1910s, Head had acted as Hearst's personal representative in Europe. As such, she had overseen the publisher's extensive acquisitions of European art objects and antiquities at auction, and had directed the purchase (and the eventual dispersal) of Hearst's St. Donat's Castle in Wales and its contents.

70. In an effort to stave off the dissolution of his holdings, nearly two years earlier William Randolph Hearst had called upon JPK to oversee the restructuring and refinancing of his crumbling empire. Since then, however, JPK's departure for London coupled with infighting within the Hearst organization had resulted in JPK's supersession in favor of Hearst's longtime counsel, Clarence Shearn.

I am not kidding myself about all this talk of candidate for President.[71] I am going to wrap up this job as best I know how and do as much good as I can, and then I am going right back and go into business, and spend my time sharp-shooting at those gentlemen who now think they are your boss.

I was intensely interested in Cissy's letter and also in the boss's editorial.[72] They were masterpieces, but he also ought to write an editorial calling on business not to be looking for an opportunity to watch the failure of this Administration so that there will be a possibility of a clean sweep in 1940, because, if the President increases the debt four billion dollars and it doesn't catch on, it just means more trouble to try and work out of. The trend of the world isn't back to Conservatism, it's going toward Progressive Liberalism, with intelligent management. One question I ask myself — will the world be any better and will America be safer and happier and more prosperous if Great Britain is destroyed? Think it over. I am thinking about it.

I miss you very much. My best to all.

Yours sincerely,
Joseph P. Kennedy

Joseph P. Kennedy to Drew Pearson: *Telegram*

GROSVENOR SQUARE, MAY 3, 1938

DEAR DREW I KNOW YOU AND BOB DONT WANT TO HURT ME UNLESS YOU HAVE DEFINITE REASONS YOUR STORY ON THE CLIVEDEN SET[73] IS COMPLETE BUNK THERE IS NOT ONE SINGLE WORD OF TRUTH TO IT AND IT HAS DONE ME GREAT HARM YOU KNOW I WOULD NOT MAKE THIS FIRM DENIAL UNLESS IT WAS SO IT IS UNFORTUNATE WHEN I AM WORKING AS HARD AS I CAN TO KEEP THIS SITUATION STRAIGHT THAT THIS KIND OF STORY SHOULD BE PUBLISHED THE REPERCUSSIONS OVER HERE HAVE BEEN EXTREMELY BAD I DONT KNOW WHAT YOU CAN DO ABOUT IT BUT THOUGHT I SHOULD TELL YOU[74]

KENNEDY

71. JPK's "private and confidential" political letters to politicians and members of the press had given rise to speculation (which would find its way into print over the coming months) that he would be a Democratic candidate for the presidency in 1940. Upon hearing of JPK's expressed attitude toward his possible candidacy, William Randolph Hearst responded, "Ambassador Kennedy would make a very strong candidate. He may not want to consider the matter himself, but other people are considering it seriously — and if he could get the country out of this mess he would have no right to refuse."

72. On April 7, Cissy Patterson, publisher of the *Washington Herald,* had printed an open letter to the president calling upon him to curb his "hostile attitude toward legitimate business," his "shifting policies" and his "insistence on discredited tax methods and other laws which prevent the earning and retaining of fair and honest profits" in the face of the current recession. Hearst's hearty concurrence appeared likewise upon the editorial pages of his own papers throughout the country.

73. Since late 1937, Claud Cockburn, the former *London Times* correspondent in Washington and current *Pravda* correspondent in London, had made a series of assertions regarding "pro-Nazi intrigues centering on Cliveden," the Astors' Buckinghamshire estate. Drawing upon the claims that Cockburn had made in his leftist London news sheet, *The Week,* Pearson and his partner Bob Allen opened their nationally syndicated "Washington Merry-Go-Round" column of April 22 with the statement, "Latest American to be wooed by the Clivedon [sic] group is genial Joe Kennedy, new Ambassador to Britain. Reports are that Joe has been taken in just a bit by the Clivedon charm, not on the Nazi-Fascist theories, but on the idea of cooperating with the Tories of Great Britain."

74. JPK's dismay at the columnists was short-lived, apparently; he would send them an installment of his latest "Private and Confidential" political bulletin later that day. "As a matter of fact, I have never been to Cliveden, and I have seen very little of the persons who go to make up that so-called 'set,'" he informed Pearson and Allen in the short personalized section of the letter that otherwise touched on the budget, the Anglo-Irish agreement and the aftermath of the *Anschluss.* The Astors, he said, "have never asked me to do anything, have never suggested anything whatever to me, and have done nothing more than to show me the ordinary and formal courtesy which all Englishmen display toward a new Ambassador."

Joseph P. Kennedy: *Diary*

May 5, 1938

At luncheon at Lady Astor's today, the talk turned on the Court presentations. She asked George Bernard Shaw[75] if he approved of my decision. "Certainly not", the old gentleman replied. "We don't want the Court to have only selected riff-raff." Lindbergh[76] was there and spoke most intelligently of most of [my (?)] speeches here, which he appears to have followed in some detail. He seemed to be particularly struck at the warning I sounded before the Association of Chambers of Commerce to the effect that the democracies must look to themselves for help.

Joseph P. Kennedy to Lady Astor

London, May 10, 1938

Dear Lady Astor:

Well, you see what a terrible woman you are, and how a poor little fellow like me is being politically seduced.[77]

O weh ist mir!

J.P.K.

Rose Kennedy: *Diary*

May 11, 1938

Lunch at Prime Minister Neville Chamberlain's home at 10 Downing Street. Told me that only until a short time ago, there was a grill over the balcony in the House of Commons as it was believed a plain uncovered view of ladies would be too distracting. Prime Minister has several characteristics like Joe, though Joe has told me not to compare them to people. Firstly, both had a business background, both love to walk with their wives for recreation, thirdly, both take music for recreation. I found that he talked easily and he does not smile as often or with as much gaiety as Joe, nor has he such a spontaneous laugh as the President.

Joseph P. Kennedy to Jay Pierrepont Moffat[78]

Private & Confidential London, May 17th, 1938

Dear Pierrepont:

Henlein's surprise visit was the chief topic of interest this week, and we have all been busy trying to find out what he did and said here.[79] The British are more concerned than they allow to appear over him and his Sudeten Germans. It is feared here that these people may provoke by their extreme conduct some incident which will end up in fighting.

75. Irish-born dramatist, journalist, critic, Fabian Socialist and 1935 Nobel laureate for literature, George Bernard Shaw (1856–1950).
76. In the wake of the kidnapping and murder of his eldest child, aviator Charles Augustus Lindbergh (1902–74) had emigrated to Europe with his family in 1936. Although the Lindberghs were currently making arrangements to move to France, they spent much of the spring of 1938 in England.
77. He had sent her the recent Pearson and Allen clipping, presumably.
78. Jay Pierrepont Moffat (1896–1943), chief of the State Department's Division of European Affairs, 1937–40. The letter constituted the latest installment in JPK's series of "private and confidential" political letters.
79. Konrad Henlein (1898–1945), the leader of the Sudeten German minority in Czechoslovakia who had

It appears that Henlein, in talking with British political figures here, moderated his tone considerably from his Carlsbad speech and tried to convince them that he is a reasonable man, pushed on by extremist followers whom he must placate.[80] The men he interviewed impressed on him the imperative need for keeping his and his party's demands within the field of negotiability. Some of them told him things they would do in case of a putsch in Bohemia which were far in advance of anything the Government has been willing to promise the Prague authorities.

The Sudeten German leader left the impression that he and his lieutenants, if not their followers, have learned a good deal by watching the progress of events in Austria since the Anschluss. They have now decided that they would be much better off if they were in control of a practically autonomous portion of Czechoslovakia than they would be if they were swallowed up in the Greater Reich. Also, they realize that their part of the country would be the first theater of battle, if things came to war.

He told the politicians here that he and his party would be satisfied by autonomy for the Sudeten Germans in the municipal and county councils, with their territory exactly delimited; they will accept any foreign mediation in the situation, even that of the League of Nations; they want created a central office to look after the affairs of Germans in Czechoslovakia, but they are willing to abide by the democratic system of voting for and in parliament; they want the central government to retain direction of foreign affairs, the army, the judiciary and the national finances; they want a "proper proportion" of the national budget, after providing for the costs of the above-mentioned services, to be expended under the direction of the autonomous local governments; they accept a neutral judiciary, with no party judges such as they have in Germany; they advocate renunciation of the alliance with the Soviet Union, but are willing to campaign for that in the ordinary parliamentary way.

Granting of these concessions by Prague would "awaken a new loyalty" in the members of his party, who now favor outright Anschluss with Germany, Henlein said. The rank and file are still under the influence of the enthusiasm generated by Hitler's annexation of Austria, he implied, but the leaders of the movement have been won pretty well away from that idea by the fate of Seyss-Inquart et al.

According to Jan Masaryk, the Czech Minister here, all of the points Henlein outlined in London are acceptable to the authorities in Prague, with the exception of giving up the Russian alliance. Prague is determined to hang onto this until something better turns up to take its place.

Of course, Henlein may have sung a different tune when he got to Berlin. In some unofficial quarters here, the circumstances and results of his trip are regarded as encouraging. These observers are convinced that he came without pre-arrangement with Hitler, and that Berlin is too busy with other matters just now to do anything very serious about the German minority in Czechoslovakia. It is plain that the Czechs themselves have not yet abandoned hope that the British and French may be able to stave off the Germans from actual annexation of any part of their territory.

---

long maintained secret ties to the Reich, had spent the period of May 12–14 in London. During informal meetings, he had reiterated the Sudeten demands for autonomy from Prague, but had assured British government officials of his hope for a peaceful solution.

80. Over the course of April and May, on orders from Berlin, Henlein had proffered a number of demands that he knew would be rejected by the Czech government. His agitation on behalf of the German minority crescendoed in his speech at Carlsbad on April 24 when he demanded, among other concessions from Prague, the establishment and recognition of a separate Sudeten state in which ethnic Germans would assume full autonomy including the freedom to espouse and practice the "ideology of the German race." Additionally, he insisted on full reparations for what he characterized as the injustices that the Sudeten Germans had suffered at the hands of the Czechs since 1919.

As for Hitler's visit to Italy, the news filtering through is scarce outside of what was permitted to be published in the papers.[81] It would appear that Mussolini preserved his bargaining position and is more than ever resolved not to put all of his eggs in the German basket.

At Geneva, the British carried out their pledge to Italy in the matter of securing the possibility of recognition by League members of the Italian conquest of Abyssinia. The uninspiring role that Lord Halifax had to play there aroused a considerable amount of criticism here, but the critics were cynical rather than constructive. They admitted, by implication, that there was little else that could be done.

All usual indices on the economic side here continue to point downward. There is no indication that the current slow and steady decline will be checked in the next two months. The forecasters say that a definite reversal of the movement will depend on American economic and European political developments. Pending these, they see no reason to expect anything but perhaps temporary spurts from time to time.

With best wishes, I am,

Sincerely yours,

Rose Kennedy: *Diary*

May 17, 1938

Gave dinner in honor of Foreign Minister Lord and Lady Halifax. He was at one time Vice-Roy of India. He is about ___ years old, is said to be a very devout churchman of Church of England, is scholarly, brilliant, has great charm.[82] Had shad roe sent over from America which arrived frozen and in very good condition and tasted delicious. Surprised how many people were familiar with it and enjoyed it. (Lady Halifax is often Lady-in-Waiting to Queen)

After dinner we had a moving picture, "Test Pilot", with Myrna Loy and Clark Gable. Ass [sic] made with collaboration of Army machines and there were some spectacular shots made of spectacular maneuvers. Colonel Charles Lindbergh, who sat next to me said the aeronautical display was very authentic and well worth seeing. He came with his wife[83] and mother-in-law, Mrs. Dwight Morrow. This is second time I have met him — first time being at Cliveden, home of Nancy Astor. He acts very shy, smiles in a boyish sort of way and seems to retire to a corner where he stays most of the time. Anne is all poetry and light, simple, natural and lovable with an enchanting smile. Mrs. Morrow is an alert, keen, pleasant woman who pleased me enormously by saying that even though she was a Republican she was glad to see Joe here.

Joseph P. Kennedy to James Roosevelt

Private & Confidential London, May 31st, 1938

Dear Jimmy:

The momentary lull in Central Europe has not caused anyone here to think that the Czechoslovak business is settled. The hard part lies ahead, of course, and the For-

81. Hitler and a number of high German officials had spent the week of May 2–9 on an official visit to Rome and Naples. Although the subject of Hitler's meetings with Mussolini went undisclosed, each had reaffirmed his commitment to the Rome-Berlin Axis in public statements during the visit.
82. Halifax was fifty-five at the time, and an Anglo-Catholic.
83. Anne Spencer Morrow Lindbergh (1906–), author, diarist, aviator and daughter of former senator from New Jersey, ambassador to Mexico and J. P. Morgan partner, Dwight Whitney Morrow.

eign Office takes only what comfort it legitimately can from the fact that things have gone along thus far without greater friction.

Arthur Sulzberger,[84] who is here for a few days, was in Prague just before the first balloting last week-end, when such alarm was felt in London, and he brings rather encouraging news based on talks he had there. He reports that the Czechs are confident that they will effect a peaceful and enduring arrangement with the German minority.

They seemed to him to feel that the Germans are bluffing. He found somewhat the same sentiment in Paris. He is convinced that there would have been no German movement into Czechoslovakia over the last week-end, even if the British Foreign Office had not made such energetic diplomatic representations.

However, the British firmness did awaken considerable gratitude in French official circles. It was felt that, whether immediately imperative or not, the warnings conveyed in Berlin served notice on the Germans that Great Britain could not be included completely out, to borrow Sam Goldwyn's gem.

The German official press has taken much the same view, but has twisted the sequence of events to show that the British were merely seeking a cheap and easy opportunity to make a meaningless gesture in order to secure prestige in the eyes of the smaller countries and France. This is indignantly denied here, of course, and Government-inspired editorials have appeared praising the initiative of British diplomacy.

I gathered that Arthur Sulzberger and other publishers have now decided to make Prague their Central European news headquarters. The Czech government has no objection and continues to offer complete freedom from censorship. However, it would probably be wise if the American news gathering agencies refrained from routing their Austrian news through Prague, so as to avoid chances for German recriminations against the Czech government for circulating false news about the Greater Reich.

We seem to be living through one crisis after another these days, and no one appears to have any idea of how long this fumbling can go on without getting out of hand. The British certainly wish someone could tell them. Living dangerously is all very well in its place, but it can get on the nerves of placid British bureaucracy.

The declining economic situation in Great Britain had something of an airing in the Parliamentary debates this week, but I thought that it was somewhat glossed over by Government spokesmen. Reports we get indicate that retail sales are feeling the blast now. Selfridge's, for example, is buying on the expectation that sales will be off five per cent. during the coming months, and Harrod's is counting on twelve per cent.

Because movements, either up or down, are so much more gradual here than they are in the United States, our experts tell me that this trend would correspond to a falling off of between fifteen and twenty-five per cent. in American retail sales. In other words, they are beginning to feel the draft here.

In the City, they have given up hope that the rearmament expenditures can prevent a recession, and are counting now only on a cushioning effect. The heavy industries, especially steel and coal, are beginning to feel seriously the decline in public purchasing power in the face of rising prices, and temporary layoffs are expected. No one I have seen looks for any improvement during the summer months. Rather, they seem to think that the same slow and steady decline will continue for several months.

There is a certain fatalism in their attitude. They are so convinced that the United States holds the key to economic recovery that they seem to think they can do little about it. As the purchaser of half of the world's raw products, the United States, by

84. Arthur Hays Sulzberger (1891–1968), publisher and president of *The New York Times*.

pulling in its horns as it is now doing, can and does affect markets throughout the world, the British say.

Because American purchases of rubber have been curtailed, the market for British manufactures in the Malay States is considerably less broad than they would like to have it, for example. Instances of this kind could be multiplied indefinitely and tend to lend a certain semblance of reason to current British economic hopelessness.

The minor shakeup in the British Cabinet seems to have been well received by the public.[85] Chamberlain appears to keep his pulse on the finger of public opinion pretty well and the Opposition still has little on which to base an electoral revolt.

With best wishes, I am,

Sincerely yours,

Seeing you soon, boy. I arrive this morning of June 20. The only appointment I have is June 22 (Harvard Class Day), so let me know "what and when" do I see the President and who else. I am full of news. Mr. and Mrs. Loening arrive June 9.[86] *Joe*

Joseph P. Kennedy: *Diary*

Notes Given by JPK to His Secretary While in U.S. on Leave, June 1938[87]

I went to call on Lord Baldwin[88] at his house at 10:30. I found him in his study, a room filled with bookcases from floor to ceiling, smoking a pipe. He sat at his desk and I sat in a sofa.

I told him I would like to have Edward's abdication cleared up for President Roosevelt, so he told me the following:

He said first of all, he was still a friend of King [*sic*] unless Mrs. Simpson had changed the Duke's mind. He said, "To understand the whole affair you must understand that by some peculiar twist of the Duke's mind, he has no sense of what he should do — that is, a moral cell in his mind. He was never impressed with the fact that he owed something to his country, his family, or any one else. He just felt that the thing he *wanted* to do was the right thing to do."

"To go back", says Baldwin, "Windsor hoped he might get out of being King while he was Duke [*sic*]of Wales, but never had the courage to discuss it with his father. Then came his father's illness, which although he had been ill, took a serious turn rather suddenly."

On the Saturday preceding his father's death, he died on Sunday or Monday, Wales came to town and talked with Baldwin, and when he finished, he took Mrs. Simpson to dinner at a night club. This shocked Baldwin immensely. Well, the King died and Wales was in. The trouble started almost immediately. Wales made up his mind he would

---

85. The resignations of Lord Swinton as secretary of state for air, and of W.G.A. Ormsby-Gore as colonial secretary and their respective replacements by Sir Kingsley Wood (former minister of health) and Malcolm MacDonald (former dominions secretary) on May 16 had resulted in a general reshuffling of Chamberlain's cabinet.

86. The former chief aeronautical engineer of the U.S. Army Air Corps during World War I, Grover Loening (1888–1976) had resigned as aeronautical adviser to the U.S. Maritime Commission in February.

87. He would sail aboard the *Queen Mary* on June 15, remaining in the United States until June 29 in order to return to London for the embassy's Fourth of July celebrations.

88. Lord Stanley Baldwin, Earl Baldwin of Bewdley and Viscount Corvedale (1867–1947), had been prime minister and first lord of the Treasury at the time of the abdication crisis. Baldwin had counseled Edward VIII and had presented the news of the king's renunciation of the throne to the House of Commons in December 1936.

make her Queen and had his first discussion with Baldwin about the woman, who shortly after began divorce proceedings against Simpson.[89] It was while these proceedings were on that Baldwin came into it actively, because it was still within the province of the government to step in and prevent the divorce.

In the meantime, King was neglecting his duties. He was going to Sandringham with just her and no secretary. Official government papers were being neglected and no attention was being paid to government business. Again he was putting cabinet papers in his pocket, which were never supposed to leave his room and hands, and taking them to Mrs. Simpson's house and going over them there. This was brought to Baldwin's attention and he was requested to speak to the King. He said, "When I do, he will say two things, and until I can answer them, I cannot do it."

1. He will say, "I've been denied a normal married life and association of a woman in my house to make my life happy, as you have with Mrs. Baldwin, so I come to Simpson, sit at my desk and she reads and knits, and it is homelike."

2. "Who told you I do this?" "And he would sack any one naturally who told the Cabinet."

Baldwin said, "I will not complain but will try to reason."

He went to see the King and the trouble started. King did not make a real issue until the divorce was settled. Then he said he was going to marry her and make her queen. Baldwin pointed out this was impossible because she was not the type. Wales said then, "Ok, I can have her as my mistress, but not as my wife. That's fine hypocrisy."

Baldwin then said; "There is an obligation on the King as head of British Empire to choose a queen who definitely meets the obligations of her position. The King and Queen are symbols of the Empire — not just the King. If a king wants to sleep with a whore, that's his private business, but the Empire is concerned that he doesn't make her the queen."

He said the King made up his mind if he could not marry her he would abdicate, and having come to that decision, he was "like one who had seen the Holy Grail." He went around with his arms in the air rejoicing.

On the last Saturday Baldwin was with him for seven hours — with the family (boys). There had been *no* drinking. Wales, in spite of story all during period, did not drink and when he and Baldwin were alone, they took their first drink. Baldwin said at this stage when the decision was arrived at, he was helped by the physical cowardice of Mrs. Simpson. He told the King that if he was to abdicate, the crowd might wreck vengeance on Mrs. Simpson. King asked, "Why? She certainly wasn't to blame." Baldwin said; "Yes, but the crowd usually blamed the woman." The King immediately went to 'phone and called her and urged her to leave the country. He had no trouble. She was frightened. Baldwin said at this point he was convinced that had she stayed she might have persuaded King to stand pat and there would have been hell to pay. Remember the British public knew nothing of it. Baldwin also said in all of preliminary discussions King felt he would have popular press, but Baldwin persuaded him otherwise.

At the high ball when he finished talking with Mrs. Simpson, the entire family was depressed but King was jubilant.

Baldwin told of letter from present King at Christmas following crowning saying he hoped the British people would give him time to pay for the fatal error of his brother.

---

89. Her second husband, Ernest Aldrich Simpson, an American shipping magnate living in London.

Joseph P. Kennedy: *Diary*

I asked him about general conditions in England. He said they were getting progressively worse. He hoped that they would not get as bad in England as they were in America. They were getting advantages out of the munitions spending (pump priming — he called it), but he realized unless we picked up, he saw trouble ahead.

I asked him how he was answering questions. "What do I do with the capital I have to invest?" He answered he did not know. He was adviser to many people but now he did not know how to turn.

I then told him I had talked to Lord Baldwin about Edward's abdication but I wanted to get the financial picture, and Baldwin said to get it from Peacock who was Edward's financial adviser, "Peacock being a Canadian and very able."

Peacock then told me he succeeded Lord Ravelstohme,[91] senior partner in Barings as adviser to the late George V, and also acted as adviser to Edward, then Prince of Wales. About a year before Edward became King, he, without telling Peacock why, had suggested getting his money into securities outside of England, giving as his only excuse, "See what happened to King of Spain." However, he started to set up a trust that was not too straightforward in the certain provisions for Mrs. Simpson, but in a roundabout way. Peacock said he objected to this on the ground that if it became known it would reflect badly on Wales and told him so, saying at the same time, "After I have told you what the dangers are, if you still want it done, it will be carried out." Wales said he wanted it done. Peacock told me this to show that Wales had in mind to get out of England long before the abdication. He had all funds from the Duchy of Cornwall and this meant as much as 60 thousand £s a year. This was all invested and very wisely (a great part of it in American securities, which of course, were not suffering.) This, with what he had in cash and his interests in Sandringham and ____ [sic] amounted to about £1,000,000. This figure confirmed later by Sir Horace Wilson, Chief of Cabinet.[92] The settlement also included as a result of negotiations between Baldwin[93] and Chamberlain[94] for the Government, and Peacock for Edward, a grant from the government of approximately £25,000 a year free from tax. Baldwin said, however, that if a hostile debate sprung up in Parliament, this might have to be given up. Peacock said that the present King at this time practically underwrote it for Edward out of his Privy Purse, so that if Edward didn't get it from Parliament, the King would give it to him. Well that's what happened. It looked like a nasty debate was going to start in Parliament, and Baldwin gave up the idea. Peacock advised Edward that he thought Baldwin had done the best he could and agreed with Baldwin that it should be given up in Parliament.

Peacock said the present King had been very fair and square to Peacock, though he represented Edward and had to battle for his cause. I asked him if any deal had been made with Edward about staying out of England. He said the only mention had been made by Baldwin who had said to Peacock it would be very embarrassing if Edward should come back to England very soon, and asked Peacock to ask Edward if he would

90. Sir Edward Robert-Peacock (1871–1962), Canadian-born director of both the Bank of England and of Baring Brothers, as well as receiver general of the Duchy of Cornwall.
91. That is, Lord Revelstoke.
92. As chief industrial adviser to the British government since 1930, Sir Horace John Wilson (1882–1972) had developed a reputation as a brilliant mediator of labor disputes and had come concurrently to serve Baldwin (as he had MacDonald, and would Chamberlain) as a personal adviser.
93. Then prime minister.
94. Then chancellor of the Exchequer.

stay out temporarily. Peacock asked how long and Baldwin said, "Two years." Peacock thought that reasonable and put it up to Edward who readily agreed.

I told Peacock I heard he now wanted to come back. "How about that?" Peacock said, yes that was so. He was still advising him along with his lawyer, named ____ [sic]. The main difficulty was Wallie. She completely dominated him and he did whatever she said. To prove this, only last week the tax department of government, in a mad desire to be fair and more than just, were working on his taxes. They called him up in Paris about a settlement, and after explaining it all to Edward, heard her say over telephone, "Make no concession whatsoever." He then returned to the telephone and bit their heads off saying he would agree to *nothing*.

The bitterness behind all this on her part is based on the fact that she is not accepted as Her Royal Highness.

Peacock says the four women are to blame for that: Queen Mary, the Queen, Duchesses of Kent and Gloucester. They will not agree she should be called this, and he has steadily complained bitterly about this. His mother continues to write him nice letters but consistently refuses to mention this in the letters and only last week he wrote back to her he appreciated the letters but what was she going to do about H.R.H. for Wallie? Of course, the women of England would go insane if they had to curtsy to Wallie. So it looks as if this might be a great stumbling block to peace between Edward and the family.

I asked him about Edward's sending back the present Kent sent him for his wedding. Peacock said he didn't want any present from Kent or even have him call on him unless the Duchess came with him. Hence that break — "I knowing [sic] that Kent hated her and called her a bitch to me."

Peacock said that while he was King they all had evidence Wallie was having an affair with a young man, and of course this embittered the Cabinet more than ever. Peacock as friend of Edward is convinced they would have gladly taken an American for queen but not Wallie.

He said after the abdication had been decided on, he went home one night with the Duke of York who was terribly worried about taking on the job, and York said to him: "You know I can't do this job like my brother. Just see how he carried off the dinner tonight. That was the night all the men of the family were there with [illegible] . . . one there and handled himself marvelously. That's what a King must be able to do, but I never could do that."

I told him Kent had told me that the King was considerably embarrassed raising money necessary to give Wales for the purchase of Sandringham and the other one (?) [sic]. Peacock said this was true but was a real man about it.

Joseph P. Kennedy: *Diplomatic Memoir*

During the last few weeks[95] in public and in private considerable discussions had been taking place [concerning] the possibility of my being the Democratic nominee for President in 1940. It broke publicly in late May in an article by Ernest K. Lindley in *Liberty*. The idea was picked up by a number of newspapers including the Boston *Post* and *Sunday Advertiser*, the New York *Daily News*, the Washington *Herald-Times* [sic], and a host of papers of smaller circulation too numerous to mention.

95. JPK had returned to the United States on June 15.

No one can lightly turn away a serious suggestion from his friends that he is worthy of succeeding to the presidency of the United States. There were many reasons that militated against my candidacy for that office, including my Catholic faith, but even these might [*perhaps*] be overcome. But I ~~knew that the time was not propitious~~ [*did not desire the Democratic nomination*]. Mr. Roosevelt had made no announcement as to his attitude on a third term. I knew that many of his closest advisors were urging him to break with tradition and run for the third time in 1940. There was little doubt that he had the matter under consideration. Mr. Roosevelt also had a quality — a failing, some have called it — of resenting the suggestion that he was to be succeeded and cooling perceptibly towards a man who might be considered by his friends, a worthy successor. For many years Mr. Roosevelt had been my chief; he still was. I wanted no such false issue to arise between us and endanger both an official relationship of some importance and a personal association which to me had been heavy with meaning.

Another action of my well-intentioned friends had also caused me considerable personal embarrassment. The names of the recipients of honorary degrees from Harvard University are a closely guarded secret prior to Commencement. The popular June pastime of Boston newspapermen is guessing who these people will be. When it was announced that I was returning to the United States to see my son be graduated from my alma mater, it was a good guess that at the same time Harvard would confer an honorary degree on me. Indeed, had I not known to the contrary, I would have jumped to that conclusion myself for I could have thought that my varied and long services for the Government might have been suitably recognized in this manner. Others did jump to that conclusion, the Boston Post headlining the story one day, the other Boston newspaper following the next day, copies to the rest of the United States. To a query from the press over the trans-Atlantic telephone, I denied any knowledge of the fact. I added, in response to another query, that the award of an honorary degree to Mr. Justice Louis D. Brandeis — Harvard's second most eminent graduate who for some reason still obscure had never been awarded a degree — required no endorsement on my part; he more than deserved it on his merits.[96] To some proper Bostonians such a remark was obviously lesse majesté; but I have never seen any reason to apologize for it.

The press literally stormed me when I arrived in New York harbor on June 20, 1938. I told them that there was no truth in the rumor that I had come back to deal with the war debt or that I had negotiated or was interested in the negotiation of a tripartite agreement for the devaluation of our currencies. I added that I had no particular belief in the efficacy of monetary manipulation in the present situation. "The day of devices," I said, "is done."

"But," I went on to say, "I am far less bearish on the economic situation today than I was a year ago. So far as America is concerned, it seems to me that we have cried our eyes out." On the general international situation I said little, save to indicate that it was full of warlike tensions and that we should count ourselves happy not to be in daily fear of bombardment from the skies. "We, at least, are not teaching our children to make gas masks." I praised the efforts of Chamberlain to see through negotiation a more enduring peace.

The inevitable question of my candidacy for the presidency was put. My reply to that was as unequivocal as ~~I thought~~ I could make it. "I enlisted," I said, "under President Roosevelt in 1932 to do whatever he wanted me to do. There are many problems at home and abroad and I am happy to be busy at one abroad just now. If I had my eye on another job it would be a complete breach of faith with President Roosevelt."

96. Brandeis made it a habit not to accept honorary degrees.

I spent a goodly portion of the next day with the President at Hyde Park. He was interested in my personal experiences with and reactions to the English scene. He did not then or later express any particular criticism of Chamberlain's objectives or techniques. Indeed, as he pondered the Czechoslovakian crisis and the inherent possibilities of its blowing again into flame he thought of what part he might play to help in averting the fact of war. He was less sanguine then as to a renewal in the immediate future of his earlier plan. The existing crises were too immediate and had engendered too much heat. But he thought that a plea for a calm and rational approach to the problem coming from him might at the appropriate time have an effect. He told me to let Chamberlain know that he was ready to make such a plea if and when the time should come.

I left Hyde Park that evening for Cambridge, missing my first connection to eat a dish or strawberries and chat with Mrs. Roosevelt. It was class day at Harvard and apart from passing comment to the press praising Chamberlain for his handling of the Anglo-Eire negotiations, I gave myself over to the antics that attend graduation. I could not stay for the commencement ceremonies themselves for my son, John, was ill and I took the opportunity to spend a day with him at our summer home on Cape Cod.

It was on June 22, 1938 that an incident occurred which heralded a beginning to a series of misunderstandings, too often fostered by others, that was to plague my relationship with President Roosevelt. The facts, although not within my personal knowledge, seem to rest on unimpeachable authority. Nor was I to know about these happenings until four days later, during which I had a second occasion to see and dine with the President. But on that Tuesday of June 22, Stephen Early, the President's Secretary, gave out a story to William C. Murphy, Jr., of the Philadelphia *Inquirer* and Walter D. Trohan of the *Chicago Tribune* to the effect that the President was annoyed with me partly because of my presidential boomlet and partly because I had given out inside information about foreign affairs before I had given it to the President himself.[97]

The two stories appeared the next day. They are similar in character. Trohan's Washington dispatch of June 22, 1938 is the fuller of the two. It spoke of "the chilling shadow of 1940" falling across the friendship between the President and myself because there was "positive evidence that Kennedy hoped to use the Court of St. James as a stepping stone to the White House in 1940." It spoke of my general letter to my friends as a "political letter," replete with inside information, designed to egg my friends into initiating a campaign in my interest, and charged me with wanting to take a press agent back with me to London in order to keep my name before the American public. The Murphy story had little circulation beyond his immediate paper but the Trohan story was immediately noticed by the press in the Chicago *Tribune* territory. Editorials, blurbs and news-items appeared within a day or so in the Detroit *Free Press*, the Port Huron (Mich.) *Herald*, the Flint (Mich.) *Journal*, the Eau Claire (Wis.) *Telegram*, the Elkhart (Ind.) *Truth*, the Boone (Ia.) *News Republican*, and the Lawrence (Kan.) *General World*, to mention only a few. The Trohan story was to die down after that flurry, to be revived a few months later in the midst of the Munich crisis by the Alsop-Kintner combination.

I knew nothing about the incident until Saturday, June 25. Meanwhile I had the occasion during the intervening days to see Secretaries Hull and Morganthau and others at the State Department. These discussions were general in character, though I did take the occasion to render a report to Secretary Hull severely criticizing certain aspects of our foreign service. My short experience with the staff furnished me in the Embassy was that far too much time was spent by its members in attending teas,

97. In his "private and confidential" political letters.

receptions and other gala occasions and then picking up chit-chat about affairs that was relayed back to the State Department as information. I thought their training in this respect was far less adequate than that of the average American newspaperman, and on several occasions when I was informed that Chamberlain or Halifax or Simon thought this and that or had said so or so, I responded that I would call them up and ask them whether it was true. On occasion, I did. Accurate reporting, I pointed out to the department, required closer contact with the sources and more of the business of plain trudging. Shirt-sleeve diplomacy, in which I have always held a profound belief, must start with rolling up one's shirt-sleeves.

On Saturday,[98] following a pleasant dinner the night before with the President at the White House, I learned for the first time of Early's action. It was a true Irish anger that swept me. The President and Secretary Hull were away and I could reach no one until Monday. That Monday morning I saw Mr. Hull and offered to resign. He sought to calm me down and I recall him telling me that I should not be so disturbed because, as he said, "He (the President) does those things. He treats me twenty times as badly." I did not need to have him tell me that he too had been prominently mentioned as the Democratic candidate for 1940. An angry interview with Early brought a half-hearted denial and a further interview with the President, with whom it was not my habit to mince words, brought a denial that he had had anything to do with it. In his way he assuaged my feelings and I left again for London, but deep within me I knew that something had happened.

[James Landis]

Joseph P. Kennedy to Frank Buxton[99]

London, July 11, 1938

Dear Sir:

My attention has been called to an article which appeared recently in your paper to the general effect that I had at one time said James Roosevelt had secured my appointment as Ambassador to Great Britain, and that recently I denied this.[100]

The tenor of this article is completely inaccurate.

In the recent interview to which reference was made, I was asked to comment on the accuracy of an article appearing in the *Saturday Evening Post*. I told the reporters that, if the rest of the *Saturday Evening Post*'s article was as inaccurate as were the references to my relations with Jimmy Roosevelt, the whole article must be an unadulterated lie.

At no time have I ever said anything to the effect that young Mr. Roosevelt secured or did not secure my present appointment. I am quite prepared to stand on my interview given in Boston on January 24th.

Very truly yours,
Joseph P. Kennedy

---

98. June 25.
99. Frank W. Buxton (1877–1974), Pulitzer Prize–winning editor of the *Boston Herald*, 1929–47.
100. While embarking for London on June 29, JPK denied to the press assertions which journalist Alva Johnson had made in the most recent edition of the *Saturday Evening Post* to the effect that the president's son James Roosevelt had "helped Kennedy to reach the two real positions which he now holds—that of Ambassador to London and that of premier Scotch-whiskey salesman in America."

Joseph P. Kennedy: *Diary*

I decided to let the newspapers know of the rescue of the nuns, for a variety of reasons.[101] I wanted to emphasize that the Jews from Germany and Austria are not the only refugees in the world, and I wanted to depict Chamberlain and Halifax as human, good-hearted men, capable of taking an active interest in such a bona fide venture. I also wanted to give them credit for sending the warship after the poor women.

Joseph P. Kennedy to Cordell Hull: *Diplomatic Dispatch*

656, July 20, 8 P.M.

The following is a strictly confidential telegram for the Secretary of State:

This morning I talked with the German Ambassador.[102] Dirksen told me that recently at Hitler's request Wiedemann had to come to London to tell the British Foreign Secretary about the difference of opinion which existed on various matters in the party; he and Hitler are close friends.[103] The German Ambassador implied that he did not wish further to discuss that subject with me but tomorrow we are going to endeavor to get it from Cadogan.[104]

What was particularly made clear to me was that Dirksen thought that it was now the time for Britain to make a proposition to the Germans; that Hitler was very much in the mood to make an agreement and while Benes[105] was not at all trusted by the Germans on the Sudeten German question, he was of the opinion that negotiations for an agreement between Germany and England should begin and it was implied by him that he hoped there was some way that the United States could urge the English to start.[106]

This morning his manner was a revelation to me. Definitely he gave me the impression that Hitler was decidedly in the mood to start negotiations with the English.

---

101. The following day, twenty-eight Spanish Sisters of the Sacred Heart would arrive in Marseilles aboard a British destroyer, six of their original number having died in Nationalist air raids during the previous spring.

102. A former ambassador to the Soviet Union, 1928–33, and to Japan, 1933–38, Herbert von Dirksen (1882–1955) had succeeded Ribbentrop as the German ambassador in London on May 5.

103. Hitler had served under Fritz Wiedemann (1891–1970) during World War I. The two had formed a close attachment, and Wiedemann had come to serve both in a number of unofficial diplomatic capacities and as a foreign affairs adviser to the führer prior to the Second World War. The following year Wiedemann would become the German consul general in San Francisco.

104. Sir Alexander George Montagu Cadogan (1884–1968), permanent undersecretary of state for foreign affairs, 1938–46.

105. Edvard Beneš (1884–1948), former foreign minister and current president of Czechoslovakia.

106. In his own dispatch to the German Foreign Ministry, von Dirksen characterized their exchange regarding an Anglo-German settlement and Czechoslovakia as follows:

> I took the occasion to explain to Kennedy the present status of Anglo-German relations and to point out that we were striving for a settlement with England but saw no reason — after Chamberlain's declaration of March 23 [24?] in the House of Commons — for us to take the initiative.
> I further took the opportunity to inform Kennedy of the highly unsatisfactory progress of the negotiations between the Czech Government and the Sudeten Germans; the Czechs had no sincere desire to reach a real settlement but, by making some fictitious concessions, were only maneuvering in order not to lose the sympathy of the world. I told Kennedy that Germany had no confidence in Beneš (to which he replied that neither did the rest of the world) and I explained to him that British influence upon the Czechoslovak Government was insufficient also because the British Minister in Prague, Newton, did not have a thorough grasp of the details of the problem and his sympathies were one-sidedly with the Czechs. Kennedy received this also with lively interest.

He said that the one point that will stop Hitler from coming to an armaments agreement with England would be that the United States and England would be unable to arrange for Russia, Poland and Czechoslovakia to be included. He said that Germany will be perfectly willing to come to an agreement with France and England and Italy also will come in, but naturally the Germans are distrustful of Poland, Russia and Czechoslovakia. As far as Hitler is concerned an armaments agreement can definitely be accomplished if the above three countries can be included.

KENNEDY

Mr. Johnson

Joseph P. Kennedy to Malcolm Bingay[107]

Private & Confidential London, July 22, 1938

Sir:

Now that the excitement over the article of the 23rd of June in The Detroit Free Press has died down, I wonder if you would mind my writing you a note explaining to you that the whole article is a malicious article and that, although my attorney advises me that it is completely libelous, in view of the fact that I have received such kind consideration from the American Press, I do not propose to take advantage of it and even ask you not to publish this letter. I feel, however, that because you have been so kind to me in the past, you should at least have a chance to have the facts.

First, as far as my sensitive Irish nature permitted me to judge, I saw no signs of a frigid atmosphere between Mr. Roosevelt and me and, confidentially, I might also add that I went home primarily on a personal matter for the President and while there spent most of my time, at his request, with Mr. Lamont of Morgan's and Mr. John L. Lewis, working on the steel wage cut,[108] so, if the President has a very frigid feeling toward me, he at least did not make it evident to me.

As to the "secret circular, which Kennedy has been forwarding to selected Washington correspondents," I never sent any letter that contained "information on the progress of British debt and trade negotiations which have not been reported to the State Department." I wrote to a dozen of my friends who have been my friends for a great many years, but I am sure that nobody would believe I had been writing anything that would be unethical, but, in order to make sure that there couldn't be any criticism, you will be interested to know that a copy of every letter I wrote went to Senator Pittman, Chairman of the Senate Committee on Foreign Relations, Judge McReynolds, Chairman of the House Foreign Relations Committee, J. Pierrepont Moffat, Assistant Secretary of State, and Mr. James Roosevelt of the White House, so that's that.

The statement that I have directed a presidential boom from London is an absolute falsehood. I have never in my life discussed the possibility of being a candidate for anything.

I now quote from your article — " 'Joe Kennedy never did anything without thinking of Joe Kennedy,' a high Administration official said. 'And that's the worst thing I can say about a father of nine kids. He'd put them in an orphanage one by one to get himself into the White House.'" As to whether Joe Kennedy ever did anything without

---

107. Malcolm Wallace Bingay (1884–1953), editorial director of the *Detroit Free Press*, 1930–40.
108. Fearing further damage to the ailing economy, FDR had asked JPK to intervene with J. P. Morgan partner and U.S. Steel director, Thomas Lamont (1870–1948), in an attempt to forestall by ninety days the wage cut that would by necessity accompany a beleaguered U.S. Steel's recently announced price cut.

thinking of Joe Kennedy, that, of course, is anybody's opinion, but I am inclined to believe that the higher-ups of the Roosevelt Administration are the last ones that should have any such opinion.

The statement that I put my children in an orphanage is, of course, so scandalous that I won't even pretend to answer it. I am sure you must feel some chagrin at publishing such a thing. I am sure you know my children are all in London, seemingly enjoying themselves with their father and mother.

I quite realize that when anyone takes a job in public life, he leaves himself open to all kinds of attack, but for the past five years I have given the best I have to the United States Government and my judgment and what I have learned is always available. I feel that attacks like this that include my children are beyond all rhyme or reason.

I am not writing this for publication, as I do not want it published, but I do want to set myself right with your paper.

Very truly yours,

Joseph P. Kennedy

Copy sent to — Col. Robert Rutherford McCormick,[109] The Honorable Frank Murphy, Henry J. Haskell[110]

Joseph P. Kennedy to Cordell Hull: *Diplomatic Dispatch*

RUSH — 838 — *August 30, 5 p.m. Strictly Confidential for Secretary Hull*

The Prime Minister with whom I have just talked had just concluded a meeting with the Cabinet, and he is leaving for Balmoral for four days to join the King and Queen. He looks quite unwell.

The gist of the conversation is that he is very much disturbed about the situation in Czechoslovakia. All the information that he gets with the exception of the report from Gwatkin,[111] Runciman's aide,[112] is that Herr Hitler has made up his mind to peacefully take Czechoslovakia if possible, but with arms if necessary. The advice is that it is the belief of Hitler that the French are not ready to fight and that Great Britain does not want to go in. If the matter were just to be decided between the Czechs and the Sudetens Runciman feels that it could be settled amicably, but unfortunately it rests with Hitler.

I inquired whether he thought Hitler was affected by the speeches from the United States or the one of the other night of Sir John Simon's. Psychologically he thought the two speeches in the United States — the President's and the Secretary of State's — and Simon's — had had an excellent effect, but he is advised that very little of the proper information gets to Hitler any more, so far as world peace is concerned; he is kept high up on a mountain peak, so to speak, by a ring around him; the group that want to go to

109. Upon receiving his copy of the letter from JPK, McCormick, whose *Chicago Tribune* had published Trohan's original article on its front page, responded: "The reporter has produced for me the sources of his information . . . [h]e leaves no doubt in my mind that he had complete authority for everything he said." "You are the victim," McCormick concluded, "not of the reporter, but of your political associates."

110. Editor of the *Kansas City Star.*

111. Frank Trewlawny Ashton-Gwatkin (1889–1976), former Foreign Office delegate to the Imperial Conference at Ottowa in 1932 and to the World Economic Conference of 1933, as well as economic adviser to Foreign Secretaries Simon, Hoare, Eden and Halifax.

112. In late July, Halifax had asked former cabinet minister Walter Runciman, first Viscount Runciman of Doxford (1870–1949), to act as an independent mediator in the intensifying Sudeten dispute.

war which he thinks unfortunately includes Ribbentrop[113] are advising him that now is the time to add increased prestige to the cause of Germany, since France is not prepared to go and Great Britain will not come in.

I asked the Prime Minister whether he had as yet made up his mind to go to war if the French went, and he replied that he was very much afraid that they might be forced into it but that he definitely would not go until he was absolutely forced to. He also said that he had an agreement with France that they would not declare war before consulting Great Britain. He said they had been very loath to give this commitment even though the choice was between breaking their treaty obligations or fighting a war they knew they would lose, but the Prime Minister said that the British convinced the French that they were entitled to this agreement if they were expected to go along.

Henderson[114] had advised Chamberlain that no more speeches should be made because instead of giving courage to the moderates to fight against a war in Germany, it was having the effect of urging them to get into it.

In spite of all this, Chamberlain said that he is still hopeful that war will be averted. Hitler's speech will come on Tuesday the Prime Minister thinks and the matter will remain as is until then. Henlein and Benes were to meet today but up to four o'clock here the Prime Minister had had no word. The Prime Minister opposes those in his own Cabinet who believe that Herr Hitler must be struck at now or else his prestige will increase so much it will be impossible later to stop him. This Chamberlain feels is not necessarily true; that the anschluss lost Hitler a great deal of public opinion in the United States and he will not believe that the smaller countries — Bulgaria, Yugoslavia, Rumania, and others — are willing to have themselves regimented as the Austrians have been.

It is my own impression that he regards war as about an even chance; that even if Herr Hitler strikes my own belief is that his influence will be to keep the French out; if the French do go it will still be some time before he goes, but his own opinion is that he will have to. He says that he is advised Hitler believes that if they march into Czechoslovakia, the war will be over before you can say the word "knife." The Prime Minister does not agree with that at all, figuring the Czechs will give Hitler a battle and that public opinion will be aroused and force France and Great Britain into the fray. The Prime Minister says today public opinion in England is definitely against going to war for the Czechs but what it will be if France declares war is another matter. He still has very definitely in his mind that it is quite easy to get into war but what have we proved after we are in and he is always hopeful that if he stays out something may happen for the good of the world. Today Chamberlain is still the best bet in Europe against war, but he is a very sick-looking man; he is worried but not jittery.

KENNEDY

The Ambassador

Joseph P. Kennedy to Cordell Hull: *Diplomatic Dispatch*

846, August 31, 5 p.m. For the Secretary, Strictly confidential.

Have just seen Lord Halifax. He told me that this morning he received a cable from Runciman which is not so encouraging. Benes, Runciman says, is not going through as he should and Runciman told the Foreign Secretary to twist Benes' tail, which the For-

---

113. Joachim von Ribbentrop (1893–1946) had served as German ambassador to London from 1936 until February 1938, when he had returned to Berlin in order to replace Constantin Freiherr von Neurath as foreign minister.
114. Sir Neville Meyrick Henderson (1882–1942), British ambassador to Berlin, 1937–39.

eign Secretary has just done with a cable. Yesterday the Czech proposition was given to Henlein and they have asked until Thursday or Friday to give an answer to Benes. I hope to have a copy of the proposition from Masaryk tonight or tomorrow.

Public opinion here is definitely against going to war for the Czechs. The Foreign Secretary says that the French do not want to fight either. The Foreign Secretary asked me what American reaction would be if the Germans invaded Czechoslovakia, with the Czechs fighting them, and Great Britain did not go along. I told him a great deal would depend on the attitude the President would take as to whether he thought Great Britain should be encouraged to fight or whether he would contend that they should stay out of war until the last possible minute. The Foreign Secretary said he would keep in touch with me on this problem because obviously they cannot prepare for this emergency without tipping their hand to the Germans. I asked the Foreign Secretary if, with the information he has up to the minute, he thought the Germans were bluffing, to which he replied that he does not think it is quite a bluff. He thinks that Herr Hitler hopes to get all he wants without a fight and that by taking advantage of the situation as he thinks he sees it, it might be a good a time as any to march.

I inquired as to how the situation in Spain was coming. There were no new developments he said. He thought that if the matter of Czechoslovakia was settled and out of the way they would look forward to peace for some time. What is causing all the trouble with the Italians and the Spanish situation, he said, is that both the English and the Italians, when they signed the agreement, believed that within two months the war would be over. The Foreign Secretary therefore does not take the hostile attitude toward Italy that some people think he should perhaps take because, while Italy agreed to furnish only supplies and equipment to their people who were fighting in Spain at the time the agreement was signed, he now thinks that they are doing that and probably adding on enough to offset what they think Spain is getting from Russia and France. He wishes it were not so but feels it is no reason to have a row about yet.

I talked with the Foreign Secretary about the Jewish situation. He said he was not very well up on it except that he had been told by Winterton[115] that they could do something about placing Jews in Kenya and Rhodesia, but just how many they cannot tell yet. The Foreign Secretary believes that as settlement is attempted on Austrian and German Jews, other countries who want to get rid of their Jews will be encouraged to throw them out, hoping that France, England and America will find some way of taking care of them.

I judge that Vansittart is back more or less in favor here and is being consulted a great deal on moves that are being made.[116]

This morning Lord Halifax reiterated that they are instructing everybody not to make any more speeches on the Czech-German situation, as he believes that all has been said that should be said. He and Chamberlain feel very strongly that silence on their part and hoping on our part will get the best results.

I would appreciate some opinion from you as to policy of handling the attitude of the British if Germany marches and the English decide not to. I think that the Prime

115. Edward Turnour, sixth earl Winterton and later Baron Turnour (1883–1962); chairman of the Intergovernmental Committee for Refugees, 1938–45, chancellor of the Duchy of Lancaster, 1937–39; deputy to the secretary of state for air, and vice president of the air council and assistant to the home secretary, 1938–39.

116. Sir Robert Gilbert Vansittart, later first Baron Vansittart (1881–1957). An early and vocal critic of the growth of Nazism, Vansittart spent nearly eight years as permanent undersecretary of state for foreign affairs. He had been replaced by Sir Alexander Cadogan in early 1938, however, and given the specially created (although largely ineffectual) position of chief diplomatic adviser to His Majesty's government.

Minister and the Foreign Secretary would appreciate your reaction and judgment, as far as the United States goes, as to what should be done on this.[117]

KENNEDY

The Ambassador

Joseph P. Kennedy to Cordell Hull: *Diplomatic Dispatch*

868, September 5, 8 p.m.

I have just talked with Lord Halifax. Runcimans' report of the interview of Henlein with Hitler was this morning received by the Foreign Office. According to the account of this interview which Ashton-Gwatkin was given by Henlein yesterday, it passed off rather encouragingly and Hitler was as friendly as they could have expected. The message to Hitler which Runciman sent through Henlein was to the effect that he was prepared to recommend a settlement based on the plan of Benes for cantonization and the Carlsbad speech of Henlein. This is said to have been accepted in principle by Hitler. The Foreign Secretary says that so far, in the negotiations, the Sudetens have made it very clear that the issue rises or falls on the eight Carlsbad points, which must be conceded. However the Sudeten leaders have said that while insisting on these points in principle, they would be willing to work out the details of them so that they will be practicable for both sides. Hope was expressed by Henlein that he could still work something out with Benes and have it concluded in time to report to the conference of the Sudetens which is to be held around October 16th. I asked the Foreign Secretary if he thought the tension would last till that time, and he replied that he thought it probably would. He said that from all his information he is now convinced Hitler himself has not made up his mind whether he wants to go to war and the personal opinion of Halifax is that he does not want to at this time.

The Foreign Secretary leaves on Friday for Geneva where he says he will make a blustering speech on Tuesday, which will not amount to anything.

An official of the Foreign Office in conversation with a member of the Embassy staff this afternoon in addition to an outline of the information given above said Ashton-Gwatkin had been told by Henlein that he, Henlein, had spoken in terms of warm approval and commendation to Hitler of the work of the Runciman mission. According to this official of the Foreign Office, Runciman was anxious to secure from Hitler through Henlein some expression of approval of or acquiescence in Henlein's commendation and the latter reported that Hitler did express approval of the work of Runciman. The official also said that Henlein was asked by Hitler what the basic line of his policy was, to which Henlein promptly replied that primarily he wanted no war and Hitler is said to have agreed to this. Hitler was told by Henlein that the situation resolved itself into two alternative lines of policy (1) autonomy within the State and (2) a plebiscite which would inevitably mean the incorporation into Germany of the Sudeten area; and that he preferred to pursue his aims within the limits of number one policy. Hitler merely expressed great skepticism to this.

The official[s] of the Foreign Office said that they naturally feel some satisfaction at the general attitude that Hitler is reported to have taken with Henlein at this interview and particularly that nothing was said by Hitler to indicate a desire for the present negotiations between the Czechs and Henlein to be discontinued. In the view of the For-

---

117. The following day the secretary responded that his own and the president's recent speeches accurately reflected "the attitude of this Government toward the European world situation," and that as a result, "it would not be practicable to be more specific as to our reaction in hypothetical circumstances."

eign Office this reported attitude of Hitler is the most favorable and important development of the past few days, coupled with the realization which they believe Benes has now reached that the situation is acutely serious and that if any successful agreement is to be worked out Benes must make drastic concessions.

On Saturday the Foreign Office sent a long telegram to the British Ambassador at Washington containing a résumé of the British information and the situation as it appears here, for communication to the Department of State. A further telegram, it was stated, will be sent tonight to Sir Ronald Lindsay[118] bringing the matter up to date.

KENNEDY

Mr. Johnson

Franklin Roosevelt to Joseph P. Kennedy

<u>PRIVATE</u> September 7, 1938

Dear Joe:-

As you know, we were all greatly disturbed by the appearance of an "exclusive" message of advice from you which was published as having been given to the Boston American and then passed on to the other Hearst papers.[119]

I know that the Secretary wired you about it and the other day I saw what you sent to the Secretary. It is not a question of "getting along reasonably well with the agencies"[120] — for, of course, you do that but it does involve the use by an American newspaper or single news agency of a "special interview" or "special message of advice" to people back here.

I know you will understand.

As ever yours,

Robert Kennedy, 12, to Rose and Joseph P. Kennedy

IMPERIAL HOTEL, CORK

Dear Daddy and Mother,

To start letter off we had a very calm crossing and nobody was sick. When we got up we went up on deck and looked at the beautiful scenery. We noticed a black light house. I think it is about the only black one in Ireland or the world. It is a wonderfull fishing place and people come over from England to fish there. The name of it was Bally-Cotton Light House. We then were invited up to the bridge. Eunice and Miss Dunn had thier cameras and I had Eunice's other one. All of them worked very well.

When we arrived at Cobh we went to church it was very big and crowded. The mass was over in about 30 minutes. We went at two thirty to The Blarney Castle. We were very tired when we had reached the top of 108 steps. We all kissed the Blarney stone and wished on the wishing stone. It was much harder when we looked at it then we thought it was going to be but when we tryed it, it was allright

Well I guess that all the news

Love
Bobby

---

118. Sir Ronald Charles Lindsay (1877–1945), British ambassador to the United States, 1930–39.
119. In a front-page exclusive, Hearst's *Boston Herald American* of August 31 had quoted JPK as appealing for calm in the intensifying crisis, "[k]eep cool—things aren't as bad as they may seem."
120. The press agencies, that is.

Joseph P. Kennedy to Cordell Hull: *Diplomatic Dispatch*

893 — September 10, 1 p.m. For the Secretary of State — Strictly Confidential

Halifax and Cadogan were seen by me separately. The message, Halifax says, was prepared last night, to be delivered to Ribbentrop not to Hitler, saying that if the French went the British had practically decided to go. Word was received after the message had gone with this statement that Henderson was in conference with Hitler, so they tried to send word to Henderson to hold up temporarily until they had the result of the conversation with Hitler, any action on their message. Finally last night they got Henderson on the telephone and found that he had not seen Hitler but most strongly he urged upon them not to insist on his delivering the message. What his point of view is they don't know, but he has sent his point of view to Cologne with a messenger. A plane has been sent by the British to Cologne to meet the messenger and the plane is expected back in London about four o'clock this afternoon, and immediately after he and the Prime Minister have this information, Halifax will communicate with me.

The British secret information is that Hitler is prepared to march, and with that in mind, preliminary steps were taken with the Admiralty yesterday. The opinion of the British is still that there are three alternatives for Hitler: (1) to stir up trouble in the Sudeten area and march in to put down bloodshed (2) try to get public opinion on his side by calling for a plebiscite and (3) to march and bomb Prague. If they were doing business with a normal man, they all reiterate that they would have some idea what might happen, but they are doing business with a madman.

Their advice from their confidential sources is that Hitler cannot stand out very long; that the Generals are a bit disturbed at the regime. That Hitler has reached his decision and that he has made up his mind that this is as good a time as any to strike are their secret advices. Cadogan and Halifax think their advices are more than likely correct.

Again Halifax asked what would be America's reaction, I said I had not the slightest idea; except that we want to keep out of war. Then he asked me why I thought Great Britain rather than the United States should be the defender of the ideals and morals of the democracies — merely for the sake of argument and not in a nasty way — and I told him that the British had made the Czechoslovak incident part of their business, the allies of the British were connected with the whole affair, and where we should be involved, the American people just failed to see. Later Cadogan said he was in complete sympathy with this opinion and wished in Heaven's name it could be maintained by them.

The French, Halifax said, had advised him they felt they could make trouble for the Germans on the Siegfried Line; that the French were not at all convinced the Germans were as invincible as they sounded.

This morning, my own observation is that much against their will, the British are veering away from the stand of keeping out; that unless Henderson has very good arguments and his opinion is very strong, they are inclined to hand a stiff note to the Germans. Of course there cannot be any good in a war, Halifax said, except that a short one might mean the end of this impossible Naziism which will very likely make it impossible for democracies to live unless destroyed. I asked Halifax how the Prime Minster felt and he said last night as the Prime Minister went out he said, "This really isn't as much fun as shooting grouse." So I feel they sense great danger in the air, but they are quite calm. Later Cadogan told me it is quite possible nothing terribly important may be said by Hitler at Nuremberg and the meeting may pass off quietly, but they do not believe by any manner of means that that is the end.

It is difficult to be entirely consistent in reporting these bulletins daily as with shifting events and information the top-side people are changing their minds every few hours as to procedure. We are staying here all day and I will send you another message as soon as I hear from Halifax again.

KENNEDY

The Ambassador, Mr. Johnson

Rose Kennedy: *Diary*

[Cannes] September 14, 1938[121]

Decided I should leave early in the morning on the 8:50 plane. However, no seat on the plane so I am going to go by sleeper to Paris tonight. I think I should be in London as Joe has Teddy on his mind and, also, these crises in world politics. Everyone fearing war and blaming Hitler. The French all took part in the last war and are still eligible and are almost frantic at the spectacle of another one. Secretary of Golf Club enlisted and wounded at age of 17. Still on list. Woman at bathing lost her husband before.

Joseph P. Kennedy: *Diary*

September 14, 1938

I was called to Downing Street this morning and told of the Cabinet's decision for Mr. Chamberlain's direct intervention with Hitler.[122] The announcement of his flying visit to Berchtesgaden was not made until ten o'clock tonight, and came as a great surprise to the newspapers and the general public. Apparently it had been a secret well kept during the day.

Joseph P. Kennedy to Cordell Hull: *Diplomatic Dispatch*

TRIPLE PRIORITY 923, September 14, 4 p.m. FOR THE SECRETARY OF STATE.
Strictly Confidential and private. No distribution.

The Prime Minister has just seen me. He went into a room with me as he came out of a Cabinet meeting and told me the following:

If a crisis should arise and war seemed imminent, he has been thinking every night what he could possibly do to stall it off. He came to the conclusion last night and sent word to Hitler that he would like to go to Berlin to see him, without asking the Cabinet's permission, because he thought the thing had arrived at that serious state. While I was there today he told the Cabinet and their unanimous approval was received. He felt, he said, that any plans Runciman might now present, which is what the French wanted done, would, under these trying times, probably not be sufficient.[123] He felt it absolutely imperative, with that in mind, to send a message last night to Hitler and ask if he would see him and go over the situation with him. No answer has, up to now, been received. However, he feels that Hitler cannot refuse to see him for fear of the reaction throughout the world psychologically. He had great fear, he said, as to misconception regarding the British Prime Minister going to see Hitler, but the time had come, he felt, when the fact that all efforts of his were bent upon preventing war should be demonstrated to the world.

---

121. The Kennedy family had spent most of the month of August in the south of France. Rose had stayed on after the children had returned to school in England.
122. At the annual party rally at Nuremberg on September 12, Hitler, accompanied by Henlein, had threatened German military intervention on behalf of the Sudeten German minority.
123. Indeed, consistently frustrated by German inventions of Czechoslovak outrages and atrocities against the Sudeten minority, the independent mediator was to return to London two days later.

I asked him what he considered the greatest danger, to which he replied very frankly that it was the request of Hitler for a plebiscite. He feels that that would be rather an astute move on the part of Hitler in that he would try to make the democracies fight against democratic principle. He said that he had considered that and had arrived at two answers: first he will suggest to the German Chancellor that the Sudeten area take local autonomy for a five year period and that the German army be demobilized at once; at the end of that time borders, other problems and elections could well be held under the auspices of an international body. If the German Chancellor completely repudiates that on the ground that he wants immediate action, the Prime Minister will suggest that it might possibly be done after six months. The great trouble with this is that Herr Hitler will be winning a victory without bloodshed and make the next crisis whenever and about whatever it comes, much easier for him to win out. This is realized by Mr. Chamberlain but he plans to say that he is ready to talk economics, colonies or any other big plan for the peace of the world, without definite commitment at this time, but if Hitler wants to talk business he will try to get the approval of the British public. He will tell the German Chancellor that he has come to try to formulate a settlement for world policy and that Czechoslovakia is after all a small incident in that big cause. If that is turned down Great Britain will have tried everything and have made every suggestion that they can and he will then tell Herr Hitler that he will fight on the French side. The Prime Minister told me that the French had not been advised of this yet for fear of a leak but he has been informed during the last 48 hours that they are becoming less and less anxious to fight and he feels certain they will throw their hat in the air when they hear of this plan.

The Prime Minister is now waiting to hear from Hitler and asked me to wish him luck and pray for him as he went out of the room.

KENNEDY

Rose Kennedy: *Diary*

September 15, 1938

Arrived in Paris about 9:30. Was told that Chamberlain was on his way by air to Berchtesgaden to talk to Hitler. Everyone ready to weep for joy and everyone confident that issues will be solved.

Several comment on fact that Joe has been on hand constantly and has aided [Chamberlain (?)] by his presence. Feel that he has given great moral support. First air flight of Prime Minister who is almost seventy years old. Unprecedented move in diplomacy but the gravity of that situation seemed to warrant it. Sir Horace Wilson went with him as interpreter.[124]

Position much more acute and more urgent than P.M. had realized. Hitler determined to march in and risk a world war if Sudeten Germans did not have the right of self determination and could not achieve it by their own efforts. Told Chamberlain if he could give him assurances that British Government accepted principle of self-determination, he would be ready to discuss ways and means.

---

124. To the dismay of some factions within the Foreign Office, Wilson's closeness to Chamberlain coupled with his advocacy of appeasement had resulted in his assumption of an increasingly important role in foreign affairs (and in Anglo-German relations, particularly) over the course of 1938. The chief industrial adviser would accompany Chamberlain not only to Berchtesgaden, but to the prime minister's subsequent eleventh-hour meetings with the führer at Godesberg and Munich.

P.M. returned to London next day to report and after conference M. Daladier[125] and M. Bonnet[126] were invited to fly to London and discuss it on September 18. Everything looks as though it was moving to peaceful solution.

Joseph P. Kennedy to Cordell Hull: *Diplomatic Dispatch*

950 — September 17, 1 p.m. <u>Strictly Confidential — For the Secretary of State</u>

I asked Cadogan to receive me although the Cabinet is still meeting and urged him to give me some information for immediate despatch to you. The Prime Minister, he says, found the German Chancellor in a mood which he describes as very bad. The people surrounding him had just announced another Sudeten incident in which it was alleged three hundred Sudeten-Germans had been annihilated. The English Prime Minister asserted that he knew nothing of such an incident and suggested to Hitler that until the report was confirmed he should take nothing for granted. After this bad start, the essence of the conversation was that Hitler insists upon the recognition of the principle of self-determination at once. In reply, Chamberlain said he was not prepared to agree to any such proposal before an opportunity to consult with the British Cabinet and perhaps with the British Parliament had been afforded him. Then Chamberlain was told by Hitler that since the British Government knew the Nazi ideas concerning race, it would not be necessary to reiterate them. Hitler insisted, however, that immediate action of some sort be taken. In reply the Prime Minister insisted that he must return to England and Hitler agreed that unless an extremely big incident occurred in the German areas of Czechoslovakia the Germans would not march, although the Prime Minister was convinced that orders to march were on the point of being given when he arrived at Berchtesgaden. Just what comfort Chamberlain can get from this undertaking I don't know, because the British have evidence, Cadogan says, that preparations have been made for stirring up an incident spectacular enough to furnish an excuse for the Germans to attack Czechoslovakia.

Hitler was then told by Chamberlain that if the British Government and people would not accept the principle of self-determination and if the Germans went to war, the British would have no alternative but to join the French against Germany. The German Chancellor replied that he was perfectly willing to take on a world war.

Cadogan saw the French Ambassador just before receiving me. I am now about to see Corbin[127] and hope Halifax will receive me after the Cabinet has concluded its sitting. I learned from Cadogan this morning that Halifax expressed it as his opinion that it was most unlikely that the Cabinet would reach an agreement this morning and that an adjournment until later in the day would probably have to be made.

From a very good source this morning I learned that there are many rumblings among Cabinet members. Some members are not pleased that the Quote Inner Cabinet Unquote consisting of Halifax, Hoare[128] and Simon, is in constant conference with the Prime Minister. Secondly, it was intimated that there may be dissensions in the Cabinet if the principle of self-determination is forced down their throats by Chamberlain.

Shortly I will telegraph you the reactions of the French Ambassador and as soon as I can see Halifax I will send you an account of my talk with him. I will also make an

---

125. Edouard Daladier (1884–1970), prime minister of France, 1933, 1934, 1938–40.
126. Georges Bonnet (1889–1973), French foreign minister, 1938–39.
127. The French ambassador, 1933–40, Charles Corbin (1881–1970).
128. Sir Samuel John Gurney Hoare, later Viscount Templewood (1880–1959), home secretary, 1937–1939.

attempt to see the Prime Minister if it is possible either tonight or tomorrow. Nevertheless, if he is having a row in the Cabinet, it is my judgment that he will not wish to talk about the matter with an outsider. My discussions reported above and what I have heard from other Cabinet members in the past day lead me to believe that self-determination or war is going to be the issue and the anti-Chamberlain group, I think, will be left with the responsibility of declaring war. In spite of the fact that the Labor leaders until now have cooperated very well, Cadogan does not venture a prophesy as to the future.

KENNEDY

The Ambassador

Joseph P. Kennedy to Cordell Hull: *Diplomatic Dispatch*

970, September 19, 6 p.m.

STRICTLY CONFIDENTIAL — FOR THE SECRETARY OF STATE

At this moment I have returned from seeing the Prime Minister. The information he gave me does not add much to the note, the substance of which was cabled you today, which has now been sent to the Czechoslovak President. He did say, however, that a personal message had been sent to Benes informing him of Runciman's view that the last Czechoslovak offer for a settlement of the Sudeten problem was not entirely hopeless and that a separation of the Sudeten region was the only solution possible under the present circumstances.

In the meantime, the German Chancellor has been informed by telegraph that Chamberlain would visit him probably on Wednesday.[129] Hitler has replied that this plan was agreeable to him, adding the query whether Chamberlain could issue a statement concerning their next meeting tonight. To this Chamberlain answered that he could not give out this information until some indication of what Benes' reply would be had been received from Prague.

Yesterday the French impressed Chamberlain, he said, as coming over with their tongues out seeking for some excuse to avoid actual warfare. During the conference sad words were spoken about Czechoslovakia a number of times but the conclusion always was Quote We must be realistic Unquote. Just before the end of the conference, Daladier was asked by Chamberlain what the former proposed to do if Benes were to answer no. When Daladier answered that he supposed he would have to march because of the Franco-Czech treaty, Chamberlain asked Quote Since you have already gone on record as asserting that you do not believe in the principle of war, how are you going to reconcile a call for war with that fact Unquote. To this Daladier replied that he had not thought of that angle.

It is my own impression that England does not propose to fight on the Czech issue unless all over the world a terrific rise of public opinion occurs.

Another thing that Chamberlain told me was that the British Ambassador in Berlin had visited Göring[130] to impress upon him that if German troops were ordered to march by Hitler while these negotiations were going on, Great Britain would regard it as an insult. The British need not be afraid of that unless a catastrophe occurs, Göring

---

129. September 21.
130. Field Marshal Hermann Wilhelm Göring, (1893–46), commander in chief of the German air force, 1933–45.

278

said. When I asked the Prime Minister what he thought such a catastrophe might mean, Chamberlain replied he thought it might be defined as a military coup by the Czech army. This he does not think at all unlikely because it is conceivable that the Czech army may refuse to agree to the terms of the settlement which Benes himself might agree to. Were this to happen, Chamberlain is convinced that Hitler would march.

The whole plan has been objected to by some members of the British Cabinet and Chamberlain appreciates that the rape of Czechoslovakia is going to be put on his shoulders. Nevertheless, since war is the only alternative, he says he can see no justification in fighting for a cause which would have to be settled after the war was over along more or less the same lines as he is trying to settle it at the present time. Chamberlain looked rather worn out and seemed quite worried, I thought. This morning I gathered that Winterton, Elliot,[131] Oliver Stanley[132] and Duff-Cooper[133] were not at all enthusiastic concerning the whole proposal and that the Minister of War[134] would possibly incline to their side. However, they have supported Chamberlain on the general principle of trying to work out the problem.

Chamberlain will leave for Germany on Wednesday if the reply he gets from President Benes permits that step.

KENNEDY

Joseph P. Kennedy to Cordell Hull: Diplomatic Dispatch

983, September 21, 5 p.m. <u>STRICTLY CONFIDENTIAL</u>

At this moment I have returned from seeing Sir Alexander Cadogan in the Foreign Office. A translation was being made when I arrived of the communiqué from Czechoslovakia and it was brought in before I left. After reading it he prepared to communicate it to the Cabinet which is at present sitting in the Prime Minister's house. It is unsatisfactory. The Czech president reports that he is at loggerheads with the chiefs of the political groups in Czechoslovakia. Although he hopes to get them in alignment later on today, he is unable to accept the plan proposed by the French and British. Cagodan's disturbed frame of mine was evident. Later on today or tonight he will let me know exactly what transpired with regard to this last communication.

At this morning's conference with the Prime Minister, Cadogan told me that the question was discussed of what Chamberlain's attitude should be if the Hungarian or Polish minorities problem was brought up by Hitler. The Prime Minister determined that nothing but the Sudeten situation would be discussed by him inasmuch as it had been made clear by Hitler that the Sudeten problem was a racial problem — a point of view with which Chamberlain sympathizes somewhat. Chamberlain will break up the meeting and come back to England if Hitler insists on discussing these new problems. I judge that public opinion here is slightly opposed to the Prime Minister's plan. Moreover unless Chamberlain returns with some commitments from Hitler there will certainly be opposition in the Cabinet. The commitments include a larger percentage of votes in the Sudeten region to carry the plan, demobilization, some outlines of Hitler's

---

131. Walter Elliot (1888–1958), minister of Health, 1938–40.
132. Oliver Stanley (1896–1950), president of the Board of Trade, 1937–40, and younger son of the earl of Derby.
133. Alfred Duff Cooper, later first Viscount Norwich (1890–1954), first lord of the Admiralty, 1937–38.
134. (Isaac) Leslie Hore-Belisha (1893–1957).

future action and two or three other commitments which have not yet been worked out. The Cabinet is likely to split if Chamberlain does not get these commitments.

Cadogan told me, when I put a question to him concerning the guarantee of the Czechoslovak State after the Sudeten territory was ceded, that Great Britain would participate in such a guarantee for protection against aggression but that the British Government did not eliminate from discussions some peaceful means of settling the other minority problems. Thus, in my judgment, this guarantee probably means little or nothing.

In my opinion the British Government are deceiving themselves by believing that a war at some time in the future is not inevitable. The Prime Minister and his advisers always hope that before war actually takes place something will happen. I have it from Chamberlain that he does not believe that it will ever be possible for England in peacetime to reach the states of preparedness for war that Germany has reached for in that country the whole influence of the State is behind war preparedness. Thus, we have a more or less official intimation that Britain needs something more than just time for catching up with Germany in armaments.

At the direction of the Cabinet the leaders of the House of Commons are still sounding out public opinion and the impression I gain is that the public reaction does not particularly support the Cabinet's ideas. The Prime Minister feels deeply that a war would be the end of civilization as we know it and that Communism or something worse would be likely to follow war.

At about seven p.m. I am planning to see some of the Cabinet Ministers and I will telegraph if anything transpires.

When we attend gatherings here the English guests spend much time making excuses to us for Great Britain's actions and while they would fight if war broke out, nevertheless, they would strongly object to having to fight for Czechoslovakia. As I see it it is pretty hard here to win public opinion to your side. It's a question of being damned if you do and damned if you don't, I guess.

KENNEDY

The Ambassador

Rose Kennedy: Diary

September 21, 1938

Czechs agree to Anglo-French plan and now there are criticisms that England has sacrificed the Czechs. Especially are these reproaches hurled at the English in U.S.A. by the Jews who hate Hitler so desperately. Looks as though danger of war was past. Czechoslovak Government accepted in hope of averting a general disaster and saving Czechoslovakia from invasion.

Col. Lindberg has an insatiable desire for sweets so am sending him some from Cape Cod, no liquor for either. Col. Lindberg and Anne Lindberg came to lunch with Joe and me alone. He was rosy cheeked, fresh looking with very wavy hair which falls naturally without much combing. Has a wonderful smile which comes easily and lights up his entire face. She is small, gentle, terribly sweet in looks and manner with a wistful expression, all of which makes you seethe to know that anyone had hurt her so tragically. She is always neatly, simply dressed and wears clothes of the latest fashion, but always in a sort of subdued way. I should say no make-up or lipstick. The Colonel gave us a rude awakening by declaring from his observations that Germany could turn out dozens of planes to England's one, that he had no confidence in Russia's manhood material,[135] that Germany had excellent army though perhaps not so many good leaders since the purge.[136]

Joseph P. Kennedy to Thomas Corcoran:[137] *Telegram*

GROSVENOR SQ. 9-22-38

UNDERSTAND ALSOP AND KINTNER HAVE WRITTEN VICIOUS ARTICLE SUPPOS-EDLY INSTIGATED BY FRANK KENT[138] AND BARUCH I AM DEPENDING ON YOU TO SEE THAT THESE THINGS DONT START IT IS VICIOUS PROPAGANDA AND AS YOU KNOW ABSOLUTELY UNTRUE[139]

JOE

Joseph P. Kennedy to Cordell Hull: *Diplomatic Dispatch*

997, September 22, 8 p.m.

STRICTLY CONFIDENTIAL — FOR THE SECRETARY OF STATE

I venture to transcribe below the substance of an interesting talk I had yesterday with Colonel Lindbergh regarding the present relative air strength of the Great European Powers as he sees it, which he has confirmed today in a memorandum. Lindbergh has had unusually favorable opportunities to observe the air establishments of the countries he discusses and has in fact just returned from a trip to Russia. You may feel that this confidential expression of his personal opinion will be of interest to the President and to the War and Navy Departments.

Special Gray.[140] Quote Without doubt the German air fleet is now stronger than that of any other country in the world. The rate of progress of German military aviation during the last several years is without parallel. I feel certain that German air strength is greater than that of all other European countries combined, and that she is constantly increasing her margin of leadership. I believe that German factories are now capable of producing in the vicinity of 20,000 aircraft each year. Her actual production is difficult to estimate. The most reliable reports I have obtained vary from 500 to 800 planes per month. The quality of German design is excellent and the extensive

135. The Lindberghs had made several trips to Germany since 1936, gathering aviation intelligence for the U.S. military. Colonel Lee, the U.S. military attaché for air in London, had suggested that they make a similar assessment of the Soviet air force in late August 1938.

136. A pair of dubious sex scandals touching the German minister of war and the army chief of staff (both of whom hesitated to risk war with Britain) had provided Hitler with the pretext not only for retiring sixteen generals and transferring forty-four others, but also for assuming supreme command of the armed forces in his own right on February 4, 1938.

137. The joint drafter of the Securities Act of 1934 and special counsel to the Reconstruction Finance Corporation was also JPK's Washington counsel.

138. One of the earliest syndicated columnists, the *Baltimore Sun*'s Francis Richardson Kent (1877–1958) published his "Great Game of Politics" column in more than 140 papers nationwide by the mid–1930s.

139. In their syndicated "Capital Parade" column of September 20, the journalistic duo of Joseph Alsop and Robert Kintner accused JPK of a growing Anglophilia: "He is one of the prize exhibits at Cliveden, and the wonderfully impressive and exciting English world has taken him to its bosom. He regards Neville Chamberlain as a very great man, and loves every instant of his London life." In a similar article published the previous day in the *Washington Star*, they asserted that "[w]hile Kennedy is loved in London, he is no longer popular at the White House." The president, they went on to say, was well aware of JPK's indiscreet private comments both about him and about the administration. Roosevelt, they contended, "resents it, and rebukes it while he can."

140. At the time the State Department classified its coding system by colors; the gray code was only moderately confidential, and allowed for relatively easy (and therefore rapid) encryption and decipher.

research facilities which have been built in that country are a guarantee of continued progress in the future. The Germans long ago established their ability in the design, construction and operation of aircraft. I believe they have the greatest ability of any European nation in the field of aviation. In fact I believe that the United States is the only country in the world capable of competing with Germany in aviation. At present however Germany is rapidly cutting down the lead we have held in the past. In numbers of fighting planes she is already ahead of us. In time of war, her weakness would undoubtedly lie in her supply of raw materials. PARAGRAPH. Germany now has the means of destroying London, Paris and Prague if she wishes to do so. England and France together have not enough modern war planes for effective defense or counter-attack. France is in a pitiful condition in the air. England is better off but her air fleet is not comparable to Germany's. France is probably now building in the vicinity of 50 planes per month; England probably in the vicinity of 200 first-line aircraft. I understand that France hopes to have about 2500 first-line planes by the spring of 1940. PARAGRAPH. Czechoslovakia has no completely modern aircraft except those obtained from Russia. I saw a number of Russian-built bombers on the field at Prague. The Czechoslovakians have excellent machine guns and anti-aircraft guns. PARAGRAPH. It is not possible to estimate the Russian air strength. The Russians have copied American factories and purchased American machinery of the most modern type. If operated on American standards these factories might place Russia next to Germany in military aviation. The production is certainly much less on Russian standards. Judging by the general conditions in Russia, I would not place great confidence in the Russian air fleet. However Russia probably has a sufficient number of planes to make her weight felt in any war she enters. Her aircraft are not the best but their performance is good enough to be effective in modern warfare. I believe the Russian weakness lies in inefficiency and poor organization. PARAGRAPH German military strength now makes them inseparable from the welfare of European civilization, for they have the power either to preserve or to destroy it. For the first time in history a nation has the power either to save or to ruin the great cities of Europe. Germany has such a preponderance of war planes that she can bomb any city in Europe with comparatively little resistance. England and France are far too weak in the air to protect themselves. ENDQUOTE.

KENNEDY

Mr. Johnson

Joseph P. Kennedy to Cordell Hull: *Diplomatic Dispatch*

1006, September 23, 6 p.m.
STRICTLY CONFIDENTIAL — FOR THE SECRETARY OF STATE

I have just had a conversation with Cadogan. The Foreign Office has not yet been informed of the text of Hitler's reply; nevertheless, Mr. Chamberlain has it according to their information. The conversation I had over the telephone had to be somewhat cryptic but I gather that the German reply is not very satisfactory. Therefore Mr. Chamberlain has again communicated with Hitler requesting him to prepare a written memorandum of his ideas. Cadogan was rather vague about the whole thing because the telephone communication became disturbed at this point.

Because Mr. Chamberlain is not planning to leave Germany[141] tonight Cadogan is of the opinion that the conversations may continue. The result so far is not satisfactory, is the way he summed it all up.

I will be in constant communication with them throughout the evening and as soon as I learn anything I will let you know.

KENNEDY

The Ambassador, Mr. Johnson

Joseph P. Kennedy to Cordell Hull: *Diplomatic Dispatch*

1011, September 24, 1 p.m.

My conversation with Cadogan is just finished. The Foreign Office has just received Hitler's answers which Cadogan believes to be absurd. Not only does Hitler want what has been willingly offered to him but apparently he is demanding much more. When the communications are made public Cadogan is convinced that public opinion will turn against Hitler bitterly and completely. Not that public opinion is not anti-Hitler today but many people still want peace. The Foreign Office feels that it will be apparent to everyone that the British policy was right inasmuch as every possible opportunity has been taken to demonstrate the British belief that Hitler still had some sanity left and to preserve the world from war with its horrible results. Of course Cadogan is waiting to get the Prime minister's report. But his own opinion is that the answers sent by Hitler prove the man insane and that all that is left to be determined is England's future course of action. That question of policy must wait until the Prime Minister has come back. From the tone of Hitler's communication Cadogan judges it probable that Hitler will march in spite of everything in a short time.

Halifax has gone to the airport to meet Chamberlain. Thereafter there will be a small conference between Halifax, Hoare, Cadogan, Simon and perhaps others. A meeting of the Cabinet at 5:30 is being called. In the circumstances I suppose I will not have further authentic news before 8:30. Sometime later I will try and see Chamberlain and Halifax. Chamberlain is very tired, Cadogan said, and may not be able to see anyone.

I have just been told by Oliver Stanley that a proposal is on foot [*sic*] to have the Prime Minister broadcast in England and possibly to the United States something along the following lines: Quote I have made as many concessions as my reason and my conscience would allow. There are many people who say that I have gone too far. In spite of all efforts to preserve sanity and peace in the world I tell you now that I do not believe Hitler intends to cooperate Unquote. Cabinet members, among whom is Stanley, think that public opinion would be tremendously influenced by such a statement. They are of the opinion that the die is cast and that it is now only a question of a short time.

We are attempting to keep you informed as thoroughly as possible. Am I missing anything?

KENNEDY

The Ambassador

---

141. Godesberg.

Joseph P. Kennedy: *Diary*

TRANSATLANTIC TELEPHONE CONVERSATION BETWEEN SECRETARY HULL (WASHINGTON) AND AMBASSADOR KENNEDY (LONDON), SEPTEMBER 26, 1938, 9:30 a.m.

Secretary: What is going on this morning?

Ambassador: You got my first message on Cadogan?[142]

Secretary: No, we haven't seen it yet.

Ambassador: I sent it quite a while ago. I have just seen Halifax and these two things are very secret. Chamberlain has told Daladier that if the French go, they will definitely go. He gave me this assurance definitely this morning. Also they have sent a note to Warsaw to the Poles telling them that they will have to take what is offered them because it is fair and if they don't take it, they will regard it as an unfriendly act. The Prime Minister will broadcast tomorrow night and is considering broadcasting to America. Parliament is called for Wednesday and the Prime Minister will make a speech Wednesday afternoon. They expect to pass legislation very quickly which will enable them to conduct war if Hitler does not back down before that. They are very happy about the President's message.[143] It had a very, very good effect. I have sent you a message on that and also Daladier's reply to the President's message. It is on my wire now. Bonnet just gave it to me before he went back.

Secretary: A reply to the President's message?

Ambassador: Yes, Bonnet just gave it to me before he went back. That is about the set-up. Hore-Belisha said there wouldn't be a war if Hitler would back down on the strength of the message and it would give him a chance to back out. On the strength of the President's message and also the message sent to Horace Wilson by airplane this morning, both those two messages might make Hitler back out. They will not permit it to be given out in the press.

Secretary: Is Great Britain making any counter-proposition?

Ambassador: No, they are merely sending them word that they are standing pat and will not accept Hitler's demands. They will ask him to negotiate it as they originally suggested. I feel sure that this thing can be worked out but not on his terms. The Cabinet told (?) Chamberlain that if he (Hitler) turns it down, they will go. I sent you a telegram this morning (a message by Wilson). This is not a counter-proposition but is merely telling him approximately what the President said. This is no agreement; it asks him to appeal to reason and negotiate it.

Secretary: How do you feel and how do the British feel about the results of the meeting yesterday and last night?

Ambassador: This is what happened. The Cabinet finally swung around to the point that they would go through with the French and fight. Chamberlain would give up the idea of battling any further and run the risk of losing the country. This was definitely decided at the meeting this morning. They are all one unit. Even the dissenting members agreed to go along.

Secretary: Do they understand that the French are in very good shape to fight?

Ambassador: No, they understand that they are not in good condition to fight. They feel as they always do that they can rise to the occasion. There will be a terrible

142. Dispatch No. 1011 of September 24.

143. Shortly after 1:00 A.M. that day, Washington time, Roosevelt had appealed to Germany, Czechoslovakia, France and England for peace. He reminded the heads of state that "the United States has no political entanglements," and appealed to them not to break off negotiations, for "so long as negotiations continue differences may be reconciled. Once they are broken off, the reason is banished and force asserts itself. And force produces no solution for the future good of humanity."

time for a while. In addition to that, they had a talk with the French this morning. They made a direct proposition that if the French decided to go, they would go along too. They were told definitely that Great Britain would go. There would be no more equivocation from now on. They are moving up their battleships, you know about that?

Secretary: Yes, I know a little about it.

Ambassador: They are calling territorials. They have called them to arms.

Secretary: I see.

Ambassador: We are going to have quite a time here because of all the people that are trying to get out. I will keep you posted. I might send you a message tonight asking you to get in touch with the Maritime Commission to see about ships. We ought to have them. I will get in touch with the British Government to see if they would take big ships or if they can make any more sailings. I understand they are willing to have the NORMANDIE make one more trip. They will not make any promises after that. We will be in a terrible way to get people out of here. There are 1,800 people on the waiting list for the QUEEN MARY for Tuesday from here alone. If they take that ship off, that will leave us with a terrific problem. I am urging them to make one more trip if they can.

Secretary: They don't feel that the Germans are liable to make any move until the next few days?

Ambassador: It all depends on Hitler's speech tonight and if, after the President's message and Chamberlain's message today, he indicates that he is not going to back down, they will call the Army and Navy at once.[144] They feel that, if his speech tonight, after these two talks, is not any good, they figure it is on. You see, Chamberlain's message asks Hitler to go back to negotiations on the original proposition. At least, they settled nothing on the second conference, and they asked him on the first conference to negotiate and see if he could arrive at something without plunging the world into war.

Secretary: Have you anything else in mind?

Ambassador: Nothing of a political nature. There will probably be nothing until eight o'clock. Have you received the three or four telegrams sent a long time ago? Have you any suggestions?

Secretary: I have nothing in mind just at the moment.

Ambassador: We will have to start thinking about how we are going to organize. There are an awful lot of people here who all want to go home. There are so many transient people here. It gives us quite a problem.

Secretary: Have you received a long instruction about setting up a separate unit to take care of Americans?

Ambassador: We haven't received any instructions but we are talking it over.

Secretary: This was about setting up a separate unit. It should be on the boat arriving today.

Ambassador: You mean a separate organization for Americans?

Secretary: Yes. I have just this minute received your three messages that you spoke of. I thank you very much. We are still delighted to have your fine cooperation.

Ambassador: Thank you very much. Your telegram gave me very great courage. It made me feel very happy.

Secretary: We will send you another one some of these days if you keep on.

Ambassador: Thank you very much.

---

144. That evening at the Berlin *Sportpalast*, Hitler would denounce the Czechoslovak state as having been engendered "with a single lie, and the father of this lie was named Beneš." He went on to threaten that if Czechoslovakia did not liberate the Sudetenland and its German population at once, "we will go and fetch . . . freedom for ourselves."

Rose Kennedy: *Diary*

Took golf lesson from assistant who did not help me much. Played nine holes which is skirted by road so I heard too many cars for my pleasure. Am told the Queen's course is most attractive and quiet and as it used to be a nine hole course, I can easily play the first "5" and the last "4." Cannot seem to find quiet walks here in the woods or surrounding country like we have at home at the Mt. Washington Hotel for instance. There also do not seem to be any specially attractive places to sit out of doors. There is no porch on the hotel, only the main doorway, room for six chairs, quite public and too noisy to read or write.

French Ministers informed us if Czech were attacked, France would support her and England said she would feel obliged to support her.

Sir Horace Wilson sent to Berlin with a personal message for discussions between German and Czecho representatives in presence of Britishers as Prime Minister was deeply impressed with the fact that in Hitler there is a deep rooted distrust and disbelief in sincerity of Czechs. No result obtained.

Speech of Prime Minister on radio which we listened to. His voice filled with sadness, with loathing of war, with discouragement as to result of his efforts but still urging people to keep calm, to cooperate quietly and with confidence and not to give up the last shred of hope.[145]

Joseph P. Kennedy: *Diary*

September 27, 1938

At 1:50, while I was lunching at home with Teddy, 10 Downing Street called and informed me that Sir Horace Wilson was leaving at 1:45 and was due in London at 5:15. He had seen Hitler this morning and Hitler had remained "obdurate." They regard the situation as almost hopeless.

I then called the Secretary and gave him this message and also told him I was to see the King at 4 o'clock to deliver the personal letter from the President. I also talked with him about the general situation, as I saw it, and urged upon him the need for getting ships here to get the Americans out, because the panic would be great. I urged him to have the "Honolulu" stay so we could get our wives and the wives of men in business here out as soon as possible. He quite agreed and said it was absolutely necessary.

He asked me my opinion on what had been heard from the Dominions. I told him that Massey[146] thought public opinion in Canada and Australia was definitely behind Chamberlain but, up to date, the Governments had taken no action.

145. That evening the prime minister had told a national radio audience,

> [h]owever much we may sympathise with a small nation confronted by a big and powerful neighbour, we cannot in all circumstances undertake to involve the whole British Empire in war simply on her account. If we have to fight it must be on larger issues than that. I am myself a man of peace to the depths of my soul. Armed conflict between nations is a nightmare to me; but if I were convinced that any nation had made up its mind to dominate the world by force I should feel that it must be resisted. Under such a domination life for people who believe in liberty would not be worth living; but war is a fearful thing, and we must be very clear, before we embark on it, that it is really the great issues that are at stake, and that the call to risk everything in their defense, when all consequences are weighed, is irresistible.

146. (Charles) Vincent Massey (1887–1967), former Canadian minister to the United States, 1926–30; first Canadian-born British high commissioner for Canada, 1935–46, and later, governor-general of Canada, 1952–59.

I called to see the King this afternoon at 4 o'clock, taking a letter from President Roosevelt, who had requested me to present it in person. The King read the letter in my presence. It was two full pages and had to do with an invitation for him to come to America if he went to Canada.

He asked me to sit down and discussed the foreign situation. He looked very well and said he felt much better than he had in the spring. He spoke about how inconceivable it was to have another war twenty years after the last one; how he was obliged to stay at the telephone and then made an interesting remark, seemingly as though it slipped out, — "One of the minor calamities of the war will be his return." This was a reference to the Duke of Windsor, about who he had been talking, I saying I had seen him at Cannes and that he looked very well, and the King saying he had heard he was a great deal less nervous. He also thanked me very much for getting the letters back.

He seemed very amused at the stories they had told of my trying with Chamberlain to bluff the Germans, and particularly the story which Halifax and I worked up that we would cause the Germans considerable confusion by the constant trips to Downing Street and the King laughed at the remark that I would go down there, even if we only read the newspapers.

He told me he had been listening to the broadcast of the launch of the "Queen Elizabeth" and said he was much more nervous listening to it than he could possibly have been being there.[147] He also told me he had listened to Hitler's speech, although he didn't understand German. He told me he had had a terrible time with his French in Paris; that he would learn an expression from the man on his right, and immediately pass it on to the man on his left, so, if they thought he spoke French, that is the way he spoke it. He also told me Paris was not as much of a strain as people thought, because everything was planned out until he turned out the light and went to bed.

After talking 45 minutes and waiting for him to give the signal to leave, I suggested that I had taken a lot of his time and had better be going. He said, "By no means," that he didn't often have a chance to talk to Ambassadors. He inquired very kindly about Mrs. Kennedy and the children.

Rose Kennedy: *Diary*

September 27, 1938

Today individual, brooding, silence was as general as un-smiling, un-emotional faces. Everyone [sic] unutterably shocked and depressed falling [sic] from the Prime Minister's speech that his hopes for peace are shattered and that war is inevitable.

Went to Glasgow to Exposition which is not popular among visitors, especially, yet I felt I should go as I am so near.[148] Motored from Gleneagles which took about one and a half hours. Went on a little steam car with seats on both sides to the painting exhibit where we saw several Raeburns, among them the Great McNab, loaned by John Dewar and Sons. Also two lovely Raeburns of women. Also, saw one by Elwes[149] of his wife[150]

147. That day in Edinburgh, accompanied only by the two princesses (international events had precluded the king's attendance) the queen christened and launched the *Queen Elizabeth*, the largest passenger liner ever built.
148. The British Empire Exhibition, boasting pavilions "illustrating every facet of life" in every British dominion, including a full-scale Scottish Highland village, had opened in Glasgow's Bellahouston Park in May.
149. Simon Edmund Vincent Paul Elwes (1902–1976), Scottish Catholic society portrait painter.
150. The former Honorable Gloria Rodd, daughter of Lord Rennell.

(he is son of woman[151] who came to tea with Cardinal Hinsley as her other son is Secretary to Cardinal). Regretted I had no time for exhibition of Scottish silver which they say is much cruder than English silver and much coarser in feeling. Should have loved to see the Scotch village called the Clachon, but no time.

Went on to Launching of Queen Elizabeth. Queen came without King as the times were so uncertain. She was dressed in grey with a smart small hat and looked much thinner than in the spring. Little Princess Margaret Rose saw me in the group, smiled, told Princess Elizabeth who immediately told the Queen who again looked over and bowed. I did not stand near at the launching as I felt the Scotch people should have first consideration.

September 28, 1938

Joe phoned this morning. Said I should go home tonight as we must make some sort of plans for the children as war was imminent. Everyone depressed and sober. Waiters chattering in groups. Some of the reserves called out.

Took golf lesson. Then played first four holes and last three on Queen's course which was wonderful. Beautiful large greens. Grass wet and heavy underfoot. Had to wear a large rubber as the ground heavy with dew and moisture.

Lunched in rather a subdued atmosphere as few people at hotel, though the races are on at Perth (horse). Took ride to Perth and visited Frazer's tweed shop, a rather small shop filled in second room with all sorts of tweeds. Said to be the last for tweeds. While there, the proprietor told us that the four great Powers were to go to Munich to discuss peaceful ways of settling the controversy. From the depths of despair we were moved to a new hope. Everyone showed gladness. The girls in the office, the waiters, etc. Of course most people had left the hotel. Some had even entirely packed and my maid had left, but I decided to stay at least over the weekend.

Joseph P. Kennedy to Cordell Hull: *Diplomatic Dispatch*

1073, September 28, 6 p.m.

Have just returned from the House of Parliament and by now you have the whole speech with the dramatic finish where Mussolini asked Hitler to postpone action and Hitler notified Chamberlain of the meeting tomorrow. Chamberlain of course is leaving tonight or tomorrow morning.[152] The President can feel that God was on his side and that he was on God's side.

I was sitting in the gallery with Grandi;[153] on the other side of the division rope was the Duke of Kent, then Baldwin, and then Halifax. While Chamberlain was making his speech a messenger delivered an envelope to Halifax; he opened it and showed it to Baldwin and immediately got up and went down stairs. Shortly after a messenger brought the papers in to Sir John Simon, who was sitting on the front bench and he showed them to Sir Samuel Hoare. They held the papers until Chamberlain had practically finished his speech and then handed them to him. When the Prime Minister read out the replies of Hitler and Mussolini, the cheers in the House from both sides were terrific. Everybody feels tremendously relieved tonight. It may be that England will thank Chamberlain but certainly their second choice will be the President while the rest of the world will have real appreciation of this last hour drive of his. A number of Am-

---

151. Lady Winefrid Elwes, daughter of the eighth earl of Denbigh.
152. To meet Hitler at Munich.
153. Dino Grandi, conte di Mordano (1895–1988), an early and eager proponent of Italian Fascism, Mussolini's former foreign minister, 1929–32, and Italian ambassador to London, 1932–1939.

bassadors and Ministers spoke to me at the meeting of the President's wonderful appeal.

The only discordant note was that Masaryk riding back with me from Parliament said "I hope this doesn't mean they are going to cut us up and sell us out."

I told Sir Alexander Cadogan, with whom I have just talked, that never again did I expect to be entertained in a theater after being here when the Prime Minister first made his flight to Germany and also being present at the finish of this dramatic speech in Parliament. The President's appeal had unquestionably done the trick, Cadogan told me, saying that the pressure on Hitler today must have been very great. Cadogan said that as far as he knew this was the first time Hitler's time schedule for accomplishing things had been held up five minutes and that since this definitely delays his program, he is very hopeful. Cadogan said that foreign affairs move so rapidly now that the old-time diplomat feels himself unable to keep up with things and quite out of place.

Well, as they say on the radio "Signing off" and will try to get six hours sleep which I haven't had for seven days.

KENNEDY

The Ambassador, Mr. Johnson

Rose Kennedy: *Diary*

[Scotland] September 29, 1938

Joe called. Said everything was packed at Home though no one wanted to go except Teddy who wants to go to North America to have his tonsils out because he thinks if he does he can drink all the coco-cola [*sic*] he wishes and all the ice cream.

Talked to Kathleen who went to the horse races at Perth yesterday which is a big drawing card here now. Called at Lord Forteviot's Castle yesterday[154] and saw her for a moment as she was just returning from a cocktail party after the races. The driveway is magnificent. Must be over a mile and a half long with magnificent old spreading trees on either side, sheep grazing and the castle, a large part of which was destroyed by fire and has now been restored. Bright and attractive, new looking, no details, as I made such a hurried visit.

Everyone expects Prime Minister's visit to be crowned with success though preparations for war are still being carried out. Trenches are being dug and gas masks fitted. All sorts of warnings are broadcast about taking care of the masks, as carelessness is apt to result in deficiency in the mask. One reason I suppose, why they have not been given out before.

Jean Kennedy, 10, to Rose and Joseph P. Kennedy

Convent of the Sacred Heart. Roehampton Sept 29, 1938

Dear Mother & Daddy,

Miss Dunn came up to day. She brought us a half of a cake. Eunice ate most of it. Mother Burent has said that as long as we are here it is safe. I here that the war is very bad. I am getting a long fine at school. We play a game called net ball. It is a lot like bas-

---

154. Dupplin Castle, seat of John Dewar, second Baron Forteviot, chairman of the Distillers Company and a director of John Dewar and Sons, whose products JPK's Somerset Importers represented in the United States.

ket ball. But you don't run with it. It is great fun. I am working very hard. Everyone is fine. Love to all,

Jean

Rose Kennedy: *Diary*

[Scotland] September 30, 1938

Everyone feels quite relieved and happy.[155] Chamberlain arrived home last night and he was given a wonderful reception by the people and received a stupendous oration when he appeared with the King and Queen. We all feel that a new psychology for settling issues between different countries has been inaugurated and that henceforth war may be out of the question.

Chamberlain's words from Henry IV, "Out of this nettle, danger, we pluck this flower, safety." Words as he departed for Munich. Also quoted this Chinese proverb on his last birthday, justifying achievements of old men in politics, "One decrepit camel still bears the burden of many asses."

Prime Minister went to school at Rugby and to Mason College, Birmingham.

Joseph P. Kennedy, Jr., 23: *"Charles Lindbergh"*

EMBASSY OF THE UNITED STATES OF AMERICA [PARIS],
SATURDAY OCTOBER 1[156]

MET COLONEL LINDBERGH FOR DINNER AND HE IMPRESSED ME A GREAT DEAL. HE IS MODEST AND SHY, AND NEITHER SMOKES NOR DRINKS. HIS INTERESTS HOWEVER ARE NEARLY COMPLETELY WRAPPED UP IN HIS ARTIFICIAL PUMP[157] AND FLYING. HE HAS A SMALL HOUSE ON AN ISLAND OFF THE COAST OF BRITTANY WHERE HE LIVES QUITE A PART FROM THE WORLD.[158] YOU CAN WALK TO SHORE ONLY AT LOW TIDE. HE ALSO CAN WALK TO CAVELS [SIC] ISLAND AT LOW TIDE. HE IS TERRIBLY OUTSPOKEN AGAINST THE NEWSPAPERS AND SAYS THAT THEY KEEP HIM FROM LIVING IN AMERICA. HE THOUGHT THAT CHAMBERLAIN HAD PURSUED THE RIGHT COURSE DURING THE PRESENT CRISIS: AND HAD THE GREATEST OF PRAISE FOR THE GERMAN AIR FLEET. HE SAID THAT THEY WOULD HAVE COMPLETELY WIPED OUT ALL THE CITIES IN FRANCE AND ENGLAND. HE FELT THAT TO DESTROY THE CULTURE OF EUROPE FOR THE SAKE OF AN ERROR MADE IN THE TREATY OF VERSAILLES WAS RIDICULOUS. HE SAID THAT RUSSIAN AVIATION WAS

---

155. On September 30, Chamberlain had returned from Munich, having secured "peace for our time," the declaration of Anglo-German cooperation that both he and Hitler had signed that morning. He told the expectant crowds at Heston Airport and later at the House of Commons that the agreement was "symbolic of the desire of our two peoples never to go to war with one another again."

156. Joe Junior was spending several weeks working at the American embassy in Paris under Ambassador William Bullitt.

157. The inoperable and ultimately fatal heart condition of Anne Morrow Lindbergh's elder sister, Elizabeth, had had a profound and lasting effect on Lindbergh himself. In late 1930, Lindbergh met, and began collaborating with the Nobel laureate for medicine, Dr. Alexis Carrel, in an effort to create what Lindbergh would come to call the "glass perfusion pump." The apparatus, a pressurized container upon which Lindbergh improved over the course of his life, was designed to maintain organs outside of the body for extended periods of time (during operations, for example). By 1935, Lindbergh had begun to publish his findings, which had resulted in a number of collateral discoveries, among them new means of both cultivating blood cells and separating blood into its component parts.

158. The Lindberghs had purchased the small, remote island of Illiec secretly from Dr. and Mrs. Carrel, who owned the nearby island of St. Gidas.

Joseph P. Kennedy: *Diary*

October 3, 1938

I have just been listening to the opening of the debate on the Czechoslovak situation. I heard Duff-Cooper defend his resignation with what I consider a most ordinary defense.[159] I heard the Prime Minister explain the Munich Conference and I felt he showed the great weakness in his armor: first, that England permitted Czechoslovakia to believe they intended to do something and waited as long as he did before anything happened; second, he talked about his agreement with Hitler as being one for world peace and at the same time pointed out that England must continue to rearm. I am afraid that this last argument will come back to plague him before many months have passed.

I listened to Attlee make his argument in answer and I am again impressed with the mediocrity of the men in charge of the Parties in England.[160] We have got men in every house of representatives in the United States that could make better arguments and advance their cause in much better shape.

London, October 4, 1938

In my opinion the English and French were feverishly working for peace because they knew that they were not prepared and they knew that Hitler very likely was. Knowing this condition and knowing that Hitler was ready to pull the trigger to start the war at any time, I have tried, in my own mind, to decide on what it was that at the last minute made Hitler listen to the Roosevelt and Mussolini appeals. I have come to the following conclusion:

(1) In the first place the Nazi party is pretty smart. They have their ear to the ground and although no one of the German people was allowed to express his opinion, they probably learned that there was a heavy ground swell of public opinion in the real German people against the war.

(2) Mussolini injected himself into the affair, at the last minute, in the manner in which he did because although he had secretly mobilized — probably to the extent of 1,500,000 men — he felt sure that if Hitler went ahead with his plan that France and England must fight. He figured they certainly would not try to break down the Siegfried Line but would try to go through Northern Italy while the English fleet bombed the Italian Coast. He had there the incentive of protecting his own country. Probably he also

159. In what the *New York Times* described as both "the first break in the chorus of acclaim that welcomed Mr. Chamberlain back home" and "the first indication to most Britons that the entire cabinet was not solidly back [*sic*] of the Munich settlement," Alexander Duff Cooper resigned as first lord of the Admiralty on September 30, citing a profound distrust of the government's foreign policy. On October 3, Duff Cooper expounded upon his views before the House, contending that "it was not for Czechoslovakia that we should have been fighting if we had gone to war last week," but rather, Britain should have fought "in order that one great Power should not be allowed, in disregard of treaty obligations, of the laws of nations and the decrees of morality to dominate by brutal force the Continent of Europe."

160. As a result of the Munich Agreement, the leader of the opposition declared, "[Hitler] has destroyed the last fortress of democracy in Eastern Europe, he has opened a way to the food and oil resources which he requires in order to consolidate his military power. He has successfully divided and reduced to impotence the forces which might have stood against the rule of violence."

figured that if anything happened to Hitler he was out the window too. Acting as he did at the request of the British to do everything in his power for peace he is now assured of a loan from England which is what he greatly needs. Abyssinia having turned out to be a complete bloomer in what was supposed to yield.

(3) Chamberlain undoubtedly had an influence with Hitler for the reason that Hitler could see in the marvelous reception accorded Chamberlain by the German people their wish to keep out of war and their great respect for Chamberlain who was not for one minute allowing diplomacy to bog down entirely and who really made the only warlike or prepared gesture he could in the mobilization of the British fleet.

(4) Hitler probably drew the conclusion as other Germans whom I have met have drawn that the United States Government's declarations were not so strong on the moral side as they sounded but were expressions rather suggesting that the United States would eventually have to come in with the democracies and they all remember what that did before.

Joseph P. Kennedy to Cordell Hull: *Diplomatic Dispatch Draft*

October 5

The feeling of relief which began to sweep through the length and breadth of Great Britain on [*last*] Wednesday afternoon has now been largely supplanted by a mood of analysis, a questioning of the pros and cons of the past in terms of probabilities for the future. The debate now taking place in the House of Commons is of course stimulating this reaction.

Since the European political outlook is by no means clear and assured it may be worthwhile for us to look the past in the face for the lessons it may hold for the future. So I am setting forth some of my own tentative conclusions in this respect.

As I see it four immediate main causes produced the avoidance of a European war last week.

In the first place, the German man and woman in the street did not want it to take place. And the ground swell of public opinion in Germany which found legitimate expression in such demonstrations as those made before Chamberlain's hotel were not personal tributes to him but expression of the German people's will to peace. The strength of this reaction of the German public was not lost upon the Nazi leaders.

Secondly, Chamberlain's bulldog persistence was an important contribution, for without it the diplomatic machinery of negotiation would have broken down and none of the other powers immediately concerned was able to or willing to take the initiative to keep in being the interchanges which could lead to an amicable settlement. Therefore if Chamberlain had ceased his efforts events would have been in the saddle and ridden away.

Thirdly, Italy which with the approach of war regained its middle, balance-of-power position was able to intervene decisively on the side of peaceful settlement. Hitler was under obligation to Mussolini because of the Austrian annexation and in turn Mussolini was somewhat indebted to Chamberlain in the matter of the Anglo-Italian rapprochement agreement. Furthermore Mussolini, besides fearing an unrestrained Germany, was no doubt aware that Italy from a strategic viewpoint constituted the most suitable target for an Anglo-French attack both by land and by sea. Therefore Mussolini preferred to avoid these pitfalls and to attempt to obtain new benefits both in freedom of action and in opportunity by bringing moderating pressure to bear on Hitler at the decisive moment.

Lastly and by no means least was the President's message to Hitler and the subsequent follow-up diplomatic exchanges. The last message particularly hit the nail on the head at the right time. In appraising our intervention in this recent situation for the benefit of future use I think we should take into account the fact that it was effective but not because the most detached and powerful country in the world had neutral good offices to offer at the decisive moment. For better or for worse we have not been and are not now regarded in Europe as maintaining an unprejudiced neutral position because of public utterances made in the United States since the rise of Hitlerism in Germany. And in this instance although we preserved the form that we did not quote in any way imply any opinion as to the merits of the dispute unquote in point of fact, regardless of how we conceived our intervention, it was effective because it was conceived in Europe, from its manner and urgency, as a definite and significant indication of how quickly America would come in on the side of England and France to the then pending European war. In effect our intervention was taken as falling into the same category of action as for example the mobilization of the British fleet.

It seems to me in view of the average American's desire for non-involvement in a European war and in order to meet any similar future crisis we should now try to get back to a middle position where we will have as an unprejudiced neutral good offices as such to offer. In the present state of the world, in which power politics dominate and in which the efficacy of diplomacy is conditioned by armed strength alone, we have to face the fact that whereas the offer of our good offices or the exertion of our so-called moral influence in any future crisis may not be sufficient to prevent a conflict, on the other hand we will have avoided definite dangers which the alternative attitude would hold. There seem to me to be three main dangers. In the first place, a danger of kidding our potential friends; *i.e.,* although the heads of the Governments of England and France might understand perfectly clearly, both from our envoys and their own in the United States, the real attitude of the American people as regards involvement in a European war, nevertheless the British and French publics might well be led to hold a contrary view of the facts which in turn could lead them to press their leaders for a course of action that otherwise they might not desire. As a matter of fact if the average Englishman did not in his heart of hearts count on our helping him in the last analysis, British public opinion might well press the British Government more forcefully to take steps to repair the really lamentable condition of their state of preparation against an attack. Secondly, if Germany comes to regard us as a potential enemy such a decision may well weigh in the balance against her agreeing to some form of armaments standstill arrangement. On the contrary she might think it wise to increase her efforts, taking our military strength into account. Thirdly, we run the grave risk of creating an emotional background among our own people, of arousing them towards action which would hold nothing for them but incalculable material and personal loss.

May I add one other thought, it is that with the virtual exclusion of Russia from Europe, England, and France have lost a potential ally and it will be even more than ever before in their interest, in order to meet any future crisis, to be able to call the new world in to redress the balance of the old.

KENNEDY

The Ambassador

Joseph P. Kennedy to Cordell Hull: *Diplomatic Dispatch*

GRAY 1196, October 17, 6 p.m. FOR THE SECRETARY OF STATE

I have to make a speech at the Navy League Dinner on Wednesday night.[161] I have struggled with this for ten days and am sending you the result of my work. Save as much of it as you can for me.[162] (end Gray)

QUOTE Mr. Chairman, My Lords, Ladies and Gentlemen:

Lord Lloyd[163] tells me that I am the first Ambassador invited to speak at the annual Trafalgar Day Dinner. Needless to say I appreciate the compliment you have paid me and through me the country I am privileged to represent at the Court of St. James's.

As pleased as I am to be here, I must confess that your invitation has involved me in definite difficulties. The representative of a foreign Government, addressing the people of the country to which he is accredited, is always presented with certain difficulties. Normal diplomatic procedure, as most of you have undoubtedly discovered, does not consist of a vigorous exchange of ideas in public. Furthermore, an Ambassador must bear in mind the attitudes of the people of two nations, which do not necessarily coincide. Meanwhile, those whom he is privileged to address expect him to say something.

This dilemma applies with particular force to me on this occasion. Three weeks ago we passed through one of the greatest crises of modern times. It is still in our minds. We expect people to talk about it. To talk about anything else would be like discussing the weather just after we had escaped from a burning house. Yet, for some of us, the observations which we can, with propriety, make on the fire are exceedingly limited.

From which you will gain the impression, I hope, that I have had something of a time trying to decide what I could say that would be of interest to this gathering and still would be appropriate to your circumstances and to mine.

I do not want to talk about the Navy. The record of past dinners shows that you have heard a great deal about the Navy — from men who know all there is to know about the subject.

The first thing then that suggested itself as of topical interest was armaments. For armaments are a matter not unconnected with the Navy and one which concerns all of us at this time. Recent events will undoubtedly further stimulate the already frenzied race for arms. Considering what we have been through, it is hard to quarrel with the decision of any nation to build up its military forces. In fact we can only commend such action on the part of those sincerely committed to a policy of peace. Nevertheless, the armament burden is approaching a point, it seems to me, where it threatens sooner or later to engulf us all in major disaster.

The arms race, if unchecked, presents us with two terrifying possibilities. One is war, the other is economic collapse.

This is the terrible dilemma presented to the leaders of all nations. Failure to arm may mean domination by a stronger Power or group of Powers. Further rapid rearming will eventually bring economic ruin to all concerned as surely as would a world war. I know that no one nation can stop this vicious circle of misdirected energy, but we

---

161. The annual naval commemoration of Nelson's victory at Trafalgar.
162. The following day, Jay Pierrepont Moffat, chief of the Division of European Affairs at the State Department, would record in his diary that "Kennedy sent in a speech he is planning to make to the Navy League tomorrow night. He had spent about ten days on it and wanted us to vet it in one. A large part of it is an endorsement of the Chamberlain philosophy of government, but being expressly advanced as the Ambassador's personal views there was nothing to do but pass it" verbatim.
163. George Ambrose Lloyd, first baron Lloyd of Dolobran (1879–1941), president of the Navy League, former governor of Bombay, 1918–23, and high commissioner for Egypt and the Sudan, 1925–29.

are going to have to get together, and that soon, if we are to maintain a standard of living anything like that which we now enjoy. The arms burden in the final analysis comes out of the livelihood of the workers of the world. It falls with equal weight on the people of every land regardless of forms of government. For this reason the American people look forward to the day when the leading nations of the world will realize that the present course must inevitably lead them to disaster.

I consulted my wife on this as a possible subject for my speech. "You cannot talk like that to the British Navy League" she exclaimed. "You had better try something else, dear."

So that was that. I had another idea.

It has long been a theory of mine that it is unproductive for both democratic and dictator countries to widen the division now existing between them by emphasizing their differences, which are self-apparent. Instead of hammering away at what are regarded as irreconcilables, they can advantageously bend their energies toward solving their remaining common problems and attempt to re-establish good relations on a world basis. The democratic and dictator countries differ ideologically, to be sure, but that should not preclude the possibility of good relations between them. After all, we have to live together in the same world, whether we like it or not.

The nations of the world have always embraced many forms of government, races and religions. Surely we should be able to surmount a difference in political philosophy.

Here, I thought, was something that could and should be said. Certainly no one can object if we turn the searchlight upon ourselves.

I reckoned without my wife.

"That's all very well" she said "but it seems to me that if you want to talk about that idea in any really useful way you would have to produce concrete suggestions to bring home your point, and you know perfectly well that if you try to do that you will find yourself discussing issues which a diplomat should not raise."

That was also that. I had a further idea. I thought that I might say a few words about Mr. Chamberlain. I had the privilege of seeing a great deal of your Prime Minister during the long days and nights of the crisis. I am sure that no one, not even those who disagree in principle with his policies, can fail to appreciate Mr. Chamberlain's courageous devotion to the welfare of his country and to peace. He was forced to make one of the gravest decisions of our time. It is not for me to comment on his decision — history will show whether or not he made the right decision. But I *can say* that so completely was he convinced, both by his conscience and by his reason, of the paramount importance of peace, that his all but superhuman efforts to keep the door of peace open, must command the respect and admiration of all of us.

"You are absolutely right", says my wife the critic, "but . . . have you thought how this would sound back home? You know, dear, our Ambassadors are supposed to lose all powers of resistance when they get to London and see things only through English eyes."

Again, that was that. I decided not to talk about the Prime Minister. But what could I talk about? I could not very well talk about the Army at a Navy League dinner, and there is not much for me to say about the A.R.P.[164]

For a while I was tempted to fall back on my nine children. They are always good for five minutes. I could also enlarge on the hole-in-one for which I had the good fortune to make at Stoke Poges.

"You have talked about the children too much," came from their mother. "They are

164. Air raid precautions.

295

fine children and there are nine of them, but you cannot expect everyone else to be as interested in them as you are. And, as for the hole-in-one, what has that to do with international affairs, with the Navy, or with anything else of interest to an intelligent audience?"

That was the last straw! I am sorry, Ladies and Gentlemen, but it appears that I shall have to fall back on the Navy after all. Even though my tenuous connection with it merely arises out of the fact that during the war I was connected with the management of an American shipyard and more recently I served as Chairman of the United States Maritime Commission. Frankly I do not know what I can say that has not been said before, but with your permission I shall pass on a few thoughts that occur to me on the relationship of our two countries arising out of their necessity to maintain a strong position at sea.

It might appear incongruous, at first glance, for a representative of one great naval power to toast the Fleet of another. It is, in my opinion, a perfectly logical procedure in this case.

Great Britain and the United States, after more than a century of rivalry, seem to have reached an understanding with regard to naval matters that really means that each of us has come to appreciate the aims of the other and that we have decided to substitute cooperation for the costly competition of the past. Neither navy has assumed any obligation to assist the other in time of trouble. On the other hand, we can rid our minds of the thought that we shall ever again be enemies.

I do not think that I am revealing any technical secrets when I say that, in the up-building of the American Navy, we have ignored the possibility that our vessels might have to meet the vessels of Britain. This is not an alliance in any sense of the word, not even a negative alliance. It is just common sense. When military men plan their air forces, their armies and their navies, they naturally take into account all contingencies. They have to do that; otherwise they wouldn't be good military men. Fortunately our two countries, in planning for defense, have not had to give any consideration to each other as potential enemies.

This is, I believe a relationship unique in the annals of naval history. Here are two nations bound by no treaty of alliance that actually welcome every ship launched by the other. So far as Great Britain and the United States are concerned, the navy is an incentive not to discord but to peace.

The feeling about merchant shipping, I am sorry to say, has not been quite so harmonious. However, I feel sure that here, too, we shall eventually find a basis for understanding. We have come to an agreement on naval limitation; we are developing trans-Atlantic aviation on a cooperative basis; there is no reason why we should not get together on the mercantile marine.

The United States has found it necessary to maintain a modest fleet in foreign trade. Our reasons are the same as those which govern the shipping policy of Great Britain. Only last year Winston Churchill told you, in his address at the annual dinner, that Britain "cannot rely for necessities upon foreign tonnage." The same is true — to a lesser degree, of course — of the United States. Even more important, so far as we are concerned, is the problem of naval auxiliaries. We are spending on the Navy this year in the neighborhood of 200 million pounds. It would be stupid on our part to make this colossal expenditure, which, incidentally, has the hearty approval of your people, unless we are also prepared to provide the auxiliary support without which the fighting force would be helpless.

We in American realize that shipping is, for us, an uneconomic industry, and that we should maintain no more vessels than are considered absolutely necessary for purposes of trade and defense. The fact that we have to subsidize some of our ships is, in our opinion, irrelevant. All nations, including Britain, subsidize, in one way or another, industries considered vital to the national welfare. It would be cheaper, as a matter of pure economics, for us to let you carry our goods, just as it would be cheaper for you to buy our motor cars instead of making them yourself. Unfortunately, the world isn't organized on a purely economic basis and we sometimes find it necessary to do things for ourselves which could be done better and more cheaply by the people of other nations. This is especially true of shipping, which has ceased to be a business in most countries and has become, instead, an adjunct of national defense.

I do not believe that Britain has any cause for worry over the maritime policy of the United States. Our aims are really very modest. I hope that the time will come when we shall see eye-to eye on merchant vessels as we do on naval vessels. I appreciate the desire of company officials on both sides of the Atlantic to make a good showing for their stockholders, but we must recognize that though we are competitors, there is no reason why we cannot be friendly competitors. We try to understand your need for a *great* merchant fleet. We hope that you will try to understand our need for a *small* one.

In that spirit, I am happy to participate in your annual dinner, and to pay tribute to your endeavors on behalf of British seapower. I now join the Royal Navy and the Merchant Navy, as they are always joined, in peace and in war, and give you the toast, "The Royal and Merchant Navies."

KENNEDY

The Ambassador, Mr. Johnson

Joseph P. Kennedy to Cordell Hull: *Diplomatic Dispatch*

1259, October 28, 5 p.m. FOR THE SECRETARY PERSONALLY.

While I do not like to bother you with this, I am somewhat embarrassed by being questioned practically every day in connection with the King's trip by the King's Secretaries and by the Foreign Office. I hear about Lindsay's despatches and of the discussions that are taking place between the President and Lindsay. The Foreign Minister told me today, for example, that Lindsay's message had come up through the Department with various notations calling attention to the fact that until the President's letter is written, which Lindsay says is coming along, nothing need be decided. Lord Halifax said he thought a letter should be written by the King to the President and he wanted to know what I thought. I do not know how the President would like them to think over here nor do I know what is in his mind, but opinions are being continually expressed here by people who think they know something of the United States which causes the confusion. If the President wanted me to be aware of any discussions he is having I suppose he would inform me, but I would know nothing about the King's trip whatsoever if I were not advised by the Foreign Office. Because I imagine my contacts and prestige here would be seriously jeopardized I hate to admit knowing nothing about it.

Possibly nothing can be done about this and although it is difficult I can continue to look like a dummy and carry on the best I can.

KENNEDY.

The Ambassador

Joseph P. Kennedy to Dr. Sara Jordan

London, November 4, 1938

Dear Dr. Jordan,

It was nice of you to drop me a line about Jack and I feel very much encouraged. I worry a good deal more about him than I do about international affairs or anything else, so your letter came as especially good news.[165]

We are all very well and while we haven't got to the point where everything is quiet, we are hoping it will be very soon.

With kindest regards and best wishes,

Sincerely yours,

Joseph P. Kennedy to Doris Fleeson

London, November 9, 1938

Dear Doris,

Thanks for the clipping.[166] In fact, it was the only one that arrived on that boat that wasn't from Heywood Broun,[167] Walter Lippmann[168] or Hugh Johnson.[169] If those boys knew how many people read their columns, they would ask for more money, because I am sure the entire population and, by the way, 75% of the letters were from Jewish people, wanted to be sure I wouldn't miss it.

Oh well, I have been getting along pretty well anyway and I am perfectly happy to take a pasting on that idea of mine. I feel that the present plans, both in the United States and Great Britain, aren't getting a helluva long way towards the settlement of world conditions and spending money isn't going to help out in the long run. So I have an idea that maybe if Mr. Hitler enjoyed some good trade with us, he would be so busy trying to protect it he wouldn't have time to think about fighting with everybody. Somebody told me that was commonsense and not good politics, but we shall see.

Seriously, Doris, it was awfully nice of you to write me. I don't know who spread poison around the White House as far as I am concerned, but when I heard, the other night, from my father-in-law that somebody had just been in to see him and told him that Miss LeHand was saying very unkind things about me, I practically gave up. I thought Missy knew me well enough to know that I don't shift like the wind and that anything I have to say I say to the parties concerned. However, this is really the only

---

165. Jordan, chief of gastroenterology at the Lahey Clinic of Boston, had written to tell him that "Jack is looking better than I have ever seen him look, and having relatively little difficulty."

166. *New York Daily News* Washington correspondent Doris Fleeson (1901–1970) had sent a copy of her latest "Capitol Stuff" column (coauthored by her current husband, John O'Donnell), which revived the notion of a Kennedy presidential candidacy in 1940. The clipping had arrived amidst a barrage of protest against JPK's recent Naval Day speech.

167. In a recent syndicated column that reached an estimated one million readers daily, the *New York World Telegram's* Heywood Campbell Broun (1888–1939), who had been two years ahead of JPK at Harvard, proposed throwing the ambassador into Boston Harbor "so that his Americanism might be restored by resting a while among the alien tea."

168. In his "Today and Tomorrow" column of October 22, Lippmann had lamented JPK's lack of diplomatic discretion in expressing his personal views publicly, and suggested the speech had been "designed to please . . . the voters at home."

169. The former (controversial) head of the National Recovery Administration 1933–34, Hugh Samuel Johnson (1882–1942) had served briefly as a Works Projects administrator for New York City in 1935 before breaking acrimoniously with the administration and becoming a columnist for the Scripps-Howard papers. Johnson had dedicated his column of October 25 to attacking JPK's recent address, asking, "what agreements with Hitler would be worth the ink and papers to express them?"

news I had that got me down. What anybody else on that Executive Staff feels interests me not one damn bit.

I am hoping to get back for a vacation some time after Christmas and I think I can give you a story then. At least, I can give you some impressions about this place that I think will interest you very much indeed. You know I always thought you were a swell person and your letter proves it.

My best to you and John,

Sincerely,
Joseph P. Kennedy

Joseph P. Kennedy to T. J. White

London, November 12, 1938

Dear Tom,

It was good of you to write me. I was distressed to hear that you have had such a bad time, but can't say that I am surprised. Anyway, I am tickled to death that you are getting better.

Now, regarding my speech that caused all the excitement; I made it with premeditation and since I never have had any political ambitions, it strikes me that it is well somebody said it. You know and W.R.[170] knows that I am not any more influenced by the English than I was the day I arrived here. They haven't shown me anything that makes me wish I was their friend beyond their great courtesy to me, or that they have anything to offer the United States that is of any particular value to us. I believe that unless England and France are prepared to fight and endanger civilization by trying to correct the present civilization, then there is no point in staying on the side lines and sticking your tongue out at somebody who is a good deal bigger than you are. As far as the United States goes, we ought to mind our own business, but that means minding our own business and not one minute kicking the dictators' head off and the next suggesting that they cooperate along certain lines. It is my theory in doing business with individuals or with nations that you must either keep away from them altogether or, if you are going to stick your tongue out at them or slap them on the wrist, you have better be prepared to punch them in the jaw.

I have no more sympathy with Hitler's ideas than anyone in America, but I asked myself, what am I going to do about it? If I am going to war with them to stop them, fine, that's one thought; if I am going to cut them off economically, fine, that's another thought; but, if I am just going to stick my tongue out at them, then I am not with it at all.

75% of the attacks made on me by mail were by Jews and, yet, I don't suppose anybody has worked as hard for them as I have or more to their advantage.

Now as to the tie-up with the British. How, in the name of Heaven, is anybody going to know what's going on or use his influence for whatever it amounts to, unless he gets along well with the people of the country to which he is accredited? To me it is just a lot of nonsense. My speech, if anybody reads it, said that we don't agree with totalitarian states, but we ought to try to get along with them the best way we can. If that isn't good policy for the United States, I don't know what is. I don't know whether they will ever be able to work out a deal with Hitler and I don't know whether trying to get along with him is going to bring good results or not, but we have tried the other way and we are going to spend ourselves into economic chaos, which will mean great sor-

170. Hearst.

row to all and destruction of the present standard of living. Therefore I say let's see what we can do with this method. It certainly isn't going to cost the United States anything. Then, if it doesn't work out, we have tried every possible method of trying to come to an adjustment and maybe the alternative is war to hasten the destruction of civilization.

Incidentally, don't let anybody feel badly that I talked out of turn, because this entire speech was submitted to the State Department and was approved and O.K.'d by them.[171] Of course, I would like to answer these attacks in the way I feel I could answer them, but that isn't diplomatic, I am told, but I won't be here all the time and my heart is almost broken watching us gradually lower ourselves into an abyss it will be very difficult to get out of.

If you see W.R. please tell him about this letter of show it to him. I would like him to know how I feel. I am not writing to anybody else and this is just for your confidential information and his.

Sincerely yours,

Joseph P. Kennedy to Charles Lindbergh

London, November 12, 1938

Dear Colonel Lindbergh,

I was very pleased to hear from you and, of course, I have been keeping up with you in the newspapers. I don't know which is the worst — the Russian attacks on you or the columnists' attacks on me for my Navy Day speech.[172] However, I think we both are a good deal more honest in our convictions than the critics.

I am hopeful that something can be worked out, but this last drive on the Jews in Germany has really made the most ardent hopers for peace very sick at heart.[173] Even

---

171. The October 21 diary entry of Jay Pierrepont Moffat, chief of the State Department's Division of European Affairs, sheds some light not only on the department's approval of (or rather failure to correct) the draft of the Trafalgar Day speech that JPK had submitted, but also upon the confusion that its delivery had created:

> The Secretary is very upset over the effect of Kennedy's recent speech. He loses his amiability and wishes that all Ambassadors would forego all speeches. He says that every time our foreign policy has run off the rocks it has been because of a speech made by one of our Ambassadors abroad. He thinks we should have definitely called Kennedy off in advance, despite his claim that he was advancing a "pet theory of his own."

> The Secretary asked Sumner why he did not see the danger of the speech. Sumner replied that he had been thinking of Mexico and had assumed that the Secretary himself had given attention to the matter and had initialed blind. The Secretary then said that I had not appeared unduly perturbed when I discussed the matter with him. This is not strictly accurate as I told him there would undoubtedly be repercussions, but that I thought the phrase "a pet theory of my own" would keep the Department and the Secretary our of the range of editorial attack. The truth of the matter is that the Secretary dislikes calling down Kennedy and Bullitt as they have a way of appealing to the White House over his head . . . However, a "goat" is needed and I shall have to be the goat. In the long run, however, no one is going to be hurt unless it be Mr. Kennedy himself.

172. A recent issue of the leftist London news sheet, *The Week*, had reported not only derisive comments that Lindbergh was alleged to have made at Cliveden regarding the Russian air force's inferiority to the *Luftwaffe*, but also fictitious claims of the aviator's having recently rejected an offer to head the Soviet Aviation Administration. Soon after, *Pravda* published an open letter written by a number of high-ranking Soviet air force officers denouncing the American aviator. The *Pravda* piece had been picked up subsequently in the United States, first in the leftward-leaning press and then in mainstream publications, resulting in a barrage of criticism not only of Lindbergh's reported claims but also of his recent acceptance of the Service Cross of the German Eagle from Hermann Göring.

173. The *Kristallnacht* pogrom had swept Germany, Austria and Bohemia on November 9 and 10. Distraught over the plight of some seventeen thousand stateless Jews (including his parents) who had been recently deported from Germany, seventeen-year-old Herschel Grynszpan assassinated Ernst vom

assuming that the reports from there are colored, isn't there some way to persuade them it is on a situation like this that the whole program of saving western civilization might hinge. It is more and more difficult for those seeking peaceful solutions to advocate any plan when the papers are filled with such horror. So much is lost when so much could be gained.

I hope you will let us know when you come to London, as Rose and I look forward to seeing you both. Tell Mrs. Lindbergh that everyone is talking about her beautiful book.[174]

All kinds of good luck to you and may your stay in Germany be pleasant and interesting and do let me hear from you from time to time.[175]

With warmest regards,

Sincerely yours,

Joseph P. Kennedy, Jr., 23:
"Answer to Lippmann Editorial Against Dad"[176]

Nov. 14

Mr. Lippmann [*sic*] article shows the natural Jewish reaction to the speech of the ambassadors calling for some kind of cooperation between the democratic and fascists [*sic*] nations. The ingenuity with which criticism of the speech is hidden behind the criticism of Mr. Kennedy's desire to say something when he speaks. Mr. Lippmann would prefer the Ambassador to speak of anything except those things which are vital to the welfare of the world at the present time. If the duty of an ambassador is to merely report the policies of the government to which he is accredited, and to make no effort to make his ideas felt, I suggest that the Ambassadors of the US should be some unemployed office boy, who could ably transmit the releases of the foreign government to his own government.

The insinuation in Mr. Lippmann's article is that the ambassadors who are not appointed by the Secretary of State have no responsibility in that direction and therefore their speeches are made with regard to increasing political prestige back home. It is easy to make a statement like this, but I venture to ask if a speech like the one the ambassador delivered on the subject of cooperation with the dictatorial states is one which would increase his prestige at home. With the natural hostility toward dictatorships in the US at the present time I would say that this would have quite the opposite effect. It represents what he regards as the only possible policy to follow. Either you have to be

---

Rath, the third secretary of the German embassy in Paris on November 7. By November 9, the pre-orchestrated Nazi pogrom had begun, resulting in orgiastic anti-Semitic violence that included the looting and destruction of synagogues, Jewish businesses and homes, as well as the internment of tens of thousand of Jews in concentration camps.

174. *Listen! The Wind.*
175. In his letter to JPK, written hours before the outbreak of violence on *Kristallnacht*, the aviator had noted that he and his family planned to spend the coming winter in Berlin. "I am extremely anxious to learn more about Germany," he told JPK. "I believe a few months spent in that country would be interesting from many standpoints." Following the events of early November, however, the Lindbergh family would remain in France.
176. In his "Today and Tomorrow" column of October 22, entitled "The Ambassador Speaking," Lippmann argued that JPK had ventured far beyond his ambassadorial mandate in expressing his own views publicly on Trafalgar Day. Unlike their career State Department colleagues, Lippmann contended, "amateur and temporary diplomats take their speeches very seriously. Ambassadors of this type soon tend to become each a little state department with a little foreign policy of their own."

prepared to destroy the fascist nations, a course which very people in the States advocate at the present time, or you might as well try to get along with them. I know this is extremely hard for the Jewish community in the US to stomach, but they should see by now that the course which they have followed the last few years has brought them nothing but additional hardship. If the different nations of the world can come to some agreement political or economic with the fascist nations a great deal will be accomplished. If some kind of a financial arrangement could be made with Germany, transfers of capital by the Jews could probably be affected. This would go a long ways in solving the very serious problem of refugees.

With this in mind I beg to ask Mr. Lippmann whether he thinks an intelligent man even though he is ambassador should not air his views with the complete approval of the State Department. Only by the exchange of views can progress be made and if we take that right away from out ambassadors I propose that we recall our ambassadors and substitute any third rate clerk. Also this would abet the criticism that the ambassador is being taken in by the country to which he is accredited. If the Ambassador acts in a belligerent enough manner he will find that he will have no contact with the English and therefore can look out for the interests of America without being taken in. Or as a better suggestion let us recall all our ambassadors and rely for information on the daily press, for then no taint of the Anglophile will be found in the state department.

Yes Mr. Lippmann you have a fine case, but I would like very much to read your at criticism of a speech which violently debased the dictatorships. Not being Psychic I hesitate to guess but I think I would be safe in saying that you would praise the ability of such an able ambassador who could foresee the fact that Dictatorships can't live with democracies and that the course of the US should be the complete destruction of those dictatorships.

Joseph P. Kennedy to Cordell Hull: *Diplomatic Dispatch*

1330, November 18, 5 p.m. FOR THE SECRETARY — CONFIDENTIAL

Last Sunday Mrs. Kennedy and I had lunch with Malcolm MacDonald[177] and two friends of his at his country estate. Palestine and the atrocities in Germany were naturally discussed as well as other subjects. MacDonald was asked by me why England, which had all the land, did not show more interest in Intergovernmental relief, that Rublee[178] would have something to go on if England offered some of the land; then the problem of raising the money to get the refugees out would be secondary to having a place to put them. I told MacDonald that it looked to me like everyone was feeling sorry for the Jews but that nobody was offering any solution. This item was one of a great many discussed.

I saw Lord Halifax the next day and he told me the British were doing a lot. MacDonald had evidently discussed this with him. He told me very confidentially that they were now admitting 75 Jews a day, but for fear it might cause trouble they did not

---

177. A son of former prime minister James Ramsay MacDonald, at the time Malcolm John MacDonald (1901–1981) served concurrently as both secretary of state for the colonies and as secretary of state for dominion affairs.

178. In July, President Roosevelt had appointed Washington attorney George Rublee (1868–1957) director of the Intergovernmental Committee on Refugees. Comprised of members from the United States, Scandinavia, South America, Great Britain and France, the committee sought both to repatriate refugees from the Reich and to negotiate an emigration agreement with the German government, permitting Jews to leave German territories without being stripped of their personal property.

want their own people to know. Rublee said, when I told him this that he and Pell[179] knew it; and the whole matter was being looked into by the British and that Lindsay had been asked to enquire of you whether the quota the United States had for British subjects could be used and transferred to Jews. I repeated to the Foreign Secretary what I had said to MacDonald: Speed up Lord Winterton, and get some land and then find out who felt badly enough to give funds. I told Halifax that I had been told by Myron Taylor[180] that Baruch had said to him that if they had a good place to put the Jews the Jews in the United States could raise one hundred million dollars. These conversations were repeated to Mr. Rublee.

When I saw Neville Chamberlain at a dinner to King Carol of Roumania[181] I urged speed to get some place.

Except what the Prime Minister said yesterday I know nothing more about what they propose to do. If I had any news of any description concerning this matter which I thought would be of interest to you, you would have had it as you always do from me. If any contribution has been made by me it is that I have urged the British to do something for the Intergovernmental Committee quickly but then for the past four months I have been doing that.

Today I saw the Prime Minister and introduced Senator Reynolds at the latter's request. No official business was mentioned.

KENNEDY

The Ambassador

Joseph P. Kennedy, Jr., 23: *"November 21"*

Today in the House the Prime Minister came out with his offer to settle the Jews in the colonies and mandates of Great Britain. Just one week ago Dad urged upon Malcolm MacDonald the need for speed in this great problem, and everyone thinks that it was largely due to his efforts that this gesture has been made. Dad thinks that now it will really be seen whether the righteous indignation aroused all over the world and especially in the United States, will be backed up by cold cash. The baby is tossed right into the laps of the people themselves for the real concern now is money. If the Jews come through and especially the other people this problem can be cleared up.

Dad doesn't think they will put up the necessary money, but he thinks he has done his part, and the rest is up to the others.

The papers have played up his part to a great extent and as a result the State Dept. got kind of peeved and sent a wire trying to find out what the hell was going on. Dad sent a very good wire back saying that the only thing he was doing was urging speed, but his real usefulness I think was putting the problem strongly before MacDonald and urging that England do this in order to help Anglo American Friendship.

I don't think he is too crazy about the job at this point and the other day spoke about quitting. He is afraid that they are trying to knock him off at home, and may

---

179. American career diplomat, Robert Thompson Pell (1902–1969), Rublee's aide and vice director of the Intergovernmental Committee.
180. Roosevelt had appointed Myron Charles Taylor (1874–1959), who had recently resigned as chairman of the board of U.S. Steel, chief of the American delegation to the conference on refugees in Evian-les-Bains, France, in July 1938.
181. Having renounced his throne (temporarily) in order to live with his mistress in Paris, Carol II of Rumania (1893–1953) had reclaimed his birthright in 1930. He would reign with increasing autocracy for a decade before abdicating in 1940. The British royal family had received Carol, a great-grandson of Queen Victoria, at Buckingham Palace on November 15.

make a monkey out of him in some diplomatic undertaking. None of them kept him informed about the Kings invitation, and he had to bluff his way through.

Joseph P. Kennedy to John Boettiger

London, November 25, 1938

Dear John:

Your letter came like a bolt out of the blue.[182] All I have been having poured into me for the last three months is how Roosevelt is off me, how the gang is batting my head off, and that I am persona non grata to the entire Roosevelt family. Well, of course I know a lot of this is hooey, but it is damned annoying three thousand miles away. When I add up my contributions to this cause over the past five years — and I do not mean monetary ones — I get damned sick that anybody close to the Boss finds it necessary to do anything but say a good word. It has taught me one lesson: I am going to stay on the sidelines for a while and mind my own business and let the boys worry about their problems. I am planning to go home the 30th of December, and I will see O'Leary then and find out what is going on.[183] As I told you before, I am twice as disgusted with that advertising crowd as you are, but it is damned difficult to pay attention to a business three thousand miles away, but if I have any time or any energy left by the time I get home I am going to see what I can do about it.

We read in the news over here that you are expecting a new arrival in the spring and that makes us very happy. I am sure that you and Anna must be terribly glad, so Rose and I send our love to you both, and I am looking forward to at least having a word with you on my return.

Sincerely,

Joseph P. Kennedy, Jr., 23: *"Visit to Plymouth"*

Dec. 6

Dad and I went to Plymouth as the guest of the board of Trade there. We were met at the station by Lord Astor and the Lord Mayor both of whom are very charming. In the different town shops the mayoralty reverts in successive years to candidates from the three leading parties so all of them get a chance at it. Politics doesn't enter into the office nor does the salary which is very low. This present Lord Mayor is a worker in the dockyards.

We were shown around the city and saw the place where the Pilgrims left on the Mayflower. We also went out on the moors and saw Dartmouth Prison. Very few people ever escape from this prison where the most serious prisoners are sent.

Lady Astor is full of vim and vigour and vitality. She has a marvelous personality and is most amusing. She is hipped on the idea of Anglo-American cooperation and would like us to come into the war at the beginning to save lives. She is indignant with the press and all the stories of the Cliveden set which she says is a lot of hog wash. In her speech that night she was most amusing. She pretended that Dad and she were

---

182. Boettiger, publisher of the *Seattle Post-Intelligencer* and the president's son-in-law, had written JPK on October 28, asking "how goes the great 'war-buster?'" and adding, "[f]rom all I hear—and that is plenty—you have done a grand job. There are plenty of brickbats flying around, but that is an old-fashioned American custom that always comes as a reaction to anything unpleasant."

183. Boettiger had included a copy of his recent letter to Ted O'Leary, president of JPK's Somerset Importers, attempting to persuade him to advertise Somerset's scotches in the *Post-Intelligencer.*

only friends for the evening, that really the southerners had no use for the Yankees and it is only on conditions like these that the U.S. showed a united front. She ballyhooed the press, spoke indirectly about letting the Jews in, and really got away with wholesale murder.

Dad got a tremendous reception and the crowd rose and sang for he s a jolly good fellow. He joked about Lady Astor, and said how sorry we were that Lord Astor had taken her away from America. His speech went well. While at the Astors he got a telegram asking whether it was true that he has tipped off Scotland Yard that there was a plot afoot to assassinate Prince Paul of Yugoslavia. All in all it was a fine and enjoyable trip.

Joseph P. Kennedy to Charles Lindbergh

London, December 8, 1938

Dear Colonel Lindbergh,

I am leaving Saturday for what I hope is going to be a two months vacation. I am a little dizzy watching the present international situation and want to get to the United States to see what's happening there. Judging from what I know to be the actual conditions over here, I am a little uncertain as to just where America is heading. Hence the trip.

I am not at all happy about the situation as it is. As I've said to you before, I don't know just what England can do to satisfy Hitler. If ever a man was willing to work out a deal, it was Chamberlain, but I do not doubt that he is rather despondent about the outlook now. The doctrine I preached in my Navy Day speech of trying to work out something with the totalitarian States seems to be, at least temporarily, out of commission. But I do believe that, unless something is worked out, it is hard to tell what is going to happen to civilization.

In some ways I am rather sorry you are not going to Berlin, because I think you are probably the only contact the United States now has on speaking terms with Hitler, but, considering everything, I suppose it is all for the best that you are going to be in Paris and, I hope, in London after I get back.

Tell Mrs. Lindbergh that I saw Lord Halifax last night and he asked me to thank Mrs. Kennedy for having sent him Anne Lindbergh's book; that he hadn't read anything so charming in years. Please give her the affectionate regards of the Kennedys and with warmest regards to you, I am,

Sincerely yours,

Joseph P. Kennedy, Jr., 23

Dec. 10, 1938

After ten months of carrying out his ambassadorial duties, Dad is rather tired of his work. He claims that he would give it up in a minute if it wasn't for the benefits that Jack and I are getting out of it and the things Eunice will get when she comes out next Spring. He doesn't like the idea of taking orders and working for hours trying to keep things out of his speeches which an Ambassador shouldn't say.

He also doesn't like the idea of sitting back and letting the Jewish columnists in America kick his head off. The papers have made up a pile of lies about him, and he can't do anything about it but claims that he is going to let a few blasts when he gets back there in a couple of days.

Every place you go you are impressed by the way that every one is trying to get us in fighting for dear old England. Dad wants to have a study made to see just where we would be if something happened to the British Empire, both economically and politically. If we possibly could exist without them I think Dad would speak against us being drawn into a war.

In regard to the Jewish business he is afraid that if they do settle the Jewish side of it the other countries especially Poland will throw out all of theirs. With all the work he has done he is indignant that some papers have kicked his head off claiming that the government at home had to prod him to get anything done. He thinks there might be a tremendous Jewish reaction in the United States. Also that many people who are very indignant now wouldn't put up much money to get them settled. He is alarmed that the country should get so worried up by the treatment of the Jews, for if they can be roused to fever heat on this question, there doesn't seem to be much possibility of keeping them out of war.

Joseph P. Kennedy to Rose Kennedy: *Telegram*

PALMBEACHFLO 28-XII-38[184]

ASSOCIATED PRESS TODAY PICKED YOU AS OUTSTANDING WOMAN OF THE YEAR FOR SELLING THE WORLD THE AMERICAN FAMILY JACK AND I ARE BASKING IN YOUR REFLECTED GLORY HE HAS GAINED FIVE POUNDS MY LOVE TO ALL = JOE

Robert Kennedy, 13: *Composition*

A Portrait of myself

I am thirteen years old, and about five feet two inches tall. I have got alot of freckles. I have hazel eyes, and blond hair which is plenty hard to keep down because I have som many licks, and so much of it. I am not very fat, but fat enough. I weigh about one hundred pounds. I take about five and a half shoe.

I have a pretty good character as a on the whole, but my temper is not too good. I am not jelous of any one, I have got a very loud voice, and talk alot, but sometimes my talk is not very interesting. Mr. I have quite good tastes for food, but there is alot of things I don't like at all for instence cabbage, fish pie, Brussels sprouts, colif flower, and pears. I love allmost every thing, Cholcet. I like the cinema very much, and go very often. I go to the Theatre once in a while, and like it quite well. I like football, but I like American football much better. I don't like cricket very much I like baseball alot. Going swimming is one of my favorite sports. I like skiing one of the best, and I think I ame the best at this sport out of all the thing I do. I can't dive very well, but like it to a cirten exstant. I think this is a portrait of my self.

Joseph P. Kennedy: *Diary*

My conversation with President on Feb. 9, 1939 after his hurried call to me to leave Palm Beach and go to England 2 weeks ahead of time.[185] (He told me he was dis-

---

184. JPK was spending the Christmas holiday in Palm Beach with Jack, while Rose had taken Joe Junior and the younger children to St. Moritz, Switzerland.
185. During his nearly two-month holiday in the United States, JPK had met with the president on several occasions to discuss European affairs. On January 10 both JPK and William C. Bullitt, JPK's counter-

turbed because of the message Herschel Johnson had sent the State Department that Chamberlain was hoping I would not extend my vacation because of the conditions being as they were over here.

Chamberlain told me when I got over that he was afraid that things were happening so fast over there that any one would get out of touch very quickly and staying away was dangerous for them as well as me.)

The President had a very bad cold and saw me in his study.

Mrs. R came in while I was there to read him her column, "My Day," that had reference to her accepting a book from the Spaniard that was [a] copy of their wonderful prints.[186] The President made several suggestions.

He also told me that Baruch was mad with me because he had come to London on his way home and left word at Embassy he was there and I had sent around a fourth assistant secretary to his hotel to say if we could be of service to him let us know.

I said there wasn't a word of truth in the whole story. He never even notified me he was in London and if he had of course I would have seen him. He was just too damn jealous. The President said he knew that and he had got a great laugh out of the whole story. He only regretted if it were true I had no secretary lower than a third to send around.

He reiterated his disgust at the way Baruch had, on leaving the White House months before, given out a statement about the arming of Government and managed to "let slip" that he was willing to pay certain expenses of getting ready.[187] Roosevelt told me this story when I first came home but told me again.

He also told me that before Baruch went to Europe in July[188] he had talked with him about general plan of Industrials getting together an organization similar to war [sic][189] and for Baruch to be thinking it over.

When the Crisis got tough, Baruch wired him he was prepared to take this work on and wanted President to call meeting of Replogle,[190] Johnson,[191] Liggett,[192] and Farn-

---

part in Paris, had testified secretly before the House and Senate Military Affairs Committees, emphasizing the superiority of the German military in Europe.

186. The following day, the United Features Syndicate would publish the first lady's thoughts on receiving a book of Goya prints "as a remembrance from the people of Spain." "A few people who believe that the Loyalist Government of Spain is Communistic and anti-religious have written me during the past weeks denouncing my acceptance of such a gift," she told her readership. "I have told them that the gift had not been proffered me. It has now [sic] been made to Mrs. Eleanor Roosevelt, a person, and comes from the people of Spain and I accept it with deep appreciation and gratitude. These men, women and children have suffered much and yet they want to give something as a token of their appreciation for what has been done to alleviate their suffering."

187. Leaving his meeting with FDR on October 13, 1938, Baruch had made the uncharacteristic gesture of seeking out the press, thereby giving the impression (as the New York Times put it) "that he spoke with the knowledge and consent of the President." Recently returned from Europe, Baruch touched upon the "tragic unpreparedness of France and Great Britain" and the potential for the United States to fall into a similar "humiliating position" should the president's defense-expansion initiative languish.

188. 1938.

189. FDR had called Baruch, who was vacationing in Scotland at the time, about heading a remobilization effort patterned after Woodrow Wilson's War Industries Board, of which Baruch had served as chairman during the First World War. According to diarist and Secretary of the Interior Harold Ickes, the president found the financier's suggestions for manning the organization (with a number of Baruch's cohorts) laughable.

190. Jacob Leonard Replogle (1876–1948), chairman of the board of the Warren Foundry and Pipe Corporation and former director of Steel Supply for the War Industries Board.

191. Baruch's influence had helped to launch Hugh Johnson (another former member of the War Industries Board) to the head of the NRA in 1933. Johnson had since renounced the administration, however, and had become a bitterly anti-Roosevelt, Scripps-Howard syndicated columnist.

192. It is unclear whom he means.

ham,[193] ____[sic] and his old group. And President said that they certainly were an "old group," and under those conditions if President wanted to accept them he would come home. President completely ignored the request and said he did nothing and Baruch came home and went to Washington on his own and then gave out the "arming story."[194] I said that none of that gang was worth a damn and told him the Kent, Swope, Kennedy story on the bellyaching speech in New York.[195]

(I would like to add here a story that President told Baruch and me in his study in June about the Jews. He told us both that if there was a demagogue around the type of Huey Long, who took up the cause of anti-Semitism, there would be more blood running in the streets of New York than there was in Berlin.)

I told President I didn't want to go to London unless I had his confidence. That he knew how I felt about things and people and I had never made a public statement against him or his policies and what I said privately wasn't as bad as I had said to him personally. He knew the way I felt about him and I wasn't the kind to be any good unless I was on good terms. He said that he knew all that and not to worry — people just liked to make trouble.

Sam Hoare at Granard Dinner for Queen Mary,[196] said jokingly:

1. "Bonnet was o.k. in France today because the French Government had bought (attaché) Bonnet.

2. Cripps[197] a Communist but honestly planning for a revolution.

3. The Communists had given up their Frontal attack and were active in subversive attacks through Liberals and papers. Daily Worker gets £25,000. a year to keep it going."

(Note: Chamberlain at Astor's. Hole in his stocking with dinner suit.)

Joseph P. Kennedy, Jr., 23, to Joseph P. Kennedy:
"DEAR DAD: An Ambassador's Son Writes from Spain."

Perpignan, France, February 10th

Dear Dad:

Well, I'm on my way — and on my own. Now I'll be able to see for myself conditions in Spain as they really are. It's a great opportunity. I only hope that I can do justice to it. If my experiences today are any criterion of what I'm going to see, it ought to be an eye opener. I'll do my best to give you the picture as I see it. It won't be literature, but I promise you that it will be the truth.

Arrived here at Perpignan this morning, came down from Paris on the night train. I had to hustle as my trip was arranged in a day. Have exchanged my diplomatic pass-

193. He refers, possibly, to industrial engineer and economist Dwight Farnham (1881–1950).
194. Of October 13.
195. Addressing the Economic Club of New York in late 1937, JPK had told business that it was time "to get behind [the administration] now and stop bellyaching and try and do something for the cause." JPK left the controversy concerning Frank Kent, Herbert Bayard Swope and himself otherwise unrecorded, however.
196. Evidently this diary entry was written sometime later than February 9, as the earl and countess of Granard hosted a dinner for Queen Mary on March 3, 1939.
197. MP for Bristol East, future British ambassador to the Soviet Union, 1940–42, and Beatrix Potter's nephew, Sir (Richard) Stafford Cripps (1889–1952). In mid-January Cripps had been expelled from the Labour Party's executive council in the wake of the procedural controversy arising from his advocacy of the defeat of the Chamberlain government by a united front of Liberal, Labour and Communist parties that he had long envisioned.

port for a regular passport. Now the State Department won't be involved if I get into trouble. It seemed pretty lonely at the station in Paris, without even one brother or sister to see me off.

Perpignan is a half-pint French seaport on the Gulf de Lyon. It is not far from the Spanish border. Today Gilbert,[198] one of the fellows from the American Consulate here, was going out to Argeles to repatriate some members of the International Brigade and he took me along to visit the concentration camp.[199] That gave me my first glimpse of the war, as I watched the beaten Catalonian army come pouring over the French frontier. It was a grim sight.

Most of them were badly clothed. Some of them were limping; others trudged wearily along with their belongings on their backs. Hungry, tired, unshaven, they were making their way back to the camp. Ever to be fighting again seemed the last of their desires. Some looked terribly sad. Others joked back and forth. A few even sang — or tried to. Truckloads of them were strung along the road. It was no uncommon sight to find a truck overturned and abandoned in the ditch. Many men were eating and sleeping by the roadside. They were of all conceivable sorts. Many looked the type that would — and could — fight. Others looked like misfit intellectuals who'd never seen a gun in their lives — let alone fired one. Members of the International Brigade I talked to later had nothing but contempt for these Catalonian troops, whom they claimed, weren't worth a damn.

The Argeles concentration camp is right on the sea. The entrance is well guarded by sentries of the French Army and nobody gets in without a pass. Passes for civilian visitors are scarce as hen's teeth. I had to put up an energetic — but not very fluent — French sales talk before I got one.

Once safely inside, we came first to the place where the hospital cases are kept. It's terribly sad to see so many men — many of them pitifully young — without arms and legs, crippled for the rest of their lives. I thought no provision had been made for the wounded, but I'm told the Loyalist Government has set up funds abroad to care for the poor guys. I hope it's fixed so no shyster can get away with the dough; otherwise these fellows will be sunk for fair.

There's no organization at all about this camp. No one seemed to know where the members of the International Brigade were quartered, or if there were any of them there at all. We had to search for nearly an hour before we found the "I.B.", as they call it down here.

The I.B. camp consists of small straw shelters, erected by the men themselves, each housing from two to five persons. There are no sanitary arrangements whatsoever. The nearest ditch is the only available place. Some of the men have no shelter of any kind and are forced to sleep in the open, with just their ragged coats over them. It gets terribly cold here at night, too. Last night four chaps got tight on bad wine and lay down without any covering at all. This morning they were found dead.

198. Charles Gilbert (1907–87), U.S. vice consul at Barcelona, January–February 1939.
199. Comprised largely of Communists but also of those committed to stemming the spread of Fascist aggression in Europe, the Republican International Brigades had at their height been represented by troops from at least fifty countries that numbered more than thirty-five thousand in total over the course of the Civil War. For a variety of reasons (among them the volunteers' dwindling numbers due to casualties, attrition and the declining fortunes of the Republican effort generally) Prime Minister Negrín had requested the League of Nations' assistance in removing foreign troops from Loyalist Spain at the time of the Munich crisis. Although the repatriation of foreigners had begun by late 1938, the process was slower and more confused in Catalonia than elsewhere, continuing into February 1939 due to the influx of refugees heading toward France in flight of Franco's advancing Nationalist army.

There are many hot scraps, with the men fighting among themselves. You see, some want to go back to Franco Spain[200] — which they are free to do. Others, who are devoted heart and soul to the Republican Government, regard these men as worse than traitors. The arguments turn into wild free-for-alls in no time. And nobody outside the immediate fight seems to care or give a thought, not even the guards.

The guards are mostly Senegalese. They're good soldiers and plenty tough hombres. The Guardia Mobile are supposed to be pretty cruel, and they're unpopular as hell. The color question adds to the discontent, but most important is the fact that these colonial troops understand no Spanish and very little French. That causes a lot of undue harshness to be dished out to the prisoners.

I saw an occasional woman in the camp, but most of them are stuck off in a camp "for women only."

The food here consists of bread — and that's all. One loaf is given to three men and they "divvy it up." That doesn't make for good feeling either. Today there was a wild rumor that meat was to be distributed. The men lined up for hours, three abreast. But no meat appeared. The lines collected only bread, as usual. Even that was guarded by gendarmes with rifles.

American and English members of the International Brigade are better cared for than the rest. With their bread they get meat — occasionally. Horse meat, of course. I got my first taste of it here. I expect — if I'm in luck to see more of it. It doesn't taste so bad. But you might tell Bobby I advise him to stick to ice-cream cones or even spinach. They're much more enjoyable.

The International Brigade men tell me they haven't had guns in their hands for five months, due to the Republican Government's decision to dispense with foreign volunteers. They didn't know where they were going while they were retreating and thought that they might fall into Franco's hands any minute. That, they said, might not have been very healthy for them. They were separated from the rest of their group and didn't have a ghost of an idea where they were. One of the fellows mentioned the paradox of it all: here they are helping to uphold British imperial interests in Spain and most of them are Communists!

They talk a great deal about the bombing of women and children. They're dead against that. Apparently there has been a lot of it in this war. Many of the I.B. men have families at home who are supported by various trade unions.

Tonight I leave for Marseilles. There I hope to get a ship for Valencia, from which I can probably get transportation to Madrid. Everything I have heard and seen so far indicates that the war is a horrible mess. Not a very soothing thought to go to sleep on, but I'll have to say "Good night" anyway. Just to contradict the customary post-card message, I *don't* wish any of you were here.

Love
Joe

---

200. With German and Italian military aid, Nationalist forces had celebrated a number of victories in northern Spain during the course of the previous year under the insurgent leader Generalissimo Francisco Franco (Bahamonde) (1892–1975). Having captured Bilbao in June 1937, the Nationalist army had crossed the River Ebro and penetrated deep into Catalonia by the end of 1938, occupying Barcelona on January 26, 1939.

Joseph P. Kennedy, Jr., 23, to Joseph P. Kennedy

Valencia,[201] *February 15th*

Dear Dad:

The port of Valencia is one of the most devastating things I've ever seen. The damage is beyond description.[202] Not merely the floating derelicts, like those I saw in Barcelona, but the complete destruction of all that part of the city which borders on the port. Every house within a radius of half a mile is a litter of wreckage.

It's just plain suicide to stay there any length of time. Incredibly, some people still live there, but it's like a deserted village that's been battered to death by bombs. Outside of the men who work there, I saw hardly a living soul. Some little old ladies sat hunched outside the low entrance of a bomb shelter, known here as a "refugio." I wonder why they stay. Men at the docks, and sailors on ships at the port, get their wages increased two hundred percent while there. Maybe the old ladies haven't anywhere else to go; maybe they don't care what happens. Poor, helpless people.

Going along the streets of the city near the port, where misdirected bombs may fall at any time, I saw every few hundred yards home-made refugios. They're just rough tunnels or dug-outs under the tumbled bricks and masonry, hardly more than uncertain protection from shrapnel. But people go right on living in them — without comfort and in perpetual danger.

Only a short distance from the port, outside the immediate danger zone, everyone seemed undisturbed and happy enough. I saw children — no bigger than Teddie [*sic*] or Bobby — laughing and playing games. It made me sick. The sound of those little kids' voices . . .

Later Wednesday

After breakfast this morning, walking through the city's streets, Wallner,[203] the American Consul here, pointed out that there'd probably be no bread today, for the people were not queued up for it. There are many days when the bread ration is cut off, and the lines form to buy whatever may be offered in its place. It's a mystery to me how the scrawny dogs, which prowl around the garbage cans in vast numbers, manage to exist.

On our way back, Wallner suddenly said, "Here they come!" He was listening. I'd never have noticed the sound against the noisy background of the city, but Wallner's ears were sharpened by experience. Now I heard the sirens going in various parts of the city to warn of the approach of enemy aircraft.

People were already hurrying to take shelter in refugios or in the basements of nearby houses. Some raced to the refugios, then stood outside, ready to duck in if the going got tough. The dug-outs are bigger and better than the home-made ones near the port. Some of them go as much as thirty feet below the surface; many have lights and ventilating systems to keep the air clean.

We heard nothing for about five minutes, then the anti-aircraft guns began. We saw the white puffs of the exploding shells high against the blue sky. But none seemed

---

201. From Marseilles he had traveled to Barcelona, where he had found passage to Valencia aboard the British destroyer HMS *Havoc* on February 12.
202. Count Ciano, the Italian foreign minister (and Mussolini's son-in-law) had ordered the aerial bombardment of the port city, at the time the Loyalist capital, in August 1937. Between July 18 and 23, 1938, joint Nationalist and Italian forces, attempting to isolate Republican Madrid, advanced from Teruel to Valencia, again pummeling the latter without taking it. Valencia would fall to Nationalist forces in March 1939 following the flight of the Republican government.
203. Woodruff Wallner (1909–1983), U.S. vice consul at Valencia, 1938–39.

very close to the little black specks of planes and the latter kept on coming as if they didn't give a damn. No bombs fell and, after a bit, people commenced coming out of their shelters. Then it started. They'd begun bombing the port.

The noise was terrific. It made our ears ache. The buildings vibrated like drums. The planes must have been lost in the sun or hidden by high clouds for we didn't catch another glimpse of them. I'd have felt more comfortable knowing where they were.

A few people stayed out on the square. I noticed one man who kept right on with his work, shining shoes. The rest either huddled behind stone pillars or were out of sight in refugios. Some people won't go into the refugios because they're not allowed out again until the release whistle sounds, which may be some time after the planes have gone. The din lasted for about five minutes; then complete silence. As abruptly as the streets had cleared, they filled up again. A few minutes after the raid Valencia was back to normal. The boot-black kept on shining shoes.

The thing that got me was the feeling of absolute helplessness. There's not a thing you can do about it all. I don't wonder any more that people develop a sense of fatalism after going through this day after day. I guess I'd acquire it myself in a little while.

The Valencia papers are just two-page affairs, but they're full of the stuff manufactured to appeal to man's finer sentiments. Phrases like: "The Fatherland is worth every sacrifice" and "The State needs the help of every man!" They only carry short bits of news from the outside world. When Barcelona fell they held the news back for several days, then released it with the phony explanation that the high command thought it best to retire a short way in order to consolidate their position. I wonder how many people swallowed that. Today's papers say that the Communist paper in Madrid has been banned indefinitely. A hint for the populace here of a new attitude toward the Communists. How's anybody going to recognize truth when it's forever wearing a mask of propaganda in print!

I've heard it's no cinch getting from here to Madrid. It may take some very practical diplomacy. I'd better start working on it right away if I'm going to manage it tomorrow. If all goes well my next letter will be written from Madrid. Here's hoping. Don't worry about me. It's not really very dangerous, and I'll take care of myself. My love to you all,

Joe

Joseph P. Kennedy, Jr., 23, to Joseph P. Kennedy

Madrid, February 16th

Dear Dad:

This is written from our Embassy — and I'm the only American in it.[204] Left Paris just a week ago today, but I've seen enough suffering to last me a year. This will be a sloppy account of things; they've been coming at me too fast. It's all a jumble of quick impressions, each more vivid than the last. One thing I am sure of: If anyone wants to give real charity, this is the place. I can hardly believe it's true. The suffering — the terrible conditions — people dying every day.

I arrived in Madrid on a military bus at four-thirty this afternoon. Left Valencia shortly afterwards. It was terribly difficult getting any kind of transportation. The railroad had broken down because the Nationalists have cut the main line. A trip that took

204. The diplomatic community, including historian and U.S. Ambassador Claude Gernade Bowers (1878–1958), had relocated across the French border in Saint-Jean-de-Luz in November 1936, when a Nationalist victory over Madrid appeared imminent.

only seven or eight hours before the war now prolongs itself into two or three days. I finally worked it through the military commandante, but seats in the buses were at a premium and I was lucky to get one.

I was only allowed to have one small suitcase, but I slipped the driver a package of cigarettes, worth a handful of paper money, and he let me take a small box of food, too.

The bus was jammed full of soldiers, but when I passed out cigarettes, I was everybody's friend and things went very well. While we changed buses, one of the soldiers, who knew a little English, came up and talked with me.

Returning from leave, he had to wait at Valencia for three days trying to promote a ride to Madrid. He'd been at the front for eight months and was heartily sick of the war, just as they all were. The Reds killed his brother when the revolution broke out, and while he'd been away his father had gone blind from lack of food. He didn't think Franco would do anything to people like him, only to those who were guilty of killing others. He thought this perfectly just. He said an awful lot of them didn't have their heart in the work and had been forced to go out and fight. Like many of the rest, my pal had some food with him, the gift of friends in Valencia. He insisted I share it, so we swapped groceries.

Every few miles along the road are control stations where travelers are checked; being an army bus, we didn't have to stop. We had no trouble at all on the way. Someone did drop a cigarette once and the truck caught on fire. We all hopped out and ran to get sand to smother it. Apart from that, there were no other incidents.

Women must have special passes to enter Madrid as it's considered part of "the front." Before we got near the outskirts of the city, two women who were on the bus were asked to show their permits. One had none, and, with her two small children, she was thrown off in the middle of nowhere. She'd been hoping to sneak in without a pass but she didn't get away with it. We tried to get the driver to help her but he said there was nothing he could do. I looked back as we drove on and she was just standing in the road, the kids clinging to her draggled skirt, looking after us helplessly.

I found our Embassy easily enough for there's a big sign with letters a foot high outside the locked gates. It's run now entirely by Spaniards, to whom it was entrusted after the official departure on Thanksgiving Day, in '36. All the employees brought their families into the Embassy then and they organized a little self-sufficient community of their own here.

A skinny Spanish chap named Ugarde is in charge. He's kind of bald and about thirty, I'd say. Only a foreign clerk before the outbreak of the revolt, he suddenly found himself looking after all the Americans left in Madrid, solving their troubles, settling their quarrels. Now, in his semi-ambassadorial position, he handles all Embassy matters, sees the local officers in charge and makes the reports. He's a Republican, and very "left" but his own brother-in-law's a rabid Communist. Sounds like the brother-against-brother hoke in American civil-war movies — only this is real — and *now*.

I was surprised to find two sheep grazing on the Embassy lawn and, in back of the barn, half a dozen cows left by a farmer who feared they'd be confiscated by the Government. The Embassy agreed to give them protection provided he'd sell milk to the staff and also give them first choice of the beef if he slaughtered any of his precious herd.

Here at the Embassy they have five or six hens, a pig and some lambs, besides the "refugee" cows, so they're comparatively well off. By buying so much a day everyone's entitled whatever can be picked up by journeys out into the country in the official Embassy car. You have to go about two hundred and fifty miles to obtain fresh eggs, vegetables and chickens — in fact to find anything besides the regulation menu diet of lentils and salt fish. Besides, none of the farmers want the paper pesetas and usually you have to bring them clothing, soap, sugar or tobacco, for which there's always an eager demand. The chickens, carefully guarded on the Embassy roof, are used on extra special occasions. Eggs are scarce and they're purchased in big lots whenever possible; on good days, as many as a hundred dozen or so in one trip's not an unusual haul. Rumors of food float around here like rumors around the London Embassy during a crisis.

After Valencia, the physical appearance of Madrid comes as quite a shock. There, the people seemed relatively happy and they could eat rice and oranges that grow abundantly near the city. Here, they're entirely dependent on transportation from the port of Valencia, and that's almost completely broken down. Buses are few and far between; trucks, which formerly kept the service going, need new parts that it's impossible to obtain. So they stand idle and useless. The people look miserably hungry and depressed.

The big number of queues in the streets reminds me again of Russia. I don't think anyone outside has any idea of the severity of the food problem in Madrid. It's terrible. Hundreds of people are actually starving to death every day, and everybody's hungry all the time. The amount of food rationed out isn't nearly enough, and unless you have "pull" or some friends in the country you're just damn-well out of luck.

One strange phenomenon is the growth of barter meeting-places. In little groups of a couple of hundred, these poor people barter among themselves the few things they have. This is strictly against the law and the police try to break it up; but no matter how often they're scattered, the bartering groups form again in no time at all.

There's practically nothing to buy in the shops. No razor blades or soap or paper or string; none of the things we've come to take for granted as common necessities. Some of the bigger department stores have a few counters — down in their basements — of odds and ends, which they sell cheaply enough. I managed to buy a felt hat which only cost me a few cents. But most of the smaller shop-keepers have hidden their valuable stuff and won't sell. They're sure the war is lost and very soon this "red" currency won't be worth a cent, so they're waiting 'till Franco comes in and they can get some good money for theirs.

Already there's an entirely different price for the pesetas issued before the Revolution, which Franco says he'll recognize and exchange, peseta for peseta, with his money. I haven't seen any coin in circulation. I hear it disappears nearly as soon as it's issued. Now they give us little cardboard plaques with ordinary postage stamps on them. I don't know yet just what you can do with them.

The benches along the street have all been destroyed and used for firewood. There's no heating in the houses — "central" or otherwise. I've noticed that already. Today I saw them chopping down a beautiful tree on one of the main streets. When it fell, about fifty people let out a screech and rushed for it, some with tiny hatchets. A guard tried to push them off with the butt of his gun, but he hadn't a chance. The tree was literally torn to pieces and disappeared in no time. Some old women stood around, grabbing for the chips that flew with each blow of the axes. Further on I watched another old woman chopping up a piece of furniture in order to have wood to burn.

I just heard that the Government is moving towards the seacoast. We've had no shelling in twenty-four hours, which may mean it's true, for they probably made an agreement that shelling is to stop if the Government gets out. That'll be a great relief to the civilians, who've been horribly affected by the continual air-raids. Most of them, I understand, go down in the cellars and wait there all night. Maybe I'll get an uninterrupted night's sleep. I could do with one. I'll let you know in the morning.

Joe

Joseph P. Kennedy, Jr., 23, to Joseph P. Kennedy

Madrid, March 8

Dear Dad,

Monday morning we awoke to find soldiers on every street corner and heard that, on the night before, Casado and the other members of his military Junta had spoken over the radio, disclaiming the Negrín government and setting up a new Council of National Defense.[205] It appeared the city was under complete military control and the war was over. The soldiers inspected all documents, picking up bearers identified as Communists. By mid-day they had about 1,200 in jail. Everything seemed to be going perfectly, and the Fascists were elated, congratulating themselves on the ease with which the Casado takeover had been accomplished. There was only one trouble spot, the Ministerial Building near the Embassy, where it was said about 70 Communists had installed themselves, along with hostages taken from passing cars during the night. One of the hostages is believed to be Besteiro's[206] niece.

Everyone seemed relieved to see soldiers in the streets, and I am sure most people thought the war was over in spite of a declaration by Casado that the Loyalists will fight until they get a worthy peace. Crowds of people chased after newspaper boys and the price of a paper rose to four cigarettes.

In the afternoon, artillery was in position for an attack on the Ministerial Building. From a hill above the city, we watched shells crash against the structure, and thought that the surrender would soon be complete.

Some Falangi[207] went out to the hospital prison in the afternoon and got their chief, a likable young-looking fellow with a fine face. Not as dynamic as Benini[208] but a good figurehead. He had been in prison since the outbreak of the war.

We had a good scare yesterday afternoon following a report that the Communists had taken Hacka[209] and were on their way here.

The Government announced that it completely dominated the situation, and any persons found on the streets after 11 o'clock would be regarded as *factiosos*. Nevertheless, shooting in the streets last night was terrible.

Things were quiet all morning until about 11, when shooting broke out. The noise was terrific. Government cavalry rushed up but were beaten back. There are two bodies in the street near the Embassy.

In the afternoon, men surrounded a nearby house. We can't tell from here whether they are Government troops or Communists.

The Nationalist radio has attacked one Junta, describing it as a tool of Besteiro and the democracies. An announcement on the government station said that Republican

---

205. Hoping to stem further Republican bloodshed, Colonel Sesigmundo Casado López (1893–1968), commander of the Loyalist armies in central Spain, had been attempting secretly for some time to sue Franco for peace. As the Nationalist army (now holding all but the center and southeast of the country) advanced on the capital, Casado and his junta revolted against Republican Prime Minister Dr. Juan Negrín (1892?–1956) on Sunday, March 5. Negrín and his ministers would flee shortly afterward. The coup would split Loyalist Madrid, pitting Communists (loyal to Socialist Negrín) against Casado's supporters in street skirmishes that would last nearly a week.

206. Foreign minister of Casado's new National Council of Defense, Marxist-Socialist theoretician, former professor of logic at the University of Madrid and speaker of the Spanish *Cortes*, 1931–33, Julián Besteiro y Fernández (1870–1940).

207. Falangists or members of the extreme Nationalist, anti-Marxist *Falange*. Founded in 1933, the party had been taken over by Franco and his brother-in-law Ramón Serrano Suñer in 1937.

208. The *nom de guerre* of the director of the local *Falange* Council, whom Joe had met about a week earlier. In a letter of March 1, he told his father, "I was greatly impressed by Benini's earnestness, and by the logic and clarity of his thinking."

209. That is, the town of Jacka in Aragon to the northeast of Madrid.

planes were on the way here but none showed up. Meanwhile, the porter's son, who belongs to a Communist brigade near here, said all the officers have been arrested.

Salamanca radio[210] said last night that troops from the Ministerial Building had surrendered but I heard this morning that they had been reinforced and are still there.

Cannons and machine guns have been mounted, and trenches dug, in front of the Department of Safety. Junta troops are a little more confident than they were yesterday. The Communists are in control of the Air Force but the position of the *carabineros* is unclear. It is rumored that the Communists want peace.

Roberto's[211] friend called up last night, saying the head of the sanitation department wanted refuge.

I visited the French Hospital. Everyone was quite calm. They said yesterday was the crucial day, that the war will be over in 15 days.

Today is like the calm before a storm. There are no people to speak of in the streets; the only sound to be heard is the occasional crack of a rifle.

Joe

Joseph P. Kennedy: *Diary*

March 12, 1939, Sunday

Day of Coronation[212]

I got up at 6, a beautiful sunny day. We all left in four cars. Rose and I and Galeazzi in one. We arrived at St. Peters at 7:30. Drove up through narrow driveways to what seemed an adjoining building to St. Peters. We went upstairs and Galeazzi stayed down to get the children into the right place. While up there waiting a Mr. Matthews, son of former Mayor of Boston, now librarian in Vatican Library,[213] came up to tell us how sorry he was not to have us to take through, they had set him aside to put Galeazzi there. Finally we went into St. Peters and then proceeded to stand set up in outside portico.

We sat in the front row. In the middle was the Crown Prince and Princess,[214] she the only one in white, all other women in black. On his left was the Crown Prince of Luxembourg,[215] a youngster whom I was to meet with his father[216] the next day at Gandolfo.[217] His sisters go to school at Roehampton.[218] Then deValera[219] and then

---

210. Salamanca radio was Nationalist controlled.
211. In a letter of February 21, Joe described Roberto, the custodian of the all-but-deserted U.S. consulate, as "a Basque and his three brothers are fighting for Franco. He himself escaped military duty by 'drinking blood and acid' — at least that's his story. I don't quite know his system, but from the sound of it I'd take the army! He also had some friends do a little 'arranging.' He has pals on both sides and will, if he can, do favors for any of them. But he says, bluntly, that the Leftists should now suffer as he and his wife have suffered."
212. JPK was to serve as the United States representative at the coronation of Eugenio, Cardinal Pacelli, as Pope Pius XII.
213. Papal chamberlain, 1932–39, and a contemporary of JPK's at Harvard, Sullivan Amory Matthews (1890–1942). Matthews was the son of Nathan Matthews, mayor of Boston, 1891–94.
214. King Victor Emmanuel III's only son, the prince of Piedmont, later Umberto II of Italy and his wife, the former Princess Marie-José (Charlotte Sophie Amélie Henriette Gabriele) of Belgium, King Leopold III's sister.
215. Jean (Benoit Guillaume Marie Robert Louis Antoine Adolphe Marc d'Aviano) (1921–) had come of age in January, becoming hereditary grand duke of Luxembourg, hereditary prince of Nassau, and prince of Bourbon and Parma.
216. Prince Félix (1896–1970), consort of Grand Duchess Charlotte of Luxembourg.
217. The papal country villa.
218. The Convent of the Sacred Heart outside of London, which Eunice, Pat and Jean Kennedy also attended.
219. Éamon de Valera (1882–1975), prime minister of the Irish Free State and later prime minister and president of the Republic of Ireland.

Rose and then me. Rose, deValera and I talked all the time, principal subject England should permit Northern Ireland come in with Southern and, if necessary, let them all return their privileges. I never understood this but I could see he was whipping himself into his campaign for U. S. He thought there would be many Irish against him in U. S. A.

He also told us of his trip to Zurich to have his eyes fixed. They were getting very bad. (Get copy of broadcast for description of whole ceremony).

After first move I noted Ciano[220] and several members of his staff who came after de Valera and immediately ahead of us in the procession. We made our first move to where we saw the Cardinals kiss toe and ring. Then we moved to final seats in St. Peters where we were opposite Pope's throne when mass was said. Here we heard that Ciano was mad because England's representative[221] was ahead of him in Procession. Said "Italy" was insulted. After watching him march through the church giving Fascist salute and bowing and smiling, I was convinced he was a swell-headed Muggo.

After Mass we went to outside and sat high up on roof on Pope's left as he faced crowd and then saw him crowned. Six hours and never tired.

That afternoon went to Colonnas, the first Catholic family of Rome, all the Cardinals, Ciano and I first saw Countess Ciano.[222] He passed off quickly with women and she with a couple of men. Very old beautiful house. They escorted Cardinals in with lighted candles. Very interesting.

Monday, March 13, 1939

Woke up at 8 to get ready for audience with Pope at 11:30.

Got the family all together in three cars with Miss Dunn and Miss Hennessey,[223] the Moores, Houghton, Gowen[224] and Mrs. Kennedy, French maid. Guided by Galeazzi, started for Vatican. On arrival we were photographed. Moore was delayed in third car so we left the children to wait for them and Rose. Galeazzi and I started up. We went through the rooms with guards drawn up and finally arrived at outside waiting room. Norfolk who had been to see the Pope came out while we were waiting. The children arrived with countless packages of holy things and rosaries for their numerous friends to be blessed by Pope.

Finally my arrival and I went with Galeazzi. The Pope was in his old office. He had not moved to the Pope's quarters as yet. We went into the room and genuflected and then to my amazement as he was sitting behind a table he got up and I went to meet him he advanced a few steps towards me. I knelt and kissed his ring and then stood up. He smiled, motioned me to sit down and then sat down himself. He told me how happy he was to see me. He recalled his visit to the house[225] and his picture taking with all the children surrounding him. How nice they all were and how he "rejoiced" that President had sent me to Rome. He then thanked the President for what he had done, recalled his pleasant visit to Hyde Park and then talked about recognition of Vatican. I told him Hierarchy were against it because I thought they were afraid they would lose power. He said, "No, of course not." "Let America send representative to Vatican and delegate could remain at Washington." I told him I would help but he should have some

220. Galeazzo Ciano, count of Cortellazzo (1903–1944); Italian foreign minister, 1936–43; former Fascist minister for press and propaganda, 1935–36; and, since 1930, Mussolini's son-in-law.
221. The leading Anglo-Catholic layman and earl marshal and hereditary marshal of England, Sir Bernard Marmaduke FitzAlan-Howard, sixteenth duke of Norfolk (1908–1975).
222. The former Edda Mussolini (1911?–1995), the duce's only daughter and close adviser. She would denounce her father and renounce his name after her husband's arrest and execution in 1944.
223. The children's nannies.
224. Franklin C. Gowen (1895–1981), second secretary of the U.S. Embassy in London.
225. Pacelli had visited the Kennedys in Bronxville during his trip to the United States in November 1936.

one speak to Cardinals.[226] He was cheerful, most kind and showed a real affection for me. After I had been there for 20 minutes (and by the way, I crossed my knees while the Pope was talking and Monsignor Hurley[227] told me, in a talk I had with him afterwards, that Lord Halifax when he visited the Pope in January crossed his knees and acted most reverently but the Europeans would never cross their knees) I got up to go because I knew the family were waiting. Galeazzi, wanting to put in a boost for his friend Bishop Spellman of Boston,[228] said to Pope "You know, the Ambassador comes from Boston" and I took the hint and made a speech for Spellman and the Pope said "He is a good man and a good friend."

Then the family came in and all knelt and kissed the ring and he talked with Rose and remembered Teddy and Rose told him she was going to have a tablet to commemorate his visit to Bronxville. He recalled his visit and said how he enjoyed it. Said Teddy was a smart boy. Then he walked over to the table, a thing a Pope never does and got a white box with rosary which he gave to Rose with his blessing. He talked to her so much and so kindly and intimately I thought she would faint. He then gave rosaries in white casings to all the children. After 15 minutes we all knelt for his blessing and as we withdrew he said "Pray for me." (Galeazzi said afterwards he hadn't got used to saying "us" not "I" or "Me." Popes always say "We" or "Us.") We all went out after he had blessed the rosaries, etc. and we had to send Gowen back with large bunch the children had forgotten.

(Add children's and Rose' impressions to mine — here).

After we left we went down to the new Secretary of State, Cardinal Maglione,[229] who received us all and spoke French. He thanked Roosevelt and us and congratulated us on family and said he was a ninth child so Rose trotted out Teddy to meet him. She talked French and then he blessed Teddy and told him he, the Cardinal, had done well as a ninth child so Teddy would. He blessed us and then we went into Sistine Chapel and saw the beautiful works of Michael Angelo and Raphael and Galeazzi showed us where the Cardinals were locked up for the election of the Pope. He also told me in great confidence that he had been selected to make a thorough search of the premises to make sure that no dictaphones were hidden and he said he found a very small one when he noticed a connection to wires above. No one but Pacelli and he knew this. He also told me that it was generally understood that 26 of Foreign Cardinals all but one whom he suspected was O'Connell voted first ballot for Pacelli and 10 Italians. The next ballot had 40 (he needed 42) and on third ballot all.

We then had our pictures taken and went home to lunch after the most thrilling day of our lives.

In the afternoon went to tea at Gandolfo, the Pope's summer residence. A beautiful spot but very cold. We went in grounds first. Galeazzi told me not to wear a silk hat so when I got there practically every one else had on a silk hat, so in order to look respectable I had to go around with my hat off and almost froze to death. The photographers wanted a picture so they got Cardinal Hinsley to pose with me and just then Jack

---

226. Since 1934 Pacelli had been working with a number of Catholics within the Roosevelt administration to restore relations (which had been severed in 1867) between the United States and the Holy See.
227. Joseph Patrick Hurley (1894–1967), American-born attaché to the Papal Secretariat of State, 1934–40, later papal nuncio for Yugoslavia and archbishop of St. Augustine, Florida.
228. Francis Joseph Spellman (1889–1967), auxiliary bishop of Boston under Cardinal O'Connell (with whom Spellman's relations were strained), had arranged Pacelli's meeting with FDR through JPK in 1936. In April 1939, the newly elected pope would name Spellman archbishop of New York.
229. The former papal nuncio to both Switzerland and France, Luigi Cardinal Maglione (1877–1944) had succeeded Pacelli on March 11 over the objections of the Fascist government.

came up and started to kiss the Cardinal's ring sort of going down on his knees and click went the camera. Jack said if that ever appears in U.S.A. good-bye to Martin Luther Cannon.[230]

After walking around for a while we went up to the house. Beautifully done inside. When we got to the room in which they were serving tea on a tray on the long sea table was a bottle of Gordon's Gin with the label like ours in U.S.A. and a bottle of Canadian Club Whiskey. It looked very funny in the Pope's house and 50 Cardinals around.

On going out the Crown Prince of Piedmont was coming down the stairs and we met at foot of stairs. Gowen who was with me stepped up, told him who I was and introduced us. He was very pleasant and said [sic] (See Gowen).

We then went back to hotel and I got ready for dinner at the Phillips', American Embassy. When I got to hotel found a note from Phillips[231] asking us to be there at 8:50 and please be in the receiving line.

We arrived and quite a nice looking group of young as well as old people there. Phillips explained he had to have these young attractive Italian girls there for Ciano or else he just wouldn't come.

Small group at dinner divided into four tables.

After dinner I started to talk with Countess Ciano and it lasted the whole evening. (See my cable to Department).[232]

1. She wanted to know if we would fight. I said "Positively." I felt if we didn't there was no point in telling her so. She was attractive and said she would have to come to England and I said I would give her a party.

Ciano sat on a stool opposite us part of the night surrounded by three or four young girls. She didn't act as if she cared a darn. I had a few words with Ciano before he left. He told me how much Musso thought of Phillips. Phillips said if he did he had a poor way of showing it. He never could see him. All the time he was talking he was looking around as if he had St. Vitus dance.

March 15, 1939

Was called at 6 o'clock to dress for Teddy's First Communion to be given by Pope at 7:30 Mass at Vatican. Galeazzi called for us at 7, Jack, Eunice and Pat (who had arrived night before at midnight from Naples to come back for Communion)[233] Teddy and I. Teddy in a blue suit and a white rosette on his left arm. We arrived at Vatican and went immediately to Chapel which the Pope is still using, which he used while still Secretary of State. It was a small room with red walls and a beautiful small altar with a white background. White-yellow flowers decorated the altar and in the left hand corner a statue of Blessed Virgin with a crown of electric lights and small Stations of the Cross in white marble-like material. Teddy's kneeling bench was in front and we knelt on his left facing the altar and three nuns on his right. In front of him was a candle lighted and lilies twined around it. After mass the valet gave the candle to Teddy for souvenir.

After we arrived the Pope walked in looking neither to the right or left and proceeded to put on his vestments standing in front of the altar. The vestments were red and he wore red shoes.

His valet acted as altar boy.

I noticed when the wine and water were served to him he poured a good deal of wine and then used a gold spoon to put the water in the chalice.

230. Jack's current girlfriend, Frances Anne Cannon, was Protestant.
231. William Phillips (1878–1968), U.S. ambassador to Italy, 1936–41.
232. His Dispatch No. 374 of March 17.
233. They had been touring Pompeii.

When it came time for Communion he left the altar, came down to Teddy and gave him his Communion. His touch was so light when he put the Host on his tongue he didn't quite know it was there. I knew this was so because when he put it on my tongue I had a like experience.

After mass he took off his vestments and knelt down at his (Prior?) [*sic*].[234] He reached into his left-hand pocket, took something out then looked at it and put it back. He prayed, so sincerely for quite some time then turned towards Blessed Virgin statue and prayed to that. After another short while he reached into his pocket again and went through same performance as before. This time I noticed it was a small watch of black enamel and red covers. One of those flat ones you press and both top sides open and the watch is seen, then you press both back and it is closed. It looked funny to be using this kind of watch and also to be timing your prayers. Galeazzi said afterwards he always uses exactly the same time to the minute every day.

In the meantime the nuns had taken away the vestments and brought out a long white box and three red ones and left them on a chair and signaled to the Pope they were there. The nuns left and we were alone. After he finished praying he got up, went over, got the boxes and came over to Teddy. He smiled and said to Teddy "This is a souvenir of your First Communion" and then he blessed him. Galeazzi beckoned us over around Teddy and he gave me three red boxes, one for Miss LeHand, one for Frank Murphy[235] and one for me. Souvenirs of coronation. He then said to girls "I had such a nice time in your Villa in New York" and when Galeazzi had told him the girls had traveled all night to be there he said "I thank you very much." His simplicity is miraculous. To Teddy, as he blessed him, "I hope you will always be good and pious as you are today." He said how glad he was to see me again and blessed us all. Then turning to Teddy he made the Sign of the Cross on his forehead, we all knelt and he Genuflected before the altar and went out. Just before he left us he said "Pray for me."

He is awe-inspiring, majestic, kindness personified and with the humility of God. Galeazzi then took us into his office where there was a long desk with silver inkstands at each place. We then went back to hotel.

I went shopping — bought some jewelry and a watch for Galeazzi.

Gave Galeazzi 50,000 Lire for Pope. Went to station. Bishop Hayes[236] and his assistants, Monsignor Hurley, Bill Phillips and his group at station to see me off. Phillips introduced to French Ambassador at Rome while train was pulling out.

Joseph P. Kennedy to Joseph P. Kennedy, Jr., 23: *Telegram*

MARCH 15, 1939

STAY AS LONG AS YOU LIKE USE YOUR JUDGMENT CABLE ME IN LONDON IN CASE OF
NEED LOVE

DAD

---

234. Prie-dieu?
235. The former governor of Michigan and recently appointed U.S. attorney general.
236. James T. G. Hayes (1889–1980), the American-born bishop (later archbishop) of Mindanao in the Philippines, 1933–51.

Joseph P. Kennedy: *Diary*

Arrived Paris on Rome express at 8 A.M. Met by Offie,[237] driven to Ritz Hotel to see Rose, heard she had gone to church. Went to Madeleine Church, found her there praying with her eyes closed.

Took her back to hotel and then went to Bullitt's for breakfast. Talked with Bullitt. He said March 13 had marked the end of our civilization.[238] Deplorable act of Germans. Roosevelt had said on phone "I have the evening papers in front of me with headlines "Chamberlain washes his hands" and said "You know the last well known man about whom that was said" and Bill answered "Yes." "Pontius Pilate."

Roosevelt indignant with Germans and displeased with Chamberlain.

Went to airport with Offie. Told me of change in personnel in Paris.

Flew to London, went to Chancery and then to see Halifax. (See cable to Department).[239]

Discussed chance of taking Mussolini away from Hitler. He thought they had done all they could and I told him unfortunately our relations with Italy hinged on recognition of Abyssinia and since that was obtained as result of aggression and we were condemning that in Hitler at the moment it didn't seem practical but I still felt it was the one step that might be taken to help before going to war.

Saw the Rumanian Minister (see cable to Department).[240]

Saw Roy Howard. Told him I was bearish and thought we would eventually have to have some form of dictatorship in U.S.A. to solve our own difficulties.

He spoke about how Roosevelt treated him as a boy in discussions. Never acted as if he needed his advice.

Saw Dillon of Dillon Read[241] — just lightly went over situation.

Had dinner with Lonsdale[242] at Embassy.

Joseph P. Kennedy to Cordell Hull: *Diplomatic Dispatch*

354, March 17, 10 p.m. For the Secretary, strictly confidential.

I had a long talk with Countess Ciano during my visit to Rome and I reported to Ambassador Phillips three outstanding points in the two and a half-hour's conversation I had with her. First, she could not see any reason for the democracies fighting Fascist Italy. Fascism suited Italy, having lasted for seventeen years, and had been of great benefit to the Italians. Its chief disrepute had come from its close tie-up with Herr

---

237. Carmel Offie, third secretary at the American embassy in Paris and Ambassador Bullit's personal secretary. A 1956 FBI memorandum would report that in 1939, Bullitt had stated that during JPK's tenure in London, the latter called Offie "every day and sometimes four times a day to ask [his] advice on important issues, which advice Kennedy followed."

238. Despite Hitler's protestations prior to Munich that the Sudetenland would be the last of the Reich's acquisitions, in the early morning hours of March 13 German troops had crossed the boarder into Bohemia and Moravia without opposition. By evening Hitler had arrived to claim Prague.

239. In his Dispatch No. 352 of 6:00 P.M. on March 17, JPK related his conversation with Halifax over whether the British "proposed to release the gold which is being held in England for the account of Czechoslovakia."

240. The Rumanian minister had asked his opinion of whether the British would fight for Czechoslovakia or, if not, whether Rumania should "make the best deal she can" with the Germans.

241. Clarence Douglas Dillon (1909–), who had been elected vice president and director of the brokerage of Dillon-Read and Company the previous year. Although a Republican, Dillon would serve as secretary of the treasury during both the Kennedy and Johnson administrations, 1961–65.

242. Playwright and screenwriter Frederick Lonsdale (1881–1954).

Hitler. Secondly, she said that after all if the United States, France and England all stuck together, there was nothing left for the Duce to do but play along with Hitler for his own protection. Third, she made it very clear by implication that the Italians were deeply concerned over the loss of the friendship of America and since there are a number of enthusiasts for America around Mussolini, I believe there is a good deal in what she said.

I had lunch with the Minister of Agriculture, whom I met with a very close friend of mine.[243] He outlined to me his plan of handling wheat in Italy and said that during his visit to Germany last week, where they are arranging to send many Italian laborers to work in the fields, he found that the German business man and farmer were definitely not in good shape. From his conversation I gathered that up to now Italy has not stored very much wheat for its protection, although they have urged the farmers to plan well beyond the demands of Italy so as to provide for substantial storage.

He felt that trouble between countries because of a difference in government was unthinkable. He said that the people of Italy definitely did not want to go to war; their problem was entirely economic.

I also met Count Ciano. On Sunday at St. Peter's I sat next to him for five hours; I saw him at a tea with his wife and attended a dinner at which he was present. I have no idea how able he is in his office, but a more pompous ass I have never met in my life. Every time it was necessary for the distinguished guests to march through St. Peter's most of his time he spent in giving the Fascist salute and trying to share honors with the Pope. I should judge that at the tea which we attended there, there were about forty Cardinals. Most of his time he spent rushing girls into the corner for conversation and he could not talk seriously for five minutes at the dinner for fear that the two or three girls, who are invited in order to get him to come, might get out of sight. As a result of my observations of Ciano and the gossip that Mussolini now has a German sweetheart, I came away believing that we would accomplish much more by sending a dozen beautiful chorus girls to me than a fleet of airplanes and a flock of diplomats. If, in spite of his tendencies, Ciano becomes a great Secretary of State, then I have lost all judgment of men.

The speeches of the President drive them absolutely crazy. My Italian friends tell me that every time the President says anything, none of the members of the Cabinet or the Government in Rome are fit to converse with for the balance of the day.

KENNEDY

The Ambassador, Mr. Johnson

Joseph P. Kennedy to Neville Chamberlain: *Telegram Draft*

March 18-1939

Affectionate greetings on your birthday. I count upon your courage never failing and your strength increasing I have been one with you in your striving for peace and have nothing but admiration for the convictions you so eloquently expressed last night Opinions may change but underlying conviction changes only to deepen Cordially Joe Kennedy

---

243. Galeazzi?

Joseph P. Kennedy to Missy LeHand

London, March 27, 1939

Dear Missy,

The signature cards of the President, which you sent me after I dashed out of town, evidently arrived here in good order, but, somehow or other, were mislaid in the shuffle and came to light only the day before yesterday. I am putting them up as prizes to the youngsters for improvement in work. If they get certain grades, they get signature cards; if they don't, they are out of luck.

I received a wire this morning telling me that Jimmy is sailing on the 1st of April.

Don't forget that, provided there is peace in the world, you and Betsy must give me at least one chance to entertain you before I leave this job. So, come early.

Always my love and deepest thanks.

Sincerely,

Joseph P. Kennedy, Jr., 23, to Joseph P. Kennedy

Madrid, March 28

Dear Dad,

A young man returning from the front around Madrid reports that soldiers were told to go home in the morning but ordered back to their trenches in the evening. During the day, he says the men had been talking to soldiers from the other side.

This morning I learned the Nationalists had planned to enter the city this afternoon at four o'clock.[244] Shortly before noon a large car drove by bearing a Nationalist flag and a bunch of young fellows yelling *"Arriba España," "Viva Franco,"* etc. In a few minutes, Nationalist flags were everywhere and people were greeting each other in the streets with the Fascist salute. The city came to life — with parades, flags, shawls hung from windows and balconies, pretty girls appearing from nowhere, crowds hanging onto the sides of cars, women and men weeping with joy. We were touched by the expressiveness in their voices and the look in their eyes, by occasional sad faces, by a woman in black holding two children with a bitter look on her face.

The long siege was over. Nationalist planes stunted overhead, with everyone clapping for them. Men with machine guns in hand clung to the sides of passing cars. The radio station changed hands. People appeared in Nationalist dresses and shirts, embraced each other on the street. There was widespread singing of the Nationalist anthem.

Refugees from the embassies ventured out for the first time. In the *Presidente* people were busy congratulating each other and signing *laissez passers* for autos and civilians. Officers who came over from the other side were given a magnificent welcome as they passed through the streets sitting on the tops of trucks or standing on the running boards of cars.

Lights were to be left on last night until two o'clock although there really wasn't much light on the Castellana. For the first time, the telephone doesn't seem to work. The Nationalists have already started arresting people; they came yesterday and took one of the guards from here. He was probably denounced. Roberto hid Espinoza[245] for

---

244. Casado had surrendered Madrid on March 26.

245. A former member of the *Cortes* and leader of the Republican Union, Espinoza was, as Joe put it in the miscellaneous notes that he compiled on the various "Personalities" whom he encountered in Spain, "a true democrat as we know one. He saved a lot of the Right from being slaughtered. Scared to death

323

the first few days. Everything seemed to go off incredibly well. Fish merchants have been told they can bring their wares into Madrid, so for the next few days we ought to be able to get fresh fish.

Joe

Joseph P. Kennedy, Jr., 23, to Joseph P. Kennedy

Irun, April 4 Last!

Dear Dad,

I'm in an awful mess here so I thought I would write you this note and let you know what's what in case I get interned for a couple of days. I'm just rattling this off and giving it to a fellow who's crossing over into France, so it will be short.

I left Madrid yesterday with a newspaper fellow and arrived last night in San Sebastian after an uneventful trip. We nearly ran out of gas crossing the Sierra Mountains as there was no gas to be bought in Madrid and we just had to take a chance with what we had. But Providence was with us. There doesn't seem to be any shortage of food in this part of the country; in fact, the stores look completely normal. It is hard to believe that people around here were aware that a war was going on for nearly two and a half years.

I came to Irun this morning with my letter of introduction to the frontier authorities and, to my surprise, they made a terrific fuss. They nearly went crazy when they found I had entered by a Loyalist port and refused to let me go until they had permission from Burgos.[246] This meant I had to go back to San Sebastian and tell contacts there my sad story. They promised to fix it up right away. I returned to Irun. That was 11 o'clock. At one o'clock the frontier station closes 'til four for lunch. At four no word had been received. I spoke to my keepers again. Now they were regarding me with actual hostility. None of them knew that the U.S. had recognized Franco so I was almost as unpopular as Joseph Stalin.[247] At seven o'clock they received word to pass me. Joyfully, with my bags under my arms, I started for the bridge which crosses from Irun to France a couple of hundred yards down the road. At last, I was going to get out. Well, I got down to the bridge and the boys decided to go through all my luggage and, in addition, to search me. Of course, they found some money from the Republican side, which was utterly worthless and which I was bringing home to Bobby as a souvenir. Well, when they found this they went crazy. They really thought they had found something. Officials crowded around, questioning me n a manner which could only be interpreted as "We know you're a dirty Russian spy, but speak up." After going through the story which I had related many times to the authorities at military headquarters, they decided I would have to go back. When I got back, the faces of officials lit up as if to say they knew all along something was fishy and that they wouldn't have to let me go except for those stupid people in Burgos.

---

of the first few days when the fascist [*sic*] came in. Didn't mind being judged. Burning all of his papers including a beautiful colored copy of the Constitution. One of the very few. Got refuge and then turned himself over to the police."

246. The seat of Franco's government since 1938 and the administrative center for the insurgent Nationalist army since 1936.

247. The United States had recognized Franco's nationalist government on April 1; France and Britain had already done so on February 27.

I took all my things to the censor and he started going through my wallet and duplicates of some of the letters which I sent to you. He also found some Communist newspapers from Madrid, along with some of the regular newspapers published there. When he found a pass allowing me to visit the Front he said, "Ah, signed by the Reds." He started reading all the cards on which I had telephone numbers, etc., and as he knew very little English, and had to spend about five minutes on each card, I envisioned having to stay here for several days.

It takes so long to send a wire from this side that I decided to drop you this note in case they try to jail me as a spy. The censor's looking at me pretty suspiciously but I told him I was going to send this to some of my friends in Madrid and will go downstairs and give it to an English fellow who has kindly offered to take it over into France. I'm so darned mad — just when I thought this country might amount to something. That's the great danger here, that petty army officials will remain in power for many years at the expense of the Spanish people. If you can put in a good word for me with the Duke of Alba[248] unofficially and explain my predicament, it might do your devoted son a little good. The censor looks like he's ready to give me the third degree now.

Love,
Joe

Rose Kennedy: *Diary*

April 7, 1939

Stores all closed and everyone away for holiday extending over Monday. Went to play golf at Addington with Joe at 10:30 A.M. and when we finished about one o'clock, he had a tense look as he had received word the Italians had marched into Albania and it might mean war.[249] He came home, went to Foreign Office. Chamberlain is in Scotland for a much-needed rest, and there is an aeroplane waiting to fly up to get him if necessary. Had quiet supper with children, talk to Joe Jr. who has shown me some of the purchases he made in Spain, mostly odd pieces of linen, bedspreads, doilies, odds and ends, nothing of value. The most interesting thing he brought in was a candlestick made of covers of milk bottles. Could plainly distinguish milk cover on bottom. Said he never received message from Father telling him to come to Pope's Coronation, but had heard on the radio that we all were there except him as he was in Madrid. He has been working on some of his magazine articles today and deciding what to do as *Cosmopolitan Magazine* has made him an offer. His father thinks he should write a book as the fact that a person who has written a book gives him a certain prestige. Went to church with Rose, Joe Jr. Later Kathleen arrived from some English friends who she said were upset about war news and thought she was so lucky to be American. Also said two or three people had threatened playfully to shoot her or some of us as ____[sic] as stated in the Senate one day that could they imagine U.S.A. not in war if American Ambassador or some of his family were shot [sic]. Therefore, perhaps some Englishman may take it upon himself that one or two of us be accidentally (?) killed in a supposedly German air

---

248. Formerly the Nationalist representative in London, Don Jacobo Fitz-James Stuart y Falco, seventeenth duke of Alba (1878–1953) had become the Spanish ambassador upon the British recognition of Franco's government.

249. That morning, Italian forces had taken the Albanian ports of Durazzo, Valona, San Giovanni di Medua, and Santi Quaranta, forcing the Albanian king, Zog I, and his government to flee to Greece two days later.

raid. Everyone stunned and shattered by news of Italians advance, especially on Good Friday. It seems their technique always calls for their coups taking place over the weekends. Feel so sad for the Prime Minister as Mrs. Chamberlain said he was so looking forward to the long holiday in Scotland as Monday is also free. Now a plane is waiting to take him back although he is actually coming by train.

Joseph P. Kennedy: *Diary*

[Windsor Castle] Friday, April 14, 1939

Dentist — Message — President — Chamberlain and message back to U.S.A.[250]

Message to Mussolini. He "gave editor more hell than anyone in a long time." Attlee agreement — Dalton-Attlee-Rumania "a poor specimen."

Showed old map. "If this continues much longer will need a new map, opening it and folding it."

"Thankful about Navy" going to Pacific Saturday.[251] Got message on Peace from Roosevelt. Sent it to Halifax and Prime Minister. Had it read to B.B.C. and U.S. newspapermen for clarification.

Brought copy out to Windsor. Gave it to General Child[252] on arrival for King to read. Later Child told me King had given to Queen. "You must read that before dinner" so Child said the King and Queen would probably be late.

Dinner — sat on Queen's right. Lovely and charming as ever. She had on a gold dress and when she sat in chair she laughed and said "I have a hard time fitting into these chairs with these new dresses, but tonight I don't seem to overflow."

She talked about the present situation. How changed it was and how serious and only a year ago we were talking about presentations at Court.

She wanted still very much to go to U.S.A. no matter how dangerous it was because not to go would give satisfaction to the enemies. What a woman.

We talked about the Duchess of Windsor and I told her the story of Hillman[253] coming to me in Rome to tell me the Duchess of Windsor had sent for American newspaper women to use the article criticizing Mrs. K. for snubbing her and playing the English game.

I told him when the article was written I wanted merely to add "I know of no job that I could occupy that might force my wife to dine with a tart." Nothing has been heard since. The Queen laughed and said it served her right.[254] She said she understood

250. The following day, the appeals for peace that Roosevelt had addressed to both Hitler and Mussolini in light of the recent instances of German and Italian aggression would be broadcast worldwide. The president reminded the dictators that "throughout the world hundreds of millions of human beings are living to-day in constant fear of a new war," and challenged them "to give assurance" that they would refrain from military actions against other nations for a period of ten years.

251. On April 11, fearing the Royal Navy's inability to reinforce its battleships in the Far East while attempting to contain Italy in the Mediterranean, Halifax had urged FDR to order the U.S. fleet to reassemble in the Pacific.

252. Brigadier General Sir Hill Child (1868–1958), master of the Royal Household, 1936–41.

253. William Hillman (1895–1962), chief of staff of foreign correspondents for the Hearst papers, 1934–39, and European manager of the Hearst International News Service, 1936–39.

254. Lord Halifax would record what he described as JPK's "coarse story" more extensively in his own diary on Friday, July 19, 1940:

When [JPK] went over to America some months ago Mrs. Kennedy was in Paris, and was asked to dine to meet the Windsors. She telephoned to Joe Kennedy for his advice, and he told her that, as he was Ambassador, and they were what he called "in with the other set" in London, he thought she had better keep out of it, which she did. A week or two later, however, Bill Bullitt asked her to dine to meet them, adding that the Duke had expressed a wish that all the guests should curtsey to the Duchess. To this Mrs. Kennedy thought she must go, but telephoned to Sir

that they (W's) were talking about her and the King, but their conscience was clean. She deplores their action.

She laughed about being caught in U.S. or Canada in event of war. I suggested moving to U.S., we'd love to have her.

I asked her if she knew that the motif in big ballroom at Buckingham Palace on ceiling was the Swastika. She was astounded and said "No." I said Madam Maisky[255] had pointed it out to me. After dinner I talked with King. He talked same way about U.S. trip. I talked [sic] how cheerful he appeared. He said he was a bit depressed in his room yesterday.

He told me he has to send for Prime Minister and all the excitement about his going to London rather irked him.

He said the problem of Windsors annoyed him.

Sunday morning, April 15 [16], 1939

We went to 11 o'clock Mass. On our return Rose put on her walking shoes and a blue scarf over her head and we went for a walk. While returning we saw a couple in front of us, he in a gray top coat and she in a light blue coat with a hood over her head. It was the King and Queen. They saw us and came to join us, smiling pleasantly as usual.

I walked with the King, Rose with the Queen. I told the King I was going to write the last 6 months and dedicate to him as "The man who has the most to lose and shows it the least." The Queen took him by the arm and blushed and said "That would be most kind of you."

They invited us to go back to the Castle through their entrance and Queen stopped to show Rose some lovely white flowers. She picked one and gave it to her. The King looked at the card alongside where it was growing and said, "why must these simple flowers have such long names just like medical terms." (I had often thought the same thing myself but never asked the question).

"Incidentally", said the King, "If you have a pain in your chest the doctors say in your sternum. Strange, I call it."

We came in dressed for lunch and the Prime Minister and his wife were there.

He greeted me effusively and said, "Well, that was a great job Roosevelt did, the message and order to the Navy."

He asked me if I knew of it when I called on him yesterday. I said "No." "The President had spoken of it the week before when I talked with him, but I had recommended waiting awhile." The Prime Minister said he was glad he didn't know and could so say.

I asked him what he thought would happen. He thought Hitler's answer would be evasive and probably delayed. He felt that it had put them both on the spot.

John Monck to ask about the curtseying, which, of course, she was told that she ought not do, so she didn't. A little later the Kennedys were at Cannes, in the neighbourhood of the Windsors, and one morning a young American lady newspaper correspondent brought along to Kennedy an article based on an interview with the Duchess, in which Mrs. Kennedy was depicted in [a] very unfavourable light, and the general impression given to American readers that the Kennedys were undemocratic snobs, only concerned to lick the boots of Royalty. The correspondent asked whether Mrs. Kennedy had any comment to make which might be published with the interview, to which Joe replied that she had none, but that he had one to make, and asked the young lady whether she had a paper and pencil, and would she write it down. The comment was this: "I know of no position that I could hold which would involve my wife in any obligation to dine with a tart." Joe then asked the young lady to be sure that she published it with the article and on the strength of the interview the newspaper correspondent returned to the Duchess, and the article never appeared. Fairly downright diplomacy.

255. The wife of the Soviet ambassador in London.

I asked him what he would do if Italy refused to take troops out. He still contends Musso will move them out and pointed to Ciano's speech Saturday night as indicating their intention.[256]

I asked him about Russia. He said they hesitated to come to any definite plan with Russia for fear it might frighten the Balkans but once they were tied up he would close with Russia, which he feels he can do.

Extra on queen.

In my conversation with the Queen at dinner talking about Italy I mentioned Musso's daughter. She said she had met her once and thought she was "tough." I agreed.

After dinner with King.

Wanted to go to U.S.A. Had fought before, could do it again.

Brought up question of Windsor. I said I thought King and Queen had improved their position immensely in year.

He felt so too. It was embarrassing to contemplate. Said he tried to talk with Edward in '36 but she always prevented it and, of course, when she left it was too late.

Spoke of Chamberlain as *my* Prime Minister. He said he (King) had to send for him. Of course Prime Minister could ask for appointment but, laughingly he said, "I had to tell him I want him to come." He is remarkably gay and courageous.

Sitting next to Princess Beatrice[257] at dinner. Told me by Grandi being away she drew Maisky at Palace dinner for French President.[258] Never would meet him before because she was cousin of Empress of Russia.[259] He rushed his wife up later.

Told also story of his predecessor who was at Palace one night with his wife, when one of old Empress' lady-in-waiting, wearing her picture as an honor (she was now married to some Minister) met this woman. The Soviet Ambassador's wife asked whose picture she was wearing. She answered "Her Empress of Russia" and with that the Soviet Ambassador's wife spat on the picture. Princess Beatrice asked the Russian lady what she did then. She said "I drew myself up and spat back at her." (How is that for the Palace).

Beatrice also said Von Dirksen's wife was strange. At the dinner she asked Beatrice to introduce her to Archbishop of Canterbury. "You know," she said, "He hates all Germans." Princess Beatrice said "No, just the leaders." Von Dirksen said "I want to meet him but I am handicapped because I don't speak English too well and I suppose he speaks it fluently." "Yes", says Beatrice "I think he does."

On the King's visit, he thought the thing to do was to keep planning to go and we can call it off at a minute's notice, if necessary.

(He looks frightful — thin, tired, walks like a sick old man and his color is bad).

256. The previous evening, as a precursor to the official ratification of the union between Italy and Albania, the Italian foreign minister had addressed the Italian Chamber of Deputies, visiting Field Marshall Hermann Göring and more than a hundred defeated Albanian chieftains. In his speech Ciano attempted both to justify the recent Italian occupation of Albania and to quell international fears of further Italian expansion. He added that the Italian legions presently in Spain were soon to make a "triumphant return home after the deserved pride and honor of marching through the streets of Madrid past Generalissimo Francisco Franco."
257. Beatrice Marie Victoria Feodora (1857–1944), the king's great-aunt and Queen Victoria's youngest and last surviving daughter.
258. Albert François Lebrun (1871–1950), last president of the Third Republic, 1932–40.
259. The German-born Czarina Alexandra Feodorovna (who had been shot along with her husband, Czar Nicholas II, and their children by Bolsheviks in Ekaterinberg in 1918) had been Beatrice's niece, the daughter of her elder sister Princess Alice Mary Maud.

(See Monday's paper for account of band concert and trip to Balloon Barrage).[260]

At luncheon — I sat between Queen and Princess Elizabeth, who by the way handles herself beautifully. We talked, she called across table to the King (Papa).

She talked about Snow White, how she loved Dopey and knew his song in French. Thought he would look pretty funny working as an Italian.

Liked Mr. Smith, my riding instructor, who is teaching her to jump.

Queen and I discussed the political situation, she saying how hard it was to make any plans due to uncertainty.

Somebody at table discovered a ladybug and Princess Elizabeth suggested it was good luck and sent it along to the Prime Minister. So it came along on a gold spoon, one from another, and I handed it to the Queen and then she tried to tip it out on the Prime Minister's shoulder, most gently, but the bug refused to stay, but after many attempts finally did and then went slowly up. The Prime Minister said "It will probably go down my neck" and with that the Queen took it off with the spoon and it passed cross the table.

In the afternoon we returned from Barrage. I traveled in car with Princess Beatrice and Mrs. Chamberlain. The Princess was most interesting telling us about dictation from Victoria and one time when Queen was having trouble with Gladstone, whom she did not like at times, Princess Victoria said to the Queen "Why don't you tell him just what you think and do what you please." "I would, if I were Queen." Victoria smiled and said "Isn't it lucky you're not Queen." She told us all about the fear of the Royal Family in Russia long before the Revolution and guards practically standing in her room while she slept and dressed.

The influence of Rasputin grew because strangely enough the Empress' child got better several times when Rasputin visited him.

Sunday Evening. [April 16]

Jimmy Roosevelt was out to dinner, sat next to the Queen and had long talk with King afterwards. They both told me how much they liked him.

I walked with Queen through Windsor later looking at the pictures. She told me that she had told Jimmy how remarkable it was the confidence that the British had in me and how it was shown today when the King and Queen and Chamberlain were to enter the *secret* room of the Balloon Brigade the King immediately said "Have Mr. Kennedy come in."

This gesture spoke more than words could ever speak.

I thanked her and said "I know one shouldn't say this to a queen, but may I say you look particularly beautiful tonight in that dress." She blushed, said she was so pleased and I added I hoped she would wear that dress in U.S.A. She was pleased because she loved the dress but they had told her she had worn it too much. However, after what I said she was going to take it to U.S.A.

---

260. That day, JPK had accompanied the king and queen, the prime minister and Mrs. Chamberlain and the Princesses Beatrice and Helena Victoria (the king's aunt), to Hook, Surrey, to inspect a balloon barrage. "The royal visit was symbolical of Britain's interest in tightening her defenses," the *New York Times* reported.

Joseph P. Kennedy to Paul Murphy

London, April 18, 1939

Dear Paul:

I am enclosing two copies of a group of letter, an outline of future letter, and a clipping from the London *Evening Standard,* all of which I wish you would hand to John Kennedy.[261] The letters are a series that young Joe wrote to me during his recent visit to Spain, and which, after consultation with many experts over here, are deemed excellent material for the Saturday Evening Post or the Cosmopolitan Magazine.

I have talked with Wesley Stout, Editor of the *Saturday Evening Post* about a series of articles on Communism by young Joe, but Stout told me he already had a series on that subject and consequently was not sure he could use these, so Joe is going to do a series of articles on Communism for the Hearst newspapers, but these letters could run in about three installments, and I think would prove very interesting. I have gone through all this material and young Joe is now engaged in whipping it into shape, but has only had time to fix up the detail[s] of the first six.

As I said before, I want you to give these to John Kennedy of NBC, because he knows Wesley Stout, who I want to read them so that he may decide whether or not he wishes to buy them. I also wish John Kennedy to show copies to Harry Burton of the Cosmopolitan Magazine, who will know about them because Bill Hillman, the representative of the International News Service in London, has cabled them that they are on the way, and see whether he is interested in them, then we can decide, if both want them, who is offering the best price.

Whatever money is received from either of these young Joe is to give to charity, as I do not want him competing with newspaper men on the strength of being the Ambassador's son; this you can make clear to both parties. However, it does not stop him from wanting to get the best possible price should they be interested. My interest in the matter is to see young Joe get out on his own with what I consider a very worthwhile contribution in the form of these letters and some other articles he is going to do that will not conflict at all with these letters, but will give him international publicity.

I want to get a reply by cable as soon as possible after you receive this material, so if possible get hold of John and ask him if he will do it at once, because I don't want these things to get stale.

If John Kennedy should not be available I would suggest that you call Arthur Krock in Washington and get his advice as to whom you will get to do this at once.

Sincerely yours,

JOSEPH P. KENNEDY

Joseph P. Kennedy to Franklin Roosevelt and Cordell Hull: *Diplomatic Dispatch*

529, April 20, 10 p.m. CONFIDENTIAL FOR THE PRESIDENT AND SECRETARY.
On my way to Edinburgh with speech all international affairs omitted, talking about flowers, birds and trees. The only thing I am afraid of is that instead of giving me the freedom of the city they will make me queen of the May.

KENNEDY

---

261. That is, newsreel announcer, NBC radio political commentator, and editor of *Collier's Weekly* and *The Commentator,* John Bright Kennedy, who had authored the *American Magazine*'s 1928 feature on JPK.

Rose Kennedy: *Diary*

April 21, 1939

Princess Elizabeth's birthday.[262]
Joe sent her a drawing in color of Snow White signed by Walt Disney. The current impression is that she especially is spoiled and someone asked me if Princess Margaret Rose had an impediment when she spoke. To me they both are natural, simple, solicitous of one another, and it does seem as though they have a difficult time always accompanying their parents now to some maneuver or public demonstration. The Queen with her usual facility for meeting people spoke to Joe Jr. and another boy and discussed his trip in Spain.

Joseph P. Kennedy to Geoffrey Dawson[263]

London, May 1, 1939

Dear Geoffrey,
This is the first draft of the article on the fall of Madrid by young Joe. If it seems to be of any interest to you at all, we will whip it into shape and let you have it.

He is doing a number of articles for American magazines and French papers, but hasn't submitted this article to anybody and I thought the standing he would get out of it, if it were your type of thing, would be more than worth while. However, it is not worth printing if it isn't something of real interest.

It is the only copy I have, so I would appreciate it if you would send it back to me.
Yours sincerely,
Joseph P. Kennedy

Joseph P. Kennedy to Sumner Welles: *Diplomatic Dispatch*

606, May 4, 2 p.m. For the Under Secretary — strictly confidential.
I had a call this morning from Berlin from Mooney who is in charge of General Motors Export business and head of the German plant. He invited me to dine with him in Paris Saturday night. Another party at the dinner will be a personal friend of Hitler and high in influence in the Reichsbank.[264]

I plan to go by plane Saturday afternoon at five o'clock, returning here Sunday morning.

This man is in the inner circle, from what Mooney said. As I understand this person has an influence half way between Ribbentrop and Poole, is there any particular information regarding financial and political matters which you would like me to try to obtain.

---

262. She was thirteen.
263. (George) Geoffrey Dawson (1874–1944), editor of the *Times* of London, 1912–19, 1923–41.
264. A series of talks regarding both General Motors German operations and a substantial gold loan that Hitler had requested from the United States had brought James David Mooney (1884–1957), a vice president of the General Motors Corporation and president of General Motors Overseas, into contact with a number of high Nazi officials during the spring of 1939. Among these was Helmuth Wohlthat, an American-educated economist and special assistant to Reich Marshal Göring. Although Welles would not grant JPK permission to travel to meet Wohlthat in Paris, Mooney would propose an alternative meeting in London, which would take place on May 9.

The dinner is to be private and no one will know about my presence there and I will return Sunday morning early. Do you perceive any objection to my going and have you any suggestions to make?

KENNEDY

Rose Kennedy: *Diary*

May 4, 1939

Very busy all day preparing for the dinner for the King and Queen. The flowers arrived from Paris about 1:30. As we found, we could get more unusual flowers there and much less expensive, Offie had them flown over by plane. Everyone was rather nervous until they arrived because it always takes quite a long time to arrange them, and get the right colors for the right rooms. The flowers for the table were particularly lovely. They were like baby orchids, some white and some orchid color. They were called moth-orchids, or fillanopsis [*sic*]. I did not want the press to get the idea that I was decorating the table with orchids, which would should [*sic*] too nouveau riche, or too extreme, so I called them "fillanopsis" to the press. As we had old-fashioned strawberry shortcake, the strawberries also came from Paris by plane, as we thought they would be better. Everyone seemed very calm and confident but I know everyone in the house was terribly excited, including myself and the Ambassador.

During the day men from Scotland Yard came up to interview our butler to find out who the men were who were helping out in the evening. The butler, who has been in London for a long time, had chosen men who had all served at Buckingham Palace, so Scotland Yard was reassured and there were no detectives present. I suppose they are especially careful at this time because of the Irish terrorists in the I.R.A.

The six youngest children were seated at a small table at the end of the room. The conversation was naturally quite informal. I told the King about the shad roe which we had had sent from America for a big dinner last year and which had not arrived on time as the boat was twelve days late. Therefore, at the last moment I had to substitute filet of sole. As menus had already been printed for shad roe, we had had to leave them. And one English lady was quite astonished to find that shad roe tasted so like her own filet of sole and so I had to explain the difficulty.

We also talked about the King's coming visit to America. The menu was purely American, and the Virginia ham had come from America, as had the shad roe.

At the end of the dinner the Queen and I left the table, I giving a slight curtsey as I left the King; and as the ladies left the room, they each curtsied towards the King. We then went to the French room. The Queen and I went upstairs to my bedroom for a minute for a little powder. I showed her my reflector mirror, something she had never seen before. She asked me if I got up in the morning to see the children off, and I said I used to in what I called the good old days, but that now I was usually up late at night and rested in the morning. To my astonishment and humiliation, she said she usually got up, half-dressed, to see her children, and then went back to bed again.

When we joined the ladies for coffee, she chatted with two or three of them, and I brought up two or three of the American ladies with whom she chatted about seven or eight minutes. We followed the regular procedure of the hostess, bringing up different ladies to speak to her for a few minutes each. Lady Halifax, who was lady-in-waiting, had already told me in advance with whom she would chat. After about twenty-five minutes, we were joined by the gentlemen, and we went in to the pine room which had been arranged for the cameramen and had two pictures taken, one serious and one laughing.

The Queen had on a beautiful pink satin gown with paillettes, a crinoline style which she wears, the same length all around, I had on a turquoise satin dress, also with paillettes which, when I was near the Queen, seemed to become entangled in her paillettes. Consequently, in the picture mine were rather pulled to one side.

Then we went into the back room for the film. We had two of Walt Disney's, and "Good-Bye, Mr. Chips" which was long, as it had not been cut, — to use moving picture parlance — but excellent and marvelously acted.[265] I think it was an American picture made over here. It was quite sad, and after it was finished, it was very plain to see that the Queen had had a little weep, as had had most of the people.

After that we stepped into the hall where we had something to drink. Again they chatted with a few of their friends and then went downstairs. They shook hands with almost everybody as they left. I said good-bye in the hall and the Ambassador went to the car with them. After a minute's interval, the other guests said good-night and the party was over.

May 9, 1939

Lady Astor's Dinner and Dance

Joe and I went to Lady Astor's dinner at her town house, 4 St. James' Square, arriving about 8:20, as the Duke and Duchess of Gloucester were going to be there. The house was beautifully decorated with spring flowers from her garden at Cliveden, and there were a great many flowering shrubs. Their Royal Highnesses arrived promptly and went around the circle as usual.

I went down to dinner with the Duke of Devonshire, Under-Secretary of State for Dominion Affairs,[266] and we talked about his trip to Africa, where he was going to make an extended speaking tour. There were about 50 people to dinner; about half of them were debutantes, as the party was really given in honor of Lady Astor's niece, Dinah Brand. Quite a few of the ladies wore simple tiaras, although I noticed during the evening that the jewelry was not as elaborate as a year ago, when Lady Astor had a dinner in honor of the King and Queen; I suppose, being a debutante's party, everything was on a simple scale. Lord Astor was on my right and I chatted with him. I always enjoy him very much, as he is very easy to talk to and has a very engaging smile.

After dinner we went upstairs and the other guests from other dinner parties began to arrive about 10 o'clock. Kathleen had been to dinner at the Duchess of Buccleuch's[267] and Joe, Jr. had been at Lady Airlie's.[268] The party was soon in full swing. It was quite interesting, as all the representatives of London Society were there. Anthony Eden arrived, dapper as usual, and Lady Patricia Ramsay was still quite beautiful and, though not as girlish-looking, she is very stately.[269] The Duke and Duchess of

---

265. Robert Donat's performance as the public schoolmaster, Mr. Chipping, would beat out Clark Gable's Rhett Butler for the 1939 Best Actor Academy Award. Produced by MGM in Britain, *Goodbye, Mr. Chips* was the most expensive film produced in England to date.

266. Edward William Spencer Cavendish, tenth duke of Devonshire (1895–1950), parliamentary under-secretary of state for dominion affairs, 1936–40, and Kathleen Kennedy's future father-in-law.

267. The former Vreda Esther Mary "Mollie" Lascelles, one of the major lights of interwar London society and the duchess of Gloucester's sister-in-law.

268. The former Lady Mabell Frances Elizabeth Gore, eldest daughter of the fifth earl of Arran (1866–1956), author, editor, and lady of the bedchamber to Queen Mary.

269. The king's cousin, the former Princess Patricia of Connaught (1886–1974), had broken with tradition in renouncing her royal title to marry Captain the Honourable Sir Alexander Robert Maule Ram-

Kent came on from the Buccleuch's dinner and Joe danced with the Duchess. She wore a pink frock with a parure of light blue turquoise — I believe a wedding gift from Queen Mary. The combination of light pink taffeta and turquoise was lovely. One of the prettiest debutantes I noticed was Lady Sarah Churchill, the daughter of the Duke and Duchess of Marlborough.[270] Mild drinks were served, as Lady Astor is very much opposed to strong drink of any kind.

We left about 1:00 or 1:30 and the girls came along a little later.

Joseph P. Kennedy to Wesley Winans Stout

London, May 10, 1939

Dear Mr. Stout,

Your dropping me a note about the Baruch incident touched me more than almost anything that has happened to me since I have been here.[271] The fact that, as busy as you are, you bothered to comment on this state of affairs pleased me to no end.

When I was home, the President told me he had had a story planted with him to the effect that Baruch was mad because, when he arrived in London on his way back to America, he rang up the Embassy and I sent around a fourth assistant secretary to ask whether I could do anything for him. I told the President the story was completely untrue. There may be some truth in the Customs incident, however, because, when we sailed from America last June on the same boat, one of Baruch's friends mentioned that it was an outrage that Mr. Baruch had to go through the ordinary line of American visitors, considering the important position he held in the United States. At that time I thought it was merely a facetious remark and paid no attention to it.

I haven't the faintest idea where it all started, unless, as Freddie Lonsdale once said — "More people die from jealousy than from cancer." There is a small group in New York, consisting of Swope[272] and Baruch and a few others, who, I am afraid, would like to have me feel it incumbent upon myself to call upon them for advice and suggestions and if I would do that, I would be the fair-haired boy. In fact, last Friday night it was intimated to me from Washington that Baruch would be very pleased if I would call him on the telephone, because he could give me some valuable suggestions on how I should conduct the present barter negotiations between Great Britain and the United States.

Well, I can't keep up with all this conniving. I have got too much to do with really important things and if the boys want to knock my head off, it's just too bad. I am in receipt this morning of Walter Winchell's[273] column saying "there is no statute that prohibits our Ambassadors from speculating — get it?" Unfortunately, there isn't any way one can answer this kind of rotten insinuation, but, if the trend of public affairs is going to be toward more bureaucracy or Federal control, and I am afraid I am one who believes that is the tendency whether we like it or not, the question of getting men to give up their own personal interests and business and work for the Government is going to

---

say of the Royal Navy in 1919. Lady Patricia was an accomplished watercolorist and an avid sportswoman (who had been among the vanguard of ladies to ride astride rather than sidesaddle).

270. Sarah Consuelo Spencer-Churchill (1921–), daughter of John Albert Edward Spencer-Churchill, tenth duke of Marlborough, not to be confused with her second cousin once removed, actress and writer Sarah Millicent Hermione Churchill, the third of Winston Spencer Churchill's children.

271. On April 25, Stout had written JPK to say that "[r]ecently the rumor reached us from Washington that Baruch was annoyed with you. The reason advanced was that you had failed to clear him through the Customs on his latest visit to England."

272. Publicist Herbert Bayard Swope had been Baruch's former assistant at the War Industries Board.

273. Radio personality and inventor of the modern gossip column, Walter Winchell (1897–1972).

become more difficult. When I went to work for the Government in 1934, I made up my mind that I was through with stock markets, etc., regardless of what the cost might be and even during the year I was out of Government service I adhered religiously to that idea, and, in spite of the fact that I have called the turn on the markets, not only privately to the President but publicly in interviews on my return from Europe last summer, I have never speculated in a share of stock in the last five years. Johnson's attack one me, of course, is one that is made on all ambassadors; that is, becoming pro-British, but I fail to see how a man can serve his Country without being on friendly terms with the nation to which he is accredited.[274] They must respect and believe you; otherwise your efficiency is handicapped. I think the greatest shock many people have had is that they thought I could probably do a good job in business in America, but this one would be way beyond anything I had been trained for.

Besides doing the ordinary routine of this job, I have had only one interest and that is, the best interests of the United States are served by peace in Europe and not by war and my efforts have been towards that every hour of every day that I have been here. I am handicapped by my position, in that I cannot say what I think and I cannot resign and say what I think until at least the situation becomes more quiet, so that the interests of our Country will not be injured even for the shortest period of time.

You may think from this long protest that I have let these matters get unduly under my skin. Well, perhaps I have let them more than I should but it is only because I don't have a chance to hit back and because I have never seen a more complete misunderstanding of what is to me the best interests of the United States.

You were good enough to write me about this Baruch situation and I am, as I said, deeply indebted to you, because I regard it as an act of real kindness and friendship. I just want to give you one assurance: I read the Post every week and I want you to know that your anxiety for America and mine are the same. I have nine children and I have young friends and I regard them all as my hostages for my devotion to the interests of the United States, first, last and always.

Again thanking you, I am,

Sincerely yours,
Joseph P. Kennedy

Joseph P. Kennedy to John B. Kennedy

London, May 12, 1939

Dear John:

I have just sent the enclosed wire to Paul[275] and I know by this time he has passed it on to you.

After we got your letter — and it was a splendid letter — I had a talk with young Joe and we decided that in view of everything the best thing to do was to give up the idea of trying to have anything published at this time, but to get his letters in shape and to add it to it his trip to Italy and Germany and possibly Russia and Spain which he contemplates starting next week. Then, on the basis of all these spots, make up a book along

274. Likening JPK to his World War I–era predecessor, Walter Hines Page ("a British Ambassador in Washington"), bitterly anti–New Deal syndicated columnist General Hugh Johnson had testified at the neutrality hearings before the Senate Foreign Affairs Committee on April 24 that JPK was allowing himself to be taken in by London society to the likely detriment of American neutrality in the event of another European war.
275. Paul Murphy.

the line of the letters you have seen. I think this will do him a lot of good and I believe it will make interesting reading. That's for the business.

I had great qualms about bothering you to interest yourself in this matter but, after all, it was of vital interest to me and I could think of no one whose judgement I could trust, or whom I felt was more interested in the Kennedy family than yourself, so if I have added to your worries and work just put it down to that I turned to you ahead of everyone. I also want you to know that although I am three thousand miles away, I am deeply grateful for your many kindnesses to me which I constantly hear about.

So, with my deepest appreciation and warmest regards, I am,

Very sincerely,
Joseph P. Kennedy

Joseph P. Kennedy to Benjamin Cohen: *Telegram*

1 GROSVENOR SQ. MAY 16, 1939

YOUR CABLE SHOCKS ME[276] IMMEDIATELY TOOK UP MATTER WITH MACDONALD WHO DENIES STORY COMPLETELY TOLD ME ONLY THING EVER MENTIONED WAS DISCUSSED WITH WEIZMANN[277] AND PRIME MINISTER WEIZMANN CAME TO SEE ME THIS MORNING DENIES MACDONALDS STORY AND IS SHOCKED THAT AMERICAN ZIONISTS ARE REPEATING THESE UNFAIR STORIES ~~ABOUT ME~~ IT IS RATHER A PECULIAR SLANT FOR THE ZIONISTS TO TAKE AT THIS LATE DATE AFTER MY WORK FOR THEIR CAUSE HOWEVER I AM GETTING USED TO THIS TYPE OF EXPERIENCE

KENNEDY

Joseph P. Kennedy to Dr. Solomon Goldman

London, June 2, 1939

Dear Dr. Goldman,

I can't tell you how pleased I was to receive your cable.[278] I was really frightfully upset by the one I got from Ben, because, while realizing he sent it in the most friendly spirit, it seemed to me that it was another of those unfortunate things that happened to me no matter how much work I did on the Jewish problem, as witness the lying article

276. The day before, Cohen, joint drafter of Securities Acts of 1933 and 1934, had cabled "I THOUGHT I SHOULD CONFIDENTIALLY LET YOU KNOW FOR YOUR PERSONAL INFORMATION THAT ZIONISTS HERE HAVE BEEN INFORMED THAT MALCOLM [MACDONALD] HAS TOLD SOMEONE IN LONDON FRIENDLY TO THE ZIONISTS THAT YOU HAVE GIVEN MALCOLM TO UNDERSTAND THAT THERE IS NO NEED TO WORRY ABOUT AMERICAN REACTION TO THE NEW PALESTINE POLICY THAT ALTHOUGH JEWS WOULD SHOUT IT WOULD HAVE NO SERIOUS EFFECT ON AMERICAN OPINION." In February 1939, the British government had hosted a conference in London on the future of Palestine. Relations between invited Palestinian delegates and Zionists having deteriorated irrecoverably by March, however, the British government had established its own policy in the form of the MacDonald white paper, which it was to make public the following day, May 17. The white paper would reverse the Balfour Declaration of 1922, declaring the creation of an "independent Palestine state" (rather than a Jewish state in Palestine) to be government policy. Further, the white paper limited Jewish immigration to seventy-five thousand per year for the next five years after which no further Jewish immigration would be permitted ("unless the Arabs of Palestine are prepared to acquiesce"). The document would provoke outrage from Zionists and those sympathetic to the Zionist cause throughout the world.
277. Chemist, president of the World Zionist Organization and future president of Israel, Chaim Weizmann (1874–1952).
278. Rabbi Solomon Goldman (1893–1953), president of the Zionist Organization of America, 1938–40, had recently become chairman of the National Emergency Committee for Palestine, which sought to rally public opinion against the MacDonald White Paper. In his wire of May 18, Goldman expressed appreciation for what he described as JPK's efforts on behalf of Zionism and suggested that JPK "IGNORE ALLEGATIONS BROUGHT . . . BY INTERESTED PARTIES . . ."

in the "Nation" last year, after I had been of real service in getting the British Government to take action.[279] Ben's wire coming at the conclusion of another episode in the Jewish question seemed to me to be very unfair. Therefore your wire was a very pleasant relief.

If you see Ben tell him I quite understand the reason for his sending it and that I am appreciative of his interest, but that I was very much upset to think that was the result of all my efforts. Perhaps you will hear some day from Dr. Weizmann the aftermath of the whole situation.

I talked with Winston Churchill about the whole problem the other day and he told me he was not at all sure that the League would support the Government's position, but we will see.[280]

Again thanking you, I am,

Sincerely yours,

Joseph P. Kennedy to Cordell Hull: *Diplomatic Dispatch*

807, June 9, 1 p.m. The following message is Strictly Confidential for the Secretary of State:

During a conversation which I had with the Prime Minister last night he stated that he does not regard the situation in a favorable light at all; that it would not surprise him if Hitler would make a move[281] some time between now and the first of August. The most important thing that could be done, he considers, would be for France to make some gesture to Italy with regard to their demands. He is very much surprised, he stated, that the French Premier is so decidedly against even a discussion and he thinks that the determining point in trouble starting may be the failure of the French to make some gesture. After Monday he is contemplating writing a personal letter urging Daladier to do something.

In reply to the critics who say that the Duce is so bound up with the Germans that the Democracies in their desire for peace could not possibly be aided by any gesture of the French, he states that he does not feel it any stranger for him to think that Mussolini would be anxious to have some sort of deal with the French than was his prediction that the Italians would withdraw during the month of May from Spain. He said that most of his associates did not at all support his idea that the Italians would evacuate and that most of his associates also do not support the idea that Mussolini would welcome in his heart an agreement with the French. The gesture made yesterday to Germany by himself and Halifax in their statements to Parliament was Chamberlain's reply to German accusations of encirclement and the charge that the British would be averse to making any concessions whatsoever, once having attained a strong political position, and a hint to the French, at the same time, to get busy and help in cooperation.

---

279. " . . . [I]t required sharp prodding, along with Hitler's latest tornado of anti-Semitic terror to persuade Mr. Kennedy to bestir himself" on behalf of refugees from the Reich, *The Nation* contended in its the November 26, 1938 edition. The anonymous special correspondent who wrote "Kennedy and the Jews" noted that George Rublee, director of the Intergovernmental Committee on Refugees, had found JPK polite but unhelpful until the recent *Kristallnacht* pogrom. "Mr. Chamberlain himself has consistently opposed letting the refugees impair an improvement of Anglo-German relations," the correspondent concluded, " . . . Ambassador Kennedy, in his eight and a half months in London, has time and again demonstrated convincingly his slightly grim determination to collaborate with the British Prime Minister."
280. Winston Churchill too had denounced the white paper in the House of Commons; on August 17 the Permanent Mandates Commission of the League of Nations would reject the British plan by a vote of four to three before submitting it to the greater League Council.
281. Against Poland.

He is most annoyed by the Russian situation.[282] He is not at all certain that the Soviets have the faintest idea of signing the pact and he, on the other hand, if they do not accept the latest proposition, is not at all certain that he will not call the whole thing off.

The reception of the King and queen in America overwhelmingly delights him[283] and he again paid tribute to the President in saying that the President's attempt to save the world from war can never be forgotten, no matter how history is written.

As a summary of my last night's conversation with him: he felt that everything was being done by him that could be done to put him in a strong position to trade with Hitler, but he is not confident that Hitler, in the back of his mind, has not decided to take England on. In reply to my question when he thought the time would come, he answered "In August — probably just in time to spoil our vacations." It is rather on his inability to get anything out of Germany that indicates the slightest cooperation and not on any new information that his apprehension is based.

KENNEDY

Joseph P. Kennedy, Jr., 23: *Notes*

June 10, 1939[284]

Before Mr. Hull and Mr. Roosevelt ask me to go over and fight because an American ship is sunk or some tourist is killed by the Germans, I want them to answer me the following questions.

What do they think would be the economic and political effect of German domination of Europe and having licked England and France?

How much trade would we lose and how would it effect us?

What might be the political repercussions in South America?

Would the break up of the British Empire in itself be most dangerous for [us] or could we still retain our trading position to Germany after such break?

Would a policy of government planning with reciprocal agreements with South American colonies be enough to assure us of a decent standard of living if we withdrew from European politics?

Could not the loss in the level of the standard of living by withdrawing ourselves be made up by the putting to work of millions of unemployed as Germans have done?

Do we want to get frightfully aroused by the treatment of the Jews when Cat[holics] and others were murdered more cruelly in Russia and in Republican Spain and not a word of protest came?

Do we want an increasing anti-Semitism in our country brought about by the production of forty thousand Jews and political undesirables in our country from Europe having turned over our full quota to these in many cases very citizens? If you have seen like I have the type of people who are thronging our consulates getting visas and having gotten them can immediately get their families a preferential place on the quota. Do we

282. Since mid-March the British and French had been engaged in negotiations with the Soviets in an effort to arrive at a pact of mutual assistance in the event of further fascist aggression on the Continent. Negotiations had advanced only haltingly, however, due to disputes over the specific terms and guarantees that such a tripartite agreement might entail. By the first week in June discussions had reached a standstill. The British and French were unwilling to subject the independent Baltic states to possible Soviet encroachment by guaranteeing to protect them from Axis aggression.
283. The king and queen had arrived on American soil on June 7, crossing the border from Canada at Niagara Falls.
284. Joe Junior would spend much of the summer traveling throughout the Continent with Kick and their friend Hugh Fraser. On June 10 they were in Hungary.

want these people when we have eighteen million unemployed and a budget whose relief expenditures have made for a deficit of _____ [*sic*] billion of dollars?

Are we going to fight for the liberties of the people of the world when is really none of our damned business but is up to the people in those countries themselves? Are we going to guarantee liberty in every country the world and if there isn't that liberty are we going to march in? Are we going to yell bloody murder when the Italians go into Ethiopia and Spain and the Germans in Czechoslovakia and then do nothing about it except to call the English cowards for not fighting?

Are we going to continue to accept newspaper reports which always try to state the worst of all the dictatorships for that is the best news? How many prominent newspaper men and ministers I have spoken to who have said that I think this or that policy is a good idea but when I tell them at home they refuse to play it up or tell me that I am a nice fellow but just don't know.

Does it ever occur to people that there are happy people in Italy and Germany? Did it ever occur that contrary to the workers tales of woe about labor treatment in the Italian and German system the worker is by far the best off and it is rather the middle class which bears the burden. What I want to know is from a selfish point of view. I know it is terrible the way the Jews are being prosecuted but the Chinese are being bombed and Catholics were killed in Spain, but as far as I am concerned that is none of my business unless my country wants to dominate the world and impose its conditions of justice on all people and be prepared to support its laws at any time so that freedom and justice will be assured.

In other words in these days of power politics I want to know what he in it [*sic*]. I want to know if this is going to hurt my country, I want to know if it is impossible to live in a world with the dictator countries. I want to know the effect on South America.

If the experts of the US abroad believe this to be the case I think some prominent statement should come out with it at the risk of his political career and lay all the cards on the table so the American people can decide. But this I demand to be done before the outbreak of a war. America might be a deciding force in preventing war only if she is prepared to back up her statements. The speeches that Mr. Hull and the President have made and the tone of the American press have convinced many people in Europe that America will be in at the first shot or at least material will be forthcoming. The Gallup poll has shown this to be the case.[285] If this be the case let us take a positive policy let us immediately say that we feel that American interest will be threatened by German domination of Europe. If that is so then we should demand the repeal of the Johnson Act and immediately earmark credits for Rumania and Poland and whatever countries regard as of strategic importance in the stopping of the aggressors.[286] Even though we should stipulate that we would not send armed men though I [think?] we should if we decide that it is of our vital interest to interfere the mere fact of giving arms and munitions now would have a terrific effect in bolstering the morale of the countries involved. Having lost faith in England after Munich the fact that America's material is at their

---

285. "By January of this year, in the fading light of the Munich agreement," pollster George Gallup (1901–1984) had concluded in *The New York Times Magazine* on April 30, "44 persons in 100 had come to expect war during 1939, and a majority thought the United States would eventually be drawn in . . ." Further, Gallup noted that the results of the American Institute of Public Opinion's latest poll indicated that following the recent German occupation of Czechoslovakia, 82 percent of the American public had come to favor selling food supplies to the British and French and 57 percent favored selling "war materials" as well.

286. The precursor to the neutrality laws of 1935–39, the Johnson Act (passed into law in April 1934) had placed an embargo upon private loans to governments that had defaulted on their debts either to the United States or to American citizens.

disposal to stop aggression would be all that is needed. Especially in the case of Poland who is at fever pitch and needs only material and a financial loan to help them to remain strong.

If then we decide that the policy of isolation is working against our best interest I think immediately we ought to take a positive policy abroad. It is a revelation to visit some of the centers of Europe especially in the Balkans and see the hates and jealousies that exist between these people and which could be whipped up to fever pitch in just a few hours. Bulgaria Drobubja and an outlet through Greece. Rumania's refusal because of the Bessarabia Transylvania claims and the fact that England doesn't want the Slavs of the Mediterranean. Also because of the fear that they might unite with the Italians whose Ethiopian port is far away. Into these lands of jealousies and hates America would have to impose its good offices. It would be a terrific job but I think that America would do a lot and the increased feeling of security of having America to guarantee the peace of Europe would be a deciding factor.

If America decides against this policy and decides to stay out of Europe I am for one not prepared to fight having been drawn in at the last moment. War is a terrible and horrible thing and everything should be done to prevent it. I am entirely unsympathetic to the idea of blu [sic] and if my country takes part in European affairs I think that we should be prepared to fight if another country challenges us. It is this which gives the dictators power, and as far as guts are concerned I am confident that we have it plus. The only thing is that we live better and have much more to lose but to me it is better to fight now than lose in the end. I have not decided myself whether America should enter into the field of foreign affairs or whether it is [in] our interest to do so, however what I feel and strongly that unless we clarify our foreign policy we may find ourselves in the same position as the last war and being drawn in after the damage has been done and having lost the opportunity of using out terrific power to forestall a war. I myself object very much [to] the Americans urging the English to fight and calling them cowards when we are prepared to do nothing ourselves. Also if we are prepared to do nothing why then do we make the speeches for liberties and freedom etc. which has made the English and French man on the street confident that we will be with them and when the German at the same time realizes the difficulty in foreign policy in the US and knows that the President would have a lot of trouble urging us into war and probably a lot in getting us to sell raw materials to the democratic nations. When our cash and carry policy will start us selling goods but will cause us to stop as soon as the [cash?] is exhausted. When we are spending millions and millions on armaments and our military men start talking about an attack from two sides. If we really believe it why don't we do something about it and if we don't why don't we shut up and mind our own business. Why recall our ambassador and make the Germans furious and lose the opportunity to have any influence of German policy and put a chargé d'affaires there whom the Germans pay no attention to.[287] Why have we kept our ambassador at home when the English have sent theirs back so that he at least may have some influence. Why did we send an Ambassador to Germany a few years ago who did nothing but criticize the country to which he had been accredited[288] to when the real job of the am-

287. On November 14, 1938, in the immediate aftermath of *Kristallnacht*, the president had called upon the United States ambassador to Germany, Hugh Robert Wilson (1885–1946), to return home "for consultation." Wilson would never return to Berlin and the president would appoint no successor after his eventual resignation in August 1939.
288. Historian William E. Dodd, Wilson's immediate predecessor in Berlin, 1932–37. Dodd had recognized the Nazi menace early on, and, to the detriment of his diplomatic career, had expressed his contempt for both the regime and its ideology publicly on several occasions. He had been recalled in December 1937.

bassador is to keep his govt. informed and he must be on good terms with the govt. and pretend that he likes them. Why do the newspaper columnist knock your head off when you try to see as many people in the govt. as you can and say that you are pro English or pro French.

I have now visited nearly every country in Europe in my years abroad. It is true that some only for a few days but it has been long enough to open up some of the problems which are facing Europe today. I had always thought that we should stay out of war and that being a rich nation we can live by ourselves. If we can do it I hope we can but we can't and the State Dept has enough diplomats and economists in the country to lay the problem before the American people then I think we should have real policy in Europe entirely fitting for the greatest power in the world rather than a half hearted mamby pamby policy skipping one way then to the other no one knows what will happen if there is a war.

Joseph P. Kennedy, Jr., 23: *"Poland"*

June 10 1939

Although any day may see open warfare break out between this country and Germany, to the casual observer conditions here seem completely normal. It would seem that the Poles have no nerves at all and are showing a marvelous display of courage in the face of overwhelming odds. They have no fear of Germany and are ready to fight to death for their independence. Their spirit is unbeatable and the number of men that they can put under arms is very great, but the equipment of these men is the weak link. It is most difficult for one of the poorest countries in Europe to compete in war equipment with Germany. It is on this point that I can't understand the policy of England. It has been often complained that England is trying to get people to fight for her and now that she has found them she has given them no great economic or military support.

The German minister is carrying out a campaign here as they have been carrying out in the different capitals for making the other heads of missions completely jittery. They cite the fact that England can give no aid, that they let the Czechs down and they would let this country down, that this country come under the domination of Moscow, and that the complete superiority of German military strength makes resistance impossible. It has had quite an effect and is most successful propaganda.

Rose Kennedy: *Diary*

[New York] June 11, 1939

King and Queen with President and Mrs. Roosevelt at church.[289] Queen had on short dress and Mrs. James Roosevelt, the President's mother and also the President's wife had on long skirts. When we go to Windsor Castle, the Queen's lady-in-waiting always advises me how the Queen is going to dress. Whether she wears a print or a suit, an important evening dress or a lesser one, which makes it easy for all of us. Great argument on whether it is befitting for the President to serve hot dogs at a picnic to King and Queen of which they have many. Everyone unanimous in their praise of the King and Queen, especially of the Queen. Her charm, her kindness, her understanding, her

---

289. As the State Department had not given JPK leave to accompany the royal couple on their visit to the United States, he had remained in London.

constant smile which puts everyone at ease. Then, too, the unexpected incidents, the fact that they mingled with the crowd on different occasions, the fact that they spoke to the newspaper reporters on the train and saw the press at the White House, their willingness to fulfill at the social engagements under sweltering heat and overcrowded programmes. Then, too, the King's slim, straight, almost boyish face and figure, his simplicity, unaffected charm, his readiness and even eagerness to cooperate.

Joseph P. Kennedy, Jr., 23: *"Berlin"*

Berlin, June 18

One is immediately impressed here by the lack of talk about war. In nearly every other place I have been this is the only conversation but here they appear unconcerned about it. It seems it was the same way in September. The propaganda on encirclement is very strong and may serve [*to unite*] Germany as sanctions did in Italy. The material condition of the people seems nominally good. There is a shortage of coffee and they say flour is difficult to obtain. It is hard if you are entertaining to get good things and in large enough quantities. However it is far from bad and it is thought that they are canning tremendous amounts in case of war. Although there is grumbling amongst the workers there seems no possibility of any [*kind*] of a revolt even if they were led into war. In the last analysis the German does what he is told. ~~As far as I can gather the average German is very much against the policies of the Nazis and~~ the German worker complains of the numerous taxes he has to pay. Also there are collections from time to time in the restaurants by the brown shirts which takes more and more from them. Hitler is regarded by many people as a God and there is no doubt of the difference between him and the rest. The next fellow to him now seems to be Göring followed by Ribbentrop and Himmler.[290] There is a great feud going on between Göring versus Himmler and Ribbentrop. The latter are the most dangerous element. It is this element which is saying that England will not fight and [*are*] convinced that if there is a war that Germany can win within a few months. The Danzig question[291] would be a good question to fight upon because the Germans have [hate?] the Poles and they all know that Danzig is 100 per cent German. As one noted Former German diplomat said to me the other night the Poles will never get anywhere because they have not the element of Souplesse. He said that the Poles will have to choose between either Germany or Russia. They have now chosen the latter and it will certainly go hard with them.

They are tearing down the great statues [*& swastika*] *signs* which line the streets here so it doesn't look like they expect a victory parade for some little time.

Went in to see two officials in the Economic Ministry yesterday. They both had spent some time in America. It was like trying to squeeze information out of a stone. When I asked them about Germany rights is [in?] Eastern Europe they said it was a po-

---

290. Heinrich Himmler (1900–45), reichsführer-*SS* and chief of the Gestapo since 1936, as well as architect of the Reich's expanding racial purification policies and apparatus.

291. In order to provide Poland with a port, the Treaty of Versailles had designated (the predominantly ethnically German) Danzig a free city within the Polish Corridor (lands ceded from Germany to Poland, separating East Prussia from the rest of Germany). The existence of the Polish Corridor had been a source of deep German resentment since its creation nearly two decades before. In the wake of the German occupation of Czechoslovakia, on March 31 Chamberlain had guaranteed Polish independence from Nazi aggression. On April 3, Hitler had secretly ordered the army to commence preparations for the seizure of Danzig and war with Poland by September 1.

litical question and although they thought there was also room for England there they thought that it was primarily theirs. They said that the duties the US was imposing ag[ainst] their goods was political and not economic and pointed to the fact that the 25 per cent countervailing duty had gone on three days after the German troops had gone into Prague. The fellows [in the Embassy] say that it wasn't political though political events had hastened the putting into effect of the laws. ~~One of them said that world trade was a necessity but said that German economics had opened up entirely new ideas.~~ He said that they followed out Keynes' theory of underconsumption and by rapid turnover and increased purchasing power they had accomplished many things. He criticized the tie up of money in the US and said that he thought the only solution was more and more govt. control. When I asked him who bore the burden he said that it was evenly distributed and it was done by state loans and by taxation. It seems to me that they can go on as long as they have decent crops. However all their savings are soon becoming exhausted as can be seen by the fact that I B Farbisher floated a loan not many months ago at five per cent and only half of it was subscribed. Also to meet the duties on the bonds might be quite difficult and might necessitate printing more money. However there are so many tricks left at their disposal that the end is not in sight and they can probably continue like this for many years. They have had the further advantage of obtaining the agricultural goods before they pay in machinery which has given them a considerable advantage. Now the danger might [may] be the inferior goods which they are now forced to export as most of the good mechanics are in the army.

There is a tendency with the terrific shortage of labor to replace most of the easy positions by women. A young girl who wanted to take a vacation the other day went to police headquarters to get her visa and was asked whether she was working or not. She said no that she was on a vacation. They said get a job in two weeks or we will get you one.

I should think Hitler is backed by at least 80% of the people. Many of them disagree with the policy against the Jews but on the whole are with him.

One of the fellows in the Economic Ministry . . .[292]

Rose Kennedy: *Diary*

[London] July 4, 1939

I went to the 4th of July dinner where I sat next to the Duke of Kent. One of the amusing things he told me was that they had heard that when the King and Queen were in Hyde Park, they heard a terrific noise in the middle of the night and one of the equerries went downstairs to see what was going on and found the four sons dancing around Mrs. Roosevelt saying: "At last we have heard you tell a funny story!" He also said the English people were very much shocked and surprised at the President's wife writing a daily column. "My Day" has come out here in the "Evening Standard" describing the King's and queen's visit over there and the festivities.

We had the 4th of July party this year and we received in the dining room. We had not had the party last year. Fortunately it was warm outside, although many days here are too cold or too rainy to enjoy being outside. The entire group was very nice looking and quite representative, I thought, of an American gathering. There were quite a number of people from Boston.

292. The original document ends here.

Banquet: Sat next to Duke of Kent who told me accidentally he had seen Kennedys at every table at 400 Club which is supposed to be rather gay and not a place for Kathleen.[293] Joe reprimanded Kick for being there and a few nights later, the Duke apologized for telling on her (to Kathleen).

Eunice Kennedy, 17: *"A Weekend at Blenheim Palace"*

The "deb" luncheon was over at last, yet this one had not been as dull as usual. The chief topic of conversation had been the coming ball at Blenheim Palace which was to present Lady Sara Spencer Churchill to English society. Lady Sara had invited me to spend the week-end during which the grandest ball of the season was to be held. Without a moment's hesitation I accepted, and during the remainder of the luncheon lost myself in joyful anticipation of the great event.

June the 8th[294] finally arrived, and four o'clock in the afternoon I was ready to depart for the famous Blenheim Palace. Having received every beauty treatment available, I listened patiently to suggestions and instructions from numerous members of my family. At last, I hopped into the car and with baggage and maid and we were off!

As I drove through the lovely countryside, I recalled with some remorse my listless attention at history class. How vivid it all was now! Blenheim was in Bavaria, wasn't it? And the Duke of Marlborough won a great victory over the French in Louis XIV's War of the Spanish Succession? At least I knew more than the man in the famous poem.[295]

Soon, we passed through the Blenheim gateway, on top of which is a stone pedestal engraved with the Marlborough crest, — a helmet topped by three feathers, and I could see the ungraceful [*sic*] palace loom in the distance. A short drive up a winding approach, and I was standing at the foot of a long flight of steps that lead up to that imposing stone structure, which looks like a giant sentinel guarding the peaceful countryside. There is something very English about the way it retires from the rest of the world behind a grey stone wall and a gateway which alone gives indication of its character. It is no ordinary country house; it is a national monument raised to commemorate the victory from which it takes it name, and given by grateful Queen Anne and her people to the man who is still considered to be the greatest English military genius, John Churchill, the first Duke of Marlborough.

Lady Sara and the Duchess of Marlborough[296] greeted me warmly, and as it was quite late, I was escorted to my room to prepare for the ball. I walked through the many long stone corridors, decorated on either side with paintings of famous ancestors, the work mostly of Sir Christopher Wrenn.[297] Also I could see butlers and maids rushing

---

293. That is, the Embassy Club in Old Bond Street, otherwise known as The 400 Club. At the time, parents of debutantes and recent postdebutantes feared their daughters' attendance at the most fashionable of the London nightclubs might appear "fast."
294. Sarah Spencer-Churchill's' coming-out ball, one of the last and most spectacular of its kind, took place, in fact, on July 7, 1939.
295. In "The Battle of Blenheim" by Robert Southey (1774–1843), ". . . everybody praised the Duke/ Who this great fight did win./ 'But what good came of it at last?' Quoth little Peterkin./ 'Why that I cannot tell,' said he/ 'But 'twas a famous victory.'"
296. The former Honorable Alexandra Mary Beatrice Cadogan, Viscount Chelsea's daughter and a niece of Sir Alexander Cadogan, current permanent undersecretary of state for foreign affairs.
297. Sir Christopher Wren (1632–1723), the architect of St. Paul's Cathedral, did not in fact design Blenheim Palace (nor did he paint any of the portraits which it contained). In celebration of the duke of Marlborough's victory over Prussian, Bavarian and French forces at Blenheim during the War of the Spanish Succession in 1704, Queen Anne commissioned Wren's colleague, architect and playwright Sir John Vanbrugh, to design the palace for the conquering hero.

about completing final touches for a magnificent ball. Quickly I prepared for dinner, for tardiness was one American custom not accepted by the British.

At nine o'clock a terrific din, loud enough to re-echo in London, announced dinner. Slightly nervous, yet very excited, I made my way through the hallway now clustered with servants whose eternal thrill was to sit and watch the aristocracy arrive. I found myself not the first to enter the reception room, where great battles are still being won in Brussels tapestry and heavy gilded mirrors are still hanging on the crimson walls. After waiting a few moments for royalty, (who, incidentally arrive ten minutes after ~~the older people according to rank filed into the banqueting room, while the younger group, regardless of~~ other guests), the older people according to rank filed into the banqueting room; while the younger group, regardless of rank, entered a smaller dining room. Although royalty dined with us in the person of the young and handsome Prince Frederic of Prussia[298] — and though there were numerous now stolid butlers dressed in knee breeches and powdered wigs, nevertheless, dinner remained quite informal. Again, I noticed a custom different in America. One must have patience and "bon appetit" and endurance to survive an English ten course dinner which includes appetizers, soup, fish, game, greens, dessert, sweets, savory and side dishes. And this night, was a gala night! Blenheim chefs daily prepare 20 meals for guests and staff. "How does the English youth remain so slim?" I questioned myself. When dinner was over, the ladies withdrew to the Duchess' cream and gold sitting room and the gentlemen were left to talk and joke over their brandy.

Within a few minutes, the music started, the men joined their partners, and gallantly filled their names upon the programs of fluttering debutantes. I noted with interest another exception to the rule. No "cutting-in" is permitted at these dances. The Big Apple, the foxtrot, and the Lambeth Walk were danced to the lively swing of an American orchestra. Round and round we glided in a ballroom of flowers; lilies, pink and white hydrangeas took the place of the 20,000 valuable books — for the library was converted into a ballroom for this occasion. Gloxinias and malmaisons had the spotless white marble wall as an exquisite background, and huge brilliant chandeliers sent sparkling light into every corner of the room. Guests continued to arrive until at midnight more than 600 persons waltzed to the Blue Danube.

The ladies made a beautiful picture with their bouffant dresses, brilliant tiaras and glittering jewels, while the men were equally handsome with their shinning decorations always worn in the presence of royalty. One of the loveliest figures was that of Madame Balsan, the mother of the Duke of Marlborough.[299] She wore an exquisite white brocade gown with a diamond collar and her sapphire jewels accentuated the beauty of the grey haired, dignified lady.

At one o'clock the guest gradually began to diminish [sic]; some enjoying supper in the banqueting room, while others strolled outside to enjoy the beautifully light[ed] terraces and fountains overlooking the lake. As the dawn crept over the Easter [sic] skies, the houseguests closed the party with a breakfast of coffee and "hot dogs"! And then exhausted, yet happy, tumbled into bed.

The best part of Saturday was unknown to me for like everyone else, I appeared for luncheon at 2:00 P.M. We discussed every aspect of the party, and the possible im-

---

298. Prince Friedrich Georg Wilhelm Christoph (1911–1966), youngest son of Prince Wilhelm, last crown prince of Germany, was studying at Cambridge at the time.

299. New York heiress Consuelo Vanderbilt (1877–1964) had married the ninth duke of Marlborough in 1895. By 1906, after having two sons together, the couple had become estranged; they divorced in 1920. The following year she married again, this time to Lieutenant Colonel Jacques Balsan, and began to devote herself to charitable work.

pending war. After lengthy debating, each of us decided upon an afternoon sport, either tennis, golf or riding. I chose tennis, but was rather a failure as my weary muscles refused to move. After tea, we played prisoner's base and relays all of which I had learned in primary years; yet it was great fun.

In the evening there was an experimental blackout because of the constant fear of war. The very suitable game of hide and seek was thought of, and from nine o'clock until twelve thirty, fleeting shadows rushed through Blenheim, here and there knocking someone or something down. In an attempt to hide, I gracefully fell down six steps, — uninjured except for a broken flashlight, which I considered as part of my person for the time being. I ask now, where is [sic] the cool humourless English! Certainly this weekend they were hard to find.

Sunday morning dawned with the inevitable Sunday rain. The Blenheim bus took me and several others to Church; the rest planned to go in the afternoon. Upon returning, I finished the morning with a game of croquet, and a friendly religious argument.

At lunch I noticed the napkins, like my bedroom sheets, were embroidered with the crown and an elaborate "M." Later I went bike riding with the Count of Rosslyn[300] over the extensive grounds of Blenheim. Occasionally we greeted Sunday excursionists who are allowed to use parts of the grounds as a park. We paused a moment at the statue of Marlborough mounted on a 130 ft. pillar upon which is inscribed the Acts of Parliament, and a record of the Duke's four campaigns. Mooing cows grazing peacefully in the meadows in unmilitant contrast. Swiftly, we rode through acres of land preserved for hunting and shooting, and on past the nine small lodges at the Blenheim frontier, then by the kennels and the huge farmyard. At twilight we turned back. I again, saw the castle on the hill cold and somber, yet warm with human associations.

All the houseguests supped early, and reluctantly I left Blenheim Palace with memories of a glorious week-end and glowing appreciation of true English hospitality.

Joseph P. Kennedy to Franklin Roosevelt

London, July 20, 1939

Dear Mr. President,

I think you are up to date on everything I know about the international situation, but I thought you would be interested to get my observations on the political situation in England.

My own belief is that the Chamberlain Government, coming down the last stages of a hectic career, is having some difficulty with their representatives, but not nearly enough to challenge their leadership. The attempt to put Churchill in the Cabinet, supported by the Opposition Conservatives in Chamberlain's own Party backed by some of the prominent newspapers, reached a high about last Sunday and has been rather going down hill.[301] The demand is very much like the demand there is in the United States: when there is dissatisfaction if anybody brings out any kind of an idea backed

---

300. Lord Loughborough, Anthony Hugh Francis Harry St. Clair-Erskine (1917–1977), who would succeed his grandfather as sixth earl of Rosslyn and Baron Loughborough two months later.

301. "In March [1939]," Churchill recalled after the war, "I had joined Mr. Eden and some thirty Conservative Members in tabling a resolution for a National Government. During the summer there arose a very considerable stir in the country in favour of this, or at least for my and Mr. Eden's inclusion in the Cabinet." By summer, he continued,

[a]s the weeks passed by almost all the newspapers, led by the *Daily Telegraph* (July 3), emphasised by the *Manchester Guardian*, reflected this surge of opinion. Thousands of enormous posters were displayed for weeks on end on Metropolitan hoardings, "Churchill Must Come Back." Scores of young volunteer men and women carried sandwich-board placards with similar slogans up and

by a newspaper campaign, it receives considerable impetus, but, unless it is very sound, falls of its own weight.

I talked to Eden about this. Of course he feels that the Government should have been broadened a long time ago. By that he means representatives of Labor, representatives of the anti-Chamberlain group in his own Party, and representatives of the Liberal Party. But Chamberlain's idea always has been that the difficulties for which he would want an All Party Cabinet would be for international reasons and, since the program he is carrying out is practically the one that they have all wanted, if he broadened it at this time he would merely make his international policies the subject of continual football playing.

I talked to Lord Baldwin about what he thought of the political situation and he felt strongly that, after all, Chamberlain was responsible to the Country and that if Churchill were admitted to the Government, he would, being entirely different from Chamberlain, so irritate Chamberlain that it might mean a very serious situation and result in a very bad mess.

Today I talked with Chamberlain about it. He told me he is unwilling to admit Churchill, because he does not believe in the first place that he could deliver nearly one-tenth as much as people think he could; he has developed into a fine two-handed drinker and his judgment has never been proven to be good. Chamberlain is also convinced that if Churchill had been in the Cabinet, England would have been at war before this.

There is one issue, however, that is giving Chamberlain a good deal of concern, and that is a demand throughout the Country for an increase in old-age pensions and up to the minute he has not been willing to do anything on this because of the increased cost. He told me today that he was giving it very careful consideration and thought he would probably have to do something in order that the Party would not run the risk of being licked on an issue that the world would not at all understand.

I would think that, on the basis of the present situation and their willingness to patch up their fences before they go to a national election, which may be in October, assuming there are not international difficulties, the Conservative Party under Chamberlain would win quite easily.

I thought you would be interested in getting this brief survey of the political situation.

With my warmest regards, I am,

Sincerely yours,
Joe

Joseph P. Kennedy to Joseph Patterson[302]

London, July 20, 1939

Dear Joe,

The cigars arrived in good shape and I will see that they are well appreciated.

---

down before the House of Commons. I had nothing to do with such methods of agitation, but I should certainly have joined the Government had I been invited.

302. Joseph Medill Patterson (1879–1946), editor and publisher of the *New York Daily News*, the first viable American tabloid. Between 1914 and 1925 Patterson had served as publisher and coeditor (with his cousin, Colonel Robert Rutherford McCormick) of the *Chicago Tribune*. Patterson's sister Eleanor (or "Cissy") was owner, editor and publisher of the *Washington Times Herald*.

I can't tell you how pleased I was with the comments on Joe and Jack. After all, I am most anxious that they should know their responsibilities as citizens of the United States and the heads of the Kennedy clan. Therefore, I have devoted much time and attention to trying to make them aware of what's going on in the world. But the fact that you and Mrs. Patterson noticed some real development and were kind enough to mention it pleased Mrs. Kennedy and me no end.

I was delighted that you both could be with us for a while and see the goings on over here. I am sure it has given you some new angles on the problems as they are. I have one parting suggestion: Please do all you can to keep the United States financially strong. That's their best hope for their future.

With all our best,

Yours sincerely,
JPK

Joseph P. Kennedy to Cordell Hull: *Diplomatic Dispatch*

*1031, July 20, 6 p.m. The following is strictly
confidential and personal for the Secretary of State:*

Wohlthat, Göring's right-hand man, and I have just had a long talk on economic questions. Hitler, he told me, has definitely decided in his own mind that his ultimate victory will be made possible by the mistakes the British are making. To his own group, Hitler has admitted that his major mistake was the taking of Czechoslovakia in March, which was prompted entirely by military considerations. Hitler, Wohlthat feels, intends to wait the British out and see the effect of the mistakes they are incurring, such as the complete failure of the discussions at Moscow, the inability to recognize the Polish needs, Rumania and other countries, the way the Tientsin affair is being handled,[303] and the building up of the encirclement idea throughout Germany which is permitted by the speeches being made in England. Hitler believes all of these things will make his problem that much easier if permitted to run their course. It is Hitler's belief that the British will not take the gamble of plunging the world into war over anything as small as the Danzig incident and any move that England and her allies would be willing to stop by force of arms at the risk of a general world war will not be made by Hitler. Two important impressions were received by me from my conversation with Wohlthat; first, Wohlthat thinks that because Hitler believes his position is being improved by the tactics of the British every day, he is not disposed to strike quickly; and secondly the military authorities, and Herr Wohlthat was a former member of the German General Staff, say that it does not make any difference, if it is necessary to fight, whether Germany strikes today, in one month or three or six months. He also said that in appraising the actions of the British the German General Staff have come to complete agreement with Hitler that there is nothing left for Germany to do but fight if the British continue

---

303. The murder of a Japanese bank official by a Chinese terrorist in the British concession at Tientsin on April 9 had given rise to increasing tensions among the British, Japanese and Chinese factions within China. British hesitation in handing over the four suspected Chinese coconspirators to Japanese justice had prompted the Ministry of War in Tokyo to authorize a blockade of the British concession by mid-June. Late in June negotiations had reached an impasse. On July 24, Sir Robert Craigie, the British ambassador in Tokyo, would enter into talks with the Japanese government, which by early August would ease tensions sufficiently to avert armed conflict for the time being.

go the way they are going, but they must first of all pick their spot and then not worry about the outcome.

When I asked Wohlthat if it were possible that Hitler realized that the economic situation of the whole world is becoming precarious, he said that he does, but that now while the political movements of the British make his problem that much easier, no economic problem need by considered.

I realize of course that, after all, while Wohlthat is high in Göring's confidence, nobody knows Hitler's mind, and that the idea is one that cannot be dismissed of getting propaganda over to me. I received the important impression from him that Hitler is not disposed to hurry or to worry about economics, nor to make any conciliatory moves as he feels his position is improving so much politically by the bad tactics of the British. He feels that however bad his economic condition is becoming his political position is improving proportionately due to British stupidity.

KENNEDY

Joseph P. Kennedy: *Diary*

July [20] 1939

I went to see Prime Minister before I went away on vacation. He said he would have been disappointed if I had not. He thought the situation looked much better. He told me Wohlthat was after all Göring's man and nobody was *close* to Hitler. And after all he decided everything. (See my wire to Washington.)

I told him from his point of view of preventing war was unfortunate that the Neutrality Bill hadn't passed.[304] He said, "Yes, but after all everything had broken against him except as yet we hadn't gone to war." He said he had no intention of putting Churchill in Cabinet. In the first place he would not be near as good a man as people thought and 2nd if he were there he thought England would be in war long before this.

Reminding me of what Baldwin had said, "If he was a lot of trouble outside the Government he was 20 times more trouble inside and I've served with him in a Cabinet."

(Halifax at luncheon I gave him at Embassy on being questioned on Russian negotiations said, it was very strange because they were *not* negotiations. The British and French came to meeting with Molotoff.[305] Told him what their Gov't had to say and

---

304. By summertime the administration's proposals to repeal the 1937 Neutrality Act's arms embargo and implement a modified "cash and carry" policy for belligerents attempting to purchase arms and munitions from the United States had foundered in Congress. After contentious debate on the House floor on June 29, the bill presented by Representative Sol Bloom, acting chairman of the House Foreign Affairs Committee, had passed but had emerged so much diluted as to be almost unrecognizable. On July 11, the Senate Foreign Relations Committee had voted twelve to eleven to postpone consideration of Chairman Key Pittman's bill and all other proposed neutrality legislation until the start of the next session in January. Neither the message that the president sent to Congress on July 14 (arguing that "the arms embargo plays into the hands of those nations which have taken the lead in building up their fighting power") nor the special meeting of senators that he convened at the White House four days later had prompted Congressional reconsideration of the neutrality issue before the summer recess, however.

305. The chairman of the Council of People's Commissars, 1930–41, and an unflinching supporter, aide and confidant of Stalin, Vyacheslav Mikhailovich Molotov (1890–1986) had succeeded Litvinov as people's commissar for foreign affairs in May. Unbeknownst to the British and French (with whom the Soviets would continue to negotiate a pact of mutual assistance throughout the summer), Molotov was simultaneously engaged in talks with the Germans that would culminate in the Nazi-Soviet Nonaggression Pact in late August.

Molotoff said nothing — no argument, no discussion — just nothing. Halifax added it was "It was pretty hard to negotiate on that basis."

Joseph P. Kennedy: *Diary*

Friday, July 21, 1939[306]

Last night Rose and I had dinner with the Kents for the King and Queen and Prince Paul of Jugo Slavia[307] and his wife.[308] Rose has the list of guests.

I sat on the Queen's right and Duke of Kent on her left. As at all parties I have observed her at dinner she passed up the soup and then she also started to pass up the fish. Kent sold her the idea she should try some and she then took a little piece. She then had some of all the rest of the dinner except the ice. She drank champagne and at the finish drank a glass of Cointreau.

In our conversation she again made it clear she liked Betsy Roosevelt very much. She said in their ride with President on his farm Betsy had lost her hat three times. She didn't like Ethel Dupont[309] very much. She thought her kind of snippy. She liked the Roosevelt boys very much although she hadn't seen much of Elliott, who had only come for a short time she thought.

She didn't think too much of the women of the New Deal but again reiterated how kind all the people had been to them. She said Secretary Wallace[310] had shown up at meetings with a 3-day growth of beard on his face and she didn't like Hopkins[311] although her recollection of him was very faint. She said Mrs. Roosevelt had been most considerate of Hopkins' daughter.[312]

They had never seen a hotter place than the White House. She said after the lawn party at the British Embassy she had come back to her room and was so exhausted she actually had to lie on the floor in her room. She again spoke of how charming the President was and I think she considered him the tops of all.

She again reiterated that the President had told her and King that he realized he was moving too fast but he saw no alternative. She thought it a mistake for him to come to England now because of political situation in USA. He told the king and Her on their way to RR Station he absolutely did not want to be a candidate.

(The King before dinner called me aside and asked me about the letter I had written to the president about the German submarines in the Atlantic.[313] Said he knew

---

306. That day JPK would leave London to meet his family in the south of France, where he had rented the *Domaine de Ranguin* outside of Cannes.

307. Prince Paul (1893–1976) acted as regent of Yugoslavia after the assassination of his brother, King Alexander I, in 1934 until his own overthrow in 1941.

308. Princess Olga of Greece, the duchess of Kent's sister.

309. A week after graduating from Harvard, Franklin Delano Roosevelt, Jr. (1914–1988), the fourth of the six Roosevelt children, had married heiress Ethel du Pont (1915–1965) in Wilmington, Delaware, on June 30, 1937.

310. Henry Agard Wallace (1888–1965), secretary of agriculture, 1933–40. Later, Wallace would serve as vice president, 1940–45 and as secretary of commerce, 1945–46.

311. Former director of the Works Progress Administration and Federal Emergency Relief administrator, Harry Lloyd Hopkins, secretary of commerce, 1938–40.

312. When Hopkins's second wife, Barbara, died of breast cancer in 1937, Eleanor Roosevelt had taken the couple's five-year-old daughter, Diana (1932–) under her wing, even offering to become the child's guardian in the event of her father's death. During the royal visit, the first lady had made a particular point of introducing Diana to the queen while the latter was in evening dress. The queen's "spangled tulle dress, with her lovely jewels and her tiara in her hair made her seem like someone out of a story book," the first lady reported to Hopkins later.

313. On June 1, JPK had written the president that Admiral Godfrey of Naval Intelligence had recently told him "in very great secrecy" that

nothing about it and asked me to keep him posted if I heard anything one way or the other. Said his people had not told him about the incident.)

Queen said she thought President had a real affection for me although she had the impression from some, we fought quite a bit.

She said she had 2 hours at Hyde Park with Morganthau and it was quite enough. She was not at all impressed. She enjoyed the "hot dogs" and when I said how upset people were over here about Mrs. Roosevelt writing all about the visit, she said the trouble was they didn't understand about her writing.

I told her Collier's wanted to pay her £30,000.00 for 5 articles. She laughed and said, "I certainly could use the money but guessed it was impossible."

Talked over broadcast of Mrs. Helen Reid, who had been trying to get the Queen to broadcast over *Herald-Tribune Forum* in October.[314] (See letter of Halifax.) The Queen told me that Hardinge[315] had spoken to her but she thought she shouldn't do it now. It wouldn't seem the right thing. But of course if anything turned up in Sept. or Oct. and it was thought wise she would be glad to.

I told her Queen Mary had been to the Embassy at dinner. And she said, "Yes, I wrote her a note and told her how lucky she was to meet so many interesting people. When I got out all we met from the beginning of the season to the end are Crewes and Londonberrys etc. — dinner after dinner." She said Queen Mary had had a fine time.

She told me when she got to Baltimore and stepped off the train, a woman approached her with a bouquet of flowers and the Queen almost fainted. The woman was a dead ringer for Mrs. Simpson and the Queen said, "I didn't know what to think. I knew she came from Baltimore and after I realized it couldn't be she, I thought it might be her sister. Anyhow I had a few uncomfortable minutes."

I then told her how anxious I had been for the King and Queen to get to USA as quickly as possible. I recognized how attractive they were and I realized how completely mistaken America was in its judgment of them. In addition and by far most important I realized how difficult it was for them both to have Windsor sitting on the side lines and people talking about their coming back to live and I recollect that rainy day last September when the Queen was christening the Queen Elizabeth, I had gone to the Palace with the invitation to the King and Queen from President Roosevelt to come to USA. It was raining hard and it certainly looked like war. The King had said to me, "He'll have to come back of course if there is war" (meaning Windsor) and a more troubled man didn't exist.

She thanked me again for all I had done and said they always wanted to go to USA and when they got Roosevelt's invitation, they felt free to go.

---

there is no question but that there are six large submarines operating in the Atlantic; that two of them are relieved from time to time by two others from Germany; that they are being supplied by ships which they think have their bases in Brazil.

The danger, Godfrey says, is that if trouble were to start, the British would have to furnish convoys immediately for all of their ships engaged in trade with North and South America. He wondered whether it would be possible to have the Pan American air pilots keep on the watch for the bases for these supply ships and also whether a hint could be passed to the Brazilian Government that these things were taking place.

314. In 1930, Helen Rogers Reid, vice president and advertising manager of the *New York Herald Tribune* (and the wife of its owner Ogden Reid), had founded the annual Forum on Current Problems, at which a number of prominent speakers discussed current affairs and world events in the ballroom at the Waldorf-Astoria in Manhattan.

315. Sir Alexander Hardinge, later Baron Hardinge of Penshurst (1894–1960), private secretary and adviser to both Edward VIII and George VI, 1936–43.

I told the Queen that Halifax had had a message from Danzig (see my despatch next evening to Hull)[316] and I felt well and if I hadn't been dining with the Queen I would get tight. She said, "by all means do it. Don't by any chance let dining with the Queen stop you."

I told her I had received a letter from Doris Fleeson of *New York Daily News* saying the Queen had made a great success but she thought the King had made an even greater one. As I said a woman if she is pretty and charming had a great start but the King was in a tough spot. But he handled himself marvelously well. She thought so too and was much pleased.

When we were finishing dinner Kent passed around quill toothpicks and King gave one to Rose and they all started picking their teeth (if American children saw this there would be plenty of discussion back home — almost like picking up asparagus and eating with their fingers.) I looked over at Marina[317] and she promptly picked up her napkin and held it in front of her mouth.

When dinner was finished the ladies left the room after a long talk and Kent went round the table and asked the King whom he wanted to talk with. The King evidently said, "The Ambassador" because Kent called me around and asked Halifax to come and talk to Prince Paul. I went around and the King, Kent and I sat down together. The King asked me if I minded the cancellation of the Lawn Party. I said frankly I didn't and the King laughed and said it had been the first cancellation he ever knew of.

Kent then said he had met a Massachusetts man at the installation of Masons at which he was elected to succeed Duke of Connaught. And the King said it was most interesting because never to anyone's knowledge had a woman's name been mentioned at such a meeting but today the Massachusetts man had spoken of the King and "Her Majesty Elizabeth." The King was much pleased and thanked the gentleman personally.

The King then said he had never heard Kent speak before, because of course they have never gone to meetings where the younger brother had spoken. He started to give him advice on speaking. He should speak louder. He should work with his (King's) vocal teacher. Kent said he read from his notes but the King said he got the first and last word of a sentence and put in his own words. (He must do this before he starts. I don't think it possible for him to do it after he once has it on paper.) I said Kent had done a fine job at 4th of July speech, and Kent said mine was fine. The King said, "I don't suppose you have any trouble with your speeches — you have never had a defect of speech." Rather pathetic but quite courageous.

King then started to tell me how difficult it had been growing up. Kent joined in this. How unfair and unreasonably the King had always been — continually throwing up to him that he had a defect and made him so self-conscious. Kent said he had been treated worse because of course Wales had his own money so he was the only one left to develop on his own because he was independent of the King. It was apparent from both of them that they just missed hating their father. (Lady Oxford had already told me before how cruel the King had been to the boys.) I rather got the inference here that Wales had sort of been tough on York.

316. He refers most likely to his Dispatch No. 1041 (sent not the next evening but at 10:00 A.M. the following day before leaving for vacation) in which he recounted his observations of the previous evening's dinner. Additionally JPK noted that Halifax had received a wire from Albert Forster, the Nazi gauleiter of Danzig, informing the foreign minister that Hitler had not increased his demands on the city during his visit there that day. Forster went further to say that the führer "'was in no hurry and thought the Germans and Poles should play down all discussions of agitation in their newspapers and see whether anything might work itself out automatically." "The foreign minister was pleased, but Prince Paul was very distrustful," JPK remarked.

317. The duchess of Kent, the former Princess Marina of Greece and Denmark (1906–68).

The King while drinking his brandy then told me that Canterbury's speech the Sunday after Abdication sounded o.k., but when it was read it was the cruelest thing that ever happened to him. Canterbury said first King was sickly and second he had a defect in his speech. King said he was so stunned it took him along time to get over it.

He then turned to me and said, "I hope I have changed people's minds by making the Canadian & USA trip which certainly couldn't be made by a sick man. And I hope that my last speech at Guildhall persuaded people that I have improved that." He said one very interesting thing. He said, "I made that speech straight at Churchill" (I don't know what was behind this unless something Churchill had said when Wales gave up the throne.) I commented I had seen Churchill while speech was being delivered and he was impressed and had said so to me on leaving the Guild Hall.

King told me that the first use of the word, "His Majesty" was made by Napoleon I and words in "God Save The King" changed from original when Queen Victoria reigned to "Glorious."

Kent told a story that he was visiting at King's school at Canterbury the Archbishop of Canterbury spoke for 35 minutes (which bored him to no end) and then finally introduced him as Duke of "York." ("The old fool," said Kent.) I nudged him and said, "I'm not York," but Canterbury just laughed.

We had a very gay talk. I told the King I had told the Queen that while she had had a glorious success the King had had a greater one because he started way behind her. He was pleased and so was Kent.

After dinner Halifax hurried away and I talked to Prince Paul who is very pessimistic about the whole situation. (See my wire.)

When the queen was leaving, she joined Paul and me and he told her he saw no hope for anything good and I said the Queen might help the cause because the people of 2 nations love her. Paul sees the end of all that is good.

Franklin Roosevelt to Joseph P. Kennedy

Hyde Park, N. Y., July 22, 1939

Dear Joe:-

I suppose you know of the latest "Krock" in the Times about you, and I think you begin to agree with me that that particular gentleman, with his distorted ideas of how to be helpful, has done you more harm in the past few years than all of your enemies put together.[318]

---

318. In his July 18 piece, entitled "Why Ambassador Kennedy Is Not Coming Home," Krock argued that although JPK had for some time considered resigning and returning to the United States for personal reasons, the recent intensification of the European situation had prompted the president to urge him to stay on "until next fall at the earliest." Moreover, Krock argued, the president feared that JPK's departure at that time "would quickly engender rumors of differences of opinion." The piece also raised the issue of administration leaks about JPK to the press:

> The young New Dealers have long ceased to approve of Mr. Kennedy. For several weeks this year they engaged in a propaganda campaign against him, funneling—through willing newspaper channels—a series of reports that he was in White House disfavor because he wanted to make terms with the dictators, because he had "gone British," was a member of the Cliveden (appeasement) set in Great Britain, and spoke somewhat less than adoringly off the record of his chief. Except that Mr. Kennedy was being dragged toward the doghouse by the tales these counselors were bringing to the President, none of these statements was true. But they were sedulously circulated for quite a while.

I tried to correct the impression by telling several people the other day that I have complete confidence in you, that you have never mentioned leaving London, that you are doing a good job there, and that in these critical days I count on your carrying on.

It is true that some people are getting things printed like the enclosed, which you have doubtless seen, but things like this have small distribution and are so frankly hostile and silly that they do no harm. Krock, on the other hand, has never in his whole life said a really decent thing about any human being without qualifying it by some nasty dig at the end of the praise.

He is, after all, only a social parasite whose surface support can be won by entertainment and flattery, but who in his heart is a cynic who has never felt warm affection for anybody — man or woman.

It is a pity that the Republicans as a whole and some weak-kneed Democrats have made it impossible to pass the Neutrality Bill at this session. In any event, the responsibility is definitely pinned on them, and I feel, with you and the British Government, that the delay has given comfort to the aggressor nations. The other night I got them to agree at least to take the matter up in January. In the meantime, all we can do is to pray that another actual crisis will not arrive.

Drop me a line to tell me your inside thoughts about the present situation. Joe Davies is pretty pessimistic.[319]

My best to Rose and the children,

As ever yours,
F.D.R.

Joseph P. Kennedy to Franklin Roosevelt

Cannes, 9th August 1939

Dear Mr. President,

Your letter made me happy — not only what you said but the whole tone of it. By now you will have received my last wire despatch and my two letters.[320] They constitute my latest thoughts, with any degree of accuracy, on the present situation. But, in the mood of your letter, I should like to add some personal observations and comments.

The chief thing I have noticed in the South of France, on the part of caddies, waiters and residents, is a very strong anti-Semitic feeling. Beyond that, and a general sense of wary waiting for almost anything to happen, I can contribute nothing to an understanding of the international state of affairs.

As I told you when I was home, over here one feels out of touch with conditions at home, and reading these rotten reports by columnists anyone "with a temperament like mine" feels very unhappy. I am sure you know that no job in the United States Government appeals to me in the slightest degree except as it affords an opportunity to work for you. I have said repeatedly that in the two important positions I held in the United States I never received one word of dictation or even suggestion as to the policy

319. In his July 18 attempt to persuade the Senate not to abandon the issue of neutrality revision until the next session, Roosevelt had called upon U.S. ambassador to Belgium Joseph Edward Davies (1876–1958) to repeat the account of a rapidly worsening European situation that he had earlier that day presented to the president himself.

320. Dispatch No. 1041, of July 21, describing the dinner for Prince Paul, and JPK's two characteristically "bearish" letters of July 20, describing first his observations of the political situation in Britain and, second, what he viewed as "the makings of the worst economic conditions the world has ever seen" (the latter of which does not appear in this volume).

I should adopt, and that it is only working under such conditions that I should be at all happy.

I realize that certain friends of mine have occasionally put me in very embarrassing positions. At such times I have felt it silly to be in a place where I could not straighten matters out with my boss at a minute's notice.

About my position in England my only thought was to wonder whether my experience and knowledge were not being completely wasted. After all, I recognize that in this day and age an Ambassador may be hardly more than a glorified errand boy.

I do get a bit discouraged for, although I have worked harder and longer hours in this job than on any job I ever held, it seems that three quarters of my efforts are wasted because of the terrific number of things to be done which seem to have no close connection with the real job at hand.

Of this one thing, though, you may be sure. Regardless of any personal inconvenience, as long as I am of any assistance to you, I shall remain for whatever time you like.

I had a talk with Steve[321] when he was in London and I dare say he told you what I said.

When I was a youngster, my father taught me two principles: gratitude and loyalty. About the first, he told me that I should never let any act of kindness go by without in some way returning it. Because he said, 90% of people seem to forget favors and kindnesses done them. Of the second principle, he said, no matter how you may fail in ability you can make it up by being unfailingly loyal to your friends.

I have tried to live up to those two principles and, to you personally; I owe a debt on both counts.

That I have carried out your assignments to me in a way that merited your approval pleases me no end.

Have a good holiday, and remember that whatever you want to do, I always "stay put."

Again my warm appreciation for your letter and your thoughts, and many thanks from the entire Kennedy family.

Sincerely
Joe

Joseph P. Kennedy, Jr., 24: *"Unity Mitford"*[322]

Munich, August 21, 1939

The city is terribly calm and no one would think there was a prospect of war. The people looked very serious but there was no feeling as there was in London and in Paris during the last crisis. At noon over the radio came the announcement that Ribbentrop

321. Early, the president's secretary.
322. The fourth of Lord Redesdale's daughters, who, by 1939 were becoming as well known for the extremity of their political inclinations as for their beauty, wit and literary proclivities. The Honourable Unity Valkyrie Freeman Mitford (1914–48) had first come into contact with Hitler at the Nuremberg rally of 1933 through Sir Oswald Mosley, the leader of the British Union of Fascists who had since become her brother-in-law. By 1939 Mitford had lived in Germany for several years, during which she had come to know and, indeed, idolize Hitler; he in turn regarded her as "the perfect Aryan type." Less than two weeks after meeting Joe Junior, distraught at the state of war by then in existence between Britain and Germany, Mitford would shoot herself in the head. The bullet lodged in her skull but having recovered sufficiently to travel, Mitford would be returned to England in 1940. She would die of related complications in 1948 at the age of thirty-three. Unity Mitford's youngest sister, Deborah, had come out with Kick the previous year; later the two would marry brothers.

was going to Moscow to conclude the terms of the Russian non-aggression pact.[323] Everyone smiled knowingly and it could be seen that they attached a great deal of importance to it.

Unity Mitford is one of the most unusual women I have ever met. She is not at all pretty, with very bad teeth and terribly fat, however with a certain fine Aryan look. She doesn't impress you with personality but rather seems to be in a state of high nervous tension in which she has no great interest in other things but thinks only of the Führer and his work. She never refers to him as Hitler but always as the Führer and looked at me rather funnily when I called him Hitler as if I was taking his name in vain. She says that the international situation was the result of a complete misunderstanding. She said that Hitler had a tremendous admiration and fondness for the British and would do them no harm unless they forced his hand. I asked why and she said on the purely racial question, the only reason they are playing ball with the Italians is because the English won't try to play ball with them. She says he hates the Japanese and is afraid that they might dominate the world. She hadn't heard about the Russian agreement but was delighted for now she said the Poles and the English won't fight. She thought that the situation in England and the United States was due mainly to Jewish propaganda and the only way to clear it up was to throw them out. Of course she felt sorry for them but you had to get rid of them. When I asked her about marching into Czech she said that the Führer had to do it. Of course he had provided not to but conditions had changed so much that he had to do it. The important thing was race and the Poles and the Czechs are not a great race and unfortunately they must be under the domination of the others. Anyway, she said they will be better off under Germany, maybe not now but you will see in a few years.

She believes Hitler to be more than a genius; those who know him well consider him as a God. He can make no mistake and has made none. He spends as much time in looking after detail as he does on great things. He picked out all the pictures for this exhibition. He can work for a week without sleep and not show it. Why should England want Eastern Europe? It is rightly German and they should have it. England can have its empire. Even though England got beaten in battle the Germans would give England its empire for they could not run the world by themselves. The English could teach the Germans how to live. It would be much better if the English got defeated. She has been afraid to go to England lately for fear there would be a war and that she would be caught there. She said the feeling at home is very strong against her.

She is the most fervent Nazi imaginable, and is probably in love with Hitler

---

Joseph P. Kennedy: *Diary*

[London] August 24, 1939[324]

At 10 o'clock in the morning Sir Horace Wilson called up. I haven't heard from him for a year on 'phone. I just can't make myself like him. He seems so damn supercilious and at the same time makes me feel he does not like Americans. Asked me if I had any word from President as to what he might do.[325] I told him I had talked with Bid-

323. The pact would be signed three days later.
324. The announcement of the Nazi-Soviet Nonaggression Pact had brought JPK back from the south of France unexpectedly early, on August 22.
325. That day Hitler elevated the gauleiter of Danzig, Albert Forster, to the position of chief of state.

dle and had planted the idea of getting the Poles to talk but that the President would not be arriving back in Washington until 1 p.m. "Please let me know at once if you will as the P.M. is anxious to know."

He called up later after lunch but we had no word. He called me at 10 o'clock at night. I said I had an appointment to speak to White House at 11 p.m. I asked him if he wanted me to advise him and then added that since there was nothing could be done why not let me notify him in the morning. I realized that what had to be done must be done right away.

About 12 o'clock I got the White House and Welles sitting with the President listened to my conversation. First of all, I asked Welles if he understood the import of my request for President to get in touch with Poland. He said, yes, but it could not be done the way I suggested. I said I didn't care how it was done so long as something was done and quickly. He said it would be done tonight — "whatever is going to be done." He asked me what I thought of the Italians' message and I said I thought it was lousy.[326] He seemed surprised and asked why. I said first, the idea of addressing anything to King of Italy, whom people here had considered as nonentity for years did not make the dramatic hit that Roosevelt's style usually did. He said they had to address it to King as head of the State. I said nevertheless, it did not go over as far as England went. Everybody appreciated President's efforts but it wasn't a smash.

The next morning on my desk I received the telegraphic copies of wires to Hitler and Poland — not in code — for release at 10 a.m.[327] I called up Wilson about 9:45 and read them "slowly" (as he requested) in the 'phone. He thanked me and said, "God bless you" and hung up.

Later in the day news despatches carried word of Neville Henderson being summoned by Hitler for conference and then the word he is flying to London.[328]

We try the foreign office for some word as to what this means.

Sterling of course had been breaking due to Gov't decision to withdraw support. So in answer to England's notice to us we received assent from Johnny Hanes, Acting Secretary,[329] which seemed to say, "Well England's done it without discussing it beforehand much, so what the Hell!"[330]

---

326. Late that night the president had appealed to King Victor Emanuel of Italy to influence Germany and Poland to settle their differences peacefully.
327. Roosevelt sent a similar appeal to both Chancellor Hitler and President Moszicki of Poland to resolve their disputes without resorting to war.
328. Ribbentrop's announcement of the Nazi-Soviet Nonaggression Pact on August 21 (three days before its signing) had prompted an emergency meeting of the British cabinet at Downing Street on August 22. By nightfall, the ministers had drafted a personal message to the führer in the form of a warning that Britain intended to honor her obligations to Poland. By midday on August 23, Ambassador Henderson delivered the message during the first of two meetings with Hitler; at the second he would receive the reply.
329. Undersecretary of the Treasury John Wesley Hanes, Sr. (1892–1986), was a former member of the SEC, 1937–38, as well as a former governor of the New York Stock Exchange.
330. JPK expanded upon the issue in his Diplomatic Memoir:

> On August 24, in an effort to check the flight of funds from London, the Bank rate was raised from 2 to 4 percent and, in an attempt to avoid exchange control, the British the next day withdrew their support of sterling. Under the Tripartite Agreement they were under a duty to discuss the subject with our Treasury before taking action. Events moved so fast, however, that on the afternoon of August 24 the Treasury without consultation determined to act the next morning and apologetically notified us of their intention. John Hanes, who while Morganthau was touring Europe was Acting Secretary of the Treasury, when he learned of the proposed British action at first, literally blew his top. I reached him by telephone, explained the circumstances and the fact that the action had not been premeditated, calmed him down with the end result that he gave out an appreciative statement to the press.

Butterworth[331] relayed this to British Treasury and in the afternoon, Sir John Simon called me on 'phone to explain the reason they hadn't discussed it with us was because affairs had moved so quickly this week that they had tried to protect the pound but they were losing so much gold that they just couldn't stand it any longer. They were now down to about 2 billion (France now had a little more than they — about 2½ billion). He also said they had received nice note from French telling them ok and congratulating them for not putting on exchange control. Simon asked me to explain to the Gov't and Mr. Morganthau, who they said they could not contact, just what their problem had been. As I agreed they were up against a tough chain of events I said I would be glad to. And I promptly called Johnny Hanes in Washington and explained the facts. Johnny understood my explanation and gave out a nice statement in Washington. What was worrying them was the fact that the Oct. 1936 statement made it imperative to throw England out as under present state gold could not be earmarked any longer.

I also pointed out to Johnny that if the worst happened over here I wanted to be consulted on any step taken on handling British securities if by any chance they didn't consult me first and also any suggestions as to handling their gold.

He said he would be delighted and would more than appreciate my help.

(To go back). While Simon was asking me to speak to Treasury I asked him what was new on Henderson's visit to Hitler, he said a message had been received but was being decoded, but from what he could gather "The door was not completely shut." I thanked him and hung up. There was constant agitation all that afternoon wondering what Hitler had said and Welles called up to ask if I had heard anything.

About 6:30 o'clock Butterworth and I went to the Foreign Office to turn over to the British the final authorization to sign the Cotton and rubber Agreement and while there was asked Sir Mounty what was new on Hitler and he told us that Henderson had called on Hitler. I said he was about 6 hours late.

I then went down stairs and asked to see Cadogan. After about 10 minutes I saw him and asked him what was new and he said that 2 messages were still being decoded. I asked him if he had any idea and he said that he had had a 'phone conversation with Henderson and got the idea that there were some hopes of working something out but he could not give me any idea until the messages had been decoded. I asked him if he would call me up when they were decoded, as the President was very anxious. And since he had been of great help on the letters to Poland and Germany they should keep him posted. Fine, he said he would.

I went back and sent a short message to Washington and then went home. After dinner I tried to locate both Cadogan and Halifax, but could not. At 10 o'clock I decided to call Sir Horace and try to force a showdown. I located him at #10 and I asked him if he had any news and he said he had a lot, but didn't think he could give it over the 'phone. I immediately said, "Would you like me to come around?" He said that would be fine — could I possibly do that. I said, "I'll be there in 10 minutes."

I jumped up. Jack Kennedy[332] was with me and we called a taxi (we had no cars that night at 14 Prince's Gate)[333] and speeded off to 10 Downing St. When we arrived,

331. The financial attaché of the American embassy.
332. The former RKO representative in London, now JPK's private secretary at the embassy.
333. The American ambassador's residence.

there was quite a crowd outside and I could hear the murmurs go through — "The American Ambassador."

I rang. They promptly let me in, and walking down the long corridor, I ran into Sir John and he thanked me for the message I had sent telling him I had straightened out his matter in Washington. He introduced me to his granddaughter Pat, aged 15, a fat girl who bears a great resemblance to Lady Simon. I said, "What's new?" He said, "There's still hope — you know, he said, I went through one war I don't want to go through another." He said, "You're going to see Wilson, well I must be going back to No. 10." I said, "How is your golf game"? He replied, "You know I've been playing pretty well — well, we must have a game, Good-night!"

Then Wilson's secretary brought me into his office and after a few minutes Sir Horace came into his office out of the Cabinet Room carrying some papers in his hand. I was sitting in the chair alongside of his desk and he came over and handed me the papers and said, "We thought the best way was to let you read the despatches as they came and then come into the Cabinet Room."

I changed glasses and proceeded to read. First, there came Henderson's report of Hitler's state of mind, and then the text of the conversation between him and Hitler, then the memorandum given to him by Hitler outlining the proposition for the British Cabinet. And then a short memorandum on some items Henderson had forgotten in his 1st and long memorandum.

Incidentally this was the memorandum that contained the item that Hitler omitted from his report of the conversation that "why both with Poland because he, Hitler and the Russians, had their plans to practically cut it up." Well after I read them all I said was, "okay" and he said come along. So I followed him into the Cabinet Room.

Chamberlain was sitting in the PM chair dressed in a dinner jacket. Across the table sat Halifax in his regular business suit. And on his right sat Cadogan in evening clothes. The P.M. asked me to sit down next to him and Wilson sat down on my right.

The P.M. turned to me and said, "What do you make of it?" I said, "If it weren't for Henderson's additional memorandum of Germany-Russia cut up of Poland, I would be convinced that Hitler was disturbed and really wanted to either try some new tactics of driving a wedge between the Poles and England or he had the wind up."

I noticed in front of each of the men that they had a copy of each of the telegrams that I had read and they were variously marked and underlined and alongside was a sheet of foolscap on which each was making notes. I noticed as I talked or made a suggestion they underlined the parts I had reference to.

P.M. asked me various opinions of the text and what I thought Hitler meant. And then we proceeded to discuss it. (See my report to Washington which I wrote out in longhand when I got back to Chancery).[334]

We then talked on the possibility of the answer. I said I felt strongly he could not quit on Poland no matter what else happened. He would jeopardize not only the honor of Britain, but would completely break his political party. They all agreed on that.

I then suggested that the answer contain a suggestion that if he accepted a reasonable Polish settlement perhaps he could get U.S. and other countries to get together on an economic plan that certainly would be more important to Germany than what he could possibly get out of getting anything in Poland. I said, "You must pass the hat before the corpse gets cold." Meaning, get U.S. now to say what they would be willing to do in the cause of International Peace and Prosperity, in which we would probably be the largest

---

334. His Dispatch No. 1262, which would be received in Washington the following morning at midnight.

beneficiary. I said, U.S., if a proper plan would be sold them, might very well put in between 1–2 billion in gold on the ground they would get it back many times over if an international economic settlement could be made.

Well, we talked it all out for another half hour and then I rose and as I went by the P.M.'s chair I put my hand on the back of his shoulder and said, "Don't worry, Neville, I still believe God is working with you."

(Halifax told me the next day that Henderson had told him that Hitler had worked himself into a frenzy while he was talking with him against the Japanese because they were displeased over his Russian Pact). (He must think he is God).

When I left No. 10 I thought to myself that incident has probably been the most important thing that has ever happened to me. Here I was an American Ambassador, called into discussion with the P.M. and Foreign Secretary over probably the most important event in the history of the British Empire. I had been called in before the Cabinet and had been trusted not only for my discretion but for my intelligence. It was a moving experience. The next day I said so to Cadogan and told him I felt greatly complimented to have been asked into that terribly important meeting and he said, "We are very happy to have an Ambassador here that we feel we can trust — whose judgment we respect and appreciate to give us another point of view."

It is now Tuesday night and the British have not yet given out the text. And the answer which went forward last night was just about what we had discussed at our meeting including the economic paragraph for bait.

Saturday I spent the morning in the office seeing people and sent a small addition to my wire of night before. Had lunch at Claridge's and came home to bed and went out to Croyden to meet Rose on her way from Cannes.

Joseph P. Kennedy: *Press Release*

American Embassy, London, August 24, 1939

The following statement was today issued by Ambassador Kennedy at the American Embassy:

The international situation has reached a point which makes it advisable for American travelers to leave England.

We feel that it is our duty to warn those Americans now in England that, by remaining longer, they are running the risk of inconvenience and possibly danger. They are also contributing to the anxiety of those at home and will, if an emergency develops, make it harder to care for those compelled to remain. Moreover, we must remember that a large body of foreign tourists would be a considerable burden, in the event of trouble, upon the resources of a country faced with grave problems of its own.

All those who do not have any important reason for remaining are, therefore, urged to return to the United States without delay. Accommodations are now available on most vessels. The same may not be true in another day or two.

This notice is addressed at this time particularly to tourists. All Americans who do not leave are requested to register immediately at the nearest American consulate if they have not already done so.

Joseph P. Kennedy to Sumner Welles: *Diplomatic Dispatch*

1223, August 24, 11 a.m. PERSONAL AND CONFIDENTIAL
FOR THE PRESIDENT AND THE SECRETARY OF STATE.

Sir Horace Wilson called me this morning and told me he saw no hope of avoiding war unless the Poles were willing to negotiate with the Germans. As things stand now that is the place to apply pressure. The British are in no position to press the Poles strongly, but if anything is to be accomplished action must be taken at once, as the Prime Minister feels the blow is fairly near.

KENNEDY

Joseph P. Kennedy to Sumner Welles: *Received Diplomatic Dispatch*

RUSH 1262, August 25, midnight.

I have just been at 10 Downing Street with Prime Minister, Halifax, Cadogan, and Horace Wilson. They have discussed with me the Henderson interview.

Hitler seemed calm and earnest. He pointed out that he always wanted a deal with Great Britain but he was not deterred by Great Britain's actions of yesterday. He was indignant with the Poles for their persecutions of his people, firing on airplanes, et cetera, and if they said they did not, it showed they had no control over their subordinates. He was going to have his rights in Poland even if it meant a great war, from which England would suffer much more than Germany. He now had Russia to back him up with supplies and therefore he could go on.

If, however, he could get straightened out in this Polish business he would make a deal with England that would guarantee the British Empire forever. He would limit armaments and then Germany and England could proceed to economic satisfaction. Henderson kept pointing out that England could not make any deal that the Poles did not want, and Hitler said he did not want England to break her word and in the next breath said that Poland had no future anyway because Russia and Germany would settle Poland. This last remark was said to Henderson but was left out of report of meeting which Hitler sent to Henderson after the meeting which purported to be the gist of the conversation. Hitler urged Henderson to fly home to persuade Britain to accept his proposition which was:

One. That Poland adjust her differences with Germany at once. Two. England agree and urge this and in return Germany would agree to respect and even fight to preserve the British Empire.

Three. Hitler would limit armaments, go back to peaceful pursuits, and become an artist, which is what he wanted to be. (Aside by Kennedy, he is now but I would not care to say what kind.)

Four. If this was not agreed it was going to be a war worse than fourteen-eighteen.

Writing this out it looks like a ridiculous proposition to make Great Britain quit or cut away from the Poles but to hear the text as read it seems much more reasonable.

Chamberlain and others do not know just whether the proposition is (one) throw sand in their eye while he marches in or (two) whether he really does not want a fight with England or (three) whether it is a proposition on which something can be done. They are going to listen to Henderson in the morning and then probably say.

We certainly will not agree to permit Poland to be carved up by you and Russia.

Nor are we willing to force Poland to make concessions based on these probably ridiculous charges of cruelty but we are willing to help negotiate a fair deal and perhaps with all other powers work out some economic future for the world.

Incidentally Hitler asked for a settlement from Britain on the colonies but on a time basis and as he said by fair negotiation.

They are not going to give this message to either (?) [*Sic*] or French until they have thought it out very carefully and have heard Henderson.

During the conversation Wilson asked whether the President had received any answer from Hitler. I said I had not heard of any.

Chamberlain held up Henderson's wire and said, "This is the answer."

KENNEDY

Joseph P. Kennedy: *Diary*

Friday, August 25, 1939

I thought I would add a few notes of my visit to Chamberlain on Wednesday 23 that were not contained in my wire to Washington.

He looks like a broken man. He said he could think of nothing further to say or do. He felt that all his work had come to naught. "I can't fly again because that was good only once."

He urged me strongly to do what I could on my plan to interest Roosevelt to work on Spain which, being Catholic, certainly could not like the Russian-German Pact, Italy which did not want to fight, and Japan might be brought in too because of the Russian Pact. He felt strongly the Japanese and Polish were the two fronts to concentrate on. He of course was shocked at the conduct of the Russians and I told him of the Hearst editorial praising his conduct and he was quite pleased. He reiterated that he had never believed in them or trusted them but was really forced into discussion by force of misguided public opinion.

He thought the war would proceed for a while. Then both sides seeing they could not accomplish anything would discuss peace, come to an agreement, that they might be coming to now [*rather than*] after "millions of young men are dead and our financial and economic position almost destroyed."

He was visibly moved.

Joseph P. Kennedy to Sumner Welles: *Diplomatic Dispatch*

Telegram sent August 26, 1939
PERSONAL FOR THE UNDERSECRETARY

Following is Joe's account of his visit to Germany that I spoke to you about "I have just come back from a trip to Munich, Berlin and Hamburg and I am sure that the German people do not want a war and are pretty well convinced that there will be no war. Firstly, they think that the signing of the Russian pact will make England back down and that a war with Poland will be just a question of a week or ten days. Some of them told me that before signing of the pact with Russia they thought that a general war might result. Now they were sure that it wouldn't. It is hard to believe that they are so confident that there will be no war. I think that the mounting of anti-aircraft guns in Berlin made some impression upon the people but on the whole they don't realize the seriousness of the situation. In Hamburg where connections with the outside are much closer, the fact that the British ships steamed out and the constant influx of Danish papers which are widely read has made them fully conscious of the danger, but I did not meet one who believed that war would result. They felt that even if British stood behind Poland that the Führer would find some other way out of it. The Russian pact has had a terrific psychological effect in that now they are confident that England and France can do nothing. Most of them are baffled but they feel that it was a very clever diplomatic move. Many of them ridiculed it and I have seen the closed fist given in salute quite openly amongst friends. The press have done a complete about face and are now praising the scenery in the Crimea and the immense potential business with the Soviets. All of this yet they have not caught up with it in time to stop a moving picture disclosing the Russian element in Spain which is being shown in some of the theatres as propaganda against the Red Government. It has been such a turn about that I don't think that the Germans will swallow it whole. However it is so important strategically that for the time being they are accepting it on this basis and shaking their heads. The anti-Polish campaign is beyond description. Every edition of the newspapers has a more gruesome tale to tell of Polish outrages against the Germans, of planes being attacked and of German soldiers tortured. In the news-reel about ten minutes was given over to showing the real German background of the city of Danzig. The Nazi banners, the Fascist salute and the goose-stepping soldiers were all featured. After this they showed the women and children who had been turned out of their homes by the Poles. With tears streaming down their cheeks they bawled into the microphone their tales of grief. Even children told theirs. In the middle of their speech they would break down in a flood of tears and the effect of this must be most powerful. Hitler has gone so far with his people now that it is impossible for him to back down. The people are behind him and I don't think there will be any reaction against him even though he leads them into war at least for some time. They dislike the Poles anyway, they feel that Danzig is a German town, they have Russian backing and they have faith that Hitler won't lead them on the wrong course. This is supported by the most powerful propaganda I have seen anywhere and you may be sure that if war breaks out the Poles will be shown to be the aggressors and it will be the duty of every German to stop them."

KENNEDY

Joseph P. Kennedy: *Diary*

August 27, 1939, Sunday

Stayed in bed, read the papers, went to 12:00 noon Mass, had lunch, went back to office. Had a call from Welles — anxiously awaiting news. I told him there was none until Cabinet met. At about 5 Cabinet broke up I 'phoned and asked for Halifax. He came on the line and I said, "I'd like to see you." He said, "I'd like to see you but I'm terribly tired and am going home to bed for a couple of hours." And I said, "Why don't I come down and get you and drive you home." He said that would be fine — come down in about 10 minutes to the back door and I said, "Fine, when I get there I'll send word up to you."

As I was driving the Chrysler I jumped in and dashed off. When I got down to the back door there was a tremendous crowd and I drove the car in and jumped out and amid cheers for U.S.A. walked into the door and asked the man to tell Halifax I was there.

While I was waiting Vansittart came in and then along came my old friend the black cat of 10 Downing Street — of last years fame.

Halifax came down and I told the detectives to get the crowd out of the way as I had to back the car up. Well, we both went out the door together. Halifax remarked jokingly as the crowd cheered, "The 2 popular men in England." I went alongside and got in on driving side and Halifax went other side. He is so tall he had great trouble getting into the seat alongside of me. He took off his hat and put his bags and umbrella on the back seat and I started off with the crowds cheering and the detectives waved me back when all of a sudden my bumper caught under the mudguard of a car at right angles to me and I was stuck. They waved me forward slowly and waved me back. I couldn't budge. The crowd laughed — were very gay. Halifax and I both laughed heartily. Finally the police asked about 8 or 10 strong young Englishmen to come over and lift the car, which they did and so amidst the crowd's cheers they lifted the car up and put me on the road. Then Halifax said, "Let's drive ahead and then go round to the left. The police can clear the way." We did and off we went with every one giving us a cheer. Halifax is definitely popular. While we were stuck, people stuck their heads in the window — men and women — with "God Bless you!" "Please don't let us go to war." "You'll save us we know" "I don't want to send my boy except to fight for Britain not for Poland" etc. As we drove away Halifax said, "Quite a sight, the great British Public lifting the car of the American Ambassador to safety."

Halifax was definitely tired. He said he was going to have a nap for 2 hours and then have dinner with "Alex"[335] and Neville Henderson to go over the ground carefully. We drove home slowly and he gave me the story (see cable).[336]

Joseph P. Kennedy to Henry Kittredge[337]

London, August 30, 1939

Dear Henry,
    I have wired you today as follows: —

"Deeply appreciative of your help with Robert. With due regard for the uncertainties of situation here I am planning to enter him September nineteenth and am writing you today."

Of course, by the time you have received this letter, the whole situation here may have changed, but it still has many difficult points.

Bobby has never been away to school. He will be fourteen years old in November and has had the unfortunate experience of having attended a great many schools, due to my moving around so much. The fact also remains that he has been here a year and a half now and, of course, may be out of touch with the requirements of St. Paul's School. I think he is reasonably smart, with a great lack of concentration, which has been a serious handicap to him so far. However, he is earnest and industrious and anxious to get along, so if you can be a little patient with his first experience away from home and the fact that he has had, as I say, great difficulties in that he has been changed from school to school, and that he has not been instructed primarily for American school requirements, you will be doing a great service for me and the boy.

I am planning to send him with his brother Jack, who is returning to Harvard this fall, possibly the end of next week. He will be in Boston on the 18th of September to attend his Grandfather's fiftieth wedding anniversary and will go right from there to Concord. If there were any instructions that might not reach me in time by mail, you could

335. Cadogan.
336. In his Dispatch No.1289, JPK reported that the British Government was "very anxious" to promote "good relations" between itself and the German Government, "but of necessity . . . they [could not] compromise with any terms that do not protect their commitments to Poland," and would therefore attempt to continue negotiating.
337. Henry Crocker Kittredge (1890–1967), JPK's Harvard classmate, was at the time acting rector of St. Paul's School in Concord, New Hampshire.

cable me, at my expense, because, even if censorship is put on, they will still take wires for the American Ambassador.

Mrs. Kennedy will probably be in America around the 18th and will of course come to see you, if that would be of any advantage whatsoever.

I am deeply appreciative of your kindness in helping me out at such short notice and, always having had such great admiration for St. Paul's and having a justifiable pride in the fact that you are running the establishment, I hope Bobby will be able to make the grade and go along with you.

With warmest regards,

Sincerely yours,

Joseph P. Kennedy: *Diary*

Sunday, September 3, 1939

I left the country[338] intending to go to Church — then the office and at 12:00 to go to Parliament to hear what I thought would be the speech of the Prime Minister declaring war.[339] I thought after hearing Greenwood's[340] speech and Sinclair's[341] Saturday night complaining of P.M.'s action in even considering Mussolini's offer[342] of peace and Jack Kennedy's telling me of spending the evening with some of the young fliers who were disgusted with Chamberlain because again he seemed to be hesitating. These boys and all of the rest of the Country and those smart people in USA who wanted England to fight will soon see what Chamberlain was trying to save them from. It is a terrible thing to contemplate but the war will prove to the world what a great service Chamberlain did to the world and especially for England. If he had permitted Hitler to go to war at Munich he first of all would not have had:

1. Public opinion with him. A great many people in England and especially in the dominions were not at all convinced that Hitler's demands on Sudetenland were not fairly reasonable.

2. The French for 6 weeks previous to Munich had been urging the British to work out something, as they were committed by treaty to Czecho, they weren't at all anxious to fight.

3. England's condition to meet an air raid attack was almost pathetic. They couldn't have licked a good police force attack in the air. Anti aircraft guns and organization was pathetic. The Germans would have come over and slaughtered the people.

---

338. J. P. Morgan, Jr., had lent Wall Hall, the abbey he had restored in Hertfordshire, to the U.S. government for the use of the American ambassador.

339. On September 1 the German army had crossed the Polish border, and German aircraft had begun bombing Polish cities. Additionally, Forster, the Nazi leader of Danzig, had signed into law an act of union linking the city to Germany. Poland had called upon the British and French to honor their guarantees of her independence as a result. The British and French governments in turn had issued ultimatums to Germany (which, for lack of response, would be repeated the following day) to remove its forces from Polish soil by noon at the latest on September 3 in order to prevent war.

340. An early and outspoken critic of Nazism, Arthur Greenwood (1880–1954), acting Labour Party leader, had questioned the delay in fulfilling Britain's obligations to Poland, which by then had exceeded thirty-eight hours.

341. Liberal Party leader Sir Archibald Henry Macdonald Sinclair, later first Viscount Thurso (1890–1970), had seconded Greenwood's sentiment, to the cheers of his colleagues, by arguing that "the sitting of this House would not have been held in vain if it had demonstrated to the world that the British Parliament would not tolerate delay in the fulfillment of our honourable obligations to Poland."

342. On August 31, Mussolini had proposed a conference to revise the Treaty of Versailles to the British and French governments.

Well, Rose and I came in the car. I got off at Farm Street and as there was no Mass at 10:30 o'clock, Rose went immediately to the Brompton Oratory. (Where she said later there were very few men, nothing but women.)

I came immediately to Chancery where Johnson informed me of the ultimatum Britain had sent Germany that war was on at 11 o'clock[343] unless Germany answered the note England had sent them.

At the same time the broadcast announced that Chamberlain would broadcast to the nation at 11:15. I cleaned up my desk, sent for a small radio from the house in a hurry and had it set up. (Copy of P.M.'s speech here) I listened to the speech in my office with several of the staff. It was terribly moving. And when he got to the part of his "efforts have failed", I almost cried. I had participated very closely in this struggle and I saw my hopes crash too. Immediately Chamberlain stopped speaking, I picked up the receiver and asked for the P.M. I was astounded that he should come right on the 'phone but he did at once. I judge it was Horace Wilson who answered the 'phone because he said, "hold the line for the Prime Minister."

I said, "This is Joe, Neville, and I have just listened to the broadcast. It was terrifically moving." He said, "You heard it?" And I said that it was great, really fine and it was terribly, terribly moving. I said, "Well, Neville, I feel deeply our failure to save a world war." He said, "We did the best we could have done but it looks as though we had failed." I said, "It does indeed, Neville, but my best to you always." He replied, "Thanks, Joe, my best to you always and my deep gratitude for your constant help — Goodbye — Goodbye."

I hung up. His voice still quivered, deeply moved after his broadcast and he spoke to me with real feeling.

Almost as I finished talking and was getting ready to go down to Parliament to take part in the proceedings, people rushed around saying the air raid warning was sounding. And sure enough it was. I urged every one to get out and they went to Molyneaux, the dressmaker across the street, who had a reasonably good basement. The car drove up with Rose in it and I told Joe and Jack to take her at once to Molyneaux.

People rushed into Embassy but as we had no air raid shelter (see Messersmith's letter of Feb. 24)[344] they congregated in the entry until I had some of our staff take them to Molyneaux. A number of Americans started right then and there to holler for boats and a lot of women were panicky. And I noticed quite a few white faces amongst the men. Comments such as, "He didn't wait long" — "Isn't that like Hitler to hop in 25 minutes after war was declared?" I went over to Molyneaux's to cheer people up and found most of them in pretty good shape.

Well, it was over and finished — a good dress rehearsal. This war is definitely not going to have the long run they predict. The woman and children at home in *all* belligerent countries are going to have a terrific moral pressure on the men fighting. All countries will be damn sick of it pretty soon because their wives and children will all be subject great danger.

Well, Joe, Jack, Rose and I rushed down to Parliament at 11:45 and when we got there and were just taking our places at 12:05 another warning came and we all went down to shelter in House of Parliament. This proved to be very short and the all clear whistle came quickly and we all marched back.

---

343. The time at which the British ultimatum was set to expire; the French ultimatum would expire at noon.
344. Assistant secretary of state for administration (and later, Truman's ambassador to Cuba, Mexico and Argentina), George Strausser Messersmith (1883–1960) had presumably refused JPK's request for funds.

I took my seat with the other Ambassadors and Mr. Chamberlain started to read his statement, when one of the attendants came up to me in the balcony and waved me out for a very important telephone call. When I got to the stairs he told me it was the President. It was then 12:25 — London time, 6:25 — Washington.

I got myself a private office and was surprised and pleased to hear Missy's voice. It was sad and she told me how she was thinking of me and really was terribly sweet. Asked me to call the President, as he wanted to talk to me. She said how proud she was of the way I was doing this job over here and the President was too. I thanked her and said I hoped I'd see her soon. She was crying. When I got back up stairs, Chamberlain had finished and Greenwood was speaking (Get speeches and list of speakers from daily papers.)

We left and I came back to Chancery and then went home to Embassy to lunch. I then sent Rose back to country and I came back to Chancery, listened to King's speech (his method of delivery is becoming better and better). (I imagine he is worrying now about Windsors coming back).

I talked to Hull — gave him the news of War Cabinet[345] — told him of our 2 air-raid warnings and answered miscellaneous questions. He sounded to me like a tired old man (one thing I forgot to say was that when I was leaving Parliament I ran into Beverly Baxter,[346] who thanked me for all I have done. He said he had left his wife and children in Canada and I said, "Will you leave them there." He said, yes, he thought so. He went on and Nancy Astor who had heard him said, "Why should he leave his wife and children in Canada — let them come home here and work like every one else." She was sobbing at the prospect of losing 5 boys, but plenty game.

I also ran into Dalton, the opposition leader.[347] He said, "Now all is fine, I was worried last night that there was no attention being paid to Article 1 of Treaty with Poland."[348]

Joseph P. Kennedy to Cordell Hull: *Diplomatic Dispatch*

1393, September 3, 11.20 a.m.

The Prime Minister has just broadcast that no undertaking having been received from the German Government to withdraw its troops from Poland, Great Britain is in consequence at war with Germany.

KENNEDY

---

345. Chamberlain's peacetime cabinet had resigned to be replaced by a streamlined wartime counterpart, according to the model established in 1916. Most of those ministers who remained were taken from the previous cabinet with the exceptions of Lord Hankey, who was to serve as minister without portfolio and Winston Churchill, who was to be first lord of the Admiralty.
346. Canadian-born editor, journalist, drama critic and author, (Arthur) Beverly Baxter (1891–1964) had been elected as a conservative MP from Wood Green in 1935, after serving Lord Beaverbrook as managing editor of the *Daily Express* and *Sunday Express*, 1921–29, and as editor in chief and director of the *Daily Express*, 1929–33.
347. Economist, Labor MP for Bishop Aukland and former chair of the party's national executive committee, 1936–37 (Edward) Hugh John Neal Dalton, later Baron Dalton (1887–1962), had been an early proponent of British rearmament.
348. According to the Agreement of Mutual Assistance between the United Kingdom and Poland, concluded on August 25, "[s]hould one of the Contracting Parties become engaged in hostilities with a European Power in consequence of aggression by the latter against that Contracting Party, the other Contracting Party will at once give the Contracting Party engaged in hostilities all the support and assistance in its power."

Joseph P. Kennedy to Cordell Hull: *Diplomatic Dispatch*

1443, Sept. 4, 12 midnight. Strictly Confidential. Personal for the Secretary.

I asked Halifax, when I saw him this evening, how he felt about the whole thing. He said his feeling reminded him of a dream he once had in which he was being tried for murder. When he was finally convicted and found guilty he was surprised at the feeling of relief that came over him. Now it was very much the same. He had planned in every way to stave off a world war and had worked himself into a sad state of health. Now that he had failed he found himself refreshed for the new struggle. One of the things he was greatly worried about over the past few weeks was that war might break out anyway on some issue that Poland would not accept, that would be infinitesimal in the entire negotiation, and that England and the world might be plunged into a war over something that he, Halifax, would feel in his heart was not issues but the result of a major mistake in political tactics. He felt, at any rate, that England's position was quite clear.

As to the situation today:

A large squadron of planes flew at 25,000 feet over Hamburg and other German cities last night and dropped five or six million leaflets in Germany. They were fired on but no planes came to fight them. Some of the leaflets evidently flew into Holland from where there were cries today that her neutrality was being broken. All the planes swore they were not near Holland. Probably the wind took the leaflets there. Tonight they are going again.

As to their own bombing, they are very carefully watching to not give the Germans an opportunity to say that the British are killing women and children first and Germany is finally forced to fight back. The French wanted to make a raid by air last night, but the English persuaded them to wait until the heads of their general staff had gone over the matter and made arrangements for both countries to work together on bombing plans. The generals return tonight or tomorrow morning.

The position is a very difficult one: the Poles want help and the French are "leaning on the Siegfried Line" with two million men. What, as the French, are the English going to do?

In the first bombings on the Western Front, the British feel there is great danger on world public opinion, particularly the United States, on the course taken by either side. As a matter of fact, I think a good deal of this war's strategy is directed with one eye toward the United States.

Now as to the present position in Poland. Lord Halifax said that at the Cabinet meeting this morning, General Ironside[349] stated the Germans were adopting tactics that were wholly unexpected by the Poles. May I suggest that a map of Poland be used to follow this outline. The Poles expected the Germans to press forward across the Corridor, after they had taken Danzig, which, of course, they knew would require no strategy at all, and the Poles planned to fall back to the Vistula and make their stand there. The Germans, however, advanced only slightly at this point. They marshaled 37 divisions near Krakow and proceeded to cross the line in parallel columns. One important thing to consider in this strategy, Ironside said, was the fact that the Germans must get through the peaks of the mountains, following a difficult crossing, soon. If the Poles make it too tough for them, so that it requires a couple of months to make any headway, the Germans will encounter considerably [*sic*] difficulty in advancing or retreat-

---

349. The recently named chief of the Imperial General Staff, General Sir William Edward Ironside (1880–1959), later field marshal and first Baron Ironside, had visited Warsaw in July to confer with high-ranking Polish government and military officials.

ing, so even if it did surprise the Poles there is a possibility of some real good coming out of this change of German tactics. To the Army this description may make some sense, but as neither Halifax nor I have the slightest knowledge of tactics, it means nothing to us.

As Halifax talked it became more and more apparent that what Britain depends on more than anything else to end the war before the world collapse is Germany's internal collapse. They have definite confidence in their secret service reports that the gasoline and oil supply is definitely not over four months, that there is a definite feeling in Germany against war, that if it got too tough economically Hitler would be out. How this will turn out remains to be seen.

The British tactics are to try in every way to propagandize Germany that the fight is against Nazism and not against the German people, etc. etc.

Now as to Mussolini. Britain is being constantly told by the Balkan States that as soon as Hitler has polished off Poland, Italy will show her true colours and join Hitler. This is not Halifax's thought. All his secret advices are that Mussolini does not want to fight with Hitler and if he attempts to lead the Italian people in a fight against the British he is afraid of a bad internal situation.

Halifax said there was in England a certain group of hot heads who wanted to deliver an ultimatum to Mussolini to within ten days fight or stand with England. Halifax and, I think, Chamberlain are against that on the ground that it would be another sanction mistake and might easily be the move to lose the sympathy of the Italian people. Unless Italy makes some hostile move they are going to consider her, for the present time at least, as an honest neutral.

Lord Perth,[350] at the meeting between himself and the British and Dominions press correspondents regarding censorship, said two things are forbidden:
1. To speak slightingly of Mussolini;
2. To speak of drawing America into the war.

KENNEDY

Joseph P. Kennedy, Jr., 24: *"Sept 4, 1939"*

The war has gone on with no outstanding developments except one which broke like a bombshell early this morning. It seems the Cynthia [*sic*] a British ship carrying over three hundred Americans was torpedoed off the Hebrides without warning.[351] As far as we know now most people were taken off by a life-boats except those killed by the explosion. It ought to cause tremendous feeling in the US, and may make for a new neutrality bill. I don't know why the Germans do things like this especially in not following out the submarine agreement signed by the different nations. The Admiralty rushed boats but did not arrive 'til 12 o'clock today and I think by that time most of the people had been picked up.

There have been no outstanding reports on the war, and it doesn't look like the Germans have let themselves go. They have made only occasional attacks on Warsaw

---

350. The first secretary general of the League of Nations, 1919–33, James Eric Drummond, sixteenth earl of Perth (1876–1951), had served as the British ambassador in Rome from 1933 until April 1939. At the outbreak of war he had become chief adviser on foreign policy at the newly created Ministry of Information.

351. The previous day the British liner *Athenia*, bound for Montreal with 1,347 aboard (including 311 Americans) had been torpedoed some 200 miles west of the Hebrides. Of the 221 survivors, 109 were United States citizens. In a statement issued to Alexander Kirk, the American chargé at Berlin, the German Government denied any involvement or responsibility.

and have not followed out the idea of everyone that it would be rapid march into Warsaw. Not much news comes through on the ticker and I suppose the censor cuts things up quite a bit. Roosevelt made a speech last night in which he said that the US was going to follow a course of neutrality and that he was going to try his best to keep us out of war. I suppose that the events of today will make for a change in the neutrality bill provision.

I think for myself that the war will not be a long one. I don't think that the human being will be able to withstand the terrific force of this war and that something must crack. I also think that many people who thought that Hitler was God and could get them through anything will wonder if they start getting licked and he will probably have a serious internal problem on his hands. There was an air raid warning last night and every body had to run for shelter but it seems that it was another mistake. It was probably made to familiarize the people with what they are supposed to do.

Joseph P. Kennedy to Cordell Hull: *Diplomatic Dispatch*

No. 1519, September 8, 2 p.m. FOR THE SECRETARY OF STATE

The telephone conversation the *Herald Tribune* reports was held by me with Max Truitt.[352] Of course I am sure nobody needs to tell you that I gave out no such statement. I have made an investigation and find that when the call came through I was called to Harvey Klemmer's[353] office and Frank Kelly of the *Herald Tribune* was able to hear what I said to Max. I certainly would not give out a statement that would not only be embarrassing to the Government but to Truitt, one of my dearest and best friends, who I know is working day and night to get ships. With hundreds of people around in all offices in the Embassy, it is amazing to me that there have been no leaks before and, when you consider that there have been none since I arrived here, this was an unfortunate occurrence.

Everything in the report I said and a lot more because I felt I could say it to my friend and steam him up to get me some action but certainly the statement was never meant for public consumption.

Of course I know you realize the situation is bad here but I am sure you do not realize how bad it is. There are a great many newspapermen trying to get their wives and children and friends on boats and it is very difficult and people are constantly complaining that no ships are being sent from America. We are doing our best to keep them quiet but when you are bombarded by the Press every minute of the day and night as to what you are going to do about it, ~~you have to give some kind of an answer~~ the press is going to publish something and I am sure there have been no statements by me that would be embarrassing to the Government. Privately I have said plenty to Truitt but also I have brought the matter to your attention and to Mr. Welles' attention in order that you will all know exactly where the pressure comes from.

Yesterday my son Jack went up to Glasgow to ~~see~~ contact the people rescued from the *Athenia*. He came back with the very definite impression that they are in a terrible state of nerves and that to put them on a ship going back to America for seven days without a convoy or some kind of protection would land them back in New York in such a state that the publicity and criticism of the Government would be unbelievable.

---

352. Senator Alben Barkley's son-in-law and former Maritime Commission counsel, Max O'Rell Truitt (1904–1956) had been appointed a maritime commissioner when JPK had left for London.
353. Harvey Klemmer (1900–1992), the United States Maritime Commission representative in London.

Also remember that a great deal of attention is being paid to these people and they are beginning to feel terribly important and they are having an awful lot to say, most of which the censor is not permitting to go through, particularly criticism of our Government.

With the danger of submarine warfare outlined in my 1518, September 8, 12 noon, a critical situation might well arise with Americans sailing on British boats. All I am working for is to get them out as quickly and safely as we can with as much credit to the United States Government as possible.

KENNEDY

Kathleen Kennedy, 19: *"Lamps in a Blackout"*

Blackout, blackout. England must be blacked out, and on the night of September 19,[354] issuing her final defense commands, England lay in dark, silence while smiling moon and twinkling stars shone over her like lights of an anticipated victory.

It is an eerie experience walking through a darkened London. You literally feel your way, and with groping finger make sudden contact with a lamppost against which leans a steel helmeted figure with his gas mask slung at his side. You cross the road in obedience to little green crosses winking in the murk above your head. You pause to watch the few cars, which with blackened lamps, move through the streets. With but a glimmer you trace their ghostly progress. You look, and see no more, the scintillating signs of Piccadilly and Leicester Square, the glittering announcements of smokes and soaps. Gone are the gaily-lit hotels and nightclubs; now in their place are sombre buildings surrounded by sandbags. You wander through Kensington Garden in search of beauty and solitude and find only trenches and groups of ghostly figures working sound machines and searchlights to locate the enemy. Gone from the parks are the soapbox orators and the nightly strollers. But yet the moon shines through and one can see new beauties in the silent, deserted city of London. It is a new London, a London that looks like Barcelona before the bombs fell.

In our household, the first night of the blackout was one of excitement and mistakes. Young Ted ripped the black curtain, which is used by homes and hotels alike, to prevent the least ray of light from shining through. Within five minutes three air-raid wardens called, to complain of great streaks of light shining through the window. Consequently the hall light was extinguished, and Jean sprained her ankle in falling downstairs. Joe returned from an exploring trip with a very swollen, black eye. No one believed his story of walking into a lamp post, until we read in the next morning's paper, of hundreds bumping into trees, falling on the curb, and being hit by autos with such results as broken legs fractures, and even death. Thus, now one hears tap, tap, tap, not of machine guns, but of umbrellas and canes as Londoners feel their way homeward, for it is a perilous task. Now it surprises none to hear more people have been killed in the darkness than in battle- during the first month of the war.

As I lay dreaming of peace and the brilliant lights of New York, a series of piercing blasts shook me from my bed. I seized my gas mask and offering my soul to the Lord, ran downstairs where the rest of the family stood ordering one another about, and trying at the same time to put on gas masks. Having been joined by the servants, we all dashed to the air-raid shelter across the road. Air-raid wardens were running through the

---

354. The date is an apparent typographical error because Kathleen, Eunice, Bobby and their mother had embarked for New York aboard the United States liner *Washington* on September 12.

street issuing orders and bustling people into the underground dugout. Within 15 minutes the streets were cleared of men, women, children and animals. Everyone was quite calm as they seemed to trust in God and their country for protection. However, the ladies looked most unlovely with their creamed faces and paper curled hair. One stout matron was more upset about leaving her Pekinese dog behind than about the German bombs. Another woman promised to enter the convent if only she were spared. (I wonder if she did.) After 40 minutes, the all clear signal sounded and everyone murmured a prayer of thanks. An auxiliary fireman said that planes had been seen off the East coast, which later turned out to be English. Back I went to bed not the least bit angry that I had been aroused by a false alarm.

May England soon have her midnights changed to mid-day with lights of victory and until then may the moon and starts and the brilliant lamps of courage and faith shine gloriously in the blackout!

Joseph P. Kennedy to Franklin Roosevelt

Personal and Confidential, London, September 10, 1939

Dear Mr. President,

Since the war is a week old, I would like to give you a few of my impressions as to what is taking place here.

First of all, the high Government officials are depressed beyond words that it has become necessary for the United States to revert to its old Neutrality Law.[355] They contend, at least for the time being, that all they want to do is to buy equipment already on order or whatever other equipment they may need, for which they are willing to pay cash and carry away. They feel as they did when the new Neutrality Bill was licked — that America has talked a lot about her sympathies, but, when called on for action, have only given assistance to Britain's enemy. All of this, of course, you know and I merely reiterate it because I suppose one of my jobs is to let you know what the people in power here are saying. However, this hasn't yet reached the stage of bitterness because the war hasn't yet been fought on this front. And such anti-Americanism as exists is carefully concealed.

There is no question that the war is going to be conducted with eyes constantly on the United States. Unless the war comes to a standstill and it is a stalemate between the Germans and the French on the Maginot and Siegfried Lines, the English are going to think of every way of maintaining favorable public opinion in the United States, figuring that sooner or later they can obtain real help from America. I talked with Commander Critchley, who was General Critchley in the last war, and who is now in charge of all training of the Royal Air Force,[356] and he is thoroughly convinced that, since the Siegfried Line is at least ten times stronger than any German line was during the last war and the Maginot Line even a great number of times stronger than any French line was during the last war, the fight will be in the air and it will not be decisive for either side, even though he admits that the German air force is probably better than the British. However, no one really knows what the effect of air bombardment will be. The British admit that within three days after the outbreak of war, the Germans had not only done great damage to Poland's communications, but had destroyed all aircraft producing centers and many aerodromes. To my mind it is a very open question as to

355. On September 5, the president had issued two neutrality proclamations, the second of which invoked the arms embargo provision of the 1937 Neutrality Act.
356. Brigadier General Alfred Cecil Critchley (1890–1963).

what will be the effect on this country of air bombardment, coupled with submarine warfare.

There is another part of informed opinion that feels if Russia kept out as an ally of Germany, England and France could lick Germany, and that some way will be found to get at Germany through one of the neutral States. Of course, when you mention this to anybody in official quarters, they hold up their hands in horror, but if Russia indicated support of Germany, Italy might then decide it was the stronger side and might well kick up herself. Then England might just dig in for protection instead of even contemplating some way of getting at Germany. There is no question that the active forces, particularly in the army and air forces, were anxious to take a shot at Italy, and the Admiralty would be also if they had better control of the submarine warfare carried on by Germany, which might be notably aided in the Mediterranean by the large Italian submarine fleet.

As it stands so far, outside of the rush at the American Embassy and the mad desire of the Americans to get home, the most noticeable thing in London is the blackout, and the service in the high-class hotels is probably a little worse, but beyond that there is no real indication of war.

The place where the real works are going on is in the economic and financial departments. There the best brains in England have been concentrated. Every means which can be used to gain the main objective is being considered. At the moment there is a lot of hasty improvisation, but they have executive powers and the manpower. There is no question that Mr. Hull's Trade Agreements program is completely out of the window. England is as much a totalitarian country tonight from an economic and trade point of view as any other country in Europe — all that is needed is time to perfect the organization. All trade will be directly or indirectly controlled by the Government and I expect in due course to see a great deal of it conducted by barter or compensation arrangements. The British have a line on every country in the world from which they can get the supplies they need and the Government controls the shipping to transport them. They have in many cases predominant resources of commodities in the Empire which they can virtually take over and use for bargaining to get other goods they need. They have already taken over the surplus wool supplies in Australia, for example. It seems to me that we should make a careful survey of the supplies of raw materials of which we have a surplus and study our competitive position vis-à-vis other producers with whom England may make compensation or special agreements. In making this survey we should also keep in mind the agreements England may make with our principal markets for these goods. We should also consider the importance that the British Fleet and the ships they can charter will have on world trade and their ability to buy and sell goods if certain provisions of our Neutrality Bill make it difficult for our ships to function.

I think that we will have to exercise the greatest caution in any piece of legislation that we pass so its far-reaching ramifications may not result in doing our own economic situation untold harm. As long as we are out of war and the possibility is still present that we might ever come in, England will be as considerate as she can not to upset us too much. Because, of course, she wants to drag us in. And my own impression is that if by any chance she should succeed, the burden will be placed more completely on our shoulders by 100% than it was in 1917.

Incidentally, we must remember that England and France have approximately four and a half billion dollars worth of gold and that, if we are willing to accept this gold, we are left with practically the whole world's supply and there won't be the slightest incentive in the world for these countries to resume trading with gold as a standard. It strikes me that we should let them spend their gold last and we should first take over all other assets, particularly those in the United States, against the supplies which they must purchase from us.

This all adds up into one suggestion: That we should be on our guard to protect our own interests. In the economic and financial field the best possible brains should be concentrated on the problems which the European war is bound to raise. I remember Schwab[357] saying in 1915, after a conference in Washington between the representatives of labor and industry, that labor always seemed to be able to put it over industry's representatives. I asked him why, and he said, "Joe, because that's their problem 365 days of the year." That's the way I feel about the economic and financial picture here. It is their problem now twenty-four hours a day and we have got to think, and think most intelligently, to be able to maintain the right kind of trade and to maintain the strength of our financial system.

With warmest personal regards, I am,

> *Sincerely yours,*
> *Joe Kennedy*

Joseph P. Kennedy to Cordell Hull and Franklin Roosevelt: *Diplomatic Dispatch*

1578, September 11, 2 p.m

I had a visit of an hour alone yesterday with the King and Queen and this morning in my office one of three-quarters of an hour with Sir Samuel Hoare.[358] It was very evident to me as a result of my talk with the King that the one problem which is desperately worrying him is that within a relatively brief period, possibly three or four weeks, Poland will have been liquidated by Herr Hitler and then certainly a proposal will be made by him to France and England to put a stop to this war and to arrive at some understanding. This problem will be discussed by me in this message on the basis of my talk with Sir Samuel.

As regards the Queen, the return of the Duke and Duchess of Windsor appears to be the problem that affects her because it was quite evident to me that his arrival in England is worrying the King. I was told by the Queen that the Duke is returning immediately but merely for a brief period. She stated that it was naturally terribly embarrassing to have a "former King" in the vicinity. Likewise it appears to me that the situation will not be solved, for the time being at least, inasmuch as she refuses to receive the Duchess. This is not being quoted by me as a matter of vast historical significance but rather because it will have a certain effect subconsciously on the King and Queen both in arriving at a conclusion as to what answer should be made to Hitler.

As I have stated, Sir Samuel Hoare visited me this morning and we had an extended conversation. He is positively of the opinion that the gravest fact confronting the world today will be the proposal to abandon the fight which he feels will without question be presented within the next month or so by the Reich to Britain. He analyzes the situation in the following manner: neither the Germans nor the French can make progress against each other to any appreciable extent. He stated that the French

---

357. Charles Schwab, the chairman of the board of Bethlehem Steel and director general of the U.S. Shipping Board's Emergency Fleet Corporation, under whom JPK worked as assistant general manager of the Fore River Shipyard from 1917 to 1919.

358. The former home secretary had become lord privy seal in Chamberlain's wartime cabinet.

Army's progress at the present time is virtually like the Lancers — three steps back and three steps forward; that it is very improbable, except at the cost of unbelievable slaughter that either one of the belligerents could pierce either line of defense. Of course the Navy is able to patrol the seas but the consequences of this will not be made manifest until some time in the future. Meanwhile only war in the air remains. He stated that at the present time Germany has two bombers to England's one although he has the feeling that the English have more fighters than the Germans. It will be a struggle in the air to determine whose morale will be the first to collapse. Almost all of England's bombers have been sent to France but they are still being retained under the command of the British. Sir Samuel feels that the problem will originate from a situation somewhat similar to the following: the French after they have suffered a number of losses will demand that the English bomb the Ruhr and other localities. As soon as that commences women and children are certain to be killed in spite of the fact that English aviators would have the most strict orders not to do anything of this nature; right away reprisals would occur and regardless of all the defenses in England the Reich is able to make these reprisals extremely grave. It is positively the feeling of the General Staff that the only way of meeting the attacks of the Germans is to continue sending their bombing planes in attack on the Reich and in view of the fact that the quantity thereof is extremely restricted the question arises whether they will be able to last very long. Meanwhile Germany will make attacks on the different plants in England and although no direct hits are scored production will be so hampered by continual aerial raids that it is very improbable that a quantity of bombing planes sufficient to supplement the terrible losses can be produced. If they obey France's proposal of sending over the bombing planes, this will be the case. If, according to their conviction, the bombing planes are to be preserved until great capacity is attained and until they have a greater quantity, then France becomes restless and says why should we fight for the preservation of England?

Sir Samuel is aware that if any Party here considered any sort of an understanding with the Reich it would necessarily at the present time have the consequence of putting the Party out of power and I gathered the impression this morning from him that it is not at all out of the question that an issue may be made of that by this Party. It was not so much what he told me; but this was the inference I made. Lord Trenchard[359] who is regarded very highly by all here has the feeling that if they send British bombing planes over the Reich, the morale of the Germans would collapse rapidly, much more quickly than that of the English. That, of course, is a gamble that may have to be made, but I feel that the war cabinet at the present does not feel that the risk is justified.

The statement was issued on Saturday night on Sir Samuel's responsibility that the English look upon this as a war which will last three years, on order to keep up their morale and to prevent any disturbing criticisms of the Government's policies from making too much headway. It is my conclusion from conversation on Saturday with His Majesty that this is a problem which is worrying the Government very much. They know that if the war continues or if a Government is maintained on a war basis, it signifies entire social, financial and economic breakdown and that after the war is over nothing will be saved. If the war were stopped, on the other hand, it would provide Herr Hitler with so much more prestige that it is a question of how far he would be carried by it.

359. Hugh Montague Trenchard, first Viscount Trenchard, (1873–1956), marshal of the Royal Air Force.

His Majesty and Sir Samuel realize the very serious danger that France may have the feeling that the English are not contributing as much as they are and may commence to get disgusted with the war in spite of their very strong courage and determination at present. In passing Sir Samuel made the statement to me that it is his understanding that in France Bonnet was going to be put out of office.

I considered that this news would be of extreme value to you in determining your course of action. It appears to me that this situation may resolve itself to a point where the President may play the role of saviour of the world. As such the English Government definitely cannot accept any understanding with the present German Chancellor but there may be a situation when President Roosevelt himself may evolve world peace plans. This occasion may never arise but, having been quite a practical person all my life, I am of the opinion that it is quite conceivable that President Roosevelt can manoeuver himself into a position where he can save the world although I have not been of this opinion up to the present.

If the war goes on and air raids between the two countries as well, of course it is conceivable that Soviet Russia or Italy or other nations may decide to enter and then the situation might be without hope.

I am transmitting this to you because I am of the opinion that above all other important questions in the world this is the one that President Roosevelt should be considering to evolve in his own mind what might be undertaken at the psychological moment possibly to bring peace to the whole world without increasing Hitler's prestige.[360]

KENNEDY

The Ambassador

Joseph P. Kennedy to George VI

September 14, 1939

Sir,

I was greatly touched by your gracious and friendly letter.[361] I realize how heavily burdened you are with cares and responsibilities. May I reaffirm here my deep appreciation and affectionate esteem?

Feeling as strongly as I do about the economic results for all of us of this war, I wish I might, as you say, emphasize them to the people of the United States. I can, however, only express my personal convictions to individuals in my own country. This I have

---

360. Postmaster general and Democratic Party chairman, Jim Farley recalled the president referring to JPK's Dispatch No. 1578 as "the silliest message I have ever received. It urged me to do this, that and the other thing in a frantic sort of way."
361. On September 12, reflecting upon the conversation that he had had with JPK over tea on September 9, the king had wondered,
    When referring to the fact that England would be broke at the end of this war and that your country, the United States of America, would be broke as well, is it not possible for you to put this fact before the American people? As I see it, the USA, France and the British Empire are the three really free peoples in the World, and two of these great democracies are now fighting against all that we three countries hate and detest, Hitler and his Nazi régime and all that it stands for. You were speaking about the loss of prestige of the British Empire under the changed conditions in which we live since the last war. England, my country, owing to its geographical position in the World is part of Europe. She has been expected to act and has had to act as the policeman, and has always been the upholder of the rights of the smaller nations. The British Empire has once again shown to the World an united front in this coming struggle.

done to the President and to numerous other important men — and this I shall continue to do.

I much appreciated our talk the other day. You were most considerate in explaining the British viewpoint. The people of America, like the people of the British Empire, abhor war. They have watched, with sympathetic interest, the attempt of your Government to find a peaceful solution for the tragic situation which has now burst into open conflict.

As you say, England must, of necessity, feel herself a part of Europe. The United States are not faced with that same necessity. The President's action in calling a special session of Congress to consider revision of the Neutrality Act is an indication of what many Americans want — to help England and France economically, but not to send American troops to Europe.[362]

Today's situation, of course, does not affect us. Try as we may, we cannot dodge the fact that the present conflict is charged with grave dangers for the future of every person now on this earth. There is no telling what may arise from this conflict and the chaos which may follow.

Of this you may rest assured, whatever strength or influence I possess will be used every hour of the day for the preservation of *"that life"* we all hold so dear, and in which cause you and your gracious Queen help to lead the world.

With real admiration and regard, believe me, Sir,

Most respectfully,
JOSEPH P. KENNEDY

Joseph P. Kennedy: *Diary*

Friday night, Sept. 15, 1939

I had put a call in for the President in the afternoon and said I wanted to talk with him at 10 o'clock. The call was accepted.

At 10 the President came on. "Hello Mr. President." "Hello, Joe." "I have a few things to discuss and it won't make any difference even if the Germans listen in."

"1st. Before the war you mentioned to the Dutch and Netherland Minister in Washington about a neutral shipping lane. Are you still interested in that because Cartier, the Belgian,[363] came into see me this afternoon?" "Yes, but I think you should work on that over there — they should be able to work something out." "Fine", I said, "I'll tell Cartier."

"2nd. I said, "I'm interested in Tom Woodward's appointment to Maritime Commission. He has done a fine job and that job needs him now more than ever."[364] He said, "I know he's a good man, but I'm being pressed to appoint a West Coast man." I said, "Okay, but put him on next year in Wiley's place."[365] He said, "Yes, fine."

"3rd. I said, "I hear indirectly that Baruch is trying to get an appointment of some kind that has to do with Britain's purchases in U.S.A. and is being helped by Churchill. I want to know if you know about it and whether it is anything you are interested in."

362. The day before, the president had summoned Congress to convene in special session on September 21 in order to consider a repeal of the arms embargo to belligerents in light of recent events in Europe.
363. Baron Emile de Cartier de Marchienne (1871–1946), Belgian ambassador to London and dean of the Diplomatic Corps at the Court of St. James's, 1927–46.
364. Thomas M. Woodward, a lawyer from Pennsylvania who had worked with the U.S. Shipping Board.
365. Maritime Commissioner Admiral H. A. Wiley intended to retire the following year.

He ignored the question completely and said, "Your know the Senate vote on Neutrality is coming along fine and we need those votes up there," which was another way of saying, "Baruch has some friends in the Senate and we want to keep them in line until this Neutrality fight is over." I said, "Okay, I understand." He said, "That's fine."

I then asked him if he had received the message I sent him that afternoon.[366] He said, "The one from the young fellow (meaning the result of my conversation with Hore-Belisha)?" "Yes, I got that. What you need to do is to put some steel up their backbone. That's what is necessary." (I still don't believe he understands the almost desperate position of the British) I said, "Okay, did you read Chamberlain's speech the other day?" He said, "Yes, that's what's needed." A little more ordinary talk and — "Goodbye, Joe."

Joseph P. Kennedy: *Diary*

Sunday morning, Sept. 17, 1939

At 10 a.m. Lord Beaverbrook called me on 'phone at Watford to tell me that the Russians had crossed the borders into Poland. He was frightfully disturbed. He said, "This puts a terrible new aspect on the war." He said, "All my papers, my money, and everything else I own is yours to do as you wish with. There are only 3 men in England who know what the real situation is: first you — second, Hore-Belisha — and 3rd — (You may be surprised) — Winston Churchill."

I said, "Of course, you know I am against my country coming in and fighting?" He hastened to say, "Of course, I do not expect you to do any such thing. You know I've never advocated that or suggested it. What we need now is you to get your President to see what plans can be worked out to save this catastrophe." I said, "I'll come to see you anywhere, anytime." When I hung up, I said to myself. "How true my cables this week to the President."

It is more apparent than ever we must hold our position of strength, in order to be a determining factor in this peace settlement. We must help to arrive at a settlement that gives Germany *not* the position of a victor. That should be the direction of all our actions and legislation.

I then put in a call for Bullitt. I got him around 2 o'clock. His first question was, "When are you fellows over there going to declare war on the Bolshies?" I just talked to Tony[367] on 'phone at a town in Rumania where he had gone to telephone and was returning to Poland right away. (Monday's paper indicated that town was where most of Diplomats were.)[368] He reported unbelievable bombing. In fact, Tony said that the Germans had deliberately tried to bomb him and Margaret.[369] They had bombed open towns and had even dropped germs, etc. in tubes to kill women and children. (I don't know how much is true. I don't consider Bullitt entirely calm in either his judgment or at least in his reporting to me.)

"And all this time when bombing was going on, Bullitt says, not one shot was fired by the British — and the French are damn sore about it." (Maybe they are but Hore-

366. In his Dispatch No. 1666 of 5:00 P.M. that day, JPK had related his conversation with Leslie Hore-Belisha, the secretary of state for war, over lunch. He had found the minister "extremely downcast" both about the domestic and the international situations.
367. Biddle, the U.S. ambassador to Poland.
368. The Polish Government and President Moscicki had fled there as well.
369. Copper heiress, journalist and international hostess Margaret Thompson Shulze Biddle (1896–1956).

Belisha didn't indicate that when he told me Gamelin[370] was in accord with their policy.)

I said, "What about the Neutrality Bill — did Lindbergh have any effect on it?" "That son of a bitch. He wants to be the Führer in the U.S." Evidently he had dealt the President's Campaign an ugly blow.[371]

Bullitt went on, "I don't think you or I should go to U.S.A. for the Bill but if there is a filibuster, I am going home and stop at nothing. You've never seen me in a fight. I'll lay that opposition low. I'll drag Borah's[372] p[r]ostate over the front page of the papers." (My own feeling is he'd better calm down and start working for the U.S. not acting or talking like a damn fool.)

Offie got on the 'phone later and I said, "You boss is quite excited." He said, "He'll cool down."

Joseph P. Kennedy to Rose Kennedy

Wall Hall, Watford, Monday evening. [September 18, 1939]

Rose darling,

Well, my family gets smaller and smaller. Joe left on the *Mauretania* with a convoy, Jack leaves tomorrow by the clipper,[373] bringing this letter with him and the rest of the gang leave Southampton Wednesday afternoon.

Last Saturday morning I went up to visit Mother Isabel[374] and had a nice talk about Rose. She agrees she is much better off there so Rose is coming here tomorrow night and staying here until next Monday, when she goes up to Mother Isabel's.

I told Rose on the phone, she was going to be the one to keep my company, and as this house was very handy to her new school I would invite some of her girl friends and herself down to spend every other weekend with me and I would have a picture show at the house. That tickled her no end. So we will see how that works out. I think I will have the Moores stay over, perhaps at Sunningdale until I see how serious this bombing turns out and then if it gets real bad they can take her home. And in the meantime the Moores can take Rose out every once in a while and between us all she will be really happy and enjoy herself.

I also thought I would install a telephone at Mother Isabel's so there would be a connection up there if I wanted to talk. It won't be very expensive. I also told her to get

---

370. General Maurice Gustave Gamelin (1872–1958), chief of staff of the French Army, 1935–1940, and supreme commander of the Allied Armies, 1939–40.

371. Invoking both Washington's farewell admonition against entangling foreign alliances and the Monroe Doctrine, Lindbergh had expressed his conviction that the United States should not be drawn into the European war in a nationwide radio broadcast on the morning of September 15. "This is not a question of banding together to defend the White race against foreign invasion," he argued, never referring directly to the Neutrality Act. "This is simply one more of those age old quarrels within our own family of nations—a quarrel arising from the errors of the last war—from the failure of the victors of that war to follow a consistent policy either of fairness or of force."

372. William Edgar Borah (1865–1940), Republican senator from Idaho, 1906–40. In recent weeks Borah, along with his Senate colleagues Vandenberg, Clark and Nye, and a number of prominent figures such as Lindbergh and Father Coughlin, had been part of the isolationist radio campaign seeking to prevent the repeal of the arms embargo. The radio drive had provoked enormous popular support nationally.

373. That is, Pan-American Airways' flying boat, the *Yankee Clipper*, which had made its first commercial transatlantic flight in April.

374. The mother superior at Belmont House, the Montessori school where Rosemary was in training in Hereford.

an extra girl to exercise with Rose and as that would rest Miss Gibbs[375] and give Rose a change. So that's that! Don't give it a moment's thought at least for the present.

The weather is still lovely and I really love this place. I went to another golf course near here where we were all invited to become honorary members and the course is lovely. The cook is still grand and old Begley and his staff are getting more friendly.

The war situation still looks terrible for Great Britain. I saw Neville today and I don't want to write much about but Jack will tell you as I let him read my dispatch. The Russians going into Poland with the Germans, I feel is disastrous for the English, and I think just as strong as ever that if England has a chance to make an honorable peace she had better do it before she gets busted every way.

I think the people who know don't like the situation at all but the difficulty is going to be to find a basis to settle on.

If by any chance U S A doesn't change present neutrality law then the position of the French and British I think will be nothing short of ~~desperate~~ disastrous.

I received a 4 Page letter from the King written in long hand and it will be a classic for the Kennedy's in days to come. I showed it to Joe & Jack and they will tell you about it.

I talk to Bullitt occasionally. He is more rattle-brained than ever. His judgment is pathetic and I am afraid of his influence on F.D.R. because they think alike on many things.

I ordered the alligator bag and will get it to you somehow.

Now darling, as to me. With all of the family safe in America I have no worries. I will miss you terribly but that can't be helped. With the state of the world I doubt if I could be happy in business as long as I had any money to live on and support my family.

This position at the minute is probably the most interesting and exciting in the world, and in addition I may be of some help in helping to end this catastrophic chaos. The strain of being away will not be felt badly until Christmas and by that time it should be very clear that the job of ambassador can function for a few months without my being here.

I have all the dep'ts organized and we could easily function efficiently without me being here. So around Dec. 1 you might suggest to Johnny Burns he might drop a line to Franklin that he should send for me to come home. After all Joe Grew came home from Japan when Hell was popping in the Far East and when we were parties [sic] to negotiations.[376] While here I will not be doing anything. So until the winter comes I will be optimistic.

Get the children set in a way you will be happy and then take it easy.

I am passing up all luncheons & dinner on ground of being too busy, so I expect to be leading a normal life.

Well darling, drop me a line and tell me all the news, there ought to be a few laughs over there and remember you're still the most attractive woman in the world.

All my love, always,

Joe

---

375. Rosemary's companion, Dorothy Gibbs.
376. The U.S. ambassador to Japan, 1932–41, Joseph Clark Grew (1880–1965), and his wife (a grand-daughter of Admiral Perry) had returned to the United States for five months' furlough on May 19, 1939. The same day, at the International Settlement in Shanghai, French and Chinese blue jackets and a regiment of American marines had cooperated in a show of force intended to dissuade the Japanese from attempting to take control of the area.

I should appreciate it if no one remove pictures
from this book. If you do so, it will not be
so interesting for other people.

Personally, I should like to keep all the pictures
to look at myself, because as you know we lost
all the moving pictures of you children.

Many of these pictures have been lost in the past,
due to the clamor of newspapermen, so please do
not remove any more.

Thank you.

                    Rose Kennedy

The notation that was included in family photo albums from the 1950s onward.

Dear Jean,

This is a copy of picture that some old friends of the family sent me. I don't know how old I was. It is a rather striking costume. What I would like you to observe is the sharp piercing eyes, the very set jaw and the clenched fist. Maybe all of this meant something.

Dad

Joseph P. Kennedy, circa 1910.

"America's Youngest Bank President,"
a twenty-four year-old Joseph P. Kennedy
in 1914.

Rose Kennedy and her sister Agnes Fitzgerald on their trip to California, 1923.

Rose with Eunice, Kick, Rosemary, Jack and Joe, circa 1923.

When I look back now, I wonder at the colossal size of the job & I think that when we stood as a blushing radiant gay young bride & groom [it was lucky] we were not able to look ahead & see nine little helpless infants with our responsibility to turn them into men & women who were mentally morally & physically perfect . . .

—Rose Kennedy, "Early Life"

The film industry financier.

After having sat in your chair for the past four days, and using your office and your efficient secretary, I am beginning to think I am a "picture" man.

—Joseph Kennedy, the new president of Robertson-Cole Pictures, to Joseph Schnitzer, his vice-president in charge of production and distribution, in February 1926

The newly assembled Securities and Exchange Commission, July 19, 1934.

Jack, Joe Senior, Rose and Kick bound for Europe in September 1935.

The newly appointed ambassador to the Court of St. James's has a last chat with the president's son James Roosevelt before embarking.

Jimmy Roosevelt managed to get to my cabin and I took him into the bedroom for a brief chat. Even there, the photographers had to snap us as we sat on the bed trying to make sense.

—Joseph P. Kennedy,
Diary, February 23, 1938

Rose Fitzgerald Kennedy, 1938.

Kick, Rosemary and Rose on their way to be presented at Court, 1938.

I often bought my clothes in Paris . . . However, when came to be a question of buying a dress for Court my friends urged that I buy it in London, as the English dressmakers knew the type to be worn at Court, understood the importance of the train, etc. I finally selected one for my elder daughter Rosemary and myself at Molyneux, a beautifully embroidered lace dress in silver and gold beads . . . For Kathleen, when shopping in Paris, we found a lovely white net, trimmed with silver croquettes and a girlish net train.

—Rose Fitzgerald Kennedy,
autobiography draft

"Ambassadorial Grin," 1938.

Joseph P. Kennedy, U.S. Ambassador to England, who landed in New York June 20 for a visit to the United States, grins broadly while being interviewed. Kennedy said he would not see the Democratic presidential nomination in 1940. He is shown here on the deck of the Queen Mary.

— AP photo caption

Jean, 10, Rose and Teddy, 6, St. Moritz, Switzerland, Christmas 1938.

At 11:30 went down to have some photos taken by about ten photographers who snapped me skating with Teddy and Jean. Rather disappointed in my clothes as my hat from Schiaparelli failed to arrive.

—Rose Kennedy, Diary, December 26, 1938

Joe Junior, 24, and custodian Francisco Ugarde at the American Embassy in Madrid, 1939.

A skinny Spanish chap named Ugarde is in charge . . . a foreign clerk before the outbreak of the revolt, he suddenly found himself looking after all the Americans left in Madrid, solving their troubles, settling their quarrels.

—Joseph P. Kennedy, Jr., to his father, March 16, 1939

Kathleen Kennedy and the Marquess of Hartington, circa1939.

In July 1944, she would write her mother, "I suppose I really always expected to marry Billy. Some day—some how."

Joseph P. Kennedy leaving No. 10 Downing Street, March 8, 1940.

Jack, 23, at his graduation from Harvard College, June 1940.

At 9 the next morning Jack phoned and urged us to come out at once. [We stopped at Spee Club for our tickets.] Jack popped out and we got at the Quadrangle where our seats were. They were the worst in the place; three rows from the back on the extreme left; however, we had the brave idea of moving back against the college wall where it was sunny. As it happened, all the dignitaries [& the graduates] passed along that particular section on their way to the platform so we had a marvelous view of everyone. Kick was sure he had chosen the seats for this, but I am sure he got them at the last minute.

He was really very handsome in his cap and gown as he had a tan, which made him look healthy, and he has got a wonderful smile.

—Rose to Joseph Kennedy,
June 24, 1940

Radio address of Ambassador Joseph P. Kennedy over the NBC Red Network, Saturday, January 18, 1941.

"To Train for His Wings"

BOSTON. MASS . . . *Joseph P. Kennedy, 25, son of the former United States Ambassador to Great Britain, today started training as an airplane pilot at the Squantum Naval Air Station. After passing his examination he and a group of other trainees were shown about the field and given a few pointers about the airplanes.*

—Boston Globe, July 15, 1941

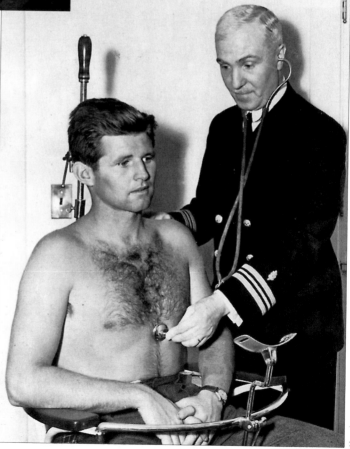

Joe Junior in training to become a navy pilot at the Squantum Naval Air Station, a short distance from the Fore River Shipyard, where his father had worked as assistant general manager during the First World War.

Joe Junior receiving his commission from his father at the Jacksonville Naval Air Station, May 1942.

Joe Junior escorting Kick to her wedding, London, May 6, 1944.

I picked up Lady Astor, Mrs. Bruce and Kick the next morning and off we went to the town hall. The Devonshires were already there, and after wading through the reporters we got to the room, and the ceremony was held. This consisted of the signing of the contract and the witnessing. The Duke and I were the witnesses. The whole thing took about ten minutes. Kick looked very pretty, and she repeated her statement without a falter. I think I was more nervous than she.

—Joe Junior to his parents,
May 8, 1944

Billy, Kick and Joe, following the ceremony, May 6, 1944.

They posed for pictures, which seemed better than have the photographers take them anyway, and turn in awful ones. I saw no point in looking extremely grim throughout so I looked as if I enjoyed it.

— Joe Junior to his parents,
May 8, 1944

Twenty-nine-year-old congressional candidate John Fitzgerald Kennedy with his namesake and grandfather, former Boston Mayor John Fitzgerald, 1946.

INCREDIBLY BAD WEATHER CONDITIONS HAVE MADE IT INADVISABLE FOR ME TO ATTEMPT TRIP TO WASHINGTON MAY TODAY MARK THE BEGINNING OF SERVICE THAT WILL MAKE YOUR NAME SOME DAY A HOUSEHOLD WORD THROUGHOUT THE COUNTRY FEELING PRETTY GOOD. GRANDPA =

—John Fitzgerald to John Fitzgerald Kennedy
on the day of the latter's swearing-in for
a first term in the U.S. House of
Representatives, January 3, 1946

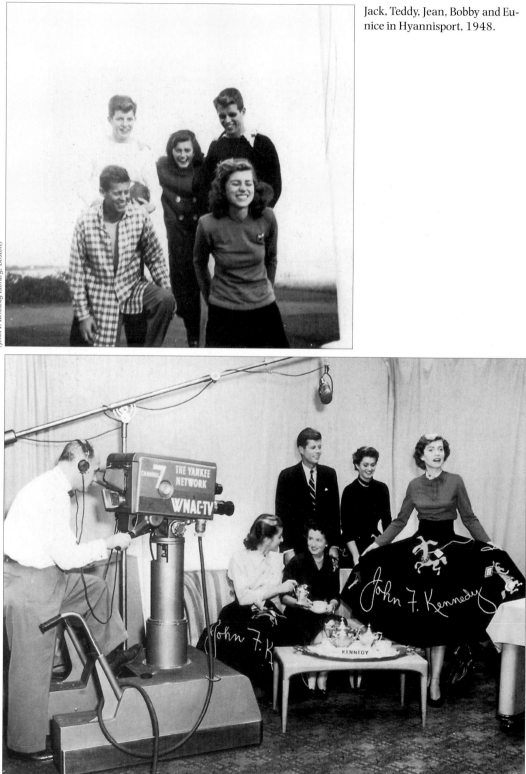

Jack, Teddy, Jean, Bobby and Eunice in Hyannisport, 1948.

Senatorial candidate John F. Kennedy with his sisters Pat, Jean and Eunice and their mother, Boston, 1952.

Former Ambassador Joseph P. Kennedy with the former Jacqueline Bouvier, Hammersmith Farm, Newport, Rhode Island, September 12, 1953.

Jack and Jackie on their honeymoon.

AT LAST I KNOW TRUE MEANING OF RAPTURE JACKIE IS ENSHRINED FOREVER
IN MY HEART THANKS MOM AND DAD FOR MAKING ME WORTHY OF HER YOUR
LOVING SON JACK=

Kathleen Kennedy, 19, to Joseph P. Kennedy

United States Lines, On Board S. S. Washington, *Sept. 18, 1939*

Dearest Daddy

I still can't believe that we are actually landing in New York today, this afternoon at 4:00. It can't be eighteen months since we were on this boat going in the other direction. It all seems like a beautiful dream. Thanks a lot Daddy for giving me one of the greatest experiences anyone could have had. I know it will have a great effect on everything I do from herein.

The Dillingham family have been aboard. The girl, who is at Sarah Lawrence, has been able to give us all the dope so it sounds like a great place. The two boys couldn't be nicer and are at Harvard. The trip has been great fun in spite of the fact that there are no movies or swimming etc. and that are ten people standing in whatever direction you want to go.

The weather has been perfect which has helped considerably. Robert Craigie[377] & Leslie Nast[378] couldn't have been nicer or more fun to have along.

I can't get excited about landing but I suppose it will come when we sight that Statue of Liberty.

Everybody said they didn't think the Germans would torpedo this boat with us on board —

Take care of yourself. Love to everybody

from
Kick.

P.S. The spelling & writing are terrific. But blame the rolling boat

---

Joseph P. Kennedy, Jr., 24, to Joseph P. Kennedy

Cambridge, Sept 27, 1939

Dear Dad:

Just a short note to tell you that I am all set here at Cambridge and have already started on the big grind.[379] I saw Burns and he went over the profs with me so I think I have a pretty good group. We have an apartment right near the law School so it's most convenient.

I went on John B. Kennedy's radio program for a few minutes the day I arrived back, and it was pretty good fun. I didn't say anything and only spoke about what I had been doing over there and about the evacuation of Americans.

I thought what might interest you is the feeling here as it has struck me in the short time since I have been back. Every one is unanimous in wanting to stay out of war. Joe Gargan[380] is the only one who thinks we should join immediately for he is afraid that the Russo-Germ combination will be too strong and if they get beaten he says that these Germ and Russian organizations here will really do a job on us. Gargan is the only person who has argued that far ahead. The rest of the people are praying that we will stay out.

Father Coughlin seems to have as much influence as anyone on the neutrality bill fight. I listened to him last Sunday and he is for us staying out altogether. Not selling the

---

377. Presumably the half American son of Sir Robert Craigie, the British ambassador to Japan, 1937–41.
378. The young daughter of publisher Condé Nast, whose passage to the United States JPK had arranged.
379. He had recently begun his first semester at Harvard Law School.
380. His first cousin, the son of his maternal aunt, Agnes Fitzgerald Gargan.

belligerents anything. He condemned the empirical designs of England and France and said why should we fight so they could preserve their ill-gotten gains. He has flooded the Congressmen with telegrams against the repeal of the embargo for he says this would be the first step in involving us. I think a lot of people don't understand the bill and a lot of people have been able to capitalize on it by stating that the repeal of the embargo would involve us in war.

Unless something drastic happens I think that the feeling will be altogether to stay out. Many newspapers have come out against the repeal of the embargo but educated opinion seems to think that the embargo will be withdrawn.

Everyone seems to think that Roosevelt will run for a third term and will be re-elected.

That's about all the news. Best to Ed and the others

Love

Joe

PS: The Atlantic Monthly printed this month one of my Spanish letters.[381]

Will you ask Eddie to buy a half a dozen Dunhill $\frac{1}{2}$ pipes no hurry for them and also to get me a golf bag?

Please tell Stevens[382] that two of my watches, one the one that opens from both sides and the other with an attachment for a key, weren't in with my things. Does he know anything about it?

If you are interested I will write you every couple of weeks letting you know the feeling around here. The stuff I have sent you in this letter is not my own belief but the feeling of the people, as you know. Just in case someone reads the letter.

Joseph P. Kennedy to Franklin Roosevelt

London, September 30, 1939

Dear Mr. President,

Referring to my cable to you and your answer regarding the possibility of peace proposals,[383] I feel nevertheless that I should write you as I see this picture at the minute. I also ask you to read this in conjunction with my cable to September 30th, telling of my interview with Montagu Norman. As you remember, this interview was bitterly bearish and with most of it I am in complete accord.[384]

Russia and Germany have today served notice of their intentions. In talking to John Simon last night, he said two things had struck them very forcibly: (1) The ability of the Russians to mobilize and move their large army, because up to now they had

---

381. "Here They Come," his February 15 account of the devastated port of Valencia appeared in the "Under Thirty" section of the October 1939 issue.
382. The butler at the American Embassy in London.
383. To JPK's Dispatch No. 1578 of September 11 (in which he had suggested that the president might "maneuver himself into a position where he can save the world") Hull responded for the president that "this Government, so long as present European conditions continue, sees no opportunity nor occasion for any peace move to be initiated by the President of the United States." Furthermore, Hull informed him, "[t]he people of the United States would not support any move for peace initiated by this Government that would consolidate or make possible a survival of a regime of force and aggression."
384. In his Dispatch No. 1873 of 1:00 P.M. that day, JPK had characterized the chairman of The Bank of England as "pessimistic to put it mildly," and added,
> [Norman] said that as far as Europe is concerned the financial and economic situation is worse than tragic, and that England is now busted. He told me that Simon and the officials of the Treasury felt that England could go on spending for three years before chaos hit the country. Norman thinks two years at the most.

rather been under the impression that the Russians could not do very much outside of their own country; (2) The very conclusive proof that the Prime Minister's attitude in delaying making a deal with Russia that involved the independence of the small Baltic States was a worthwhile one, because Russia had proven by its move into Poland and its might claw over Rumania that that is just the kind of tactics they intended to adopt towards the Baltic States, given half a chance. However, Simon said, having double-crossed everybody, they will probably turn around and start all over again, so it is not known just exactly what form a new tie-up with Germany might take. He thinks they will know better when the Turkish delegation returns from Moscow.

As to the Italian situation, he says it is very definitely to Britain's advantage to keep Italy at peace. In the first place, it permits free movement of ships in the Mediterranean; it gives them much less to worry about with regard to Malta, Gibraltar and Spain; it permits the French to move their troop freely from Algiers without danger of submarining; it makes it unnecessary to move troops up from India and it makes Egypt and Palestine much more comfortable by being a long way from the scene of action. So it is much to their advantage to keep Italy out of the trouble. Simon added, "Of course, if they go in with Germany, we are prepared to move at a minute's notice", but it was very apparent from listening to him that this is one spot they hope to keep peaceful.

As to the German situation on the Western Front, he is still of the opinion that Germany may definitely move through Belgium and Holland, or, what is much more serious, the present peace offer. I asked him, as I asked Halifax, "Just what are you fighting for now? You can't restore Poland to the Poles, can you?" He said, "No, not all of it." I said, "Well, then, that will be a failure; you can't talk about aggression and permit Russia to retain half of Poland and have its claw over the Balkan States as well as the Baltic States" and he said, "Possibly not." I told him that as to the removal of Hitler, people from Germany in the last few days had told me that if Hitler goes, chaos will result and Germany might, in the absence of food and the possibility of desperate economic outlook, very well go communistic and be a menace to Europe, because, after all, beating them isn't going to solve the problem of eighty million people who have no economic resources and nothing very much to look forward to; that the cost to England and France will be so great that it will reduce them to a mere shell of their present selves. Simon said he agreed and so does the Prime Minister that that is the long-distance outlook. He said they had an immediate problem, however, which there does not seem to be any way of sidestepping; if they were to advocate any type of peace, they would be yelled down by their own people, who are determined to go on.

Now there is no question in my mind that the British can see no way they can give up the struggle even though they are more and more confused in their own minds just what they are fighting for and what they will attain even if they win.

The topside people don't relish the possibility of the Russian submarines, of which there are a very considerable number, joining the German submarine fleet, and they don't like the prospect of Russian flyers and Russian airplanes going up with the German, with the possibility always that Italy might hop in feeling Germany looked like a winner. Topside people don't like leaning on the Turks, who, Simon told me, were continually blackmailing England for financial and economic assistance. There is also a prevalent idea amongst a number of English newspaper men, who feel that the French may decide that they don't like the looks of things and ask themselves, what are we fighting for, the echo will answer, "the British," and they'll say, "no more for us." Montagu Norman, in speaking of the French, felt this would probably not happen, because the French always acted much better when things got tough.

On the other hand, many important people are saying, what has England and France to look forward to? The defeat of Germany; O.K; that will take some time and England and France will go bust, as well as lose millions of lives, and then what do they propose to do with eighty million Germans who have a communist neighbor — Russia?

Well, you say, I know all that, so what? I answer that by saying, we all keep repeating in the United States that we don't want any part of this mess. Well, we certainly won't want any part of it if we think clearly of what happens even if the Allies win and the problems that will have to be met in the arrangement of Europe and also the bills that will have to be met to keep the beaten countries functioning. And we are all vitally concerned in what happens to the United States if the fight goes to a finish and the Allies are beaten. The prospect of our best customer beaten and finished as a Power and the attendant difficulty of arranging our place in the world with Powers who know we hate them.

Some people are saying here, the United States will get all this business from the Allies and of course they want the war to go on. I answer that by pointing out the temporary fillip we get to our own economic structure is only a pleasant interlude before chaos that is to follow if this war goes on.

"Well then," America says, "we demand an end to this aggression and this complete disregard of international law." Mind you, they speak of something that is happening in Europe and in the same breath say, of course, you over there settle it, we don't want any part in it. And I don't disagree with this point of view entirely, but, if this is the case, that by continuing a hopeless struggle means the complete collapse of everything we hope and live for, then it seems to me that perhaps another thought should be given to the whole problem by the American people. I have yet to talk to any military or naval expert of any nationality this week who thinks that, with the present and prospective set-up of England and France on one side and Germany and Russia and their potential allies on the other, England has a Chinaman's chance.

So you ask, what do you suggest I do? I answer, at the minute do nothing but consider two things: How you can point out to the American people just what the position of England and France is and what their possibilities are to achieve the aims we all hoped they would attain and by pointing out that, since we do not intend to get in the war, we must be considerate of our friends who are in it. Secondly, I would start thinking how you can help save face for the Allies and yet at the same time be the factor in getting the position of the United States a topside one as a result of your intervention.

England and France can't quit whether they would like to or not and I am convinced, because I live here, that England will go down fighting. Unfortunately, I am one who does not believe that is going to do the slightest bit of good in this case.

The whole problem needs a mastermind and that soon if you don't want the world's greatest calamity to fall on our friends and subsequently on us. Please don't think I am unduly pessimistic. I'm not, but I feel as your friend on the job I must urge you to give this your consideration.

Sincerely yours,
Joe

Joseph P. Kennedy to Franklin Roosevelt

London, September 30, 1939

Dear Mr. President,

Although such officials as Vansittart anticipated that the signing of the Russian-German Agreement meant, as I reported in my telegrams of the time, the fourth division of Poland,[385] nevertheless, when the event took place, it created a great shock here. But the facility with which the Anglo-Saxon can play power politics while talking in terms of philanthropy is triumphing. Whereas at the beginning of the war the protection of the independence and preservation of the territorial integrity of Poland was headlined as the immediate cause of the war and the reason for attempting to overthrow Hitler, now the restoration of Poland — certainly Russian Poland — is being pushed gently but very firmly into obscurity.

Of course, the real fact is that England is fighting for her possessions and place in the sun, just as she has in the past. I got out the Times' editorial of August 5, 1914 and compared it with the one on September 4, 1939, and they are practically identical, except for the substitution of the word "Nazi" for "Junker." Regardless of the God-awful behavior of the Nazis, surely the fact is that the English people are not fighting Hitler — they are fighting the German people, just as they fought them twenty-five years ago, because forty-five million Britons controlling the greatest far-flung maritime empire in the world and eighty million Germans dominating continental Europe haven't learned to live together peacefully.

I personally am convinced that, win, lose or draw, England will never be the England that she was and no one can help her to be. Technological changes, like the invention of the airplane and the increase in industrial power of other countries, have conspired with the decline in English ability and forcefulness to push her well past the peak and down to another level.

There are signs of decay, if not decadence, here, both in men and institutions. For example, no one in power over the past dozen years has really told the English people where they stand politically, economically and financially — and they are reaping the result of that now. Furthermore, the Parliamentary machine is not operating to throw up real, able leaders. Many people doubt, and I share those doubts, whether the Chamberlain Government can survive a single serious reverse, and who is to replace the Prime Minister? Possibly Halifax, possibly Churchill. But for all Halifax's mystical, Christian character and Churchill's prophesies in respect to Germany, I can't imagine them adequately leading the people out of the valley of the shadow of death. And after that, who is there? It is the question that all the English are asking themselves and the answer seems to be that there is no adequate person within the parliamentary ranks. And therefore it would not be surprising if the maelstrom of war had to cast up extra-Parliamentary leaders.

I am afraid that I can't conceive [of] the results that this war will bring as running counter to the evolutionary process. England passed her peak as a world power some years ago and has been steadily on the decline. War, regardless of the outcome, will merely hasten the process. And even the concomitant changes which the war will bring to all the world, such as the breakdown of the international mechanism of trading and the substitution of barter and other state control arrangements, were really

---

385. Since 1772, Poland had already been partitioned four times by her Prussian, Austrian and Russian neighbors. Upon the meeting of their respective forces at Brest-Litovsk on September 18, 1939, the German and Soviet governments had begun to establish a line of demarcation for their territorial claims, thus partitioning Poland for a fifth time.

started when Russia began to operate in this wise a couple of decades ago and have been the development of the future ever since.

Nor do I think this war is a holy war, despite the fact that most of the people I see here sincerely believe that it is and they talk in public and in private equally sincerely about the awfulness of force in international affairs and how it must be forever done away with, as if force hadn't always been the underlying basis in most all international dealings of any vital, life and death importance, and as if any means had been found for peacefully settling vital, life and death international disputes. I regret it, but I can't honestly believe that such will not still be the case long after Hitler's "body lies amouldering in the grave." I sometimes feel that, living as we do in a sparsely inhabited country with great natural resources and no natural enemies, we attach too much importance to, say, the Alabama Claims settlement as a precedent in international procedure.[386] Enlightened nations, particularly those where the pressure for existence isn't all-powerful, can emulate the behavior of more civilized individuals. But where there are two hungry dogs to eat a bone sufficient for one, arbitration doesn't decide the issue.

In this connection, let me say two things about democracy — the only form of government I want to live under: first, that the so-called democracies of Europe have conducted themselves in such a way as to make autocracy flourish. By forcing democracy upon the conquered nations after the last war, they aligned democracy and the status quo together. By resisting change, they ensured that all the forces within those countries making for change should of necessity take on an anti-democratic character. Just as the force making for change after the Treaty of Vienna had to take on an anti-autocratic, i.e., democratic character.[387] Since the dynamic always triumphs over the static, Fascism and Communism were left to move ahead. And moving ahead they are! Secondly, democracy as we now conceive it in the United States will not exist in France and England after the war, regardless of which side wins or loses. In fact it hardly does now. France is ruled by a dictatorship which has just this week made illegal one of the largest Parliamentary parties,[388] and England, which has always had a concentration of power in the so-called governing class, will certainly not be a democracy in our sense of the world, in the post-war world to come.

All this and more leads me to believe that we should curb our sentiments and sentimentality and look to our own vital interests. It may not be convenient for us to face a world without a strong British Empire. But whatever we do or don't do, we shall have to face it. Neither we nor any other Power can re-create what has disappeared, and the leadership of the English-speaking world will, willy-nilly, be ours. Certainly it is going to be a hard, difficult and dangerous world in which to live, and the United States will only be able to thrive in it by pulling itself together as a nation and being ready and prepared to protect its own vital interests. These, to my mind, lie in the Western Hemisphere.

With my warmest personal regards,

Sincerely yours,
Joe Kennedy

---

386. In settling the United States' so-called *Alabama* claims against Britain, the Treaty of Washington of May 1871 had established precedent for the use of arbitration in the peaceful resolution of international disputes. The treaty had awarded some $15.5 million in gold to the United States for damages inflicted by five warships, including the *Alabama*, which Britain had sold to the Confederacy between 1862 and 1864, despite her neutrality proclamation of 1861.
387. The Treaty of Vienna of 1815 had established the new (or in some cases restored the preexisting) territorial and ruling orders on the Continent in the wake of the Napoleonic Wars.
388. On September 26 the French Government had dissolved the Communist Party. Two months earlier the government had extended its own term to June 1942 in an attempt to avoid the disruption of the previously scheduled 1940 election.

Joseph P. Kennedy to Franklin Roosevelt

London, September 30, 1939

Dear Mr. President:

I have been a witness to the swift evacuation of England's schoolchildren, and its long-term implications may, in my opinion, do much to reshape the population distribution and social structure of this old country.

During the two days preceding Great Britain's entry into war, and the two succeeding days, over three-quarters of a million schoolchildren with their teachers, nearly half a million mothers and children under five, 11,000 expectant mothers, 5,000 blind adults and about 1,000 cripples were moved from London and thirty-four other densely populated vulnerable areas and scattered over the length and breadth of England, Scotland and Wales.

The plan was based on the possibility of a "blitzkrieg" breaking loose from the air without warning and was designed to take care of a maximum of three million people. Actually only a million and a half were moved, the remainder being away, making their own arrangements, or being unwilling to go. Incidentally, had the "blitzkrieg" come at this time, I would have had a terrific job in getting 10,000 Americans to places of safety since the British transport authorities had informed me that the evacuation of women and children would have priority over all other demands.

The objectives of the scheme, which had been in preparation since the crisis of September 1938, were (1) dispersal, to save as many lives as possible without disturbing essential work, (2) the preservation of the morale of the civilian population, enabling the country to develop its maximum war capacity at the outset by removing from the minds of workers fear as to what was happening to their children, (3) the assurance of continued care and education for the children despite disorganization and (4) insulation of the children from the psychological shocks of air bombardment.

The movement was carried through without a single casualty and with a minimum of mistakes and inconvenience. The ECONOMIST hails it as "the first triumph of the war." Practically every individual evacuated is housed in a private home. Every effort has been made to keep families together, to house neighbors in the same communities and to fit individuals into suitable environments wherever possible. Special arrangements were made for groups of blind, crippled and mentally defective children.

In general, the Ministry of Health did a magnificent job of planning and execution, but they had, of course, several headaches. Eastside and Westside were suddenly brought into too close contact. Many children had never been off pavements, many were dirty and some had a liberal supply of insect life. (The B.B.C. has seized the occasion for a nation-wide drive against head-lice). The evacuees were billeted in the homes of middle-class shopkeepers, county families and clean self-respecting rural artisans.

Of course, following English traditions, the inevitable collisions received an airing in the press. The subject of vermin was discussed pro and con in many letters to editors, not only in the provincial press but in the London TIMES. But the children, especially the younger ones, have shown great adaptability and have responded quickly to soap and kindness. The receiving communities have given ample evidence of their desire to do something for the country and to share their own greater measure of safety with those less fortunately placed.

The worst problems have arisen with the mothers who were evacuated with young children. There are lurid tales of some of these spending mornings in bed with a packet of cigarettes and a newspaper and the rest of the day at the nearest pub. Perhaps evacuation appealed most to the less domesticated mothers and these have found the greatest difficulty in fitting into the new households. It is not surprising that there has been a steady flow back to the cities of perhaps 30 per cent of the mothers evacuated, despite continued public appeals that they stay where they are. What is more surprising is that so many have remained and appear to be settling down to country life, if not with enthusiasm at least with a resigned determination to put up with a lack of sidewalks, movies and street cars.

The schools in the evacuation areas are closed and the teachers are for the most part with the children in the country. The local schools in reception areas are frequently working two shifts, a morning one for the local children and an afternoon one for the visitors. While there will inevitably be disorganization of formal education, the children are learning a lot they would never get from books. The Government recognizes that evacuated mothers cannot remain away from home indefinitely and nursery schools for all children over six months are being set up as rapidly as possible. As fast as these are opened the mothers are advised to return home. Special clinics have been started and extensive arrangements made for medical care of the children by local doctors.

Of course inevitable adjustments will come only as slowly and of their own accord. Evacuation has meant the artificial severance of family and trade ties. These migrants must be placed on as nearly a self-supporting economic footing as possible. The Government is spending a million pounds a week, and yet the Government allowance of 10s.6d. a week for full board and lodging if there is only one individual and 8s.6d. if there are more than one, is proving inadequate. Country families are dipping into their own pockets to make the youngsters more comfortable, happy and healthy.

The contemplated course of development in the next several months will be towards (1) increased allowances for certain classes of billeted refugees, (2) official canteens, possibly even official markets, (3) greater requisitioning of public buildings to ease the strain on overcrowded private dwellings and (4) the erection of about fifty national camps to replace the more overcrowded billets. There is an urgent need also for an immediate overhaul of the rural and small town drainage systems, water supplies and medical services in some reception areas.

There is in all this, however, the potentiality of a broad new social order. The policy of population dispersal forced upon the authorities by the air raid danger offers some hope of permanently gathering the population into a larger number of smaller communities and eliminating the great congested urban centers of London and the Midlands cities which were created by a series of industrial revolutions. There will be also an opportunity of organizing these communities so that industry and agriculture will better supplement each other.

If the war lasts any length of time a new social solvent will have been assimilated into country life. The health of the under-privileged classes of children will be immeasurably improved while the inhabitants of the smaller towns and villages will have had their horizons widened. As Geoffrey Crowther, editor of the ECONOMIST, said: "The springboards of a healthy and national decentralisation and recasting of our social structure may even now be being fashioned by the threat of German bombers."

With warmest regards,

Faithfully yours,
Joe Kennedy

P.S. Evacuation has, of course, produced a crop of stories relating to the reactions of the slum dwellers to country life. I've been too busy to garner many, but there are a couple which are reputed to be authentic.

One of the developments of evacuation has been the difficulty in getting the East End Londoner used to the quiet of the country village. One Cockney mother turned up at the local billeting officer's headquarters with her child and announced: "I'm goin' back to Lunnon. Them there Germans will at least make some noise with their bloody bombs. I fair get the creeps with the bloomin' quiet out 'ere. I'd rather take a chance with the 'Uns droppin' them h'eggs than feel like a corpse already in the dead quiet out 'ere."

One little boy sent to village in Surrey was asked by his hostess to go into the garden and pick some flowers for the table. Half an hour later she found him in the garden looking furtively about, but no flowers had been picked. She asked him why he hadn't done what he was told. The reply was: "I'm waitin' for that there copper on the corner to move along so as I don't get pinched."

A little girl of ten billeted on a well-to-do county family was given a lovely bedroom to herself and shared the attention of the family nurse.

When bedtime came the first evening, the nurse showed her the bedroom and left her to undress. Returning half an hour later, she found the light out but no one in the bed and the room apparently deserted. A thorough search, however, revealed the child half-asleep under the bed.

After pulling her out, the nurse naturally inquired what had frightened her so badly that she had to hide there. "I'm not frightened", said the little girl, "Our room is very small so Mamma and Papa sleep on the bed and I always sleep underneath."

Robert Kennedy, 13, to Joseph P. Kennedy

St. Paul's School

Dear Daddy,

Here I am at St Paul's working plenty hard. On weekdays we get up at 7:00 o'clock, breakfast at 7:30 plenty early. We go to bed about 9:30.

I am glad to get back to American sports. We have started practicing football.

I am not used to this kind of a school yet but I guess I will be in a few days. I have talked to Mother twice on the telephone and she told me about Jack coming home on the clipper.

Tell some one over there to write me and give me the news

We had quite a lot of fun on the boat coming over. There were people sleeping in the swimming pool gym and in part of the lounge. They had words and they didn't have any movies.

My studies are getting along quite well. My algebra I am ahead in but I am still staying in the Second form I am doing first form latin.

I hope you arn't working to hard send my love to every one

Love Bob

Edward Kennedy, 7, to Joseph P. Kennedy

Dear Daddy

Mr. Jimmy Murphy who used to work for Jack Kennedy[389] in London is going to take me and Paul Murphy's little boy to see the horSe show of the World's Fair. It is in Conn. I think I am going to get a pony there and where do you think I could keep it?

---

389. That is, JPK's private secretary and the former RKO representative in Britain.

Maybe in the little tool house. Louis said he would take care of it. It he doesn't have a name, I would like you to name him. How are you and Stevens[390] and Rosemary and Mr. Bingley. Give my love to Eddie and Mrs. Moore and Jack Kennedy and Mr. Seymour.

Please Write us another

Love from
OXOXOXOXOX Teddy OXOXOXOX

Joseph P. Kennedy to Cordell Hull: *Diplomatic Dispatch*

1893, October 2, 6 p.m. For the Secretary, strictly confidential.

Today at luncheon with Churchill I received the impression that any peace terms that Hitler might offer would be rejected. There may be a slight hope that if the latter asked for an armistice pending a discussion of terms, it might be agreed to principally because Great Britain feels the time could be used to great advantage. Churchill told me that there are rumblings from France that a much bigger army should be sent by the English, but the truth of the matter is that for the last three years the Government here somehow forgot to order the necessary material to equip a large army, so they cannot send a large army because there is not enough equipment for it.

Up to date, he says, there is no evidence that Germany is bringing up troops on either the Belgian or Dutch borders that would indicate any contemplated violation of the neutrality of either of these two countries, but that the Germans are massing large forces behind the Seigfried Line. As I talk to them it becomes more and more apparent that they are definitely apprehensive of the air strength of Germany, but in no event will they first start bombing into Germany. There is no intention of their fighting the Russians now or later on. I see an argument already arising that the part of Poland the Russians have is really all Russian. Churchill does not feel that Russia's power to move out over the world is nearly as dangerous as Germany's, and for that reason Germany under the present regime of the Nazis must be finished off.

It appears to me that there is a feeling that if women and children are killed as a result of these bombings in this country that the United States will tend more toward their side. Churchill remarked that after all if Germany bombed Great Britain into a state of subjection, one of their terms would certainly be to hand over the fleet and if England attempted to scuttle the fleet the German terms would be that much worse; if they got the British fleet they would have immediate superiority over the Untied States and then her troubles would begin.

No one in authority, I judge, likes this particular picture at all, but a bold front is being kept up pending developments of the winter. It is their contention that all they want is an opportunity to buy in America through a revision of the Neutrality Act, but this I do not believe at all. If the Germans do not break and throw out Hitler, after the Neutrality Act passes every hour will be spent by them in trying to figure how we can be gotten in.

KENNEDY

The Ambassador

---

390. The butler at the American embassy.

Joseph P. Kennedy to Rose Kennedy

Wall Hall, Watford, Oct. 2, 1939

Rose darling

I got your letter today along with 2 from Kick, one from Eunice and one from Pat. The other day I had one from Bobby. So I'm doing fairly well.

I've given you most all the news, because outside of working all day and drinking a bottle of JP Morgan's milk for my lunch — nothing happens to me.

Yesterday being completely fed up listening to Seymour[391] & Jack Kennedy, I went off by myself to see Nancy Astor.

She was the same as ever, Lady Reading[392] was there, Mrs. Dawson[393] and 2 or 3 other people who, following the true British custom, were not introduced.

Of course they all wanted to know when America was coming in and of course I told them they weren't coming. So perhaps, dear, you went home at the height of your husband's popularity.

The thing she[394] is worried about is that she has $50,000 in U.S. to use for her poor relatives; but now she hears she can't give dollars away anymore and so the Gov't are going to take what she has there and give her pounds for American cash. And is she mad!!

She thinks Waldorf should be Minister of Agriculture and she is very disappointed in Chamberlain's appointments to date. She says that there is beginning to be an undercurrent for a change of Prime Minister and Churchill seems to be in the lead.

If he does, then I certainly think England's march down hill will be speeded up.

Churchill has energy and brains but no judgment.

By the way he called me up this morning in a terrible state of the slip up he made in his broadcast last night in the closing paragraph he made reference to the South and Slavery in a comparison with the Nazis.[395] Of course that isn't what he meant to say

---

391. In 1927, JPK had hired James Seymour (1895?–1976), then director of Publicity at Harvard, after working with him on the Business School film lecture series, to serve as an assistant at FBO. During the early and mid-1930s, Seymour had dabbled in screenwriting at Warner Brothers before joining JPK at the embassy in London as an assistant and press secretary.

392. Having chaired the Personal Service League to assist those hard hit by the Depression from 1932 to 1938, Stella, dowager marchioness of Reading (1894–1971), had founded the Women's Voluntary Service in 1938. The WVS had originally served as a means of recruiting women into the field of air raid precautions before the outbreak of war, but by the early 1940s the organization would grow to evacuate, feed, clothe, house and generally assist those displaced by the war. In 1958, Lady Reading would be created a life peeress, and would be the first woman to take her seat in the House of Lords as Baroness Swanborough.

393. The former Margaret Cecilia Lawley, the wife of Geoffrey Dawson, editor of the *Times*, and daughter of the sixth Baron Wenlock, governor of the Transvaal, 1902–1905.

394. Lady Astor.

395. On October 1, the first lord of the Admiralty had given the first month's summation of the war. "Of all the wars that men have fought in their hard pilgrimage," he told his radio audience,

> None was more noble than the great Civil War in America nearly eighty years ago. Both sides fought with high conviction, and the war was long and hard. All the heroism of the South could not redeem their cause from the stain of slavery, just as the courage and skill which the Germans always show in war will not free them from the reproach of Nazism, with its intolerance and brutality. We may take good heart from what happened in America in those famous days of the nineteenth century. We may be sure that the world will roll forward into broader destinies. We may remember the words of old John Bright [nineteenth-century radical British statesman, orator and Anti-Corn Law League member] after the American Civil War was over, when he said to an audience of English working folk: "at last after the smoke of the battlefield had cleared away, the horrid shape which had cast its shadow over the whole continent had vanished and was gone forever."

but that's what happened. He asked me what he should say, I told him nothing until I got a line on things in U.S.

I had Max Truitt get the President on it and he sent back "he was very pleased" so I told Churchill he was lucky and say nothing. Of course he is delighted. So there you are helping all I can but never giving up the idea of <u>Peace</u> on which I work every day — and we will get it, too.

I've had Rose to the doctor and chiropodist, have had a phone installed, Put my radio out in her house and am having her & Miss Gibbs here for the weekend. So she is happy as can be.

She has plenty of clothes but if she needs anything, Miss Scanlon will take care of her.

I'm running true to form, I'm sick of everybody and so I'm alone tonight by choice. Its funny that nobody in the world can be with me very long without boring me to death. I just can't help it. You are the only individual in the world that I love more every day.

I'm sorry I'm not there on our 25th[396] to say they have been great years is understatement. They've been the happy years that poets write about. I would like to live every day of them over again with you, but wouldn't want to live one more without you.

So Darling, we'll celebrate when I get home.

I love you devotedly. This job without you is comparable with a street cleaner's at home.

All my love,
Joe

Joseph P. Kennedy: *Diary*

Thursday, October 5, 1939

Churchill called me first thing this morning and asked me to come to Admiralty. I went down there and he said he wanted to read me the letter which I had sent to him from the President which came in the pouch yesterday sealed.

It said:

"Dear Churchill:

I am delighted you are back at the Admiralty, takes me back to last war when I was with the U.S. Navy. Want you to feel if you want to send me anything personal just drop me a line and send it to me by pouch."[397]

(This is the gist of the letter. Another instance of Roosevelt's conniving mind, which never indicates he knows how to handle any organization. It's a rotten way to treat his Ambassador and I think shows him up to the other people. I am disgusted). However, we will see later on.

Churchill introduced me to Pound, the First Lord,[398] and Admiral Keyes[399] who were just leaving. He wanted to talk about the Panama Conference and then he pulled

---

396. Their wedding anniversary on October 7.
397. Churchill had asked JPK to respond, "The Naval person will not fail to avail himself of invitation and he is honored by the message," thus launching the now-famous secret correspondence between the president and the first lord of the Admiralty.
398. Admiral of the Fleet Sir (Alfred) Dudley (Pinkman Rogers) Pound (1887–1943), first sea lord of the Admiralty and chief of Naval Staff, 1939–43.
399. Sir Roger John Brownlow Keyes, former admiral of the fleet, 1930, and MP for Portsmouth North, 1934–43, and later first baron Keyes of Zeebrugge and of Dover (1872–1945), would be recalled from

down the maps of U.S. and South America and said he hoped U.S. would not extend the line beyond what they could patrol.[400] (See my cable).[401]

He kept smiling when he talked of "neutrality" and "keeping the war away from U.S.A." I can't help feeling he's not on the level. He is just an actor and a politician.

He always impressed me that he'd blow up the American Embassy and say it was the Germans if it would get the U.S. in. Maybe I do him an injustice but I just don't trust him.

Joseph P. Kennedy to Franklin Roosevelt: *Telegram*

GROSVENOR SQUARE, OCT. 9, 1939

YOUR DEAR REMEMBRANCE WAS BRIGHTEST SPOT IN DAY WHICH ROSES PRESENCE HERE WOULD HAVE MADE PERFECT DEEP THANKS AND AFFECTIONATE REGARDS TO YOU BOTH

JOE KENNEDY

Joseph P. Kennedy to Rose Kennedy

Wall Hall, Watford, Monday, Oct 11, 1939

Rosa darling,

Well darling, it was a great treat to talk to you on Saturday. I was beginning to think I was an outcast on a desert island not being able to talk with you because after all, I didn't write letters because I would much rather talk to you.

Well last week I said to myself, this is an interesting job but no matter how interesting it is, if I know I *can't* talk with you, I *want* to 100 times more. So I call up Lord Halifax and go to see him, and tell him I've got to be permitted to talk to the U.S.A. I've got more sense than to discuss the war, in a way to help the Germans, but must keep track of my family. Mail is terribly delayed and very unsatisfactory with the Clipper stopped. He tells me then that of course he sympathizes with me but it requires Cabinet action, because no one is permitted to talk to USA at all. I said I didn't much care what action had to be taken, I wasn't going to be much help to anyone if I didn't get that privilege. Well anyhow I have it with a warning not to let the Germans know anything, because they have a most powerful Radio Station on the top of the Bavarian Mountains where they listen in on all our conversations. So that's that!! You'll be hearing from me.

Things are getting very dull here and from a business point of view when the Peace offer is turned down,[402] I do not expect to have anything to do certainly after this month.

---

retirement in 1940 to act as director of combined operations, 1940–41 and as special liaison to King Leopold of Belgium in 1940.

400. At the Pan-American Conference, concluded the day before in Panama, the United States and her Latin American neighbors had agreed to remain neutral, to take steps to preserve hemispheric financial stability and to delineate a jointly guarded zone of neutrality between 300 and 1,000 miles off the Atlantic Coast of the Americas.

401. In his Dispatch No. 1892 of October 2, JPK had informed the president, the secretary of state and the acting secretary of the navy that he had been told "by the First Lord of the Admiralty to-day that he was creditably informed that the *Admiral Scheer*, the German pocket battleship, sank the British merchantman, which was sunk on September 30th at 2 p.m. off Pernambuco. The *Admiral Scheer* may be moving in the direction of the Caribbean or perhaps to Capetown."

402. Rumors of a German peace offer had been circulating in the British and American press since the beginning of the month. Despite his September 11 message to JPK that the U.S. "would not support any move for peace," since mid-September the president had in fact been in contact with Hermann Göring

Bullitt wrote Roosevelt about 2 weeks ago and said he was going home for Christmas and Offie says it is all understood and he is leaving about Dec 10.

My own feeling is that when there seems to be nothing coming from here after Nov. 1 it will be quite easy to get home. The job is now a complete bore and with you all away, well its just too awful. If I didn't have this house in the country, I'd go mad.

Rose and Miss Gibbs came down Saturday & went home Monday. She is wonderful and Mary Moore who was here said she had never seen such a change in her life. She is completely happy in her work, enjoys being the boss here and is no bother or strain at all.

Mother Isabel has hired another woman to walk with her and fill in for Miss Gibbs and it is working wonderfully. She gets 1 pound a week.

It becomes definitely apparent now that this is the ideal life for Rose. She is contented completely to be teaching with Mother Isabel. She is happy, looks better than she ever did in her life, not the slightest bit lonesome, and loves to get letters from the children telling her how lucky she is to be over here, (tell them to keep writing that way).

She is much happier when she sees the children just casually. For everyone peace of mind, particularly hers, she shouldn't go on vacation or anything else with them. It certainly isn't a hardship when everyone, especially Rose, is 1,000 times better off.

I'm not sure she isn't better staying over here indefinitely with all of us making our regular trips, as we will be doing, and seeing her then.

I have given her a lot of time and thought and I'm convinced that's the answer. She must never be at home for her sake as well as everyone's else.

As to the situation here, they would love to have peace but naturally they want to be sure that's what they are getting and not a 6 month interlude. If the terms that Hitler gave out were his last words then we are going to see the war go on. Everybody would love to see it over with if that meant the end of war. I still don't think it will be a long war.

I'm sorry you had trouble with Bobby. Whatever you do will turn out OK, so don't worry. [403]

I don't see anyone anymore as of course there is no gathering anyplace.

I am enclosing wires I received. I've answered all there.

When the heads of great countries wire you it is rather satisfactory. I'm convinced more than ever that you, not I, made the 25 years a success.

I'm writing this in bed so it's a little worse than ordinary.

Well darling that's all I know, I'll be talking to you soon. My love always

Joe

(through American businessman William R. Davis) regarding the possibility of a settlement negotiated by the United States. On October 6 Hitler had unveiled a peace plan before the Reichstag, but despite the fact that discussions between Göring and Roosevelt would continue for several days more, nothing would come of them.

403. Concerned about Bobby's religious education, she had moved him from the Episcopalian St. Paul's School to the Catholic Portsmouth Priory in Rhode Island.

Joseph P. Kennedy to Joseph P. Kennedy, Jr., 24, and John F. Kennedy, 22

London, October 13, 1939

Dear Joe and Jack,

I was delighted to get your observations and, from everything I hear from America, you are quite right. There is a very definite feeling here, underground, that they would like to have Churchill as Prime Minister pretty soon and Eden as Foreign Secretary,[404] but Chamberlain's speech in Parliament yesterday swept the boys right back in their corners again.[405] The Country wouldn't have stood for any other kind of a speech, but it is still amazing how hopeful people are that something will still be worked out.

The more figures I get on the economic and financial position of Germany, the less I am inclined to believe that the break will come in that direction. I think, if it comes at all, it will come from the psychological point of view — that the communist influence is creeping on them too quickly and too strongly, and that there isn't much hope that Germany will come out with anything even if they win. Russia seems to be the big beneficiary to date.

It still looks like Italy will play it safe and probably be right on hand with the victor — whoever he may be.

I haven't changed my opinion at all about this situation. I think that it will be a catastrophe financially, economically and socially for every nation in the world if the war continues and the longer it goes on, the more difficult it will be to make any decent rearrangement.

The picture of you on the "Mauretania" appeared in the evening News here and Lady Reading told me she had heard a lot of favorable comment from the English about your sailing on a British boat. I thought you handled your newspaper interviews especially well. You kept off the danger points and I should think it made very good reading both in the United States and in England. I think also it was very nice getting your letter in the *Atlantic Monthly*. It gives you a very good standing and I think you can follow it from there and get yourself a good reputation.

I saw Lady Astor and I hope somebody is remembering to send her that gum and candy she wanted. If you will send it to me, I will see that she gets it all right.

I saw Tony Loughborough[406] yesterday. He expects to be going to the Front any time now. Beyond that, I haven't seen anybody to speak with.

I hear from Offie occasionally. All he seems to have is the latest social dirt. I told him his friend Beth Leary turned out to be a fine bitch, but I didn't know anybody who would be surprised at that, unless it were himself or Bullitt; everybody else had known it for years.

He tells me that he and Bullitt are planning to go back sometime around the 10th of December to spend Christmas at home. When I asked him if he has received permission yet from the president, he said "No" but it is generally understood.

404. At the outbreak of war Chamberlain had passed over Anthony Eden for a cabinet post, choosing him instead to head the Dominions Office as secretary of state.

405. Acceptance of Hitler's recent peace proposal, Chamberlain told the House of Commons, could only be based on "recognition of his conquests and his right to do what he pleases with the conquered." "It would be impossible," the prime minister added, "for Great Britain to accept any such basis without forfeiting her honour and abandoning her claim that international disputes should be settled by discussion and not by force."

406. Their friend, the twenty-two year-old earl of Rosslyn.

I expect that all my work will be pretty well cleaned up at the end of this month and I am hoping to fly back from Lisbon around the middle of December, but I can't be sure of course until I see how things develop over the course of the next three or four weeks.

Margaret Biddle's daughter is going to be married tomorrow to some Polish Count or something,[407] so it looks like there will be one Pole anyway who won't worry about what happens to his fatherland; he is stepping in very soft. Tony evidently got out of Poland with nothing but the suit of clothes on his back, because we have ordered him a tuxedo and a couple of suits in England, which we are sending over to him. We hope they fit.

I got a nasty toss off the horse day before yesterday bright and early in the morning and was lucky I didn't break my neck.

Stephens insists that he remembers packing your two watches in a wood-inlaid box and the box was put in your suitcase. I suppose you have found them by now.

Show this letter to Jack, because it is about all the news I have and it is much easier to write to one of you at a time and have the other read the letter.

Let me hear how you are going. I suppose it is pretty tough. And have Jack write me and let me know how he is working out.

Everybody wants to be remembered to you both.

Joseph P. Kennedy to Robert Fisher[408]

London, October 23, 1939

Dear Bob,

I can't tell you how happy I was to get a letter from you. It arrived about a week ago, so evidently it took about fifteen or seventeen days to get here.

I have to smile to myself every once in a while when I think of the idea that I was coming to England for a nice rest — to finish off an otherwise hectic career. Since I got off that boat a year ago last March, I haven't had what I could consider one quiet week. Of course, I am thoroughly convinced that if it had been quiet, I would have been so bored I would have gotten out of here long ago, so it all goes to prove that no matter what happens, one is never satisfied. It isn't that the work is so terribly hard now; it's really the atmosphere one works in. I mean — seeing youngsters, whom you had to the house for dinner with your own daughters, going off to war and some of them already killed in airplanes; seeing business shot to pieces; seeing, with the vision or imagination I think I have, what's going to happen to America, even though they never get into the war [sic], and, of course, they shouldn't. It all makes you sick at heart, because, when it is all said and done, no good can come from any agreement settled by a war.

What my future plans are I can't tell. I am sure there shouldn't be any reason why I can't get home for Christmas, but I am not saying I can and I won't make any application until I get a look at the situation here. If my presence here is needed, of course I will stay.

I am terribly lonesome without the family, because you can't have all those kids around for a year and then not have anybody in one fell swoop, so all these factors contribute to a damned disagreeable life, although an interesting one.

---

407. On October 15, after fleeing Poland, Boyce Thompson "Peggy" Schulze, the stepdaughter of the American ambassador in Warsaw, would marry Prince Alexander Hohenloe in Paris. The couple would divorce a decade later, after which the former princess would marry singer and radio personality Morton Downey.

408. JPK's Harvard classmate, former all-American football player and Harvard football coach.

I read in one of the New York papers that arrived today that young Bob was the outstanding candidate on the football team. You must get a great kick out of that. From all I gather though, the Harvard Varsity Team this year will be almost a total flop. I am sorry for Torb McDonald, because he is a very nice boy and especially because he is a room-mate of Jack's. I imagine Harlow will blame it on McDonald or somebody else. I will never forgive that gentleman as long as I live.[409]

I am delighted about Tommy.[410] It is a great satisfaction after all these years that he really has got himself in a comfortable spot. Please give him my best and tell him how happy I am about it.

As to what's going to happen as far as bombing goes here, nobody knows, but they are ready for everything. My own belief is that unless your name is on one of those bombs, you are going to be all right. I have made arrangements to move my organization to different parts of England, but I must remain on the job until the last of the Government Departments have left London. Bombing doesn't bother me very much with all the family out of here.

I hope your health is much better and that you are really getting lots more fun out of life, from a health point of view, than you were when I saw you last.

Give my love to Louis and my best to all those husky Fishers and remember, when I do get back, I will have plenty of interesting stories to tell you.

With my warmest regards,

Sincerely,

Joseph P. Kennedy to John B. Kennedy

London, October 26, 1939

Dear John,

I have already told you how deeply appreciative I am of your interest in Joe and I was particularly pleased to hear that he appeared on your Radio Hour. I was also very happy about that small article of his in the *Atlantic Monthly*. I believe that young Joe has great possibilities if he goes along the right lines and his experience over here should have furnished him with a great deal of material that should be more interesting to the American public than 95% of the stuff they read and hear about from people who base their opinions on what they read rather than on what they observe.

This is just a note to thank you again and to say I sincerely hope I will have an opportunity reasonably soon to thank you in person.

Sincerely yours,

Edward Kennedy, 7, to Joseph P. Kennedy and Edward Moore

Dear Daddy

We had a Halloween party lost week Afterwards Igot dressed up like a ghost and went all the way down the road I didnt scare because you said not to scare anyone because they may have a weak heart. How is Rose the Moore's jack Kennedy and Mr. Seymour

Love from
Teddy

---

409. Harvard's football coach, Dick Harlow, had not played the Crimson's second string at the Yale Game two years earlier, preventing young Joe, then a senior, from ever earning his varsity letter.
410. Thomas Campbell, their fellow 1912 alumnus.

Dear Eddy,

We had a party. We Have been to the Worlds Fare — 5 time Wee are fime
Love from
Teddy

Joseph P. Kennedy to Franklin Roosevelt

London, November 3, 1939

Dear Mr. President,

I thought you would be interested in getting some of the leaflets that were dropped by the British Air Force in Germany; you might like them for a scrap book. Strangely enough, at the minute they are very scarce in England. I guess they took all they had on their flying expeditions. I suppose you have heard the story about one of the airmen who returned a couple of hours after his colleagues on one of these leaflet-dropping parties and the Commander said to him, "Where have you been all this time?" "Well," said the young airman, "things were so quiet over there, I started tucking them under the doors." The purpose of this being to demonstrate their complete disregard of the German anti-aircraft fire.

Make no mistake, there is a very definite undercurrent in this country for peace and I think that it is going to make itself felt by pressure on the Government to set forth definitely their war aims, because the group who are anxious for peace feel that when those aims are set forth, it will be apparent to the world, and particularly to the English and French, that they are fighting for something they probably never can attain. It is by no means a popular war and although everybody hates Hitler, they still don't want to be finished off economically, financially, politically and socially, which they are beginning to suspect will be their fate if the war goes on very long. My own impression is that if the war stays in the state it is now, this undercurrent will get stronger and stronger here. Of course, it is impossible to set forth in despatches or in cables just what I sense from my close observation of the Treasury's position and my talks with the top-side people, but perhaps I will have a chance to tell you that personally.

One of the things I have particularly in mind is your slant on the Churchill situation. Remember, Churchill has in America a couple of very close friends who definitely are not on our team. This is a very important aspect of the situation, if by any chance there is a change of Government in this Country.

There have been a great number of things done for important interests in America during the last two months right here in London, and they will be important to know when we consider what the political criticisms are likely to be over the course of 1940.

I am enclosing a letter from Lord Beaverbrook and we are sending by the same pouch a couple of pictures that he is sending you. He was terribly impressed by his talks with you and he definitely considers that only one man can save the world, not only in attaining peace, but in planning for the future, and that man is yourself. If he had his way, he would like to turn over the British Empire to you to straighten out. I think I know what your answer would be — that you have troubles yourself straightening out the one you've got. At any rate, at the minute, you are a combination of the Holy Ghost and Jack Dempsey.

Incidentally, Beaverbrook told me that in his conversations with you, you were most complimentary in discussing me and I am deeply grateful to you for this. One's influence on this Country is primarily dependent on how they think one stands with the President.

There isn't much political news nowadays to be elicited from any of the Cabinet Ministers, because there just isn't any news. Until Germany indicates some new line of action, things will be very dead here.

With my warmest regards to you all, I am,

Sincerely yours,
Joe

Joseph P. Kennedy: *Diary*

November 8, 1939

Went to see Prime Minister at House of Commons at 4 P.M. He was delayed because he had to sit on bench until Churchill had made statement on Navy.

(See my report to Department).

Said he tried to put himself in Hitler's place when he was trying to guess what Hitler was going to do. He admitted this was difficult.

Very grateful to Roosevelt for Neutrality Legislation[411] and told me he could never thank me enough for all I had done for him.

I told him Apostolic Delegate's Secretary, an Italian, had told me Mussolini had gone back to the Catholic Church. We both thought this highly significant. His interest in ungodly nations like Germany and Russia must be antagonistic.

We talked domestic affairs. I told him he didn't need propaganda in United States because Gallup poll showed 95% with Allies. So, short of going to war, propaganda couldn't help England.

He said "But I don't want their soldiers, I don't want them to fight in this war. This is an economic war."

I said what he needed was propaganda for the Chamberlain Government.

He said "These newspapers are terrible, but I suppose more people are interested in tearing people down than in building them up."

I said I thought a swell job had been done and if bombs had dropped all the things that people were complaining about would have made Chamberlain look more efficient.

We then got on to Churchill. I said not as Ambassador, but as one who had seen what he had tried to do, I wanted him to remain as Prime Minister until success — peace had crowned his work. He was deeply touched.

I could see he bitterly distrusts Churchill and is well aware he is after his job.

He thinks he is better in the Cabinet than out. Easier to handle. He didn't think there was one man in his Cabinet who would vote for him for Prime Minister. I said I thought that was true. I didn't know about Belisha. I had never discussed it with him. Chamberlain said Belisha and Churchill were fighting *all the time*. He had his hands full to keep them apart.

He felt that people were getting on to Churchill. He couldn't keep up this high pace all the time.

He spoke very feelingly of it all. He hates it all but is "tough" and is not going to let Churchill get away with it.

He said he was much pleased that the Dominion Representatives who came here believing England was not ready, had told him how pleased they were.

411. After considerable bitter congressional wrangling in late September and October, the president had signed the Neutrality revision into law on November 4.

He then said what I've said many times about the picture business, "You can't convince people 3000 miles away." "You've got to get them here."

We chatted for a while then as I was leaving he said "Please keep in touch with me."

Joseph P. Kennedy to Will Hays: *Telegram*

NOV. 12, 1939 12:30 A.M.

I HAVE JUST SEEN MR. SMITH GOES TO WASHINGTON.[412] STOP. I CONSIDER THIS ONE OF THE MOST DISGRACEFUL THINGS I HAVE EVER SEEN DONE TO OUR COUNTRY. STOP. TO PERMIT THIS FILM TO BE SHOWN IN FOREIGN COUNTRIES AND TO GIVE PEOPLE THE IMPRESSION THAT ANYTHING LIKE THIS COULD HAPPEN IN THE UNITED STATES SENATE IS TO ME NOTHING SHORT OF CRIMINAL. STOP. I AM SENDING A COPY OF THIS WIRE TO THE PRESIDENT OF THE UNITED STATES.

JOSEPH P. KENNEDY

Joseph P. Kennedy to Harry Cohn[413]

London, November 17, 1939

Dear Mr. Cohn,

Replying to the cablegram which I received from you and Mr. Capra[414] regarding "Mr. Smith", I am afraid that we are looking at this picture through different eyes. I haven't the slightest doubt that the picture will be successful in America and I have no doubt that, financially, it will be successful here and will give great pleasure to people who see it. It is my belief, however, that, besides giving people entertainment, it will give an idea of our political life that will do us harm. I have felt it to be my business since I have been Ambassador here to try to correct completely erroneous impressions that the English people have regarding customs and manners in the United States.

I do not question that in "Mr. Smith" you have made a sincere attempt to attack crooked politics, but I am also convinced that the picture will definitely discredit American Government and American civilization in the eyes of the English public. In the United States we are accustomed to violent attacks on public servants and muckraking exposures of officials, but in England this is not nearly so much the case.

In your picture a Governor, Senators, the Press and Radio are all taking orders from crooks. I disagree that "the picture develops theme of true Americanism showing how under our democratic procedures least experienced of people's representatives could arise in highest legislative halls, expose political chicanery and through existing Senate rules with sympathetic aid of presiding Senatorial officer make justice triumph over one crooked Senator." The mere fact that "Mr. Smith" talks for twenty-four hours isn't the thing that finally persuades the Senate that they should back him up. It is the moral conscience of an old associate of his father that finally breaks the filibuster. It is not the strength of our Government that makes this break. It is one man's conscience.

---

412. Frank Capra's comedic melodrama about Jefferson Smith, a Boy-Scout-leader-turned-senator who finds himself unwittingly embroiled in congressional corruption (starring James Stewart, Jean Arthur and Claud Rains) had been released on October 19.
413. Harry Cohn (1891–1958), president of Columbia Pictures, 1932–58.
414. Producer and director Frank Capra (1897–1991) had won three directorial Academy Awards in earlier collaborations with Harry Cohn for *It Happened One Night* in 1934, *Mr. Deeds Goes to Town* in 1936 and *You Can't Take It with You* in 1938.

In foreign countries this film must inevitably strengthen the mistaken impression that the United States is full of graft, corruption and lawlessness and contains very little in politics that is creditable. For instance, today I am disgusted, in reading all the English newspapers, to see that Al Capone's release from the penitentiary receives front page notice,[415] while only one paper gives an obituary notice concerning a man who has given many years of his life to service in the Supreme Court of our Land — Mr. Justice Butler.[416] I have been in England long enough to get the feel of the people here and it is amazing, the impression they have about our Country being run by gangsters and crooked politicians.

The technical excellence of the film increases the danger of making our Government seem to be run entirely by dishonest interests. I have a high regard for Mr. Capra and for his sincerity and creative genius. I know of no man in Hollywood whose work has given me greater pleasure or who I think has made a greater contribution to the production of motion pictures, but his fine work makes the indictment of our Government all the more damning to foreign audiences. He makes it appear a vivid, living truth and, to an uniformed public, it becomes a sweeping condemnation of a general condition. I feel that to show this film in foreign countries will do inestimable harm to American prestige all over the world.

I regret exceedingly that I find it necessary to say these things. As one who has been in the business and who has been vitally interested in its success, I am the last one to offer gratuitous criticism, but I do feel that the producers of California must assume their responsibilities much more earnestly than they have to date, in order that the prestige of our country will not suffer. I know they never intend this shall be the case. The fact remains, however, that pictures from the United States are the greatest influence on foreign public opinion of American mode of life. The times are precarious, the future is dark at best. We must be more careful.

Sincerely yours,
JOSEPH P. KENNEDY

Joseph P. Kennedy: *Diary*

November 28, 1939

Lunch with King and Queen

When I called up Alex Hardinge[417] last week to say good-bye through him to the King and Queen I was surprised that afternoon to receive from Lascelles[418] an invitation to have lunch with them on Tuesday. Previously I had gone to the opening of Parliament at House of Lords. The crowd was small, just the Lords, the Cabinet standing at the Bar, the Ambassadors in the gallery and no pomp. What a difference over last year. Lord Chatfield[419] carried the crown like a cigarette girl carries her tray. Incidentally, the

415. Gangster Alphonse Capone (1899–1947) had been convicted of carrying a concealed weapon in 1930. While serving his sentence, he was indicted and convicted of tax fraud and conspiracy to violate federal prohibition laws and sentenced to eleven years in jail. He had been released the previous day, November 16, however, having been diagnosed with advanced syphilis in 1938.
416. The *New York Times* had published conservative Associate Justice Pierce Butler's obituary the previous day.
417. The private secretary to the king.
418. Sir Alan Frederick "Tommy" Lascelles (1887–1981), assistant private secretary to George V and, since 1936, to George VI.
419. Alfred Ernle Montacute Chatfield, first Baron Chatfield (1873–1967); minister for Coordination of Defense, 1939–40; and former admiral of the fleet, first sea lord and chief of naval staff, 1933–38.

King at lunch said it didn't look like the real crown, it looked too big, but he was assured by the Queen it was and that it had to be "dug out" at Windsor where the jewels were.

When I arrived at 1:15 I was shown upstairs to the King's small reception room where he was waiting in an Admiral's uniform. He was most gracious, shook hands and invited me to sit down with him. We talked about how busy he was. The shipping situation: I told him the Argentine Ambassador had said it took $4^1/_2$ months now to make a round trip from London to Argentine where it used to take $2^1/_2$ months. He was amazed and repeated to Queen later at lunch. He didn't look very well, thin and drawn, and stuttered more than I had ever seen him.

After we had talked a few minutes the Queen came in with the Duke and Duchess of Gloucester. She is a nice little thing but terribly shy. He, the Queen calls "Harry," is a pleasant fellow but certainly doesn't impress one.

Queen was sweet as usual, inquired anxiously about Rose and children and said it was lovely I was going home for Christmas. Said then we were having lunch in adjoining sitting room and said "Why does it seem so much pleasanter when you eat in some other room than the dining room."

Gloucester sat on her right and I on her left. I just remembered Queen came into room first because when the Gloucester came in they both kissed on both cheeks and Duchess curtseyed to both King and Queen.

The first course was melted fried cheese and egg, I think. I couldn't tell exactly. I ate it.

Before lunch they drank sherry and the King asked me if I had taken to drink yet. I said "No, but the temptation was becoming greater every day." The Queen said "I hope you still eat chocolate because I've ordered chocolate pudding for you." I beamed and said I was delighted.

The next course was something I didn't recognize, but I took a small piece and the Queen noticing my hesitancy said it was hare and perhaps I wouldn't like it, after all it was an acquired taste, like in the United States they gave them terrapin and neither she nor the King could manage that and she added again "that man who had his head on my shoulder most all the time for two meals, Bankhead, the speaker,[420] kept urging her to eat it.

(King then turned to the Gloucester and said Tallulah Bankhead's father).

"If you don't like that we have pheasant." I tasted it and said "I'm sorry, Madam, I don't like it." She laughed and said "What an honest man." She ordered me pheasant and with some puree of either cabbage or brussels sprouts and potato. I staggered through.

The dessert was a chocolate pudding, not very good.

Then we had some cheese, the Queen took small piece of roquefort cream and so did I.

She again referred to Morgenthau being pleasant but not very keen. "I had him as my partner almost all afternoon at Hyde Park" (this to the King).

She admitted British Empire fighting for its life but tried to add the high moral tone of fighting for all other countries.

I maintained United States should not send soldiers, she agreed and thought I should say so.

---

420. William Brockman Bankhead (1874–1940), Democratic representative from Alabama, 1917–40 and speaker of the House, 1936–40. Bankhead's brother, Hollis Bankhead II, served as senator from Alabama from 1930 to 1946 (as their father had done previously.)

She was disappointed at Lindbergh talking about the "crown."[421] I stuck up for Lindbergh. He was honest and not Pro-Nazi.

Wanted to know if Roosevelt would want Third Term. All English hope so. Regretted their trip had been so short in U.S.A.

(I think both of them conscious they might lose their throne if this war goes on too long. She doesn't fool herself.)

Sent their love to Rose and children and said she might send that to both Roosevelts. Asked how the Roosevelt children were behaving, they were all so attractive.

Do come and see them when I got back.

I said good-bye and left.

Casey — The Australian Delegate[422]

On sheet of paper.

Some facts.

His talk on airplanes convinced me bottleneck of production, aluminum, checked this through _____ [sic] and Air Ministry, can't clear.

Saw Winston Churchill at the Admiralty at 5 o'clock. He looks pasty. Asked me to have a whisky and soda. I declined. He acted like he wanted one.

Showed me the charts of sinkings and showed how well off they were. Gave me copies to show the President.

Asked me to get President's opinion on mines off Norway to stop Germans bringing ore down and keeping in Norway territorial waters. I agreed to send him wire. "Eunice would like to go to party" (if O.K.) "Eunice would not like to go to party" (If President thought it would cause big upset in U.S.A.) (See Churchill's letter to me.)

Disturbed over the mines, but not discouraged. "We'll cope with it."

He belittled the losses caused by sinkings only 100,000 tons and said, although the loss of time on convoy system was large now he planned to get it down to 20% over normal (Leith Ross[423] said now it was 50-100% delay.)

I also talked over my plan of taking over for U.S. ships all English lines between non-belligerent ports and also having our ships handle all long runs. Like getting wheat in Australia and taking it to Halifax, dropping there and reloading on British boats, the same with lumber. It would cut down number of ships required for long runs. He is heartily in accord.

Edward Kennedy, 7, to Joseph P. Kennedy

Dear Daddy,

it snowd on Friday and give my love to Rose I hope not many- bombs have drop near you sir james come on Sunday. we have bot some pansies flowers and I am takeing care of them. my reading is beter in school

love Teddy

421. In a second radio address regarding neutrality on October 13, Lindbergh had contended that "[w]e desire the utmost friendship with the people of Canada. If their country is ever attacked, our navy will be defending their seas, our soldiers will fight on their battlefields, our fliers will die in their skies." He went on to ask, "[b]ut have they the right to draw this hemisphere into a European war simply because they prefer the Crown of England to American independence?"

422. The Australian minister of Supply and Development, Richard Gardiner Casey, later Baron Casey (1890–1976), had been sent to London for the current Imperial Conference. In 1940 he would become the first Australian minister to the United States.

423. Sir Frederick Leith-Ross, director general of the Ministry of Economic Warfare, 1939–42.

On Friday December 8, trip to Washington.[424]

Arrived at Washington Station at 7:30 a.m. Met by newspaper men (see my interview).[425] Went to Carlton Hotel, shaved, changed my clothes, had breakfast, arrived White House at 9 A.M.

Was again interviewed and photographed. (See picture entering White House).

Waited in Red Room for 15 minutes. Then went up to President's bedroom. He was in bed; looked terribly tired; was most cordial in his reception. He was eating his breakfast and making his own coffee in glass bowl. I proceeded to talk at once.

Told him of shipping plan, Southern Pine prospect,[426] showed him the schedules sent to him by Churchill, and then discussed the situation as I saw it. Very bearish. Told him of my statement to press on 3rd term. He then told me he would not be a candidate. He thought we could get a good man and win with him. I said, "Absolutely no."

I then went over the sale of British securities and the disastrous possibilities on the U.S. markets. How essential this should be watched for fear it might come next fall at a particularly bad time near election. He was intensely interested and said we must discuss this later.

We talked for an hour and I asked him then about what Churchill wanted to know about laying mines off Norway Coast. I went over to his mahogany tallboy and drew Norway as I saw it and pointed out where Churchill wanted to lay mines, provided U.S. wouldn't object too much. Roosevelt recognized the location even with my very vague map drawing on blank wood, and said that, since we did practically that during the last war when we laid 350,000 mines, it ill became us to complain now. Also, he said that Norway's protest then was merely perfunctory. So I took this as a go ahead and so cabled Churchill in the code we agreed upon.

I told President that Churchill felt this mine would be a prime move in shutting off ore from Germany and thus help to end war.

Missy came in and I went out with her after making 4:30 date to come back to see him.

My talk with Missy was about Jim's and Betsy's divorce.[427] She said President was worried and hoped to get it settled up. Was much surprised at how little money Jim had.

---

424. JPK had left England on November 29. His diplomatic memoir records that "[t]he strain of work at the Embassy was beginning to have its effect on me. In slightly over two months I had lost some fifteen pounds. Sleep was at a premium; the telephone rang at all hours with its insistent demands. I was advised by my physician to return to the United States for the type of thorough check-up that I was accustomed to get at the Lahey Clinic in Boston."

425. In a brief statement supporting another Roosevelt candidacy in 1940, he told the assembled crowd of reporters that

> [t]he problems that are going to affect the people of the United States — political, social and economic — are already so great and becoming greater by the war that they should be handled by a man it won't take two years to educate . . . First and foremost, we know from what we have seen and heard that President Roosevelt's policy is to keep us out of war, and war at this time would bring to this country chaos beyond anybody's dream. This, in my opinion, overshadows any possible objection to a third term.

426. JPK was scheduled to visit the Maritime Commission later in the day in order to discuss the possibilities both of using idle American merchant vessels to trade with British possessions outside of the war zone, and of supplying American lumber to countries whose imports of Scandinavian pine had been interrupted by the war.

427. James Roosevelt had moved to California in October 1938 to work for Samuel Goldwyn, and since then had lived apart from his wife of ten years and their two young daughters. He would file for divorce officially in February 1940.

Went over to see Cordell Hull. He was most cordial. Said I had done a great job and he had told every one the same thing. Spent great deal of time explaining difficulties with American Lobbyists to hold to Trade Agreement policies. I told him I was working on Chamberlain, Halifax, and Simon to do better by us. No point of sucking around Italy, Turkey, and Rumania, et als, and be careless of what happens to U.S. He said that would help.

Told me that he had outlined the Neutrality Policy that was finally carried. "If you knew the trouble, right within our own family to agree to the policy we adopted, you would be surprised", he said.

He is not 100% in his heart on the Roosevelt group. He kept saying, "You and I have always seen this thing the same way." He brushed off the mention of him as candidate for President but impressed me he was a candidate. We went up to Carlton Hotel in his car. He told me he was working 17 hours a day.

Saw Welles. Thanked him for his favors. Told me ours was the best objective reporting he had seen in the Department.

At 4:30 went to see the President. I forgot to write he invited me to his press conference and was most friendly. Talked of my shipping plans and gave me a good break (see newspaper a/c).

Sitting at the Press Conference I was impressed that he was tired. He didn't flash the way he used to, and also I felt what a tremendous variety of subjects he must cover. And he must know his business.

Well at 4:30 I went in and we sat at his desk.

He said, "Did you see me finish off another candidate for President this morning? That relief question in Ohio finishes Bricker and yet I never mentioned his name."[428]

I said, "what about this 3rd term, you'll have to run."

"Joe, he said, I can't. I'm tired. I can't take it. What I need is one year's rest. That's what you need too. You may think you're resting, but the subconscious idea of bombings, wars, etc., is going on in your brain all the time. I just won't go on unless we are in war."

He added, almost as an aside, "Even if we are in war, I'll never send an army over there. We'll help them with supplies."

I said, "What about Hull, personally, I thought he couldn't come to a decision."

He said, "I'll tell you a story that you must keep to yourself. When the other day it was absolutely apparent that the Russians were about to attack Finland, I was at Warm Springs, Cordell called me up and said that his reports from abroad indicated Russia would march and he thought we should prepare a statement and offer to mediate between them. He read me the statement and I said, "Okay, it seems to be all right but it should be timed just right." This was in the morning. He did not give it out until after 6 o'clock that night and it was then 1 o'clock in Russia before it got there. Well, at 3 o'clock, the Russians started to bomb the Finns, with the result that our offer of mediation appeared in the morning papers along side of the bombing. And needless to say it turned out to be a bad flop and our prestige suffered.

I said, "Exactly. Well then, whom have you got?" He dodged this by saying that we

---

428. "Without mentioning Governor Bricker by name," the *New York Times* reported, "the President indirectly accused him of attempting to balance the State budget at the expense of home relief clients who were beyond the scope of WPA aid." John William Bricker (1893–1956), the staunch Republican anti–New Deal isolationist governor of Ohio, 1939–45, would nevertheless announce his candidacy for the presidency in May 1940, only to lose the party nomination to Wendell Willkie that summer.

had much better young men than England did. We had Carmody,[429] who was doing a great job, McNutt[430] who is a go-getter if he has a definite assignment. "But, he added, he is only good if he has a definite assignment." Hopkins, who has gained 16 pounds and hasn't got cancer, in spite of what Mayo's said. Frank Murphy, (I said, "Is Frank doing a good job?") He said "Fine, he is doing a swell job." Bob Jackson is a fine fellow and most able.[431] "Yourself", he added very generously. Bill Douglas.[432] Take that group. England has nobody as good as that.

My own impression, Douglas is only potential candidate among that group.

I'm convinced he doesn't want it but wants his own man and expects to give him help and advice after 1st year when he is rested.

We then started talking about the Cabinet.

"Now Hull is probably the best man and the only man to run this job with the possible exception of Frank Polk, who I suspect is probably rusty, to run the State Department."

"Now as to the Treasury, Old Henry is doing a pretty good job. We are doing our financing cheap and all in all that department is going okay."

I interrupted to say that the financing was certainly not essential criterion as to whether the Treasury was doing well. It was the underlying philosophy, such as the gold and silver policy and taxes, etc. He said that there were 2 schools in gold. Lamont,[433] who by the way I got to line up the mid-Western and far-Western manufacturers on the Neutrality Bill. Baruch, et als, who say that for centuries, gold has always been good. (Churchill's treatment of Roosevelt–Birkenhead[434] snippy.)[435]

I countered, "Yes, if any one else has any. But we're going to have it all and we've built up a policy of not taking any goods in we have to pay for, so we'll have it forever."

Joseph P. Kennedy to Rose Kennedy

London, March 14, 1940

Dear Rose,

I thought I had better dictate this [&] get it in the pouch that is closing this afternoon, if I am to get any news to you.

As to the trip over, it was really quite pleasant. The *Manhattan's* food, as the last time, was excellent. It really is better than on the French boats and way ahead of the British boats. I went to bed before the ship left the dock and continued to run a temperature for about three days — not much at any time, but still enough to make me stay in bed. We didn't have much sun, so only on the last two days did I go on deck then it was

---

429. John Michael Carmody (1881–1963), Federal Works Agency administrator, 1939–41; former Rural Electrification administrator, 1936–39; member of the National Labor Relations Board, 1935–36; chief engineer of the Civil Works Administration and then of the Federal Emergency Relief Administration, 1933; and chairman of the Bituminous Coal Labor Board, 1933.

430. Former one-term governor of Indiana, Paul Vories McNutt (1891–1955) had resigned as U.S. high commissioner to the Philippines in July 1939 to head the new Federal Security Agency.

431. Solicitor general of the United States, Robert Houghwout Jackson (1892–1954) would succeed Frank Murphy as attorney general in 1940.

432. The former counsel to and 1937 chairman of the SEC had earlier that year been appointed to the Supreme Court to replace Justice Brandeis.

433. Herbert Hoover's treasury secretary and J. P. Morgan partner, Thomas W. Lamont.

434. Statesman, MP and lawyer, Frederick Edwin Smith, first earl of Birkenhead (1872–1930), was attorney general at the time of the First World War.

435. JPK would expand upon this Churchill-Roosevelt-Birkenhead anecdote in his diary entry of March 28, 1940.

very windy, but rather pleasant. I went down to dinner one night — the Saturday before we landed. There were about half a dozen people on the boat who requested interviews, but nothing very interesting. Clare Luce and Miss Case of Vogue[436] were on the boat. Clare is writing a running story for LIFE, but I don't know what news she got on the trip.[437]

We landed in Naples on Monday,[438] noontime, and we had three or four hours before the train went to Rome. I took Ding-dong[439] and we dashed up to Pompeii and we looked the place over. Then we took the fast trolley to Rome and arrived there in the evening, where I saw Bill Phillips and went over the situation and had dinner at Alfredo's, where Jack and I and Marie Bruce[440] had dinner last year, and went to bed. The Excelsior was crowded and they had quite a time getting me a room. I finally got on the first floor, practically on the street. All the people around the Hotel were asking for all the Kennedys and Clare Luce told me that at a newspaper luncheon she went to in Rome, one of the newspapermen had said he had been told by his papers to get pictures of the Kennedys, but, my God, he could never get that crowd together; one minute he would get a report that some were in one part of the city and the next minute, that some were in another part.

The next day I spent quite a while with Phillips at the Embassy and saw Myron Taylor[441] and Galeazzi in the afternoon. Galeazzi is fine, but is terribly tired and working very hard. I didn't try to see the Pope, because my time was limited, I had no clothes, and I didn't really think that it was quite politic because Taylor had just arrived. In the evening I went to the Opera to hear Mascagni direct Cavalleria Rusticana on the 50th Anniversary of its performance in Rome.[442] It was a very dressy audience. The Queen was in a box, but I was so far away from her that I couldn't see her. The performance was lovely and of course there was a good deal of excitement. I never saw so many homely women in my life and there wasn't one smart dress or more than five thousand dollars worth of jewelry in the whole place.

I left Rome early in the morning and took the Simplon Express, which goes by way of Lausanne. In the meantime I had acquired a sore throat again, so promptly, upon getting in the train, went to bed again and stayed there until we arrived at Milan in the afternoon about 4:30. Of course, when I got to Milan, there were two things I wanted to see — da Vinci's "Last Supper" and the Cathedral. We hired a guide and a car — Jack and I — and rushed out to see the "Last Supper" and found that the place was locked — at 4:30 — and we couldn't get in. That didn't please me very much, so I went back to try to find the home of the head of the Museum and finally located it and managed to get him up and around and he sent somebody back with us, so we had a private showing. Then we saw the Cathedral, took a walk and got back on the train.

436. Margaret Case, society editor of American *Vogue*.

437. Playwright and former *Vogue* and *Vanity Fair* editor Clare Boothe Luce (1903–1987), wife of *Time, Life* and *Fortune* publisher Henry Luce, was en route to Europe to serve as a special war correspondent for *Life*. Later that year her observations would be published collectively as *Europe in the Spring*. Mrs. Luce would go on to represent the Fourth Connecticut District, Fairfield County, in Congress, 1943–47, and to serve as U.S. ambassador to Italy, 1953–57.

438. March 4.

439. JPK's personal secretary, "London" Jack Kennedy.

440. A close friend of Rose Kennedy's from London.

441. The president had recently appointed the former chairman of the board of U.S. Steel and head of the American delegation to the Intergovernmental Conference on Refugees at Evian-les-Bains in 1938 to act as his personal representative to the Vatican.

442. In 1889, the Sonzogno Publishing Company had awarded the opera and its twenty-six-year-old composer, Pietro Mascagni (1863–1945), first prize for new operatic compositions. *Cavilleria rusticana* had opened at the Costanzi Theatre in Rome to phenomenal success in 1890.

When I got up in the morning, some Frenchmen had told Stevens[443] that they had noticed a lot of French detectives on the train, so we guessed that Mr. Welles was aboard.[444] That interested me very much, so I dashed back and there he was, so I had the extreme good fortune of riding up to Paris with him. The train was a couple of hours late arriving in Paris. We arrived in Paris minus a couple of trunks and immediately flew over to England. There were plenty of newspapermen and photographers on hand and I gave an interview, which you probably saw in the papers. One of the boys wrote I had said that America didn't know what the war was all about. I didn't say that, of course. I said, there were many phases of the war they didn't understand, but, anyway, that's the way they printed it and they have been giving me a terrible hiding ever since.[445]

There is a very definite anti-American feeling here in the city and while the topside people all deny it, it unquestionably is so. I dropped out Saturday to see Nancy Astor and in one breath, while she was denying there was anti-American feeling, she was proving to me by what she said that there was plenty. Tell Kick that Jakie[446] was there and said he was glad the Americans weren't doing anything, because they really wanted to win this war without America taking credit for it. Anthony Eden was there and he said he did not think there was any anti-American feeling because of this situation but because a lot of people felt America should have helped Finland.[447] This was about as poor an excuse as I ever heard.

Well, anyway, Welles arrived on Sunday and I have been spinning ever since. We have had two or three conferences with the Prime Minister and Halifax and saw Churchill, Lloyd George,[448] Eden, Attlee, Sinclair and all the rest. They treated Welles exceptionally well here. By that I mean they were courteous, gave him plenty of space in the papers and told him they saw there was no hope until they licked the Nazi régime. Welles is very intelligent and is hoping that out of all the mess some plan may be devised that can save the world from this devastating war. There is always a hope, but the chances look like about one in a thousand. Opinion is very much divided here as to whether there will be an air attack soon or not. The real weight of intelligent opinion is that before long Hitler will make some move; although, in the next breath, they strangely enough feel that his wisest move would be to do nothing. However, we shall see.

Up to date there doesn't seem to be any shortage of anything. When I went to Sir John Simon's the other day they didn't serve any butter, but, both in Rome and in London, the ordinary person in a restaurant can seemingly get all he wants.

Now that Welles has gone, I am trying to catch up on my diary, clean up my mail, see my own staff, and move to a new house. As it looks now, I will go out to Dodge's

443. JPK's valet.
444. On February 17 the president had dispatched Undersecretary of State Sumner Welles to Italy, Germany, France and England in order to assess "the views of the four governments . . . as to the present possibilities of concluding any just and permanent peace."
445. Asked by reporters about the state of isolationist sentiment in the United States upon his arrival at Heston Airport on March 7, JPK responded that "[i]f you mean by isolation a desire to keep out of war I should say that it is definitely stronger. I think it is stronger because the people understand the war less and less as they go along."
446. The Astors' fourth son, twenty-one-year-old John Jacob Astor (1918–).
447. In violation of the nonaggression pact the Soviets had signed with the Finns in 1932, Soviet forces had attacked Finland on November 30, 1939. In the early morning hours of March 13, Moscow had concluded severe peace terms with the Finnish government.
448. David Lloyd-George (1863–1945), later Earl Lloyd-George of Dwyfor; prime minister, 1916–1922; and Liberal MP for Caernarvonshire, 1890–1931.

place.[449] It is not an English type of house; it's the most modern thing you can imagine — rather big, but I think will be quite comfortable. At any rate, I expect to be in some place next week and then probably do some writing from then on until I find out just what I am going to do.

It is very difficult when you go out to meals to keep your stomach right and while it has been reasonably good, it of course is not as good as it was in America. In addition to that, without any exercise, I have gained quite a little weight, so I think, beginning next week, I will start putting myself in condition.

That's about all the news, dear. I will write you next week.

Joseph P. Kennedy to Rose Kennedy

March 14, 1940

Rosa darling,

I have dictated the news to you but I thought I would write a few observations.

1st I don't think any of the children should come over. They have friends here now, but you would be surprised how much anti-American they have become and if the war gets worse which I am still convinced it will, unless Welles & Roosevelt pull off a miracle, I am sure they will all hate us more. So for Kick to see her old friends and get into a discussion about U.S. and the war might undo all the pleasant memories she has.

For the most part this would be true of the boys too. If you came over, you'd be annoyed, but it wouldn't be so important.

I feel it strongly against me, not with the topside people but with a lot of others. However we can see later on. I thought you should all consider this.

Welles is working very hard to get a plan that may prevent a war of devastation, as he calls it. He was impressed with Mussolini and his desire to help. Hitler he didn't like particularly but he thought he was in a mood to make a reasonable peace and the French and English somewhat in the same frame of mind. We ought to know something before the end of the month.

I told him how anxious I was to be at home if I can do it gracefully. I just never will be happy over here without you and the children. The interest of the job outside of a visit like Welles' is in people['s] imagination. There is nothing to do except stagnate. However I can stand it for a while and home I come.

Tell Kick I have written her everything I know in these 2 letters, except that I brought the 2 pictures down to Antony [*sic*] Eden to autograph and he will send them to her directly. He asked about Joe and spoke of him in high and affectionate tones.

I have arranged for Eddie and Mary to go to Rome on business for Welles and it will give them a vacation at Easter. I judge they've had a tough time with colds etc.

Rose met me when I came home and I had dinner with her. She has got a little fatter but her disposition is still great and Mother Isabel tells me she shows improvement all the time I'm riding out to see them both tomorrow. I'm thinking over her future plans. Of course a lot depends on what is going to happen in England in the war. We'll see.

Well darling that's all the news. I love you and perhaps I'm getting old enough now so that not even work interests me. I just need my family. Love

Joe

---

449. St. Leonard's in Windsor, the sixty-room country estate that American automotive heir Horace Dodge, Jr., had allowed JPK to use rent free.

Joseph P. Kennedy, Jr., 24, to Joseph P. Kennedy

[Harvard Law School] CAMBRIDGE, March 17, 1940

Dear Dad:

Not much news since you left. The papers yesterday carried the story of the purported rift between you and the English Government, but outside of that things are moving smoothly.

Work goes on as always with the boys really starting to put on the pressure for there is only about two more months to go. We have started to review and I am counting on Judge Burns to give me a few pearls of wisdom.

Some so and so has protested me as not being a registered voter and the papers have carried a story about it. Burns says that it is OK, and though I am not familiar with the requirements I think I am OK as I am a registered voter of Cambridge. I don't know how long you have to be one, which might be the only catch.[450]

Kick came up one weekend for the Pudding[451] Dance and seemed to have a good time.

Jack rushed madly around the last week with his thesis and finally with the aid of five stenographers the last day got it in under the wire. I read it before he had finished it up and it seemed to represent a lot of work but did not prove anything. However he said he shaped it up the last few days and he seemed to have some good ideas so it ought to be very good. He is ready to run for Florida in about four days

I have decided I will not go to Winnipeg for Hopwood's wedding as it would make too long a trip from Florida and we only get week's vacation.

Boston politics are still as bad as ever and it looks from the headlines of the last few days as if they are getting pretty close to Dever.[452]

That's about all the news. Best to Ed, London, and Harvey, Jim etc.

Love
Joe

Joseph P. Kennedy to Rose Kennedy

March 20, 1940

Rosa darling,

You would never believe the way public opinion in this country has turned anti-American and incidentally anti-US Ambassador Kennedy.

The things they say about me from the fact I've sent my family home because they were afraid, to the fact that I live in the country because I am afraid of being bombed etc. etc. All rotten stuff but all the favorite dinner parties at Mayfair go right to work

---

450. In February, James A. Farley, postmaster general, Democratic National Committee chairman and Roosevelt's 1932 and 1936 campaign manager, had entered himself in the upcoming Massachusetts Democratic presidential primary. Over the past few years Farley's relations with the president had deteriorated as his objections to a Roosevelt third term had mounted. Joe Junior had recently placed his name on the ballot for election as a Farley delegate at the Democratic National Convention that summer in Chicago.

451. Harvard's Hasty Pudding Club.

452. John Patrick Connolly, former clerk of the Massachusetts Superior Civil Court, was at the time standing trial in Boston on bribery and job-selling charges. On March 13, Connolly had alleged that he had resigned in order to prevent his superior, Massachusetts Attorney General Paul Andrew Dever (1903–1958), from being "dragged into the case." Neither Connolly's eventual conviction nor the Curley administration's unwavering animosity toward Dever would sully the attorney general's reputation as "champion of the little fellow" or prevent his landslide reelection victory in September, however.

hauling the U.S. Ambassador down. It's for that reason it would be silly for you or the children to come over. It might spoil your pleasant impressions.

Walter Lippmann is around saying he hasn't liked the US Ambassador for the last 6 months. Of course the fact he is a Jew has something to do with that. It is all a little annoying, but not very serious.

I have been feeling pretty well but I find it very difficult to be as careful about my food as I should. You just can't keep to the diet as you do at home.

The thing that keeps me up is the fact that I expect to get home in a reasonable time. When I see if Welles and the president don't see any chance of peace then I'll go to work. The real basis of my difficulty is nothing else but being away from the family, and knowing you can't see them when you want to.

I went out last Friday to Boxmoor to see Rose Mary and she was fine. I had a talk with Mother Isabel about her staying here and Mother Isabel says she is already working on it and she is selling Rose the idea to stay. So depending on what happens here I think we can work that out.

I invited her in to Claridge's to have lunch with me Tuesday before the Chiropodist's appt. She looked fine and she got along OK. I really don't have any trouble with her when she is alone. She's not 100% of course, but no real difficulty.

She's gone away to Hereford for Easter and she is very happy. I've sent sugar & supplies to Hereford, Kensington & Boxmoor, so I'm keeping them all happy.

Everybody hates the war but don't see how they can get out of it. I'm more than ever convinced it's the end of everything.

Tell Kick & Eunice I've sent out all the records & gum etc. Tell Joe, Brendan Bracken[453] & Arthur Greenwood, the Labour Leader both asked for him. Tell Jack, Tony[454] and Jack's gang all want to see him but they think he's crazy if he comes over.

So darling that's all the news, except the old story, I love you and miss you. 3 months with you all the time makes me miss you all the more. Love to all.

Joe

Joseph P. Kennedy: *Diary*

March 28, 1940

Miscellaneous Items

In my talk with President Roosevelt in December at White House in discussing Winston Churchill he said "I always disliked him since the time I went to England in 1917 or 1918. At a dinner I attended he acted like a stinker. Birkenhead finally made him act properly. I'm giving him attention now because of his possibilities of being P.M. and wanting to keep my hand in.

In regard to helping the British in the war Roosevelt said "I'm willing to help them all I can but I don't want them to play me for a sucker."

Churchill in my conversation the other night in which we discussed the reshuffling of lines in the Pacific said among other things "For goodness sake don't let the Presi-

453. Brendan Rendall Bracken, later Viscount Bracken of Christchurch (1901–58); MP for North Paddington, 1929–45; and Churchill's parliamentary private secretary at the Admiralty. A close and longtime associate of Churchill's (as well as a faithful supporter not only of Churchill's attitude toward appeasement but of Churchill himself during the "wilderness" years), Bracken would become minister of information in 1941.
454. The twenty-two-year-old earl of Rosslyn.

dent come out with a peace plan it will just embarrass us and we won't accept it. In fact I would fight Chamberlain if he proposed to accept it."

He also asked whether Roosevelt would run for 3rd term. I said probably if it were necessary to keep things right in U.S. He said of course we want him, but we must be careful US doesn't know that. He implied it would be almost worthwhile to stir up things by July in the war so Roosevelt would run.

He is plenty warlike, he loves his position, he likes the idea the Germans hate him and except for the title he is more pleased than to be P.M.

My visit to Halifax, March 29.

Halifax asked what Welles thought about possibility of peace. I said he thought there was a bare chance. He asked what reaction Welles had to Chamberlain's suggestion that the English made their guarantee of disarmament in event of peace to U.S. "a unilateral agreement so to speak. Of course he said we expect to hold the balance of power as I said to Welles," said Halifax. "I immediately said, "I don't remember that point." He passed that by.

I think they wish they could get a secure peace but unfortunately see no hope.

He said I always picture Roosevelt as a man of too high class to gamble with the fate of the world by doing anything to help himself politically. I agreed completely.

He asked what I thought of him running for a third term. I said I thought he might if he saw the US possibly involved, but only if the situation in the war in Europe was in a hectic state. (He like Churchill acted as if it were necessary they'd raise hell to get him in.) The British Gov't acts as though they had private advices that Roosevelt would go if they put on a show over here. They might.

I can't help but remember what Roosevelt said to me over a year ago. (He would be a bitter isolationist, then help with arms & money & then depending on the state of affairs get in. I'm very leery.)

Rosemary Kennedy, 21, to Joseph P. Kennedy

the poplars, boxmore, Herts, Cowper Road, Saturday [April 4(?), 1940]

Darling Daddy,

Many thanks for coming tosee on Friday. <u>You</u> were darling.

(turn over) I hope you liked every-thing here. — And . the . chats with me, and Mother . Esbelle [*sic*]. Just. liked to know if you would like me to stay with you at. Easter. Or go to Hereford. It is up to you. Mother says I am such a comfort to you. Never . to leave you . Well Daddy . I feel honour because you chose me to stay . And . the others suppose are wild . — Let . me know tuesday about the arrangements . or . Sunday night when you . telephone me. I . would to talk to you very much.

to . talk to

<u>*me.*</u>

Much, Love,

<u>*Rosemary*</u>

<u>*E.D.M.*</u>

PS I am so fond of you. And . Love you very much. Sorry . to think that I am fat you . think) —

Joseph P. Kennedy to Rose Kennedy

London, April 5, 1940

Dear Rose,

The more I think of the possibility of your coming over for three weeks or a month, the better I like it. I think that as the weather gets better the Clipper will go fairly regularly and if that's the case, it's by far the pleasantest way. In addition to that, I expect that towards the first of May there will be a direct service by air from Lisbon to London, taking about eight hours. If, however, you wouldn't want to make it that way, the boat trip is pleasant and you could stop off in Paris for a few days before coming over to London and I probably could get over there to see you.

I still feel strongly about the children coming in June. As it stands now, aside from the question of the disagreeable arguments they would get into, there is nothing to do but spend practically every night in a night club. It is the only place where youngsters get together now. So I doubt very much whether any of them would have a very satisfactory time. In addition to that, there is always the possibility that trouble might start and settle the question automatically.

As it stands now, the great difficulty seems to be where the battle will be joined up between Germany and the Allies. Hitler evidently feels that, because of the political unsettlement in France and the changes in Cabinet in England,[455] there are internal political conditions in both countries that eventually make it unnecessary for him to assume the great risk of deciding where he wants to fight a battle. It is not at all unlikely that the Reynaud Government will fall and that reasonably soon. There is no question that under the leadership of the British the Allies only want to wage an economic war and this is all right for Hitler, because up to date he has not felt the stress of the blockade. The great difficulty will come when the American production of airplanes added to the French and British will give the Allies absolute air supremacy and at that time Hitler will definitely be in hot water, but that won't happen until 1941 and he may be prepared to gamble for the balance of this year. In the meantime, of course, I imagine he will start attacking the convoy system, which action has speeded up quite considerably in the last two weeks.

Of course, all of this is subject to change without notice, because nobody has the slightest idea of what's going through the minds of the General Staff in Berlin and it is not at all unlikely that he may decide to enter Holland and the fat will be in the fire.

Conditions in England haven't changed much at all. There is still a feeling that America should stop talking about the mistakes the Allies are making and, unquestionably, a great many of the people feel that we are making money out of the war. On the other hand, great groups of people are restless because nothing seems to be happening and, because of their inherent confidence in the British ability to win through, they can't understand why the Allies don't turn loose on the Germans and settle it up once and for all. Much easier said than done, however.

I haven't changed any of my bearish opinions. I think that on the 23rd of April, when the British bring in their new budget, they may have to finally decide just how they are going to pay this bill and when the world knows the sacrifice the people will

---

455. The secretary of state for war, Leslie Hore-Belisha, had resigned on January 5 amidst what Chamberlain described as "strong prejudice against him" within the British high command, and had been replaced by Oliver Stanley. On April 3, the lord privy seal, Sir Samuel Hoare, had been made secretary of state for air, replacing Sir Kingsley Wood. On March 20, French Premier Edouard Daladier too had resigned amidst criticism of his conduct of the war and had been succeeded by his minister of finance, Paul Reynaud.

have to make to pay a bill for the war, the people in America will be less and less interested in getting into one.

I was out riding in Windsor Park the other day and met the King and the two Princesses. Princess Elizabeth asked about you and Princess Margaret Rose smiled that cute little smile of hers. They both look exceptionally well. We talked, all of us on horseback, about fifteen minutes. The King looked rather tired, but who wouldn't?

Eddie caught a bad cold in Rome and finally was taken down with it in Paris. A great many people have the "flu" and he had rather a bad attack. I wasn't at all sure that he was getting along all right, so I flew over there and brought him and Mary back with me and put them out in the country. Of course, he looks terrible, but I think he is pulling along all right. He doesn't want to go home, of course, because he figures we will all be going home pretty soon and he would rather stay so that we can all go back together.

I wasn't at all disturbed about the German White Paper,[456] because, in the only version I have seen of it there was a reasonable account of my interviews with both Raczynski[457] and the Commercial Attaché. Of course, I think he got confused about young Joe, because the conference was long before the war and I don't know what Joe and Jack were going to do with public opinion.[458] The only talks there were going to give were to try to explain to the American public some of the things going on over here, but that was all knocked out when war was declared. I think, on the whole, my conversations were reasonably well reported and of course there was nothing in them that was anti-American. Naturally, I never said that I would insist on the Prime Minister doing anything and of course I would never take any instructions from anyone except Roosevelt or Hull. I wish they would have a congressional investigation and call me home to testify. There is nothing I would like better.[459]

Rosemary is out at Hereford and I talk with her a couple of times a week. She seems to be getting along very well. She is very happy and she is looking forward to the time when she can come back and act as hostess at Windsor.

456. On March 29, the German Foreign Office had released a series of diplomatic documents that Nazi troops had captured from the Polish Foreign Office after the fall of Warsaw the previous September. Bound in white, these "Polish Documents Bearing on Events that Led up to the War" were a compilation of diplomatic dispatches and memoranda that various Polish diplomats had sent from Washington, London and Paris between September 1938 and the first weeks of the war in September 1939. Collectively, the documents appeared to undermine the sincerity of the United States policy of neutrality in the European conflict. Ambassador Bullitt, the documents asserted, for example, had suggested that although the United States would not begin the war on the Allies' behalf, it would "finish" the war with them. The Polish ambassador and commercial attaché in London had described JPK as pressuring the Chamberlain government to assist Poland against the Nazi menace "with cash." Further, the documents cast the president as generally hostile to the totalitarian powers despite the current professed American attitude of nonintervention.
457. Count Edward Raczinski (1891–1993), Polish ambassador in London, 1934–45; later acting Polish foreign minister, 1941–45; and president of the Polish government-in-exile, 1979–86. "I read [the White Paper] with some apprehension," Raczinski noted in his diary on June 20, 1940, "but they contained nothing liable to compromise myself or the Embassy or to impair relations with our British hosts. All that has happened to me is that my photograph appeared in the *Völkischer Beobachter* — along with Kennedy's, of all people — as a 'war-monger.'"
458. The White Paper included a report by Jan Wszelaki, the Polish commercial attaché in London, recounting that "Ambassador [Kennedy] stated that his two sons, who recently had traveled all over Europe, had an opportunity to see and learn a great deal and intended to make a series of lectures on the European situation [in the United States] generally and in single States."
459. On April 1, both Representative Hamilton Fish and Senator Robert Reynolds had proposed closer congressional examinations of the White Paper. In typical form, "President Roosevelt, who went for a ride in the spring sunshine, had nothing to say," the *New York Times* reported, "and Secretary of State Cordell Hull had nothing to contribute to the controversy."

The Olivereiras left here this week and they are terribly disappointed and hope to see us all in America next September.

Well, I guess this is about all the news and perhaps after you have read it to the children, you might send it up to Joe and Jack, because I haven't much else to say to the boys and it will save sending an extra letter in the pouch.

Joseph P. Kennedy to Rose Kennedy

April 5, 1940

Rosa darling,

It was great hearing you last night, I had just been to a Sibelius Concerto, with Jim Seymour, for the Finnish Relief Fund. Not too good.

My tummy had been pretty good until I went to Paris and of course I ate the wrong things. I can't understand why I can't eat a few things I shouldn't. However I'm paying for it now and I hereby take a new resolution not to eat any thing I shouldn't.

The news all seems to be Roosevelt won't run so automatically I'm out. The only thing is how soon? I hear now the Germans are going to put out another lot of reports on me as well as others. Strangely enough Göring[460] told Welles I was the best and fairest Ambassador in Europe. They want Roosevelt licked because they feel they couldn't be worse with anyone else.

Well darling I guess it's right nothing is perfect in this life and I just don't like being so completely away from you. Yet knowing myself as I do when I've been home 6 months I'll want to get going again. Maybe old age and a bad stomach will change me. I don't know. I guess I'm a restless soul: Some people call it ambition. I guess I'm just nuts! Nevertheless, I love you so much

Joe

Joseph P. Kennedy, Jr., 24, to Joseph P. Kennedy

Palm Beach, April 5, 1940

Dear Dad:

The vacation is just about over, and soon back to the law School for the last two months of the grind and they ought to be honeys. I am typing this as I think on the finals I shall have to type as I don't think the Profs will be able to get through my papers as my handwriting is worse than ever.

There isn't much news and I know you probably have most of the news from down here. Grandpa left today and looked very well but says that he doesn't feel very well. He had been feeling pretty well up until a couple of days ago when he took a look at the stock market and saw that one of his stocks had dropped four points and from then on his stomach started to go badly.

All the papers have been full of the German White Paper as you know and the preponderance of newspaper comment feels that the papers discovered were authentic. I think it was a very smart idea not to make any comment. Johnson wrote a terrific edi-

---

460. In January 1940, Field Marshal Göring, already chairman of the Cabinet Council for the Defense of the Reich since the Polish invasion, had been made head of the new Council of Economic Warfare.

torial the other day against Bullitt, Cromwell[461] and Biddle but made no comment on you, it was really a scorcher.[462]

From the accounts in the paper of your conversation with the Polish attaché it would seem that you are in a very good position. There is nothing that can be criticized and your comments shaped up very well with the future events.

Everyone has been very well and we have had plenty of sun. Teddy is fatter than ever but looks as healthy as it is possible to look. Jack finished his thesis[463] and Arthur Krock thought it was excellent.

Nothing new on the convention except election will be on the 30th of April and I've got to figure some way to prevent myself from being the last on the ballot. There was some criticism of me not being on the voting list but that was straightened out OK and the protester finally got his only consolation in stating that it was sending a child on a mans job.

The death of Jay O'Brien yesterday was quite a blow to Palm Beach.[464] I saw him in the theatre just before he died and was talking with him and he seemed perfectly OK, however it seems that he had had heart trouble before and was out playing golf the last three or four days which were scorchers. My golf by the way is as good as usual.

From the comment in the paper it looks like Dewey will get the Republican nomination OK and it is still a mystery as far as the Democratic one goes.[465] At the present time it doesn't seem that anyone could be elected except Roosevelt. The Republicans are rather afraid that Hull would be nominated for that would take a lot of the wind out of their sails. Farley has come out and said that his name will be presented at Chicago regardless of what happens.

That's about all the news. My best to Ed and Mrs. Moore and all the others. Will write you from college if anything interesting appears.

Love
Joe

Edward Kennedy, 8, to Joseph P. Kennedy

April 8, 1940

Dear Daddy,

We are up in Bronxille now. the day that we left we had a dead skunk in the pool so we went to a boys. it was a sulphur pool. we had a very nice trep home. we saw the eclipse yesterday. the moon past the sun it got dark

How is Rose and the moores?

Love
Ted

---

461. James Henry Roberts Cromwell (1898–1990), United States Minister to Canada, January–May 1940.

462. In a series of personal attacks on the president's "glamour boys" in his column of April 2, 1940, the bitterly anti-administration Hugh Johnson excoriated Bullitt, Biddle and Cromwell as much for what he described as their diplomatic amateurishness as for their having married heiresses.

463. *Appeasement at Munich (The Inevitable Result of the Slowness of Conversion of the British Democracy from a Disarmament to a Rearmament Policy)* would form the basis for his first book, *Why England Slept*, which would be published in the coming autumn.

464. Investment banker, real estate entrepreneur, amateur steeplechase jockey and former Olympic bobsled star and official, J. Jay O'Brien had died of a heart attack in his home on Palm Beach.

465. The popular racket-busting New York District Attorney Thomas Edmund Dewey (1902–1971) had narrowly lost the New York gubernatorial race in 1938 and would go on to be edged out of the Republican nomination in July by Wendell Willkie. He would later serve New York as a three-term governor beginning in 1942, and would twice win the Republican presidential nomination, to run against Roosevelt in 1944 and against Truman in 1948.

John F. Kennedy, 22, to Joseph P. Kennedy

SPEE CLUB, CAMBRDIGE, MASSACHUSETTS

Dear Dad:

Just got back to-day from the South. It was great down there — the weather was about the best I've ever seen. An awful lot of people were down — three girls to every man — so I did better than usual — the girls (sisters) — having a bit of a battle at first but finished up the week in a blaze of glory.

Pat has Elliot Van Vleck on his ear — and Eunice had some flyer from Duke who was visiting the Loenings around all the time. It was quite a blow about Jay O'Brien. Joe and I had been talking with him that afternoon on the golf course and he had seemed fine. Mother was in great shape — and seems to be feeling fine. Bobby has increased in strength to such a degree that I seriously believe he will be bouncing around plenty in two more years. He really is unusually strong and that school seems to have done him an awful lot of good as he has improved immensely as everyone has noticed, — in every way. He looks 100% better too.

I am sending my thesis — the delay has been that it has to be retyped as the 1st two copies had to be handed in and this copy is not too clear. Arthur Krock read it and feels that I should get it published. He thinks that a good name for it might be "*Why* England Slept" as sort of a contrast to Churchill's "*While* England Slept." The conclusion I have now was done for college and can & should be changed although I could keep some of the ideas. Krock felt it should be brought out in the spring — May or June — but it would depend on

1st When you resigned &

2nd If you thought it was worth it —

3rd If you stayed on thru the summer it could be published while you are in office

You can judge after you have seen it — as I get finished on May 10th with my divisionals — I thought I could work on re writing it and making it some what more complete and may be more interesting for the average reader — as it stands now — it is not any where polished enough although the ideas etc. are O.K. I think. Jack Daly also read it & thought it should be done

Whatever I do, however will depend on what you think is the best thing — Jim Seymour might be able to assist me in some way on the English if I went ahead —

Harvard's base ball team looks none too good but Torb has been batting 400 for the 1st 8 games so that much of the talk on the football season is being wiped out

Planning to put the boats in the water and am going down shortly to look at the Davilis — Will probably have to put it in the water as it is pretty dried out — but I think that we may be able to rent it if we don't use it.

That's about all the news — Please let me know what you think about the thesis as soon as you can — Am sending it to an agent Krock gave me — and see what he thinks — the chief questions are

1. Whether it is worth publishing if polished up.

2. If it can be published while you're still in office.

Best to all

Love
Jack

Joseph P. Kennedy to Rose Kennedy

London, April 26, 1940

Dear Rose,

While I am still trying to get up courage to tell you to come on over, I thought that, since it is still a fifty-fifty chance that you had better not come, I had better give you the situation as I see it today.

The Norwegian invasion by Hitler was a staggering blow to the British, although, strangely enough when it happened, Churchill and others were rather optimistic in thinking that Hitler had overstepped himself.[466] I must say that I did not share that optimism, not through any military knowledge, but because of a hunch. The Germans are demonstrating that control of the air from their bases in Denmark is a very important factor in maintaining supremacy in Norway. The British have land men and supplies and they haven't the airplanes to protect them and, as a matter of fact, they haven't many aircraft guns to help them, so the German air force is continuously attacking the transports and the troops and their supplies as fast as they are landed. The result of this is that the British are not making a very good job of it.

The[ir] only hope now is that Sweden and Germany will get into a war and that, besides giving the Allies the additional force of the Swedish army, will give them some air bases to start operating from. But, frankly, I am not really too optimistic about this, because the difficulty seems to be that, even were the British to put airplanes in the Swedish airports, unless they got there quick enough and a force large enough to smash the Norwegian air bases the Germans now hold, they still would be in trouble. The real truth has not yet come out as to what value the air force is against convoys, cruisers and battleships, but I am not one of those who believe it is not terribly effective.

The danger of course of a German victory in the Scandinavian countries would be the devastating effect it would have on the neutrals in the Balkan States and on Holland Belgium and I don't think Mussolini would need much more, even with the opposition of the King and the Pope, to rush to the aid of the victor and were he to do that, it would be another bad mess for the Allies.

All these complications added to an unprecedented budget which the British people must meet even after only nine months of war bear out what I always told you — that this war means absolute chaos. To all those in America who are anxious to help the Allies, I can only say frankly, I don't know just how it could be done. At the minute they don't need credit because they still have well over two billion dollars worth of American securities they haven't sold, in addition to the gold they still have. We can't send an army over here because we haven't got one prepared; we are sending them airplanes as fast as we can make them with all our latest improvements; we can't send the Navy because the big percentage of the Navy is in the Pacific and we are continually making faces at Japan, so that if we move the Navy out of there the Japanese might very well walk into the Dutch East Indies and walk off with everything in the Pacific. So it is easy enough to say we should do something but the real difficulty is — what? My sympathies are completely with the Allies, but they must not run away with my judgment of what can happen to the United States. We may have to fight Hitler at some later date over South America, but we had better do it in our own back yard

---

466. On April 9, German troops had crossed both the Danish and the Norwegian borders, occupying Copenhagen and forcing the Norwegian government to flee Oslo. By the following day, Germany had installed a new Nazi puppet government under the former Norwegian Minister of Defense Major Vikdun Quisling. Over the subsequent weeks, Norwegian and British air, sea and land forces had attempted to fight off the German invasion with heavy losses on all sides, resulting in the eventual disintegration and abandonment of the Allied assistance effort in early May.

where we will be effective and not weaken ourselves by trying to carry on a fight over here.

My great difficulty in trying to make up my mind about your coming over is — if Italy gets into the war that will be the end of boats running between the United States and Italy and that means one would have to travel on a belligerent ship in order to get home, unless we could get you down to Lisbon some how by plane, but it might be more difficult than we can foresee, and, while I would rather have you here more than anything in the world, I don't think you would be very happy when the gang all got out of school if you weren't there to superintend them. However, I am hoping every day that some move will be made that will help me make up my mind.

Rosemary is fine. Her disposition is great and there is no question that she is getting along very well. She has gotten fat again and I am trying to get after her to go on a diet. I am not hopeful, but at least I can try.

The weather is very much nicer now and for the last week or ten days my stomach has been feeling very much better. Of course I am on a diet that would shame a one-year-old baby. I gradually am cutting out things that I have been eating all my life, but I guess that's what I've got to do.

The thing that worries me now is that it is going to [be] physically difficult to get home with Italy getting into the war. However something will turn up I hope. It's terribly interesting, but it's Hell to be here without all of you. I get blue about once a week and then I am most unhappy but I am trying to be sensible & watch the weeks go by.

I get news that you are more beautiful than ever. Maybe you do better away from me. All my love.

Joe

Joseph P. Kennedy, Jr., 24, to Joseph P. Kennedy

CAMBRIDGE, May 4th, 1940

Dear Dad:

Well, the only great excitement over here was the election and Grandpa thought I did quite well, so I guess the Kennedy name is a pretty good vote getter. There were only four of us running on the Farley ticket in this district and two others who were unpledged. The two unpledged got no votes to speak of. I came second about 100 votes behind Brennan who was a Cambridge man who got 2,250.[467] I beat a state senator[468] by about 200 votes and old Dan Coakley was way behind with only about 1,200.[469] They say that he was pretty broken up about doing so badly. The fellow who beat me was running for another office and hence had quite a few henchmen voting for him. The voting was very slight. In all the districts I did very well, and the reason I didn't win was because in a district like Cambridge Brennan beat me by 200 votes which was only natural, though I was a good second. In the other districts with the exception of Brookline where the state senator came from, I was first. In Brookline I was again a close second. So over all the result was very satisfactory. I don't know how well I should have done, but Grandpa was very pleased about it and he knows the situation pretty well.

467. James H. Brennan, the current Democratic nominee for Massachusetts attorney general.
468. Edward O'Hearn Mullowney (1903–1983).
469. The seventy-five-year-old Massachusetts executive councillor, Daniel Henry Coakley (1865–1952), had made a long and lucrative career of cronyism, fraud and extortion within Boston ward politics. A former prosecutor and attorney in private practice, Coakley had been disbarred in 1922. In 1941 he would be impeached by the state legislature for "misconduct and maladministration" in the granting of pardons as governor's councillor.

In the delegates at large the count has not been officially tabulated but Curley won in Boston. There was not much interest in the thing as it was such a sure-fire result, and only about 25% of the people voted.

Farley was on here about a week ago and I went into his banquet in town. I didn't think that he made a very good speech, all he said was that our foreign policy was OK. As I said to you over the phone it kind of looks like Roosevelt is going to run. There is no one else. McNutt faded out like a summer day. The only person I can see is Douglas, and no publicity is being given him. Hull stated categorically that he will not run, but he seems to be the only one except Roosevelt. The Republicans would have a hard time beating him. Thus the only combination which could loom up with the exception of Roosevelt would be Hull and Farley.

By the time this letter reaches you a great deal will have happened over there, I suppose. The general opinion here is that the English blundered. From the beginning I thought they would have a devil of a job, but I think they made a mistake in impressing upon people that Hitler made a strategic blunder and giving the impression that their fleet was doing a lot of damage. I think if they had impressed upon everyone the difficulty of their maneuvers that it would have been a much less severe blow, when they decided to withdraw. I don't see how people could have expected much when the Germans got such a terrific jump on them.

People over here still feel the same way. However every once in a while now you hear people talking about the need to go over now and not wait till it is too late. They are getting the idea that the English will have their hands full and feel that the only way to prevent Hitler from dominating the world is to go in now. There are three or four professors here who feel that way.

The atmosphere around here is really something now. It seems that we have more work all the time, and still have to do all our review work. I don't know how the dickens I am going to learn all this stuff in the next three weeks, but I suppose every one else is in the same position. I have decided to definitely type my exams as I am much faster now and have bought a new typewriter. Though as you can see I am far from perfect still it is much easier to read than my handwriting and I can do it a little faster than I can write.

Jack takes his divisionals tomorrow, or rather Monday and then is through for the year.

Grandpa is still making speeches and going strong. His latest remark is that Curley tried to sell the Boston Common but he stopped it.

Cousin Con[470] called me the other day and said that he had been meaning to write but was afraid to write anything political and didn't think it was the appropriate time to write anything funny. I told him that you would be delighted to hear from him.

That's about all the news. My best to everyone there. Give Rose my love.

Love
Joe

---

470. Cornelius Fitzgerald.

Rose Kennedy to Joseph P. Kennedy

May 8, 1940

Dear Joe,

I have been quite busy as I have told you making plans for going away. It has been a bit more complicated than usual because I have not had my usual standbys. Eddie is away, Kikoo is no longer with us, Miss Hennessey is ill and Mrs. Waldron[471] has another position. I have had to think not only of the present "status quo," but of the future plans of moving to the Cape, Class Day,[472] Eunice's tennis tournament in the West etc. There have been changes to be made in the house preparatory to the summer plans, and there have been more clothes to buy for Class Day. Then too, the Clipper schedule was not very inspiring. There has been much uncertainty and delay; however, I am gradually getting set, and it now looks as if I would go about the 15th.

I am going to the "Allied Ball" Friday night with Mr. and Mrs. Walker, the French Ambassador, and several other French dignitaries. It should be quite interesting and a glamorous occasion for New York. Kick is going with the Beverly Bogert, and I tried to get Eunice a beau but was unsuccessful.

Eunice is terribly interested in swimming [*& is captain.*] The other day her team was in a meet and beat all the upper classmen. In June, she goes to Ohio for a tennis tournament.

Pat received your wire on her birthday, and was thrilled. When she thanked Margaret for the cake, she said she remembered the first cake she ever made Pat, and that you carried Pat out to the kitchen on your shoulder to thank her, and that Pat could barely gurgle a "thank you".

Ted went to the circus last week with some friends from school and had a wonderful time.

Eunice, dressed in her Cannes shorts for the tennis tournament, was finally ushered off the field by an astonished coach. She raced to the gym, borrowed the conventional attire, including bloomers & long hose. Her bloomers loosened & to the snorts & laughter of the team — she had to be ushered off the field again & tighten up the borrowed attire. Her legs are so long that her stockings (which she must wear for the sake of the propriety of the nuns) do not reach to her shorts & the gap is now the subject of concern & of comedy at the games.

She went to the circus with a pal & bought, what the vender told her, was a lazy lizard. During the performance, she took a peek into the box & the lizard jumped out — slithered onto some one's shoulder & under someone's dress. One woman shrieked her mother would have a shock & Eunice's pal was so hysterical she jumped onto the railing. However — the reptile was retrieved, & Eunice insisted on getting back her 35 cents because she felt the man had deceived her about the little pet, & he was a bit nervous himself.

All my love.
Rosa

---

471. Her secretary.
472. The day preceding commencement at Harvard.

Joseph P. Kennedy: *Diary*

Last night (May 8th) I went to the House of Commons to hear the closing debate on Norway. A. V. Alexander[473] was speaking when I arrived and he asked a great many questions of the First Lord of the Admiralty about the conduct of the war in Norway. Not a particularly impressive speech. Churchill proceeded to answer him. We can see his answer in the record.

The House on the whole was in a belligerent mood. The one subject of conversation seemed to be the Prime Minister's break in the afternoon, when discussing the question of the vote of confidence he had said he would depend on his friends. All the Opposition had taken this up to prove that he was more interested in having his friends stand by him personally than in the good of the Country. There were constant interruptions of Churchill's speech. Churchill seemed to be quite able in his answers and handled the Opposition in very good shape, except for a couple of times when he lost his temper. One couldn't help but feel all the time, however, that he saw in the distance the mantle being lowered for his shoulders and that he didn't want to have anybody too mad with him.

In the gallery, where I sat between Maisky and Corbin, the Belgian Ambassador said it was his opinion that the Government majority would be 130 and everybody felt that was quite likely, so that when the announcement was made of the majority being only 80,[474] everybody was shocked. (See my cable of today).[475] The Prime Minister looked stunned and while he appeared to carry it off, he looked to me like a definitely beaten man.

I saw Dalton and Lady Astor in the lobby afterwards. Lady Astor immediately started for Halifax for Prime Minister. I then saw Beverly Baxter who seemed to be very pleased and happy that I had no ill-will for him on account of the article he had written about me. He said he had received a number of letters from America, which said it was a very bad way to treat a man who had done as much for England as I had, but he was very glad that I wasn't sore.[476]

I then went to Beaverbrook's house to get his slant on the situation. He felt that Chamberlain would have to go — if not right away, very shortly. He definitely favors Churchill.

I called the President on the telephone and told him roughly what had happened. He said he was surprised that 44 of the Conservatives had voted against Chamberlain.

---

473. Albert Victor Alexander (1885–1965), Labour MP for Hillsborough, had been first lord of the Admiralty under Ramsay MacDonald, 1929–31, and within three days would take up the post again for the duration of the war.

474. Eighty-one, in fact.

475. In JPK's Dispatch No. 1148 of noon on May 9, he reported that

   [t]he size of the majority of the vote last night, although in numbers a victory for the Party, definitely indicates failure. Two choices open to Chamberlain. (1) He can remain as Prime Minister and make drastic changes in his cabinet. (2) he can resign and suggest for the Premiership either Halifax or Churchill.

476. In his "Diplomatic Memoir" JPK went on to characterize the reaction of the British press to his remarks and its impact upon his standing in London.

   Those remarks, which I believe correctly summarized American thinking at that time, were not received graciously by the British press. In fact, the press lashed out at me quite bitterly. Beverly Baxter, writing in the *Sunday Graphic* and confusing my function as the American Ambassador to Britain with that of Lothian as the British Ambassador to the United States, bitterly criticized me for not telling the American Public what I believed the British war aims to be. Others reiterated Baxter's criticism and it soon became evident that a coolness had developed towards me in those circles, official and otherwise, whose main use for America was to embroil her in the war.

He said he thought there wouldn't be any more than 25. He was also sorry to see the ill-will that had sprung up. He thought this was disastrous in war times, which reminded me of what Corbin had said to me in the gallery — it seems to silly to be handing out vital information and furnishing propaganda to Hitler as this debate was doing. The President told me he was very much upset as he had just heard that Germany had delivered an ultimatum to Holland. I told him I was pleased to see the big votes he was getting in the States. He said, "Yes, everything is going fine," but they were keeping him altogether too busy. He asked how I was feeling and I said "All right" and I rung off.

Subsequently I told Churchill and Sam Hoare that the President had told me about the ultimatum. Churchill said, "A terrible world this is getting to be." Hoare said, "There really doesn't seem to be much hope anywhere, does there?"

There is a very definite undercurrent of despair because of the hopelessness of the whole task for England.

About 2 o'clock I called up John Cudahy, the ambassador in Brussels, and told him about my talk with the President and asked him what had happened. He said that some action in Holland was construed as an ultimatum of Hitler's but that he did not believe it should be and that he doubted whether the Germans would do anything last night or today, but it was quite probable that something would happen before the end of the holidays. This morning the Foreign Office called up, wondering if I could add anything to what I had given them last night, but I told Johnson to tell them that was all I knew and told them about Cudahy's statement.

May 10, 1940

At 6 o'clock this morning my telephone rang and they said it was Secretary Hull. I held on five minutes and then the Secretary came on and asked me if I knew of anything that was going on. I said, "Nothing." He said they heard from Cudahy who said the Germans had attacked Holland, and Belgium, and that there was great concentration of airplanes over Luxembourg. I told him that naturally I had heard nothing at that hour of the morning that affected the English, but that I would get busy and let them know at once.

I immediately called the Admiralty and got the map room and they indicated that the only news they had was that Holland had been invaded. I told them then of my conversation with Hull. They were very grateful but again it struck me that they didn't have the slightest idea of what was going on. I am sure they had no knowledge of either Luxembourg or Belgium.

I immediately got dressed and came to the office and put in a call for Gordon at The Hague and got him about 9:10.[477] He told me that things were very bad there; that he had been told they expected a battle within an hour; that he could not get into a suburb not more than ten minutes from the Embassy to evacuate some Americans. He understood that magnetic mines had been laid by the Germans in all the Dutch harbors and at Rotterdam they could not evacuate two ship loads of British subjects for that reason; that the Germans were landing in parachutes and in sea planes. At 4:03 the bombing took place and one dropped very close to the Embassy. He said he had sent telegrams 155 at . . . [sic], 156 at 6 o'clock, 157 at 6 o'clock, 158 at 7 o'clock, and 159 at 8 o'clock and hoped he could get an acknowledgment. He also said if the Dutch banks opened he proposed to get as much money as he could in order to have it on hand and he hoped that would be satisfactory. I told him I had no authority, but said he was the best judge of what was necessary to be done.

---

477. George Anderson Gordon (1885–1959), United States minister to the Netherlands, 1937–40.

I then got Cudahy about 9:30. He told me of his conversations with Hull. He said that at 2 o'clock the Luxembourg Foreign Minister had told him of great concentration of German planes; Brussels had been bombed at 5:30 and a building alongside the Embassy had been blown up; that an air raid warning was taking place as he was talking to me. He said there had been no warning or notice to the Belgian Government from the German Government before the attack, but at 8:40 the German Ambassador called on the Foreign Minister and handed him the German memorandum and the Foreign Minister refused to accept it and proceeded to give him a piece of his mind. Cudahy was then trying to get through to Washington at the request of the Belgian Foreign Minister to notify Berlin and the United States that Brussels was an open city and there were no troops there. He said he had no authentic news of fighting but understood there was a battle going on along the Meuse.

I called Rome at 9:30 and got Reed.[478] He said they had no news and there was no news in the morning papers and the only word they had was from the radio.

I called up Halifax after my talk with Gordon and again after my talk with Cudahy and gave him the information. I asked him what the British were doing and he said, "We are moving all ways — air, navy, and army".

I talked with Sumner Welles and gave him all this information. He said they hadn't been able to get through to anybody, not even Paris, and he was very anxious to keep in touch with these countries and to know what was going on. He told me that the message I sent him yesterday on the political situation was helpful and he appreciated it very much.

Joseph P. Kennedy to Franklin Roosevelt and Cordell Hull:
Diplomatic Dispatch

1211, May 15, 2 a.m.

At one o'clock I had just left Mr. Churchill.[479] Tomorrow morning he is sending you a message saying that he considers the chances of the Allies winning is [*sic*] slight with the entrance of Italy.[480] The German push he said is showing great power and the French are definitely worried although they are holding tonight. The French are calling for more British troops at once but the Prime Minister is not willing to send more from England at present for the reason that he is convinced the England will be vigorously attacked within a month. He needs help badly is the reason [*sic*] for the message to you. I inquired what the United States could do to help that wouldn't leave us holding the bag for a war which the Allies expected to lose; that if we had to fight it seemed to me that we would do better fighting in our own back yard. "You know our strength," I said. If we wanted to help all we can, what could we do? You don't need credit or money now; the bulk of our Navy is in the Pacific Ocean, our army is not up to re-

---

478. Edward Lyndal Reed (1895–1962), counselor of the U.S. Embassy in Rome, 1937–41.
479. Churchill, now prime minister, had formed a new coalition government following Chamberlain's resignation on May 10. Chamberlain would stay on as lord president.
480. Italy would declare war on France and Britain on June 10.
  On May 16, Churchill would write FDR that "[a]lthough I have changed my office, I am sure you would not wish me to discontinue our intimate, private correspondence." The new prime minister went on to say, "[i]f necessary, we shall continue the war alone and we are not afraid of that." He reminded the president, however, that "the voice and force of the United States may count for nothing if they are withheld too long," and went on to ask that the United States declare nonbelligerency, aid Britain with "everything short of actually engaging armed forces," and loan her "40 or 50" destroyers as well as aircraft, submarines, munitions and steel.

quirements and we haven't sufficient airplanes for our own use. So what could we do if this is going to be a quick war all over in a few months. It was his intention, he said, to ask for whatever airplanes we could spare right now and the loan of 30 or 40 of our old destroyers. Regardless of what Germany does to England and France, he said, England will never give up so long as he remains in power in public life, even if England were burnt to the ground; he said, "Why the Government will move, take the fleet with it to Canada and fight on." This is something I think I should follow up; there will be some conversation of what England will do eventually if the Germans carry on. Mr. Churchill called in Eden[481] and the first Lord of the Admiralty Sinclair[482] and they are very low tonight although they are tough and mean to fight.

KENNEDY

Joseph P. Kennedy: *Diary*

May 15, 1940

I went to the theatre last night with Gowen and Bill Hillman. After the theatre I stopped off at Beaverbrook's house, where he told me that he had just taken a job in Churchill's Cabinet.[483] He was sorry that he had to run away but he had an appointment with Churchill at 12 o'clock.

I stayed behind for a few minutes talking to some people and the telephone rang and it was Beaverbrook on the telephone asking me if I could come right away to the Admiralty; that Churchill would like to see me. I left immediately and went to the Admiralty House, where there were a number of soldiers on guard. I understood later that there were 175 soldiers alone guarding the Admiralty. When I went inside Eden was there talking to Dave Margesson.[484] I spoke to them both and started to the room where the Prime Minister was and Archie Sinclair was there and was most friendly in his greetings.

I then proceeded to read to the Prime Minister and Beaverbrook, who were sitting together, the telegram I had received from Phillips, indicating his worry over the Italian situation.[485] I later paragraphed the telegram by dictation and left a copy with Churchill. (See my confidential wire on gist of conversation with Churchill.)

I couldn't help but think as I sat there talking to Churchill how ill-conditioned he looked and the fact that there was a tray with plenty of liquor on it alongside him and he was drinking a scotch highball, which I felt was indeed not the first one he had drunk that night, that, after all, the affairs of Great Britain might be in the hands of the

---

481. Eden had become secretary of state for war on May 12.
482. The Liberal Party leader, Sir Archibald Sinclair had in fact replaced Sir Samuel Hoare as secretary of state for air; A.V. Alexander had replaced Churchill as first lord of the Admiralty.
483. The publisher had become minister of aircraft production the day before.
484. Captain (Henry) David (Reginald) Margesson (1890–1965), later first viscount Margesson, Conservative chief whip, 1931–40. "Without question," JPK had informed Hull on May 8, "the Party organization headed by David Margesson . . . who handles it like a cheer leader or like the Tammany bosses used to handle Tammany, is the best organization in the British Government."
485. In his diplomatic memoir, JPK recalled that
    on May 14, Ambassador Phillips in Rome cabled me that he had just seen Count Ciano and that the Italian Foreign Minister speaking with the utmost frankness had told him that whereas the chances of Italy remaining out of the war a week ago were fifty-fifty, the chances of her participation in the war were now ninety to ten. Ciano also had said that Mussolini had been greatly impressed by Germany's successes in Belgium and Holland . . . Mussolini's mind was now made up in favor of entering the war.

most dynamic individual in Great Britain but certainly not in the hands of the best judgment in Great Britain.

He was frankly worried about the situation but, as usual, he was clinging to the theory that, regardless of anything, we will never be beaten.

In discussing the French demand for soldiers he said, "I have seen so many battles that I realize that always in the beginning they want more men, but as the battle develops their demands become less and less." "So that's going to be my attitude toward the French." He said he thought that within a month there would be bombs and murder and everything terrible happening to England but it still would not deter them.

He sent for the First Lord and told him about the Italian situation and that he was going to ask Roosevelt for some destroyers and the First Lord agreed that that would be of great help because they could fit them up with the Asdic system[486] and use them in the Mediterranean and thus release their destroyers for other kind of work. The first Lord of course admitted that things were very quiet on the oceans at the minute but they expected renewed submarine attacks, particularly if Italy went in.

Churchill also said, "We are going to be in a terrible situation in regard to steel with Narvik cut off[487] and with trouble in the Mediterranean it looks like Spain might very easily be cut off and we will have to buy steel from the United States." I said they were in a position to buy it yet and the question of credits would come up when they started to feel the pinch. Churchill admitted that probably was right.

He got a scotch highball for the First Lord and the two of them sat down with me while we discussed the prospects. I would say that a very definite shadow of defeat was hanging over them all last night.

Churchill said he would discuss the whole matter with the Cabinet this morning and he asked the first Lord to get in definite requests that he could forward to the President and he would let me have a message to send to Roosevelt the first thing this morning.

In a telephone conversation I had with Sumner Welles yesterday, I told him I had just talked with Phillips, Cudahy and Gordon; that Phillips said the situation was acute and therefore he was planning to get the Americans out of Italy, but as there was no more room on American ships coming into that Country, he saw no point in anybody trying to get to Italy on boats and if Italy came in he supposed he would have to get his people over to Lisbon.

I told him Cudahy wanted to have Norman Davis[488] to help out with the Red Cross because the refugee problem was becoming very serious; that Gordon was worried about getting Americans out of Holland because, since there were no facilities and American boats in which to get them out, he didn't know what he could do about it.

So I recommended to Welles that either they send a ship to Ireland or get permission to travel on belligerent ships out of England. This morning I received their wire and I am taking issue with it shortly.

I called up Lord Halifax this morning and told him of this wire and that I wouldn't want to do anything until I talked with him, and that I did not see how they were going

---

486. The Allied Submarine Detection Investigation Committee device, the then secret apparatus for the detection of submarines using sound echoes; the British analogue to SONAR.

487. Allied forces would recapture the crucial northern Norwegian port of Narvik on May 28, but would be forced to withdraw again on June 8 in order to focus on Dunkirk.

488. Norman Hezekiah Davis (1878–1944), chairman of the American Red Cross, 1938–44.

to send an American boat into Bordeaux unless they changed the Neutrality Act but that I was not aware of the plans yet because I hadn't got the cable from Paris.

London, May 16, 1940

Last night at 12 o'clock Gowen called me and said the Prime Minister wanted to talk with me on the telephone. I called him and he wanted to know whether his message had gone forward to the President. I told him it had — instantly.[489]

He told me not to be too depressed about the situation; that he thought it was a little better last night. He said, "We have all got to put on a good front." I said there was no trouble about putting on a front, but I couldn't help my inner thoughts based on the facts.

He asked me if I had heard anything from the Barbary Coast Pirate (meaning Mussolini). I said I had no news from Rome at all.[490] He asked me what I thought the President would do on his request and I said — anything he could do that wasn't a complete violation of the law he would attempt. He asked when I thought we would get an answer and I said I didn't know, but I was sure as quickly as he could possibly send it.

I saw Kingsley Wood yesterday afternoon — the new Chancellor.[491] He told me that Montagu Norman had suggested he should have a talk with me as soon as possible. He told me he was very friendly with Norman and in that respect differed from Simon's relationship with Norman. He said he had talked with the chief of the Air Staff that morning and said he hoped he was keeping enough planes to protect England and the Air Chief assured him he was. He told me of a significant thing: that one of the German pilots captured was a boy 20 years old who had only 20 hours flying experience. He thought they weren't too well prepared with mature pilots.

He agreed with me that for the present England didn't need credits; that that was a problem for the future and I said when it became a problem that was the time to take it up. To take it up now merely looked to Americans who understood the financial situation that it was an excuse to get us into the war, because they realized England didn't need money or credit at this time.

London, May 16, 1940

I saw Chamberlain this afternoon. He is definitely a heartbroken and physically broken man. He looks ghastly; and I should judge he is in a frightfully nervous condition.

He asked me if I had seen that they were trying to get rid of him out of the government. I said, "Yes." He said: "Of course, I have no interest in holding office merely as an office-holder unless I can do good for my country." He said, "When Churchill asked me to come in and I came into the government with him, he remarked 'now we are together. I was with you when you were Prime Minister and now you are with me when I am Prime Minster.'" "Of Course," said Chamberlain, "as a result of this agitation he may say to me, and that is exactly how I would feel: 'This agitation is growing so much it is bad for the country;' and in that even," Chamberlain said, "Of course I will go." I said, "Why don't you answer these criticisms?" He said, "I can't do that and remain in

489. Later that day the president would respond that he would be "most happy" to continue corresponding with the "former Naval Person." He assured Churchill that the administration was "doing everything within [its] power to make it possible for the Allied Governments to obtain the latest types of anti-aircraft in the United States." He informed Churchill, however, that with regard to the requested destroyers, it would be unwise to broach the subject in Congress at that time, and in any case the United States could not spare them.
490. The previous day the president had appealed to Mussolini to keep Italy out of the war.
491. The former secretary of state for air, Sir Kingsley Wood (1881–1943), had replaced Sir John Simon as chancellor of the Exchequer.

the government, because I must of necessity attack some of my present colleagues." I said, "You must answer this question of rearmament," and he said, "It amazes me to hear some of these critics now complaining that we are not armed, when almost two years ago at Munich when they knew the armament conditions, they were critical of me for making the Munich arrangement."

He didn't seem bitter. He seemed more brokenhearted.

He evinced a real interest in Jack's forthcoming book and asked me for a copy.

I asked him if he thought the French would stick, and he said, "positively not." He was unqualified in his opinion that they would quit, and that soon.

Chamberlain.

He told his wife when war started, he knew nothing of military tactics and he was disposed to resign and let a younger man more versed in military matters take up the job. But since nothing happened, he held on. Now it is so military and since Winston thinks he understands war, perhaps it is better he should take on.

Joseph P. Kennedy to Franklin Roosevelt and Cordell Hull: *Diplomatic Dispatch*

1237, May 16, 1940, 6:00 p.m., For the president and the Secretary: Most Secret and Personal.

In order to try and strengthen the French moral[e] Churchill has flown to Paris. The situation is deadly acute. The French are not even fighting on the Line.[492] My friend[493] does not believe if the French persist in the present course of action that England can fight on alone. There will therefore be another fight in the Government because Churchill said he will fight until England is burned to the ground. Refer to my 1211 of May 15 last 2:00 a.m.

Air bombardment of the civilian population, the English feel, is the real reason for the French funk. The Ruhr was bombed last night by the English and today there was a row in the Cabinet over the sending of more planes to France. It was Churchill's wish to send a substantial number of squadrons though this would leave the position rather precarious here. A compromise was finally reached on sending four squadrons. Some people in the Government feel that this was too many at this time since the Germans will definitely return last night's engagement unless they decide to finish off their present job in Belgium and later on take care of England.

The President might start considering, assuming that the French do not stiffen up, what he can do to save an Allied debacle. It is not beyond the realm of reason that this crack up can come like a stroke of lightening. In consequence any action must be conceived now if it is to be effective.

It is the view of my friend that nothing can save then from absolute defeat unless by some touch of genius and God's blessing the president can do it.

This is absolutely reliable information.

KENNEDY

The Ambassador

492. That is, the Maginot Line.
493. Periodically JPK sent the assessments of this anonymous friend, whom he regarded as an "unimpeachable source," to the department.

Joseph P. Kennedy to Neville Chamberlain: *Draft*

May 18

Dear Neville,

Your picture so nicely inscribed arrived last night.

I really wanted this picture to hang in my house to remind me constantly of a man who worked with all his capacity to keep peace in the world, and with whom I am most happy to have been associated with in the 2 most eventful years of my life.

My warmest regards to Mrs. Chamberlain and my sincere wish that you will continue in your efforts.

Joseph P. Kennedy, Jr., 24, to Joseph P. Kennedy

CAMBRIDGE, May 18, 1940

Dear Dad:

Since I last wrote you a great deal has happened and I thought you might be interested in knowing what people are thinking and talking about.

Everyone is unanimous in thinking that Roosevelt made a marvelous speech.[494] Some wonder what we are going to do with 50,000 planes, and suspect that it is Roosevelt's intention to get the country into war immediately after the election, whereas to others it is a natural defensive measure. You would be surprised to see how panicky the people here are getting about the possibility of invasion. Some of them have asked for muskets for protection against parachute troopers and you would think that the war was in their backyard.

Also the change in attitude toward the war has been remarkable. Overnight the people turned strongly sympathetic to the allies, and now many people are saying that they would just as soon go to war, and that they will have to go anyway and why not now. Also there is a kind of feeling here that we are bound to be in the war, like a mysterious force which is ever bringing the country closer.

Roosevelt increased his prestige a great deal by the speech and I think that he could win easily today. How he will be if there is a reaction against spending all that money is hard to tell. People are most enthusiastic now, but if there is a reaction it is likely to be a strong one. The Republicans have hopped on the preparedness bandwagon, and want to know why the money already spent by the Democrats was not used for defense purposes. Dewey looks far ahead of the others, however a lot of people seem to think that if he doesn't get the nomination at the beginning that they will knock him off. Willkie[495] has increased his popularity a great deal, but seems a pretty dark horse. It

---

494. "We stand ready not only to spend millions for defense, but to give our service and even our lives for the maintenance of our American Liberties," the president had told both houses of Congress on May 16 while requesting some $286 million in order to fortify American defenses against possible attack. Citing recent events in Europe and the unpreparedness that had permitted such rapid German expansion there, Roosevelt called for an immediate acceleration of the of the Army, Navy and Marine Corps rearmament programs. He noted in particular that he "should like to see this nation geared up to the ability to turn out at least fifty thousand planes a year." "Rarely, if ever before," *The New York Times* commented, "has Mr. Roosevelt received such an ovation as that which greeted his appearance before the joint session of Congress."

495. By the mid-1930s Wendell Lewis Willkie (1892–1944), president of the utility conglomerate Commonwealth and Southern Corporation, had become an articulate and nationally known opponent of New Deal measures such as the Public Utility Holding Act and the Tennessee Valley Authority. A former Democrat, Willkie had changed party affiliations a year earlier and would become the Republican presidential nominee that summer.

looks like Taft[496] is next to Dewey. No Democrat is getting any play, and it looks like Roosevelt or nothing.

Not much news at the law school. Have been working pretty hard, and everybody is a jumble of nerves. Some of the fellows are really a wreck, but so far I have been holding body and soul together and praying for the best.

Jack has been down at the Cape. Talked to Mother and the children all seem well. Everyone is most sympathetic to your job over there, and say how difficult it must be.

Some of this job of rebuilding the defense program would be right up your line, and might be a possible reason for bringing you back.

Love

Joe

Joseph P. Kennedy: *Diplomatic Memoir*

I was in Windsor . . . Saturday,[497] when Herschel Johnson of our embassy telephoned to say that he must speak to me immediately. A representative of Scotland Yard had called on him, Johnson said, to tell him about the conduct of a code clerk in our Embassy. Johnson's language was guarded by I gathered enough from what he said to learn that one of our clerks was suspected of having given our confidential information to sources allied to the Nazis. It was already late in the evening and since it seemed wise not to converse at length over the telephone I asked Johnson to be down at Windsor in the morning.

Johnson had an extraordinary story to tell the next day. A Captain Maxwell Knight of Scotland Yard had been to see him about Tyler Kent, a code clerk in our Embassy, who had been sent to us by the State Department from Moscow about a year ago.[498] Scotland Yard, Knight said, had first noticed Kent because of his association with members of the Right Club. That Club was reported to be a fifth column organization engaged in pro-German propaganda and said to have contacts abroad, even in Germany.[499] Its leader was Captain Archibald Ramsay, a Conservative Member of Parliament and a member of one of the socially prominent families.[500] Captain Ramsay was associated with an Anna de Wolkoff, the daughter of an ex-Admiral of the Imperial Russian Navy who had fled with his family to England from the Bolsheviks in 1919. She worked in a fashionable dressmaker's shop and her attractive and interesting personality had given her numerous contacts with important official and diplomatic persons.[501]

Scotland Yard had originally become interested in Kent because of an encounter between him and a naturalized Swede of German extraction that occurred last October, this Swede, Ludwig Ernst Matthias, was known to the Yard officials a Gestapo agent

496. In 1938 Robert Alphonso Taft (1889–1953), the eldest son of the former president and an outspoken opponent of the administration, had been elected to the U.S. Senate from Ohio.

497. May 18.

498. The son of the former American consul at Newchang, Manchuria, Tyler Gatewood Kent (1911–1989) had entered the Foreign Service in 1934. He had served in Moscow until July 1939, when he had become a cipher and code clerk in London.

499. In a secret memorandum of May 30, 1940, Herschel Johnson, councillor of the Embassy, would report to the department that "[t]he Right Club, according to Captain Knight, is a definitely 'Fifth Column' organization which under the cloak of anti-Jewish propaganda conducts pro-German activities, has contacts in British Government offices and also in several foreign Missions."

500. The openly anti-Semitic Unionist MP for Peebles and the Southern Division of Midlothian, Scotland, Captain Archibald Henry Maule Ramsay (1894–1955) would maintain his seat in the House of Commons even after his arrest, conviction and imprisonment under section 18B of the Defense Regulations.

501. Surviving records list her as Anna Wolkoff (1902?-1976?).

and for this reason they had had him under close surveillance during his October visit to London. He had been observed after a visit to Kent's rooms leaving with a bulky manila envelope under his arm. Some time later information came into the Yard to the effect that Anna de Wolkoff was using Kent as one of her chief sources of information and had been seeing a great deal of him. Indeed, the information which Captain Knight gave him as having its source in Anna de Wolkoff, Johnson said, had been checked with the Embassy despatches and telegrams and much of it could have had no other possible origin. Johnson said that Scotland Yard was preparing to arrest Anna de Wolkoff on Monday morning and would search Kent's rooms at the same time provided that we would waive any diplomatic immunity that might prevent such a search.[502] Neither of us had any hesitancy about permitting such a search and we notified the Foreign Office to that effect.[503]

The next morning the Scotland Yard officials, accompanied by Mr. Gowen, the Second Secretary of our Embassy, and armed with search warrants knocked on Kent's door. Twice a voice shouted, "Don't come in." Inspector Pearson, however, crashed the door open. Kent was found inside with his mistress, a Russian-born woman who had married a British subject. Both were scantily attired. They were ordered to dress and the woman, who was known to the Police, was allowed to go home. A series of documents were brought back to the Embassy.

Kent was shortly after interrogated in my presence. Over fifteen hundred Embassy documents were found in his possession. They consisted mainly of telegrams sent between the Embassy and the State Department, but there were also copies of letters, telegrams to our other Embassies in Europe, and miscellaneous documents. Much of the material related to non-confidential and apparently harmless matter[s], but among the material were the true readings of telegrams to the State Department in our most confidential codes and about the most secret subjects. Many of these had originally been coded and copied by Kent himself. A goodly portion of the material had been placed by Kent in separate subject files, such as "Germany," "Russia," "Churchill," "Halifax," "Jews," and a key to the abbreviations used in the dispatches had been prepared. Kent also had in his possession two excellent photographic plates of two cables that I had sent containing messages from Churchill to Roosevelt. Among other articles found in his possession were duplicate keys to the Code Room and a heavy leather-bound, pad-locked volume of which he claimed he had no key and which when broken open was found to contain the names of the members of the Right Club. He denied any knowledge as to the contents of that volume but admitted that it had been given to him by Captain Ramsay for safe-keeping.

The interrogation of Kent by the Scotland Yard officials was not too deftly conducted, but it produced enough to warrant his further detention. I was naturally distressed by the incident and by the failure (that I had no hesitancy in commenting on) of

502. The Tyler Kent case constitutes the only known instance of an American ambassador's waiving an embassy employee's diplomatic immunity (thus allowing that employee to be tried under foreign jurisdiction.) Kent would be charged both with larceny and with violating the Official Secrets Act of 1911. He was tried in late October in camera, that is to say in closed court. The proceedings, testimonies and documents in question (including the secret correspondence between Roosevelt and Churchill) would therefore remain secret. Had Kent's diplomatic immunity been maintained, he would have been deported and tried openly in the United States, thus revealing the documents and secret correspondence to an as-yet noninterventionist American public and Congress in the months leading up to the 1940 election. On November 8 Kent would be sentenced to seven years' imprisonment on the Isle of Wight.

503. With regard to JPK's waiver of Kent's diplomatic immunity, Hull would inform the Embassy that "[t]his Government has no objection to formally charging the offender with violations of British law," and added, "[i]n the circumstances, publicity in connection with such charges might not be helpful."

431

the Scotland Yard Officials to bring their suspicions about Kent to our attention months before. Their failure had led us to continue Kent in our employ in the most confidential of all positions, and had led to the dissemination of much confidential information as well as spreading broadside data in the form of true readings that would make insecure our most secret codes. Kent's explanation for purloining these documents was not convincing. He claimed that he had done so only "for his own information" and because he thought they were "interesting." One fact, however, that a quick check of our records disclosed was that Kent only a short time before his arrest had applied for a transfer to our Embassy in Berlin. Realizing that the whole matter deserved a very thorough investigation that could only be effectively carried out by the British police and that the evidence pointed to an offense under British law, I agreed to waive any further immunity for Kent and he was taken off by the Scotland Yard officials to Brixton Prison.

More material on Kent's activities was developed shortly afterwards. Captain Ramsay, Anna de Wolkoff, and a Mrs. Nicholson were arrested at the same time and also confined to prison. Mrs. Nicholson had in her possession a rough pencil copy of the President's message to Churchill of May 16, which she in turn had made from a copy in the hands of Anna de Wolkoff. Anna de Wolkoff and Captain Ramsay were shown to have been frequent visitors to Kent's rooms and to have read some of the dispatches in his possession. Early correspondence in Kent's possession, originally sent through the diplomatic pouch to Moscow, showed that he and other associates in the Embassy in Moscow had been engaging in petty smuggling, while other articles in his possession indicated the pursuit of a course of conduct in his associations in London and elsewhere that, to be charitable, could not have qualified as morally acceptable in normal society.

With the State Department's acquiescence, Kent remained in Brixton Prison pending trial on such charges as might finally be preferred. His arrest, however, threw our entire communications into confusion. Our existing codes were no longer safe, and their violability imperiled the secrecy of our diplomatic communications throughout all of Europe. It was days and weeks before the situation could be completely restored and in the meantime we had to resort to one stratagem after another to deal with transmitting to the Untied States the flood of information that was pouring in on us as the Germans were making their rapid advance through the broken French and British lines to the Channel ports.

Joseph P. Kennedy to Rose Kennedy

Monday Morning, May 20, 1940

Rosa darling,

I just got your letter from Whigham,[504] I'm heartbroken, but you just couldn't be here.

The situation is terrible unless the French can push to the sea and with the British who are falling back from their position, stop this drive of the Germans. I think the jig is up. The situation is more than critical. It means a terrible finish for the Allies.

I'm planning to get Rose and the Moores out either to Ireland or Lisbon. We will be in for a terrific bombing pretty soon and I'll do better if I just have myself to look after.

---

504. Presumably her letter of May 13, in which she told him,
> I was finally ready to go on the 10th and they said they would take me on the 13th, but of course the way the picture looked from here, as well as it looked over there, it seemed like taking too many chances. I am still hoping I may go a little later, which will be better for me.

The English will fight to the end but I just don't think they can stand up to the bombing indefinitely.

What will happen then is probably a dictated peace with Hitler probably getting the British Navy, and we will find ourselves in a terrible mess.

My God how right I've been on my predictions. I wish I'd been wrong.

Well darling it's certainly been a great adventure. It's getting near the finish.

Love to all and take care of yourself. I'll probably be home sooner than we thought.

Love to you my darling,

Joe

Joseph P. Kennedy to Rosemary Kennedy, 21: *Telegram*

DEAR ROSEMARY I AM SORRY I AM NOT THERE TO SEE YOU GET YOUR DEGREE YOU HAVE WORKED VERY HARD AND I AM VERY PROUD OF YOU AND I LOVE YOU A LOT

DAD

Joseph P. Kennedy to John F. Kennedy, 22

London, May 20, 1940

Dear Jack:

I have shown your thesis to various people around here. Everyone agrees that it is a swell job, and that you must have put in some long hard hours assembling, digesting and documenting all of this material.

Most people, I believe, will agree with the fundamentals of your thesis. However, one or two of those who have read it complain that you have gone too far in absolving the leaders of the National Government from responsibility for the state in which England found herself at Munich. These people agree that no good purpose can be served by making scapegoats out of Baldwin and Chamberlain; on the other hand, they feel that you have gone too far in putting the blame on the British public.[505]

The basis of this criticism is that the National Government was in absolute control from 1931 to 1935, and that it was returned to office in November 1935, with another huge majority. This mandate, it is contended, should have been used to make the country strong. If the country supported such a policy, well and good; if not, then the National leaders should have thrown caution out of the window and attempted to arouse their countrymen to the dangers with which Britain obviously was confronted.

One of the men who read the thesis was especially critical of your treatment of Baldwin on page 99. He contends that if, as you imply, Baldwin did not believe in the policy he was pursuing, it was his sacred duty not only to plump for the policy he did believe in but to go to the country on that issue and not on another. To say that Baldwin went to the country on one issue in order to gain strength to support another does put him in the role of deceiving the public and playing politics with the country's welfare.

There are some, of course, who do not believe that Baldwin was himself sold on the idea of rearmament until it was too late. They point out that those who did attempt to warn the people of the German menace were systematically ridiculed and eventually

---

505. "To blame one man, such as Baldwin [prime minister 1935–1937] for the unpreparedness of British Armaments," Jack had asserted in his preface, "is illogical and unfair, given the conditions of Democratic government."

forced — or at least allowed — to leave the Government. These people say that stupidity and passivity on the part of the National leaders might be explained away, but how are we going to justify their outright opposition to the demands of Churchill, Eden, Cooper, Lloyd George and others for a rearmament program that would restore to Britain their prestige and the security she once enjoyed. In other words, they think you are letting Baldwin off too easily.

An ex-minister in the Chamberlain Government, with whom I have discussed this question recently, lays Britain's failure to rearm to two factors:

(1) The National leaders, especially Chamberlain, underestimated the rapidity of German rearmament;

(2) They always expected to be able to make a deal with Hitler.

Germany got a head start on the Allies before they were able to comprehend what she was about. She probably got this head start not so much through the manufacture of actual implements of war, but through laying a foundation for their manufacture. The German locomotive industry, for example, was turned over to the manufacture of tanks instead of rolling stock for the deteriorating German railways. Germany was especially smart in getting tooled up for aircraft production. It takes a couple of years to get factories organized for the production of munitions on a large scale. Germany got the jump principally through getting everything set for a large-scale output rather than through the output itself, even though the latter certainly was considerable. It was easy for the Allied leaders to overlook this preliminary preparation, as it is difficult to keep track of manufacturing in a foreign country and to know whether an automobile plant is being tooled to produce engines for the "people's car" or to produce engines for 'planes.

There is no doubt that many people here thought that England and Germany should be, and could be, friends. When they found that it was impossible to do business with the Nazis, it was too late to catch up in the arms race. They may have been guilty of bad judgment, but they certainly tried to get along with the German Reich.

I believe that the basis of your case — that the blame must be placed on the people as a whole — is sound. Nevertheless, I think that you had better go over the material to make sure that, in pinning it on the electorate, you don't give the appearance of trying to do a complete whitewash of the leaders. I know that in a Democracy a politician is supposed to keep his ear to the ground; he is also supposed to look after the national welfare, and to attempt to educate the people when, in his opinion, they are off base. It may not be good politics but it is something that is vastly more important — good patriotism. I do not see how we can take any other line if we hope to make Democracy work.

It seems to me that this would be a good line to follow: The National leaders failed to rearm, and they were caught at Munich. They had to shut up because they couldn't put up. It would be very simple to blame the leaders and to say that they should have been prepared. However, Britain is a democracy and at that time Britain was definitely a pacifist democracy. The leaders moved slowly, just why we don't know. Perhaps they underestimated the danger; perhaps they were afraid to jeopardize their political position; perhaps they misread the temper of the country (it is quite possible that the people would not have objected to a real rearmament program); perhaps the leaders thought that they could best contribute to the national defense by keeping the country's internal economy on an even keel and not destroying it, as was done in Germany, by colossal expenditures on armaments. The chances are that all of these reasons contributed to the sorry state in which Britain found herself in September 1938. Why not say that British national policy was the result of British national sentiment and that everyone, leaders and people alike, must assume some share of the responsibility for what happened. It is not fair to hang it all onto the leaders; it is equally unfair to absolve them of all responsibility. For some reason, Britain slept. That means pretty much all Britain, leaders and people alike.

You might point out the difficulties our own President has had in seeking to awaken the country to the dangers of aggression. To say that democracy has been awakened now by the horrible events of the past few weeks does not prove anything; any system of government would awaken at a time like this. Any person will wake up when the house is burning down. What we want is a kind of government that will wake up when the fire first starts or, better yet, one that will not permit a fire to start at all.

The American Congress has repeatedly cut the President's requests for defense appropriations. And Roosevelt was strong. The English leaders didn't fight for rearmament. Roosevelt fought but Congress resisted and sometimes licked him. Now that the world is ablaze Congress may give him the treasury but we can't escape the fact that democracy in America, like democracy in England, has been asleep at the switch. If God hadn't surrounded us with oceans three and five thousand miles wide, we ourselves might be caving in at some Munich of the Western World. We should profit by the lesson of England and make our democracy work. We must make it work right now. Any system of government will work when everything is going well. It's the system that functions in the pinches that survives.

A thing to remember always about defense is that the complex machinery used today takes a long time to produce. It takes a year to tool up for an airplane, and it takes two or three years to produce a battleship. America is just starting on this business of national defense. I am sure that, isolationist or not, practically everybody is now convinced that we had better be strong as hell if we want to survive in the world of to-day.

I am having a mimeographed copy edited here and will get it on the next Clipper. You might also be trying to improve the writing. After you are satisfied with it, ask Arthur Krock to go over it again. If Krock is willing, let his agent handle the publication.

I suggest that, when you are going over the material again, you check your reference[s]. We have found several mis-spellings of names and a couple of wrong dates. For example, I believe that you had Baldwin making in 1939 a speech which was really made four or five years ago.

The point has been made that your use of the word "warning" is incorrect. "Warning" requires an object; in other words, you have to warn somebody.

JPK

Princess Elizabeth, 14, to Joseph P. Kennedy

Windsor Castle May 22nd 1940.

Dear Mr. Kennedy,

Thank you very much indeed for the lovely pictures from "Pinocchio." They are so cleverly done. I think I like the one of Pinocchio's head best, or perhaps the one of them all on the raft.

We saw the film the day before my birthday and we all liked it very much. I think I prefer it to "Snow White.["]

I am so sorry for the delay in thanking you but in the muddle of leaving Royal Lodge to come down here, the pictures were not given to me till yesterday.

I hope you, Mrs. Kennedy and the children are well.

Yours very sincerely,

Elizabeth

Rose Kennedy to Joseph P. Kennedy

Saturday, June 1

Joe darling,

We are waiting for Rose & there has been much delay — as you know. I wanted to get the last word from Eddie before I wrote.

I am thinking of you — darling, and just wishing you were along, but I am hoping and praying that somehow or other, I shall see you soon. I suppose we are infinitely better off than thousands of other people. I do hope your tummie is not too awful — but of all places to be! There seems not much more to be said. It was such a wonderful experience, and as I said to the children — Friday — so few youngsters their age have seen the old Europe. But you are so important to me — my darling — so do take care of yourself the best way you can & we shall just keep on praying.

All my love always,
Rosa

Joseph P. Kennedy to Arthur Goldsmith:[506] *Telegram*

JUNE 4, 1940

JACK CABLED ME GRADUATING WITH HONORS THOUGHT YOU MIGHT DIS-
CREETLY WHISPER TO WINCHELL THAT THIS IS SECOND OF THE KENNEDY BOYS TO
GET HONORS AT HARVARD INCIDENTALLY JACKS THESIS ON BRITISH APPEASE-
MENT TO BE PUBLISHED BY HARPERS NEXT WEEK RECEIVED MAGNA MAYBE YOU
COULD WORK UP LITTLE BOOST FOR HIM HE IS IN BRONXVILLE
JOSEPH KENNEDY

Joseph P. Kennedy to Joseph P. Kennedy, Jr., 24

London, June 6, 1940

Dear Joe:

I am sending this note to the Cape because I imagine that by the time it gets to America you will be down swimming and sailing; and if ever a boy was entitled to a good vacation you are the one. I can't tell you how pleased I have been with your superlative effort this year at the Law School. It was a terribly tough thing to go back to that kind of work after a year in Europe, and the fact that you stuck with it is a great tribute to you.

I had been hoping and praying that I would be back so that I could be with you on your twenty-fifth birthday, because on that day you take over your interest in the Trust and you become owner of a considerable amount of securities and money. In addition to that you are now arriving at the point here you have a responsibility to the family. Of course I am completely confident nothing is going to happen to me in this mess, but one never can be sure, and you don't know what a satisfaction it is for me to know that you have come along so well, and I have such confidence that come what may, you can run the show.

The situation today is a serious one. If the French break — and the consensus of opinion here is that they will — then I should think the finish may come quite

---

506. JPK's Harvard classmate and a New York stockbroker.

quickly.[507] The British, of course, will fight, but only through pride and courage. With the French out of the way and the Germans in control of all the ports I can see nothing but slaughter ahead. I am arranging to send everybody away with the exception of about ten of us, of which number Ding Dong is one, who will stay and sleep at the Chancery. I am going to try to keep this place operating as long as they leave the building standing up.

The story about the bomb missing Bullitt is a fake.[508] Duff Cooper[509] was at the luncheon and he said he saw no signs of a bomb, and of course I think that is just another instance of trying to stir up public opinion without a firm basis. God knows there are enough real reasons why America should arm, and arm quickly, without stirring up their emotions.

Tell Jack I talked with Chamberlain yesterday and he is very anxious to read Jack's thesis. He said he would regard it as a very important document, even from his point of view. Laski also wrote me this morning that he wants to read it.[510] I think Jack did a swell job and I hope the book comes out well for him.

Well, you will be hearing from me from time to time, and in the meantime take care of yourself and have a good rest.

Love to all,
J P K

Edward Kennedy, 8, to Joseph P. Kennedy

PORTSMOUTH PRIORY SCHOOL, PORTSMOUTH, RHODE ISLAND

Dear Daddy

We are down in cap-card mother has gone to jacks graduain. joe is here. The wether is very dad. Would you get me the kings autograh for me I will send you an other lettor soon

love Teddy

507. On May 16, German forces had broken through the French lines at Sedan, resulting in a reshuffling of the French cabinet. On June 3, the *Luftwaffe* had begun bombing Paris, and by June 5, German forces had started their offensive between Laon and the coast of the English Channel, thereby launching the Battle of France.
508. It had been reported that the U.S. ambassador to Paris had narrowly escaped with his life when an aerial bomb hit the French Air Ministry during the German air raid on Paris on June 3.
509. Duff Cooper, who had resigned his position as first lord of the Admiralty over his opposition to the Munich Agreement in 1938, had been appointed minister for information on May 12.
510. After reading the published version two months later, Laski, the political theorist under whom Joe Junior had studied at the London School of Economics in 1934–35, would comment that

> The easy thing for me to do would be to repeat the eulogies that Krock and Harry Luce have showered on your boy's work.
>
> In fact, I choose the more difficult way of regretting deeply that you let him publish it. For while it is the book of a lad with brains, it is very immature, it has no real structure, and it dwells almost wholly on the surface of things. In a good university, half a hundred seniors do books like this as part of their normal work in their final year. But they don't publish them for the good reason that their importance lies solely in what they get out of doing them and not in what they have to say. I don't think any publisher would have looked at that book of Jack's if he had not been your son, and if you had not been Ambassador. And those are not the right grounds for publication.
>
> I care a lot about your boys. I don't want them to be spoilt as rich men's sons are so easily spoilt. Thinking is a hard business, and you have to pay the price for admission to it. Do believe that these hard sayings from me represent much more real friendship than the easy praise of "yes men" like Arthur Krock.

Joseph P. Kennedy: *Diary*

My Notes, June 10 — Conference with Churchill

On Friday last I asked for appt with Churchill Saturday. It was made for 6 p.m., tonight. This morning it was moved to 7 p.m. and subsequently cancelled. In talking to Beaverbrook, I expressed my resentment at this because I feel it was personal.

Beaverbrook immediately said Randolph[512] was a [sic] s.o.b. and he and his father had had a bitter fight last week. (Bracken had told me this at lunch.) that the old man had left the dinner table because he said his son had a poisonous tongue. Evidently I was berated as well as Eden. I told Beaverbrook to hell with him, I didn't give a damn.

Anyway, a little later appt was put on by P.M. for 7:30. I saw Archie Sinclair and Neville came out of Cabinet room. Neville says US can have a great moral effect if they come in even though they can't help at this time.

On entry to room, my first visit since Churchill P.M. He got up very graciously offered a high ball. I said I don't drink and what's the news.

"Mussolini's name will go down through centuries as a jackal and a betrayer of all things good and fair. Hitler was a gentleman compared with him."

I asked if the French would quit. No he thought not. A good new general had come in. A Colonel when war started now a general and advisor to Reynaud.[513]

Reynaud assured him France would not quit even if Paris went to part of army.

I asked him about help to France.

"We can't give them anything that will take away our capacity to make war."

We lost everything in France and after all, they gave the orders. If they had given them sooner we could have fallen back and saved more than our skins." "America will come in when they see England bombarded" he said. "How about these destroyers, we need them badly."

(He looked well, and kept reiterating we will fight to the end and give Hitler plenty of trouble.)

I said well you certainly picked a nice time to be Prime Minister. He said "They wouldn't have given the PM ship if there had been any meat left on the bone."

I judge when he gets with his friends he says plenty.

But after all he said "Hitler has not won this war until he conquers us. Nothing else matters. And he isn't going to do that."

We'll hold out until after your election and then expect you'll come in.

I'll fight them from Canada. I'll never give up the fleet. Maybe some other government may."

[June 12, 1940]

My view of situation this a.m.

The condition of Britain's preparedness affecting her ability to fight the kind of war Hitler wages still appears to be appallingly weak. I am of the opinion that outside of some air defense, the real defense of England will be with courage and not with arms.

---

511. That day, having already crossed the Seine in their push toward Paris, German forces had broken through the French line along the Marne.
512. Journalist Randolph Frederick Edward Spencer Churchill (1911–68).
513. General Maxime Weygand (1867–1965), Marshal Foch's former chief of staff and chief of staff to the French Army, 1931–35, had succeeded Gamelin as Allied commander in chief on May 19.

No matter what action USA takes towards this war, it is only fair to say that short of a miracle that this country after, and, if and when France stops fighting, will hold on with the hope that the U.S. will come in. Churchill said quite definitely to me he expects U.S. will be in right after election, once the people in the U.S. see the towns and cities of England after what so many U.S. cities and towns have been named, bombed and destroyed, they will rise up and want war.

The people here are kept buoyed up by the inference in the papers and the judicious clipping from the *NY Times*, *Herald Tribune* and political speeches. This morning an American correspondent of an English paper mentioned that all it needs in an "incident" to bring the U.S. in.

If that were all that was needed, desperate people will do desperate things. The point of all this is the fact that the preparedness for carrying on a war from here on is pitiful and we should know this in the light of any action we in America might see fit to take. A course of action that involves us in any respect that presupposes the Allies have much to fight with except courage is as far as England goes I think fallacious.

London, June 13, 1940

I saw Churchill at 8:00 o'clock last night when he handed me the message to go to the President and also talked to me about destroyers. He had just returned from Paris where he, accompanied by Mr. Eden, secretary for war, and Gen. Sir John Dill, chief of the Imperial General Staff,[514] had attended meetings with Reynaud, Marshal Petain and Gen. Weygand, and I waiting for him until he had returned from his visit to the King.

He did not look so well as he did the other night, but after all, an air trip from France now takes two hours and a half, even for a Prime Minister. He still was not quite frank with me about the situation and hastens to remark on all occasions that England is going to fight to a finish. He said the French would not give up their fleet; they would turn pirates before that. Both he and Halifax reiterated that if the French were beaten to their knees and had to give up their fleet the British would still fight on. The only alternative might be, to save the French people from further punishment, for the French to scuttle their ships, and both Churchill and Halifax regarded this as extremely likely. I couldn't help pointing out that regardless of what happened, that if the French and British fleets, reasonably intact, sailed away from these ports and the governments of both countries still functioned, it would be very difficult for Germany to pick up much strength economically with the big navies of the world molesting their foreign trade, because while the navies might not be effective within 200 miles of the shore, they would be effective away from Germany and her air bases.

Churchill showed me a cable from Lothian,[515] which he asked me not to comment on, to the Government, in which Lothian said he had heard from an "authoritative source" that the President was not impressed with Churchill's and Britain's demand for destroyers and wanted to know a great deal more about England's position in this respect. He told me that he regarded destroyers as much more important than planes because of the terrific problem of protecting the Island from invasion and at the same time keeping trade routes open.

514. Sir John Greer Dill (1881–1944) had succeeded Ironside as chief of the Imperial General Staff on May 27. He would serve in that capacity until 1941, when he would head the British Service Mission in Washington.
515. Philip Henry Kerr, eleventh marquess of Lothian (1882–1940). Chamberlain had appointed the former journalist and private secretary to Lloyd George (and frequent visitor, contemporary press accounts reported, to Cliveden) ambassador to the United States in 1939.

Once again he asked me to have a scotch and I saw one for him resting on the table back of him to be drunk when I had left.

Yesterday afternoon about 6 o'clock Chamberlain's Secretary 'phoned to inquire if I would come at once to see him. I went about 7 o'clock. When I arrived in his office Kingsley Wood was there. Chamberlain said, "Joe, I have been very much upset to hear from Kingsley of your conversation with him this morning (the conversation referred to being that I felt I was not getting information as to what was in the government's mind that I was entitled to get)."[517] I told Chamberlain that I felt very strongly about the whole matter, that I quite appreciated that Churchill was busy, but so was Reynaud but the latter had found the time to keep our Government informed through Bullitt almost daily. I said I had had a talk with Halifax the night before and had said the same thing to him, and repeated that the only information I had obtained was that the British were going to stop Italian ships. I remarked that fortunately that had not been my experience previous to the change of administration, but nevertheless, I felt my government was entitled to more consideration. "After all," I said, "the United States is not trying to get England into a war."

Chamberlain deplored the fact and said it was unfortunate I had not been kept posted, and we talked over the danger of the French quitting and saying that they could not get further support. Chamberlain said he recognized that and the facts in the case were so very different, for after all the British Army in Belgium had not received an order for a week, and that previous to the fighting at Dunkirk there were still no orders given them and they just struggled along as part of a French army without receiving any orders. To show how ridiculous their requests were, he said that Weygand had said the French Army could not stand up much longer with only 50 divisions against 150 but at the same time begged for one division to be sent over. Chamberlain pointed out how absurd this was, that instead of having 50 divisions against 150 they were to have 51. He assured me that anything I wanted to get in the future he would help me to get it.

On my return from Chamberlain's office I found the message from the President which he wanted me to deliver to the Prime Minister at once, this being a copy of his wire to Reynaud.[518] Also instructions to me to say that he could not send any of the fleet to Ireland because he had a squadron in Lisbon, a squadron in South America and a patrol on the Atlantic as far as Trinidad, and that he thought it was advisable the balance of the fleet be kept in Hawaii.[519]

I telephoned Churchill's office and ascertained that he was arriving back from Paris about 8:30 and that he would then have his dinner, and I said that I would be around the Embassy at 9:30 waiting for a call from him. I told his secretary that I had

516. The French government had been forced to relocate to Tours on June 11 as German forces advanced on Paris. On June 13 the government had moved again to Bordeaux.

517. He refers probably to a conversation that he had had with Kingsley Wood two days earlier in which he informed the chancellor of the Exchequer that he
   was sick and disgusted at coming down there and not being kept posted on current financial matters. I said it was getting to be apparently the policy of the present government to see how little I could find out. [Kingsley Wood] was much upset and promised to keep me advised on everything and said he would get hold of Churchill and everybody to see that I am brought up to date.

518. On June 10, Reynaud had appealed personally to the president for material support to the Allies. "Your message . . . has moved me very deeply," the president responded in his wire. "As I have already stated to you and to Mr. Churchill, this Government is doing everything in its power to make available to the Allied Governments the material they so urgently require and our efforts to do still more are being redoubled."

519. On June 12, the Former Naval Person had wired the president, "[w]e are worried about Ireland. An American Squadron at Berehaven would do no end of good I am sure."

had an answer to his cable to the President. I left Johnson to prepare the message and I went to the Coq d'Or for dinner. While there Johnson called me to say the Prime Minister would see me at Admiralty House at 9:30 sharp, for he was due for a Cabinet meeting immediately afterwards. Johnson came along in a taxi and off we went. When I arrived at Admiralty House the Prime Minister was just sitting down to dinner with his wife and two daughters. He introduced me to his two daughters and I gave him the message, or rather, since he was eating his dinner, he asked me to read it to him. I read it and he was visibly excited. He felt that this answered Reynaud's speech and there was no reason why this should not keep the French fighting. He then read it himself three or four times during dinner and was visibly moved by, I think, excitement, but possibly by champagne, which he was drinking, and told me he would immediately convey to Reynaud that his understanding of this message was that America assumed a responsibility if the French continued to fight and finally moved out their government. This was the point that he stressed most strongly. In other words, while he didn't say "I am entering the war," this was a commitment. However, he felt, and to be honest I felt, that Roosevelt certainly knew what he was doing, and as it is impossible to judge from here to what heights American public opinion had risen, I felt, as Churchill did, that this was a commitment and that Roosevelt knew what he was doing.

During the dinner he described to me the appalling conditions in France, an outline of which I sent in my cable of last night.[520] One of the things I neglected to put in my cable was that in the minutes of the two Supreme War Council meetings the British brought up the fact that the French had from 200 to 500 trained German pilots as prisoners in France, and the British thought that it was absolutely imperative that these pilots be moved to England for fear that the French might release them and thus supply Germany with that number of trained pilots again. Reynaud said he would take the matter under immediate consideration.

The Prime Minister ate quickly a very substantial meal composed of an entree, followed by fish, jellied chicken and strawberries, and then rushed away to the Cabinet with a request to me to return to 10 Downing Street at 11:30. I found Johnson and Gowen waiting for me outside in a taxi. I dropped Johnson off at Pruniers and then decided to walk home since it was then about 10:25. It started to rain, however. Got another taxi, got home, drank my bottle of milk and had a sponge cake; sent for Jee,[521] and tried to lie down for a few minutes. At 11 o'clock a telephone call came to immediately go to Downing Street. When I arrived there the Prime Minister came out of the Cabinet Room and I could see he was visibly excited. He had had the Cabinet agree with him that this was an exceptional message and its repercussions meant a great deal to England, but he said he had two problems: first of all, was he right in saying that the President's Charlottesville address was not an answer to Reynaud's message of June 10th?[522] I said I hadn't the slightest idea, he would have to use his own judgment. The second was, could I arrange to get permission from the President to print this latest message to Reynaud. He requested me to call the President on the telephone and ask him and suggested that it be done right there. I said I was perfectly willing to do that.

520. "Reynaud told Churchill that Weygand was insisting on an armistice," JPK reported in his Dispatch No. 1643 regarding the meeting between the prime minister and the French premier in Tours on June 13. "The French Army could not fight any longer - there was nothing but death and destruction ahead for all France." Further, Reynaud had requested that Churchill release France from her March 28 agreement not to sign a separate peace.
521. JPK's valet.
522. Addressing the Class of 1940 at the University of Virginia on June 10, the president had excoriated Mussolini for effectively stabbing Britain and France in the back, and called for both immediate rearmament and material assistance to the Allies.

They put the call through and I talked to the President and the President told me, or rather indicated, that he didn't think the message should be printed, but it was not with great firmness that he said that. He said Hull objected to printing it because he thought it was too much of a commitment. I said, "Have you heard anything about what happened in France today?", and he said "No." I said, "Very well, I will send you quickly an outline and then you can consider whether you still think that the message should or should not be printed." He then went on to say that he saw a great opportunity for an economic tie-up with South America and with other countries not involved in this struggle, that would make it, with the assistance of the French fleet, most difficult for the Germans to ultimately win the war. This latest thought coming at this time seemed to me to be out of key because of the imminence of the critical situation in Paris.

I told Churchill then that I was going to the office to send a message. He urged me to write it out there. I said it couldn't be done because it must go in code. He then asked me if I would show him what I was reporting, and I said "certainly"; and then he said that when I returned he might ring the President up himself and tell him how necessary it was to print the message.[523]

In the meantime he had 'phoned me the minutes of the meeting, and there is no question but what he put on an elegant, eloquent show. Beaverbrook later described his speech to Reynaud and the French as being unqualifiedly the greatest oration made in the history of the world. He pointed out their weaknesses, avoided recriminations, but was firm in his determination that France should and must stick and promised that England would.

It is interesting to point out here that after I had dictated my memorandum I had talked to Beaverbrook about the engine construction of Rolls Royce, at which time he said he was anxious to tell me about his trip to Tours with the Prime Minister.[524] While I was waiting to have it typed I dashed down to his house. He outlined the situation as follows: "We arrived at Tours — you will remember that it was at that City Hall that the Duke and Duchess of Windsor were married, and it was in this locality that the Duchess was waiting to marry the Duke while the British Empire decided against it." He add here parenthetically that Churchill, in describing the telephone call that he had received the night before from Reynaud asking him to come to France at once, said that Reynaud suggested over the telephone that he arrive at Tours at 2:45 p.m. Churchill had hastened to add that it indicated complete lack of understanding of the whole situation when you consider that any spy or fifth-columnist might have listened in to this conversation and the Germans would have been more than pleased to have knocked Churchill off. He said that they decided to completely ignore these instructions and go earlier, which they did, guarded by, he said smilingly, nine Spitfires, and of course when they arrived in Tours there was no one to meet them, so they dug up some cars and went to the Mayor's office. To get back to Beaverbrook: He said Reynaud looked like a broken man; he was no longer sure of himself, and his expression and face looked like defeat. However, after he had described all his problems and stated that he wanted to

---

523. JPK's dispatch regarding the minutes of the meeting in Tours also informed the president that

> The arrival of your note to Reynaud . . . gave the British Cabinet great courage and Churchill feels that it is sufficiently strong to warrant the French fighting on. I called you on phone [sic] at Churchill's insistence to ask you if your note could be published because Churchill said that morale in France must be bucked up in order to keep them in the fight and he thinks your note will do it.

Before closing, JPK interjected, "[t]hough I realize the tragedy of the present moment and how important it is for the success of these poor people that their morale should be bucked up . . . I nevertheless see in the message a great danger as a commitment at a later date."

524. That day German forces had occupied Paris.

make peace, Churchill started his wonderful oration and really left Reynaud and the French bucked up. (In fact, Churchill told me that when he left, Herriot,[525] who had attended the meeting along with the Chairman of the other House of Deputies, said that regardless of what Roosevelt says or America proposes, we are going to fight on!) But Beaverbrook and Churchill both made it clear that this hypodermic might last for a few days, but unless something strong came from the United States it could not last long.

I rushed back from Beaverbrook's and then I received a call from the Prime Minister asking if I would come and see him, and I immediately dashed down there. He didn't ask me for what I had sent, but instead presented me with an outline that he wanted to send to the President, so I brought that back. I had suggested to him while I was there that I would get it on its way at once to the President and that if he wanted to call him about 2:30 he could have a talk with him, but Churchill said that in spite of the fact that he had had an hour and a half's sleep in the plane coming back, he thought he would be sound asleep long before that time.

I got back to the Chancery about 1:45 a.m., sent for Johnson and another code clerk and put the boys to work. I then went home and to bed, and about 4:30 the telephone rang and the President was on the 'phone. I judge that Hull was listening on the extension. He told me that he had only received two parts of my report and none of Churchill's since I had advised them both were coming. He made it clear to me, however, that he did not want the text of the note published and again reiterated that if the French Navy broke away from the French people in the event of an armistice, the United States would see to it that they were fed and supplied, and for me to get both these pieces of information to the Prime Minister this morning. I was a little sleepy and this is my best recollection of the conversation, except that when Hull got on the 'phone I asked him if there were any information that he wasn't getting, and he said that as far as he knew everything was coming all right. At 9:20 a.m. today the Prime Minister called up and I told him both of these facts.

In the meantime, Gowen had telephoned my house that we had received the wire confirming these instructions, and I so informed Churchill. Churchill was visibly affected by this refusal. He was also affected by the fact that Steve Early, according to the London "Times," seemed to have said that the Charlottesville speech was an answer to Reynaud and hoped I could get a correction on that. I said I thought that would be a great mistake for it would focus too much attention on the whole matter and I judged that since the President's mind was made up not to publish the Reynaud reply, that the more attention was drawn to the failure of the President to answer Reynaud the worse it would be for the cause. Churchill, in a very subdued voice, said if that were the case all would be lost in France. My impression is that all will be lost in France anyway, and I am sure that publication of the President's reply would have only delayed the demise very slightly and merely temporarily.

On my return to the office I found the very firm wire of the President and some time during the day I am planning to have further word with Churchill.[526]

525. Edouard Herriot (1872–1957), president of the French Chamber of Deputies, 1936–40. Despite reports of his resignation on June 17, Herriot would maintain his position within the Pétain government until the marshal's dissolution of both houses of Parliament (over Herriot's objections) in 1942. He would be arrested and interned in Germany for the duration of the war, and after being liberated by Soviet forces, would return to France to be elected mayor of Lyons and president of the Radical Party in 1945. The same year, he became president of the National Assembly of the Fourth Republic.

526. "As I asked Ambassador Kennedy last night to inform you," the president had responded to the prime minister, "my message of yesterday's date addressed to the French prime minister was in no sense intended to commit and did not commit the Government to military participation in support of Allied governments." He added that only Congress had had the Constitutional right to make such commit-

John F. Kennedy, 22, to Joseph P. Kennedy

SPEE CLUB, CAMBRIDGE, MASSACHUSETTS

Dear Dad:

This will be rather short as exams are coming up. I think I should get by but I don't know about honors yet as there seems to be considerable I have to learn.

Mother told me you didn't think it best I came over which is probably right as it would be a short time and I guess I shall go to the Cape. Regarding my thesis — I suppose the best plan is that someone looks it over, suggests new ideas on how it can be improved, and then send it back and I will work on it with someone around here as regards getting my English polished up. I think the best plan would be to air-mail it as I should try and get it published as soon as possible as I should get it out before the 1. issues becomes too dead and 2nd before everyone goes away for the summer. I should like to get some thing in the conclusion about the best policy for America, ~~but~~ as learnt from a study of Britain's experience, but of course don't want to take sides too much. Is "Why England Slept" OK for a title — and will Churchill mind? What should I do about publisher — keep Krock's agent or can you fix it? Thanks very much for the assistance. Please remember me to Jack Eddie & Jim & Tony. Love to Rosie —

Love
Jack

P.S. I have a copy over here.

Joseph P. Kennedy to Cordell Hull: *Diplomatic Dispatch*

1680, June 16, 9 p.m.[527]

PERSONAL AND STRICTLY CONFIDENTIAL FOR THE SECRETARY

I saw Halifax at 7 p.m. He said early this a.m. they had message here from Reynaud saying that French proposed asking President of the United States to ask Germany for an armistice and Reynaud wanted to know if the British would agree to let the French make a separate peace provided the French agreed not to include the French Fleet as one of the terms of agreement.

British answered that agreement was not with a man or an administration (this in answer to the statement that Reynaud said that if the British did not agree to the separate peace Reynaud would resign and then a Government might come in that would agree to everything that Hitler wanted). However, the British would agree to let the French make a separate peace provided the French Fleet sailed at once for British ports and then the British would fight on. They also told Campbell[528] in separate agreement to have the Polish, Czech and Belgian Governments come here. Also have the French air force come here or go to North Africa and all other troops outside of France do the same thing.

Later on the French gold arrived here with some Frenchmen who said Herriot,

---

ments, and for that reason, he was unable to permit the message to be published. "I believe it to be imperative," he concluded, "that there be avoided any possible misunderstanding . . ."

527. Reynaud's government had fallen that day; President Lebrun had called upon the elderly Marshal Philippe Pétain to form its replacement. Additionally, the Germans, having captured Verdun the previous day, had broken through the Maginot Line.

528. The British ambassador to France since November 1939, Sir Ronald Hugh Campbell (1883–1953), had vacated his post that day in Bordeaux.

Mandel[529] and others wanted to fight on and if Reynaud got some stiffening from England he would stick.

So the British drew up a declaration of union between France and England — all partners now — what you have is mine and what I have is yours. All damage done to France England pays her share. A noble sentiment but just does not mean much. (Halifax agreed it didn't but if it kept the French fighting it was worth while). So the armistice proposition has been held up pending finding out Reynaud's reaction to the Declaration of Union.

These are high spots so you can get it in a hurry. Lothian will fill in all the details.

KENNEDY

Joseph P. Kennedy: *Diary*

London, June 24, 1940[530]

Yesterday, at 8:15 p.m., I delivered the Red Cross Speech, copy in files.[531] I then went to see Beaverbrook at 8:30. He said he had told the Prime Minister he was on the way to see me and I rather got two impressions: 1. they would like to sell me the idea of backing the General de Gaulle Committee, which is to formulate a new French Government here.[532] The General is the one who has really been going along with Churchill in all his ideas; in fact, when Churchill told Weygand he could not send him any help and explained that he needed his soldiers and air force for protection at home, Churchill told me de Gaulle said he agreed with him. This Churchill regarded very highly. Also, Beaverbrook again pointed out that he had talked to Churchill about whether there was any possibility in the event of invasion of the British Government moving to Canada. Beaverbrook reiterated what he had said before — that Churchill said he hadn't the slightest idea of moving. They will go to Cheltenham and they have no plans beyond that. He also made it clear that he thinks it not at all unlikely that if Great Britain is beaten that Germany will take the fleet, or what they have left of it, and sail up the St. Lawrence, setting forth the case that Canada had declared war on them and must be occupied as part of the indemnity price. Beaverbrook seemed very optimistic about the production of airplanes, saying last week was the biggest week in England and that he was not at all worried about the airplane handling its position. He said if the Germans had come over three or four weeks ago and knocked out the Derby works, they would have ruined their production, but now they have managed to spread it around, so they can't be knocked out quickly. He didn't talk like his old self. He talked as a Minister of the Churchill Government should, I suppose, and seemed to be doing his best to sell me on the idea that things were still all right, although he finished up by saying, "After all, if we don't think we are going to win, there is no point in going on" to

---

529. Georges Mandel, French minister for the Colonies, 1938–40.
530. Two days earlier, Marshal Pétain had signed the armistice with Germany in the same railway carriage in Compiègne where the Germans had surrendered in 1918.
531. The brief address, pleading that "[w]e cannot give too much, or give too soon!" to England in her state of seige, had been delivered in the United States as part of the Red Cross broadcast over the NBC network.
532. Charles-André-Marie-Joseph de Gaulle (1890–1970), the brigadier general of the French Fourth Armored Division whom Reynaud had made undersecretary of state for defense and war only two and a half weeks earlier, had come to England on June 17 to head the Provisional French National Committee, that is, the French government in exile and the command center for military resistance.

which I agreed. He talked about the United States coming in and what a great moral uplift it would be, and that it would give something for the people to hope for.

At 10:40 last night the telephone rang and it was Churchill. If I had to make a judgment after listening to him talk, I would think that he was slightly cockeyed. He started in to sell me the idea that General de Gaulle was going to form a provisional French Government and he expected the United States would recognize it and that there was going to be a great deal of support for it from the fleet and French Colonial Empire. In fact he said "Everything looks good to me tonight." Considering the despatch that we sent from the Foreign Office on the situation of the fleet, he would have to be drunk to think it was good. He said, "we haven't had any answer on our destroyers yet, have we?" and I said, "No, we haven't" and he said, "We have got to get those, because if we don't, we will all go down the drain together, because if we are not successful, you will be taking orders from the Germans unless you have the British fleet to support you." I didn't add at this point what Dr. Dunning, the osteopath, said the other day: "I am damned sick of those American politicians saying that the British fleet has been protecting us for the last twenty years; Who the hell have they been protecting us from? And it seems to me that on the first occasion they are called upon to protect anybody, it is themselves and they don't seem to be able to do that."

Churchill went on to say that party politics will be the death of us, just like it has been a great body-blow to them. I told him I understood Laval had been elected Vice President and he said, "You mean the corrupt Laval?[533] His type is the sort of mayoralty position in the middle of France instead of anything important; I hope he gets put under six feet of soil." He then went back and referred to the new French Committee of DeGaulle and said, "Keep your eye on this Committee, because the United States must recognize it, because it represents the soul of France, and remember all the time, after us, you will get it."

Rose Kennedy to Joseph P. Kennedy

Hyannisport, June 24, 1940

Dear Joe,

We went up to the Class Day on Wednesday; Rose, Eunice, Bob, and I, and were joined by Kathleen up there. We went directly to lunch in the Yard. Jack was as usual entirely irresponsible when he talked to me Tuesday night. He thought we could go to Dutchland for lunch. We arrived about 15 minutes ahead, and Torb came out and took us to a couple of gates where we were checked up for tickets which we did not have and he referred them to Jack. We had a hurried lunch, and Jack was greeted by several of the waitresses who served him solicitously, and seemed anxious that he should have something good to eat; however, he decided he should leap out and get something suitable for his tummy, and then decided everything was in a rush any way and that he should be on his way to join his class. We then swallowed our lunch and made for the stadium and had no tickets again and bought some and clammered up the stairs. The festivities there were as usual. There was a speech made suggesting the probability of the present graduating class going into war and there was considerable hissing. Otherwise, everything went on as usual. I did not see anyone I knew.

After that, Rose and I went to the O'Keefe wedding, which was small but very thrilling for Rose. I met Jack Hannon, who has stood the test of time better than most of

---

533. Twice a former premier, 1931–32 and 1935–36, Pierre Jean Marie Laval (1883–1945) had become deputy prime minister (*vice-président du conseil*) of Pétain's government the previous day.

his contemporaries, probably because he still has his hair.[534] He was as charming and genial as always and we reminisced and laughed a good deal. After the wedding we went back to the Ritz where we had dinner and were joined by the other 3 darlings who had been to tea in the yard; an afterthought of Jack's but proved to be a very enjoyable occasion. At that point he was none too sure of time etc. for Commencement, but Arthur Goldsmith had given me a program which helped considerably.

At 9 the next morning Jack phoned and urged us to come out at once. [*We stopped at Spee Club for our tickets.*] Jack popped out and we got at the Quadrangle where our seats were. They were the worst in the place; three rows from the back on the extreme left; however, we had the brave idea of moving back against the college wall where it was sunny. As it happened, all the dignitaries [*& the graduates*] passed along that particular section on their way to the platform so we had a marvelous view of everyone. Kick was sure he had chosen the seats for this, but I am sure he got them at the last minute.

He was really very handsome in his cap and gown as he had a tan which made him look healthy and he has got a wonderful smile. After graduation, we returned to his room where after waiting several minutes and not finding him, we left and went in town. After that, I did some shopping and came home. It was the day of Marie O'Connell's wedding and I am sorry I did not ask you to send her a wire as you were her god-father. I am also sorry I did not go there. It would have been a rush as it was the same time as graduation. I suppose everyone was there, though I have not the details yet.

Dave is going to N.Y. Wednesday to close up the house, and I am asking Marie Green and her family down to stay a week at the garage. She will probably give me all the news.

Kick spent the weekend in Long Island after the boat race in New London. Jack expects to come home tomorrow. I believe he was going to make some inquiries about his book today in N.Y. Ted and Jean have been playing with the Southgates who are staying at the McLaughlin cottage at the end of our road. As you know, they are very charming children.

Grandpa[535] was down until today. He seems pretty well, although he is of course getting older all the time.

Joe is back again and has been sailing with Jack Daly a little. He will be on his way to the Convention on July 13. That is the day of Anne McDonnell's wedding to Henry Ford.[536] I am going to try to get him to go to that first. It is going to be a big affair.

The weather has been very cool, in fact too cold for bathing. The last few days seem more like fall, just cool and lovely, but a little chilly. It really is a wonderful spot, and we probably appreciate it more after having been over so many parts of the world.

Everyone seemed to think your speech was excellent and the newspaper commentator at 6 spoke very favorably of you.

I believe you said you had got to church all right. At this time of my life there need to be no mental reservations.

> *All my love dearest.*
> *Rosa*

---

534. Her maternal uncle, John Edwards Hannon (1877–1951).
535. Her father, that is.
536. In what was described at the time as "the wedding of the century," Anne McDonnell, a close friend of Kick's from the Convent of the Sacred Heart at Noroton, was to marry automotive heir Henry Ford II. Ford, a Protestant, had converted to Catholicism against his father's wishes.

John F. Kennedy, 23, to John F. Fitzgerald

July 10, 1940

Dear Grandpa:

Just a note to ask you to suggest to whom I can send early copies of my book for publicity purposes. I should appreciate your giving me the names of the newspaper editors and any others you might suggest. I should be grateful for an early reply.

Love,

Robert Kennedy, 14, to Joseph P. Kennedy

Dear Dad,

I got your letter this morning. Thank you very much it was very interesting.

We all went to Edgertown last weekend and had alot of fun. Billings went over and he led the singing with his <u>wonderful voice</u>. While he was down here we sang the song that Pepsi Cola has for advertising. He just sat there with a grim face.

We have all been sailing here. I came in 2nd in the July series and Eunice is doing quite well now.

I was in bed for a few days because I had some boils on my knee but they are almost all gone now though I am not able to go in swimming.

Pat has a new boy friend who is 6 feet 7 in. She likes him very much We are making up songs about him like this.

6 feet 7
Straight from Heaven

Father Downing is not making any more sermons because he was in an auto accident so we don't get yelled at in the middle of mass any more.

This is about all the news except that some of us may go to Nantucket next weekend.

Love From All
Bob

Joseph P. Kennedy to James Farley: *Telegram*

JULY 19, 1940

YOUR THINKING OF SENDING ME A WIRE ABOUT YOUNG JOE IN THE MIDST OF THE HECTIC SITUATION IN CHICAGO TOUCHES ME VERY MUCH STOP[537] AS YOU CAN IMAGINE I HAD HEARD ABOUT THE STRUGGLE TO GET HIM TO CHANGE HIS VOTE AND WAS DELIGHTED HE TOOK STAND HE DID STOP AFTER ALL IF HE IS GOING INTO POLITICS HE MIGHT JUST AS WELL LEARN NOW THAT THE ONLY THING TO DO IS TO STAND BY YOUR CONVICTIONS AM MOST HAPPY TO SAY HE NEEDED NO PROMPTING IN THIS RESPECT MY BEST WISHES THAT GOOD LUCK FOLLOW YOU IN YOUR NEW UNDERTAKING WARMEST REGARDS

JOE KENNEDY

---

537. Having lost his challenge to Roosevelt's renomination at the Democratic Convention in Chicago the night before, the postmaster general and Party chairman wired JPK, "I WILL EVER BE THANKFUL TO YOUR SON JOE FOR HIS MANLY AND COURAGEOUS STAND AT LAST NIGHTS CONVENTION."

Joseph P. Kennedy, Jr., 24, to Joseph P. Kennedy

OSHKOSH, WISCONSIN, July 22, 1940

Dear Dad:

I am up here visiting Tom Schriber after the Convention, and I thought I would give you some of my reactions.

Even before the Mass delegation left Boston there were arguments as to whom they would support, Farley or Roosevelt. It appears that Burke[538] and Coakley worked out the arrangement to support Farley, and they claim that there was a tacit understanding that if Roosevelt ran, then the delegation should be released. However I went over the documents quite carefully, and it seems that the wording was such that Burke presumed that if Roosevelt ran then Farley would withdraw. Burke should have gotten it in writing from Farley that if Roosevelt went, then Farley would release the delegation. Although there were accounts in the newspapers setting forth this arrangement at the time, still there was nothing definite upon which you could depend. Given this ambiguity, the delegation had all they needed to start playing local politics. Some of them thought it would give them the support of the Irish back home. Others went just the opposite to their political enemies. It was soon evident that no agreement could be reached. We had a caucus the first night and it was the stormiest session that I have ever seen. They called each other liars and thieves and claimed that Coakley was selling the delegation down the river. Well from then on, the delegation divided.

I went to see McCormack whom I knew was very friendly to you, and as you know he was strongly for Roosevelt.[539] Coakley and Clem Norton[540] made up the rest of the Roosevelt leaders, and they all claimed that Farley was sore, and had put them in the hole. On the other hand there were those who felt that they had pledged themselves and that they were bound by this pledge. Then I spoke to Burns, and the first day he thought that I should vote for Roosevelt, and I said that I thought that I would vote for Farley. Then I guess he spoke to you, and when I last left him, he was undecided for he thought that Farley was going to try to double-cross Roosevelt. I had seen Krock previously, and he thought that I should stick with Farley, and later after the voting sent me a nice note. Well I was still undecided, but rather favored Farley when I ran into Walsh, and his support of Farley was all that I needed. Of course someone demanded a poll of the delegation so I gave my vote orally. A lot of people came up to me afterwards and said that they thought I had done the right thing, and now I am more than ever convinced that it was the right thing.

So much for that. Now the convention. From the administration's point of view, it must have been very disappointing. The first few days there was none of the enthusiasm, which they had thought, would be evident. This apathy led them to move up the nominations one day in advance. Barkley was the one picked to put over the speech.[541] Well, Kelley the mayor of Chicago had his men planted over the floor and in the gallery,

---

538. William "Onions" Burke (1906–1975), chairman of the Massachusetts Democratic Committee, 1939–44.

539. Joe's fellow Massachusetts delegate, U.S. Representative John William McCormack (1891–1980). McCormack would be elected majority leader in September 1940, and in 1962 would become speaker of the House.

540. Boston School Committeeman Clement A. Norton (1894–1979), a former beau of Joe's mother. Norton was (as contemporary press accounts described him) a "perennial" Democratic Boston mayoral candidate and an intimate of James Michael Curley.

541. Senate Majority Leader Alben William Barkley (1877–1956) of Kentucky, later vice president under Truman.

and when Farley mentioned Roosevelt's name there was quite a demonstration.[542] However it didn't seem at all genuine. They had set up microphones across the street and obtained different people to yell into it, Arizona wants Roosevelt, Mississ. — wants Roosevelt etc., etc. They got a band going and you can imagine the show that they could put on. The delegates however did not seem to get very excited, nor did the gallery. This went on for about a half hour. Barkley continued with his speech. At the end of it, something went wrong with the microphone, and the demonstration which they had planned went flat. Barkley tried his damnedest in a subtle way to get them going again, but not for about five minutes did he succeed, and in the meantime the delegates sat looking at each other like sheep. Finally they got it going again, but there was no fooling anyone, they all knew it was a put up job.

On Wednesday night with the nominating speeches you would have been surprised at the amount of applause which Carter Glass got, when in nominating Jim Farley he came out against the third term. You know the rest. Farley was delighted with the number of votes which he obtained, and then all the candidates made it unanimous for Roosevelt.

On Thursday night the nominations for vice president took place. The report during the day was that all the candidates had withdrawn due to the insistence by Roosevelt on the nomination of Wallace.[543] That night Wallace came in for a terrific booing. Everyone seemed to be against him, including the galleries. McNutt got a terrific hand when he refused to run, and it looked like he might have been the one if Wallace had not been chosen. Jesse Jones got a surprisingly small hand,[544] though personally I favored him. Bankhead couldn't keep up to Wallace. There were numerous speeches by ordinary delegates who demanded the floor, and much to the distaste of Barkley and Byrnes, stated that this shouldn't be a rabbit convention and they should be able to nominate a real democrat. It was easy to see that everyone was sore.

On the original ballot of our delegation I had voted for Bankhead, for Walsh said that we could vote for whomever we wanted. However someone challenged the vote, and as Mass had passed the first time Wallace was already elected, so I thought that would look badly if I went against the administration twice so I voted for Wallace, although I think that he will be a liability on the ticket.

Well that's about the story. Here's the reasons as I see them for the lack of enthusiasm at the convention.

1. Everyone was sore that they had been kept in the dark so long as to Roosevelt's intentions. They knew that he was going to do what he did, but they resented having to say please Daddy, please run.

2. Sore that Farley and Roosevelt had broken off and that they had sent Hopkins to handle the campaign. Farley was terribly popular out there.

3. Dictating to the delegates whom they had to vote for. (Wallace)

4. Against Wallace for he was formerly a Republican and because his policies are not in favor [*sic*]

5. A sentiment, whose force is difficult to estimate against a third term.

542. Mayor of Chicago and head of the local machine, Edward Joseph Kelly (1876–1950) had orchestrated the Roosevelt draft movement at the convention with Secretary of Commerce Harry Hopkins.

543. Iowa-born plant geneticist, self-taught economist, reputed mystic, former Republican and secretary of agriculture, 1933–40, Henry Agard Wallace (1888–1965).

544. Reconstruction Finance Corporation chairman, 1933–45, and Federal Loan Agency administrator, 1939–45, Jesse Holman Jones (1874–1956) would succeed Hopkins as secretary of commerce in August upon the latter's resignation due to failing health.

These are the principle reasons why everyone was pretty sore. Added to this was the fact that the administration didn't want men like Farley and Garner[545] to get a complimentary vote on the first ballot.

Although it is much too early to make predictions I am not at all bullish on the Democratic chances. I wouldn't make an even money bet right now. If this Democratic Party was together, even then they would have a tough time, but these combination of factors makes it look awful black to me.

I spoke to Jimmy Byrnes about the possibility of you coming home to manage the campaign, but he thought that you should stay over there. It doesn't look like it is going to be easy to get you back over here.

Grandpa said that he had cabled you my marks. I was pretty well satisfied with them, but thought in a couple of courses I had done better. The average however was what I expected.

I am leaving for California next week where I am staying with Killefer for a while, and then I am going to drive to Mexico with him.

Love, and take care of yourself,

Joe

Joseph P. Kennedy to Robert Kennedy, 14

London, July 23, 1940

Dear Bobby,

Well it was nice finally hearing from you. I was really quite surprised that all during the Spring I didn't hear how you were getting along at school, but I suppose you were so busy you just didn't get around to writing. It is, however, a very good practice to write somebody at least every week. I don't like to find fault with your penmanship, because I am such a terrible writer myself, but a little practice on that and on spelling would be a great help to you.

As far as things are concerned over here, we are expecting that Hitler will really go to work and bomb the whole place out this week.[546] It seems to me that it is entirely to his advantage to finish the war off quickly. He has two elements of danger if he doesn't. First of all, all the territory he has conquered contains millions of people who may find it difficult to eat this winter and when people are starving, there is no limit to what they will do. In addition to that, he is never sure that, once the political campaign in the United States is over in the Fall, he won't have the United States giving aid to England in ways that even we do not see now. So for these two reasons, if for no other, I am inclined to believe he will try to finish the war off quickly. Whether he can or not depends entirely on the strength of his air force. The English people have been led to believe that England is a fortress, well protected, and that the Germans can never successfully get here because of the strength of the British Navy and because of the great number of men they have under arms here. On top of that, they have been led to believe that their air force can take care of any attacks that Hitler might make. Personally I am of the opinion that is the spot against which he will make his great drive. If he can beat the air

---

545. "Worst damn-fool mistake I ever made was letting myself be elected Vice President of the United States," former speaker of the House John Nance "Cactus Jack" Garner (1868–1967) would proclaim after leaving office in 1941. The plain-spoken Texan had come to be increasingly at odds with the administration over issues such as court packing, and had broken ranks entirely over the third-term issue, offering himself as an alternative.

546. The *Luftwaffe* had been making daylight bombing raids on Britain since the beginning of the month.

force, the Navy and the Army will not be of great value to England. So we are like the fellow sitting in the theatre waiting for the curtain to go up. We should know very soon.

Take good care of yourself and let me hear from you.

Love,

Joseph P. Kennedy to Joseph P. Kennedy, Jr., 24

London, July 23, 1940

Dear Joe,

I didn't get your letter of June 12th until ten days ago and of course I was glad to hear that the examinations were finished. Since then I had the wire from Grandpa that you had a 71B. I think that's a swell record and that you have done a great job.

It was rather interesting about the Convention and Johnny Burns calling me up. I agreed with your point of view completely and told him that while I was ready and willing to offer any advice, I didn't want you to be put in a position where any decisions you made must be dependent on how they affect me, because that isn't fair to you. After I have given you my best judgment, you are the fellow who has to make up his mind. Anyway, I think that incident will stand you in good stead. After all people do appreciate a straightforward opinion, and that includes those you oppose. I am enclosing a copy of a telegram I received from Farley.

I am also enclosing a letter from Warren. I did something for someone in his family and he sent me this letter. I thought you might like to follow it up sometime.

I have written Bobby the news, because I want him to feel that he is part and parcel of the family and I do wish, if you can, you would give him and Teddy as much personal attention as possible this summer. If I were home, I would do it, but it is up to you and Jack to carry on for a while. It really means a great deal to them to have older people interested in what they do and say.

After we have a good bombing here, if the war does hang on, I am really going to go home, because my activities thereafter will be most limited and I will not be making any contribution either to the country or to myself by remaining here, but of course that will depend entirely on how gracefully I can make an exit.

Love,

Joseph P. Kennedy: Diary

Memorandum of Telephone Conversation between the President and Myself at 3:00 p.m., August 1, 1940.

Last night at 12:20 the telephone rang and they told me the President was calling from overseas. When it came time to talk with him the circuit was so bad that the President decided to talk with me at 3 o'clock today. The conversation went along somewhat as follows:

FDR: Hello, Joe.

JPK: Hello, Mr. President.

FDR: How are you?

JPK: I am fine.

FDR: I wanted to ring you up about the situation that has arisen here so that you would get the dope straight from me and not from somebody else. The sub-committee of the Democratic Committee desire you to come home and run the Democratic campaign this year, but the State Department is very much against your leaving England.

JPK: That's very nice of the State Department and I am also very flattered by the sub-committee.

FDR: Yes, they were very anxious to have you and you know how happy I would be to have you in charge, but the general impression is that it would do the cause of England a great deal of harm if you left there at this time and I didn't want you to hear that you had been named and that your name had been turned down by me.

I thanked him very much and said that, as far as I was concerned, I wouldn't take the job even if it were offered to me, because I felt, in all justice to the position I held here, I should stay as long as there was any prospect of the British going through a bad bombing. I said, if, of course, at the end of this month Hitler hasn't indicated any intention of doing so, then I am seriously considering going home; that, as far as I can see, I am not doing a damn thing here that amounts to anything and my services, if they are needed, could be used to much better advantage if I were home.

FDR: That's where you are all wrong. I get constant reports of how valuable you are to them over there and that it helps the morale of the British to have you there and they would feel they were being let down if you were to leave. In addition to that, the people in our country who are already complaining that we are not doing enough in Great Britain feel well satisfied with you being in England.

JPK: Well that's all very good but nevertheless I am not at all satisfied with what I am doing and I will take a look at it for another month and then see what my plans are.

I am damn sorry for your sake that you had to be a candidate, but I am glad for the country.

FDR: I am damn sorry too, but there wasn't anything else to do. I am not intending to campaign at all. There is enough to be done right here and I am well pleased with the way the defense legislation is going through.

Then with the usual "Take care of yourselves" and "Goodlucks" we rang off.

During the above conversation the President also said, "Things are better there now, are they?" and I said, "Yes, if you mean they are willing to fight with broken bottles."

Joseph P. Kennedy to John F. Kennedy, 23

Secret London, August 2, 1940

Dear Jack,

I am enclosing a clipping from this morning's *Express* about the book. I think you got the one from the *Telegraph* some time ago. I am very anxious to read the final copy. I am sure if it reaches the problem as they now visualize it in England, the book will have quite a sale and at least will get a very good standing. Chamberlain, Halifax, Montagu Norman (governor of the Bank of England), and Harold Laski have all asked me about it. So, whether you make a cent out of it or not, it will do you an amazing amount of good, particularly if it gets a good standing. You would be surprised how a book that really makes the grade with high-class people stands you in good stead for years to come. I remember that in the report you are asked to make after twenty-five years to the Committee at Harvard, one of the questions is "What books have you written?" and there is no doubt you will have done yourself a great deal of good.

Now as to the situation here: The whole crux of the matter is, as I have said to you before, the strength of the German air force. All their attacks to date have been piddling affairs, except for the attacks on the convoys. If they have the strength they pretend to have and they come over and knock off the British air force, it will not make the slightest difference what land precautions the British have made. No country today can stand up unless it has air parity with another country, assuming that the other country can get its airplanes in to fight, which of course the Germans can do very easily now because they have practically all the bases up and down the whole west coast of Europe.

I believe there are three reasons why Hitler will not depend entirely on the blockading of England. First of all, he has had his own radio tell his own people that England was weak and demoralized and practically a push-over any time he wanted to invade it. Now that propaganda would be all right if it only went to the outside world, but, having told his own people that he could do it, it seems to me that he is in a position where he must go ahead or back down. Second, he always has to have in mind, if the war lasts any length of time, that Roosevelt might get the United States into the war, even through the back door, and the additional impetus that that would give the British cause might be dangerous to Hitler. Third, the economic position of the conquered countries is getting progressively worse and just what this may lead to is such an unknown factor that I doubt very much if the group behind Hitler want to take that on as an additional burden to a military war. So, with all these factors having some influence on him, if he has air supremacy, it seems to me it is up to him to go after England and beat it.

In the meantime, of course, England is suffering great losses on the seas. The destroyer problem is a precarious one for them because they are losing them altogether too fast. In addition to that there is no doubt that Germany's fast motor boats, submarines and dive-bombers are seriously handicapping the progress of imports and exports to this country. So, even if Germany does not polish it off, England is faced with a very serious situation the coming winter. Of course, if the Italians could fight worth a tinker's damn, that whole situation would be wiped out at once, but the Italians are scandalously bad. If Great Britain could take them on for a decisive battle anywhere, I think it would please the English no end.

I am writing mother about my plans, so you can exchange information.

Now that you've got the book off, get a good rest. You have the brains and everything it takes to go somewhere, so just get yourself in good condition so you can really do things.

Love,
Dad

Joseph P. Kennedy to Rose Kennedy

London, August 2, 1940

Dear Rose,

I have tried to divide up all the news among the children, so after you have read all the letters you will be up to date.

I have the exceptional chance to send these letters by Bill Donovan who is returning by Clipper on Saturday and I should think you would have them by Tuesday, which of course is marvelous.[547]

---

547. The president had sent Colonel William Joseph "Wild Bill" Donovan (1883–1959), future head of the wartime Office of Strategic Services, to London on a confidential fact-finding mission to make an evaluation both of the effects of the recent German bombings and of the British military and intelligence services.

First of all, I have been feeling surprisingly well, considering everything. I have gained four or five pounds and everybody thinks I look much better than I did last fall. I have kept pretty religiously to the diet and have been able to stop taking belladonna and only take the tresetin tablets occasionally.

The big difficulty, of course, is being lonesome, but I have to keep my mind off that or I'd throw up the job and go home. I am enclosing the notes from my diary of my conversation with the President yesterday. This gives you a pretty good idea of what the situation is. I am rather amused, considering the rather bitter reception I got from practically everybody when I returned — my crime at that time being that I thought America should not get into the war. Of course, you know I always felt they shouldn't, because I knew they couldn't lick anybody, but you can't go around telling about your country's weaknesses. However, now I am the fair-haired boy again.

Last night I went to the opening of Clare Boothe's show — "Margin for Error" — and when I came in the theatre I got a big hand. In the meantime, the Government officials, realizing that most of my predictions have worked out 100%, right now regard my judgment rather highly. However, I am not fooling myself and I haven't the slightest doubt that they would turn around tomorrow and throw me in the ash can. It has nothing to do with the individual, it is just what happens to public opinion.

After having worked as hard as I have the last six years and a half, I don't want to do anything that would reflect on the family. After all that's why we went into this and I don't want to spoil it for the sake of a month or two. The boys are doing so well. While I am thoroughly disgusted with the way Roosevelt is handling this situation, as far as this Embassy goes, there is nothing much I can do about it. He hasn't the slightest comprehension of organization. He sends people over here to get reports that he already has in his office made by his own people and the fact that he sends them here over my protest would, under ordinary conditions, make me resign.

In a conversation with Sumner Welles he told me that when Bullitt started to go to Lisbon to return home, the President had ordered him back because he did not feel this was the time to leave France without a representative, particularly since Bullitt had always professed his great friendship for the French people. Nevertheless, Bullitt went straight on home. Then I saw where Phillips went home and of course all the other Ambassadors — from Holland, Belgium, Norway and Denmark — are all back home. Joe Davies,[548] who is very friendly, said he would love to have me home and would do everything he could to get me home if I wanted to go, but that I am building up a terrific amount of good-will by being the only fellow to stay on the job.

My own feeling is that the reason Roosevelt rang me up to discuss the matter was that he is afraid I will walk out because of my dissatisfaction with things and he wanted to "soft-soap" me. At any rate I will see what the situation looks like this month. The trouble is that people think you do a great deal more than you really do and that you are much more important than you are and therefore they would expect you to stay, thinking your task is Herculean, whereas the truth of the matter is, I could name a hundred people who could carry on the detail of the office. As to the psychological effect, both here and abroad — that I don't know.

When Corbin, the French ambassador, decided to close up his house, I took over what French wines he had in his cellar and sent them to America. There weren't many, but they were very good and I am having O'Leary[549] put them in storage with champagne I sent over when the war started. We can always use them for the weddings.

---

548. The former ambassador to Belgium was now special assistant to the secretary of state.
549. The president of JPK's Somerset Importers.

In addition to that, I took over his French chef. After all, aside from the cooking at Wall Hall, I found that English cooks can't purée vegetables, and I thought I would have a fling for myself since it wasn't going to be for long and get myself a great cook. Well, I did, and he is terrific. I think he could purée a bale of hay and make it taste like chocolate ice cream. He is having quite a time making those egg muffins and broiling bacon so that I can eat it. He told Stevens the other day he couldn't understand how anyone could eat bacon when all the good was out of it. I agreed with him, but it is still better than anything I can get from anybody else.

I have sent the details of the four pictures I bought to Paul Murphy and I am sure they are in New York somewhere. They are really very lovely little pictures and I am sure you will be crazy about them and they are by a very good man. I have also sent you the silver. It was picked out by Christies' expert and they sold it to me out of the Red Cross Sale without going to auction. I bought the tea set put up by the Queen and everybody here was delighted and there was a lot of publicity about it. Of course I paid about twice as much as it was worth, but I thought it would be most interesting for the family. After I bought it I received a very sweet note from the Queen, in which she said she was delighted that I had got the set and she felt it looked so lonesome the way it was that she was arranging to have a tray made for me to go with it which she was presenting to Mrs. Kennedy and me as a token of her friendship for us both. So I am waiting for the tray and when it comes I will send the stuff over to you.

Another day I went down to the Red Cross Sale and bought, at rather high prices, one of the best volumes with miniatures and letters of Napoleon and his entire family, and another volume of the Duke of Wellington and several of the great statesmen of that time. These purchases caused quite a furore, but they will be of intense interest to the boys. I also bought quite a number of books — some of them quite old — but all of them very good — at ridiculously low prices. The things that bring the highest prices are jewelry and old silver. Your diamonds are now worth 50% more than they were when you were here.

I am waiting for the sample for Palm Beach. I have gathered a great many pieces of material. I can't imagine the one you picked out in the living room at Palm Beach; it just doesn't seem to me to be bright and cheery enough, but if I can't do any better, I will get it as near that as possible. When I get the sample I am sure I can get expert help. The best material here would probably not cost more than $2.00 or $2.25 a yard, so, if I can get what you want, it will save a lot of money.

I am not very much impressed with the idea of taking evacuées. It is all right while the excitement lasts but having another child in your house eventually gets to be an awful bore. Incidentally, you have to assume responsibility for the child up to its 21st birthday and you have to pay all its bills because they cannot send any money out of here. So that the fact that we offered to take Stella Jean[550] and she has twice accepted and twice postponed it, I think lets us definitely out and I think it is much better that it should be that way. The whole plan is not thoroughly understood in the United States and I think will bring a lot of grief after the excitement is over.

I have written Kresel[551] on the Rosemary matter and I think that can be straightened out right away.

As to the war situation, I don't believe there is a practical chance of invasion, unless Hitler can defeat the British air force. If he can do that, then I don't think he will

550. Stella Jean Gordon, Jean's classmate at the Convent of the Sacred Heart at Roehampton.
551. Isidor Jacob Kresel (1878–1957), JPK's New York attorney.

have to fight hard for the invasion. I think then that the people here will decide it is hopeless. Of course the long-range view is still frightful as far as England goes and they should have great difficulty with the food question next winter if things continue as they are now. The morale here of course is excellent at the minute because they are confident that Hitler can't beat the air force and therefore can't invade. They imagine that the food situation in Europe will finally catch up with them.

I think my poor old friend Chamberlain is finished, although it isn't known, of course, that he has cancer of the bowel. They haven't told Mrs. Chamberlain yet.

Well, darling, I guess this is all the news and I must get this off.

Love to you all.

Joseph P. Kennedy: *Diary*

London, August 6, 1940

I had lunch with Brendan Bracken today and he told me a couple of interesting stories. He said that Churchill called at the Palace the other day to make his weekly visit on the King. The attendant asked if he would mind seeing the King in the garden and when he got to the garden the King was shooting at a target with a rifle and told Churchill if the Germans were coming, he was at least going to get his German and Churchill said if he felt that way about it, he would get him a Tommy gun so he could kill a lot of Germans and he is getting him one.

Bracken also told me about Ironside,[552] who, he said, was a damned old fool; that he had been urging Churchill to fire him for a long time, but the thing that finally made them decide to fire him was that outside of Oxford the police had arrested a parachutist and Ironside told Marlborough, who is his aide, to get his car right away, that he was going to leave the War Office and go down to see the parachutist. When he got there he saw an old fellow hanging around on a bicycle and he said, "Who is he?"; there was a lot of mumbling and he said, "Arrest him; lock him up in Oxford jail for further examination." He said, "Who lives in that house over there?" and they said a Mr. Wilk a farmer who has lived down here for 20 years. He said, "Bring him in," so they brought Wilk in, but he was a tough guy, so Ironside said, "What connection have you got with Germany?" The old man said, "Don't be ridiculous, I haven't any" and Ironside said, "Don't talk that way to me; we have ways of finding out things, if you don't want to tell us" so he said, "Arrest this man and lock him up and search the house from top to bottom; open the mattresses and everything." Then he said, "Has this man got anybody working for him of foreign extraction" and, by mere chance he had two Czechs who had been put in there by the Department of Agriculture. So he said, "Have the two Czechs brought here." When they came he said, "Ah! I know what you fellows are up to." He first talked to them in German and they didn't understand that, and then in Czech. They protested they didn't know what he was talking about and he said, "Lock them up." Then he came to the "parachutist" and they brought the "parachutist" in guarded by twelve men with bayonets. Ironside threw out his chest and stuck his fingers in his belt and proceeded to interrogate the fellow in German, but the fellow doesn't answer one word. "Ah! said Ironside, won't talk, eh? We know how to treat people like you." He turned around to the other officers and said, "He won't talk." The

---

552. Ironside, the former chief of the Imperial General Staff, had been made commander in chief of the Home Forces on May 26.

"parachutist" then said, "I'll talk if you talk to me in a language I can understand" and it turned out that the fellow was a drunken Canadian who was away without leave from the Canadian Division; he had gotten in a bus to rejoin his detachment and finally got off at some pub in Brayton and when in there, being drunk, went up to the bar and hollered for more liquor, saying, "If you don't give me some liquor, I'll clean the place out, I'm a parachutist." So they pinched him. So this was the story of Ironside's discovery of the parachutist and he got himself into a hell of a mess because Eden had to send for Farmer Wilk and apologize and give him plenty of money to square him. So with this evidence they fired Ironside out.

John F. Kennedy, 23, to Joseph P. Kennedy

HYANNISPORT

Dear Dad:

I've had Paul send some clippings over on the book — It's doing very well and is still on the *N.Y. Herald Tribune* list of best-sellers and last week was no 1 in Boston, and no. 2 in New England.

Everything here is fine, we hear terrific stories from England which was chiefly why the publisher accepted the 200 pounds as it seems to us that the last thing an Englishman would want to do now is to read why he slept.

Am not doing any writing just now — merely a book review, although I've had offers from the *Readers' Digest* etc. I feel that unless I took an active part in something, I should merely being stringing along on the book — and if I did take a part, I would the position of an "amateur", which I believe, is in a large measure responsible for the favorable write-ups. However, I am waiting to see what goes on.

Even if it does little more, it has gone twice what the publishers had thought it would. I have gotten nice letters from Roosevelt, Hull, Lothian, and a lot of people in Boston whom I sent it two which seems to have done a lot of good.

Health is OK, but they seem to feel I should take the year off. I will give Stanford a try and will take it very easy and see how it goes for a couple of months.

All the kids are fine — Teddy is very fat, Bobby has really turned into a great kid as everyone remarks. They all did very well in the races and won most of the prizes.

As I said on the phone — politically its hard to tell, Willkie has dropped a lot, but he may just be saving up, he hasn't yet found any issue that he can dramatically break with Roosevelt on, as he can't talk spending when the country voted 10,000,000,000 for defense. Will write soon again.

Love
Jack

Joseph P. Kennedy to Cordell Hull: *Diplomatic Dispatch*

2613, August 7, 8 P.M. Personal and Secret for Secretary Hull

The least, it seems to me, that can be done for the American Ambassador in London, is to let him, subject to the State Department's policy, run his own job. I have previously complained about Mowrer's appointment[553] and I protested Donovan's

---

553. At the request of the new secretary of the Navy, former *Chicago Daily News* publisher Frank Knox (1879–1948), Edgar Mowrer (1892–1977), the eminent *Daily News* foreign correspondent, had accompanied Donovan on his mission to London to record their observations. After returning home Mowrer would write a series of articles and speeches for Donovan based on their findings.

appointment. In both cases, I informed the State Department, that over here, the newspapermen were familiar before I was with their appointment. I casually mentioned that an Admiral had been appointed as my Naval Attaché. This was known to the British Departments and Cabinet while I knew nothing about it. From the British, I hear that he is over here for the purpose of staff talks. I was advised on Saturday night that two Generals are to come here, without any consultation with me, as my Military Attaches. Also this has been known for a week to the War Office and when we ask them for what purpose they are coming, they reply that they are coming for staff talks.

Now there is probably a good reason why it is necessary to go around the Ambassador in London and take up the matter with the British before he knows about it. However, I do not like it and I either want to run this job or get out. At this time, this job is a delicate one and to do the job well, requires that I know what is going on. Not to know what is going on causes embarrassment and confusion. I want to know, in other words, what is going to happen before the British are notified. Not to tell me, is very poor treatment of me, and is bad organization.

Across the entire front page of to-day's Daily Herald blazons that the secret envoy of President Roosevelt sees the Premier and King and then goes on to say he came over here to make a report for Roosevelt. I know, of course, that you cannot help what the newspapers say, but let me tell you now that there are several American newspaper men to-day that know about the arrival of the Generals and Admirals. They know that they are coming over here for staff talks and these men represent interests in America that are prepared to charge that Roosevelt is carrying on negotiations with the British to get us in war and these men are the evidence. I am naturally upset when I consider that information that they are here for staff talks must have come from the British.

There isn't very much that can be done about this now except that you could give me some idea of what story I am to tell when these gentlemen arrive here. Its perfectly silly to say that they are to be my Naval or Military Attaches because over here, no one is going to believe that and I don't think they will in America. However, the least we can all do, and that includes the British, is to have a story that will fit the occasion and I would like to be advised on it.

Incidentally, my situation has not been made much easier by the Cudahy interview.[554]

KENNEDY

The Ambassador

---

554. On August 6, while visiting JPK, John Cudahy, the American ambassador to Belgium who had left his post in mid-July, had made a number of off-the-cuff remarks to the press regarding the German invasion of Belgium. Asked, for example, whether he viewed the invasion "as a minor atrocity," Cudahy responded, "I was a soldier in the last war and I say this frankly, they behaved better than the American soldiers would have behaved." To a question regarding whether any "action against the Jews" had occurred, he replied, "[t]he Germans showed great restraint."

Joseph P. Kennedy to Brendan Bracken

London, August 8, 1940

Dear Brendan,

I am enclosing the posters I talked to you about at lunch today. I realize it is an imposition to ask that the Prime Minister autograph all these, but I know that unless I give one to each of the children I will get into plenty of trouble. It's bad enough having to explain Ambassador's stray remarks, let alone try and define myself in my own family.

But, seriously, I think it is an exhortation the children might well have in front of them for the rest of their lives and I know that the posters will be framed and regarded highly.

Yours sincerely,

Joseph P. Kennedy: *Diary*

London, August 14, 1940

I just took a telegram with the message from Roosevelt to Churchill about the terms on which the Americans would give the British destroyers.[555] Churchill apologized for not being able to see me at 3:30, which is the time I asked for an appointment, because he said he has a sleep then.[556] He was smoking a cigar when I entered and asked me if I would have a scotch highball and said he would have one. He said after his sleep he was good until two o'clock in the morning.

He read over the statement of the President and said nothing until he came to the part where a 99 year lease was mentioned and said, this war will go on till then unless Hitler is beaten and he said, "I think the more we get together with you people, the better it will be for the world. I said, "You mean a sort of "Union Now"?[557] and he said, "Well, something along those lines; otherwise there is no hope for civilization. He said we will let them have anything they want on these Islands that the President speaks about and those points can be adjusted very easily. As to the fleet going to protect the Empire, of course I don't want to say anything that will give people the idea we are in muddy waters, because I would be telling you wrong if I said I didn't think we had Hitler licked, but I am seeing the Admiralty tonight and I will have a statement for you tonight. We will get around it somehow.

I told him that young Jack had finished his book and it was receiving almost universal approval in the United States and that it had paid very great tribute to the Prime Minister and he evinced a great interest in it and I said I would send it around to him this afternoon. He said he realized that he was able to say a lot of things during that pe-

---

555. "It is my belief," the president told Churchill, "that it may be possible to furnish to the British Government as immediate assistance at least 50 destroyers" in addition to a number of motor torpedo boats and several classes of aircraft. "Such assistance" he added, "would only be furnished if the American people and the Congress frankly recognized that in return therefor the national answer was made and security of the United States would be enhanced." The president requested the government's assurance that in the event of Britian's inability to defend herself on the seas, the fleet would be sent out of German reach to other parts of the empire. Additionally, the United States would be granted the right to use a number of naval and air bases throughout the empire "for training and exercise purposes with the understanding that the land necessary for the above could be acquired by the United States through purchase or through a 99 year lease."

556. "Imagine," JPK would comment on the incident in his Diplomatic Memoir, "this was the message Churchill had been waiting for for weeks, and on which he said the fate of Civilization might well depend, and he had to have his afternoon nap!"

557. Journalist Clarence Kirshman Streit (1896–1986) had published his "Proposal for a Federal Union of the Democracies" in *Union Now* in 1938.

riod when he was unsaddled because if they had saddled him he would have had to jump when the ringmaster said jump and therefore he was probably able to make a better record than he would have otherwise. He didn't think there was any satisfaction in trying to attach blame to individuals like Baldwin and Chamberlain because people just didn't believe the truth in those days about Hitler.

He said they dropped 30 tons of bombs on Turin and Milan last night and gave them a good dose. He said the Italians were fighting a little better than was expected in Somaliland and of course their position was very much like a main building in a house and the French were the equivalent of girders which started to fall out while the house was being constructed and the British were expected to get the house in shape without the girders, but he was confident that they would do it. In fact he was confident about everything. He felt that Hitler would invade and soon, but that he would get a very terrible reception. In fact the only thing that disturbed him was that Hitler might not invade and Churchill would be in a bad way in that he had built up the defenses and army to fight Hitler. He said the British soldiers would probably want their money back, because they won't be satisfied with the show.

I pointed out to him that Roosevelt's position was very difficult; the country was definitely hoping that England would win; they had taken on the responsibility of the Monroe Doctrine for the entire North American Continent and they had told the American public that they had no strength so they must appropriate 5 or 6 billion dollars to build a navy. So, with all these factors, it was pretty difficult to let England have 50 destroyers unless he could persuade the American public that the British fleet would not go to Hitler. Churchill said he quite understood that and was perfectly willing to do it, except that he must not strike a note of discouragement for his own people. He said, "You know that I was the only one who wasn't discouraged at the outlook when I took this job and now most people are coming around to my way of thinking. We are going to beat this man."

Joseph P. Kennedy to Joseph Medill Patterson

Personal and Confidential. London, August 22, 1940

Dear Joe,

Your letter of July 22nd about young Joe arrived here this week. I can't tell you how happy I was to receive this message from you.[558] One is always surprised — although I suppose one shoudn't be — when a busy man with lots on his mind has time to do as kind a thing as this: first of all to note the fact that Joe was even alive and second, that any action he took at the Convention was worthy of your notice, and, third and most important, that you took time to write me about it.

I judge that great pressure was brought to bear on him, because Johnnie Burns called me from Chicago the night before and said that Joe had affirmed his intention to vote for Farley and that some of Roosevelt's friends thought I should be notified about it. Of course I told Johnnie that Joe would have to make his own decision and that I thought it would be manifestly unfair for me to mix in it one way or another. I thought that if he intended to go into public life, he might as well find out now if calling the play as he saw it was going to cause him difficulty. I wrote him a letter when it was all over

---

558. The founder, publisher and editor of the *New York Daily News* had written JPK on July 22 to say "what an excellent impression . . . Joe Jr., made on the delegates and spectators," at the convention and added, "I am sure he can have a political future if he wants one."

and praised his stand. Jim Farley, from the thick of the campaign in Chicago, sent me a wire commending Joe for showing plenty of guts, so I was happy.

Perhaps you would like to have my observations on the situation as I see it today. I remember well the last time I saw you before I left America. The immediate cause of a dispute that day between Bullitt and me was whether the United States should continue to loan money to other countries. I said I thought it was like pouring money into a sieve. I still think so. In fact, I think everything they are giving to South America will go the same way. If, however, our rich country can afford to give this money away — in the interests of foreign policy — why that is one thing. I just don't think it makes sense. We are spending money like nigger rich, without those who have the control of the spending having the slightest idea of what this long-range program is going to mean to the people of the United States. Now that doesn't mean that we shouldn't arm and that we shouldn't prepare, but, while we are doing that, we ought to have a well formulated policy as to what our economic future is to be. I grant that this is very difficult to approximate, but while you are trying to estimate the future, it certainly shouldn't be difficult to remain practical at all times.

The situation on this Island is as I have felt it was for some time. If Germany can knock off the British Air Force and gain supremacy in the air, then I don't believe that all the plans made for the protection of England will amount to a tinker's damn. I believe that the Germans will invade the Island whenever they please, provided they attain air supremacy, which, at the moment, they are certainly having great difficulty doing. If the last two weeks' attacks on England are part of the Blitzkrieg, then it is definitely a failure so far. If they haven't air strength enough to defeat or immobilize the British Air Force, then it strikes me that this Island will continue as long as it is possible to get ships into the country and their resources in the United States permit them to purchase supplies. In the meantime, of course, things are becoming worse for them around the Mediterranean and I am not particularly hopeful as to their prospects there.

As I see it, we are going to be faced more and more with the argument that England is our line of defense and that will serve as a reason for every action we want to take, even up to the declaration of war. They need destroyers, because their Navy isn't powerful or big enough to protect the Mediterranean, the British Isles and the trade routes. They will need money to pay for the supplies they buy in the United States after next spring. To me, whatever our country wants to do of its own free will is fine, but if we ever enter this war we will be signing a blank check, not only for our resources but for our manpower and our social and political life. Don't misunderstand me. There is nobody in the world who would rather see the Germans beaten than I would, but it strikes me that my job here is to keep as realistic as I can and to call the picture as I see it, which I am doing every day in my despatches to Washington.

It is rather dismal here with my entire family in the United States and I hate to have Mrs. Kennedy burdened with the whole responsibility, but I have resisted invitations to come home, because I felt I couldn't leave here until I had seen the bombing through. After that, we will see.

With warmest regards,

Sincerely yours,

Joseph P. Kennedy to Franklin Roosevelt: *Diplomatic Dispatch*

2913, Twenty-Seventh of August at 6 P.M.
FOR THE PRESIDENT. PERSONAL AND CONFIDENTIAL.

Regarding our last telephonic conversation you will recall that I informed you that I did not care to return home until I had seen how England withstood the attack by Germany. Except for the above reason, I informed you at that time that I did not think my work here important enough for me to remain. You were kind in saying that the people in the United States feel that their interests were being well protected here and that it was important for the morale of the English that I remain here.

Regarding the negotiation of destroyers and bases, I am sure you must be aware of the very embarrassing situation I feel myself in in this connection. While realizing that Washington handled the matter entirely, on the other hand I can find no commonsense explanation when I consider the amount of information furnished the British Ambassador in Washington by the British Government and the lack of information furnished to me on matters of vital importance to me. I would have no knowledge whatsoever of the situation had it not been for the fact that the Prime Minister had seen fit to send some cables back through me and also has furnished me with supplementary data. You may properly say there is no reason for my knowing anything about it but if I am not acquainted with facts of vital importance to both countries I fail to see how I can function with any degree of efficiency. Mowrer and Donovan who were appointed only recently on special missions and two Generals and an Admiral were assigned as observers without consulting me and the event was known in important British circles even before I was informed.[559] Rarely, as a matter of fact, am I ever advised when important conversations are held in Washington with the British Ambassador. While vice versa Lothian is informed by his government in all talks or events of which there is a mutual importance. Of course it has been impossible for me to make any contribution to the destroyer-bases discussion seeing as I do not know any of the facts, except second hand, but there was a possibility that I might have been able to make some contribution.

I have been fairly active in any enterprise which I have taken up for the last twenty-five years. Frankly and honestly I do not enjoy being a dummy. I am very unhappy about the whole position and of course there is always the alternative of resigning, which I would not hesitate to do if conditions were not as they are.

KENNEDY

Joseph P. Kennedy: *Diary*

London, September 2, 1940

The Prime Minister came to dinner with Lord Beaverbrook and General Emmons[560] and Brigadier General Strong[561] and Admiral Ghormley.[562] The Prime Minister arrived about 15 minutes late, and I should judge he had been having a little sleep. When he sat down, he suggested that we call this the "Destroyer Dinner" in

---

559. Without consulting JPK, the president had recently dispatched a group of high U.S. military officials to London both to act as military observers and to finalize the destroyers-for-bases negotiations.
560. Lieutenant General Delos Carleton Emmons (1888–1965), chief of the U.S. Army Air Corps.
561. George Veazy Strong (1880–1946), chief of the U.S. Army War Plans Division, 1938–40, and special War Department observer.
562. Robert Lee Ghormley (1883–1958), U.S. naval observer in London, 1940–42.

honor of the destroyer deal. Ghormley had told me earlier in the day the British had informed him the agreement was to be signed at six o'clock the following day. Of course nothing had been said to me about it and Roosevelt's conduct in this closing phase of the negotiations was just as inconsiderate as during the entire negotiations. The only thing that was apparent was that Roosevelt, through Lothian, had immediately sent back word to Churchill that it would be very embarrassing to him if Churchill made any statement that he had originally desired to give these bases without any consideration whatsoever. Churchill told me he had received this request and of course had assured Roosevelt that he would do nothing to embarrass his position. Churchill reiterated in front of everybody that he had wanted to give the bases, not trade them, but he said, "I will say nothing now, but will stand on my speech in Parliament and will never discuss the details until after the U.S. election, but probably before the next British national election. Beaverbrook joined in again saying that he never wanted this kind of a deal to be made because, while it would elect Roosevelt President, it would make the British look very silly for having made this kind of agreement for what are probably a lot of old, decrepit destroyers. I made it clear in the presence of all that I had never been asked about the condition of these destroyers and I didn't know much about them anyway, but the deal seemed to me to be an "as is" deal. Churchill then asked Ghormley whether they were overhauled, whether they had any submarine detectors, etc., depth bomb machinery, but Ghormley gave him very little encouragement as to their condition. Beaverbrook finally said, "Will they be able to come across the ocean on their own power?" and I said, "Perhaps."

It became apparent, however, that there were ulterior motives behind Churchill's seemingly generous desire to give the bases without consideration, because he said, "I always expected if I made such a gesture, you would have to give us something and of course I believe that the something is going to be, sooner or later, big financial credits or gifts" and I think that's what was in Beaverbrook's mind when he said, "Let's give the bases and not let America think she is settling for these old worn-out destroyers." Churchill said that of course England will have to have credit and money and then, strangely enough, he went on to say that immediately after the last war if he had had the power, he would have repudiated the American debt on the grounds that by the British forcing the battle in 1918 they had finished the war and if it had gone over to 1919 the United States would have lost at least 500,000 men. Therefore, England, having made her contribution in manpower, we should have made ours in money. Later on he said Baldwin and Chamberlain made monkeys of themselves by negotiating the kind of deal they did and then finally repudiating them.

It becomes apparent to me that if Churchill was able to find a ground for repudiating the debt in 1918, he certainly will find no difficulty in repudiating this one. Of course, he said, that before they ask us for money they will give us everything they have — gold rings, silver — whatever we take and then we will have to pay.

He told Strong that what he wants is 250,000 rifles or the original order of 875,000, of which to date he has only received 563,000, and approximately 175,000,000 rounds of ammunition; he also wants flying boats badly and Beaverbrook says that what comes ahead of all these things are machine tools, which they ordered and which they must have.

Churchill gave us the impression that he was terribly optimistic as to what will happen. He feels that Hitler cannot gain superiority in the air and therefore cannot invade successfully, although it is very apparent that he sees a likelihood of invasion attempted within a comparatively short time at Dover.

Beaverbrook said they were stronger in the air now than they ever were and that they had twenty times more reserve planes than they had in June.

Churchill added that he wished Roosevelt were at the dinner with us so that he could tell him how much he appreciated his efforts and how strong he thinks England is.

Churchill told Beaverbrook to tell the newspapers not to hazard the guess that the United States will be in the war soon as the result of the destroyer deal. He made it very clear to him that this would be a very disastrous thing to say because he did not believe it would be true. (Sir Walter Layton[563] told me when he came the following day that the papers had all been advised, even though they said they would not have said that at all.)

The deal was to be announced on September 3rd — one year from the declaration of war. My own impression is that Roosevelt will gain a lot of prestige from the destroyer deal, provided the United States does not find out that he gave away the destroyers for something he could have had for nothing.

One of the other things that was discussed was the great progress the British were making on locating the night bomber, which Emmons agreed the British will have worked out in the course of the next few months.

Churchill asked me how many people I thought had been killed by air raids in this country. I hazarded 750 and the rest of the party guessed from 500 to 600. Churchill said, actually about 780 had been killed, which he said was a surprisingly small number. He thought it extremely likely that the Germans may double the force of the air attacks in September but that the British Air Force could handle that.

We opened the box of cigars that Tony Loughborough had sent me and as the P.M. liked them, I gave him the box and said that would even up the destroyer-bases deal.

Churchill said a great deal about getting pilots trained in the American air fields, but Beaverbrook contended that unless they get military training, the other training was of no value. It was very apparent, watching Churchill and Beaverbrook, that Beaverbrook has very great influence with Churchill and is more than likely to have great weight in any ultimate decisions. (I noticed that, when Churchill came into the Abbey the other day, although I was talking with Halifax, he didn't appear to be very gushing in his greeting to Halifax, but this may have been my imagination).

Joseph P. Kennedy to Franklin Roosevelt and Cordell Hull:
Diplomatic Dispatch

> *3038 September 6 12 midnight. FOR THE PRESIDENT AND SECRETARY*
There's hell to pay here tonight[564]
> *KENNEDY*

The Ambassador

---

563. Sir Walter Thomas Layton (1884–1966), later Baron Layton, economist, journalist and director general of Programs at the Ministry of Supply, 1940–42.
564. That day London had endured the most extensive air raids of the war to date; the bombings would intensify in the weeks to come.

Joseph P. Kennedy to Rose Kennedy

Dear Rose:

The record with the children's voices arrived just on the 6th,[565] and I have played it at least twenty times already. I can't say that any of my children's voices have improved in tone quality since I heard them last, but there is still plenty of pep in the sound. And incidentally your piano touch was never better.

Gladys Scanlon[566] got the dress and I am sending it by General Emmons who is sailing from here this week, so that you should have it by the end of next or surely the beginning of the following week. I am addressing it c/o Paul Murphy.

As to Queen Mary's picture, I have already written Miss Dunn but I am sure that in all the excitement at Christmas we put it in the drawer with some cartoons in the tall desk in the drawing room at Bronxville. I think you will find it there. Let me hear from you if you don't, and I will see what I can do about getting another one.

To give you the social items before the war situation, I had the Prime Minister at 14 Prince's Gate with Lord Beaverbrook the other night for dinner with General Emmons, General Strong and Admiral Ghormley who have been assigned here as observers, and we had a very nice dinner prepared by the French chef. And on Sunday night the Duke and Duchess of Kent came out to Windsor — they are living right handy there — and we had a picture. I had the Generals and the Admiral too, and Nancy Astor came over after dinner. She's getting nervous and quite a bit fidgety, but she is still terribly nice. She sent me a little snuffbox of great age for my birthday. She still hears from Joe, and she thinks the family is marvelous but that I am terrible because I don't run over there all the time. But I can't take it all the time. I took her out on the golf course and gave her such a licking that she won't dare talk golf to me any more.

I bought quite a lot of French wine from French Ambassador Corbin and sent it to you in America last week, and got the very good news on my birthday that the Germans had sunk the ship. So that's that.

Now I suppose you have been frightfully nervous reading about all the bombing. If one wasn't in very good shape physically it would unquestionably get one down sooner or later. The bomb at Windsor fell about 250 yards from the house. We were out looking at the searchlights and the anti-aircraft fire when we heard it coming and dove into the bushes. It struck with a dull thud.

The last three nights in London have been simply hell. Last night I put on my steel helmet and went up on the roof of the Chancery and stayed up there until two o'clock in the morning watching the Germans come over in relays every ten minutes and drop bombs, setting terrific fires. You could see the dome of St. Paul's silhouetted against a blazing inferno that the Germans kept adding to from time to time by flying over and dropping more bombs.

14 Princes Gate has just missed being hit. One of the bombs hit the barracks, you know, facing Rotten Row; one last night dropped in the bridle path opposite the house; and Herschel Johnson was almost killed the other night when the house next door to his was completely demolished. It seems they are looking for two power plants and the headquarters of the A.R.P. The latter were in the Natural History Museum which they finally got Sunday night, setting fire to it. Because they are working against Kensington, I have moved out of there completely. Last night, after I had looked the situation

---

565. His fifty-second birthday.
566. JPK's secretary at the embassy.

over, I slept in the air raid shelter at the Chancery and did very nicely for myself. When I have to stay in town I am planning to sleep there and the rest of the time go out to Windsor. Windsor is reasonably quiet, and unless some stray bomb happened to hit you, you would be very well off there. As to the chances of danger —

While I was dictating this, the air raid siren went off at one o'clock and everybody rushed down to the cellar. We have put in a system here along with the Government of sending observers to the roof, in order to carry on as long as we can without having to take to the air raid shelter.

As I said, as to the prospects of danger, even though it sounds terrible, the chances of anything happening to one are still one in a million. It is amazing to see all these flares and all these bombs dropping and yet as you ride through the streets there is little indication of their effects except in the devastated areas. I am completely a fatalist about bombing accidents. I don't think anything is going to happen to me, and for that reason it doesn't worry me the slightest bit. I am still riding horseback every morning. I play golf on Saturdays and Sundays. My stomach is quite good. The only thing that gives me any concern at all is getting home. There is a very definite feeling in the minds of both the Prime Minister and Beaverbrook that Hitler will try an invasion very soon. Barges and ships are lined up at all the ports from Norway to the southern point of France, and if he can demoralize transportation and the air fields and has the strength to further cripple the Air Force, I should think he would be in here very soon. If he comes with any strength, then the battle will be terrific, and the whole story will be whether he can bring up his reserves. If he can, England will have a tough time. If he can't, it will mean a major defeat for Hitler. With all my desire to get home, I feel I must see this through. I have talked with Beaverbrook, Halifax, Montagu Norman about my going home and while they all appreciate how anxious I am to see you folks, they would regard my leaving as tragedy. Of course they all say go home for a little while and come back, but that doesn't suit me at all. When I go home I want to stay home. I don't want to do anything that will harm the British, but on the other hand I have no misgivings about finishing my job here just as soon as I see whether this prospective invasion will work or not. I have you and the children and what is left of my business to try and work on, and I really feel that after the last six, important years of my life dedicated to Government service, I am tired. If you ride horseback with German aeroplanes overhead, shoot a golf game with a battle going on, and eat all your meals and do all you sleeping under the strain of the present situation, that, it seems to me, should entitle you to a rest for a while. That's the way I feel. So I think that towards the end of this month it should become clear whether the invasion is a possibility or not; and by that time there will have been enough concentrated bombing on all of us in London so that certainly nobody in America could think I had left before I had seen a big part of the show. I'll be very interested to get your reaction on this.

I am enclosing some signed statements of excerpts from Churchill's two famous speeches. I am only sending you half of them for fear something might happen to this mail. I will send the other half with the next mail. I had them all signed for the children as I think they will be important historical documents.

My group of three — Burgess, Gee and Stevens[567] — are still taking very good care of me; and I want to tell you that this man Stevens is really the wonder of the world. If I ever go home and he doesn't come with me, I really won't know what to do with myself. He certainly makes one's life worth living.

Love
Joe

567. JPK's household staff.

Joseph P. Kennedy to John F. Kennedy, 23

Dear Jack:

It was nice to hear your voice ringing out on that record that you sent us and it made me plenty homesick. I couldn't be more pleased that you got away with such a marvelous start with the book and I think you are very wise in not attempting to write other articles until this book has had a long run, because, since the critics think this is all right, there is no sense in opening yourself up to attack on some other article you might write which might not go over so well. You will have plenty of time to do that.

I am enclosing some of the clippings I have at hand and I have a good many others that I will send to you later on. I haven't had a chance to get many letters for you because I have used the book to put before reviewers rather than important people, but I am sending one of the copies to Edward Halifax and I will try to get something out of him. Of course it is going to be fairly difficult to get letters from people who were in the government you criticize, for they can't be expected to agree with you, so that may hold that point up.

Bilainkin has written a couple of very praiseworthy articles and I loaned him your graduation picture to use in connection with an article in the "Illustrated" this week.[568] I will send it to you when it comes out.

Tony comes out and stays with me whenever he gets a day off, to play golf with Ding Dong, Seymour and me. Ding Dong and I usually beat Tony and Seymour, and as you can imagine, there is plenty of talk about this. Kick will tell you of the incident that happened last Saturday night. I had the Duchess of Kent for dinner Sunday and she said she had been reading about the book you had written and asked if you were not very young to do it. I said my experience was that my sons were very precocious! She can take that any way she likes, but she was very nice about both you and Tony. I think you are both very strong there.

For a man with a weak stomach these last three days have proven very conclusively that you can worry about much more important things than whether you are going to have an ulcer or not. The Germans every once in a while give a very clear indication that they have been only fooling when it comes to bombing, because they fly over, certainly at night almost at will, and they could be dropping a great many more bombs than they are. After all the run from the French coast over here isn't much more than twenty-five minutes, so the boys can make a good many trips in seven to nine hours at night, whereas the British have to go all the way to Berlin, which is a long grind, and then only drop a few bombs. There are a lot of angles to this war that are not thoroughly understood yet by the people. I have suggested to Joe that all you children exchange letters so you will get all the slants on it.

As regards the newspaper reports on censorship, I am inclined to hold them very lightly. There is no question but what they are covering up a great deal in the English press, and there is also no question but what the censors are changing a good deal of copy. For instance, Bill Hillman wanted to broadcast the fact that he had been down to Dover and had seen no British ships going through the Channel. The censors refused to let him say that and suggested that he should say he saw no enemy activity. It is things like that which give me great doubts as to the complete reliability of the reports out of here. On the other hand I don't think the Germans are telling the truth either, but what percentage of fact you take of either I don't know. The people here keep saying their

---

568. Geroge Bilainkin (1903–1981), diplomatic correspondent for Britain's Allied Newspapers.

chin is up and that they can't be beaten, but the people who have had any experience with these bombings don't like it at all. After all, it remained for London to receive the worst bombing since Rotterdam and remember that this city is attempting to function while all this is going on, whereas Warsaw and Rotterdam were evacuated.

I am feeling very well. Haven't the slightest touch of nervousness. But I can see evidences of some people beginning to break down. Herschel Johnson was almost killed Sunday night when the house next door to him was blown right off the map. The Natural History Museum in Kensington was practically gutted by bombs and fire Sunday night, so all in all Jack, it is a great experience. The only thing I am afraid of is that I won't be able to live long enough to tell all that I see and feel about this crisis. When I hear these mental midgets [*U.S.A.*] talking about my desire for appeasement and being critical of it, my blood fairly boils. What is this war going to prove? And what is it going to do to civilization? The answer to the first question is nothing; and to the second I shudder even to think about it.

The second air raid warning is going off while I am dictating this to you at 4 o'clock in the afternoon, but until it gets really tough I am carrying on.

Good luck to you Boy, and I hope to see you soon.

Love
<u>*Dad*</u>

Joseph P. Kennedy to Robert Kennedy, 14

London, September 11, 1940

Dear Bobby:

I thought you might be interested to get my opinion as to the present situation here. There is no question but that there is a very definite feeling that within the next forty-eight or seventy-two hours Germany will try an invasion. There are evidences that they have accumulated a number of barges and ships to move their forces all along the French Coast. There is also an indication that their guns, which they are firing from the French Coast and the shells from which land in Dover, will be the sort of rainbow effect over the channel that they will send their fleet under for protection. There is also evidence that the Germans are magnetic mining all the harbors that the British naval forces might be in, so that they will have difficulty in getting out. So to all intents and purposes Hitler gives every indication of attempting to invade. However, there are some flies in that ointment. One is that everything that Hitler has done so far, aside from what he has told the world he proposes to do in his book "Mien Kampf", has never lacked an element of surprise, and his preparations for invasion seem so obvious that one hesitates to believe that this is his method. Of course, on the other hand, if he really plans an invasion, he will find it most difficult to hide ships in which he intends to move his troops in some dark alley, for the British reconnaissance 'planes are constantly looking for signs of any activity from the Germans. The second reason why one may doubt the possibility of invasion is that to date he has not been able to beat the R.A.F. fighters, as he would have to do, in order to feel sure that his ships could successfully close the Channel. Now it may be that he has a terrific air force ready to launch with his invasion plans, but this we will have to wait for and see.

Hitler's attacks on London and on the transportation systems here are naturally slowing up all the war effort, and it may be that he will concentrate on this in the next two or three days and nights in order to make it very difficult to move men and materials to various parts of this country. After all, London is the key to the whole place, and if they render this part helpless it will be a great boon for their prospective invasion.

Up to date neither the British nor the Germans have been able to counter night bombing raids, but the British are working on a discovery that may be very helpful in stopping the German night bombers, but I am afraid it will not be much use to them for some months.

The Government here is still very popular, and Churchill is, of course, the God of all. Now how long that will last when people, like those in the East End of London to-day, are homeless and jobless, it is difficult to say. My opinion is that the people who just see this bombing from afar and who aren't direct sufferers from it, are standing up very well, but those who have lost their homes, their friends and their jobs, are not much different from other poor unfortunates who have suffered this air attack. Therefore, what the future of the Government here will be one can't say, at least for the time being.

The censorship here on all articles going to the United States and even appearing in the British papers is terribly strict. You never hear anything on the air or read anything in the papers that indicates just how bad England is off or what the probable results of the war might be. As a result the people have an optimism that is away beyond the facts. I have never been able to figure out how, if the Germans make up their mind to join with Italy and come down into South-eastern Europe and fight Turkey and gain the benefits of the oil wells and the use of the Suez Canal, the British can possibly stop them. It now takes almost two and a half to three months to get any forces from England down around the Cape of Good Hope and up into the Egyptian territory, and in addition to that until they find out what Hitler is going to do about invasion they have been very loath to send any men down there. Should Italy and Germany get control of these oil fields the prospect for England becomes darker by the minute.

The whole problem will finally be dropped in the lap of the United States, because as the manufacturing facilities here are destroyed or disorganized, we in the United States will have to furnish more supplies, and that means that England will have to have more money, and they can't get more money unless we give it to them, so after the election we in the United States will be faced with the problem of how far we are willing to go in a financial way to help Great Britain. In other words, if we say, "We will help England", she probably will continue the struggle, but if we say, "This is hopeless," England must of necessity quit. So you see, within a very few months we will have the settling of the whole matter right in our own hands.

Well, I am terribly sorry I have not had a chance to see you this summer Bob, but I do hope you will put in a good effort this year. It is boys of your age who are going to find themselves in a very changed world and the only way you can hold up your end is to prepare your mind so that you will be able to accept each situation as it comes along, so don't, I beg of you, waste any time. Do all the things necessary to get yourself in good physical condition and work hard.

Love,

Joseph P. Kennedy to Edward Kennedy, 8

London, September 11, 1940

Dear Teddy:

I certainly don't get all of those letters you keep telling me you write to me and I should think you would make your plans to write me at least once a week, because your sisters do very well and you and Bobby are the worst correspondents I have in the family. In addition to that it is very good practice for you to write, so I hope that you will plan to send me a regular letter for as long as I am here. Incidentally I certainly was thrilled to hear all your voices on the radio. You are a great little cheer-leader, and that Hip! Hip! Hooray! Couldn't have been better.

I don't know whether you would have very much excitement during these raids. I am sure, of course, you wouldn't be scared, but if you heard all these guns firing every night and the bombs bursting you might get a little fidgety. I am sure you would have liked to be with me and seen the fires the German bombers started in London. It is really terrible to think about, and all those poor women and children and homeless people down in the East end of London all seeing their places destroyed. I hope when you grow up you will dedicate your life to trying to work out plans to make people happy instead of making them miserable, as war does today.

I was terribly sorry not to be with you in swimming at Cape Cod this summer, but I am sure you will know I wanted to be, but couldn't leave here while I had work to do. However, I am looking forward with great pleasure to our swims at Palm Beach this winter.

I know you will be glad to hear that all these little English boys your age are standing up to this bombing in great shape. They are all training to be great sports.

I thought you might be interested to know, and you might tell this to all your brothers and sisters, that the other night when I was going to the Concert to hear some music at Queen's Hall and afterwards going to have dinner with Duff Cooper, the Cabinet Minister of Information, I dashed home to 14 Prince's Gate, put on my dinner jacket and then left to go to the concert. When I got to Queen's Hall I found out the concert was cancelled, and then I went back to my office, and after sitting there three-quarters of an hour I noticed by the merest chance that I had forgotten to shave for a couple of days, and I was going out to a dinner party without having shaved. So you can see how busy I am. I am sure everybody will laugh at this.

Well, old boy, write me some letters and I want you to know that I miss seeing you a lot, for after all, you are my pal, aren't you?

Love
Dad

Joseph P. Kennedy to Rose Kennedy

Wed, Sept 11, 1940

Well Darling, I've dictated the news but I want you to know that I love you and miss you terribly. The excitement of this life of course keeps one going and because a great many eyes are on me all the time, I must act gay, etc. All the papers are again playing me up and saying how right I've been and I'm enclosing an editorial from the *Express*. So the Kennedys are OK again.

Don't worry about me please, I'm going to take care of myself in every way I can and still do my job.

I just wish I could be with you and help with the children.

Well it won't be long now I'm sure.

All my love
Joe

Joseph P. Kennedy: *Diary*

At 12 o'clock today I received another telephone call from the balloon barrage headquarters who have been on the lookout for German planes to let me see just where they are met in the London area. I was told there was a squadron of 200 coming, and I rushed over. By the time I arrived at headquarters practically all of them had been turned back. There were about 8 or 10 British fighting squadrons in the air, about 100 planes. I asked how many balloons were now in use in the London area and was told about 350; there had been up to 500 or 600, but they have been losing them at the rate of about 30 a night from shrapnel from the British anti-aircraft guns. I was told that most often they don't come down with one hit but that after four or five they blow out and come down. The greatest loss is the gas and the time taken in manning the balloons. It seems that in one of their stations a high explosive bomb landed right on the spot where the balloon was being flown from. They filled up the hole and covered it over, and the very next night another high explosive bomb landed in the identical spot. I believe the chances this would happen are a million to one.

Last night (September 23rd) Churchill's office called again and said he had another message for the President which he would send over and it could go this morning after I had read it.[569] This is the second message that has been sent this week, and both were fixed up and sent over at night. Since Churchill became Prime Minister there is no question but that the bulk of the work and planning takes place at night.

I called to see Chamberlain on the 17th, which was the first time I had seen him since his operation. He looked quite well and seemed to have a good deal of his old steam. When he returned he told me that he said to Churchill that he would not be able to take up his regular work, that he didn't feel fit; and Churchill told him not to pay any attention to that, that he wanted him for his counsel and needed him for that very badly. I had been suggesting that it was necessary that he be there because of the financial problems I saw arising and because I had no very great confidence in the financial canniness of the present War Cabinet. He said he told me about the incident because what I said seemed to agree with what Churchill had suggested to him. He also added: "You know, Joe, it's a pretty bad Cabinet we've got." I told him that Jack Garner had told me when I left to come over here that in his forty years of political life he had never seen a Cabinet in Washington that was as destitute of brains as the Roosevelt Cabinet, and Chamberlain said: "He should come over and take a look at ours." I said: "I still think this war won't accomplish anything. We are supposed to be fighting for liberty and the result will be to turn the last of the Democracies into Socialist, Communist, or Totalitarian States." Chamberlain said "Absolutely. Do you know what kind of a committee they want me to act as chairman of? Well, it's one to discuss the set-up of Europe after the war. Did you ever hear such nonsense. However this committee hasn't met yet, and I tell you that it won't meet. These long-haired specialists at Oxford think they know all about the problems of the world today. How in heaven's name can anyone tell what Europe will look like when this war is over when nobody has the slightest idea under what conditions this war will end?"

569. On September 23, 1940, a joint Free French and British force under General de Gaulle attacked the Senegalese port of Dakar in order to prevent the establishment of a German base there. In his message the prime minister requested that the president send additional American warships to the African ports of Monrovia and Freetown, and added that the president should "put it across" to the Pétain government that "a declaration of war would be very bad indeed for them in all that concerns the United States."

After commenting on the American situation, Chamberlain said "Willkie seems to me to have made a great many mistakes but his reference to Munich and Roosevelt is absolutely ridiculous.[570] It just shows that people, even people in high places, still don't understand the true situation in Europe."

I reiterated what I had said before, that he was most needed to work on what I think is the most important problem of the entire war for England, i.e. the United States' attitude toward credits to be extended to England. It is apparent to me from my talks with Kingsley Wood, Walter Layton, Montagu Norman, Catto[571] and Chamberlain that this is the problem that will make or break England. If England cannot get the money from the United States, then as far as the war is concerned it is all over, because they need the manufacturing output of America so badly and they will not have the money to pay for it after another year. Chamberlain of course said that the Cabinet took it for granted they were going to get what they wanted, and in this they have been encouraged by Roosevelt and Morgenthau. I said it wasn't going to be nearly as easy as that unless the war situation caused a complete shake-up in the people's mind. But, after all, Johnson[572] who was the author of the Johnson Act was going to be almost unanimously re-elected in California, and he had a fair amount of brains and was a fellow who couldn't be cast aside very easily; as against that, Roosevelt and Morgenthau had never had any great financial experience and I felt that they had plenty of trouble coming ahead. When I mentioned Morgenthau's name, Chamberlain said "I thought by this time Morgenthau might know something." I said "Well, of course he's learned some, but he had no background to start with." Chamberlain then said "Of course I see a great deal of trouble in the immediate future. In a short while after this bombing and the disarrangement of their lives, people will begin saying 'What are they fighting for?' Of course the answer now will be 'To beat Hitler', — probably the only answer they'll get now, whereas at the beginning of the war we were going to put all the States back where they belonged. Of course that is still our intention, but the immediate problem is to beat Hitler. Well, when he starts having trouble in his own country we must be ready to work then for peace. This isn't the time, even though Hitler keeps throwing out feelers, as in that incident in Sweden the other day. The difficulty is that there isn't anything new in any of them. The old principle of 'You keep yours and I'll handle mine' isn't satisfactory at this time because you can't be sure his ultimate intention is only to handle his own and not to mix into yours again."

I can't help but feel that Chamberlain is not carried away with the prospects of England; but, like everyone else, he sees nothing can be done at the moment.

I again say, how fortunate it might be for civilization if, instead of making enemies of every country in the world for the United States, we had made friends; then our influence would have amounted to something. As it is now, as it has been ever since I arrived here, they all regard us as a terrific influence but in their hearts no country likes us at all.

570. Attacking the president's handling of foreign affairs during a speech in Rock Island, Illinois, on September 14, the Republican nominee asked, "[w]as it extraordinary skill when he promoted the Munich pact? Was that an extraordinary demonstration of human knowledge and understanding when he telephoned Hitler and Mussolini and urged them to sell Czechoslovakia down the river?"

571. Thomas Sivewright Catto, first Baron Catto (1879–1959), financial adviser to the chancellor of the Exchequer.

572. The former progressive Republican governor of California, Hiram Warren Johnson (1866–1945) had been, despite his party affiliation, a New Deal supporter in the Senate during Franklin Roosevelt's first term. Johnson's staunch isolationism had distinced him from the administration over the course of the late 1930s, however.

Getting this message from Churchill this morning makes me wonder again just why it is that he sends me any of them. The one this morning thanks Roosevelt for his statement on Dakar and also thanks him for the information and the word on rifles. It is of course apparent that we here are being kept completely in ignorance of what Roosevelt is doing. It is by far the most unsatisfactory method of doing business that I have ever seen, and if it weren't for the possibility of invasion I would resign today; in fact I would have resigned a month ago. However, later on we will see.

I am interested to find out, and I will if possible, just why it is Churchill sees any reason at all for keeping me advised; because if he didn't send me these cables occasionally I would have no conception whatsoever of what is going on. I am at a loss however to understand why he wants to keep me posted. Of course there is no question but what he is taking his lead from Washington and he knows quite well that I have no standing at the moment. Why he bothers to count me in is a mystery.

Robert Kennedy, 14, to Joseph P. Kennedy

BRONXVILLE

Dear Daddy,

Thanks an awful lot for your letter, it was very interesting There hasn't been much doing here except that my boils have finally gone away.

We read in the paper this morning that a plane crashed very near you and that it came so close that you could see the fuzz on his face and count the buttons on his coat. It said that over here now you are called 'The worst bombed Ambassador.[573]

We have had pretty good weather over here althoogh it is raining today. Everybody around here seems to be for Wilkie but the Kennedys are in there fighting for Roosevelt.

Everyone asks me Why you didn't run for President and I ask them if they'd vote for you. They all say they would.

Teddy is getting thinner. He only weighs about 90 pounds now.

Pat and I went to the World's Fair about a week ago. I thought it was wonderful. I thought general Moters was marvelous

We received alot of prizes for sailing during the years mostly due to Eunice. Jean and Teddy did vey we good also

We all have had a wonderful vacation though we have missed you an awful lot.

Every time the King and Queen or Churchill come on the screen in the movies the people Yell and cheer for all they're worth. The three of them are very popula over here.

Well Daddy this is about all the news. I'll write you again at school.

Love
Bob

Rose Kennedy to Joseph P. Kennedy

Tuesday [October 7, 1940]

Joe dear,

I am at Johni's[574] Office & we have gone over the whole situation. Between you & me, it is the same old story. They think the Pres. Does not want you home before the

---

573. On October 2 the *New York Times* reported JPK's "Close Escape from Crashing Nazi Plane." The previous day, a Messerschmitt 109 had crashed near JPK's country residence following a dogfight over Windsor, missing the house "by inches."
574. Former SEC and Maritime Commission Counsel John J. Burns, that is.

election due to your explosive — defeatist, point of view, as you might so easily throw a bomb which would explode sufficiently to upset his chances. I wanted to go to the W.H. as a wife, say I am worried about your health, think you have done enough — guarantee to chloroform you until after the election, & say you should be brought home. Johni says there would be repercussions — such as that you had sent me etc. However, if it were more than 3 weeks, I should certainly do it. Everyone's opinion is that you have done more than your share — and this is a changed picture from last spring when they said you could not take it, for instance the clients who come to E. Arden, the clients of Saks etc. You cannot tell about Father's or Archbishop Spellman's point of view as Johni has influenced them all.

Well, anyway it will not be long.

All love,

Rosa

Franklin Roosevelt to Joseph P. Kennedy

THE WHITE HOUSE, WASHINGTON October 17, 1940

Dear Joe:

I know what an increasingly severe strain you have been under during the past weeks and I think it is altogether owing to you that you get a chance to get away and get some relief. The State Department has consequently telegraphed you by my desire to come back for consultation during the week commencing October 21. I am very anxious to have an opportunity of talking over with you personally a good many aspects of the present situation and to get from you your last reactions with regard to the war in England.

I need not tell you that a great deal of unnecessary confusion and undesirable complications have been caused in the last few months by statements which have been made to the press by some of our chiefs of mission who have been coming back to this country. In your particular case the press will be very anxious to get some statements from you and no matter how proper and appropriate your statements might be, every effort will be made to misinterpret and to distort what you say. I am, consequently, asking you specifically not to make any statement to the press on your way over nor when you arrive in New York until you and I have had a chance to agree upon what should be said. Please come straight through to Washington on your arrival since I will want to talk with you as soon as you get here.

Yours very sincerely,

As ever

F.D.R.

Joseph P. Kennedy: *Diary*

October 19, 1940

<u>Conference with Chamberlain at his Home in Country</u>

Hore Belisha — didn't get along with ~~many~~ [*army*]. They lost confidence in him. Has handled himself well.

Winston wanted L. G.[575] in Cabinet. Neville first said, "No", and then "Ok." Prejudices must be dropped by both. L. G. Wants to be the Petain — form a new Government.

---

575. Lloyd George.

Neville not U.S. come in.

Turks etc., want things now, not later. Hence, what good is U.S.A.

Glad Churchill locked him out.

Moved by messages from people.

Ulcer in stomach — has three months.

Friday — operation Monday.

Wants to die.

How much he thinks of me.

Bevin[576] not liked by Parliamentary Labour — Attlee.

Anderson[577] might be P.M.

Morrison a bluff.[578]

Bevin got sense — better than Attlee to work.

Made up his mind on vote as there was no unity he must resign unless labor came in. He called then for a formal statement.

They said must get instructions but indicated they would not come. He then wanted to make Halifax P.M. and said he would serve under him. Edward, as [is] his way, started saying, "Perhaps I can't handle it being in H of Lords and Finally Winston said, "I don't think you could". And he wouldn't come and that settled it. Neville offered to serve under either.

Would not have liked Winston throwing Halifax out for Eden when Neville went as that would have looked "old crowd being thrown out."

Winston has had rows with Amery,[579] Duff-Cooper — doesn't know what to do with Sinclair[580] and Boothby.[581]

Winston listens to Beaverbrook — no judgment. Should listen to Anderson. Should have Kingsley Wood in Cabinet. Wood not strong enough Beaverbrook said. Exchequer not important in war.

Touching speech about me. We've always seen eye to eye. I'll tell you — I haven't told my wife. I want to die. I saw my father live 8 years after a stroke and often wish he were dead.

I haven't had many successes in my life but I've made real contributions I think. Nothing to look forward to — I don't want to be a burden. Worrying only about my family. Can't do work. Can't visit friends.

Unnatural bowel movement. Nausea — new attack.

Fine today — I'm glad because I see you.

Halifax and he never had a disagreement. Except little things as between men.

Thought King was happy because he was really 1st. P.M. He said to me, "I remember you always said you would stay after me. I said, "true", "Invasion prospect and bombing made me stay this long."

576. Trade unionist, Labour MP for Central Wandsworth and minister of Labour and National Service, Ernest Bevin (1881–1951).

577. The home secretary and minister for home security, Sir John Anderson, later first Viscount Waverly (1882–1958), had replaced Chamberlain as lord president on October 3.

578. Labour MP for Hackney South Herbert Stanley Morrison, later Baron Morrison of Lambeth (1888–1965), had replaced Anderson as home secretary and minister for Home Security. Morrison had been among the active parliamentary supporters of Chamberlain's ouster in May.

579. Leopold Charles Maurice Stennett Amery (1873–1955), Conservative MP for Sparkbrook, Birmingham, and secretary of state for India and Burma.

580. The former Liberal Party leader had become secretary of state for air in May.

581. Robert John Graham Boothby, later Baron Boothby (1900–1986), parliamentary secretary to the ministry of food, Conservative MP for East Abredeenshire and former parliamentary private secretary to Winston Churchill during the latter's tenure as chancellor of the Exchequer, 1926–29.

Clasped my hand in his two and said, "This is Goodbye, we will never see each other again." Terrible feeling.

No pain from his ulcer until it was too late.

"You always said I was a tough guy."

Norway failure made Churchill P.M. "True", says Neville, smiling sadly.

Mrs. C. came back from telephone — Lord Harder sent his regards — don't let him disturb Neville's rest.

Mrs. Chamberlain — "I was always sorry little boy didn't come back to see the black cat.

When I told him of Bevin plan for future of Britain he said, "I can't see any plan with the results so uncertain and as for Europe, how can one plan until they know where Russia will be?"

When we talked of slowness of preparation he said, "A Democracy will not wake up until the danger is imminent." "Leaders have to wait until public opinion is formed and then try to be a little ahead. I did that with Conscription but to do a lot of these present things the country would not have accepted them. They look all right as we look back but people would not accept them then. I was slow to put money into broad preparation because to do so would have taken it away from commercial business which was the life of England."

Last visit I made to Prime Minister pronounced "fanatic" as fern'-a-tic, speaking of Hitler. (Also)

Speaking of Eden — he can't come into Cabinet (as he thinks) from his own point of view unless he agrees with Chamberlain's policy and admits his was wrong, or else the Prime Minister admits that his policy (the Prime Minister's) is wrong and I'm certainly not going to admit that.

Joseph P. Kennedy to Neville Chamberlain

October 22, 1940

Dear Neville,

Your letter reached me as I was leaving today for Bournemouth. Here I am tonight getting ready to fly at daybreak tomorrow

Before I go, I must tell you what I feel in my heart about you.

I have met in my life two men whom I ~~have~~ felt had dedicated their lives to the real good of humanity without any thought of themselves. The first one was the present Pope, the other was you.

Your conception of what the world must do in order to be a fit place to live in, is the last sensible thing we shall see before the pall of anarchy falls on us all.

For me to have been any service to you in your struggle is the real worth while epoch in my career.

You have retired but mark my words the world will yet see that your struggle was never in vain. My job from now on is to tell the world of our hopes.

Good luck, Neville, may God watch over you and bring you the peace you richly deserve

Now and forever

Your devoted friend,
Joe Kennedy

Joseph P. Kennedy: Diary[582]

Account of Ambassador's Trip to United States on Clipper October 22, 1940

We left London on [*Monday*] night[583] after lunch with an air-raid siren blowing as if to send us off.

A nice ride down to Bournemouth through the forest.

We arrived, took a walk, heard that Lord Derby had been in an automobile accident, called him up and found him okay.

Truitt called from Washington to tell me good luck and the ship was being delayed. Worked after dinner and answered my mail. Had a fairly good night with a bomber still over head.

Got up at 6 a.m. and waited downstairs for Jee to come back and drive up to airport, as he had taken Ding Dong and Hillman out earlier. Jee got lost taking them out, so we used Keatley's car, pressed a chauffeur standing by to show us the way and off we went. Arrived okay. The Captain of flying boat said we would have to leave promptly at 8 a.m. because we were picking up a fighter escort that would pick us up at a fixed point.

Well, we got on board. They turned over the engines and found that the right-end one wasn't functioning. Captain came back and reported that probably the spark plugs were wet. They were changing them and we'd be off in a few minutes. Well, we didn't get away. When the plugs were changed they found the magneto was bad so we finally got away about 9:30, and of course, we never met the fighter escort. We went west about 350 miles and then went south. Of course, if the Germans wanted to, they could knock off this ship any time they wanted to. Up to date, however, all civil planes of all belligerents have been immune.

The Captain told me of an incident the other day on a flight to Lisbon that the German plane was flying from Lisbon and the English flying to. As they approached one another they recognized one another as being belligerents and they both dived down in opposite directions — each trying to get away from the other. But as it turned out that both were commercial nothing happened.

On my arrival in Lisbon I was met by Wilson[584] and handed a note from Roosevelt specifically requesting me to come to the White House and make no statements to the newspaper men. I was, of course indignant, but could understand Roosevelt's position particularly when I came home and saw what the status was.

I went to the Minister's house but he and his wife were away. Had dinner with Jack and Bill Hillman. I talked with Wilson the Counselor there. He told me that nobody could get a visa to get out except Jews and that Pell[585] had already written to the President explaining the situation but had received no action. He said that they were asked to give visitors' visas to Jews whom everybody knew were bad citizens. He was quite stern about it. I said that they would not be able to do anything like that in London. It's

---

582. Although this account is taken from JPK's 1940 diary, it appears to have been written somewhat later, as the rough draft of the Diplomatic Memoir's version of the events of October 21–30. For the sake of continuity and readability I have broken the entry (which treats a period of several days) into several segments in order to insert other relevant documents at appropriate points.—AS

583. October 21.

584. Warden McKee Wilson (1892–1973), first secretary of the U.S. embassy at Lisbon.

585. Herbert Claiborne Pell (1884–1961), minister to Portugal, 1937–41, and father of the future Rhode Island senator.

really a disgrace that this thing is going on. I am delighted that we wrote that telegram to Breck Long[586] about Sol Bloom's[587] request. It at least puts us on record.

My observation at Lisbon is that they should have a lot of bright fellows there to meet all the people coming down from France and Germany to get a lot of good information. It's the only listening post left in Europe. I advised the President to do this — also Welles.

Also, saw Monsignor Hurley, who is now a Bishop, on his way to St. Augustine. He had just left the Vatican. He said the Pope was all right physically, but mentally depressed. The Church is receiving terrific blows everywhere. The youth of the European countries are rapidly getting away from the Church. I asked him about the Fascist Cardinals in Italy and he told me that the Cardinals who had direct contact with the people and had dioceses were naturally patriotic Italians as well as church members and it was not surprising that they were with their country. Italians who did not have churches and were not at the Vatican any more believed that it was necessary to work with the Fascists in order to maintain their influence, while others felt that the Church's position made it necessary for them to be on that side. He said that the Italians did not like war and it would be bad for the church whatever way it came out. I asked him if he thought there would be any possibility of the Italians taking the treasures of the Vatican. He said he thought they would never do that, but some day the Germans might when they decided to have a row with the Italians which would come one of these days.

We finally took off from Lisbon a day late and arrived at Horta after a reasonably rough trip, where we remained one day. We made a tour of the Island and attended a little church for benediction the night we were there. Surprisingly enough, however, in spite of the fact that there was a Portugese ship in the harbor, there was only one man in the Church.

Franklin Roosevelt to Joseph P. Kennedy: *Telegram*

OCTOBER 25, 1940

I HOPE ROSE AND YOU WILL COME TO WASHINGTON IMMEDIATELY AFTER YOUR ARRIVAL IN NEW YORK TO SPEND SATURDAY NIGHT AT THE WHITE HOUSE. I SHALL HAVE TO LEAVE WASHINGTON SUNDAY AFTERNOON TO BE GONE TWO DAYS AND I SHOULD LIKE TO HAVE THE OPPORTUNITY OF SEEING YOU BOTH SATURDAY SO THAT I CAN TALK WITH YOU BEFORE I LEAVE.

BEST REGARDS, FRANKLIN D. ROOSEVELT

Joseph P. Kennedy: *Diary*

Arrived in Bermuda,[588] where I received another memorandum from Roosevelt urging me to come with Rose to the White House to spend Saturday night. Evidently this was sent before they knew that we would be a day late. However, I thought I had better call him on the telephone, which I did. As the telephone doesn't function there until 1:00 p.m. on Sundays, they had to send out and get an operator and open up the board. I got Missy on the telephone and she was glad to hear my voice.

She turned me over to the President whom they evidently had to awaken. The Pres-

---

586. Now assistant secretary of state.
587. Sol Bloom (1870–1949), Democratic Representative of New York and chairman of the Committee on Foreign Affairs. JPK's papers shed no light on the congressman's request.
588. On October 25.

ident was very pleasant and said that he was going to New York next day and would be tied up campaigning and would not be able to see me. However, he urged Rose and me to come down immediately on arrival.

Joseph P. Kennedy: *Diary*

*"Rough pencil notes made by Mr. Kennedy on an envelope
addressed to him in Hamilton, Bermuda"*

[October 25, 1940]

Questions on Clare Boothe's book in last chapter indicate the scope of the one problem of international relations.[589] It's not all black and white.

I'm against getting into war through the back door. But you can't have a nation condemning every act of European and Eastern nations without sooner or later getting into trouble.

You can't say you don't want to go to war if you listen with great intolerance to somebody like Col. Lindbergh who points out what he thinks are the dangers.

If the U.S. people keep their heads no President can lead you anywhere you don't want to go.

You can't have newspapers demanding we do something and then condemn the President because he does. He may have to give his judgment based on all the information he has. His obligation is to give the facts to the people and then let them decide.

The only sure way to get in this war, no matter who is President, is to shilly dally about defense.

The only price we pay Great Britain for giving us time is to furnish them equipment. It's a small price.

Being rich and appropriating money won't get us anywhere. How many planes can you put in the air tonight? That's all that counts. Democracy is on time. Since war began it hasn't given a very good account of itself. Get busy.

Franklin Roosevelt to Joseph P. Kennedy

THE WHITE HOUSE, WASHINGTON Sat [October 26, 1940]

Dear Joe

Thank the Lord you are safely home — I do hope you & Rose can come down Sunday p.m. — we expect you both at White House — I go to N.Y. at Midnight for an awful day on Monday

Affec
FDR

Joseph P. Kennedy: *Diary*

We proceeded to New York where I arrived at about 2:30 p.m.[590] Immediately upon arrival Max Truitt handed me a personal letter from the President asking me to come to Washington at once. After I had seen the children, we went into another room

---

589. Clare Booth Luce's firsthand account of her travels on the war-torn Continent between February and June, *Europe in the Spring,* had been published in the United States in mid-September.
590. On October 27.

— Rose, Judge Burns, Connie Fitzgerald, Eddie Moore and Ted O'Leary. We talked the situation over as to whether or not I would be for or against the President. I told them that I had many personal grievances, but questioned as to whether or not they were sufficient grounds on which to take a definite stand. At any rate, Rose and I took the five o'clock plane to Washington and were met at the airport by the White House car. We arrived just before seven. They announced that cocktails would be served in the Study and dinner at 7:15.

I went into the Study alone and Missy was there. She was very glad to see me. I shook hands with the President, who was very gracious. Shortly after Rose came in and after that Jimmy Byrnes and his wife.

I showed the President the Chamberlain letter[591] and told him a little about the difficulties in England. Nothing was said about my relationship or anything on it.

Six of us went into dinner on the Upper Floor right off his Study where we had scrambled eggs and sausages, toast and rice for dessert.

When we were about half through the dinner, Jim Byrnes, acting as though a wonderful idea had just struck him, said he thought it would be a great idea if I would go on the radio Tuesday night on my own. He thought it absolutely essential that I go and most necessary for the success of the Roosevelt campaign. He constantly referred [sic] to the President on this matter and he agreed it was necessary. I didn't say, Yes, Aye, or No. The President worked very hard on Rose, whom I suspect he had come down because of her great influence on me. He talked to her about her father. All through dinner, Byrnes kept selling me the idea, but I made no comment, because I wanted to talk alone with the President before making any decision. After going back to the Study, and it still looked as if they had no intention of leaving me alone with the President, I finally said, "Since it doesn't seem possible for me to see the President alone, I guess I'll just have to say what I am going to say in front of everybody."

"In the first place, I am damn sore at the way I have been treated. I feel that it is entirely unreasonable and I don't think I rated it." I said, "Mr. President, as you know, I have never said anything privately in my life that I didn't say to you personally, and I have never said anything in a public interview that ever caused you the slightest embarrassment; in fact, the only speech of mine that was ever criticized was the Navy Day Speech in London, which the State Department had approved and ran out on when I was criticized." I said, "Last year, when there was a great doubt amongst a great many people when I came back from London, I definitely came out for you for a Third Term. I wrote you a letter from Cannes and told you what I was willing to do and in spite of all that, you have given me a bad deal. First, because Donovan was sent to London without consulting me. Secondly, your sending a general there and Britain's knowing about it before I did. Thirdly, carrying on negotiations on destroyers and bases through Lothian and not through me: And fourthly, the State Department's never telling me about what was going on."

I went on to say, "All these things were conducive to harming my influence in England, and if I had not gone to the British Government and said, 'If you don't let me know all about this, your country is going to find me most unfriendly toward the whole situation.' So I smashed my way through with no thanks to the American Government."

591. He refers probably to Chamberlain's last letter to him of October 19, in which the former prime minister noted, "I should imagine there can have been few cases in our history in which the two men occupying our respective positions were so closely in touch with one another as you and I." Chamberlain continued, "I found in you an understanding of what I was trying to do . . ."

Roosevelt promptly denied everything. He said that Knox wanted to send Donovan there and he asked the State Department to clear those things up with me. Welles denied knowing anything about it. Somebody is lying very seriously and I suspect the President. He said that he could not understand why the State Department did not keep me informed and was quite disgusted with them. He said that those career men always did things wrong. He went on to tell me that during the first part of his term he had found out that a great many of the career men would bring material to Castle from the State Department and when he found it out through the Federal Bureau of Investigation, he stopped it.[592]

I asked him how it was that Alsop had the contents of one of my cables in his column. The President couldn't understand that. Also told him that Britain had refused to give us any more war reports because of a leak. He was surprised and couldn't understand it. I then told him how Breck Long called me on the telephone at 2:00 a.m. and put Alsop on the line to talk about the evacuation of children. At this he was really surprised and indignant. However, he disclaimed any responsibility, and protested his friendship for me. Rose chimed in at this point and said it was difficult to get the right perspective on a situation that was 3,000 miles away. So the discussion went on and on. Finally I said that I had a great sense of responsibility and obligation and would make a speech, but wanted the situation cleared up between us before making such a decision. I said that I would write the speech without saying anything to anybody and say just what I felt. They agreed and suggested that I go home on the same train with the President and his party. This I refused to do pointing out that if I did that, my attitude would be perfectly plain to every one and there would be no surprise; in fact, it would definitely leave an impression that I was not likely to go against him. They agreed there was something in it. I said that I would not go to the rally on Monday night. They urged me to go to Boston on Wednesday, but I made no commitment.

I returned to New York and worked very hard on my speech on Monday and Tuesday (see telegrams from Clare Boothe and others for colorful reference).[593]

After the speech, I received telephone calls from Long, Frank Walker, Biddle, Boake Carter, who said he was glad the speech was not on all three systems, because it would have done a lot of harm.

Joseph P. Kennedy: *Radio Address*

SPONSORED BY OWN FAMILY, AMBASSADOR KENNEDY
URGES RE-ELECTION OF PRESIDENT ROOSEVELT
Following is the text of the talk by Joseph Patrick Kennedy, Ambassador to Great Britain, delivered tonight, Tuesday, Oct. 29, 9 P.M., EST, over 114 stations of the Co-

592. The former U.S. ambassador to Japan, William Richards Castle, Jr. (1878–1963), had become an increasingly outspoken opponent of the Roosevelt administration's foreign policy after the end of his tenure as Herbert Hoover's undersecretary of State from 1931 to 1933.

593. His friend, staunch Republican Clare Boothe Luce, had written,

I want only for you to know, when you make that radio address tomorrow night, throwing as you will, all your prestige and reputation for wisdom, your experience abroad and into the scales for F.D.R. you'll probably help to turn the trick for him. And I want you also to know that I believe with all my heart and soul you will be doing America a terrible disservice. I know too well your private opinions not also to know that half of what you say (*if* you say it) you *really* won't believe in your heart. Perhaps I am doubting you *too* soon. Perhaps I will deserve to be smacked for doubting you, but I'm so *terribly* frightened for this country.

lumbia Broadcasting System, under sponsorship of Mrs. Kennedy and the nine Kennedy children, in which he urged re-election of President Roosevelt:

Good Evening my fellow Americans:

On Sunday I returned from war-torn Europe, to the peaceful shores of our beloved country renewed in my conviction that this country must and will stay out of war. Tonight I desire to give to you, my fellow countrymen, my views on what I consider to be the position of the United States of America in a world crisis which inevitably — win, lose, or draw — gravely will affect the destinies of every man, woman and child. The impact of this conflict will be felt even by our children's children. This evening I am going to tell you briefly what I think of the world situation as it affects America. Since early 1938, mine has been a ringside seat.

Doubtless there are some who will look askance when an Ambassador to the Court of St. James speaks over the radio in the last week of a Presidential campaign. But it is for the very reason that I serve as Ambassador to England that I am addressing you in order that you may have an accurate report and my estimate of the future on the eve of this, probably the most critical election year of our existence.

The events of the last few years are confusing, even to the best informed minds. There are some things, however, that are as clear as crystal. The people of America are dedicated to the cause of peace. They want a chance to work out their own problems, and if possible, to help in the realization of the age-old dream of a world without war. The American people overwhelmingly repudiate the philosophy of Blitzkrieg — that force is the sole arbiter of man's destiny. But the world, sad to relate, is not of our making.

Heretofore the technique of diplomacy has been used to advance a policy of a particular government. There was no more difficult art in the realm of human affairs, and a country's success in the world was, to a great extent, measured by the skill of its diplomats.

In place of negotiations and peaceful methods of adjustment the dictator countries have discovered a new weapon — unbridled force and terrorism towards nations large and small. Unfortunately, from the society of nations reason has fled. Diplomacy has almost become the lost art.

The other day in talking to a fellow diplomat in London I pointed this out. He said, "Ah, but let any nation win a few battles. You would be surprised how important their diplomacy would then become." Yes, I think that is true. And it emphasizes my point, that diplomacy is no longer the instrument it was — it has to give way to power.

The thing that matters most now is not in the field of diplomacy — not at all — what counts in this hour of crisis is what we in the United States of America are prepared to do in order to make ourselves strong. On that point there can't be, and I am sure there is not, the slightest disagreement in this country. Even the most staid isolationist is now alive to the danger facing any nation in the modern world. The realization that oceans alone are not adequate barriers against revolutionary forces which now threaten a whole civilization has not come too late. We are rearming. We are re-arming because it is the only way in which American can stay out of war. If we re-arm fast enough, America will stay out of war. It is today our guarantee of peace.

While we shall not be involved in this war, we are bound to be seriously affected by it. All during my first year in England I felt strongly that if England got into the war, in the long run it would be most unfortunate for the interests of our people. And I always hoped for a lasting peace.

And speaking about peace, in the last year I have read a lot of irresponsible writing, most of it of a critical nature, about the Munich Pact. The criticism in my judgment is not justified. Mr. Chamberlain hailed it as "peace in our time" and was cheered by thousands of people who had the dread of the war in their hearts — a war that comes to them now, night after night, in a relentless shattering of bombs, of death and destruction. He and nearly every one in Great Britain knew that Munich was but an armistice, a last opportunity given to the Allies to make up, in part at least, for their tragic failure to understand the peril to their very lives as nations. Can anyone imagine what would have happened to England if the blitzkrieg of the summer of 1940 had occurred in September of 1938?

About a year ago on my return from England after having seen the failures of the diplomats and the outbreak of a force which has conquered so many peoples, I said American should keep out of war. And after my experiences of the past year — I am more convinced than ever that America should stay out of this war.

The American people are overwhelmingly in favor of avoiding war and at the same time giving all aid short of war to Great Britain. There is no conflict on that issue among the candidates for the Presidency. The Republicans have expressly approved of this policy.

From the day I went to the Court of St. James until this minute I have never given to one single individual in the world any hope whatsoever that at any stage or under any conditions could the United States be drawn into the war.

Unfortunately, during this political campaign there has arisen the charge that the President of the United States is trying to involve this country in the World War. Such a charge is false. Consider the contradiction between first getting us into war and, secondly, desiring to give all assistance possible to Great Britain. The truth of the matter is that there is no more harmful step which could be taken from the viewpoint of Great Britain than our declaration of war. It is clear that the minute war is declared our armed forces will take over, and in all probability they would resolve all doubts about shipping material to England in favor of keeping it here for our Army and our Navy. Such a declaration of war would also greatly increase our responsibilities in the Western World. Our obligations to preserve the integrity of the Monroe Doctrine would be expanded; and these increased obligations would further drastically limit our power to give effective aid to England.

If we declare war, our own best interests would be harmed. England's valiant fight is giving us time to prepare. Without assistance from us the British will find it much more difficult to carry on. Viewing the problem then from either the British or the American angle, declaring war would be foolish.

If President Roosevelt were as wicked as his opponents charge, which he is not, and even if he had undisclosed commitments, which he has not, the facts are against our participation in this war.

Yesterday I received a letter from a colleague who was with me in Washington, and who is head of one of the great industries. He said it was my duty, regardless of any friendships I might have, to inform the American people if, as he believed, there was a secret commitment beyond what the American people had been made aware of and unknown to the Congress a commitment by Roosevelt to Great Britain to lead us into war.

Mr. Roosevelt has already denied that, and I, as the Ambassador of the American people in London, who would certainly become aware of this fact in one way or another, can assure you now with absolute sincerity and honesty that there has been no such commitment.

So far as war is concerned, what do we do if we declare war? The thing which most people are afraid of is that we will send an army to help the British. Mr. Walter Lippmann in a recent article said, and very rightly so, "It would be absurd to consider sending an army to Europe." Where would an army disembark, with Hitler holding nearly all the ports of continental Europe?

When one considers the tonnage required to move a soldier with the type of equipment that it is necessary to have in this kind of a war, the problems of transportation alone become staggering. We can't compare a movement of troops today with the movement of troops of the last war. This is a machine war. This is not a war of men — but a war of industries. Moreover, there are not available to this government now, or in sight, shipping facilities adequate to transport a modern army to Europe. And how would they land and where would we secure the needed protective planes.

Only this morning the British Admiralty confirmed the report that the Empress of Britain of 48,000 tons was sunk within the range of German bombers. To suggest, yes, I say to even suggest, that our boys will soon be on the transports in this kind of war, under these conditions, is completely absurd.

Another factor is that England is not now looking for manpower. She has not even called up all the men she has eligible. I repeat, this is a war, not of men, but of machines. Modern warfare requires a particular skill that is not furnished on the drill field. The time element for training a mechanized army properly would be so great that an American expeditionary force is just not in the cards.

There is thus no sense to a declaration of war. Congress should pause a long, long time before declaring war. No irritants, no incidents, should blind us to what happens when war is declared. Democracy — our freedoms — all become jeopardized. The British Parliament only last May passed the Emergency Powers Act which gives to the government the power to take over every person and all property — that is — to go totalitarian. That's what happens when war is declared.

The problem of attacking us presents the same difficulties to any belligerent that our attacking them does. I have seen an outnumbered, but brave band of RAF fliers and about 20 miles of water keep back the German invader. The answer still rings out — speed in re-armament.

Three thousand miles of ocean, while handy, in and of itself is not enough protection for us. But with an adequate Navy we are assured of a greater measure of safety. We must also remember that while the British Navy remains unconquered and while the British Nation continues to fight its gallant battle for its existence and its ancient democratic way of life, we are given time, precious time, so that we can make ourselves strong and thus have that one guarantee which no form of diplomacy can afford.

The British fleet, therefore, is highly important to our national existence, and the American people must have felt very relieved when the President received public assurance from the Prime Minister. Lord Lothian referred to it in a communication to Secretary Hull in which he said that the settled policy of His Majesty's Government in the United Kingdom was "never to surrender or sink the British Fleet in the event of the waters surrounding the British Isles becoming untenable for His Majesty's ships," but would be sent overseas for the defense of other parts of the Empire.

This represented a real victory for the American people. Those of us who know the stuff of which Churchill and the British leaders are made, those of us who know the courage and the calibre of the officers and men of the Royal Navy, can feel completely assured that surrendering the fleet to Hitler is a thought so fantastic that it is beyond the basis of belief. We know that under those circumstances the fleet will never be used for the purposes of conquest of the nations of the new world.

Again I repeat, there is no valid argument for putting America into war. We can be strong, unprovocative, resolute, fair with the democracies, hostile to the aggressors, and sympathetic with the oppressed without bringing to our shores that miserable thing that does nothing but destroy — war.

But to do this we must be strong. I have heard a great deal since I returned home about the worry of a great many people that the defense program is "bogging down." It is particularly unfortunate that this charge has been injected into a political campaign when national teamwork is necessary. It is charged that the President has failed us in re-armament, despite the fact that he has drafted, regardless of affiliation, the best brains of the country to serve the nation.

Unfortunately, it is true that a democracy such as ours is difficult to rally when it is neither desperate nor frightened. England had the same experience. Even after it learned that Germany was "arming to the teeth," England proceeded confidently but leisurely to the task of getting prepared.

A study of this was made by my son, while he was in England. His conclusions published in a volume entitled "Why England Slept" reveal that all the elements of Great Britain were shortsighted in their failure to appreciate the peril and to prepare accordingly.

The very advantages which a democracy has for the long run, namely, fundamental vitality, voluntary co-operation and a capacity for sustained and grueling effort, become disadvantages in the task of preparing for a war that it thinks may never happen.

If we now lack the crusading effort for re-armament, and I hope we do not, it is certainly not to be laid at the door of the White House. The President has provided a program and the nation's best specialists, and a Democratic Congress has provided ample funds.

If blame there be, we all must share in the inherent weakness of our democratic system where force and propaganda have no place, even in the vital job or rearming.

If I appear to take an unduly pessimistic view of the world situation, and, if as some of my critics say, I am "steeped in gloom," let me ask you, what is there in the world picture that gives any excuse for gaiety. A large part of the productive capacity of the world is devoted to the cause of killing; millions are facing starvation; millions are facing disease. Great peoples are being sacrificed. The greatest war machine in the history of mankind is geared to a high pitch of efficiency by every technique that science could devise, serving in the cause of a man who believes that war is a noble cause and that world domination is his destiny. Gloom, under such circumstances, is nothing more than "facing the facts."

The lessons of this war are ours for the taking. Machines today are more important than men. I have always been of the opinion that if Mr. Chamberlain had had 5,000 first-line planes at home when he conferred at Munich, we would have truly seen "peace in our time." Already the lessons have been learned. Peace and good-will on this hemisphere, greater and still greater plane production, a powerful and still more powerful Navy, and a trained, competent and larger Army — all are being translated into effective results by our national government. In short, the country must realize that it must get itself in shape.

This administration has been wise in bringing to Washington experts from the field of industry to assist in the mobilization of this country to insure a lasting peace. Modern warfare is not like anything of the past. It is a grinding clash of industries. Today war is the battle of productive systems. In modern war the machine is the key. Infantry manpower alone may be overcome with shocking suddenness by the streamlined implements of destruction.

We are informed today about the new methods of warfare. Various departments of our government have sent men to England. They are over there now in order that they may learn from bitter British experience how peace can be assured for this nation.

Every phase of a nation's life in modern warfare is being studied in order that we may be prepared. For example, the New York City Fire Department has sent over a squad to study the technique of fighting fires in city areas caused by incendiary bombs. The Army and Navy have had trained observers at the front watching and learning the lessons of modern war — all that we may be found ready for any contingency.

Under my supervision the experts at the Embassy in London have prepared a survey of the entire British economy as of the opening of the second year of the conflict. Every important phase of British life has been critically appraised. This has been done in order that the American people may know what the problems are when modern war breaks out, and what steps should be taken in our own defense.

The studies have embraced such grave problems as production difficulties, the overhead cost of the war, questions of planning, of exchange control, of food control, the all important issue of the labor front, prices, cost of living wages, agriculture, overseas trade and transportation. This was done to the end that the costly experiences for Great Britain would not be endured in vain — in order that our nation would have more than a vague unscientific notion of what modern war means. We have considered the problem of citizen morale, because we know that in total warfare everyone is "in the trenches." We have given particular attention to the problem of air raid warnings and shelters to learn from the experience of the British people what might benefit our countrymen.

All these steps have been taken by the President with a firm purpose to assure the security of the nation. When the sad tale of the transformation of Europe is told, it will be a story of the dictators' secret preparations and the democracies' easygoing slumbers. But happily for us this Administration was on the alert, and the American people realizing the new peril responded to the vision and foresight of the President.

It is all too clear that there are tremendous domestic problems which must be solved before the United States can see its way out of this maze of gloom. But my own feeling is that all these problems have taken a new turn by the horrors of war.

Once when Chairman of the Maritime Commission, I was talking to a noted economist. I had asked him to look over some phases of an economic survey we were making which was to form a basis of a Merchant Marine Policy for the United States. One of the problems was to decide what would be the results of a certain action under war conditions.

"Kennedy," he said, "when war comes in, economics go out the window."

And so I am afraid that the domestic issues are to a great extent dependent for their solution or lack of solution on where we stand in this horrible war.

The President must watch every move abroad to judge by what action he can serve the United States best. Events move so quickly — the man of experience is our man of the hour.

Thus in this atmosphere charged with war and revolution when the social order of the whole world is being challenged, not only by fighting armies but by new techniques of revolution, psychological, physical and economic, the people of America must make a solemn decision. Which of two men will lead the destinies of our people for the next four years?

It is true that there have been disagreements between the President and me — I have disagreed sharply with him on some issues. And I have disagreed with him on methods employed in carrying out objectives on which we agreed. I am certain that if he has had the time to study my work, as I have his, that he has found things done by me with which he disagreed. But such is not uncommon. I am positive every employee is not always in agreement with his employer, and certainly the opposite is true.

However, these are times, as you all know, which clamor for national unity — times when national teamwork is vital and when only fundamental disagreements should be considered. Happily, on these great, momentous questions of foreign policy, trade, commerce and the future of our American way of life I find little basis for disagreement with the President.

It is true that there is nothing in our Constitution which limits the term of service of our President. It is true that the tradition represents the preference of earlier Presidents. Nonetheless, in normal times, I might be persuaded that the best interests of the country called for no third term. But the third term is the least of the many considerations which the American people should take into account in exercising their choice a week hence. The gigantic issues which must be faced, arising out of the world crisis, make the third term opposition seem insignificant by comparison. The question still remains — which of the two men can best serve the nation.

The present war in Europe, as I have said, will affect seriously every man, woman and child in this country. There will be maladjustments in this world greater than ever before seen. There will be required of our President wisdom and talent, diplomatic foresight, courage and great ingenuity. There will, more than all this, be required of our President for the next four years experience in domestic and especially in foreign affairs.

The problems that he must face are staggering just to comprehend. In the field of agriculture, what is to be done with the surpluses of the North American continent? In the field of labor relations, America will need leadership of great stature. The President must have the trust and confidence of the toilers of the nation. Finances will be disorganized and foreign trade may be completely transformed.

No matter who is President, make up your minds, the problems will be terrific. There is no chance of our achieving perfection by picking a President. Mr. Roosevelt will not have all the answers — probably no human being can have sound answers even for a fraction of the acute issues that may confront us.

Many of my listeners on the radio are specialists in various fields. How would you answer some of the following questions? If you are in foreign trade, what about your lost markets? What about the problem of securing foreign exchange? Just think of what has happened to the motion picture industry when the war has cut off almost a third of the revenue. Shall we go to the barter system? If so, by what route? Can an individual trader compete when his competitor in a totalitarian government? No man can know all the answers — no man can fail to make serious mistakes.

It is wrong not to appreciate thoroughly the limitations set by the world-wide dislocation. Many of these problems will remain even if peace comes tomorrow.

But we must make our choice next week on what qualities are revealed to us by the contenders.

About a year ago on my return from London I referred to the gigantic problems which the war had brought to the American people and said that a newcomer would need two years of training before he could govern adequately. It is still true, only more so.

But two years will be too late. Don't forget the world is on the move at a speed never before witnessed. Already Hitler's conquered nations make the advances of Napoleon appear puny. It is later than you think. Denmark was conquered in a matter of hours;

Norway, in days; Belgium and Holland, in weeks, and the proud and honorable France fell in a month. We do not have the time to train a green hand even though he comes to his task full of goodwill and general capacity but lacking in vital governmental experience. It is not an answer to our problem that strong men, able men, may be summoned to Cabinet posts. Ultimately decisions on burning questions of policy will have to be made by the Chief Executive. A new hand cannot give to these problems that careful, thorough and intelligent attention which they must immediately have if our nation is to be secure.

As a servant of the American people I feel that they are entitled to my honest conclusions. In my years of service for the Government, both at home and abroad, I have sought to have honest judgment as my goal. From the other side I sent reports to the President and the Secretary of State which were my best judgment about the forces that were moving, the developments that were likely and the course best suited to protect America. After all, I have a great stake in this country. My wife and I have given nine hostages to fortune. Our children and your children are more important than anything else in the world. The kind of America that they and their children will inherit is of grave concern to us all. In the light of these considerations, I believe that Franklin D. Roosevelt should be re-elected President of the United States.

(End)

Franklin Roosevelt to Joseph P. Kennedy: *Telegram*

1940 OCT 29 PM 10 18

WE HAVE ALL JUST LISTENED TO A GRAND SPEECH MANY THANKS. LOOKING FORWARD TO SEEING YOU ALL TOMORROW EVENING=[594]

FRANKLIN D ROOSEVELT

John F. Kennedy 23, to Joseph P. Kennedy: *Telegram*

SANFRANCISCO CALI 1940 OCT 30 AM 7 40

PROUD TO HAVE SPONSORED YOU THANKS FOR THE PLUG LOVE=

JACK

Kathleen Kennedy, 20, to Joseph P. Kennedy

[October 30, 1940]

Dear Dad,

The Pres really went to town for you tonight in Boston admidst terrific cheers from the crowd "that Boston boy etc"

Ed called to say to be sure & tell you.

It's great to be famous —

Goodnight from your 4th hostage

---

594. The president was to deliver his final speech of the campaign on October 30. "I have said this before but I shall say it again and again and again," he would tell his audience at the Boston Garden, "[y]our boys are not going to be sent into any foreign wars. They are going into training to form a force so strong that, by its very existence, it will keep the threat of war away from our shores."

Joseph P. Kennedy, Jr., 25, to Joseph P. Kennedy

HARVARD LAW SCHOOL, CAMBRIDGE, MASS. Sunday [November 2(?), 1940]

Dear Dad:

I have spent the last week thinking over the situation, and at this point I think that I would prefer to join the Navy Air Corps, rather than the Naval Reserve.

I know that there will be a great deal more risk in this, but I think that it will be a lot more exciting, stimulating, and will do me more good when I get out.

I understand from my trip to Washington, that they intend to cut down the period of enlistment from four to two years, and in any case, I am confident, that if the crisis ends, which doesn't look like much of a possibility right now, that I can get a discharge.

It seems to me, that I can get out of the air corps, just as soon as I could get out of the Naval Reserve for they are going to have to have men to take charge of all the Navy ships which they are now building.

The advantage of the Reserve are two, One, I get a chance to finish next year, and 2ndly there isn't so much risk. As far as next year is concerned, if things are going the way they are, no one back here will feel very good with everyone in the army navy etc, and it looks like most of the fellows will be in one of the services, except those very few with high numbers. Also I think in that Jack is not doing anything, and with your stand on the war, that people will wonder what the devil I am doing back at school with everyone else working for national defense.

As far as the danger is concerned, it doesn't bother me very much. Quite a few fellows from law school are going in, and I think that you have a pretty good chance. The main reason for my wanting to go in, is that there is a chance for some individuality. There are thousands upon thousands of naval reservists, and you are just one of a flock, whereas here if you've got anything, I think there are numerous possibilities, and not only in the flying end.

As far as the family is concerned, it seems that Jack is perfectly capable to do everything, if by chance anything happened to me. Also everyone seems pretty well grown up, thus I should think that from that end, it would be OK.

I have not yet definitely made up my mind, nor do I know that I can pass my physical exam for the ~~navy~~ [*air corps*] however I thought that I would send you my thoughts.

~~Admir~~ Kirk[595] has arranged for me to take a physical exam which will be merely preliminary, and I thought that I could then find out, what are my chances for getting in either branch of the Navy.

The class of V7 has not yet opened up, so though I have all the material on hand, it has been impossible for me to do anything about it.

Would like to hear any ideas you have on it.

Love

Joe

595. Alan Goodrich Kirk (1882–1963), naval attaché and naval attaché for air at the American embassy in London, 1939–41. Afterward, Kirk would serve as director of the Office of Naval Intelligence in Washington, 1941–42; as chief of staff to the commander of U.S. naval forces in Europe, 1942–43; and as commander of the Atlantic Fleet's Amphibious Force in 1943. That year he would lead the U.S. Task Force's invasion of Sicily in July and go on to command the task force during the invasion of Normandy in 1944. He would serve as U.S. ambassador to Belgium, 1946–49, and to the Soviet Union, 1949–52.

Joseph P. Kennedy: *"Notes Dictated by Ambassador for His Diary"*

November 4, 1940

On Saturday, at Frank Murphy's[596] request, I dropped in after the Notre Dame Game at the Ambassador Hotel to talk with him. He still doesn't enjoy doing business with books — he enjoys people. Later, when I said that Rose and I were going to have dinner at Twenty-One and asked him to join us, he said with great regret, "I am practically a prisoner, I can't go to any of those places."

He had an interesting story, however, to tell about my speech. He said that about a week or ten days ago, he had been approached by Frankfurter while sitting on the Bench as to what could be done to save the Catholic vote, which was rapidly leaving Roosevelt. Murphy told Frankfurter that the only thing that could be done was to get me to make a speech. Frankfurter said, "He's too gloomy". "Nevertheless," said Murphy, "he's the only one who can do it."

He said that a day or two after he received a call from the President asking him to come to the White House. When he got there, he found Frankfurter, Douglas, and Hopkins, and they entered into a discussion as to how they could get me to come out for them.

Douglas and Murphy agreed that I was absolutely important to get. Frankfurter appreciated that I was, but hated to ask me. The President said that young Joe had been making good speeches and they hoped to get him to go on the radio. There was a lot of conversation and it was left to the President to get in touch before (as they said) Krock could get me, and see if I would come out.

The picture, as Murphy sees it, is a serious one. He said that Frankfurter is continually saying that he heard from England on the telephone — I imagine from Laski if he hears at all — and that it was Frankfurter and Ben Cohen who wrote the Attorney General's opinion on destroyers and bases. Murphy regards the Jewish influence as most dangerous. He said that after all, Hopkins' wife was a Jew; Hull's wife is a Jew; and Frankfurter and Cohen and that group are all Jews, and Jackson, Attorney General,[597] is sympathetic with the Communists.

Murphy said, "We can't have both Catholics and Communists — we must have one or the other." He regards Roosevelt as a tired man and thinks the element around him can do anything they want with him. Frankfurter, so Murphy says, engineered Stimson's appointment.[598]

November 6, 1940

My interview with President at 12:15 a.m. November 6 (day after Election).

I went in to see Missy and she went in to see if President could see me. I went in and he looked tired but shook hands and said, "Well you've got it — I certainly don't begrudge you the next four years."

---

596. The former U.S. attorney general and Michigan governor had recently been appointed an associate justice of the Supreme Court.

597. Robert Houghwout Jackson (1892–1954), attorney general of the United States, 1940–41. In July 1941 Jackson would be confirmed an associate justice of the Supreme Court, and in May 1950 would affirm the constitutionality of the Taft-Hartley Act's oath of nonmembership in the Communist Party. From the summer of 1945 to the fall of 1946, Jackson took a leave of absence from the Court in order to act as chief counsel for the United States in the prosecution of German war criminals at Nuremberg.

598. As a young lawyer Frankfurter had served under U.S. attorney for the Southern District of New York, Henry Lewis Stimson (1867–1950), 1906–1909. Stimson went on to serve as secretary of war under Taft, 1911–13, and as secretary of state under Hoover, 1929–33. Seeking broad-based support in the upcoming election, Roosevelt had appointed the Republican secretary of war for a second time in June 1940.

He was happy but I thought detected a note of bitterness when he read me Hugh Johnson's wire of congratulation. The President said, "Wouldn't that make you sick?"

I said, I think I should hand you my resignation at once — I've told you how I feel being Ambassador without anything to do — If there is a chance of peace or some situation that makes the U.S.'s position difficult there I'll go back in 24 hours' notice, but to sit there doing nothing and have whatever has to be done, done through British Embassy in Washington, I want to come home."

He said, "I understand and I appreciate your feeling against the State Department (It's funny he insists that all my misunderstandings are the result of the State Department's actions not his — I don't think that's true.) "However, he said, I don't want to leave London in charge of chargé [sic]. — I don't want to have to pick a new man, and you stand so well with British, so go take a good vacation, I know you won't go back, but stay around U.S. until I have a chance to look into this situation over here (the inference being he might have something for me to do in Washington — This is sort of a follow-up on his remark to Rose the night I got back — Not to let this fellow think he is going to get away from me and loaf.")

I said, "Okay — I'm going West[599] — I'll see you when I get back."

Joseph P. Kennedy to Franklin Roosevelt: *Resignation Draft*

My dear Mr. President,

I feel that the situation in Europe has ~~come to~~ [*reached*] a point where I can with propriety and without neglect of ~~my~~ responsibility, ask to be relieved at the earliest date you can fix. My ~~person aff~~ personal affairs require that I return as soon as possible and give them my undivided attention. But even so I should not please them as a reason for retirement as Ambassador to Great Britain if I did not sincerely feel that conditions are favorable for that step.

Already, for reasons which are obvious, I have remained here longer than it was my original intention to remain. It has been a marvelous experience, for which I shall always be deep[*ly*] grateful to you. It has given me a sense of having in some small degree served you, our country and the cause of world peace. I have applied myself to this job with whatever capacity I may possess, and I believe I may now [fairly] ask you to give it into new and fresher hands.

So far as service to you is concerned, which I want to render as long as you want me to ~~do~~ and think ~~that~~ I can, I am certain that [*present*] conditions ~~will~~ make me a more valuable aid as an unofficial citizen at home than as your Ambassador here.

I hope you will find it possible to ~~agree with my ag~~ accede to my request and let me know that you have, for I should like to make my plans as early after this writing as can be ~~arranged.~~

With deep gratitude for the opportunity you have given me, and every assurance of loyalty and admiration, I am,

Yours faithfully,

---

599. On November 13 he would leave for California to discuss the recent renewal of the British Film Exchange Agreement with a number of studio heads and afterward visit William Randolph Hearst at Wyntoon, the publisher's retreat outside of San Francisco, with Jack.

Joseph P. Kennedy: *Diary*

November 9, 1940

It is with great sorrow I hear of Neville Chamberlain's death.

I had lunch with *him* 3 weeks ago yesterday. He, with the great nobility of character and bravery of spirit which I had always found in him, called me into a room after lunch and told me privately he would not live long. He said, "Since my illness makes it impossible to be of further service to my country, my great concern is not to be a burden to my wife and family so perhaps God in his mercy will take me soon."

I had hard work to keep from crying because I was closer to Neville Chamberlain than I was to any one in England.

History will record his real struggle for the rights of humanity and England will come to recognize that all his efforts were for England's salvation. In America he was misunderstood but in my relations with him he never was bitter of criticism but chiefly grateful for America's help.

He was noble. He was kind and fair and brave. The world and particularly England will miss his counsel.

No sacrifice was too great for him to make for his country. He really gave his life that England might live. The world will miss his sane counsel.

Joseph P. Kennedy to William Randolph Hearst

November 26, 1940

Dear Mr. Hearst,

I have landed back in New York after a reasonably pleasant trip home, and after having had a few hours to myself to think the whole situation over, I feel that I want to write you again and say what a great satisfaction it is to me to have your friendship and confidence.

There have been a great many times in the last six years in my three government jobs when I wondered whether anything that an individual does is of any real value, and I have added things up to make sure that I am not taking myself too seriously. That feeling, however, always gives me the re-action that I should come back and spend more time with my family and interest myself again in my personal affairs.

And in many of those disappointing times, whether you know it or not, you and your papers have been a real consolation to me. I don't think that I have ever really acquired the kind of hide that I have been told is necessary in politics. Then again, maybe it's because I don't like to have my younger children reading things that are not pleasing to them.

From this you can easily gather that I am quite sensitive at times as to what happens to my public career, but your helpful talks and your confidence have been a great factor in my deciding to stay on. I find myself now in quite a confused state of mind. I should hate not to go back to England if there were to be a serious break in the situation. And I should hate to be in America if England found it necessary to sue for peace, because I feel that our position would then be influenced a great deal by the attitude England would take in her peace arrangements.

On the other hand, if the war is to go on for a period of months, and if I do go back, I shall merely sit down and do nothing pending something's happening in the war area. I really have no fear of bombs, and I am sure the British people would respond very happily to my return. Also, it would probably be good for the morale of the American people. That's one side of the picture.

The other side is that I feel I know the situation abroad, and am in the best position to answer anybody who might be in America. For instance, I know that I have the complete answer to the British request for more financial aid. And there are a great many problems that are coming up which I feel I can aid greatly here in the States.

I saw Mr. Hoover[600] at his request and he was kind enough to say that he thought all the things I had said and done in the last ten months had been of more help in keeping America out of the war than anything else.

I am leaving Mrs. Kennedy and the children entirely out of the picture. I am sure that they look with great apprehension on my return, and yet I feel that whatever I thought best would meet with their approval. And unless my efforts were being used over there I feel that the responsibility of bringing up nine children is too much for Mrs. Kennedy at this time. If you have some time I wish you would tell me what you think. I realize that in the last analysis the judgment is to be mine, and the decision must be mine, but it would be helpful to get your slant.

Jack and I had a great time at Wyntoon and they couldn't have been nicer to me at the house at the beach for which I am very grateful to both you and Marion.

If I decide that I am not going over there, I shall of course, be a free lance from the middle of December on, and I want you to know that I shall only be too glad to be of service to you on any of your problems that you think I can help work out. I have a very great desire to see the Hearst problems worked out satisfactorily to you as quickly as possible, and if I can make any contribution I am yours to command.

I expect to be in Bronxville until next Sunday night and after that, I shall be in Palm Beach until Christmas.

Again with my very deep appreciation of your kindness in the past for my real pleasure of seeing you again, I am

Yours very sincerely,
Joseph P. Kennedy

Joseph P. Kennedy: *Diary*

Sunday, November 30, 1940

Justice Bill Douglas called to see me.

Said columnists were sons of bitches.[601] Roosevelt always spoke well of me. He was afraid he would be nominated for Vice-President. Wanted me for Co-ordinator of De-

---

600. The former president.

601. Surprisingly, the notation constitutes one of the few (if oblique) references among JPK's papers to his recent disastrous interview with the *Boston Globe*'s Louis Lyons. In July 1936, shortly before the publication of *I'm for Roosevelt*, Lyons had interviewed JPK for "Kennedy 'Sticks His Neck Out,' Asks Business To Back New Deal." Reminding the ambassador of the widespread publication of the flattering article, on November 8, 1940, Lyons wrote, "[t]he *Globe* hopes I can persuade you to talk to me a little for our people—just as a traveler home from the wars, not political talk." The following day Lyons joined Ralph Coughlan and Charles Edmondson of the *St. Louis Dispatch* at JPK's suite at the Ritz in Boston. By oversight, JPK had failed to secure Lyons's previous agreement (as he had with Coughlan and Edmonson) that his remarks should be regarded as off the record. Producing the resulting article exclusively from memory, Lyons quoted JPK on a broad variety of subjects ranging from the war to contemporary personalities. "I'm willing to spend all I've got left to keep us out of the war," Lyons reported him to have said. "People say I'm a pessimist. I say, What is there to be gay about? . . . Democracy is finished in England." Eleanor Roosevelt was "a wonderful woman," but "she bothered us more on our jobs in Washington to take care of the poor little nobodies who hadn't any influence." The queen, by contrast, had "more brains than the cabinet." From the *Boston Globe*'s front page on November 10 the article had been reprinted and excerpted both around the country and in Britain, unleashing a torrent of criticism and recrimination upon JPK for many weeks to come.

fense which he said is not functioning. Told me Wallace was a crackpot and a mystic. He sends code messages to Madame Zenah [*sic*] who reads the stars. Talks about Roosevelt, says he's a crackpot.

During the campaign Paul Block's publishers had these letters of Wallace to the Madame and they'd show he was nuts.[602]

There was a meeting at the White House. Douglas was there. They decided that the only chance was to say they were forgeries and dare the papers to print them. They got away with it, but they're still looking up whether they can force him to resign and fill the place in the sequence of the Cabinet. What a fine mess! Hopkins to blame for his choice.

Welles on Sunday begged me not to get out in a row because soon, I would get back in the Government.

Roosevelt should accept my resignation for my good reasons. Bullitt was a bastard and dangerous and so was Frankfurter, who "read all the papers and made suggestions to Roosevelt — *He's a* Jew chiseler."

Hull said be stiff and get out — "I've had lots of trouble with the crowd around President — Columnists try to belittle me — try not to give me any credit, such as Pan American situation."

"I'm working out Japanese situation — If I make a mistake it will be terrible!"

I asked Welles who gave Alsop & Kintner the material for their White Book. He said, "Instructions came from White House."[603]

Joseph P. Kennedy: *Diary*

December 1, 1940

On Sunday, December 1, I went to Washington and saw the President at White House.

I arrived and usher said papers had been calling up but my appointment was not scheduled. He took me to Red Room and said President was behind on his appointments and Mr. Morgenthau was with him. I sat down and shortly the clock in Red Room struck 3 and then the one in the Blue Room struck 5. If the Republicans heard it they'd say even the clocks as well as the inhabitants of the White House were wrong.

602. Late in the 1940 campaign a cache of letters potentially damaging to the president's reelection had fallen into the hands of a number of antiadministration publishers, among them Paul Block, who had unearthed Associate Justice Black's connection to the Ku Klux Klan three years earlier. The cryptic, mystical letters had been written, purportedly, by the president's running mate to an astrologer named Zenda. Zenda herself was reputed to be a close associate of Dr. Nicholas Roerich, a White Russian artist, world peace advocate, sometime botanist and mystic with whom Wallace had been in contact since the beginning of his tenure as secretary of agriculture in the early 1930s.

603. In late March the columnists had published a counterpart to the "Polish Documents Bearing on Events that Led up to the War" that the German Foreign Office had recently released. *The American White Paper: The Story of American Diplomacy and the Second World War* chronicled the development of American foreign policy since the invasion of Poland in September 1939 and recorded its "disappointments and successes." Focusing largely on the disappointments of the president's efforts at peace to date, the pair made a case for a more directly interventionist American role henceforth. Although Alsop and Kintner never quoted directly from confidential documents or sources, the content of the *White Paper* made it evident that they had had access to classified information. Describing JPK's announcement to the president of Chamberlain's declaration of war, for example, they reported that

Being easily emotional, Kennedy had read it with unashamed tears in his eyes. Still deeply moved, always bearish, and more appeasement-minded tha[n] any other American policy-maker, Kennedy was in a state of unrelieved despair when he recited the gist of the speech to the President . . . He kept saying, "It's the end of the world, the end of everything."

About 3:15 I was ushered up. The President was sitting at his desk and looked badly. We shook hands. He said he was sorry to drag me down on a Sunday but he was anxious to get away early Monday morning. He had a cold, a temperature and he thought pleurisy in his throat.

I said that I hated to bother him but I did want to get fixed up on my resignation. I hated to be sitting in Florida and have London bombed. People might well say, "Why doesn't he go back?" The President said, "I understand and I don't want to send you back — you've done enough but as I told you after Election, I don't know whom to send and I don't want to leave London in chargé d'affairs hand." He said, "You resign but remain as Ambassador until your successor is appointed." So if anything comes up I can talk to you about it." I said, "That's okay just so long as I'm out."

I then read him what I intended to say and he suggested adding — "I'll stay until successor appointed."

I then suggested sending Tony Biddle, although I knew the State Department didn't consider him heavy enough. I said, "He's done a good job for you in Poland and France — He and his wife were good friends in the Campaign, and the British appreciate his help in Poland." He said, 6 or 8 years ago he was considered a playboy, but I think he has outgrown it and I think Margaret's a peach." He asked, "Would Halifax talk to him frankly?' I said that I felt sure he would. He said, "How about Churchill?" I said, "If there is a Chinese nigger, Churchill would talk to him now if you sent him." He laughed at this.

I said, "Mr. President — Churchill is keeping this fight going only because he has no alternative as Churchill the fighter, whether there is any hope in the future or not, but his real idea is that he'll get the U.S. in and then U.S. will share the problems." I said, "Mr. President, there is no doubt in my mind that Churchill has no particular love for the U.S. nor in his heart for you." "I know," said the President, "He is one of the few men in public life who was rude to me: (This is story he told me last year.)

He said, "I've gone over their financial position and they're all right for quite a while — They've got plenty in the South and holdings all over the world — And besides Belgium and Holland have American holdings." "Mr. President", "I've said all this before — And they also have Norway, Holland, Belgium gold and French which they will get their hands on if they lose."

"The problem seems to me if the Germans close these West Coast ports what can they do. We can't get anything in and with England licked the party is all over. As I see the picture you have 2 alternatives — To become greater than Washington or Lincoln or to become a horse's ass." He said, "I have a 3rd alternative — to be the one responsible for making the U.S. a small and unimportant power." I said, "That puts you in my second class."

I sensed for the first time he is more worried about the future than he has been and possibly he recognizes the truth of what I have been telling him about Europe. Sumner Welles bore out these ideas when I saw him Monday morning. He said that the President spoke in glowing terms of the jobs I'd done and Welles felt he was trying to think out the future course of the U.S. He hoped no one including Hopkins was going with him while he was thinking things out.

He asked me how Jack was. He said he had a theory that stomach trouble of these kids was due to drinking. I said that mine didn't drink. He said, "Well that explodes that theory."

I told him Jack had been turned down by Draft Board and I was trying to get him with General Emmons. He then brought up how blind Elliot was and how, "those bastards of newspaper men made up that story about him during the campaign." He said,

"I don't call them 'sons of bitches' because that reflects on some one else — They're bastards."

He wanted to be remembered kindly to Rose and family. He said he wanted me available to discuss any matters that might come up.

I said how did he think he could get defense up so that England could get real help and our defense would get better with Perkins talking about short working weeks.

He said, "Now wait a minute — If 2,000,000 unemployed come off the unemployed rolls then I'll go to a 6-day week". I said, "But, Mr. President, these unemployables are not equipped to work in the capital goods industry." "Well," he said, "Put them in lower form of industry and move each class up to top". I said, "That's okay except it takes time and you've got to help England *now* and you've got to get defense up *now*." (I judge he's thinking that over.)

He spoke of "damn fool" Talbot who evidently made a statement during campaign about South America. He said, "I've got to keep S.A. in line. Canada will do what she's told, but S.A. must be worked with." I said, "What are you doing about fitting their economy into ours?" He said, "I'm working on it all the time — people don't understand all the problems." I agreed.

Navy won't stagger work — took me three months to show them how to do it. Glenn Martin[604] said he just couldn't do it. I said, "Try and see." He did and now it's working.

He said, "I've got a funny story about the Navy you'll enjoy."

"I've got this little dog and I thought I might have a box built for him on the ship. I told them about five feet square and about six or nine inches off the ground that he could jump into. Well, what do you think they did? They met me and said, 'We've improved your idea.' They had made the box five feet square and about three feet in the air so that only a great Dane could jump in (President's dog being a little black one.)" "But", said the Navy, "We've put a post in the middle of the box he can use like a telegraph pole. That, said the President, was a stroke of genius." "Ah!" said the President, "That's fine, but my own opinion is he'll use the four legs of the box and just not bother trying to get up in the box to use the one that's there." He is tickled with this story.

I remember when he told me he was ill. I said, "for God's sake don't let anything happen to you and then have to take Wallace — You're responsible for him and he has no experience." He said, "That's right — I'll be careful."

Joseph P. Kennedy: *Press Release*

December 1, 1940

Ambassador Joseph P. Kennedy, made the following statement today. "On November 6, I tendered to the President my resignation as his Ambassador to the court of St. James's.

"Today the President was good enough to express regret over my decision, but to say that, not yet being prepared to appoint my successor, he wishes me to retain my designation as Ambassador until he is. But I shall not return to London in that capacity.

"My plan is, after a short holiday, to devote my efforts to what seems to me the greatest cause in the world today, and means, if successful, the preservation of the American form of democracy. That cause is to help the President keep the United States out of the war."

604. Glenn Luther Martin (1886–1955), aviation pioneer, developer of the MB-2, B-10 and B-29 bombers, and president of the largest aircraft manufacturer and military aircraft supplier in the nation.

John F. Kennedy, 23: *Memorandum*

Palm Beach, December 6, 1940

Memo for: Joseph P. Kennedy
From: John F. Kennedy

Dear Dad:

I received the letter from Simon and I am writing him myself and sending Luce one of the three pamphlets as he was quite bitter about Simon, and may find it of some interest.

I also received a rather unusual letter from Londonderry, a copy of which I am enclosing. I am also answering that. And lastly I received a very interesting letter from Liddel Hart. (Enclosure)[605]

I am sending along to you a rough outline of some points that I feel it would be well for you to cover. It only shows an approach to the problem, it is not meant to be a finished form. Part of it is in article form; in other parts I have just mentioned points you might answer. I don't present it in the form of a finished article as I first of all don't know what your view-point is on some questions, and secondly I think the article should be well padded with stories of your experiences in England in order to give it an authenticity and interest.

Some points such as my mention of Alsop and Kintner you may want to leave out and undoubtedly you will prefer another approach to such questions as this, but it may serve to give you a different angle. I think it is right for you to do the article, at least one, in order to clear the record which has been somewhat twisted by Pearson and Allen and Alsop and Kintner, although I saw where Boake Carter wrote a couple of what I thought were very good articles on your views.

(Not written after article) I have just finished reading Alsop and Kintner's latest attack on your appeasement tendencies, which really makes no sense whatsoever.[606] I mention it further along — but I must say that I can't judge whether or not it is better to just dismiss them. While it may sound important to us — to the average person it merely makes a vague impression. It might be merely better to ignore them and just stick to the central theme of answering the appeasement charge without going into anything specific. However, I have included something about them just in case you decide to use it.

AS I SEE IT

On November 6, the day after the election, I resigned from a post that I have held for nearly three years, that of the American Ambassador to the Court of St. James. In the statement which I gave when the resignation was made public I said that I would devote my efforts to aiding the President to keep out of the war. And this I propose to do.

For this reason I have decided to set down for the people of America what I really believe and feel about the great problems that face this country. The problems facing America today are not academic. They demand concrete answers, and rightly or wrongly they must be answered soon. As the decisions to be made in the next few years will have a far-reaching effect on our lives and the lives of our children, I feel that the

---

605. Lord Chancellor Simon, former minister of state for Air Lord Londonderry, and military strategist and historian Sir Basil Liddell Hart (1895–1970) had sent Jack their criticisms of *Why England Slept*, which had recently been published in England.

606. "When Joseph P. Kennedy announced he was laying down his office to fight for the cause of peace," Alsop and Kintner had asserted the previous day, "he really meant he was going to talk appeasement all across the United States. His former associates at the State Department are firmly convinced of it."

American people, from whom the ultimate decisions must come, should have and must have all the facts before them. All view-points must be considered. Colonel Lindbergh and William Allen White[607] must both be given fair and impartial hearings if the American people are to have a fair voice in determining what sort of country they are to live in.

For my own part I have always felt that the art of diplomacy was far too shrouded in mystery. This tendency to treat diplomacy as a sort of Machiavellian poker game in which only experts could sit in on has been in a great measure responsible, I think, for the fatal inertia of the democracies during the last tragic years. How foolish it is to expect the people from whom the ultimate decisions must come to take the vigorous and forceful action necessary to match the dictators when they have been lulled into a false sense of security and complacency until the last hysterical moment.

The views that I now set down are not new to me. I have held them since the tragic days of Munich. The war has only cemented them. And I have emphasized them in every conversation I have had since then with both American and British leaders. Now that I am a private citizen I feel that the American people should hear them. Since returning home especially, I have repeatedly emphasized these views to newspapermen all through the country. I have spoken to them on every possible occasion. Of necessity the conversations have been off the record. My official position forbade any direct interviews.

Throughout my public career during the last seven years I do not recall ever having refused to talk to the newspapermen on any subject. This has not been a one-sided bargain, however, by any means. The best-informed men that I have met in twenty-five years of a varied career are not statesmen, diplomats, or college professors, but American newspapermen.

During the last two years, however, I have tried especially to give newspapermen all the background that circumstances and my job permitted. I have felt that their responsibility is great, as it is upon them that the American people depend for their knowledge on the problems facing them. The manner in which the settlement of Munich was treated in this country demonstrated to me powerfully the danger that lack of adequate information could bring.

(Dad: You might work in here some of your own ideas of Munich and background of it. That is, what you thought; how you felt it would be serious danger to America if there was a war at that time; that America's own defenses were completely down as well as England's; that England might have been bombed into submission over night due to her complete lack of defenses and America would have been in an exposed and dangerous position. You might put in here that it was worth any risk for America to have a Europe at peace, and therefore, you supported Chamberlain. You felt that Munich was misunderstood in America and that the bitterness of the attacks on England for not fighting has given America a great moral responsibility in this present war, which she should not have undertaken. You cannot blame many Englishmen for feeling that they have been let down, that we were continually urging them to fight as we did in October, 1938. This, I think of course, was a mistake. We should not have taken such a critical view point without more knowledge.)

Through the last months it has been more and more evident that Munich was inevitable due to the complete lack of preparedness. But in this country at the time the settlement was attacked with a bitterness seldom equaled. It was attacked as a failure of

---

607. William Allen White (1868–1944), editor of the influential *Emporia* (Kansas) *Gazette* and chairman of the Committee to Defend America by Aiding the Allies.

British diplomacy to provide security where it should have been attacked as a failure of British democracy to provide adequate armaments. It might have been a trumpet call to America to awaken, but the press wasted its energy in a bitter attack on the individuals involved. That taught me a vital lesson and since then I have always tried to give as thoroughly as circumstances would permit, any information that I could that would help news men get nearer the truth.

I have had many such talks since returning home. From several of these rumours have sprung that I am a defeatist, that I am an appeaser. Joseph Alsop and Robert Kintner in their column said that I hold views unacceptable to 90% of the American people. I do not think that I do, but I am setting my views down here sincerely and with complete frankness. I think that the American people can decide whether or not my views agree with theirs much more accurately than Mr. Alsop or Mr. Kintner.

I must confess at the outset that my views are not pleasant. I am gloomy and I have been gloomy since September, 1938. It may be unpleasant for America to hear my views but let me note that Winston Churchill was considered distinctly unpleasant to have around during the years from 1935 to 1939. It was felt he was a gloom monger. In the days of the Blitzkrieg the optimist does not always do his country the best service. It is only by facing the reality that we can hope to meet it.

It is not easy for me to discuss what should be our attitude towards England without emotion — purely from the point of view of what is best for America. I have lived in England for many months. My wife and I have many friends there. My children have gone to school there. I have seen the English stand with their backs to the wall and not whimper. I have seen the grim determination with which the man in the street met the news of the disasters of May and June. I have seen the soldiers coming back from the hell that was Dunkirk with their thumbs still up. I have heard the story of the fight of the grenadier guards. (Here you might tell that story you were telling me about the guards signing and driving the Germans out of the town losing so many men.) I have seen the boys who were friends of my children die in the air. I have seen the sprit of the Londoners through 244 air raids. I repeat, therefore, it is not easy for me to discuss the situation from a purely American point of view but I feel I must, I feel that the situation today is so fraught with peril and disaster for us [*that*] we must take the course, for many it may be the hardest, of looking at the situation completely from the point of view of what is best for America.

Dad: Here's sort of a general introduction. You will probably want to approach some of the points I have brought out in it in a different way but the points themselves may be of interest. In regard to Alsop and Kintner, you may not want to take direct issue with them as they have 365 days a year to strike back. If you do hit at them I think it would be well to do it not in the form of attacking them for personal reasons but rather because they have by their malicious and untrue attacks misinterpreted the truth and have thus done a disservice to the people of the United States, who need the truth so badly. Here is a paragraph on them:

I must confess also another reason for wishing to set down what I really think and this is a more personal one. I have lately noted several bitter attacks on me in a gossip column taking me to account for being an appeaser and a defeatist. I give these columnists who have attacked me credit for complete sincerity. I believe that when Joseph Alsop and Robert Kintner devoted a whole column to discussing a newspaper interview they felt they were giving the truth. I cannot understand it quite so clearly when they fail to even mention it when the interview was denied and repudiated by me. I believe also that when Joseph Alsop and Robert Kintner attacked me in their column of August (I am not too sure of the date of this or of its accuracy but it can be checked) complaining about a wire I had sent to the State Department a previous week, that they felt they were doing a real public service. That the wire in question was confidential to the President and Secretary of State is not the important matter, or that they were able to gain access to a confidential wire and felt free to make a public news story of it is also not the really important matter.[608] The important point is that they completely misquoted it, I trust unintentionally, and thus gave the American people a completely untrue version of what the American Ambassador to England who was supposedly in the best position to observe what was happening in England, really felt. I believe in this that their disservice was great and that theirs is a severe responsibility. To misinform the American people for the benefit of a story is, I believe, in these times a grave offense. Now that they have seen fit to release the wire and place a completely false implication on its contents I will show where they were wrong and what effect this might have. (Here, if you have it, you might see fit to compare what Alsop and Kintner said about the wire and what the wire really said and show the danger that this misinformation might cause. I am rather vague about it as you mentioned it briefly in the plane, but you might be able to work something out from these lines.) The wrong, I believe, has not been done so much to me as it has been done to the people of the United States when they are desperately trying to learn the truth of the situation, A situation puzzling even to those who have a great many more of the facts before them. To me it is of grave and serious concern that this matter should have been handled with such a complete disregard for the actual truth. In the same way and for the same reason I take serious issue with some of the later stories which brand me as an appeaser and a defeatist on the basis of a newspaper interview which I later denied. The original story was given an entire column, the denial not a single line. It is thus also to nail these particular stories for the lie that they are that I set down ~~what I really think~~ [*the situation as I see it*]. The American people have the right to know.

Point #2

In order to show why it is necessary for you to write an article on why America should not enter the war it might be well to bring in Hiram Johnson's statement in San Francisco, December 4, that America is definitely headed for entry into the war; that it is inevitable.[609] This will answer any of those who claim that there is no need to write such an article, that both candidates promised to keep us out and none of the American people wish to go in. You might bring in that during the next few months the pull towards war is to become stronger and stronger and that the American people must have the arguments of those who think we should go in and those who think we should not go in right out on the table before them.

Point #3

In giving your reasons why America should not go into the war I would not state that Britain does not want it as you did in your speech because I imagine that they will be asking for more direct aid in the near future.

608. He seems to refer not to any of Alsop and Kintner's August columns, but to their October 7 piece, which touched upon the administration's circumvention of its ambassador in London during the military fact-finding mission in August, and noted that "[o]nly last week [JPK] virtually warned the State Department, in one of his despatches, that the British Empire was too weak and too near defeat to be of any value as an ally."

609. "Only a miracle can keep U.S. out," the isolationist California senator had told the *New York Times*. "[W]e are going to get into it. There isn't any doubt in my mind. We [are] edging nearer and nearer every day."

Point #4

It is well to remember also that while many people, the more vociferous ones, might be sore because you are not pro-British enough, there are others such as the Father Coughlan group who are sore because you are too pro-British in that you feel we should give them money as a form of insurance. While they may not be nearly as important, I believe that these people also are entitled to an explanation of why you feel that Britain should get this money. There is still a considerable group of complete isolationists. You should explain to them how and why you differ.

Point #5

I imagine that you will have to explain your views on the Johnson Act and about the advisability of loaning money. It would seem to me that the British undoubtedly should be forced to pay as ~~well~~ [long] as they can but it should also be brought out exactly how much money we are spending and will spend throughout the long years to come on defense, which we will save if Britain wins the war or achieves a deadlock, and secondly how important it is that Britain goes on fighting in order to give us time to prepare ourselves both economically and defensively for the future.

Point #6

It might also be worthwhile to mention your views on whether you feel that the British are liable to say to hell with it if they see we are being completely selfish or if they see we are definitely not coming in. This might be a reason for giving more aid.

Point #7

Of course it will have to be mentioned whether you feel that England can hold out and if so for how long. You can avoid a direct prophecy as you have before by stating that you cannot judge this unless you know Germany's strength. You can put in a boost by saying you know the bombing won't make them quit.

Point #8

You might bring out how important it is that we start immediately to organize our economy for the post war world and how thoroughly we must become adjusted to the change, not just a few experts in Washington, but the whole country. This is worth quite a bit of space.

Point #9

It must be remembered continually that you wish to shake off the word "appeaser". It seems to me that if this label is tied to you it may nullify your immediate effectiveness, even though in the long run you may be proved correct. Lindbergh may prove a good example of this. I don't mean that you should change your ideas or be all things to all men, but I do mean that you should express your views in such a way that it will difficult to indict you as an appeaser unless they indict themselves as warmongers.

Point #10

You might bring out in the point that you have always told the British frankly where you stood, that you have never given any Englishman the slightest hope that America would ever come into the war. You have done this for two reasons — because you believed that it would be disastrous for America to come into the war and that Americans were firmly against it, and secondly because you felt that you would be doing the British just as great a disservice. It would have been much easier during the trying days of the summer to have held out some hope — but you thought it would have been a disservice to both the country to which you were accredited as well as the country from which you came. You might also make some mention that the diplomatic wires when released will bear you out.

Point #11

I have not copy [*sic*] of Bevin's speech, but of course you will want to bring it in.[610] The impression that people should have if possible, after reading your article is how right you have been from the beginning. This will make them more anxious to hear from you in the future. Of course, this will have to be subtly expressed, as otherwise it will open you too wide to cracks from these wise-apple columnists that you are more interested in telling how right you've been than in helping the American people.

If you ever think that perhaps you are giving the impression that you feel you know it all, you can always imply that it is not that you are so smart, but merely that after all you have been closer to the situation than anyone else in this country for three years. In showing how you always looked out for America's interest you might show that at Munich you agreed closely with British policy, and were very popular, yet during this last winter you became quite unpopular because of your firm stand against America's entry and your statements that America would never come in and couldn't if she wanted to. You felt that while it hurt you temporarily in the long run you feel and felt before you left that the British appreciated that you had played fairly with them by telling them the truth as you saw it. In the same way you think that in the long run this country will be glad you are telling them the truth.

Point #12

As another approach to Alsop and Kintner, etc., you might just ~~discuss~~ [*mention*] them, treating what they say as insignificant, that you don't care what they say, in the long run you have confidence [in the people]: that you will continue to tell the truth — that you will submit to the judgement of your country, if not received favorably now, then in the future. You answer Alsop and Kintner merely because the situation now is so acute that you feel what you [*really*] think should be on the record. But you don't give a damn what they say about you personally.

Point #13

In reading Alsop and Kintner's latest remarks and their continual use of the word appeasement without amplifying its meaning, I received the impression that they, like so many other Americans, are guilty of throwing around the term when they never have stopped to think exactly what it meant. It might be a good idea to try to get a definition of what they mean. This is necessary because no one — be they isolationist, pacifists, etc., — no one likes to be called an appeaser. Is Hiram Johnson an appeaser? They would probably answer no — Well, is Lindbergh an appeaser — Yes. But where does the difference in their beliefs lie — Johnson must express himself better, because he has avoided the label — yet in essence they both stand for the same thing. The word appeasement of course started at Munich; the background of it seems to be the idea of believing that you can attain a satisfactory solution of the points in dispute by making

---

610. In a radio broadcast of November 24, the minister of Labour and national service had asked that the United States give Britain a "resounding answer in a roar from the planes built in your factories, the guns, the ships and the full resources of your production . . ."

concessions to the dictators. But you do not believe this — you predicate your views on other grounds. Where I think Lindbergh has run afoul is in his declarations that we do not care what happens over there — that we can live at peace with a world controlled by the dictators — or at least that is the impression he has given.

I would think that your best angle would be that of course you do not believe this, you with your background cannot stand the idea personally of dictatorships — you hate them — you have achieved the abundant life under a democratic capitalistic system — you wish to preserve it. But you believe that you can only preserve it by keeping out of Europe's wars, etc. It's not that you hate dictatorship less — but that you love America more.

The point that I am trying to get at is that it is *important that you stress how much you dislike the idea of dealing with dictatorships,* how you wouldn't trust their word a minute — how you have no confidence in them — but that you feel that they can best be fought off, internally as well as externally, if we build ourselves up strong economically and defensively, and we can only do that by following the procedure you advocate.

In that way you can prevent their fastening the word appeaser on you. You could take the word appeasement apart and question what it means. Does it mean fighting for the Dutch East Indies, etc. Stress the danger of speaking in such broad generalities, try to give a fair definition of what Alsop and Kintner mean by appeasement and then show how you couldn't possibly believe in it. If, however, it means getting us into the present war — you must plead guilty — it would be great if you could get from some others who hold as they do — a definition of what *exactly* they mean, and then answer it.

Point #14

You might bring out that many of the people who want to get us into war — argue that Hitler has piece-meal gobbled up Europe's democracies — and that we should avoid their mistake and get in and help while we still have England. It would seem to me that the fallacy in that argument lies in the difference between Norway's or Belgium's position and ours. We must not always identify ourselves too closely with others' experiences and try too vigorously to make them apply to ours.

Point #15

In talking about the gloom charge — it might be well to mention that you don't enjoy being gloomy. — It's much easier to talk about how pleasant things are. The only advantage of doing so is that you hope that it may prove of some value to the country. You believe that the optimists in England and France did their countries a profound disservice. It is not that you believe that come hell or high water — everything is going to be bad. I think you have to show some hope for the future — or otherwise people will say — "Oh well — no matter what we do — he says we are doomed." Rather you think that by preparing for the worst — you may be able to meet it. You might bring it home by saying you have seen plenty of optimists cleaned out in the stock market before you went into the diplomatic service — and you have seen plenty of optimistic statesmen cleaned out since then.

It seems to me that you've got a wonderful point here, provided you make it appear that you are not gloomy for gloom's sake. You can bring out those French optimists who believed in the Maginot line, etc. You might bring out that it is necessary for politicians to stress the bright side of things — they are in politics and must get the people's vote — you don't care what people think — you are interested only in the long-run point of view of what is best for this country.

Point #16

I noticed in Alsop and Kintner's latest article that they said that you okayed Lyons' story twice. I should think it would be easy to disprove this. The Globe itself might help you out.

Point #17

It is well to remember that businessmen are always distrusted as being the prime appeasers, due to the fact that this was the group that promoted it in England. This is why I emphasize that you will have to disclaim any [*similar*] beliefs ~~from the point of view of~~ "having confidence in the dictatorships," [*etc.*] This, of course, will not interfere or in any way change what your views [*really*] are. It is merely a point that you should emphasize.

Dad: Here then I have set down some ideas. I hope that they are of some good — I wish I was down there so that I could be of more help and could go over it with you directly.

I think it is important that you write in a very calm and a judicious manner, not as though you were on the defensive.

I plan to get down there around December 19. I am going to the Political Science Conference for a week — fly to New York — see Dr. Jordan and then come South. Have been feeling better lately and am looking forward to getting down.

Love,

Jack

P.S. My address from Sunday, December 8, to Saturday, December 15, will be: Institute of World Affairs — Mission Inn–Riverside.

If there is anything further I could do — let me know there & will get right to work. — I have just read it over — and I'm not too sure I've been of much help, but I hope so.

John F. Kennedy, 23, to Joseph P. Kennedy

Flying the Mainliner

Dear Dad:

This is just a supplementary note on the article which I think might be considered.

It seems to me that our actual aid to Britain is pretty small, and that the defense program calling for more and more planes is falling behind; and the concern over this seems to be chiefly in some of the columns — and is on the academic side. We seem to be in the same psychological pattern that England was during the year from ~~1939 to~~ Sept 1938 — to Sept. 1939. As Munich awakened England — so the events of the month of May awakened us. But like England we are rearming in much the same leisurely fashion that England did — note the lack of genuine legislation empowering the defense commission — Of course the reason we are so confident as a nation is that we know, especially after watching England hold out during the summer that *we* cannot be *invaded* — *We* are safe. We are failing to see that if England is forced to give in by summer due to our failure to give her adequate supplies *we* will have *failed* to meet *our* emergency as did England before us. As England failed from September 1938 to September 1939 to take advantage of her year of respite due to her feeling that there would be no war in 1939, we will have failed just as greatly.

Now as this affects your position I realize that aid for Britain is part of it but in your message for America to stay out of the war — you should not do so *at the expense of having people minimize aid to Britain.* The danger of our not giving Britain enough aid, of

505

not getting Congress and the country stirred up sufficiently to give England the aid she needs now — is to me just as great as the danger of our getting into war now — as it is much more likely.

If England is defeated America is going to be alone in a strained and hostile world. In a few years, she will have paid out enormous sums for defense yearly to maintain her armaments — she may be at war — she even may be on the verge of defeat or defeated — by a combination of totalitarian powers.

Then there will be a general turning of the people's opinions. They will say "why were we so stupid not to have given Britain all possible aid. Not present attitude towards England's do-nothing attitude at Manchuria. Why did we worry about money etc. *We should have put in more legislation.* We should have given it to them outright — after all — if we voted $13,000,000,000 for defense in 1940 at home we should have been ready to give England money — they were definitely another arm of our defense forces" (In discussing loans to Britain — it might be well to bring out that a loan does not leave the country — that it is spent here — as is W.P.A. — a simple point — but often not re-alized)

Just as we now turn on those who got us into the last war, Huns, Nazi etc. (Which after all may have been the best thing when all the accounts are added up) — so in the future they may turn on those who failed to point out the great necessity of providing Britain in the crucial months of 1940-41.

Of course I do not mean that you should advocate war — but you might explain with some vigour your ideas on how vital it is for us to supply England. You might work in how hard it [is] for a democracy to get things done unless it is scared and how diffi-cult it is to get scared when there is no immediate menace — We should see that our immediate menace is not invasion, but that England may fall — through lack of our support. Therefore you are gloomy in the hope that you can get the country stirred up — the situation is acute — America must get going.

Of course no one wants war — the anti-war is the most ~~important~~ popular now — But so it was with Chamberlain & the others — in the future as we look back — we may be shocked at our present lack of vigour.

The reason I advocating [*sic*] the strength of this point is that while you do believe in aid for Britain — there is must [?] popular force [?] (*Time* Magazine) that you are ap-peaser & against aid — this you have to nip —

In other words — I'm just saying what you've been saying all along — but I feel you should say this part stronger. You may be able to give some samples [?] between En-gland and our position.

Was an usher in Jack Moffet's wedding yesterday. It was good fun — every one in San Francisco was there & I must say — you have more supporters there than I've ever seen in my life. *Everyone* was swooning with admiration — so I guess while some people read the columnists & pay attention to them there are plenty that don't. Clarence Lin-der — the newspaper man who was up at Hearst[611] — has been giving you a terrific build-up from what I understand also —

On my way to the Round Table Conference —

Love

Jack —

---

611. Clarence Richard Lindner (1890–1952), publisher of the *San Francisco Examiner* and vice president of the Hearst Consolidated Publications.

Joseph P. Kennedy to Arthur Houghton

Palm Beach, Dec. 21, 1940

Dear Arthur:

I had received most of the news from Hays, and when I think of those sterling patriots, Sam Briskin[612] and Harry Cohn, having criticism, it does make me laugh. I am glad that Mr. Cohn understood that I gave him a brush-off at Cannes, because that is just exactly what I meant to give him. There is nothing in my life that requires me to associate with the like of him. Reassure him that I have no intention of getting into the picture business. I wouldn't care to divide up any of the responsibility that those boys will have to assume when this situation really gets bad.

As far as Briskin's opinion of Hays is concerned, the General probably has more important people in the United States thinking well of him than any other citizen. If they will remember rightly I had a very good reason for being able to say something to the industry because in two years I had gotten them, at least, $15,000,000 more than they were possibly going to get,[613] and that is a lot of money for those boys to get there hands on.

So on the whole, I understand, they are going to give Hays a contract, and I should judge from the way the Jewish boys are carrying on, at least, the unimportant Jewish boys, that they are quite nervous about the conditions and they have reason to be. The cry that has gone up from the boys about me is probably based on the fact that the smart British interests have taken over the Jewish boys, because they have organization and have sold them an idea they already had, that they must work for England, even if it means getting us into the war.

Strangely enough the Briskins and the Cohns, the Silverbergs and the Griffiths all leave me cold. They have lots more to worry about than I have.

I read with interest your story about Fox, and it looks to me like the boys haven't changed a bit and the reckoning is coming one of these days; I would suggest to them also that they be very careful about their pictures because whether they like it or whether they don't, the Legion of Decency is going to get tougher and tougher; you can put that right in your pocket.

I think you can call up Marlene[614] and just make it clear by inference that you know a lot of work has been done on her case, and just how is she feeling about all.

The children arrived yesterday and I am expecting Jack to-day. I expect to get up to New York sometime after the holidays, at least for a short while, depending on what happens in this war business.

Take care of your health and start practicing a little golf because we expect you to be with us when Green gets back.

Best wishes for a Merry Christmas and a Happy New Year to you all.

Sincerely yours,
Joseph P. Kennedy

---

612. Samuel Jacob Briskin (1897–1968), executive in charge of Production at Columbia Pictures.
613. Out of the recent British film negotiations, that is.
614. Dietrich.

Joseph P. Kennedy to R. Douglas Stuart, Jr.[615]

Palm Beach, Fla. Dec. 23, 1940

Dear Mr. Stuart:

Thank you for your letter of the 19th.

I enjoyed talking with you and Hanford very much indeed. As I told you when you were down here, I am, first of all, handicapped by the fact that I am still Ambassador and on two occasions the President has requested me not to withdraw as Ambassador designated. Until I am completely free I can make no commitments as I told you. However, I am expecting that my successor will be appointed any day now.

I quite agree with you that the sand seems to be running out on us, but how are you going to attack a plan until you know what it actually is. You might have an opinion on this latest outline of the President, but when it comes up, presented to Congress, it may be completely different. So it strikes me that whatever I have to say will probably be delayed until sometime in January. Just as soon as I have my own plans definitely in mind I will get in touch with you.

I have been talking to some people down here who are forming an America First Committee and I have also been talking to a young man who is prepared to finance five broadcasts in this state.

I expect to be in New York sometime after the 5th or 6th of January.

With warmest personal regards, I am

Sincerely yours,
Joseph P. Kennedy

---

615. Director of the America First Committee.

PART V

Semiretirement

Having consolidated his fortune in Hollywood and on Wall Street, Joseph Kennedy had managed to salvage it from dissolution at the close of the 1920s. He had established himself as a consultant sought after by some of the major media conglomerates and figures of the day. He had won over his critics in Washington, taken on the plum American post abroad, and (although not without consequences for his relations with Roosevelt) had been noted as a contender to be the first Irish Catholic president of the United States. If the thirties had been for him a decade of aspiration, hard work, legitimization and overall success—political, financial and social—the forties would usher in the loss and destruction of much that he had worked for and much that he held dear.

The president's acceptance of his ambassador's resignation in December 1940 would signal the end of Joseph Kennedy's official public career, and all but complete the erosion of whatever residual good will existed between the two men. Having assured the American public that "[y]our boys are not going to be sent into any foreign wars" immediately before the election, and now safely ensconced for a third term, the president would exhort his radio audience shortly before New Year's Eve to become "the great arsenal of democracy." Easing from neutrality toward commitment and hoping to encourage the American public to do likewise by supporting Lend-Lease, he would argue in his most successful fireside chat that "[w]e must apply ourselves to our task with the same resolution, the same sense of urgency, the same spirit of patriotism and sacrifice as we would show were we at war."

Since his return from London, Kennedy's speech on behalf of the third-term election, his apparent diatribe to Louis Lyons and his reported comments regarding the Reich to Hollywood studio executives had engendered widespread confusion regarding his views and a barrage of criticism in the media nationwide. In the weeks immediately preceding the Lend-Lease hearings in late January 1941, he would find himself excoriated in columns syndicated from coast to coast in which he believed his views to be misunderstood, mischaracterized and exaggerated. Alsop and Kintner, for example, accused him of intending to "peddle appeasement all across the United States." *Life* characterized him (along with the Lindberghs and Hugh Johnson) as central among the isolationist "Foes" of Roosevelt's foreign policy. Nevertheless, supporting (incongruously his critics charged) both aid to Britain and continued American neutrality, and having recently returned from London where he had witnessed firsthand the horrors of war, the former ambassador's support would be courted by those on both sides of the Lend-Lease divide. Hamilton Fish invited him to testify as the first opposition witness at the hearings; America First encouraged him warmly to join up. On the other side of the issue, despite the president's reported pronouncement, shortly before Thanksgiving 1940,[1] that he never wanted "to see that son of a bitch again" as long as

---

1. The story of the reported closed-door late-November meeting in Hyde Park (over whose occurrence historians have disagreed) comes down, Gore Vidal contends, through Eleanor Roosevelt. No documentary evidence to confirm (or indeed to deny) its having taken place survives among either the Roosevelt or the Kennedy papers. A memorandum in the Kennedy papers, cataloging the dates of JPK's "Conversations with Roosevelt" between 1938 and the president's death in 1945 notes that at the close of 1940 the two men met on November 6 ("Interview with FDR day after election") and December 1 ("Conversation with FDR at White House"), but makes no mention of any interim meeting at Hyde Park.

he lived, Kennedy would be called to Washington first in early December 1940 and then in mid-January 1941 for friendly chats regarding his upcoming public statements on H.R. 1776. The purpose of the Washington meetings with the president and State Department officials was merely, he suspected, "to butter [him] up." "I don't think the President has gone out of his way to help me by calling off his 'Hatchetmen,'" he complained to the undersecretary of State regarding the recent treatment he had received at the hands of the press, and added with characteristic plainspokenness, "I'm sore." In an effort to clarify his opinions to the American public, he arranged to give a nationwide radio address outlining his position on January 18, and went on to testify before the Senate Foreign Relations Committee on January 21. His more than five hours of testimony, intended to delineate once and for all his stance, "all aid to Britain short of war," and his reservations regarding the extensive powers the bill would vest in the president, would be broadly regarded as confusing and equivocal, however. His statements would do little to dampen the media firestorm surrounding him. Nevertheless, inasmuch as he had been courted by the bill's supporters as well as its detractors in the weeks leading up to the hearings, his seemingly conflicted testimony would be claimed as a minor victory by both camps.

In the weeks and months ahead the former ambassador retreated to private life. He felt keenly the sting of both the ostracism of his former Washington colleagues and the public and journalistic opprobrium to which he was by now regularly subjected on both sides of the Atlantic. Despite the ongoing friendship of a few loyal friends and associates in Washington (most of them relatively conservative Irish Catholics like himself), he would find his political influence rapidly waning and himself persona non grata in the capital. Although he had argued against voluntary or premature intervention on Britain's behalf, he had for some time encouraged rearmament and preparedness in the face of the aggression that he had come to believe the Axis would eventually direct at the United States. Learning of the Japanese assault on Pearl Harbor, therefore, he offered his services to the president despite his personal feelings. "IN THIS GREAT CRISIS," he wired Roosevelt on December 7, 1941, "ALL AMERICANS ARE WITH YOU. NAME THE BATTLE POST. I'M YOURS TO COMMAND."

The telegram would initiate a period not unlike the uncertain eighteen months he had spent in the aftermath of the 1932 election, when he had waited with mingled anxiety and resentment for the presidential nod. This time there would be no presidential nod, nor indeed would there be any presidential response to his telegram for some months to come. While the former ambassador grew increasingly isolated, hurt, resentful and vocally critical of the chief executive and the administration, he nevertheless attempted vainly for many months through those Washington connections that he had maintained to secure a post that he felt would be commensurate with his talents, experience, previous contributions and stature. By and large, however, the positions suggested were nebulously defined managerial posts of secondary importance in the shipping, shipbuilding and defense industries. The president had made the offers anticipating correctly the responses they would receive. "I think you know that if I am given a job cleanly and concisely I will work hard to get you the results you want," Kennedy wrote him in response to one offer in March 1942, "but running around without a definite assignment and authority, I'd just be a hindrance to the program." For the duration of the war, therefore, the former ambassador would remain isolated outside of the administration fold.

If he had suspected Louis Howe's influence in his exclusion from participation in the New Deal in 1933 and early 1934, nearly a decade later he would envision his enemies within the administration multiplied manyfold. His written ruminations from the early 1940s are replete with notations regarding the antagonism, supposed and actual, of various influential members of the administration. Even those like Frankfurter, Hopkins and Cohen, with whom he had at one time been on cordial terms, he now lumped together with the likes of Perkins, Rosenman, Ickes and Morgenthau as "a lot of bastards." He believed the most leftward-leaning elements within the administration to have long been hostile to him for his conservatism. Jewish members of the administration, he insisted, were resentful of what he held were his distorted and misunderstood efforts on behalf of refugees several years earlier. Thus his enemies in Washington and their influence on the president, he believed, had barred his path to meaningful participation in the war effort. Suspecting as much, and having heard of some of his former friend's resentful diatribes, Felix Frankfurter would record in his 1943 diary his own views on the reasons why the former ambassador had been offered no significant wartime post. Kennedy, as Frankfurter characterized it,

> was not only venting his gorge against the New Deal, but more particularly his personal resentment against Harry Hopkins and me, who he, in his foolish and ignorant way, blames for his exclusion from participation in the conduct of the war. I don't suppose it ever enters the head of a Joe Kennedy that one who was so hostile to the war effort as he was all over the lot, and so outspoken in his foulmouthed hostility to the President himself, barred his own way to a responsible share in the conduct of the war.

Though effectively forced into retirement from public life, the former ambassador was not inactive during the early 1940s. In 1941, with the older children out of the house and their younger siblings away at school, he sold the Bronxville house where they had grown up, dividing his time for the most part between Hyannisport and Palm Beach. He continued on in a number of his preambassadorial business interests. To augment the family's wartime rations he kept a farm on Cape Cod. In 1943 he bought a "small interest" in Hialeah Racetrack in Miami and backed a Broadway drawing room comedy. As the former Hollywood financier grew increasingly suspicious of leftward-leaning thought and those who espoused it, he volunteered his services to the FBI. "He feels," Agent Edward A. Soucy reported to Hoover in December 1943, "that he is in a position to secure any information the Bureau may desire from his contacts in the [film] industry with reference to any individuals who have Communistic sympathies." His diplomatic contacts, the former ambassador suggested, might also be of use to the Bureau. Nevertheless, the Bureau would only occasionally make use of his offers, information or contacts over the coming decades.

"I am withstanding all efforts to get me to make speeches or to write articles, because I don't want to do anything that won't help us all win the war and get out of this mess, and they expect criticism from me, so I am suffering in silence," he lamented on New Year's Eve, 1942, in a letter to Lord Beaverbrook, by now one of his few remaining friends in Britain.

His views did not go entirely unexpressed, however, despite his public silence. In a variety of ways, direct and indirect, he made clear his disgust with the administration and the conduct of the war. Despite the mutual hostility and suspicion that had grown up between Kennedy and Roosevelt, the president would make a personal plea for his former ambassador's support of the administration candidate, Congressman Joseph Casey, in the Massachusetts Senate race of 1942. With the counsel of his cousin, veteran Boston politico Joe Kane, and the help of the local Hearst press, Kennedy not only supported Casey's principal opponent, former Mayor John Fitzgerald, but indeed orchestrated his father-in-law's campaign to capitalize on antiadministration sentiment and general war weariness. "[Fitzgerald] made his fight completely on the inefficiency of the war effort, the bungling and the confusion in most everything they did in Washington, and spared the bureaucracy and the planning not a bit," an ebullient Kennedy would write William Randolph Hearst shortly before the September primary. "We've had a lot of fun," he added, with no real expectation of winning. Almost eighty years old, Fitzgerald would come in second in a field of four Democrats with some 30 percent of the vote to Casey's roughly 40 percent.

Kennedy's irritation with the administration would express itself in other ways as well. His correspondence from the period is rife with criticism of the conduct of both the war and of the domestic situation, giving him ample opportunity to attack those former colleagues and associates whom he held responsible. As an Allied victory came within view at last, he would rail against Roosevelt's and Churchill's settlement on unconditional surrender at Casablanca in 1943, believing it likely to draw out the conflict and cost many more American lives. The Morgenthau Plan to reduce postwar Germany to a demilitarized agrarian state would provoke disgust perhaps not unmingled with his feelings about the plan's progenitor, his old nemesis, the secretary of the treasury: "I was shocked beyond words to see Morgenthau at Quebec taking up state matters with his plan for Germany since I knew that Morgenthau had never been able to answer one question in ten years before the House or Senate Committee without referring to his so-called experts."

Despite the deterioration of their relationship, Roosevelt himself had begun to make overtures to his former ambassador shortly before the fourth-term election. Their meeting in October 1944 would be their last. After nearly four decades of antagonism and friendship, both political and personal, Kennedy would be "shocked beyond words" to see his old chief. Further, "[t]he terrible realization came to me," he recalled, confronted with a president who would be dead by the following spring, "that the Hopkins, Rosenmans, and Frankfurters could run the country now without much of an objection from him." Asked by the party chairman whether he might make a speech on the president's behalf as he had done with such success four years earlier, Kennedy's uncharacteristically restrained response (as he recorded it) was simply, "with one son in the hospital, one son dead, and my son-in-law killed, . . . I didn't think it would be very helpful to Roosevelt."

After returning from London in the wake of the declaration of war in 1939, the children had returned to their respective schools or had begun at new ones. Joe had rejoined Jack in Cambridge to matriculate at Harvard Law School for the fall term of 1940. Kick finished off her studies at Finch College for Women in New York. In the spring of 1941 Eunice would embark on a cruise to South America with her mother; they met up with Jack in Rio. In 1942 Eunice would transfer from the Catholic Manhattanville College in New York to Stanford; her mother would join her there in taking classes for enrichment and relaxation in the fall and winter. Pat would attend Rosemont in Philadelphia. Having been moved from his father's choice, the Episcopalian St. Paul's School in Concord, New Hampshire, to his mother's, the Catholic Portsmouth Priory in Rhode Island, Bobby would once again transfer, this time to Milton Academy in the fall of 1942, where he would complete high school. Jean and Teddy spent the winter of 1940–41 in school in Palm Beach before going off to boarding school themselves. Jean would first attend Eden Hall, a Convent of the Sacred Heart school in Philadelphia, afterward following in her elder sisters' footsteps by transferring to Noroton. Teddy would attend Riverdale in New York and Fessenden in Massachusetts before following Bobby to Milton.

Rosemary had flown home from England via Lisbon with the Moores in the spring of 1940. She spent that summer as a junior counselor, teaching arts and crafts at Camp Fernwood in Massachusetts before beginning to do a little teaching at St. Gertrude's School of Arts and Crafts in Washington, D.C. in the fall. Assisted as she always had been by tutors and companions, she wrote her parents with some effort, but no little regularity, a series of careful, disjointed, affectionate notes and letters over the course of 1940. After that point, however, her correspondence ends, and she seldom appears except obliquely in the surviving family letters and papers.

Her parents had, throughout her life, tried to avoid institutionalizing Rosemary. They had consulted over the years with a variety of medical and psychiatric experts without arriving at an entirely satisfactory treatment, educational program or, indeed, diagnosis for her pronounced learning disabilities and her delayed emotional development. Her parents—her mother in particular—had long been forced to improvise with little or no medical or psychiatric guidance in discovering the most suitable schooling and special care for Rosemary in the absence of an established treatment for mental retardation. In 1939 they had sent her to Belmont House, a Montessori school in Hertforshire, to take a little vocational training in teaching small children. They also hoped she might benefit from the patience, attention and care of Mother Isabel, the school's mother superior, and Dorothy Gibbs, Rosemary's particular companion there.

The benefits of Belmont House on her had been such, apparently, that her parents deemed it worth the risk of her staying at the school even after the declaration of war and the return of her family (with the exception of her father) to the United States. Mary Moore, who had watched her grow up, remarked that "she had never seen such a change in her life" as Rosemary had shown after only a few months at Belmont House. Shortly after Rosemary's return home, her mother too noted the "great improvement" that had resulted, evidently, from Mother Isabel's and Miss Gibbs's ministrations. "It becomes definitely apparent now that this is the ideal life for Rose," her father noted of her progress in October 1939. "She is contented completely to be teaching with Mother Isabel. She is happy, looks better than she ever did in her life, is not the slightest bit lonesome, and loves to get letters from the children [i.e. her siblings] telling her how lucky she is to be over here, (tell them to keep writing that way)." The intensification of German aerial aggression and her father's contemplated departure from England in 1940, however, would bring an end to her productive stay in Hertfordshire and necessitate her return both to the United States and to her family.

Indeed, her family—her siblings specifically—presented another reason for Rosemary's distance from home. As the Kennedy children had grown up, they had become increasingly active, social and accomplished, widening the likewise increasingly evident gap between her abilities and theirs. Despite her siblings'—and particularly Eunice's—efforts at her inclusion, as an adolescent and a young woman Rosemary had developed a growing (and apparently painful) awareness that their capacities and independence were not hers. "She is much happier when she sees the children [her brothers and sisters] just casually. For everyone's peace of mind, particularly hers, she shouldn't go on vacation or anything else with them," her father had decided while they were both still in England. "I have given her a lot of time and thought and I'm convinced that's the answer. She must never be at home for her sake as well as everyone's [*sic*] else."

Although her life in the decade following her return from London goes all but undocumented, Rosemary apparently began to lose ground in Washington despite the progress she had made at Belmont House. Her independence curtailed both by her condition and by the restrictions placed upon her by her parents and by the nuns among whom she lived, Rosemary came increasingly to experience episodes of unpredictable rage. Encouraged, apparently, by the publicized results of Dr. Egas Moniz's relatively new, Nobel Prize–winning surgical technique for subduing aggression, her father began to explore the prefrontal leukotomy's applicability to Rosemary's case sometime in 1941. It is uncertain who performed the operation, when it took place, at what facility, or indeed where she lived until she arrived at St. Coletta's School in Jefferson, Wisconsin, in 1949. Almost no mention of Rosemary survives among her father's papers after the end of 1940.

What is clear is that the operation had failed. Rather than impart the serenity that contemporary medical literature and press accounts boasted, the operation had caused Rosemary to regress. Her father would be horrified that his efforts to improve his child's condition and alleviate her manifest unhappiness with what he had believed to be the best available treatment, had produced results so utterly unintended. He concealed Rosemary's condition, telling her siblings, acquaintances and old friends who inquired about her that she was "teaching in the Midwest." Ostracized, increasingly embittered and isolated, he experienced after the failure of Rosemary's operation the first in a series of crushing personal losses that would only be compounded over the course of the decade.

Although young Joe had been active in galvanizing antiinterventionist sentiment on campus during his two years at Harvard Law School, he realized that war was imminent and, hoping to avoid being drafted when the time came, he volunteered in the summer of 1941. He began his training in the naval aviation cadet program south of Boston in Squantum, not far from the Fore River Shipyard where his father had worked during the First World War. In July 1941 he reported to the Jacksonville Naval Air Station to build upon the foundation of his aviation training; his father would pin his wings to his uniform at the graduation ceremony the following May. From Jacksonville he would report to Banana River, Florida, to begin flying.

Jack, who had been taking classes at Stanford, attempted to enlist in naval officers' training shortly after his elder brother had signed up. The younger brother's bad back, the result of an old football injury compounded by a backward fall from a chair some years earlier, caused him to fail the physical. After working out over the summer he passed his second exam with the intervention of Admiral Kirk, the former naval attaché at the embassy in London. He was commissioned an ensign in late September 1941 and assigned to report for duty at the Office of Naval Intelligence in Washington, D.C.

His stint in the capital writing intelligence digests placed him near Kick, who was currently working and writing under Frank Waldrop, the editor of Cissy Patterson's *Times Herald*. Through Kick he met Inga Arvad. The beautiful Danish feature writer had an obscure past and suspected Nazi connections (a photo taken at the 1936 Olympics placed her on the dais with the führer himself). The relationship would provoke not only nationally syndicated cracks from Walter Winchell and prompt the couple's scrutiny and surveillance by the FBI, but also bring about Jack's rapid reassignment to the Charleston Navy Yard as well. "Disgusted" with desk jobs, in July 1942 Jack reported to the U.S. Naval Reserve Midshipman's School at Northwestern University in Chicago, where he became interested in the new Motor Torpedo or PT Service after hearing a talk by John Bulkeley and John Harlee, heroes of the recent bestselling *They Were Expendable*. He reported to Harlee's new Motor Torpedo Training School in Melville, Rhode Island, in October. Although initially assigned an instructorship rather than active duty upon graduation, with the intervention of Senator Walsh of Massachusetts, Jack was on his way to the Solomon Islands by March 1943.

In July 1943, Kick arrived in London to begin work at the Hans Crescent Club for the American Red Cross, where her days were filled with morale-boosting activities for homesick American servicemen and her evenings with renewing old acquaintances, particularly Billy Hartington's. In August the elder Joe Kennedy would reveal at last the news that had weighed heavily upon him for some days: Jack had been missing in action. "Dad knew he was missing for two weeks," Rose informed her scattered children in one of her signature round-robin letters on August 25, "although he gave no sign— for which I am very thankful—as I know we should all have been terribly worried. He just complained about his arthritis and I said it was funny he was nervous now, little knowing what he had to be nervous about."

In fact, a funeral service had been held for Jack and the crew of the PT 109 in Tulagi after the events of the night of August 1–2. Jack's time in Tulagi, although punctuated by a few scrapes with the enemy, had been relatively quiet until the beginning of August, when the PT 109 was cut in half by the Japanese destroyer *Amagiri* in the Blackett Straight. Of the original crew of thirteen, eleven had managed to survive the destruction of their boat. Together in the darkness they swam ashore on a nearby island, Jack towing his crewmember Pat MacMahon (who had been immobilized by severe burns) in a life jacket attached to a line clenched between his teeth. For several days Jack and the other crew members—exhausted, injured and hungry—had attempted to swim toward Furguson Passage in order to attract the attention of passing PT boats. Meeting at last with two well-disposed native islanders, Jack and his crewmate George Ross presented them with a coconut carved with a message indicating the survivors' location and their need for immediate help. Early in the morning of August 8, a week after having set out, the eleven surviving crewmembers of PT 109 returned to the safety of Rendova Harbor aboard the PTs 157 and 171.

"Of course the news about Jack is the most exciting thing I've ever heard. There wasn't a very big piece in the English newspapers but quite big enough for me to gather that he did really big stuff," Kick would write from London in the aftermath of her brother's ordeal, her own trials just beginning. At twenty-three her name had been associated romantically with a number of young men, both English and American. Since meeting the Anglican marquess of Hartington, the duke of Devonshire's eldest son, five years earlier, however, judging by her letters and diaries from the intervening period, no one appears to have rivaled him in her affections. "Imagine," she wrote her father after moving to Manhattan and starting a course in home economics at Finch College in October 1940, "if I had married Billy and there was no war it would be a castle and not a 3 room apartment." Alluding to an eventual return to London, she wired Billy, whom she had not seen in a year, her Christmas wishes for 1940: "DEAREST BILLY: HAPPY XMAS GREETINGS. MISS YOU. HOPE THE NEW YEAR BRINGS US TOGETHER AGAIN. GOD BLESS YOU ALWAYS. LOVE. KICK." She would count herself "so anxious to go back that I can hardly sit still" upon hearing of his engagement to someone else in late 1941. "I have never been engaged before, thanks to you," he wrote her by way of explanation after a long silence. "It was a very long time before I gave up all hope of marrying you."

The engagement did not last, however. Upon Kick's return to London two years later the pair renewed not only their relationship, but their discussions of marriage as well, despite the divide between their religions and upbringings. Over the course of the winter and spring of 1944 with the (somewhat clandestine) help and support of her father, Kick made unrelenting, but ultimately unfruitful efforts through clergymen and theologians of both faiths to discover some means of marrying outside of her Church while still remaining part of it. Finally, in early May she agreed to marry Billy without the blessing of the Catholic Church and conceded to his request that their children be brought up as Anglicans. At some point, she hoped, a dispensation might be made retroactively that would permit her once again to practice the religion in which she had been raised. One month to the day before D Day she and Billy were married in a London registry office amidst a wartime hodgepodge of guests—Red Cross girls, aristocrats, GIs and some of the leading lights of London café society. Having waited six years to marry, their feelings for each other had weathered separation and war. Many months of soul-searching, trial and isolation had culminated, therefore, in Billy's placing on Kick's finger the ring on which he had inscribed, "I love you more than anything in the world."

The happy few weeks that Kick and Billy finally spent together as a couple before his return to the Coldstream Guards and the front would also serve as the line of demarcation between the trials of the previous months and the grief and loss that were shortly to come.

The union had been controversial, even among those who were close and sympathetic to the pair. "Kik [sic] Kennedy's apostasy is a sad thing," her friend Evelyn Waugh pronounced with all the zealotry of the convert. He was at the time finishing *Brideshead Revisited,* concerning in part the young, impetuous Julia Flyte, who marries outside of the Church, divorces and finally repents of her dissolution by returning to Catholicism. "It is second front nerves [that] has driven [Kick] to this grave sin and I am sorry for the girl," Waugh wrote his wife a few days after the wedding. "Letters continue to pour in from irate Catholics saying I have sold my soul for a title. Billy is very busy answering them all," Kick reported to her mother three days after the ceremony. Indeed, the Catholic laity and clergy alike had been particularly opposed to the marriage. Over the course of the month of May her mother had received a number of unsolicited letters, many, like Father Hugh O'Donnell's, offering nuptial condolences: "May the Blessed Mother give her the necessary grace to see the error of her ways before many weeks have passed." The announcement of their engagement had left Rose "disturbed horrified—heartbroken," according to notes she kept of her thoughts at the time. In an effort to avoid "emotional upset," she had taken some time to think at The Homestead, and after learning that the wedding had in fact taken place she retreated to her room at home, afterward entering the hospital briefly to collect her thoughts and remove herself from the aggressive intrusions of the press. She had not only worried about the possible "blow to family prestige" and the "mighty repercussions" that Kick's example might have for other young Catholic women, certainly, but also she considered her own failings in properly guiding her daughter by "allowing her to drift into this dilemma." Most of all, after a lifetime of the devout practice of Catholicism, she worried for her child's soul since Kick could no longer be an active participant in her faith. Over the next few months, after the initial shock had worn off, Rose would become more than reconciled to the existing situation, writing Kick by the end of June that "as long as you love Billy so dearly, you may be sure that we will all receive him with open arms."

Although her father had made sincere efforts to help Kick in her dilemma, given her distance from home, young Joe had been her only immediate source of family support in making the decision to marry Billy. Joe had arrived in England in September 1943 to join the VB-110 squadron in Devon in joint operations with the RAF to fly Liberator anti-U-boat bombers. On his leaves he had provided Kick with moral support, acted as an intermediary for her with the duke and various members of the clergy, kept their father informed of the latest developments, attempted to soften the blow for their mother and saw to the legal and financial ramifications of the marriage. He had also fallen in love. Pat Wilson was the beautiful, Australian-born, Protestant, previously divorced wife of a British Army officer currently stationed in North Africa. She was also the mother of three small children. Perhaps not surprisingly, Pat seldom appears in Joe's extensive letters home.

Over the spring and summer of 1944 he would write repeatedly that although he had finished his missions and was eligible to return home, he and his squadron had volunteered to stay on. On July 26, he would tell his parents, "I am going to be doing something different for the next three weeks. It is secret, and I am not allowed to say what it is, but it isn't dangerous so don't worry." He had volunteered to pilot a PB4Y Liberator bomber that had been gutted to accommodate twenty-two thousand pounds of explosives. Joe and his copilot, Wilfred Willy, were then to lock the aircraft on its target, the German fortifications lining the Belgian coast, and bail out.

On the afternoon of Sunday, August 13, while the younger Kennedy children sat downstairs at the Hyannisport house listening to "I'll Be Seeing You" on the Victrola, two priests came to the door asking to speak to Mr. Kennedy. They brought with them news that young Joe was missing as the result of an explosion of operational flight 12.

Upon hearing the news of Joe's loss, Kathleen returned home to be with her parents. Difficult as losing him had been for her and indeed for the entire family, none of them took it as hard as their father. As the months following his death grew into years, he would remain inconsolable, admitting later that he had never been able to finish the memorial collection of essays, *As We Remember Joe*, that Jack had edited and compiled while at the Chelsea Naval Hospital in Massachusetts in the wake of his own ordeal in the South Pacific. For the father, expressing himself on the subject of Joe's death would always be difficult; to the vast influx of condolence mail that the family received, he responded, by and large, with the same note typed and sent by secretaries. For many years to come, although many observed him hardening and growing increasingly conservative, he would always reserve special consideration and kindness for grieving parents, and would express himself to them in an uncharacteristically tender and self-revelatory fashion.

Having been home for almost a month in the wake of Joe's death, Kick was out shopping with Eunice in New York when she received word from a messenger to return to their father's suite at the Waldorf-Astoria at once. Billy had been shot and killed in Belgium on September 10. Having waited six years and endured exhausting personal and spiritual reflection and public controversy in order to marry, they had spent little more than a month together as husband and wife. Nevertheless, "If Eunice, Pat & Jean marry nice guys for fifty years," she wrote her parents during the course of her return to England, "they'll be lucky if they have five weeks like I did."

The twenty-four-year-old dowager marchioness of Hartington would remain in England after Billy's death and live there until the end of her own life. She resumed the practice of the faith in which she had been raised, once again receiving communion in her widowhood. She continued working at the Red Cross for the duration and began to resume her old social life, becoming, as one friend put it (to Kick's delight) something of "an institution" in early postwar London. Over the course of the three years following V-E Day, she would again be associated romantically with a number of men on both sides of the Atlantic, but settled upon the dashing, Irish-born Lord Peter Fitzwilliam. If marriage outside of the Church had been impossible to maneuver and difficult to sell to her parents, her mother in particular, then a second marriage to an already-married Protestant was out of the question. In an effort to persuade her father, on May 13, 1948, she and Fitzwilliam chartered a plane to the south of France. They intended to spend a few days on the Riviera before meeting her father in Paris, where he was scheduled for meetings. Although a storm was closing in over the Rhône Valley, they had decided to take off anyway.

Having read the news over the wire of the crash in the mountains outside of the town of Privas and of the death of all aboard, Joseph Dinneen of the *Boston Globe* tracked Kennedy to the George V Hotel in Paris in the early hours of May 14 to ask whether he had heard the news about Kick. He had not until that moment. "To Kick," he managed to scribble half an hour later. "No one who ever met her didn't feel that life was much better that minute. And we know so little about the next world we must think that they wanted just such a wonderful girl for themselves. We must not feel sorry for her but for ourselves."

The war had arrived at a moment when all of the Kennedy children were not only old enough to be literate, but also to find themselves scattered throughout the world. Wartime restrictions on the private use of expanding telecommunications technology had forced the entire family to set their activities and reflections to paper, not only for one another but also, as it turned out, for posterity. Their wartime correspondence forms a kind of protoworldwide web of letters, telegrams, V-mail and postcards stretching from the Solomon Islands to Britain. It would grow to be most voluminous immediately before its sharp diminution. "The infrequency of my letters is due to the glorious transatlantic telephone," Kick both enthused and apologized to her family in August 1946. If such was the case with regard to Kick, arguably the most enthusiastic and expansive of the Kennedy correspondents, then there was an even more precipitous decline in the self-documentation of the rest of the family. Their correspondence would only diminish further over the coming decades.

By the end of the 1940s the Joseph Kennedy papers were becoming more and more one-sided. That is, rather than house both incoming and outgoing letters (in effect written conversations, personal and professional), the correspondence increasingly came to refer to unrecorded telephone conversations, thus leaving some of his insights and instructions impenetrable to posterity. "I have told Jack of our talk about getting out the vote and Jack agrees that that and that alone is the only problem," he wrote Cardinal Cushing of Boston in May 1958, without elaborating on a subject that would be of primary importance to Jack two years later. With the elder Kennedy now readily accessible to his children by telephone and ever-improving rapid transportation, he found less of a need to maintain his accustomed written personal advice or reflections on the present political situation and the state of the world. By the 1950s he corresponded regularly and extensively, for the most part, only with his friends Max Beaverbrook in London and Enrico Galeazzi at the Vatican. Although he would continue the practice that he had developed after coming into the Roosevelt camp of recording conversations with notable figures and memorable events at which he had been present, as his stature in Washington diminished these too would decline in regularity.

His activities were uncharacteristically diffuse compared with the bursts of focused reorganizational or regulatory work that had characterized his professional life in the 1920s and 1930s. He established a foundation in memory of young Joe, the focus of which would gradually evolve from underprivileged children to mental retardation. He chaired a commission to establish a state Department of Commerce in Massachusetts in 1945. He began to make investments in the Texan oil and gas industry, and entered into a flurry of real estate deals, most notably the purchase of the Chicago Merchandise Mart in 1945. In 1946 he sold his interest in Somerset Importers. He served as a member of both Hoover Commissions to reorganize government, and went on to serve on an intelligence oversight committee for President Eisenhower.

His attentions, however, seemed to be less occupied by his own present than by the recent past and by his surviving children's futures. He became involved in writing a number of historical tracts presenting revisionist views on both the events leading to the war and his former associates in Washington and London. In a 1948 letter to the editor of the *New York Times*, written shortly after the appearance of *The Gathering Storm*, the first volume of Churchill's memoirs, he took exception to what he described as the former prime minister's "cavalier treatment of recorded facts" with regard to the foreign policy of the Chamberlain government. In 1950, with his old SEC colleague Jim Landis, he coauthored *The Surrender of King Leopold*, challenging Churchill's and Reynaud's accusations of the Belgian monarch's perfidy in surrendering his forces to Germany a decade earlier. By 1955 Landis had finished ghostwriting the diplomatic memoir that had been in the works in one form or another since 1938. The result chronicled not only the ambassadorship, but also presented an account of the president's duplicity both to his ambassador and to the American people on the issue of neutrality.

It has sometimes been said that the aging ambassador left his memoir unpublished in order to avoid branding his sons with the stigma of his prewar attitudes, supposed or actual. Nevertheless, he would remain outspoken and unapologetic about his prewar views until the end of his life, believing, for example, that Chamberlain and other "peacemakers" like him would be vindicated by history. Moreover, if he had been an isolationist arguing for economic appeasement while still advocating aid to Britain short of war in the late 1930s, his tendencies toward vocal conservatism, retrenchment from internationalism and seeing to American needs and weaknesses first and foremost would only grow in the years to come. He supported the British postwar loan only reluctantly, arguing eventually that the United States should present the $4.4 billion as an "outright gift," without expectation of repayment, given Great Britain's postwar financial straits. He had little confidence in the Marshall Plan, railed against the Truman Doctrine and saw only "a hopeless instrumentality for world peace" in the United Nations. "Is it 'appeasement' to withdraw from unwise commitments, to arm yourself to the teeth and to make clear just exactly how and for what you will fight?" he asked at the University of Virginia Law School Forum in December 1950, during a short-lived cease-fire in Korea. Having stated in 1940 that he could not sympathize with advocates of appeasement, he would assert a decade later in Charlottesville, "If it is wise in our interest not to make commitments that endanger our security, and this is 'appeasement,' then I am for 'appeasement.'"

Likewise, his views on the domestic situation, grounded, as always, in his economic opinions, grew increasingly bleak and conservative. In the booming postwar American economy he saw an overriding need to "keep our heads above water." A friend of Senator Joseph McCarthy's, under whom Bobby had worked in the early fifties, said Kennedy's papers from the period are infused with a deepening suspicion of the encroachment of left-wing ideology both abroad and at home.

"[O]ne day, because there is a world to be lived in," he had told a friend about the acceptance of (or rather, resignation to,) the loss of a child, "you find yourself a part of it again, trying to accomplish something—something that he did not have time enough to do." The grieving father emerged somewhat from the fog of his bereavement by the late forties and early fifties, finding his course again, as it is often said, in his surviving children and their political careers. "Old man Kennedy" (to use his phrase) was greatly reinvigorated by his renewed participation in the backroom politics on which he had been nursed from his infancy in the wards of Boston and on which he had come to thrive during the early Roosevelt campaigns of his middle age. The increased use of the telephone, the decline in his correspondence generally and his long-cultivated circumspection and reticence in recording controversial aspects of his life appear to have conspired to ensure that the archive he left to document his role in Jack's campaigns— advisory, financial or otherwise—would be fragmentary at best.

He had begun spending his summers on the Riviera in the late 1940s, initially for relaxation. As Jack's name became associated with national political office between 1956 and 1960, the elder Kennedy's vacations in Eze-sur-Mer would serve to some degree as a means of escape from the intrusions of the press. They would permit him also to make the conspicuous gesture of absenting himself from the inner circle. Far from home again at moments crucial and historical to his family, for a few months each summer he would once more engage in regular and expansive correspondence with his children. He would write with particular regularity and focus to his sons and sons-in-law, congratulating Bobby on the latest probe of the Permanent Subcommittee on Investigations and offering Jack his advice now on political strategy instead of penmanship, untidiness or dry-cleaning bills. And yet such letters, coupled with the campaign bulletins brimming with paternal pride at Jack's latest primary win, which he sent to Galeazzi and Beaverbrook, constitute the bulk of his written reflections on the role he played in Jack's ascent to the national stage. No correspondence survives (if ever any existed) between the candidate's father and Mayor Daley of Chicago, for example. Very little survives to document the details of his growing and lasting disgust with the Catholic hierarchy (particularly with Cardinal Spellman, with whom he had previously been on friendly terms for decades) for what he felt was their tepid reception of Jack's candidacy. No ledgers of his widely rumored and strenuously denied campaign expenditures appear among his papers.

Seven decades of work, strategy, public acclaim and controversy had culminated in luxurious elder years, throngs of grandchildren and a son at the White House. The ward boss's son had emerged from the Catholic middle class to follow the previous Protestant and patrician model of upward mobility and legitimization in the United States. He had made his fortune in banking, film production, speculation, liquor importation, consultancy, real estate and, likely, other means that go unrecorded in his own papers. He thus permitted himself and his progeny the independence to participate in the civic life of the nation that had made their many advantages possible. He would survive almost half of the children in whom he had invested so much of himself. He would in turn be survived by an enormous body of documentation, as characteristic of him for what it demonstrates explicitly as for what it leaves unsaid. His reticence on issues such as his personal relations with Gloria Swanson and women other than his wife, the practices that allowed him to augment his growing fortune on the unregulated market in the 1920s and early 1930s and the negotiations that resulted in Somerset Importers' readiness to supply the American public with spirits at the very moment of the Twenty-first Amendment's ratification (to name only a few) is indicative of an individual who was as much a product of the advancement of media-related technologies as he was their proponent and exploiter. His earliest surviving papers underscore his marked fascination with technological advances in fields ranging from film to advertising to the dissemination of news and opinion, whether in the form of stock tickers or syndicated columns. He realized quickly that the orchestrated interplay of such rapidly evolving and expanding technologies might generate profit, favorable publicity and celebrity. He made use of such advances not only to generate much of his early fortune, but also much of his growing notoriety in middle age as well. His expanding renown had prompted him to consider his place in history and record his reflections on significant events and personalities. At the same time, his growing reputation seems to have prompted him to edit carefully the record that he would leave of himself.

On the afternoon of December 19, 1961, while playing golf in Palm Beach after seeing Jack off at the airport, he felt unwell and unlike himself. At home he passed up medical attention, collapsing soon after, and was rushed to St. Mary's Hospital. The massive stroke he had suffered would leave him cognizant, but largely unable to speak or move until his death eight years later.

Joseph P. Kennedy to Stephen Early

Palm Beach, January 3, 1941

Mr. and Mrs. Joseph P. Kennedy regret that they cannot attend the buffet luncheon at the White House on Monday, January 20th, immediately after the Inaugural Ceremonies at the Capitol.

Joseph P. Kennedy: *Diary Notes*

January 21, 1941

On Tuesday, January 14, 1941, I received a telegram from Hamilton Fish requesting me to appear before the Foreign Relations committee of the House to testify on the Lend Lease Bill.[2] Being uncertain as to what procedure I should follow I called up Sumner Welles and told him I had received it and asked him if he had any opinion on it. He said he thought I would probably have to go, but he would talk it over with Mr. Hull and let me know in the morning. Incidentally I said, "I am planning to go on the radio and broadcast Saturday night —I am sick and tired of being attacked by both sides and think I am at least entitled to state my position clearly — I don't think the President has gone out of his way to help me by calling off his 'Hatchetmen' and I'm sore."[3] He urged me to do nothing and he would call me in the morning.

On Wednesday,[4] he called at 10:00 a.m. as he had talked with the President. He agreed that I should go to the hearing, but hoped I would come to the State Department and talk it over with him, Hull, and Asquith of the Legal Department. This was sort of a repetition of his talk the previous day when he urged me to come to Washington to talk over my broadcast talk and I had refused pointblank to do it. "However", he added, "The President, when I spoke to him last night, said he was very anxious to see you and have a long talk with you either Thursday or Friday and he would like to have you come down." I said, "What is this for, to butter me up?" And Welles said "Oh, no, he mentioned it himself." I said, "Well, if the President says he wants to see me, of course, I will come at once and I will be there tomorrow morning about 10:30 or 10:45." "Very well, said Welles I shall arrange an appointment and will let you know when you can call at the State House."

I proceeded with my speech and later that afternoon Herbert Hoover's secretary called and asked if Mr. Hoover could come in and see me. He did and I read my speech to him. He said that he thought it one of the finest speeches he had ever heard. He felt strongly that the proposed legislation was a direct influence on getting us into war and must be stopped. He told me that Willkie's announcement had made practically no difference to the Republicans, and as far as he could find out, not more than six had been

---

2. On January 10, House Democrats had introduced H.R. 1776, the Lend-Lease Bill, "An Act to Further Promote the Defense of the United States." The bill empowered the executive to "sell, transfer title to, exchange, lease lend, or otherwise dispose of . . . any defense article for the government of any country whose defense the President deems vital to the defense of the United States." Further, it left the terms of "payment or repayment in kind or property" to the president's discretion. The president's own Dutchess County congressman, staunch isolationist Republican Hamilton Fish (1888–1991) had contacted JPK, stating that he assumed JPK would "appear in opposition either to fundamental principles or to some parts of the bill." JPK had responded that he had "no comment" on Fish's assumption.

3. In an effort to clarify his opinions and repudiate what he described as "many false statements regarding my view on foreign policy" before his testimony on the Lend-Lease Bill, on January 18 JPK would broadcast a recapitulation of his belief that "we ought to stay out of war" but afford "England all possible aid."

4. January 15.

affected.[5] He thought the Republicans were going to stand quite solidly against the bill and if the Democrats could marshal 50 or 60 votes against the bill they would kill it in the House. I told him I was going down to have a talk with the President and expected to broadcast on Saturday night. I went out to dinner and on my return I received a telegram from Welles asking me to come down earlier as my appointment was at the White House and had been made for 10:15 Thursday morning. As there was great doubt as to whether or not the planes would go because of bad weather I took the 12:50 train and arrived in Washington in the morning.

After a shave and bath I went to the State Department where I saw Welles. I told him of my indignation at my treatment. He said that he agreed but didn't think I should have any feeling against the President because he was always friendly. I said, "Be that as it may, strange things have happened."

I told him that I disagreed with Secretary Hull's attitude on the invasion of America.[6] He thought it was a mistake because he said one of the South American countries might be influenced by the Nazi factor and go over to the German side. I said, "What are the rest of the South American countries going to do?" He said, "I think they will re-arm against him." I said that they are not in that mood. I rather think that we are wasting our time loaning them $500,000,000 to keep their trade going. As a matter of fact I think all we need are bases for our own airplanes which could fly down before the Germans could land any appreciable force. So I'm not very much persuaded.

He asked me to go in and see Mr. Hull and we had a short talk.

I then went over to see the President. I waited for 15 minutes and was finally ushered into his bedroom and found he was in his bathroom in his wheel chair. He was attired in sort of grey pajamas and was starting to shave himself. I sat on the toilet-seat and talked with him. I told him of indignation at the treatment I had received. He said no one had received worse treatment than he had in the last eight years. He told of the repeated attacks made on Elliott.[7] I said "That's all well and good, but as far as I am concerned I'm getting it on both sides." He agreed that that was true and he saw no objection to my making a speech. I mentioned that the Germans had never dropped a bomb on the British shipyards. He said that perhaps I had better not put that clause in because the British might not want the Germans to know it. I replied that they know everything now, but if he didn't want me to put it in, of course, I wouldn't. I told him that I was for all aid to Britain short of going to war.

I told him I thought the Lend Lease Bill could be forced through by him but I thought it would leave a very bad taste; that it was a request for power that the American people would not grant unless they understood it better. He admitted that he has asked for a lot hoping to get something. He said, "Tinkham[8] says that I can give the Navy away under this Bill". "And, he added, I could stand on my head under this Bill if

5. On January 12 the recent Republican nominee had endorsed the Lend-Lease Bill provided a time limit be placed on the extensive powers that it proposed to grant the president. Congressional reaction to Willkie's stance had been mixed; few Republicans had followed his lead.

6. On January 15 Hull had argued that "[w]ere Britain defeated and were she to lose command of the seas, Germany could easily cross the Atlantic—especially the South Atlantic—unless we were ready and able to do what Britain is doing now."

7. Since his father's election in 1932, Elliott Roosevelt had been the subject of ongoing criticism focusing on his position as manager of some of the Hearst radio interests and his divorce and rapid remarriage in 1933. The press's derision had reached a new tenor in late 1940, however, when Elliott had been commissioned a captain in the Air Corps Reserve despite bad eyesight and a lack of aviation experience.

8. The isolationist Republican representative of the Tenth Massachusetts District, George Holden Tinkham (1870–1956).

I wanted to, but I don't propose to do either." I said "That's one of the difficulties the country worries about — they are not sure that you want to keep out of war." He replied "I have said it 150 times at least. For the last seven years I have been going to get them into every war that has taken place in Europe and I haven't done it yet." (I didn't think then that this was a very effective argument but said nothing). He added "I have no intention of going to war." (I don't know whether it was due to my own suspicions but it sound as convincing as it did before when he said that same thing [sic]).

I said that I thought it most important that the fellows on our side (Democrats) make amendments to the Bill rather than have them forced by the opposition which would then give the opposition too much strength. He told me he was willing to accept the amendment by old Jim Wadsworth which permitted a joint committee of the House and Senate to keep posted on what was going on. He pointed out to me that the Constitution set up the President as the executive officer; therefore the power could not be delegated to a Congressional body. However, on a thing like this he said he was willing provided the Committee was not too big so that everything he told them would not be in the newspapers the next day.

I asked him if he had made up his mind as to the man he would send to England and he said that since Bevin and that group were becoming very powerful there, it might be well to send somebody over there who spoke their language. And he had in mind sending Winant, former governor of New Hampshire, but people have told him he would have to study very hard to go into the Bevin class.[9] He added that he thought of sending Averell Harriman as minister who could talk production problems with their executives.[10] Personally, I don't know what training he has for that sort of job.

Then he said that the State Department wanted him to send Messersmith.[11] At this I hollered "Murder!" As I thought it would be a disgrace to send him over there and, in addition, I thought it a very serious blow against Johnson[12] who was there now and had done a good job. "Why not raise him to the rank of Minister" I asked. He said he thought that a good idea and said that Britain had two ministers there was no reason we couldn't. Then he said "I thought I would send Tony[13] over as Ambassador at large to represent us in London with Belgium, Norway, Denmark and Holland." I said that I didn't think Tony would accept it. I told him of a talk I had had with him last week when this subject had been considered and he said he wasn't interested and was considering going into politics in Pennsylvania. He asked, "What do you think he will do in that?" I replied "I don't know, but understand that he has 350,000 Polish votes pretty solidly behind him and that's a good start. He replied, "That is but a step — After all, we picked out the rich man, Earle, and made him Governor and while administratively he did well, he made rather a sad record."[14] So I got the impression that the president is not very highly in favor of Tony's going into Pennsylvania politics.

9. The president had appointed John Gilbert Winant (1889–1947), a moderate Republican sympathetic to labor, director of the International Labor Organization in Geneva in 1935. The president would appoint the former governor and U.S. senator to be JPK's successor as ambassador to the Court of St. James's on February 11, 1941.
10. Railroad heir, investment banker and Union Pacific chairman of the board, William Averell Harriman (1891–1986). A former Republican, Harriman had served as special assistant administrator of the NRA in 1934 and was currently chief of the raw materials branch of the Office of Production Management. In March 1941, the president would appoint him special representative to Great Britain and the Soviet Union (with the rank of minister) in order to expedite the implementation of the Lend-Lease Act.
11. The former assistant secretary of state was currently serving as ambassador to Cuba.
12. The counselor of the embassy was currently acting U.S. ambassador in London.
13. Biddle.
14. George Howard Earle III (1890–1974), the current U.S. minister to Bulgaria. A former Republican, Earle had switched party affiliations and made substantial contributions to the Roosevelt campaign af-

We then talked about Father Drought of the Maryknoll Fathers[15] who had come to see me with a plan that might be of some help in straightening out the Japanese situation. Father Drought said that he could get personal authorization from the Japanese Prime Minister, which would permit him to talk with the President provided it did not go through the State Department, and he thought the plan he had in mind would adjust the situation. The President evinced great interest in it and said he would like to see him Tuesday. He asked me to make an appointment. He seemed very anxious to work out something with the Japanese. And contrary to the impression gathered from Hull's public speeches he thought Japan entitled to Manchuria and thought they should have access to the oil in Java and Sumatra.

He was pleased with his talk on Wheeler and said he thought everybody realized that he used the wrong consonant when he said "dastardly".[16]

I told him that I couldn't understand the British sheet[17] and he said he was disgusted with them too. He said they had been telling him they could only pay their bills through March, but when pressed harder admitted they could pay through the year.

He said that his reports from Germany were most mixed up. From one side he hears that the German morale is very high and then he hears that they want only peace. He said that one of the funniest statements he heard was that the Germans would stick to Hitler as long as he stayed lucky. He didn't convince me that he hadn't a grave doubt as to the English people staying in the fight, but nothing definite he said gave that impression.

I told him that it was too bad that all the fine jobs like Stimson's, Patterson's,[18] Knox's and Forestall's,[19] had to be given to fellows who didn't bear much of the brunt of his campaign. He said that the difficulty was, unfortunately, there were no good administrators among the Democrats and pointed out to me that he is now going away out to California for a fellow named Pauley of whom he had never heard, but who built up a small business like a 15 million dollar one, to be an aid to Patterson in the War Department.[20]

He told me that he would like to have a long talk with me about the Irish situation, merely repeating what Welles had said to me that I was the only one who could straighten out the Irish problem. That was all that was said on the subject.

We talked about Jimmy and the fact that he would have to be careful about losing too much money in the moving picture business. He said that he would talk with him and then talk with me later.

---

ter meeting FDR through Biddle in 1932. In 1933 Earle was appointed U.S. minister to Austria, returning to the U.S. the following year to run as a Democrat in the Pennsylvania gubernatorial race with the backing of Pittsburgh bosses Joseph Guffey and David Lawrence. In 1938, Earle and his administration would face charges of corruption that overshadowed the successes of his "little New Deal," thus effectively ending his hopes of election to the U.S. Senate.

15. The Very Reverend James Matthew Drought (1896–1943), vicar-general of the Roman Catholic Foreign Mission Society.

16. During a radio debate on January 12, the leading Senate isolationist, Burton Kendall Wheeler (1882–1975) of Montana, had declared that the Lend-Lease Bill would stand to "plow under every fourth American boy." On January 14 Roosevelt responded angrily that he found the statement to be "the most untruthful, . . . most dastardly, unpatriotic thing that has ever been said."

17. The British balance sheet, that is.

18. Former Second Circuit Court of Appeals Judge Robert Porter Patterson (1891–1952) had become undersecretary of war in 1940.

19. Undersecretary of the Navy James Vincent Forestall (1892–1949) would succeed Knox as secretary in 1944.

20. Self-made oil magnate Edwin Wendell Pauley (1903–1981) would become petroleum coordinator for the administration of Lend-Lease supplies to Britain and the Soviet Union later in 1941.

His whole attitude was very friendly. I said numerous times that I couldn't understand why so many people were so anxious about our not being friends. He said he paid no attention to this, but he wouldn't have been human if he hadn't.

He told me that he was about an hour late on his appointments, but when I talked with Early, he said the President had come back from our meeting very happy and pleased with our talk and didn't care how late he was with the appointments. I asked Steve who it was who was so anxious to cause trouble and he said, "Oh, there are a lot of 'kissers' around here who go out of their way to start rumors thinking they can get in — termites — he called them." "But, he added, if there is anything you want me to do let me know."

After I left the President I went over to see Hull. I told him of my talk with the President and he seemed more than delighted at my remarks about the Democrats getting positions.

He said he knew nothing about the bill but did think they could have gotten four or five men around the President to print a bill that would have had everything the President needed and all this trouble could have been avoided.

He had telephoned me before I went to see the President and said he had talked with the President and told him that a limitation on money was most important. The President said that Hull had talked with him about that and he had agreed with the "old man".

Hull said that if I was going to make a speech not to break down the psychology by being tough.

He said in talking with Norway at 8:19 Hitler had given instructions for the best broadcasting man to leave for Paris that he had a most important announcement to make. This man went to Paris accompanied by Schreiber, [*sic*] American announcer for Berlin.[21] They waited for the announcement but it never came. It was probably an announcement to the effect that Laval would take over the government from Petain and turn it over to Germany. It did not come off and since then by our strong attitude we have built up a resistance in France that may be important.

He stated that it is quite true about the Japanese. If we show an inch of weakness their fleet would be on the way to the Dutch East Indies and Singapore.

I said that I did not entirely agree with the invasion of America and he said one of the countries in South America might go bad. "Well, I said, if that's true we'll have to go down and beat the hell out of them before Germany can land troops — if this country is going to take a tailspin at the mere mention of Hitler's name we had better close up right now."

I saw Burton Wheeler in the afternoon. He was delighted because Roosevelt had talked because he thought they were making headway and he was going to fight to the bitter end on the Bill which he thought represented public opinion.

The Sunday night before Harry Hopkins went to Europe he came to the Waldorf to see me. I gathered from his conversation that the President was displeased with the way England was acting toward America about the war situation and Trinidad and the bases, and I felt strongly (as I do when talking with Roosevelt) that he is not sold on the British at all. I don't think Hopkins is any regular man. I think he will just go over there like Willkie.

---

21. He refers, apparently, to journalist William Lawrence Shirer (1904–1993), who had been broadcasting from Europe for CBS since 1937 and whose *Berlin Diary* would be published later that year.

When we were discussing the question of British government spending I told the President that Bevin admitted to me the day he had lunch with me that he had gone to the British Cabinet and said, "Never mind the present policy; we are trying to find out where to spend it; let's go out and spend and put the responsibility up to America." I told him that Beaverbrook had told me that this thing had happened and Beaverbrook admitted there was no other policy to follow. The President said, "Would you trust either of them?" I said, "Well, not too much but I would have much more confidence in Beaverbrook than in what any one else told me, but I would always be gun-shy of both of them."

Joseph P. Kennedy to John Boettiger

Palm Beach, Feb. 10, 1941

Dear John:

I am terribly sorry that we didn't get together while you were here. I would so have liked to had a chance to talk with you, but evidently you were in Washington all the time I was in New York and as my visit to Washington was only one day and that a very busy one, I missed everybody.

I am more than appreciative of your letter because you show what I have always known you possessed an understanding of the other fellow's point of view. When I saw the President the other day before I made my radio speech I told him that I had been put in a most unenviable position, in fact he added that it was the truth that both sides were attacking me, and I told him then I had to clear my position; and if I had fallen into this state on my own account it might have been different, but I hadn't, his hatchet men were great contributors toward my difficulty.

I also said that I didn't think it was fair to wind up seven years of service in his Administration with a bad record and I had gone in for everything he wanted and this time I had to do something for the Kennedy family. I tried to be as fair as I could as the testimony before the House Committee and if you read it sometime you will be convinced that under the circumstances I got out quite well.[22]

Now, if my statements and my position mean that, outside of the ever-loyal Boettigers, I am to be a social outcast by the administration, well so be it. I will be sorry but if that's the way it is, it's just too bad. I will, at least, have the satisfaction of having fulfilled all my obligations.

At any rate, I am delighted that you and Anna were sweet enough to send me a note and I appreciate it more than I can tell you.

I do not look forward with any great hope for our future but I am convinced that a country as great as ours can do lots better than anybody thinks we can do if we unite and put our shoulders to the wheel and boy, we are going to have to do it to come out of this mess with anything but grief.

My love to you both.

As always,
Joseph P. Kennedy

---

22. In the course of five hours of testimony (which many regarded as rambling and equivocal), JPK had reiterated his views on aid to Britain and American involvement in the war before the House Foreign Affairs Committee on January 21.

Rose Kennedy to Joseph P. Kennedy

S. S. Brazil Tuesday [May 13, 1941]

Joe dearest,

Well, here I am on the go again, and I must be a gypsy at heart, because I do get such a thrill out of it all, no matter how uncomfortable I may be — which was the case yesterday where I felt the reaction from my typhoid inoculations.[23]

The boat is comfortable. The food good. Neither compares with the European travel standards of the old days. But there is no vibration so we can read & sleep with no quivering and quaking, and that is a joy on a long trip. We three have made up our minds to the long cruise idea of 12 days, and we do not find it monstrous at all, but on the contrary, relaxing and restful to realize that we can do absolutely nothing. The group aboard is disappointing — none of those sleek Latins, — men or women, but just stocky — swarthy pater familiases & the maters. We girls took one look & are resigned to a health cruise, but we are never going to tell of our chagrin, but pretend to P. Beach that it is all a secret.

I talked to a priest who was quite illuminating about the country at BA, & I am to meet the wife of the Chinese minister to-day, who knows Mme. Khang Kai-chek [sic] well.[24] If Eunice or I inquired about the celebrities aboard the first day or so, the answer was usually: "I hear Mme. K- is here with a couple of her daughters." — which always makes it so difficult to wear my old clothes in case I ever was considering the idea.

Mrs. Simpson at Barbadoes is going to entertain us to-morrow, and if we are lucky, we are going to have flying fish for lunch. Think what you all are missing! We are also taking lessons in the Conga & Rhumba. We were going to take Spanish, but as we had not time for all the attractions — I decided the Conga was more practical.

Be sure to look at the little house & order the piazza twice the ordinary length so there is room for a reclining chair. Much — much love darling & give all the children a hug & kiss for me.

Rosa

My fur cape is unsatisfactory — ask Paul if I send it back by air — is insurance O.K. Jaeckel is not so generous since Richard has gone & I want no disaster. Write me Rio —

Joseph P. Kennedy: *Diary*

July 7, 1941

Monday afternoon saw Frank Murphy — said the President had been sending for him and wanted him to be Attorney General but that the Palace Guard of Ickes, Frankfurter, Corcoran, and Hopkins did not want him as such even though they had hoped to get him off the Bench.

He said Black hated Frankfurter. On the morning of Hughes' resignation Frankfurter passed him a note while on the Bench — Jackson Chief Justice.[25]

Murphy said he knew Roosevelt had promised Jackson the job so he felt that Roosevelt realized the difficulties of his present situation by doing 3 things:

1. Sending for Murphy

---

23. She and Eunice had embarked on a tour of South America; they would meet Jack in Rio de Janeiro.
24. The Protestant, Wellesley-educated sociologist, director of the Chinese New Life Movement and wife of the Nationalist Chinese president, Madame Mayling-Soong Chiang Kai-shek (1899–).
25. Chief Justice Charles Evans Hughes (1862–1948), former governor of New York, 1916 Republican presidential candidate and secretary of state under Harding, had retired on July 1 to be replaced by Associate Justice Harlan Stone. The president had appointed former Attorney General Jackson an associate justice in June 1940.

2. Turning down Jackson.

3. ?

The Frankfurter group trying to shake Hull out and put in Bullitt, Patterson, or Acheson as Secretary of State.

Hoover told Murphy he had placed the affidavits on Roosevelt's desk on Welles' improper relations with nigger porters.[26]

The four men who followed me to Europe:

Hopkins[27] had a Jew wife and 2 Jew children. *Harriman* a Jew wife. *Cohen* a Jew.[28] *Fahey* — lawyer — a Jew mother.[29]

Frankfurter has control of Justice and War. His relation with Stimson over a long period.

Ickes wants to be Mayor of Chicago, hence he got Knox in. He asked Murphy to help him.

Roosevelt thinks Hopkins [is] doing great job. He is tired and no longer keen.

Murphy doesn't want to get out of public life hence he does not want to become Attorney General because he figures all Democrats will be licked 3 years from now.

Joseph P. Kennedy, Jr., 26, to Rose Kennedy and Joseph P. Kennedy

U.S. Naval Air Station, Jacksonville, Florida, Friday [September 5(?), 1941]

Dear Mother and Dad:

I have just finished my first two weeks of what is known as indoctrination. The purpose of this course is to teach you something about the Navy. You read about the makeup of the various fleet[s], battle dispositions, the positions held by the various men, in fact as much as you can in two weeks about the entire navy. The purpose is to make you a naval officer as well as a flyer, and they do a pretty good job in a short time. We have about eight hours of classes, and then at night we have to prepare our stuff just like at school. At the end of the week we have quizzes on it. It is not terribly difficult, but there is a terrific amount of stuff to cover. I think I got through it pretty well. We also have had three hours of marching a day, which was rather difficult to take, and then we got marked on this. There is one thing about this Navy in that they keep a record of every time you make a move. Every mark you ever get, anything you ever do, all goes into your record.

We don't get out at all during the week for the next four weeks, however, you don't mind it much, as you have so much work to do. To add to this however, I have a watch tomorrow night, which is Sat. night, and must stand watch till midnight. I am going out on a yacht on Sunday, which will be pretty nice.

We start flying the 1st of December. They have started a new policy down here, of flunking out one of three, which makes me rather doubtful. About 80% of the boys here have done quite a bit of flying before they came in.

26. In the early morning hours of September 18, 1940, a number of Pullman porters would later attest to FBI agents, the undersecretary of state had offered money for sexual acts aboard the presidential train during the return trip to Washington from Speaker Bankhead's funeral in Alabama.

27. Hopkins had been put in charge of implementing the Lend-Lease program in March 1941. In that capacity he had traveled to England in mid-July to report on the program's progress. He had conferred with the king and the war cabinet, and offered immediate aid to Soviet Russia, which had been invaded by German forces on June 22.

28. Cohen, one of the principal drafters of the Lend-Lease Bill, had been sent to London as a legal adviser at the American Embassy in order to facilitate the program's implementation.

29. As assistant solicitor general, Charles Harold Fahey (1892–1958) had helped negotiate the destroyers-for-bases deal in 1940. He would be appointed solicitor general in November 1941.

When are you coming south? No word has come through as to how long we will get for Xmas, and I suppose it depends somewhat on the international situation. Last year, they got about 5 days to a week. They let half the station off for Xmas, and the other half for New Years. Thus it looks like I will be home for either one or the other, but not for both.

Dave Gardner came down from Atlanta yesterday, and I am delighted. I only wish Tom Killefer could get over here, but there doesn't look like there is much chance for it.

Some one sent me some brownies and cookies, and they were excellent. If it was Margaret let me know, and I will write her a letter.

If Dad has any of those spare Dunhill pipes around, I wish he would send me one. Also how about that check for the typewriter?

That's about all the news around these parts. If any of the family were going to be together at any time, I would call. I can be reached by phone any evening except Sat and Sun, before nine o'clock at bldg. 70I down here.

Love

Joe

Joseph P. Kennedy to Kathleen Kennedy, 21

1941 SEP 14

WHEN I WAS IN PRIVATE BUSINESS I ALWAYS HAD A SIGN ON MY DESK WHICH READ AFTER YOU'VE DONE THE VERY BEST YOU CAN THE HELL WITH IT ANYWAY I AM PROUD OF YOU FOR TRYING ALL KINDS OF GOOD LUCK LOVE=

DAD

Kathleen Kennedy, 21, to Joseph P. Kennedy

Times Herald, Washington, D C. October 20, 1941[30]

Dear Daddy,

I have just had lunch with Dinah Brand[31] and I am nearly going mad. She said that everyone she say [saw?] sent all sorts of messages to me and that there just never been [*sic*] such a missed girl as I am. I am so anxious to go back that I can hardly sit still. I received a letter from Andrew and Debo[32] pleading with me to come back and save Billy[33] from Sally Norton[34] who apparently has got him in the bag. No one wants him to marry her and all told Dinah to tell me to come back and save him. Apparently they are going to announce it in Jan. I haven't heard from him for simply ages and that no doubt is the reason. Offie says he could fix the visa up

Love and kisses

Kick —

---

30. Kathleen had recently begun work as the assistant to the executive editor, Frank Campbell Waldrop (1905–1997), at Cissy Patterson's *Times Herald*.
31. Lady Astor's niece, the daughter of Robert Henry (later first baron) Brand and the former Phyllis Langhorne of Virginia.
32. Lord Andrew Robert Buxton Cavendish (1920–), later the eleventh duke of Devonshire, had married the Honourable Deborah Vivien Freeman Mitford (1920–), the youngest of the second Baron Redesdale's famous daughters six months earlier.
33. *I.e.*, the ninth marquess of Hartington, William John Robert Cavendish (1917–44), heir to the duke of Devonshire and Andrew Cavendish's elder brother.
34. The Honourable Sarah Katherine Elinor Norton (1920–), Lady Mountbatten's goddaughter and the only daughter of the sixth Baron Grantley, had come out with Kick and Debo Mitford in 1938.

Kathleen Kennedy, 21, to Joseph P. Kennedy

Times Herald, WASHINGTON, D. C., Wednesday

Dear Daddy,

Enclosed you will find latest contribution from your Washington correspondent. Hope this is clearer.

Received letter from Billy last night. He said he was engaged and that apparently he had quite a tough time with his parents as they did not think that the Nortons were respectable enough. The Duchess[35] and Mrs. Norton had a tremendous fight but things have settled down and they are going to announce it in Dec. Some of the quotes from the letter: "I have never been engaged before, thanks to you." "It was a very long time before I gave up all hope of marrying you." "What sense of humor I have I owe to you." "Please keep writing," etc. Rather sad, don't you think?

The cocktail party was a great success and quite a number of people showed up and everyone seemed to have a very good time. Jack went to the Fight For Freedom with Page[36] last night. He is coming to dinner tonight as Miss McCammon puts on such a nice meal. He is thinking of making a deal with her of coming twice a week. A good idea .

Mr. Waldrop and the City Editor came to the party. Every one said it was a great surprise as Mr. Waldrop rarely goes to Parties

How did you like Mrs. Heffron? Going to Middleburg Sat. for some races and a dance with George Meade.

Love to all
Kick

Joseph P. Kennedy to Franklin Roosevelt: *Telegram*

DECEMBER 7, 1941

DEAR MR. PRESIDENT. IN THIS GREAT CRISIS ALL AMERICANS ARE WITH YOU. NAME THE BATTLE POST. I'M YOURS TO COMMAND

JOE KENNEDY

Joseph P. Kennedy: *Diary*

January 7, 1942

Approximately a day before New Year's I received a wire from John F.,[37] saying that he had talked with John McCormack and he was going to have a real talk with the President about calling me back on the Defense Program. On receipt of this wire, the day after New Year's, I called McCormack's office in Washington. He wasn't there. Neither was his secretary, but I left a memorandum with the girl in the office in which I said that I appreciated Mr. McCormack's interest, also Mr. Fitzgerald's and I didn't want to appear ungrateful, but I definitely did not want McCormack to speak to the President

---

35. Billy's mother, the duchess of Devonshire, the former Lady Mary Alice Gascoyne-Cecil, daughter of the fourth marquess of Salisbury.
36. *Times Herald* reporter, Paige Huidekoper, a friend and contemporary of Kathleen's, who had worked at the embassy in London during JPK's tenure.
37. His father-in-law.

about me — that I had already sent him a wire on the Sunday the Japs bombed Hawaii and had offered my services in any capacity he could use them. And since he knew my work, knew me, and knew I was available, the President was the one to decide as to whether or not he wanted me. I wrote John F. along the same lines.

On last Monday (January 5) I received the following telegram:

"ANXIOUS TO HAVE TALK WITH YOU. SUGGEST YOU CALL ME AS SOON AS POSSIBLE".
(signed) John W. McCormack

I called McCormack immediately and this is the gist of his conversation: He, Barclay, Wallace, and Rayburn were at the White House getting ready for the President's speech on the following day. When the conference was over he had a chance to talk with the President alone and while he had received my telephone communication, nevertheless, he had taken it upon himself to talk with the President about me. He told the President that he was speaking entirely on his own initiative, but hoped the President was contemplating calling me back on the Defense Program. McCormack said that he had seen me the Monday before when I was in Washington to see the children and he was convinced that the real affection I had always for Roosevelt was still there, and he thought the President needed me. The President at once replied that as far as he was concerned personally he had a great affection for me, but I was of course a tough Irishman and very stubborn. Also, that he was very much surprised to find out that I was practically the only important man in the country who had not sent a wire to him offering his services in this emergency.

McCormack said, "Why, Mr. President, that can't be true because I saw in the papers from word given out by the White House that a telegram had been received from Joe in which he offered his services. And I have reason to believe that Joe got a letter of acknowledgment from Steve Early." The President replied, "I can't understand that at all — I shall look into it at once." And made a note on paper.

Then McCormack said, "Of course, I never say anything about my talks with you, but how do you feel about my telling this to Joe?" The President replied, "By all means tell him." "And with that in mind, said McCormack, I am calling you."

Also, he suggested my writing a letter to the President telling him about my telegram and offering my services, suggesting that I might go to see him. I immediately told McCormack that I didn't think that the right thing to do. I said, "I have already offered my services. The record is there and if I did ask to go and see him and sat down with him, I wouldn't know what to take up with him or what to say. Again, I think his time too valuable to spend in dilly dallying."

McCormack kept urging me but I made no commitments whatsoever. John F. kept urging me saying that after all Roosevelt was Commander-in-Chief and that we must do everything possible to win the war. I said, "There's no doubt about that, but I want to do the thing the right way." At any rate, I left it hanging fire, but when I hung up I had definitely decided not to write.

(See date of December 7, 1941 for copy of Mr. Kennedy's telegram to President and copy of Mr. Early's reply dated December 9, 1941)

Rose Kennedy to Robert Kennedy, 16

[Palm Beach] January 12, 1942

Dear Bobby:

I was so disappointed in your report, which I shall send you later. The mark in Christian Doctrine was very low and I wrote to Mr. Brady[38] about it, as certainly in a Catholic school you should be taught that above everything else and you should apply yourself to that subject.

I have kept your report to show to Dad, as it arrived very late due to our failure to notify Mr. Brady of our change of address. As soon as your Dad has seen it I will send it to you.

Please get on your toes. After all, you might as well do a good job in your school-work as well as every place else. You have a good head and certainly you ought to use it. You owe it to yourself as well as to me to make the most of your advantages. Remember, too, that it is a reflection on my brains as the boys in the family are supposed to get their intellect from their mother, and certainly I do not expect my own little pet to let me down.

I hope your father got up to see you, but I did not have a chance to ask him yesterday.

Rose Kennedy to Robert Kennedy, 16

January 12, 1942

Dear Bobby:

I really think it would be a very good idea if you went to dancing school in Providence. I know that you loathe them, but after watching the children the other night, I can see where practice every week would make a lot of difference in your confidence and in your dancing ability.

I feel that unless it handicaps your studying, you really should go for the next few months and I am writing a letter to Mr. Brady, suggesting it. However, I shall leave it to your judgment to make the final decision as I realize that Providence is quite a distance from the school and it may be difficult or out of the question.

Joseph P. Kennedy: *Diary*

[New York] January 17, 1942

Beaverbrook said that because of the conditions of the fleet after the result of the bombing in Pearl Harbor,[39] the fleet was going to be moved from the Atlantic to the Pacific where it would be about the middle of February. (I checked on this with Joe Patterson who told me he had said to Beaverbrook that he understood out of a fleet which numbered 8, 3 ships of our Pacific Fleet were sunk and 4 were badly damaged, which practically put the Pacific Fleet out of commission. Beaverbrook would neither confirm nor deny this, but intimated that Joe wasn't far wrong with the additional comment that 250 of our planes had been destroyed.)

38. Headmaster of Portsmouth Priory School.
39. The secretary of state for Air was currently in New York and, like JPK, was staying at the Waldorf-Astoria.

However, in view of Secretary Knox's statement that Hitler was the real enemy I don't know whether or not this can be true unless Knox is trying to fool the Germans into thinking that the Fleet is still going to be left in the Atlantic. I should imagine though that they would have to go through the Canal, and if so, the Germans will have some evidence of it.

Beaverbrook considered our position very serious. He looked for bombings on the West Coast. Also, in the East, but here he expected "token bombings." He said we had practically no defense and no anti-craft guns.

I asked him if there was any chance of his staying. He said he didn't think so because Churchill did no want him to leave his side. As an instance, he cited the time it was agreed Beaverbrook should go to Russia as an English representative and Churchill got nervous and almost insisted that he stay in England.

He said that when my name was mentioned in his discussions with Roosevelt he always told him of the great affection he held for me. Beaverbrook said at the time of the August meeting between Churchill and Roosevelt it was practically admitted by Roosevelt that I was an important factor in his re-election.[40]

Beaverbrook asked me with that baby stare of his how Hopkins and I got along. I replied, "All right as far as I know", but I am convinced that he knew it's Hopkins who is keeping my services from being employed, and he just wanted to know my re-action. When he said he was going to look into the matter when he went to Washington I asked him not to because they are very well aware of what I can do and that I am ready and willing to do it — and that's all that's needed.

He is disappointed at our production and amazed at our complacency. He urged Patterson and me to point out to the American people that it is possible for us to lose, with a view to arousing them to real action.

He was convinced that England would not be bombed very much more, because he said the last time the Germans sent 200 bombers over Liverpool, 36 were brought down, and no country could stand that kind of punishment. There ran through all of his conversation the confidence that whatever Britain did was superior. How he can feel that way in the face of everlasting criticism of their policy of their army and navy and their production, is beyond me. But that's what makes them what they are. He pointed out to me very, very carefully that as far as *Great Britain* was concerned they had delivered to Russia everything they had promised, and the inference was very plain that the United States had done no such thing.

Clare Luce told me yesterday that the oil man (her friend in Washington) said that Hopkins had practically given the Russians everything connected with our oil refinery processes, which would permit the Russians to have everything we now have when they cease to be our allies. Also, that we had agreed to lay oil pipelines through Iraq and Iran. And after the war is over, no matter in what tough shape the British are now, they would have their eye on that trade.

When Patterson left, Beaverbrook told me that Roosevelt had told him Patterson was taken back into the fold, and added as a matter of great interest, "You know Patterson has become a Roman Catholic" and that may be the cause for a lot of things. Patterson told me when I went to lunch with him the following day that Beaverbrook

40. From August 9 to 11 Churchill, Roosevelt and a number of high British and American government and military officials had met on board ship off the coast of Newfoundland in order to formulate the Atlantic Charter, a "joint declaration of broad principles " which were to guide each nation's "policies along the same road."

had told him the same thing and added that he wished he could go back wholeheart-edly, but since he was divorced from them, he couldn't.

When I returned from Lisbon, I got the impression that deep down in his heart Roosevelt had a decidedly anti-Catholic feeling. And what seems more significant is the fact that up to this time he has not appointed a prominent Catholic to any important post since a year ago last November. This seems to tie in with the observations I made in my diary notes when I met him the night of my return. Charles Driscoll the Columnist[41] told me that Alice Longworth[42] said her father, although a great friend of Archbishop Ireland, was anti-Catholic, and this feeling was firmly imbedded in the Roosevelt family.

Doris Fleason, in off-the-record notes taken at the time Churchill was in Canada, had it that Darlan[43] would like to give up the French Fleet, but the officers and men wouldn't submit. That Typhus was prevalent in the German Army. That Hess had wound madness and had come to England with a peace proposal saying that Hitler was not unfriendly to England.[44] That Hess had once met the Duke of Hamilton when he was Steward to the King (one who poured the King's wines) and in that way could get the proposal over. Hess was very incensed with the treatment he had received when he felt he had come to do England a good turn. Churchill had every intention of fortifying the places open to German and Italian attack, but couldn't do it due to lack of men and supplies. For this reason they chose Libya rather than Singapore because they thought they could drive them out of Africa in short time. At present it looks like a wrong guess by Churchill.

After my conversations with Clare Luce (who had been in Washington and contacted all the important people) and with Joe Patterson (who had had many talks with Beaverbrook) I am thoroughly convinced that the British have taken over Roosevelt. It is not at all likely that by spring if the Russians have not made peace with Germany, they will serve notice on England and America for more men and equipment. And when we have no more supplies and men, trouble will result. In addition, if we continue to be divided in the Pacific, it will be possible that China (if she hears through Knox that Germany is the real enemy) will make a deal with the Japs, and that will be bad.

I still have very little confidence in the business ability of Churchill and Roosevelt to decide these terrific matters. When you consider the Japanese situation, our attitude toward them, and that Roosevelt knows they have been preparing for 20 years, our unpreparedness is nothing short of insanity.

41. Charles Benedict Driscoll (1885–1951), the late O. O. McIntyre's successor as author of the popular syndicated "New York Day by Day" column.
42. Alice Lee Roosevelt Longworth (1884–1980), columnist, eldest daughter of Theodore Roosevelt and widow of the former speaker of the House, Nicholas Longworth.
43. (Jean Louis Xavier) François Darlan (1881–1942), deputy premier of the Vichy government, 1941–42, and former commander in chief of the French Navy, 1939–40.
44. As Germany prepared to invade the Soviet Union on the afternoon of May 10, 1941, Hitler's intimate, Nazi Party leader (Walter Richard) Rudolph Hess (1894–1987), had taken off alone in a Messerschmitt 110 and flown to Scotland. Upon bailing out and landing, Hess demanded that the farmer who found him take him to the duke of Hamilton, whom Hess had met in Berlin at the 1936 Olympics. Hess informed Hamilton that he was "on a mission of humanity and that the Fuerher did not want to defeat England and wished to stop the fighting." The party leader had been imprisoned briefly in the Tower of London before being transferred to a mental institution, where he would remain until his trial and life sentence at Nuremberg in 1946.

John F. Kennedy, 24, to Rose Kennedy

WASHINGTON, D.C.[45]

Dear Mother:

I enjoy your round-robin letters.[46] I'm saving them to publish — that style of yours will net us millions. With all this talk about inflation and where is our money going — when I think of your potential earning power — with you dictating and Mrs. Walker beating it out on that machine — its enough to make a man get down on his knees and thank God for the Dorchester High Latin School which gave you that very sound grammatical basis which shines through every slightly mixed metaphor and each somewhat split infinitive.

Now, in regard to the chair, you can have any chair I've got. I've got two very nice brown ones which are in my living room — but if you want one I will send it down and move the very dark one from my bed room which will be fine. Just let me know — but, I'll keep it if you don't need it.

My health is excellent — I look like hell, but my stomach is a thing of beauty — as are you, Ma, — and you, unlike my stomach — will be a joy forever.

Love
Jack

Joseph P. Kennedy to Kathleen Kennedy, 21

[Palm Beach] January 26, 1942

Dear Kathleen:

Jack was here and had beautiful weather and the rest did him a great deal of good. We're waiting to hear from him as to what his plans are in Charleston and what they propose to do with him.[47]

Now that you've moved into the house, I want to make a suggestion. There are two things very essential for you to come out with from your experience in Washington. One is a general knowledge of things and people that you would probably not get anywhere else. Secondly, that you look well, and that can only be done by getting fresh air whenever you can and getting to bed early nights. You are only twenty-one and your type is very susceptible to fading very fast — and you wouldn't want to do that.

Why don't you just lay out a schedule for yourself and say — I'll go out not more than one night a week and have people in not more than one night a week and the rest of the time take care of ~~your~~ myself.

I don't want to preach, but I can assure you that this is the best advice I could give you.

Love
Dad

---

45. Since late October Ensign John F. Kennedy had been posted at the Office of Naval Intelligence in Washington, D.C.
46. In an effort to consolidate her correspondence during wartime, Rose began sending what she called "round-robin" letters (with slight variations, depending on the recipient) to each member of her scattered family.
47. On January 24, he had reported for duty at the District Security Office in Charleston, South Carolina.

Joseph P. Kennedy to David Sarnoff

PERSONAL *Palm Beach, February 2, 1942*

Dear David:

I've been thinking down here at Palm Beach — and there isn't much else to do outside of swim and play golf — that since my two boys are eventually going to make their homes in Massachusetts, if they get through this war successfully, I would be interested in purchasing any radio station that you might have for sale in Boston or Massachusetts.

I don't know whether you have one or whether you ever contemplated selling one separately, or whether the price you would have to get for it would be too great, but there is no harm in dropping you this note because my energy from now on will be tied up in their careers rather than my own.

I think of you often, working so effectively as you do, and feel rather badly that I'm such a loafer, but I can't interest myself in private business. Until I can be of some use in the war effort, I guess I'll just sit back.

Again with my warmest regards, I am

Sincerely yours,
Joseph P. Kennedy

Rose Kennedy: *Round-Robin Letter*

Palm Beach, February 16, 1942

Dear Children:

Joe and Jack do not seem to have any particular news other than what I told you last week. Jack finds his present post rather irksome as he does not seem to have enough to do and I think will be glad of a transfer if such is in the offing.

Kathleen has been transferred to the Play Department; that is, she has a column and is giving her opinion of plays and pictures. I am a little confused as to whether it is both or one, but anyway, that is the general idea. My suggestion would be that she have a *nom de plume*. My second suggestion would be that she have a decent picture taken, but she and her father seem to think both of these matters are okay. She is quite thrilled at the idea of people watching for her column and I am quite crushed to think that my three or four children got into print with works of their brains and I was never allowed to edit one little word. I believe it is the Bible which says — "The twig cannot be greater than the root from which it has sprung."

I have not heard a single word from Eunice. I suppose there is a letter coming in the slow way.

Clare Boothe went to Cairo on Friday. She was at Miami for a day or two, held up by motor trouble in the plane. I believe there were sixteen Generals with her scheduled for different parts of the fighting fronts. I understand she was going to South America and then to Africa, and I believe is going to be in a plane for about eight days before she arrives at her destination. She also had misgivings as to her reception in Cairo, as I believe TIME pictured King Farouk[48] in a rather inauspicious fashion last week. Your father spent several hours with her and enjoyed it thoroughly. Among other things, they planned to have Eunice and her daughter[49] make some arrangements for the Easter

---

48. Farouk I (1920–65), last reigning king of Egypt, 1936–52.
49. Anne Clare Brokaw (1920–1944), Clare Boothe Luce's only child from her first marriage, which had ended in divorce in 1929.

holidays. I believe they see one another frequently at Stanford. Harry is to go to London a little later at the invitation of Lord Beaverbrook. They stopped in at Harry Richman's in Miami, by the way. You remember how moved your dad used to become in London when Harry would sing — "Your Broadway and My Broadway." Those days now seem so happy and carefree.

Pat was to spend last weekend with Kathleen, and Kathleen is coming down over her birthday with Nancy Tenney, so we should have some news of Pat. I believe she says she never receives letters from any of you, but I know how busy you are and I try to give you all the news in this round robin affair. I also send copies to Grandpa and Eddie Moore, so please remember this when writing to them.

I should like Pat and Bobby to go away for the 22nd as they both have a long weekend. Perhaps they could go some place in the country for skiing and winter sports. I am a little envious of them myself as I always have a nostalgic feeling whenever I think of any winter resort.

Teddy is the same and is very busy. He assists at Mass and the Priest invited him to breakfast last Sunday. Teddy said he informed him that he had already had his breakfast with the Priest. I think he has put on the ten pounds which he lost at Riverdale. He dances very well, has remarkable rhythm, and shakes his head like a veteran when he does the conga. He only fell down once last week, so he is improving. He has a little dancing partner, just the proper height, and as they are the two youngest in the class, it is just as well that they prefer each other.

Dad seems quite well, although his knee has been bothering him and he has not been playing as much golf. He is working a little bit trying to straighten out the financial difficulties at St. Mary's Hospital, which are colossal. Mrs. Pierrepont is no longer here as she rented her house this year so she could be north with one of the boys.

Hugh Dillman and Mrs. Huntington are still raising money very successfully for the Good Samaritan and there is quite a bit of feeling I believe. Dad went to see Mr. Bradley yesterday afternoon as he is terribly impressed by the unselfishness and devotion of the Sisters, but he is flabbergasted and a bit disheartened by their woeful lack of knowledge of the financial responsibilities in connection with such an undertaking.

Miss Hennessey is still here, although I have not seen her. She was asking for London Jack, but dad is not expecting him down this year.

Miss Dunn bought a radio with the money we gave her so she seems to be quite settled. I thought perhaps the war would make a difference with her husband and that she might have to come East, but she seems to be all right.

The Dalys are still here but Jack has been feeling very low. I suppose his business has worried him a bit.

Grandpa and Grandma and Aunt Rose arrive on Tuesday, so we will probably never have a dull moment.

Lent will be here this week and I am glad to say they are going to have a nine o'clock Mass this year. I do not believe we will stay much after Easter as I am anxious to go west to see Eunice, but that is still a few weeks away yet.

Much love to you all and come down whenever you can.

Mother

Rose Kennedy to Joseph P. Kennedy, Jr., 26

February 19, 1942

Dear Joe:

I heard from your grandfather that you were not going to eat candy in Lent. I feel rather strongly that you should eat all the sweets which you like and can get as you have lost considerable weight and I don't think you should give up candy at this particular time, as it seems as though you need it.

My suggestion would be that you say a Rosary occasionally or stop a Coca-Cola or two. The church is also rather against having too many people give up candy as it puts a good many people out of work, so you can see it is quite as salutary for your soul to make sacrifices other than sweets.

This is just an idea, Joe, which I wanted you to realize. Anyway, you know I am thinking about you and always hoping that you are having the best possible break whether it is worldly or spiritual.

Grandpa was delighted to have seen you and we are all hoping that we shall see you here soon.

John F. Kennedy, 24, to Kathleen Kennedy, 22

March 2

To Kick:

Without meaning any criticism of your very excellent character, I have noted that with you, popular opinions are frequently accepted as true opinions. There is nothing particularly wrong in this, it's safe and you've got plenty of company, which you like. But I think you'll find that the majority are only occasionally well-informed and that your own judgment is frequently better, and will always be more "Christian than opinion is mans." So don't bum rides on other peoples opinions. It's lazy at best — and in some cases [*it's*] much worse.

Joseph P. Kennedy to Franklin Roosevelt

Palm Beach, March 4, 1942

My dear Mr. President:

I hesitate to take up your time to set forth the enclosed facts, but I feel that our relationship in the past certainly justifies my writing to you.

I tried to reach you on the phone on Monday, but they told me you were unavailable and that if I'd leave my number you would get in touch with me later on. Not having heard from you and knowing how very busy you are, I am taking the liberty of restating my position.

John McCormack told me some six or eight weeks ago of his talk with you and of your surprise at not having heard from me when war was declared. I hoped that when he told me you were going to look up the telegram I sent, you would find the record as McCormack outlined it. Since then I have heard indirectly from Alben Barkley, who said you were still of the same opinion. Therefore, I am taking the liberty of enclosing copy of my telegram which I sent on the Sunday of the Pearl Harbor attack, and a copy of Steve's answer to me.

I don't want to appear in the role of a man looking for a job for the sake of getting an appointment, but Joe and Jack are in the service and I feel that my experience in these critical times might be worth something in some position. I just want to say that if you want me, I am yours to command at any time.

With my warmest personal regards, I am

Very respectfully,
Joe Kennedy[50]

John F. Kennedy, 24, to Kathleen Kennedy, 22

District Security Office, Navy Yard, S. C. March 10, 1942

Dear Kick,

Enclosed find a letter I wrote to a disciple of the New Deal. The book was interesting though biased, and might be of some interest to you, or Betty, as it gives very clearly the attitude of mind of the ruling class of the Etats-Unis.

After reading the papers, I would advise strongly against any voyages to England to marry any Englishman. For I have come to the reluctant conclusion that it has come time to write the obituary of the British Empire. Like all good things, it had to come to an end sometime, it was good while it lasted. You may not agree with this, but I imagine that the day before Rome fell, not many people would have believed that it could *ever* fall. And yet, Rome was ready for its fall years before it finally fell, though people, looking only at it through the rosy tinted glasses of its previous history, couldn't and wouldn't see it.

It was the same way with France. She's been a second rate power ever since Sedan in the 1870's but it wasn't until May 1940 that its fundamental weaknesses could be seen, stripped naked without the protection of the rosy glasses and the mist of its Napoleonic tradition.[51]

It's the same with England. Singapore was only the symptom,[52] the cause goes back long before Chamberlain or Churchill. It goes back, I think, fundamentally, far beyond any special event. It goes back to a state of mind, really, which is a phase of its organic growth. When a nation finally reaches the point that its primary aim is to preserve the status quo, it's approaching old age. When it reaches the point where it is willing to sacrifice part of that status quo to keep the rest, it's gone beyond being old, it's dying — and that is the state of mind England reached some time ago. From a purely psychological viewpoint, the advantage that a country which is on the make, with not much to lose and plenty to win will have over a country like England, is obvious. In a war like today's, tradition and a way of life and a great past history are merely excess baggage that impedes movement, and make the way easy for the enemy. We've reached the same stage, ourselves. Of course, we are in a somewhat better position — we've got an old man's mentality, but unlike England, a young man's body, so we might pull through.

You might dispute the above, which is mostly theoretical. Well, look at it from a practical point of view. In the first place, any time the Prime Minister of a country will

---

50. On March 7 the president would respond, "[i]t is mighty good to get your letter and I am very certain I did not get your telegram of December seventh. This was probably because several thousand came in at the same time and were handled in the office without my ever seeing them." Roosevelt added that he was "of course, sure that [JPK] wanted to do everything possible to help," and suggested vaguely that the former assistant general manager of the Fore River Shipyard "could be of real service in stepping up the great increase in our shipbuilding—especially in getting some of the new production underway."

51. The battle of Sedan of September 1, 1870, marked Napoleon III's final defeat by the German army in the Franco-Prussian War.

52. On February 15 some seventy thousand British and Australian troops had been forced to surrender the port to Japanese forces.

admit to his own people that another country is going to save them— it's on the toboggan. The main ties that have kept the British Empire together in the past are the defensive, the financial, and what might be called the social ties, (in the latter, we might include common language, tradition, and all that other paraphernalia that the British have employed so successfully). Well, the first link, the defensive, finally snapped at Singapore. Do you think that the Australians will ever trust their national safety to a British cabinet in London again? Responsibility like that is only given to those who can handle it. The financial tie, with the British Empire already in hock to the United States can't possibly survive a war as tough as this is going to be.

The "social tie" went down for the last time with the rise of Sir Stafford Cripps[53] to power. He may only be a symbol, but he's red right down to his underwear, and the old school tie won't see much service in the future. That tie will be gone because any resemblance after this war to the English way of life or its technique in governing to what we know today will be purely coincidental. If we really fight this war through as we say we're going to, it will take such an effort that we'll never be able to turn the clock back. In addition, what gives manners and techniques their fashion is the success with which they are applied, and I'm afraid that the English will find it difficult to give living proofs of the success of their formula.

Now, those aren't very happy thoughts, are they? But it's good practice for my typewriter, and they're probably not right. I wouldn't bet that they weren't, though.

Love,

Joseph P. Kennedy to Franklin Roosevelt

Palm Beach, March 12, 1942

Dear Mr. President:

It gave me great joy and pleasure to receive such a nice reply to my note.

Of course, I will do any job that you want me to do. Yesterday upon receipt of your letter, I called Jerry Land[54] and asked him exactly what kind of a job he had in mind, what results he would expect, and what authority I would have to get the results. He was rather indefinite about it but said he would have a meeting yesterday and let me know today.

He has just called me on the telephone and said three things have occurred to him and his advisors. First, that I would start a new shipbuilding company. Second, that I would go around and help the management in four or five of the weak shipyards, and third, that a wage board would probably have to be set up in the country and that I would be a fine fellow to be chairman of it.

Now the first of these might have been practical ten months or a year ago, but it certainly isn't today and I don't want to get into private enterprise and have a relationship with the government. Secondly, a whole organization could be set up that would strengthen shipyard management, and it certainly wouldn't take me to do that. And the third seems to be really none of the shipping groups' business, so I don't think that for the time being there seems to be any position in this organization in which I could get you any real results.

---

53. The former Labour MP was currently British ambassador to the Soviet Union.
54. Rear Admiral Emory Scott Land (1879–1971), head of the War Shipping Administration and JPK's successor as chairman of the U.S. Maritime Commission, 1938–46. Land was a longtime friend of the president's and a cousin of Charles Lindbergh's.

I have watched this shipbuilding program very carefully and I realize that it won't make any difference how near the production of this country gets to your desires for thousands of aeroplanes and thousands of tanks if we do not have ships in which to transport them. And I am not at all sure that I am very far off when I say that while the program has done well to date, it may run into serious difficulty by the middle of the summer.

After I read your letter I hoped that what they contemplated was divorcing the shipbuilding construction from all the rest of the shipping program and just make that a full time job, but perhaps when things get tougher in the summer they may get around to seeing that possibility.

I think you know that if I am given a job cleanly and concisely I will work hard to get you the results you want, but running around without a definite assignment and authority, I'd just be a hindrance to the program.

It is a great satisfaction for me to know that you will use me if the proper occasion arises. I'll be there when it does.

With my warmest personal regards and appreciation, I am

Very respectfully yours,
Joseph P. Kennedy

Joseph P. Kennedy: *Diary*

April 10, 1942

Received a telegram from Joe Eastman.[55] Called him on 'Phone asked him what was nature of job. He told me he wanted me to take charge of all rubber transportation down to private auto. I said I'll be there.

I arrived Monday, April 13. He outlined job — according to papers in file. Definitely a rotten job in that I know nothing about transportation. Eastman admitted that and said Nelson and Henderson had both sidestepped it.[56]

I listened to the story and said I'd think it over and talk to him on Tuesday.

At the airport before I came in to see Eastman I had seen Max Truitt and decided to call up President and see if he would see me. I first tried to get Steve Early, who they said was out (he later told me he had gone to Bowie to see the races). Then I asked for Gen. Watson.[57] After some delay they said he was out (I wasn't convinced on this). Then I asked for Grace Tully. They said she had just gone in with President but her assistant would talk. I said, "Okay" and I proceeded to tell her that in his letter to me the President had said he had hoped to see me soon and therefore I was up to see Joe Eastman and was going home Tuesday, if he had a chance, I would like to see him. I realized he was terribly busy and I would quite understand if he couldn't see me. I would be at Max Truitt's office for an answer.

At 8 o'clock that evening Grace, very friendly, called up and said President would love to see me but as I was going Tuesday and he had a press conference and Pan American meeting, he had no time but if I was going to be here Wednesday — "Well", I said, "If he can see me Wednesday, I'll stay." "Fine", said Grace, "I'll let you know". Tuesday morning she telephoned. Said President would see me at 12:45 Wednesday.

55. Joseph Bartlett Eastman (1882–1944), director of Defense Transportation, 1941–43.
56. Donald Marr Nelson (1888–1959), chairman of the War Production Board, 1942–44. Leon Henderson (1895–1986), economist, and as director of the Office of Price Administration, 1941–42, the wartime "rationing czar."
57. Major General Edwin Martin "Pa" Watson (1883–1945) had replaced James Roosevelt as the president's secretary in 1939.

I later went to see Eastman and he showed me memorandum from White House signed by Coy[58] saying about as follows:

"I have spoken to the President about Joe Kennedy's becoming associated with you. He says it is perfectly satisfactory to him but he doubts if you can get him as he has been offered 2 jobs by the Maritime Commission and turned them down." I then explained to Eastman the President's letter to me and my letter back to him. I then told Eastman I would see him after I saw the President. (I'll leave out seeing and talking with other people until recount visit with Roosevelt).

At 12:35 I arrived at White House Gate where they have my name on list. The photographers were waiting. I went and asked for Steve. He was friendly as usual and I told him of Coy's note to Eastman. He advised clearing this up because he said he thought President had these 2 jobs in mind. We talked a little and President sent word at 12:45 he was ready to see me. Steve took me in through Grace's room and turned me over to Grace who opened door to President's office. Pa Watson was standing at his desk and President was writing a note in long hand to Stimson. I shook hands with Watson. The President smiled but made no attempt to shake hands. He said, "I've got to get this letter off to Stimson and I have to write everything in longhand because he gets all upset if he thinks any one sees anything." So President addressed the envelope in his own writing marking it private and confidential and then wetting the envelope with his tongue sealed it and told Watson to send it over. Then Watson had a memo. Evidently from Stimson saying he wanted to talk to President on matter he had neglected to talk to him about. President turned to me said, "I have fine Sec'y of War, but he talks so much when he's here." "Anyway", said President, "Tell him I can't see him."

Watson went out and President turned to me. He looked badly but his voice and manner were gay.

He started right off reminiscing about last war. Spoke very critically of way Navy did things then. Spoke of trying to get Sterling engine a try — Navy against. Finally got Army engineers to witness trials. This lead to general criticism of way Navy does things. Spoke of taking up old pipe and laying it across Florida for oil as he said he was going to stop tankers from going through Florida Straits because the loss was so great. He wasn't going to bother with Navy engineers as Army was so much better at getting things done. He was keen on old men down Maine making wooden tankers.

He said Navy had new combination of ship and plane knocking off sub. and started to tell me about in great secrecy, but I said, "If this isn't known please don't tell me because some time it might slip out". He acted surprised at this.

He then entered into a tirade against Pro-Nazi John O'Donnell kicking up the fuss about McArthur's command.[59]

Then he said that Cissy, Joe and Bertie[60] were a little crazy — they'd always been, he said. I said Beaverbrook and I thought he could get Joe back — that Joe was sore because when he called there after Pearl Harbor, Roosevelt had him in his office and kept him standing there for 15 minutes. Roosevelt got mad and said, "That's of course a damn lie. He sat right there (pointing to his left) and Steve sat over there."

58. Wayne Coy (1903–1957), special assistant to the president and liaison officer for the Office of Emergency Management, 1941–43, assistant Budget director, 1942–44, and future chairman of the FCC, 1947–52.

59. Columnist John Parsons O'Donnell's (1896–1961) unflagging vitriol toward the administration and the conduct of the war would prompt the president to award the *New York Daily News* Washington bureau chief the Nazi Iron Cross at a press conference eight months later.

60. That is, the Pattersons' cousin, Colonel McCormick of the *Chicago Tribune*, whose lifelong enmity toward Roosevelt was reputed to have begun at Groton, where the publisher had been a year ahead of the president.

"What really happened", he said, "Joe sent word he'd like to help after Pearl Harbor and he wanted to make up for his attacks before. Well, when he got here he didn't say a word about how sorry he was for what he had done but merely said he wanted to help — So I just lit into him and told him how much he was responsible for a lot of misunderstandings and when he denied this I suggested he read his own editorials of the 6 months preceding Pearl Harbor." (At this point I was sure he had not taken me back to the fold because remembering he hadn't shaken hands with me nor asked about the family, I was sure that dig "about not being sorry" went for me as well as Patterson.) (Well I'm not sorry, so to hell with it.)

I then managed to break into a long dissertation about how easy he was taking it. Now he only worked 1 night a week and didn't see anybody. "In fact," he said, "I don't work as hard now as I did before the war." (That to me is bunk.)

He spoke very disparagingly of Navy [sic] and said Jerry Land when asked by him this morning where he got the information he gave out that Navy was taking over the Merchant Fleet, Land said Admiral King[61] said so. Roosevelt said, "I called King and asked him about it and King said, "I never said that". "I said I was just making a study of the whole matter." Roosevelt said to me, "Things like this upset labor." (He certainly has this on his mind.)

I then went on to explain Eastman's proposition. He at once said that would be no good for me.

Then I referred to the 2 jobs that he said I had been offered. I took them up as I had in my letter to him:

1. Start a shipyard and he at once said that was foolish even to consider.

2. He said they had offered me a job to buck up all shipbuilding. I said, "Nuts, they had not but offered me 4 or 5 small yards as in my letter". He said he completely misunderstood that.

He said Jerry had no business to go up on hill and talk labor policy and then said the trouble with Land and Wiley was they had no imagination but Wiley was better than Land. I said they'd all asked for me and I knew them. He said then he had to talk to Jerry and work me into shipbuilding.

After I had again suggested splitting up shipping and shipbuilding, he said, "You won't mind what they give you for a title will you?" I said, "No, provided they give me the power". (In all this discussion he didn't act like he'd ever read my letter — I don't understand it.)

I stayed about 35 minutes and told the reporters when I came out (see papers).

I felt he called me because it was good politics. He had no friendly feeling and when I heard from Father Sheehy[62] later that *Farley* had been there 2 times and had notified the White House he was in town but they never noticed him. I was convinced he will put me to work not particularly to help the war effort, but to help his politics.

As Jesse Jones and Frank Murphy said, "He needs you damn bad politically — don't sell yourself cheap."

61. Admiral Ernest Joseph King (1878–1956), commander in chief of the U.S. fleet and chief of Naval Operations.
62. Maurice Stephen Sheehy (1898–1972), chaplain of the Naval Air Station at Jacksonville, where Joe Junior had been stationed.

Joseph P. Kennedy to William Randolph Hearst

Hyannisport, September 16, 1942

My dear W.R.:

Again I am writing you as I have so many times in the past twenty-five years to express my deep appreciation for your whole-hearted cooperation and kindness in things in which I have been interested.

We have just finished the campaign in Boston. Walter Howey and the boys on the papers were most kind to John F. We've had a lot of fun. We had a candidate — the only one we could get to run against Casey, the hand picked candidate of the administration — John F. Fitzgerald, eighty years old, out of politics for twenty odd years. Against him were all the Congressmen, ex-Mayor Curley, Mayor Tobin of Boston,[63] all of the government employees and W.P.A. workers who were put on the line, all those looking for contracts and commissions, and yet I'll be very much surprised if we don't make a very good showing. If Casey wins, I'm sure he won't be a majority candidate.[64]

John F. made all the speeches himself, covered the entire State, and was on the radio practically every day for three weeks. He made his fight completely on the inefficiency of the war effort, the bungling and the confusion in most everything they did in Washington, and spared the bureaucracy and the planning not a bit.

The magnificent support of the papers was the real helpful thing in the campaign, yet we never put them in the position of having to take a stand on any embarrassing subject or to write anything that wasn't in every news column in the United States.

The political situation in the east is definitely anti-administration. The results in Maine, no matter how they may be covered up, demonstrate very clearly the feelings of the people. George Lane is a partner of mine, so I know very well what the situation was. If Casey wins, I don't see how a Republican can be licked in this State, even though the Catholic Church will wage a terrible fight against the Birth Control amendment, which should bring a lot of Democrats to the polls.[65] However, there are a great many things going on here that I'm going to make it my business to come out and tell you.

My daughter, Eunice, has gone back to Stanford University today, and Mrs. Kennedy is planning to go out there this fall to take some courses, and it is my intention to get out there around the first of November, so I should like to come up, if I may, to spend a few days with you and bring you the picture as I see it traveling around.

In the meantime, I wanted to hurry to thank you for your cooperation. All I can say is to repeat something that I wrote you before. If I had to be out on the ocean in a small boat with nothing in sight and no signs of ever getting through, I'd like to have you for my shipmate.

My love to Marion and you.

Sincerely yours,

---

63. Maurice Joseph Tobin (1901–1953), mayor of Boston, 1937–44; later governor of Massachusetts 1945–48; and secretary of labor under President Truman, 1949–53.
64. The day before, Representative Joseph E. Casey had beaten Fitzgerald for the Democratic Senate nomination 76,366 to 53,579; the administration's candidate would lose the election to Republican incumbent Henry Cabot Lodge in November, however.
65. On November 4 the proposal to "allow registered physicians to produce contraceptive care to married persons for the protection of life and health" would be defeated by 186,351 votes.

Rose Kennedy: *Round-Robin Letter*

Hyannisport, October 9, 1942

Dear Children:

I have been home all the week and it has been lovely here. I have been working in my own little way, trying to get all your clothes sorted out etc. Dad came home from New York on Wednesday, as it was our twenty-eighth anniversary.

We expected darling Teddy home over this weekend, but it seems the little angel got into a water fight in the laboratory and "after he knew his way around he got full of biscuits" and got himself into a little trouble, so he was put on bounds for two weeks. It seems quite unfair because I am sure the boys who were there before provoked him to mischief. Also, these are our last two weekends when he might come home as we now expect to close the house about the 19th. I suppose he has learned his lesson, but a little too late.

Bobby did not expect to get off for the holiday, as I can quite understand that they are steeping their brains in study. He will have to keep on his toes to get used to the new school and the new masters and the new requirements because everyone is going at a rapid clip in order to get into college as soon as possible.[66]

Joe wrote to us this morning and it seems his latest concern is over a new mustache, which he is raising. He has promised to have some photos taken later and so you will see him all in his mustache glory. He is still busy with his students and general flying business.

Jack, you know, is a Lieutenant, j.g. and of course he is delighted. His whole attitude about the war has changed and he is quite ready to die for the U.S.A. in order to keep the Japanese and the Germans from becoming the dominant people on their respective continents, believing that sooner or later they would encroach upon ours. He also thinks it would be good for Joe's political career if he died for the grand old flag, although I don't believe he feels that is absolutely necessary.

Dolly von Standen was down over last weekend and seemed to be a very pleasant, happy-go-lucky girl. I say happy-go-lucky, as when she left here Sunday night she was not quite sure whether she would get a sleeper on the train to New York, or whether she would get the midnight train for Boston, where she would awaken her brother, but neither predicament seemed to upset her very much.

Torb MacDonald has been in a dreadful mess again. It seems some woman, who signed herself "A Conscientious Taxpayer" complained that one Torbert MacDonald was using a Navy Station Wagon to call at a certain number on a certain street every day. The woman resented the fact that her tax money was put to such a use. The above-mentioned street number turned out to be Polly Carter's house. Torb disclaimed that he had ever called for Polly in the Navy Station Wagon, but he had to get the affidavit of two policemen on the beat, plus numerous other legal signatures in order to explain it to the Navy. It was all very complicated and upset his weekend no end. It seems he is always in some sort of physical or mental dilemma.

Kathleen wanted very much to get to Hot Springs this weekend. It seems Zeke thought of going down, too. She was trying to get Betty or Charlotte to go with her, but they had other plans and I could not allow her to go down there without a chaperone. We scanned the register for some mutual friend but could find no one and so I do not know what her present plans are. She said everyone and his brother was to be at LaRue in New York this weekend. Your father, by the way, said New York is a mad house. You

---

66. He had begun his junior year at Milton Academy near Boston in September.

cannot get near the Copa Cabana. They are just standing on the street so the maitre d'hotel cannot see you even if you have an ambassadorial air. On some instances, even the beaming countenance of Ted O'Leary can not affect an entrance and so it is all too complicated. Jack is going over this weekend and your father has warned him [*and*] as usual has been making life easy for him by preparing the way at the various hot spots.

I do hope you will have a good time this weekend, Pat. I do not blame you for being bored and I wish you knew a few exciting swains in Cambridge or New Haven. It is really not your fault that you do not, as we really should make a few contacts for you and then you might follow them up. I am certainly going to do something about it pretty soon, as there is no reason why you cannot be having your share of debutante excitement. By the way, I hear you are an excellent bridge player and I cannot understand how you accomplished that art.

I am sorry if you have to wear your old clothes, Jean, and I am quite ashamed that I have not been able to buy you any new ones, but I am going to New York in about another week. Your father and I are going to visit the Convent and I hope I shall have the pleasure of meeting Reverend Mother, as I missed her last year. I also hope I shall hear words of praise for your application and industry. And please do not put on a lot of weight. It is so silly at school to eat that long bread roll, etc.

Mrs. Daly is here as usual, and arrives nightly with her little bag. She always brings a gift and is so generous. Her latest kind deed was to ask her sister-in-law to send Joe a cake from Georgia. Marie made one for Jack down here, but someone came in the front door and she had to remove the frosting before it was finished and so the cake could not be sent but was presented to me. Our Josephine also made an angel cake here last Sunday to send to Jack but there were not enough eggs in it so I got that. Josephine also made another one on Tuesday, during which Stevens slammed the back door and spoiled that one, whereupon it also was given to me. I have had angel food the last week until I must be ready for the golden gates.

Pat, do keep up your good work because as I said, there is always a record of your marks sent for every college year to whatever school or position you are taking. When I was applying for a secretary myself, I had complete records from Simmons College and Boston University of applicants who had studied there, their courses and their marks during the four years, with recommendations from their Professors or teachers as to their eligibility.

Much love to you all. *Off for the 4 o'clock mail*
Mother

Joseph P. Kennedy to Robert Kennedy, 16

Hyannisport, October 14, 1942

Dear Bobby:

It was nice to talk with you the other night and it was interesting also to get your letter.

I wouldn't be too discouraged about the football team. After all, the value of playing football isn't primarily playing on the first team — it's the opportunity to meet a lot of nice boys and to get the practice of playing teamwork. Of course, it's nice eventually to get on the team and I'm sure you will do that, even if it isn't this year. Remember that Joe alone made his football team and that in his senior year. Jack didn't make it at all.

There's one point, however, that I'd like to clear up in your mind. Mother told me that Jack advised you to sort of sit back and let the boys come to you rather than for you to go to the boys. Now I don't know exactly what he meant by that, but I'm sure if it means waiting a little bit aloof, I think it is a big mistake. Every boy has a different personality and nobody can outline exactly how he should handle his social relations with other people. He has to depend upon himself for that, but I think as a matter of general policy, it is much better to be sociable with everyone and make your intimate friends after you have appraised their various values, but for goodness sake don't stand off. Try to cultivate as many people as you can and know as many people as you can. That's all life is — whether it's in business or a profession or anything. The contacts you have made from boyhood on are the things that are important to you in your own life's development.

You have a lot on the ball and you have a personality that will make friends, so by all means hop in there and meet everybody, be pleasant to everyone, and don't stand off. That's much more likely to make a bad impression. Go to games with your friends in the school; arrange to take some to luncheon when you go out to lunch, etc., etc. But for the next two years that's probably going to be your life and you might as well have as many friends as you can. Make them in the school; don't try to make them on the outside.

I'll see you next week before I go to New York, and of course I'll be back again to see you before I leave for the South.

All kinds of good luck.

Love,

John F. Kennedy, 25, to Rose and Joseph P. Kennedy

[Motor Torpedo Squadron][67]

Dear Mother and Dad:

Haven't heard from you since I left the States. Letters take quite awhile to get here — but let me know what is going on. Has Kick gone to Europe yet — received a V—mail letter from her from Palm Beach — but she didn't say what she was going to do. Those V—mail letters aren't really worthwhile — as ordinarily they take considerably longer than airmail.

As to conditions here — they are not too bad — though if this is the dry season — the wet season must be considerably damp. Rains every day for four or five hours — solid rain — every thing gets soaked — and on my blue uniform — a green mold has grown almost 1/4 of an inch thick — However the food isn't bad at all — and the waters are very calm which make it ideal for the boats. They have really done an exceptional job — sunk or damaged severely — 10 destroyers — 2 cruisers and one submarine — and this with only a very few boats. Bulkely incidentally is in a different part of the South Pacific — is on a staff — and I understand doesn't like it a bit. Kelly arrived here the other day — and told me that there was no such girl as Peggy — E. B. White [sic] merely took 5 nurses that Kelly knew at Corregidor — and took the best characteristics of each. That's his story anyway.[68]

Have my own boat now — and have as an executive officer a 220 pound tackles from Ohio State — so when the next big drive comes — will be well protected. We go out

---

67. Jack had assumed command of PT 109 on Tulagi in the Solomon Islands on April 25, 1943.
68. Motor Torpedo Squadron 3 Lieutenant Commander John Duncan Bulkeley (1911–1996) and Lieutenant Robert Bolling Kelly (1913–1989), heroes of William L. White's best-selling *They Were Expendable*. Bulkeley had interviewed Jack for PT service in Chicago in 1942. Kelly had recently taken command of Jack's PT squadron. A year earlier Kelly's evacuation of General MacArthur's forces from Corregidor, under Japanese attack, had won him a Silver Star.

on patrol every-other night — and work on the boats in the day-time. They get us up at 5:45 — and the black-out begins at 6:30. The black-out is total — as the huts we live in have no sides. They have just opened up an officers club which consists of a tent — the liquor served is an alcoholic concoction which is drained out of the torpedo tubes — known as torp juice. Every night about 7:30 — the tent bulges — about 5 men come crashing out — blow their lunch and stagger off to bed. This torp juice which is the most expendable item on the island makes the prohibition stuff look like Haig & Haig — but probably wont do anyone any permanent harm — as long as their eyes hold out.

Went over to visit George Mead's grave the other day. He is buried near the beach where he fell — it was extremely sad.[69]

Have hopes that Torb & Cy may be up here by June which will make it very pleasant.

Love to all

Jack

You might send this along to Grandpa & Grandma

John F. Kennedy, 25, to Rose and Joseph P. Kennedy

[Received May 10, 1943]

Dear Mother and Dad:

Sorry that I haven't written sooner, but have been unable. In addition am so bound by censorship that I can't say much now. Had some difficulty getting here — and frankly don't understand why Dad's stomach improved when he was in England.

I have learned, however, that what they say about the Japs is true — or at least in one case. The other day we went to pick up a Jap pilot that had parachuted into the water. We pulled along side of him to a distance of about 20 yards. He was young looking, powerfully built — short black hair. He suddenly threw aside the life belt he was wearing, pulled a pistol and started firing. We let go with everything but he didn't seem to get hit until finally an old soldier aimed with his rifle and took the top of his head off. He leaped forward and went out of sight. That I understand is the usual story with the officers. With the men, however, there would seem to be no such desire for the glorious death.

Our life here isn't too bad. We live in tents — no hot water or anything, but the food is better than Irver Hall in Chicago, though there is still no sign of all those steaks that "the boys in the service" are getting.

Came out with a fellow called Pennoyer — whose grandfather is J. P. Morgan. In addition to having a fine set of cigars with J.P.M. on the band — which would undoubtedly have pleased brother Joe — but which seemed to me inferior to say Robert Burns — he had lived a good bit of his life out at Wall Hall. Evidently the whole Morgan family has lived in some awe of Butler Bingley and he was extremely interested in Bingley's reaction to the nine Kennedys.

Roger Cutler, who used to be in charge of Joe's group, is out here, though I haven't had a chance to see him yet. I understand that he spoke out of turn down in Jax and that they sent him out with the Amphibian forces.

That's about all the news. Saw Harry Willis who is okay, but will give you more dope about him when next I write. Haven't heard from home as yet. How about some-

---

69. Lieutenant George Houk Mead, Jr. (1917–1942), a summertime neighbor of the Kennedys' in Hyannisport, a beau of Kick's, a contemporary of Jack's, and a Yale man, had been shot by an enemy sniper during the Solomon Islands offensive in August 1942.

one writing. Suggest Mother read "Blind Date with Mars" by Alice Leone-Moats[?] — the part about Russia will interest her extremely.

Love to all

Jack

Note to children: Please write to Jack as frequently as possible, using V-Mail stationery, a few sheets of which are enclosed. Write on one page only, but if it should be more than one page put each page in a separate envelope. Also send regular letters (not V-Mail) to Joe, who is in Norfolk as you know.

Dad

Rose Kennedy: *Round-Robin Letter*

May 13, 1943

Dear Children:

I am now at the Plaza in New York trying to get a little shopping done and having a gay whirl. Dad has been taking me to the best shows as he says he cannot tell when I will change my mind and decide to go to the Cape, so he wants to be sure I have seen all the top ones.

We saw OKLAHOMA last night. The Duke and Duchess of Windsor were there and I never felt more sorry for anyone. Between the acts the rumor went around that they were in the theatre. They were back about three-quarters of the way on the left-hand side four or five rows behind us. Everyone turned around and stood up and looked at them and talked and laughed and made quite a hub-bub. I thought they would take a look and then pass along but the American people certainly want to get their money's worth so they just stood there and stared and gabbed until the curtain went up for the second act.

Madam Chiang Kai-Shek is also here at the Waldorf so between us all there are quite a few celebrities in town.

The weather has been rainy and quite disagreeable and if it continues I shall not go to the Cape until the sun shines. Dave is coming up on the 16th and I may hop down around the 27th or 28th if Bobby is ready. Dad's plans will not permit him to go until later as he is going to make a speech at Oglethorpe University the last of May.[70]

Kathleen telephoned to dad yesterday and said there had been quite a clean sweep as far as all the busy little Red Cross Assistants were concerned. Betty has been sent to Richmond and Kathleen may fade out of sight any hour. I'll let you know when she definitely passes out.

Eunice is full of ideas about going to Mexico for the summer but I have told her she must come home.

We saw Joe in Washington, who looked very well and seemed much more calm than when he saw us in Palm Beach, where I think he was just recovering from the Puerto Rico influences.[71]

Mr. and Mrs. Daley are back in Boston and will go to the Cape in a minute's notice. Marie has been having quite a hard time with her knee but now seems to be all right.

Dad, Morton Downey and Ted O'Leary are going to the circus tonight. They invited me but I thought I would give all the boys a night off.

---

70. "Do not despair of America," JPK would tell an audience of two hundred at the university's commencement exercises in Atlanta on May 29.
71. Lt. (jg) Joseph P. Kennedy, Jr., had reported for temporary duty in San Juan on May 1.

I am going to call the Dali exhibition and if I like his work I may have him do my portrait as Joe Jr. was incensed the last time I saw him that I had not had it done.

I received Mother's Day cards from Eunice and Bobby, which are now sitting on my bureau. I had told the girls not to send me any flowers as my plans were so upset and it is so difficult to do things these days. I was amazed and very much delighted yesterday on receiving a lovely basket full of the sweetest spring flowers. It seems Jack had written to Paul Murphy and asked him to send it to me for Mother's Day. He also enclosed a card, "To Mother with Love. Sorry I am not there to give these personally." It was in his own handwriting so imagine how thrilled I was. He certainly is having a great experience. I suppose you all read the article on the P.T. Skippers which was in LIFE on May 10.

Much love to all of you.

Mother

John F. Kennedy, 25, to Rose and Joseph P. Kennedy

MOTOR TORPEDO BOAT SQUADRON TWO [May 15, 1943]

Dear Dad and Mother:

Received your letter to-day — and was glad to hear everyone was well. Things are still about the same here — we had a raid to-day but on the whole its slacked up over the last weeks. I guess it will be more or less routine for another while. Going out every other night for patrol. On good nights it's beautiful — the water is amazingly phosphorescent — flying fishes which shine like lights are zooming around — and you usually get two or three porpoises who lodge right under the bow — and no matter what the speed — keep just about 6 inches ahead of the boat. Its been good training as I have an entirely new crew — and when the showdown comes — I'd like to be confident they know the difference between firing a gun and winding their watch.

Have a lot of natives around — and am getting hold of some grass skirts — war clubs etc. We had one in to-day — who told us about the last man he ate. "Him Jap, him no good." All they seem to want is a pipe and will give you canes — pineapples — anything including a wife. They're smartening up lately — when the British were here — they had them working for 17¢ a day — but we treat them a heck of a lot better. "English — me no like" — is their summation of the Brit. Empire.

I was interested in what you said about MacArthur's popularity. Here he has none — is in fact, very very unpopular. His nick-name is "Dug-out-Doug" — which seems to date back to the first invasion of Guadalcanal. The army was supposed to come in and relieve the marines after the beach-head has been established. In ninety-three days — no army. Rightly or wrongly — probably wrongly — MacArthur is blamed — he is said to have refused to send the army in — "he sat down in his dug-out in Australia." (I am quoting all Navy & Marine personnel) — and let the Marines take it.

What actually happened seems to have been that the Navy's hand was forced due to the speed with which the Japs were building Henderson Field — so they just moved in ready or not. — The Marines took a terrific beating but gave it back. At the end the Japs wouldn't ever surrender till they had found out whether the Americans were Marines or the Army — if Marines they didn't surrender — as the Marines weren't taking prisoners. In regard to MacArthur — there is no doubt that as men start to come back — that "Dug-Out-Doug" will spread — and I think would probably kill him off. No one out here has the slightest interest in politics — they just want to get home — morn-

ing—noon—and night. They wouldn't give a damn whether they could vote or not —
and would probably vote for Roosevelt — but just because they knew his name.

As far as the length of the war — I don't see how it can stop in less than 3 years —
but I'm sure we can lick them eventually. Our stuff is better — our pilots and planes are
— everything considered way ahead of theirs — and our resources inexhaustible —
though this island to island stuff isn't the answer. If they do that the motto out here
"The Golden Gate by 48" won't even come true. A great hold-up seems to me to be the
lackadaisical way they handle the unloading of ships — they sit in ports out here weeks
at a time — while they try to get enough Higgins boats to unload them. They ought to
build their docks the first thing — they're loosing ships in effect by what seems from the
outside to be just inertia up high. Don't let anyone sell the idea that everyone out here
is hustling with the old American energy. They may be willing to give their blood but
not their sweat — if they can help it — and usually they fix it so they can help it. They
have brought back a lot of old Captains & Commanders from retirement and stuck
them in as the heads of these ports — and they give the impression of their brains being in their tails as Honey Fitz would say. The ship I arrived on — no one in the port had
the slightest idea it was coming — it had hundreds of men — and it sat in the harbor
for 2 weeks — while signals were being exchanged. The one man, though, who has
everyone's confidence is Halsey[72] — he rates at the very top.

As far as Joe wanting to get out here — I know it is futile to say so — but if I were
he — I would take as much time about it as I could. He is coming out eventually — and
will be here for a sufficiency — and he will want to be back the day after he arrives — if
he runs true to the form of every one else.

As regards Bobby — he ought to do what he wants — you can't estimate risks —
some cooks are in more danger out here than a lot of flyers.

Was very interested to hear what your plans were — and the situation at home. Let
me know the latest dope whenever you can. Whatever happened to Timilty?[73] Jerry
O'Leary is out here — to the South of where I am — but I hope he will get here some
one of these days. He has command of a 150 ft. supply boat.

Feeling O.K. the back has really acted amazingly well — and gives me scarcely no
trouble and in general feel pretty good. Good bunch out here — so all in all it isn't too
bad — but when I was speaking about the people who would just as soon be home — I
didn't mean to use *they* I meant "*we*".

I figure should be back within a year though — but brother from then on it's going
to take an act of Congress to move me — but I guess that Act has already been passed
— if it hasn't it will be.

By the way — could you send me out a simply — fairly small camera — and as
much film as you can muster — Just wrap it up plain — and just ship it along — I hope
I get it — as it will be great to have out here —

My best love to everyone
Jack

P.S. Mother — got to Church Easter — they had in a native hut — and aside from
having a condition red "enemy air-craft in the vicinity" — it went on as well as St. Pat's.

---

72. As commander of the South Pacific force, Admiral William Frederick "Bull" Halsey, Jr. (1882–1959),
    had eradicated the threat of Japanese resistance from Guadalcanal between November 1942 and Feb-
    ruary 1943 and would orchestrate the Solomon Islands offensive in 1943–44.
73. JPK's friend, Boston Police Commissioner Joseph F. Timilty, had been indicted along with six other high-
    ranking police officials in late March for conspiracy to permit gambling. On July 2, Timilty's indictment
    would be quashed.

P.P.S. As far as Joe going around with Lorelle[74] — I think he'll be lucky if he's alive to get out here.

P.P.S.S. Please send me a couple of fountain pens — and some needles for victrola records — One thing about this place — if you loose something — it's lost — and you can't get another one.

P.P.P.SS. Air-mail is better than V-mail

If any of the pictures taken this last winter come out very well — shoot them here.

John F. Kennedy, 26, to Kathleen Kennedy, 23

[JUNE 3, 1943]

DEAR KIK:

THANK YOU FOR YOUR LAST LETTER—BUT HOW ABOUT CUTTING DOWN ON TERSE TELEGRAPHIC COMMUNIQUÉS—AND SITTING DOWN AND WRITING A LETTER. YOU SHOULD BE ABLE TO DO IT —CISSY WAS PAYING YOU 40 CLAMS A WEEK FOR THAT COOL LIMPID STYLE.

AS TO THE SITUATION UP HERE — I'VE MOVED FROM MY NATIVE VILLAGE UP THE LINE SOMEWHAT, AND AM LIVING ON ANOTHER ISLAND—WITH THE JAPS NOT FAR AWAY—AND WITH FLIES AS THE WILD LIFE AND NOT MOSQUITOES. THAT BUBBLE I HAD ABOUT LYING ON A COOL PACIFIC ISLAND WITH A WARM PACIFIC MAIDEN HUNTING BANANAS FOR ME IS DEFINITELY A BUBBLE THAT HAS BURST. YOU CAN'T EVEN SWIM— THERE'S SOME SORT OF FUNGUS IN THE WATER THAT GROWS OUT OF YOUR EARS—WHICH WILL BE ALL I NEED. WITH PIMPLES ON MY BACK—HAIR ON MY CHEST AND FUNGUS IN MY EARS I OUGHT TO BE A NATURAL FOR THE OLD SAILORS HOME IN CHELSEA, MASS. RAN INTO OLD JAKE PEEPOT[75] THE OTHER DAY. I WAS ZOOMING ALONG LOOKING FOR A BOAT THAT I HAD HEARD THAT JERRY O'LEARY WAS COMMANDING WHEN I LOOKED UP AND THERE HANGING FROM THE RIGGING WAS THE POT. HE LOOKED AS HEARTY AS EVER BUT I ONLY HAD TIME [FOR] A QUICK WORD AND HAD TO LEAVE. LOCATED JERRY O'LEARY WHO IS IN COMMAND OF A NICE LITTLE BOAT— I TOOK HIM OVER TO THE OFFICERS CLUB AND GAVE HIM SOME OF MY LIQUOR CHITS AND HE POLISHED OFF FIVE SCOTCHES WITH NO VISIBLE EFFECT EXCEPT HE COULD HARDLY STAND BY THE TIME I GOT HIM OUT. HE WAS DUE TO TAKE HIS BOAT OUT THAT NIGHT — BUT AS IT A BOAT THAT IS SUPPOSED TO GO UP ON BEACHES — HE COULDN'T GO WRONG. I HAVEN'T SEEN HIM SINCE — HE'S PROBABLY UP ON SOME JAP ISLAND AS THE OPENING GUN OF THE BIG DRIVE.

HE SPEAKS VERY FONDLY OF MARRIED LIFE — BUT THEN THEY ALL DO OUT HERE. I THINK I MAY HAVE TOLD YOU THAT THERE IS SOME POSSIBILITY OF CY AND TORB COMING UP HERE WHICH WOULD MAKE IT EXCELLENT. THEY HAVEN'T GOTTEN OUT THIS WAY AS YET. I READ IN LIFE MAGAZINE AN ARTICLE BY JOHNNY HERSEY ON PTS OUT HERE.[76] IT DIDN'T HAVE THE WILD WEST STUFF OF THEY WERE EXPENDABLE, BUT IT WAS A MUCH TRUER PICTURE. THE GLAMOUR OF PTS JUST ISN'T EXCEPT TO THE OUTSIDER. ITS JUST A MATTER OF NIGHT AFTER NIGHT

74. Lorelle McCarver, later the first Mrs. William Randolph Hearst, Jr.
75. John Pierrepont (1917–), a Yale contemporary of Jack's.
76. *Time* correspondent (and later, Pulitzer Prize–winning novelist) John Richard Hersey (1914–1993) had been assigned to the South Pacific in 1942; his "PT Squadron in the South Pacific" had appeared in the May 10 edition of *Life*. Hersey had married Jack's former girlfriend, Frances Ann Cannon, in April 1940.

PATROLS AT LOW SPEED IN ROUGH WATER-TWO HOURS ON- THEN SACKING OUT AND GOING ON AGAIN FOR ANOTHER TWO HOURS. EVEN WITH THAT HOWEVER ITS A HELL OF A LOT BETTER THAN ANY OTHER JOB IN THE NAVY. YOU'VE GOT NO IDEA OF THE MONOTONY OF SOME OF THE JOBS WHICH FELLOWS HAVE TO DO WITH NO RECOGNITION OR EVEN THE OCCASIONAL STIMULANT OF GETTING YOUR PANTS SCARED OFF. AS A MATTER OF FACT THIS JOB IS SOMEWHAT LIKE SAILING IN THAT WE SPEND MOST OF OUR TIME TRYING TO GET THE BOAT RUNNING FASTER- AL-THOUGH IT ISN'T JUST TO BEAT DALY FOR THE KENNEDY CUP -ITS THE KENNEDY TAIL-THIS TIME . . . .SPEAKING OF JOHNNY HERSEY I SEE HIS NEW BOOK "INTO THE VALLEY" IS DOING WELL..HE'S SITTING ON TOP OF THE HILL AT THIS POINT-A BEST SELLER-MY GIRL-TWO KIDS-BIG MAN ON TIME- WHILE I'M THE ONE THAT'S DOWN IN THE GOD DAMNED VALLEY. THAT I SUPPOSE IS LIFE IN ADDITION TO FOR-TUNE KNOWS GOD, SAY I.

MY FONDEST TO ALL-IF YOU ARE IN ENGLAND BY THE TIME THIS TO YOU GETS, SAY HELLO TO TONY, BABY,[77] ETC.

> LOVE
> JACK

Joseph P. Kennedy: *Diary*

June 17, 1943

I saw Lord Beaverbrook the night before last as a result of his telephone call to me at Cape Cod that he was going to Washington and would like to go over things generally with me before he went home.

We met in his apartment at 8 o'clock and had dinner alone.

He spent the entire hour and three-quarters upbraiding me for my position in the politics of this country. He said I should do one of two things, I should either join the Roosevelt administration at once or I should come out against Roosevelt in a speech saying that I was against him and why, but that if he were nominated I would not bolt and I would support him. This was the sum substance of the first attack.

I let him talk and said, "Now, let's take the first one." "I am of the opinion that if I wanted to go to Washington tomorrow and see Hopkins I could readjust my entire position and probably be offered a real job. Is that true?" He said "Completely." He said that there were a great deal of positions there that he compared with the man that is holding carrots in front of a rabbit, that if he doesn't bother jumping at the little carrot they increase the size of the carrot and while they offered me the small carrots if they could get me in they would offer me a big carrot. I asked him whether he had had any conversations with Roosevelt on his trip with him last week-end. He said "No", but he knew exactly how he felt. (We must remember that Beaverbrook tries to be straight-forward but very debonair and when he said Roosevelt didn't discuss it and yet he knows how he feels it is a little difficult to reconcile because I think he has discussed me a number of times with him). I said, "Well, how does he feel?" He said "He is a candidate for the fourth term and he, of course, wants you in and would be very happy to get you in and would pay a big price if you went in." I said "Let's take up the second thing and that is that I will take the position against him but not the party." That, of course, is the biggest lot of bunk

---

77. Stella Cárcano, another of Jack's old girlfriends, the elder daughter of Don Miguel Angel Cárcano, Argentine ambassador to the Court of St. James's.

that there is because I have yet to see anybody who does not think that Roosevelt can win the Democratic nomination in the Convention. Therefore, all this would be is making a speech against him, cutting down my own influence because I would be tied up to Roosevelt whether I liked it or not after the Democratic Convention. Well, he hemmed and hawed about this and came back with I hadn't done what I should do and a lot of stuff and that I should run for an elective office. I said that if the war weren't on I had no desire at all to return to public life. The political career of my two sons, if that is what they want to follow, is the only concern of mine now. I can honestly say that I have no further desire for public office. This rather surprised him because he said when a man is your age and is getting tired of making money and there is nothing else he can do that the only way he can stop from being frustrated is to go into public life. I let him talk and said I never heard more bunk because I could get all the thrills and excitement watching the careers of my children. I do not have to have it centered on me any more, I have had mine. That stopped him and he finally said, "We would like to see Roosevelt re-elected. We know he is our friend and we naturally feel that we would be much better off with him than anybody else." He said "Of course, I like Roosevelt very much" and I said "That's a damn lie, you never liked him and if you like him now you like him because he is giving you everything you want." He didn't terribly dispute that except to say "I like him". My own opinion was that he wanted to get me in and was making it clear to me that I could make a deal with them, but I feel that now is not the time to do anything.

I asked him how Roosevelt and Churchill got along and he said "I will tell you a secret if you won't repeat it," so I am just having this for my own file. He said, "Churchill is a terrible bore. I have known him for 33 years and while he is a great vitality of the nation he is still a hell of a bore. When Roosevelt and he went to Camp Rapidan together and he kept repeating or talking Roosevelt opened the stamp book and started to work on the stamps, letting Churchill continue to talk. This annoyed Churchill so much that he stalked out of the room in a huff and sat outside and smoked his big black cigar, peeved, while Roosevelt continued to work on the stamps. Finally I came along and went into the room and, of course, I understand how to handle Roosevelt, I think, better than Churchill and can get him talking and so all I have to say is "Now, who do you think represents the best ideal of Democracy, Jackson or Jefferson" and, of course, with that he closes the stamp book and talks on that and while that discussion is going on Churchill walks back into the room. This is an interesting and only side light I have on how the two boys are getting on together, but where the opinion of the world is that every visit is spent in big discussions you have a general idea of what is going on. Beaverbrook said "I had two fights with him while on the ship going over, when he didn't speak for a day and one in Washington when he didn't speak to me until the following morning when he opened up the conversation by remarking that we haven't changed much, we still argue and fight, but it only shows that we are vital people and we must continue in our regular way.

The aftermath of the story was that when Roosevelt sent for Beaverbrook last Thursday for a week-end party to go traveling somewhere, as they got in the car Roosevelt said to Beaverbrook "Well, on this trip I am not taking my stamps." Believe me, there will be a row between Churchill and Roosevelt one of these days and I can imagine what they say about each other.

I reminded Beaverbrook that I had a long conversation with Roosevelt before I resigned about both Churchill and Beaverbrook and at that time neither stood particularly high in his regard, but at that time I knew that he didn't stand very well with them, so it was all even.

I asked him about the war and while he said he couldn't give me a definite time that the attack was coming against the Italians and, of course, that means Sicily and Sardinia.[78] He doesn't look for the war to be over this year unless the Germans in their two-prong drive to Moscow are stopped by the Russians. In that event it might very well cause the internal collapse of the Germans.

He said that he had no knowledge of the Russian situation, that the British staff had repeatedly said that the Russians would collapse and now they have changed to the idea that they will beat the Germans, so Beaverbrook says that they were wrong then and are wrong now. Anyway, he doesn't take any stock in his own staff, but unless the Germans destroy the Russian army then the Germans are definitely in for trouble.

I judge that the Channel attack was off, Churchill being definitely against that. He, Beaverbrook, is not convinced that the bombing is as effective as this country is made to believe, that the German bombing of England was in a small concentrated area whereas in Germany the manufacturing facilities are all well scattered, but, of course, it is causing trouble and it may be a contributing cause of the collapse. I asked him what he thought of the chances of the Russians and Germans coming to an agreement and he said that there was a river of blood that would always stop them getting together as there was too much damage done by the Germans for the Russians to ever forgive them.

I asked him about the China situation and he was rather bitter. He confirmed the Madame Chang Kai-Shek, Roosevelt and Churchill discussion about the meeting, but he was indignant that she should ask Churchill to come to New York. He said it was a hell of a gall for her to consider as after all she was not an official representative and why should Churchill call on her. Anyway, he thought very little of her. In fact he said she was a Lesbian and her girl friend was a 26 year old girl, Soong, who she had with her. I thought to myself that it certainly didn't portend any great feeling between two countries if the top-side people feel the way they do.

He also talked about that he thought neither Roosevelt nor Churchill ever had any affairs with women, as was being discussed about Princess Martha.[79] She was at the week-end party with them and he thought that they liked to have women around and talk to them and all that sort of thing, but that was as far as it went. They have had nothing in their head but power.

He didn't think Churchill had changed much, but I told him that there was a very contrary opinion, that he had become very arbitrary and Beaverbrook admitted that that happened to all of them sooner or later.

I introduced Downey and Kathleen to him and we talked on a few generalities after they arrived. He is convinced that Roosevelt will be nominated and elected and that Willkie will probably get the nomination of the Republicans,[80] this after he had talked with all the important people in the last month.

June 17, 1943

I have had three rather long visits with Madame Chiang Kai-Shek.[81] She strikes me as a most interesting and attractive woman. There are definitely two facets to her per-

78. The amphibious Allied invasion of Sicily would begin on July 10; American forces would capture Palermo by July 23.
79. In the wake of the German invasion of Norway in 1940, King Haakon VII's daughter-in-law and niece, Crown Princess Martha, had taken asylum in Washington with her three children. The princess and the president's close friendship, frequent visits and evident fondness for each other had provoked speculation as to the true nature of their relationship.
80. The 1940 Republican candidate would withdraw after his defeat in the Wisconsin primary. Governor Dewey of New York would be the Republican nominee for 1944.
81. Madame Chiang had arrived in the United States in November for medical treatment. Since then she had

sonality, one is that statesman, the manager of the airplane business, assistant to the Generalissimo in his stand against Communism and the bribes of the Japanese. Her stand for a better world after the war is her real platform. She believes that unless each individual of himself helps to make himself better that civilization is doomed. She repeatedly stated to me that she would never ask for help for China if she didn't believe that the victory of China would work for a better world, otherwise she would rather see China destroyed. The other definite side of her character is a charming female. She smiles. She appeared to be horrified when I told her she had sex appeal and immediately asked if I meant like Gypsy Rose Lee. I said not exactly that, but if she wanted another word, charm. I said I thought that it helped her to sell herself to the American public, but she said that women like her as well as men and I said her charm did that for the women but her appeal helps her with the men. She always appeared to be horrified but I secretly thought she rather liked it.

On my first visit she read me two of her stories that she had written when she was 19, one rather a staid one and one rather a naughty one. She is having them published by the Viking Press. She reads beautifully and on my last visit she read me her two broadcasts, one to the Occupied Nations and one to the American soldiers. She seems to have the rareness of William Randolph Hearst of getting over definite ideas in punchy words. She told me she writes all her own speeches and does all her own research work. She said she has no head for business and does not understand figures. She told me that when I told her a friend of mine had been in back of her Chinese secretary at the Chase Bank, when he had cashed checks and had put thousands and thousands of dollars in his pockets. I said it shouldn't have been done in this way, he should have gone to a private office in the bank, because in this way it became a matter of gossip as she raised money for the orphans but spent ridiculous amounts on herself.

She admitted to me that Roosevelt had called her twice to go to Washington to meet Churchill but she had declined. Beaverbrook told me last night that she had told Roosevelt that it was the place of the gentleman to call on the lady, but Beaverbrook thought that was ridiculous that a head of a British War Office should call on a woman who had no official standing. At any rate, she was secretly pleased that she didn't go and stood out against Mr. Roosevelt's pressure. She feels definitely that the British are not at all interested in China winning. She deplored their action in closing the Burma Road. She said that completely demonstrated the opportunism of Churchill. She felt that the British position, after the war was won in Europe, would be that while they would help us with their Navy and Air Force their real position would be as arbitrator between Japan and ourselves. She feels that the British really do not want the Chinese or Americans to lick the Japs but wants to maintain the present status quo in the Pacific.

She told me that the Japanese had made a peace proposal to the Chinese and she outlined it. I think it would be a very difficult proposal for the Chinese to withstand. They offered to get out of a lot of the occupied territory, stop the bombing and turn back a lot of their facilities for feeding the people. She admitted that it put the Generalissimo's position in a rather difficult spot because they had been telling their friends that they were going to get help from the Democracies and since that hadn't turned up the crowd around the Generalissimo might rise up and say "We have had enough of this, let's make the deal and end the war and then if the Allies win — why Japan will be

---

remained in the United States (at one point living in the White House) in order to rally support for the Chinese cause.

licked — and our position will be good anyway and if the Japanese win we are not worse off than we are today." I asked her then what would be the excuse for not accepting the Japanese terms and she said "Our honor", meaning hers and the Generalissimo's, I think. I told her that I understood Roosevelt had told somebody that the Chinese haven't fought for two years and she got rather indignant and said "How could we fight, we never had air support, we never had artillery, we have nothing but small arms and with that we can't make an attack." Claire Luce thinks that a great many of the communiques of these great victories are mostly "phony", what actually happens the Japanese just walk out and then walk back because they have about everything they need and the Chinese just issue these in order to make people still aware that they are in the war.

She came to this country because of her physical condition. She believed she had cancer of the stomach but this turned out to be false. She is terribly susceptible to the heat and really gets in a bad state, her skin breaks out and she looks, I think, with great apprehension to her return, but the Generalissimo has sent for her repeatedly and she says that he needs her very badly. From time to time he resents the fact that she isn't more of a woman and less of an executive. She said when those occasions arise she leaves her work and takes him for a walk in the gardens and when they return, after they have talked everything over, he is in a better mood.

She doesn't drink, but she smokes rather incessantly and she has beautiful flowers around her at all times. When we moved from her living room to her study, where she was told it was much cooler, because the heat was oppressive, she immediately told her secretary to move in four or five vases of flowers. It really did make quite a change in her study.

She said that she would go to see the President on her return from Ottawa, thank him for his kindness and then leave for China and I could see that she abhorred the fact.

She said before she goes home she was going to have an ice cream soda even if it would upset her terribly, so she finally decided she would have it right there and then and ordered two strawberry sodas, so they sent to Schrafft's and back they came and we had them. She had no ill effects that I could see before I left, but she promised herself some.

The big point in her discussion with me at all times was that she believed that the mind of man must change and work for a better world. She said she had temptations like everyone else, but she made up her mind that if she gave in to them it was like dropping a pebble in the pool, that the shock went out all over the pool and so it was that if you did something you shouldn't do it affected not only yourself and those immediately around you but those that had confidence in you. She thought that in spite of the opportunism of leaders and the faking of their ideals that she had hopes that they would all work for a better world.

I said how did she reconcile the fairness to all nations in the willingness of Churchill and Roosevelt to give Stalin the Baltic States, Finland, Poland, etc. She said she thought that Roosevelt means to do the right thing and while he had to agree in a measure to these things in the face of Stalin's position, nevertheless when the war was over and Russia would be so busy rebuilding her nation that the power of the United States would see that justice was done to all the nations of the world and with that as a starting point we would start the new world. When I expressed skepticism she chided me severely saying that if you did not have that to look forward to there wasn't much to one's life or to the life of civilization. She told me that she had tried to pattern her life on that principle, that she had never had a lover except her husband because only in that way could she keep her mind on this great work. I told her that a friend of mine had read her articles on religion in this month's *Reader's Digest* and he was convinced that there was some measure of insincerity in it. She bristled at this and said that the article had been written for the Forum in 1932, long before this all started and that she felt that way long before the pressure of war made her feel the way she does now.

She gave me a very good picture for Rose and myself and said "I picked out the smiling one rather than the severe one because I am always happy and that is the way you know me and I thought you would recognize it better than the sober one."

She is a remarkable woman and has done a remarkable job. It would be a terrible calamity were she to go back and the Generalissimo should fail, because in that event she might easily lose her life.

I asked what she proposed to do after the war and she told me run a newspaper and write editorials and hope that they would have some world-wide circulation. She told me she had been approached here by a syndicate for three articles a week and she asked me how much I thought she had been offered. I said possibly $10,000 a week and she said a million and a half dollars. This sounds almost incredible, but in this day and age it may not be unlikely because of the international force of her personality and her ability.

We must follow her career closely.

John F. Kennedy, 26: *Round-Robin Letter*

June 24, 1943

Dear Family:

May I first express my appreciation for the manner in which you have kept in contact with your broken-down brother & to know that all nuns & priests along the Atlantic Coast are putting in a lot of praying time on my behalf is certainly comforting. Kathleen reports that even a fortune-teller says that I'm coming back in one piece. I hope it won't be taken a sign of lack of confidence in you all or the Church if I continue to duck — I was interested to see in Teddy's last letter that Pat was on the "virage of going to Calaphoney" — which I should certainly think she should enjoy.

Mother, you will be pleased to know that their is a priest nearbye [*sic*] who has let all the natives go — and is devoting all his energies to my salvation. I'm stringing along with him — but I'm not going over to easy — as I want him to work a bit — so he'll appreciate it more when he finally has me in the front row every morning screaming halleluyah — Please have Teddy check the spelling of the last word — as I don't believe there should be a y in it.

Admiral Halsey inspected us yesterday and I tried to look broken-down so he would send me home — but he said we were a "fine looking crowd" — which was obviously a lie — and said it was "a privilege for us to be where we are" — which made me edge away from him in case God hit him with lightning.

The war seems to be turning in our favor — some of the scores coming of here [*sic*] which sound unbelievable — err on the side of conservatism — Our planes are getting better — their pilots greener — but we shall see.

May not be able to write very often for a while — but am in good shape.

Much love

Jack

Kathleen Kennedy, 23: *Round-Robin Letter*

June 27th, 1943

Dearest Family:

This is going through the pouch, I hope! After talking to you on Wednesday,[82] I went back to the hotel and got myself together. At 7:00 P.M. promptly one of the hottest days of the year, dressed in winter uniforms, raincoats, gas masks, wearing tin helmets, carrying 35 pound musette bags, over bags and another one in the hand, not to mention the canteen and First Aid Kit strapped to the waist — we boarded the *Queen Mary*. There are eight of us in a cabin and when I say on top of one another I do mean on top of one another! We didn't leave New York until the following day at noon after nearly 18,000 troops had been packed in all over the ship. They are sleeping in the hallways, decks, etc. It really is the most pathetic looking sight in the world to see the way they are living.

There are about 160 Army nurses and they are certainly a lot of tough babies. There are also about 300 Officers of every nationality. Most of the Red Cross girls don't pay much attention to them, as it certainly isn't any compliment to be sought after when the ratio is so uneven.

We eat twice a day — 9:00 A.M. and 7:00 P.M. People keep from getting too hungry by eating crackers and chocolate which is plentiful. The weather has been perfect and tomorrow we land in the port of Glasgow and proceed from there in a troop train to London.

We have had Mass every afternoon at 3:30 — a wartime measure and guess where we have it — in the Synagogue. I have been serving Mass, as the soldiers didn't seem to show up. We are allowed to go to Communion then and yesterday we had Mass on the deck under the most crude circumstances.

The girls are quite nice but you certainly get sick of a lot of giggling females and they still like to sit up until about 1:30 A.M. every night.

Mother, you wouldn't recognize this boat as the same one you made that comfortable luxury cruise on in 1936. The only lounge available to the officers is the one main one and you can imagine how crowded that is at all hours of the day. And the deck space is about 40 feet long for walking. I pace 400 or 500 times a day trying to eke a mile out of it.

I really am becoming quite excited at the thought of seeing England again and I am quite prepared for the changes. This arrival certainly is going to be different from our last one. This life on an Army troop transport has been an eye-opener. It seems to unreal and far removed from anything I've ever known that I can't believe I'm a part of it. Sometimes it almost feels like a dream.

I still haven't any idea about my assignment, but hope like anything it will be London for a while.

Have had tea etc. with British Staff Colonel aboard. Apparently his niece used to go to Roehampton with Eunice and Pat.

Today it is windy and wet. We are really getting near England. No one really knows I'm coming. What a shock they'll get when I get on the other end of the phone.

About a half-hour after each sharp swerve we are informed that this good ship has just missed a sub. There's another one. It was probably about nine miles to starboard.

---

82. June 23.

Tell Eunice I shall keep her constantly informed of all happenings as maybe she could join me after graduation — or Dad, do you think you could go through another session with the Red Cross.

Please tell everyone to write — American Red Cross, APO 887 c/o Postmaster, New York.

Love to all and eat a lot of ice cream for me on Sunday.

Much love,

Kick

July 3rd

Just a quick P.S.: Everything wonderful and it certainly doesn't seem like four years. Lots of people out of town and to say that those I've seen were surprised is putting it mildly. Still haven't any idea about definite assignment, but hope and pray it is London. If it is, will move in to Jane Kenyon Slaney's flat with her, which is perfect. Tim McInerny[83] has been wonderful and has given me lots of useful advice. Certainly glad I brought an evening dress. As much gaiety here as in New York.

Had steak for dinner last night, which is probably more than you all can say.

My other letter may not get by censors but hope it does. I guess it really shouldn't be quoted. Write me c/o Tim and he'll see that I get it.

Much love to all.

Kick

Kathleen Kennedy, 23, to John F. Kennedy, 26

PIMLICO HOUSE, HEMEL HEMPSTED. July 3, 1943

Dearest Jack —

At the moment I am sunning myself in the Gore's garden — still recovering from a rather hectic trip over. That's about all I can say on that point!

London seems quite unchanged — food is very good — blitzed areas are not obvious — Americans every place who pay through the eyes and get all the good things such as steak which I had my first night in London.

Have seen Janie — she looks marvelous and is quite determined to get out to India to join her husband — she's absolutely mad about him. Sissy & David Gore[84] have two wee ones now. Talked to Tony on the phone — am going to get down to see them tomorrow Lady Astor wrote me a note of welcome but she's at Plymouth at the moment. There are a great many in the country on maneuvers etc. Everyone is very surprised & I do mean surprised to see me. There's much more anti-Kennedy feeling than I imagined and I am determined to get my stories straight as I think I'll get it on all sides — People are tired— not quite as many as ever — but things are terribly gay. Party about every week. I haven't any idea what my assignment but would like a public relations job in the central office in London. You know Jack how good I'd be there. Failing [that,]

83. Former *Boston Post* editor and Pulitzer Prize–nominated columnist Timothy Anthony McInerny (1902–1965) had joined the U.S. Army in 1938.
84. Kick's close friend Sylvia Lloyd-Thomas (d. 1967) and William David Ormsby-Gore, later Lord Harlech (1918–1985), had married in 1940. Ormsby Gore (second son of the fourth Baron Harlech and Lady Beatrice Gascoyne-Cecil, daughter of the fourth marquess of Salisbury) was a cousin of Billy Hartington and Andrew Cavendish. In 1950 Ormsby Gore would be elected a Conservative MP for Oswestry, Shropshire, and would serve as foreign secretary, 1957–61. Harold Macmillan would appoint Ormsby Gore, close friend of Jack's since the late 1930s, ambassador to the United States in 1961.

I'll be assigned to some Recreation Club somewhere in England hours 12-2 and one day off a week. This is war!

Tim McInerny is here and most helpful about fixing me up. If I do stay here will probably share an apartment with Jane

The Naval officers about town do nearly nothing and are rather a disgrace — I think.

The Carcanos don't get on very well with the English and go about mainly with South Americans — Will call them when I get a moment write me

---

Kathleen Kennedy, 23: *Round-Robin Letter*

July 14, 1943

Dearest little Kennedys:

I haven't heard a word from any of you but expect all letters to take a very long time these days. I long to see the clippings announcing my arrival in this country as I heard they used a most peculiar picture.

The job is going very well. Slowly but surely I am catching on as to what exactly I am up to. I simply can't get over how nice everyone is. I must say that I expected old friends to be kind but they have exceeded all expectations. Anytime anyone ever says anything against the British in front of me they'll hear about it. Yesterday Lord Beaverbrook rang up and asked me down for the weekend but of course weekends are impossible for me, which is very sad. However, I am going to dine with him next week even though he said, "this admirer is the combined age of all your other admirers."

Lady Astor also rang up and asked me to come to Cliveden. She said Jakie had been invited to stay with the Duchess of Kent but refused until he found out whether or not I was coming to Cliveden. Lady Astor insisted that I promise to ring her up anytime I could and wanted to come and stay at Cliveden and she's coming to visit the Club next week. Am having dinner with the Biddles tonight.[85] I guess they got Pop's letter. Oh, another thing Lady Astor is doing. There's a big ball this Saturday, the biggest of the summer, where all the young folks are going. She said she was going to ring up Mr. Gibson[86] and insist that I be allowed to go in the cause of Anglo-American unity, which at this point is anything but good. Mr. Gibson arrived back the day before yesterday and yesterday I went into have a visit with him. He is still sour, but was very kind.

After work last night Tony Rosslyn and I went out for a few hours to the 400 and of course ran into lots of old pals. Tim calls every day to see how I'm getting on and really is a kind soul. Tried to get in touch with Bob Hope the other day. He's out on tour at the moment but Captain Eddie Dowling[87] said he'd try to fix up something when he returned. Captain Eddie asked for Daddy.

I have made a solemn resolution not to discuss anyone while I'm here because people do nothing but gossip these days. They are just so sick of the war that in order to get away from it they spend their time ruining people's reputations.

---

85. Between 1941 and 1944, Anthony Drexel Biddle was stationed in London as U.S. ambassador or minister to the exiled governments of Poland, Belgium, Norway, Greece, the Netherlands, Czechoslovakia and Yugoslavia.
86. Banker Harvey Dow Gibson (1882–1950), commissioner of the American Red Cross in Britain, 1942–45.
87. Playwright, actor, director and Pulitzer Prize–winning producer Eddie Dowling (1894?–1976). An ardent Roosevelt supporter, Dowling had worked on the 1932 campaign and had served as chairman of the Democratic Stage, Screen and Radio Committee.

Did I tell Eunice that Elizabeth Scott[88] is a Wren. Also, I saw Mary Pratt last night who asked for her. She is definitely a popular figure around London.

Marie Bruce rang me up and wanted to hear all the news about the family. She is living in a small flat now and longs to do anything she can for me. As soon as I get a minute I am going to go and see her.

I am beginning to think this letter sounds terribly conceited. It's not really but I just want you to have all the news but I'd hate to have it read out loud to anyone outside the family.

Billy and I went out together for the first time in London last Saturday. It really is funny to see people put their heads together the minute we arrive any place. There's heavy betting on when we are going to announce it. Some people have gotten the idea that I'm going to give in. Little do they know. Some of those old Devonshire and Cecil ancestors would certainly jump out of their graves if anything happened to some of their ancient traditions. It just amused me to see how worried they all are.

I saw the Carcanos at Church last Sunday. I don't think they like it very well and according to Marie Bruce they are terrifically impressed with the Lords.

The boys around the Club are very nice but most of them are so homesick and heartily dislike the British and everything about them. The warm beer, the climate (I've slept with three blankets every night) the soldiers, etc. Tony Rosslyn says he tries to impress his men with the good things about the Americans and I'm trying to do the same thing around here but it's an uphill job.

July 15th

The party at the Biddles was great fun. I'd never met him before and it certainly is true what everyone has always said — he could charm a bird right off a tree. They have quite a small house and we had a buffet supper consisting of all the things I've been yearning for ever since I arrived: lobster, ice cream, chocolate cake, chicken salad, etc. Capt. Eddie Dowling was there and we went after that ice cream in a big way. Prince Bernhard was about.[89] Of course, stupid Kick had no idea who he was, and made no attempt to curtsey. He asked me if I was a member of the famous Kennedy family. I remembered afterwards what a great friend he was of the Princess in Palm Beach. Mr. and Mrs. Gibson told me about Lady Astor calling them and saying I must go to the party Saturday night. Any minute I expect to be isolated to the Isle of Man. The gayest spot of the evening was the appearance of Lieut. Commander James Van Alen, who is still mumbling about the note Daddy gave him to Prof. Laski. He says the hardest job Tony Biddle's Naval Attaché has here is pouring out the cocktails every evening. We were also happy to find out that Ambassador Biddle was getting everything he needed in the food line because he's got a tough war to fight.

That's about all the news at the moment. Received your cable last night. Will send a photo in my uniform as soon as possible.

Love to all,
Kick

---

88. Lady Elizabeth Montagu Douglas Scott (later the duchess of Northumberland) had become a member of the Women's Royal Naval Service.

89. The German-born Prince Leopold Frederick of the Netherlands (1911–), consort of Crown Princess Juliana, had renounced his German citizenship when he married in 1937, and had fled to England with his family in May 1940 shortly before German forces occupied Holland. With his wife and children safely in Canada, Bernhard had been named British-Dutch liaison officer in London in 1940, and would become commander in chief of Dutch forces in 1944.

Kathleen Kennedy, 23 to John F. Kennedy, 26

July 29, 1943

Dearest Jack:

I am enclosing a letter from Tony. Need I add it [*sic*] I read it. He is a nice person in fact one of the nicest, and he really has been kind to Sister Kick. In fact everyone has been more than kind — it's been sort of overwhelming. In our country one would take such hospitality for granted more or less but coming from the English it's quite unexpected and very, very comforting. I feel that my devotion to the British over a period of years has not been without foundation and I feel this is a second home more than ever. No one with the exception of Mr. Aurean [*sic*] Bevan,[90] MP from Wales has mentioned a thing about Pops which fact has quite amazed me. In Washington hardly a night would pass that someone didn't ask about them, make remarks etc., and they were Americans. Now here are the British who are directly concerned and not a peep out of them. Of course a lot of it I can put down to British reserve which feel that some things are better left unsaid but mostly I blame it on their ability to make friends which last all their lives . They are slow about it as first but once made then its lasting — wholly and completely.

I have just returned from a day and a half spent in the country with Billy at Eastbourne. Its right on the East Coast has been blitzed quite badly but the family continues to go there during the summer months. For 24 hours I forgot all about the war. It's the most lovely spot and all the fruit which one never gets in London at your disposal. Peaches sell for $1.50 apiece over here and I returned to London clutching a dozen under my arm. Billy is just the same, a bit older, a bit more ducal but we get on as well as ever. It is queer as he is so unlike anyone I have ever known at home or anyplace really. Of course I know he would never give in about the religion and he knows I never would. It's all rather difficult as he is very, very fond of me and as long as I am about he'll never marry. However much he loved me I can easily understand his position. It's really too bad because I'm sure I would be a most efficient Duchess of Devonshire in the post-war world and as I'd have a castle in Ireland, one in Scotland, one in Yorkshire and one in Sussex. I could keep my old nautical brothers in their old age. But that's the way it goes. Everyone in London is buzzing with rumors and no matter what happens we've given them something to talk about. I can't really understand why I like Englishmen so much as they treat one in quite an off-hand manner and aren't really as nice to their women as Americans but I suppose it's just that sort of treatment that women really like. That's your technique isn't it? Went out with William Home the other night.[91] He is a Captain now and is still spouting about what a lot of nonsense the war is. He stood for Parliament from Windsor and did amazingly well as an Independent Candidate. It's quite ridiculous for him to stand up in his uniform and spout about the uselessness of war when he is supposed to be doing nothing but living and learning about just that. He's very good company but that's about as far as it goes. He marches about in a beret looking quite fantastic. Ran into Toni Tichborne at lunch. She looks just as sweet as ever.

90. Aneurin "Nye" Bevan (1897–1960), trade union activist, Labour MP and later, architect of the National Health Service as minister of Health, 1945–51.
91. Playwright William Douglas-Home (1912–1992), third son of the thirteenth earl of Home and brother of future Conservative prime minister, Alec Douglas-Home. William Douglas-Home had enlisted in 1940, despite his philosophical objections, and would stand for election three times during the course of the war as an outspoken antigovernment independent candidate. In 1944 he would be court-martialed and sentenced to a year of hard labor for his refusal to participate in the British advance on the French port of Le Havre, which, he argued, had needlessly endangered thousands of civilians due to the British insistence on unconditional German surrender.

Lady Anderson, wife of Sir John Anderson who is in the war cabinet was staying with the Devonshires while I was there. Apparently she is a great friend of the Carcanos so I am going to meet them there one day next week. I haven't heard much about them since I arrived and I think they see mostly Americans like Angie Duke[92] and Jock Whitney.[93]

I have written lots of letters to Mother and Daddy which I hope they have sent out to you with all the news about Lady Astor etc. It certainly is going to be a tough job to get the British out to your part of the world to do any fighting. Imagine some of these boys who have been out in the Middle East for four years or more going on now to fight in the Pacific. You're probably wondering why they don't send some of the boys like Lord Hartington and Rosslyn don't go but apparently there is a great thing over here about keeping the experienced men in battle

Well, take care Johnny. By the time you get this so much will have happened. The end looks nearer now than ever. Write to me: American Red Cross A.P.O. 887 Postmaster, New York. God bless you.

Much love
Kick —

John F. Kennedy, 26: *Round-Robin Letter*

[received August 10, 1943]

Dear Dad & Mother & Brothers & Sisters:

I'm sorry that I haven't written sooner — but I've been extremely occupied with the South Pacific phase of this total—global—war. I have finally seen what I came 10,000 miles to see — and to the question was it worth coming 10,000 miles to see — the answer — with a quick look up into the air — is yes — but I must admit that a 10,000 mile trip in the other direction to see peace would be a heck of a lot more worth-while.

I can't tell you in much detail about where I am or what doing — but will try to give you a rough idea.

First I would like to say that the note of optimism of Germany this year — the Japs a year or so later to me seems like over—optimism of a very high order. It may be true about the Germans — but I can't believe it about the Japs. They are, I think, with the possible exceptions of a couple of Marine divisions — the greatest jungle fighters in the world —Perhaps not the most skillful — but they make up for this by an unbelievable determination to die rather than quit. Supremacy in the air does not hold the whole answer in the land warfare here — as I've seen the Japs absorb an unbelievable amount of punishment from the air for days — and then when we move in — and it appeared as though there could not be a leaf left alive — they kick the hell out of us. All soldiers fight better with their backs to the wall — witness us at Bataan — and the Japs will

92. The scion of two prominent American families, Angier Biddle Duke (1915–1995), future ambassador to El Salvador, Spain and Denmark and chief of protocol under Presidents Kennedy and Johnson, was currently serving with the Air Force Air Transport Command.
93. An heir to one of the United States' largest fortunes, future ambassador to the Court of St. James's and editor and publisher of the *New York Herald Tribune,* John Hay Whitney (1904–1982) had arrived in London in May to serve as public relations director of the Combat Intelligence Division of the Eighth Army Air Force. The philanthropist, financier, art collector, six-goal polo player and noted breeder of thoroughbreds had recently finished his service as special adviser and consultant on motion pictures to the State Department after leaving the chairmanship of Selznick International Pictures, during which time the company had produced *Rebecca, A Star Is Born, Prisoner of Zenda* and *Gone with the Wind.* In March 1942, he had married Betsey Cushing Roosevelt.

have theirs all the long way back across the South Pacific — or through the "roads" of Burma — The one bright gleam on the stark horizon is that we are knocking them stiff in the air — they (the fliers) are the boys doing the job.

As far as I go myself — which has been in the last few weeks — a good deal farther than I would choose to go — I find that this life is not exactly what the Dr. (Jordan) ordered. If she could have put in the last week with me — she would have had that bed turned down for me at the Baptist[94] — and as a matter of fact — she probably would have had one turned down for herself. —

The living conditions here are rugged — nearly as rugged as Daly — and much more rugged than me (or is it I, mother). We live on the boats — eat canned army rations (beans, fried Spam!) and go out nearly every night — Try to grab a little sleep in the day. So far we have been lucky. The first night out they came the closest. We were well up in there — and lying to thinking that this wasn't too tough — when suddenly I heard a plane looked up — and said it looks like one of our new ones to my exec. The next minute — was flat on my back across the deck. He had straddled us with a couple. The boat was full of holes — and a couple of the boys were hit — but are doing O.K. — They've bothered us quite a bit — but we've had only minor hits on our boat since then. They usually drop a flare — of terrific brilliance — everything stands out for what seems miles around — you wait then as you can't see a thing up in the air — the next minute there's a heck of a craaack — they have dropped one or two. All in all, it makes for a certain loss of appetite.

Most everyone stands up to it pretty well — there is no doubt about it — Americans are not quite the nonchalant heroes that we have been led to believe. That concept of "I'll handle this — I'm dummy this hand" — may read good — but its not actually true. This is probably because Americans have not been sold this war enough so that they would rather be dead than see us lose an island. They fight this war like they would play foot-ball. Those that don't like the game simply won't show up for practice — or if they are made to — are not worth a damn — Those that play — play like the devil — and do a great job — what is all the more to their credit is that we don't seem to have the same burning fervor for the cause that the Japs do. What is interesting though is that some of the mildest most unassuming fellows — stand up & do the best job — and another pleasant surprise — the tougher it gets — the less beefing you hear — I heard more beefing back at Melville, R.I.[95] than I've heard the last few weeks. All in all its an education — and there is an undeniable interest & attraction to it.

I myself am completely — and thoroughly convinced that nothing is going to happen to me. I think this is probably the way everyone feels — someone else — yes — themselves — no. Feeling that way — makes me anxious to see as much of it as possible — and then get out of here and get back home — The more you see here — the quickest you get out — or so they tell us.

As the real curse of war is being stuck in some isolated spot with nothing to relieve the monotony for months — I feel I'm lucky to have this chance.

Am starting my sixth month out of the states — a few more and I'll be ready to let Bobby relieve me — I'll go back and get married — and have a son — and when he grows up — he can come out and relieve Bobby. Teddy better stay home — and join the WPB.[96]

94. The New England Baptist Hospital.
95. The site of the Motortorpedo Boat Squadron Training Center.
96. The War Production Board.

Back has stood up fine; the rest of me is O.K. also. On reading back over the letter I may have caused you some worry — don't am in an excellent spot — in the best duty I could possibly be in the Navy — and we have the boat going very fast. We can always get away.

Love to all

Jack

How about those victrola needles — and that small camera & film — you can put the needles in an airmail letter.

Have not seen Jerry lately but he's around someplace — Saw Jack Pierrepont yester-day. He has rotten duty — and is moaning like the devil. Am serving under Kelly (They were expendable) now. He does a good job — and am fortunate.

John F. Kennedy, 26: *Round-Robin Letter*

[Postmarked August 13, 1943]

Dear Folks:

This is just a short note to tell you that I am alive — and *not* kicking — in spite of any reports that you may happen to hear. It was believed otherwise for a few days — so reports or rumors may have gotten back to you. Fortunately, they misjudged the durability of a Kennedy — and am back at the base now and am O.K. As soon as possible I shall try to give you the whole story.[97]

Much love to you all

Jack

Joseph P. Kennedy to Edward Kennedy, 11

October 5, 1943

Dear Teddy:-

I got your telegram and I was pleased to note that you are still the only child of the Kennedy family that pays for his telegrams.

I don't know whether it would be worth while to go all the way down to the Cape and back again the same day, but I am going to talk with Mother and we will make some plans for you for that day anyway. I will let you know when I see you on Saturday.

I also got your report from school and, boy; it is the worst one you ever had. In the fifth of your class you didn't pass in English or Geography and you only got 60 in Spelling and History. That is terrible — you can do better than that. You wouldn't want to have people say that Joe and Jack Kennedy's brother was such a bad student, so get on your toes.

Love,

---

97. A few days earlier, Motortorpedo Squadron 2 had held a funeral mass for Jack and his crew, whom they believed to have died when the Japanese destroyer *Amagiri* plowed through the hull of PT 109 in the early morning hours of August 2. Although the Navy Department had notified JPK during the course of the week that Jack was missing in action, he believed that Jack was still alive and did not inform his family until after Jack and the surviving crewmembers had been rescued on August 7.

November 17, 1943

Haven't had a minute to write since last Saturday but there's lots to tell. The party went off very well; at least I think it did. We couldn't possibly have jammed another soul into the house and they all stayed until the bitter end at 1:00. I must say, that I didn't have a very good time, as I was so nervous about everything. At nine when I arrived on the scene the band looked very cross and brightened a bit at the mention of a drink. People swarmed in, it was the first party London had had for the young for two years. There were about a dozen girls who hadn't been to a party since the beginning of the war. Everybody brought some drink, so we were never short on that end. The room was about the size of our living room in Bronxville, there was a hall outside and also a staircase where people could sit. In the large room we had about six tables with flowers in the middle and a large table at one end with the buffet consisting of sandwiches and little cakes (all disgusting). The band consisted of six pieces and then I had a little man come in about eleven with an accordion. No one would stop talking when he played so he became rather upset. Joe Jr. arrived with his entire squadron who were feeling no pain.[98] I'll send you names of the other people on another sheet of paper.

Before dinner I was putting on my dress at Marie Bruce's when Irving Berlin rang her up and wanted her to go to a party that same evening.[99] I had just persuaded her to come to mine for a little while. She told him I was giving a party and to come along. Then I spoke to him and told him he must come. At about ten he arrived. Of course people don't pay such attention to celebrities over here as they do at home and when he walked in the door he might have been Joe Snooks for all the glances he got. I planted him at a table with the Duchess of Devonshire, hoping she'd strike up a lively conversation. Marie Bruce hadn't arrived and Joe had just gone to fetch her and I was praying that she would arrive very soon. Sheila Milbanke[100] suddenly appeared and as he [*sic*] had known Berlin on his [*sic*] honeymoon I know he'd well taken care of in her hands. Then Marie Bruce appeared looking extremely well. I asked Berlin to render us a few pieces and he was very reticent. However he finally agreed and got up saying he had known the family for years and he would do anything for one of us. (Please thank him again Daddy when he gets home). He played his new piece "My British Buddy" which was extremely appropriate for the occasion and then a lot of his old ones. We all sang with him so it made everything go very well. The climax came when someone requested "Over There" which he said he didn't write but he'd finish up his performance with. He sat with Marie a while longer and then Joe conducted his thin, shivering little shape back to Claridge's. Before departure he gave two tickets to Marie and myself for yesterday's performance which the King and Queen attended. The show was even better than it was at home and very exciting to be there with them. He really puts "My British Buddy" over and has everyone singing it as they leave the theater.

The party ended at 1:00. We wanted the band to stay on but they refused. It was probably just as well as the party ended on a high note. However we had an incident before it was all over. Lord Edward Fitzmaurice, a young Guardsman of 21, had rather too much to drink and set a match to Elizabeth Cavendish's new evening dress. She is Billy's younger sister and it was the first party she had ever been to so we were all afraid it

---

98. Joe had reported to the First Naval Squadron in Devon under the Coastal Command of the RAF in September.
99. The composer was touring with his review, *This Is the Army*.
100. The earl of Rosslyn's mother, Margaret Sheila Mackellar Milbanke of New South Wales, who had divorced Rosslyn's father, Lord Loughborough, in 1926.

might have scared her away from other parties. She stayed on and told her mother "before I was set on fire the boys didn't pay much attention to me, but afterwards I was very popular". An American boy put the flames out. I was very relieved that it hadn't been the other way around. Angie Laycock said that she said to her brave husband General Laycock,[101] "why don't you do something about putting those flames out"? He replied "I thought it was a fireworks display".

I really think everyone had a good time and I have received lots of letters saying, "why aren't more parties like that given".

Sunday I went out with the gold team from here when they played Cambridge University. We won all our matches and at the luncheon I was asked to make a speech. I disgraced you. I arose, laughed and had to sit down. I really must learn how to make a speech because I get such stage fright.

Monday Joe and I did some shopping, called on Mr. Borum[102] and a few of the old folk at the Embassy. We lunched with Lady Halifax and Richard.[103] It was rather interesting as they had a man there who had just been to Moscow with Anthony Eden. He told us all about the religious revival and what it meant. It was very interesting, especially to Joe and myself having been there. Wednesday I lunched with a girl who is one of the directors in Public Relations. She said the director, Mr. MacHarrie had asked for me in his department and Mr. Gibson had said No. The reason being that I hadn't been over here long enough. However, she thinks that there might be some hope later on. Last night I took the lady who is directing Hospitality for American soldiers in the British Isles to meet the Duchess of Devonshire who directs it for the Dominions. They got along terribly well, and Mrs. De Paula I think would be a very good person to help run it. I really would like that and so we shall see what happens. Last night Joe and I dined with the Biddles. Mrs. Biddle was ill but Tony was there as big as life. There was more brass around. A Miss Hall, who used to be an interior decorator at home was there. She is here with the Red Cross. We had a delicious dinner as usual. Shortly after dinner Joe and I went to join some of his pals. A General dropped us off. He was very nice but as Joe said "I hate to think of him giving orders". We all went on to the 400. Joe seems to be having a good time but no special girl friend. Goodness it makes a difference having him over. He is in wonderful spirits.

Marie Bruce has been wonderful to me so try and send those things I mentioned. I have given her some things in the food line.

That's about all the news at the moment. Tell everyone how much I love their letters and that I am sorry not to be able to answer each one of them.

Think of you all often, especially as Xmas draws near.

Much love to all from
Kick

101. The former Angela Claire Louise Ward, daughter of MP William Dudley Ward, and her husband, Major General Robert Edward "Lucky" Laycock (1907–1968), chief of Combined Operations, 1943–47. In 1941, as commander of the "Layforce" commandos, Laycock had overseen a series of spectacular, extremely dangerous missions in the Middle East, including the raid on what was believed to be Rommel's Libyan desert headquarters. Escaping into the desert and surviving for more than forty days on rain and berries, Laycock had been one of two members of the original fifty-man force to escape capture or death.
102. The former special disbursing officer at the Embassy during JPK's tenure.
103. Richard Frederick Wood (1920–), later Baron Holderness, third son of Lord Halifax, who had become the British ambassador to the United States in 1941.

Joseph P. Kennedy, Jr., 28, to Rose Kennedy and Joseph P. Kennedy

England, Dec. 5, 1943

Dear Mother and Dad:

My giant constitution, nurtured from babyhood by coca colas, nut sundaes and Hershey bars, which drew such derogatory remarks from JP Sr. as "wait till you're thirty years old," has once more shown its remarkable power, by passing through the crisis of a severe cold and bellyache, and placing well on the road to recovery. It would be over flattering it to say that it shook it off with no difficulty whatsoever, for several days found me shivering in my bunk, and dragging myself to my plane, but all in all, it did quite well.

It is essential that I continue to feed it on that to which it has been accustomed, so it is with sincere regret that I notice the lack of Xmas packages for JP, Jr. amidst the towering bundle of packages for other men. I am expecting a strong finish later in the month.

I have had quite a time getting Xmas presents. I talked with Kick about it, and she said there is nothing over here that is worth the money asked except the scarfs, and she said that she had sent everyone these. Practically everything is rationed, so pass the word to all the little Kennedys, that they can't expect much from Brother Joe on this Xmas, but wait till he gets home.

The Seabees[104] have arrived here, and I think they will make this spot a little more livable. They are working well, and they seem to be a good outfit.

It looks like we will be working on both Xmas and New Years. I wish I could spend Xmas with Kick, but at this point it looks quite impossible. She thought she might be able to get down here sometime before Xmas, and I thought she might come down the day after tomorrow. I have been trying to get in touch with her today but without success. The difficulty with our system of days off, is the uncertainty of it. We only get one off, if we fly, and the flights are frequently canceled due to bad weather, so you cant plan much in advance.

They had a dance here last night, and recruited some army nurses from town. They certainly were no beauties, and I gave up early in the evening. We have really been flying a great deal, and it tires the devil out of you. When you get any time off, you usually spend it in your bunk.

It looks now as if my next leave will be the middle of January. Getting leave is the only thing to look forward to, and getting a week off in every eight isn't bad at all.

I now wear long underwear constantly so I'm really back to my boy hood days. Overshoes and a big coat all the time. We have been taking some pictures which ought to be ready in about a week, and I shall send them over to you.

I haven't had any mail for quite a time now. The rumor is that they sank the last ship with the mail, and packages. It is probably untrue, but if true, it probably had all my packages from home. That's all the news. Hope you all have a wonderful Xmas. Certainly wish I were going to be there.

Love
Joe

---

104. The naval construction battalions (or CBs), which had been sent to the North Atlantic since early 1942 to build naval air stations, seaplane bases and storage and repair facilities in anticipation of an eventual Allied invasion of the Continent.

John F. Kennedy, 26, to Rose and Joseph P. Kennedy

Dec 7, 1943

Dear Mother and Dad:

Not much news except that I have received fairly definite dope that I'm heading back in the very near future — which is certainly great to hear. I'll know definitely when in a week or so — but I should get back sometime in January according to the present arrangement. I am going to get sent to Melville as an instructor but there is a P.T. school at Miami that I'd like to get sent to — naturally. When I get definite word on what the plans are I will write and give you the definite dope —

Much love
Jack

Joseph P. Kennedy to Kathleen Kennedy, 23: *Telegram*

1943 DEC 28

DEAR KICK WE ARE ALL AT PALMBEACH AND I KEEP THINKING WHAT FUN IT WAS TO HAVE YOU HERE WITH ME LAST YEAR AND WE ALL ARE PRAYING YOU WILL BE WITH US NEXT XMAS GIVE JOE OUR LOVE AND WISH HIM AND ALL OUR FRIENDS A MERRY XMAS AND A NEW YEAR THAT WILL BRING US ALL PEACE ON EARTH WE ALL SEND OUR LOVE TO YOU BOTH DAD

Rose Kennedy: *Diary Note*

He is really at home — the boy for whom you prayed so hard — at the mention of whose name your eyes would become dimmed — the youngster who you would think dead some nights & you would wake up with sorrow clutching at your heart. What a sense *of* gratitude to God to have spared him. What joy to see him — to feel his coat & to press his arms [*& know he's here*] to look at his bronze tired face which is thin & drawn. He can't eat his old full meals but has to stop & say with an apologetic nod to Margaret the [*life long*] old cook who has fixed up his favorite lunch. Just can't take it yet Margaret Seems nervous When he goes to Patio he Keeps running in & out several times — When he races to Miami he [illegible] his hand through his hair — Barry Shannon[105] — familiar with horse racing lingo — says — he's like a race horse who has been highly geared — you have to unwind him slowly & gradually.

Still he has not changed too much — He still is late at meals — He still is vague on his plans — he still overflows his bathtub & ruins my bedroom rug. So he has not the [illegible] indelible stamp — no [illegible]

Joseph P. Kennedy to Harry Hogan

Palm Beach, February 21, 1944

My dear Harry:

I have just today heard of the loss of your boy. As one father to another, who, although he has not had the total loss, has had his boys missing in action, I can feel in a small way how you must be suffering.

---

105. Charles Barry Shannon (1891?–1946), publisher of the *Palm Beach Post and Times* and owner of the Idle Hour stud farm.

Regardless of what some of us older fellows feel about the war, the reasons for it, and what it is to accomplish, we all know that our youngsters have had a firm determination to make the world a better place. It is small satisfaction for you, but God in His justice, will soften the blow.

With my deepest sympathy to you and your family.
Sincerely yours,

Kathleen Kennedy, 24: *Round-Robin Letter*

February 22, 1944

Dearest Family:

Just arrived back from a most exciting week in Derbyshire and three very restful days in Yorkshire.

Left here Feb. 12th for York and Richard met me at the station. He has got his wooden legs now and is most efficient driving a car etc.[106] Of course it is a terrific effort for him to walk and it will take a long time before he is able to cover any distance but he'll do it sooner or later. We drove to his sister, Anne Feversham's house.[107] It is situated in a Dale and is most attractive but was terribly cold. In fact I have never felt such cold. Anne's husband has just come back from the Middle East but was not there over the weekend. She is very attractive and was terribly sweet to me. Had my breakfast in bed every morning and she took wonderful care of me. Richard is in good spirits and when he is not staying with Anne he lives by himself at Garrowby, his home. I don't think it's very good for him to be alone so much but he doesn't want to go about until he can really manage himself. It would be very nice if you could write Lady Halifax and thank her for all the hospitality various members of her family have extended to me. If Eunice ever gets to Washington she should be sure and go to the Embassy because they would be delighted to see her.

Tuesday afternoon Feb. 15th I went to Derbyshire. Before Election Day, the 17th, the papers were full of news of the election. In fact it aroused so much publicity that three newspaper correspondents had arrived from America to cover the election and Walter Graebner from *Life* was up there.[108] Billy had a meeting with the press every morning and the papers were full of it all day. When I arrived we decided that news of me wouldn't add any votes and I'd be well out of it so I was known as Rosemary Tong, the village girl. Wasn't allowed to open my mouth, although I did go canvassing for votes one afternoon with Billy's sister. We gave all the ~~villagers~~ a good pep talk and found out later that the town voted solid Conservative. Tuesday evening Billy had to speak in six different towns, his mother spoke five other places and there were two MPs from London who had arrived to make speeches for him. I drove around with Billy and sat in the back to hear the crowd's comments. He was asked every sort of question from the Beveridge plan[109] right on down to "Why isn't the park at Chatsworth plowed up?" "Why didn't your father pay more death duties?"[110] "What do you know about being

---

106. Lord Halifax's youngest son, Richard Wood, had been badly wounded in the Middle East.
107. Halifax's youngest daughter had married the third earl of Feversham in 1936.
108. Author and war correspondent Walter Graebner (1909–), London bureau chief for the Luce publications.
109. Economist, writer, civil servant and master of Balliol College, Oxford, William Henry Beveridge (1879–1963) had published his blueprint for the postwar welfare state in November 1942. Although the Beveridge Plan had received only a tepid response from the national government, its proposals for social insurance and national health care had met with widespread public enthusiasm and would underpin the Labour government's postwar social legislative program.
110. Billy's grandfather, the ninth duke of Devonshire, had died in May 1938.

poor?" "Why didn't the Conservative Party interfere in Spain?" Billy has been in the Army for the last four years and hasn't had much chance to keep up on every political bill that has passed the House of Commons. He did awfully well. His speeches were absolutely terrific and they never stuck him on a question. He had everything against him, every vote he got, he got despite who he was, not because. Churchill wrote him a letter which didn't help, his father pulled a few fast ones which made every one rather mad. In short Billy had everything against him. His own personal charm was the only thing he had in his favor. When he started out the odds were twenty to one against, the eve of the poll it was even money. Various Conservative leaders who came down to help with the election said whoever polled 11,000 votes would win. Billy polled over 11,000 but Charlie White[111] polled over 16,000. Everyone was amazed at the size of the poll. The eve of the poll Billy had the ground floor of the town hall in the largest city in the constituency and Charlie White; his opponent had the top floor. When Billy started his speech Charlie White's boys hooed, hissed stamped on the floor and Billy just spoke louder. The various MPs who came were shaking their heads over the actions of the people of West Derbyshire.

We all used to sit up far into the night discussing trends, elections and the world in general. I just sat and listened and thought how lucky I was to be there. It really was something to see and definitely marked a turning point for the Conservative Party. First I want to tell you about Mr. George Muff, Labour MP from Leeds. He spoke for Billy because of the Party truce, which everyone now considers, exists in name only. Mr. Muff was absolutely charming; he spoke of Daddy as "holy Joe". He told me of an incident when Daddy broke all the laws of the House of Commons. During the tricky days of Munich one day Chamberlain was speaking in the House. Daddy was in the visitor's gallery. Lord Halifax arrived and sent down the note to Chamberlain informing him of Hitler's desire to see him at Munich. When Chamberlain announced this to the House the MPs all started cheering and then cheers came from the visitors' gallery. It was Daddy. Of course people in the gallery are never supposed to register any emotion. When he started everybody else joined in including the Lords on the other side of the Chamber. Mr. Muff said it was wonderful to see and has never happened since. Captain W.W. Wakefield[112] was there [*Derbyshire*]. He is charming. David Eccles a new MP who is supposed to be brilliant also came.[113] They all said they would come along to the Club[114] any time and talk to the boys.

I don't know how much of the election was put in the American papers but I just want to say something about Billy's opposer, Charlie White. He hates the Cavendishes like poison, he stood against Billy's uncle and was defeated, he is very well known in the district and he has held various public offices around that section for years. He looks absolutely repulsive, a bit like Mayor Hague.[115] The Commonwealth Party, which consists of a hundred young political organizers, preaching socialism ran his campaign. They know just what the working people want to hear and they give it to them. There is no doubt about it, there is a terrific swing to the Left. People want to hear

111. The local alderman, Charles Frederick White (1891–1956), was standing as an independent socialist Common Wealth Party candidate.
112. William Wavell Wakefield, later first Baron Wakefield of Kendal (1898–1985), Conservative MP for Swindon, 1935–45.
113. Connoisseur, financier, Conservative MP for Chippenham, 1943–62, and future cabinet minister, David McAdam Eccles later first Baron and first Viscount Eccles, (1904–1999).
114. She had been living and working at the Hans Crescent Club since mid-November 1943.
115. As the longtime Democratic mayor of Jersey City, New Jersey, Frank Hague (1876–1956) controlled one of the most powerful and notoriously corrupt political machines in the United States from 1917 to 1947.

about how much money they are going to get out of the Beveridge plan not how much money the Tory government is spending on the war. It's all very upsetting. However most people recognize the fact. They say the pendulum will swing to the Left but it always swing back. I hope so.

The day of the polling I rode around with Billy when he visited the various polling booths. Everyone felt very confident and you could see they all thought he was wonderful and that he would get in. The day after polling day Billy, his three agents, his mother, his sister and myself assembled with Charlie White and his stooges in the town hall to watch them count the votes. We were locked in for three hours while each ballot box was opened and the votes counted. What a nervous three hours it was as we watched and poor Billy had to walk around looking pleased and not too disappointed. There's no doubt about the secrecy of the ballot and it was a most interesting thing for me to see. When the results were ascertained the press was allowed in. The clerk read out the results and then Billy, Charlie White and a farmer who had entered the race at the last moment and who had won a little over 200 votes went out on the balcony. Billy made a good speech and when we left people cheered him tremendously. He didn't really mind very much although the large majority was a surprise as White had gotten the Liberal vote. No matter what happened he was going back to the army but it just leaves a bad taste. His father was most disappointed and kept saying; "I don't know what the people want." Billy just said "I do, they just don't want the Cavendishes." I think it shook his father a bit to hear it from Billy. However he still would never admit the fact to himself.

Billy's mother was nicer than ever and is absolutely wonderful on the platform. She understands the situation completely.

Received a lovely old leather book from the Duke for my birthday. The Duchess said she had nothing to do with it, and when I opened it up I knew why. It was the Book of Common Prayer of the Church of England. I laughed and thanked him very much. Had a long chat with the Duchess and she is very sympathetic about the other situation. She said to me, "It's a shame because you are both so good and it would please everyone so much". I told her about your cable, which was a great joy. She longs to make things easy. Please try and discover loopholes although I keep feeling that the particular parties involved would make any compromise impossible. The Catholics would say it would give scandal. This situation, Daddy, is a stickler.

Never mind about Mrs. Bruce's refrigerator. Speaking of Mrs. Bruce she has been wonderful and still is. Don't know what I'd do without her. Please write if you already haven't.

Now, more about the election. Everyone is discussing it every place, including even the German radio so you can see the way things are going. I could hear people discussing in on the train. I must say I haven't ever spent such an interesting week. That's really the way I like to spend my time

Lady Astor was coming this week to my Quiz the British [show] but now she can't make it. I called Oren but he couldn't do it, he suggested Roger Putnam who is a Lieut. Commander in the Navy over here. I had a long talk with him and he's coming along to do it. It's a small world isn't it?

Please save the enclosed clippings, as I shall want them later.

None of the clothes have arrived as yet and am eagerly awaiting them.

Please tell Jack that Baby is still nuts about him.

Thank you for the cable about Chuck. Gosh I hope he's all right. We've [the family] been so lucky so far that it scares me.

Love to all. Write soon.

P.S. Have just read in the paper about some new job for Daddy.[116] Is it true and is he going to take it?

Everyone here asks me about the coming election. Of course they all think the country could not possibly go on without Roosevelt. I launch into a long speech [about] what Roosevelt hasn't done and what a bad idea it would be to give him another four years in the White House. I'm not exactly sure on the points I should emphasize so it would be wonderful it you could write down a few things. Thanks Daddy I don't think you would mind too much unless you are now working for the old man.

Have just talked to Joe on the phone. He sounds very well and may be up in two or three weeks' time.

Am having lunch with Kitty Charlton today so should have plenty of gossip.

Alfred Clark, Dodo's husband rang me up yesterday. He said he had just heard from Dodo in Palm Beach that she had seen a lot of Jack!! Does our heroic brother think himself more attractive with the marks of battle upon him?

Rose Kennedy to Kathleen Kennedy, 24

PALM BEACH, February 24, 1944

Dear Kathleen:

I know your father has written you all the news, but I just wanted to add a couple of tidbits.

There is no news about Agnes and Hartie.[117] Galleazzi's pal said of course the authorities were always the same and frankly I do not seem to think Dad can do anything. He feels terribly sympathetic and so do I and I only wish we could offer some suggestions. When both people have been handed something all their lives, how ironic it is that they can not have what they want most. I wonder if the next generation will feel that it is worth sacrificing a life's happiness for all the old family tradition. So much wealth, titles, etc. seem to be disappearing. But I understand perfectly the terrific responsibilities and the disappointment of it all.

It is Lent now and I am praying morning, noon and night, so do not be exhausting yourself and running your little legs off going to Church, as your first duty is towards your job. The little verse — "Do your duty, that is best; leave unto the Lord the rest" may be Protestant or Catholic, but it really teaches us that our first responsibility is towards our immediate job.

We had a letter from someone in Boston whose third cousin watches you go to Communion frequently, so the news has been carried across the waters.

I am sorry about sending you a red suit but I did not know that you already had a red coat over there and I thought the rose suit would be pretty under your mink coat.

Father Keller is down here and they are giving him a luncheon Thursday. I have not talked to him yet, but his book — MEN OF MARYKNOLL — is a great success.[118]

---

116. A number of recent press reports had indicated that the president had offered JPK the post of secretary of commerce. "A reliable source," had told the *Boston Herald,* for example, that JPK was "giving serious consideration" to the offer in Palm Beach.

117. To prevent censors and telegraph clerks from understanding the issues at stake in Kick's and Billy Hartington's efforts to marry, the family adopted the code names "Agnes" for Kick (her middle name as well as the confirmation name that she had taken in honor of her maternal aunt), and "Hartie" for Billy, in their correspondence.

118. Maryknoll Father James Gregory Keller (1900–1972) had coauthored the account of Catholic missionary work in the Far East with Meyer Berger of the *New York Times.* The following year Keller would found the Christopher Movement to "make every person a missionary" within the domestic realms of government, education, law and the media.

Admiral Willson[119] was up here to lunch today and says that Mary's husband might be sent to Miami later and that she will be down this way.

Nancy Tenney is marvelous — looks tremendous, feels magnificent, and is a matter of great interest to Jack and Bobby.

Dodo Potter's baby is adorable. Bobby was teaching him to swim in the pool yesterday. To watch her and Bobby handle the baby made me ready again to see Dr. Jordan, so I do not know what I will do when all the little grandchildren start to swim in the pool.

Have you heard the song, "Mares eat oats and Dotes [*sic*] eat oats and Little Lambs eats Ivy" (only the words are all run together).

Ann Bullitt's engagement to Lt. Brewster was broken and she suddenly married Casper Townsend, and the paper said, "She was unable to communicate the news to her father in time for last night's wedding."

I guess that's all, dear Kathleen. I certainly wish I might see you. We are all going to Hialeah[120] Saturday. No one seems to be very lucky on the horses except bobby, who looked 21 and picked a couple of winners.

Much love to you.

Kathleen Kennedy, 24: *Round-Robin Letter*

March 22, 1944

Dearest Family:

Daddy's letter of March 10th arrived yesterday.[121] Very interesting most enlightening. It's so hard to realize what people are really thinking at home just by reading the papers. He sized it all up — for the first I've really realized that to be a realist in these days one risks being called a pessimist.

Tim called me yesterday and gave me a message from mother to the effect that a lot of people read my letters other than those for whom they are written. To tell you the truth such a fact is a little putting-off. In fact, I wonder if you get all my letters. From now on I think I shall number them, at the top. This one is Number 1. In any case I sincerely hope they have done no one any harm.

Today a sale starts at Christie's of the furniture from Wall Hall. Marie Bruce was going over this afternoon to mark any of the stuff and I shall go tomorrow to see if there isn't some little thing I can pick up which would be fun for us all to have. In any case I should very much like to have a look at all that stuff again.

Sunday I wended my way to Churchdale. Please look at confidential matter enclosed for further details of that visit. However quite a funny thing happened on the journey. I got into a first class carriage for six — I was not in uniform. In the carriage was an Englishman, his wife, two American Lieutenants, and an English Army Cap-

---

119. The former naval attaché at the London Embassy had been promoted to the rank of vice admiral in 1942, and was currently serving as a deputy with the Joint Chiefs of Staff.
120. JPK had purchased what he described to the *New York Times* as a "small interest" in the Miami racetrack in May 1943.
121. "Your letter on the election was one of the finest letters I have ever read," he had written her, and it was most enlightening because while the American papers gave terrific publicity to Billy's contest, they have played down the significance of all these elections. In fact, a few days later when Churchill['s] candidate was elected in some spot, the information was given out to really indicate to people that it was the candidate in a former election that lost but this one won because Churchill was with him. Of course, it is all a lot of dribble, like most of the stuff we're getting out of England.

tain. Before very long the younger of the two Lieutenants brought out a Hershey bar and passed it all around. Is usual in such a case no one likes to take anybody else's food because everything is so strictly rationed. However the American insisted, and we all [had] a small piece. A half an hour passed. The same young American produced a box of chocolates. The English couple was overcome. Such remarks as "That's the first box of chocolates we've seen since the war" issued forth. When he passed them around the second time after a lot of chatter about how good the food was that the American army had sent over — the English Army officer buried himself behind T.E. Lawrence's "Seven Pillars of Wisdom" and said to me in a whisper "There come those damn chocolates again." At once I understood what he felt and what a lot of people must feel about Yanks in this country. I could observe the whole thing quite impartially and look objectively at the effect that quite unconsciously that young American was producing. It seems a shame but there's absolutely nothing that can or could be done about such a state of affairs. It's nothing serious but it's there — the friction I mean.

I left the carriage after about an hour as Elizabeth Cavendish was on the train and I wanted to sit with her. When I came back to the carriage just before I got off the train (I'd left my suitcase there) the English man said to me "I've just had a dispute with those Americans about your name. They guessed I couldn't possibly know it and as I never forget a face I knew I did. It is Kennedy, isn't it?" I said yes it was. He continued "I remember seeing your face five years ago and then again the other day. However you wouldn't know me from a hole in the ground".

Rather terrifying. I might have said anything. But as Brother Jack would probably say, I was very flattered.

Today I Lunched with William Douglas-Home who has just put himself to stand for Parliament at Clay Cross, Derbyshire. This is his third try and this time he is standing as the Atlantic Charter candidate against the Government's Labour man. The seat is a safe Labour seat [as safe as any seat is nowadays] as it is the center of the mining district. However, he has high hopes. He is quite sincere in his motives and feels very strongly about the Atlantic Charter being applied to Germany and the other defeated states as well as the victorious ones. He is anti-unconditional surrender. Hughie Fraser[122] was with us today and said that William would probably voice the sentiments of a lot of people in this country but it would be disastrous if he got in. I told you Jakie Astor wrote and said that to be one of my suitors he found it was necessary to stand and fail for parliament. Quite funny.

Received a delicious box of candy from Aunt Loretta yesterday. It really was kind of her to think of me on my birthday.

Wrote and told Shellie Milbanke to look up Byron Foy.[123] I think he would [be] just her cup of tea.

Haven't talked to Joe this week but will probably do so tomorrow.

The five-pound boxes arrive every week and they are a great blessing. I'm especially fond of the juices, Kleenex.

122. The younger son of the fourteenth Lord Lovat, the Honorable Hugh Charles Patrick Fraser (1918–1984) was a former president of the Oxford Union, and had traveled with Kick and Joe to Spain in the summer of 1939. Later in 1944 he would distinguish himself in Operation Pegasus, rescuing those left behind following the Battle of Arnhem. The following year he would be one of four Roman Catholics to be elected Tory MPs, serving eventually as parliamentary undersecretary of state for the colonies, 1961–62; secretary of state for air, 1962–64 and minister of defense for the RAF, 1964. In 1956 he would marry Lady Antonia Pankenham; he and the writer would be divorced in 1977.
123. Byron Cecil Foy (1893–1970), president of the De Soto Motor Corporation, had resigned in 1942 to join the Army Air Force.

Please tell Bill Hearst that I have seen Lee Carson of INS.

Much love to all from Kick

This typewriter is terrible

THIS IS FOR MOTHER AND DADDY ONLY

Sunday I went to Churchdale for two days. The Duchess, with my full knowledge, asked a very great friend of hers, Father Ted Talbot[124] to come and stay to talk to me. (He, by the way, is Lord Halifax's greatest friend.) Her idea was for him to explain what the Cavendish family stood for in the English Church, the impossibilities of Billy permitting his son to be brought up a Roman Catholic. He also took a great deal of trouble to explain to me the fundamental differences between the Anglican and Roman Churches. Of course I explained that something one had been brought up to believe in and which was largely responsible for the character and personality of an individual is a very difficult thing for which to find a substitute. Further, I explained that I had been blessed with so many of this world's goods that it seemed rather cheap and weak to give in at the first real crisis in my life. Of course both the Duchess and Father Talbot don't for a minute want me to give up something. They just hoped that I might find the same thing in the Anglican version of Catholicism. When I left Churchdale on Tuesday, yesterday, I felt most discouraged and rather sad. I want to do the right thing so badly and yet I hope I'm not giving up the most important thing in my life. The Duchess is so wonderful and kind. She wants me to consider wherever they are as a home and really couldn't be kinder. She is writing Mother. Poor Billy is very, very sad but he sees his duty must come first. He is a fanatic on this subject and I suppose just such a spirit is what has made England great despite the fact that Englishmen are considered so weak-looking etc. If he did give in to me his father has told him he would not be cut off, in fact nothing would happen. They, meaning Mother and Father, would just make the best of it. That makes things even more difficult. I am going to quote a bit from the Duchess' letter to me which arrived a few minutes ago — "I am no good at saying things so I am writing to say how you are always in my thoughts and how I feel for you alone here without your mother and father when you are going through so much and have had such overwhelmingly difficult things to decide about. It is desperately hard, that you should have all this great unhappiness with the second front always at the back of one's mind. I know how lonely you must feel and almost forsaken but we must trust in God that things will come out for the best in the end. I do hope you know how much we love you and if there is even the smallest thing we can do to help you have only to say — and always please come and see me at any time if you feel like it and come and stay. There is always a bed for you — you have only to telephone."

That really is a kind letter. This Friday I am going to see Bishop Mathew,[125] a friend of Father d'Arcy's,[126] about a dispensation. I suppose it will practically impossible.

You two have been wonderful and a great strength. I'm sure Mother's prayers are helping all the time.

Write soon. Much love again.

.

---

124. The Reverend Edward Keble Talbot (d. 1949), former superior of the Community of the Resurrection, 1922–40, and chaplain to the king, 1920–45.
125. David James Matthew (1902–1975), auxiliary bishop of Westminster, 1938–46.
126. Martin Cyril d'Arcy (1888–1976), Jesuit, writer, lecturer in philosophy and master of Campion Hall at Oxford. A friend to many of London's literary and intellectual luminaries, including T. S. Eliot and Bertrand Russell, d'Arcy had converted both Edith Sitwell and Kick's friend Evelyn Waugh to Roman Catholicism. The following year he would become the Jesuit provincial for England.

Joseph P. Kennedy to Kathleen Kennedy, 24: *Telegram*

PALMBEACH FLO 1944 APR 3

CONTINUE WRITING LETTERS AS ALWAYS THEY ARE WONDERFUL STOP NOBODY
SEES ANYTHING CONFIDENTIAL STOP I FEEL TERRIBLY UNHAPPY YOU HAVE TO
FACE YOUR BIGGEST CRISIS WITHOUT MOTHER OR ME STOP YOUR CONFIDENTIAL
MEMORANDUM WORTHY OF CHESTERTON MAGNIFICENT STOP WITH YOUR FAITH
IN GOD YOU CANT MAKE A MISTAKE STOP REMEMBER YOU ARE STILL AND ALWAYS
WILL BE TOPS WITH ME LOVE

= DAD JOSEPH P KENNEDY

Kathleen Kennedy, 24: *Round-Robin Letter*

April 4, 1944

Dearest Family:

Tim has just called with the information that he is on his way home very soon. Will try and give you all the latest news in this rather rushed letter.

Returned from Cliveden this morning where I have been for the last four days. Had an attack of laryngitis last week and was in bed for four days, then to the country to recuperate. While I was sick I stayed with Marie Bruce which certainly quickened my recovery, as she was so very solicitous. She gave me delicious food and I got plenty of peace and quiet. However by the end of the week I think she was thanking her lucky stars that she hadn't given birth to one child, let alone nine. Mother, I think she shakes her head when she thinks of you and how gay and attractive you still are. She had to go to bed for three days when I departed. Lady Astor was her usual kind self. She took wonderful care of me. Don't ever worry about me not being looked up. I have quite a few generous souls who have given themselves that particular job. Joe came down on Sunday for the night. We took a long walk and he seems very well and in good spirits but I think he becomes slightly dejected when he thinks of the future and how much valuable time is slipping [*away*] during the war. This is a natural feeling and one that all the boys of his age have. Today I kissed him good-bye and he took the cigars back to his base with him. He had a very enjoyable leave, and lived in style at the Dorchester. The party at Cliveden was small compared to most Cliveden parties. All the boys were there and Barbara Astor who has just had a miscarriage.[127] Her little son, David is adorable with bright red hair. Even though she has a baby Barbara has been called up. She had a job in a Ministry here in London. However, now she has decided to do the housework and live in the country for the summer. That's the way it works. If you have servants you must do an official job or otherwise do the housework. Lady Astor gets peppier every day and she was furious the other night because we just wanted to sit and she longed to play games. She decided on one called "Subjects" and poor Joe had to talk on "Jam" for two minutes. Needless to say his public speaking didn't put up a very good showing. Mr. Barrington Ward, Editor of the *Times* was there and the Lady who is the head of our WAACs and a man who was [*under Dad*] and still is Agricultural Attaché. The food really was too delicious. As Aunt Nancy gives everyone her sweets it would be a tremendous gesture if you would send her a box of caramels or something of the sort

---

127. The Astor's third son, Michael Langhorne Astor, had married Barbara Mary Colonsay in November 1942. Colonsay was the daughter of Mrs. John Dewar's first marriage; in 1933, JPK had negotiated U.S. distribution rights for Dewar's whiskeys through Barbara Astor's stepfather, John Dewar, chairman of the Distillers Company.

twice a month. Any little goodie would be nice as she is the soul of generosity. Of course she still hopes I'll marry Billy and keeps telling me I'll only be happy in England.

Now about that little Matter! Joe very kindly went to see the particular Bishop who has been advising me. He will write you about the interview. Billy also went to see him. I received your cable about possible concessions. I understand perfectly why there aren't any. The Bishop told me that it would put the Church in a very difficult position for us to get a dispensation and it would be better if we went ahead and got married and then something might possibly be done afterwards. Of course he wouldn't guarantee that anything could be done, but I'm quite sure that if we wait to see about a dispensation we might wait years.

Of course the Dukie is very worried about having A Roman Catholic in the family. In fact, he's a fanatic on the subject. In their eyes the most awful thing that could happen to our son would be for it to become a Roman. With me in the family that danger becomes immediate even though I would promise that the child could be brought up as an Anglican. The Church would not marry us and the result would be that I would be married in a registry office. I could continue to go to Church but not Communion. How long this state would continue would be impossible to say. I certainly am not going to count on everything being made okay — I shall only hope for it. If I do marry Billy within the next two months, please be quite sure that I am doing it with the full knowledge of what I am doing and that I'm quite happy about it and feel quite sure that I am doing the right thing. As My Bishop said, "No one can say that you are committing a sin because a sin is done from a selfish motive. What you are doing is done entirely from a non-selfish motive."

What the Red Cross is going to say is another question, but I don't think they will mind too much. I thought I'd say I'd work later on as a volunteer. Mr. Gibson wrote me today about a clipping which appeared in the Washington Star saying I had taken part in British politics — it was a most uncomplimentary little piece. Mr. Gibson said he was sure that I had not done anything wrong but wished to get the matter straightened out. If it's not one thing it's another!

My best love to all and a very happy Easter to everyone.

much love from Kick

P.S.: Feeling happy & well — Don't worry! Sorry you'll have to face the McDonnells

April 5th

Billy just called last night and said that there wasn't much hope of getting any more leave. That's our latest difficulty. Goodness, when will they ever stop.

Spring is in the air and that means summer is just around the corner. I'm in need of a new bathing suit so by the time it gets over here it will be summer. If possible I want one with quite long legs to cover my big fat ones, dressmaker is the best kind. The rose suit hasn't arrived as yet, but hope for it soon. I wore the black silk skirt last weekend and it was a great success. Any cute little shorts would be a good idea too and one dirndl dress. You know those Austrian kind I always used to wear with the frilly blouses.

Love again to all

Kick

Kathleen Kennedy, 24: *Round-Robin Letter*

April 24, 1944

Dearest Family:

The censor has gotten after me again so I'm afraid you haven't heard from me in some time.

The box of clothes arrived about two weeks ago and they are all awfully nice with the exception of Mother's evening dress, which I am going to give to some deserving British soul. The dress is really too old for me. Sent Joe's stuff off with one of his roommates.

In my last letter I think I told you that I asked the King's secretary, Tommy Lascelles, to find out about the mirror which Mother sent to the Queen. Today the following letter arrived from him. It speaks for itself "The mirror certainly reached the Queen safely; and equally certainly a letter was sent to your mother within a few days of its arrival. But the letter seems to have gone astray — maybe through enemy action — and a copy of it is being sent out at once to Mrs. Kennedy. Mind you, let me know if this too fails to turn up!" By now that letter should have reached you.

Returned late Sat. evening from three days in Yorkshire staying with Jean Lloyd.[128] She lives in a small house there, does all her own work, has no phone and lives in a very domestic life. The evening I arrived she has just broken her foot so for three days I was most efficient around the house. Billy, stationed right near there, came out every evening with lobsters and champagne to keep us going. It really is fantastic when I think of how Jean lived before the war at Cortachy Castle and how easily she has taken on this role. Neither she or her husband think they will ever go back to the luxury of pre-war days and have quite gotten used to the idea of having one servant and running their lives on a very inexpensive scale. Most of the young people think the same way here and one may say, "well, they ought to", but it's awfully easy to talk that way but difficult to really get down to it. Billy doesn't ever expect to live at Chatsworth I don't think really but he won't give up all hope. He is in tremendous spirits and not at all gloomy about the future! He has been sending for rings from all the jewelry stores in London. I have definitely decided to marry him but of course the date depends on a lot of things. We are not going to announce it as I think that will only make things very tricky. However no matter what I shall let you know in advance, as I would not dream of doing it otherwise. You understand that the ceremony would have to be performed in a registry office which is rather sordid but the only thing to do as I wouldn't have an Anglican service. Speaking of Anglicans I am going to pay a formal visit to the Archbishop of Canterbury[129] at Lambeth Palace next week. I am not dreading it a bit as he is so very nice. I spoke to Billy's mother on the phone last night and she says she thinks she can fix up so I can get down to Eastbourne.

Everything is lovely here in London now and my only regret is that I can't get to the country a bit more. Things at the Club have been rather quiet, but things are picking up a bit this week. Some G.I. just told me that I was like a lovely picture that hadn't been developed. What a compliment.

Please tell Jack that I saw Blair Clark the other night. He had just arrived. Mr. Waldrop wrote me a very funny letter with the front page of the Toledo *Blade* reproduced for my enjoyment. The front page needless to say had a small article about my political activities.

Just talked to Joe. He was very well and is getting off this weekend.

Much love from Kick

---

128. The former Lady Victoria Jean Marjorie Mabell Ogilvy, eldest daughter of the ninth earl of Airlie.
129. Dr. William Temple (1881–1944), archbishop of Canterbury, 1942–44.

Rose Kennedy: *"Notes on My Reactions at Kick's Marriage"*

The Homestead, Hot Springs, Virginia

Personal Reminiscences Private

K — sent cable Sat April 29th that she would marry in a registry office — Joe phoned me said he hadn't slept — Naturally I was disturbed horrified — heartbroken — Talked for a minute on our responsibility ~~for~~ in allowing her to drift into this dilemma then decided we should think of practical way to extricate her. I said I would think it out & then call him later.

Later we decided we would send a cable about like this Heartbroken — think-feel you have been wrongly influenced — Sending Archie Spell's[130] friend to talk to you. Anything done for Our Lord will be rewarded hundredfold —

Joe decided to see Archbishop who talked to him about three hours but not all about Kick — said he was having difficulties with many of the young people — they adopt attitude they can do something later etc. — Did not seem unduly excited — I thought it would have such mighty repercussions in that every little young girl would say if K- Kennedy can — why can't I? — why all the fuss, then everyone pointed to our family with pride as well behaved — level headed & deeply religious. What a blow to the family prestige — No one seemed to be as excited about that as I & I was sick & supposed to keep from any emotional upset so I prayed with all my heart & tried to imagine where a *[illegible]* from there — Kick would be still a Red Cross woman and Lady H.

Joe told me I had done all that could be done — He called LH[131] to see if he could &_____ but said impossible. He also said he had often discussed the whole situation with K— & for us to discount [?] no matter what she said there — that He was positive she would be in only as a Cath. as she had argued it out several times with him — that she had something up her sleeve & would pull it off as she was much smarter than any of the D.[132] I would like Joe to fly to her but he seemed to think that was impossible al-tho' now I know he should have gone over a month or 2 ago —

I have sent another cable

Rose Kennedy to Kathleen Kennedy, 24: *Telegram Draft*

Archie Spell~~man~~ has made investigation — ~~All cases~~ there & here. Can you write or cable what concessions your friend ~~can~~ will consider — ~~may be contained in letter to Mother~~ Hoping for some solution but looks extremely difficult.

All our love & affection

Mother

The Marquess of Hartington, 26, to Rose Kennedy

April 30, 1944

Dear Mrs. Kennedy,

I do feel so ashamed at not having written to you before, and I hope you won't think too harshly of me for my bad manners. The situation has changed so much from day to day, and I'm afraid I've kept on putting off writing to you until we could reach a decision one way or the other.

I have loved Kick for a long time, but I did try so hard to face the fact that the reli-

---

130. Archbishop Spellman's.
131. Lord Halifax.
132. The Devonshires.

gious difficulties seemed insurmountable, and I tried to make up my mind that I should have to make do with second best. I felt too that if she could find someone else she could really be happy with, it would be much better & more satisfactory for her.

But after Christmas I realized that I couldn't bear to let her go without ever asking her if we couldn't find a way out and I knew that time before I should have to go and fight was getting short.

I could not believe, either, that God could really intend two loving [?] people, both of whom wanted to do the right thing, and both of whom were Christians, to miss the opportunity of being happy, and perhaps even useful, together because of the religious squabbles of His human servants several hundred years ago.

I do feel extremely strongly about the religion of my children both from a personal and from a national point of view, otherwise I should never have asked Kick to make such sacrifices in agreeing to their being brought up Anglican.

I know that I should only be justified in allowing my children to be brought up Roman Catholic, if I believed it to be desirable for England to become a Roman Catholic country. Therefore, believing in the National Church of England, as I do very strongly, and having so many advantages, and all the responsibilities that they entail, I am convinced that I should be setting a very bad example if I gave in, and that nothing would justify my doing so.

I do feel terribly keenly the sacrifices I'm asking Kick to make, but I can't see that she will be doing anything that is wrong in the eyes of God. My first worry has been to decide whether she could really be happy with me, having made these sacrifices. Obviously if I felt she could not, and if I felt that she would live with a sense of guilt, I should not be justified in asking her to marry me. But I do think in my heart that she is so holy and good that God will continue to help her and that she can be happy, and I know that selfish though it sounds, I should never be happy or be much good without her.

I will try with all my power to make her happy, and I shall never be able to express my gratitude to you and to Mr. Kennedy for your understanding and goodness in giving your consent.

Please excuse this dopey & after reading over, pompous letter, I think we both feel a bit punch drunk after the emotional battering of the last few months.

I shall never be able to get over my amazing good fortune in being allowed to have Kick as my wife; it still seems incredibly wonderful.

Please try not to think too harshly of me for what must seem to you a tyrannical attitude. I promise that both Kick & I have only done what we really believed in our hearts to be right.

> Yours ever,
> Billy

Kathleen Kennedy, 24, to Rose and Joseph P. Kennedy

May 3, 1944

Dearest Mother & Daddy —
Enclosed is Billy's letter to you. Since he has written it your various cables have arrived. They make me feel very sad but somehow I cannot feel I am doing the wrong thing. I saw the apostolic delegate[133] yesterday. He was very gentle and kind —

---

133. Archbishop William Godfrey (1889–1963), since 1938 the first apostolic delegate to Britain since the Reformation and wartime chargé d'affaires for the Holy See to the Polish government in exile. Godfrey would be created a cardinal in 1958.

Marie Bruce is most upset about your cable. She has been more than kind. Please do not be angry with her.

You both have been so wonderful to me all my life — given me every advantage and whatever I have or am stems from you both. Many thanks.

Please try and understand and pray that everything will be all right in time. I'm sure it will be.

Billy is so pleased and so kind. It would delight your heart to see how solicitous he is.

Joe comes tomorrow. He is a great strength.

I shall write you next week a long, long letter and give you all the news.

All love to everyone

From Kick

Archbishop William Godfrey to Archbishop Francis Spellman: *Telegram*

LONDON MAY 4 1944

THANKS CABLE HAVE DONE AS REQUESTED EFFORT IN VAIN STOP MOTHER COULD TRY AGAIN WITH ALL HER POWER STOP AM CONVINCED THIS ONLY CHANCE

ARCHBISHOP WILLIAM GODFREY

Kathleen Kennedy, 24, to Joseph P. Kennedy: *Telegram*

LONDON 1944 MAY 5

RELIGION EVERYTHING TO US BOTH WILL ALWAYS LIVE ACCORDING TO CATHOLIC TEACHING PRAYING THAT TIME WILL HEAL ALL WOUNDS YOUR SUPPORT IN THIS AS IN EVERYTHING ELSE MEANS SO MUCH PLEASE BESEECH MOTHER NOT TO WORRY AM VERY HAPPY AND QUITE CONVINCED HAVE TAKEN RIGHT STEP LOVE TO ALL=

KATHLEEN KENNEDY

Archbishop Francis Spellman to Archbishop William Godfrey: *Telegram Draft*

[May 6, 1944]

Will you kindly call on ~~Eileen~~ Kathleen Kennedy care of Marie Bruce 49 Hill St. London explaining that her mother is greatly distressed news of ~~prospective~~ contemplated ~~marriage~~ action and if possible persuade her to postpone this step.

Joseph P. Kennedy, Jr., 28, to Rose Kennedy: *Telegram*

LONDON MAY 6, 1944

EVERYTHING WONDERFUL DONT WORRY SHE IS VERY HAPPY WISH YOU COULD HAVE BEEN HERE LOVE=

JOE KENNEDY

Marie Bruce and Lady Astor to Rose Kennedy: *Telegram*

1944 MAY 7 PM 3 29

DEAREST ROSE YOU WOULD REJOICE IN THEIR YOUNG HAPPINESS STOP ONLY GRIEF
YOUR SORROW KATHLEEN LOOKED LOVELY PALE PINK

MARIE BRUCE NANCY ASTOR

Joseph P. Kennedy, Jr., 28, to Joseph P. Kennedy: *Telegram*

1944 MAY 7 PM 4 34

THE POWER OF SILENCE IS GREAT=

JOE

Kathleen Kennedy Hartington, 24, to Joseph P. Kennedy: *Telegram*

LONDON 1944 MAY 8 AM 9 14

=MOST DISTRESSED ABOUT MOTHER PLEASE TELL HER NOT TO WORRY YOUR CA-
BLE MADE MY HAPPIEST DAY WIRE NEWS COMPTON PLACE EASTBOURNE SUSSEX
HAVE AMERICAN PAPERS BEEN BAD ALL LOVE KICK

KATHLEEN HARTINGTON

Joseph P. Kennedy, Jr., 28, to Rose and Joseph P. Kennedy

England, May 8, 1944

Dear Mother and Dad:

I arrived back from London this morning after three days there. Everything went over quite well considering the problems. I think the best way to give you the picture is to take it chronologically.

Kick called me all last week asking whether I had heard from the family, and whenever she heard from you she would call me and ask me what I thought. Once she had definitely made up her mind to do it, I did the best I could to help her through. She was under a terrific strain all the time, and as the various wires came in she became more and more upset. It is extremely difficult over here to tell exactly what everyone there thought about it.

I went to see the Devonshires' lawyer and read over the marriage settlement. He asked me about her income etc., and I gave it to him from what I remembered of the trust. Customarily the wife places her money with the husband, but in this case with the vagueness of my knowledge, he decided to leave her money alone. The Duke is making approximately the same settlement on her as was made by his father on the present Duchess. Billy is to receive an income of 6,000 pounds clear without taxes, [*except income tax*] which in reality amounts to half of this when the [*income*] tax are paid. If he is killed, Kick receives an income of 3,000 pounds a year until she remarries in which case it is cut down to a thousand pounds per year. If Kick becomes the Duchess she gets an increased income of 5,000 pounds. The children receive a lump sum of 25,000 pounds, and an income of 1,000 pounds a year for education and maintenance. All this is conditional on them not becoming Catholics, which would automatically cut them out of the gift and the income.

587

From this you will see that Billy receives no capital. I was surprised at this but in view of the war and the tax question, from a financial point of view this seems to be a wise decision. If he ever needs capital for anything like buying a home, he asks the corporation which is in charge of his father's estates, and they advance the capital to him. I think the Duke will wait until after the war before giving any great amount of capital. The amount of money which Billy will receive [*above the 6000 pounds*] depends entirely on the Duke, and there is nothing automatic about it.

Kick did not sign a paper saying that she would bring the children up as Anglicans, though I think the Duke did want her to do it. I think she told them that she would not interfere with their religion, but this can be worked out sometime in the future. The Duke and Duchess wanted to have the blessing of the Archbishop of Canterbury on the wedding, but I didn't think much of the idea. The Archbishop wrote to the Catholic Bishop and asked him whether they might both say a few words of blessing, but the Bishop declined. The Duke's idea on this is that it would lift the marriage from a purely civil ceremony to something which would have the blessing of God. Kick has probably given you the full story on this.

The lawyer seemed very nice, and I don't think he put anything over on me, and didn't impress me at all that he would try. Kick must name a trustee and I suggested Wilkinson.[134] Some time during the year a list of Kick's holdings will have to be sent to him, because for purposes of English income tax, the incomes of both parties are considered. You are probably aware of the tax problems involved and will have some ideas. In any case, I can talk with you about it, when I get home.

I then went to the Colonial Office and saw the Duke. He is a shy old bird, and was as jittery as an old duck. The conversation was rather strained, but he said that he wanted the family to know, that neither he nor his family had made any attempt to get Kick to become an Anglican. He said that it would be far more satisfactory to have both of them in the same church, and with that in mind, he suggested that she explore the possibilities of the Church of England and see whether she could possibly become one. He said she honestly told him that she couldn't, and as far as he was concerned it was finished. He said it was quite impossible for them to change, as they were so closely allied with the Church of England, and I think I understand his problem. We then spoke about the blessing by Canterbury, and I said that I didn't think it was a good idea. He said it would be completely secret, and it would make the Duchess feel so much better. We left it at that, and Kick will have to decide. We then went over to the Lawyers and Kick signed the marriage settlement.

The newspapers had picked it up in the meantime, and were trying to get hold of Kick. She stayed with Mrs. Bruce and had no interviews. At the last minute they invited everyone to the reception, and there was quite a conglomeration.

I picked up Lady Astor, Mrs. Bruce and Kick the next morning and off we went to the town hall. The Devonshires were already there, and after wading through the reporters we got to the room, and the ceremony was held. This consisted of the signing of the contract and the witnessing. The Duke and I were the witnesses. The whole thing took about ten minutes. Kick looked very pretty, and she repeated her statement without a falter. I think I was more nervous than she.

We then went to the reception, and everyone seemed delighted. The Duchess was marvelous, and I like her very much. She is the one who is so much in favor of it. The

<hr>

134. Douglas Wilkinson, one of the distillers with whom JPK had negotiated for Somerset's U.S. distribution contracts in 1933.

reception lasted a couple of hours, and Kick has probably told you who was there. She got some beautiful presents.

They posed for pictures, which seemed better than have the photographers take them anyway, and turn in awful ones. I saw no point in looking extremely grim throughout so I looked as if I enjoyed it. You have probably seen the pictures.

As far as publicity was concerned over here, I think we got off pretty well. Only one paper had much of a discussion about it, in which they quoted Honey Fitz, and said that Mother was too ill to comment. Outside of this, there was only a picture and some small description of the marriage. I suppose Boston went wild.

Billy is crazy about Kick, and I know they are very much in love. Everyone talks about it. I am much more favorably impressed with him, than I was the last time I was over here. I think he really has something on the ball, and he couldn't be nicer. I think he is ideal for Kick.

Somehow, I think things will work out OK. It doesn't look so now, but I am sure something will happen. This didn't influence me on any advice that I gave Kick. As far as Kick's soul is concerned, I wish I had half her chance of seeing the pearly gates. As far as what people will say, the hell with them. I think we can all take it. It will be hardest on Mother, and I do know how you feel Mother, but I do think it will be all right.

That's about all I can think of at present. I will write a fill-in later. I have finished my missions, and was due to start back in about two weeks, but volunteered to stay another month. I persuaded my crew to do it, which pleased me very much. We are the only crew which has done it. It looks now as if I will be home about the first week in July.

Give my love to all the family, and I can say from what I have seen that Kick handled herself like a champion.

Love
Joe

Kathleen Kennedy Hartington, 24, to Rose Kennedy

Compton Place, Eastbourne, Sussex May 9th

Dearest Mother —

A telegram arrived from Daddy this morning with the news that you are well. I was very worried about a newspaper report here that you were very ill. They made out that it was because of my marriage. Goodness mother — I owe so much to you and Daddy that nothing in the world could have made me go against your will. However, I felt that you expected the action I took and would judge that it was the course to make under the circumstances. Last week was most difficult. The clergy of both churches were after me and now every morning letters arrive condemning my action. They don't bother me a bit and I only hope and pray that things will not be too difficult for you and the rest of the family with the McDonnells etc. Please don't take any responsibility for an action, which you think bad (and I do not). You did everything in your power to stop it. You did your duty as a Roman Catholic mother. You have not failed. There was nothing lacking in my religious education. Not by any means am I giving up my faith — it is most precious to me. Billy wants it to remain as such. We would have been married in the Church if they had consented to perform the ceremony without B's signing the paper. This they could, and would not do. As I have said before, 15 years ago our marriage could have been solemnized in the Church — the boys being brought up in the father's religion — the girls in the mother's. However, then a rule was made like the one in our country — which put a stop to those marriages. Bishop Mathew whom I have consulted so often told me that perhaps at a later date our marriage could be made valid. Until that time I shall go on praying and living like a Roman Catholic and hoping. Please, please do the same.

On Wed. Last I spent the afternoon with Dr. Temple the Arch of C and the evening with Archie Spell's friend the Papal Delegate — The former was charming and was so desirous to be helpful that he asked Bishop Mathew to join with him in saying a few prayers for us. He said he expected Bishop Mathew to turn down his request (which he did) but it was nice of him to offer. The Papal Delegate was absolutely charming and made me feel very sad about Mother.

Of course it was too bad that the papers made such an issue of the religious question. However, I must admit that I expected it. I hope they weren't too bad in Boston. As soon as any photographs arrive I shall send them along — You've probably seen quite enough of them!!!

Now for news of the wedding: Marie Bruce saved my life. She took full charge of buying me what little trousseau I had. Of course all those sort of things were terribly expensive but I did get a few and so many people gave me things. I can't tell you how generous and kind most people were. I wore a pink crepe dress which Marie had copied from one of my plain American black dresses. It turned out very well and couldn't have been prettier with those aqua-marine clips. The hat was made of pink and blue plumes with a pink veil. Marie feels very badly about being in your bad graces, as she loves you more than anyone else in the world. Please do write her and make it all right as she was only doing what she thought right. She, Lady Astor and Joe came to the squalid old registry office

May 10th

Mr. Brand wrote me this morning that he is going to America the end of the week, so I am giving him this letter, a piece of wedding cake and a copy of the local paper which appeared today with some pictures.

Joe was absolutely wonderful. He arrived in London the day before the "Big Event" and was very efficient with lawyers, marriage settlements etc. He was in tremendous form throughout and quite conscious after seeing his face plastered all over the papers that he was "finished in Boston" — He may be home soon and I shall go down & see him before he leaves for U.S. Sat morning Joe, Marie and Aunt Nancy Astor took me to the Registry Office. When I arrived the press reporters and crowds of people were waiting outside. (By the way we got lost on our way there).

I hopped out with Joe and we ran in. In the small room where we were married Billy, his best man, the Duke of Rutland,[135] his mother, father, two sisters, and grandmothers, Salisbury & Devonshire were waiting. The ceremony was very short. We went directly to the reception held at Eaton Square. The chef at Claridge's supplied an enormous chocolate wedding cake and the Dukie-Wookie supplied the champagne. We sent out telegrams the day before, thinking & hoping many would not come but over 150 showed up including: Laura Corrigan,[136] Lady Cunard,[137] Mr. & Mrs. Harvey Gibson

135. Charles John Robert Manners, tenth duke of Rutland and marquess of Granby (1919–).
136. The Wisconsin-born, American steel magnate's widow, Laura Mae McMartin Corrigan (d. 1948), had launched herself in London society after the First World War, having been snubbed in Chicago and New York (she was reputed to be a former waitress). Entertaining on a grand scale, she became one of the doyennes of interwar London society. Corrigan had spent the first years of the war organizing a women's group in France to provide amenities to soldiers and had returned recently to London, where she had founded the Wings Club to provide lodging and aid to Allied air officers.
137. Maud Alice "Emerald" Burke (1872–1948), of New York, had married Sir Bache Edward Cunard, grandson of the founder of the steamship line, in 1895. Living in London for the rest of her life, she would become a legendary hostess and avant-garde arts patron, as well as the mother of writer, eccentric and civil rights activist Nancy Cunard.

(in fact I invited everyone including porters etc. from the Club, needless to say they all showed up). Mrs. Biddle (they gave me the most terrific ruby sapphire clip from Cartier's). One man there thought all the Red Cross girls (30 strong) were my sisters. He had heard I had a lot "but I didn't think she had that many". I completely forgot about asking Admiral Stark[138] or Kirk. I shall write them. It was all so rushed. The reception was certainly a funny collection. A few G.I.s who became rather tiddley on the champagne carrying on long conversations with Lady Cunard who looked more terrifying than ever. I must say, I enjoyed every minute of it and I shouldn't have thought I was very well married without it.

Letters continue to pour in from irate Catholics saying I have sold my soul for a title. Billy is very busy answering them all.

I am so sad that I cannot send every member of the family a piece of wedding cake but they won't let one send foodstuffs out of the country.

My engagement ring is a beautiful square cut sapphire with diamonds on each side. The Dukie gave me a diamond bracelet. Billy gave me an enormous old diamond clip, which I wouldn't wear much until after the war but it really is absolutely lovely. Boofie and Fima gave me a gold, diamond & pearl pin — apparently lots of presents arrived, but I won't know what they are until next week.

I never realized how many friends I had in this country (some of them are just impressed but most of them are genuinely pleased). Please tell Jack that the Carcanos were so pleased and the entire family was at the reception, bubbling over.

We are down here enjoying the most wonderful weather and having a good rest after the hectic week until this weekend. After that Billy goes back to the ~~reception~~ army and I may be able to see him quite often. I am returning to the Hans Crescent Club. Mr. Gibson was <u>delighted</u> to have me back. I'm not returning until the end of this month. Will probably rest down here until the 1st of June so cable me all the news here. When I do return to the Club I am going to be a volunteer & live with Marie Bruce. I think it would be too difficult the other way. I think you'd better keep writing letters and sending any packages to the Club.

Daddy cabled that Mother is busy buying me clothes. I shall wear civilian things more and I do need the following things: a bathing suit (very badly) size 14 long in the legs — a pair of nice gabardine shorts, a few cotton dirndl dresses and a pretty light summer dinner dress. ~~Any~~ a nice pink dressing gown (can't get anything nice here), a pair of gold & silver evening sandals 7 AA, a pair of moccasins. Eunice knows the kind everybody wears.

The pineapple juice arrived last week and it's simply delicious.

I'd like to give B— a nice wedding present but haven't found anything as yet.

Please do not be sad about anything. I'm very, very happy and quite certain about what I have done. My only regret is that none of you were here for the 1st Kennedy marriage. What an event!!! I missed you all so much. You have no idea! Please keep writing & often. I think you knew I'd marry B— some day.

All love in the world to you all. Grandpa & Grandma the Moores etc. I wanted to send them all some wedding cake.

Let's hope & pray that we'll all meet soon.

Much love

K.

---

138. Harold Raynsford Stark (1880–1972), commander of U.S. Naval Forces in Europe, 1942–45. The former chief of Naval Operations, 1939–42, Stark had come under criticism for his role in the events leading up to the attack on Pearl Harbor.

Kathleen Kennedy Hartington, 24: *Round-Robin Letter*

May 18, 1944

Dearest Family:

I have now become a camp follower. Am living in a small hotel near to where Billy is stationed. It's very comfortable and we have the prize suite. I wouldn't compare it to Daddy's set-up at the Waldorf Towers, but as I have often said it takes all sorts of experience to make life worthwhile. Billy is their first Marquess and they all take the greatest delight in calling him that at the top of their lungs on every occasion. He has a motorbike to go back and forth to camp and I have my bike to get around on during the day.

By now you should have the letter I sent over with Mr. Brand with all the news of the wedding. I hope Daddy and Mother have seen him to talk to as he was at the reception.

We really did have the most lovely honeymoon as the weather was perfect throughout and I haven't felt so well for years. I was as brown as a berry, much to everyone's envy as it happens so seldom in this country.

Billy had to go off the Friday after the wedding and then I joined him in London the day before yesterday. We spent one night with his grandmother Salisbury at Hatfield. The house is a hospital now but still quite lovely. Billy's uncle, Lord Robert Cecil, the great League of Nations man was there and although very old, is wonderful to listen to.[139] All the old relatives and servants continue to give me the eye, but now I feel I can stand anything. We came down here last night and as today was Ascension Thursday I was up bright and early for Church.

Went into the Hans Crescent Club on Monday and I must say it felt very odd to go back as an old married woman. Although I tried to invite everyone there were quite a few people left out who were rather hurt. It was all so rushed I couldn't do any more. Ran into Admiral Kirk having lunch at Claridge's. Of course I had forgotten him too. I apologized profusely and he said he was going to write Daddy and tell him how well I was looking.

Will spend most of my time here answering letters and telegrams. Received some awfully nice ones including ones from: Mrs. Joe Davies, Morton Downey, the Truitts etc. Please tell Bobby his telegram was the best one I got and Billy agrees wholeheartedly on this point.

As I am going back to the Hans Crescent the end of this month to carry on with my work I am not going to do any functions etc. in Derbyshire with the exception of opening a Red Cross Carnival in Derby. They asked Mrs. Biddle to do it and then wrote me. As I don't want to get involved in all that until after the war I am just going up there once and will then tell them that I must do my American Red Cross work.

I am rather upset about the money situation. I know it all becomes very complicated now that I have married an Englishman. Do I have to pay taxes both places etc.? Between Daddy and the Dukie something should be worked out. The Duke is located at the Mayfair hotel if you want to communicate with him.

This morning a letter arrived from Richard Wood enclosing a letter from Lady Halifax about Daddy's conversation with the ambassador. Lady Halifax was awfully kind

---

139. Edgar Algernon Robert Gascoyne-Cecil, first Viscount Cecil of Chelwood (1864–1958), principal drafter of the League of Nations Covenant. The former foreign secretary, 1918; lord privy seal, 1923–24; and chancellor of the Duchy of Lancaster, 1924–27, had been awarded the Nobel Peace Prize in 1937.

about me and I do hope Lord Halifax was some help to Mother. He understands the situation so well, I feel. Richard really is the soul of honesty and I think is one of the best and most understanding friends I have in all this world.

Just went downstairs to the phone as Marie Bruce called with the good news of your cable. Gosh, it was good to get it. I really was terribly worried about Mother and am so [glad] to hear that she is well and happy. Please tell her not to fuss about the clothes because the competition in the way of well-dressed women isn't much.

We have received some of the funniest letters. Yesterday one came from the London editor of *Life* wanting to do a picture on the greatest gesture for Anglo-American relations since the Atlantic Charter. Today one came from *Vogue* to do an artistic study of me. I must say the publicity isn't very pleasant when they make those nasty cracks but it's extremely flattering when they make so much of our wedding. I can hardly wait to see what the *Times Herald* says about their former office girl. Mr. Waldrop will have a few cracks I feel sure.

Invited the Wilkinsons to the wedding and I thought of possibly having Tom as a trustee over here. Sir James is a bit old, I think. The other alternative was Mr. Brand. He ~~undurstras~~ banking etc. so well.

Talked to Joe on the phone the other night. I suppose you know he volunteered to stay another month although most of his squadron are going home. His crew got together 30 clothing coupons for the wedding. Billy is 6 ft. 4 in case there was any chance of picking up a Vicuna dinner jacket for him in a maroon color anyplace in New York. He's very thin. I haven't really given him a proper wedding present yet and thought possibly of the coat.

The diamond bracelet which his father gave me really is too lovely and the envy of all. His father is very nice, but very difficult in ways. The funny thing is that he thinks Billy has given in as the one thing he has always dreaded is that one of his sons should marry an R.C. Even though his present daughter-in-law has acquiesced to his demands he always sees within me a sort of evil influence. I shall just have to prove myself over a period of years, I suppose.

Billy and I talk a lot about going to America immediately after the war. Needless to say he's pretty nervous about it, and is secretly hoping that it won't be possible for a year. I have already told him what each relative will say to him. He had a bit of it at the wedding when an American sergeant came up to you [*sic*] and said "Listen, you dog [*sic*] damn limey, you've got the best god damn girl that America could produce." Speaking of sergeants, some of our wedding pictures are very funny because all the porters and Red Cross people were so anxious to have their pictures taken that they crowded around whenever there was a camera in sight. The result is that the Marquess and Marchioness are surrounded by the strangest-looking group of wedding guests that has ever, ever been.

Please give my love to all and a kiss for everyone

Kick

Billy sends nervous love to all his new sisters- and brothers-in-law. Please send mail to same address —

Kathleen Kennedy Hartington, 24: *Round-Robin Letter*

May 23, 1944

Dearest Family:

Am still situated at the Swan Hotel, which gets funnier and funnier every day. Little did we know what we were in for when we arrived in this town.

There never has been a funnier assortment of people in one spot than in this hotel. The little bellboy, a native of Dublin informed me that his name was Kennedy and we might be related. Every time Billy or I stick our noses out of our room — there he [is] waiting to march in front of us, flinging open doors and saying "this way Marquess" at the top of his lungs. Last night we went to call on the Chef, as he had put us up such a delicious picnic on the Sunday. The Chef told me a long sad story about how he almost came to work for us in the Embassy days. He said one of the secretaries had gotten the letters mixed up so he never came. The food here is exceptionally good and much better than any London restaurant. Last night he christened the desert after Billy by calling it "croute Cavendish," I must say it was most disgusting but we had to grin, eat and bear it. There is another old retired Army man here who has had his house taken over by the Americans so he lives here. He collects prints and happened to have one of the 3rd Duke of Devonshire. He has already given it to us as a wedding present. Yesterday the priest from the local Catholic Church came to see me. He used to be at Maidenhead where we used to go from Cliveden and he has been here since the war. I must say I have never met a nicer man. He confessed that he was unorthodox, but he said he admired my courage and he sympathized with my stand. He went on to say that I would be amazed at the number of people who also felt the same way. He told me not to worry and he was quite sure that prayer and trust in God's holy will would bring everything right. He said that even in a small village like this the same problem arises all the time with Church of England people refusing to sign the paper. I must say I was rather dreading the interview but he certainly turned out to be a nice man. I told him if I stayed around here any length of time I should like to do any work for him I could. We are going to invite him to dinner one evening.

On the eight o'clock news this morning they gave a short summary of Daddy's speech in Boston.[140] It sounded very good. Whatever you say makes a terrific difference.

There was a nasty article [*about us*] in the weekly news magazine "News Review" here but I hear it is owned by the Labor people so that explains it. It quoted from an article written by Helen Kirkpatrick.[141] She really is an awful woman. I think I shall write her a letter when I read the stuff. She never has been nice to our family. I'm going to tell Aunt Nancy.[142] She'll give her a piece of her mind.

Joe rang me up from London the other day. He was up on day's hop and I am going to have dinner with him up there tomorrow night. He is on a week's leave and sounds very well and happy. Every one over here thinks he is so handsome and so nice.

Vogue magazine has written for a picture by Cecil Beaton. Goodness only knows what that will look like.

No letters have arrived from you all as yet. Joe said he hadn't gotten any either. I'm longing for them and hope they arrive soon.

---

140. The previous evening he had addressed a Boston audience "on the occasion of the celebration of National Maritime Day."
141. Helen Kirkpatrick, later Millbank (1909–98), foreign correspondent, and later war correspondent for the *Chicago Daily News,* 1939–47.
142. Lady Astor.

We think we may be [*here*] another month so I wrote Mr. Gibson yesterday and asked for another month's leave. I don't think I can fail to get it, as I am a volunteer now.

Marie Bruce has fixed up my room in her flat so I shall live there during the week and probably go to Eastbourne on the weekends.

The days go very quickly here and it really is pleasant not having anything to do. However, if I do stay here I am going to work at an American Airman's Rest home, which is quite close. The pilots go there after a particularly exhausting time, and have a glorious time playing tennis, golf etc. That would be my work — playing with them.

As Billy's Pa owns half of Eastbourne he has already given orders for a Kennedy Street which runs into Astaire Street. I have chosen to have flowering cherry trees up and down. Adele says Astaire Street is a very bad slum section so we hope to get something better than that.[143]

I am feeling better now than I have since I left America. This is the first really good rest I have had for a year. Have put on some weight and am getting plenty of sleep. MARRIED LIFE AGREES WITH ME!

That's about all the news for the moment. Billy sends love to all. My love to everybody. There never was a nicer family. I am feeling extremely sentimental about you all now so please write soon. Those letters really matter. My very best love to Mother and pray just like I do every morning and evening and no matter what the McDonnells think just tell them not to judge anybody. God does that.

All love to all from Kick

P.S. Looking forward to that bathing suit and shorts.

Rose Kennedy to Kathleen Kennedy Hartington, 24

Hyannisport, Massachusetts, June 30, 1944

Dear Kathleen:

Here it is the fourth of July again, and another summer is almost half over. It seems almost impossible. Everything I start to tell you, I think perhaps your father has already written you.

We are all looking forward now at having Joe home and we only wish you and Billy were going to be along too. I answered the Duchess' letter a few days ago. As I said, it didn't arrive here until about a month after it was sent. I answered by air-mail so she should have it reasonably soon. It was a very enthusiastic, understanding note and it made us very happy to know they all love you so dearly.

I hope Billy felt we were giving him an equally warm welcome into our family. Of course, when I wrote to him, it was directly after the wedding, and at that time I was a little bit stunned because none of your letters, which you had sent to Tim, had arrived on time and it was all quite a surprise and shock. I really didn't expect that you would be married until after the invasion or at least until I knew more definitely of your plans. However, that is all over now, dear Kathleen, and as long as you love Billy so dearly, you may be sure that we will all receive him with open arms. I guess I told you that Joe liked him better every time that he saw him, which was a great satisfaction to all of us.

143. In 1932 Adele Marie Astair (1898–1981) had left both the musical comedy stage and her dancing partner (and brother), Fred, to marry Lord Charles Cavendish (the duke of Devonshire's younger brother and Billy Hartington and Andrew Cavendish's uncle). Throughout the war she worked at the well-known Rainbow Corner Red Cross Canteen in London.

Your younger sister, Eunice, is in New York this week visiting Ann Resor. I wish she were better looking, and I think Jack might like her as she is quite bright and interesting and has a most attractive voice.

We went up last week to see Gloria Swanson open in Cambridge. I believe the name of the play is "Goose for a Gander," and it looks as though she really has a success at last. It was written by a youngster named Kennedy, and some of those Bostonians who are perennially rooting for a Kennedy thought that Jack had written a play, so they were congratulating us again. Now, when anyone steps up to me with a gleam in his eye and a warm smile on his lips, I know he is going to say one of three things: Isn't it wonderful about your daughter's marriage, or isn't it marvelous about the story of your son's exploits in the Pacific, or isn't it wonderful of you to send us that case of Scotch!! I believe the most enthusiasm is apparent over the last remark. Wylie Reynolds at Palm Beach donated a $100,000 worth of war bonds when the case of Scotch was auctioned at the Paramount Theater. I suppose the bank took the bonds and Wylie took the Scotch, but anyway the bonds were sold.

The Harrises are around working for the devastated Sacred Heart Convent. I have had no messages from any of that clan. Nancy is still showing a great stamina and has kept right on nursing the baby. They thought I was wonderful to do that a generation ago, and I expect in this generation it is unheard of, so I am duly impressed.

Jack is quite elated to have the operation on his back over, as the doctors believe that was really the root of his trouble. His tummy was a bit upset yesterday, but I am sure he will get that straightened out.

I am leading a very quiet life, taking care of mine. I have dismissed all of my usual problems of the household and the children and just read books all day in my little house, which is really a very pleasant change instead of being a "glamour house-keeper."

Etsie picked you up two summer dresses, which she says are very attractive, and we are getting you moccasins. We should have sent them before, but they wouldn't except the coupon without the book so we missed Meloy. I wish you would say once in a while what colors you like or Billy's reaction to one or two things as I am sure you do not like everything, and I should like to follow the lines which you like. Dodo Potter picked the bathing suits. Now they have little skirts which go over them like a sarong, but I didn't see them in town.

Madame Lopez has taken a house down here with her baby and three or four maids. She is now Mrs. Deheeren, some relation to Charles Munn. I have not seen her yet, but they tell me she has not been well since her baby has been born. She is up in the island in one of Mr. Humphrey's houses.

I hope you like some of the crepe, etc., I sent you. I bought it in a rush as I thought it was going off immediately. If you don't use it now, I am sure you will use it later, and after all, you are only a bride once! Have you ever thought of wearing woolen gabardine slacks in the country? They are so warm and quite smart if you are small. I don't believe I can send you a warm suit unless the suit fits properly, especially in England. It is hopeless. It seems to me Etsie is about your size, and I can try if you like.

We never heard whether you got the rose flannel suit, which you asked me for when you were working in the Red Cross.

Do you ever see Molly Buccleuch? We were so sorry to have missed her daughter last year. She sent a post card, and Eunice was away at the time; but if I had read the post card, I would have easily had her down over the weekend. Please explain to Molly how to get in touch with Mr. Murphy. I believe I wrote to her myself, but I am not sure the letter was sent as your father did not think it was quite cordial enough, and I was going to rewrite it. Therefore, I am not quite sure what happened to it.

Jean is coming home today as she has been visiting the Carneys in Chicago. She knows Jean Carney at Noroton, and Jean's brother was the one who collaborated with Chuch Spaulding when he wrote "Love at First Flight." I probably shall have some news of the Colmans as they live next to the Carneys, I believe.

Give my love to Marie, dear Kathleen. I have told her that we hope to see her as soon as the war is over, which we think may be soon— that is, the European war.

Do you want any music or records? I guess that is about all the news.

Much, much love to you,

Kathleen Kennedy Hartington, 24, to Rose Kennedy

July 6, 1944

Darling Mother —

This letter is just meant for you. It's a birthday letter — Hope it arrives by July 23rd.

By now I hope you are happy about my marriage. I suppose I really always expected to marry Billy. Some day — some how.

However, you and Daddy know that I never would do anything against your will. You two have been so wonderful to me as well as to every member of the family. The older I get and the more I see makes me realize this and a lot of other things. First, that you are the most unselfish woman in the world. Any house where we have all been has been difficult to run and you have always put us before any of your own desires or pleasures. We all have happy personalities and get along with people far easier than most people— This is due to the happy atmosphere which has always surrounded us.

When I see some homes I marvel at you more and more.

Certain qualities I have — people admire. They are all traits that you have instilled in me.

In the matter of my marriage — I knew you would be upset, but I felt sure you would see the ultimate good. I knew you would never forbid anything if you felt it meant my happiness. It must have been hard for you to resign yourself to the idea of my doing something quite against all your principles — I repeat, the one thing I don't want you ever to think is that my religious or moral education has ever been lacking. You have done more than enough to show me the gateway to Heaven. Please God I can do half as well for the little Cavendishes

I miss you so much and long to see you. We have so much to talk about. There wasn't anyone to really take your place at the time of the wedding and it seemed so odd that at the time, the moment, the period of one's life which one has looked forward to for so long, the dearest person in the world wasn't there —

Please have a wonderful birthday. Think of me and always remember that if I spend the rest of my life trying to repay you for everything it will be very little.

All love to you
from
Kick

Joseph P. Kennedy, Jr., 29, to Rose Kennedy and Joseph P. Kennedy

Dear Mother and Dad:

No doubt you are surprised that I haven't arrived home. Here's the way I figured. I am going to get my leave anyway, and every month I stay over here, I get an additional two and a half days. The duty now is very calm, and for foreign duty it is ideal. I figure I might as well stay over here for a while, then go home, have my leave, and get shipped off to some spot which I don't like half as well. I have been having a wonderful time, and the real danger has gone. It's very much like flying training hops now.

I am going to be doing something different for the next three weeks. It is secret, and I am not allowed to say what it is, but it isn't dangerous so don't worry. So probably I won't be home till sometime in September. I imagine you are a bit disappointed that I haven't gone home, but I think when I tell you the whole story, you will agree with me.

I had a wonderful birthday party. I stayed with Pat Wilson[144] and Kick was there. She had some people over for dinner including Rothermere, the newspaper man.[145] There was champagne, and a delicious dinner, so I really enjoyed it. It wasn't at all like a birthday at home, but if I were going to have it any place but home again, I would take a duplication of last night.

The big thing in my life at present is that I am starting to get grey. I hope I shall have some brown strands left by the time I arrive. I'm getting on, and I had better get a gal while there is some life in the old boy.

Kick came down here last week for a few days, and then we went to Torquay for a while. We went swimming a couple of days, but the weather has been terrible. She looks marvelously. She is terrified of the Doodles[146] as is everyone else, and I think she is smart not to work in London.

I don't know whether I told you in my last letter that Bob Hancox is here. He is the fellow with whom I used to room at Banana River and Norfolk.

That's about all the news from here. The Kennedy clan on this side of the Atlantic is doing OK.

Love,
Joe

P.S. At last I am a full Lt.

Joseph P. Kennedy, Jr., 29, to Rose Kennedy and Joseph P. Kennedy

[August 4, 1944]

Dear Mother and Dad:

I haven't received a letter from you people for quite some time, but I presume that you thought I had left for home. As I explained in the last letter, I am working on something different. It is terribly interesting, and by the time you received this letter, it will probably be released, but at this point is quite secret. Per usual I have done nothing, but it is far more interesting than patrolling over the bay.

Don't get worried about it, as there is practically no danger. The only bad feature is that it has cut into my social life a great deal. We are in the country, and I have spent all

---

144. Joe had become romantically involved with the young, Australian-born wife of Major Robert Filmer Wilson, who was currently stationed in Libya with the British Army.
145. Former Conservative MP Esmon Harmsworth, Viscount Rothermere (1898–1978), had taken control of the *Daily Mail* and the *Evening News* (originally headed by his uncle, Lord Northcliffe) in 1932.
146. Doodle bugs, German aerial bombs.

my time on the base. It has given me a good chance to rest up, so now I am the picture of health. I hope you are not too disappointed about my not coming home.

I am going to get the thirty days leave anyway, and as I enjoy it more over here, than any future duty I might get, it seems wise to stay on. Also, as it looks like Germany is folding up, it would be nice to be here at the end of the war. I hate missing the Cape, and had looked forward to it, but in weighing all factors, I thought it would be better to stay over here. When I tell you the whole story I think you will agree. All the boys who did go home, now wish they had stayed over. They have been at a rotten base in the States shaking down new crews to go off some place, and old England looks pretty good to them.

I don't know how long I will be working with this outfit. It might be for a week, and it may be longer. I will try and give you more dope in the next letters.

Bob Holbrook (Bunty Holbrook's cousin) is over here working on the same deal with the Army. Will write you if there is any further news. My address is the same in regard to mail.

Love,

Vice Admiral Randall Jacobs to Rose Kennedy: *Telegram*

WASHINGTON D.C. AUG 13/44 4:30 PM

THE NAVY DEPARTMENT DEEPLY REGRETS TO INFORM YOU THAT YOUR SON LIEUT. JOSEPH PATRICK KENNEDY JR. U.S.N.R. IS MISSING RESULT EXPLOSION OPERATIONAL FLIGHT 12 (TWELVE) AUGUST 1944 IN THE PERFORMANCE OF HIS DUTY AND SERVICE OF HIS COUNTRY.

Rose Kennedy: *"Joe Jr.'s Death"*

One Sunday afternoon about 2:00, after we all had lunched outside on the big porch at Hyannis Port picnic style, Joe went to take his usual nap. The youngsters had gathered in the big living room chatting quietly so as not to disturb their father, and I sat reading the papers. Suddenly, there was a knock at the front door and I answered it myself and I saw a clergyman there who asked to see Joe. This request was not unusual and I invited him in, said perhaps he would join us for a short time, until Joe had finished his siesta. However, he said, "No, he could not wait. His message was urgent, and it concerned Joe, Jr., who had been reported missing as of yesterday." I flew upstairs, hesitated, stumbled, and finally broke the tragic news of Joe's death to his father. He leaped from the bed, went downstairs, saw the clergyman, told the children in the next room, and then together we wept silently a few minutes on the death of our first born who had shown such promise and had always been such a joy to us and to the other children. Joe then said, "We must carry on like everyone else. We must continue our regular work and take care of the living, because there is a lot of work to be done." I think he referred especially this time to Lord Halifax who had been Prime Minister [*sic*] when Joe had been Ambassador to London, and, who at the moment of our tragedy, was the Ambassador from England to Washington. He had lost one son in the War and another had lost his two legs. And still, like so many other British fathers whom we knew, he continued bravely, uncomplainingly, working probably harder than ever in order to keep his mind so occupied that he would not dwell on the sorrowful, heart-breaking picture of seeing so many of the bright, gay, well-educated young men, who the year before had so confidently talked and planned their futures in the professions or in politics, to see them all killed in the skies or in the trenches. What makes it more devastating is that the men who grew up, and played, and visited our children comprised a great percentage of the men killed, as they were all of that generation — all the right age and many of them were so well-educated and well skilled, that they had the qualities which made them such successful pilots and there was terrible toll exacted on the pilots over Britain in those days. In our house, it was Joe; across the street, the husband of my daughter's best friend; or, down the street, another classmate. So all around us, here and in England, our friends as well as we were all visited with the same terrible tragedies. They used to say the leaders who planned the War never suffered personally; but, in World War II, many members of the Government here and abroad, lost their sons and they worked, and prayed, and wept like the fathers and mothers of the humblest men in the ranks.

We did carry on our regular daily commitments. Joe worked even harder at his work and at his golf, and in the following year, undertook a big assignment for Governor Tobin of Massachusetts. He was chairman of a commission to study the establishment of a State Department of Commerce. He rode through the different towns of Massachusetts, inspecting them, and making speeches. It was a long, somewhat tedious program, as it entailed a lot of motoring, and he often left at dawn, returning late at night to Hyannis Port. But, it occupied his mind and so I was glad that he was doing it.

Kathleen Kennedy Hartington, 24, to Marie Bruce: *Telegram*

TELL BILLY AM STAYING WITH FAMILY AND SEEING DENTIST.[147] IF POSSIBLE CHANCE OF HIM RETURNING WOULD LEAVE AT ONCE. MOTHER AND DADDY ARE INSISTING ON THAT. BILLY KNOWS THAT WOULD BE WHAT I WOULD WANT TO DO. IF HE ISN'T COMING AT ONCE I WOULD LIKE TO STAY WITH MOTHER UNTIL END OF MONTH ALL THE OTHER CHILDREN LEAVING FOR SCHOOL SEPTEMBER 21 AND JACK MUST GO BACK TO HOSPITAL. IT'S STILL QUITE SAD BUT NOTHING WOULD STOP ME COMING HOME IF BILLY HAS CHANCE TO GET BACK. MISS YOU ALL VERY MUCH PLEASE READ THIS TO DUCHESS AND PLEASE ASK HER TO TELL DUKE. DADDY RECEIVED HIS LETTER AND WAS DEEPLY TOUCHED AND GRATEFUL.

KICK

Franklin Roosevelt to Joseph P. Kennedy: *Telegram*

PLEASE TELL KATHLEEN I AM THINKING OF HER IN HER CRUSHING SORROW[148] MRS ROOSEVELT JOINS ME IN HEARTFELT SYMPATHY=

FRANKLIN D. ROOSEVELT

The Duchess of Devonshire to Kathleen Kennedy Hartington, 24

[September 13, 1944]

My darling Kick,

We heard the news this morning in a telegram which was addressed to you. We had not heard from Billy for nearly three weeks so I had been very anxious for he was always so wonderful about writing and saving as much anxiety as he could. We have heard no details, but of course I will send you on all we hear the moment it comes.

147. She had returned to the United States for Joe's memorial service.
148. Billy had been shot and killed in action in Belgium on September 10.

I want you never, never to forget what complete happiness you gave him. All your life you must think that you brought complete happiness to one person. He wrote that to me when he went to the front. I want you to know this for I know what great conscientious struggles you went through before you married Billy, but I know that it will be a source of infinite consolation to you now that you decided as you did. All your life I shall love you — not only for yourself but that you gave such perfect happiness to my son whom I loved above anything in the world.

May you be given strength to carry you through these truly terrible months. My heart breaks when I think of how much you have gone through in your young life.

Your loving

I opened my letter again to tell you that we have just heard that Billy was killed instantly in the fighting after they went through Brussels, I think on the Albert Canal. It is such a great weight off my mind that he died instantly and did not suffer at all. I know it will help you, too.

Kathleen Kennedy Hartington, 24: *Diary*

Sept 20th 1944

So ends the story of Billy and Kick!!!

Yesterday the final word came. I can't believe that the one thing that I felt might happened should have happened — Billy is dead — killed in action in France Sept 10th. Life is so cruel — I am on my way to England. Writing is impossible.

Kathleen Kennedy Hartington, 24, to Rose and Joseph P. Kennedy

CHATEAU FRONTENAC, QUEBEC Wednesday [September 20, 1944]
Darling Mother and Daddy —

We depart tonight some time — I am so glad to be going.

Now I understand your sorrow for Joe much better. When a brother dies, a sister is very sad but she doesn't have the gnawing pain which one gets when one loses a part of oneself — that was Joe to you both — And Billy to me.

Remember I told you that he got much holier after we were married. Now he is the one to bring me closer to God — what a funny world.

On July 26th B. wrote me a letter. "I have been spending a lovely hour on the ground and thinking in a nice vague sleepy way about you & what a lot I've got to look forward to if I come through this all right. I feel I may talk about it for the moment as I'm not in danger so I'll just say that if anything should happen to me I shall be wanting you to try to isolate our life together, to face its finish, and to start a new one as soon as you feel you can. I hope that you will marry again, quite soon — someone good & nice" —

I like to think about what he said and though it makes me sad to write this I just want you both to know what B's orders were.

I don't mind feeling sad 'cause why should I mind.

If Eunice, Pat & Jean marry nice guys for fifty years they'll be lucky if they have five weeks like I did —

Tell Jack not to get married for a long time. I'll keep house for him.

Thank[s] to all —

All love
K.

601

Rose Kennedy to Kathleen Kennedy Hartington, 24

Hyannisport, September 25, 1944

Dear Kathleen:

This is just a note to [*tell*] you, what I am sure you feel, that I have been thinking about you day and night ever since you left and praying for you and loving you more and more.

I was so exhausted that I spent Friday night at Noroton, and the nuns were so sympathetic.

I have been to Mass for Billy frequently. In fact, I am on my way now (7:15 a.m.). After I heard you talk about him and I began to hear about his likes and dislikes, his ideas and ideals, I realized what a wonderful man he was and what happiness would have been yours had God willed that you spend your life with him. A first love — a young love — is so wonderful, my dear Kathleen, but, my dearest daughter, I feel we must dry our tears as best we can and bow our heads to God's wisdom and goodness. We must place our hand in His and trust Him.

I hope you have helped the Duchess, and I am sure she has helped you, probably because you are thinking of one another and you're thinking less of your own grief.

I am now home from Mass, and the house if full of workmen so I shall say good-bye for today. Pray hard and work hard to help everyone.

With my heartfelt love and affection.

P.S. We are arranging some Masses for your dear husband.

Kathleen Kennedy Hartington, 24: *Round-Robin Letter*

Sept. 23rd—

Dearest Family:

The realization of Billy's death has come to me very acutely here and I should probably have spared myself a great deal of agony if I had remained in America. However, I am so terribly pleased that I came and the Duke and Duchess were so glad and I couldn't have borne not being able to talk to them all about Billy. The letters about him have been perfectly wonderful and I found letters here from various people, long before he was killed saying how well he had done during the whole course of the summer. In fact we think there is a very good chance of him getting a D.S.O. Everyone is so kind and I keep reading pathetic little articles about poor Lady Hartington that I feel everyone is suffering for me. The Duchess is so wonderful and I do love her so very much. The Duke is awfully kind and they are going out of their way to spare me every agony. They sent off a cable Monday and are so upset that it never arrived. We are investigating it on this end and you might do the same there, please. We are having a service for him at Chatsworth next Saturday so I am afraid that will make me very sad. Its funny those first few days after the news I just felt very numb — it was lucky it came gradually and now that I am here and every thing reminds me of him so much. I just feel terribly, terribly sad. I know that Daddy said I had a lot of problems that might never have been worked out and that perhaps later in life I might have been very unhappy. That's all quite true, but it doesn't fill the gap that I now feel in my life. Before it had its purpose, I knew what it would be. Now I feel like a small cork that is tossing around. I know that there are hundreds like me, and lots more unfortunate, but it doesn't heal the wound. The nice Bishop, who was so helpful before I was married, wrote the following: "Having borne you both so much in mind I am very anxious that you should begin again swiftly and easily the use of the Sacraments and the full practice of your faith. I have always been convinced that the reason why you took the line you did about the marriage was because you wanted your husband to be happy in what might prove the last portion of a short life." Isn't that nice? I am going to see him this Tuesday and he is going to say mass for Billy and Joe at which I shall receive Communion. I hope that makes Mother as happy as it makes me.

I am not sure what I shall do — nothing for awhile anyway and then I should like to do a job for the British and Americans. I won't go to Paris; it's too far away for the moment. I can't get over how kind everybody is.

Now a bit about my trip: It was perfectly wonderful. We left Quebec at seven, make a stop for two hours and a half luncheon and we arrived at Plymouth at about 8:20. There were seven of us in the Clipper, Sir Alan Brooke,[149] two aides, Sir Charles Portal[150] and two aides. They all kept opening up important looking boxes and rushing around always clutching a very, very secret looking brief case. I had an enormous suite and the dinner served on board Wednesday night consisted of: soup, meat vegetables, ice cream. They had lots of drink and champagne for dinner. I must say the last thing I thought I'd be doing last week at this time was watching the Chief of the Air Staff and the Chief of the Imperial Staff drinking champagne in mid-Atlantic. I must say I am most impressed with the efficiency of the British after that trip. At our two stops enormous groups of generals and Air-Marshals were drawn up to attention and then out of the plane stepped me. We were whisked off in low high-powered cars to eat costly and rationed food. We finally decided that we might pretend that one of the "higher-ups" was very ill and that I was the nurse of one of them. I was especially pleased when Lord Portal asked me sign his Short Snorter's bill. I signed — in between The King and General Giraud.[151] So you can see I shall never be in better company. We came up from the Coast on a private train five of us with luncheon served aboard. The Duke and Mrs. Bruce met me at the station as the Air ministry had kept them in close touch. Sir Charles Portal was unbelievably nice. We had lots of long chats and he said any time I wanted an air passage or anything done quickly in the US he would arrange it.

It might also interest you to know that Captain Charlesworth took me up to Quebec and planned my trip without ever getting his boss's permission. They just knew he wouldn't refuse and apparently Lord Halifax also sent a special message that there shouldn't be any doubt about my going. Sir Charles told me this and how terrified the Captain and his aide were when they came to them with the news that a young woman was coming with them. I spent a lot of time up in the cockpit watching the landings and take off, which was terribly exciting and Portal took great pleasure in showing me everything about an airplane. When we arrived at Plymouth we found that the weather had cleared at the place we were supposed to land so we all piled back on the plane again and went on to meet the private train. I came practically straight down here. Debo is here and the two girls. They are all wonderfully brave. What you and mother went through has only now just been brought home to me as I feel such a funny pain all the time and that must be just what you had.

Apparently the Red Cross thought I was going to come back and sent all my mail

---

149. Field Marshal Alan Francis Brooke, first Viscount Alanbrooke of Brookeborough (1882–1963), chief of the Imperial General Staff, 1941–46.

150. Air Marshal Charles Frederick Algernon Portal, first Viscount Portal of Hungerford (1893–1971), chief of the British Air Staff, 1940–46.

151. The former commander in chief of French forces in North Africa, General Henri Honoré Giraud (1878–1949) had served as copresident of the French Committee of National Liberation with de Gaulle for several months in late 1943.

and several parcels back to the Cape so please be on the watch for them and if it isn't too much trouble send them back again. I'll expect the other things in a week or two. Please don't forget about the box of Eliz Arden things I left under the bed and also my pearls. I meant to buy something for Pat Wilson which I never did, so would Eunice be very kind and go to Bonwit's and buy one of those black evening sweaters with the sparkles on them about a size fourteen, in fact please buy two of them with the round necks. I'm sorry to be writing for things already. The Duchess isn't wearing black and as I shall be in the country for the next month or so I shall not either.

Please write soon lots of letters. I thank God every night I married him and I think it must have been God's way of making Billy's life, though short completely happy. All my love and many thanks for everything. All love Kick

P.S. I just wanted to quote from a letter written by James Willoughby (Lady Astor's son-in-law) who has just lost a foot in battle, written to the Duchess well over a month ago, long before anything happened. "I thought that I must write and tell you how very well Billy was doing out in France as I was working with a battle group of the 5 Coldstream and Irish Guards before I had to retire from the battle owing a tank running my legs. We all advanced together for two days during which time the Coldstream suffered very heavy casualties, 2 Commanding Officers being wounded in 12 hours and Billy was left in Command. Billy was magnificent, he never lost his head or his good spirits in spite of the hard time his Battalion was having, no sleep, no food and continual casualties and kept up the spirits of his men the whole time. On the last day we were counter-attacked continuously from 6 o'clock in the morning until 10 o'clock at night and Billy's Battalion had to stand the brunt of the attack. Again he organized the defense in the most cool headed manner, and the position was held in spite of the most determined efforts by the Germans to capture it". There are so many others from different people about how well he had done long before he was killed. That's what makes such a difference.

I should also like to quote a bit from a letter from a friend of Billy's to the Duchess. She received it yesterday and though it makes me very sad to look at them I long to. "Since the Seine we have been working with Billy's battalion and the morning before he died during an attack on Beverloo I saw him walk across to one of his sections as calmly as if he had been in the garden at Compton Place. That same morning he had been standing on the back of one of our tanks directing the fire on to those German tanks and was largely responsible for their destruction. All the time, under fire. Many of our guardsmen asked me who was the officer from the 5th Battalion, for it was impossible not to be inspired by his presence. I hope it may be of some little consolation to know that he died instantly and yesterday Bill Anstruther-Gray and I visited his grave by a little chapel in Heppen. He lies with five other guardsmen and the local people have make it all very beautiful with flowers and a private hedge. I am thankful, too, that he lived to see the welcome we received all the way across France and Belgium for the look of happiness in the peoples faces made us all realize that almost any sacrifice is worth while."

Please send a copy of this to all the brothers and sisters. Since they didn't know Billy very well they might like to know how well he had done. The Duke told me this morning that he had sent daddy copies of some of Billy's letters [from] France about the battles. Please keep them all.

One of the officers told me last night that he definitely would have gotten the D.S.O. for commanding the Battalion so well during a bad time but apparently they don't award them posthumously.

Write soon, lots of letters and pray.

All love again, Kick

P.S. Have just had Mother's cable from the Cape. Sent you off one about new A.P.O. number 413 — It doesn't mean anything except that its changed from 887. The letters continue to come in. All one in the same vein of Joe's — What a leader Billy would have been and how brave he was thru out the whole battle.

I have so much to be proud of.

Joseph P. Kennedy: *Diary*

DIARY NOTES ON THE 1944 POLITICAL CAMPAIGN

Bob Hannegan, Chairman of the Democratic National Committee,[152] was brought to my room at the Waldorf by Morton Downey and former Senator, Jack Hastings.[153] He came with the idea of getting me to come out for Roosevelt. He admitted, starting off, that he had heard a great deal about my difficulties with the group behind Roosevelt and made no bones about the matter that he despised the group also. I related to him some of my feelings about Hopkins, Rosenman,[154] and Frankfurter, besides telling him that they were all trying to kick him out, and he went almost as far about them as I did. Of course, he made it clear that Truman[155] was his friend and the first time he met me, he insinuated that Roosevelt was not as well as they thought and that it was extremely likely that Truman would be President, would throw that gang out bodily, and would want fellows like myself to come back into the Government and make it work.

He asked me if I would be willing to see Roosevelt, and I said, "Of course, if Roosevelt asked me to go there, I would go."

However, I didn't want any misunderstanding that my trip meant I was for him because I was seriously contemplating making a speech for Dewey. He admitted that my speech four years ago had been a turning point in Missouri, and when I told him that I was getting ready to make a speech four years from that night, and with one son in the hospital, one son dead, and my son-in-law killed, that I didn't think it would be very helpful to Roosevelt, Hannegan amusingly said that I had better get ready to support his four young children because if I made that kind of a speech, he would have to jump out the window. He left me with no misapprehension about my attitude but said that I would hear from him again.

The following Saturday, October fourteenth, the White House called the Waldorf, but I had left for Cape Cod. The White House also called Paul Murphy at Somerset on the following Monday, October sixteenth, asking where I was, and Paul said that I was at Cape Cod.

On Tuesday last, October twenty-fourth, about three o'clock in the afternoon, the telephone rang at the Waldorf, after the operator at Somerset had told me that the White House was trying to get me, and it was Grace Tully, the President's secretary. She

---

152. Former Missouri ward boss and Internal Revenue collector Robert Emmet Hannigan (1903–1949) had become chairman earlier that year (amidst some controversy) with the help of his longtime associate and fellow Missourian, Senator Truman. As chairman, Hannegan in turn had been instrumental in replacing Henry Wallace with Truman as the 1944 Democratic vice presidential nominee. In 1945 Hannegan would become postmaster general.

153. John Ambrose Hastings (1900–1964), former New York State senator and cohort of Mayor Walker, had come under the scrutiny of Judge Samuel Seabury during the latter's investigations into New York graft and corruption in the early 1930s.

154. Former New York State Supreme Court Justice Samuel Irving Rosenman (1896–1973), special counsel to President Roosevelt, 1943–45, and later to President Truman, 1945–47.

155. Harry Shippe Truman (1884–1972), Democratic senator from Missouri, 1934–45; vice president, 1945; and president, 1945–53.

asked how I was, how Rose and the children were, and said how terrible everything was for us. Then she said, "Are you going to be down this way, and if you are, the President would like to see you."

I said, "No, I had no intention of being down that way. I had not been in Washington for about a year and as there was nothing there which required my attention, I looked conspicuous by being there with nothing to do."

She said, "That is too bad because the President would like to see you." I said, "Do I understand that he *wants* to see me?"

She said, "Yes," and I said, "Well, if he does, I shall be glad to come. When does he want me?"

"Thursday, October twenty-sixth at 12:30."

"Where?"

"At the White House."

I then said, "You know, when I put my foot in the White House, it will create some considerable comment."

She said, "That will be all right."

I said, "Now Grace, so that there will be no misunderstanding, I think that most of the fellows around the President are a lot of bastards, and in order that no one will have any misunderstanding about how I feel, I wanted to tell you that."

She said, "I know how you feel. Come along."

And I said, "Very well."

I took the early morning plane Thursday (7:25) and arrived in Washington about ten o'clock. Mrs. Truitt met me at the airport and drove me out to see Max, who was home ill with a cold. He told me (and I imagine through Jimmy Byrnes, one of the President's secretaries) that they were all scared to death to have me down there, that they were all afraid of what I might say or do. But both Max and Hannegan subsequently said that the President was the only one not disturbed because he felt I wouldn't do anything unfair. Of course, my impression is that those rats down there have been doing unfair things to so many people that it runs in their normal procedure.

I thought while I was there I would call up Lord Halifax, as the Embassy was not far away, and say hello to him before I went to the White House. He was very busy but said that he wanted to see me and made 11:45 as the appointment. I walked over to the Embassy where I saw Lady Halifax first, who looked about the same as always and was as charming as ever. She asked very solicitously about Kathleen. Then Edward came along and suggested that we sit out in the garden. We picked up a couple of chairs and sat in the corner. I told him why I had come down, and he asked me if I were going to make a speech for Roosevelt, and I said, "Positively not. I had no confidence in the outfit, I didn't think Roosevelt was well enough to carry on, and I thought we had the makings of an unholy mess."

He asked me who I thought would be Secretary of State if Hull didn't come back. I thought I saw no one but Stettinius,[156] which would be a horrible thing for the country as I consider him completely incompetent.[157] Halifax's expression and complete silence on this statement on this were more eloquent than words. I told him I had no confidence in Roosevelt's peace proposal because I felt in the last analysis, Joe Stalin

---

156. Roosevelt had appointed former chairman of the board of U.S. Steel, Office of Production Management (OPM) Director and Lend-Lease Administrator Edward Reilly Stettinius (1900–1949) undersecretary of state in 1943.

157. Hull, the longest serving secretary of state, would resign on November 30 to be succeeded by Undersecretary Stettinius, who in turn would be succeeded by James F. Byrnes after Roosevelt's death in April 1945.

would decide on what basis the world line-up would be made. Halifax was afraid that was probably true but he hoped that by working together, the United States and England could make Stalin not want more than he should have. Halifax said that, to date, he has demanded only the Baltic States, Poland to the Curzon Line, and Bessarabia.

I said, "Do you in your right sense believe that is his limit?"

Halifax said that he hoped it was but he didn't think it would be.

I said, "Aren't you in for trouble in Iran already?"

"Most likely."

Then I remarked, "Remember Chamberlain saying to me when negotiations were taking place with Russia to attempt to line them up on the side of England in the event of trouble with Germany, what a travesty it was on World idealism to think of agreeing to let Russia absorb the three Baltic states and go to war which would ruin the world because Germany wanted the Polish corridor."

Halifax shook his head and said that it was indeed strange.

I said, "I still believe the day will come in history when the British will tip their hats passing the statue of Chamberlain because they will realize that he was making a fight to preserve England."

He said that he agreed with me completely that history will make a rightful place for Chamberlain.

I said, "He will never be condemned for Munich. He will be criticized for being part of a government which didn't prepare to meet this menace, but his action at Munich will be approved."

Halifax said, "You know, one night while talking to the President, I asked him what really was his attitude towards Munich, and he said it was typified by the message sent by him to Chamberlain. It consisted of just two words, "good man.""

Halifax continued by saying that Roosevelt asked him if he had ever seen the message and he said that he hadn't and that there was no record of it in the foreign office. Halifax then asked me (and cautioned me never to say that he had asked me) if that actually were the case.

I said that it was true and that I had delivered the message to Chamberlain. Halifax couldn't understand why, with all the attacks which were being made on me as an appeaser, instigated by the Roosevelt group, I knew this statement of his and had never used it. My answer to that, of course, was that once having got into the war, I felt that there wasn't any sense in dividing up public opinion. Let's win the war and I'll take care of the record later on myself[.] Halifax told me that if he had to make a list of six men on whom England must depend after the war, one of the six would have been Billy Temple, the Archbishop of Canterbury, who died that day.

I left him about quarter past twelve and hurried to the White House. On my arrival I was shown into Grace Tully's office where we had a pleasant few minutes talking about Missy LeHand and what a wonderful girl she had been for that job.[158] After a few minutes President rung and I went in to see Roosevelt.

If I hadn't been warned by the stories of his illness and the fact that Archbishop Spellman told me he looked very badly, I would have been shocked beyond words. He sat behind his desk, and his face was as gray as his hair, put out his hand in a very friendly manner, and asked me to sit down. During the entire conversation, I was convinced that he is far from a well man. He is thin; he has an unhealthy color. His hands shake violently when he tries to take a drink of water. About 10 per cent of the time that he is talking, his words are not clearly enunciated. He seems to have none of his old-time pep

158. The president's close companion and former secretary had died in July.

but a great deal of his old charm. My overall impression is that Roosevelt is a sick man. The terrible realization came to me that the Hopkins, Rosenmans, and Frankfurters could run the country now without much of an objection from him.

In speaking about Kathleen's husband, he spoke of him as Billy Harkshire or some name like that. He said the news came when they were in Quebec, and he asked Churchill what kind of a boy he was, and Churchill told him he was one of the most promising lads in England. However, Roosevelt did not have his name right once, and that for Roosevelt is unheard of — his memory was his next greatest asset to his charm. Also, during the entire conversation, Roosevelt kept talking about $10,000 when he meant $10,000,000.

He started off the interview by asking me whether I thought he should make a speech on the employment problem after the war. He said that Kaiser[159] had come in with a plan for building airships just as Ford builds automobiles at $1,600 a piece and for having air fields all over the country, housing, and so forth and so forth. He asked me what I thought, and I said that it would be a great mistake to attempt to outline a plan for post-war employment which was based to great extent on theory because the Republicans would tear the speech apart and tell the country — "See, Roosevelt is still depending upon theory and not on practical ideas to put the boys back to work, and that would be very disastrous."

Roosevelt said that he was of that opinion, too. He asked me what I thought of the election, and I told him that I thought it was close and that the odds of 3-1 in his favor were too high for the evidence as we all saw it. He thought so too. However, I did say that the 3-1 odds were the greatest argument that he had today for re-election because it gave a lot of people confidence who were for him. If the Republicans brought the odds to 7-5 in the last few days of the campaign, I thought he would be licked. I said that I thought Massachusetts was 7-5 in his favor and that New Jersey was 7-5 against him. He thought that was right, but Hague had told him he was never as confident of carrying New Jersey as he is this year. He added, of course, Hague isn't always a good prophet. I told him that in my opinion the so-called 5 per cent vote that had yet to make up its mind was for the first time, not an independent vote, but was the old line Democrats — the Irish, and the Italians — all of whom should be in the Democratic columns but this year were off for two or three good reasons: First, they felt that Roosevelt was Jew-controlled. Second, they felt that the Communists were coming into control. (He countered that by saying that there was no Communist Party in the United States, which struck me as being a very weak answer.) Third, that this group, along with many others, felt that there were more incompetents in Roosevelt's Cabinet than you could possibly stand in this country. When I said that the Irish and Italians were off, he said the English were to blame for the Italian situation. Then he asked me if the Irish were off because of the Free State situation, and I said that I had not heard that discussed and thought it was rather the Communist and Jew idea. I added at this point that I was with the group who felt that the Hopkins, Rosenmans, and Frankfurters, and the rest of the incompetents would rob Roosevelt of the place in history that he hoped, I am sure, to have — because they would make such a horrible mess of it before they got through. Roosevelt said that lots of the present group working in Washington would be looking up train schedules November eighth. He also said he was very much displeased with Jones' sending out the list of surplus material at that time. He should have waited until after the election. (Hannegan later said that Roosevelt was quite disgusted with Jones.)

159. Industrialist, engineer and government contractor, Henry John Kaiser (1882–1967).

Roosevelt went on to say "Why, I don't see Frankfurter twice a year." And I said to him, "You see him twenty times a day but you don't know it because he works through all these other groups of people without your knowing it."

I said, "Of course, I am sore and indignant because of the way I have been treated. The last blow was when Jack was recommended for a medal by all his officers in direct command, which was two degrees higher than what he finally received. He was reduced by Halsey's group for reasons unknown to me, but which I suspect were because I was *persona non grata* to the powers that be in Washington — the result being that he received only the same honor that members of his crew received."

Roosevelt said, "Well, those things happen. In fact, Elliott was recommended for the Congressional Medal of Honor. The board turned it down because they felt it would look as if he had been given it because he was the President' son. (I remarked to myself — and God knows, it would have been!) He also said that Elliott should have been made a General now, but that was held up for the same reason. My own guess will be, however, that he will get it pretty soon after the election.

I said that it was a strange state of affairs when no group in the United States wanted any of his cabinet to come to their place to make a speech. In fact, I was of the opinion that there wasn't one man who could ever get five votes in Congress for any bill he was interested in. He said that he thought that was true, but he thought Ickes was doing a good job and that Ickes probably could get some votes in Congress from the group he represented. I suppose by that he means the lunatic fringe.

I said that I was shocked beyond words to see Morgenthau at Quebec taking up state matters with his plan for Germany since I knew that Morgenthau had never been able to answer one question in ten years before the House or Senate Committee without referring to his so-called experts.[160]

Roosevelt added, "I don't know anybody who has less political sense than Henry. That plan of his caused me great trouble throughout the country."

I said, "I don't know why you confine it to political sense. He never had any financial brains either, and you know that because you have discussed it with me many times. (Later that afternoon when I saw Jimmy Byrnes, he told me that Eisenhower had told him that neither Generals Patton,[161] Patch,[162] Holmes,[163] nor himself had ever seen this Morgenthau plan, which he got from a Jew named Bernstein, who used to work in the Treasury Department.[164] Eisenhower told Byrnes it had cost thousands of American Boys' lives. Jimmy added that a Sergeant who spoke German translated some of the German broadcasts, and every one of them pointed out what the Morgenthau plan meant to the German people. As Eisenhower said, where the Germans had been surrendering by the thousands, they were now fighting for every inch of the way.)

Of course, I can't help but feel that since Roosevelt knows this, to continue a man in office who had done our boys that much damage is an unpardonable crime. Roosevelt said that the conditions in Italy, which he admitted were chaotic, were entirely

160. The secretary of the treasury had unveiled his plan for a divided, demilitarized, agrarian postwar German state at the conference in early September.
161. General George Smith Patton (1885–1945) had commanded the Third Army in its push across northern France that summer.
162. Seventh Army Commander Alexander McCarrell Patch (1889–1945).
163. Brigadier General Julius Cecil Holmes (1899–1968), assistant chief of staff for personnel at Allied Force Headquarters, 1942–44, and adviser to General Eisenhower, was also the architect of the Allied plans for the military governance of occupied territories.
164. Economist Dr. Edward M. Bernstein (1904–96), assistant director of monetary research at the Treasury Department, 1940–46.

due to British mishandling of the situation. He didn't specify what it was, but he showed supreme disgust with it. He said that he had tried everything he could think of to win back the Italians for himself but he only had one thing left which was going to be put into effect right away — to permit Americans to send packages to their friends in Italy.

He then started to describe de Gaulle to me. I said, "Will you please remember that I saw more of de Gaulle than you ever saw because I saw him when Churchill brought him back from Paris after France fell, and there are reports in the State Department files about my interview with him.

Roosevelt said, "Did you ever hear of my difficulty with him?" And I said, "No."

"When Churchill and I met at Casablanca to discuss the French situation, we thought we had better have Giraud and de Gaulle. Giraud was ready, but de Gaulle was in England. Churchill said that he would send for him, which he promptly did, but de Gaulle refused to come and Churchill so reported to me. I told him I thought it was essential that he should be there and to try again. This time Churchill cabled Eden to try to persuade him to come but again de Gaulle refused, and Churchill so reported again. Then I said that I would get him here, and Churchill asked how? I said, "Tell him to come or we will stop his pay, which was the money that the British were feeding to the free French." "That brought him down and right away," Roosevelt concluded. "Then he came in to see me and started on the great discussion about how France in one of its great periods of crisis had been saved by this woman touched with the hand of God, Joan of Arc. De Gaulle said, "I am the Joan of Arc of France at the present moment."

Roosevelt said, "I couldn't stand much of that and suggested he come back the next day."

The next day he came back, and Roosevelt, talking about the needs of France, found de Gaulle saying, "I am prepared to cope with those. I am a Clemenceau."[165]

Roosevelt said, "Why, Clemenceau was a tough politician of the old school who would stop at nothing to attain his political ends. That being my understanding of Clemenceau, will you tell me how you are going to combine Joan of Arc and Clemenceau in your own good self?"

Roosevelt added, "That was the end of a beautiful friendship, but it will all iron itself out."

When I told Roosevelt that I didn't take much stock in any plans I had seen for post-war peace because I thought Stalin was, after all, the dominating influence in the world, he said, "Well, he doesn't always get what he wants." He said that he is demanding sixteen representatives on the Council Assembly of the United Nations, and I said, "Well, if he went through with that argument, Brazil would have to have 27 or 37 and I, meaning Roosevelt, would have to have 48, and that stopped the argument.

However, I hastened to add, "But it hasn't been settled, has it?"

He said, "No, it hasn't."

I was remembering my meeting with Halifax a few minutes ago when I was talking about Stalin. I said, "Of course, the United States will certainly not go to war now against Russia to enforce any position for England or for ourselves, and I remember Halifax adding, "You won't go to war and neither will we." I still think Uncle Joe knows that and will go after what he wants.

After this situation, we reverted back to a discussion of politics, and Roosevelt mentioned that he thought that handling his speech in a very light manner was good.

165. As French premier, 1906–9, 1917–20, Georges Eugène Benjamin Clemenceau (1841–1929) had represented France at the Paris Peace Conference in 1919.

I disagreed completely by saying that so many families had lost boys in the war that they didn't want such light treatment. He thought they would probably figure he is a good-natured man with the speech that way, but I said that it was delivered in a facetious manner. He could see in my attitude, I am sure, an unwillingness to commit myself, and I am sure he didn't want to be turned down so when I started to go, I said to him, "Now, the press will, of course, want to know what took place in here and I am perfectly willing to tell them. However, I imagine some of it might be unfair so if you are agreeable, I shall merely say that you asked me to consider some of the aspects of Kaiser's post-war plan and make that the main subject and handle politics the best I can."

He said, "That will be fine. I won't have to see the press until next week and that will be o.k. Of course, I am going to make a trip in New England through Hartford, Bridgeport, Springfield, and then come into Boston to wind up my campaign," (and I believe this was to be the cue for me to say, "Well, I'll be seeing you there," but I didn't.) I went out and the press reports will take care of my interview.

I don't believe I have stressed heavily enough my bitterness, which I certainly made clear to him, at his group and their attitude towards my offer of service for four years. I repeated this again and again. The only comment I got on the interview was that Frank Walker followed me in, and Roosevelt told him that he had a very pleasant interview but was very distressed that he had received no commitment from me as to help.

After I saw the President, I had lunch and went to see Jimmy Byrnes. Jimmy told me the Morgenthau-Eisenhower story. I told him that Roosevelt had told me that Jimmy Byrnes was a tower of strength to him and I had said, "Well, if he is, all his friends are out against you for the way you have treated him."

Jimmy said, "If I am a tower of strength, I have only seen him once since the last of July and that was the other day to report to him on my European trip."

Byrnes is still bitter and is getting out on the fifteenth of November and said he only stayed that long because he had forced the President to issue a statement that he was going to appoint somebody in Byrnes' place. Otherwise, he would have tried to keep him on and refused to accept his resignation. Byrnes was delighted that I had said what I did about Kaiser because he said that he is a swell-headed gentleman backed by Sam Rosenman as Sam Rosenman's wife is, of course, for Kaiser. Byrnes says that the cancellation of ships that had the approval of both Land and Vickery[166] was stopped by Rosenman because it would have affected Kaiser's Vancouver plant.

He thought the impression I had given that I was checking up Kaiser's statement would deflate Kaiser and would irritate Rosenman, so my perfectly innocent, as I thought, remark made most of the people in Washington very happy who hate Rosenman and Kaiser both. Byrnes said that he was going to make this one speech, but it looked to me as if it were simply a gesture and not because his heart was in it. He said that Cordell Hull had told him he had asked Roosevelt if any State matters were to be taken up in Quebec and Roosevelt told him, no, and then sent for Morgenthau. He said that Hull was bitter most of the time because he said he had no control over State matters.

In discussing Roosevelt's health, which was very bad, Byrnes said that on the day the Supreme Court came to visit Roosevelt — it is the custom for each Justice to talk to Roosevelt personally — that he was in such bad shape that Justice Roberts[167] said

166. Howard Leroy Vickery (1892–1946), vice chairman of the U.S. Maritime Commission, 1942–45, and deputy administrator of the War Shipping Administration since June 1942.
167. Owen Josephus Roberts (1875–1955), Hoover appointee to the Supreme Court.

to Byrnes, "I think this is cruel. This man is in no shape to talk, and we should get him out."

He and Byrnes bundled him out, and when Byrnes told that to McIntyre, he said that Roosevelt was perfectly all right and that he had a Navy dietitian who had just made him thin. When Byrnes met Harry Hopkins and spoke about Roosevelt's difficulty in talking, Hopkins said it was new dental work that he had done, but Byrnes didn't take any stock in that.

Byrnes also said he didn't know what he was thinking of because he had promised Churchill six billion six hundred million dollars on Lend Lease after the war, and this was confirmed when I talked to Admiral Willson in New York, who told me that at Quebec Churchill had asked for one billion six hundred million, and that he heard that Roosevelt had given him six billion six. Byrnes also said that Roosevelt's condition at Quebec was very bad, and at the Press Conference, Churchill had to take it over.

In my discussion with Archbishop Spellman, who came to see me at the hotel after his return from abroad, he said that he was very discouraged and disheartened about what he saw in Europe and most disconsolate about the Pope's position in Italy. He said that the Pope was really very discouraged about the way the world was going.

He told me two anecdotes to describe the hate which was rampant — Of a woman who hated her daughter-in-law so much that she conspired to have her own son killed so that her daughter-in-law would be bereft — Of a man crossing the street in Rome almost struck down by a taxicab driver, who pulled his cab up sharply and started to abuse the pedestrian, calling him everything he could think of. The man turned his sad eyes towards the taxicab driver and said, "You don't know what a favor you would have done me if you had hit me and killed me."

"Those incidents, Archbishop Spellman said, typify the feeling in Europe."

On Sunday afternoon at Hannegan's request, I went to Boston to meet Harry Truman. Truman came to see me in my room and begged me to make a speech. They both believe Roosevelt won't live long, particularly Hannegan. He has made this statement to me a number of times before, and they felt that Truman will be President and will kick out all these incompetents and Jews out of Washington and ask fellows like myself and others to come back and run the government. Truman assured me that that is what he would do. He said that he disliked Mrs. Roosevelt very much and that she had snubbed him when she was out west.

I couldn't help but think if the world knew that the candidate for Vice President and the Chairman of the Democratic National Committee were sitting in my room telling me that they hated the crowd that ran things in Washington and wouldn't keep them there five minutes, and that Roosevelt wouldn't live long and they would run things right — no wonder I am not going to do anything. Every time I would make the point — and I did to Truman — that I couldn't in conscience come out for Roosevelt when I have so little confidence in what they do, they both finished up by saying that knowing my experience, they didn't blame me a bit, but they still hoped I would come out for him.

And if I haven't made it strong enough before, I state again — both Truman and Hannegan discussed what they would do when the President died.

Joseph P. Kennedy to Francis T. Leahy

Palm Beach, February 13, 1945

Dear Frank:

You are correct. Your letter was entirely unsatisfactory to me and confirms my judgment about the lack of sportsmanship and a sense of fair play of the "Globe." It is inconceivable to me that this is the same newspaper which my father and the Irish Catholics of his day respected so greatly.[168]

There seems to me little sense in your comment that if the "Globe" had not published the article, other newspapers would have gone ahead anyway. In the first place, regardless of the syndicate arrangement of Lyons, he was and still is in essence a "Globe" employee and his relationships with other papers are indirect. In the second place, I still hold the judgment that no reputable paper would have carried the article without getting in touch with me personally for a clearance. Therein lies the essence of the act of injustice perpetrated against me and my family by the "Globe." It is the core of my complaint and nothing has been said or written to satisfy me or to exonerate the "Globe."

I shall be kind to Dinneen. He is mistaken.[169] Insofar as the "Globe's" position is predicated on the story of Dinneen, I assure you it has not a leg to stand on. Can it be that Dinneen asserts that I discussed this article before publication or does not Taylor[170] and all of you know that Dinneen never read the article to me until after it had been published? From Dinneen's recollection of that conversation, it should be clear that I had never expected that Lyons would treat my statements as an interview for the record. The editorial judgment involved was in itself a breach of confidence since any well-disposed editor would have sensed the explosive nature of Lyons' comments and would not have permitted the publication without expressly calling me on the phone. The testimony of the other newspapermen is lightly disregarded in the "Globe's" correspondence for the reason, I suspect, that no amount of ingenuity can square Lyons' conduct with the testimony of Messrs. Coghlin and his associate. It strikes me as a case of where the "Globe" decided to go ahead anyway, and when it found it had violated an elemental principle of journalism, the employees of the "Globe" closed ranks even to the point of injustice.

Believe me you are mistaken in your own personal judgment that the article was not to be condemned. Quite apart from any relationships I may have had in England, the article was raw in its misrepresentation. If the "Globe" cared to have confirmation of my complete ignorance of the plan for publication, they can get such from Judge Burns with whom I talked the Sunday of publication and expressed my amazement and disgust at the violation of the newspaper code.

The advertising discussion was always beside the point. My present resentment against the "Globe" for its inexcusable misconduct made the continuance of my commercial relations impossible.

---

168. In a letter of January 18, Leahy, the *Boston Globe*'s counsel, had written JPK to say that "the advertising manager of the *Globe* asked me to pacify you if I could, so that the Globe would again receive advertising from Somerset." Somerset had discontinued advertising in the *Globe* in the wake of Louis Lyons' publication of November 10, 1940, containing the inflammatory remarks that JPK believed had been made off-the-record.

169. *Globe* reporter Joseph Dinneen had called JPK on the morning of the interview's publication "to find out whether [JPK] said the things [he was] charged with saying and had authorized the interview." Dinneen had reported to Leahy that "he had read the article to [JPK], that [JPK] had confirmed it."

170. William Osgood Taylor (1871–1955), editor and publisher of the *Globe*, 1921–55.

I had hoped in the light of Mr. Taylor's letter and your kind intervention, the "Globe" would find it desirable to do the decent thing in some way consistent with saving their face. It is apparent that my hopes reflected a belief in the integrity and courage of the "Globe" which they do not possess.

I appreciate your kindness in trying to straighten this out and I appreciate the problem had great difficulties because of Dinneen's conduct. However, I must continue to believe that by the "Globe's" failure to deal forthrightly with a gross breach of propriety it has forfeited the respect of fair-minded citizens.

Sincerely,

[John J. Burns]

Joseph P. Kennedy to Henry Luce

February 15, 1945

Dear Harry:

Jack is preparing a final draft on this article. Do you think you can use it?

With warmest personal regards, I am

Sincerely,

Joseph P. Kennedy to Joseph Medill Patterson

Palm Beach, February 19, 1945

Dear Joe:

What a wonderful article you had written about young Joe and Jack!

It seems to close the book on young Joe, but I doubt very much if it will ever be closed for his mother and me.

Thank you so much.

Sincerely,

Joseph P. Kennedy to Joseph Kane[171]

Palm Beach, March 19, 1945

Dear Joe:

I am indeed grateful to you for your very complete outline of Bobby's situation. I can quite understand his embarrassment if he isn't able to get a shot at this war along with a great many of his contemporaries. He will always be disturbed about that, I am sure, but on the other hand, he may not get in it no matter which of these courses he follows out because the best advices from Washington seem to be that they will finish it off against Japan this year. Therefore, I should like to have him get as far along in his school as possible and then get him out as reasonably soon after the war as I can. I want Bobby to have a college education and then really get busy. With Joe gone and Jack still a long way from being well, there is plenty of slack for Bobby to take up so the R.O.T.C. doesn't seem to hold as much horror as Bobby seems to think it does, particularly if he doesn't have to spend five years there after the war.

I received a notice from the War Shipping Board about my boat and I have sent it up to Johnnie Ford. You two can decide whether it is worth while taking it on.

I talked to Krock the other day and told him that I couldn't think of anything worse

171. Longtime Boston Democratic politico, Mayor Tague's former secretary and JPK's cousin.

for the Jewish people than to have Rosenman abroad making an economic survey, Lubin to be our sole member of the Reparations Committee,[172]Lehman handing out relief all over the world, Baruch now going over to take a look at the situation, Frankfurter being mentioned as the Judge on the court to try the criminals, Mr. White[173] and Mr. Bernstein handling the Bretton Woods hearings before Congress, and Mr. Oscar Cox, Chief Adviser to Stettinius.[174] Now that is only part of those whom I know about, but it certainly does not look any too good on paper.

Do let me hear from you. Your letters are always so stimulating.

With my warmest personal regards,

Very sincerely,

Joseph P. Kennedy to Kathleen Kennedy Hartington, 25

Copy of letter to Kathleen. Please destroy this after you've read it.

May 1, 1945

Dear Kick,

The cable censors have just called me and told me I have been addressing your cables wrong, so it's possible that I've been sending you some messages, none of them important, that you never got. I was particularly anxious to know whether you got the dress that I sent special and whether you ever received the clippings of Billy that I received from the White House and also the President's autograph. I never heard whether you received them or not, and I was anxious about them.

I received your last letter about your return from Paris and the Anderson dinner.[175] Mother and I were talking it over last night and decided that nobody in the world twenty-five years of age has had the kind of life you've had or as interesting. If you haven't kept a good diary of all this material, you've robbed yourself of another thrill you should have and that is writing a book. I'm sure you could make enough out of that to buy all the clothes and jewelry you want in Paris for many a year and, in addition, have a most interesting contribution to make to our literary field.

Now as to the situation here. Roosevelt's death, of course, was a great shock to the masses.[176] They had been lead to believe that the horrible-looking pictures of him that were appearing were the result of a very strict diet that he'd been put on, but you remember when I wrote you about my visit with him I told you then that he was far from a well man. Well evidently he'd been slipping very badly, and it becomes more and more apparent to all of us that Hopkins and the rest of them were really running this country for the last year and a half, and, if I do say so, damn near ran it into the ground.

There is no doubt that there was real sorrow on the announcement of his death and for two or three days after. Now you rarely, if ever, hear his name mentioned, and

---

172. On March 12, brain trust economist Isidor Lubin (1896–1978), who had been serving as director of statistical analysis to the Combined Chiefs of Staff had been appointed to represent the United States at the Allied Reparations Committee meeting scheduled to be held in Moscow.

173. Harry Dexter White (1892–1948), assistant to the secretary of the treasury, 1943–45. In 1948 White would die of a heart attack shortly after defending his innocence against charges of passing wartime secrets to Soviet agents before the House Un-American Activities Committee.

174. Oscar Sydney Cox (1905–66), deputy administrator of the Foreign Economic Administration.

175. In a letter of April 22, Kick had reported on her luncheon ten days earlier at the Paris apartment of Chancellor of the Exchequer Sir John Anderson. "I sat in between Mr. Churchill & Sir John," she reported. "Wasn't it lucky for me? He certainly lived up to all my expectations but I must say for the first time in my life I was pretty nearly speechless."

176. The president had died at Warm Springs, Georgia, on April 12.

there is also no doubt that it was a great thing for the country. He had stirred up a hatred in the minds of at least half the country, and no matter whether he proposed anything good or bad, half the country would be against it and half for it. He had lost control of Congress, as I wrote you he would, and had been licked on almost every suggestion he had made. Whether we'll ever get a chance really to do anything constructive as a result of the San Francisco Conference[177] is still in the lap of the gods, but there would have been a fight if Roosevelt were present to ratify anything. Of course, I can easily understand England's feeling sorry for him because he did everything that a man could do for that country, but I don't think that it made any very great impression in America to read that Churchill, when speaking of him in Parliament with tears in his eyes, talked of what a great friend Roosevelt had been to England and mentioned some of the nice things he had done. He mentioned Lend-Lease, and at this point, the American papers reported that the House of Commons broke into applause, and many a person said in America, "Why the hell shouldn't they? They got 16 billion dollars." That type of feeling, as I repeatedly said to you, is becoming more and more evident, but I'll discuss that later in the letter.

Truman has made a great hit so far. I always remember what President Hoover told me that Boies Penrose, who was the great Republican leader of thirty-odd years ago in Pennsylvania,[178] said: "Never pick a fight with a new President for at least six months". That seems to be the slogan of everybody in the country at the present minute. The strong opposition papers to Roosevelt, such as the Chicago *Tribune, Times Herald* and *Daily News*, all are backing up Truman, and at the present moment he can do no wrong. The Jews are crying that they've lost their greatest friend and benefactor. It's again a clear indication of the serious mistake that the Jews had in spite of their marvelous organizing capacity. They made all their bets on one man rather than on some real social improvement. Then the man dies, and their hope for social improvement dies with him. On Saturday when Truman put Ed Pauley on the Committee for Reparations, replacing Lubin, that started the screeching all over again. Fundamentally, what has happened in this country is that the people believe that the day of free spending and the power of certain groups to control the future life of this country are finished, and for that reason everybody is pitching in to help Truman make a success. In fact, last night at a dinner the fellow who got the biggest laugh said that he understood there was a club being formed in Washington of those who "don't know Truman," and it was getting very difficult to find any members. So at least for the next three to six months the honeymoon will be on, and we may be able to get some constructive things done.

As to Truman, I know him very well and knew him as a Senator in Washington. I wrote you that he came to see me in November to try to interest me to come out for the ticket. I should say that his greatest attributes at this time are, first of all, his common sense; second, his desire to get things done well by getting the best people as advisors; and third, his advocating Americanism as the Mid West knows it and not as the elements in New York want it. The closest man to him is Bob Hannigan, who is just going in as Postmaster General. He was chairman of the Democratic National Committee and is a very close friend of mine. Truman's Senate advisors are very likely to be Senators George[179] and Barclay, with Senators Hatch[180] and Wheeler being reasonably close; on

177. The United Nations Conference of International Organization had convened on April 25, drafting and ratifying the organization's charter by June 26.
178. Boies Penrose (1860–1922), U.S. senator, 1897–1921.
179. Walter Franklin George (1878–1957), Democratic senator from Georgia, 1922–57.
180. Carl Atwood Hatch (1889–1963), Democratic senator from New Mexico, 1933–49.

the Republican side, Vandenberg[181] and Austin.[182] He's a man who will follow the Democratic Party machine very closely, and the New Dealers are likely to be out of luck. I think he'll make lots less concessions to Russia than Roosevelt would have been willing to make. He's quite friendly with Britain, but it will take him a long while to get as friendly as Roosevelt was.

As to what my plans might be, I'm not sure he'll offer me some kind of job. If it's anything I can do, I'll probably take it on the basis that everybody should help if they can. The only thing I'm seriously considering is whether I might not say to him that I'd like to help any way I can; but if he's going to give me a job, I'd rather have him give it to Jack and maybe make him the minister to some country or Assistant Secretary of State or Assistant Secretary of the Navy, or something of that sort. I haven't mentioned it to Jack yet, but I'm thinking it over. I'm going to write Jack today and ask him what he thinks about it. At any rate, I'm in a much better position to express an opinion than I was with the group around Roosevelt. They didn't want judgment; they merely wanted prejudices.

Now as to the general reactions on the international situation. The Russians have made themselves thoroughly unpopular in this country due to their tactics. The American public now begin to see, with Roosevelt out of the way, that the Russians just tell us to go to hell and really mean it; that they're not at all concerned about our position; and that they feel confident that they can dictate a policy to the world that will serve their best interests. Unless there are fundamental changes in the attitude at the San Francisco Conference, you may, conversationally, get the idea of world peace, but, practically, it will always be in the lap of the gods. It's a horrible thing to contemplate, with the death of all these boys and with the world economically and socially in chaos, that we haven't anything to look forward to in the line of peace for the world as the pay-off for everyone's sacrifices. That's the least we should all be working for.

Jack is out at the Conference writing articles for the Chicago *Herald American*, and I'm arranging to have the articles printed in some of the other Hearst papers. I talked with him Sunday night, and he was quite thrilled with the job. He was back at Mayo's ten days ago, and they advised another operation on his back, but I think he'll have it done in New York.

The most serious job of public relations or propaganda, as you wish, that needs to be done in this country today is the one that must be done for the English. As I've repeatedly told you, there's a bitter anti-English feeling throughout the United States, and to me it's the silliest thing in the world to have that feeling at this time because it merely plays into the hands of the Russians, whom very few people like. It seems to me that some very serious consideration should be given to the idea of getting across to the American people the fact that regardless of any differences we have with the British, we are much more natural allies with them than we could ever possibly be with the Russians. In the case of the English, the American people aren't able to describe very definitely why they dislike them; but in the case of the Russians everybody can describe why he dislikes them. For people like myself who know that England must depend for her economic rebirth on the attitude of the United States towards loans and economic competitive agreements, it's more than essential for England and America to be working hand in hand. If they miss the opportunity, they'll rue the day.

Well that's about all the news, dear, on the political situation. Eunice is working very hard in the State Department in the Prisoner of War Section, but I think that after

181. Arthur Hendrick Vandenberg (1884–1951), senator from Michigan, 1928–51.
182. Warren Robinson Austin (1877–1962), senator from Vermont, 1931–46.

the San Francisco conference, when Stettinius will probably resign and Jimmy Byrnes go in as Secretary of State, she may get an even better job. By the first of July I think that all the Cabinet will be changed except Wallace, [183] Stimson, and Forrestal.[184] Pat will be twenty-one on Sunday, but is postponing her party until later on at the Cape. Bobby has been with me the last five days here in New York and is courting very strongly a little twenty-one-year-old, nice but a little on the quiet side — he denies it seriously. Jeanie was up last weekend and expects to graduate in another month. Teddy weighs 152 and is as good-natured and irresponsible as ever. Mother is feeling a little better, but after reading your letters has made up her mind that she doesn't think you'll come back very soon, and she thinks that she'll probably just move over there. I think she can hardly wait to get to London and Paris.

Harvey Klemmer,[185] whom I don't trust, told Max Truitt that you discussed with him whether you should stay in England or not and whether the Duke wanted you to stay and what Nancy Astor would say in the matter. There isn't any way you can know that Klemmer is a blabber-mouth, but he is.

Well, darling, this is about all the hot news; things will get pretty interesting around here from now on, and I'll keep you posted. Have a good time. Tell me about whether you ever bought the house and if there's anything I can do.

Love,

P.S. Fred Carroll, formerly Vice President of the Stoneham Bank of Boston, has been appointed to succeed Harvey Gibson. He's talked with me about the job, and I suggested he take it. He's going over there without Mrs. Carroll. He's a great friend of all our friends in Boston. All you've got to do is make yourself known to him and tell him what you want. He'll do anything you ask, I'm sure.

I had dinner with Basil O'Connor, the head of the Red Cross, a couple of nights ago, and I think the Red Cross units will be in Europe in strength for at least another year.

Joseph P. Kennedy to Edward Kennedy, 13

May 8, 1945

Dear Teddy:

I received your report for May fourth. You certainly fell down badly from the previous report and dropped to the 4th/fifth rather than the second. You can do better than this. Coming down the last stages of the lap, a good runner doesn't quit at the finish — that's the time he puts on the speed! So get busy.

Love,

Kathleen Kennedy Hartington, 25: *Round-Robin Letter*

May 12, 1945

Dearest Family —

What a week this has been! I really feel that I have lived five years rather than five days. When I arrived back from Yorkshire Monday everyone in London was in a terrific

---

183. The president had allegedly offered Wallace the cabinet post of his choice in consolation for the former vice president's replacement by Harry Truman on the 1944 Democratic ticket. Wallace had chosen Commerce, thereby forcing the removal of his rival, Jesse Jones, both from the cabinet and from the Reconstruction Finance Corporation, and provoking a bitter fight over his confirmation in the Senate.
184. James Forrestal (1892–1949), secretary of the navy, 1944–47.
185. The former U.S. Maritime Commission representative in London.

state expecting the V-Day announcement at any moment. Then finally on the 9:00 o'clock news they announced that the PM would speak Tuesday. With that London settled down to tremendous celebrations. Bob & Angie Laycock had come to play bridge at my flat with an American who has been out in the Pacific. Bob said to him I hope you notice the way we are observing VE day with the minimum of noise etc. At the moment bedlam broke loose and never stopped for two days

Of course there were no taxis etc. and one was forced to walk everywhere. Tuesday night David & Sissy Gore & Hugh Fraser (who is standing as a Conservative candidate at the next election) went & stood with the enormous crowd in front of Buckingham Palace. I must say that it was a most moving sight. They all shouted "We Want The King" and finally they appeared in the flood-lit balcony, the Queen wearing her tiara etc. People cheered & screamed etc. Noel Coward was standing right in back of us in the crowd giving out autographs — Then we watched an enormous bon fire in Green Park & on to Piccadilly which was absolute bedlam. Fire-works, dancing in the street. It really was the most tremendous spectacle as long as one didn't get swamped in it.

Wednesday night I dined with the Dutch who is quite well but feels as we all do that one must really now settle down to facing life without the best ones, who will never come back. During the war everybody lived in a state of flux but now we must all settle down & make definite plans. That is what is difficult. On Wednesday I lunched at the House of Commons & we climbed to the top of Big Ben & surveyed the crowd from there. Most exciting, but most tiring. Yesterday I lunched at Lady Anderson's & met: Megan Lloyd-George (old LG's daughter)[186] Mme Massigli, wife of the French Ambassador. She is very cross about Claire's stories on France. Apparently they (the stories) stopped a lot of food, etc. from going to France. Shane Leslie (the Irish writer) was there too. He is charming & a great friend of M. Bruce's I am going to Ireland the end of July to visit Lismore.

Daddy's interesting letter of May 1st arrived yesterday. I had been longing to hear all the latest.

Jack sent a telegram from San Francisco saying he had just lunched with Betty Biggs & Richard. Am so glad.

Staying at Dytchley now — Ronnie[187] sends best

All love from
Kick

John F. Kennedy, 27, to Rose and Joseph P. Kennedy

The Palace Hotel, San Francisco, May twenty first, nine[teen] hundred and forty-five. Dear Mother & Dad:

Here is the book on Joe — a good deal later than I had planned. Its lateness is in some ways a blessing — as it made it possible to include several recent events affecting Joe.[188]

---

186. Megan Lloyd-George (1902–1966), the former prime minister's youngest daughter, was the current Liberal MP for Anglesea. She would join the Labour Party in 1955.

187. The Anglo-American Arthur Ronald Lambert Field Tree (1897–1976) was a grandson of Marshall Field as well as the conservative MP for the Harborough Division of Leicestershire, 1933–45; parliamentary secretary to the Ministry of Town and Country Planning, 1945; and a former adviser on American affairs to the Ministry of Information, 1940–43.

188. Over the previous few months Jack had compiled and edited a series of short essays on Joe written by friends, family members and acquaintances; he titled the compilation *As We Remember Joe*.

The book, I am afraid — may make you sad. I hope that that sadness will be mitigated by the realization — clearly brought out in the book — of what an extraordinarily full and varied life Joe had.

The book is a gift from all of the children. Five hundred copies have been printed — and the other envelope contains a list of the names of people to whom it is to be sent.

If you have any changes or anyone to add please list them and send them to Mr. Edgar Sherrill — University Press — Cambridge — Mass — Mr. Sherill, incidentally, has taken a most personal interest in the job.

I have arranged to send some to Kick.

Much love
Jack

Joseph P. Kennedy to Arthur Houghton

Hyannisport, May 26, 1945

Dear Arthur:

I received your note today. It was delayed because it was addressed to Nine Rockefeller Plaza, New York, so I didn't get it until this morning.

Of course, we were shocked beyond words to hear the news about Andy. I have often wondered just what my reaction would have been if young Joe had been married and had a widow and a child as close to me as Andy's are to you.

The father has the problem of keeping the mother reasonably happy, but in your case there is the additional problem of seeing the baby and worrying about the widow. I feel for you very, very much indeed.

I have told you so many times before that when you are our age, I don't think you ever get over the shock. However, I believe it is a little keener for the parents if the boy has not married because, in a sense, when they get married, they sort of start their own life; but while they are single, we still look upon them as little children.

I won't offer you that hocus-pocus that some people offer — that he died for a great cause — I don't believe he did. I believe he died like young Joe as a result of the stupidity of our generation. The one thing he did die a martyr to was his own conscience. He wanted to do the right thing because it was his idea of the thing to do, and for that — and that alone — he died. That is the satisfaction which you and I will always have.

I saw Will Hays the other day and had a long talk with him about pensions for the group. It came up quite easily because he was discussing the company when pensions came in. He said that the real reason against pensions was that Paramount and Fox hadn't adopted a plan for their own companies and were against it.

I said I thought that all of the employees had stolen enough over a period of years (stolen probably isn't the word) but, at least, got enough so that they could be very comfortable; yet, what about his own organization?

He agreed with me, but I doubt very much if he would battle to put it through; nevertheless, I am going to keep after it.

I received a letter from Paul Mallon[189] telling me that he thought Snyder, now head of RFC and a very close friend of Truman's,[190] will be made Secretary of the Treasury

---

189. Paul Raymond Mallon (1901–50), author of the syndicated "News Behind the News" column, 1932–47.
190. Federal Loan Administrator John Wesley Snyder (1895–1985) would become director of the Office of War Mobilization and Reconversion in July 1945 and secretary of the treasury in 1946.

and that Ed Pauley, when he returns from his Reparations job in Europe, will get Snyder's place. It sounds possible.

I think, up to date, things are going very much better in the feeling towards the government now as against Roosevelt, but the problems are still there.

Well, boy, my heart is with you all, and I know there is nothing one can do or say except that your friends feel for you deeply.

With warmest personal regards.

Sincerely,

John F. Kennedy, 28: *Travel Diary*

[July 24, 1945]

Arriving in Ireland from England, you see sharply the blessings of peace. The people are cheerful there is none of that chronic fatigue that sharpens tempers in London. Food is plentiful, what rationing there is is applied with Irish tolerance and good humor, there are none of the queues of London.

In Dublin there are few cars, petrol is difficult to get, but the people walk or ride their bicycles. The streets are scrupulously clean and the famous doors of Dublin are freshly painted and the brass is shining.

But the appearances are superficial. Ireland which has escaped the devastation and the bombing of Europe has had its casualties. More than 250,000 thousand of its population crossed to England to serve in the armed forces or to [sic] in the factories. How many of these went direct into the armed forces has not been disclosed, but the fact that residents of Southern Ireland received seven Victoria Cross while people in the North received none has caused some satisfaction among the people in the South.

In direct contrast to the political situation Irelands economic ties with England are closer than they have ever been.

Joseph P. Kennedy to Bartholomew Brickley

Hyannisport, October 12, 1945

Dear Bart:

This Tyler Kent case will have to be brought out in the open some day either by a Senate investigation, a suit, or something. I received this letter when I arrived home last night.

Of course, the fellow was absolutely a bad one and he will never dare bring anything to trial because they've got too much on him. As far as withdrawing anything I have ever said about him, the answer to that is "nuts."

I thought you might have it, however, because sooner or later it will have to come in the open. He has received sympathy on the basis that he was supposed to have been put away because he knew things between Churchill and Roosevelt. That is all pure unadulterated bunk!

My warmest personal regards.

Sincerely,

Joseph P. Kennedy to Cissy Patterson

Hyannisport, November 26, 1945

My dear Cissy:

All the Kennedys have delegated me to answer your very sweet note to us. We have just finished a very happy Thanksgiving in that we had all the children back for Thanksgiving dinner. Of course, as you say, we miss Joe terribly.

It does seem ironical that somebody who opposed the war as bitterly as I did should lose his oldest son, his son-in-law, and have his second son badly banged up.

I still find it very difficult to get over Joe's death. God in His wisdom ordained so well that the young soon forget the sorrow of the death of older people, but I don't think that the older people ever get over the death of the younger ones.

At the minute it does seem that it is rather too much to hope for that the world will be any better as a result of the sacrifices of all these fine young men — but then again, I never thought it would be.

Kathleen is home and she will be in Washington next week. She is looking forward with great pleasure to seeing you. After all, she always feels a great sense of gratitude to you for having given her the opportunity of writing that column.

Jack has been making a number of speeches for the Community Chest Drive here and has been writing some book reviews for the local papers and also is doing some lectures on the European situation for charity.

I think it is extremely likely that he will run for Congress when Curley gets through. With his background, brains, and his courage, he would do a good job if anybody could. I hope, for his peace of mind, that he does.

As you may suspect, I have only been in Washington three times since 1940 — and then, in all cases, only for the day. It just wasn't any place I wanted to be.

We plan to go south around the seventh or eighth of December and to be there most of the winter. Do tell us if, by any chance, you are coming that way.

This again seems to be an opportunity to thank you most sincerely in the name of all the Kennedy's for all the kindnesses you have shown us in the papers over the last ten years. You have never let one opportunity go by that meant saying or doing something nice for the family. It is silly to try to say "thank you" for such friendship, but we all know it and sincerely appreciate it.

With the best from us all, I am

Most sincerely,

Joseph P. Kennedy: *"Memorandum of Conversation with Winston Churchill at Hialeah Race Track on January 31, 1946"*

I was sitting in my box with Mrs. Kennedy, Pat, and Eunice when Colonel Clarke, Churchill's host, [191] asked me if I didn't want to come over and have a little chat with Winston. I said, "Fine, a little later in the afternoon."

Finally, I went over and sat in the box. He started off by saying to me, "I have always been very grateful to you for that correction you made in that speech you gave about the South. [192] You saved me from a great embarrassment."

---

191. Canadian paper, pulp and shipping magnate Frank Clarke (1887–1967) had earlier hosted Churchill at the Quebec Conference in 1943. During his visit to the Clarkes' winter home in Florida, Churchill would accept an honorary degree from the University of Miami in late February.
192. On October 1, 1939.

Of course, I didn't mean what the speech seemed to say but I can easily understand why it might have been interpreted in such a way. (I am not sure what this speech was, but Miss Walsh can look it up.)

Churchill also said, "I remember that one of the last times we met we were having dinner during an air raid. It didn't bother us very much, though, did it?"

Then he remarked, "You had a terrible time during the war; your losses were very great. I felt so sad for you and hope you received my messages." I thanked him and said that I had.

He then said, "The world seems to be in a frightful condition." I said, "Yes. After all, what did we accomplish by this war?" He turned sharply, saying, "Well, at least, we have our lives," and I replied, "Not all of us." With that he dropped the subject at once.

Churchill said he was getting ready to make a speech in the United States and that he would stress the fact that although we must all cooperate with Russia, it is essential that the United States and England work closely together. After all, with their populations, they have approximately 175,000,000 whites and the Russians have about 195,000,000. He thought that if England and America stood firmly together, there would never be another war. After all, the war could only come from the Russians, and they would not hazard one with the United States and England together.

Churchill thought Anthony Eden should have been elected Secretary General of the UNO Security Group because he was far and ahead the most able man. However, while he had much respect for the Belgians, who had given him a great reception when he went there, he couldn't see any reason for electing Spark the head of the organization. Certainly the Belgians were never willing to take a step to help the British when war was declared and only became really excited when they were invaded. The same held true for Lie, the new Secretary General of Norway.[193] They wouldn't take any position until it was too late.

I told Churchill that I favored the British loan as a gift rather than as a loan.[194] He said he thought that it was necessary for the British to make concessions on their bases and all other possessions of theirs to make them available for the United States. We, in turn, would do likewise, which, by the way, would make our Navy twice as effective as it would be without the bases. He thought that England desperately needed the loan, and if she didn't get it, the very Left Wing of the Labor Party would point out the injustices of the capitalistic system of the United States and it would not be long before it would be wiped out in England. Then another force would be created to help wipe it out in the United States.

Churchill said he realized that to all intents and purposes, his political career was finished. I interrupted him and said that he was very fortunate that he had been defeated. He smiled and said he wasn't sure but that was right.

He said he intended now to enjoy himself as best he could until he died. Of course, it was apparent that he really didn't mean that, but that was what he said.

193. The former Norwegian foreign minister in exile, Trygve Halvdan Lie (1896–1968), would be appointed the first secretary general of the United Nations the following day.

194. After many months of negotiation, before the new year the U.S. had agreed to lend Britain some $4.4 billion over fifty years at 2 percent to replace Lend-Lease.

Joseph P. Kennedy to Edward Kennedy, 13

Palm Beach, January 31, 1946

Dear Ted:

I am sending $50 up to the school with instructions to let you have what you need. Your letters are coming through all right, but your penmanship hasn't improved much.

You still spell "no" know. Now know means if you understand something, but if someone says, "Are you going swimming?" and you say "no" it is *no* — not know. Skating is not "scating"; it is *"skating,"* and tomorrow you spell wrong. You spell it "tommorow"; it is *"tomorrow."* You spell slaughter as slauter. It is *"slaughter."* You really ought to do a little more work on the writing and the spelling. You are getting pretty old now, and it looks rather babyish.

The weather has turned out to be a little nicer now, although it isn't nearly as good as last year. The Commish[195] and I get down to the races every week, but we still lose a little every day so we don't bet very much.

Pat is down here with us and Kathleen has gone back to New York for a while. We are thinking now that we will keep the house open for your vacation since you come around the first of April but we can work that out as time goes along.

I am sorry to see that you are starving to death. I can't imagine that ever happening to you if there was anything at all to eat around, but then you can spare a few pounds. Margaret is sending some cookies.

Take good care of yourself and drop us a line.

Love,

Kathleen Kennedy Hartington, 26: *Diary*
February 27th, 1946

Motored down from Palm Beach to Colonel Clarke's house in Miami Beach to meet Mr. & Mrs. Winston Churchill and to watch the latter receive his degree from the University of Miami. Seymour Berry[196] and I arrived about 9:15. Leslie Hore-Belisha and his wife Cynthia were already there in the small living room of the house where the former Prime Minister was spending his vacation. We hadn't been in the house long before Winston appeared downstairs with an enormous cigar, bare-footed in his dressing gown complaining as to whether quarter to ten meant quarter to or past. Mrs. C-calmed him, he went upstairs and we (the party included General and Mrs. Anderson, Col. Clarke and Sarah Oliver[197]) talked for about half and hour. Then escorted by 20 motor-cycle policemen we drove to the Orange Bowl Stadium. We marched in the official entourage followed by members of different Florida Universities. I sat on the platform in between Seymour and L. Hore-Belisha. Afterwards we drove back to the Clarke's, picked up our suits and bathed at the Surf Club. Winston presented a very comical sight, bobbing around in the surf. He adores the water although I must say I wouldn't enjoy swimming in quite such a public spot every day. He asked about Daddy and when I said he sends you best regards, W.C. replied, "he makes an exception in my case." Daddy took umbrage at this remark. We then all went upstairs for the big official luncheon. I sat at the main table next to John Erskine who wrote "Private Life of Helen

---

195. Timilty.

196. John Seymour Berry (1909–), later second Viscount Camrose, eldest son of the *Daily Telegraph*'s owner and editor in chief, William Berry, first Viscount Camrose.

197. Actress Sarah Millicent Hermione Churchill Oliver (1914–82), Churchill's second daughter.

of Troy," which supposedly made him an expert on the subject of women.[198] There were about 20 short speeches and we arose from lunch about 4:00 p.m

Mrs. Churchill is so gracious and with overwhelming charm.

Joseph P. Kennedy to Arthur Krock: *Telegram*

FEBRUARY 28, 1946

DEAR ARTHUR: THIS IS APPROXIMATELY WHAT I THINK ABOUT THE LOAN. IT NEEDS PUNCH AND POLISH. WILL YOU LOOK IT OVER, SHAPE IT UP, AND THEN SEND ME WHAT YOU THINK WILL DO THE MOST GOOD FOR US.

OF NECESSITY I HEARTILY FAVOR A LOAN TO BRITAIN. THE QUESTION IS, NOT WHETHER THEY HAVE THE RIGHT TO DEMAND IT, THEY HAVEN'T. BUT IS IT TO OUR INTEREST TO GRANT IT? ENGLAND, AFTER ALL, IS OUR BEST CUSTOMER IN FOREIGN TRADE. THE ENGLISH PEOPLE AND THE ENGLISH WAY OF LIFE IS THE LAST EUROPEAN BARRIER AGAINST COMMUNISM. WE MUST HELP THE ENGLISH GOVERNMENT TO HOLD THAT LINE. I QUITE AGREE WITH PRACTICALLY EVERYTHING THOSE WHO OPPOSE BRITAIN'S AID HAVE SAID. ENGLAND FOUGHT FROM '39 TO '42 TO SAVE ITS OWN SKIN. AS MR. CHURCHILL LATER SO ELOQUENTLY SAID, "DURING THOSE YEARS I WAS WORKING, HOPING, PRAYING, NIGHT AND DAY, THAT THE UNITED STATES WOULD ENTER THE WAR."

SO THAT WE OWE THEM NOTHING [SIC]. WE HAVE ALREADY SPENT ABOUT 250 BILLION DOLLARS IN A WAR THAT WE WERE TOLD WAS TO SAVE CIVILIZATION. WE HAD BETTER GIVE FOUR MILLION MORE, EVEN THOUGH WE CAN ILL AFFORD GIVING AWAY ANY MORE MONEY TO HELP 47,000,000 ENGLISHMEN WHO DEFINITELY ARE IN A BAD WAY ECONOMICALLY. THEY ARE FINE PEOPLE. LET'S NOT DRIVE THEM INTO THE HANDS OF COMMUNISM.

IT IS, HOWEVER, TO OUR INTEREST TO HELP THEM MAINTAIN NOW THE BALANCE OF WORLD TRADE AND WORLD SALVATION: ONLY, LET THERE BE NO BEGUILING OF THE AMERICAN PEOPLE EITHER; FINANCIAL AID TO BRITAIN BY ANY NAME IS STILL A GIFT. LET'S ADMIT IT AND DO IT GRACIOUSLY.

JOSEPH KENNEDY

Joseph P. Kennedy to Joseph Kane

Palm Beach, March 11, 1946

Dear Joe:

I have read your letter with its very clear outline of Jack's position. Personally, I think I would rather see him Lt. Governor. Now mind you, I don't say that I would rather see him "run" for Lt. Governor. I would rather see him Lt. Governor, but I realize his greatest weakness is his lack of experience.

Therefore, since he would have an easier chance to win in Congress, I believe I am inclining more toward that idea. However, I understand he will be down next Monday, and we will have a chance to discuss it then.

I feel it is most important to find out as soon as possible just when the primaries are going to be. You might send me word on that as quickly as you can.

---

198. Musician, novelist and professor of both English literature at Columbia University and music at Juilliard, John Erskine (1879–1951).

As far as my statement on the British loan is concerned, that is exactly how I feel. With the exception of a few Coughlinites, I am sure the statement won't hurt Jack in that district, and it certainly will help him with the Canadians and English in the state at some later time.

This next issue of LIFE will have my big article on foreign policy.[199] It can't possibly hurt him, and I think you will like it very much.

When I get back the first week in April, I think I can make a statement on that Commerce Committee which will scare the hell out of the Republicans. They are playing right into Tobin's hands.

The young men with their wives and families who want jobs — those who know that industry is failing in Massachusetts — are all going to be awfully mad with any opponent of this bill before it is finished. Of that I am sure.

I plan to be in New York about the twenty-eighth or ninth of this month and will be on the job from then on.

With my warmest personal regards,

Sincerely,

Rose Kennedy: *Round-Robin Letter*

April 11, 1946

Dear Children:

I still have a lot of trouble with bills down here. For instance, there is a bill from Peck & Peck, and we had to call up to find out that one skirt was for Kathleen and a blouse was for Eunice. We did not know whether it was down here or in New York. We got a bill from Dr. Peters in Boston, and we do not know whether it is Teddy or Jack or both. Someone has bought jewelry in Burdine's, and we have no idea what it is or who it is. We have a bill from the Golf Shop for gloves, cash advanced, balls, etc., and we know nothing about that. We got a bill from Newberry's Pharmacy for three prescriptions of which no mention has been made, but Miss Mac thought she recognized one number as Eunice's medicine.

We got a bill from Schwarz with a Bronxville, N. Y. address on it for purchases in February. We had to call up to find out who bought it and what year it was. This happens every month. I have asked you repeatedly to either notify the stores or even notify Miss Mac as it takes us endless time and discussion. Please check carefully in New York as I have written them all notes and I am afraid it is going to be embarrassing from now on as I have just told them I would not be responsible.

Love,

Joseph P. Kennedy to Lord Beaverbrook: *Telegram*

HYANNISPORTMASS 22 JUN 46

DEAR MAX YOUNG JACK WAS NOMINATED FOR CONGRESS TUESDAY.[200] I AM SELL-ING OUT SOME OF MY BUSINESS INCLUDING THE LIQUOR AND WILL NOT KNOW MY

---

199. "The U.S. and the World" in which JPK argued that "[t]o prevent World War III we should keep our military forces strong, work closely with Great Britain, support Nationalist China, encourage a Western European bloc—and tell the Russians exactly where we stand," would appear in the March 18 edition.
200. Out of a field of ten candidates, Jack had won the Democratic primary for the Eleventh Massachusetts District with 40.5 percent of the vote on June 18.

Kathleen Kennedy Hartington, 26, to John F. Kennedy, 29

GARROWBY, July 13 — 1946

Dearest Jack —

This letter has been coming for ages. It's just to tell you how terrifically pleased I am for you. Everyone says you were so good in the Election and the outcome must have been a great source of satisfaction. Its nice to know you are as appreciated in the 11th Congressional District as you are ~~in the~~ among your brothers & sisters. Gee, aren't you lucky? The folks here think you are madly pro-British so don't go destroying that illusion until I get my house fixed. The painters might just not like your attitude!

Lord & Lady Halifax send you many congratulations. I have been staying with them for the past week, and there's nothing they don't know about the eleventh congressional district. Tonight is a nervous moment as the decision comes out about the Loan. Lord H— has a dog called Truman so he can go out & kick that about if the news is bad.

William[201] still has not sold a play but continues to be optimistic and has started writing another. Hugh goes off to Nuremberg with two Socialists at Parliamentary Recess — He's written a good article which I shall send you.[202] Dined with Hugh & Michael Astor in the House of Commons the other night — During dinner there were three divisions[?]!!! Betty seems well. She wanted to cable you. Everyone agreed her husband nice but a bore. Janie fights with Max Aitkin[203] every day but continues to live with him and plans to marry him in August. Daily Telegraph had no mention of your Election, which is *a bit* hard, isn't it? Sent $50.00 to George Meade scholarship fund. Enough, do you think?

Write soon 4 Smith Square S.W.1. and my best love to you from

Kick

P.S. Nothing new has been added but no danger of anything old taking me away! Get it?

Joseph P. Kennedy to Sir James Calder[204]

Hyannisport, July 31, 1946

My dear Jim:

It was nice hearing from you, and I talked with Kathleen in London yesterday and she said you still looked as well as you did the first day we knew you and hadn't gotten a day older.

I can think of two things which you could do — you could come over here this summer and stay at the Cape or you could come over in the winter and stay with us in Florida. I am sure both of these would do you a world of good.

---

201. Douglas-Home.
202. Fraser had been one of four Roman Catholics to be elected in the general election of the previous year; he had been the single successful Tory candidate for Staffordshire.
203. John William Maxwell Aitken (1910–) Lord Beaverbrook's son and heir, would marry Kick's friend, Jane Kenyon Slaney Lindsay on August 15.
204. Chairman of the Distillers Company.

Now, as to my getting out of the liquor business: There are quite a number of reasons for it. All of them made my final determination, and not any one of them would have been reason enough to get out.

First of all, I was annoyed that Somerset received less Haig than the other major companies. I thought the excuse they gave us was a perfectly ridiculous one. When you consider that I was willing to put $3,000,000 in Scotch back in '39 when the other companies could have bought it and didn't, it seems to me to have been sufficient reason to have received top consideration.

Second, I have been continually disgusted with their handling of the Gordon gin situation over here and have made no secret of it to any representatives of the Distillers Company I saw.

Third, the Somerset organization, for the last five years, has been merely an order-taking organization and lacked the punch which a real organization needs to keep it going. O'Leary and Delehanty are too old to start a new drive when Scotch becomes plentiful — at least, that is my opinion.

I don't feel that at sixty years of age I would be up to it.

Fourth, in Jack's campaign for Congress they made the real issue my support of the British Loan and said the only reason for it was that I had a franchise from Haig & Haig. It occurs to me that from here in it is going to be necessary for me to take a great many positions for England as against Russia, and it is silly to have wrong interpretations put on my actions.

Fifth, my franchise for Haig & Haig runs out next year, and it has been continually told to me that the English were annoyed with me and would not renew the contract. In fact, O'Leary came back the last couple of times with the definite feeling that things, as far as I was concerned, were not too friendly.

Sixth, I thought this new group had business relations with Distillers Company before and that they could furnish all the alcohol you need for Gordon gin under present conditions, which might be an advantage.

Seventh, I could get a price now for my stock in which I could make a capital gain and it would probably net me more than I could make out of the company in the next ten years. As none of my children are at all interested in business, it seemed now is the time to sell out.

I knew that Jasbon and Reinfeld were keeping the Distillers group advised of every move that was made so I didn't bother to send them any word. Also, they stopped shipping me whiskey with a telegram to the effect that I had a large enough supply on hand. This, I think, was a hell of a gall on their part considering for the last five years I have sold all of the Scotch that they sent here and what I had in stock is what might have been left from my overwhelmingly large purchase in '39 and '40.

In addition to that, with the uncertainty of gin and no demand for rum, I had to keep some Scotch or I would have been out of business any month that the government took a position [sic] gin and you cut down your shipments on Scotch.

I feel that I did a very good job for Distillers and gave a good deal of standing to their company. I am glad to be out of it now because I don't like arguments when I am fifty-eight years old.

That is roughly the picture. There are lots of odds and ends, which I don't care to write — some to do with England and some to do with my own organization — but when I see you I will tell you about it.

As to the economic conditions here, they are not good. Truman was left with plenty of bad situations as a result of Roosevelt's negotiations, but he has made most of them worse with his inexperience and his completely unqualified group of advisers.

I have been asked to take two or three jobs but I just don't feel up to it. I am not worried about inflation over here, although I do look for a higher scale of prices for a long time to come. Labor has established itself so that it has great political strength which will help to keep prices up. Make up your mind, though, that our production possibilities are enormous and it won't be very long before you will see a lot of these items which are now scarce — like radios, fireless cookers, etc., etc., in bargain basements.

I think the liquor business will be a cut-throat affair, and outside of scarce Scotch and aged bourbon, the price will go down very fast and very low unless they make a better domestic Scotch than they are making now. I don't think it will affect the high quality of the Distillers Company, but the cheaper bars and places like that will probably use it, which will limit the amount that the English brands will get.

Jack is taking a rest and Bobby has gone to South America to visit some of my friends in Argentina and Brazil. Eunice is working hard and Pat is working hard, and the rest of the youngsters are at home.

On the second anniversary of Joe's death on the twelfth of August, we are planning to make a donation of $600,000 to the Franciscan Nuns to establish, in memory of young Joe, a Convalescent Home for crippled children and mentally deficient ones. I have established a charity foundation in his memory and I think I will give some time to that from now on.

Well, that is about all the news. It will give us great pleasure to see you. You know that you will always be most welcome.

With affectionate regards, I am

Very sincerely,

Kathleen Kennedy Hartington, 26: *Round-Robin Letter*

4 SMITH SQUARE, LONDON, S.W.1. October 18-1946

Dearest Family —

I am enclosing a letter which I received the other day from Lady Norman. The house sounds all too wonderful.[205] However Tony Pulitzer can give you first hand information about it as he saw it this past summer. I am writing to her to the effect that I have sent this letter on to you. If there is anything else you want me to do please let me know.

Last Monday night I dined with Margaret Biddle. Sat next to Ed Beattie[206] who asked a lot about Daddy. The next day she had a very small, informal cocktail party for the Duke of Windsor to meet the American newspapermen. I was the only outsider & it was most interesting. Herbert Mathews, *N.Y. Times* etc.,[207] all the top people. The Duchess was certainly putting her best foot forward. I was very struck by the Duke's youthful look. In fact that was the only thing most of them agreed they had discovered by the meeting. That same night Eric & Laura Dudley who have given them Ednam Lodge (where I stayed for Ascot week this year) gave a dinner party at Claridge's. It was the first dinner since their arrival where politicians of the Government and the Opposition were present. I should think there were 20 and it was held in a private dining

205. JPK had been considering renting a house on the French Riviera from the wife of the former governor of the Bank of England.

206. United Press war correspondent Edward William Beattie, Jr. (1909–), had reported on the British Expeditionary Force in France and on the Battle of Britain before being captured by German forces in France in late 1944 and held as a prisoner of war until 1945.

207. *New York Times* war and foreign correspondent Herbert Lionel Matthews (1900–77) had become chief of the London bureau in 1945.

room. With the exception of Baby Carcano Ednam & Billy (Eric's son)[208] I was the only young person present. I sat on Eric's left, the Duchess of W. was on his right. On my other side was Anthony Eden who couldn't have been nicer. He told all about Daddy fixing his trip to America in '34, his stay in San Francisco, & lots about the present government, Molotov etc. Emerald Cunard was on his other side & kept leaning across & saying "Anthony, don't you think Kick is pretty" — "Kick don't you think Anthony is wonderful". He is extremely fond of Daddy.

There was tremendous talk before dinner about not curtseying & then the wife of a Labor peer who is in the government came in, lost her head & curtsied. Of course there are a lot of parties being given for them but all the entertaining is being done by the Cafe Society Element in London. None of the other people see them, which group includes my mother & father-in-law. They feel that being too cordial makes difficulties for the present King. The Royal Family is certainly not receiving her. She looked wonderful the night of the dinner with the most terrific jewels. Of course at the moment all the headlines are screaming that 2 million dollars worth of jewels were stolen from her. Of course that won't increase their popularity.[209] The Duke was most awfully sweet & kind to me & he seems so pathetic — She looks as though she can handle any situation —

Thursday evening Christopher Hollis who is one of the most outstanding Catholic writers in England today as well as a member of Parliament came to have a drink with us. Eunice gave him an earful on exactly what was wrong with his latest book.[210] He is taking us to lunch in the House of Commons on Tuesday and we hope to hear Bevin speak on the first day of the Foreign Affairs debate.

We lunched with Adele yesterday. She is not returning to America, anyway until after Xmas and then hopes to do so for good. Eunice longs to stay with her during our trip to Ireland so we shall hope to manage that.

Mrs. Robert Hudson who used to own my house in Smith Square came to see it the other day and I'm glad to say was most impressed by all I had done. Lady Halifax also came to call with Richard. They have taken a flat in LONDON for the winter and she does all the cooking.

Chiquita & Jakie Astor's new baby is sweet but everyone is waiting to see what is going to happen at the Baptism.

At the moment I am at Compton Place waiting for the two Princesses to arrive for the weekend. Police surround the house & everything looks terrifically glamorous. They arrive tonite Sat. & leave Monday morning. The Duchess longed to have Eunice come and stay but there was no room, and just the family is here. We all dreading it, as they have to be entertained every minute. Tonite we are going to have fireworks so ~~everything is very glamo~~ we hope & pray that it doesn't rain.

Sunday morning [October 20, 1946]

The two Princesses arrived last nite just before tea. They are very sweet but Princess Elizabeth is very royal and very hard to talk to. She has a sweet face but dresses so badly. Her evening clothes make her look much fatter than she really is.

Monday [October 21, 1946]

Arrived up from the country just before lunch. (This letter is certainly taking ages to get written). We were all exhausted by the time the Princesses left this morning as we

208. Stella Cárcano, the daughter of the former Argentine ambassador (and Jack's former girlfriend), had married William Humble Eric Ward, Viscount Ednam (1920–), heir to the second earl of Dudley (and the duke of Windsor's godson), in January.

209. On October 16, the *Times* had announced that day, a cat burglar had crept though an open window at Ednam Lodge, making off with some £20,000 to £25,000 in jewelry.

210. She was currently visiting Kick.

could never sit down when we wanted to and every time they moved we had to leap to our feet and of course, we had to get down stairs to all meals before they arrived.

Tuesday [October 22, 1946]

This is really the last installment. We have been wondering today why we haven't heard from you — Today we went to the House of Commons for lunch and hoped to get in for the foreign affairs debate but unfortunately there was too much of a crowd so we ended up in the House of Lords listening to the Health Bill. We ran into Lord & Lady Halifax as we were struggling along in the pouring rain — they were in great form and gave us a lift home.

Last night I dined with Kenneth de Courcy[211] & sat next to the Duke of Windsor who ~~repeated~~ told me the story about mother not meeting the Duchess in Paris — He was most outspoken, and asked all about his nieces at the weekend as he hadn't seen them for so long. She told a long thing about her jewelry being taken & how it had ruined her trip. At this point she hasn't got a rock to her name & said how she'd been admiring my ruby & diamond bracelet all during dinner — Its simply ruined her whole trip — Eunice came in after dinner & talked to them both.

Old Lady Airlie is coming to tea Thursday and we are going up to Chatsworth this weekend and then go to Ireland on Oct. 31st for ten days.

My very best love to all. By the way I made a stirring speech to the Y.M.C.A. at Eastbourne on Sunday. It was on America. They then asked questions ranging from "When do little boys in America start wearing long trousers?" to "What does America think of the Labor government?"

Write soon — My love to all. Please keep my letters as I am counting on them as a dairy.

All love
Kick

P.S. Have just another letter from Lady Norman — She's had another offer but is most anxious for you to have it.

Kathleen Kennedy Hartington, 26: *Round-Robin Letter*

Ednam Lodge, Sunningdale, Berks., October 27–1946

Dearest Family —

By now you have received the cable about my jewel robbery.[212] I'm afraid everything is gone with the exception of my pearls and earrings. It really is the most awful blow especially Daddy's wedding present and the lovely aquamarines. You might ask Van Cleef if they have any drawings of the aquas — or the diamond & ruby bracelet they could send over. Everything is being done by Scotland Yard but in the last week there have four or five similar robberies — All the things are insured but nothing can replace the sentimental value. The odd thing is they didn't even bother to look in Eunice's room where a mink coat was hanging in the cupboard and my short fur jacket

---

211. The shadowy Kenneth Hugh de Courcy (1909–99) had served as former honorary secretary to the right-wing Imperial Policy Group in the 1930s and had made (or claimed to have made) a number of secret missions to the Continent in the late 1930s on Chamberlain's behalf to conduct political meetings with several leaders, among them Mussolini and Schuschnigg. Between 1938 and 1969, de Courcy wrote, edited and published the arch conservative weekly newsletter, *Intelligence Digest*. Having claimed the titles of duc de Grantmesnil and chancellor of the Order of the Three Orders (with questionable legitimacy), de Courcy entertained politicians and royalty from all over Europe in lavish style at his Gloucestershire estate.

212. Her flat in Smith Square had been broken into on October 25.

was in my own room. I was silly and forgot to put them away like I usually do on weekends. However there isn't any use now in thinking of all the things one might have done. Everyone here has been most kind & helpful and Scotland Yard is busy but at the moment they don't seem to have a clue on anything.

After being questioned etc. all day yesterday I came down here last night for the rest of the weekend. Laura & Eric Dudley, the Duke and Duchess of Windsor and a young newspaperman compose the group and that's all. The Duchess continues to talk of nothing but her robbery ~~and is really nothing but a bore, really.~~ and how she has nothing left — so far I haven't seen her with the same jewel. He seems so pathetic but full of charm — They have the house adjoining La Garoupe in the South of FRANCE. I asked them all about it and everyone says it has the best bathing and the nicest property of anywhere along that coast. However, I don't know how Daddy will like having the Windsors as next door neighbors. Really, no one here takes any notice of them & the extraordinary thing is that I actually feel that she is jealous of what I, an American, have got out of England and which has always been denied to her. Old Lady Airlie who came to tea the other day told Eunice and me that Queen Mary and none of them will see her — This afternoon we drove over to Fort Belvedere where he used to live as Prince of Wales — It was so sad to see him walking about examining everything like a small child. They are leaving for America on the *Queen Elizabeth* next week.

Pam Churchill[213] was supposed to leave today but I may be able to get her to take this letter for me.

Eunice and I will try and ring you up this week. We will send you a cable when we leave for Ireland. I will be sorry when she returns to America. I really think she has enjoyed herself terrifically.

My very best love to all and lots of prayers to St. Anthony.[214]

from Kick

P.S. As I caught Brendan Bracken peering into my house the other night, I'm already accusing him.

John F. Fitzgerald to John F. Kennedy, 29: *Telegram*

BOSTON MASS 1947 JAN 3 PM 12 10

INCREDIBLY BAD WEATHER CONDITIONS HAVE MADE IT INADVISABLE FOR ME TO ATTEMPT TRIP TO WASHINGTON MAY TODAY MARK THE BEGINNING OF SERVICE THAT WILL MAKE YOUR NAME SOME DAY A HOUSEHOLD WORD THROUGHOUT THE COUNTRY[215] FEELING PRETTY GOOD. GRANDPA =

Joseph P. Kennedy to John F. Kennedy, 29: *Telegram*

WASHINGTON D.C. 1947 JAN 4 PM 1 35

YOU CERTAINLY HANDLED VOICE AND MATERIAL IN GREAT SHAPE AND NOT FOR A MINUTE OUTCLASSED BY OTHERS CONGRATULATIONS LOVE = DAD

---

213. Kick's London contemporary, the former Pamela Beryl Digby (1920–97), had married Randolph Churchill in 1939. The couple had divorced in 1946. Widowed from her second husband, producer Leland Hayward in 1971, she would marry Averell Harriman and become an American citizen. Between 1993 and 1997 she would serve as U.S. ambassador to France after more than two decades of prodigious fund-raising for the Democratic Party and Democratic candidates.
214. Patron saint of lost articles.
215. Jack was being sworn in that day; on November 5 he had been elected U.S. representative from the Eleventh Massachusetts District with 71.9 percent of the popular vote.

Charlton, Banbury May 16 — 1947

Dearest Family —

I've been back two weeks and so much has happened.

Dined with Margaret Biddle one night. She has now decided to sell her house in the country — Tony B's wife is having a baby in Frankfurt.[216] I find her absolutely miserable and very lonely. John Winant and Eden were both there. The former's book is due for publication quite soon.[217] I find him more bogus each time I see him —

Another evening I went out with Marina[218] — We dined with some Danes (never any English) and went on to a nightclub. She asked about mother Daddy and especially Jack.

Spent the weekend at Eastbourne. The Duchess, Eliz and Anne are off to Italy tomorrow. They are all very well, and thrilled with the things I brought back.

I watched the Royal Family drive in open coaches from the station to Buckingham Palace upon the return. There was an enormous crowd lining the entire route. Billy's aunt, Lady Harlech who went as Lady-in-Waiting said they had all got frightfully thin. King lost nearly 25 pounds.

Richard Wood and his bride came to see me upon their return. He has just managed to get a conservative seat and will be its prospective candidate from now on.

Went to the Ballet which was absolutely lovely with Lady Anderson — Six of us went, sat in the Royal Box and dined with Ava Anderson afterwards. General Montgomery[219] was in the group and I was popped into his car at Covent Garden to drive to the Andersons' house. The car is covered with flags, stars etc. and unmistakable and, of course, was surrounded by people longing to have a look at "Monty" — I've never seen anyone quite so keen on the admiration of the crowd. I'm sure they were all intrigued as to what I was doing. He's saluting and waving like a madman. At dinner which included David Margesson and Desmond McCarthy, the great Irish critic & writer. Montgomery described his visit to Russia how well he got on with Stalin how they both teased Molotov who will succeed Stalin. I think he has great political ambitions & is quite ruthless. Poor David Margesson was quite non-plussed by his derogatory remarks about politics, politicians, etc. John Anderson droned on about India, as one time Governor of Bengal he does know it inside out.

At the moment I am spending the weekend with Freddie & Sheila Birkenhead[220] (Seymour's[221] sister) Freddie is writing the Biography of Kipling and is most attractive.[222]

---

216. Anthony and Margaret Schulze Biddle had divorced in Paris in 1945. In July 1946, Biddle, by then chief of the Allied Contact Section of the Supreme Headquarters Allied Expeditionary Force, had married Margaret Atkinson Loughborough, a Canadian member of Eisenhower's staff.
217. Winant, now the U.S. representative to the United Nations Economic and Social Council (who had been Biddle's high school history teacher at St. Paul's), would publish his diplomatic memoir, *Letter from Grosvenor Square*, shortly before committing suicide in November 1947.
218. A commandant of the Women's Royal Naval Service since 1940, the beautiful forty-one-year-old dowager duchess of Kent (formerly Princess Marina of Greece and Denmark), had been widowed in 1942.
219. Field Marshal Bernard Law Montgomery, first Viscount Montgomery of Alamein (1887–1976); commander of the British Eighth Army in Egypt, 1942–44; commander in chief of the British Forces of the Occupation of Germany, 1945–46; and chief of the Imperial General Staff, 1946–48.
220. The countess of Birkenhead, the former Sheila Berry (1913–1992), literary biographer; lady-in-waiting to the duchess of Kent, 1949–53; and daughter of *Daily Telegraph* publisher, Viscount Camrose.
221. Deputy chairman of the *Daily Telegraph*, 1937–87, and former Conservative MP for Hitchin, 1941–45, John Seymour Berry, later second Viscount Camrose (1909–95).
222. Biographer and lord-in-waiting to George VI, Frederick Smith, second earl of Birkenhead (1907–75). Although completed in 1948, the Kipling biography would not be published until 1979, after the deaths of both Birkenhead and Kipling's daughter, who had objected to the publication of the work.

My house is getting on. Lunched with Mr. Dulanty, the Irish High Commissioner. He is charming, and mot helpful about getting my curtains. I don't think they will miss Gray!![223]

My best love to all and write very soon.

Much love —

Kick —

P.S. The lawyers are still in a state about my income tax.

P.P.S. Please tell Jack Eunice & Pat I sent Nancy Lloyd two horse prints for wedding present.

———

Joseph P. Kennedy to T. J. White

Hyannisport, October 9, 1947

Dear Tom:

By the time you have received this letter, I hope I will have had the chance to talk with you. I want to give you the story on the Krock article so that your friend, Gene, can have it. I appreciate his opinion too much not to straighten out his mind as far as I am concerned.[224]

First of all, I have exactly the same opinion that I have always had — that we are making an unholy mess of ourselves by trying to stand the tide of Communism with dollars. Second, I am thoroughly convinced that whatever money we give them is poured down the drain. Third, I am also convinced that I am part of a majority who believes this, but one of a minority that will come out publicly to defeat it.

Now what I said to Krock was this: We must, very shortly, come to a conclusion that our future lies in this hemisphere, at least until Communism has failed to deliver to the people of the rest of the world. As I have told you many times, it isn't Communism that people are affected by; it is the struggle of the have-nots against the haves because of discontent and insecurity.

I look to see Communism spread all over the world, and, the horrible part of it is, I don't think we can do anything about it. However, there are a great many people in this country, based on their own judgment or some form of idealism which they possess, that believe we should continue to help Europe. I would be perfectly willing to gamble five billion dollars for one year's trial because, if we stop giving money now and Communism spreads, there will always be a great number of people in this country who will think the world could have been saved if we sent money abroad.

The Paris Economical Conference, in their rather well-done report, superficially touched on the political status of the countries of Western Europe, and yet the question of productivity, on which all of these countries depend, is entirely based on whether the Communists, who control the unions, will go to work to save their countries. I know they won't; you know they won't. But, if realizing the condition of their country, which they have been told about by everybody, in the next year they do not increase their productivity then certainly nobody in their right mind in this country will suggest giving them more money.

223. David Gray (1870–1968), playwright and United States minister to Ireland, 1940–47. Gray, whom the Irish regarded as a fundamental Anglophile, was married to Eleanor Roosevelt's aunt, Maude Livingston Hall.

224. JPK's initial objection to American aid for European reconstruction had given way over the course of the past several months to limited support for the proposed Marshall Plan. Krock's account of JPK's "Proposal to Treat the Marshall Plan in the Nature of an Experiment" had appeared in the *New York Times* on September 14.

The second point in the Paris Conference report, which hasn't been stressed very much, is that the authors presuppose that the Russian policy against the Capitalistic countries will change and permit food to come from Eastern Europe into Western Europe. Now you and I know that this is crazy also, but the masses don't understand it. They will understand it if we give them five billion dollars for the first year and they make an unholy mess of it. I believe that the five billion dollars is a cheap investment to unite this country on a policy under which we will have to live, at least for another generation.

Now I gave all this to Krock in this form, and the interview was the way he sized it up.

Warmest personal regards.

Sincerely yours,
Joseph P. Kennedy

Joseph P. Kennedy to Lord Beaverbrook

Palm Beach, March 23, 1948

Dear Max:

I was sorry I didn't see you before you left town. I actually returned to the hotel at 10:30 o'clock and waited until 12:30 o'clock for your call, so there must have been some slip up.

I was very pleased to get your note about Bobby. He is just starting off and has the difficulty of trying to follow two brilliant brothers, Joe and Jack. That in itself is quite a handicap, and he is making a good battle against it. You were very kind to talk to him because it meant a great deal to him.[225]

Another of the nice things that you do for people was evident when I received a clipping from the paper about Jim Farley's diary and my position with Great Britain before the war. I know you knew the truth, but it is rather nice to have you tell it to quite a lot of English people.

The situation is becoming more and more hectic in this country. People are talking war and really think it is very close. It is a horrible thing to contemplate, and I shudder to think what the end of the next one would be. There are so many more places now where war could break out, as compared with the last World War, that I haven't much confidence in the situation. However, I thought I would tell you a few words about the outlook for the presidential situation and leave the world's mess as it is.

First of all, I believe that, if Wallace[226] stays in the fight, which it certainly looks like he is going to do, any Republican can beat Truman. The Democratic Party is too definitely split up to get together behind Truman.

In addition to all the political questions that are causing a rift, you have the Catholics mad because it is the first cabinet there hasn't been a Catholic in for a long time. The Jews are all indignant over the inept handling of the Palestine matter.

225. Beaverbrook had seen Bobby in London in early March while the latter was on his way to the Middle East as a correspondent for the *Boston Post*. The publisher had written JPK that Bobby was "a remarkable boy. He is clever, has a good character, energy, a clear understanding, and fine philosophy. You are sure to hear a great deal of him if you live long enough."

226. Having resigned as secretary of commerce, broken with the Truman administration and distanced himself from the Democratic Party, the former vice president had announced his independent presidential candidacy in December 1947. In July 1948 he would become the Progressive Party candidate.

With Truman a candidate, I see the Democratic Party badly split up. Even if he withdrew and some other candidate were to take on the nomination, I still think that the country wants to change after sixteen years of Democrats.

Wallace is surprisingly strong because he is advocating peace, and I would think he would get between at least six to eight million votes which, in a total vote of sixty-five million, would be very substantial. His vote, of course, will depend on how domestic prices and the international picture develop in the next six months.

As to the Republican situation, most people think that Taft and Dewey will knock one another off and that Vandenberg is the most likely compromise candidate. He has repeatedly said he would not be a candidate under any conditions, but the feeling of the insiders is that he will accept for one term if he is a compromise candidate.

My own belief is that Taft and Dewey are a little fed-up with the idea that they are going to knock one another off and make someone else President of the United States. I will be very much surprised if they don't fight it out between themselves and then arrange that one or the other will be the candidate. Dewey unquestionably has the larger popular following, but Taft has the organization. I would think Taft would go into the convention with the most delegates.

This is about the picture today; but, as it changes, I will let you know.

I am planning to go to France, on the fourteenth of April, to look at the situation, and then fly down to Italy and see the Pope.

Of course, if you are not too busy, I will just drop over and see you and chat about things before I come back to America. In the meantime, again my many, many thanks for your kindness to Bobby and to me.

Very sincerely yours,
Joseph P. Kennedy

Joseph P. Kennedy to Kick

Hotel George V, Paris [May 14, 1948]

No one who ever knew her didn't feel that life was much better that minute. And ~~probably~~ we know so little about the next world that we must think that they wanted just such a wonderful girl for themselves. We must not feel sorry for her but for ourselves.

File JPK on Kick
written by me 1/2 hr after notified of Kick's death[227]

227. Since the summer of 1946 Kick had been romantically involved with Lord Peter Fitzwilliam, an Irish peer and a Protestant, who was already married. In an effort to overcome her parents' strenuous objections to the couple's proposed marriage (following Fitzwilliam's divorce), Kick and Fitzwilliam had chartered a plane from England to France, hoping to persuade JPK to give them his blessing. Disregarding the pilot's reservations, they had taken off as a severe storm approached the Rhone Valley. *Boston Globe* reporter Joseph Dinneen received news of Kick's death over the wire and tracked JPK to Paris in the early morning hours of May 14. Calling to ask whether JPK had heard the news of her death, Dinneen in effect informed him of it.

Joseph P. Kennedy to the Duchess of Devonshire

Hyannisport, September 1, 1948

Dear Moucher:

It probably isn't news to you to know that I thought about you a great deal since I came back to America. I think that the only thing that helped me retain my sanity was your understanding manner in the whole sad affair.[228] I would like to be able to tell you that I am very much better, but I just can't.

I can't seem to get out of my mind that there is no possibility of seeing Kick next winter and that there are no more weeks and months to be made gay by her presence. I realize that people say, "You have so many other children, you can't be too depressed by Kick's death," and I think that, to all intents and purposes, no one knows that I am depressed. In fact, I have never acknowledged it even to Rose who, by the way, is ten thousand per-cent better than I am. Her terrifically strong faith has been a great help to her, along with her very strong will and determination not to give way. I am glad she has made up her mind to go to England to see you because, all during the summer, she said she would go to Paris but could not go to London.

I am glad you like the pictures reasonably well. Of course, I don't think anything but snapshots really portrayed Kick truly, but, as they were taken only a month before she died, I thought that people over there would like to have at least the last picture that any of us have. Rose is making out the list, and we will have them shipped from here. We will send you a list of people we send pictures to and then possibly will send you some other pictures for people that we have forgotten.

I still get letters from Kick's friends and received one from Ed Halifax last week. Strangely enough, I never heard from Anthony.[229] I do hope you heard from the King and Queen because, frankly, I was a little disappointed that Rose didn't hear something from them.

I received a cable from Virginia,[230] asking me to be Godfather to her child and, because of Kathleen, I said I certainly would like to be.

Jack and Bobby have returned and are so terribly appreciative of the many kindnesses extended to them by you and your family.

I just talked to Mr. Carusi, at the State Department in Washington, who is in charge of the displaced persons, and who is working on the possibility of bringing in Kathleen's two maids, but he hasn't any definite word for me yet.

I know I tried to tell you, while I was in London, how grateful I am to Edward and you for your whole attitude in those dark days. I don't know whether I made myself very clear or not, but it will do no harm to repeat again that I will never forget it and I will always be deeply grateful to you and your family.

If Andrew would like to come over for the last month of the presidential campaign, which closes November fifth, we can make all the arrangements for him. Tell the girls that we will be looking for them whenever they can come.

My very best to Eddie and my deepest affection to you.

Sincerely,

---

228. JPK had brought Kick's body back to England after her death; she had been buried at Chatsworth on May 20.
229. Eden.
230. Kick's friend and an old girlfriend of Joe Junior, the former Virginia Gilliat, now Lady Sykes.

Joseph P. Kennedy to Pamela Churchill

Palm Beach, December 21, 1948

Dear Pam:

I am terribly sorry that I have not been around New York to meet your friend, John Aguelli[231] [*sic*], to do what I could for him. I went into the hospital in Boston for a check-up right after Thanksgiving and have now come to Palm Beach. It was nothing serious, but at least it kept me there much longer than I wanted to stay.

I am afraid Palm Beach is never going to be the same without Kick. She contributed so much gayety to this place that I doubt if we will ever be content here again.

Of course, I hear about you every now and then, but usually that some rich fellow is passionately in love with you. I don't blame them, but it is about time you gave some of these Americans a chance. Unless you hurry, there won't be any rich ones left.

It looks like we are going to get the beginning of a little treatment like you folks are getting over there, as far as incomes are concerned.

I do hope you are well and that you are happy. I am looking forward to seeing you when you arrive in this country.

My best always.

Sincerely,

Joseph P. Kennedy: *"Summary of Talk between President Truman and Hon. Joseph P. Kennedy"*

On Friday, June 30th, 1950, I had a twelve o'clock appointment with President Truman. On the day previous I called Mr. Mat Connelly, the President's secretary,[232] and told him because of the Korean War situation I was not sure that the President would have time to see me.[233] He left the line, evidently to confer with the President, and came back and said that he would expect to see me as per the appointment at twelve o'clock on the following day.

I arrived at the White House at 11:50 and was immediately ushered into Connolly's room. Connolly was out at the moment and I talked to his secretary who had been there during the Roosevelt days. She told me there was a Cabinet meeting on regarding the Korean situation. About 11:55 John Steelman[234] came in and seeing me came over and shook hands and seemed delighted to talk with me. He told me what had taken place in the Cabinet, which was contained in a press release. While we were talking Mat Connolly came in and, although I have no recollection of ever having seen him before in my life, he came over and said he liked to see the Irish talking together. If Steelman is Irish, I am learning something every day.

---

231. Automotive heir and future chairman of Fiat, Giovanni "Gianni" Agnelli (1921–), who was currently vice chairman of Fiat, president of RIV Ballbearings and mayor of the town of Villar Perosa.

232. Truman's longtime aide and appointments secretary Matthew Connelly (1907–76). As a public relations consultant after the end of Truman's term in office, Connelly would be indicted and convicted of influence peddling, tax evasion and conspiracy in 1955; he would receive a presidential pardon in 1962.

233. In the early hours of the morning of June 25, North Korean forces had crossed the thirty-eighth parallel into South Korea. By the twenty-seventh, with the support of the UN, Truman had authorized the use of American air and naval forces to aid in their expulsion. On June 28, Communist forces had captured Seoul.

234. John Roy Steelman (1900–), assistant to the president to coordinate Federal Agency Programs and policies, 1946–53.

The Cabinet meeting having broken up, Oscar Chapman[235] came up and shook hands with me, as well as two or three others. While I was starting to talk with them, Connolly came in and said the President would see me.

He got up as I entered the room and stood by his chair and I thought he looked rather cross, but when he shook hands with me he smiled and was quite affable. We sat down at his desk. He told me he had been up since 4:30 that morning and that he was not going to let those sons of bitches push him around. His own impression was that he did not think the Russians would fight on this particular occasion. They are much more interested in the Black Sea and the oil peninsulas and Yugoslavia. I asked him if he didn't think they would go into West Germany and he said he was convinced they would not because they know the people of East Germany would not stand behind them. He said the Russians had loads of troops already in Bulgaria and Romania for whatever might happen in that district. We said after all the Russians have no God and no morals and he was damned if he would trust anyone who did not have both.

He realizes that these are horrible times and that the decisions he is making are going to affect all civilization, but he considers it his responsibility and he is taking it on. He said he had all the leaders of Congress and of the Foreign Relations Committee of the House and Senate, and they included some real stinkers, but he wanted them to know what he was doing and he said they all backed him up.

I said that I felt mentally very much as I did when Chamberlain guaranteed Poland because I felt that was the step that really made it impossible to leave anything further to negotiations. Truman said the reason he had to do that was because the English refused to kick up a fuss when the Japs went into Manchuria and, second, when Hitler marched into the Saar. He said that through some of the papers that had been captured through the Germans it was apparent that if the French and British had stood up to Hitler, the Germans would have retreated. Then he said Chamberlain quit at Munich and he was not going to appease.

I told him that the greatest concern I found in talking to people was that they were worried that we would be bombed and could not be protected in this country. Truman said they are right, they can't be protected and neither can the Russians. We could drop bombs on Leningrad tonight, but he has been active in two wars and he wants peace.

He then went on to say that when he went to Potsdam he was willing to loan Stalin six billion dollars (he kept saying six million but finally corrected himself after using it three or four times) but Stalin broke all the agreements before they were really settled and, all in all, he has broken thirty-two different agreements to date.

He said we must and we are going to protect the Philippines at all cost. I asked him if he didn't feel as if he was handling this like a poker game. He looked up very much surprised, but I added there had to be a great deal of bluff in this sort of thing and he admitted that he was going to make a firm gesture and didn't think the Russians would accept the challenge.

We then took up the question of the Vatican, which was my prime reason for going there. He told me that he knew the Vatican was a fine listening post and that there was no question about that. I said I thought Taylor was a horse's ass. He said he liked him. I said that was entirely a matter of individual opinion. As far as I could see his best role was giving some dinners but that the authorities in the Vatican certainly did not feel that he was availing himself of the opportunities there. He said he had received some fine information from Taylor and I said if he did he got it very incidentally.[236]

235. Oscar Littleton Chapman (1896–1978), secretary of the interior, 1950–53.
236. The February 10, 1950, edition of *US News & World Report* had asserted that in mid-January, Myron

He said that he had called a conference of the Big Four, i.e., Lucas,[237] Barkley, McCormack and Rayburn,[238] and they all agreed to send a Minister to the Vatican, but they all felt it would defeat Democratic Senators and Congressmen in the Bible Belt if it were done right away, so Truman decided to do it after the election. He pointed out that McCormack, a Catholic, was very insistent on this as a plan.

He said that Cardinal Dougherty had been down to see him and that he was a great man. I said that I thought he was in his dotage. He said he also talked this over with Stritch,[239] who approved the idea. His greatest friend was McNicholas who had just died in Cincinnati.[240] He pointedly never mentioned Spellman which rather confirmed what Connolly had told Downey that Spellman had no standing at the White House. Connolly said that during the Spellman-Roosevelt fracas Spellman had asked for an appointment and he had not given it to him.

I also said that I understood that the American office at the Vatican had been closed without consultation with the Pope, and he said that was not so. He said Taylor had notified the Pope and had notified the Delegate three months before. He said the Pope has already been notified of the plan to appoint a Minister. He is going to name a Republican Protestant. For some reason he digressed at this point to tell me that Mrs. Truman's mother is ill, and he seems to have these personal problems come up when serious government problems arise.

I also told him that the Vatican had not been very well treated on the question of money in the last Italian election. He told me that the United States spent one billion dollars on the last election there. I said if they did the Vatican did not even get the six million dollars which I understood they had been promised, and I told him that Baruch had presumably gotten the information from the State Department and had notified Spellman and had notified me. He said Baruch was no good and wouldn't trust him. He never takes a stand and is a trimmer [sic]. (I am convinced he will never get in the White House while Truman is there). Truman added that they will never have a good government in Italy until they make up their minds to take the land from the six or eight rich Italians who live in Rome and who own it all. He was very bitter on this. I said they had too many people in Italy to have them economically well off, and he said that was why he was recommending his Plan Four. He said it would take very little money and his idea was just to send experts to the various countries to show them how to improve medically and economically — killing off mosquitoes and flies and things of that sort. I said that certainly had not been my impression of Plan Four from what I had read in the papers and he vigorously said that 90 per cent of the papers were against him, but he licked them before and he would lick them again.

As far as the Vatican is concerned, he is not going to take all the abuse that the Protestants and Oxnam[241] have been heaping on him all the time for keeping Taylor

---

Taylor, the president's personal representative to the Vatican since 1939 (and former chief of the American delegation to the Evian conference on refugees in 1938) had resigned the post, and that the U.S. mission had been closed with no word to Vatican officials.

237. Senate Majority Leader Scott Wike Lucas (1892–1968) from Illinois would lose his reelection bid later in 1950.

238. Rayburn had succeeded Bankhead as speaker of the House in 1940, and would serve until his death in 1961 (except during the brief Republican majority of 1947–48).

239. Samuel Alphonsus Cardinal Stritch (1887–1958), archbishop of Chicago, 1939–58.

240. John Timothy McNicholas (1877–1950), archbishop of Cincinnati, 1925–50, and a founding member of the Legion of Decency, had died on April 22.

241. As a founding member of Protestants and Other Americans United for the Separation of Church and State, Garfield Bromley Oxnam (1891–1963), Methodist bishop of New York, had locked horns with the Catholic hierarchy over a number of issues since the early 1940s. Oxnam would spearhead the op-

there. He is going to let Congress take it from here in. He said that he had not discussed this with anybody except the Pope himself and he had hopes that it would go through all right.

He then went back to the seriousness of the world conditions but he always got back to the point that he had to take a stand no matter what the consequences turned out to be.

He was most agreeable and pleasant and was not the slightest bit rushed in getting me out of the office. I stayed there for about 35 minutes. When I left, he walked with me to the door, shook hands, and in the outer office I ran into Jim Meade[242] and others, among which were Symington, head of the National Securities Committee,[243] who shook hands, asked about the family and then said, "I'm going to get you down here to help me out." I said, "I'm too old for that kind of stuff now." But he said indeed not. Remembering that he was never very friendly with Jim Forrestal, I could never be very enthusiastic working for him no matter what the demands were.

Rose Kennedy to Hélène Arpels[244]

July 10, 1950

Dearest Helene:

Thank you very much for your letter, which I enjoyed, although it was a little short. I know you must have a lot of news for me but I am afraid you would rather spend your time with those vendeuses than in writing to an American Rose.

I hardly know where to begin but I am sure you want to know about the wedding.[245] I cannot tell you what a great success I had with my dress. Everyone said I stole the show and I was really quite embarrassed because I was standing next to Mr. Skakel and so many Boston people rhapsodized over it that I finally started to say hush hush before they spoke too loudly. Really, dearest Helene, it was a great success.

Although it was very rainy and cloudy in the morning, it turned out to be a beautiful day about 11 o'clock — sunny and warm. The garden was at its best with beautiful flowers every place and the fountain playing, and the swimming pool shining in the sun. The dress looked very appropriate and summery in such a setting and, of course, the colors were very becoming. Everyone was entranced with the sun-shade because no one else had one. The bride's family insisted that I carry flowers and I had a tiny bouquet of small white orchids made in a bracelet for my wrist; therefore, it did not interfere with the sun shade or when I put my arm through the ushers going down the aisle.

We all were delighted with the jewelry which Joe bought at the shop. I have never seen a more lovely brooch than the one Bobby gave to Ethel. It was a four leaf clover and the leaves were solid diamonds. Joe gave her a bracelet which was also very lovely, but the pin was outstanding, and you know you do not run into those every day. The happy couple are now in Honolulu where they expect to stay until about the end of this

---

position to the renewal of diplomatic relations between the United States and the Holy See following the war.

242. Former three-term New York senator and staunch New Dealer James Michael Meade (1885–1964) had been appointed chairman of the Federal Trade Commission in 1949.

243. William Stuart Symington (1901–88), chairman of the National Security Resources Board, 1950–51, and former secretary of the air force, 1947–50.

244. The wife of jeweler Louis Arpels.

245. Bobby had married Jean's college roommate, Ethel Skakel (1928–), in Greenwich, Connecticut, on June 17.

month. They say they will motor home across the country as Pat left her car in California. Teddy is in Europe at the moment and I believe I will tell him to give you a ring when he gets to Paris, although I doubt if you will be there. He arrived at about the second of August and will remain until the tenth when he sails home on the America. He has been in Rome and Switzerland and is later motoring to Oberammergau to see the Passion Play.

Eunice is taking a course in juvenile delinquency in Chicago, Pat is in New York working on television, and Jean is staying here with me. Jack has been here for the last week but is going to Washington on Monday.

I am thinking of going up to the Music Festival on July 29th to hear Koussevitzky[246] conduct. It is always very interesting and they have the concerts in a wonderful setting up in the Berkshire Mountains. From there we may motor on to Saratoga to the races for a few days, although Saratoga is really too hot in the summer for me. However, Pat has never been there and would like to go this year so I shall probably go along with her.

The season down here has been very unattractive as far as the weather is concerned. It has been windy, cloudy, damp and foggy most of the time. I have had to wear slacks and sweaters just to keep comfortable when playing golf, or even around the house. However, today is beautiful and sunny, the roses are in bloom at last, and we are getting ready for a swim and then we shall have our lunch on the porch. I only wish you and Louis were along and I would have a nice fresh compote for Louis, not those horrible canned peaches which we had in Florida.

I may go to Paris the middle of September although I am not at all sure yet. My father is still fairly well although he is confined to his bed most of the time. He certainly is not getting any better. Mother is in wonderful spirits and I go up to see her every week and spend the day.

Joe seems to be feeling fine and he is spending a lot of time in Chicago this summer and expect to go out again this week. However, he is very much interested in the work out there and so he does not mind. Arthur Houghton, whose wife died about a month ago, will join him there and then come back here to spend the rest of the summer. My nieces will also be down and so we will have a full house again with eleven or twelve people for meals all the time.

I have not really heard much gossip as I am out of touch down here. Morton Downey went to Europe as I believe Peggy[247] is over there. You probably have seen her. Bootsy[248] and Bill Hearst were going over but Mr. Hearst is very ill and I believe they are going out there instead.

I think this is about all the news, dearest Helene, but I know if we got together we could talk for hours. Do write me again soon as your last letter was very delayed.

Give my love to Louis and keep looking beautiful.

Ever affectionately,

246. Serge Koussevitsky (1874–1951), conductor of the Boston Symphony Orchestra, 1924–51.
247. Margaret Biddle's daughter had divorced her first husband, Prince Alexander Hohenlohe, in 1949 and had recently been remarried to the singer.
248. William Randolph Hearst, Jr.'s third wife, the former Austine McDonnell.

Edward Kennedy, 18, to Rose and Joseph P. Kennedy

VILLA D'ESTE, CERNOBBIO, LAGO DI COMO

Dear Mother & Dad,

I received your letter today mother and Joey and I did get to the beatification in time which you probably know now since I mentioned it in my last letter.[249]

Florence was wonderful except that the only day we were there was the feast day of Saints Peter and Paul and so therefore all the stores and museums closed at one, but we did get to all the principal places of interest and that afternoon we went out to some country club which had a swimming pool and so it ~~was~~ couldn't have worked out better. The next day we drove to Venice and had quite a bit of difficulty with the car and even our chief engineer Joey was stumped by the situation but we soon got it fixed and arrived in Venice. We had a very difficult time at first in Venice because we couldn't believe that we were unable to drive to the Hotel, but we finally managed things and after a short ride ended up at the most luxurious hotel in all of Europe. They had all sorts of men carrying our bags and baggage in as we were met way out on the dock and as Joey and I in our T shirts and me in my Khaki shorts and carrying the football and Joey in his long pants which have become very oil stained from numerous unsuccessful attempts to fix the car. Actually though the car has worked quite well and what has had to be fixed never took more than an hour or so.

The day after we arrived in Venice we took off for Trieste. At Trieste we were warned not to go near the border of Yugoslavia in the American Sector because fairly recently two soldiers were fired on and so we went to the British Roadblocks and took some pictures of the zone signs forbidding us to enter etc. and we really felt as if we had accomplished something but yesterday when we read the paper we saw that it was that day that anyone might enter Yugoslavia who had a passport and so we feel rather slighted. We were again impressed how everyone hates the British and likes the Americans. All along the houses on the outskirts of the city there are Communist posters not in this sector but in others there are posters blaming the U.S. for intervention in Korea. In Venice the Communist Youth movement is ever increasing and they all march around at night in big mobs.

We remained one more day in Venice and then drove up here yesterday and have already met numerous people who know you both.

I read the letter from Eunice explaining what she wanted and where and Joey and I have both read Communist signs in Yugoslavic, Italian advertisements in Italian and have made more out of them than we were able to out of Eunice's letter.

Love,
Ted

Rose Kennedy to Robert, 24, and Ethel Skakel Kennedy, 22

July 13, 1950

Dear Ethel and Bobby:

We were delighted to get your letters and have sent along copies to Teddy and Grandma. I am sorry but your father has both of Teddy's letters and I will try to remind him to send you a copy from Chicago. Joey also wrote quite an illuminating one which I sent along to your father also, so I am afraid you are limited to my little news package which is not very great in scope.

---

249. He was spending the summer traveling throughout Europe with cousin Joey Gargan.

It has certainly been a quiet summer on the Cape. One reason being the weather, I believe, which has been foggy and cloudy and overcast most of the time. I thought when the Gargans arrived Tuesday they might dig up a little news but they made the rounds between here and Wianno and report there are only 32 people at the Wianno Club, and that there was nothing doing here with the younger set, so you have not missed a thing up-to-date. Joe Timilty reports too that the Oyster Harbors Club is much less popular than usual.

We had a wonderful party here last weekend for Eunice's birthday. She told everyone it was going to be a birthday party and to be sure to bring a present. Your father was very embarrassed, but not Eunice, who opened everything up with plenty of comments and plenty of smiles. Frank Conniff[250] came down and also little Nimbo, who was very surprised that I did not have gray hair. Effie came also and we all like her better every visit. Bootsy and Bill Hearst were to come but were unable to make it. Jack, of course, was here and Torb arrived. We had very good pictures, and a champagne dinner Saturday night. Senator McCarthy,[251] who had been invited Saturday, joined the group Sunday. They gave him the boat treatment, i.e., throwing him out of the boat, and then Eunice, in her usual girlish glee pushed him under. To everybody's concern and astonishment, the Senator came up with a ghastly look on his face, puffing and paddling. The wonder of it all was that he did not drown on the spot because, you see, coming from Wisconsin he had never learned how to swim. You can imagine the reaction of the group! Of course Frank Cunniff said it would have made a wonderful story and the Communists would have been delighted. However, I am sure they will not try anything like that on him again, although you can never tell.

Jean started piano lessons yesterday so the house resounds with scales. She is going to New York this week end to see Effie. I asked if she had written to you but she said it was time you had written to her. We have been to the Playhouse a couple of times and this year they have started the Music Circus in Hyannis. By that I mean a company gives a light operetta in an outdoor tent. There is a stage in the middle of the tent so that the entire audience can see all the figures. The cast divides the songs and actions in different parts of the stage. There are hardly any props and the costumes are rather moth eaten; however, the affect in general is quite pleasing and this form of entertainment was very popular in Miami last year. Aldrich started it down here this summer and I believe he has another successful venture on his hands. Last Tuesday Jean and I went to the "The Chocolate Soldier" and we really enjoyed it.

Dad seems to be feeling quite well and was in very good form for the party. Of course, with this war business he is considerably worried both about you and the business.

I talked to Mrs. Skakel a week or ten days ago, as I was very anxious to have the list of gifts in case I met people in Boston who had sent one. However, I have not received the book yet, nor the pictures, nor have I heard from Mrs. Skakel lately. However, I hope to hear from her this weekend as she said she had some very good pictures. We have the complete set that were taken at the engagement party and most of them are very good. We loved the pictures of you and Ethel with the leis. We also like the snapshots although I do not see any advantage to wearing a Bandaid on your nose for a photograph; however, I am not very versed in the techniques of the younger set.

250. By the end of 1950, Frank Conniff (1914–71) would discontinue his "East Side West Side" column for the Hearst papers in order to cover the Korean War.
251. The previously little known Wisconsin Republican, Joseph Raymond McCarthy (1908–57), had come to national prominence in early February following an address in West Virginia in which he claimed to have proof of extensive Communist infiltration of the State Department.

I guess this is about all the news, especially as the lawn mower has started to hum under my window.

Much, much love to you both and come home whenever you like — the little house will always be ready.

Love,

Joseph P. Kennedy to Lord Beaverbrook

Hyannisport, November 28, 1950

Dear Max:

It has been a long time since we corresponded with one another but I hear about you quite frequently. I need some help from you now on the following matter and I think perhaps you might be able to be of real service to me.

The anti-Roosevelt press has always made something terribly diabolical about the Tyler Kent case and the only reason it did not create a smear against me was because I was able to smash back at Kent rather strongly. However, one of these days I've got to put the whole case out, and there are three or four things which would be of tremendous help to me if you could get them through some of your influences. They are as follows:

1. Minutes of the trials of Tyler Kent and Anna de Wolkoff. These trials, which were held in secret, occurred in the fall of 1941 [*sic*]. Only the sentences were made public.

2. A pamphlet put out by Captain Ramsay in defense of himself in 1944. A summary of it was published in the London *Sunday Pictorial* of October 8, 1944.

3. The list of members of the Right Club which has never been disclosed.

4. The Report of the so-called Advisory Committee, established under the Defense of the Realm Act, recommending in 1941 the continued detention of Captain Ramsay.

Of course, it may be impossible to get any of this material, but the story will never be correctly put forth unless I have it in my possession. Whether I use it or not is a different matter. Of course I would like to use it, but I would be satisfied to have it and use it for my protection when I really go after Kent. Can you help me?[252]

With my warmest personal regards, as always, I remain,

Very sincerely,
Joe
Joseph P. Kennedy

Joseph P. Kennedy to John B. Johnson[253]

December 28, 1950

Dear Sir:

When I returned from Great Britain in 1940 and endorsed President Roosevelt for reelection on his platform of keeping this country out of war, I was subjected to a deliberate smear campaign by a few Washington columnists who so outrageously misinterpreted my views that, in January, 1941, I gave a nation-wide radio broadcast to set the record straight.

252. Kent had been released from prison on the Isle of Wight in 1945 (two years before the end of his sentence) and was deported to the United States.
253. The editor and publisher of the *Watertown Daily Times* (Massachusetts). On December 13, the paper had published an editorial entitled, "Mr. Kennedy is Wrong again."

Your editorial of December 13, 1950 repeats the old charges of the irresponsible columnists and ignores my answer, as well as my subsequent speeches, which are on public record.

You state that I believed in 1940 that Germany would defeat Great Britain. That statement is absolutely false. As I explained in my speech of January 1941, a prediction can be based only on a complete knowledge of the strength and weaknesses of both sides. Without first-hand knowledge of German strength it would have been senseless to predict the final outcome of the war, nor did I attempt to do so, although I, in company with others including Churchill, recognized the enormous difficulties facing Britain at that time.

You state that I was and am an unreconstructed pacifist ready to make any concession rather than war. That is also false. Then, as now, I said we should be prepared to defend our own shores against all aggressors, giving aid to any other nation willing to resist, but not to a point which would endanger our own protection.

As for my record as a prophet, I predicted that if we entered World War II Russia would become strong while the rest of the world approached exhaustion; that to prevent defeated Germany and the other countries from going completely Communistic would be our job; that we would have to reorganize these countries, probably standing guard while the reorganization was taking place; that such a task would create great internal problems for the United States and put impossible burdens on our grandchildren. I warned that our participation in the war would not destroy totalitarianism but would only leave the world in a worse condition than before.

Sincerely yours,

Joseph P. Kennedy: *"Honorable Joseph P. Kennedy's Interview with General Dwight D. Eisenhower, Paris, France — April [1951]"*

After having dinner with Margaret Biddle and talking about Downey and Peggy, the following morning General Tony Biddle[254] called me on the telephone and said Margaret had called him up to talk about what ought to be done about the Downey situation. I told him I was delighted to hear from him but I felt that since Margaret had plenty of money she should have settled it when the divorce took place by giving him some money and have done with it. Tony said he agreed with me and then said, by the way, would I come up to the offices and see some of the topside men on Thursday of that week. I said I would and that I would call him Thursday morning and tell him just what time I would get there.

Thursday morning I called Biddle and he told me that General Eisenhower would like to see me but that he was in The Netherlands and could I come on Friday.[255] I said that I had an appointment early Friday morning and could they make it late in the day. Later on Biddle's secretary called and said that they had contacted the General and that he would be back late Thursday night and would appreciate it very much if I could make it at 10 o'clock Friday morning. Well, since he seemed to be anxious to make the appointment, I said I would be there at 10 o'clock Friday morning.

On Friday I walked up to the headquarters at the Astoria Hotel and was told by the guards at the door to go to the Securities Office, where I went. They asked me what I

254. The former U.S. ambassador to France served as foreign liaison officer for the Department of the Army in 1950–51.
255. Eisenhower had recently become supreme commander of the new North Atlantic Treaty Organization.

wanted and I told them I had a 10 o'clock appointment with General Eisenhower. They asked me for some identification. I said I was sorry but I did not carry any since I imagined the General would make arrangements for me to be met. The Sergeant said the new rule required identification but would I wait while he sent for the Captain. The Captain came in and we went through the same rigmarole and I decided this was a lot of nonsense, so I suggested that they just send word to General Eisenhower that I had been there at 10 o'clock and had gone back to my hotel. Just then General Biddle came along and yelled and shrieked how glad he was to see me. The Captain and the two Sergeants started apologizing so all was well.

I went up stairs and arrived at Eisenhower's office and he saw me at once. I had never met him before and he unquestionably is a very attractive man to meet. He was sitting behind his desk, got up and shook hands, and said let's sit over here where it is more comfortable and so we sat in lounge chairs facing one another. He started off by asking me what I had noticed in the situation there. I told him I had spent a couple of weeks trying to find out what a cross-section of the ordinary French people thought about the whole question of war and the alternative, war occupation. I told him I was amazed at how many people when asked their choice between 1) all-out war, 2) occupation by the Nazis, 3) occupation by the Russians, preferred occupation by the Nazis first, by the Russians second, and all-out war last. He thought that probably was the truth but that there had been a big improvement since '47 in that attitude. His job, as he saw it, was to make the people realize that they must improve their spiritual attitude towards this whole problem of Russia.

Eisenhower started off by saying he was against my general plan to withdraw to the North American continent. I told him that wasn't my plan if he read my speech very carefully, in that I would be willing to give some help provided Europe showed the real attitude of a desire to fight; but, in the absence of that, I thought we would be just pouring our resources down a rat-hole.[256]

Eisenhower said he could not see a plan which had us all by ourselves with all our friends gone and expect to live safely. I said that wasn't it and that there wasn't any point in arguing our points of view because I was convinced neither could persuade the other but that we should leave my point of view completely out of it and take up his.

Eisenhower then said he thought it might take ten years to put Europe in shape to fight. I looked at him in amazement at the prospect of a ten years' armament program, both spiritually and militarily, and said that ten years was an absolute impossibility; that if the American people heard Eisenhower thought it would take ten years I was convinced they would throw the plan right in the river. Eisenhower immediately saw this was a dangerous statement and said: well, let's assume it will take three years but to make that three years effective we should pour everything in in the beginning and taper off at the finish.

I then asked his opinion on this proposition: Did he recognize that the inflationary threat in every country in Europe, as well as the United States, might very well cause such state control that we would have governments in all our countries operated by the states, which would be different from Communism only by the type of management. He said he recognized this as a real danger. I pressed him a little further and asked him if he recognized this as almost inevitable. He said it was almost quite unlikely. I asked

256. Addressing Bobby's fellow students at the University of Virginia Law School in December 1950, JPK had asserted that the number of dollars that the United States had "squandered" on defense to date in Korea and Europe "could have been far more effectively used in this hemisphere and on the seas that surround it . . . We need defenses in this hemisphere," he continued, "in Canada, in the Caribbean and in Latin America."

him if he had not found out that the European countries sensed this great danger and were perfectly willing to use American soldiers and money but did not want to get too involved themselves because they might be ruined in the effort. He admitted that this might also be true.

I also asked him if the Korean War had not shown the people in Europe what happens to a country we try to defend. On this remark he looked at me rather sharply and said that was the truth. Also, wasn't it true that in all the countries on the fringe of the Soviet sphere that not a dollar had been spent for civilian defenses and nothing was being done to protect the civilian groups from the bombs that everybody talks about; and wasn't this the result of three facts: 1) the Europeans are unwilling to get excited over another war; 2) fatalism, i.e. if they are to be bombed there is nothing they can do about it; and 3) they can't possibly provide the money to do the job satisfactorily. He admitted that all these things were true also.

We both agreed that since most of the countries in Europe are faced with elections in the near future — Italy had elections in May, France in June, Germany in May, and England very likely in the Fall, and the other countries are so-so, that none of the countries are willing to appropriate very great amounts of money for war or protection because they are afraid that since the expenditures will mean new taxes the people will resent them. In addition to that there is a feeling of the people in each country that they are keeping one foot in the so-called enemy camp, i.e. the man who is not a Communist is not too unfriendly with the man who is, figuring that maybe some day he may need him as a friend. This also works very extensively against Eisenhower's wish to build up the spiritual desire of the people for freedom.

Eisenhower told me he had written to Cardinal Spellman asking him for his help in the great problem that he was facing, i.e., that the material problem was great but the spiritual one was even greater. I told him that in my contacts I was convinced that the Europeans felt that Americans are unduly excited over the European situation; that the United States makes up its mind quickly but not wisely. They believe that the United States government does not know what it is doing and that it has no long-term program that makes any sense.

I asked Eisenhower did he feel he had taken this job to lead an army into war. Eisenhower said he would resign rather than accept that kind of a proposition. He interest was to build up the morale of the Europeans, get a force together, with the help of the United States, and arrive at a point where we would be on a parity with Russia, and then we could trade. At that time I said, for the sake of discussion, let's assume that 1) you can change the psychological feeling of the Europeans and get them in line to resist the Russians; 2) let's assume that the spiral of inflation, which has been started for a cause that a great many people do not believe in and under leadership that a great many do not trust, does cause economic chaos in all these countries and eventually substitutes almost complete state control in government. Let's assume No. 1 does happen and No. 2 does not happen and you reach parity with the Russians. What do you do then? Eisenhower said if they attempt to attack any place such as Burma, or any place in the world, we will serve notice on them to stop. Assuming they won't stop, what do you do then, I asked. Then we will fight them. I thought you said you would resign rather than lead this army to war. He hesitated for an answer and I asked him what his other alternative was. He said we'll have to have a plan, one on which we could come to some agreement with the Russians because, he admitted, both countries could not stand fully armed with the world ready to go and not have something happen.

I then asked him if a deal has to be made, if we don't intend to have a war, what kind of a deal would he make. Eisenhower said he did not know; that was a matter for the politicians. But he admitted the United States should have a plan and also admitted it did not have one. I said I thought he was the man to talk to Stalin and do it now. He said he would be willing to do it and resign but that if he did resign he would be nothing but a private citizen and would have no standing. I said that as America's first citizen he certainly could talk for the American people, but in order to talk he would have to have some plan and wouldn't it be well for somebody to start thinking about a plan. He said it absolutely would be.

I asked him how he thought he could build up a spiritual willingness in the Europeans to talk about fighting for liberty when they were almost faced with the idea that in America there was a very serious division of opinion as to just how far European help should go. He thought that was very serious and very dangerous but did not know how it could be stopped.

He said everybody should understand that he was not part of the Truman-Acheson Administration and while he could not approve entirely of the way MacArthur handled his differences with the administration, he was upset by his dismissal and said it almost would make anybody in authority, like himself, feel that there was a danger of getting his own throat cut if he shouldn't see eye to eye with the administration.[257] When he made this statement he put his finger to his throat and drew it across his neck.

Eisenhower also said we cannot continue to intervene in other Koreas — Iran, etc., that in a great many of those places the uprising may have had some Communistic backing but it was the final recognization [sic] of the masses of the power of the vote and they were beginning now to avail themselves. It was like a younger brother finally arriving at a period in his life when he thought he could talk back to his older brother; and that for the United States to interfere all over the world may make it very clear we would no longer be master of our own destiny. He pointed out that even Russia would not be able to supply its satellites with arms, but I asked him if it was necessary in places like Iran for Russia to supply arms. All it needed for an uprising in places like that was a pistol shot like when the Premier was shot and the Nationalist feeling, which is becoming stronger in every nation in the world, was urging the masses to go out and get what was coming to them.

Eisenhower said that the whole problem was an immense one. He had some idea of the difficulties of it when he started but they were much greater than he possibly imagined, but he must do the best he can.

When Eisenhower talked to me about asking Cardinal Spellman to help him he said the Cardinal could not come himself just now unless it was a matter of terrific importance, but would send Bishop Griffiths[258] and Fulton Sheen.[259] I said that, of course, the real powerful factor for the upbuilding of that morale is His Holiness, the Pope. He said he knew that and hoped to enlist his efforts. When he was in Rome, on the inspection of the Italian Army, the Pope was on retreat and could not see him. I asked him,

257. On April 19, while addressing a joint session of Congress, both as a defense of his strategic aims in South Korea and as a public farewell, MacArthur had noted famously that "old soldiers never die— they just fade away." Truman and MacArthur had disagreed publicly over the administration's unwillingness to permit the UN military commander to bomb bases in Manchuria following the Chinese Army's recent repulse of UN forces at the 38th parallel. The president had relieved the general of his duties in South Korea and Japan on April 11.

258. The Most Reverend James Henry Ambrose Griffiths (1903–64), auxiliary bishop of the Roman Catholic Archdiocese of New York, 1949–64.

259. The enormous, nationwide popularity of The Right Reverend Monsignor Fulton John Sheen's (1895–1977) books, articles on faith and weekly "Catholic Hour" radio broadcasts would lead to his hosting the Life Is Worth Living show on television later in 1951. The director of the Society for the Propagation of the Faith (who had been credited with the conversions of the likes of Henry Ford II and columnist Heywood Broun), would be made a Bishop in June.

outside of the desire of the Holy Father to do good to all the world, if the Pope had any idea how badly he had been treated by the present administration in the closing of the United States office in the Vatican when Myron Taylor decided to come home. I told him the facts. He was astounded and shook his head in sheer disgust.

The conversation lasted for over an hour and while there was no mention of his political future, I was convinced he was a candidate for the presidency. He spoke of the horrible domestic policies of the Democratic party, which he said he had opposed in a couple of speeches so everybody knew he was against increasing state control; but, on the other hand, the policy of the Republicans he thought was very shortsighted. He spoke of Hoover as "the old man" and said he thought his plan would cost just as much as sending the troops to Europe.

Joseph P. Kennedy to Mary, Duchess of Devonshire

Hyannisport, June 22, 1951

[Dear Moucher,]

It was very nice hearing from you, just as it was listening to your voice over the telephone in Paris.

No matter how many years I live, I will always feel towards you the most undying gratitude for your sweet understanding of Kathleen and your great kindness to me when I was in England for her funeral.

There was some difference in the degree of love that Kathleen possessed for people, because, while it might be said she loved a great many, she possessed a special love for you. I suppose the fact that nothing in the world seems to be right these days may be the result, for some of us, of having lost those who were near and dear to us. When that kind of love goes out of ones life it is very difficult to replace it with anything else, and it is almost impossible to see with any degree of reasonableness all the good things that are left.

You have never failed to be a great inspiration to me, as I am sure you have been to your own family. One does not have to wonder why England was great when it had people like you for its backbone. I am sure that you will recover from the shock of Eddy's death[260] with the same courage and fortitude that you have shown all your life.

Please do not give up the idea of coming to visit us next winter at Palm Beach. The elections will probably be over in England; there are no social gatherings at Palm Beach and the life, I am sure, would please you and do you a lot of good, physically and mentally. And do bring anybody with you whom you would like to have. We would enjoy it more than you can imagine.

My love to all the family and my very best to you.

Joseph P. Kennedy: *"Interview with General MacArthur, June 27, 1951"*

I saw MacArthur promptly at 11:30 A.M. (His aide, Col. Bunker, comes from Wellesley, and is a graduate of Boston Latin School, class of 1920. He was originally associated with John W. Davis[261] in a law firm downtown.)

---

260. The duke had died on November 26, 1950.
261. John William Davis (1873–1955), solicitor general of the United States, 1913–18; ambassador to the Court of St. James's, 1918–21 and Democratic presidential candidate, 1924.

MacArthur is dressed now in civilian clothes. We sat down in a couple of big chairs and I told him the first thing that worried me about the situation as I saw it was that the determination of the value of his work would be the result of the 1952 election, and that I thought Eisenhower was definitely a candidate. He said that Truman, if his health is at all good, is definitely a candidate, and if any nomination [*for*] Eisenhower [*it must be Republican*]. He said that on his trip so far he has found that, except on Park Avenue, Eisenhower has become progressively weaker. He said "I like Ike. He was my Chief of Staff. He is a very charming man and very well educated." But he said that he would consider that anybody who proposed the military plan [*of the North Atlantic Pact*] that he did before the Congress of the United States was out of his mind. In fact, he said, if a corporal of mine did it I would break him and make him a private. He said that if he were to consider the man who would do the most harm [*to the U.S.*] in the next five years, he would pick Eisenhower. He said that the difficulty was that he would bring in a plan that was all set up and very well thought out and then, without being seduced or cajoled, three months later he would bring in an entirely different plan with the same conviction. He said that Eisenhower came to visit him in Japan some time ago and said that he was probably going to be a candidate for President on both parties tickets; that he thought he would get 20,000,000 soldiers to vote for him and was trying to get 15,000,000 labor votes and with that he would control the whole situation. Then MacArthur said to him, "That's all very well, Ike, but even George Washington knew better than that, that the success of America depends on two political parties. You must have an opposition party [*which*] can keep quiet when it should and be critical when it has to be." MacArthur said they sold Vandenberg[262] this idea of non-partisan foreign policy and see what happened. He said that in the last two decades the Democrats have passed legislation that within the next 2 decades would mean the redistribution of wealth in a legal manner so that there will be no possibility of private enterprise because there will not be enough capital in the hands of anybody to carry it on. He said that not being satisfied to divide the wealth of the U.S. amongst everybody, we started the Marshall Plan with the idea of dividing what was left of our wealth with other nations, hoping to bring up their standard of living; but there is no other way of doing it except by debasing our own standard of living, which we have done by inflation and high taxes. He said that the trend was completely Socialistic; that by talking about containing Communism and spending 8 ½ billion dollars, they are trying to make it appear like a good thing by spending 6 ½ billion of it in the U.S. which will make it more difficult for us to get civilian goods, and make it much easier for the European to do it because he will be getting armed by our factories and permitting his factories to make civilian goods to compete with ourselves everywhere in the world.

He said that the Chinese were all so weak that it would not be necessary to bomb them, but merely to threaten to bomb them and they would make peace; that Truman definitely has the two horns of dilemma — if he takes the cease fire he must do it with appeasement to the Chinese or the Russians; that he would not be able to do what Roosevelt did so well — make a bad deal and tell the people it was a great deal. He will attempt to do that but he will not be able to do it and realizing the powers of propaganda may try to persuade the public that this should be.

One of the great dangers of the world today is Truman's forcing higher-ups in the military forces to be subservient to his wishes. He said that Denfield had been fired,[263]

262. The former Senate Foreign Affairs Committee chairman.
263. Truman had relieved Admiral Louis Emil Denfield of his post as chief of Naval Operations in October 1949 as the result of a public dispute regarding the Navy's role in the postwar military.

Anderson had been fired,[264] and four of the topside men had been made to say and do everything Truman wants them to. He repeated what he had told Jack, that the military furnished a Praetorian Guard for the President of the United States.

Bobby asked me to ask MacArthur if he had been considered [*sic*] at all about Yalta and he replied that he had not — that it was a *fait accompli* when he was brought in on it.

Then I asked him if he had been consulted about Korea. He told me that on the morning that the decision was made on Korea, his Aide said that he was wanted on the telechron at a certain hour, and he replied that was strange as messages on the telechron were usually given to one of his aides. When he got there, State Department and high Defense officials were on the wire and told him what he was to do as far as Korea was concerned. "They gave me no suggestions, told me nothing of what had gone on or what happened. In fact, I had assumed that I had done a very good job because I had evacuated 2,100 American civilians from Korea without loss of any life. When they finished telling me what my orders were, they said 'Do you understand your orders?' I said yes. 'Do you need any further orders to make them clearer?' I said no." He said that that was the end of the orders. I asked him why he said Truman was justified in going into Korea. "I made that clearer in my Texas speech." I said that I was always of the opinion that anybody who believed in any organization to stop war like the United Nations, ought to have at least one fair try. He said, of course, that is true but the unfortunate part of that is that the United States made the decision about Korea before the U.N. took action.

He said that the North Atlantic Pact was a complete fraud; that it had no merit from a military point of view whatsoever. He doesn't believe it could ever work out and he does not believe that the principals of the military in Europe will believe that it will, and, therefore, will never be a part of anything that forces them into trouble, but will make every gesture to get money and men that will not necessarily bring them into contact with the Russians.

What do you think of the possibility of war on any basis with Russia? "Did you ever know a manager of a ball team or football team or a business that was getting everything he wanted who thought that he should change the format and take a chance on something else? That is the exact position the Russians are in. When Russia goes into a country, they change it over from bottom to top. They so work on the military that it is impossible to ever believe that a revolution could spread. To do that, it takes a great deal of time. My impression, from a military point of view, is that they have not even begun to assimilate the territories they have already taken and that they have so much to do that there is no possibility that they would take on anything, *anything* at this time to bother them with more work to do."

I asked him what he thought about the inflationary trend. He said it was, of course, merely a totalitarian method of destruction of people's savings, life insurance, etc., and is bound to come to this end if it continues. He said that when you knew it was something that everybody had belief in, there might be some sense in going broke and ruining this country and all it stood for, but you know that anybody that knows anything knows you are crazy [*following the financial plan*]. He read my speech very carefully because he remembered that in the speech I had said I would give aid if there was any

264. The Air Force had summarily suspended Major General Orville Arson Anderson (1895–1965) in September 1950. In describing his views on averting war, the commandant of the Air War College had reportedly told a journalist, "Give me the order to do it, and I can break up Russia's five A-bomb nests in a week."

help from the other side. I told him that Eisenhower had criticized that speech. He said that in addition to that, Eisenhower is the only man who has never been tested by the fire of Smeardom. He said only Pegler[265] and a few others had started to do it a little before and MacArthur said it didn't do Eisenhower any good. He wondered how Eisenhower would stand up if they really turned the guns on him, and said that, knowing his temperament, he didn't think Eisenhower would stand up at all.

He said that the Republican Party was making an awful mess of everything because they don't seem to realize the difficulties of the country and how important it is to have a well set up opposition that is intelligent. He said that the only man he had met in the Republican Party whom he thought had any brains whatsoever was Taft.

(Mr. Landis[266] at this point asked Mr. Kennedy if General MacArthur had any plans of his own.)

He is going in the middle of July and speak to the Massachusetts Legislature, and I told him it was very important. I told him he hadn't made proper arrangements for his radio talk in Texas. The oil man, Cullen,[267] he said, tried to get NBC to carry it and they said that they weren't going to carry MacArthur any more. I said that if he would go on a national broadcast from Massachusetts I'd pay for it. He is going to address the joint legislature, as mentioned above, at 8 o'clock in the evening. He said that Lodge[268] is more pro-Democrat than most Democrats were. Said he was strictly a pro-Trumanite on foreign policy.

He is going to go from time to time and place to place and make speeches on what he thinks are the issues of the day. There isn't any question—he is not a candidate for the Presidency. He will fight to the last drop of blood to keep Truman from being reelected. It is amazing how many people he sees, how many contact him and all that sort of thing.

(Mr. Fayne's[269] question: Did MacArthur touch on Malik's[270] suggestion for a cease-fire?)

He thought that the cease-fire would be carried out by the Russians only by getting some concessions which Truman is prepared to give which he will justify under some other heading. I think you can count on MacArthur's being in the field to fight and move around wherever the occasion seems to be a good one until election.

(Mr. Landis asked: "How did MacArthur explain the business that he thought President Truman was justified in going into Korea?")

He didn't have a good answer for it.

(Mr. Landis asked: "What are his theories in regard to Western Europe?")

265. The Hearst papers' caustic and increasingly conservative "As Pegler Sees It" columnist, (James) Westbrook Pegler (1894–1969).
266. Landis, former dean of the Harvard Law School and JPK's successor as chairman of the SEC, had worked as an adviser and assistant to JPK since the former's dismissal from the Civil Aeronautics Board in 1947. Landis was in the (ongoing) process of ghostwriting JPK's diplomatic memoir and had coauthored *The Surrender of King Leopold* with him in 1950.
267. Millionaire oil field developer, philanthropist and Republican Party benefactor, Hugh Roy Cullen (1881–1957).
268. Henry Cabot Lodge, Jr. (1902–86), Republican U.S. senator from Massachusetts, 1936–44, 1947–53.
269. James Fayne (1884–1972), JPK's Harvard contemporary and former Boston banking associate, had served as a technical adviser to the SEC in 1934–35. Since 1949 Fayne had worked for JPK as a financial adviser, also assisting Landis in drafting both JPK's diplomatic memoir and *The Surrender of King Leopold*.
270. The Korean truce that Yakov Aleksandrovick Malik (1906–80), the Soviet delegate to the United Nations, had recently proposed would set the stage for the cease-fire of 1953.

The plan of the North Atlantic Pact as set forth is of no strategic value to Europe whatsoever; it would not stop the Russians at all if they wanted to do business. He is aware of the fact that all those countries are tending toward Socialism, which we are too, and it is only a question of time.

I told MacArthur also of my talk with Eisenhower about a plan as to what he would do when he arrived at parity with the Russians, and Eisenhower said if they go into Malaya we will serve notice for them to get out or we will go to war. MacArthur said "It seems to me that that is the threat I am accused of using, isn't it, and now he is going to use it in three years. That is very interesting." I told MacArthur that I had asked Eisenhower what plan he had and the latter said that he had no plan—that that was the business of Truman and Acheson. MacArthur replied that the reason why they haven't got one is that they have no idea where they are heading. He said that the foreign policy here is absolutely decided in the Foreign Office in England. (MacArthur is very critical of the British.)

(Mr. Fayne asked: "Did he happen to mention that he thought this inflationary trend could be checked in any way by some reduction in the military budget?")

Yes, all budgets—military included, of course. Money being spent here is doing harm in two ways: Makes it impossible for Europeans to compete with us in order to arrive at a so-called parity, at the same time creating a much stronger inflationary force in the United States.

He has a very statesmanlike attitude not just that of a general. He said, "I don't agree with those who say a general should not be President of the United States. I do agree with those who say a general should not be President at a time like this because success in the kind of government in the United States has to come from civilian, not from military." He said if Eisenhower were elected, we would have a repetition of Grant.

(Mr. Landis asked: "Did he speak of any individuals backing him?")

No, he criticized the Republicans but spoke highly of Taft — he is going it alone. MacArthur could take everything we have said and stood for and say "I take it 100%."

I said, "Why do you think the Eisenhower Mission will fail?" He said everybody who has a responsibility in Government said it themselves that if the United States with its great potential cannot beat a second grade crowd in a small little war and cannot find a way of satisfactorily concluding that war, how will anybody be convinced that this is the group to follow for the protection of Europe or of anywhere else? Their hope of making a success of the Pact died when we made such a horrible mess of the Korean situation.

(Mr. Landis asked: "Is he personally bitter about his affairs?")

He is personally bitter about the situation but gave me his honest opinion that he is terrifically concerned over the America that he and his father and every boy has been brought up to believe in. Those that don't like me say I should be fired and those who do like me say I shouldn't be fired.

Joseph P. Kennedy to Cornelius Fitzgerald

Hyannisport, July 18, 1951

Dear Con:

I was delighted to hear from you but sorry to hear that you have to move out of your home. I know what a nuisance it is to try to get something that will be satisfactory.

I am very discouraged at the situation as it stands today because I have come to the conclusion that the people of the country are not particularly interested in what is going on except as it affects them personally. They can't understand the foreign situation; all they know about controls is that prices still go up and if they can get enough money to get by, the hell with everything. It's a pretty dreary outlook when you think they are even considering the possibility of Truman being elected with the fundamentally bad administration that he has given us by incompetent people.

I am concerned, of course, about the choice that Jack must make, but it's a little too early yet. Lodge's strongest weapon is the propaganda that he himself is very strong, but so was Saltonstall[271] when he was darn near beaten the last time he ran. Of course, if Eisenhower is the Republican nominee and Truman is the Democratic nominee, the Republicans in these state fights will be helped tremendously, at least in the Eastern states. I am against generals being elected President of the United States at this particular time because it gives too much emphasis to the fact that our future lies along the line of armaments and collective security, and the America that grew great with everything else is just a thing of the past.

Keep you ears to the ground on Jack's situation and let me know what you hear. My warmest personal regards.

Sincerely,
Joseph P. Kennedy

Rose Kennedy to Marie Bruce

July 23, 1951

Dear Marie:

We just came home from the christening last night and I knew you would like to hear about it.

Anne Skakel sent the plane over for us about 11:30 yesterday morning and Jean, Pat, Joe, Arthur Houghton and I got aboard and after a fairly good flight to Greenwich we arrived at the Chapel about 1:15. It was held at one of the Convents of the Sacred Heart which had formerly belonged to a very wealthy philanthropist and is beautifully situated in the hills of Greenwich. About 1:30 the rest of the guests arrived, among them about twelve Carmelite nuns who were on their way to found a new mission in South Africa. Most of them had not been out for ten or twelve years so I am sure they were almost as thrilled at the occasion as we were. Finally other guests came along, friends of the Skakel family and of their children, all of whom were present yesterday.

The Queen of the day finally arrived, Kathleen Hartington Kennedy, all dressed up in her new Paris christening robe which I had brought over with me in May. She behaved very well for the occasion and cried lustily during most of the ceremony. Jean was the Godmother and Danny Walsh, a former teacher of Ethel's at Manhattanville, was the Godfather. Father Connelly who married Bobby and Ethel came along for the ceremony but I am afraid nobody paid any attention to their prayers as they were more or less distracted by several little youngsters running about and emitting baby gurgles and coos. You see, there were five grandchildren of Mr. and Mrs. Skakel present, all of whom were consecrated to the Blessed Virgin after the christening ceremonies. As the five of them were under the age of four, it was really a very appropriate ceremony but strictly given over to the youngest set. There was a particularly cute baby present who had the pinkest, roundest cheeks I have ever seen. Her father is an Irishman and she certainly had the Irish complexion. She is Pat Skakel's daughter.

---

271. Leverett Saltonstall (1892–1979), Republican governor of Massachusetts, 1939–44, and U.S. senator from Massachusetts, 1945–67.

After all that excitement was over we went back to Skakel's where their house was perfectly adequate for the occasion as the trees and shrubs were in their fullest splendor, and there were three long tables out on the lawn horseshoe shape. Much to my relief we soon sat down to a gorgeous repast from soup to nuts and every thing was so good, especially the ice cream and cake. There was also a tremendous cake for the baby with a little frosted baby and cradle on it. As it was my birthday, I wore my orchids which baby Kathleen had sent me with a card enclosed saying, very diplomatically, "You are one of my two favorite grandmothers". There were numerous photographs and much rejoicing and the rain held off so we were all very happy and pleased and thrilled.

I gave baby Kathleen a blue enamel locket which Kathleen had had as a baby, and after a few more words of thanks and rejoicing we boarded the plane again and came back to Hyannis Port where we just got in ahead of the fog which was slowly coming down. It was really a wonderful day and one I knew you would want to hear about. The baby now almost weighs 1- [*sic*] pounds and seems very well. Bobby and Ethel are coming down here the end of the week and will probably stay the rest of the summer.

Pat and Jean are going up to Canada for a fishing trip and are going to stay with the Timmins. Possibly you know some of the family as Mrs. Timmins was abroad with me one year and several of the children have gone to the Sacred Heart here in the states. Eunice telephoned last night from Chicago where she is working with child delinquents. She had spent a very happy weekend in the country but she was very anxious to get all the news here. Jack is here at the moment but is going back to Congress on Tuesday. He expects to go abroad around the 20th of August and I am urging him to go to the big masked ball in Venice which, I think, takes place early in September, and which you may have read about. I am not planning to go anywhere at the moment myself. I used to go to Tanglewood to hear Koussevitzky and then on to Saratoga, but I decided not to go this year. I may go abroad later on, perhaps around the end of September. I guess this is all the news.

Much, much love,

Affectionately,

Joseph P. Kennedy to John W. McCormack

Hyannisport, August 8, 1951

Dear John:

I am very happy indeed over your two letters. Regardless of what Mr. Mackay says, my experience over 35 years with John Ford is the same as it would be with Eddie Moore — he just doesn't lie and he just doesn't make mistakes.[272]

However, that's neither here nor there; the important thing to me was that the observation did not come from your office and give credence to the fact that you were hostile to Jack. I have been around long enough to know that some people strike it off very well and some do not—which is against neither of them. As far as you and I are concerned, I have always held you in the greatest respect and affection and I have always had the greatest admiration for Mrs. McCormack, who has brought credit to everyone of us by her dignity and kindness all her life.

272. Ford, who headed JPK's New England film concerns, had reported that a member of the majority leader's staff had made disparaging remarks about Jack.

It's a strange thing that the only thing that seems to even disturb me is something said about my children. Nothing ever said about me has ever bothered me five minutes. I suppose that is the natural instinct of a parent who has always felt that the success of a family is estimated by their loyalty to one another.

You have achieved great heights in American politics. I have always felt a great pride in it because I was at the meeting that determined Rayburn for Speaker and McCormack for Leader, and I still feel that was one of the finest political moves that Roosevelt ever made. Jack is some years younger than you. He took up politics not because it was natural for him or that it was his desire, but because he felt that his brother, Joe, had made up his mind to dedicate his life to public service, and as the next oldest Jack took up a great many other obligations and desires of Joe's. I am sure there is nothing in Jack's hopes for the future that would ever conflict with your wishes. He may not follow your advice or suggestions as well as he should, but then, he doesn't follow mine and I assume that is a natural instinct. It's his responsibility and it's his future.

I have written you this way as a reason for ever having written you in the first place. I would want somebody to write me if the positions were reversed. I am very grateful to you for your prompt response.

With my warmest regards to Mrs. McCormack and to you, I remain,

Very sincerely yours,
Joseph P. Kennedy

Joseph P. Kennedy to Enrico Galeazzi

Hyannisport, October 28, 1951

My dear Enrico:

I suppose you have been kept posted accurately as to the course of the development on the establishment of the Embassy at the Vatican. There is no question that Catholics and Protestants alike have deplored the way that the appointment took place. It was the last day of the Congressional session; somebody should have known that Clark would not accept a recess appointment, and it has served no good purpose to date except to stir up some ill will.[273]

Truman got some support from an editorial in the New York TIMES which got behind the idea of the establishment of the Embassy at the Vatican. To make Clark eligible to accept the appointment, we will not only have to get senatorial approval of him as Ambassador, but we will have to get a vote of both houses of Congress to permit him to hold his Army status and still be an Ambassador.

Next year being the presidential election year, it is safe to say that all candidates in districts that have Catholic voting strength will go along with both the establishment of the Embassy and permission for Clark to retain his Army status. In a good many of the districts in which there is no great hostility chances are they will go along with the administration. I will be surprised if they will not be able to get the Republican candidates to support the bill. Eisenhower certainly made it clear to me that he wanted the Vatican's help in Europe and I don't see how he could avoid coming out in support of the

273. Although General Mark Wayne Clark (1896–1984), who had captured Rome in 1944, had accepted Truman's nomination as the first U.S. ambassador to the Vatican since 1868 a week earlier, a Reconstruction-era law barring officers from holding civilian posts had blocked his confirmation. Not wishing to retire from the military, Clark would withdraw his name from Senate consideration when Congress reconvened in January 1952.

plan, because by January I imagine they will have forced him into the position of declaring himself on his candidacy. The odds seem to be slightly better than even that he will be a candidate. His strength is almost exclusively in the eastern part of the United States but he may get support of all the anti-Taft forces.

It is still unsettled as to whether Truman is a candidate. Arthur Krock, who wrote the column I sent you, in discussing the column with me told me he thought Truman would definitely not be the candidate and would try to make Chief Justice Vinson of the Supreme Court his candidate. My own feeling is that if Vinson is the candidate, he will be beaten by either Taft or Eisenhower.

We still spend most of our time stirring the people up against Communism and Russia, but the tone of it becomes more and more political rather than international.

If you have any questions in connection with this, do let me know what they are and I will clear them up for you from the best sources.

I do hope you are well and happy and I talk of you frequently with Cardinal Spellman.

My best to you always.

Very sincerely yours,
Joseph P. Kennedy

Joseph P. Kennedy to Marshall Field III[274]

Palm Beach, December 28, 1951

Dear Marshall:
I was interested in reading the editorial in the SUN-TIMES of December 19, 1951, dealing with the speech I had delivered two days before at the Chicago Economic Club. The editorial was good enough to compliment me for having stated my position ably, and that naturally pleased me. However, I was disturbed by a few statements made in that editorial some of which are plainly wrong and should be corrected before they furnish a basis for repetition at a later day, and some of which fail to set forth my own position with accuracy.

The editorial says that during the Battle of Britain, I predicted the fall of England in three weeks. After a careful check of all my records, I cannot find that I ever made such a statement. True, I was pessimistic as to the meaningfulness of any kind of a victory that might eventuate from that war, even after Hitler's attack on Russia, for I foresaw then that the result of war would be the destruction of many of our democratic institutions and the rise of Communism. But I publicly stated in 1940 that a British victory was so essential to us that I would support measures short of war on our part which would help bring it about. Of course, Pearl Harbor in the end gave us no choice, but I wanted a policy before then that would lead to an Allied victory without ourselves being shooting participants in it. Looking back after some ten years now, I cannot feel that I was wrong in my attitude.

The editorial says that I have no plan other than to abandon Europe to Communism. This, I think, is a definite misreading of my speech. I did say that our present policies of supplying dollars and guns had not only *not* increased the number of our friends

---

274. The Chicago department store heir and liberal philanthropist, Marshall Field III (1893–1956), had founded the *Chicago Sun* (with Franklin Roosevelt's encouragement) in 1941 as an alternative local voice to Col. McCormack's isolationist, anti-administration *Tribune*. In 1948, Field had purchased the *Chicago Times* and merged it with the *Sun*.

in Europe but had actually increased the intensity of anti-American feeling in that area apart from its weakening ourselves. If this is true, obviously something radical must be done. Abandonment of this policy is a different thing from abandonment of Europe. The alternatives to this policy, as I stated, are (1) to make ourselves strong and (2) to adopt a European policy that will realistically build within those nations a will to resist the menace of Communism. Consequently, I called for a reappraisal of our policy that would lead to increasing our self-sufficiency and our armed strength, and to encouraging and fostering the desire of Europe to take steps necessary to build within herself a will to resist and re-arm—which mere dollars and guns will not do. I want Europe to be a source of strength to us, not of weakness, and I have stated that I am willing to pay a price for that. You assume that the existing policy creates a dam against Communism and anti-Americanism. The facts, however, do not substantiate you. Of course, my suggestions might also not create such a dam, but I believe they have a better chance of doing so. They may not and Europe may go Communist irrespective of anything that we can do. If so, the consequences of failure will be far less serious under my suggestions than they would be otherwise.

I think you should have noted that I made a point of the fact that Europe's will to resist should be cultivated by adjusting our policies to the development of her own sense of her destiny rather than by imposing upon Europe patterns of our making. I made this same point with regard to the Middle East and Asia. This to me seems sensible and likely to be productive. It certainly is a far cry from "abandonment." Emphasizing our security, militarily and economically, as well as the innate validity of our democratic institutions, is in accord not only with this policy of getting Europe to stand on its own feet but aligns itself with out traditional policy of relying upon ourselves. If, because of overextension, we fail to build ourselves into a strong nation, we fail the people of the whole world, for there will then be no fortress of liberty.

I would suggest that one virtue of my suggested approach is that we might thereby convince Europe that we are not planning to make her the battlefield of a future war. As you know, she fears this and fears the consequences of our present actions as much and even more than she fears the Russian threat. Those fears destroy the very thing we are seeking to achieve—the building of a will to resist. Of course, Europe may again become a vast battlefield, but if Europe knows that this will happen as a result of her own choosing, and not ours, she may well develop the will to prepare herself to make that choice. On the other hand, you can hardly expect her, as we do now, to prepare to sacrifice herself at our behest. Thirty times thirty billion dollars will not buy that. We may try but I suspect that in so doing we may find that Europe may have abandoned us and we, like Esau, will have lost our birthright.

It was very nice seeing and talking with you and I hope to see you again soon.

Sincerely yours,
Joseph P. Kennedy

Joseph P. Kennedy to Loretta Connelly[275]

Hyannisport, August 22, 1952

Dear Loretta,

First of all I must confess that I woke up too late to the fact that I did not send you any word on your birthday on the tenth of August. I am afraid I am not as thoughtful

275. JPK's sister.

as you and I don't keep notes of birthdays and other special events. In fact, I am ashamed to say I forgot to send a cable to Rose on her birthday last month. Maybe it's old age, but I am choosing to blame it on the excitement of the campaign. As late as it is, you have my best wishes always for many happy returns!

Now as to the political situation, it is definitely Governor Stevenson.[276] He is a great friend of the family and is a remarkably smart fellow. He doesn't see eye to eye with me at all on foreign policy but you can't get a candidate who agrees with you on everything, and the last thing I want is Eisenhower.

In the first place, I don't want a military man as President. All the countries that have military men swing into dictatorship pretty soon afterwards—for example, Franco, Peron in Argentina, now the general in Egypt, and you could go on like this forever. In addition to that, these fellows have no plan to stop the trend towards Socialism. Eisenhower has already come out for increasing social security, so it is just a fake. The Korean War must be stopped, but they were all responsible for getting us into it and there's no way they can get us out of it that I can see. Certainly Eisenhower can't!

They talk about what a great administrator and conciliator he is. Look at the mess the European plans are in now. He walked out right in the middle of it.

By all means let's hustle for Stevenson and the Democratic ticket. Stevenson will give an honest, able administration. We haven't had either in the last two.

Things are looking fine for Jack. I hope you saw the picture in TIME last week of the girls and Jack and Bobby. Everybody is working very hard. Be sure and write to your friends in Massachusetts to do some work amongst their Republican friends. They can do more good than all the politicians.

Take care of yourself and we'll let you know what is going on.

Love,

Edward Kennedy, 20, to John F. Kennedy: *Telegram*

IL EST FATIGUE ET TRISTE SES YEUX SONT ROUGES CE QUE VOUS FEISIEZ [*sic*] A LODGE NE DEVRAIT PAS ARRIVER AUX MORTS=[277]

ted=[278]

Joseph P. Kennedy to Sir James Calder

Palm Beach, December 31, 1952

Dear Jim:

The whole family, except Teddy, are here for Christmas. Teddy is a private in the Army stationed in Paris. We all enjoyed your letter and all send you our best for a happy New Year.

Jack is staying a few days and leaving for Washington tomorrow to be sworn in on Saturday as United States Senator. This is probably one of the jobs that I thought Joe

276. Adlai Ewing Stevenson (1900–65), governor of Illinois and Democratic presidential nominee.
277. On November 4, Jack had become the third Democrat to be elected to the U.S. Senate from Massachusetts, beating incumbent Henry Cabot Lodge 1,211,984 to 1,141,247.
278. Six months earlier Teddy had been suspended at the end of his freshman year at Harvard for having a friend take a Spanish exam for him. He had enlisted in the army two weeks later and was currently stationed in Paris as a military policeman with the rank of private first class.

would have filled, but we are more than fortunate to have Jack come along with the same hopes and ideals. His victory was, next to Eisenhower's, the most sensational in the United States because he defeated a Republican that has never been defeated for anything in Massachusetts before.

In addition to all this, Lodge brought in Eisenhower and Nixon the night before the election to make a lot of speeches in his behalf, but it was of no avail. Jack beat him by 70,000 votes with Eisenhower carrying the State by 208,000. It is little wonder that we are very happy.

Jack also is enjoying better health than he has for eight or ten years; he weighs a hundred and sixty pounds, which is about fifteen pounds more than his average for the last five years.

Bobby will probably be assistant counsel for the McCarthy Investigating Committee in the Senate. He had been with the Department of Justice up to the time he came back to manage Jack's campaign. He and his wife now have two children: a little girl named Kathleen and a baby named Joseph P. 2d.

Eunice is still following up her work on children delinquency and is going back to Chicago to resume right after Jack is sworn in. The other girls are doing various work connected with the charity work of the Church.

Teddy enlisted in the Army rather than be drafted and if there is no trouble should be out in June and will resume his studies at college.

The country seems to be very pleased with the Eisenhower election and the appointments to the Cabinet. Practically all of the appointments represent big business, so that the Republicans are in position to solidify their standing if we don't have a war and if we don't have an economic collapse. There is no sign of either one on the horizon at the minute, but within a couple of years there should be some economic difficulties. I think on the whole it is a good thing that the Republicans came in; otherwise, it would have been the end of the two-party system in this country, and it also gives us a chance to see if we can't get things done better than we have been doing them for quite a few years.

I want to digress for a moment to tell you that you would have been very much surprised and pleased to have seen the wonderful television programs that Rose and the girls put on for Jack and the remarkable speeches that Rose made. It was all the more amazing because she had always felt she would get so nervous speaking to a small group that she never attempted it, but in this campaign she spoke before thousands. She is very well and looks very well.

I am promising myself every year that I will take it easy. I haven't done too well so far, but I am hoping I will make a real effort in '53. I doubt very much if I will get over there shortly, but it may be that some of the family will be over there after the Coronation. If so, they are surely going to look you up.

Our very best from all of us and our best wishes for a happy New Year.

Sincerely yours,
Joseph P. Kennedy

Edward Kennedy, 21, to Joseph P. Kennedy: *Telegram*

ANTIBES 1953 JUN 20

HAPPY FATHERS DAY HAVING BARRELS OF FUN SEND MONEY FOR MORE BARRELS LOVE = TED

Jacqueline Bouvier, 23, to Rose Kennedy

Hammersmith Farm, Newport, Rhode Island, Monday [June 29, 1953]

Dear Mrs. Kennedy:

It seems very strange and quiet to be home—after all the dashing around of this last week. I hope Mummy will immediately start producing lists for me to go over—and wedding plans to settle on—because if I'm ever left with nothing to do—I start missing Jack.

I suppose this should really be a thank you letter for last weekend, but what I want to thank you for is something much bigger than that.

I never realized how wonderful it is to love your husband's family. I thought if you liked your in-laws—that was fine—and if you didn't it didn't matter, because your life was with your husband. Now I see that if you enjoy the family you are going to become a part of—your happiness is doubled.

As I met every Kennedy one by one, I liked them all so much. I don't think I ever knew you very well until this weekend. Now I think I'm so lucky to have you as a mother in law.

It seems to me that very few people have been able to create what you have—a family built on love and loyalty and gaiety. If I can even come close to building that with Jack I will be very happy. If you ever see me going wrong I hope you will tell me—because I know you would never find fault unless fault was there.

I do mean to thank you for this weekend too. It was such a perfect one—and I would have made a terrible mess of it if you hadn't told me how to hold my arms for photographers—and how to pick out engagement rings. I hope I shall see you soon again—either in Hyannis or over here—and please don't worry about the wedding. I think it's going to be a lot less hectic than it looked at first.

Much love,
Jackie[279]

Joseph P. Kennedy to Torb Macdonald

Hyannisport, July 22, 1953

Dear Torb:

Jack needs a rest. Unquestionably he has the best time with you. I am a bit concerned that he may get restless about the prospect of getting married. Most people do and he is more likely to do so than others.

As I told you, I am hoping that he will take a rest and not jump from place to place, and be especially mindful of whom he sees. Certainly one can't take anything for granted since he has become a United States Senator. That is a price he should be willing to pay and gladly. I understand your love and devotion to Jack and I know you wish him nothing but the best and I hope you both will have a good vacation.

With my warmest personal regards.

Sincerely,
Joseph P. Kennedy

---

279. On June 24, Janet Auchincloss had announced the engagement of her daughter Jacqueline Lee Bouvier (1929–94), former *Times-Herald* "Inquiring Camera" reporter, to Senator John F. Kennedy.

Joseph P. Kennedy to Frank Conniff

Hyannisport, August 5, 1953

Dear Frank:

You didn't disturb my golf game at all; it was nice hearing from you.

I agree with you 100 per cent on the fight for the real Democratic Party. I can't understand why people who have been brought up in Democratic tradition should use their influence to elect a lot of people whose desires, let us say, are certainly a long way from what I believe the fundamental principles of the Democratic Party are. Now I am not saying that a lot of the progressive legislation that has been passed is not good. Democratic policy, I think it is; what I do resent is the fact that a lot of people with no experience whose only claim to any political support is their so-called intellectual capacity, which when called upon to do some good for the country has fallen down miserably.

I have been thinking over a long period of time of some effective way to offset the pseudo influence of the ADA.[280] They have less than 2000 members in the state of Massachusetts and to hear all the fuss they put up, you would think they were the dominant political party in a state that cast over 2 million votes in the last election.

I certainly don't know what I can do in the New York picture but I am trying to work out some kind of an idea as to how we can at least make real Democrats an important factor in determining the future policies of this country. It can be done and certainly the columns you sent me look like a real smash in the right direction.[281] The only trouble with them, of course, is that people are only liable to read a column if somebody tells them their name is mentioned, but most columns written by newspaper writers today are getting the go-by. If the paper will adopt this kind of a firm attitude on policies or anything else as far as I am concerned, then they could make themselves the important factor that old "WR" made himself in this country. Newspapers make money when they stand for something and stand for it come hell or high water. Take the TRIBUNE and the DAILY NEWS — the two greatest money making institutions in the country. The NEW YORK TIMES was that until its editorial policy started to play footsies with minority groups.

I don't know when I'll be in New York but if I don't get down this month, I hope you and your bride will take a plane and come up. I would like to talk to you.

Again, it was nice hearing from you, and with my warmest personal regards, I am

Very sincerely yours,
Joseph P. Kennedy

John F. Kennedy to Rose Joseph P. Kennedy: *Telegram*

ACAPULCO MEX 1953 SEP 15

AT LAST I KNOW TRUE MEANING OF RAPTURE JACKIE IS ENSHRINED FOREVER IN MY HEART THANKS MOM AND DAD FOR MAKING ME WORTHY OF HER YOUR LOVING SON JACK=[282]

---

280. Americans for Democratic Action, the noncommunist labor and political movement founded in 1949 by a number of prominent liberals, among them Minnesota Senator Hubert Humphrey.
281. The Hearst papers "East Side West Side" columnist had written JPK of what he described as a "left-wing clique" within the New York State Democratic Party. Its plan, Conniff suggested to JPK, was to launch Franklin Roosevelt, Jr., to the governorship, "then in '56, controlling New York's big delegation and teaming up with other 'liberal' groups in other states . . . to force their candidate on the party for the presidency."
282. He and Jackie had been married in Newport on September 12.

Joseph P. Kennedy to Robert Kennedy, 28

Villa Les Fal Eze, Eze s/Mer A[lpes] M[aritimes], August 15, 1954

Dear Bobby:

I tried to get you on the telephone at the Cape but they told me you had left for Chicago. I can't imagine why particularly since I just got another letter from Jean saying that she was on her way back to the Cape, and Eunice was out visiting Pat; so I just imagine that we were getting truly French telephone service which means they tell you anything they want.

I was very interested in your report on McCarthy but was even more interested in mother's report on Symington's estimate of your hard work at the Cape.[283] That must have set you off in good shape!

By all means kick out all the Fitzgeralds if you want the house for a house party. They would stay with you for the rest of your life.

I had dinner with Lord Beaverbrook a couple of times and the other night Lady Diana Cooper, the widow of Duff Cooper,[284] asked me, "How much longer will McCarthy amount to anything in the United States?" That, of course, rubbed me the wrong way because it was true British pontification. I said he was the strongest man in the United States next to Eisenhower. Then I said to the small English group, "What have you got against McCarthy?" Lord Beaverbrook, who hasn't anything particular against him, said that the real objection to him was his calling Marshall a traitor.[285] He, Beaverbrook, had no objection to him saying he was a bad Secretary of State and that he had lost China for the world, but he said people just know he isn't a traitor. I said I had never heard that he said he was a traitor by condemning him for being an incompetent; but my own feeling is that Joe went further than that.

I then asked Lady Diana what she had against him. She said she thought people she talked with felt he ruled by fear and added, "You know we British don't like anybody to do things like that." I said that was poppycock. Then Sir Patrick Hennessey, who represents the Ford Company in England, said when he was in America he met a very interesting lawyer who wrote out a case against McCarthy but warned Hennessey against using his name. Beaverbrook asked Hennessey why and Hennessey added he was afraid that McCarthy might attack him or his family or what not. Biggest lot of dribble I every listened to! The only thing I regret is that they seem to be forgetting Cohn[286] in the picture and concentrating on McCarthy.

I am enclosing a clipping from the SUNDAY DAILY MAIL, which is about as big a piece of junk as you ever read. Incidentally, Lady Cooper insisted on quoting Joe Alsop who is sort of a little God to these "Café Society British." Beaverbrook, of course, is very sane and sensible; he just lets them talk so I can find out what I want to know. He is strictly a de Gaulle man here so you know where he stands on international affairs.

283. He does not appear to have saved the letters that he received in France.
284. The dowager Viscountess Norwich, formerly Diana Manners, actress, legendary beauty, socialite, writer and eccentric (1892–1986), had been widowed in January after thirty-five years of open marriage to the former British ambassador to France and wartime minister of information.

   McCarthy would be censured by his colleagues in the Senate for "contemptuous, contumacious and denunciatory" behavior on December 2, 1954.
285. George Catlett Marshall, former army chief of staff, 1939–45; secretary of state, 1947–49; secretary of defense, 1950–51; and 1953 Nobel Laureate for Peace for the postwar European reconstruction plan that bore his name.
286. Roy Marcus Cohn (1927–86), chief counsel to the Senate Permanent Subcommittee on Investigations, had been forced to resign in July in the midst of bipartisan outcry at his conduct in the events leading to the Army-McCarthy hearings currently raging in Washington.

We also got into a discussion about just where the United States and Great Britain were headed. Beaverbrook is frank to admit he doesn't understand what is going on. I asked, "Would you go to war even if you knew you possessed the edge now and would not possess it in three or ten years?" He said, "I would be willing to take any steps in China that were necessary." But since the English are in favor of recognizing China and we are not, and since Chou[287] has announced that he is going to invade Formosa, it looks to me like we will be the ones to drop the bombs and the British will hold their hands in sanctification.

Jack's article in the NEW YORK TIMES was carried in the French edition of the TIMES which appeared here last week.

My cup is filled to overflowing! Randolph Churchill came up to me at Monte Carlo and asked me how I was, and told me he was going to stay with Beaverbrook a couple of days. He did, and Beaverbrook said he was the most insufferable bore he has ever listened to and only tolerates him on account of his father. He is fat and just as repulsive as ever. Winston is expected here but they don't know when.

We have the most beautiful villa on the Riviera and while the last week in most of France has been chilly and stormy, we have had nothing but a little wind and, on the whole, it has been most pleasant.

To come back to Beaverbrook, he told me that Anthony[288] is annoyed as the devil that Churchill doesn't get through, and the other day Churchill, talking to Beaverbrook, said there is a chap named Eccles working for Churchill and he said to Max he would give him a better appointment in a year or two, and then looked at Max and chuckled and said, "Don't tell Anthony," which indicates he knows Anthony is expected to be Prime Minister but Churchill gives him no satisfaction.

Reisman has gone home presumably to take a job with Mike Todd.[289] Houghton has been in bed three days with diarrhea and everyone within a radius of twenty miles knows about it. Those who don't know him feel sorry for him; those who do, meaning me, kill themselves laughing. Mother has been in Paris a few days looking over the clothes and thinks that Jean should come some time after the first of September if she wants to get things done. I don't know why the first but Jean probably has her plans made anyway. Jeannie is the best correspondent; I have had two letters from her and the letter from Ethel had us in convulsions. I tried to get Jack on the telephone a couple of times but got Jackie both times.

If you feel sure you are going to be tied up with the Committee, don't you think you might be looking around for an assistant for me on the Hoover Commission, without any commitments until I get home? I have seen some very important people and expect to see more in September before I go back.

You might pass this news on to any of the family who are interested.

Give my love to all.

---

287. Chou En-lai (1898–1976), concurrent prime minister and foreign minister of the People's Republic of China.
288. Eden.
289. The flamboyant theatrical and motion picture producer, and self-proclaimed "lucky bum," Mike Todd (1909–58).

Robert Kennedy, 28, to Joseph P. and Rose Kennedy: *Telegram*

GREENWICH CONN 1954 OCT 8[290]

40 YEARS OH CAN IT BE. LOOKING BACK WHAT DO I SEE. OUR GREAT ACCOM-
PLISHMENT THE MART OR WAS IT THE SEC, OH NO OF COURSE NOT, IT WAS=
JUST PLAIN OLD ME.

Rose Kennedy to Joseph P. Kennedy

Saturday [July 1955] 6-30 A.M.

Dearest Joe,

Bob arrived at 10 P.M. - last night & was jubilant over the press releases, & was enthusiastic & appreciative in his acknowledgment of McCarthy's praise of Bob's work on the committee during the Peress investigation.[291] Bob got two very good notices in the N.Y. Times, which Ethel sent to me to read - but I could not find anything in the Herald Tribune. Something should be put in the Boston papers & I am going to call Frank Morrissey[292] to-day. I know you will hear about Bob investigating Harold Talbott[293] before this letter reaches you — I shall see to it that Bob writes to-day or Monday. I can't imagine Bob investigating some one as old & matured & as social as Talbott. In fact — Bob was dropping big names around like Johnnie Haines. (he was on Commission with you).[294] Folsom[295] etc. You would eat it up. He says he is still going on his trip but I was wondering about it last night.

I also am thinking of having Grandma's photo taken with me Bob & the 4 great grandchildren. It would be a good excuse for some good publicity & until I announced on my arrival that Bob had another son, no one in Boston knew it.[296]

---

290. JPK and Rose had celebrated their wedding anniversary the day before.
291. On July 15 the *New York Times* had quoted McCarthy (who had been removed from the chairmanship of the Permanent Subcommittee on Investigations after his censure in 1954) as describing the recently published Peress Report as a "great tribute to the staff of the subcommittee." In January 1954 McCarthy had instigated an investigation into the promotion and honorable discharge of one Major Irving Peress. The army dentist, a member of the American Labor Party, had invoked his Fifth Amendment right in refusing to state on an Army questionnaire whether he was affiliated with any subversive organizations.
292. Francis Xavier Morrissey (1910–), former assistant to both Massachusetts Governor Tobin and JPK, and Jack's office manager during his early congressional campaigns and career. Amidst public outcry against Morrissey's lack of judicial credentials, he would be appointed a municipal judge in Boston by Massachusetts Governor Furcolo at JPK's urging in 1958. Jack and Teddy would propose Morrissey's nomination to the federal bench (without success) in 1961 and 1966, respectively.
293. Harold Elstner Talbott (1888–1957), secretary of the air force, 1953–55, former industrialist, aviation multimillionaire and, like the Kennedys, a wintertime resident of Palm Beach. Despite having divested himself of his aviation and defense interests before taking the secretaryship, Talbott had been permitted to retain his interest in the Mulligan Company, an industrial engineering firm based in New York. In July the Permanent Investigations Committee had begun to investigate his use of his position to solicit business for the company (whose profits had risen markedly since his appointment). Talbott would resign in August.
294. In February 1953, Talbott had contacted John Wesley Hanes (1892–1987), a director of the Olin Corporation (as well as a former Securities and Exchange Commission commissioner, 1938–39, and assistant secretary of the treasury, 1939). The secretary of the air force had used official stationery, it was alleged, to arrange a business meeting between Hanes and an officer of the Mulligan Company.
295. Television marketing pioneer Francis Marion Folsom (1894–1970), president of RCA, 1948–57. RCA, it had been revealed in the probe, had not renewed its contract with Mulligan because it had been unable to secure the Justice Department's assurances that doing business with Mulligan would not present a conflict of interest.
296. David Anthony Kennedy (1955–84) had been born on June 15.

Talked to Eunice who is all set to come down — she has a sail boat now on Lake Michigan. Have not heard from Jack but Sara[297] gave him a check up on his tummie & said he was fine. Everyone else perfect. Expect to leave July 27th or July 29th.

Love
Rose

Joseph P. Kennedy to Robert Kennedy, 29

EZE S/MER, July 21, 1955

Dear Bobby:

Just a quick note. Heard from Mother that Talbott had said that his activities were no different from mine when I bought Haig & Haig while in government. I should say they were!

First of all, I bought Haig & Haig before I ever went in government. Second, there never was any question from Senator Fletcher when I made known everything I owned. Third and most important, we never did any business with the government or with anybody who ever did any business with the government. That's about as different as I can imagine.

I have known Talbott for 25 years but have never had any business dealings or social connection with him; I just knew him to say hello to.

This is just so the record is straight — McInerny or no McInerny.

Love,
Dad

Joseph P. Kennedy to Joseph Dinneen

August 6, 1955

Dear Joe:

I received your letter today and also a letter from Jack setting forth in a small way that you were contemplating this article.[298]

First of all, I think you should know that some writer prepared a lot of material on Jack's life for REDBOOK, and I think that Mr. Murphy in my office would know what his name is. Also, Mr. Gould, of the LADIES HOME JOURNAL contacted the same man about getting Mrs. Kennedy to write a story about the children, but I told the writer and his editor that I didn't think Mrs. Kennedy would be very comfortable writing an article extolling her children. Aren't these two magazines connected in ownership with COLLIER'S?

Now I have one serious question is my mind as to whether people just don't get sick of reading about the Kennedys time and time and time again. I also wonder what possible good such an article could do for any other family. I grant you that they have done a very good job to date and there could be a lot of interesting things written about their accomplishments, but I still wonder whether that is the kind of a story that has any excuse for being published, unless it would mean something to anybody who might read

---

297. Dr. Sara Jordan, chief of Gastroenterology at the Lahey Clinic in Boston.
298. Collier's had contacted the *Boston Globe* reporter about writing a feature entitled "The Fabulous Kennedys."

it. I am trying to look at this question quite objectively. If you can feel that anything would be accomplished by it, I would certainly be in favor of trying it.

Ethel, Bobby's wife, with her four children will be at Hyannis Port until the end of August. Eunice, Mrs. Shriver,[299] is there with her child now and will remain until the end of August. The present plans are for my daughter Pat and Ethel to meet Bobby in Moscow when he arrives there with Justice Douglas in September.[300] Jack and his wife will be here for the month of August and will be at the Cape sometime in September. Jean, as you know, if next to [sic] Father Keller in the Christopher Movement and she comes down to the Cape in August to visit with her sisters. Teddy is on a Pacific Ocean race to Hawaii and back and should be at the Cape around August 20th, and Mrs. Kennedy and I will be back there the end of September.

That is roughly an itinerary of what is going on, and if you and I decide we can really do something worth while with the story, you can count on my co-operation in any way that I can give it. I am sure that you have known the Kennedys for longer than any other writer that COLLIER'S could assign to this task and I know that you have a very sympathetic feeling for them.

With my warmest personal regards, I am

Very sincerely yours,
Joseph P. Kennedy

John F. Kennedy to Joseph P. Kennedy

United States Lines

Dear Dad:

I am sending you our first and last chapters.[301] I believe Mother ~~wrote~~ brought you the rest of the book. This is the final draft And if you have any thoughts that there might be something wrong with it — I wish you would write your thoughts as soon as possible to Ted[302] in Washington — & we can get it changed. In any case — I shall be talking with you.

Torb & I are going to Scandinavia for a week — He is then returning home — and I shall be coming down. Thought we would stay over at the Hotel du Cap as I think Jackie would like to be near Lee as long as Lee is there.

The trip over was very quiet but pleasant. Congressman Adam Powell[303] is the outstanding personality in the boat.

Love
Jack

---

299. In 1953 Eunice had married Robert Sargent Shriver (1915–), the former assistant general manager of the Merchandise Mart who had helped her organize a national conference on juvenile delinquency in 1947.

300. After several years of denied visa requests, Bobby and Justice William O. Douglas (formerly SEC counsel during JPK's tenure as chairman) had embarked on a tour of the Soviet Union in late July.

301. During his convalescence following a series of back surgeries in 1954 and 1955, Jack had begun work on a group of essays that would be published as *Profiles in Courage* by Harper & Brothers in January 1956.

302. Jack's legislative assistant, speechwriter and future special counsel, Theodore Chaiken Sorensen (1928–) had compiled the book's background materials and had helped prepare the preliminary rough draft.

303. Harlem congressman, author and Abyssinian Baptist Church minister, Adam Clayton Powell, Jr. (1908–72).

Joseph P. Kennedy to Theodore Sorensen: *Draft*

Dear Ted:

I have had to talk with Jack about the book. I think it is a magnificent job and will be very interesting, I am sure. I wish I could think of a better title but I can't; therefore, I suppose this one will have to do.

~~I am quite confused by the paragraph on Page 18, beginning with "Today the challenge of political courage . . . ." because I do not know what he means by it, and going through to Page 19 the end of the paragraph finishing with "more than it fears hydrogen bombs". I have read it over three times. I know there is something here that is important but I don't get it at all. I would like to have you read it over again and see if you can't make it clearer.~~ [*I have a few suggestions. On page 18*] The sentence beginning "And our public life is becoming . . ." should be stated much more simply and forcibly.

The next paragraph, "And thus, in the days ahead . . . . ." needs some clearing up. It's out of tune to me with the rest of the material just previous to it.

I think the next paragraph (first paragraph Page 19) [*beginning "Of course"*] has good basic material but it is not simply stated.

In addition to that, I think Harper's should have an excellent editorial writer go over the whole book, particularly these two chapters, with the idea of punctuation and simplifying the structure. It's a fine job as it is but I remember when Lindbergh spoke to me about the real success of his book he said he almost did not recognize it after the editorial writer at Scribner's had finished working on it — he brought so much more clarity and punch to it. I think instead of having Harper's take this book just as it is, they should have a man of top caliber do this same job on it and, if he is very good, I am sure you will have a worth-while and profitable piece of literature, and worth-while financially if properly exploited.

Very sincerely yours,
Joseph P. Kennedy

Joseph P. Kennedy to Robert Kennedy, 29

Dear Bobby:

I think that the value of the trip, besides adding stature to your background, is the articles and lectures you might give on it. However, I am rather of the opinion that for you to land there after Douglas would make the news value of your trip very slight. Getting home before Douglas would be best; getting home with him would be excellent; but getting home by yourself would not be of very great importance for the eventual buildup.

How about having Mr. and Mrs. Douglas come to Eze as our guests, and that means transportation and everything, and then get them to go home on the boat with you, if you still wanted to go home that way.

I also would try and see what you could of Poland, if it is at all possible. Remember that the thing you learn in Russia and in the Iron Curtain countries are the things people will want to hear about. Eze is pleasant but not important. I would see as much as I could of Russia while I was there. If Douglas has to go home right away and you don't want to leave that soon, then by all means I would extend the trip into Poland and any other places under Russian influence. That would give a new slant on your interview when you got to the States.

In addition to all of this, if you are going to do any articles for "Life" or the "Saturday Evening Post," I would do them jointly, if possible; at least as far as the one big article is concerned; after that each one on his own. Up-to-date the publicity has been fine for both of you, but as I have said a thousand times, things don't happen, they are made to happen in the public relations field. As much as you and Ethel would love to be in Eze and take a seven-day trip home in a boat, I think it would be a mistake unless Douglas is going to stay somewhere out of America until you get back. From your point of view, the Americans must not think of this trip just in relationship to Justice Douglas.

I can easily arrange to have the material picked up in Paris, delivered in America the next day and developed at once and have your material put in order while you are over here, if that is what you would like.

For the sake of keeping the point of view on Russia down to earth, I would suggest reading again Whittaker Chambers' book, "The Witness."[304] It will still give the idea that no matter how well the Russian people think of us, as long as their dictators hold police power, they are not going to be able to show it. American people and most people in the world now, as in '38, want peace but the leaders of all countries can get them into trouble.

These are just suggestions; there may be perfectly good reasons why they do not make sense. In any event, we would love to see you both if you can make it.

Love,

Joseph P. Kennedy to Edward Kennedy, 23

September 3, 1955

Dear Teddy:

I don't know whether you know it or not but the reports of your goings on with all these beautiful women at Cape Cod is slowly but surely driving your oldest brother insane. There was a time when I think he thought I was a little strict with you by insisting that you have something else on your mind besides girls, but after having heard from Morton Downey that he saw you at the airport with a more beautiful girl than Grace Kelly, Jack, I am sure, has changed his whole outlook on your future. He hasn't expressed it to me as yet, but from hints being dropped, I gather he feels that I should take a much stricter hand and, in other words, if there are so many beautiful girls looking around for a Kennedy, it should be for the oldest brother and not the youngest. I'll leave this matter entirely in your hands and trust you will settle it to your mutual satisfaction.

Last night we went to the Gala at Monte Carlo and Jack arrived early and dressed in my room. As usual, he arrived without his studs, with two different stockings and no underpants; so he walked off with a pair of brand new Sulka stockings of mine, a new pair of Sulka underpants of mine, and the last pair of evening studs I possessed. I gave him your letter to read about Bobby and while we thought it was hilarious, I'm not too sure that he knows how to spell Sarge's name himself; therefore, the point may have been lost. He is very happy, however, that you are now rolling in the dirt at Soldiers Field and, he hopes, in strict training. He had planned to spend quite a long time over

---

304. The former Soviet agent's account of his membership in the Communist Party and his role in the Alger Hiss trial had been published three years earlier.

here but I have an idea that he will be back, knocking at your door before long now to get your list. He is back on crutches after having tried to open a screen in his hotel room, but if he hasn't any more brains than to try that, maybe he should stay on crutches. His general attitude towards life seems to be quite gay. He is very intrigued with the constant rumors that he is being considered for the Vice Presidency, which idea I think is one of the silliest I have heard in a long time for Jack.

Well, the weather still stays beautiful but we're getting ready to leave and I figure to land back in New York on the 20th by plane. Hope things are going well and that you will make your last year at Harvard a real big one, if only for your future.

Love,

Joseph P. Kennedy to J. Edgar Hoover

Hyannis Port, October 11, 1955

Dear Edgar:

You sent me a personal note on June 7 which I saw on my return to the United States a week or so ago. I gave my office hell for not sending it to me but they said my final instructions were "not to bother you with any mail or messages for three months". So that's what happened. I want to thank you for your most kind and generous remarks.

I think I have become too cynical in my old age but the only two men that I know in public life today for whose opinion I give one continental both happen to be named Hoover — one John Edgar and one Herbert — and I am proud to think that both of them hold me in some esteem. I am all even on the rest.

I listened to Walter Winchell mention your name as a candidate for President. If that could come to pass, it would be the most wonderful thing for the United States, and whether you were on a Republican or Democratic ticket, I would guarantee you the largest contribution that you would ever get from anybody and the hardest work by either a Democrat or a Republican. I think the United States deserves you. I only hope it gets you.

My best to you always.

Sincerely,

Joseph P. Kennedy to John F. Kennedy

May 25, 1956

Dear Jack:

I have just finished talking with Clare Luce,[305] who, by the way, is still quite sick. I think it would be nice if you sent her flowers. She is one of your greatest rooters. She hopes you will not accept the nomination for the Vice Presidency. She has many arguments, not the least of which is that if you are chosen, it will be because you are a Catholic and not because you are big enough to do a good job. She feels that a defeat would be a devastating blow to your prestige, which at the moment is great, and nonpartisan. She has many good arguments and many hopes for your future. I think definitely you should see her if you can, but if not, talk to her. She has some very, very

305. Now the U.S. ambassador to Italy.

interesting sidelights for you. I could write them, but I think you should hear them from her directly. This I assure you is very, very important.

Sincerely,

Joseph P. Kennedy

P.S.: The above letter was dictated by your father on his way to the ship.[306]

John F. Kennedy to Joseph P. Kennedy

WASHINGTON, June 29, 1956

Dear Dad:

As you know, the authorization for the Vatican bill passed the Senate unanimously yesterday.[307] I think the appropriation bill will be all right too.

The office has probably sent you the article which appeared in the *New York Times* containing Governor Ribicoff's statement.[308] I did not know he was going to say what he did, but when he keynoted the Democratic Convention at Worcester he had spoken to me about it. In the meantime he had John Bailey look into the matter further and I am enclosing a copy of John's letter.[309]

Governor Roberts [*of R.I.*] seconded Ribicoff's motion and Governor Hodges [*of North Carolina*] also indicated that it would be acceptable to him. The situation more or less rests there.

Arthur Schlesinger wrote to me yesterday and stated that he thought it should be done and that he was going to do everything that he possibly could. He is going to spend a month in Stevenson's headquarters.[310]

Competition is mostly from Hubert Humphrey,[311] who had his Governor make a statement that I would not be acceptable because of my vote on the farm bill; Senator Symington,[312] Senator Gore,[313] Mayor Wagner (who doesn't seem to have much support)[314] and myself.

I have done nothing about it and do not plan to although if it looks worthwhile I may have George Smathers[315] talk to some of the southern Governors. While I think the prospects are rather limited, it does seem of some use to have all of this churning

---

306. He was departing for Europe. On January 13, acting on the recommendation of the recent Hoover Commission Report, Eisenhower had appointed JPK to an eight-member board to review the activities of the government's foreign intelligence services, particularly the CIA.

307. On June 27 the Senate had voted to authorize $964,199.35 in order to repay the Vatican for damage to Castel Gandolfo caused by American bombers during the liberation of Rome in 1944. The House had already voted in favor of the payment on June 5; the president would sign the bill on July 4.

308. At the Governors' Conference in Atlantic City on June 25, Abraham Ribicoff (1910–98) of Connecticut had reiterated the support that he had voiced for Jack's vice presidential candidacy earlier in the month at the Massachusetts party convention.

309. On a recent visit to Illinois, Bailey (of the Democratic State Central Committee of Connecticut) had told Governor Stevenson that Jack "would be helpful to the ticket from a vote-getting standpoint, much greater than many people who are being talked about for the position."

310. Joe Junior's former Harvard classmate, Pulitzer Prize–winning historian, former Office of Strategic Services deputy chief, Harvard professor, and cofounder of Americans for Democratic Action, Arthur Meier Schlesinger, Jr. (1917–). Schlesinger had been a speechwriter for Stevenson in both 1952 and 1956; he would become special assistant to the president in 1961.

311. Hubert Horatio Humphrey, Jr. (1911–78), U.S. Senator from Minnesota since 1949.

312. Truman's former chairman of the National Security Resources Board had been elected senator from Missouri in 1952.

313. Albert Arnold Gore, Sr. (1907–1998), U.S. senator from Tennessee, 1953–70.

314. Robert Ferdinand Wagner, Jr. (1910–91), mayor of New York City, 1954–65.

315. George Armistead Smathers (1913–), U.S. senator from Florida, 1950–69.

up. If I don't get it I can always tell them in the State that it was because of my vote on the farm bill.

We expect to get out of here in about three weeks and will then spend a couple weeks at the Cape before going to the Convention in Chicago. I expect to come to France with George Smathers right after the Convention.

Love,

Jack

P.S. Harriman[316] was pretty well set back during Governor's Conference and it looks sure that Stevenson will either be nominated on the 2nd [1st]or 3rd [2nd] ballot.

Joseph P. Kennedy to Sargent Shriver

[Eze-sur- Mer] July 18, 1956

Dear Sarge:

Replying to your request for my opinion as to the possible success of a Stevenson-Kennedy ticket and what tactics I would recommend for a victory, let me give you what I think of the situation away from the heat and strife of the contest in America.

First of all, previous to Eisenhower's second medical upset,[317] I would have thought that an Eisenhower-Nixon ticket could win very easily against the Democratic ticket. Since the second attack, I have come to the following conclusions:

You will remember Governor Stevenson calling me from Hobe Sound while I was at Palm Beach well over two years ago, asking me what I thought of the speech he had made attacking Eisenhower. I told him I did not think there were any votes or good-will to be gained by attacking Eisenhower, and I do not believe there are any today. I think Eisenhower is the most popular man that we have seen in our time and to make attacks on him in the coming campaign is to me a sure way to commit suicide. Strangely enough, as in Jack's case, when a man is ill and is putting up a good fight, it is almost impossible to generate a feeling against him.

If I were in the councils of the Democratic strategy board, I would have the tone of every speech indicate that you recognize that an Eisenhower who was a well man was doing a great many things of which you highly approved. Remember, Sarge, that you are going into an atmosphere where over 65 million persons are working and getting better pay than ever before, and while the farmer is complaining, it's a fantastic thing but the people in the country are used to the farmers complaining and while they don't know how much the government does for the farmers, they have a subconscious idea that on the whole they are pretty well taken care of. So you have an economic condition that is excellent; you can't offer anything to anybody from laborer to capitalist that can persuade him that you can do better by him.

In addition to that, as far as the women are concerned, they feel that war is not in the offing at any rate. So no matter how lazy Eisenhower may or may not be, or how inefficient he may or may not be, there are an awful lot of people who are very pleased with their lot. Therefore, I am convinced that Eisenhower is not the man to attack. I would concede that perhaps if he were a well man, or even as Truman says, were a full-time President instead of a part-time President, his efforts might prove beneficial to the United States; but — and here I stress the nub of my thinking — he isn't a well man and

---

316. Averell Harriman had been elected governor of New York in 1954.
317. In the early morning hours of June 9, 1956, the president had been operated on to clear an intestinal obstruction; in September 1955 he had suffered a mild heart attack in his sleep.

every family in the United States that has had sickness in its house suspects that it is being kidded when the bulletins from the White House insinuate that Eisenhower is a better man as a result of his operation than he was before.

Now, mind you, Sarge, the issues in this campaign, as in most Presidential campaigns, are never thoroughly understood by the public. How can any normal person who has just the ordinary interest in government arrive at any clear thinking on what's good or bad in policy when you find the Democrats, through Mr. Truman, asking for credit for NATO, for the Marshall Plan, for the stopping of the Communists in the Far East by the Korean War; when a few years later they read that NATO is getting weaker, that all the countries that were recipients of Marshall Plan aid are on the verge of real economic difficulties and inflation; that unrest is rampant in the Middle East; that Japan is restless under the economic barriers of the West; that real suspicion is still in the minds of the people that if Adenauer[318] should die the Western Germans would start talking to the Eastern Germans and we might well finish up with a neutral Germany.

These are only some of the problems that confuse the mind of the American public. Therefore, the campaign must be on a level that they can understand, and what I think they can understand is that the problems of the United States are enormous; that it requires all the energies of a well man to carry the burden.

In addition, I would base my entire campaign on the possibility that Mr. Nixon would become President if anything happened to Eisenhower; that Mr. Eisenhower's physical condition cannot constantly keep him able to force Mr. Dulles[319] to bring out an imaginative foreign policy and not one that has constantly caused us to lose ground. Constant motion is not the answer to diplomacy. That Mr. Eisenhower is not going to be strong enough to constantly keep Mr. Wilson[320] on his toes so that there are not public rows between the three forces of the Defense Department — the Army, Navy and Air; that in spite of the fact that Mr. Eisenhower is a soldier, something has happened because he cannot give it all the time and the energy of a well man to see that Mr. Wilson does not permit the United States to drop behind Russia in guided missiles and the latest bombers.

Mr. Eisenhower must be well in order to keep an even balance between Mr. Humphrey of the Treasury[321] and Mr. Martin of the Federal Reserve Board[322] to make sure that the row over tight money does not result in such cheap money that the paralysis of inflation will attack us. Mr. Eisenhower must be a very well man to forbid Mr. Stassen[323] from making the concessions on East-West trade that have turned out to be most devastating to our position. Mr. Eisenhower must be very well to see that Mr. Brownell[324] does not play politics, such as the suit against General Motors over a sponsored television show.

However strange it may sound, I would not try to enumerate the things that are wrong with Nixon, because that, to me, would be a glaring weakness. I have asked

318. Konrad Adenauer (1876–1967), chancellor of West Germany, 1949–1963.
319. John Foster Dulles (1888–1959), secretary of state, 1953–59, and elder brother of CIA Director Allen Welsh Dulles.
320. The outspoken secretary of defense, 1953–57, and former General Motors executive, 1928–52, Charles Erwin "Engine Charlie" Wilson (1890–1961), had coined the phrase, "What's good for General Motors is good for America."
321. George Magoffin Humphrey (1890–1970), secretary of the treasury, 1953–57.
322. William McChesney Martin (1906–98), chairman of the Federal Reserve, 1951–70.
323. The former Minnesota governor and repeated presidential candidate, Harold Edward Stassen (1907–), had been named special assistant to the president for Disarmament in 1955.
324. Herbert Brownell (1904–96), attorney general, 1953–57.

people now for a year why they don't like Nixon and why they would hate to see him President. Strangely enough, very, very few people give you a satisfactory answer. Don't you remember the night that Marshall Field and Jack Knight[325] were in your apartment and I asked them the same question and they both admitted they were trying to get that answer from a lot of people and never with much success.

But the fact remains, rightly or wrongly, that the great mass of independents do not like him. I suggest that you just hold up the spectre of Nixon as President and don't try to dot the i's or cross the t's. This can be one of the most important factors.

Everyone imagines that the attack is going to be on Nixon. Why? Because he called the Democrats communists? That's nonsense! Maybe you've got some idea of your own about this but I would say that outside of constantly reiterating that Nixon has a reasonable chance of becoming President of the United States, and ask, "How would you like that?" I wouldn't try to prove anything else.

In short, I would never attack Eisenhower; I would feel sorry that he is a part-time President because of illness, which everybody understands; that the men without him in full physical vigor have demonstrated nothing whatsoever, either economically or internationally that will secure the future for our children. This is the kind of campaign that the Republicans will not expect; this is the kind of campaign that is most difficult to answer.

I would also get the Stevenson Advisory Council to analyze the columns of Reston,[326] Lippman and the Alsops over the last year and a half for the purpose of demonstrating that you must have a well man for President; that the Government cannot cooperate in this day and age, particularly with the crowd that is operating, and be a success.

Now it strikes me that this will get the Democrats back in the fold and a great percentage of the independents. The independents follow these columnists and when you use them for authority, you are getting strong backing for your arguments.

Also remember that the Democrats starting off will have trouble getting anywhere near enough money to compete with the Republicans, but the minute "The Money" recognizes a campaign that is starting to appeal to the masses, there will be a sudden shift, I am sure.

Now this is rather long-winded but these are my thoughts. To follow any other line, I believe that while Stevenson and Jack would certainly do better than the last time, they will not win.

Three things to sum up:

1. Don't attack Eisenhower; feel sorry for him.

2. Don't attack Nixon unless you have specific points that would shock the independent voter. He thinks badly enough of him as it is. All you have to do is constantly remind him that he might be President.

3. Prove to the American public that what is happening economically and internationally promises no security for our children.

With my warmest personal regards.

Sincerely,

Joseph P. Kennedy

---

325. John Shively Knight (1894–1981), founder and chairman of the board of the Knight (later Knight-Ridder) newspaper empire.

326. A former *New York Times* foreign correspondent in London during JPK's ambassadorship, the Scottish-born political reporter and columnist James Barrett "Scotty" Reston (1909–95), who would be widely acclaimed upon his death as the most influential reporter of his generation, had become Washington bureau chief in 1953, and in 1957 would be awarded his second Pulitzer Prize.

Joseph P. Kennedy to Edward Kennedy, 24

July 18, 1956

Dear Ted:

Glad to hear everything is exciting but be careful.

You were accepted for Virginia Law School session to start September 14th.

If you like, send your article to me here. I will whip it up and sent it to Joe Smith in New York, if you wish.

Talked to Jack twice. After conversation with Bill Blair[327] on Cape on Sunday, he is giving serious consideration to the job. Last night, however, he was worried because the New York EVENING POST was coming out with an article that said he had Addison's disease. I told him he should co-operate with the reporter and admit that he had it but that the disease was not a killer as it was eight years ago, and I feel that it should be brought out now and not after he gets the nomination, if he gets it. He thought he might come over for a week to talk things over, but I doubt it.

Eunice is still handing out salami sandwiches on dry lettuce with rice pudding for dessert. Not having you and Jean to charge it to, it's really tough. Eunice is chairman of convention reception committee for all women at the delegation, so she is going back to Chicago with Ethel and Jean. Mother leaves for a week or ten days in Switzerland tomorrow. No news from Bobby so evidently there is to be no further investigations this summer.

Take good care of your pictures and your motion pictures. They will be handy for a lot of lectures, if you want to give them.

Very small crowd at the Riviera, but weather is very good. Keep that American flag all over the car but learn to duck.

Good luck and love from us all.

Love,

Joseph P. Kennedy to John F. Kennedy

July 23, 1956

Dear Jack:

I am enclosing a letter I received from Sarge. I came to a couple of conclusions. Here they are:

1) Stevenson is going to nominate his own Vice President when he gets the nominations. 2) He's definitely worried about your health, and if the other papers pick up the *Evening Post* article, that will be his excuse, if he wants it. 3) When you see what he wants the Vice President to do, you can decide how attractive it is.

I have two thoughts in mind: If you make up your mind that you either don't want it or that you are not going to get it, before either of these things happen, you should get out a statement to the effect that representing Mass. is one of the greatest jobs in the world, and there is lots to be done for your state and her people, and while you are most grateful for the national support offered you for the Vice Presidency, your heart belongs to Massachusetts. In your own words this should get out in order to have the proper effect for your candidacy two years from now, if nothing happens on the V.P.

327. William McCormick Blair, Jr. (1916–), a partner in the firm of Stevenson, Rifkind & Wirtz, 1955–61; Governor Adlai Stevenson's former administrative assistant, 1950–52; and future U.S. ambassador to both Denmark, 1961–64, and the Philippines, 1964–67.

Now if you don't see how this opportunity offers itself, because you want to ride the thing through to see whether you can get it, why couldn't I give an interview here in France to either Joe Smith of the INS, or the New York TIMES reporter, arranged by Krock or Jimmy Reston, in answer to the Periscope article in which I might say something like this:

I stand prepared to back my son's decision whatever it may be. My own impression, however, is that his choice is being swayed by his heart and his head. His devotion to Massachusetts and its people has made him most reluctant to accept any position until he has done everything he possibly can for that state. On the other hand, he has a loyalty to his friends in the leadership of the Democratic Party who feel that his record and his integrity and ability would be of great assistance to the Democratic ticket. When he does, I stand ready to support him in whatever his decision may be, and if he is nominated by his party, I am dead sure he will give a fine account of himself.

I think this statement should be got out by either you or me in some way or another the minute you make up your mind that you are not going to try the V.P. so that the full good effect will accrue to you. You or I might both add that being a U. S. Senator from Massachusetts is the finest position any young man could aim for.

Love,

Joseph P. Kennedy to Morton Downey

August 24, 1956

Dear Morton:

It would be silly for me to thank you for your kind and thoughtful note about Jack, but it would not be silly for me to thank you for all the trouble you went to as a result of my telephone calls.

Jack arrived here very tired but I think very happy because he came out of the convention so much better than anyone could have hoped. As far as I am concerned, you know how I feel — if you're going to get licked, get licked trying for the best, not the second best. His time is surely coming![328]

I am leaving here in another week or so and will be in New York on the 11th of September and I am most anxious to see you and talk everything over.

My love to Peg and you and the children.

Sincerely,

Joseph P. Kennedy to Henry Luce

Palm Beach, April 12, 1957

Dear Harry:

In cleaning out my 1933 files, I came across this receipt. You see, even twenty-four years ago when Jack was at the ripe old age of fifteen, I thought he should be reading "Time."

Could it be that the diligent support of this idea has made him as smart as he is?

Best always,
Joseph P. Kennedy

---

328. On August 17, Jack had lost the vice presidential nomination to Estes Kefauver on the second ballot.

Joseph P. Kennedy to Jean Kerr McCarthy: *Telegram*

SHOCKED AND DEEPLY GRIEVED TO HEAR OF JOE'S PASSING.[329] HIS INDOMITABLE
COURAGE IN ADHERING TO THE CAUSE IN WHICH HE BELIEVED EVOKED MY WARM
ADMIRATION. HIS FRIENDSHIP WAS DEEPLY APPRECIATED AND RECIPROCATED.
ROSE AND I EXTEND TO YOU OUR HEARTFELT PRAYERS, OUR DEEPEST SYMPATHY
AND OUR WARM AFFECTION.

SINCERELY,

JOSEPH KENNEDY

Joseph P. Kennedy to John F. Kennedy

ANTIBES, July 26, 1957

Dear Jack,

I quite understand your feeling about mixing in on anything that Senator Byrd[330]
is interested in. He is too nice a fellow, and I'm sure he'll be one of your good friends. It
does occur to me, however, that he has not yet pin-pointed this inflation idea, and as
Sarge said in his letter, Houser might furnish some magnificent material. I think it's
worth while trying to think up some way of getting into the picture before some of
those lightweights on Byrd's committee preempt the field. I am as sure of this subject as
I have ever been of anything in my career.

I went over and saw Beaverbrook the other day, and he told me that Britain's foreign trade was its best ever, but that he and the Powers That Be had grave misgivings
that inflation would soon destroy the whole setup. He regards the prospect most seriously. He said France is very rich, but most of its money has been shipped out of the
country to Switzerland to avoid inflation.

He said Harry Luce called on him about two weeks ago and said he was confident
that you would get the Democratic Nomination, and that he himself felt, to show he
had no feelings of bigotry, he would have to vote for you. Max thinks from his conversations with important people such as Sulzberger that your chances are better than
ever. He also told me that Sulzberger had written him that at a luncheon at the *Times*,
Stafford Cripps had said that he had come around to Beaverbrook's point of view on the
Marshall plan; that it was one of the worst things that had ever happened to England.
He has written Sulzberger for permission to quote, and expects to get it. He also said
that Harry was thinking lots less of Eisenhower and Dulles. He feels that the rest of the
world think we want to do the right thing, but we just don't know how. The Hoffa decision stunned me, as I'm sure it did all of you.[331] I think it is time to start some fireworks.

I am enclosing Teddy's last letter. Please have Bobby read them all.

Love to all,

---

329. McCarthy had died of acute hepatitis on May 3.

330. Harry Flood Byrd, Sr. (1887–1966), U.S. senator from Virginia, 1933–65; Finance Committee chairman, 1955–65; and chairman of the Joint Committee on Reduction of Nonessential Federal Expenditures, 1941–65. In the wake of the 1954 *Brown v. Board of Education* decision, Byrd had spearheaded
congressional resistance to integration.

331. International Brotherhood of Teamsters' executive board member James Riddle "Jimmy" Hoffa
(1913–75?) had been acquitted of charges of attempting to bribe a Senate staffer for access to the files
of the Senate Select Committee on Improper Activities in the Labor or Management Field. "There was
pandemonium in the courtroom for a few moments until marshals shouted the crowd into silence,"
the *New York Times* reported on July 20, when the verdict was announced. The committee (of which
Jack was a member, and Bobby chief counsel) had been investigating Hoffa and IBT President Dave
Beck for some months for their connections to organized crime.

Joseph P. Kennedy to McGeorge Bundy[332]

Palm Beach, February 11, 1958

My dear Dean Bundy:

I am sure that Jack has told you how I feel about Harvard and perhaps, it is strange, but what Harvard is doing for Jack has not changed my opinion one iota.

I will be very happy, however, to meet with you when I come back to Florida in April and point out possibly some things that Jack has not told you.

In my younger days, I started off by giving $25,000 to Harvard in my enthusiasm. I have lost my enthusiasm and I am quite sure that I will never regain it; however, I would be very happy to visit with you because I knew you when you were a very small boy and a very smart one and if you want to take the time to visit with me, I will be very happy to see you.

Very sincerely yours,
Joseph P. Kennedy

Joseph P. Kennedy to John F. Kennedy

Palm Beach, March 7, 1958

Dear Jack:

I think that the speech is great![333]

There are a couple of things to bear in mind. The fact that the entire audience is not made up of Washington newsmen is important because the guests will be a little slower on the uptake. That is why I have made a question of several points — for one of two reasons: either that the crowd wouldn't get it or the people whom you are talking about may consider it a little rough.

To be terribly successful, you must get yourself plenty of laughs. A lot of this is so very fast that you would have to tell it very slowly, with accent on the point and give them all a chance to laugh before passing on to the next one.

You ordinarily tell a story very well, but this is a crowd that can be entertained very easily if you keep smiling whenever you take a crack.

I am sure that you have a fine speech here.

Love,

Joseph P. Kennedy to John Knight

Palm Beach, March 11, 1958

Dear Jack:

There are no words to dispel your feelings at this time and there is no time that will ever dispel them.[334] Nor is it any easier the second time than it was the first. And yet, I cannot share your grief because no one could share mine.

When one of your children goes out of your life, you think of what he might have done with a few more years and you wonder what you are going to do with the rest of yours. You never really accept it; you just go through the motions.

---

332. McGeorge Bundy (1919–86), Jack's childhood schoolmate and future National Security adviser, was currently both teaching government and serving as dean of the Faculty of Arts and Sciences at Harvard.
333. He refers probably to Jack's speech before the Quincy Chamber of Commerce, scheduled for March 10.
334. The publisher's thirty-year-old son, Frank McLain Knight, had died following brain surgery on March 9.

Then one day, because there is a world to be lived in, you find yourself a part of it again, trying to accomplish something — something that he did not have time enough to do.

And, perhaps, that is the reason for it all.

I hope so.

Sincerely,

Joseph P. Kennedy to Edward Kennedy, 26

May 2, 1958

Dear Teddy:

If you're going to make the political columns, let's stay out of the gossip columns.

Love,

Joseph P. Kennedy to J. Edgar Hoover

Hyannis Port, May 7, 1958

Dear Edgar:

Bill Carpenter called me up this morning and asked me if I had noticed some newspaper-syndicated articles of May 5 regarding the Mike Wallace interview of Cyrus Eaton on Sunday night.[335]

I said that I had not seen them and if I had seen them, I would not have read them because anything which emanates from Mike Wallace and Cyrus Eaton automatically establishes itself as unreliable.

Bill read some of the quotes to me and I think that the only people who could find one iota of truth in any of his statements are unsympathetic to our Government. For one Wallace or Eaton, you could find millions of high-standing Americans who would deny every one of his allegations. It could be that Eaton has not recovered from entertaining the Russian Ambassador at his home a couple of weeks ago.

I am sure that you are mad enough to make fifty answers; but I am also sure that you would only be giving publicity to statements which, I am positive, have gone almost completely unnoticed. I felt just as indignant when the Wallace interview with Drew Pearson permitted Pearson to say that somebody else had written Jack's *Profiles in Courage*. I was for suing Pearson up hill and down dale in every community in the United States that had an ABC station; but the apology from ABC calmed me down.

And all the advice at that time was, "Forget it; if people don't know Jack well enough to know that he would never be a party to this, then you are wasting your time and your money to try and persuade them that Jack is worthwhile."

Certainly, with your personal record and the reputation of the F.B.I., no statement of yours is necessary. Five million Cyrus Eatons could not do you or the F.B.I. one bit of harm. Eaton has not good enough reputation — even amongst his own associates — to justify your losing one minute's sleep.

I repeat what I have said so many times before: This is the greatest organization in

---

335. On May 4 the Cleveland industrialist had told interviewer Mike Wallace that American freedoms were imperiled by government agencies involved "in investigating, in snooping, in informing, in creeping up on people . . . Hitler in his prime, through the Gestapo, never had any such spy organization as we have in this country today."

the Government and you have performed the greatest public service of any man that I know.

Best to you always.

Sincerely,
Joseph P. Kennedy

Rose Kennedy to Joseph P. Kennedy

June 19, 1958

Dear Joe:

Please do not change anything while I am away and do not add anything like the fire escape which spoils the view and the breeze.

Please do not redistribute the land as no one likes the Tenney[336] fence.

And please do not buy any more furniture.

Barbara can explain that.

Much love,

John F. Kennedy to Eleanor Roosevelt

PERSONAL United States Senate, Washington, D.C. December 11, 1958

Dear Mrs. Roosevelt:

I note from the press that on last Sunday afternoon, December 7, on the ABC television program College News Conference, you stated, among other things, that Senator Kennedy's "father has been spending oodles of money all over the country and probably has a paid representative in every state by now."

Because I know of your long fight against the injudicious use of false statements, rumors or innuendo as a means of injuring the reputation of an individual, I am certain that you are the victim of misinformation; and I am equally certain that you would want to ask your informant if he would be willing to name me one such representative or one such example of any spending by my father around the country on my behalf.

I await your answer, and that of your source, with great interest. Whatever other differences we may have had, I'm certain that we both regret this kind of political practice.[337]

Sincerely yours,
John F. Kennedy

John F. Kennedy to Eleanor Roosevelt

PERSONAL December 29, 1958

Dear Mrs. Roosevelt:

Thank you for your letter of December 18, 1958. I am disappointed that you now seem to accept the view that simply because a rumor or allegation is repeated it be-

---

336. Their Hyannisport neighbors.
337. "If my comment is not true," the former first lady would respond on December 18, "I will gladly so state. I was told that your father said openly he would spend any money to make his son the first Catholic President of this country, and many people as I travel about tell me of money spent by him in your behalf. This seems commonly accepted as fact."

681

comes "commonly accepted as a fact." It is particularly inexplicable to me inasmuch as, as I indicated in my last letter, my father has not spent any money around the country, and has *no* "paid representatives" for this purpose in *any* state of the union — nor has my father *ever* made the statement you attributed to him — and I am certain no *evidence* to the contrary has ever been presented to you.

I am aware, as you must be, that there are a good many people who fabricate rumors and engage in slander about any person in public life. But I have made it a point never to accept or repeat such statements unless I have some concrete evidence of their truth.

Since my letter to you, I assume you have requested your informants to furnish you with more than their gossip and speculation. If they have been unable to produce concrete evidence to support their charges or proof of the existence of at least one "paid representative" in one state of the union, I am confident you will, after your investigation, correct the record in a fair and gracious manner. This would be a greatly appreciated gesture on your part and it would be consistent with your reputation for fairness.

Sincerely yours,
John F. Kennedy

Joseph P. Kennedy to Enrico Galeazzi

Palm Beach, March 18, 1959

Dear Enrico,

We have been a little stirred up by some rather bitter attacks on Jack by Catholic papers as a result of LOOK magazine's article on him.[338] I dare say that you have received the clippings from Cardinal Spellman.

Cardinal Cushing,[339] however, came out and defended Jack and at least for the time being, the noise has subsided. The only result of it can be to knock a Catholic out of a chance of getting the big job. It is the same kind of pettiness we spoke about in connection with bishops and archbishops saying a Catholic could not win. They don't deserve to have a President. I myself am thoroughly disgusted and if I were Jack, I would tell them all to go jump in the lake and call it quits.

Do I understand that I definitely will have the Mercedes Benz for sometime in July? As I have not heard anything from you about my letter of February 12 regarding the car and the appointments in Rome, I wondered if you had received it all right.

There was also an article this week in LOOK on the present Pope. After reading it, I just marveled at how stupid people can get in not realizing how great Pius XII was.

At any rate, we can only get the proper perspective when we talk together again. My best to you always.

Your affectionate friend,

---

338. "Whatever one's religion in his private life may be," Jack had been quoted as saying in *Look* magazine's recent feature, "A Catholic in 1960," "for the officeholder, nothing takes precedence over his oath to uphold the Constitution and all its parts—including the First Amendment and the strict separation of church and state."
339. Richard James Cardinal Cushing (1895–1970), archbishop of Boston, 1944–70.

Joseph P. Kennedy to Enrico Galeazzi

Palm Beach, March 30, 1959

Dear Enrico,

You have a better understanding of Jack's problem than most of the Catholics in America have. Long before this discussion came up, you and I talked a great deal about the lack of support of the Catholics for Jack's candidacy. It has been there all along.

Robert Frost, the great poet of America, said last Friday when asked at a press conference, that he favored Senator Kennedy for President and that he was amazed at the lack of enthusiasm among the Catholics.

Notre Dame with Father Hesburgh,[340] and Frank Folsom are two of the group that I will never forgive or forget. In fact, I am more than ordinarily bitter about the whole subject. I doubt very much if my relations with the Church and the hierarchy, with the exception of Cardinal Cushing, will ever be the same.

I really do not care now whether Jack is elected President or not and I have told him so. I certainly will never ask the hierarchy for anything ever again — not that I have ever asked them for much. And I have always been anxious to do everything I could, but that also has ceased. I just believe that they do not deserve to improve their position one single bit.

Now, as to the car.[341] If it is not too much trouble, perhaps you would write to Mr. Hrones and arrange with him about the plate and the insurance or whatever has to be arranged. I hate to ask you to do this, but it saves your writing to me and then, my writing to Hrones. I have written him today and told him that he might hear from you.

I am really looking forward to seeing you and talking with you, but I am not interested in talking to anybody else. Fortunately, I wrote you that before this controversy arose, so it is not sour grapes.

I will write to you later as to just when I will get down to Rome, if you think that it is all right. Otherwise, I would meet you at the Riviera where you might come with your Marisa and spend a weekend with us. We have been hoping to have you down for a long time. It might be better if you came there rather than my going to Rome at all.

My best to you always.

Your affectionate friend,

Joseph P. Kennedy to Enrico Galeazzi

Palm Beach, April 17, 1959

Dear Enrico,

First of all, thank you for writing to Hrones and if there is any hitch, why let me know because I do not want you to add any bother to your present chores.

I value your suggestions and advice, but I am really more than annoyed or upset — I am downright disgusted! And I do not imagine that anything is ever going to change that. I deplore the pettiness of the hierarchy for not speaking out, at least in some measure, in Jack's defense.

340. Theodore Martin Hesburgh (1917–), the influential president of Notre Dame, 1952–87, with whom JPK had been on cordial terms throughout the early fifties; JPK had made a number of significant contributions to the institution in recent years.

341. Galeazzi had been deputized to organize JPK's transportation during the latter's planned summertime stay on the Riviera.

I have had time to think it over and quiet down—if I were ever going to quiet down—but I know now that I never will. As I have said to you in my last letter, I really do not care whether or not Jack runs and I am satisfied that Jack is less affected than I am by it all, but he is definitely upset.

No man running for the Presidency of the United States could have said less. It was just an excuse for a lot of stupid bishops and editors to say out loud what they have been saying privately for the last year and a half.

I have felt for a number of years when I had the opportunity of knowing the Holy Father and you, that the thing which kept me interested to pursue the work that I was pursuing and to do everything that I could for the Church, was my admiration and respect for both of you. I never need see any further evidence that when one is dead, a new regime looks most attractive.

It may be very well to have these ideas, but they are not the kind that I was brought up with. I am more than just annoyed or irritated or disgusted — I am all of those things and a great deal more.

You have no idea of how this agitation has developed in the discussions of the so-called Catholic intelligentsia. I was at a meeting the other day with Carmine DeSapio, the New York political leader,[342] and Shanahan, president of one of the banks.[343] And Shanahan told me that at a meeting the other night at the Maryknoll Center, three of the outstanding Catholic laymen were indignant at Jack's speech and on being pressed as to why they were indignant, the answers were so silly and ridiculous that I just gave up.

My relationship with the Church will never be the same and certainly, never the same with the hierarchy. But that will not make any difference to them, I am sure, and I can assure you that it will not make any difference to me. For the few years which I have left, I will indulge myself at least in continuing to believe that friends are friends when you need them.

Please do not upset yourself about my attitude. I would not want anything to annoy you and I will look forward, as I always do, to seeing you and spending some of the pleasantest moments of my life.

With my deep affection, I remain

Sincerely,

Rose Kennedy to John F. Kennedy

June 15, 1959

Dear Jack,

This is just a note to remind you of Church.

Love,

---

342. Carmine Gerard DeSapio (1908–99), New York secretary of state, Democratic National Committee member, Tammany boss and reputed New York kingmaker.
343. Thomas Joseph Shanahan (1902–63), Democratic fund-raiser and president of the Federation Bank and Trust Company, 1944–62.

Rose Kennedy to Jacqueline Bouvier Kennedy

June 15, 1959

Dear Jackie,

I am listing a few things below to help you and to help me:

1- Will you please remind Jack about his Easter duty; I am sure that he could go to confession some morning in Washington as the church is quite near.

2- The bed which I am now using will be moved to your house and you can decide whether or not you want to keep it.

3- Will you ask your decorator for suggestions about reading lamps — one that could be used on a stand. I would like to replace the one by Grandpa's chair in the sun room. It is very ugly and I would like to get something which is better looking.

4- Will you also ask your decorator about "Do Not Disturb" signs. I like the cellophane ones; but it is very difficult to get them. If she has a suggestion about them, I would like to order six.

5- Will you see about some old socks for Jack — for him to wear playing golf or walking in the rain, as he did not have any the other day when he was down here.

6- Please label my blue coat so that it will not be lost (I talked with you about this today.)

Joseph P. Kennedy to Herman Kahn[344]

Palm Beach, Florida, December 21, 1959

Dear Mr. Kahn:

I doubt very much that I have any papers which would be of real service to the Library. The few that I have are probably ones which my family would like to keep.

I have never made an extensive study of my papers because I have never seriously considered writing a book, although it seems to be the fashion nowadays.

If, when I do get a chance to look them over, I think that they would be at all worthwhile in this great library, I would be very glad to take it up with you at that time.

Sincerely yours,
Joseph P. Kennedy

Joseph P. Kennedy to Louis Harris[345]

Palm Beach, December 30, 1959

Dear Lou,

Thank you very much for your Christmas card and for that generous message.

I am very confident of 1960, but no small part of the great problem rests on your own good shoulders. And for my money, it couldn't be in a better place.

Best wishes to you for a Happy New Year.

Sincerely,
Joseph P. Kennedy

344. Khan, the director of the Franklin D. Roosevelt Library, had attempted to persuade JPK to deposit his papers and memoranda there. JPK's papers, including the substantial unpublished Diplomatic Memoir that Jim Landis had finished ghostwriting several years earlier, amount to approximately three hundred linear feet of material.
345. Louis Harris (1921–), pollster and founder of the Louis Harris and Associates marketing and public opinion firm.

Rose Kennedy to Eunice Kennedy Shriver

January 19, 1960

Dear Eunice,

Thank you very much for the radio. As you can imagine, I love it.

Dad went to New York yesterday and Jack returned to Washington. He really hated to leave and he says if he gets licked in Wisconsin, he will lead a lazy, happy life down here.

I do hope that Maria[346] does not go into the elevator by herself. I thought of her again the other day and the idea of her riding up and down in it really disturbs me. And as I have said to you before, it does not look well to people entering the apartment.

Much love, dear, and do come back soon,

Joseph P. Kennedy to Ted Sorenson

Palm Beach, February 24, 1960

Dear Ted:

I continually hear about Nixon's experience and I certainly think for the most part that experience is a term usually used to describe a lifetime of mistakes.

Sincerely,
Joseph P. Kennedy

Joseph P. Kennedy to Enrico Galeazzi

New York, March 9, 1960

Dear Enrico:

I am enclosing some newspaper clippings this morning after the first Primary fight in New Hampshire. Jack did much better than anyone expected him to do.[347] He is still campaigning in Wisconsin where the fight will be on April 5th. That is going to be a real tough fight — but we should win. Then he goes from there to West Virginia where the Catholics total around three or four percent. They may use the religious issue there and it may be very, very tough. In the meantime, those other Primaries will have an effect on the people who are sitting on the side lines to see who they are going to be with. It is very apparent now that if they don't give the nomination to Jack, the Democratic Party is very likely to get licked.

Rose is campaigning in New Hampshire and the girls have been campaigning in Wisconsin. Rose will be out in Wisconsin in another week or ten days. She is still a top campaigner.

Nobody quite understands how Jack is keeping up the terrific pace. He is working harder and demonstrating that he is the best campaigner the United States has ever seen.

I had lunch yesterday with the Cardinal. He is working as hard as ever and is very, very interested in Jack. I think a lot of those who have been on the side lines are amazed by yesterday's performance and may now start to think that maybe he can be elected. I haven't any doubt that the religious issue will be raised acutely — beginning in West Virginia. It will be a very, very difficult fight to win, but I have great confidence in Jack

---

346. Maria Owings Shriver (1955–).
347. He had received 85.2 percent of the vote.

as a campaigner. This will keep on now until some time toward the end of May, and then we will start counting noses and see if we can't get nominated on the second ballot. That is what we are aiming at.

The young lady that I wrote to you about is going to Italy this month with her son. She is going to place him in a school in Switzerland and then look around in Milan. I am sending you some money and would be very grateful if you would give her the benefit of your advice and make available to her the funds necessary to pay her tuition and her living expenses. I hate to bother you about it. We probably can organize it so that after she gets started there, we can put the money into her account and then we will not have to bother with it. As I said to you before, her mother, Dr. Travell[348] has been the means of Jack being in the condition that he is in and of Rose being better now after ten or twelve years of real misery. I feel sure that nothing I can do will make her mother, Dr. Travell, as happy as giving her girl this chance. Her name is Mrs. Janet McAlee. Later in the month I will let you know just what her plans are.

I know that if Jack wins this election, there will be no excuse for your not coming over here to attend the inauguration. You and Marisa will be my own personal chosen guests.

I will keep you posted if there are any sharp changes.

With my love to all,

> *Affectionately yours,*
> *Joseph P. Kennedy*

Joseph P. Kennedy to Lord Beaverbrook

Palm Beach, April 20, 1960

Dear Max,

We have a few troubles in West Virginia. Only about 3 per cent of the state is Catholic, probably the smallest percentage in the United States. And they are passing out religious leaflets up and down the line. The Baptists are the most bigoted group.

The Gallup Poll came out today and showed that Jack is pulling farther and farther ahead of all the other candidates; so that he will have a very good call on the nomination. If he is thrown out because he is a Catholic, I doubt very much if a Democrat will win.

If he gets the nomination, I do not imagine that I will see the Riviera this summer. But I will be expecting you here for the closing weeks. Marion Davies has given me her house in Beverly Hills for the Convention; so if by any chance, you think you would like to see that, why you could stay with me at her house. It might be very exciting.

The next big report will come to you from me on May 11.

> *Your devoted friend,*

Joseph P. Kennedy to Enrico Galeazzi: *Telegram*

MAY 12, 1960

DEAR ENRICO, JACK'S WIN IN WEST VIRGINIA PHENOMENAL.[349] HAS REALLY BEATEN THE RELIGIOUS ISSUE. I AM SURE YOU HAVE ALL THE PAPERS FROM YOUR FRIEND. PROSPECTS EXCELLENT.

JOE

---

348. Heart and musculoskeletal pain specialist Janet Graeme Travell (1901–97) had served as Jack's personal physician since 1955 when she began treating him for back pain in the wake of his spinal fusion. Her treatment included the use of rocking chairs for the alleviation of muscular stress in the back.
349. Jack had won with 60.8 percent of the vote to Humphrey's 39.2 percent.

Joseph P. Kennedy to Lord Beaverbrook

Hyannis Port, May 27, 1960

Dear Max,

Well, the seven primaries are over and we have won an overwhelming victory. Now, we are trying to put the group together. If we can get a break at all in Pennsylvania and a reasonable break in California, we're home.

If I were betting, I would bet that Jack will get the nomination and will have no great difficulty with Nixon. The only thing that will make it possible for Nixon to win is if they steal the nomination from Jack.

I leave for the West around June 10 and will be there until after the convention. Regardless of anything, I am planning on spending some time at Antibes after the convention which should close on July 16. And I expect to arrive at Antibes on July 18 or 19.

Your papers certainly treated Jack handsomely. The only thing troubling me was to have that lovely Miss Leibly of your staff think that Humphrey deserved better than he got. He went into the primaries for no other reason than to head up the stop-Kennedy movement. But I really suspect that she was impressed with his I-don't-know-what.

I had luncheon with Roy Howard the other day. He can't believe that you are coming for the election. And I said, "I don't know why not. He came for ~~his~~ senatorial election and attended a meeting in South Boston, so he certainly can attend some of the meetings that will make the next President of the United States."

And I added to Roy Howard, "He made up his mind whose side he was on a lot earlier than the American newspapers did."

I will be seeing you, I hope, right after I arrive at Antibes.

My best to you always,

Joe

Rose Kennedy: *Diary*

June 23, 1960

Jack on the phone constantly and particularly incensed because Meyner will not come out for him.[350] After dinner, we call up Dad. Strangely enough I had not heard from him for about ten days, and he said that it was in the bag, and that everyone got nervous about these things near the end.

As Jack's mother, I am confident that Jack will win because his father says so, and through the years I have seen his predictions and judgments vindicated, almost without exception. And, so I believe it. He also says, and has said all along, that if Jack gets the nomination he can beat Nixon.

We are all furious at Governor Brown of California[351] and Governor Lawrence of Pennsylvania[352] because they will not come out for Jack now. Their support would clinch the nomination for him. Joe has worked on Lawrence all winter through his

---

350. Robert Baumle Meyner (1908–90), governor of New Jersey, 1954–62, had bound his delegates to his own candidacy on the first ballot.

351. Edmund Gerald "Pat" Brown (1905–96), governor from 1959 to 1967. Although he had thrown his own hat into the presidential ring, leading the California delegation at the convention, Brown would turn over his votes to Jack before the first ballot, but would be unable to stop roughly half of the delegation from supporting Stevenson.

352. David Leo Lawrence (1889–1966), Roman Catholic governor of Pennsylvania and former Pittsburgh mayor and political boss, would eventually deliver sixty-four of Pennsylvania's eighty-one delegates to Jack.

man Rochesky [*sic*][353] who was at Palm Beach. The papers say that the Southern States will not support a Humphrey — Kennedy ticket, because they do not like Humphrey. He is too liberal about money and about the rights of the colored people, and they might bolt, rather than support him. That is a new angle.

Jack is home today. We all went to his house last night. Ethel, Joan, Jackie, and I. He eats ravenously of lobster and corn on the cob. According to Doctor Jordan of the Lahey Clinic, corn and lobster are the worse things for a tummy like I have and like Jack has. The roses are so beautiful now at the Cape. The fogs and the climate here seem exactly right for them. In the paper this morning, there was an article about the superb Kennedy organization. The efficiency with which it is run — the amazing results which it achieves — all this because it is first a purely family team at the center. Jack, his brothers, his brothers-in-law, and the overall strategy of their father, who I doubt will ever get credit for the constant, unremitting labor, day and night which he had devoted to making his son President. He used foresight as well. He sent Bobby on the Stevenson train in 1956 to see what was being done and how. A boring experience for Bob, and one which did not immediately pay off. Joe contacted different political bases from all over the United States during the winter of 1960 at Palm Beach. He went down to Hialeah and the other racing course constantly to have a meeting with various powers, especially with Lawrence of Pennsylvania, who has been one of the most exasperating and tantalizing forces. He did not think a Catholic could be elected.

Jack once was speaking at the Al Smith Dinner, a year or so before election. And Rockefeller was the Governor of New York and also mentioned as a possible Republican candidate for the presidency. I sat in the hall at one of the tables the night of the dinner with members of the family, but Joe would not come with us, but stayed in the back of the hall where he could sense the reactions from the speeches of the two men. ~~and probably because he was nervous.~~ Rockefeller as the governor spoke first. He was dull, ponderous, routine. Jack later spoke and everyone was tired, hot, satiated with food and drink, and in a lethargic mood. But Jack threw in one witticism after another at the immense audience. At the first spark the tired ones raised their heads, at the next they smiled, then they laughed. Then waited expectantly for the next volley and in twenty minutes, Jack had nineteen moments [*sic*] of applause. One of his first public appearances in New York and one which immediately threw into sharp relief the speaking qualifications of the two men.

Rose Kennedy: *"July 14, 1960-Morning After"*[354]

Waiting until Friday night to hear acceptance speech — Everyone said it will be anticlimactic, as there will be no excitement or waving flags or jostling crowds. Probably will transfer it to a smaller hall — Jack took almost an hour to appear last night from time he was nominated until he reached platform — sent for me so Pat & I took bows — Eunice furious to miss limelight but she was downstairs thanking Illinois delegates — Dad stayed at home & saw the whole thing on T.V. — Jack & Dave Powers here at dinner — Cook had an accident & we dined on lamb stew — six grandchildren in box 4 of Ethel's — Chris Lawford, Bobby Shriver & except Kathleen none of them knew what it

353. She seems to refer to Matthew Henry McCloskey (1893–1973), the Democratic Party treasurer, fundraiser, and Philadelphia contractor, who had made several efforts to secure Lawrence's support for Jack's candidacy over recent months, to no avail. McCloskey would be appointed ambassador to Ireland in 1962.

354. Jack had won the party nomination on the first ballot the night before with 806 votes to Johnson's 409.

was about — but evinced fatigue as they had been there for nominating speech, gone home & returned for balloting which was not till about 11 P.M — I had not approved of their coming but thought they should only go to Inauguration but Ethel wants to take them every where — which I feel is big mistake — as they become tired, restless — & the time & money is wasted, as they are too young & immature to understand the events —

Rose Kennedy: *Round-Robin Letter*

[*Antibes*] *August 23, 1960*

Dearest Children:

We received all your letters and have enjoyed them tremendously. We get a lot of news through the clippings and daily papers, the Paris versions of the Herald Tribune and New York Times and keep track of arrivals and departures of your guests. Life has been fairly peaceful since the first devastating bout with the reporters whom we first tried to evade. Then we used football tactics — then hide and seek maneuvers (the French cache cache) and we finally finished by being photographed with a Telescope lens — with Dad looking dangerous and explosive besides.

On arrival at Orly, I tried to use my U.S. Newspaper tactics with the French by being charming and even addressing them in French, explaining that your père was a controversial figure who had stayed out of the campaign at home and preferred to remain out of the picture here. However, since I declined to interview the man from *Time* as I had interviewed his colleague in Paris, he photographed me anyway with a scathing remark about my French although they were the ones who took me in a little car to the studio and begged me to answer the T.V. in French because it was rare that an American spoke French.

In the meantime Dad and Anne[355] were shut up in a little room awaiting the formalities of the Customs, etc.

In Paris at the Ritz, Dad made his exit by a rear door and met us on a street corner in order to avoid them. At Eden Roc, they bribed the personnel in front of our eyes and they hid in the shrubbery where Anne spied their blue shirts and finally they took us swimming with a telescopic lens. They came from England, Italy and Spain and awaited us at the gate by day and on the telephone at night. But now it is finished except for a few letters, seeking interviews.

Myles and his mother with Harold Lloyd Jr. have been at Monte Carlo. Went to the Gala with the three of them, as Dad declined. When I alighted from my little Mercedes, who should be clasping my hand and welcoming me, but Onassis[356] with Myles trailing, grinning weakly. Onassis was so profuse in his greeting and so solicitous about my welfare that I got an idea, he had made plans of his own to have me at his table and be photographed just like that. So, after a quick word to Myles, who admitted the tables had been merely pushed together, I informed Monsieur Onassis I was on my own. He said it was very embarrassing. I replied I could not possibly sit with him and as I had already declined other invitations, I would prefer to go home rather than cause any embarrassment. Whereupon there was a grand upheaval and we finally were placed at a small table on the side of the room. Next, came the maitre d'hotel, who has been a great

---

355. Her niece, Anne Gargan (later King).

356. In 1953 Greek shipping magnate Aristotle Socrates Onassis (1906–75) had bought up a controlling interest in the *Société des Bains de Mer,* the organization operating the Monte Carlo gambling concessions.

friend of Dad's for years. He was terribly excited and abashed — said he did not know I was in Myles' party and that I could not sit in that obscure corner and that I must be changed at once — which was finally accomplished. Fortunately, the photographers were busy with Princess Grace and missed all this. You probably read in the *Herald Tribune* — Eugenia Sheppard column — about the party. If not, read it. I am enclosing it for Pat.

I went to Paris, August 8th, on the fast Caravelle (one hour 25 minutes) with breakfast aboard. Everyone glad to see me, but no special collection. Saw Jayne Wrightsman,[357] who is here at Cap Ferrat now, visiting Mary Lasker.[358] She, as so many others, is going home early this year, in fact at the end of this week. Myles goes in September — early.

While I was in Paris, Onassis sent me four dozen red roses with a note regretting any embarrassment which he caused me — so what will he do next year?

Dad has been golfing and feeling fairly well. He entertained the crew and the officers of the destroyer named after Joe at a dinner last Friday and Saturday nights. We went to Vence, the ancient town way up in the hills and had the best dinner — best for me as I was even eating fish. Probably the story was written up at home. The officers had a lunch aboard for Anne and Dad while I was in Paris.

Gina Breed[359] telephoned from Monte Carlo and wanted me to go to Salzburg for the last week of the Festival, but I decided I had better not leave again, although I would like to go. Said the new Opera House opening was sensational.

Callas was at Monte Carlo sitting opposite Onassis and she is said to have had her nose fixed, but it still looked big and homely to me and Myles. Jayne said she (Jayne) and Charles stayed at Chatsworth which now is very attractive in the wing, which Debo redecorated, and Charles said the service was pluperfect. Marie Bruce is coming down next week. Galeazzi came up from Rome for a day. His daughter has remarried and is expecting a child in October. The Agnellis have been in Monte Carlo, but are going to Greece.

White eyelet embroidery shirts are the latest craze instead of the Italian ones, but I do not find them half so pretty.

I guess this is all the news from here. I leave for Paris August 29th where I expect to see Joan. Shall be home September 21st if Jack needs me. If not, I shall go to Vienna. Shall look for Eunice's coat later. Did not see one yet. Ethel has been wonderful about bringing children to Great Grandma, I hear, and appreciate it so much. Much, much love to all and remember you all are so lucky to have plenty of work to do because Myles really gets bored over here and does not know whether to go to Biarritz — where it rains, or to Paris where his mother is, or Monte Carlo where nothing is like the old days, except Jessie Donahue.[360]

Write soon if you expect any presents.

Affectionately,
G. Ma

Plans changed as Bob says I am in great demand as a speaker — so home early.

357. Jayne Larkin Wrightsman, philanthropist, fine art collector and Palm Beach friend of Rose's. She was the wife of petroleum producer, art collector, philanthropist and Palm Beach neighbor of the Kennedys, Charles Wrightsman (1895–1986).
358. Medical philanthropist, urban beautification advocate and art collector, Mary Woodard Lasker (1900–94).
359. Eugenie Grigorcea Breed (1892–1974), socialite, music patron and wife of William Breed, a partner of the New York law firm of Breed, Abbott & Morgan.
360. Jessie Woolworth Donahue (d. 1971), socialite and one of the three daughters of Frank W. Woolworth (1852–1919), the five- and ten-cent chain founder.

Joseph P. Kennedy to Lord Beaverbrook

September 9, 1960

Dear Max,

I was sorry to see you only once on my visit to the Riviera, but I had the idea that you had a lot of things on your mind; so, I did not want to bother you.

I came home to find the campaign not between a Democrat and a Republican, but between a Catholic and a Protestant. How effectively we can work against it, I do not know. Jack gave it a bad licking in West Virginia and we are confident that we can lick it now. But with the Baptist ministers working in the pulpit every Sunday, it is going to be tough.

All I can say is that they have a hell of a nerve to be talking about freedom for the world when we have this kind of a condition right here in our own country. It seems to me that it is more important than ever to fight this thing with everything we have. And that is what we are going to do.

When will you be over? I will be anxious to see you and talk with you.

My best as always,

Joe

Joseph P. Kennedy to Dr. J. A. H. Walker

Dear Dr. Walker:

Thank you very much for your letter.

Hope that the deadly jinx does not follow Mr. Kennedy or Mr. Nixon.

I quite agree that there are many, many people following Astrology, and of course we would very much like to have as many as possible feel that John will help America recover its leading world position.

Very sincerely,

Joseph P. Kennedy

Joseph P. Kennedy to Walter Trohan[361]

October 22, 1960

Dear Walter:

My blood pressure has gone up since receipt of your note of October 13. When NBC and NEWSWEEK prophesy Kennedy's election, I remain rather calm, but when Walter Trohan of the Chicago *Tribune* does, I'm flying.

I haven't been seeing the *Tribune* for many a day, but Eunice reads it every day and manages to keep calmer than she does when she reads the *Sun Times*, on the theory that you expect the Tribune to be very pro-Republican, but the *Sun Times* is rather like a Sunday school teacher being caught in a brothel raid.

I don't think there is really as much reason to be disturbed as a lot of people think there is about Jack's financial policies. Republicans for the most part have always been leery of any Democrat who is President. But, Walter, you and I remember that after the closing of the banks in '33, the bankers were begging Roosevelt to take them over, and

---

361. Walter Joseph Trohan (1903–), *Chicago Tribune* Washington correspondent, 1934–48, and bureau chief, 1949–69. It was Trohan who had broken White House secretary Stephen Early's story of Roosevelt's irritation at Ambassador Kennedy's political letters and "presidential boomlet" in June 1938.

it was Roosevelt who told them to hold their horses and continue as a private enterprise.

I don't know how Jack's plans are after the election, but I should think the last thing he would want to do for quite a little while is to make another speech. Between sessions of the Senate, fight on the Labor bills, his own campaign in '58, and his traveling throughout the country for his Presidential hopes, I think the time has come when he should settle down for a rest. However, I am sure he has other ideas, so he may land in Chicago. He likes challenges.

Don't be too tough on us the next two weeks, because you know and I know the country would be a damn sight better off with Kennedy than it would be with Nixon.

Best personal regards.

Sincerely,
Joseph P. Kennedy

Joseph P. Kennedy to Phyllis Long

October 22, 1960

My dear Mrs. Long:

I am very sorry that your letter of September 25 caught up with me only a week ago.

I have made a habit all my life of never giving advice on the stock market. I have seen many so-called experts try to advise some of their close friends of what said expert was doing, and my experience over 45 years has been that rarely, if ever, did the advice do the friend any good.

Second, if I had three small children and $10,000 to invest, I would certainly not consider putting it into the stock market. To make any money to be of any value in educating your children, you would have to make a play in some terribly risky enterprise, which certainly would be altogether too much of a gamble according to my ideas.

One of the greatest stock market operators I ever knew of was a man named Galen Stone. He operated at a time when it was legal to operate so-called stock market pools. Yet, he told me that over a period of 40 years he would have been just as well off it he had invested his money at 5%.

I am sure that if you had had this $10,000 invested over the last year, while the stock market has been going down, you would be a very unhappy young mother.

I am taking the time to write you this letter personally, because I think that a young mother, and the wife of a Lieutenant in our Army with three young children, should at least get the best advice I can give.

Sincerely yours,
Joseph P. Kennedy

Rose Kennedy: *Diary*

November 3, 1959 [1960]

We went to the airport Thursday to see Jack off to California on his private plane. The first time I had seen it. Jean was aboard with Steve.[362] Dave Powers, who goes to give Jack a few laughs and to look after his clothes.[363] It is the first time Dave has gone,

---

362. Stephen Edward Smith (1927–90), whom Jean had married in 1956.
363. David Francis Powers (1911–98), Jack's confidant, assistant and jack-of-all trades since the congressional election of 1946.

as he has a very possessive wife who will not let him out of her sight even for lunch, or sometimes even for breakfast with Jack, not to mention a dinner date. Joe has always had someone like a court jester around him, someone witty, light hearted; but faithful, loyal, and with sense enough to keep his mouth closed under all circumstances. And I think that Jack hoped that Dave Powers would fill this particular need in his life. Pat is to join the party out in California as Jackie is not going until Friday, because she is taking care of Caroline.

Jack looks unusually well. His cheeks have filled out amazingly since I saw him in June. He has lost that lean Lincolnesque look which I secretly like better.

Janet, our former secretary, is on the plane as hostess. She is neat, trim, efficient, enthusiastic, intelligent, experienced on account of her long apprenticeship with us.

The plane has been an inestimable help to Jack, as he has been able to cover the great distances, which would have been impossible to do if he had had to fit his schedule to the plane schedules. And he has saved himself wear and tear, as he has not had to hurry or become agitated about catching a plane when he was at a conference. And, of course, the plane often flew all during the night while he slept.

It was his Father's idea and his generosity which made it possible. But his father said he had risked a million dollars before on an adventure which he considered much less worthwhile than risking it on Jack's campaign, so why not on this campaign. And the primaries had been very expensive. Jack resents mention of his father's wealth and of his health, as witness the other evening, when he said he did not like Ruth Montgomery,[364] a journalist, who had written an article about Grandma[365] and me. And then he finished off after summarizing what I had done in the campaign by words like these, "Pa Kennedy stays at home and pulls a few strings too." These remarks annoyed Jack, as remarks of Grandpa Fitzgerald used to annoy Joe in the old days.

Again the night of the nomination when we were in California staying at Marion Davies' house. We all went into the convention except Joe who said that he would rather be at home and look at it in the living room and over television, so we all went off. Pat was on the floor with the California delegates, I was in one of the boxes with Eunice and the grandchildren. Later I was called to the platform with Jack and stood next to him while everyone cheered and waved. Jackie was not there as she was awaiting the birth of John-John. I suppose that it was one of the proudest moments of my life. However, Joe stayed at home away from the plaudits of the crowd, out of the range of the newspaper photographers. However, at Inauguration Day, he sat proudly in the box when the parade was going by and was joined later by Jack when he and Johnson sat on the reviewing stand.

Rose Kennedy to Ethel Skakel Kennedy

December 1, 1960

Dear Ethel:

While I was there, I talked quite a bit to the children separately about Thanksgiving and also about Mass.

Joe seemed to know quite a little about it.

I think in the future it might be well to review history and current events with him so that he may remember facts in that way. You might ask him questions like who the

364. Ruth Shick Montgomery (1912–), columnist for the King Features Syndicate and the Hearst Headline Service, 1958–68.
365. Her mother.

president of France is; what holidays are national holidays or church holidays, or both; the name of the Queen of England, etc.

This will give you an idea of our discussions.

Love,

Joseph P. Kennedy to Ernest Lindley[366]

December 9, 1960

Dear Ernest:

I don't think I have ever got so far behind in my correspondence as I have these last weeks. But with Jack's office force having taken about 45,000 telegrams and thousands and thousands of letters, mine finally got sifted out, and I get them now.

All I can say to you is that maybe there was a little more excitement in this campaign, but I can assure you it wasn't half as much fun as we witnessed in our cross-country runs in the '32 campaign.

I got very nice notes from Walter Trohan and our friend, Walter Brown,[367] and I really got a terrific kick out of both of them.

You, as well as anyone in the United States, know what the problems are that Jack is faced with. Only a miracle worker can solve them.

In 1932, the government didn't owe any money, so it could scatter around plenty without too much difficulty. I can hardly picture today as reasonably bright, and the foreign situation is devastatingly dark.

I have great confidence in Jack, and I know he won't fail.

It was wonderful hearing from you, and I hope our paths will cross more frequently in the future.

My kindest regards.

Sincerely,
Joseph P. Kennedy

Joseph P. Kennedy to Enrico Galeazzi

New York, January 6, 1961

Dear Enrico:

I am really disappointed that you won't be with us on the great day of the 21st, but I quite understand why you feel you can't come. I am serious when I say that I will miss you very much and so will the entire family.

Jack's appointments have made a great impression on the country. He has shown a breadth of vision and judgment that you and I knew he had but was not obvious to many people who were blinded by prejudice.

I suppose you saw the story in LIFE with a picture of me riding my horse. I was asked for reasons why I did not expect the race to be so close and I answered (1) I was wrong in expecting that we would get a bigger Catholic vote than we did and (2) bigotry played a much larger part in the campaign than we thought it would.

---

366. Ernest Kidder Lindley (1899–1979), *Newsweek*'s Washington bureau chief, 1937–61, and author of its "Washington Tides" column, had previously covered the New Deal enthusiastically for the *New York Herald Tribune* and the *Washington Post*.

367. New York State public relations executive, Walter T. Brown (1900–63), Governor Lehman's former secretary, 1935–38, and Associated Press Albany bureau chief, 1924–35.

Jack will be faced in the future with a horrible situation. The Laos problem is in an awful state. The Cuban situation couldn't be any worse. There is an undercurrent of unrest among the Western Allies and Africa is in bad shape. In the United States business is bad and there are many, many problems to be faced. Jack himself recognizes all these problems and just seems to feel that something can be done about them all. It is fortunate for us that he didn't have to take office on the day after election and have all the problems that have been swept under the rugs come out after he became President. However, all these problems have now come out and people are saying Kennedy was right in his campaign. I am worried but hopeful.

Bobby will make a great Attorney General. He didn't want to take the position but was finally persuaded by Jack and somewhat by me. He will make a great record I am sure. We haven't had many great Attorney Generals in the last forty years.

Teddy is going to live in Boston and will go to work in the District Attorney's office and continue in politics. I am going to "mind the store" by myself.

I am signing a lease for the same house for the months of July and August so at least at that time we will have, if not before, chance to talk things over.

I am very unhappy about our friend.[368] I have a very strong feeling that the time for friends to be together is when you need them most. I have never asked for many things, but I needed all the help I could get in this campaign. I don't think he gave the help he should have and I think we did as badly in New York amongst the Catholics as we did anywhere in the country. He was asked to do two or three things and he just didn't deliver. In my book we are all even for past services and I haven't any interest in the future. I think the less I see of clergy and the hierarchy, the longer I will live and the happier I will be. Their attitude towards a family that has done as much for the Church as I think we have was nothing short of a disgrace. As far as I am concerned, I am through working for them or with them, with the exception of Cushing in Boston. For him I will do anything and for anybody else, I am not interested. I know how you feel about it. You have known him much longer than you have known me, but I am not the slightest bit interested in him in the future. Don't think that I am irrational or too mad about the situation. I am just fed up with the whole crowd.

Maybe time is going to soften me up but I have had two very definite opinions in my mind. After this is over, I am more grateful than ever to all those who helped us in this fight and I dislike more intensely than ever those who should have helped and didn't.

I can never be too grateful to you for going to bat every time I asked you to — but then when didn't you?

So for a little while, my love to you and Marisa,

Affectionately,
Joseph P. Kennedy

Joseph P. Kennedy to Enrico Galeazzi

Palm Beach, February 6, 1961

Dear Enrico:

I am pleased that the messages have been straightened out. Both sides made enough mistakes to almost make it impossible to get it cleared up. However, I am glad it is settled.

368. Cardinal Spellman.

And now I am going to write you once more about our friend, and I will not write you ever again about it.

My letter to you explained how I felt. As you know, I have never been anxious to have anything to do with priests, nuns, or any of the hierarchy. This was driven into me by my father and mother, who always believed that the clergy had their place and the family had their own.

When I made my first gift for the original hospital in Boston to Cardinal Cushing, it was after I had a disagreeable experience, about which I have told you, with Cardinal O'Connell years back. You remember then that Cushing gave out a statement that I thought was manifestly unfair, and I kicked up as much fuss as I could.

During all these times, I continued my friendship with our friend, and I like to think that I contributed just as much to that friendship as he did.

I was shocked by his attitude in the presidential campaign. I was shocked at the reception Jack got at the Al Smith dinner, and with many other incidents about which I have written you.

That last fit of temper in which he came out publicly against the Task Force Report on Education, and on which report the President had not expressed any opinion whatsoever, and considering that Eisenhower has personally made this recommendation for the last five years, and our friend has never opened his mouth, I consider it another exhibition of the judgment of a man who should know better.

As far as I am concerned, I am disgusted, and I prefer not to have any further contacts.

Now I realize that you are his closest friend, and I don't want to put you in the middle of any arguments and disputes, and quite understand your feeling that because of your great love for the church and your friendship with so many of the hierarchy, you might be annoyed at my attitude. I have great love and devotion for you—I will always have it, and I would never do anything that would cause you embarrassment, so if we can continue our friendship without any further mention of your friend, there is nothing in God's world I would like better. But if my attitude makes you unhappy, I will quite understand it, and my friendship for you will never die.

Affectionately,

Rose Kennedy: *Recollection of the Bay of Pigs Crisis*

Wednesday [April 19, 1961]

Phoned Joe who said Jack had been on phone with him most of the day as well as Bobby. At end I asked him how he was feeling & he said "Dying" — the result of trying to bring up Jack's morale after the Cuban débacle.

That night we went to dinner at Greek Embassy — very formal reception on our arrival — Ambassador came down steps to meet President much as we had come outside to meet King when he came to Embassy — Many photos on our arrival. I wore pink chiffon dress made by Greek designer Desses in Paris & everyone seemed to like it. Jackie in white satin sheath of Cassini & Hairdresser came to White House before dinner to give it a combing out.

After dinner we chatted entirely with women for a while & then joined me for a short time, as Jack wanted to leave & then said Good night in car & rushed to office. Jackie walked upstairs with me & said he was so upset all day & had practically been in tears — felt he had been misinformed by C.I.A. — which Allan Dulles was the head of.

Felt so sorry for him — Jackie seemed so sympathetic & said she had stayed with him until he had lain down as she had never seen him so depressed except once at time of his operation —

I left Thursday A.M- without seeing him again & arrived in N. York where I looked at furs — a Russian sable cape for wear in cool weather & fall & perhaps Austria & a white mink for festive occasions when Jack visits de Gaul.

Rose Kennedy to Joseph P. Kennedy

Hotel Ritz, Paris, September 19-1961

Joe dearest,
How can I have all this and you —
And still have Heaven, too!
Home for Christmas

Love to all
Rosa

Rose Kennedy to Robert Kennedy

Chez Balenciaga [Paris]

Dearest Bob,
I think you should work hard and become President after Jack —
It will be good for the country
And for you
And especially good for you know who.
Ever your affectionate & peripatetic

Mother

Rose Kennedy: *"Thanksgiving 61"*

[November 23, 1961]
All children & grandchildren came down except John Jr. sick with cold & Pat 3 youngest. Pat & Eunice here (Peter[369] in Europe making a picture) Smiths with Joan & Ted, Paul Fay[370] & family & newspaper correspondent Anne Chamberlain at Ethel's — (she opened annex usually reserved for maids) Arrived Caroline (plane) about 4 P.M- Thursday & 4 or 5 cars rushed over to pick them up & luggage — Little houses for secret service men occupied again — police on road to question sight seers & Jack had to motor from Otis Field instead of helicopter o/o weather. Everyone at our house for drinks & Joe had fresh oysters — lobster tails etc. served with drinks — Oysters came from here & Rosenbloom sent lobster etc. from Baltimore. We all had dinner here except Jack & Jackie who went home. Jackie probably likes to be alone for a change. She has a crowd so much — Afterwards a movie but several walked out as it was long & everyone tired. I had just given a lecture in Winchester very successfully on England & introduced a few slides from White House with comments — so I am planning to lecture especially in French sections introducing pictures of Jack & Jackie in Paris in order to

369. Pat had married actor Peter Lawford (1923–84) in 1953.
370. Undersecretary of the navy, Paul Burgess "Red" Fay, Jr. (1918–), had first come to know Jack at the Motor Torpedo Boat Squadron Training Center in Melville, Rhode Island in 1942.

interest French. I can do this at French clubs, & thus get to know people & make an entrée. Called Mr. Lewin of New Bedford Standard Times who knows New Bedford & Fall River so well & he is eager to help — This idea especially useful now with view to interesting people for Ted's campaign who hopes to ~~work~~ be candidate for Senate next fall 1962 — Weather very bad but we managed to play golf Thursday A.M some of them skating on Kennedy Rink[371] — I wore 2 sweaters — snuggies under my slacks — my rain rubber short jacket — cream on face — managed to play two balls on six holes. Last night Thanksgiving everyone here to dinner — oysters first with drinks in sun room for turkey (I omitted soup) — squash (Dad insisted) altho I frowned on having squash & sweet potatoes as too much the same color — Special dessert which Jack likes of meringue built up with cream & chocolate ice cream — cook a French woman whom we had in France last summer called André — fortunately our waitress & her sister (who comes to help in kitchen) are French Canadians & understand French — Frank [sic] Fay gave a toast or two Jackie's two Filipinos came over to help serve —

Friday A.M- drizzle poured rain from 11-30 AM but the youngsters played a little touch football in afternoon — Sandy down who has charge of games in summer. Jack working all day with McNamara — Secretary of Defense[372] & others who arrived in three helicopters landing on golf course as our lawn was probably too low & soggy — Then we sent fish chowder to three different houses where various ones ate it, but as it was a working lunch — McNamara did not go to ~~Ethel's~~ to lunch but ate with others probably in town — which means they consulted & worked during lunch — Bad weather Saturday rain & drizzle but all went skating as rink reserved for family for hour or so in A.M- I played golf — Afraid to start skating as if I fall or strain wrist — feel it is not worth it as time is so short At our house every night for dinner. Celebrated Bob & Sargent's birthday on Friday with lobsters — ice cream etc. Sang after dinner while Joan played piano. She is wonderful as she can transpose — plays by ear & can play any song they start to sing — Jack gets great kick out of seeing Ted dance as Ted has great sense of rhythm but he is so big & has such a big derrière it is funny to see him throw himself around — Lots of discussion about "the Twist" — the new dance which has great vogue at the moment throw your hips around — NO one knew much about it but Jackie at end in a Schiaparelli pink slack suit gave a three minute performance to the jungling-rumbling music of Joan. Jack sits with cigar (small ones usually) just looking on & smiling especially at Ted dancing. Has good color (uses sun lamp if necessary) & of course has filled out considerably & looks in good form — Actually he has no exercise so his face looks almost chubby — Joe Sr. had an attack about ten days ago & is not at all himself but quiet — complains about a lack of taste in his mouth & feels blah — he says — For first time — I have noticed he has grown old — Sargent noticed & said was plain he was not himself. Doctor Travell here with Jack & says cold wind & air bad for Joe but he keeps going out.[373]

---

371. The Hyannis skating rink, donated by the family in memory of Joe Junior.
372. Robert Strange McNamara (1916–), secretary of defense, 1961–68, and former Ford Motor Company executive.
373. JPK would feel unwell while playing golf in Palm Beach on December 21. His niece Ann Gargan would take him home where, after declining medical attention, he would collapse. The stroke he had suffered would incapacitate him until his death in 1969.

NOTES

Abbreviations

BG	*Boston Globe*	JPK	Joseph P. Kennedy
BH	*Boston Herald*	JPK, Jr.	Joseph P. Kennedy, Jr.
BHA	*Boston Herald American*	JPKE	Joseph P. Kennedy Enterprises
CH	Cordell Hull	JPKP	Joseph P. Kennedy Papers
DM	Diplomatic Memoir	KFC	Kennedy Family Collection
EEM	Edward E. Moore	KK/H	Kathleen Kennedy (Hartington)
EK/S	Eunice Kennedy (Shriver)	LC	Library of Congress
EMK	Edward Moore Kennedy	NC	Neville Chamberlain
FDR	Franklin D. Roosevelt	NYHT	*NY Herald Tribune*
FDRL	Franklin D. Roosevelt Library	NYT	*New York Times*
HK	Harvey Klemmer	PK/L	Patricia Kennedy (Lawford)
HP	Hyannisport	REFK	Rose Fitzgerald Kennedy
HUHL	Harvard University/ Houghton Library	REFKP	Rose Fitzgerald Kennedy Papers
JFF	John F. Fitzgerald	RK	Rosemary Kennedy
JFK	John F. Kennedy	SEP	*Saturday Evening Post*
JFKL	John F. Kennedy Library	WRH	William Randolph Hearst
JK/S	Jean Kennedy (Smith)	WSC	Winston Spencer Churchill

Introduction

Page

xviii "plenty of butter . . .": "Directions for Mr. J. P. Kennedy," May 22, 1920: JPKP / "'34 J. P. Kennedy Personal to John F. Kennedy."

xix "GOOD MAN.": FDR to NC, September 28, 1938: JPKP / "Roosevelt, Franklin D."

xxi "I may have lighted . . .": Arthur Krock to JPK, July 1, 1937: JPKP / "New York Office, etc." / "New York Office."

xxi "I would suggest . . .": JPK to JFK, October 1, 1946: JPKP / "To JFK from Parents."

xxii "kindly destroy . . .": JPK to Ethel Turner, December 23, 1920: JPKP / "Columbia Trust Co.—Family Finances."

xxii "appeared to be horrified . . .": JPK Diary, June 17, 1943, JPK Diary 1942–51: JPKP.

xxiii "I am writing . . .": JPK, Memorandum, February 18, 1935: JPKP / "White House."

xxiii "(Add children's . . . ,"; "(See also . . .": JPK Diary, March 13, 1939: JPKP.

xxiii "Prime Minister last night.": JPK Diary, May 23, 1939: JPKP.

xxiii "When I left No. 10 . . .": JPK Diary, August 24, 1939: JPKP.

xxiii "a great admirer . . .": JPK Diary, October 26, 1939: JPKP.

xxiii "I am not like . . .": JPK to Count Enrico Galeazzi, October 24, 1961: JPKP / "Galeazzi, Count Enrico."

xxiv "[o]ne of the greatest . . . ,": JPK to Phyllis Long, October 22: JPKP / "Long-Lyons."

xxiv ". . . was the type . . .": James Fayne Oral History: JFKL.

xxiv "If you want . . .": JPK to Lady Halifax, DM, V, 6C-D.

xxv "Nuts!": JPK to REFK, September 26, 1939 JKS.

xxv "As a parent . . .": JPK to Bill Cunningham April 19, 1959: JPKP / "C."

xxv "In looking over . . .": JPK to JFK, April 12, 1932: REFKP / "JFK, 1932."

xxv "I don't know whether . . .": JPK to EMK, September 11, 1940: JPKP.

xxvi "The Government . . .": JPK to RFK, September 11, 1940: JPKP.

xxvi "Don't get too upset . . .": JPK to KK, July 3, 1943: REFKP / "Kathleen Kennedy, 6 / '43–7 / '43."

xxvi "Everyone who comes . . .": JPK to KK, March 8, 1944: REFKP / "Kathleen Kennedy, 3 / '44."

xxvii "To Kick,": JPK, May 14, 1948: JPKP.

Editor's Note

Page
xxx   "for purposes such as . . .": §107, 1976 Copyright Act.
xxxiii "In Frankfurt . . .": Henderson, 72–74.
xxxiv *Note on the Reichsbank—*": JFK, June 1945: JPKP.

Part 1: Boston 1914–1927

Page
4   "I think he could have been a showman . . .": Mark Sullivan on JPK, August 1, 1934: JPKP / "JP Kennedy—Personal."

5   "absolutely no technical knowledge . . .": JPK to District Draft Board No. 5, February 18, 1918: JPKP / "1918–1925."

5   "Mr. Kennedy . . .": Joseph Powell to Meyer Bloomfield, February 25, 1918: JPKP / "1918–1925."

5   "We never got along then,": JPK quoted in the *Boston Sunday Globe*, September 25, 1932, 3.

5   "Roosevelt was the hardest trader . . .": JPK quoted in *Liberty*, May 21, 1938, 15.

6   "a dainty daughter . . .": unidentified clipping, REFK Scrapbook: JFKL.

6   "one of its greatest rooters,": JPK to Joseph Powell, June 30, 1919: JPKP / "1918–1925."

6   "hostile mental attitude,": E. G. Grace to JPK, December 30, 1920: JPKP / "1918–1925."

7   "As to Eastern . . .": JPK to Dr. John Bottomley, July 9, 1923: JPKP / "John Bottomley, 1924–25."

7   "I really ought . . .": JPK to Christopher Dunphy, December 31, 1920: JPKP / "JPK-D."

7   "Confidentially . . .": JPK to Alfred Wellington, August 22, 1921: JPKP / "Columbia Trust Co.—Family Finances."

7   "more and more . . .": JPK to Matthew Brush, August 20, 1923: JPKP / "John Bottomley, 1924–25."

7   "on forty-eight hours notice,": JPK to District Draft Board No. 5, February 18, 1918: JPKP / "1918–1925."

7   "Tim Reardon is obliged . . .": JPK to Alfred Wellington, October 27, 1921: JPKP / "Columbia Trust Co.—Family Finances."

8   "decennial Santa Clause": Harvard '12's Decennial Reunion, 1912 Class Report 1922, xix–xxi.

8   "Joe made a week-end trip . . .": Joseph Conway to John J. Ford, August 12, 1954: JPKP / "Maritime Commission, Housing, Financial, 1937 / Personal Misc."

9   "there isn't any money . . .": JPK to Arthur Houghton, September 19, 1921: JPKP / "Misc. Correspondence (Arthur Houghton, Vera Murray) 1919–1925."

9   "[M]y experience . . .": JPK to R.S. Cole, September 24, 1920: JPKP / "Robertson-Cole."

9   "At City Hospital . . .": REFK, JFK Childhood Health Record, 1928: JFKL / JFK / Personal Papers / I / Early Years / Child Health Record.

9   "an excellent little patient,": Anna Pope to JPK, May 14, 1920: JPKP / Unmarked Original File (6).

9   "bedbugs and cooties,": REFK Diary, February 25, 1923: REFKP / "1923 (& '26) Diary."

9   "the best little talker . . .": REFK Diary, February 14, 1923: REFKP / "1923 (& '26) Diary."

9   "about 7 months old," "The Governess . . .": EEM on JPK: Jr. and JFK: JPKP / "Kennedy, Mrs. Joseph P."

10   "regular floating palace,": JPK to REFK, August 20, 1925, JPKE.

11   "'You go ahead . . .'": JPK quoted in P.S. Harrison, "Why Joe Kennedy Called Off a Trip to Florida," *The Irish World and American Industrial Liberator*, March 17, 1928, 12.

11   "We will produce . . .": Unidentified clipping, interview with JPK on *Bigger than Barnum's*, n.d. [August 1926], n.p.: JFKL / REFK Clipping Scrapbook.

11   "'picture' man," JPK to Joseph Schnitzer, February 11, 1926: JPKP / "1926."

11   "the oldest . . .": JPK to J. J. Murdock, November 27, 1927: JPKP / "B-C-D G-H N-P Personal."

11   "revolutionize the industry . . .": JPK, "General Introduction," Kennedy, ed., *The Story of the Films*, 12–13.

11   ". . . we intend . . .": Harry Warner, "Future Developments," in Kennedy, ed., 327.

11   " as carefully . . .": JPK on Sam Katz, "General Introduction," Kennedy, ed., 13.

12   "I'm writing your story . . .": John B. Kennedy to JPK, August 27, 1927: JPKP / "1927."

12   "With newspapers . . .": JPK to Nathan Gordon, October, 24, 1924: JPKP / "Columbia Advertising - Notes Payable."

12   "[A]s I have said . . .": JPK to RFK, August 24, 1955: JPKP / Untitled.

13   "[u]nusual tribute . . .": Johnny Walker on Red Grange, *Exhibitors' Herald*, n.d., n.p.: JFKL / REFK Clipping Scrapbook.

13   "a fine manliness,": JPK on Red Grange, unidentified clipping, n.d., n.p.: JFKL / REFK Clipping Scrapbook.

13   "IT SEEMS TO ME . . .": House of Lords Record Office, BBK / C / 90. Quoted with the permission of the Clerk of the House of Lords Record Office on behalf of the Beaverbrook Foundation Trust.

Letters

Part II: New York and Hollywood 1927–1932

Letters

Part III: Washington 1933–1937

Letters

Page
149   JPK to JFK, February 6, 1935: REFKP / "SEC Chronological File, February 1935."
149   JPK: Memorandum, February 18, 1935: JPKP / "White House."
150   "to stand idly . . .": FDR quoted in Tully, 157–61.
151   "A debased currency," Justice James Clark McReynolds quoted in the *NYT*, February 19, 1935, 16.
151   JPK to KK February 20, 1935: JPKP / "Kennedy, Kathleen."
151   ". . . put over festivities . . .": JFK 1935 Scrapbook: JFKL.
152   KK to REFK and JPK, n.d. (February 21, 1935): JPKP / "Kennedy, Kathleen."
152   KK to JPK, n.d. (February 22, 1935): JPKP.
153   JPK, Jr., to JPK, April 19, 1935: JPKP.
153   REFK, "Jean's First Communion," n.d. (April 28, 1935): JPKP.
153   Paul Murphy to Dr. Paul O'Leary, May 7, 1935: JPKP.
154   JPK to Sam Rayburn, June 28, 1935: JPKP / "R–RD."
154   Arthur Krock: Memorandum, n.d. JPKP.
157   JPK to Burton Wheeler July 8, 1935: REFKP / "SEC Chronological File, July 1935."
159   FDR to RFK, July 12, 1935: FDRL / PPF 207 / "JPK 1933–38."
159   RFK to FDR, July 19, 1935: FDRL / PPF 207 / "JPK, 1933–38."
159   JPK to FDR, September 6, 1935: FDRL / OF 1060 / SEC 1935.
160   JPK to George Steele, September 6, 1935: JPKP / "Kennedy, Jack."
160   JPK to Cissy Patterson, September 23, 1935: JPKP / SEC Misc (Unfiled).
161   JPK to Ogden Mills Reid, September 23, 1935: JPKP / SEC Misc (Unfiled).
161   "a real blow . . .": C. Norman Stabler, "Kennedy Out of SEC Post," *New York Herald Tribune*, September 21, 1935, 1.
161   REFK, Recollection, n.d.: REFKP / "John F. Kennedy—Early Years."
161   JPK to FDR, February 10, 1935: JPKP / "White House."
162   REFK, "Visit to Churchill" n.d. (1935): JPKP / Unmarked File (Rose Kennedy).
163   JPK to James Farley, October 9, 1935: JPKP / "Farley, James A."
163   JPK to JPK, Jr., October 14, 1935: JPKP / "Joseph Kennedy, Sr."
164   JPK to JFK, November 11, 1935: JPKP.
164   JPK to Robert Worth Bingham, November 11, 1935: JPKP / "B."
165   KK to REFK and JPK, November 17, 1935: JPKP.
166   KK to REFK, January 7, 1936: REFK / "Family Correspondence—Personal Between Kathleen Kennedy & Mother & Father."
166   JPK to JFK, January 11, 1936: JPKE.
167   JPK to RFK, January 11, 1936: JKS.
167   RK to REFK and JPK, January 12, 1936: REFKP / "Rosemary."
168   JFK to REFK and JPK, n.d.: JPKP.
168   JPK to KK January 18, 1936: JPKP.
169   KK to REFK and JPK, January 19, 1936: JPKP.
169   JPK to FDR, January 20, 1936: JPKP / "White House."
170   JPK to KK, January 20, 1936: JPKP.
171   JPK to Robert Rutherford McCormick, January 31, 1936: JPKP / "F–Misc."
172   KK to REFK, February 8, 1936: JPKP.
174   JPK to Louis Ruppel, February 11, 1936: JPKP / "R (Misc.)"
174   JPK to EK, February 11, 1936: REFKP / MS 77-29 / 3/8 / "Eunice."
175   JPK, Jr., to JPK, n.d. (1936): JPKP / "Kennedy, Joe, Jr."
176   JPK to Missy LeHand, February 25, 1936: FDRL / PPF 207 / "JPK 1933–38."
176   JPK to JPK, Jr., February 27, 1936: JPKP.
177   JPK to EK, PK, and JK, February 27, 1936: REFKP / "Eunice."
177   JPK to RFK, and EMK, February 27, 1936: JPKP / RFK.
177   RK to REFK and JPK, March 1, 1936: JPKP.
178   KK to REFK and JPK, March 29–30, 1936: JPKP.
179   JPK, Jr., to JPK, April 11, 1936: JPKP.
180   JPK to JPK, Jr., April 13, 1936: JPKP.
181   KK to JPK, April 15, 1936: JPKP.
183   JPK to JFK, April 25, 1936: JPKP.
183   JPK to JFK, April 28, 1936: JPKP.
183   REFK to JPK, n.d. (May 3, 1936): JPKP.
184   RFK to JPK, May 11, 1936: JPKP / RFK.
184   EMK to JPK, n.d.: JPKP.
184   JPK to Adolph Sabath, June 2, 1936: JPKP / "Paramount Report."
185   JPK to Missy LeHand, June 15, 1936: FDRL / PPF 207 / "JPK 1933–38."
186   JPK to Arthur Krock, June 24, 1936: JPKP / "K (Misc.)"
186   JPK to Robert S. Allen, August 8, 1936: JPKP / "Political Misc."

Part IV: London 1938–1940

Page

223–24   "[I]n many quarters . . .": DM, I, 6.

224   ". . . discussed the foreign situation in general . . .": JPK, 1938 Diary, February 22, 1938.

225   "The President has given me . . .": JPK (Harold Hinton) Diplomatic Memoir Draft, n.d.: JPKP / "Articles."

225   "To tell you the truth . . .": DM, I, 11-12.

227   Waugh and Kick's dowry: JKS.

227   "I feared that the admitted fact . . .": DM, III, 8.

227   ". . . entirely too isolationist . . .": Hull quoted in Koskoff, 127.

227   "I got the feeling . . .": JPK Diary, March 18, 1938: JPKP.

227   "[i]t has long been a theory . . .": JPK to Cordell Hull, draft of Trafalgar Day speech: 1196, October 17, 1938: JPKP / "1938, Oct. to Dept."

228   "in every walk of life . . .": DM, V, 6.

228   "Mr. Roosevelt . . . had a quality . . .": DM, IX, 3.

228   "deep within me . . .": DM, IX, 9.

228   "I cannot go . . .": JPK quoted Whalen, 283.

229   ". . . do nothing but complicate . . .": JPK diary, July 17, 1940.

229   "I would have no knowledge . . .": JPK to FDR, dispatch 2913, August 27, 1940: JPKP.

229   "Frankly and honestly . . .": JPK to FDR, dispatch 2913, August 27, 1940: JPKP.

230   "you could send an American to London . . .": Senator James F. Byrnes to Arthur Krock, December 13, 1937: JPKP / "Buckley-Byrnes."

230   "[T]he more I see . . .": JPK to Sen. William Borah, April 24, 1938: JPKP / "B."

231   "Sympathize,": JPK, Radio Address, NBC Red Network, January 18, : JPKP / 27.

231   "I hate to think . . .": JPK to John F. Fitzgerald, April 7, 1938: JPKP / "John F. Fitzgerald."

232   "the German Ambassador . . .": JPK Diary, June 13, 1938.

232   Von Dirksen's lack of fluency in English: JPK Diary, April 15, 1939.

232   "RUSH PACIFIST LITERATURE,": JFK to James Seymour, February 13, 1940, PRO / FO / 24251 x 9191.

233   MacDonald's diaries on birdwatching: Letter to the Editor from J. M. Fewster, assistant keeper of Archives at the University of Durham, April 29, 1994.

233   JPK Diary, July 20, 1938: JPKP.

233   "Jew influence . . .": JPK Diary 1938–39, October 4, 1939.

233   "hasn't liked the US Ambassador . . .": JPK to REFK, March 20, 1940, JKS.

233   "75% of the attacks . . .": JPK to TJ White, November 12, 1938: JPKP / "White, Thomas Justin."

234   "It is no secret . . .": JPK to Joseph Dinneen, quoted in Whalen, 388.

234   "Democracy is finished . . .": "Kennedy Says Democracy All Done in Britain, Maybe Here," Louis Lyons, BG, November 10, 21.

Letters

Page

235   JPK to John Cudahy, January 10, 1938: REFKP / "Cudahy-Cutler."

235   JPK to William Gonzales, January 10, 1938: JPKP / "USMC, Chronological File, from Dec. 14, 1937–Jan. 15, 1938."

235   "genius of adaptability . . .": William E. Gonzales, "Unstartled by Ideas," The State, December 15, 1937, n.p., clipping in: JPKP / "Goldheim-Grace."

235   JPK to FDR, January 13, 1938: FDRL / PSF 37 / Kennedy.

236   JPK, Diary, February 18, 22, 1938: JPKP.

237   "When Joe went to England . . .": REFK, "Knee Breeches"; REFKP / "Married Life, 1914–41."

237   JPK to James Roosevelt, March 3, 1938: FDRL / James Roosevelt / Box 40.

238   "the epidemic of world lawlessness . . .": FDR, Keesing's, October 5, 1937, 2766.

239   "After Joe K. told me . . .": Rabbi Stephen Wise to FDR, March 4, 1938: FDRL / PSF 37 / Kennedy.

239   JPK Diary, March 4, 1938: JPKP.

240   JPK to FDR, March 11, 1938: FDRL / PSF 37 / Kennedy.

243   .CH to JPK, March 14, 1938: FDRL / OF 3060 Kennedy, J.P., 1938–41 / Box 1 / Cordell Hull.

243   "I thought it would be wise . . .": JPK, DM, III, 8.

243   "To give some picture of the situation . . .": Pilgrims' Speech Draft, JPK to CH, March 10, 1938: JPKP / "1938, March–April to Dept.", 2.

244   "Obviously, another factor . . .": JPK, Pilgrims' Speech Draft, JPK to CH, March 10, 1938: JPKP / "1938, March–April to Dept.", 2.

244   "The lack of interest . . .": Pilgrims' Speech Draft, JPK to CH, March 10, 1938: JPKP "1938, March–April to Dept.", 2.

244   "Nothing constructive . . .": Pilgrims' Speech Draft, JPK to CH, March 10: JPKP / "1938, March–April to Dept.", 2.

244   "It must be realized . . .": Pilgrims' Speech Draft, JPK to CH, March 10, 1938: JPKP / "1938, March–April to Dept.", 3.

Page
245   JPK Diary, March 18, 1938: JPKP.
245   "On the second hole . . .": 1938–39 Diary, March 5: JPKP.
245   JPK to CH, March 18, 1938: JPKP / "1938, March–April to Dept."
245   "I agreed with Kennedy's position . . .": FDRL / OF 3060 / Box 1 Kennedy, JP, 1938–41.
246   JPK to Arthur Krock, March 21, 1938: JPKP / "Political Letters of JPK."
247   JPK to Arthur Krock, March 28, 1938: JPKP / "Political Letters of JPK."
248   "the fundamental basis . . .": "The Prime Minister's Speech," *Times*, March 25, 1938, 7.
248   "I could not find . . .": Clement Attlee quoted in "Mr. Attlee, 'A 1914 Situation,'" *Times*, March 25, 1938, 8.
250   JPK Diary, April 4, 1938: JPKP.
250   JPK Diary, April 9, 1938: JPKP.
251   West Fulham by-election results, *Keesing's*, April 7–8, 1938, 3015.
252   REFK to PK, April 10th, 1938: JPKP.
252   JPK Diary, n.d. (April 10, 1938): JPKP.
254   "the world's greatest gentleman,": George VI on Morgan, quoted in Chernow, 431.
254   JPK to T. J. White, April 27, 1938: JPKP / "White, Thomas Justin."
255   "Ambassador Kennedy would make . . .": WRH to T. J. White, NYOF / 13 / White, Thomas Justin.
255   "hostile attitude," Cissy Patterson quoted in the *NYT*, April 6, 1938, n.p., clipping in: JPKP / 13 / "White, Thomas Justin."
255   Hearst's concurrence, *New York Journal and American*, April 7, 1938, n.p., clipping in: JPKP / "White, Thomas Justin."
255   JPK to Drew Pearson, May 3, 1938: JPKP / "Pearson, Drew and Allen, Robert."
255   "Pro-Nazi intrigues," Cockburn quoted in Sykes, 336.
255   "Latest American," Pearson and Allen Washington Merry-Go-Round, "Lady Astor's Pro-Fascist Clivedon [*sic*] Group is Wooing Joe Kennedy," draft, April 22, 1938, dipping in: JPKP / "Pearson, Drew and Allen, Robert."
255   "As a matter of fact . . .": JPK to Pearson and Allen, May 3, 1938: JPKP / "Pearson, Drew and Allen, Robert."
256   JPK Diary, May 5, 1938: JPKP.
256   JPK to Lady Astor, May 10, 1938: JPKP / "Astor, Viscountess Nancy."
256   REFK Diary, May 11, 1938: JPKP / "1938 Diary."
256   JPK to Jay Pierrepont Moffat, May 17, 1938: HUHL / Jay Pierrepont Moffat Papers / MS Am 1407 / v. 41. By permission of the Houghton Library, Harvard University.
258   REFK Diary, May 17, 1938: JPKP / "1938 Diary."
258   JPK to James Roosevelt, May 31, 1938: FDRL / James Roosevelt / Box 40.
260   JPK Diary, June 1938: JPKP.
262   JPK Diary, June 13, 1938: JPKP.
263   JPK, DM, IX, 5–9: JPKP.
266   JPK to Frank Buxton, July 11, 1938: JPKP / "American Newspapers, 7–9 / '38."
266   "helped Kennedy to reach . . .": Alva Johnson, "Jimmy's Got It," *SEP*, July 2, 1938, 60.
267   JPK Diary, July 20, 1938: JPKP.
267   JPK to Department, July 20, 1938: JPKP / "1938, July to Dept."
267   "I took the occasion . . .": *German Documents*, 722–23.
268   JPK to Malcolm Bingay, July 22, 1938: JPKP / "American Newspapers, 7–9 / '38."
269   "The reporter has . . .": R. R. McCormick to JPK, August 13, 1938: JPKP / "American Newspapers, 7–9 / 38."
269   JPK to CH, August 30, 1938: JPKP / "1938, July to Dept."
270   JPK to CH, August 31, 1938: JPKP / "1938, July to Dept."
272   "the attitude of this Government . . .": CH to JPK, 492, September 1, 1938: FDRL / PSF 37 / Kennedy.
272   JPK to CH, September 5, 1938: JPKP / "1938, Sept. to Dept."
273   FDR to JPK, September 7, 1938: JPKP / "Roosevelt, Franklin D."
273   "Keep cool . . .": JPK quoted in the *BHA*, August 31, 1938, 1.
273   RFK to REFK and JPK, n.d. (September 1938): JPKP.
274   JPK to CH, September 10, 1938: JPKP / "1938, Sept. to Dept."
275   REFK Diary, September 14, 1938: JPKP / "1938 Diary."
275   JPK Diary, September 14, 1938: JPKP.
275   JPK to CH, September 14, 1938: JPKP / "1938, Sept. to Dept."
276   REFK Diary, September 15, 16, 1938: JPKP / "1938 Diary."
277   JPK to CH, September 17, 1938: JPKP / "1938, Sept. to Dept."
278   JPK to CH, September 19, 1938: JPKP / "1938, Sept. to Dept."
279   JPK to CH, September 21, 1938: JPKP / "1938, Sept. to Dept."
280   REFK Diary, September 21, 1938: JPKP / "1938 Diary."
281   JPK to Thomas Corcoran, September 22, 1938: JPKP / "Corcoran, Thomas and Cohen, Benjamin."

Page

281   "he is one . . .": Alsop and Kintner, "Capital Parade," *BG*, September 20, 1938, 14; *Washington Evening Star*, September 19, 1938.

281   JPK to CH, September 22, 1938: JPKP / "1938, Sept. to Dept."

282   JPK to CH, September 23, 1938: JPKP / "1938, Sept. to Dept."

283   JPK to CH, September 24, 1938: JPKP / "1938, Sept. to Dept."

284   JPK Diary, September 26, 1938: JPKP.

284   "the United States has no . . .": FDR to Adolph Hitler, September 26, 1938 in Domarus, 1197–8.

285   "with a single . . .": Hitler quoted in Dallek, 265.

286   REFK Diary, September 26, 1938: JPKP / "1938 Diary."

286   "[h]owever much . . .": NC, radio broadcast, September 27, 1938, in Chamberlain, 175.

286   JPK Diary, September 27, 1938: JPKP.

287   REFK Diary, September 27, 28, 1938: JPKP / "1938 Diary."

288   JPK to CH, September 28, 1938: JPKP / "1938, Sept. to Dept."

289   REFK Diary, September 29, 1938: JPKP / "1938 Diary."

289   JK to REFK and JPK, September 29, 1938: JPKP.

290   REFK Diary, September 30, 1938: JPKP / "1938 Diary."

290   "symbolic of the desire . . .": NC quoted in Watt, 29.

290   JPK, Jr., "Charles Lindbergh", October 1, 1938: JPKP / "JPK Jr. Mss—England."

291   JPK Diary, October 3, 1938: JPKP.

291   "the first break . . .": Duff Cooper resignation letter to Chamberlain, *NYT*, October 2, 1928, 1.

291   Duff Cooper, explanation of resignation to the House of Commons, October 3, 1938, *The First World War and Its Aftermath*, 1020.

291   "[Hitler] has destroyed . . .": Clement Attlee quoted in *Keesing's*, October 3, 1938, 3259.

291   JPK Diary, October 4, 1938: JPKP / "Material for Current Speeches (Pamphlets & Congressional Reports)."

292   JPK to CH, October 5, 1938: JPKP / "#2, U.S. Embassy, (London) Reports, 1938."

294   JPK to CH, October 17, 1938: JPKP / "1938, Oct. to Dept."

294   "Kennedy sent in a speech . . .": Jay Pierrepont Moffat Diary, October 18, 1938, 1-2.: HUHL / MS Am 1407 / v. 41. By permission of the Houghton Library, Harvard University.

297   JPK to CH, October 28, 1938: JPKP / "1938, Oct. to Dept."

298   JPK to Dr. Sara Jordan, November 4, 1938: JPKP / "J 1938."

298   "Jack is looking better . . .": Dr. Sara Jordan to JPK, October 25, 1938: JPKP / "J 1938."

298   JPK to Doris Fleeson, November 9, 1938: JPKP / "F, 1938."

298   " so that his Americanism . . .": Heywood Broun quoted in Beschloss, 178.

298   "designed to please . . .": Walter Lippmann, "The Ambassador Speaking," "Today and Tomorrow," October 22, 1938.

298   "what agreements . . .": Hugh S. Johnson, "Stay Strong," *Boston Evening American*, October 25, 1938, 23.

299   JPK to T. J. White, November 12, 1938: JPKP / "White, Thomas Justin."

300   "The Secretary is . . .": Jay Pierrepont Moffat Diary, October 21, 1938, 1: HUHL / Am 1407 / v. 41. By permission of the Houghton Library, Harvard University.

300   JPK to Charles Lindbergh, November 12, 1938: JPKP.

301   "I am extremely anxious . . .": Charles Lindbergh to JPK, November 9, 1938: JPKP / "Charles A. Lindbergh."

301   JPK, Jr., 23: "Answer to Lippmann Editorial Against Dad," November 14, 1938: JFKL / RFK / Pre-Administration Personal Files / (JPK, Jr., Files) / "Editorial on JPK, Sr."

301   "amateur and temporary diplomats . . .": Walter Lippmann, "The Ambassador Speaking," "Today and Tomorrow," October 22, 1938.

302   JPK to CH, November 18, 1938: JPKP / "1938, Nov. to Dept."

303   JPK, Jr., "November 21," November 21, 1938: JPKP / "JPK Jr. Mss–England."

304   JPK to John Boettiger, November 25, 1938: JPKP / "B."

304   "how goes the great 'war-buster?'" John Boettiger to JPK, October 28, 1938: JPKP / "B."

304   JPK, Jr., "Visit to Plymouth, " December 6, 1938: JPKP / "JPK Jr. Mss– England."

305   JPK to Charles Lindbergh, December 8, 1938: JPKP / "Charles A. Lindbergh."

305   JPK, Jr., December 10, 1938: JPKP / "JPK Jr. Mss–England."

306   JPK to REFK, December 28, 1938, JFKL / JPK / Exhibit Items - Formative Years / 1/2 / "JPK-REFK Telegram."

306   RFK, Composition, n.d. (1939): JPKP.

306   JPK Diary, n.d., : JPKP.

307   "A few people . . .": Eleanor Roosevelt on receiving Goya prints, Franklin D. Roosevelt Library, Papers of Eleanor Roosevelt, "My Day," February 10, 1939.

307   "tragic unpreparedness . . .": Bernard Baruch quoted in the *NYT*, October 14, 1938, 7:2.

307   FDR on Baruch: Ickes, 470, 474.

Page

308 "to get behind . . .": quoted in Beschloss, 152.
308 JPK, Jr. to JPK, February 10, 1938. JPKP / "Spain."
311 JPK, Jr. to JPK, February 15, 1939: JPKP / "Spain."
312 JPK, Jr. to JPK, February 16, 1939: JPKP / "Spain."
315 JPK, Jr. to JPK, March 8, 1939: HK, JPK, Jr.
315 "I was greatly impressed . . .": JPK, Jr., to JPK, March 1, 1939: HK, JPK, Jr.
316 "a Basque . . .": JPK, Jr. to JPK, February 21, 1939: HK, JPK, Jr.
316 JPK Diary, March 12, 13, 15, 1939: JPKP.
320 JPK to JPK, Jr., March 15, 1939: JPKP / "Telegrams, 1939."
321 JPK Diary, March 17, 1939: JPKP / "Pope Pius XII - Coronation."
321 "every day . . .": William Bullitt quoted by Agent L. V. Boardman, FBI Memorandum, January 16, 1956, 1, 3.
321 "proposed to release . . .": JPK to Department, 352, March 17, 1939: JPKP / "1938, Mar. to Dept."
321 "make the best deal . . .": JPK to Department, 353, March 17, 1939: JPKP / "1938, Mar. to Dept."
321 JPK to CH, March 17, 1939: JPKP / "1938, Mar. to Dept."
322 JPK to NC, March 18, 1939: JPKP / "Chamberlain, Neville."
323 JPK to Missy LeHand, March 27, 1939: FDRL / OF 3035, OF 3059, OF 3060 / Kennedy, J.P. Box 1 / 1938–41.
323 JPK, Jr., to JPK, March 28, 1939: HK, JPK, Jr.
323 "a true democrat . . .": JPK, Jr., on Espinoza, "Personalities": JPKP / "Spain."
324 JPK, Jr., to JPK, April 4, 1939: HK, JPK, Jr.
325 REFK Diary, April 7, 1939: JPKP / "1939 Diary."
326 JPK Diary, April 14, 16, 1939: JPKP.
326 "throughout the world . . .": FDR's peace appeal to Hitler and Mussolini, *Keesing's*, 1939, 3530.
326 "coarse story,": Halifax Diary, University of York, Borthwick Institute, A7.8.5, 202–204, Friday, July 19th, 1940. Used with the kind permission of the present Lord Halifax.
328 "triumphant return . . .": Ciano quoted in the *NYT*, April 16, 1939, 37:1.
329 "The royal visit . . .": *NYT*, April 17, 1939, 3:2.
330 JPK to Paul Murphy, April 18, 1939: JPKP / "Paul Murphy—London, 1938–39."
330 JPK to FDR and CH, April 20, 1939: JPKP / "1939, Apr. to Dept."
331 REFK Diary, April 21, 1939: JPKP / "1939 Diary."
331 JPK to Geoffrey Dawson, May 1, 1939: JPKP / "D."
331 JPK to Sumner Welles, May 4, 1939: JPKP / "1939, May. to Dept."
332 REFK Diary, May 4, 9, 1939, : JPKP / "1939 Diary."
334 JPK to Wesley Winans Stout. May 10, 1939: JPKP / "S."
334 "[r]ecently the rumor . . .": Stout to JPK on Baruch, April 25, 1939: JPKP / "S."
335 General Hugh S. Johnson on JPK's anglophilia, quoted in Harold Hinton, *NYT*, April 25, 1939, 12:3.
335 JPK to John B. Kennedy, May 12, 1939: JPKP "JPK, Jr."
336 JPK to Benjamin Cohen, May 16, 1939: JPKP / "Corcoran, Thomas and Cohen, Benjamin."
336 "I THOUGHT I . . .": Cohen to JPK, May 15, 1939: JPKP / "Corcoran, Thomas and Cohen, Benjamin."
336 JPK to Dr. Solomon Goldman, June 2, 1939: JPKP / "G."
336 "IGNORE ALLEGATIONS . . .": Rabbi Solomon Goldman to JPK, May 18, 1939: JPKP / "G."
337 "Mr. Chamberlain himself . . .": Anon., "Kennedy and the Jews," *The Nation*, November 26, 1938, 555.
337 JPK to CH, June 9, 1939: JPKP / "1939, June. To Dept."
338 JPK, Jr., Notes, June 10, 1939: REFKP / "Travel Essays, 1939—Hungary."
339 "By January . . .": Gallup poll results, *New York Times Magazine*, April 30, 1939, 2.
341 JPK, Jr., "Poland," June 10, 1939: JPKP / "Travel Essays, 1939—Poland."
341 REFK Diary, June 11, 1939: JPKP / "1939 Diary."
342 JPK, Jr., "Berlin," June 18, 1939: JPKP / "Travel Essays, 1939—Germany."
343 REFK Diary, July 4, 1939: JPKP / "1939 Diary."
344 Debutantes at The 400 as "fast," Lambert, 151–53.
344 EK, "A Weekend at Blenheim Palace", n.d. (June 1939): JPKP. Reproduced with the kind permission of Eunice Kennedy Shriver.
344 ". . . everybody praised . . .": Robert Southey, "The Battle of Blenheim."
346 JPK to FDR, July 20, 1939: FDRL / PSF 37 / "Kennedy."
346 "In March . . .": Churchill, *Gathering Storm 1*, 356–58.
347 JPK to Joseph Patterson, July 20, 1939: JPKP / "P."
348 JPK to CH, July 20, 1939: JPKP / "1939, July. To Dept."
349 JPK Diary, July 20, 1939: JPKP.
349 "the arms embargo . . .": *Keesing's*, July 19, 1939, 3644.
350 JPK: Diary, July 21, 1939, JPK Diary, 1938–39.
350 "spangled tulle . . .": quoted in Lash, 581.

Page

350   "in very great . . .": JPK to FDR on German submarines, June 1, 1939: JPKP / "Roosevelt, Franklin D."

352   "was in no hurry . . .": Forster on Hitler to Halifax quoted in JPK to CH, Dispatch No. 1041, July 21, 1939: JPKP / "1939, July. To Dept."

353   FDR to JPK, July 22, 1939: JPKP / "Roosevelt, Franklin D."

353   "Until next fall . . .": Krock, "Why Ambassador Kennedy Is Not Coming Home," *NYT*, July 18, 1939, 18:5.

354   JPK to FDR, August 9, 1939: FDRL / PSF 37 / "Kennedy."

354   "the makings . . .": JPK to FDR, July 29, 1939: FDRL / PSF 37 / "Kennedy."

355   JPK, Jr., "Unity Mitford," August 21, 1939: JPKP / "JPK, Jr., Mss–Germany."

356   JPK Diary, August 24, 1939: JPKP.

357   "On August 24 . . .": JPK, DM, XXXIII, 4.

360   JPK: Press Release, August 24, 1939, : JPKP / "#2, German-Polish Crisis: Evacuation of US Citizens."

361   JPK to Sumner Welles, August 24, 1939: FDRL / PSF 21.

361   JPK to Sumner Welles, August 25, 1939: FDRL / PSF / "Safe Kennedy."

362   JPK Diary, August 25, 1939: JPKP.

362   JPK to Sumner Welles, August 26, 1939: JPKP.

363   JPK Diary, August 27, 1939: JPKP.

364   "but of necessity . . .": Dispatch No. 1289, August 27, 1939: FDRL / PSF 21.

364   JPK to Henry Kittredge, August 30, 1939: JPKP / "K–1939."

365   JPK: Diary, September 3, 1939: JPKP.

365   "the sitting of this House . . .": Archibald Sinclair quoted in the *Times*, September 4, 1939, 3.

367   "[s]hould one . . .": Article 1 of the Anglo-Polish Treaty, August 25, 1939: *British War Blue Book*, Misc, No. 9 (1939), No. 19, Art. 1.

367   JPK to CH, September 3, 1939: JPKP / "1939, Sept. 1–15. To Dept."

368   JPK to CH, September 4, 1939: JPKP / "1939, Sept. 1–15. To Dept."

369   JPK, Jr., "Sept. 4, 1939": JPKP / "JPK Jr. Mss - England."

369   *Athenia* passenger figures, *NYT*, September 5, 1939, 4.

369   German denial, *NYT*, September 5, 1939, 4.

369   *Athenia* survivor figures, *NYT*, September 6, 1939, 4.

370   JPK to CH, September 8, 1939: JPKP / "1939, Sept. 1–15. To Dept."

371   KK, "Lamps in a Blackout," n.d. (September 1939): JPKP / "Kennedy, Kathleen."

372   JPK to FDR, September 10, 1939: FDRL / PSF / "Safe: Kennedy."

374   JPK to CH and FDR, September 11, 1939: JPKP / "1939, Sept. 1–15. To Dept."

376   "the silliest . . .": Farley's recollection of FDR's reaction to JPK dispatch quoted in Beschloss, 191.

376   JPK to George VI, September 14, 1939: JPKP.

376   "When referring . . .": George V to JPK, September 12, 1939: JPKP / "King and Queen (Britain), (Also Other Members of the Royal Family)."Quoted with the kind permission of Her Majesty the Queen.

377   JPK Diary, September 15, 1939: JPKP.

378   "extremely downcast . . .": JPK to CH, 1666, September 15, 1939: JPKP / "1939, Sept. 1–15. To Dept."

378   JPK Diary, September 17, 1939, : JPKP.

379   "This is not . . .": Lindbergh's radio address, *NYT*, September 15, 1939, 9.

379   JPK to REFK, n.d. (September 18, 1939): JKS.

381   KK to JPK, September 18, 1939: JPKP.

381   JPK, Jr., 24, to JPK, September 27, 1939: JPKP.

382   JPK to FDR, September 30, 1939: FDRL / PSF 37 / "Kennedy."

382   "this Government . . .": CH to JPK, 905, September 11, 1939: FDRL / PSF / Safe / "Kennedy."

382   "pessimistic to . . .": JPK to Dept. 1873, September 30, 1939: JPKP / "1939, Sept. 15–30. To Dept."

385   JPK to FDR, September 30, 1939: FDRL / PSF 37 / "Kennedy."

387   JPK to FDR, September 30, 1939: FDRL / PSF 37 / "Kennedy."

389   RFK to JPK, n.d.: JPKP.

389   EMK to JPK, n.d.: JPKP.

390   JPK to CH, 1893, October 2, 1939: JPKP / "1939, October, To Dept."

391   JPK to REFK, October 2, 1939: JKS.

391   "Of all the wars . . .": WSC Broadcast, October 1, 1939, Churchill and Gilbert, 195.

392   JPK: Diary, October 5, 1939: JPKP.

392   "The Naval person . . .": JPK to Dept. 1914, October 4, 1939: JPKP.

393   "by the First Lord . . .": JPK to Dept. 1892, October 2, 1939: JPKP.

393   JPK to FDR, October 9, 1939: JPKP / "Correspondence from Paul Murphy's File, 1938–39."

393   JPK to REFK, October 11, 1939: JKS.

393   "would not support . . .": CH to JPK, 905, September 11, 1939: FDRL / PSF / Safe / "Kennedy."

395   JPK to JPK, Jr., and JFK, October 13, 1939: JPKP.

395   "recognition of . . .": Chamberlain's reply to Hitler's peace proposal, *Times*, October 13, 1939, 8.

396   JPK to Robert Fisher, October 23, 1939: JPKP / "F."

Page

397   JPK to John B. Kennedy, October 26, 1939: JPKP / "JPK, Jr."
397   EMK to JPK and EEM, n.d.: JPKP.
398   JPK to FDR, November 3, 1939: FDRL / PSF 37.
399   JPK Diary, November 8, 1939: JPKP.
400   JPK to Will Hays, November 12, 1939: JPKP / "Mr. Smith Goes to Washington."
400   JPK to Harry Cohn, November 17, 1939: FDRL / PSF 37.
401   JPK Diary, November 28, 1939: JPKP.
403   "[w]e desire . . .": Lindbergh's second radio address, NYT, October 14, 1939, 10:4.
403   EMK to JPK, n.d.: JPKP.
404   JPK: Diary, December 10, 1939: JPKP.
404   "The strain of work . . .": DM, XXXXVII, 13: JPKP.
404   "[t]he problems . . .": JPK on Roosevelt third term, NYT, December 9, 1939, 1.
405   "Without mentioning," Felix Belair, Jr., "Roosevelt Blames Governor of Ohio in City Relief Crisis," 1, December 9, 1939, 1:4.
406   JPK to REFK, March 14, 1940: JPKP / "JPK, Personal, London"
408   "the views . . .": FDR on the purpose of the Welles mission quoted in Dallek, 216.
408   "If you mean by isolation . . .": JPK quoted in the NYT, March 8, 1940, 8:4.
409   JPK to REFK, March 14, 1940: JKS.
410   JPK, Jr., to JPK, March 17, 1940: JPKP.
410   JPK to REFK, March 20, 1940: JKS.
411   JPK Diary, March 28, 1940: JPKP.
412   RK to JPK, April 4(?), 1940: JPKP.
413   JPK to: REFK, April 5, 1940: JPKP / "Kennedy, Mrs. Joseph P."
414   "Ambassador [Kennedy] stated . . .": White Paper quoted in the NYT, March 31, 1940, 32.
414   "I read . . .": Raczinski, 51.
414   "President Roosevelt, who went for a ride in the spring sunshine . . .": NYT, April 2, 1940, 12:3.
415   JPK to REFK, April 5, 1940: JKS.
415   JPK, Jr., to JPK, April 5, 1940: JPKP.
416   EMK to JPK, April 8, 1940: JPKP.
417   JFK to JPK, n.d., JFKL / Kennedy Family Correspondence / MS 80-10 / 1/2 / "JFK Family Letters Owned by PKL."
418   JPK to REFK, April 26, 1940: JPKP.
419   JPK, Jr., to JPK, May 4, 1940: JPKP.
421   REFK to JPK, May 8, 1940: JPKP / "Kennedy, Mrs. Joseph P."
422   JPK Diary, May 9, 10, 1940: JPKP.
422   "[t]he size of the majority . . .": JPK to the Department, 1148, May 9, 1940, 1: JPKP.
422   "Those remarks . . .": JPK, DM, XXXX, 6–7: JPKP.
424   JPK to FDR and CH, May 15, 1940: JPKP / "1940–March to Dept."
424   "[i]f necessary . . .": WSC to FDR, 1216, May 15, 1940, 1-2: JPKP.
425   JPK Diary, May 15, 16, 1940, : JPKP.
425   "Without question . . .": JPK on David Margesson, Dispatch No. 1140, May 8, 1940, 1: JPKP.
425   "on May 14 . . .": JPK, DM, XXXXIV, 7: JPKP.
427   "most happy . . .": FDR to WSC, May 16, 1940: JPKP / "From the Department, May 1940."
428   JPK to FDR and CH, May 16, 1940: JPKP / 1940–May to Dept.
429   JPK to NC, May 18, 1940: JPKP / "Chamberlain, Neville."
429   JPK, Jr. to JPK, May 18, 1940: JPKP.
429   "We stand ready . . .": NYT, May 17, 1940, 15.
429   "Rarely if ever . . .,": NYT, May 17, 1940, 1.
430   JPK, DM, XXXXIV, 14–18: JPKP.
430   "The Right Club . . .": Herschel Johnson, Secret Memorandum to the Department, May 30, 1940: JPKP.
431   "This Government has no objection . . .": CH to JPK, 944, May 22, 1940, 1: JPKP.
432   JPK to REFK, May 20, 1940: JKS.
432   "I was finally . . .": REFK to JPK, May 13, 1949: JPKP / "Kennedy, Mrs. Joseph P."
433   JPK to RK, n.d. (1939): JPKP / "Telegrams, 1939."
433   JPK to JFK, May 20, 1940: JFKL / 1979–93 Exhibit Book.
433   "To blame one man . . .": JFK, "Appeasement at Munich," ii.
435   Princess Elizabeth to JPK, May 22, 1940: JPKP / "King and Queen (Britain), (Also other members of the Royal Family)." Used with the kind permission of Her Majesty The Queen.
436   REFK to JPK, June 1, 1940: JPKP / "Kennedy, Mrs. Joseph P."
436   JPK to Arthur Goldsmith, June 4, 1940: JPKP / "G, 1940."
436   JPK to JPK, Jr., June 6, 1940: JPKP.
437   "The easy thing . . .": Harold Laski to JPK, August 8, 1940: FDRL / PPF 207 / 1939–45.
437   EMK to JPK, n.d.: JPKP.

Page

438   JPK Diary, June 11–14, 1940: JPKP.

440   "was sick . . .": JPK Diary, June 12, 1940: JPKP.

440   "Your message . . .": FDR to Reynaud, 1179, June 13, 1940, 1:00 p.m., 1: JPKP.

440   "We are worried about Ireland . . .": WSC to FDR, 1622, June 12, 1: JPKP.

441   "Reynaud told Churchill . . .": 1643, June 14, 1940., 1: JPKP.

442   "The arrival of your note to Reynaud . . .": 1643, June 14, 1940, 2–3: JPKP.

443   "As I asked Ambassador Kennedy . . .": FDR to WSC, 1202, June 14, 1940, 1–2: JPKP.

444   JFK to JPK, n.d.: JFKL / JFK / Personal Papers / 4B / "Gene Schoor—Young John F. Kennedy."

444   JPK to CH, 1680, June 16, 1940: FDRL / PSF / "Safe 3: Kennedy."

445   JPK Diary, June 24, 1940: JPKP.

446   REFK to JPK, June 24, 1940: JPKP / "Kennedy, Mrs. Joseph P."

448   JFK to JFF, July 10, 1940: JPKP / "'40 K (Misc) to John F. Kennedy."

448   RFK to JPK, n.d.: JPKP

448   JPK to James Farley, July 19, 1940: JPKP.

448   "I WILL EVER BE THANKFUL . . .": James Farley to JPK, July 19, 1940: JPKP / "Letters, etc. for Ch. 14."

449   JPK, Jr. to JPK, July 22, 1940: JPKP.

451   "Worst damn-fool mistake . . .": John Nance Garner quoted in the *NYT*, November 8, 1967, 1.

451   JPK to RFK, July 23, 1940: JPKP.

452   JPK to JPK, Jr., July 23, 1940: JPKP.

452   JPK Diary, August 1, 1940, : JPKP.

453   JPK to JFK, August 2, 1940, JPKE.

454   JPK to REFK, August 2, 1940, NYOF / JPK / I / "Kennedy, Mrs. Joseph P."

457   JPK Diary, August 6, 1940 JPK: Diary.

458   JFK to JPK, n.d.: JPKP / "'40 K (Misc) to John F. Kennedy."

458   JPK to CH, 2613, August 7, 1940: JPKP / "1940, August. To Dept."

459   "I was a soldier . . .": Cudahy interview transcript, 2624, August 9, 1940: JPKP.

460   JPK to Brendan Bracken, August 8, 1940: JPKP.

460   JPK Diary, August 14, 1940: JPKP.

460   "It is my belief . . .": FDR to WSC, 2316, August 13, 1940: JPKP.

460   "Imagine . . .": DM, XXXXVIII, 11: JPKP.

461   JPK to Joseph Medill Patterson, August 22, 1940: JPKP / "Letters Etc. for Ch. 14."

461   "What an excellent impression . . .": J. M. Patterson to JPK, July 22, 1940: JPKP / "Letters Etc. for Ch. 14."

463   JPK to FDR, 2913, August 27, 1940: JPKP / "1940, August. To Dept."

463   JPK Diary, September 2, 1940: JPKP.

465   JPK to FDR and CH, 3038, September 6, 1940: JPKP / "1940, September. To Dept."

466   JPK to REFK, September 10, 1940: JPKP.

468   JPK to JFK, September 10, 1940: JFKL / JFK / Personal Papers / 4A / "Kennedy, Joseph P. Sr.—Letters to John F. Kennedy, 1940–45."

469   JPK to RFK, September 11, 1940: JPKP.

470   JPK to EMK, September 11, 1940: JPKP.

471   JPK to REFK, September 11, 1940: JPKP.

472   JPK Diary, September 24th, 1940: JPKP.

472   "put it across . . .": WSC to FDR, 3181, September 24, 1940: JPKP.

473   "Was it extraordinary skill . . .": Wendell Willkie quoted in the *NYT*, September 15, 1940, 1.

474   RFK to JPK, n.d.: JPKP / "'40 K (Misc) J. F. Kennedy."

474   "Close Escape"; "by inches," *NYT*, October 2, 1940, 4:2.

474   REFK to JPK, October 7, 1940: JPKP / "Correspondence from Paul Murphy's File, 1938–39."

475   FDR to JPK, October 17, 1940: JPKP / "White House."

475   JPK Diary, October 19, 1940: JPKP.

477   JPK to NC, October 22, 1940: JPKP.

478   JPK Diary, n.d. (October 22, 1940): JPKP.

479   FDR to JPK, October 25, 1940: JPKP.

479   JPK Diary, n.d., : JPKP.

480   JPK Diary, n.d. (October 25, 1940), : JPKP.

480   FDR to JPK, October 26, 1940: JPKP / "White House."

480   JPK Diary, n.d: JPKP.

481   "I should imagine . . .": NC to JPK, October 19, 1940: JPKP.

482   "I want only . . .": Clare Boothe Luce to JPK, October 28, 1940, JPK Diary, 1940–41: JPKP.

482   JPK: Radio Address, October 29, 1940: JPKP.

489   FDR to JPK, October 29, 1940: JPKP / "White House."

489   "I have said this before . . .": FDR speech at the Boston Garden quoted in the *NYT*, October 31, 1940, 1.

Page

489 JFK to JPK, October 30, 1940: JPKP / "K."

489 KK to JPK, October 30, 1940: JPKP / Unmarked File.

490 JPK, Jr., to JPK, November 2(?), 1940: JPKP.

491 JPK: "Notes Dictated by Ambassador for His Diary", November 4, 6, 1940, JPK Diary, 1940–41: JPKP.

492 JPK to FDR, Resignation Draft, n.d.: JPKP / "Roosevelt, Franklin D."

493 JPK Diary, November 9, 1940: JPKP.

493 JPK to WRH, November 26, 1940: JPKP / "H."

494 JPK Diary, November 30, 1940: JPKP.

494 "[t]he Globe hopes . . .": Louis Lyons to JPK, November 9, 1940, JFKL / JPK / MS 77–23 / 51 / "L."
Lyons Interview with JPK, BG, November 10, 1940, 1.

495 "Being easily emotional . . .": JPK quoted in Alsop and Kintner, American White Paper, 68.

495 JPK Diary, December 1, 1940, : JPKP.

497 JPK: Press Release, December 1, 1940: JPKP / "White House."

498 JFK, Memorandum, December 6, 1940: JPKP.

498 "When JPK announced . . ." Alsop and Kintner, "Peace or Appeasement," BG, December 5, 1940,
14.

501 "Only last week . . .": Alsop and Kintner, "Advice Ignored, Kennedy Determine to Come Home," BG,
October 7, 1940, 2.

501 "Only a miracle can keep us out . . .": Hiram Johnson quoted in the NYT, December 5, 1940, 12.

503 "Resounding answer . . .": Ernest Bevin radio address, NYT, November 24, 1940, 9:5.

505 JFK to JPK, n.d.,: JFKL / JPK / JFK Personal Correspondence—Xerox Copies / "JPK, Sr—Xerox Folder
VI."

507 JPK to Arthur Houghton, December 21, 1940: JPKP / "'40 H-Misc. to Insurance."

508 JPK to R. Douglas Stuart, Jr., December 23, 1940: JPKP / "40, A to BMT."

Part V: Semiretirement 1947–1961

Page

511 "[y]our boys . . .": FDR speech at the Boston Garden quoted in the NYT, October 31, 1940, 1.

511 " arsenal of democracy,": FDR Fireside Chat, December 29, 1940 in MacArthur, ed., 196–7.

511 "peddle appeasement . . .": Alsop and Kintner, December 5, 1940, NYHT.

511 "to see that son of a bitch . . .": FDR quoted in Gore Vidal, New York Review of Books, November 18,
1971.

511 "Conversations with Roosevelt," n.d.: JPKP / "Roosevelt, Franklin D."

511 "I don't think . . .": JPK Diary, January 21, 1941: JPKP / "#2, Czech Crisis (London Times Outline)."

512 "ALL AMERICANS . . .": JPK to FDR, December 7, 1941: JPKP / "White House."

512 "I think you know . . .": JPK to FDR, March 12, 1942: JPKP / "White House."

512 "a lot of bastards,": JPK, DIARY NOTES ON THE 1944 POLITICAL CAMPAIGN, JPK Diary, 1942–51:
JPKP.

513 "was not only venting . . .": Felix Frankfurter quoted in Beschloss, 252.

513 "He feels . . .": Agent Edward A. Soucy to J. Edgar Hoover, December 27, 1943, FBI, 94-37808.

513 JPK to Lord Beaverbrook, December 31, 1942: JPKP.

513 "He made his fight . . .": JPK to WRH, September 16, 1942: JPKP / "H, 1944–42."

514 "I was shocked . . .": JPK, DIARY NOTES ON THE 1944 POLITICAL CAMPAIGN, JPK Diary, 1942–51:
JPKP.

514 "The terrible realization . . .": JPK, DIARY NOTES ON THE 1944 POLITICAL CAMPAIGN, JPK Diary,
1942–51: JPKP.

514 "with one son . . .": JPK, DIARY ON THE 1944 POLITICAL CAMPAIGN, JPK Diary, 1942–51: JPKP.

515 "she had never seen . . .": etc., JPK to REFK, October 11, 1939, JKS.

517 "Dad knew he was missing . . .": REFK round-robin letter, August 25, 1943: JPKP / "Kennedy, Mr. &
Mrs.–Letters to the Children."

517 "Of course the news . . .": KK, Round-Robin Letter, August 24, 1943: JPKP.

517 "Imagine . . .": KK to JPK, October 6, 1940: JPKP / "'40 K (misc.) to John F. Kennedy"

517 "Dearest Billy . . .": KK to Billy Hartington, December 23, 1940: JPKP.

517 "so anxious . . .": KK to JPK, October 20, 1941: JPKP.

517 "I have never . . .": Billy Hartington quoted in KK to JPK, undated: JPKP.

518 "Kick Kennedy's apostasy . . .": Evelyn Waugh to Laura Waugh, May 12, 1944, in Amory, ed., 184.

518 "Letters continue . . .": KKH to REFK. REFKP / "Kathleen Kennedy, Wedding, 5 / '44."

518 "May the Blessed Mother . . .": Rev. Hugh O'Donnell quoted in Kearns Goodwin, 786.

518 "disturbed . . .": REFK, "Notes on My Reactions at Kick's Marriage": REFKP / "Kathleen Kennedy,
Wedding, 5 / '44."

518 "as long as you love Billy . . .": REFK to KKH, June 30, 1944: JPKP / "Kennedy, Kathleen."

519 JPK, Jr. to REFK and JPK, July 26, 1944: REFKP / "JPK, Jr., 7 / '44–8 / '44."

Letters

718

Page

552 "Do not despair . . .": JPK, Oglethorpe address, May 29, 1943, 4: JPKP.

553 JFK to REFK and JPK, n.d. (May 15, 1943), JPKP.

555 JFK to KK, n.d. (June 3, 1943): JFKL / Kennedy Family Correspondence / MS 80–10 / 1/2 / "Copies of 19 Hand Written Letters from Jack Kennedy to His Mother and Dad."

556 JPK Diary, June 17, 1943, JPK Diary, 1942–51: JPKP.

561 JFK, Round-Robin Letter, June 24, 1943, JFKL / Kennedy Family Correspondence / MS 80–10 / 1/2 / "JFK Family Letters."

562 KK, Round-Robin Letter, June 27 / July 3, 1943: JPKP.

563 KK to JFK, July 3, 1943: REFKP / "Family Correspondence - Personal Between Kathleen Kennedy & Mother & Father."

564 KK, Round-Robin Letter, July 14, 15, 1943: JPKP.

566 KK to JFK, July 29, 1943: JPKP.

567 JFK, Round-Robin Letter, n.d. (received August 10, 1943): JPKP.

569 JFK, Round-Robin Letter, n.d. (Postmarked August 13, 1943): JPKP.

569 JPK to EMK, October 5, 1943: JPKP.

570 KK, Round-Robin Letter, November 17, 1943: JPKP.

572 JPK, Jr., to REFK and JPK, December 5, 1943: REFKP / "JPK, Jr., 11 / '43–12 / '43."

573 JFK to REFK and JPK, December 7, 1943: JPKP.

573 JPK to KK, December 28, 1943, JFKL / KFC / KK Scrapbook.

573 REFK Diary Note, n.d.: REFKP / "Hyannisport—1975."

573 JPK to Harry Hogan, February 21, 1944: JPKP / "H."

574 KK, Round-Robin Letter, February 22, 1944: REFKP / "Kathleen Kennedy, 2 / '44."

577 "A reliable source . . .": BH, February 22, 1944, 1.

577 REFK to KK, February 24, 1944: REFKP / "Kathleen Kennedy, 2 / '44."

578 KK, Round-Robin Letter, March 22, 1944: REFKP / "Kathleen Kennedy, 3 / '44."

578 "Your letter on the election . . .": JPK to KK, March 8, 1944: REFKP / "Kathleen Kennedy, 3 / '44."

581 JPK to KK, April 3, 1944, in Edward M. Kennedy, Ed.

581 KK, Round-Robin Letter, April 4, 5, 1944: REFKP / "Kathleen Kennedy, 4–5 / '44."

583 KK, Round-Robin Letter, April 24, 1944: REFKP / "Kathleen Kennedy, 4–5 / '44."

584 REFK, "Notes on My Reactions at Kick's Marriage," n.d.: REFKP / "Kathleen Kennedy, Wedding, 5 / '44."

584 REFK to KK, n.d.: REFKP / "Kathleen Kennedy, Wedding, 5 / '44."

584 The marquess of Hartington to REFK, April 30, 1944: REFKP / "Kathleen Kennedy, 2 / '44." Used with the kind permission of the present duke of Devonshire.

585 KK to REFK and JPK, May 3, 1944: REFKP / "Kathleen Kennedy, Wedding, 5 / '44."

586 Archbishop William Godfrey to Archbishop Francis Spellman, May 4, 1944: REFKP / "Kathleen Kennedy, 2 / '44."

586 KK to JPK, May 5, 1944: REFKP / "Kathleen Kennedy, 4–5 / '44."

586 Archbishop Francis Spellman to Archbishop William Godfrey, n.d. (May 6, 1944): JPKP / "Kennedy, Kathleen."

586 JPK, Jr. to REFK, May 6, 1944: REFKP / "Kathleen Kennedy, Wedding, 5 / '44."

587 Marie Bruce and Lady Astor to REFK, May 7, 1944: REFKP / "Kathleen Kennedy, Wedding, 5 / '44."

587 JPK, Jr., 28, to JPK: Telegram May 7, 1944, JFKL / REFK (JPK) / MS 79-2 / 7 / "Kathleen Kennedy, Wedding, 5 / '44."

587 KKH to JPK, May 8, 1944: REFKP / "Kathleen Kennedy, Wedding, 5 / '44."

587 JPK, Jr. to REFK and JPK, May 8, 1944: REFKP / "JPK, Jr., 5 / '44."

589 KKH to REFK, May 9, 10, 1944: REFKP / "Kathleen Kennedy, Wedding, 5 / '44."

592 KKH, Round-Robin Letter, May 18, 1944: REFKP / "Kathleen Kennedy, Wedding, 5 / '44."

594 KKH, Round-Robin Letter, May 23, 1944: JPKP / "Kennedy, Kathleen."

594 "on the occasion . . .": JPK address, May 22, 1944. JPKP / "Maritime Day Speech, Boston, 5 / 22 / 44."

595 REFK to KKH, June 30, 1944: JPKP / "Kennedy, Kathleen."

597 KKH to REFK, July 6, 1944: JPKP / "Kennedy, Kathleen."

598 JPK, Jr. to REFK and JPK, July 26, 1944: REFKP / "JPK, Jr., 7 / '44–8 / '44."

598 JPK, Jr. to REFK and JPK, n.d. (August 4, 1944): REFKP / "JPK, Jr., 7 / '44–8 / '44."

599 Vice Admiral Randall Jacobs to REFK, August 13, 1944: REFKP / "JPK, Jr., Telegram Announcing Death."

599 REFK, "Joe Jr.'s Death," n.d.: REFKP / "Married Life II."

600 KKH, to Marie Bruce, n.d.: JPKP / "Kennedy, Kathleen."

600 FDR to JPK, n.d.: REFKP / "JPK, Jr. Condolence Acknowledgments: O'Brien-Sweeney."

600 The duchess of Devonshire to KKH, n.d. (September 13, 1944): JPKP / "Kennedy, Kathleen." Used with the kind permission of the present duke of Devonshire.

601 KKH Diary, September 20, 1944, JFKL / KFC / KK Scrapbook.

Page

601 KKH to REFK and JPK, n.d. (September 20, 1944): JPKP / "Kennedy, Kathleen."
602 REFK to KKH, September 25, 1944. JPKP / "Kennedy, Kathleen."
602 KKH, Round-Robin Letter, September 23, 1944: JPKP / "Kennedy, Kathleen."
605 JPK Diary, n.d., JPK Diary, 1942–51: JPKP.
613 JPK to Francis T. Leahy, February 13, 1945: JPKP / "L."
613 "the advertising manager of the Globe . . .": Francis Leahy to JPK January 18, 1945: JPKP / "L."
613 "to find out whether . . .": Francis Leahy to JPK January 18, 1945: JPKP / "L."
614 JPK to Henry Luce, February 15, 1945: JPKP / "45, Hyannis Finance–Kathleen Kennedy."
614 JPK to Joseph Medill Patterson, February 19, 1945: JPKP / "P."
614 JPK to Joseph Kane, March 19, 1945: JPKP / "Joseph Kane, 1945–49."
615 JPK to KKH, May 1, 1945: JPKP.
615 "I sat in between . . .": KK Round Robin, April 22, 1945: REFKP / "Kathleen—ALS, 36–40."
618 JPK to EMK, May 8, 1945: JPKP.
618 KKH, Round-Robin Letter, May 12, 1945: REFKP / "Kathleen—ALS, 41–45."
619 JFK to REFK and JPK, May 21, 1945: JPKP
620 JPK to Arthur Houghton, May 26, 1945: JPKP / "Houghton, Arthur J."
621 JFK, Travel Diary, n.d. (July 24, 1945): JPKP / "Photocopying FY '91 G-J."
621 JPK to Bartholomew Brickley, October 12, 1945: REFKP / "BA Brickley 1944–45."
622 JPK to Cissy Patterson, November 26, 1945: JPKP / "P."
622 JPK: "Memorandum of Conversation with Winston Churchill at Hialeah Race Track on January 31, 1946," n.d., JPK Diary, 1942–51: JPKP.
624 JPK to EMK, January 3 1, 1946: JPKP / "To Edward M. Kennedy."
624 KKH, Diary, February 27, 1946, JFKL / KFC / KK Scrapbook.
625 JPK to Arthur Krock, February 28, 1946: JPKP / "Krock, Arthur."
625 JPK to Joseph Kane, March 11, 1946: REFKP / "Joseph Kane, 1945–49."
626 "[t]o prevent World War III . . .": JPK, "The US and the World," Life, March 18, 1945, 117.
626 REFK, Round-Robin Letter, April 11, 1946: JPKP / "Kennedy, Mr. & Mrs.—Letters to the Children."
626 JPK to Lord Beaverbrook, June 22, 1946: JPKP.
627 KKH to JFK, July 13, 1946: JFKL / JFK / Personal Papers / 4A / "Kennedy, Kathleen—Correspondence 1942–47 & Undated."
627 JPK to Sir James Calder, July 31, 1946; REFKP / "Sir James Calder, 1944–60."
629 KKH, Round-Robin Letter, October 18–22, 1946: REFKP / "Kathleen—ALS, 81–85."
631 KKH, Round-Robin Letter, October 27, 1946: REFKP / "Kathleen—ALS, 81–85."
632 JFF to JFK, January 3, 1947, JFKL / Mus. Exhibit Docs / FY & PB / "Three Western Union Telegrams."
632 JPK to JFK, January 4, 1947, JFKL / Mus. Exhibit Docs / FY & PB / "Three Western Union Telegrams."
633 KKH, Round-Robin Letter, May 16, 1947, JFKL / Kennedy Family Correspondence / MS 80–10 / "Kathleen Kennedy Family Letters, 4–6 / '47."
634 JPK to T. J. White, October 9, 1947: JPKP / "W."
634 "Proposal to Treat . . .": Krock, NYT, September 14, 1947, IV, 3:1.
635 JPK to Lord Beaverbrook, March 23, 1948: REFKP / "Lord Beaverbrook, 1948–54."
635 "A remarkable boy . . .": Beaverbrook to JPK, March 12, 1948: REFKP / "Lord Beaverbrook, 1948–54.
636 JPK on Kick's death, n.d. (May 14, 1948): JPKP / Kennedy Family Collection.
637 JPK to the duchess of Devonshire, September 1, 1948: JPKP / "D."
638 JPK to Pamela Churchill, December 21, 1948: JPKP / "C."
638 JPK: "Summary of Talk between President Truman and Hon. JPK", n.d.: JPKP / "AB-AD, 1938."
641 REFK to Hélène Arpels, July 10, 1950: JPKP / "A."
643 RFK to REFK and JPK, n.d.: JPKP / "Bobby and Ethel."
643 REFK to RFK, and Ethel Skakel Kennedy, 22, July 13, 1950: JPKP / "Bobby and Ethel."
645 JPK to Lord Beaverbrook, November 28, 1950: REFKP / "Lord Beaverbrook, 1948–54."
645 JPK to John B. Johnson, December 28, 1950: JPKP / "JPK's Charlottesville Speech—Correspondence Answered from Palm Beach": JPKP.
645 "Mr. Kennedy is Wrong Again" Watertown Daily Times, December 13, 1950, n.p.: JPKP.
646 JPK: " Honorable JPK's Interview with General Dwight D. Eisenhower, Paris, France–April [1951]," n.d.: JPKP / "Interviews—JPK."
647 "could have been far more . . .": JPK, "An American Foreign Policy for Americans," address delivered at UVA Law School, December 12, 1950: JPKP.
649 "old soldiers never die . . .": MacArthur quoted in the NYT, April 6, 1954, 25.
650 JPK to Mary, duchess of Devonshire, June 22, 1951: JPKP / "D."
650 JPK: "Interview with General MacArthur, June 27, 1951", n.d., JPK Diary, 1942–51: JPKP.
652 "Give me the order to do it . . ." Gen. Orville Anderson quoted in the NYT, September 2, 1950, 1.
654 JPK to Cornelius Fitzgerald, July 18, 1951: JPKP / "F."
655 REFK to Marie Bruce, July 23, 1951: JPKP / "B."

Page

656 JPK to John W. McCormack, August 8, 1951: REFKP / "John W. McCormack, 1933–1960."
657 JPK to Enrico Galeazzi, October 28, 1951: JPKP / "Galeazzi, Count Enrico–II."
658 JPK to Marshall Field, III, December 28, 1951: JPKP / "F."
659 JPK to Loretta Connelly, August 22, 1952: REFKP / "Mrs. George (Loretta) Connolly, 1945–51."
660 EMK to JFK, n.d.: JPKP / "Letters from Edward M. Kennedy."
660 JPK to Sir James Calder, December 31, 1952: REFKP / "Sir James Calder, 1944–60."
661 EMK to JPK, June 20, 1953: JPKP / "Letters from Edward M. Kennedy."
662 Jacqueline Bouvier to REFK, n.d. Monday (June 29, 1953): JPKP / Untitled Folder within "JPK Jr.–RFK–Eunice–JFK" File.
662 JPK to Torb Macdonald, July 22, 1953: JPKP / "L."
663 JPK to Frank Conniff, August 5, 1953: JPKP / "C."
663 "left-wing clique", Frank Conniff to JPK, August 3, 1953: JPKP / C.
663 JFK to REFK and JPK: Telegram, September 15, 1953: JPKP.
664 JPK to RFK, August 15, 1954: JPKP / Unmarked.
664 "contemptuous, contumacious . . .": Senator Ralph Flanders quoted in DAB, 6, 405.
666 RFK to REFK and JPK, October 8, 1954: JPKP / Untitled.
666 REFK to JPK, n.d. Saturday (July 1955): JPKP / "Kennedy, Mr. & Mrs.—Letters to the Children."
666 "great tribute . . .": Joseph A. Loftus, "Army Denounced in Peress Report," NYT, July 15, 1955, 7:1.
667 JPK to RFK, July 21, 1955: REFKP / Pre-Administration—Personal / 20 / "1956 Kennedy Family & New York Office 4 / 56-5 / 56."
667 JPK to Joseph Dinneen, August 6, 1955: JPKP / "D."
668 JFK to JPK, n.d. : JPKP.
669 JPK to Theodore Sorensen: Draft, August 15, 1955: JPKP / "S."
669 JPK to RFK, August 24, 1955: JPKP / Untitled.
670 JPK to EMK, September 3, 1955: JPKP / "To Edward M. Kennedy."
671 JPK to J. Edgar Hoover, October 11, 1955: REFKP / "J. Edgar Hoover."
671 JPK to JFK, May 25, 1956: JPKP.
672 JFK to JPK, June 29, 1956: JPKP / Untitled Folder within "JPK Jr.–RFK—Eunice—JFK" File.
672 "would be helpful to the ticket . . ." John M. Bailey to JFK, n.d.: JPKP / Untitled Folder within "JPK Jr.–RFK–Eunice–JFK" File.
673 JPK to Sargent Shriver, July 18, 1956: JPKP / "S."
676 JPK to EMK, July 18, 1956: JPKP / "To Edward M. Kennedy."
676 JPK to JFK, July 23, 1956: JPKP / Untitled Folder within "JPK Jr.–RFK–Eunice- JFK" File.
677 JPK to Morton Downey, August 24, 1956: REFKP / "Downey-Dreyfus."
677 JPK to Henry Luce, April 12, 1957: JPKP / "L."
678 JPK to Jean Kerr McCarthy, n.d.: JPKP / "MacAdoo-McCarthy."
678 JPK to JFK, July 26, 1957: JPKP / "Europe, 1957."
678 "There was pandemonium . . .": Joseph A. Loftus, NYT, July 20, 1957, 1:8.
679 JPK to McGeorge Bundy, February 11, 1958: REFKP / "Buckley-Byrd."
679 JPK to JFK, March 7, 1958: REFKP / "JFK, 2 / '58-3 / '58."
679 JPK to John Knight, March 11, 1958: JPKP / "K."
680 JPK to EMK, May 2, 1958: JPKP / "Kennedy Family Correspondence, EMK and Family."
680 JPK to J. Edgar Hoover, May 7, 1958: REFKP / "J. Edgar Hoover."
680 "in investigating . . .": Cyrus Eaton quoted in the NYT, May 5, 1958, 1:7, 7:7.
681 REFK to JPK, June 19, 1958: JPKP / "Kennedy Family Correspondence, Mr. and Mrs. JPK."
681 JFK to Eleanor Roosevelt, December 11, 1958: FDRL / Eleanor Roosevelt Correspondence Papers / Gen. Corr. 1958 / 4315 / Kennedy, John F.
681 "If my comment is not true . . ." Eleanor Roosevelt to JFK, December 18, 1958: FDRL / Eleanor Roosevelt Correspondence Papers / Gen. Corr. 1958 / 4315 / Kennedy, John F.
681 JFK to Eleanor Roosevelt, December 29, 1958, FDRL / Eleanor Roosevelt Papers / General Correspondence / 4315 / Kennedy, John F.
682 JPK to Enrico Galeazzi, March 18, 1959: JPKP / "Galeazzi, Count Enrico."
682 "Whatever one's religion . . .": JFK quoted in Fletcher Knebel, "A Catholic in 1960," Look, March 3, 1959, Vol. XXIII, No. 5, 17.
683 JPK to Enrico Galeazzi, March 30, 1959: JPKP / "Galeazzi, Count Enrico."
683 JPK to Enrico Galeazzi, April 17, 1959: JPKP / "Galeazzi, Count Enrico."
684 REFK to JFK, June 15, 1959: JPKP / "Kennedy Family Correspondence, JFK and Family."
685 REFK to Jacqueline Bouvier Kennedy, June 15, 1959: REFKP / "Kennedy Family Correspondence, JFK and Family."
685 JPK to Herman Kahn, December 21, 1959: REFKP / "K."
685 JPK to Louis Harris, December 30, 1959: REFKP / "Christmas, 1959."
686 REFK to EKS, January 19, 1960: REFKP / "Kennedy Family Correspondence, Sargent Shriver and Family."
686 JPK to Ted Sorenson, February 24, 1960: REFKP / "Campaign 1960–2."

Page
686   JPK to Enrico Galeazzi, March 9, 1960: JPKP / "Galeazzi, Count Enrico."
687   JPK to Lord Beaverbrook, April 20, 1960: REFKP / "Lord Beaverbrook, 1959–60."
687   JPK to Enrico Galeazzi: Telegram, May 12, 1960: JPKP / "Galeazzi, Count Enrico."
688   JPK to Lord Beaverbrook, May 27, 1960: REFKP / "Lord Beaverbrook, 1959–60."
688   REFK, Diary, June 23, 1960: REFKP / "Campaigning, 1946."
689   REFK, "July 14, 1960—Morning After," n.d.: JPKP.
690   REFK, Round-Robin Letter, August 23, 1960: JPKP / "Requests for Books, Articles, Etc."
692   JPK to Lord Beaverbrook, September 9, 1960: REFKP / "Lord Beaverbrook, 1959–60."
692   JPK to Dr. J. A. H. Walker: REFKP / "Walker-West."
692   JPK to Walter Trohan, October 22, 1960: REFKP / "Thompson-Trohan."
693   JPK to Phyllis Long, October 22, 1960: REFKP / "Long-Lyons."
693   REFK, Diary, November 3, 1960: REFKP / "Campaigning, 1946."
694   REFK to Ethel Skakel Kennedy, December 1, 1960: REFKP / "Kennedy Family Correspondence, RFK and Family."
695   JPK to Ernest Lindley, December 9, 1960: REFKP / "Lindley-Loeb."
695   JPK to Enrico Galeazzi, January 6, 1961: JPKP / "Galeazzi, Count Enrico."
696   JPK to Enrico Galeazzi, February 6, 1961: JPKP / "Count Galeazzi."
697   REFK, Recollection of the Cuban Missile Crisis, n.d. (April 19, 1961): JPKP.
698   REFK to JPK, September 19, 1961: JPKP.
698   REFK to RFK, n.d.: JPKP / "Kathleen."
698   REFK, "Thanksgiving 61," November 23, 1961: JPKP.

BIBLIOGRAPHY

Primary Sources

The papers of Winthrop Aldrich, Harvard Business School Archives, Baker Library Historical Collections, Harvard Business School, Boston.

The *America* magazine Archives, Georgetown University Special Collections, Washington.

The papers of Anthony Eden, Earl of Avon, University of Birmingham Library, Public Records Office, Kew.

The papers of Lord (Stanley) Baldwin of Bewdley, Cambridge University Library.

The papers of Lord Beaverbrook, House of Lords Record Office, London.

Bethlehem Shipbuilding Corporation, Ltd., *Specifications for Reconditioning of Argentine Battleships "Rivadavia"* and *"Moreno."* Fore River Plant, Quincy, Mass., 1924. Fore River Shipyard Collection, Hart Nautical Collections, Massachusetts Institute of Technology Museum, Cambridge, MA.

British Cabinet papers, 1938–40, Public Records Office, Kew.

The papers of Sir Alexander Cadogan, Churchill College, Cambridge; Public Records Office, Kew.

Central Technical Department of Bethlehem Steel Company, Shipbuilding Division Quincy, MA. "List of Ships Built at Quincy Yard Bethlehem Steel Company Shipbuilding Division Quincy, MA." 1955(?). Fore River Shipyard Collection, Hart Nautical Collections, Massachusetts Institute of Technology Museum, Cambridge, MA.

The papers and diaries of Neville Chamberlain, University of Birmingham Library, Birmingham.

The Chartwell Trust papers, Churchill College, Cambridge.

The papers of Sir Winston Churchill, Churchill College, Cambridge.

Cox & Co. papers in the Lloyds Bank Archive, London.

The papers of Viscount Cranbourne, Public Records Office, Kew.

Notes by R. S. Cumming of Haig & Haig, Ltd., on his visit to the U.S., 20 May 1946, United Distillers' Archive, Edinburgh.

The papers of Lionel Curtis, Department of Western Manuscripts, Bodleian Library, Oxford.

The diaries of Geoffrey Dawson, 1938–1940, Department of Western Manuscripts, Bodleian Library, Oxford.

Distillers Company, Limited, minutes of Finance and Executive Committee meetings, 9 October, 19 November, 3 December 1935, 5 June 1939, 18, 19 June 1946, United Distillers' 18 Archive, Edinburgh.

The papers of Cornelius van H. Engert, Georgetown University Special Collections, Washington.

Federal Bureau of Investigation papers relating to Joseph P. Kennedy, Washington.

Fore River Shipbuilding Corporation Job Order List for Ships Building, 1916. Fore River Shipyard Collection, Hart Nautical Collections, Massachusetts Institute of Technology Museum, Cambridge, MA.

Fore River Plant Quincy and Squantum Works Managers' Notices, 1916–1919, Bethlehem Shipbuilding Corporation, Ltd., Fore River Shipyard Collection, Hart Nautical Collections, Massachusetts Institute of Technology Museum, Cambridge, MA.

Foreign Office papers, 1938–1940, 1944–45, Public Records Office, Kew.

The papers of Carter Glass, Special Collections Department, Alderman Library, University of Virginia, Charlottesville.

Private and confidential memorandum of Grahams & Co., 7 July 1924, Public Records Office proposals to Grahams & Co., 1 August 1923.

Harvard Business School Archives, Office of the Dean, School Correspondence, 1923–27, 1927–35, Baker Library Historical Collections, Harvard Business School, Boston.

The papers of Hon. David Gray, Franklin Delano Roosevelt Library, Hyde Park.

Haig & Haig, Ltd., minutes of the meetings of the directors, 15 December 1933, 22 October 1937, 5 May 1938, United Distillers' Archive, Edinburgh.

The papers and diaries of Lord Halifax, the Borthwick Institute of Historical Research, University of York and at the Public Records Office, Kew.

The papers of Hayden, Stone & Co., Harvard Business School Archives, Baker Library Historical Collections, Harvard Business School, Boston.

The Will Hays Papers, Part I: reels 7, 31; Part II: reels 23, 27, 29, 30, 33. Cinema History Microfilm Series, University Publications of America.

The papers of Harry Hopkins, Georgetown University Special Collections, Washington.

Hedda Hopper Collection, Margaret Herrick Library, Academy of Motion Picture Arts and Sciences, Special Collections, Los Angeles.

The papers of Leslie Hore-Belisha, Churchill College, Cambridge.

The Louis I. Jaffé papers, Special Collections Department, Alderman Library, University of Virginia, Charlottesville.

The Louis Johnson papers, Special Collections Department, Alderman Library, University of Virginia, Charlettesville.

The papers of Sara Miller Jordan, Schlesinger Library, Radcliffe College, Cambridge, MA.

Kennedy, Joseph P., *Paramount Report of 1936, Summary and Addenda*, Verticle File #22, Margaret Herrick Library, Academy of Motion Picture Arts and Sciences, Special Collections, Los Angeles.

The papers of Joseph P. Kennedy, John F. Kennedy Library, Boston.

The papers of Louis Kirstein, Harvard Business School Archives, Baker Library Historical Collections, Harvard Business School, Boston.

The Reverend John LaFarge, S.J., papers, Georgetown University Special Collections, Washington.

The papers of Lord Lothian, Scottish Records Office, Edinburgh.

The correspondence and diplomatic journals of Jay Pierrepont Moffat, Houghton Library, Harvard University, Cambridge, MA.

The papers of Walter Monckton, Department of Western Manuscripts, Bodleian Library, Oxford.

The James D. Mooney papers, Georgetown University Special Collections, Washington.

The papers of Henry Morganthau, Franklin Delano Roosevelt Library, Hyde Park, New York.

MPAA Production Code file on *Mr. Smith Goes to Washington* (Columbia, 1939), Margaret Herrick Library, Academy of Motion Picture Arts and Sciences, Special Collections, Los Angeles.

Pathé Exchange Collection, Margaret Herrick Library, Academy of Motion Picture Arts and Sciences, Special Collections, Los Angeles.

The ambassadorial papers of Hon. William Phillips, Houghton Library, Harvard University, Cambridge, MA.

The correspondence of Emil Puhl, Georgetown University Special Collections, Washington.

The Martin J. Quigley papers, Georgetown University Special Collections, Washington.

The papers of Terry Ramsaye, Georgetown University Special Collections, Washington.

The papers of Eleanor Roosevelt, Franklin Delano Roosevelt Library, Hyde Park, New York.

The papers of Franklin Delano Roosevelt, including the Official File, the President's Personal File, the Map Room File and the President's Safe File, Franklin Delano Roosevelt Library, Hyde Park, New York.

The papers of the Securities and Exchange Commission, Record Group 266, National Archives, Washington.

The papers of Edward Carl Wolfram von Selzam, Alderman Library, University of Virginia, Charlottesville.

James Seymour papers, Margaret Herrick Library, Academy of Motion Picture Arts and Sciences, Special Collections, Los Angeles.

The papers of Sir John Simon, Department of Western Manuscripts, Bodleian Library, Oxford, and the Public Records Office, Kew.

The papers of Eamon de Valera, the Franciscan House of Studies, Dún Mhuire, Killiney, County Dublin.

The papers of Robert Wagner, Georgetown University Special Collections, Washington.

War Films Hearings (1941) Collection, Margaret Herrick Library, Academy of Motion Picture Arts and Sciences, Special Collections, Los Angeles.

Walter Winchell Clippings in the Columnists' Collections, Margaret Herrick Library, Academy of Motion Picture Arts and Sciences, Special Collections, Los Angeles.

The correspondence of Helmuth Wohlthat in the James D. Mooney papers, Georgetown University Special Collections, Washington.

Adolph Zuckor Collection, Margaret Herrick Library, Academy of Motion Picture Arts and Sciences, Special Collections, Los Angeles.

Interviews

Christie, Viscountess Simon, 15 July 1994.

Page Huidekoper Wilson, 18 September 1994.

Books

Adams, Cindy Heller, and Susan Crimp. *Iron Rose: The Story of Rose Fitzgerald Kennedy and her Dynasty.* Beverly Hills, CA.: Dove Books, 1995.

Albee, Edward F., et al. *A Tribute to Benjamin Franklin Keith.* Boston: Privately published, 1927.

Alsop, Joseph, and Robert Kinter. *American White Paper: The Story of American Diplomacy and the Second World War.* New York: Simon and Schuster, 1940.

Amory, Mark. *The Letters of Evelyn Waugh.* Middlesex, England: Penguin, 1980.

Ashman, Charles R. *The Finest Judges Money Can Buy, and Other Forms of Judicial Pollution.* Los Angeles: Nash, 1973.

Asinof, Eliot. *Eight Men Out*. New York: Holt, 1963.

Associated Newspapers Ltd., eds. *News in Our Time, 1896–1946: Golden Jubilee Book of the* Daily Mail. London: Morrison and Gibb, 1946.

Barnett, Correlli, ed. *Hitler's Generals*. New York: Quill, 1989.

Beaver, Daniel R. *Newton D. Baker and the American War Effort, 1917–1919*. Lincoln: University of Nebraska Press, 1966.

Berenbaum, Michael. *Witness to the Holocaust*. New York: HarperCollins, 1997.

Berg, A. Scott. *Lindbergh*. New York: G. P. Putnam's, 1998.

Beschloss, Michael R. *Kennedy and Roosevelt: The Uneasy Alliance*. New York: W. W. Norton, 1980.

Birkenhead, Frederick Winston Furneaux Smith. *Halifax: The Life of Lord Halifax*. London: H. Hamilton, 1965.

Bjørklund, Oddvar. *Historical Atlas of the World*. New York: Barnes & Noble, 1970.

Black, Gregory D. *Hollywood Censored*. Cambridge: Cambridge University Press, 1994.

Bloch, Michael. *Ribbentrop*. New York: Crown Publishers, 1992.

Blum, John Morton. *From the Morgenthau Diaries*. Boston: Houghton Mifflin, 1959.

Blumberg, Arnold. *Great Leaders, Great Tyrants?: Contemporary Views of World Rulers Who Made History*. Westport, CT: Greenwood Press, 1995.

Bordman, Gerald, ed. *The Oxford Companion to the American Theatre*. New York: Oxford University Press, 1992.

Bourne, Richard. *Lords of Fleet Street: The Harmsworth Dynasty*. London: Unwin Hyman, 1990.

Brigance, William Norwood. *Classified Speech Models of Eighteen Forms of Public Address*. New York: F. S. Crofts & Co., 1928.

Bullock, Alan. *Hitler, A Study in Tyranny*. New York: Harper & Row, 1964.

Burk, Robert F. *Never Just A Game*. Chapel Hill: University of North Carolina Press, 1994.

Burns, James MacGregor. *Roosevelt, the Lion and the Fox*. New York: Harcourt Brace Jovanovich, 1956.

Butler, Alban. *One Hundred Saints: Their Lives and Likenesses*. Boston: Little, Brown, 1993.

Cadogan, Alexander, and David Dilks. *The Diaries of Sir Alexander Cadogan, O.M., 1938–1945*. New York: Putnam, 1972.

Cameron, Gail. *Rose: A Biography of Rose Fitzgerald Kennedy*. New York: Putnam, 1971.

Cannadine, David. *Aspects of Aristrocracy: Grandeur and Decline in Modern Britain*. New Haven: Yale University Press, 1994.

Canning, Paul. *British Policy Towards Ireland, 1921–1941*. New York: Clarendon Press; Oxford University Press, 1985.

Chamberlain, Neville. *In Search of Peace*. New York: G. P. Putnam's Sons, 1939.

Chaney, Lindsay, and Michael Cieply. *The Hearsts: Family and Empire—The Later Years*. New York: Simon and Schuster, 1981.

Chernow, Ron. *The House of Morgan: An American Banking Dynasty and The Rise of Modern Finance*. New York: Atlantic Monthly Press, 1990.

Chisholm, Anne. *Nancy Cunard: A Biography*. New York: Knopf, 1979.

Churchill, Winston. *The Second World War: The Gathering Storm*. Boston: Houghton Mifflin in association with Cooperation Pub. Co., 1948.

———, and Robert Rhodes James. *Winston S. Churchill: His Complete Speeches, 1897–1963*. New York: Chelsea House Publishers, 1974.

———, and Martin Gilbert. *The Churchill War Papers*. New York: W. W. Norton, 1993.

Ciano, Galeazzo, and Hugh Gibson. *The Ciano Diaries, 1939–1943: The Complete, Unabridged Diaries of Count Galeazzo Ciano, Italian Minister for Foreign Affairs, 1936–1943*. Garden City: Doubleday & Company, 1946.

Coit, Margaret L. *Mr. Baruch*. Boston: Houghton Mifflin, 1957.

Collier, Peter, and David Horowitz. *The Kennedys: An American Drama*. New York: Summit Books, 1984.

Curran, Joseph M. *Hibernian Green on the Silver Screen*. New York: Greenwood Press, 1989.

Cutler, John Henry. *"Honey Fitz": Three Steps to the White House: The Life and Times of John F. (Honey Fitz) Fitzgerald*. Indianapolis: Bobbs-Merrill, 1962.

Dallek, Robert. *Franklin D. Roosevelt and American Foreign Policy, 1932–1945*. New York: Oxford University Press, 1995.

Daniels, Jonathan. *Washington Quadrille: The Dance Beside the Documents*. Garden City: Doubleday, 1968.

Davis, Kenneth Sydney. *FDR: The Beckoning of Destiny, 1882–1928: A History*. New York: Random House, 1993.

———. *FDR, Into the Storm, 1937–1940: A History*. New York: Random House, 1993.

De Bedts, Ralph F. *Ambassador Joseph Kennedy, 1938–1940: An Anatomy of Appeasement*. New York: P. Lang, 1985.

———. *The New Deal's SEC: The Formative Years*. New York: Columbia University Press, 1964.

De Mowbray, Stephen. *Key Facts in Soviet History*. London: Printer Publishers in association with J. Spiers, 1990.

Dewey, Donald, and Nicholas Acocella. *The Biographical History of Baseball*. New York: Carroll & Graf, 1995.

Dinneen, Joseph F. *The Kennedy Family*. Boston: Little, Brown, 1960.

Donaghy, Thomas J. *Keystone Democrat: David Lawrence Remembered*. New York: Vantage Press, 1986.

Eden, Anthony. *Days for Decision.* New York: Kraus Reprint, 1969.

———. *Facing the Dictators: The Memoirs of Anthony Eden, Earl of Avon.* Boston: Houghton Mifflin, 1962.

———. *Full Circle: The Memoirs of the Rt. Hon. Sir Anthony Eden.* London: Cassell, 1960.

Edwards, Jerome E. *The Foreign Policy of Col. McCormick's Tribune, 1929–1941.* Reno: University of Nevada Press, 1971.

Facey, Paid W. *The Legion of Decency.* New York: Arno Press, 1974.

Farson, Robert H. *The Cape Cod Canal.* Middletown, CT: Wesleyan University Press, 1977.

Feldman, Charles Matthew. *The National Board of Censorship (Review) of Motion Pictures, 1909–1922.* New York: Arno Press, 1977.

Fisher, Charles. *The Columnists.* New York: Howell, 1944.

Freidel, Frank Burt. *Franklin D. Roosevelt: A Rendezvous with Destiny.* Boston: Little, Brown, 1990.

Frost-Knappman, Elizabeth, and Sarah Kurian. *The ABC-CLIO Companion to Women's Progress in America.* Santa Barbara: ABC-CLIO, 1994.

Gabler, Neal. *An Empire of Their Own: How the Jews Invented Hollywood.* New York: Crown Publishers, 1988.

———. *Winchell: Gossip, Power, and the Culture of Celebrity.* New York: Knopf, 1994.

Garraty, John Arthur. *The American Nation: A History of the United States.* 5th ed. New York: Harper & Row, 1983.

Gellman, Irwin F. *Secret Affairs: Franklin Roosevelt, Cordell Hull, and Sumner Welles.* Baltimore: Johns Hopkins University Press, 1995.

Gentry, Curt. *J. Edgar Hoover: The Man and the Secrets.* New York: W. W. Norton, 1991.

Gibson, Barbara, and Caroline Latham. *Life with Rose Kennedy.* Thorndike, ME: Thorndike Press, 1986.

———, and Ted Schwarz. *Rose Kennedy and Her Family: The Best and Worst of Their Lives and Times.* Secaucus, NJ: Carol Pub. Group, 1995.

Gilbert, Douglas. *American Vaudeville, Its Life and Times.* New York: Dover, 1963.

Gilbert, Martin. *A History of the Twentieth Century.* New York: Morrow, 1997.

———, and Richard Gott. *The Appeasers.* Boston: Houghton Mifflin, 1963.

Ginsburg, Daniel E. *The Fix Is In.* Jefferson, N.C.: McFarland, 1995.

Goodwin, Doris Kearns. *The Fitzgeralds and the Kennedys.* New York: Simon and Schuster, 1986.

———. *No Ordinary Time: Franklin and Eleanor Roosevelt: The Home Front in World War II.* New York: Simon & Schuster, 1994.

Grenville J. A. S. *A History of the World in the Twentieth Century.* Cambridge, MA: Harvard University Press, Belknap Press, 1997.

Gropman, Donald. *Say It Ain't So, Joe!* Boston: Little, Brown, 1979.

Guinness, Jonathan, and Catherine Guinness. *The House of Mitford.* New York: Viking, 1985.

Gunther, John. *Inside U.S.A.* New York and London: Harper & Brothers, 1947.

Hamilton, Nigel. *JFK, Reckless Youth.* New York: Random House, 1992.

Harrison, V. V. *Changing Habits: A Memoir of the Society of the Sacred Heart.* New York: Doubleday, 1988.

Hays, Will H. *The Memoirs of Will H. Hays.* Garden City: Doubleday, 1955.

Henderson, Dierdre, ed. *Prelude to Leadership: The European Diary of John F. Kennedy, Summer 1945.* Washington: Regenery, 1995.

Hersh, Burton. *The Old Boys: The American Elite and the Origins of the CIA.* New York, Toronto: Scribner's, 1992.

Hersh, Seymour M. *The Dark Side of Camelot.* Boston: Little, Brown, 1997.

Hessen, Robert. *Steel Titan. The Life of Charles M. Schwab.* New York: Oxford University Press, 1975.

Higham, Charles. *Rose: The Life and Times of Rose Fitzgerald Kennedy.* New York: Pocket Books, 1995.

———. *Trading with the Enemy: An Exposé of the Nazi-American Money Plot, 1933–1949.* New York: Delacorte Press, 1983.

Hilty, James W. *Robert Kennedy, Brother Protector.* Philadelphia: Temple University Press, 1997.

Hitler, Adolf, and Max Domarus. *Speeches and Proclamations, 1932–1945: The Chronicle of a Dictatorship.* Wauconda, IL: Bolchazy-Carducci, 1990.

Hohenberg, John. *The Pulitzer Prizes: A History of the Awards in Books, Drama, Music, and Journalism, Based on the Private Files Over Six Decades.* New York: Columbia University Press, 1974.

Holmes, Oliver Wendell, Harold Joseph Laski, and Mark De Wolfe Howe. *Holmes-Laski Letters: The Correspondence of Mr. Justice Holmes and Harold J. Laski, 1916–1935.* Cambridge: Harvard University Press, 1953.

Honig, Donald. *Baseball America.* New York: Macmillan, 1985.

Hoyt, William Glenn, and Walter Basil Langbein. *Floods.* Princeton: Princeton University Press, 1955.

Hull, Cordell, and Andrew Henry Thomas Berding. *The Memoirs of Cordell Hull.* New York: Macmillan Co., 1948.

Ickes, Harold L. *The Secret Diary of Harold L. Ickes.* New York: Simon and Schuster, 1953.

James, Dorris Clayton. *The Years of MacArthur.* Boston: Houghton Mifflin, 1970.

Jane, Fred T., ed. *Fighting Ships, 1914.* New York: Arco Publishing Co., 1969.

———. *Fighting Ships, 1919.* N.p., n.d.

Janeway, Eliot. *The Struggle for Survival: A Chronicle of Economic Mobilization in World War II.* New Haven: Yale University Press, 1951.

Jarvie, I. C. *Hollywood's Overseas Campaign: The North Atlantic Movie Trade, 1920–1950.* Cambridge and New York: Cambridge University Press, 1992.

Johnson, Donald Bruce. *The Republican Party and Wendell Willkie.* Urbana: University of Illinois Press, 1960.

Judd, Denis. *King George VI, 1895–1952.* New York: Franklin Watts, 1983.

Kapsner, Oliver Leonard. *Catholic Religious Orders.* Collegeville, MN: St. John's Abbey Press, 1957.

Kendall, Messmore. *Never Let Weather Interfere.* New York: Farrar, Straus, 1946.

Kennan, George Frost. *American Diplomacy.* Chicago: University of Chicago Press, 1984.

Kennedy, Edward M., ed. *The Fruitful Bough.* N.p.: Halliday Lithograph Corporation, 1965.

Kennedy, Joseph P., ed. *The Story of the Films.* Chicago: A.W. Shaw & Co., 1927.

Kennedy, Rose Fitzgerald. *Times to Remember.* New York: Doubleday, 1995.

Kenwood, Alun. *The Spanish Civil War: A Cultural and Historical Reader.* Berg European Studies Series. Providence: Berg, 1993.

Kessler, Ronald. *The Sins of the Father: Joseph P. Kennedy and the Dynasty He Founded.* New York: Warner Books, 1996.

Keynes, John Maynard. *Essays in Biography.* London: R. Hart-Davis, 1951.

Koskoff, David E. *Joseph P. Kennedy: A Life and Times.* Englewood Cliffs: Prentice-Hall, 1974.

Kramnick, Isaac, and Barry Sheerman. *Harold Laski: A Life on the Left.* New York: Allen Lane, 1993.

Krock, Arthur. *Memoirs: Sixty Years on the Firing Line.* New York: Funk & Wagnalls, 1968.

Lahue, Kalton C. *Dreams for Sale: The Rise and Fall of the Triangle Film Corporation.* South Brunswick: A. S. Barnes, 1971.

Lambert, Angela. *1939, The Last Season of Peace.* London: Weidenfeld and Nicolson, 1989.

Lane, Frederic Chapin. *Ships for Victory: A History of Shipbuilding Under the U.S. Maritime Commission in World War II.* Baltimore: Johns Hopkins Press, 1951.

Langer, William L., and Sarell Everett Gleason. *The Challenge to Isolation, 1937–1940.* New York: Harper, 1952, for the Council on Foreign Relations.

Lash, Joseph P. *Eleanor and Franklin: The Story of Their Relationship.* New York: W. W. Norton, 1971.

Lasky, Victor. *Robert F. Kennedy: The Myth and the Man.* New York: Trident Press, 1968.

Laurie, Joe, Jr. *Vaudeville: From the Honky-Tonks to the Palace.* New York: Henry Holt, 1953.

Lawrence, David. *The Editorials of David Lawrence.* Washington: U.S. News & World Report, 1970.

Leamer, Laurence. *The Kennedy Women: The Saga of an American Family.* New York: Villard Books, 1994.

Leib, Fred. *Baseball As I Have Known It.* New York: Coward, McCann & Geoghegan, 1977.

Lenning, Arthur. *The Silent Voice.* New York: Faculty-Student Association of the State University of New York at Albany, 1966.

Leuchtenburg, William Edward. *The Perils of Prosperity, 1914–32.* Chicago: University of Chicago Press, 1958.

Lindbergh, Anne Morrow. *The Flower and the Nettle: Diaries and Letters of Anne Morrow Lindbergh, 1936–1939.* New York: Harcourt Brace Jovanovich, 1976.

———. *War Within and Without: Diaries and Letters of Anne Morrow Lindbergh, 1939–1944.* San Diego: Harcourt Brace, 1995.

Lippmann, Walter, and Allan Nevins. *Interpretations, 1931–1932.* New York: Macmillan, 1932.

———. *Interpretations, 1933–1935.* New York: Macmillan, 1936.

Lippmann, Walter, et al. *The United States in World Affairs, Publications of the Council on Foreign Relations.* New York: Simon and Schuster, 1931 for the Council on Foreign Relations.

Low, Rachael. *The History of the British Film, 1918–1929.* London: Allen & Unwin, 1971.

Lowenfish, Lee, and Tony Lupien. *The Imperfect Diamond.* New York: Stein and Day, 1980.

Luce, Clare Boothe. *Europe in the Spring.* New York: Knopf, 1941.

Luckett, Perry D. *Charles A. Lindbergh.* New York: Greenwood Press, 1986.

Lyons, Eugene. *Herbert Hoover: A Biography.* Norwalk, CT: Easton Press, 1989.

Lyons, Louis Martin. *Newspaper Story: One Hundred Years of the Boston Globe.* Cambridge: Harvard University Press, Belknap Press, 1971.

MacArthur, Brian. *The Penguin Book of Twentieth-Century Speeches.* New York: Viking, 1992.

McBride, Joseph. *Frank Capra: The Catastrophe of Success.* New York: Simon & Schuster, 1992.

Macdonald, Dwight. *Henry Wallace: The Man and the Myth.* New York: Vanguard Press, 1948.

McJimsey, George T. *Harry Hopkins: Ally of the Poor and Defender of Democracy.* Cambridge: Harvard University Press, 1987.

McKernan, Luke. *Topical Budget: The Great British News Film.* London: British Film Institute, 1992.

McMahon, Deirdre. *Republicans and Imperialists: Anglo-Irish Relations in the 1930s.* New Haven: Yale University Press, 1984.

McNamara, Brooks. *The Shuberts of Broadway.* New York: Oxford University Press, 1992.

Madsen, Axel. *Gloria & Joe.* New York: Morrow, 1988.

Manchester, William Raymond. *The Last Lion, Winston Spencer Churchill.* Boston: Little, Brown, 1983.

Markowitz, Norman D. *The Rise and Fall of the People's Century: Henry A. Wallace and American Liberalism, 1941–1948.* New York: Free Press, 1973.

Martin, Ralph G. *Seeds of Destruction: Joe Kennedy and His Sons.* New York: G. P. Putnam's Sons, 1995.

————. *The Woman He Loved.* New York: Simon and Schuster, 1974.

Martínez Bande, José Manuel. *Los Cien Ultimos Días de la República.* Barcelona: L. Caralt, 1973.

Massachusetts General Court. *A Manual for the Use of the General Court.* Boston: [s.n.], 1943.

Mast, Gerald, and Bruce F. Kawin. *A Short History of the Movies.* 5th ed. New York: Macmillan, 1992.

Milton, Joyce. *Loss of Eden: A Biography of Charles and Anne Morrow Lindbergh.* New York: HarperCollins Publishers, 1993.

Minton, Bruce, and John Stuart. *Men Who Lead Labor.* New York: Modern Age Books, 1937.

Mitgang, Herbert. *The Man Who Rode The Tiger: The Life and Times of Judge Samuel Seabury.* Philadelphia: Lippincott, 1963.

Moley, Raymond. *After Seven Years.* New York and London: Harper & Brothers, 1939.

————. *The First New Deal.* New York: Harcourt, Brace & World, 1966.

————. *The Hays Office.* New York: Bobbs-Merrill, 1945.

Morgenthau, Henry. *The Presidential Diaries of Henry Morgenthau, Jr.* [microform]. New York: Clearwater Pub. Co., 1980.

————, and Paul Kesaris, ed. *The Presidential Diaries of Henry Morgenthau, Jr., 1938–1945.* Frederick, MD: University Publications of America, 1982.

Morris, Sylvia Jukes. *Rage for Fame: The Ascent of Clare Boothe Luce.* New York: Random House, 1997.

Nasaw, David. *Going Out: The Rise and Fall of Public Amusements.* New York: Basic Books, 1993.

Neal, Steve. *Dark Horse: A Biography of Wendell Willkie.* Garden City, NY: Doubleday, 1984.

Nicolson, Harold George, and Nigel Nicolson. *Diaries and Letters.* New York: Atheneum, 1966.

Offner, Arnold A. *American Appeasement: United States Foreign Policy and Germany, 1933–1938.* Cambridge: Harvard University Press, Belknap Press, 1969.

Oxbury, Harold. *Great Britons: Twentieth-Century Lives.* Oxford and New York: Oxford University Press, 1985.

Palmer, Frederick. *Newton D. Baker: America at War.* New York: Dodd, Mead & Co., 1946.

Parkes, Oscar, and Francis E. McMurtrie, eds. *Jane's Fighting Ships 1924.* New York: Arco Publishing Co., n.d.

Pecora, Ferdinand, and United States Congress. *Wall Street Under Oath: The Story of Our Modern Money Changers.* New York: Simon and Schuster, 1939.

Porter, David L. *Biographical Dictionary of American Sports: Baseball.* New York: Greenwood Press, 1987.

Public Affairs Information Service. *Public Affairs Information Service Bulletin.* New York: Public Affairs Information Service, 1969.

Quirk, Lawrence J. *The Kennedys in Hollywood.* Dallas: Taylor Pub. Co., 1996.

Rachlin, Harvey. *The Kennedys: A Chronological History, 1823–Present.* New York: World Almanac, 1986; distributed in U.S. by Ballantine Books.

Raczynski, Count Edward. *In Allied London.* London: Weidenfeld and Nicolson, n.d.

Ramsaye, Terry. *A Million and One Nights.* Vol. II. New York: Simon and Schuster, 1926.

Rhodes, Anthony Richard Ewart. *The Vatican in the Age of the Dictators, 1922–1945.* New York: Holt, 1974.

Robertson, John G. *Baseball's Greatest Hoaxes.* Jefferson, NC: McFarland, 1995.

Rollins, Alfred B., Jr. *Roosevelt and Howe.* New York: Alfred A Knopf, 1962.

Roosevelt, Elliott, ed. *F.D.R.: His Personal Letters.* Vol. I, 1928–1945. New York: Duell, Sloan and Pearce, 1947.

Roosevelt, Elliott, and James Brough. *A Rendezvous with Destiny: The Roosevelts of the White House.* New York: Putnam, 1975.

Roosevelt, Eleanor, and Rochelle Chadakoff. *Eleanor Roosevelt's in "My Day": Her Acclaimed Columns, 1936–1945.* New York: Pharos Books, 1989.

Roosevelt, Franklin D., Russell D. Buhite, and David W. Levy. *FDR's Fireside Chats.* Norman: University of Oklahoma Press, 1992.

Roosevelt, Franklin D., and William C. Bullitt. *For the President, Personal and Secret: Correspondence between Franklin D. Roosevelt and William C. Bullitt.* Bullitt, Boston: Houghton Mifflin, 1972.

Roosevelt, Franklin D., and Samuel Irving Rosenman. *The Public Papers and Addresses of Franklin D. Roosevelt.* New York: Russell & Russell, 1969.

Roosevelt, Franklin D., et al. *Franklin D. Roosevelt and Foreign Affairs, January 1937–August 1939.* Donald B. Schewe, series editor. New York: Clearwater Publishing Company Inc., 1983.

Roosevelt, Franklin D. *"Franklin D. Roosevelt, Diary & Itineraries, 1933–1945"* [microform]. FDR Library, Hyde Park, NY: 1933.

Roosevelt, Theodore, and Joan Paterson Kerr. *A Bully Father: Theodore Roosevelt's Letters to his Children.* New York: Random House, 1995.

Russell, Francis. *The President Makers: From Mark Hanna to Joseph P. Kennedy.* Boston: Little, Brown, 1976.

Schaller, Michael. *The United States and China in the Twentieth Century.* New York: Oxford University Press, 1990.

Schlesinger, Arthur Meier, Jr. *The Age of Roosevelt.* Boston: Houghton Mifflin, 1957.

————. *The Coming of the New Deal*, The American Heritage Library, ed. Arthur Meier Schlesinger. Boston: Houghton Mifflin, 1988.

————. *Robert Kennedy and His Times.* Boston: Houghton Mifflin, 1978.

————. *A Thousand Days: John F. Kennedy in the White House.* New York: Fawcett Premier, 1971.

————, Fred L. Israel, and William P. Hansen. *History of American Presidential Elections, 1789–1984.* New York: Chelsea House Publishers, 1986.

Schoor, Gene. *Young John Kennedy.* New York: Harcourt Brace & World, 1963.

Schwarz, Jordan A. *The Speculator: Bernard M. Baruch in Washington, 1917–1965.* Chapel Hill: University of North Carolina Press, 1981.

Scott, George. *The Rise and Fall of the League of Nations.* New York: Macmillan, 1974.

Seton-Watson, Christopher, et al. *British Documents on Foreign Affairs: Reports and Papers from the Foreign Office Confidential Print.* Frederick, MD: University Publications of America, 1990.

Seymour, Harold. *Baseball: The Peoples' Game.* New York: Oxford, 1990.

Sherwood, John M., *Georges Mandel and the Third Republic.* Stanford, CA: Stanford University Press, 1970.

Shirer, William L. Berlin Diary, *The Journal of a Foreign Correspondent, 1934–1941.* New York: Alfred A. Knopf, 1941

————. *The Rise and Fall of Adolf Hitler.* New York: Random House, 1961.

————. *The Rise and Fall of the Third Reich: A History of Nazi Germany.* New York: Simon and Schuster, 1981.

Sibley, Katherine A. S. *The Cold War.* Westport, CT: Greenwood Press, 1998.

Slide, Anthony. *Early American Cinema.* Revised edition. Metuchen, NJ: Scarecrow Press, 1994.

————. *The International Film Industry.* New York: Greenwood Press, 1989.

Smelser, Marshall. *The Life That Ruth Built.* New York Quadrangle, 1975.

Smith, Bill. *The Vaudevillians.* New York: Macmillan, 1976.

Smith, Richard Norton. *An Uncommon Man: The Triumph of Herbert Hoover.* New York: Simon and Schuster, 1984.

Sobel, Robert. *N.Y.S.E.: A History of the New York Stock Exchange, 1935–1975.* New York: Weybright and Talley, 1982.

Steel, Ronald. *Walter Lippmann and the American Century.* Boston: Little, Brown, 1980.

Stone, Fred. *Rolling Stone.* New York: Whittlesey House, 1945.

Streit, Clarence K. *Union Now With Britain.* New York: Harper & Brothers Publishers, 1941.

Swanberg, W. A. *Citizen Hearst: A Biography of William Randolph Hearst.* New York: Scribner, 1961.

Swanson, Gloria. *Swanson on Swanson.* New York: Random House, 1980.

Sykes, Christopher. *Nancy: The Life of Lady Astor.* London: Collins, 1972.

Talese, Gay. *The Kingdom and the Power.* New York: World Pub. Co., 1969.

Taylor, A. J. P. *English History, 1914–1945.* New York: Oxford University Press, I 965.

Taylor, Henry J. *Men and Moments.* New York: Random House, 1966.

Tebbel, John William. *An American Dynasty: The Story of the McCormicks, Medills, and Pattersons.* New York: Greenwood Press, 1968.

————. *The Life and Good Times of William Randolph Hearst.* New York: Dutton, 1952.

Theoharis, Athan G. and John Stuart Cox. *The Boss: J. Edgar Hoover and the Great American Inquisition.* Philadelphia: Temple University Press, 1988.

Thomas, Bob. *King Cohn: The Life and Times of Harry Cohn.* New York: Putnam, 1967.

Thomas, Hugh. *The Spanish Civil War.* New York: Harper & Row, 1986.

Thorn, John, and Pete Plamer, eds. *Total Baseball.* New York: Warner, 1989.

Toynbee, Arnold Joseph, et al. *Survey of International Affairs.* Oxford and New York: Oxford University Press, 1920.

Tucker, Sophie. *Some of These Days.* Garden City, NY: Doubleday, 1945.

Tully, Grace. *F.D.R.: My Boss.* New York: Scribner, 1949.

Tugwell, Rexford G. *The Democratic Roosevelt: A Biography of Franklin D. Roosevelt.* Garden City, NY: Doubleday & Co., 1957.

Wagenheim, Hal. *Babe Ruth, His Life and Legend.* New York: Praeger, 1974.

Wallace, Henry Agard, and John Morton Blum. *The Price of Vision: The Diary of Henry A. Wallace, 1942–1946.* Boston: Houghton Mifflin, 1973.

Wander, Meghan Robinson, and Otis L. Graham. *Franklin D. Roosevelt: His Life and Times.* Boston: G. K. Hall, 1985.

Ward, Geoffrey, and Ken Burns, eds. *Baseball.* New York: Alfred A. Knopf, 1994.

————, *How War Came: The Immediate Origins of the Second World War, 1938–1939.* New York: Pantheon Books, 1989.

————. *Personalities and Policies: Studies in the Formulation of British Foreign Policy in the Twentieth Century.* Notre Dame: University of Notre Dame Press, 1965.

————. *Succeeding John Bull: America in Britain's Place, 1900–1975.* Cambridge and New York: Cambridge University Press, 1984.

————, Kenneth Bourne, and Michael Partridge. *British Documents on Foreign Affairs—Reports and Papers from the Foreign Office Confidential Print.* Bethesda, MD: University Publications of America, 1997.

Waugh, Evelyn, and Mark Amory. *The Letters of Evelyn Waugh.* London: Weidenfeld and Nicolson, 1980.

Weber, Michael P. *Don't Call Me Boss: David L. Lawrence, Pittsburgh's Renaissance Mayor.* Pittsburgh: University of Pittsburgh Press, 1988.

Weintraub, Stanley. *Modern British Dramatists, 1900–1945.* Detroit: Gale Research Co., 1982.

Welles, Benjamin. *Sumner Welles: FDR's Global Strategist: A Biography.* New York: St. Martin's Press, 1997.

Welles, Sumner. *The Time for Decision.* New York and London: Harper & Brothers, 1944.

Whalen, Richard J. *The Founding Father: The Story of Joseph P. Kennedy.* New York: New American Library, 1964.

Wheeler-Bennett, John, *Munich: Prologue to Tragedy.* New York: Duell, 1963.

White, Graham J. *FDR and the Press.* Chicago: University of Chicago Press, 1979.

———, and J. R. Maze. *Henry A. Wallace: His Search for a New World Order.* Chapel Hill: University of North Carolina Press, 1995.

White, Theodore Harold. *Breach of Faith: The Fall of Richard Nixon.* New York: Atheneum Publishers, 1975.

White, William Lindsay. *They Were Expendable.* New York: Harcourt, 1942.

Wiener, Joel H. *Great Britain: Foreign Policy and the Span of Empire, 1689–1971: A Documentary History.* New York: Chelsea House Publishers, 1972.

Winchell, Walter. *Winchell Exclusive.* Englewood Cliffs, NJ: Prentice-Hall, 1975.

Windeler, Robert. *Sweetheart: The Story of Mary Pickford.* New York: Praeger, 1974.

Winant, John Gilbert. *Letter from Grosvenor Square; An Account of a Stewardship.* New York: Greenwood Press, 1969.

Wyman, David S., *Paper Walls: America and the Refugee Crisis, 1938–1941.* Amherst: University of Massachusetts Press, 1968.

Zeman, Z A. B., and Antonín Klimek. *The Life of Edvard Beneš, 1884–1948: Czechoslovakia in Peace and War.* Oxford and New York: Oxford University Press, Clarendon Press, 1997.

Journal, Newspaper and Magazine Articles

"All Heart." *Newsweek,* December 4, 1961, 56.

Alsop, Stewart. "Kennedy's Magic Formula," *Saturday Evening Post,* August 13, 1960, 26.

Anderson, Paul V. "Roosevelt Must Fight!" *The Nation,* April 16, 1938, 431–432.

"Archbishop Joseph P. Hurley, R.I.P." *National Review,* November 14, 1967, 1251.

Buck, Frank. "Clouded Leopard." *Colliers,* March 24, 1934.

Chambers, Andrea, Fred Hauptfuhrer, and Jerene Jones. "Mum's the Word: What's Behind the Royal Facade? A Telling Glimpse of a Very Private Woman Who is Diana's Mother-in-Law." *People,* March 7, 1983, 94.

"Common Wealth." *Newsweek,* April 19 1943, 46.

The D[istillers] C[ompany,] L[imited] Gazette, October 1925, January 1934, United Distillers' Archive, Edinburgh.

Dalleo, Peter T., and Watchorn, J. Vincent III. "Baltimore, the 'Babe,' and the Bethlehem Steel League, 1918." Paper delivered at the Eighth Cooperstown Symposium on Baseball and American Culture, Cooperstown, N.Y., June 1996.

———. "Slugger or Slacker? Shoeless Joe Jackson and Baseball in Wilmington, 1918." *Delaware History,* vol. 26, no. 2 (fall–winter 1994–95).

DeBedts, Ralph E. "The First Chairman of the Securities and Exchange Commission." *The American Journal of Economics and Sociology* 23, no. 2 (1964): 165–78.

Dieffenbach, Dr. Charles T. "Salute to a Snowman," *Christian Science Monitor Magazine,* February 14, 1948, 4.

"Dollar Lines Get Set." *Business Week,* October 15, 1938, 21–22.

"End of an Era," *People,* December 22, 1986 / December 29, 1986, 126.

"Every Man in his Humor." *Time,* October 14, 1940, 30.

Fischer, Louis. "Trotsky and Stalin." *Nation,* September 7, 1940, 191–192.

Friedrich, Carl Joachim. "Lord Halifax." *The Atlantic Monthly,* November 1939, 610–620.

"From Pillory to Post." *Time,* October 22, 1965, 24–25.

Harriman, Margaret Case. "Profiles: Dolly and Polly, Billy and Cholly," *New Yorker,* October 16, 1937, 23–27.

Harris, J. P., "The 'Sandys Storm': The Politics of British Air Defense in 1938," *Historical Research* [Great Britain], 1989, 318–336.

Hersey, John. "PT Squadron in the South Pacific." *Life,* May 10, 1943, 74–76.

Hilton, Stanley. "The Welles Mission to Europe, February–March 1940: Illusion or Realism?" *The Journal of American History,* 58 (June 1971): 93–120.

Horne, Alistair. "The Odds Were Always Against Him." *New York Times Book Review,* March 6, 1994, 6.

"How to Win a Pulitzer Prize." *The New Republic,* May 10, 1939, 23.

"In & Out." *Time,* July 4, 1949, 49.

"Joe Kennedy's Tour." *Life,* October 1, 1945, 38–39.

Johnston, Alva. "Jimmy's Got It." *Saturday Evening Post,* July 2, 1938.

———. "White House Tommy." *Saturday Evening Post,* July 31, 1937, 1.

"Kennedy Hits the Trail." *Time,* September 24, 1945, 17–18.

Kennedy, Joseph P. "Big Business, What Now?" *Saturday Evening Post,* January 16, 1937. 10.

———. "Shielding the Sheep." *Saturday Evening Post,* January, 1936, 23.

Kennedy, Paul. "George C. Marshall, Statesman 1945–1959." *New York Times Book Review,* June 28, 1987, 3.

"Kennedy vs. the C.I.O." *The Nation,* February 26, 1938, 234.

"Kennedy's Long Pants." *New York Daily News,* May 17, 1938.

Kirchwey, Freda. "Watch Joe Kennedy!" *The Nation,* December 14, 1940, 593.

Krock, Arthur. "How War Came: Extracts from the Hull Files." *New York Times Magazine,* July 18, 1943.

Lacayo, Richard. "Daddy, Where do Windsors Come From?" *People,* fall 1990, 28.

Leland, Waldo Gifford. "The Creation of the Franklin D. Roosevelt Library: A Personal Narrative." *American Archivist* 18 (January, 1955): 11–29.

"Leon Trotsky." *Nation,* August 31, 1940, 165.

Levin, Eric, and David Chandler, "Family Feud." *People,* June 2, 1986, 59.

Libby, Justin. "Hamilton Fish and the Origins of Anglo-American Solidarity." *Mid-America: An Historical Review,* vol. 76, no. 3 (fall 1994): 205–226.

"Little Specter." *Time,* July 19, 1943, 4.

Lukacs, John. "Ross Hoffman, R.I.P." *National Review,* March 7, 1980, 268–269.

McDoy, Donald R. "The Beginnings of the Franklin D. Roosevelt Library." *Prologue* 7 (fall, 1975) 137–150.

"Maritime Commission Takes Over Captain Dollar's Shipping Empire." *Business Week,* August 27, 1938, 23.

"A Measure of Freedom." *Time,* January 21, 1952, 76.

Michaelis, David. "The President's Best Friend." *American Heritage,* June / July 1983, 12–27.

"Military Ambassador." *Time,* January 31, 1944, 18.

"Morrissey Case." *Newsweek,* November 1, 1965, 100.

"Mr. Biddle Drops In." *Time,* December 20, 1943: 16.

"Mr. Frank More O'Ferrall." *The Bloodstock Breeders' Annual Review,* 1976.

"Mr. Kennedy Is Wrong Again." *Watertown Daily Times,* December 13, 1950, 2.

"Mr. Kennedy Reports." *The Christian Century,* January 29, 1941, 141+.

"My Boy Franklin." *Time,* March 6, 1933, 11.

"No Knee Pants (Joe Kennedy, the Ambivalent Ambassador)," *U.S. News & World Report,* August 27, 1990 / September 3, 1990, 63.

"One for Old Joe." *Newsweek,* October 11, 1965, 33–34.

"Only the Best?" *Newsweek,* August 7, 1961, 23–26.

Pipes, Richard. "The Seeds of His Own Destruction." *New York Times Book Review,* March 24, 1996, 9.

Podmore, William A. "The Making of the Anglo-Italian Agreement, 1937–1938." *Italian Studies* (1994) 111–124.

"Pre-Presidential." *New Yorker,* April 1, 1961, 26–27.

"Profile in Brinksmanship." *Time,* October 29, 1965, 28–29.

Pryce-Jones, David. "Not Their Finest Hour." *New Republic,* May 14, 1977, 12–16.

"Pulitzer Winners." *Newsweek,* May 9, 1938, 29.

Ramsay, Terry. "Intimate Visits to the Home of Famous Film Magnates." *Photoplay,* Joseph P. Kennedy edition, 1927.

"Red Hunt." *Time,* vol. 31, no. 9 (1938): 13.

Russell, Francis. "The Knave of Boston," *American Heritage,* August 1976, 73–80.

"Sergeant's Reward." *Time,* October 6, 1965, 33–34.

"Sorenson On Kennedy: A Long Exercise in Inhibition." *Newsweek,* October 11, 1965, 34–35.

"The Ism of Appeasement: Roosevelt Brands Foes of his Foreign Policy." *Life,* January 20, 1941.

"The Pulitzer Pattern." *The Nation,* May 14, 1938, 549.

"The Richest Boy." *Time,* February 16, 1959, 21–22.

"This Year's Crop of Winners." *The New Republic,* May 11, 1938, 2.

"Too High a Price." *Newsweek,* November 1, 1965, 23–24.

"War Debts and Peace Legislation: The Johnson Act of 1934." *Mid-America: An Historical Review* (July 1960) 206–222.

Watson, Campbell. "C. R. Lindner, Hearst Publisher, Dies in S. F." *Editor & Publisher,* January 12, 1952, 10.

Willert, Sir Arthur. "British News Controls." *Foreign Affairs,* July 1939, 712–713.

Newspapers and Magazines

The American Journal of
  Economics and Sociology
Atlanta Journal and Constitution
Atlantic Monthly
American Archivist
American Heritage
The Bloodstock Breeders' Annual Review
The Boston Daily Globe
Boston Evening Transcript
Boston Globe
Boston Herald
Boston Post

Business Week
Central European History
Chicago Tribune
The Christian Century
Christian Science Monitor
Collier's
Current History
Daily Telegraph
The DCL Gazette
Editor & Publisher
English Historical Review
Financial Times

Foreign Affairs
Historical Research
Independent (London)
Italian Studies
The Journal of American History
Le Monde
Life
Look
Los Angeles Times
Mid-America: An Historical Review
Milwaukee Journal
The Nation

National Review
The New Republic
Newsweek
New Yorker
New York Herald Tribune
New York Journal American

New York Times
People
Prologue
Providence Journal-Bulletin
Saturday Evening Post
Time

Times of London
Variety
Washington Post
Washington, D.C. Times

Government Documents and Papers

Election Statistics: Commonwealth of Massachusetts. Massachusetts Office of the Secretary of State., Boston.

Great Britain. Foreign Office. *The British War Blue Book.* Documents concerning German-Polish relations and the outbreak of hostilities between Great Britain and Germany on September 3, 1939. New York: Farrar & Rinehart, 1939.

Great Britain. Foreign Office and E. L. Woodward. *Documents on British Foreign Policy, 1919–1939.* London: HMSO, 1946.

Great Britain. Naval Intelligence Division and Alice Garnett. *Jugoslavia.* London, 1944.

Great Britain. Public Record Office and John D. Cantwell. *The Second World War: A Guide to Documents in the Public Record Office.* 2nd ed. Public Record Office Handbooks; no. 15. London: HMSO, 1993.

United States. Commission on Organization of the Executive Branch of the Government (1947–1949), and Herbert Hoover. *The Hoover Commission Report on Organization of the Executive Branch of the Government.* New York: McGraw-Hill, 1949.

United States Congress. *Congressional Record,* Washington, D.C., 1873–.

United States Congress. Joint Committee on Printing. *First Lady Jacqueline Kennedy Onassis, 1929–1994: Memorial Tributes in the One Hundred Third Congress of the United States.* S. Doc. 103–32. Washington: GPO, 1995.

United States Congress, et al. *Biographical Directory of the United States Congress, 1774–1989.* Bicentennial ed. S. Doc. 100–34. Washington: GPO, 1989.

United States. Department of the Army. *US Army Register.* Washington: GPO, 1957.

United States. Department of State. *Documents on German Foreign Policy, 1918–1945,* from the Archives of the German Foreign Ministry, Publication 3277, 3838, 3883, 4964, 5436. Washington: GPO, 1949.

United States. Department of State. *Foreign Relations of the United States. Diplomatic Papers, 1861–.* Washington: GPO.

United States. Department of State. *Principal Officers of the Department of State and United States Chiefs of Mission, 1778–1990.* Washington: GPO, 1991.

United States. Department of State. *Register of the Department of State, 1870–.* Washington: GPO.

United States. Library of Congress. Legislative Reference Service. *Events Leading up to World War II.* Chronological history of certain major international events leading up to and during World War II with the ostensible reasons advanced for their occurrence, 1931–1944. 78th Cong., 2d sess. H. Doc. 541. Washington: GPO 1944.

United States. Library of Congress. Manuscript Division. *Emory Scott Land: A Register of His Papers in the Library of Congress.* Washington: 1958.

United States. Library of Congress. Manuscript Division. *Grover C. Loening: A Register of His Papers in the Library of Congress.* Washington: 1959.

United States. Social Security Administration. *Social Security Death Master File.* Washington: GPO.

United States. War Department. Selective Service Regulations. Changes no. 1–7; January 21, 1918–July 31, 1918.

Reference Works

Anderson, Joy. *The American Catholic Who's Who.* Washington: National Catholic News Service, 1979.

Anderson, Patrick. *The Presidents' Men: White House Assistants of Franklin D. Roosevelt, Harry S. Truman, Dwight D. Eisenhower, John F. Kennedy, and Lyndon B. Johnson.* Garden City, NY: Doubleday, 1968.

Andrews, Robert. *The Columbia Dictionary of Quotations.* New York: Columbia University Press, 1993.

Alexander, Robert Jackson. *Biographical Dictionary of Latin American and Caribbean Political Leaders.* New York: Greenwood Press, 1988.

Baker, Theodore and Nicolas Slonimsky. *Baker's Biographical Dictionary of Musicians.* New York: Schirmer Books, 1978.

Balteau, J., et al. *Dictionnaire de Biographie Française.* Paris: Letouzey et Ané, 1933.

Banham, Martin. *The Cambridge Guide to Theatre.* Cambridge, New York: Cambridge University Press, 1995.

Barone, Michael, Grant Ujifusa, and Douglas Matthews. *The Almanac of American Politics.* Washington: Barone & Co., 1972.

Bawden, Liz-Anne. *The Oxford Companion to Film.* New York: Oxford University Press, 1976.

Bell, David Scott, et al. *Biographical Dictionary of French Political Leaders since 1870.* New York: Simon & Schuster, 1990.

732

Benedictine Monks of St. Augustine's Abbey, Ramsgate. *The Book of Saints: A Dictionary of Servants of God.* Harrisburg: Morehouse Pub., 1993.

Biographical Directory of the United States Congress, 1774–1989. Washington: GPO, 1989.

Blaug, Mark and R. P. Sturges. *Who's Who in Economics: A Biographical Dictionary of Major Economists, 1700–1981.* Cambridge, MA: MIT Press, 1983.

Boorman, Howard L., ed., and Richard C. Howard, assoc. ed. *Biographical Dictionary of Republican China.* New York: Columbia University Press, 1967–79.

Bordman, Gerald Martin. *The Oxford Companion to American Theatre.* New York: Oxford University Press, 1992.

Boylan, Henry. *A Dictionary of Irish Biography.* New York: St. Martin's Press, 1988.

Brady, Anne, and Brian Talbot Cleeve. *A Biographical Dictionary of Irish Writers.* New York: St. Martin's Press, 1985.

Brodney, Spencer. *Events: A Monthly Review of World Affairs.* New York: Events Publishing Co., 1937.

Brown, Gene. *The New York Times Encyclopedia of Film, 1896–1979.* New York: Times Books, 1983.

Brown, Les. *Les Brown's Encyclopedia of Television.* Detroit: Gale Research, 1992.

Brune, Lester H. *Chronological History of the United States Foreign Relations.* New York: Garland, 1985.

Buhle, Mari Jo, Paul Buhle, and Dan Georgakas. *Encyclopedua of the American Left.* New York: Garland Pub., 1990.

Buranelli, Vincent, and Nan Buranelli. *Spy / Counterspy: An Encyclopedia of Espionage.* New York: McGraw-Hill, 1982.

Burke, William Jeremiah, et al. *American Authors and Books: 1640 to the Present Day.* New York: Crown Publishers, 1972.

Buse, Dieter K., and Juergen C. Doerr. *Modern Germany: An Encyclopedia of History, People, and Culture, 1871–1990.* New York: Garland Pub., 1998.

Cannistraro, Philip V. *Historical Dictionary of Fascist Italy.* Westport, CT: Greenwood Press, 1982.

Carruth, Gorton. *The Encyclopedia of American Facts and Dates.* 10th ed. New York: HarperCollins, 1997. 1997.

Chase, Harold William. *Biographical Dictionary of the Federal Judiciary.* Detroit: Gale Research Co., 1976.

Chung-kuo, Ming Jen Lu. *Who's Who in China: Biographies of Chinese Leaders.* Shanghai: The China Weekly Review, 1936.

Cheng, Joseph K. H., Richard C. Howard, and Howard L. Boorman, eds. *Biographical Dictionary of Republican China.* New York: Columbia University Press, 1967.

Claghorn, Charles Eugene. *Biographical Dictionary of American Music.* West Nyack, NY: Parker Pub. Co., 1973.

Colby, Frank Moore, et al. *The New International Year Book: A Compendium of the World's Progress.* New York: Dodd, 1908.

Commire, Anne, and Deborah Klezmer. *Historic World Leaders.* Detroit and London: Gale Research Inc., 1994.

Corneau, Ernest N. *The Hall of Fame of Western Film Stars.* North Quincy, MA: Christopher Pub. House, 1969.

Cortada, James W. *Historical Dictionary of the Spanish Civil War, 1936–1939.* Westport, CT: Greenwood Press, 1982.

Coyle, William. *Ohio Authors and Their Books: Biographical Data and Selective Bibliographies for Ohio Authors, Native and Resident, 1796–1950.* Cleveland: World Pub. Co., 1962.

Crystal, David. *The Cambridge Biographical Encyclopedia.* Cambridge and New York: Cambridge University Press, 1994.

———. *The Cambridge Factfinder.* Rev. ed. Cambridge and New York: Cambridge University Press, 1994.

Delaney, John J., and James Edward Tobin. *Dictionary of Catholic Biography.* Garden City, NY: Doubleday, 1961.

Downs, Robert Bingham, and Jane B. Downs. *Journalists of the United States: Biographical Sketches of Print and Broadcast News Shapers from the late 17th Century to the Present.* Jefferson, NC: McFarland, 1991.

Dupuy, R. Ernest, and Trevor Nevitt Dupuy. *The Encyclopedia of Military History From 3500 B.C. to the Present.* New York: Harper & Row, 1986.

Dupuy, Trevor Nevitt, Curt Johnson, and David L. Bongard. *The Harper Encyclopedia of Military Biography.* New York: HarperCollins, 1992.

Eatwell, John, Murray Milgate, and Peter K. Newman. *The New Palgrave: A Dictionary of Economics.* New York: Stockton Press, 1987.

Echard, William E. *Historical Dictionary of the French Second Empire, 1852–1870.* Westport, CT: Greenwood Press, 1985.

Edelheit, Abraham J., and Hershel Edelheit. *History of the Holocaust: A Handbook and Dictionary.* Boulder, CO: Westview Press, 1994.

Edwards, Julia. *Women of the World: The Great Foreign Correspondents.* Boston: Houghton Mifflin, 1988.

Ekwall, Eilert. *The Concise Oxford Dictionary of English Place-Names.* Oxford: Clarendon Press, 1960.

Ewen, David. *Composers Since 1900: A Biographical and Critical Guide.* New York: H. W. Wilson Co., 1969.

———. *The New Encyclopedia of the Opera.* New York: Hill and Wang, 1971.

Falk, Byron A., and Valerie R. Falk *Personal Name Index to "The New York Times Index," 1975–1979.* Verdi, NV: Roxbury Data Interface, 1984.

————. *Personal Name Index to "The New York Times Index," 1851–1974.* Succasunna, NJ: Roxbury Data Interface, 1976.

Fest, Wilfried. *Dictionary of German History, 1806–1945.* New York: St. Martin's Press, 1978.

Filler, Louis. *A Dictionary of American Social Reform.* New York: Philosophical Library, 1963.

Findling, John E. *Dictionary of American Diplomatic History.* New York: Greenwood Press, 1989.

Fink, Gary M. *Biographical Dictionary of American Labor.* Westport, CT: Greenwood Press, 1984.

————. *Biographical Dictionary of American Labor Leaders.* Westport, CT: Greenwood Press, 1974.

Foreign Policy Association. *Foreign Policy Reports.* New York: Foreign Policy Association, 1931.

Frankel, Benjamin. *The Cold War, 1945–1991.* Detroit: Gale Research, 1992.

Friedman, Leon, and Fred L. Israel. *The Justices of the United States Supreme Court, 1789–1978: Their Lives and Major Opinions.* New York: Chelsea House, 1980.

G. and C. Merriam Company. *Webster's American Military Biographies.* Springfield, MA: G. & C. Merriam Co., 1978.

Gale Composite Biographical Series, ed. *Who was Who in the Theatre, 1912–1976.* N.p.: Ominigraphics, 1978.

Gänzl, Kurt. *The Encyclopedia of Musical Theatre.* New York: Schirmer Books, 1994.

Garland, Henry B., and Mary Garland. *The Oxford Companion to German Literature.* Oxford and New York: Oxford University Press, 1997.

Garraty, John Arthur, Mark C. Carnes, and Societies American Council of Learned. *American National Biography.* New York: Oxford University Press, 1999.

Garraty, John Arthur, and Jerome L. Sternstein. *Encyclopedia of American Biography.* New York: HarperCollins, 1996.

Gilbert, Mark, and K. Robert Nilsson. *Historical Dictionary of Modern Italy.* Lanham, MD: Scarecrow Press, 1998.

Gordon, Bertram M. *Historical Dictionary of World War II France: The Occupation, Vichy, and the Resistance, 1938–1946.* Westport, CT: Greenwood Press, 1998.

Gorman, Robert A. *Biographical Dictionary of Marxism.* Westport, CT: Greenwood Press, 1986.

Graff, Henry F. *The Presidents: A Reference History.* New York: Scribner, 1984.

Green, Jonathon. *The Encyclopedia of Censorship.* New York: Facts on File, 1990.

Gutman, Israel. *Encyclopedia of the Holocaust.* New York: Macmillan, 1990.

Halliwell, Leslie, and John Walker. *Halliwell's Filmgoer's Companion.* 11th centenary ed. London: HarperCollins, 1995.

Hamilton, David. *The Metropolitan Opera Encyclopedia: A Comprehensive Guide to the World of Opera.* New York: Simon and Schuster, 1987.

Handlin, Oscar. *Al Smith and his America.* The Library of American Biography. Boston: Little, Brown, 1958.

Herzberg, Max J. *The Reader's Encyclopedia of American Literature.* New York: Thomas Y. Crowell Co., 1962.

Holli, Melvin G., and Peter d Alroy Jones. *Biographical Dictionary of American Mayors, 1820–1980.* Westport, CT: Greenwood Press, 1981.

Hsing, Cheng Yüan and Hsin wen chü. *China Handbook.* New York: Macmillan, 1944.

Hutton, Patrick H., Amanda S. Bourque, and Amy J. Staples. *Historical Dictionary of the Third French Republic, 1870–1940.* Westport, CT: Greenwood Press, 1986.

Ingham, John N. *Biographical Dictionary of American Business Leaders.* Westport, CT: Gaunt Greenwood Press, 1983.

Institut zur Erforschung der UdSSR and others. *Who Was Who in the USSR: A Biographic Directory Containing 5,015 Biographies of Prominent Soviet Historical Personalities.* Metuchen: Scarecrow Press, 1972.

Istituto della Enciclopedia Italiana. *Dizionario Biografico Degli Italiani.* Roma: Istituto della Encyclopedia Italiana, 1960.

Jackson, George D., and Robert James Devlin. *Dictionary of the Russian Revolution.* New York: Greenwood Press, 1989.

Jacobs, Arthur. *The Penguin Dictionary of Musical Performers.* London and New York: Viking, 1990.

James, Edward T., et al. *Notable American Women, 1607–1950: A Biographical Dictionary.* Cambridge, MA: Harvard University Press, Belknap Press, 1971.

Jentleson, Bruce W., and Thomas G. Paterson. *Encyclopedia of U.S. Foreign Relations.* New York: Oxford University Press, 1997.

K. G. Saur Verlag. *Internationaler Biographischer Index.*

Kane, Joseph Nathan. *Presidential Fact Book.* New York, Random House, 1998.

Katchmer, George A. *Eighty Silent Film Stars: Biographies and Filmographies of the Obscure to the Well Known.* Jefferson, NC: McFarland & Company, 1991.

Katz, Ephraim. *The Film Encyclopedia.* New York: HarperCollins Publishers, 1994.

————. *The Macmillan International Film Encyclopedia.* London: Macmillan, 1994.

Keegan, John. *Who Was Who in World War II.* London: Arms and Armour Press, 1978.

————, and Andrew Wheatcroft. *Who's Who in Military History: From 1453 to the Present Day.* London and New York: Routledge, 1996.

Kern, Robert W., and Meredith D. Dodge. *Historical Dictionary of Modern Spain, 1700–1988.* Westport, CT: Greenwood Press, 1990.

Kernfeld, Barry Dean. *The New Grove Dictionary of Jazz.* London and New York: Grove's Dictionaries of Music, Macmillan, 1988.

King, David James Cathcart. *Castellarium Anglicanum: An Index and Bibliography of the Castles in England, Wales, and the Islands.* Millwood, NY: Kraus International, 1983.

Kinkle, Roger D. *The Complete Encyclopedia of Popular Music and Jazz, 1900–1950.* New Rochelle, NY: Arlington House, 1974.

Kirkendall, Richard Stewart. *The Harry S. Truman Encyclopedia.* Boston: G.K. Hall, 1989.

Klingaman, William K. *Encyclopedia of the McCarthy Era.* New York: Facts on File, 1996.

Kuehl, Warren F. *Biographical Dictionary of Internationalists.* Westport, CT: Greenwood Press, 1983.

Lane, Hana Umlauf. *The World Almanac Book of Who.* Englewood Cliffs, NJ: World Almanac Publications, Prentice-Hall, 1980.

Langman, Larry. *Encyclopedia of American Film Comedy.* New York: Garland, 1987.

Laqueur, Walter. *A Dictionary of Politics.* New York: Free Press, 1974.

Lehane, Brendan. *The Companion Guide to Ireland.* London: Collins, 1985.

Leiter, Samuel L. *The Encyclopedia of the New York Stage, 1930–1940.* Westport, CT: Greenwood Press, 1989.

———. *The Encyclopedia of the New York Stage, 1940–1950.* Westport, CT: Greenwood Press, 1992.

Leung, Pak-Wah. *Historical Dictionary of Revolutionary China, 1839–1976.* Westport, CT: Greenwood Press, 1992.

Leventhal, F. M. *Twentieth-Century Britain: An Encyclopedia.* New York: Garland Pub., 1995.

Lewytzkyj, Borys, and Juliusz Stroynowski. *Who's Who in the Socialist Countries: A Biographical Encyclopedia of 10,000 Leading Personalities in 16 Communist Countries.* New York: K. G. Saur Pub., 1978.

Lichtenstein, Nelson, et al. *Political Profiles.* New York: Facts on File, 1976.

Lippmann, Walter, and John Morton Blum. *Public Philosopher: Selected Letters of Walter Lippmann.* New York: Ticknor & Fields, 1985.

Longford, Frank Pakenham, and John Wheeler Wheeler-Bennett. *The History Makers; Leaders and Statesmen of the 20th Century.* New York: St. Martin's Press, 1973.

Lowery, Charles D., and John F. Marszalek. *Encyclopedia of African-American Civil Rights: From Emancipation to the Present.* Westport, CT: Greenwood Press, 1992.

Lyon, Christopher, and Susan Doll. *The International Dictionary of Films and Filmmakers.* Chicago: St. James Press, 1984.

McBrien, Richard P., and Harold W. Attridge. *The HarperCollins Encyclopedia of Catholicism.* San Francisco: HarperSanFrancisco, 1995.

McEwan, Peter J. M. *Dictionary of Scottish Art & Architecture.* Woodbridge, Suffolk, England: Antique Collectors' Club, 1994.

McGuire, William, and Leslie Wheeler. *American Social Leaders, Biographies of American Leaders.* Santa Barbara, CA: ABC-CLIO, 1993.

McKerns, Joseph P. *Biographical Dictionary of American Journalism.* Westport, CT: Greenwood Press, 1989.

McRedmond, Louis. *Modern Irish Lives: Dictionary of 20th-Century Irish Biography.* New York: St. Martin's Press, 1996.

Mahoney, M. H. *Women in Espionage: A Biographical Dictionary.* Santa Barbara, CA: ABC-CLIO, 1993.

Martí, José, and Philip Sheldon Foner. *Political Parties and Elections in the United States.* Philadelphia: Temple University Press, 1989.

Matray, James Irving. *Historical Dictionary of the Korean War.* Westport, CT: Greenwood Press, 1991.

Melchinger, Siegfried. *The Concise Encyclopedia of Modern Drama.* New York: Horizon Press, 1964.

Melton, J. Gordon and Gale Research Inc. *Religious Leaders of America.* Detroit: Gale Research, 1991.

Millgate, Linda. *The Almanac of Dates: Events of the Past for Every Day of the Year.* New York: Harcourt Brace Jovanovich, 1977.

Mills, A. D. *A Dictionary of English Place-Names.* Oxford and New York: Oxford University Press, 1998.

Milne, Tom. *The Time Out Film Guide.* 3rd ed. London and New York: Penguin Books, 1993.

Monaco, James, James Pallot, and Baseline (firm). *The Encyclopedia of Film.* New York: Perigee Books, 1991.

Montague-Smith, Patrick W. *Debrett's Correct Form.* London and New York: Debrett's Peerage Ltd., Viking Press, 1970.

Morris, Dan, and Inez Morris. *Who Was Who in American Politics.* New York: Hawthorn Books, 1974.

Morris, Jan. *The Oxford Book of Oxford.* Oxford and New York: Oxford University Press, 1978.

Mossman, Jennifer. *Pseudonyms and Nicknames Dictionary: A Guide to Aliases, Appellations, Assumed Names.* Detroit: Gale Research Co., 1987.

Nash, Jay Robert, and Stanley Ralph Ross. *The Motion Picture Guide.* Chicago: Cinebooks, 1987.

New York Public Library. *The New York Public Library American History Desk Reference.* New York: Macmillan, 1997.

North, S. N. D., Francis Graham Wickware, and Albert Bushnell Hart. *The American Year Book.* New York: T. Nelson & Sons [etc.], 1910.

Northcutt, Wayne. *Historical Dictionary of the French Fourth and Fifth Republics, 1946–1991.* Westport, CT: Greenwood Press, 1992.

Olsen, Kirstin. *Chronology of Women History.* Westport, CT: Greenwood Press, 1994.

Olson, James Stuart. *Historical Dictionary of the 1920s: From World War I to the New Deal, 1919–1933.* Westport, CT: Greenwood Press, 1988.

———. *Historical Dictionary of the New Deal: From Inauguration to Preparation for War.* Westport, CT: Greenwood Press, 1985.

Osborne, Charles. *The Dictionary of Composers.* London: Bodley Head, 1977.

Osmanczyk, Edmund Jan. *The Encyclopedia of the United Nations and International Agreements.* Philadelphia: Taylor and Francis, 1985.

O'Toole, G. J. A. *The Encyclopedia of American Intelligence and Espionage: From the Revolutionary War to the Present.* New York: Facts on File, 1988.

Pallen, Condé Bénoist, and John J. Wynne. *The New Catholic Dictionary.* New York: The Universal Knowledge Foundation, 1929.

Palmer, Alan Warwick. *The Penguin Dictionary of Modern History, 1789–1945.* 2nd ed. Penguin Reference Books. Harmondsworth, Middlesex, England, and New York: Penguin Books, 1983.

Palmer, Robert J., and Council on Foreign Relations. *Foreign Affairs 50-year Index.* New York: R. R. Bowker Co., 1973, for the Council on Foreign Relations .

Perkins, George B., Barbara Perkins, and Phillip Leininger. *Benet's Reader's Encyclopedia of American Literature.* New York: HarperCollins Publishers, 1991.

Plan, Suzy, and Library of Congress. Congressional Research Service. *Respectfully Quoted: A Dictionary of Quotations Requested from the Congressional Research Service.* Washington: Library of Congress, 1989.

Polmar, Norman, and Thomas B. Allen. *Spy Book: The Encyclopedia of Espionage.* New York: Random House, 1997.

Porter, David L. *Biographical Dictionary of American Sports.* Westport, CT: Greenwood Press, 1988.

Prest, John M. *The Illustrated History of Oxford University.* Oxford and New York: Oxford University Press, 1993.

Prokhorov, A. M. *Great Soviet Encyclopedia.* New York: Macmillan, 1973.

Ragan, David. *Who's Who in Hollywood, 1900–1976.* New Rochelle, NY: Arlington House, 1976.

Rees, Philip. *Biographical Dictionary of the Extreme Right Since 1890.* New York: Simon & Schuster, 1990.

Rigdon. Walter. *The Biographical Encyclopaedia & Who's Who of the American Theatre.* New York: J. H. Heineman, 1966.

———. *Notable Names in the American Theatre.* Clifton, NJ: J. T. White, 1976.

Roberts, Frank Cecil. *Obituaries from the Times, 1951–1960.* Reading, England. Westport, Newspaper Archive Developments Ltd., 1979; distributed in North America by Meckler Books.

———. *Obituaries from the Times, 1971–1970.* Westport / Meckler, 1975.

———. *Obituaries from the Times, 1971–1975.* Westport / Meckler, 1978.

Robinson, Alice M., Vera Mowry Roberts, and Milly S. Barranger. *Notable Women in the American Theatre: A Biographical Dictionary.* Westport, CT: Greenwood Press, 1989.

Roller, David C., and Robert W. Twyman. *The Encyclopedia of Southern History.* Baton Rouge: Louisiana State University Press, 1979.

Room, Adrian. *Dictionary of Place-Names in the British Isles.* London: Bloomsbury, 1989.

Ross, Ishbel. *Ladies of the Press: The Story of Women in Journalism by an Insider.* New York: Harper, 1936.

Ross, Martha, and Bertold Spuler. *Rulers and Governments of the World.* New York: Bowker, 1977.

Roth, Mitchel P. *Historical Dictionary of War Journalism.* Westport, CT: Greenwood Press, 1997.

Rubio Cabeza, Manuel. *Diccionario de la Guerra Civil Española.* Barcelona: Planeta, 1987.

Secchia, Pietro. *Enciclopedia dell'antifascismo e della Resistenza.* Milan: La pietra, 1968.

Shale, Richard. *Academy Awards: An Ungar Reference Index.* New York: Ungar, 1982.

Shatzkin, Mike. *The Ball Players: Baseball's Ultimate Biographical Reference.* New York: Morrow, 1990.

Shukman, Harold. *The Blackwell Encyclopedia of the Russian Revolution.* Oxford and New York: B. Blackwell, 1988.

Sifakis, Carl. *The Dictionary of Historic Nicknames: A Treasury of More Than 7,500 Famous and Infamous Nicknames From World History.* New York: Facts on File, 1984.

Slide, Anthony. *The American Film Industry: A Historical Dictionary.* Westport, CT: Greenwood Press, 1986.

———. *The Encyclopedia of Vaudeville.* Westport, CT: Greenwood Press, 1994.

———. *The Vaudevillians: A Dictionary of Performers.* Westport, CT: Arlington House, 1981.

Snyder, Louis Leo. *Encyclopedia of the Third Reich.* New York: McGraw Hill, 1976.

Sobel, Robert. *Biographical Dictionary of the Governors of the United States, 1789–1978.* Westport, CT: Meckler Books, 1978.

———. *Biographical Directory of the United States Executive Branch, No 1774–1977.* Westport, CT: Greenwood Press, 1977.

———. *Biographical Directory of the United States Executive Branch, 1774–1989.* Westport, CT: Greenwood Press, 1990.

Spiller, Roger J., and Joseph G. Dawson. *Dictionary of American Military Biography.* Westport, CT: Greenwood press, 1984.

Standard and Poor's Corporation. *Standard & Poor's Register of Corporations, Directors and Executives.* New York: Standard & Poor's Corp., 1973.

Taft, William H. *Encyclopedia of Twentieth-Century Journalists.* New York: Garland, 1986.

Taylor, Stephen. *Who's Who in France*. Paris: J. Lafitte.

Teed, Peter. *A Dictionary of Twentieth Century History: 1914–1900*. Oxford and New York: Oxford University Press, 1992.

Thomson, David. *A Biographical Dictionary of Film*. New York: Alfred A. Knopf, 1994.

Trager, James. *The People's Chronology: A Year-by-Year Record of Human Events from Prehistory to the Present*. New York: H. Holt, 1994.

Truitt, Evelyn Mack. *Who Was Who on Screen*. New York: R. R. Bowker Co., 1983.

University of London. Institute of Historical Research. *Dictionary of National Biography*. London: Oxford University Press, 1975.

Van Doren, Charles Lincoln, and Robert McHenry. *Webster's American Biographies*. Springfield, MA: G. & C. Merriam Co., 1974.

Vronskaya, Jeanne, and Vladimir Chuguev. *A Biographical Dictionary of the Soviet Union, 1917–1988*. London and New York: Saur, 1989.

Wagner, Lilya. *Women War Correspondents of World War II*. Westport, CT: Greenwood Press, 1989.

Ward, A. C., and Maurice Hussey. *Longman Companion to Twentieth Century Literature*. Harlow: Longman, 1981.

Wearing, J. P. *The London Stage, 1930–1939: A Calendar of Plays and Players*. Metuchen, NJ: Scarecrow Press, 1990.

Weatherford, Doris. *Milestones: A Chronology of American Women's History*. New York: Facts on File, 1997.

Weinreb, Ben, and Christopher Hibbert. *The London Encyclopedia*. Bethesda, MD: Adler & Adler, 1986.

Wigoder, Geoffrey. *New Encyclopedia of Zionism and Israel*. Madison, NJ: Fairleigh Dickinson University Press, Associated University Presses, 1994.

Wistrich, Robert S. *Who's Who in Nazi Germany*. London: Weidenfeld and Nicolson, 1982.

Young, Peter. *The World Almanac Book of World War II*. Englewood Cliffs: World Almanac Publications, Prentice-Hall, 1981.

Zentner, Christian, and Friedemann Bedurftig. *The Encyclopedia of the Third Reich*. New York: Macmillan, 1991.

General Reference

The American Bench Judges of the Nation. Minneapolis: Reginald Bishop Forster & Associates, 1977.

American Council of Learned Societies. *Dictionary of American Biography*. New York: Scribner, 1997.

The Annals of America. Chicago: Encyclopaedia Britannica, 1968.

The Annual Obituary. New York: St. Martin's, 1981.

The Annual Register: A Review of Public Events at Home and Abroad. London: Rivingtons, 1864.

ASCAP Biographical Dictionary. New York: Bowker, 1980.

Biography and Genealogy Master Index. Detroit: Gale Research Co., 1988.

Brewer's Theatre: A Phrase and Fable Dictionary. London: Cassell, 1994.

Brittannica Book of the Year, vol. 1938–Chicago: Encyclopaedia Britannica, 1938.

Burke's Genealogical and Heraldic History of the Peerage, Baronetage and Knightage. London: Burke's Peerage, 1938.

Burke's Presidential Families of the United States of America. London: Burke's Peerage, 1975.

Burke's Royal Families of the World. London: Burke's Peerage, 1977.

Columbia Encyclopedia, 5th ed. New York: Columbia University Press, 1993.

Congressional Quarterly: Biographical Directory of the American Congress, 1774–1996. Alexandria, VA: CQ Staff Directories, 1997.

Congressional Quarterly's Guide to the US Supreme Court. Washington: Congressional Quarterly Inc., 1990.

Contemporary Authors. Detroit: Gale Research Co., 1981.

Debrett's Peerage, Baronetage, Knightage, and Compaionage. Kingston upon Thames: Kelly's Directories, 1993.

Dictionary of Literary Biography. Detroit: Gale Research Co., 1978–1999.

Encyclopedia of American Biography. New York and West Palm Beach: American Historical Society, 1965.

Harvard Business School Yearbook, 1928.

Illustrated Souvenir of the Palace of Arts: Empire Exhibition, Scotland-1938. Glasgow: McCorquodale & Co. Ltd., 1938.

The International Who's Who. London: Europa Publications Ltd., 1935–1999.

Keesing's Contemporary Archives. London: Keesing's Limited., 1931.

Leaders in Education. New York: R. R. Bowker, 1932–.

Marquis Inc., *The International Authors and Writer's Who's Who*. Chicago: Marquis Who's Who, 1976.

Marquis Inc., *Who's Who in America*. Chicago: Marquis Who's Who, 1976.

———. *Who Was Who in America*. Chicago: Marquis Who's Who, 1984.

New Catholic Encyclopedia. Palatine, Ill: McGraw-Hill / J. Heraty, 1981.

The National Cyclopedia of American Biography. Clifton, NJ: J. T. White, 1937.

The New Encyclopaedia Britannica, 15th ed. Chicago: Encyclopædia Britannica, 1991.

New International Yearbook. New York: Funk & Wagnall's, 1936.

The New York Times Biographical Service. New York: Arno Press, 1970–.

The New York Times Current History. New York: The New York Times Co., N.d.

New York Times Film Reviews. New York: 1968.

The New York Times Index. New York: The New York Times Company. N.d.

New York Times Theater Reviews, 1973.

The Official Washington Post Index. Woodbridge: Research Publications, 1979–.

Ragan, David. *Who's Who in Hollywood.* New York: Facts on File, 1992.

The Times Index. Reading, England: Newspaper Archive Developments Ltd., 1973.

Treaties and Alliances of the World: An International Survey Covering Treaties in Force and Communities of States. New York: Scribner, 1968.

Who Did What: The Lives and Achievements of the 5000 Men and Women—Leaders of Nations, Saints and Sinners, Artists and Scientists—Who Shaped our World. New York: Crown Publishers, 1974.

Who Was Who Among English and European Authors, 1931–1949. Detroit: Gale Research Co., 1978.

Who was Who Among North American Authors, 1921–1939. Detroit: Gale Research Co., 1976.

Who Was Who in the Theatre, 1912–1976. Detroit: Gale Research Co., 1978.

Who's Who, 1849–. London: A. & C. Black, 1849–.

Who's Who Among English and European Authors, 1978.

Who's Who in American Politics. New York: R. R. Bowker, 1968.

Who's Who in New England. Chicago: Marquis, 1949.

Who's Who of American Women: A Biographical Dictionary of Notable Living American Women. Chicago: Marquis Who's Who. 1971.

INDEX

Abbott, Gordon, 18
Abyssinia, 258, 292, 321
Academy of Motion Picture Arts and Sciences, 90
Ace of Clubs, 38n
Acheson, Dean, 122, 531, 649, 654
Adams, Charles Francis, 65, 83
Addison's disease, 676
Adenauer, Konrad, 674
Adjusted Compensation Act (1924), 133n
"Administration and Business, The" (J. P. Kennedy), 186n, 188–89
Admiral Scheer, 393n
Africa, 696
Agnelli, Giovanni "Gianni," 638, 691
agranulocytosis, 163n
Air Corps Reserve, U.S., 525n
Airlie, Mabell Frances Elizabeth Gore, Lady, 333
Aitken, John William Maxwell, 627
Alabama claims, 386
Alanbrooke, Alan Francis Brooke, Lord, 603
Alba, Don Jacobo Fitz-James Stuart y Falco, Duke of, 325
Albania, 325–26, 327, 328
Albee, Edward Franklin, 53n, 60, 62, 68, 74, 76
Alden, J., 89
Alexander, Albert Victor, 422, 425
Alexander I, King of Yugoslavia, 350n
Alexandra Feodorovna, Czarina of Russia, 328
Algic affair, 215–16
Algiers, 383
Allan, Elizabeth, 167
Allen, Robert Sharon, xxi, 113, 186–87, 228, 255, 256
Allied Newspapers, 468n
Allied Reparations Committee, 615, 616
Allied Submarine Detection Investigation Committee (Asdic) system, 426
Alsop, Joseph, xxi, 281, 482, 495, 498, 500–501, 503–5, 511, 664, 675
Amagiri, 517, 569n

America First Committee, 508, 511
American Broadcasting Company (ABC), 680, 681
American Correspondents' Association, 240
American Institute of Public Opinion, 339n
American International Corporation, 17n, 38n
American Labor Party, 666
American Liberty League, 121, 133n
American Magazine, xxi, 12
American Medical Association (AMA), 134
American President Lines, 217n
American Red Cross, 517, 520, 552
Americans for Democratic Action (ADA), 663, 672n
American White Paper, The: The Story of American Diplomacy and the Second World War (Alsop and Kintner), 495, 498, 500–501, 503–5
Amery, Leopold Charles Maurice Stennett, 476
Anderson, Ava, 567, 619, 633
Anderson, John, 476, 567, 615, 633
Anderson, Orville Arson, 652
Anglo-American Press Association, 247
Anglo-American Trade Agreement, 223
Anne, Queen of England, 344
Anschluss, 230, 240–41, 246, 255n
Anstruther-Gray, Bill, 604
anti-Semitism, 232–34, 298, 338–39, 354
Appeasement at Munich (J. F. Kennedy), 232, 410, 416, 417
Arbuckle, Fatty, 68n
Argentina, 5–6, 402
Army-McCarthy hearings, 664n
Arnhem, Battle of, 579n
Arpels, Hélène, 641–42
Arpels, Louis, 641n, 642
Arthur, Jean, 400n
Arvad, Inga, 516
Ashton-Gwatkin, Frank Trewlawny, 269, 272

Association of Chambers of Commerce, 256
Astaire, Adele Marie, 595n
Astaire, Fred, 595n
Astor, Barbara Mary Colonsay, 581
Astor, David, 581
Astor, John Jacob, 408, 630
Astor, Michael Langhorne, 581n, 627
Astor, Nancy Witcher Langhorne, Lady, 232, 250, 255, 256, 258, 281n, 300n, 304–5, 308, 333–34, 367, 391, 395, 422, 466, 563, 564, 567, 576, 581–82, 587, 588, 594, 618
Astor, Waldorf, Lord, 250, 304
Astor, William Vincent, 156
As We Remember Joe (J. F. Kennedy), 519, 619–20
Athenia, 369, 370–71
Atherton, Ray, 164
Atlantic Charter, 536n, 579, 593
Atlantic Gulf and West Indies Steamship Lines, 195
Atlantic Monthly, 382, 395, 397
Atlas Corporation, 208
Attlee, Clement Richard, 248, 291, 326, 408, 476
Auchincloss, Janet, 112, 662n
Austin, Warren Robinson, 617
Australia, 286, 373, 542, 543
Austria, 248, 270, 527n
Anschluss and, 230, 240–41, 246, 255n
Awful Truth, The, 82n
Axis powers, 231, 258n, 338n
see also Germany, Nazi; Italy; Japan
Ayers, Russell Romeyn, 83–84

Bacon, Gaspar, 125
Bailey, John, 672
Baker, Mimi, 165
Baker, Newton, 66
Baldwin, Stanley, 260–63, 288, 347, 349, 433, 435, 461, 464
Balfour Declaration, 336n
Balsan, Consuelo Vanderbilt, 345
Balsan, Jacques, 345n
Baltic States, 560, 607
Bankhead, Tallulah, 402

744

137, 138, 139–41, 171–72,
195–96, 200–201, 204,
207, 208, 209, 334–35,
511, 523, 693
fortieth wedding anniversary
of, 666
French Riviera residence of,
522, 629, 632, 636,
664–65, 669, 676, 683,
692, 696
golf played by, xviii, 30, 167,
226, 235, 245, 295, 296,
325, 467, 468, 523, 539,
600, 663, 691, 699*n*
health of, xiii, xviii, 455, 466,
467, 468, 540, 642, 644,
691, 699
Hollywood deals of, xx, xxiv,
xxvii, 8–13, 23, 25–31,
44*n*, 45*n*, 46–64, 68–91,
112, 114, 139–41, 204–7,
209, 214, 233, 234, 507,
511, 513
horseback riding by, 107,
235, 245, 329, 396, 467,
695
Hyannis Port home of,
xxvi, 30*n*, 64, 98, 108,
141*n*, 175, 186, 224,
231, 513, 548, 599–600,
644, 664, 668, 670, 681,
689
Irish background of, xvii–xviii,
xxvii, 57, 67, 115, 202,
203, 207, 211, 511, 512,
534, 608, 613, 638
isolation of, 512–13, 529,
533–34
JFK's political career and, xv,
522, 617, 622, 625–27,
628, 632, 657, 660–61,
662, 671, 678, 681–97
JPK Jr.'s death and, 519,
521, 522, 599–600, 601,
614, 620, 622, 629,
679–80
Kick's death and, 520,
636–38, 650
as liquor distributor, xx, 3, 8,
12, 28, 33–34, 107–9,
135, 213–14, 266*n*, 521,
523, 596, 626–29, 667
marriage of, 3, 4, 9, 119,
143, 392, 522–23, 660,
666
media coverage of (non-
ambassadorial), xvii,
xx–xxii, 3, 5, 11, 12, 57,
108, 112–15, 137, 138,
160, 161, 171–72, 180,
186–87, 199–213, 215,
522, 545, 546, 611,
634–35, 645–46, 667–68,
690
memoranda of, 127–29,
136–39, 190–91,
199–211, 224

mentoring relationships of,
xxiii–xxv
military service avoided by, xv,
4–5, 15–18
music enjoyed by, 212, 256,
407, 415
Palm Beach home of, xxvi,
30*n*, 98, 108, 123–24,
127–28, 134, 148, 152,
166–67, 170, 181, 217,
219, 224, 231, 235, 306*n*,
456, 471, 513, 523, 538,
539, 573, 624, 638, 689,
698–99
papers of, xvii, xviii–xx,
xxvii–xxxvi, 61, 233–34,
479*n*, 511*n*, 516, 520–21,
685
in Paris, 321, 520, 636,
646–50, 690
personality of, xiii–xiv, xviii,
xxvii, xxviii, xxix, xxxv, 256
physical appearance of, xiii,
xxviii, 217
political career of, xvii,
xxii–xxiii, xxvi, xxxv, 57,
58, 66–67, 103, 107, 113,
210, 219–20, 228, 240,
255, 263–66, 268,
298–99, 406, 493, 499,
511–14, 521, 529,
556–57, 600, 629, 692*n*
presidential aspirations of,
228, 255, 263–66, 268,
298–99, 406, 511, 692*n*
public image of, xiii–xiv, xvii,
xx–xxiii, 12, 114–15,
137–41, 171–72,
199–211, 511–12, 523
radio broadcast of (1940), vii,
481, 482–89
radio broadcast of (1941),
524–25, 529, 645–46
real estate ventures of, 202–3,
521
Riverdale home of, 54*n*, 64
secrecy of, xx, xxvii, xxx, 57,
522–23
semiretirement of, xxxv, 234,
511–699
as shipyard assistant general
manager, xv, xvi, xxv, 3,
4–5, 15–22, 23*n*, 57, 65,
112, 140, 200, 203–4,
209, 374*n*, 516, 542*n*
speeches of, 141, 149,
216–17, 521, 524, 552,
556, 557, 594, 605, 606,
612, 646, 647, 652–53,
658–59
stroke suffered by, xiii, xxi,
xxxv, 523, 699*n*
twenty-fifth wedding anniversary of, 392
war service denied to,
533–34, 536, 541–46,
556–58, 577

wealth of, xxxi–xxxii, 179,
180, 223, 436, 511, 521,
523, 626, 694
in Winthrop, Massachusetts,
202
writings of, xix, 114, 173,
185–87, 188*n*, 208–9,
494*n*, 521, 626
Kennedy, Joseph P., as ambassador, 223–508
Anglo-American relations
and, 227–31, 243*n*,
246–47, 281*n*,
334–35
Anglophilia ascribed to, 238,
281*n*, 335, 353*n*
anti-Semitism ascribed to,
232–34, 298
appeasement supported by,
224, 227–28, 229,
231–32, 234, 236,
248–49, 253, 264, 265,
269–97, 469, 483–84,
495*n*, 498, 499–500, 502,
503–5, 506, 511, 521,
575, 645–46
appointment of, 109, 115,
217*n*, 218–20, 223–24,
235–37
in Bermuda, 479–80
Blitz as viewed by, 241,
432–33, 451–54, 462,
463, 465–72, 474, 476,
478, 484, 487, 500,
525
British economy as viewed by,
238, 241–42, 246, 249,
259, 357–58, 373–74,
376–77, 404, 413–14,
418, 426, 473, 487, 494,
496, 502
British military situation as
viewed by, 227, 242, 246,
433, 438–39, 451–52,
453, 454, 456–57, 462,
496, 502
British political situation as
viewed by, 241–43,
346–47, 385–86, 398,
411–12, 433–35, 455
British response to, 223–24,
226, 227–28, 230, 232,
237*n*, 245, 410–11, 453,
455, 481, 493–94, 501–3,
563, 635
codes used by, 281*n*, 431,
432, 443
correspondence of, xviii, xix,
xxi–xxvi, xxx–xxxi,
223–508
court presentations discouraged by, 226, 230, 238,
240, 245, 256, 326
credentials presented by,
239–40
death threats against,
325–26

McCloskey, Matthew Henry, 688–89
MacColl, Jim, 173
McCormack, John William, 41, 449, 533–34, 541, 640, 656–57
McCormick, Robert Rutherford, xxi, 46, 113, 171–72, 269, 347n, 545, 658n
McCullogh, Charles, 10
MacDonald, James Ramsay, 262n, 302n
MacDonald, Malcolm John, 233n, 260n, 302, 303, 336
McDonald, Torbert, 397, 548, 644, 662, 668
McDonnell, Anne, 447, 595
MacFarland, Grenville, 29
McGuirk, John, 53
McInerny, Timothy Anthony, 563, 564, 667
McIntyre, Marvin Hunter, 138, 139, 150, 190, 236, 612
McIntyre, O. O., xxi
McIntyre, Ross, 129
McKee, Joseph Vincent "Holy Joe," 122
McLean, Edward B., 35
MacMahon, Pat, 517
Macmillan, Harold, 563n
McNamara, Robert S., 699
McNicholas, John Timothy, 640
McNutt, Paul V., 406
McReynolds, James Clark, 151, 228, 236, 268
Maginot Line, 372, 428, 444n, 504
Maglione, Luigi Cardinal, 318
Maine and New Hampshire Theater Companies, 12, 36n, 45n, 75n, 76n
Maisky, Ivan Mikhailovich, 242–43, 328, 422
Malaya, 654
Malcolm Cottage, 64
Malik, Yakov A., 653
Mallon, Paul Raymond, 228, 620–21
Malloy, Joe, 37
Malta, 383
Mameaux, Albert Leon "Al," 20, 21, 22
Manchester Guardian, 110, 346n
Mandel, Georges, 445
Manhattan, 237, 406
Manhattanville College, 514
"March of Time," 216
Margaret Rose, Princess, xviii, xxv, 252, 288, 331, 414, 630
Margesson, David, 425, 633
Margin for Error (Luce), 455
Maritime Act (1936), 114, 216n
Maritime Commission, U.S., 285, 404n
  JPK as chairman of, xxi, xxv, xxvii, xxx–xxxi, 57, 65, 67, 114–15, 194–97, 198, 200, 211, 212–13,

215–16, 217n, 223, 235n–36n, 296, 487
Marlborough, Alexandra Mary Beatrice Cadogan, Duchess of, 344
Marlborough, John Churchill, 1st Duke of, 344, 346
Marlborough, John Spencer-Churchill, 10th Duke of, 457
Marsh, Oliver, 74–75
Marshall, George C., 664
Marshall, Tully, 63
Marshall Plan, 521, 634n, 651, 658–59, 664n, 674, 678
Martha, Princess, 558
Martin, Glenn Luther, 497
Martin, William McChesney, 674
Marwood estate, 112, 154–56
Marx, Harpo, xviii, 189
Marx, Karl, 136
Mary, Queen Consort of England, xvi, xviii, 288, 308, 331, 334, 456, 466, 494n, 583, 619, 633, 637
  JPK's meetings with, 245, 250–54, 286, 287, 326–29, 332–33, 350–53, 374, 401–3, 414
  U.S. visit of, 297, 332, 338, 341–42, 343, 350–53, 402, 403
Mary, Queen of Scots, 251
Maryknoll Center, 684
Masaryk, Jan, 247, 257, 289
Mascagni, Pietro, 407
Massey, Vincent, 286
Mathieson Alkali Works, 25
Matthew, David James, 580, 590
Matthews, George C., 111, 138, 139
Matthews, Herbert Lionel, 629
Matthews, Sullivan Amory, 316
Matthias, Ludwig Ernst, 430–31
Maugham, W. Somerset, 51–53, 70
Mauretania, 379, 395
Mayer, Louis B., 62, 74–75
Maynard, Joseph, 191
Mayo Clinic, 126, 134, 145, 617
Mayor of Casterbridge, The (Hardy), 99
Mdivani, Louise Astor Van Alen, 174
Mdivani, Serge, 174
Mead, George Houk, Jr., 533, 551
Meade, James Michael, 641
Meekins (U.S. embassy staff), 240
Mein Kampf (Hitler), 469
Mellon, Andrew, 115
Men of Maryknoll (Keller and Berger), 577
Merchandise Mart, xxxv, 521, 666, 668n
Merchant Marine, U.S., 194n, 211, 212–13, 215–16, 242, 296–97, 487, 546

Merchant Marine Act (1936), 194n
Merchants National Bank, 27n
Merry Widow, The, 62, 74n, 77, 88n
Messersmith, George Strausser, 366, 526
Metro-Goldwyn-Mayer (MGM), 29n, 71n, 210n, 252n
Metro-Goldwyn Pictures, 53n
Metro Pictures, 29, 46n
Mexico, 300n
Meyner, Robert Baumle, 688
Miami, University of, 622n, 624
Michelangelo, 318
Middlesex Republican Club, 26
Midnight Follies, The, 44n
MI5, 232
Milbank, Jeremiah, 59, 83, 139–40
Milbanke, Margaret Sheila Mackellar, 570
Millard (U.S. embassy staff), 239–40
Miller, Sara, 9
Milton Academy, 514–15, 548n
Ministry of Health, British, 387
Ministry of Information, British, 369n
"Miss Thompson" (Maugham), 51n
Mr. Deeds Goes to Town, 400n
Mr. Smith Goes to Washington, 400–401
Mitford, Deborah Vivien Freeman, 355n, 532, 603
Mitford, Unity Valkyrie Freeman, 355–56
Moffat, Jay Pierrepont, 228, 256–58, 268, 294n, 300n
Moffet, Jack, 506
Moley, Raymond Charles, 111, 125, 134, 136–37, 138, 139, 156n
Molnár, Ferenc, 31–32
Molotov, Vyacheslav Mikhailovich, 349–50, 630, 633
Molyneaux, Richard, 254
Monck, John, 326n–27n
Moniz, Egas, 516
Monroe Doctrine, 379, 484
Monrovia, Liberia, 472n
Monte Carlo, 690–91
Montessori schools, 226, 379n, 515
Montgomery, Bernard Law, 633
Montgomery, Dave, 15n
Montgomery, Ruth Shick, 694
Mooney, James David, 331–32
Moore, Edward E., 9–10, 78–81, 108, 382, 398, 481, 540
  JPK's relationship with, 6, 29–30, 33, 36, 37, 41n, 48, 66, 98n, 102, 107, 112, 155, 190n, 191, 207, 226, 235, 236, 237, 252, 379, 409, 414, 432, 656

Seth Parker, 126
Seven Pillars of Wisdom, The
    (Lawrence), 579
Seventh Heaven, 77n
Seymour, James, 391, 415, 468
Seyss-Inquart, Arthur, 241, 257
Shakespeare, William, 290
Shanahan, Thomas Joseph, 684
Shanghai, 380n
Shannon, Charles Barry, 573
Shaughnessy, Frank C., 138
Shaw, George Bernard, 256
Shawmut Bank, 26, 30
Shea, Francis, 175
Shearn, Clarence, 254n
Sheehan, Joseph Raymond, 112,
    217
Sheehan, Winfield Richard, 52,
    75
Sheehy, Maurice Stephen, 546
Sheen, Fulton John, 649
Sheppard, Eugenia, 691
Sherrill, Edgar, 620
"Shielding the Sheep" (J. P.
    Kennedy), 173
Shinkwin, J. J., 27
Shirer, William L., 528
Shriver, Eunice Kennedy:
    at Blenheim Palace, 344–46
    childhood of, 36, 51, 143, 273
    education of, 174, 514, 547
    in England, 226, 289, 305,
        344–46, 630, 631–32
    health of, 127, 135
    JPK's correspondence with,
        174, 177, 196, 391
    marriage of, 668
    postwar years of, 630,
        631–32, 642, 644, 656,
        661, 667, 676, 691, 692
    return to U.S. (1939), 371n,
        417, 421, 514, 552, 596,
        604
    Rose's correspondence with,
        539, 553, 686
    in South America, 514, 530
    at State Department, 617–18
Shriver, Maria Owings, 686
Shriver, Sargent, 668, 670,
    673–75, 678, 699
Shubert Theatres Corporation,
    60
Sibelius, Jean, 415
Sicily, 558
Siegfried Line, 291, 368, 372,
    390
Sills, Milton, 12, 49n
Silverman, Sid, 89
Silverman, Sime, 89
Silver Purchase Act (1934), 128,
    137n
Simon, John, 227, 232, 266,
    269, 277, 283, 288, 358,
    359, 382–83, 405, 408,
    427, 498
Simpson, Ernest Aldrich, 261
Simpson, Wallis Warfield, *see*
    Windsor, Duchess of

Sinatra, Frank, 13
Sinclair, Archibald Henry Mac-
    donald, 365, 408, 425,
    426, 438, 476
Singapore, 528, 537, 542
Sistine Chapel, 318
Sitwell, Edith, 580n
Skakel, Anne, 655
Skakel, Pat, 655
Skolsky, Sidney, 239
Slaney, Jane Kenyon, 563, 564,
    627
slavery, 391–92, 622–23
Smathers, George Armistead, 672
Smith, Alfred E., 65, 77,
    121–22, 689, 697
Smith, H. G., 16
Smith, Jean Kennedy:
    birth of, 65, 74
    as Catholic, xxvi–xxvii
    childhood of, xxvi–xxvii, 153,
        174, 184
    as editor's mother, xiv–xv,
        xxvi–xxvii, xxviii
    education of, xxvi–xxvii, 515
    in England, 226, 289–90, 371
    JPK's correspondence with,
        177, 191, 196, 289–90,
        665
    marriage of, 693n
    postwar years of, 642, 644,
        655, 656, 668, 676
    return to U.S. (1939), 447,
        515, 549, 596, 618
    Rose's correspondence with,
        191, 289–90
Smith, Joe, 677
Smith, Stephen Edward, xv, 693
Snyder, John Wesley, 620–21
Société des Bains de Mer, 690n
Society for the Propagation of
    the Faith, 649n
Solomon Islands, 517, 550–56,
    561
Somaliland, 461
Somborn, Gloria, 86
Somerset Importers, 12, 108–9,
    127n, 184n, 213–14, 289n,
    455n, 521, 523, 605,
    613n, 628
SONAR, 426n
Sonzogno Publishing Company,
    407n
Sorensen, Theodore C., 668, 686
Soucy, Edward A., 513
South America, 442, 462, 497,
    525, 528
Southey, Robert, 344
Soviet Aviation Administration,
    300n
Soviet Union:
    air force of, 280, 282,
        290–91, 300n, 383
    British relations with, 293,
        328, 338, 349–50
    economy of, 242–43
    French relations with, 293,
        338, 349–50

German invasion of, 531n,
    558, 658
German relations with,
    242–43, 355–56, 357,
    361, 362–63, 373, 384,
    385, 405
JPK Jr.'s visit to, 110–11, 113,
    134, 136
navy of, 383
nuclear weapons of, 652n
Poland invaded by, 342, 378,
    380, 382–83, 385, 390,
    607
rearmament of, 290–91,
    382–83
RFK's visit to, 668, 669–70
U.S. military support for, 531n,
    536
U.S. relations with, 560,
    606–7, 610, 617, 623,
    626n, 639, 646, 648–49,
    651, 652, 653, 654, 658
war declared by, 376
Spain, Fascist, 362, 383, 426
Spanish Civil War, xix, 226, 233,
    241, 249, 251, 267, 271,
    307n, 308–16, 328n, 337,
    339, 363
    JPK Jr.'s views on, 308–16,
        323–25, 330, 331,
        335–36, 382
Spargo, William, 36, 37
Spaulding, Chuck, 597
Spee Club, 417, 444, 447
Spellman, Francis Joseph Cardi-
    nal, 318, 584, 586, 590,
    607, 612, 640, 648, 649,
    658, 682, 696–97
Spring, Sam, 53
Stabler, C. Norman, 161n
Stalin, Joseph, 242–43, 324,
    560, 606–7, 610, 633,
    639, 649
Standard Oil, 71n
Stanford University, 514, 516,
    547
Stanley, Oliver, 232, 279,
    413n
Stark, Harold Raynsford, 591
Stassen, Harold Edward, 674
State Department, U.S., 297,
    307, 309, 341, 406, 496,
    526, 527, 567, 610, 640,
    644n, 652
    codes used by, 281n
    JPK's relationship with, xix,
        xxiii, 227, 229, 231, 232,
        246, 265–66, 268, 300,
        302, 341n, 453, 458–59,
        475, 481, 482, 492, 498n,
        500–501, 512, 524, 525
    Kent affair and, 232, 430–43,
        621, 645
    Prisoner of War section of,
        617–18
Stealers, The, 25–26
Steel, John, 41
Steele, Bob, 20

763